Contents

www.philips-maps.co.uk

First published in 2007 as Philip's EasyRead Europe by Philip's, a division of Octopus Publishing Group Ltd
www.octopusbooks.co.uk
Carmelite House, 50 Victoria Embankment
London EC4Y 0DZ
An Hachette UK Company · www.hachette.co.uk

Eighth edition 2018, first impression 2018

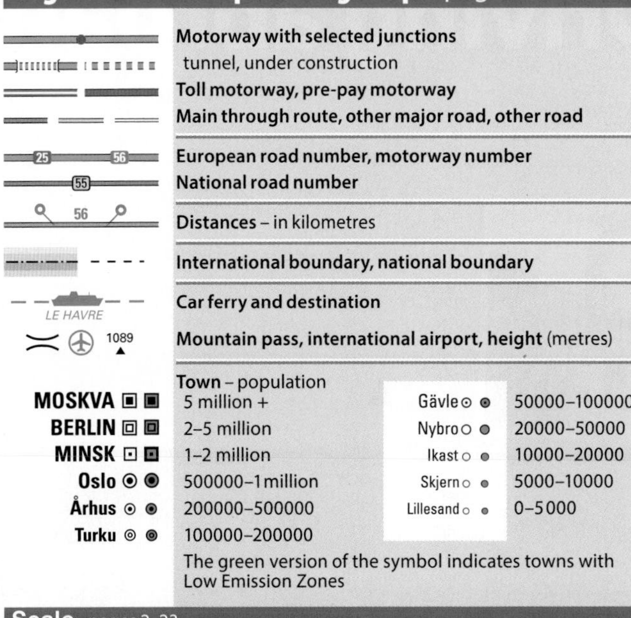

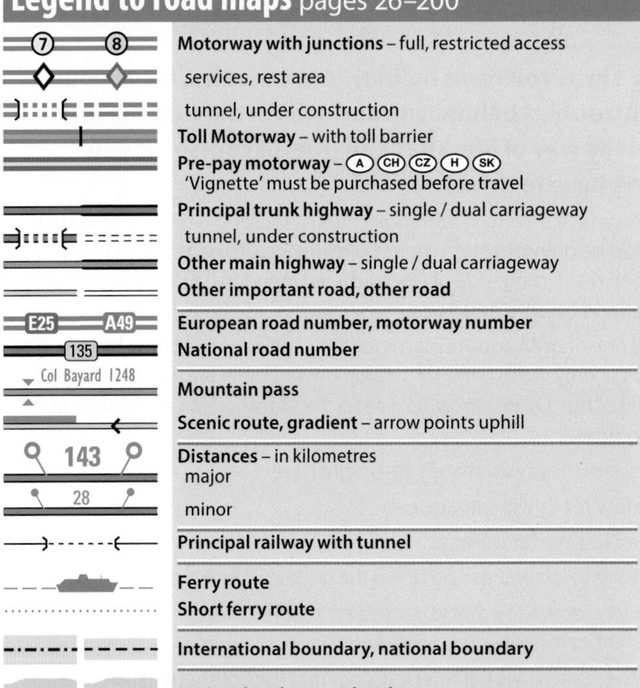

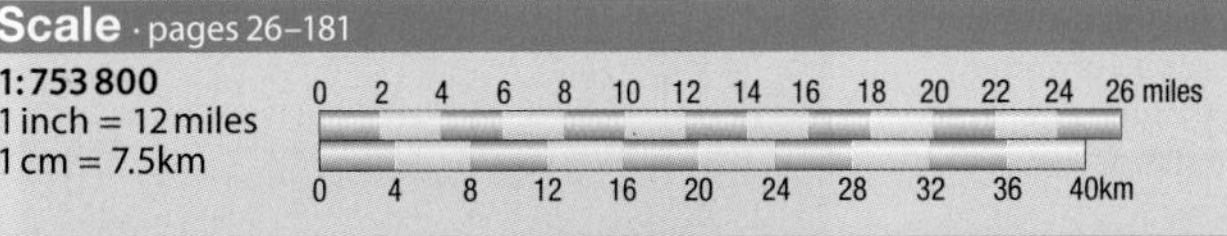

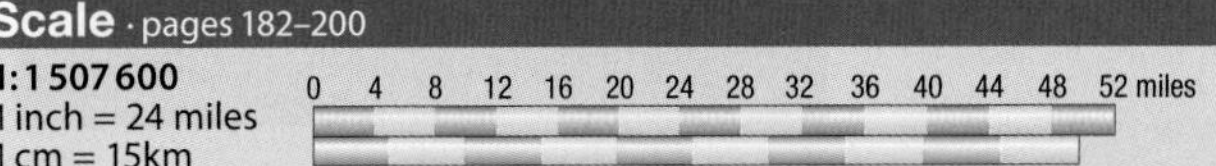

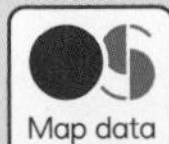

 This product includes mapping data licensed from Ordnance Survey®, with the permission of the Controller of Her Majesty's Stationery Office © Crown copyright 2018. All rights reserved. Licence number 100011710.

 is a registered Trade Mark of the Northern Ireland Department of Finance and Personnel. This product includes mapping data licensed from Ordnance Survey of Northern Ireland®, reproduced with the permission of Land and Property Services under delegated authority from the Controller of Her Majesty's Stationery Office, © Crown Copyright 2018.

All rights reserved. Apart from any fair dealing for the purpose of private study, research, criticism or review, as permitted under the Copyright Designs and Patents Act, 1988, no part of this publication may be reproduced, stored in a retrieval system, or transmitted in any form or by any means, electronic, electrical, chemical, mechanical, optical, photocopying, recording, or otherwise, without prior written permission.

All enquiries should be addressed to the Publisher.

While every reasonable effort has been made to ensure that the information compiled in this atlas is accurate, complete and up-to-date at the time of publication, some of this information is subject to change and the Publisher cannot guarantee its correctness or completeness.

The information in this atlas is provided without any representation or warranty, express or implied and the Publisher cannot be held liable for any loss or damage due to any use or reliance on the information in this atlas, nor for any errors, omissions or subsequent changes in such information.

The representation in this atlas of any road, drive or track is not evidence of the existence of a right of way.

The maps of Ireland on pages 26 to 30 and the urban area map and town plan of Dublin are based upon the Crown Copyright and are reproduced with the permission of Land & Property Services under delegated authority from the Controller of Her Majesty's Stationery Office, © Crown Copyright and database right 2018, PMLPA No 100503, and on Ordnance Survey Ireland by permission of the Government © Ordnance Survey Ireland / Government of Ireland Permit number 9130.

Cartography by Philip's, Copyright © Philip's 2018

*Independent research survey, from research carried out by Outlook Research Limited, 2005/06

Photographic acknowledgements:
Pages II and III: all photographs by Stephen Mesquita

Legend to route planning maps pages 2–23

Motorway with selected junctions, tunnel, under construction
Toll motorway, pre-pay motorway
Main through route, other major road, other road
European road number, motorway number
National road number
Distances – in kilometres
International boundary, national boundary
Car ferry and destination — LE HAVRE
Mountain pass, international airport, height (metres)

Town – population
MOSKVA	5 million +	Gävle	50000–100000
BERLIN	2–5 million	Nybro	20000–50000
MINSK	1–2 million	Ikast	10000–20000
Oslo	500000–1 million	Skjern	5000–10000
Århus	200000–500000	Lillesand	0–5000
Turku	100000–200000		

The green version of the symbol indicates towns with Low Emission Zones

Scale · pages 2–23
1:3 200 000
1 in = 50.51 miles
1 cm = 32km

Legend to road maps pages 26–200

Motorway with junctions – full, restricted access, services, rest area
tunnel, under construction
Toll Motorway – with toll barrier
Pre-pay motorway – A CH CZ H SK 'Vignette' must be purchased before travel
Principal trunk highway – single / dual carriageway
tunnel, under construction
Other main highway – single / dual carriageway
Other important road, other road
European road number, motorway number — E25 A49
National road number — 135
Mountain pass — Col Bayard 1248
Scenic route, gradient – arrow points uphill
Distances – in kilometres, major 143, minor 28
Principal railway with tunnel
Ferry route
Short ferry route
International boundary, national boundary
National park, natural park

Airport	Ski resort
Ancient monument	Theme park
Beach	World Heritage site
Castle or house	Spot height 1754
Cave	Sevilla World Heritage town
Other place of interest	Verona Town of tourist interest
Park or garden	City or town with Low Emission Zone
Religious building	

Scale · pages 26–181
1:753 800
1 inch = 12 miles
1 cm = 7.5km

Scale · pages 182–200
1:1 507 600
1 inch = 24 miles
1 cm = 15km

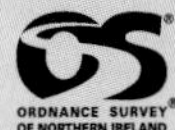

Driving abroad –
a cautionary tale

by Stephen Mesquita,
Philip's On the Road Correspondent

15/06/2016 07:10:39 LS300W   *******

At last, you're on holiday. You can relax, leave your troubles behind you and soak in the sun, the food and the way of life. That's all true, of course – if you don't have to drive.

When you're driving in a strange country, relaxing is the last thing you should be doing. In fact, when you're driving on roads you don't know – and on the 'wrong' side of the road – you need to pay attention at all times and be ultra defensive.

Take one of my favourite places to visit – the very end of the heel of Italy. If you're only used to the UK's roads, driving there is a whole different kettle of fish. Or *'un altro paio di maniche'* (another pair of sleeves), as it should be.

These are the idyllic images you might have :

- Empty roads with great views.
- Timeless pastoral scenes.
- Village locals wandering down the middle of the street.
- Driving down to empty beaches for a swim before breakfast (only if you're really keen).

But the reality's a lot different. It's not that the Southern Italians are any better or worse drivers than we are. But there are different laws, different conventions, different road conditions and different driving styles.

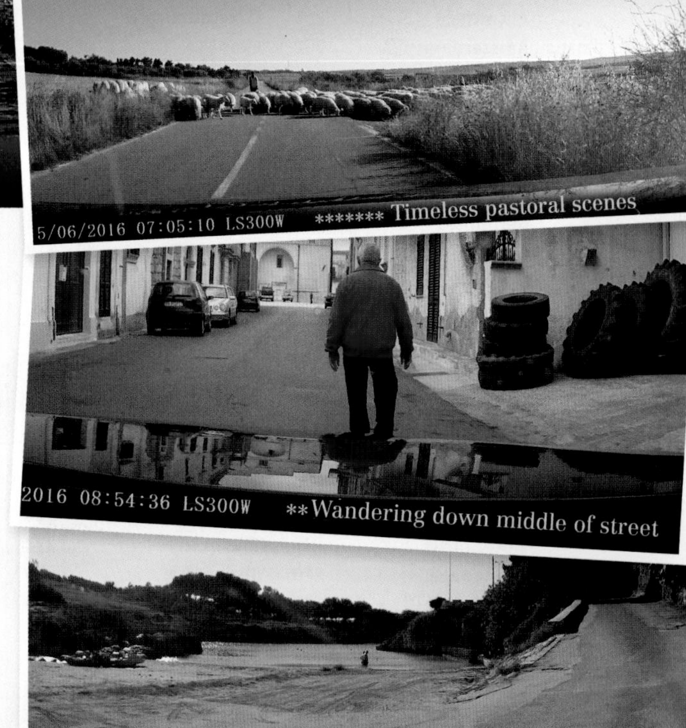

5/06/2016 07:05:10 LS300W   ******* Timeless pastoral scenes

2016 08:54:36 LS300W   ** Wandering down middle of street

15/06/2016 07:01:38 LS300W   *******   Empty beaches

So here is my survival guide. Of course, this is only one small region of Europe. But I'm sure that wherever you're driving, some of this may ring bells – and perhaps even be useful.

Here are my Top 10 Tips from last year's holiday, illustrated with real-time dashcam video...

1 Being overtaken

Overtaking is more of a national sport on the continent than it is in the UK. What's disconcerting is the way that the overtaking car pulls in so sharply after overtaking. It takes a bit of getting used to but it's generally not (quite) as dangerous as it looks.

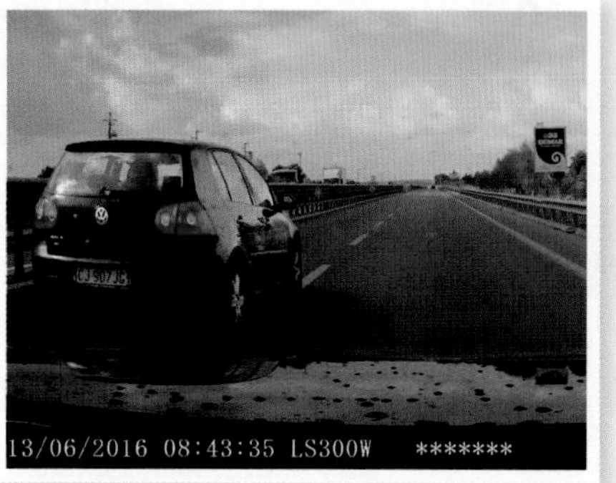

13/06/2016 08:43:35 LS300W   *******

2 Tailgating

It's probably no worse than in the UK; but tailgating can still be intimidating and distracting. If you feel threatened, try to pull off the road if it's safe to do it. Or try my favourite ploy – go round a roundabout twice to escape your tailgater.

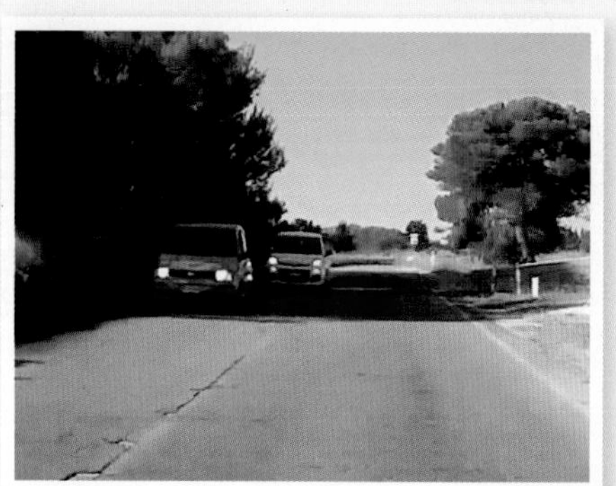

3 Motorway Slip Roads

Beware short slip roads on to motorways. They give merging motorists little chance to join the traffic at anything other than a snail's pace, leading them into narrow lanes of fast traffic. Not for the faint-hearted. Check your mirror as often as you can.

4 Oncoming traffic driving on your side of the road

On narrow country roads, this is a hazard everywhere. It's probably worse in the UK than it is in Southern Italy. But, as the picture shows, it can produce some heart-stopping moments.

5 Pulling out of side roads and hoping

Pulling out of side roads and hoping. A lot of this goes on at crossroads in small towns and villages. Given the configuration of the roads, there's not much you can do about it – except be very cautious, even when it's your right of way or, as here, the traffic lights only work at certain times of day

6 Petrol stations

Many country petrol stations are unmanned. Those that are manned sometimes charge you more for the privilege of having someone serve you. It may be worth it: the unmanned ones are not easy to operate. In a richly comic episode, I had to seek assistance to discover that I had paid for €40 of petrol at a pump some distance from the one at which my car was parked.

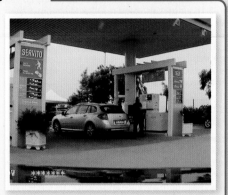

7 Parking Meters

In this region, almost every town has the blue road markings which indicate that, if you want to park here, you'll need to buy a ticket. You'll need coins – many don't accept notes or credit cards. No change is given. If you're lucky, as you put the coins in, the expiry time is shown. If you're unlucky, this panel will be dirty or scratched so that you can't read it. The times you need to pay for vary from town to town, depending on the time of year (always in the tourist season) and the time of day (siesta time is sometimes not charged). A crash course in the language is recommended. In 11 days, I spent over €65 on meters.

8 Sat Nav – beware of speed limits

Even though I'm an atlas publisher, I would strongly recommend you take a sat nav – as well as this atlas, of course. It really reduces the stress of navigating on unfamiliar roads (it's not so good for route planning). But beware if your sat nav tells you the speed limit – those on the screen seem to bear little resemblance to the signs at the side of the road.

9 Speed limits Part 2

Even relying on the roadside signs, it can be hard to work out the speed limits. Can you work out what's happening here (answer at the foot of the page)?

10 Cameras

These pictures cost me €200. They show me at the wheel of my stylish Fiat 500 (that's what the website said anyway) being distracted by two cyclists as they went through a red light. The red light is hidden in the hedge. This deserted spot in the middle of the countryside boasts the only traffic camera ever seen in the region. I stupidly had my eye on the cyclists, not the light. First I received a bill from Hertz for €47.90 – which I innocently thought was for the 'offence'. But no, it was for supplying my name and address (with almost every word misspelt) to the local authority. A year later, a bill arrived from said local authority, for €145 if paid within 5 days (or €220 if not).

And I haven't even got to that most thrilling part of your holiday 'At the Car Hire Desk' (damage waiver rip-off's, not getting the car you ordered, should you photograph the car, and is it worth having another driver), documentation (the code you have to get now from the DVLA if you're hiring a car) and taking a spare pair of glasses. And do watch how much you drink. See the next section for all the rules and regulations for each country, including the alcohol limits. If in doubt, don't drink and drive. Now turn over and read the driving laws of the country you're going to. Buon Viaggio.

Answer to point 9: the speed limit is normally 90kph but it's 50kph when it's foggy or visibility is less than 100m.

Driving regulations

Vehicle A national vehicle identification plate is always required when taking a vehicle abroad. Fitting headlamp converters or beam deflectors when taking a right-hand drive car to a country where driving is on the right (every country in Europe except the UK and Ireland) is compulsory. Within the EU, if not driving a locally hired car, it is compulsory to have either Europlates or a country of origin (e.g. GB) sticker. Outside the EU (and in Andorra) a sticker is compulsory, even with Europlates.

Documentation All countries require that you carry a valid passport, vehicle registration document, hire certificate or letter of authority for the use of someone else's vehicle, full driving licence/International Driving Permit and insurance documentation (and/or green card outside the EU). Some non-EU countries also require a visa. Minimum driving ages are often higher for people holding foreign licences. New exit checks at the Eurotunnel and ferry terminals mean that drivers taking vehicles from the UK should allow extra time. Drivers of vehicles over three years old should ensure that the MOT is up to date, and take the certificate with them.

EHIC cards are free and give you entitlement to healthcare in other EU countries and Switzerland. *www.gov/european-health-insurance-card*

Licence A photo licence is preferred; with an old-style paper licence, an International Driving Permit (IDP) should also be carried. In some countries, an IDP is compulsory, whatever form of licence is held. Non-EU drivers should always have both a licence and and IDP. UK (except NI) drivers should check in advance whether a hire company will wish to check for endorsements and vehicle categories.

If so, visit *www.gov.uk/view-driving-licence* to create a digital code (valid for 72 hours) that allows licence details to be shared. For more information, contact the DVLA (0300790 6802, *www.dft.gov.uk/dvla*)

Insurance Third-party cover is compulsory across Europe. Most insurance policies give only basic cover when driving abroad, so you should check that your policy provides at least third-party cover for the countries in which you will be driving and upgrade it to the level that you require. You may have to take out extra cover at the frontier if you cannot produce acceptable proof of adequate insurance. Even in countries in which a green card is not required, carrying one is recommended for extra proof of insurance.

Motorcycles It is compulsory for all motorcyclists and passengers to wear crash helmets.

Other Minimum age requirements are for foreign drivers. They are not always the same as the age restrictions for nationals. In countries in which visibility vests are compulsory, one for each person should be carried in the passenger compartment, or panniers on a motorbike, where they can be reached easily. Warning triangles should also be carried in the passenger compartment.
• The penalties for infringements of regulations vary considerably from one country to another. In many countries the police may impose on-the-spot fines (ask for a receipt). Penalties can be severe for serious infringements, particularly for exceeding the blood-alcohol limit; in some countries this can result in immediate imprisonment
• In some countries, vignettes for toll roads are being replaced by electronic tags.

Symbols

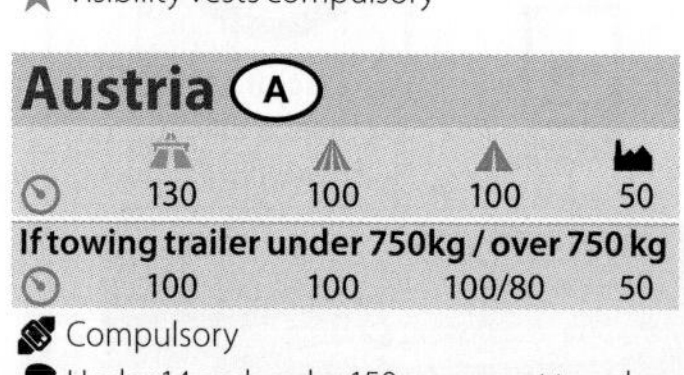

᚛	Motorway
⚠	Dual carriageway
⚠	Single carriageway
🛣	Surfaced road
🛤	Unsurfaced / gravel road
🏙	Urban area
⊘	Speed limit in kilometres per hour (kph)
🔒	Seat belts
👶	Children
🍷	Blood alcohol level
△	Warning triangle
⊞	First aid kit
💡	Spare bulb kit
🧯	Fire extinguisher
⊖	Minimum driving age
📋	Additional documents required
📱	Mobile phones
LEZ	Low Emission Zone
◑ᙆ	Dipped headlights
❄	Winter driving
★	Other information

The publishers have made every effort to ensure that the information given here was correct at the time of going to press. No responsibility can be accepted for any errors or their consequences. Please note that driving regulations may change, and that it has not been possible to cover all the information for every type of vehicle.

Andorra (AND)

⊘	᚛	⚠	⚠	🏙
	n/a	90	60/90	50

🔒 Compulsory

👶 Under 10 and below 150 cm must travel in an EU-approved restraint system adapted to their size in the rear. Airbag must be deactivated if a child is in the front passenger seat.

🍷 0.05% △ Compulsory

⊞ Recommended 💡 Compulsory

🧯 Recommended ⊖ 18

📱 Not permitted whilst driving

◑ᙆ Compulsory for motorcycles during day and for other vehicles during poor daytime visibility.

❄ Winter tyres recommended. Snow chains compulsory in poor conditions or when indicated.

★ On-the-spot fines imposed

★ Visibility vests compulsory

Austria (A)

⊘	᚛	⚠	⚠	🏙
	130	100	100	50

If towing trailer under 750kg / over 750 kg

⊘				
	100	100	100/80	50

🔒 Compulsory

👶 Under 14 and under 150cm cannot travel as a front or rear passenger unless they use a suitable child restraint; under 14 over 150cm must wear adult seat belt

🍷 0.049% • 0.01% if licence held less than 2 years

△ Compulsory

⊞ Compulsory 💡 Recommended

🧯 Recommended

⊖ 18 (20 for motorbikes over 50cc)

📋 Paper driving licences must be accompanied by photographic proof of identity.

📱 Only allowed with hands-free kit

LEZ Several cities and regions have LEZs affecting HGVs that ban non-compliant vehicles, impose speed restrictions and night-time bans.

◑ᙆ Must be used during the day by all road users. Headlamp converters compulsory

❄ Winter tyres compulsory 1 Nov–15 Apr

★ On-the-spot fines imposed

★ Radar detectors and dashcams prohibited

★ To drive on motorways or expressways, a motorway sticker must be purchased at the border or main petrol station. These are available for 10 days, 2 months or 1 year. Vehicles 3.5 tonnes or over must display an electronic tag.

★ Visibility vests compulsory

Belarus (BY)

⊘	᚛	⚠	⚠	🏙
	110	90	90	60*

If towing trailer under 750kg

⊘				
	90	70	70	

*In residential areas limit is 20 km/h • Vehicle towing another vehicle 50 kph limit • If full driving licence held for less than two years, must not exceed 70 kph

🔒 Compulsory in front seats, and rear seats if fitted

👶 Under 12 not allowed in front seat and must use appropriate child restraint

🍷 0.00%

△ Compulsory

⊞ Compulsory

🧯 Recommended

🧯 Compulsory ⊖ 18

📋 Visa, vehicle technical check stamp, international driving permit, green card, health insurance. Even with a green card, local third-party insurance may be imposed at the border

📱 Use prohibited

◑ᙆ Compulsory during the day Nov–Mar and at all other times in conditions of poor visibility or when towing or being towed.

❄ Winter tyres compulsory; snow chains recommended

★ A temporary vehicle import certificate must be purchased on entry and driver must be registered

★ It is illegal for vehicles to be dirty

★ On-the-spot fines imposed

★ Radar-detectors prohibited

★ Road tax imposed at the border

★ To drive on main motorways and on-board unit must be acquired at the border or a petrol station in order to pay tolls. See **http://beltoll.by/index.php/en/**

Belgium (B)

⊘	᚛	⚠	⚠	🏙
	120[1]	120[1]	90[2]	50[3]

If towing trailer

⊘				
	90	90	60	50[3]

Over 3.5 tonnes

⊘				
	90	90	60	50

[1]Minimum speed of 70 kph may be applied in certain conditions on motorways and some dual carriageways. [2]70 kph in Flanders. [3]20 kph in some residential areas, 30 kph near some schools, hospitals and churches.

🔒 Compulsory

👶 All under 18s under 135 cm must wear an appropriate child restraint. Airbags must be deactivated if a rear-facing child seat is used in the front

🍷 0.049% △ Compulsory

⊞ Recommended 💡 Recommended

🧯 Compulsory

🧥 Motorcyclists must wear fully protective clothing

⊖ 18

📱 Only allowed with a hands-free kit

LEZ LEZs in operation in Antwerp, Brussels and areas of Flanders. Preregistration necessary and fees payable for most vehicles.

◑ᙆ Mandatory at all times for motorcycles and advised during the day in poor conditions for other vehicles

★ Cruise control must be deactivated on motorways where indicated

★ On-the-spot fines imposed

★ Radar detectors prohibited

★ Sticker indicating maximum recommended speed for winter tyres must be displayed on dashboard if using them

★ Visibility vest compulsory

Bosnia and Herzegovina (BIH)

⊘	᚛	⚠	⚠	🏙
	130	100	80	50

🔒 Compulsory if fitted

👶 Under 12s must sit in rear using an appropriate child restraint. Under-2s may travel in a rear-facing child seat in the front only if the airbags have been deactivated.

🍷 0.03% △ Compulsory

Bulgaria (BG)

⊘	᚛	⚠	⚠	🏙
	130	90	90	50

If towing trailer

⊘				
	100	70	70	50

🔒 Compulsory in front and rear seats

👶 Under 3s not permitted in vehicles with no child restraints; 3–10 year olds must sit in rear in an appropriate restraint. Rear-facing child seats may be used in the front only if the airbag has been deactivated

🍷 0.049% △ Compulsory

⊞ Compulsory 💡 Recommended

🧯 Compulsory ⊖ 18

📋 Photo driving licence preferred; a paper licence must be accompanied by an International Driving Permit. Green card or insurance specific to Bulgaria.

📱 Only allowed with a hands-free kit

◑ᙆ Compulsory

❄ Winter tyres compulsory. Snow chains should be carried from 1 Nov–1 Mar. Max speed with chains 50 kph

★ Fee at border

★ GPS must have fixed speed camera function deactivated; radar detectors prohibited

★ On-the-spot fines imposed

★ Road tax stickers (annual, monthly or weekly) must be purchased at the border and displayed prominently with the vehicle registration number written on them.

★ Visibility vest compulsory

⊞ Compulsory 💡 Compulsory

🧯 Compulsory for LPG vehicles

⊖ 18

📋 Visa, International Driving Permit, green card

📱 Prohibited

◑ᙆ Compulsory for all vehicles at all times

❄ Winter tyres compulsory 15 Nov–15 Apr; snow chains recommended

★ GPS must have fixed speed camera function deactivated; radar detectors prohibited.

★ On-the-spot fines imposed

★ Visibility vest, tow rope or tow bar compulsory

★ Spare wheel compulsory, except for two-wheeled vehicles

Croatia (HR)

⏱	🚏	⚠	⚠	🏭
⏱	130	110	90	50

Under 24

| ⏱ | 120 | 100 | 80 | 50 |

If towing

| ⏱ | 90 | 90 | 80 | 50 |

- Compulsory if fitted
- Children under 12 not permitted in front seat and must use appropriate child seat or restraint in rear. Children under 2 may use a rear-facing seat in the front only if the airbag is deactivated
- 0.05% · 0.00 % for drivers under 24
- △ Compulsory
- Compulsory 🍷 Compulsory
- Recommended ⊖ 18
- Green card recommended
- Only allowed with hands-free kit
- Compulsory
- Winter tyres, snow chains and shovel compulsory in winter
- ★ On-the-spot fines imposed
- ★ Radar detectors prohibited
- ★ Tow bar and rope compulsory
- ★ Visibility vest compulsory

Czechia (CZ)

⏱	🚏	⚠	⚠	🏭
⏱	130	90	90	50

If towing

| ⏱ | 80 | 80 | 80 | 50 |

- Compulsory in front seats and if fitted in rear
- Children under 36 kg and 150 cm must use appropriate child restraint. Only front-facing child retraints are permitted in the front in vehicles with airbags fitted. Airbags must be deactivated if a rear-facing child seat is used in the front.
- 0.00% △ Compulsory
- Compulsory 🍷 Compulsory
- Compulsory
- ⊖ 18 (17 for motorcycles under 125 cc)
- Only allowed with a hands-free kit
- LEZ Two-stage LEZ in Prague for vehicles over 3.5 and 6 tonnes. Permit system.
- Compulsory at all times
- Winter tyres compulsory November-March, roads are icy/snow-covered or snow is expected. Max speed 50 kph.
- ★ GPS must have fixed speed camera function deactivated; radar detectors prohibited
- ★ On-the-spot fines imposed
- ★ Replacement fuses must be carried
- ★ Spectacles or contact lens wearers must carry a spare pair in their vehicle at all times
- ★ Vignette needed for motorway driving, available for 1 year, 60 days, 15 days. Toll specific to lorries introduced 2006, those over 12 tonnes must buy an electronic tag
- ★ Visibility vest compulsory

Denmark (DK)

⏱	🚏	⚠	⚠	🏭
⏱	110-130	80-90	80	50*

If towing

| ⏱ | 80 | 70 | 70 | 50* |

*Central Copenhagen 40 kph

- Compulsory front and rear
- Under 135cm must use appropriate child restraint; in front permitted only in an appropriate rear-facing seat with any airbags disabled.
- 0.05% △ Compulsory
- Recommended 🍷 Recommended
- Recommended ⊖ 17
- Only allowed with a hands-free kit
- LEZ Aalborg, Arhus, Copenhagen, Frederiksberg and Odense. Proofs of emissions compliance or compliant filter needed to obtain sticker. Non-compliant vehicles banned.
- Must be used at all times
- Spiked tyres may be fitted 1 Nov–15 April, if used on all wheels
- ★ On-the-spot fines imposed
- ★ Radar detectors prohibited

- ★ Tolls apply on the Storebaeltsbroen and Oresundsbron bridges.
- ★ Visibility vest recommended

Estonia (EST)

⏱	🚏	⚠	⚠	🏭
⏱	n/a	90*	90	50

If full driving licence held for less than two years

| ⏱ | 90 | 90 | 90 | 50 |

*In summer, the speed limit on some dual carriageways may be raised to 100/110 kph

- Compulsory if fitted
- Children too small for adult seatbelts must wear a seat restraint appropriate to their size. Rear-facing safety seats must not be used in the front if an air bag is fitted, unless this has been deactivated.
- 0.00% △ 2 compulsory
- Compulsory 🍷 Recommended
- Compulsory ⊖ 18
- Only allowed with a hands-free kit
- Compulsory at all times
- Winter tyres are compulsory from Dec–Mar. Studded winter tyres are allowed from 15 Oct–31 Mar, but this can be extended to start 1 October and/or end 30 April
- ★ A toll system is in operation in Tallinn
- ★ On-the-spot fines imposed
- ★ Two wheel chocks compulsory
- ★ Visibility vest compulsory

Finland (FIN)

⏱	🚏	⚠	⚠	🏭
⏱	100/120*	80/100*	80/100*	20/50

Vans, lorries and if towing

| ⏱ | 80 | 80 | 60 | 20/50 |

*Winter/summer. Speed limits are often lowered in winter • If towing a vehicle by rope, cable or rod, max speed limit 60 kph • Maximum of 80 kph for vans and lorries •

- Compulsory in front and rear
- Below 135 cm must use a child restraint or seat
- 0.05% △ Compulsory
- Recommended 🍷 Recommended
- Recommended
- ⊖ 18 (motorbikes below 125cc 16)
- Only allowed with a hands-free kit
- Must be used at all times
- Winter tyres compulsory Dec–Feb
- ★ On-the-spot fines imposed
- ★ Radar-detectors are prohibited
- ★ Visibility vest compulsory

France (F)

⏱	🚏	⚠	⚠	🏭
⏱	130	110	90	50

On wet roads or if full driving licence held for less than 3 years

| ⏱ | 110 | 100 | 80 | 50 |

If towing below / above 3.5 tonnes gross

| ⏱ | 110/90 | 100/90 | 90/80 | 50 |

50kph on all roads if fog reduces visibility to less than 50m • Licence will be lost and driver fined for exceeding speed limit by over 50kph

- Compulsory in front seats and if fitted in rear
- In rear, 4 or under must have a child safety seat (rear facing if up to 9 months); if 5–10 must use an appropriate restraint system. Under 10 permitted in the front only if rear seats are fully occupied by other under 10s or there are no rear safety belts. In front, if child is in rear-facing child seat, any airbag must be deactivated.
- 0.049% · If towing or with less than 2 years with full driving licence, 0.00% • All drivers/motorcyclists must carry an unused breathalyser to French certification standards, showing an NF number.
- △ Compulsory
- Recommended 🍷 Recommended
- ⊖ 18 (16 for motorbikes up to 80cc)
- Use not permitted whilst driving
- LEZ An LEZ operates in the Mont Blanc tunnel and such zones are being progressively

introduced across French cities. Non-compliant vehicles are banned during operating hours.
See http://certificat-air.gouv.fr

- Compulsory in poor daytime visibility and at all times for motorcycles
- Winter tyres recommended. Carrying snow chains recommended in winter as these may have to be fitted if driving on snow-covered roads, in accordance with signage.
- ★ GPS must have fixed speed camera function deactivated; radar-detection equipment is prohibited
- ★ It is compulsory to carry a French-authority-recognised (NF) breathalyser.
- ★ Motorcyclists and passengers must have four reflective stickers on their helmets (front, back and both sides) and wear CE-certified gloves.
- ★ On-the-spot fines imposed
- ★ Tolls on motorways. Electronic tag needed if using automatic tolls.
- ★ Visibility vests, to be worn on the roadside in case of emergency or breakdown, must be carried for all vehicle occupants and riders.
- ★ Wearers of contact lenses or spectacles or lenses should carry a spare pair

Germany (D)

⏱	🚏	⚠	⚠	🏭
⏱	*	*	100	50

If towing

| ⏱ | 80 | 80 | 80 | 50 |

*no limit, 130 kph recommended

- Compulsory
- Aged 3-12 and under 150cm must use an appropriate child seat or restraint and sit in the rear. In the front, if child under 3 is in a rear-facing seat, airbags must be deactivated
- 0.049% · 0.0% for drivers 21 or under or with less than two years full licence
- △ Compulsory
- Compulsory 🍷 Recommended
- Recommended
- ⊖ 18 (motorbikes: 16 if under 50cc)
- Use permitted only with hands-free kit – also applies to drivers of motorbikes and bicycles
- LEZ More than 60 cities have or are planning LEZs. Proof of compliance needed to acquire sticker. Non-compliant vehicles banned.
- Compulsory during poor daytime visibility and tunnels; recommended at other times. Compulsory at all times for motorcyclists.
- Winter tyres compulsory in all winter weather conditions; snow chains recommended
- ★ GPS must have fixed speed camera function deactivated; radar detectors prohibited
- ★ On-the-spot fines imposed
- ★ Tolls on autobahns for lorries
- ★ Visibility vest compulsory

Greece (GR)

⏱	🚏	⚠	⚠	🏭
⏱	130	110	90	50

Motorbikes, and if towing

| ⏱ | 90 | 70 | 70 | 40 |

- Compulsory in front seats and if fitted in rear
- Under 12 or below 135cm must use appropriate child restraint. In front if child is in rear-facing child seat, any airbags must be deactivated.
- 0.05% · 0.00% for drivers with less than 2 years' full licence and motorcyclists
- △ Compulsory
- Compulsory 🍷 Recommended
- Compulsory ⊖ 17
- Not permitted.
- Compulsory during poor daytime visibility and at all times for motorcycles
- Snow chains permitted on ice- or snow-covered roads. Max speed 50 kph.
- ★ On-the-spot fines imposed
- ★ Radar-detection equipment is prohibited
- ★ Tolls on several newer motorways.

Hungary (H)

⏱	🚏	⚠	⚠	🏭
⏱	130	110	90	50*

If towing

| ⏱ | 80 | 70 | 70 | 50* |

*30 kph zones have been introduced in many cities

- Compulsory
- Under 135cm and over 3 must be seated in rear and use appropriate child restraint. Under 3 allowed in front only in rear-facing child seat with any airbags deactivated.
- 0.00% △ Compulsory
- Compulsory 🍷 Compulsory
- Recommended ⊖ 17
- Only allowed with a hands-free kit
- LEZ Budapest has vehicle restrictions on days with heavy dust and is planning an LEZ.
- Compulsory during the day outside built-up areas; compulsory at all times for motorcycles
- Snow chains compulsory where conditions dictate. Max speed 50 kph.
- Many motorways are toll and operate electronic vignette system with automatic number plate recognition, tickets are available for 10 days, 1 month, 13 months
- ★ On-the-spot fines issued
- ★ Radar detectors prohibited
- ★ Tow rope recommended
- ★ Visibility vest compulsory

Iceland (IS)

⏱	🚏	🚗	🚙	🏭
⏱	n/a	90	80	50

- Compulsory in front and rear seats
- Under 12 or below 150cm not allowed in front seat and must use appropriate child restraint.
- 0.05% △ Compulsory
- Compulsory 🍷 Compulsory
- Compulsory
- ⊖ 17; 21 to drive a hire car; 25 to hire a 4WD
- Only allowed with a hands-free kit
- Compulsory at all times
- Winter tyres compulsory c.1 Nov–14 Apr (variable)
- ★ Driving off marked roads is forbidden
- ★ Highland roads are not suitable for ordinary cars
- ★ On-the-spot fines imposed

Ireland (IRL)

⏱	🚏	⚠	⚠	🏭
⏱	120	60–100	60–100	50*

If towing

| ⏱ | 80 | 60 | 60 | 50* |

*Dublin and some other areas have introduced 30 kph zones

- Compulsory where fitted. Driver responsible for ensuring passengers under 17 comply
- Children 3 and under must be in a suitable child restraint system. Airbags must be deactivated if a rear-facing child seat is used in the front. Those under 150 cm and 36 kg must use appropriate child restraint.
- 0.05% · 0.02% for novice and professional drivers
- △ Compulsory Recommended
- 🍷 Recommended Recommended
- ⊖ 17 (16 for motorbikes up to 125cc; 18 for over 125cc; 18 for lorries; 21 bus/minibus)
- Only allowed with a hands-free kit
- Compulsory for motorbikes at all times and in poor visibility for other vehicles
- ★ Driving is on the left
- ★ GPS must have fixed speed camera function deactivated; radar detectors prohibited
- ★ On-the-spot fines imposed
- ★ Tolls are being introduced on some motorways; the M50 Dublin has barrier-free tolling with number-plate recognition.

Italy (I)

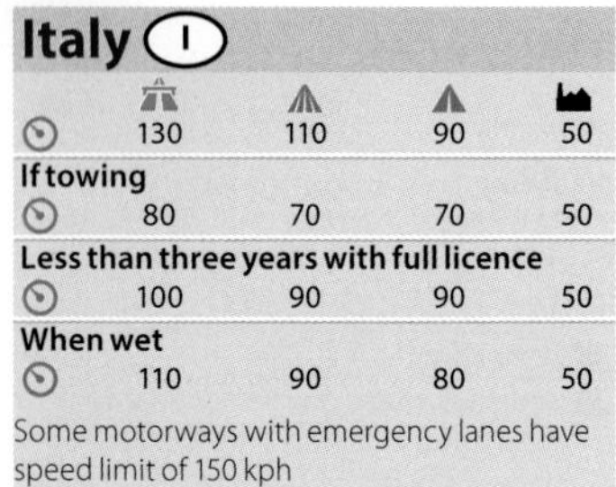

🚗 130	⚠ 110	⚠ 90	🏭 50

If towing

| 80 | 70 | 70 | 50 |

Less than three years with full licence

| 100 | 90 | 90 | 50 |

When wet

| 110 | 90 | 80 | 50 |

Some motorways with emergency lanes have speed limit of 150 kph

- Compulsory in front seats and, if fitted, in rear
- Under 12 not allowed in front seats except in child safety seat; children under 3 must have special seat in the back. For foreign-registered cars, the country of origin's legislation applies.
- 0.05% · 0.00% for professional drivers or with less than 3 years full licence
- △ Compulsory ⬜ Recommended
- Compulsory Recommended
- 18 (14 for mopeds, 16 up to 125cc, 20 up to 350cc)
- 📱 Only allowed with hands-free kit
- LEZ Most northern and several southern regions operate seasonal LEZs and many towns and cities have various schemes that restrict access. There is an LEZ in the Mont Blanc tunnel
- Compulsory outside built-up areas, in tunnels, on motorways and dual carriageways and in poor visibility; compulsory at all times for motorcycles
- Snow chains compulsory where signs indicate 15 Oct–15 Apr. Max speed 50 kph
- ★ On-the-spot fines imposed
- ★ Radar-detection equipment is prohibited
- ★ Tolls on motorways. Blue lanes accept credit cards; yellow lanes restricted to holders of Telepass pay-toll device.
- ★ Visibility vest compulsory

Kosovo (RKS)

🚗 130	⚠ 80	⚠ 80	🏭 50

- Compulsory
- Under 12 must sit in rear seats in an appropriate restraint.
- 0.00% △ Compulsory ⬜ Compulsory
- Compulsory Compulsory
- 18 (16 for motorbikes less than 125 cc, 14 for mopeds)
- International driving permit, locally purchased third-party insurance (green card is not recognised), documents with proof of ability to cover costs and valid reason for visiting. Visitors from many non-EU countries require a visa.
- 📱 Only allowed with hands-free kit
- Compulsory at all times
- Winter tyres or snow chains compulsory in poor winter weather conditions

Latvia (LV)

🚗 n/a	⚠ 100	⚠ 90	🏭 50

If towing

| n/a | 80 | 80 | 50 |

In residential areas limit is 20kph · If full driving licence held for less than two years, must not exceed 80 kph

- Compulsory in front seats and if fitted in rear
- If under 12 years and 150cm must use child restraint in front and rear seats
- 0.05% · 0.02% if less than 2 years experience
- △ Compulsory
- ⬜ Compulsory Recommended
- Compulsory 18
- 📱 Only allowed with hands-free kit
- Must be used at all times all year round
- Winter tyres compulsory for vehicles up to 3.5 tonnes Dec–Feb, but illegal May–Sept
- ★ On-the-spot fines imposed
- ★ Pedestrians have priority
- ★ Radar-detection equipment prohibited
- ★ Visibility vests compulsory

Lithuania (LT)

🚗 130	⚠ 110	⚠ 70–90	🏭 50

If towing

| n/a | 70 | 70 | 50 |

If licence held for less than two years

| 130 | 90 | 70 | 50 |

In winter speed limits are reduced by 10–20 kph

- Compulsory
- Under 12 or below 135 cm not allowed in front seats unless in a child safety seat; under 3 must use appropriate child seat and sit in rear
- 0.04% · 0.00% if full licence held less than 2 years
- △ Compulsory ⬜ Compulsory
- Recommended Compulsory 18
- Licences without a photograph must be accompanied by photographic proof of identity, e.g. a passport
- 📱 Only allowed with a hands-free kit
- Must be used at all times
- Winter tyres compulsory 10 Nov–1 Apr
- ★ On-the-spot fines imposed
- ★ Visibility vest compulsory

Luxembourg (L)

🚗 130/110	⚠ 90	⚠ 90	🏭 50*

If towing

| 90 | 75 | 75 | 50* |

If full driving licence held for less than two years, must not exceed 75 kph · *30 kph zones are progressively being introduced.

- Compulsory
- Children under 3 must use an appropriate restraint system. Airbags must be disabled if a rear-facing child seat is used in the front. Children 3–18 and/or under 150 cm must use a restraint system appropriate to their size. If over 36kg a seatbelt may be used in the back only
- 0.05%, 0.02 for young drivers, drivers with less than 2 years experience and drivers of taxis and commercial vehicles
- △ Compulsory ⬜ Compulsory (buses)
- Compulsory 18
- Compulsory (buses, transport of dangerous goods)
- 📱 Use permitted only with hands-free kit
- Compulsory for motorcyclists and in poor visibility for other vehicles
- Winter tyres compulsory in winter weather
- ★ On-the-spot fines imposed
- ★ Visibility vest compulsory

Macedonia (MK)

🚗 120	⚠ 100	⚠ 80	🏭 50

Newly qualified drivers or if towing

| 100 | 80 | 60 | 50 |

- Compulsory
- Under 12 not allowed in front seats
- 0.05% · 0.00% for business, commercial and professional drivers and with less than 2 years experience
- △ Compulsory ⬜ Compulsory
- Compulsory 18 (mopeds 16)
- Recommended; compulsory for LPG vehicles
- International driving permit; visa
- 📱 Use not permitted whilst driving
- Compulsory at all times
- Winter tyres or snow chains compulsory 15 Nov–15 Mar. Max speed 70 kph
- ★ GPS must have fixed speed camera function deactivated; radar detectors prohibited
- ★ Novice drivers may only drive between 11pm and 5am if there is someone over 25 with a valid licence in the vehicle.
- ★ On-the-spot fines imposed
- ★ Tolls apply on many roads
- ★ Tow rope compulsory
- ★ Visibility vest must be kept in the passenger compartment and worn to leave the vehicle in the dark outside built-up areas

Moldova (MD)

🚗 90	⚠ 90	⚠ 90	🏭 60

If towing or if licence held under 1 year

| 70 | 70 | 70 | 50 |

- Compulsory in front seats and if fitted in rear
- Under 12 not allowed in front seats
- 0.00% △ Compulsory ⬜ Compulsory
- Recommended Compulsory
- 18 (mopeds and motorbikes, 16; vehicles with more than eight passenger places, taxis or towing heavy vehicles, 21)
- International Driving Permit (preferred), visa
- 📱 Only allowed with hands-free kit
- Must use dipped headlights at all times
- Winter tyres recommended Nov–Feb

Montenegro (MNE)

🚗 n/a	⚠ 100	⚠ 80	🏭 50

80kph speed limit if towing a caravan

- Compulsory in front and rear seats
- Under 12 not allowed in front seats. Under-5s must use an appropriate child seat.
- 0.03 % △ Compulsory
- ⬜ Compulsory Compulsory
- Compulsory
- 18 (16 for motorbikes less than 125cc; 14 for mopeds)
- Prohibited
- Must be used at all times
- From mid-Nov to March, driving wheels must be fitted with winter tyres
- ★ An 'eco' tax vignette must be obtained when crossing the border and displayed in the upper right-hand corner of the windscreen
- ★ On-the-spot fines imposed
- ★ Tolls on some primary roads and in the Sozina tunnel between Lake Skadar and the sea
- ★ Visibility vest compulsory

Netherlands (NL)

🚗 130	⚠ 80/100	⚠ 80/100	🏭 50

- Compulsory
- Under 3 must travel in the back, using an appropriate child restraint; 3–18 and under 135cm must use an appropriate child restraint. A rear-facing child seat may be used in front only if airbags are deactivated.
- 0.05% · 0.02% with less than 5 years experience or moped riders under 24
- △ Compulsory
- Recommended Recommended
- Recommended 18
- 📱 Only allowed with hands-free kit
- LEZ About 20 cities operate or are planning LEZs.
- Recommended in poor visibility and on open roads. Compulsory for motorcycles.
- ★ On-the-spot fines imposed
- ★ Radar-detection equipment is prohibited

Norway (N)

🚗 90–100	⚠ 80	⚠ 80	🏭 30/50

If towing trailer with brakes

| 80 | 80 | 80 | 50 |

If towing trailer without brakes

| 60 | 60 | 60 | 50 |

- Compulsory in front seats and if fitted in rear
- Children less than 150cm tall must use appropriate child restraint. Children under 4 must use child safety seat or safety restraint (cot). A rear-facing child seat may be used in front only if airbags are deactivated.
- 0.01% △ Compulsory
- ⬜ Recommended Recommended
- Recommended
- 18 (heavy vehicles 18/21)
- 📱 Only allowed with a hands-free kit
- LEZ Oslo and Bergen (administered through national road-toll scheme), with plans for other cities

- Must be used at all times
- Winter tyres or summer tyres with snow chains compulsory for snow- or ice-covered roads
- ★ On-the-spot fines imposed
- ★ Radar-detectors are prohibited
- ★ Tolls apply on some bridges, tunnels and access roads into Bergen, Oslo, Trondheim and Stavangar. Several use electronic fee collection only.
- ★ Visibility vest compulsory

Poland (PL)

Motor-vehicle only roads[1], under/over 3.5 tonnes

🚗 130[2]/80[2]	⚠ 110/80	⚠ 100/80	🏭 n/a

Motor-vehicle only roads[1] if towing

| n/a | 80 | 80 | n/a |

Other roads, under 3.5 tonnes

| n/a | 100 | 90 | 50/60[3] |

Other roads, 3.5 tonnes or over

| n/a | 80 | 70 | 50/60[3] |

Other roads, if towing

| n/a | 60 | 60 | 30 |

[1]Indicated by signs with white car on blue background · [2]Minimum speed 40 kph · [3]50 kph 05.00–23.00; 60 kph 23.00–05.00; 20 kph in marked residential areas

- Compulsory in front seats and, if fitted, in rear
- Under 12 and below 150 cm must use an appropriate child restraint. Rear-facing child seats not permitted in vehicles with airbags.
- 0.02% △ Compulsory
- ⬜ Recommended Recommended
- Compulsory
- 18 (mopeds and motorbikes under 125cc – 16)
- 📱 Only allowed with a hands-free kit
- Compulsory for all vehicles
- Snow chains permitted only on roads completely covered in snow
- ★ On-the-spot fines imposed
- ★ Radar-detection equipment is prohibited
- ★ Vehicles over 3.5 tonnes (including cars towing caravans) must have a VIAbox for the electronic toll system
- ★ Visibility vests compulsory

Portugal (P)

🚗 120*	⚠ 90/100	⚠ 90	🏭 50/20

If towing

| 100* | 90 | 80 | 50 |

*50kph minimum; 90kph maximum if licence held under 1 year

- Compulsory in front seats and, if fitted, in rear
- Under 12 and below 135cm must travel in the rear in an appropriate child restraint; rear-facing child seats permitted in front for under 3s only if airbags deactivated
- 0.049% · 0.019% if full licence held less than 3 years
- △ Compulsory
- ⬜ Recommended Recommended
- Recommended 17
- MOT certificate for vehicles over 3 years old, photographic proof of identity must be carried at all times.
- 📱 Only allowed with hands-free kit
- LEZ An LEZ prohibits vehicles without catalytic converters from certain parts of Lisbon. There are plans to extend the scheme city-wide
- Compulsory for motorcycles, compulsory for other vehicles in poor visibility and tunnels
- ★ On-the-spot fines imposed
- ★ Radar detectors and dash-cams prohibited
- ★ Tolls on motorways; do not use green lanes, these are reserved for auto-payment users. Some motorways require an automatic toll device.
- ★ Visibility vest compulsory
- ★ Wearers of spectacles or contact lenses should carry a spare pair

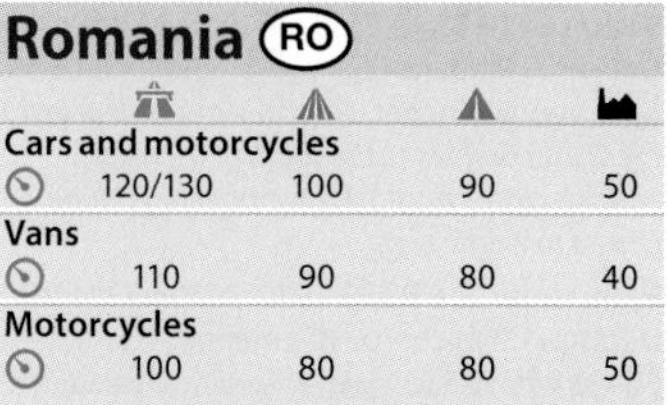

Romania (RO)

Cars and motorcycles			
120/130	100	90	50
Vans			
110	90	80	40
Motorcycles			
100	80	80	50

For motor vehicles with trailers or if full driving licence has been held for less than one year, speed limits are 20kph lower than those listed above • Jeep-like vehicles: 70kph outside built-up areas but 60kph in all areas if diesel. For mopeds, the speed limit is 45 kph.

- Compulsory
- Under 12s not allowed in front and must use an appropriate restraint in the rear
- 0.00% △ Compulsory
- Compulsory Compulsory
- Compulsory ⊖ 18
- Only allowed with hands-free kit
- Compulsory outside built-up areas; compulsory everywhere for motorcycles
- Winter tyres compulsory Nov–Mar if roads are snow- or ice-covered, especially in mountainous areas
- ★ Compulsory road tax can be paid for at the border, post offices and some petrol stations. Price depends on emissions category and length of stay
- ★ It is illegal for vehicles to be dirty
- ★ On-the-spot fines imposed
- ★ Visibility vest compulsory

Russia (RUS)

110	90	90	60/20
If licence held for under 2 years			
70	70	70	60/20

- Compulsory if fitted
- Under 12s permitted only in an appropriate child restraint
- 0.03 % △ Compulsory
- Compulsory Compulsory
- Compulsory ⊖ 17
- International Driving Permit with Russian translation, visa, green card endorsed for Russia, International Certificate for Motor Vehicles
- Only allowed with a hands-free kit
- Compulsory during the day
- Winter tyres compulsory 1 Dec–1 Mar
- ★ On-the-spot fines imposed
- ★ Picking up hitchhikers is prohibited
- ★ Radar detectors/blockers prohibited
- ★ Road tax payable at the border

Serbia (SRB)

			*
120	100	80	60
If towing			
80	80	80	60

Novice drivers limited to 90% of speed limit and not permitted to drive 11pm–5am.

- Compulsory in front and rear seats
- Age 3–12 must be in rear seats and wear seat belt or appropriate child restraint; under 3 in rear-facing child seat permitted in front only if airbag deactivated
- 0.029% • 0.0% for commercial drivers, motorcyclists, or if full licence held less than 1 year
- △ Compulsory Compulsory
- Compulsory Compulsory
- ⊖ 18 (16 for motorbikes less than 125cc; 14 for mopeds)
- International Driving Permit, green card or locally bought third-party insurance
- Compulsory
- Winter tyres compulsory Nov–Apr for vehicles up to 3.5 tonnes. Carrying snow chains recommended in winter as these may have to be fitted if driving on snow-covered roads, in accordance with signage.
- ★ 3-metre tow bar or rope
- ★ Spare wheel compulsory
- ★ On-the-spot fines imposed

- ★ Radar detectors prohibited
- ★ Tolls on motorways and some primary roads
- ★ Visibility vest compulsory

Slovakia (SK)

130/90	90	90	50

- Compulsory
- Under 12 or below 150cm must be in rear in appropriate child restraint
- 0.0% △ Compulsory Compulsory
- Compulsory Recommended
- ⊖ 18, 17 for motorbikes over 50cc, 15 for mopeds
- International driving permit, proof of health insurance
- Only allowed with a hands-free kit
- Compulsory at all times
- Winter tyres compulsory
- ★ On-the-spot fines imposed
- ★ Radar-detection equipment is prohibited
- ★ Tow rope recommended
- ★ Vignette required for motorways, car valid for 1 year, 30 days, 7 days; lorry vignettes carry a higher charge.
- ★ Visibility vests compulsory

Slovenia (SLO)

130	110¹	90¹	50²
If towing			
80	80¹	80¹	50²

¹ 70 kph in urban areas, ² 30 kph zones are increasingly common in cities

- Compulsory
- Below 150cm must use appropriate child restraint. A rear-facing baby seat may be used in front only if airbags are deactivated.
- 0.05% • 0.0% for commercial drivers, under 21s or with less than one year with a full licence
- △ Compulsory Compulsory
- Compulsory Recommended
- ⊖ 18 (motorbikes up to 125cc – 16, up to 350cc – 18)
- Licences without photographs must be accompanied by an International Driving Permit
- Only allowed with hands-free kit
- Must be used at all times
- Snow chains or winter tyres compulsory mid-Nov to mid-March, and in wintery conditions at other times. Max speed 50 kph. This limit also applies if visibility is below 50m.
- ★ On-the-spot fines imposed
- ★ Radar detectors prohibited
- ★ Vignettes valid for variety of periods compulsory for vehicles below 3.5 tonnes for toll roads. Write your vehicle registration number on the vignette before displaying it. For heavier vehicles electronic tolling system applies; several routes are cargo-traffic free during high tourist season.
- ★ Visibility vest compulsory

Spain (E)

120*	100*	90	50*
If towing			
80	80	70	50*

*Urban motorways and dual carriageways 80 kph. 20 kph zones are being introduced in many cities

- Compulsory
- Under 135cm and below 12 must use appropriate child restraint
- 0.049% • 0.029% if less than 2 years full licence or if vehicle is over 3.5 tonnes or carries more than 9 passengers
- △ Two compulsory (one for in front, one for behind)
- Recommended Compulsory
- Recommended ⊖ 18 (21 for heavy vehicles; 16 for motorbikes up to 125cc)
- Hands-free only

- Compulsory for motorcycles and in poor daytime visibility for other vehicles.
- Snow chains recommended for mountainous areas in winter
- ★ Drivers who wear spectacles or contact lenses must carry a spare pair.
- ★ On-the-spot fines imposed
- ★ Radar-detection equipment is prohibited
- ★ Spare wheel compulsory
- ★ Tolls on motorways
- ★ Visibility vest compulsory

Sweden (S)

90–120	80	70–100	30–60
If towing trailer with brakes			
80	80	70	50

- Compulsory in front and rear seats
- Under 15 or below 135cm must use an appropriate child restraint and may sit in the front only if airbag is deactivated; rear-facing baby seat permitted in front only if airbag deactivated.
- 0.019% △ Compulsory
- Recommended Recommended
- Recommended ⊖ 18
- Licences without a photograph must be accompanied by photographic proof of identity, e.g. a passport
- **LEZ** Gothenberg, Helsingborg, Lund, Malmo, Mölndal and Stockholm have LEZs, progressively prohibiting older vehicles.
- Must be used at all times
- 1 Dec–31 Mar winter tyres, anti-freeze, screenwash additive and shovel compulsory
- ★ On-the-spot fines imposed
- ★ Radar-detection equipment is prohibited

Switzerland (CH)

120	80	80	30/50
If towing up to 1 tonne / over 1 tonne			
80	80	60/80	30/50

- Compulsory
- Up to 12 years or below 150 cm must use an appropriate child restraint. Children 6 and under must sit in the rear.
- 0.05%, but 0.0% for commercial drivers or with less than three years with a full licence
- △ Compulsory Recommended
- Recommended Recommended
- ⊖ 18 (mopeds up to 50cc – 16)
- Only allowed with a hands-free kit
- Compulsory
- Winter tyres recommended Nov–Mar; snow chains compulsory in designated areas in poor winter weather
- ★ GPS must have fixed speed camera function deactivated; radar detectors prohibited
- ★ Motorways are all toll and for vehicles below 3.5 tonnes a vignette must be purchased at the border. The vignette is valid for one calendar year. Vehicles over 3.5 tonnes must have an electronic tag for travel on any road.
- ★ On-the-spot fines imposed
- ★ Pedestrians have right of way
- ★ Picking up hitchhikers is prohibited on motorways and main roads
- ★ Spectacles or contact lens wearers must carry a spare pair in their vehicle at all times

Turkey (TR)

120	90	90	50
If towing			
80	80	80	40
Motorbikes			
80	70	70	50

- Compulsory if fitted
- Under 150 cm and below 36kg must use suitable child restraint. Under 3s can only travel in the front in a rear facing seat if the airbag is deactivated. Children 3–12 may not travel in the front seat.
- 0.00%
- △ Two compulsory (one in front, one behind)

- Compulsory
- Compulsory
- Compulsory
- ⊖ 18
- International driving permit advised, and required for use with licences without photographs; note that Turkey is in both Europe and Asia, green card/UK insurance that covers whole of Turkey or locally bought insurance, e-visa obtained in advance.
- Prohibited
- Compulsory in daylight hours
- ★ Spare wheel compulsory
- ★ On-the-spot fines imposed
- ★ Several motorways, and the Bosphorus bridges are toll roads
- ★ Tow rope and tool kit must be carried

Ukraine (UA)

130	110	90	60
If towing			
80	80	80	60

If driving licence held less than 2 years, must not exceed 70 kph

- Compulsory in front and rear seats
- Under 12 and below 145cm must use an appropriate child restraint and sit in rear
- 0.02% – if use of medication can be proved. Otherwise 0.00%
- △ Compulsory
- Compulsory
- Optional
- Compulsory
- ⊖ 18
- International Driving Permit, visa, International Certificate for Motor Vehicles, green card
- No legislation
- Compulsory in poor daytime and from Oct–Apr
- Winter tyres compulsory Nov–Apr in snowy conditions
- ★ A road tax is payable on entry to the country.
- ★ On-the-spot fines imposed
- ★ Tow rope and tool kit recommended

United Kingdom (GB)

112	112	96	48
If towing			
96	96	80	48

Several cities have introduced 32 kph (20 mph) zones away from main roads

- Compulsory in front seats and if fitted in rear seats
- Under 3 not allowed in front seats except with appropriate restraint, and in rear must use child restraint if available; in front 3–12 or under 135cm must use appropriate child restraint, in rear must use appropriate child restraint (or seat belt if no child restraint is available, e.g. because two occupied restraints prevent fitting of a third).
- 0.08% (England, Northern Ireland, Wales) • 0.05% (Scotland)
- △ Recommended
- Recommended
- Recommended
- Recommended
- ⊖ 17 (16 for mopeds)
- Only allowed with hands-free kit
- **LEZ** London's LEZ operates by number-plate recognition; non-compliant vehicles face hefty daily charges. Foreign-registered vehicles must register.
- ★ Driving is on the left
- ★ On-the-spot fines imposed
- ★ Smoking is banned in all commercial vehicles
- ★ Some toll motorways, bridges and tunnels

Ski resorts

The resorts listed are popular ski centres, therefore road access to most is normally good and supported by road clearing during snow falls. However, mountain driving is never predictable and drivers should make sure they take suitable snow chains as well as emergency provisions and clothing. Listed for each resort are: the atlas page and grid square; the resort/minimum piste altitude (where only one figure is shown, they are at the same height) and maximum altitude of its own lifts; the number of lifts and gondolas (the total for lift-linked resorts); the season start and end dates (snow cover allowing); whether snow is augmented by cannon; the nearest town (with its distance in km) and, where available, the website and/or telephone number of the local tourist information centre or ski centre ('00' prefix required for calls from the UK).

The ❄ symbol indicates resorts with snow cannon

Andorra

Pyrenees

Pas de la Casa / Grau Roig 146 B2 ❄ 2050–2640m • 31 lifts • Dec–Apr • Andorra La Vella (30km) www.pasdelacasa.com • *Access via Envalira Pass (2407m), highest in Pyrenees, snow chains essential.*

Austria

Alps

Bad Gastein 109 B4 ❄ 1050/1100–2700m • 50 lifts • Dec–Mar • St Johann im Pongau (45km) +43 6432 3393 0 www.gastein.com

Bad Hofgastein 109 B4 ❄ 860–2295m • 50 lifts • Dec–Mar • St Johann im Pongau (40km) +43 6432 3393 0 www.gastein.com/en/region-villages/bad-hofgastein

Bad Kleinkirchheim 109 C4 ❄ 1070–2310m • 27 lifts • Dec–Mar • Villach (35km) +43 4240 8212 www.badkleinkirchheim.at

Ehrwald 108 B1 ❄ 1000–2965m • 24 lifts • Dec–Apr • Imst (30km) +43 5673 2501 www.wetterstein-bahnen.at/en

Innsbruck 108 B2 ❄ 574/850–3200m • 59 lifts • Dec–Apr • Innsbruck +43 512 56 2000 www.innsbruck.info/en/ • *Motorway normally clear. The motorway to Italy and through the Arlberg Tunnel are both toll roads.*

Ischgl 107 B5 ❄ 1340/1400–2900m • 101 lifts • Dec–May • Landeck (25km) +43 50990 100 www.ischgl.com • *Car entry to resort prohibited between 2200hrs and 0600hrs.*

Kaprun 109 B3 ❄ 885/770–3030m, • 25 lifts • Nov–Apr • Zell am See (10km) +43 6542 770 www.zellamsee-kaprun.com

Kirchberg in Tirol 109 B3 ❄ 860–2000m • 197 lifts • Nov–Apr • Kitzbühel (6km) +43 57507 2100 www.kitzbueheler-alpen.com/en • *Easily reached from Munich International Airport (120 km)*

Kitzbühel (Brixen im Thale) 109 B3 ❄ 800/790–2000m • 197 lifts • Dec–Apr • Wörgl (40km) +43 57057 2000 www.kitzbueheler-alpen.com/en

Lech/Oberlech 107 B5 ❄ 1450–2810m • 87 lifts • Dec–Apr • Bludenz (50km) +43 5583 2161 0 www.lechzuers.com • *Roads normally cleared but keep chains accessible because of altitude. Linked to the other Arlberg resorts.*

Mayrhofen 108 B2 ❄ 630–2500m • 57 lifts • Dec–Apr • Jenbach (35km) +43 5285 6760 www.mayrhofen.at • *Chains rarely required.*

Obertauern 109 B4 ❄ 1740/1640–2350m • 26 lifts • Dec–Apr • Radstadt (20km) +43 6456 7252 www.obertauern.com • *Roads normally cleared but chain accessibility recommended. Camper vans and caravans not allowed; park these in Radstadt*

Saalbach Hinterglemm 109 B3 ❄ 1000/1030–2100m • 52 lifts • Nov–Apr • Zell am See (19km) +43 6541 6800-68 www.saalbach.com • *Both village centres are pedestrianised and there is a good ski bus service during the daytime*

St Anton am Arlberg 107 B5 ❄ 1300–2810m • 87 lifts • Dec–Apr • Innsbruck (104km) +43 5446 22690 www.stantonamarlberg.com • *Linked to the other Arlberg resorts.*

Schladming 109 B4 ❄ 745–1900m • 45 lifts • Dec–Mar • Schladming + 43 36 87 233 10 www.schladming-dachstein.at

Serfaus 108 B1 ❄ 1427/1200–2820m • 68 lifts • Dec–Apr • Landeck (30km) +43 5476 6239 www.serfaus-fiss-ladis.at • *Private vehicles banned from village. Use Dorfbahn Serfaus, an underground funicular that runs on an air cushion.*

Sölden 108 C2 ❄ 1380–3250m, • 33 lifts • Oct–Apr • Imst (50km) +43 57200 200 www.soelden.com • *Roads normally cleared but snow chains recommended because of altitude. The route from Italy and the south over the Timmelsjoch via Obergurgl is closed Oct–May and anyone arriving from the south should use the Brenner Pass motorway.*

Zell am See 109 B3 ❄ 750–1950m • 53 lifts • Dec–Mar • Zell am See +43 6542 770 www.zellamsee-kaprun.com • *Low altitude, so good access and no mountain passes to cross.*

Zell im Zillertal (Zell am Ziller) 109 B3 ❄ 580/930–2410m • 22 lifts • Dec–Apr • Jenbach (25km) +43 5282 7165–226 www.zillertalarena.com

Zürs 107 B5 ❄ 1720/1700–2450m • 87 lifts • Dec–Apr • Bludenz (30km) +43 5583 2245 www.lechzuers.com • *Roads normally cleared but keep chains accessible because of altitude. Village has garage with 24-hour self-service gas/petrol, breakdown service and wheel chains supply. Linked to the other Arlberg resorts.*

France

Alps

Alpe d'Huez 118 B3 ❄ 1860–3330m • 85 lifts • Dec–Apr • Grenoble (63km) www.alpedhuez.com • *Snow chains may be required on access road to resort.*

Avoriaz 118 A3 ❄ 1800/1100–2280m • 35 lifts • Dec–May • Morzine (14km) +33 4 50 74 02 11 www.avoriaz.com/en • *Chains may be required for access road from Morzine. Car-free resort, park on edge of village.*

Chamonix-Mont-Blanc 119 B3 ❄ 1035–3840m • 49 lifts • Dec–Apr • Martigny (38km) +33 4 50 53 99 98 www.chamonix.com

Chamrousse 118 B2 ❄ 1700/1420–2250m • 26 lifts • Dec–Apr • Grenoble (30km) www.chamrousse.com • *Roads normally cleared, keep chains accessible because of altitude.*

Châtel 119 A3 ❄ 1200/1110–2200m • 41 lifts • Dec–Apr • Thonon-Les-Bains (35km) +33 4 50 73 22 44 www.chatel.com

Courchevel 118 B3 ❄ 1300–2470m • 67 lifts • Dec–Apr • Moûtiers (23km) www.courchevel.com • *Roads normally cleared but keep chains accessible. Traffic 'discouraged' within the four resort bases.*

Flaine 118 A3 ❄ 1600–2500m • 26 lifts • Dec–Apr • Cluses (25km) +33 4 50 90 80 01 www.flaine.com • *Keep chains accessible for D6 from Cluses to Flaine. Car access for depositing luggage and passengers only. 1500-space car park outside resort. Near Sixt-Fer-á-Cheval.*

La Clusaz 118 B3 ❄ 1100–2600m • 55 lifts • Dec–Apr • Annecy (32km) www.laclusaz.com • *Roads normally clear but keep chains accessible for final road from Annecy.*

La Plagne 118 B3 ❄ 2500/1250–3250m • 109 lifts • Dec–Apr Moûtiers (32km) www.la-plagne.com • *Ten different centres up to 2100m altitude. Road access via Bozel, Landry or Aime normally cleared. Linked to Les Arcs by cablecar*

Les Arcs 119 B3 ❄ 1600/1200–3230m • 77 lifts • Dec–May • Bourg-St-Maurice (15km) +33 4 79 07 12 57 www.lesarcs.com • *Four base areas up to 2000 metres; keep chains accessible. Pay parking at edge of each base resort. Linked to La Plagne by cablecar*

Les Carroz d'Araches 118 A3 ❄ 1140–2500m • 69 lifts • Dec–Apr • Cluses (13km) http://winter.lescarroz.com

Les Deux-Alpes 118 C3 ❄ 1650/1300–3600m • 55 lifts • Dec–Apr • Grenoble (75km) +33 4 76 79 22 00 www.les2alpes.com/en • *Roads normally cleared, however snow chains recommended for D213 up from valley road (D1091).*

Les Gets 118 A3 ❄ 1170/1000–2000m • 52 lifts • Dec–Apr • Cluses (18km) +33 4 50 74 74 74 www.lesgets.com

Les Ménuires 118 B3 ❄ 1815/1850–3200m • 40 lifts • Dec–Apr • Moûtiers (27km) www.lesmenuires.com • *Keep chains accessible for D117 from Moûtiers.*

Les Sept Laux Prapoutel 118 B3 ❄ 1350–2400m, • 24 lifts • Dec–Apr • Grenoble (38km) www.les7laux.com (in French only) • *Roads normally cleared, however keep chains accessible for mountain road up from the A41 motorway. Near St Sorlin d'Arves.*

Megève 118 B3 ❄ 1100/1050–2350m • 79 lifts • Dec–Apr • Sallanches (12km) www.megeve.com

Méribel 118 B3 ❄ 1400/1100–2950m • 61 lifts • Dec–May • Moûtiers (18km) +33 4 79 08 60 01 www.meribel.net • *Keep chains accessible for 18km to resort on D90 from Moûtiers.*

Morzine 118 A3 ❄ 1000–2460m • 67 lifts • Dec–Apr • Thonon-Les-Bains (30km) +33 4 50 74 72 72 http://en.morzine-avoriaz.com

Pra Loup 132 A2 ❄ 1500–2600m • 53 lifts • Dec–Apr • Barcelonnette (10km) www.praloup.com • *Roads normally cleared but chains accessibility recommended.*

Risoul 118 C3 ❄ 1850/1650–2750m • 59 lifts • Dec–Apr • Briançon (40km) +33 4 92 46 02 60 www.risoul.com • *Keep chains accessible. Near Guillestre. Linked with Vars Les Claux*

St-Gervais Mont-Blanc 118 B3 ❄ 850/1150–2350m • 27 lifts • Dec–Apr • Sallanches (10km) +33 4 50 47 76 08 www.saintgervais.com/en

Serre Chevalier 118 C3 ❄ 1350/1200–2800m • 77 lifts • Dec–Apr • Briançon (10km) + 33 4 92 24 98 98 www.serre-chevalier.com • *Made up of 13 small villages along the valley road, which is normally cleared.*

Tignes 119 B3 ❄ 2100/1550–3450m • 87 lifts • Jan–Dec • Bourg St Maurice (26km) +33 4 79 40 04 40 www.tignes.net • *Keep chains accessible because of altitude. Linked to Val d'Isère.*

Val d'Isère 119 B3 ❄ 1850/1550–3450m • 87 lifts • Dec–Apr • Bourg-St-Maurice (30km) +33 4 79 06 06 60 www.valdisere.com • *Roads normally cleared but keep chains accessible.*

Val Thorens 118 B3 ❄ 2300/1850–3200m • 29 lifts • Dec–Apr • Moûtiers (37km) +33 4 79 00 08 08 www.valthorens.com • *Chains essential – highest ski resort in Europe. Obligatory paid parking on edge of resort.*

Valloire 118 B3 ❄ 1430–2600m • 34 lifts • Dec–Apr • Modane (20km) +33 4 79 59 03 96 www.valloire.net • *Road normally clear up to the Col du Galbier, to the south of the resort, which is closed from 1st November to 1st June. Linked to Valmeinier.*

Valmeinier 118 B3 ❄ 1500–2600m • 34 lifts • Dec–Apr • St Michel de Maurienne (47km) +33 4 79 59 53 69 www.valmeinier.com • *Access from north on D1006 / D902. Col du Galbier, to the south of the resort closed from 1st November to 1st June. Linked to Valloire.*

Valmorel 118 B3 ❄ 1400–2550m • 90 lifts • Dec–Apr • Moûtiers (15km) www.valmorel.com • *Near St Jean-de-Belleville. Linked with ski areas of Doucy-Combelouvière and St François-Longchamp.*

Vars Les Claux 118 C3 ❄ 1850/1650–2750m • 59 lifts • Dec–Apr • Briançon (40km) +33 4 92 46 51 31 www.vars.com/en/winter • *Four base resorts up to 1850 metres. Keep chains accessible. Linked with Risoul.*

Villard de Lans 118 B2 ❄ 1050/1160–2170m • 28 lifts • Dec–Apr • Grenoble (32km) +33 4 76 95 10 38 www.villarddelans.com

Pyrenees

Font-Romeu 146 B3 ❄ 1800/1600–2200m • 25 lifts • Nov–Apr • Perpignan (87km) www.font-romeu.fr • *Roads normally cleared but keep chains accessible.*

Saint-Lary Soulan 145 B4 ❄ 830/1650/1700–2515m • 31 lifts • Dec–Mar • Tarbes (75km) +33 5 62 39 50 81 www.saintlary.com • *Access roads constantly cleared of snow.*

Vosges

La Bresse-Hohneck 106 A1 ❄ 600–1370m • 33 lifts • Dec–Mar • Cornimont (6km) +33 3 29 25 41 29 www.labresse.net

Germany

Alps

Garmisch-Partenkirchen 108 B2 ❄ 700–2830m • 38 lifts • Dec–Apr • Munich (95km) +49 8821 180 700 www.gapa.de • *Roads usually clear, chains rarely needed.*

Oberaudorf 108 B3 ❄ 480–1850m • 30 lifts • Dec–Apr • Kufstein (15km) www.oberaudorf.de • *Motorway normally kept clear. Near Bayrischzell.*

Oberstdorf 107 B5 820/830–2200m • 26 lifts • Dec–Apr • Sonthofen (15km) +49 8322 7000 www.oberstdorf.de/en

Rothaargebirge

Winterberg 81 A4 ❄ 700/620–830m • 19 lifts • Dec–Mar • Brilon (30km) +49 2981 925 00 www.winterberg.de (German and Dutch only) • *Roads usually cleared, chains rarely required.*

Greece

Central Greece

Mount Parnassos: Kelaria-Fterolakka 182 E4 1640–2260m • 14 lifts • Dec–Apr • Amfiklia www.parnassos-ski.gr

Mount Parnassos: Gerondovrahos 182 E4 1800–1900m • 3 lifts • Dec–Apr • Amfiklia +30 29444 70371

Peloponnisos

Mount Helmos: Kalavrita Ski Centre 184 A3 1650–2100m • 7 lifts • Dec–Mar • Kalavrita +30 276920 24451-2 www.kalavrita-ski.gr (in Greek only)

Mount Menalo: Ostrakina 184 B3 1500–1600m • 4 lifts • Dec–Mar • Tripoli +30 27960 22227

Macedonia

Mount Falakro: Agio Pnevma 183 B6 1720/1620–2230m • 7 lifts • Dec–Apr • Drama + 30 25210 23691

Mount Vermio: Seli 182 C4 1500–1900m • 8 lifts • Dec–Mar • Kozani +30 23310 26237 www.seli-ski.gr (in Greek)

Mount Vermio: Tria-Pente Pigadia 182 C3 ❄ 1420–2005m • 5 lifts • Dec–Mar • Ptolemaida +30 23320 44464

Mount Verno: Vigla 182 C3 1650–1900m · 5 lifts · Dec–Mar · Florina 📞+30 23850 22354 💻www.vigla-ski.gr (in Greek)

Mount Vrondous: Lailias 183 B5 1600–1850m · 4 lifts · Dec–Mar · Serres 📞+30 23210 53790

Thessalia

Mount Pilio: Agriolefkes 183 D5 1300–1500m · 5 lifts · Dec–Mar · Volos 📞+30 24280 73719

Italy

Alps

Bardonecchia 118 B3 ❄ 1312–2750m · 21 lifts · Dec–Apr · Bardonecchia 💻www.bardonecchiaski.com · *Resort reached through the 11km Frejus tunnel from France, roads normally cleared.*

Bórmio 107 C5 ❄ 1200/1230–3020m · 24 lifts · Dec–Apr · Tirano (40km) 💻www.bormio.com · *Tolls payable in Ponte del Gallo Tunnel, open 0800hrs–2000hrs.*

Breuil-Cervinia 119 B4 ❄ 2050–3500m · 21 lifts · Jan–Dec · Aosta (54km) 📞+39 166 944311 💻www.cervinia.it · *Snow chains strongly recommended. Bus from Milan airport.*

Courmayeur 119 B3 ❄ 1200–2760m · 21 lifts · Dec–Apr · Aosta (40km) 💻www.courmayeurmontblanc.it · *Access through the Mont Blanc tunnel from France. Roads constantly cleared.*

Limone Piemonte 133 A3 ❄ 1000/1050–2050m · 29 lifts · Dec–Apr · Cuneo (27km) 💻www.limoneturismo.it · *Roads normally cleared, chains rarely required.*

Livigno 107 C5 ❄ 1800–3000m · 31 lifts · Nov–May · Zernez (CH) (27km) 💻www.livigno.com · *Keep chains accessible. The traffic direction through Munt la Schera Tunnel to/from Zernez is regulated on Saturdays. Check in advance.*

Sestrière 119 C3 ❄ 2035/1840–2840m · 92 lifts · Dec–Apr · Oulx (22km) 💻www.sestriere-online.com · *One of Europe's highest resorts; although roads are normally cleared keep chains accessible.*

Appennines

Roccaraso – Aremogna 169 B4 ❄ 1285/1240–2140m · 24 lifts · Dec–Apr · Castel di Sangro (7km) 💻www.roccarasoturismo.it (Italian only)

Dolomites

Andalo – Fai della Paganella 121 A3 ❄ 1042/1050–2125m · 17 lifts · Dec–Apr · Trento (40km) 💻www.visitdolomitipaganella.it 📞+39 461 585836

Arabba 108 C2 ❄ 1600/1450–2950m · 29 lifts · Dec–Mar · Brunico (45km) 📞+39 436 79130 💻www.arabba.it · *Roads normally cleared but keep chains accessible.*

Cortina d'Ampezzo 108 C3 ❄ 1224/1050–2930m · 37 lifts · Dec–Apr · Belluno (72km) 📞+39 436 869086 💻www.dolomiti.org/it/cortina · *Access from north on route 51 over the Cimabanche Pass may require chains.*

Corvara (Alta Badia) 108 C2 ❄ 1568–2500m · 56 lifts · Dec–Apr · Brunico (38km) 💻www.altabadia.it · *Roads normally clear but keep chains accessible.*

Madonna di Campiglio 121 A3 ❄ 1550/1500–2600m · 72 lifts · Dec–Apr · Trento (60km) 📞+39 465 447501 💻www.campigliodolomiti.it/homepage · *Roads normally cleared but keep chains accessible. Linked to Folgarida and Marilleva.*

Moena di Fassa (Sorte/Ronchi) 108 C2 ❄ 1184/1450–2520m · 8 lifts · Dec–Apr · Bolzano (40km) 📞+39 462 609770 💻www.fassa.com

Selva di Val Gardena/Wolkenstein Groden 108 C2 ❄ 1563/1570–2450m · 81 lifts · Dec–Apr · Bolzano (40km) 📞+39 471 777777 💻www.valgardena.it · *Roads normally cleared but keep chains accessible.*

Norway

Hemsedal 47 B5 ❄ 700/640–1450m · 24 lifts · Nov–May · Honefoss (150km) 📞+47 32 055030 💻www.hemsedal.com · *Be prepared for extreme weather conditions.*

Slovakia

Chopok (Jasna-Chopok) 99 C3 ❄ 900/950–1840m · 17 lifts · Dec–Apr · Jasna 📞+421 907 886644 💻www.jasna.sk

Donovaly 99 C3 ❄ 913–1360m · 17 lifts · Nov–Apr · Ruzomberok 📞+421 48 4199900 💻www.paksnow.sk/zima/en

Martinské Hole 98 B2 1250/1150–1456m · 8 lifts · Nov–May · Zilina 📞+421 43 430 6000 💻http://leto.martinky.com/sk (Slovak only)

Plejsy 99 C4 470–912m · 9 lifts · Dec–Mar · Krompachy 📞+421 53 429 8015 💻www.plejsy.sk

Strbske Pleso 99 B4 1380–1825m · 7 lifts · Dec–Mar · Poprad 📞+421 917 682 260 💻www.vt.sk

Slovenia

Julijske Alpe

Kanin (Bovec) 122 A2 460/1600–2293m · 5 lifts · Dec–Apr · Bovec 💻www.boveckanin.si

Kranjska Gora 122 A2 ❄ 800–1210m · 19 lifts · Dec–Mar · Kranjska Gora 📞+386 4 5809 440 💻www.kranjska-gora.si

Vogel 122 A2 570–1800m · 8 lifts · Dec–Apr · Bohinjska Bistrica 📞+386 4 5729 712 💻www.vogel.si

Kawiniške Savinjske Alpe

Krvavec 122 A3 ❄ 1450–1970m · 10 lifts · Dec–Apr · Kranj 📞386 4 25 25 911 💻www.rtc-krvavec.si

Pohorje

Rogla 123 A4 1517/1050–1500m · 13 lifts · Dec–Apr · Slovenska Bistrica 📞+386 3 75 77 100 💻www.rogla.eu

Spain

Pyrenees

Baqueira-Beret/Bonaigua 145 B4 ❄ 1500–2500m · 33 lifts · Dec–Apr · Vielha (15km) 📞+34 902 415 415 💻www.baqueira.es · *Roads normally clear but keep chains accessible. Near Salardú.*

Sistema Penibetico

Sierra Nevada 163 A4 ❄ 2100–3300m · 24 lifts · Dec–May · Granada (32km) 📞+34 902 70 80 90 💻http://sierranevada.es · *Access road designed to be avalanche safe and is snow cleared.*

Sweden

Idre Fjäll 199 D9 590–890m · 33 lifts · Nov–Apr · Mora (140km) 📞+46 253 41000 💻www.idrefjall.se · *Be prepared for extreme weather conditions.*

Sälen 49 A5 360m · 100 lifts · Nov–Apr · Malung (70km) 📞+46 771 84 00 00 💻www.skistar.com/salen · *Be prepared for extreme weather conditions.*

Switzerland

Alps

Adelboden 106 C2 1353m · 94 lifts · Dec–Apr · Frutigen (15km) 📞+41 33 673 80 80 💻www.adelboden.ch · *Linked with Lenk.*

Arosa 107 C4 1800/1740–2650m · 16 lifts · Dec–Apr · Chur (30km) 📞+41 81 378 70 20 💻www.arosa.ch · *Roads cleared but keep chains accessible due to high altitude.*

Crans Montana 119 A4 ❄ 1500–3000m · 34 lifts · Dec–Apr, Jul–Oct · Sierre (15km) 📞+41 848 22 10 12 💻www.crans-montana.ch · *Roads normally cleared but keep chains accessible for ascent from Sierre.*

Davos 107 C4 ❄ 1560/1100–2840m · 38 lifts · Nov–Apr · Davos. 📞+41 81 415 21 21 💻www.davos.ch

Engelberg 106 C3 ❄ 1000/1050–3020m · 26 lifts · Nov–May · Luzern (39km) 📞+41 41 639 77 77 💻www.engelberg.ch · *Straight access road normally cleared.*

Flums (Flumserberg) 107 B4 ❄ 1400/1000–2220m · 17 lifts · Dec–Apr · Buchs (25km) 📞+41 81 720 18 18 💻www.flumserberg.ch · *Roads normally cleared, but 1000-metre vertical ascent; keep chains accessible.*

Grindelwald 106 C3 ❄ 1050–2950m · 39 lifts · Dec–Apr · Interlaken (20km) 📞+41 33 854 12 12 💻www.jungfrauregion.ch · *Linked with Wengen.*

Gstaad – Saanenland 106 C2 ❄ 1050/950–3000m · 74 lifts · Dec–Apr · Gstaad 📞+41 33 748 81 81 💻www.gstaad.ch · *Linked to Anzère.*

Klosters 107 C4 ❄ 1191/1110–2840m · 52 lifts · Dec–Apr · Davos (10km). 📞+41 81 410 20 20 💻www.davos.ch/klosters · *Roads normally clear but keep chains accessible.*

Leysin 119 A4 ❄ 2260–2330m · 16 lifts · Dec–Apr · Aigle (6km) 📞+41 24 493 33 00 💻www.leysin.ch

Mürren 106 C2 ❄ 1650–2970m · 12 lifts · Dec–Apr · Interlaken (18km) 📞+41 33 856 86 86 💻www.mymuerren.ch · *No road access. Park in Strechelberg (1500 free places) and take the two-stage cable car.*

Nendaz 119 A4 ❄ 1365/1400–3300m · 20 lifts · Nov–Apr · Sion (16km) 📞+41 27 289 55 89 💻www.nendaz.ch · *Roads normally cleared, however keep chains accessible for ascent from Sion. Near Vex.*

Saas-Fee 119 A4 ❄ 1800–3500m · 23 lifts · Jan–Dec · Brig (35km) 📞+41 27 958 18 58 💻www.saas-fee.ch/en/ · *Roads normally cleared but keep chains accessible because of altitude.*

St Moritz 107 C4 ❄ 1856/1730–3300m · 24 lifts · Nov–May · Chur (89km) 📞+41 81 837 33 33 💻www.stmoritz.ch · *Roads normally cleared but keep chains accessible.*

Samnaun 107 C5 ❄ 1846/1400–2900m · 40 lifts · Dec–May · Scuol (30km) 📞+41 81 861 88 30 💻www.engadin.com/ferienorte/engadin-samnaun · *Roads normally cleared but keep chains accessible.*

Verbier 119 A4 ❄ 1500–3330m · 17 lifts · Nov–Apr · Martigny (27km) 📞+41 27 775 38 38 💻www.verbier.ch · *Roads normally cleared.*

Villars-Gryon 119 A4 ❄ 1253/1200–2100m · 16 lifts · Dec–Apr, Jun–Jul · Montreux (35km) 📞+41 24 495 32 32 💻www.villars.ch · *Roads normally cleared but keep chains accessible for ascent from N9. Near Bex.*

Wengen 106 C2 ❄ 1270–2320m · 39 lifts · Dec–Apr · Interlaken (12km) 📞+41 33 856 85 85 💻http://wengen.ch · *No road access. Park at Lauterbrunnen and take mountain railway. Linked with Grindelwald.*

Zermatt 119 A4 ❄ 1620–3900m · 40 lifts, all year · Brig (42km) 📞+41 27 966 81 00 💻www.zermatt.ch · *Cars not permitted in resort, park in Täsch (3km) and take shuttle train.*

Turkey

North Anatolian Mountains

Uludag 186 B4 1770–2320m · 15 lifts · Dec–Mar · Bursa (36km) 📞+90 224 285 21 11 💻http://skiingturkey.com/resorts/uludag.html

To the best of the Publisher's knowledge the information in this table was correct at the time of going to press. No responsibility can be accepted for any errors or their consequences.

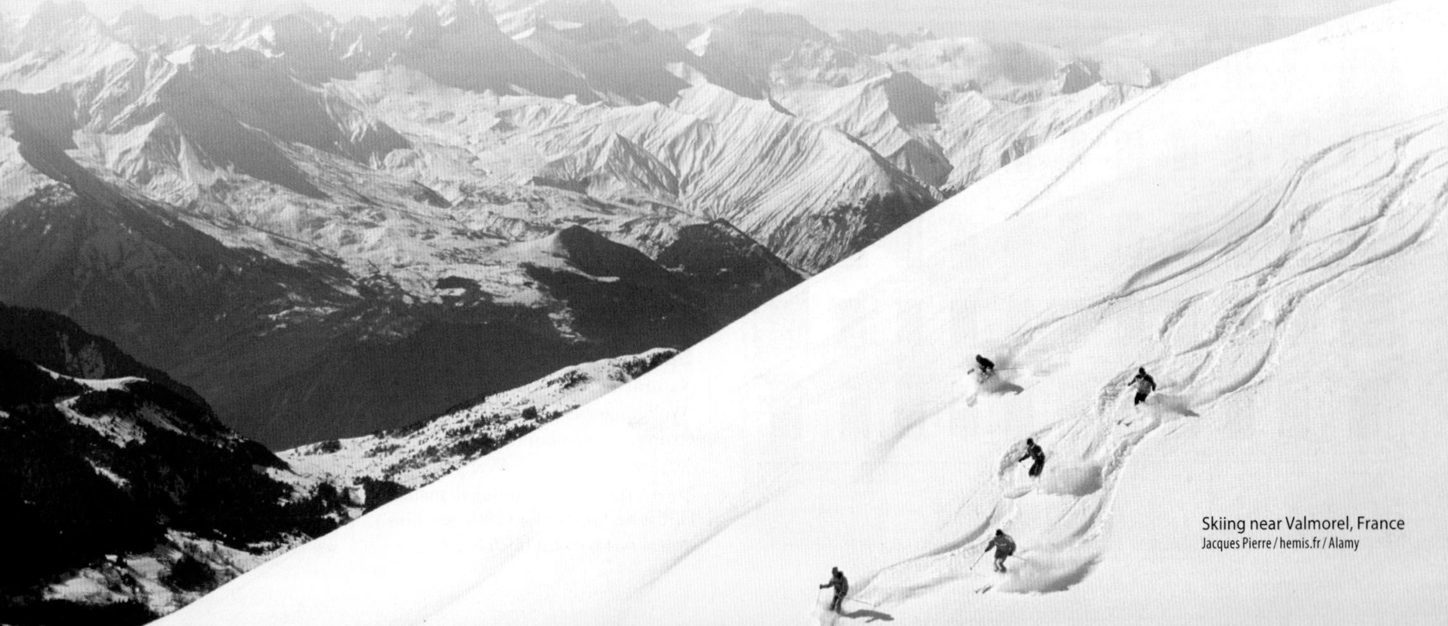

Skiing near Valmorel, France
Jacques Pierre / hemis.fr / Alamy

300 greatest sights of Europe

For entries with no website listed, use that given for the national tourist board.

Albania Shqipëria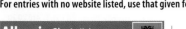

www.albania.al

Berat

Fascinating old town with picturesque Ottoman Empire buildings and traditional Balkan domestic architecture.
www.albania.al/destination/12/berati **182 C1**

Tirana Tiranë

Capital of Albania. Skanderbeg Square has main historic buildings. Also: 18c Haxhi Ethem Bey Mosque; Art Gallery (Albanian); National Museum of History. Nearby: medieval Krujë; Roman monuments.
www.albania.al/destination/8/tirana **182 B1**

Austria Österreich

www.austria.info

Bregenz

Lakeside town bordering Germany, Liechtenstein, Switzerland. Locals, known as Vorarlbergers, have their own dialect. The Martinsturm Roman to 17c tower, 17c town hall and Seekapelle, Kunsthaus modern art museum, Vorarlberger Landesmuseum, Festspielhaus.
www.austria.info/uk/where-to-go/cities/bregenz **107 B4**

Graz

University town, seat of imperial court to 1619. Historic centre around Hauptplatz. Imperial monuments: Burg; mausoleum of Ferdinand II; towers of 16c schloss; 17c Schloss Eggenberg (with Old Gallery). Also: 16c Town Hall; Zeughaus; 15c cathedral; New Gallery (good 19–20c); Kunsthaus (modern art).
www.graztourismus.at **110 B2**

Innsbruck

Old town is reached by Maria-Theresien-Strasse with famous views. Buildings: Goldenes Dachl (1490s); 18c cathedral; remains of Hofburg imperial residence; 16c Hofkirche (tomb of Maximilian I). www.austria.info/us/where-to-go/cities/innsbruck **108 B2**

Krems

On a hill above the Danube, medieval quarter has Renaissance mansions. Also: Gothic Piaristenkirche; Museumkrems; Kunsthalle (modern art). www.krems.gv.at/Tourismus/English_version/Tourism **97 C3**

Linz

Port on the Danube. Historic buildings are concentrated on Hauptplatz below the imperial 15c schloss.

▲ Melk Abbey, Austria

Notable: Baroque Old Cathedral; 16c Town Hall; Old Castle Museum; Lentos Art Museum.
www.linztourismus.at **96 C2**

Melk

Set on a rocky hill above the Danube, the fortified abbey is the greatest Baroque achievement in Austria – particularly the Grand Library and abbey church. www.stiftmelk.at **110 A2**

Salzburg

Set in subalpine scenery, the town was associated with powerful 16–17c prince-archbishops. The 17c cathedral has a complex of archiepiscopal buildings: the Residence and its gallery (19c); the 13c Franciscan Church (notable altar). Also: Mozart's birthplace; Schloss Mirabell; Salzburg Museum; the Hohensalzburg fortress; the Collegiate Church of St Peter (cemetery, catacombs); Museum of Modern Art at the Mönschberg and Rupertinum. www.austria.info/us/where-to-go/cities/salzburg **109 B4**

Salzkammergut

Natural beauty with 76 lakes (Wolfgangersee, Altersee, Traunsee, Grundlsee) in mountain scenery. Attractive villages (St Wolfgang) and towns (Bad Ischl, Gmunden) include Hallstatt, famous for Celtic remains.
www.salzkammergut.at **109 B4**

Vienna Wien

Capital of Austria, the historic centre lies within the Ring. Churches: Gothic St Stephen's Cathedral; 17c Imperial Vault; 14c Augustine Church; 14c Church of the Teutonic Order (treasure); 18c Baroque churches (Jesuit Church, Franciscan Church, St Peter, St Charles). Imperial residences: Hofburg; Schönbrunn. Architecture of Historicism on Ringstrasse (from 1857). Art Nouveau: station pavilions, Secession Building, Postsparkasse, Looshaus, Majolicahaus. Museums: Art History Museum (antiquities, old masters), Cathedral and Diocesan Museum (15c), Albertina (graphic arts), Liechtenstein Museum (old masters), Museum of Applied Arts, Museum of Modern Art (MUMOK), Leopold Museum, Belvedere (Gothic, Baroque, 19–20c); AzW (architecture); Vienna Museum.
www.wien.info **111 A3**

Belgium Belgique

www.belgium-tourism.be

Antwerp Antwerpen

City with many tall gabled Flemish houses on the river. Heart of the city is Great Market with 16–17c guildhouses and Town Hall. Charles Borromeus Church (Baroque). 14–16c Gothic cathedral has Rubens paintings. Rubens also at the Rubens House and his burial place in St Jacob's Church. Excellent museums: Mayer van den Bergh Museum (applied arts); Koninklijk Museum of Fine Arts (Flemish, Belgian); MAS (ethnography, folklore, shipping); Muhka (modern art).
www.visitantwerpen.be **79 A4**

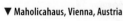

▼ Maholicahaus, Vienna, Austria

Bruges Brugge

Well-preserved medieval town with narrow streets and canals. Main squares: the Market with 13c Belfort and covered market; the Burg with Basilica of the Holy Blood and Town Hall. The collections of Groeninge Museum and Memling museum in St Jans Hospital include 15c Flemish masters. The Onze Lieve Vrouwekerk has a famous *Madonna and Child* by Michelangelo www.visitbruges.be **78 A3**

Brussels Bruxelles

Capital of Belgium. The Lower Town is centred on the enormous Grand Place with Hôtel de Ville and rebuilt guildhouses. Symbols of the city include the 'Manneken Pis' and Atomium (giant model of a molecule). The 13c Notre Dame de la Chapelle is the oldest church. The Upper Town contains: Gothic cathedral; Neoclassical Place Royale; 18c King's Palace; Royal Museums of Fine Arts (old and modern masters) Magritte Museum; MRAH (art and historical artefacts); BELvue museum (in the Bellevue Residence). Also: much Art Nouveau (Horta Museum, Hôtel Tassel, Hôtel Solvay); Place du Petit Sablon and Place du Grand Sablon; 19c Palais de Justice. https://visit.brussels/en **79 B4**

Ghent Gent

Medieval town built on islands surrounded by canals and rivers. Views from Pont St-Michel. The Graslei and Koornlei quays have Flemish guild houses. The Gothic cathedral has famous Van Eyck altarpiece. Also: Belfort; Cloth Market; Gothic Town Hall; Gravensteen. Museums: STAM Museum in Bijloke Abbey (provincial and applied art); Museum of Fine Arts (old masters). https://visit.gent.be/en/home **79 A3**

Namur

Reconstructed medieval citadel is the major sight of Namur, which also has a cathedral and provincial museums. www.namurtourisme.be/index.php **79 B4**

Tournai

The Romanesque-Gothic cathedral is Belgium's finest (much excellent art). Fine Arts Museum has a good collection (15–20c). www.visittournai.be/pratique/office-du-tourisme/article/tourist-office?lang=en **78 B3**

▼ Town Hall, Antwerp, Belgium

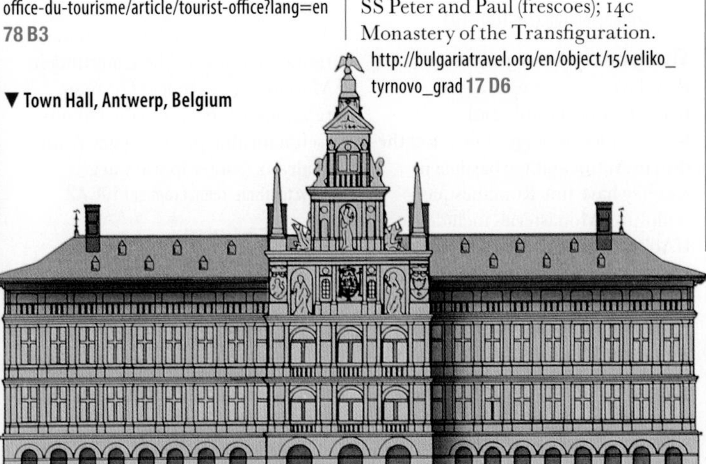

Bulgaria Bulgariya

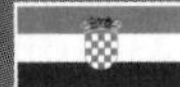

http://bulgariatravel.org

Black Sea Coast

Beautiful unspoiled beaches (Zlatni Pyasŭtsi). The delightful resort Varna is popular. Nesebŭr is famous for Byzantine churches. Also: Danube Delta in Hungary. **17 D7**

Koprivshtitsa

Beautiful village known both for its half-timbered houses and links with the April Rising of 1876. Six house museums amongst which the Lyutov House and the Oslekov House, plus the birthplaces of Georgi Benkovski, Dimcho Debelyanov, Todor Kableshkov, and Lyuben Karavelov. http://bulgariatravel.org/en/object/18/Koprivshtica

Plovdiv

City set spectacularly on three hills. The old town has buildings from many periods: 2c Roman stadium and amphitheatre; 14c Dzumaiya Mosque; Archaeological Museum; 19c Ethnographic Museum. Nearby: Bačkovo Monastery (frescoes). http://bulgariatravel.org/en/object/306/plovdiv_grad **183 A6**

Rila

Bulgaria's finest monastery, set in the most beautiful scenery of the Rila mountains. The church is richly decorated with frescoes. www.rilamonastery.pmg-blg.com **183 A5**

Sofia Sofiya

Capital of Bulgaria. Sights: exceptional neo-Byzantine cathedral; Church of St Sofia; St Alexander Nevsky Cathedral; Boyana church; 4c rotunda of St George (frescoes); Byzantine Boyana Church (frescoes) on panoramic Mount Vitoša. Museums: National Historical Museum (particularly for Thracian artefacts); National Art Gallery (icons, Bulgarian art). http://bulgariatravel.org/en/object/234/sofia **17 D5**

Veliko Tŭrnovo

Medieval capital with narrow streets. Notable buildings: House of the Little Monkey; Hadji Nicoli Inn; ruins of medieval citadel; Baudouin Tower; churches of the Forty Martyrs and of SS Peter and Paul (frescoes); 14c Monastery of the Transfiguration. http://bulgariatravel.org/en/object/15/veliko_tyrnovo_grad **17 D6**

Croatia Hrvatska

http://croatia.hr/en-GB

Dalmatia Dalmacija

Exceptionally beautiful coast along the Adriatic. Among its 1185 islands, those of the Kornati Archipelago and Brijuni Islands are perhaps the most spectacular. Along the coast are several attractive medieval and Renaissance towns, most notably Dubrovnik, Split, Šibenik, Trogir, Zadar. **138 B2**

Dubrovnik

Surrounded by medieval and Renaissance walls, the city's architecture dates principally from 15–16c. Sights: many churches and monasteries including Church of St Blaise and Dominican monastery (art collection); promenade street of Stradun, Dubrovnik Museums; Renaissance Rector's Palace; Onofrio's fountain; Sponza Palace. The surrounding area has some 80 16c noblemen's summer villas. **139 C4**

Islands of Croatia

There are over 1,000 islands off the coast of Croatia among which there is Brač, known for its white marble and the beautiful beaches of Bol (www.bol.hr); Hvar (www.tzhvar.hr/en/) is beautifully green with fields of lavender, marjoram, rosemary, sage and thyme; Vis (www.tz-vis.hr) has the beautiful towns of Komiža and Vis Town, with the Blue Cave on nearby Biševo. **123 & 137–138**

Istria Istra

Peninsula with a number of ancient coastal towns (Rovinj, Poreč, Pula, Piran in Slovene Istria) and medieval hill-top towns (Motovun). Pula has Roman monuments (exceptional 1c amphitheatre). Poreč has narrow old streets; the mosaics in 6c Byzantine basilica of St Euphrasius are exceptional. See also Slovenia. www.istra.hr **122 B2**

Plitvička Jezera

Outstandingly beautiful world of water and woodlands with 16 lakes and 92 waterfalls interwoven by canyons. Archaeological museums; art gallery; Gallery of Ivan Meštrović. www.tzplitvice.hr **123 C4**

Split

Most notable for the exceptional 4c palace of Roman Emperor Diocletian, elements of which are incorporated into the streets and buildings of the town itself. The town also has a cathedral (11c baptistry) and a Franciscan monastery. **138 B2**
www.visitsplit.com/en/1/welcome-to-split

Trogir

The 13–15c town centre is surrounded by medieval city walls. Romanesque-Gothic cathedral includes the chapel of Ivan the Blessed. Dominican and Benedictine monasteries house art collections; Ćipiko palace; Lučić palace. www.trogironline.com/tourist_info.html **138 B2**

Zagreb

Capital city of Croatia with cathedral and Archbishop's Palace in Kaptol and to the west Gradec in the Lower Town – are Baroque palaces. Donji Grad – The Lower Town – is home to the Archaological Museum, Art Pavilion, Museum of Arts and Crafts, Ethnographic Museum, Mimara Museum and National Theatre; Modern Gallery; Museum of Contemporary Art. www.infozagreb.hr/&lang=en **124 B1**

Czechia Česka Republica

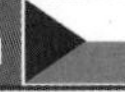

www.czechtourism.com/home/

Brno

Capital of Moravia. Sights: Vegetable Market and Old Town Hall; Capuchin crypt decorated with bones of dead monks; hill of St Peter with Gothic cathedral; Church of St James; Mies van der Rohe's buildings (Bata, Avion Hotel, Togendhat House). Museums: Moravian Museum; Moravian Gallery; City Art Gallery; Brno City Museum in Spilberk Castle. www.gotobrno.cz/en **97 B4**

České Budějovice

Famous for Budvar beer, the medieval town is centred on náměsti Přemysla Otokara II. The Black Tower gives fine views. Nearby: medieval Český Krumlov. www.c-budejovice.cz/en **96 C2**

Kutná Hora

A town with strong silver mining heritage shown in the magnificent Cathedral of sv Barbara which was built by the miners. See also the ossuary with 40,000 complete sets of bones moulded into sculptures and decorations. www.czechtourism.com/t/kutna-hora **97 B3**

Olomouc

Well-preserved medieval university town of squares and fountains. The Upper Square has the Town Hall. Also: 18c Holy Trinity; Baroque Church of St Michael. http://tourism.olomouc.eu/welcome/en **98 B1**

Pilsen Plzeň

Best known for Plzeňský Prazdroj (Pilsener Urquell), beer has been brewed here since 1295. An industrial town with eclectic architecture shown in the railway stations and the namesti Republiky (main square). www.czechtourism.com/a/pilsen-area **96 B1**

Prague Praha

Capital of Czech Republic and Bohemia. The Castle Quarter has a complex of buildings behind the walls (Royal Castle; Royal Palace; cathedral). The Basilica of St George has a fine Romanesque interior. The Belvedere is the best example of Renaissance architecture. Hradčani Square has aristocratic palaces and the National Gallery. The Little Quarter has many Renaissance (Wallenstein Palace) and Baroque mansions and the Baroque Church of St Nicholas. The Old Town has its centre at the Old Town Square with the Old Town Hall (astronomical clock), Art Nouveau Jan Hus monument and Gothic Týn church. The Jewish quarter has 14c Staranova Synagogue and Old Jewish Cemetery. The Charles Bridge is famous. The medieval New Town has many Art Nouveau buildings and is centred on Wenceslas Square. www.prague.eu/en **84 B2**

Spas of Bohemia

Spa towns of Karlovy Vary (Carlsbad: www.karlovyvary.cz/en), Márianske Lázně (Marienbad: www.marianskelazne.cz) and Frantiskovy Lázně **83 B4**

Denmark Danmark
www.visitdenmark.co.uk

Århus

Second largest city in Denmark with a mixture of old and new architecture that blends well, Århus has been dubbed the culture capital of Denmark with the Gothic Domkirke; Latin Quarter; 13th Century Vor Frue Kirke; Den Gamle By, open air museum of traditional Danish life; ARoS (art museum). www.visitaarhus.com **59 B3**

Copenhagen København

Capital of Denmark. Old centre has fine early 20c Town Hall. Latin Quarter has 19c cathedral. 18c Kastellet has statue of the Little Mermaid nearby. The 17c Rosenborg Castle was a royal residence, as was the Christianborg (now government offices). Other popular sights: Nyhavn canal; Tivoli Gardens. Excellent art collections: Ny Carlsberg Glypotek; National Gallery; National Museum. www.visitcopenhagen.com/copenhagen-tourist **61 D2**

Hillerød

Frederiskborg (home of the national history museum) is a fine red-brick Renaissance castle set among three lakes. www.visitnorthsealand.com/ln-int/north-sealand/hilleroed **61 D2**

Roskilde

Ancient capital of Denmark. The marvellous cathedral is a burial place of the Danish monarchy. The Viking Ship Museum houses the remains of five 11c Viking ships excavated in the 1960s. www.visitroskilde.com/ln-int/roskilde-lejre/tourist **61 D2**

Estonia Eesti
www.visitestonia.com/en

Kuressaare

Main town on the island of Saaremaa with the 14c Kuressaare Kindlus. **8 C3**

Pärnu

Sea resort with an old town centre. Sights: 15c Red Tower; neoclassical Town Hall; St Catherine's Church. www.visitparnu.com/en **8 C4**

Tallinn

Capital of Estonia. The old town is centred on the Town Hall Square. Sights: 15c Town Hall; Toompea Castle; Three Sisters houses. Churches: Gothic St Nicholas; 14c Church of the Holy Spirit; St Olaf's; Kumu Art Museum; Maritime Museum.www.visittallinn.ee/eng **8 C4**

Tartu

Historic town with 19c university. The Town Hall Square is surrounded by neoclassical buildings. Also: remains of 13c cathedral; Estonian National Museum. http://visittartu.com **8 C5**

Finland Suomi
www.visitfinland.com

Finnish Lakes

Area of outstanding natural beauty covering about one third of the country with thousands of lakes, of which Päijänne and Saimaa are the most important. Tampere, industrial centre of the region, has numerous museums, including the Tampere Art Museum (modern). Savonlinna has the medieval Olavinlinna Castle. Kuopio has the Orthodox and Regional Museums. **8 A5**

Helsinki

Capital of Finland. The 19c neoclassical town planning between the Esplanade and Senate Square includes the Lutheran cathedral. There is also a Russian Orthodox cathedral. The Constructivist Stockmann Department Store is the largest in Europe. The main railway station is Art Nouveau. Gracious 20c buildings in Mannerheimintie avenue include Finlandiatalo by Alvar Aalto. Many good museums: Art Museum of the Ateneum (19–20c); National Museum; Design Museum; Helsinki City Art Museum (modern Finnish); Open Air Museum (vernacular architecture); 18c fortress of Suomenlinna has several museums. www.visithelsinki.fi/en **8 B4**

Lappland (Finnish)

Vast unspoiled rural area. Lappland is home to thousands of nomadic Sámi living in a traditional way. The capital, Rovaniemi, was rebuilt after WWII; museums show Sámi history and culture. Nearby is the Arctic Circle with the famous Santa Claus Village. Inari is a centre of Sámi culture. See also Norway and Sweden. www.lapland.fi **192–193**

France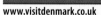
http://uk.france.fr

Albi

Old town with rosy brick architecture. The vast Cathédrale Ste-Cécile (begun 13c) holds some good art. The Berbie Palace houses the Toulouse-Lautrec museum. www.albi-tourisme.fr (French only) **130 B1**

Alps

Grenoble (www.grenoble-tourisme.com/en/), capital of the French Alps, has a good 20c collection in the Museum of Grenoble. The Vanoise Massif has the greatest number of resorts (Val d'Isère, Courchevel). Chamonix has spectacular views on Mont Blanc, France's and Europe's highest peak. **118 B2**

Amiens

France's largest Gothic cathedral has beautiful decoration. The Museum of Picardy has unique 16c panel paintings. www.visit-amiens.com **90 B2**

Arles

Ancient, picturesque town with Roman relics (1c amphitheatre), 11c cathedral, Archaeological Museum (Roman art); Van Gogh centre. www.arlestourisme.com/en/ **131 B3**

Avignon

Medieval papal capital (1309–77) with 14c walls and many ecclesiastical buildings. Vast Palace of the Popes has stunning frescoes. The Little Palace has fine Italian Renaissance painting. The 12–13c Bridge of St Bénézet is famous. www.ot-avignon.fr **131 B3**

Bourges

The Gothic Cathedral of St Etienne, one of the finest in France, has a superb sculptured choir. Also notable is the House of Jacques Coeur. www.ville-bourges.fr/_en/site/tourism **103 B4**

Brittany Bretagne

Brittany is famous for cliffs, sandy beaches and wild landscape. It is also renowned for megalithic monuments (Carnac) and Celtic culture. Its capital, Rennes, has the Palais de Justice and good collections in the Museum of Brittany (history) and Museum of Fine Arts. Also: Nantes; St-Malo. www.brittanytourism.com **100–101**

Burgundy Bourgogne

Rural wine region with a rich Romanesque, Gothic and Renaissance heritage. The 12c cathedral in Autun and 12c basilica in Vézelay have fine Romanesque sculpture. Monasteries include 11c L'Abbaye de Cluny (ruins) and L'Abbaye de Fontenay. Beaune has beautiful Gothic Hôtel-Dieu and 15c Nicolas Rolin hospices. www.burgundy-tourism.com **104 B3**

Caen

City with two beautiful Romanesque buildings: Abbaye aux Hommes; Abbaye aux Dames. The château has

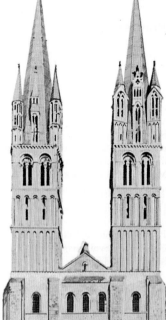

▲ **Abbaye aux Hommes, Caen, France**

two museums (15–20c painting; history). The *Bayeux Tapestry* is displayed in nearby Bayeux. www.caen-tourisme.fr/en **89 A3**

Carcassonne

Unusual double-walled fortified town of narrow streets with an inner fortress. The fine Romanesque Church of St Nazaire has superb stained glass. www.tourism-carcassonne.co.uk **130 B1**

Chartres

The 12–13c cathedral is an exceptionally fine example of Gothic architecture (Royal Doorway, stained glass, choir screen). The Fine Arts Museum has a good collection. www.chartres.com **90 C1**

Clermont-Ferrand

The old centre contains the cathedral built out of lava and Romanesque basilica. The Puy de Dôme and Puy de Sancy give spectacular views over some 60 extinct volcanic peaks (*puys*). www.clermontferrandtourism.com **116 B3**

Colmar

Town characterised by Alsatian half-timbered houses. The Unterlinden Museum has excellent German religious art including the famous Isenheim altarpiece. Espace André Malraux (contemporary arts). www.tourisme-colmar.com/en/ **106 A2**

Corsica Corse

Corsica has a beautiful rocky coast and mountainous interior. Napoleon's birthplace of Ajaccio has: Fesch Museum with Imperial Chapel and a large collection of Italian art; Maison Bonaparte; cathedral. Bonifacio, a medieval town, is spectacularly set on a rock over the sea. www.visit-corsica.com **180**

Côte d'Azur

The French Riviera is best known for its coastline and glamorous resorts. There are many relics of artists who worked here: St-Tropez has Musée de l'Annonciade; Antibes has 12c Château Grimaldi with the Picasso Museum; Cagnes has the Renoir House and Mediterranean Museum of Modern Art; St-Paul-de-Vence has the excellent Maeght Foundation and Matisse's Chapelle du Rosaire. Cannes is famous for its film festival. Also: Marseille, Monaco, Nice.
www.frenchriviera-tourism.com **133 B3**

Dijon

Great 15c cultural centre. The Palais des Ducs et des Etats is the most notable monument and contains the Museum of Fine Arts. Also: the Charterhouse of Champmol.
www.destinationdijon.com **105 B4**

Disneyland Paris

Europe's largest theme park follows in the footsteps of its famous predecessors in the United States.
www.disneylandparis.com **90 C2**

Le Puy-en-Velay

Medieval town bizarrely set on the peaks of dead volcanoes. It is dominated by the Romanesque cathedral (cloisters). The Romanesque chapel of St-Michel is dramatically situated on the highest rock.
www.ot-lepuyenvelay.fr **117 B3**

Loire Valley

The Loire Valley has many 15–16c châteaux built amid beautiful scenery by French monarchs and members of their courts. Among the most splendid are Azay-le-Rideau, Chenonceaux and Loches. Also: Abbaye de Fontévraud. www.valdeloire-france.co.uk
102 B2

Lyon

France's third largest city has an old centre and many museums including the Museum of the History of Textiles and the Museum of Fine Arts (old masters). www.lyon-france.com **117 B4**

Marseilles Marseille

Second largest city in France. Spectacular views from the 19c Notre-Dame-de-la-Garde. The Old Port has 11-12c Basilique St Victor (crypt, catacombs). Cantini Museum has major collection of 20c French art. Château d'If was the setting of Dumas' *The Count of Monte Cristo*.
www.marseille-tourisme.com **131 B4**

Mont-St-Michel

Gothic pilgrim abbey (11–12c) set dramatically on a steep rock island rising from mud flats and connected to the land by a road covered by the tide. The abbey is made up of a complex of buildings.
www.ot-montsaintmichel.com **101 A4**

Nancy

A centre of Art Nouveau. The 18c Place Stanislas was constructed by dethroned Polish king Stanislas.

Museums: School of Nancy Museum (Art Nouveau furniture); Fine Arts Museum. http://en.nancy-tourisme.fr **92 C2**

Nantes

Former capital of Brittany, with the 15c Château des ducs de Bretagne. The cathedral has a striking interior.
www.nantes-tourisme.com
101 B4

Nice

Capital of the Côte d'Azur, the old town is centred on the old castle on the hill. The seafront includes the famous 19c Promenade des Anglais. The aristocratic quarter of the Cimiez Hill has the Marc Chagall Museum and the Matisse Museum. Also: Museum of Modern and Contemporary Art (especially neo-Realism and Pop Art).
http://en.nicetourisme.com/ **133 B3**

Paris

Capital of France, one of Europe's most interesting cities. The Île de la Cité area, an island in the River Seine has the 12–13c Gothic Notre Dame (wonderful stained glass) and La Sainte-Chapelle (1240–48), one of the jewels of Gothic art. The Left Bank area: Latin Quarter with the famous Sorbonne university; Museum of Cluny housing medieval art; the Panthéon; Luxembourg Palace and Gardens; Montparnasse, interwar artistic and literary centre; Eiffel Tower; Hôtel des Invalides with Napoleon's tomb. Right Bank: the great boulevards (Avenue des Champs-Élysées joining the Arc de Triomphe and Place de la Concorde); 19c Opéra Quarter; Marais, former aristocratic quarter of elegant mansions (Place des Vosges); Bois de Boulogne, the largest park in Paris; Montmartre, centre of 19c bohemianism, with the Basilique Sacré-Coeur. The Church of St Denis is the first gothic church and the mausoleum of the French monarchy. Paris has three of the world's greatest art collections: The Louvre (to 19c, *Mona Lisa*), Musée d'Orsay (19–20c) and National Modern Art Museum in the Pompidou Centre. Other major museums include: Orangery Museum; Paris Museum of Modern Art; Rodin Museum; Picasso Museum. Notable cemeteries with graves of the famous: Père-Lachaise, Montmartre, Montparnasse. Near Paris are the royal residences of Fontainebleau and Versailles.
https://en.parisinfo.com **90 C2**

▲ Château de Chenonceaux,
Châteaux of the Loire, France

Pyrenees

Beautiful unspoiled mountain range. Towns include: delightful sea resorts of St-Jean-de-Luz and Biarritz; Pau, with access to the Pyrenees National Park; pilgrimage centre Lourdes.
144–145

Reims

Together with nearby Epernay, the centre of champagne production. The 13c Gothic cathedral is one of the greatest architectural achievements in France (stained glass by Chagall). Other sights: Palais du Tau with cathedral sculpture, 11c Basilica of St Rémi; cellars on Place St-Niçaise and Place des Droits-des-Hommes.
www.reims-tourisme.com **91 B4**

Rouen

Old centre with many half-timbered houses and 12–13c Gothic cathedral and the Gothic Church of St Maclou with its fascinating remains of a dance macabre on the former cemetery of Aître St-Maclou. The Fine Arts Museum has a good collection.
www.rouentourisme.com **89 A5**

St-Malo

Fortified town (much rebuilt) in a fine coastal setting. There is a magnificent boat trip along the river Rance to Dinan, a splendid well-preserved medieval town.
www.saint-malo-tourisme.com **101 A3**

Strasbourg

Town whose historic centre includes a well-preserved quarter of medieval half-timbered Alsatian houses, many of them set on the canal. The cathedral is one of the best in France. The Palais Rohan contains several museums. www.otstrasbourg.fr/en **93 C3**

Toulouse

Medieval university town characterised by flat pink brick (Hôtel Assézat). The Basilique St Sernin, the largest Romanesque church in France, has many art treasures. Marvellous Church of the Jacobins holds the body of St Thomas Aquinas.
www.toulouse-tourisme.com **129 C4**

Tours

Historic town centred on Place Plumereau. Good collections in the Guilds Museum and Fine Arts Museum. www.tours-tourism.co.uk **102 B2**

Versailles

Vast royal palace built for Louis XIV, primarily by Mansart, set in large formal gardens with magnificent fountains. The extensive and much-imitated state apartments include the famous Hall of Mirrors and the exceptional Baroque chapel.
www.chateauversailles.fr **90 C2**

Vézère Valley Caves

A number of prehistoric sites, most notably the cave paintings of Lascaux (some 17,000 years old), now only seen in a duplicate cave, and the cave of Font de Gaume. The National Museum of Prehistory is in Les Eyzies. www.lascaux-dordogne.com/en
129 B4

Germany Deutschland
www.germany.travel

Northern Germany

Aachen

Once capital of the Holy Roman Empire. Old town around the Münsterplatz with magnificent cathedral. An exceptionally rich treasure is in the Schatzkammer. The Town Hall is on the medieval Market. www.aachen.de **80 B2**

Berlin

Capital of Germany. Sights include: the Kurfürstendamm avenue; Brandenburg Gate, former symbol of the division between East and West Germany; Tiergarten; Unter den

Linden; 19c Reichstag. Berlin has many excellent art and history collections. Museum Island: Pergamon Musem (classical antiquity, Near and Far East, Islam; Bode Museum (sculpture, Byzantine art); Altes Museum (Greek and Roman); New National Gallery (20th-c European); Old National Gallery (19th-c German); New Museum (Egyptian, prehistoric). Dahlem: Museum of Asian Art; Museum of European Cultures; Mueseum of Ethnology; Die Brücke Museum (German Expressionism). Tiergarten: Picture Gallery (old masters); Decorative Arts Museum (13–19c); New National Gallery (19–20c); Bauhaus Archive.

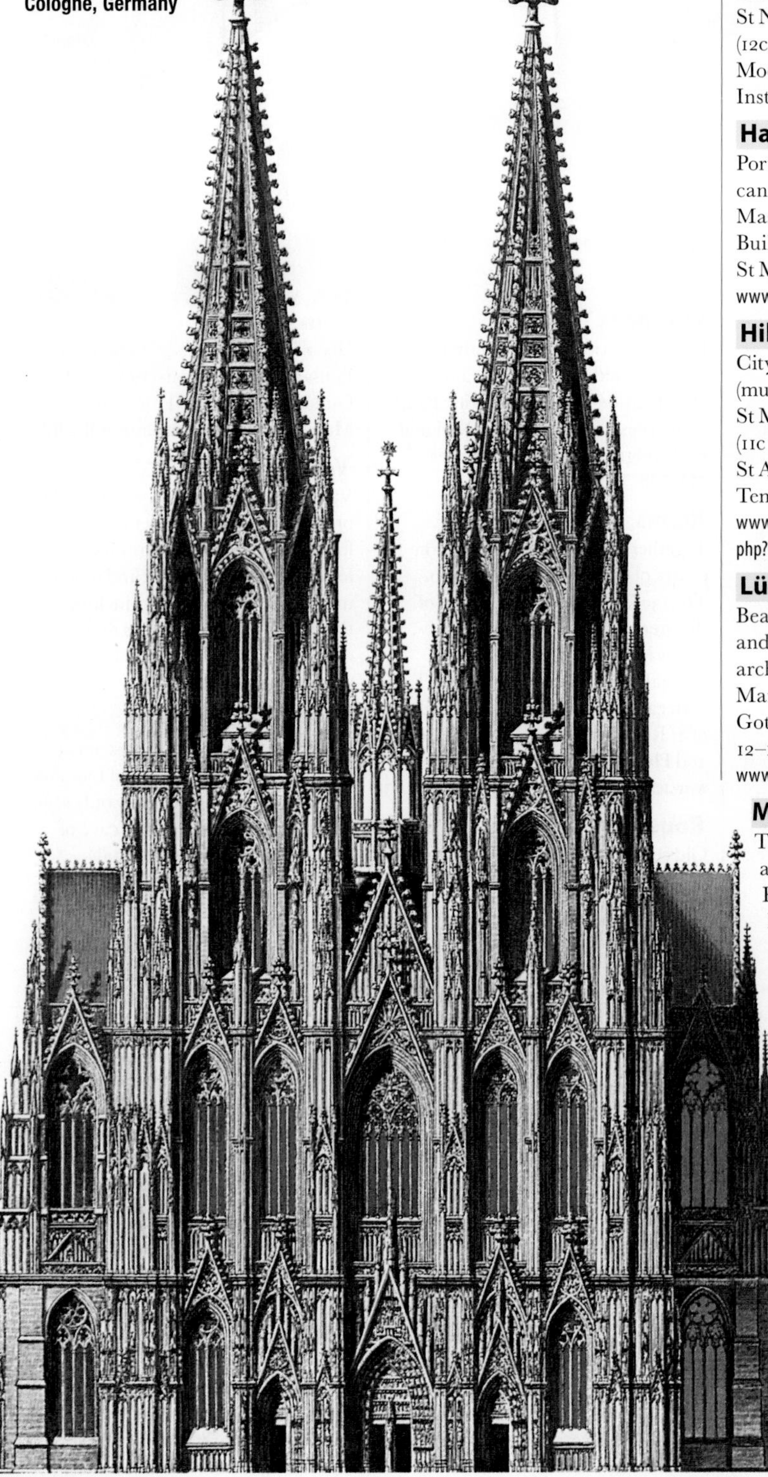

Gothic cathedral, Cologne, Germany

Kreuzberg: Gropius Building with Jewish Museum and Berlin Gallery; remains of Berlin Wall and Checkpoint Charlie House. Unter den Linden: German Guggenheim (commissioned contemporary works). http://visitberlin.de **74 B2**

Cologne Köln
Ancient city with 13–19c cathedral (rich display of art). In the old town are the Town Hall and many Romanesque churches (Gross St Martin, St Maria im Kapitol, St Maria im Lyskirchen, St Ursula, St Georg, St Severin, St Pantaleon, St Apostolen). Museums: Diocesan Museum (religious art); Roman-German Museum (ancient history);

Wallraf-Richartz and Ludwig Museum (14–20c art). www.cologne-tourism.com **80 B2**

Dresden
Historic centre with a rich display of Baroque architecture. Major buildings: Castle of the Electors of Saxony; 18c Hofkirche; Zwinger Palace with fountains and pavilions (excellent old masters); Albertinum with excellent Gallery of New Masters; treasury of Grünes Gewölbe. The Baroque-planned New Town contains the Japanese Palace and Schloss Pillnitz. www.dresden.de **84 A1**

Frankfurt
Financial capital of Germany. The historic centre around the Römerberg Square has 13–15c cathedral, 15c Town Hall, Gothic St Nicholas Church, Saalhof (12c chapel). Museums: Museum of Modern Art (post-war); State Art Institute. www.frankfurt-tourismus.de **81 B4**

Hamburg
Port city with many parks, lakes and canals. The Kunsthalle has Old Masters and 19-20c German art. Buildings: 19c Town Hall; Baroque St Michael's Church. www.hamburg-tourism.de **72 A3**

Hildesheim
City of Romanesque architecture (much destroyed). Principal sights: St Michael's Church; cathedral (11c interior, sculptured doors, St Anne's Chapel); superb 15c Tempelhaus on the Market Place. www.hildesheim.de/staticsite/staticsite. php?menuid=1067&topmenu=4 **72 B2**

Lübeck
Beautiful old town built on an island and characterised by Gothic brick architecture. Sights: 15c Holsten Gate; Market with the Town Hall and Gothic brick St Mary's Church; 12–13c cathedral; St Ann Museum. www.luebeck-tourism.de **65 C3**

Mainz
The Electoral Palatinate schloss and Market fountain are Renaissance. Churches: 12c Romanesque cathedral; Gothic St Steven's (with stained glass by Marc Chagall). www.mainz.de **93 A4**

Marburg
Medieval university town with the Market Place and Town Hall, St Elizabeth's Church (frescoes, statues, 13c shrine), 15–16c schloss. **81 B4**

Münster
Historic city with well-preserved Gothic and Renaissance buildings: 14c Town Hall; Romanesque-Gothic cathedral. The Westphalian Museum holds regional art. www.stadt-muenster.de/en/tourismus/home.html **71 C4**

Potsdam
Beautiful Sanssouci Park contains several 18–19c buildings including: Schloss Sanssouci; Gallery (European masters); Orangery; New Palace; Chinese Teahouse. www.potsdam-tourism.com **74 B2**

Rhein Valley Rheintal
Beautiful 80km gorge of the Rhein Valley between Mainz and Koblenz with rocks (Loreley), vineyards (Bacharach, Rüdesheim), white medieval towns (Rhens, Oberwesel) and castles. Some castles are medieval (Marksburg, Rheinfles, island fortress Pfalzgrafenstein) others were built or rebuilt in the 19c (Stolzenfles, Rheinstein). **80 B3**

Weimar
The Neoclassical schloss, once an important seat of government, now houses a good art collection. Church of SS Peter and Paul has a Cranach masterpiece. Houses of famous people: Goethe, Schiller, Liszt. The Bauhaus was founded at the School of Architecture and Engineering. www.weimar.de/en/tourism **82 B3**

Southern Germany

Alpine Road Deutsche Alpenstrasse
German Alpine Road in the Bavarian Alps, from Lindau on Bodensee to Berchtesgaden. The setting for 19c fairy-tale follies of Ludwig II of Bavaria (Linderhof, Hohen-schwangau, Neuschwanstein), charming old villages (Oberammergau) and Baroque churches (Weiss, Otto-beuren). Garmisch-Partenkirchen has views on Germany's highest peak, the Zugspitze. **108 B2**

Augsburg
Attractive old city. The Town Hall is one of Germany's finest Renaissance buildings. Maximilianstrasse has several Renaissance houses and Rococo Schaezler Palace (good art collection). Churches: Romanesque-Gothic cathedral; Renaissance St Anne's Church. The Fuggerei, founded 1519 as an estate for the poor, is still in use. www.augsburg-tourismus.de **94 C2**

Bamberg
Well-preserved medieval town. The island, connected by two bridges, has the Town Hall and views of Klein Venedig. Romanesque-Gothic cathedral (good art) is on an exceptional square of Gothic, Renaissance and Baroque buildings – Alte Hofhalttung; Neue Residenz with State Gallery (German masters); Ratstube. http://en.bamberg.info **94 B2**

Black Forest Schwarzwald
Hilly region between Basel and Karlsruhe, the largest and most picturesque woodland in Germany, with the highest summit, Feldberg, lake resorts (Titisee), health resorts (Baden-Baden) and clock craft (Triberg). Freiburg is the regional capital. www.schwarzwald.de **93 C4**

Freiburg

Old university town with system of streams running through the streets. The Gothic Minster is surrounded by the town's finest buildings. Two towers remain of the medieval walls. The Augustine Museum has a good collection.
www.freiburg.de/pb/,Len/225797.html **106 B2**

Heidelberg

Germany's oldest university town, majestically set on the banks of the river and romantically dominated by the ruined schloss. The Gothic Church of the Holy Spirit is on the Market Place with the Baroque Town Hall. Other sights include the 16c Knight's House and the Baroque Morass Palace with the Museum of the Palatinate.
www.tourism-heidelberg.com **93 B4**

Lake Constance Bodensee

Lake Constance, with many pleasant lake resorts. Lindau, on an island, has numerous gabled houses. Birnau has an 18c Rococo church. Konstanz (Swiss side) has the Minster set above the Old Town. www.bodensee.eu/en **107 B4**

Munich München

Old town centred on the Marienplatz with 15c Old Town Hall and 19c New Town Hall. Many richly decorated churches: St Peter's (14c tower); Gothic red-brick cathedral; Renaissance St Michael's (royal portraits on the façade); Rococo St Asam's. The Residenz palace consists of seven splendid buildings holding many art objects. Schloss Nymphenburg has a palace, park, botanical gardens and four beautiful pavilions. Superb museums: Old Gallery (old masters), New Gallery (18–19c), Lenbachhaus (modern German). Many famous beer gardens.
www.munich-touristinfo.de **108 A2**

Nuremberg Nürnberg

Beautiful medieval walled city dominated by the 12c Kaiserburg. Romanesque-Gothic St Sebaldus Church and Gothic St Laurence Church are rich in art. On Hauptmarkt is the famous 14c Schöner Brunnen. Also notable is 15c Dürer House. The German National Museum has excellent German medieval and Renaissance art.
http://tourismus.nuernberg.de/en **94 B3**

Regensburg

Medieval city set majestically on the Danube. Views from 12c Steinerne Brücke. Churches: Gothic cathedral; Romanesque St Jacob's; Gothic St Blaisius; Baroque St Emmeram. Other sights: Old Town Hall (museum); Haidplatz; Schloss Thurn und Taxis; State Museum.
http://tourismus.regensburg.de/en **95 B4**

Romantic Road
Romantische Strasse

Romantic route between Aschaffenburg and Füssen, leading through picturesque towns and villages of medieval Germany. The most popular section is the section between Würzburg and Augsburg, centred on Rothenburg ob der Tauber. Also notable are Nördlingen, Harburg Castle, Dinkelsbühl, Creglingen. www.romantischestrasse.de **94 B2**

Rothenburg ob der Tauber

Attractive medieval walled town with tall gabled and half-timbered houses on narrow cobbled streets. The Market Place has Gothic-Renaissance Town Hall, Rattrinke-stubbe and Gothic St Jacob's Church (altarpiece).
www.rothenburg.de/tourismus/willkommen-in-rothenburg **94 B2**

Speyer

The 11c cathedral is one of the largest and best Romanesque buildings in Germany. 12c Jewish Baths are well-preserved.
www.speyer.de/sv_speyer/en/Tourism **93 B4**

Stuttgart

Largely modern city with old centre around the Old Schloss, Renaissance Alte Kanzlei, 15c Collegiate Church and Baroque New Schloss. Museums: Regional Museum; Old and New State Galleries. The 1930s Weissenhofsiedlung is by several famous architects.
www.stuttgart-tourist.de/en **94 C1**

Trier

Superb Roman monuments: Porta Nigra; Aula Palatina (now a church); Imperial Baths; amphitheatre. The Regional Museum has Roman artefacts. Also, Gothic Church of Our Lady; Romanesque cathedral.
www.trier-info.de **92 B2**

Ulm

Old town with half-timbered gabled houses set on a canal. Gothic 14–19c minster has tallest spire in the world (161m). www.tourismus.ulm.de **94 C1**

Würzburg

Set among vineyard hills, the medieval town is centred on the Market Place with the Rococo House of the Falcon. The 18c episcopal princes' residence (frescoes) is magnificent. The cathedral is rich in art. Work of the great local Gothic sculptor, Riemenschneider, is in Gothic St Mary's Chapel, Baroque New Minster, and the Mainfränkisches Museum. www.wuerzburg.de **94 B1**

Greece Ellas
www.visitgreece.gr

Athens Athina

Capital of Greece. The Acropolis, with 5c BC sanctuary complex (Parthenon, Propylaia, Erechtheion, Temple of Athena Nike), is the greatest architectural achievement of antiquity in Europe. The Agora was a public meeting place in ancient Athens. Plaka has narrow streets and small Byzantine churches (Kapnikarea). The Olympeum was the largest temple in Greece. Also: Olympic Stadium; excellent collections of ancient artefacts (Museum of Cycladic and Ancient Greek Art; New Acropolis Museum; National Archeological Museum; Benaki Museum). **185 B4**

Corinth Korinthos

Ancient Corinth (ruins), with 5c BC Temple of Apollo, was in 44 BC made capital of Roman Greece by Julius Caesar. Set above the city, the Greek-built acropolis hill of Acrocorinth became the Roman and Byzantine citadel (ruins). **184 B3**

Crete Kriti

Largest Greek island, Crete was home to the great Minoan civilization (2800–1100 BC). The main relics are the ruined Palace of Knossos and Malia. Gortys was capital of the Roman province. Picturesque Rethimno has narrow medieval streets, a Venetian fortress and a former Turkish mosque. Matala has beautiful beaches and famous caves cut into cliffs. Iraklio (Heraklion), the capital, has a good Archeological Museum. **185 D6**

Delphi

At the foot of the Mount Parnassos, Delphi was the seat of the Delphic Oracle of Apollo, the most important oracle in Ancient Greece. Delphi was also a political meeting place and the site of the Pythian Games. The Sanctuary of Apollo consists of: Temple of Apollo, led to by the Sacred Way; Theatre; Stadium. The museum has a display of objects from the site (5c BC Charioteer). **182 E4**

Epidavros

Formerly a spa and religious centre focused on the Sanctuary of Asclepius (ruins). The enormous 4c BC theatre is probably the finest of all ancient theatres. **184 B4**

Greek Islands

Popular islands with some of the most beautiful and spectacular beaches in Europe. The many islands are divided into various groups and individual islands: The major groups are the Kiklades and Dodekanisa in the Aegean Sea, the largest islands are Kerkyra (Corfu) in the Ionian Sea and Kriti. **182–185 & 188**

Meteora

The tops of bizarre vertical cylinders of rock and towering cliffs are the setting for 14c Cenobitic monasteries, until recently only accessible by baskets or removable ladders. Mega Meteoro is the grandest and set on the highest point. Roussánou has the most extraordinary site. Varlaám is one of the oldest and most beautiful, with the Ascent Tower and 16c church with frescoes. Aghiou Nikolaou also has good frescoes.
www.meteora-greece.com **182 D3**

Mistras

Set in a beautiful landscape, Mistras is the site of a Byzantine city, now in ruins, with palaces, frescoed churches, monasteries and houses. **184 B3**

Mount Olympus
Oros Olymbos

Mount Olympus, mythical seat of the Greek gods, is the highest, most dramatic peak in Greece. **182 C4**

Mycenae Mikines

The citadel of Mycenae prospered between 1950 BC and 1100 BC and consists of the royal complex of Agamemnon: Lion Gate, royal burial site, Royal Palace, South House, Great Court. **184 B3**

Olympia

In a stunning setting, the Panhellenic Games were held here for a millennium. Ruins of the sanctuary of Olympia consist of the Doric temples of Zeus and Hera and the vast Stadium. There is also a museum (4c BC figure of Hermes). **184 B2**

Rhodes

One of the most attractive islands with wonderful sandy beaches. The city of Rhodes has a well-preserved medieval centre with the Palace of the Grand Masters and the Turkish Süleymaniye Mosque
www.rhodestravels.com **188 C2**

Salonica Thessaloniki

Largely modern city with Byzantine walls and many fine churches: 8c Aghia Sofia; 11c Panaghia Halkeo; 14c Dodeka Apostoli; 14c Aghios Nikolaos Orfanos; 5c Aghios Dimitrios (largest in Greece, 7c Mosaics). **183 C5**

Hungary Magyarorszàg
http://gotohungary.com

Balaton

The 'Hungarian sea', famous for its holiday resorts: Balatonfüred, Tihany, Badasconytomaj, Keszthely. **111 C4**

Budapest

Capital of Hungary on River Danube, with historic area centring on the Castle Hill of Buda district. Sights include: Matthias church; Pest district with late 19c architecture, centred on Ferenciek tere; neo-Gothic Parliament Building on river; Millennium Monument. The Royal Castle houses a number of museums: Hungarian National Gallery, Budapest History Museum; Ludwig Collection. Other museums: National Museum of Fine Arts (excellent Old and Modern masters); Hungarian National Museum (Hungarian history). Famous for public thermal baths: Király and Rudas baths, both made under Turkish rule; Gellért baths, the most visited.
www.budapest.com/ **112 B3**

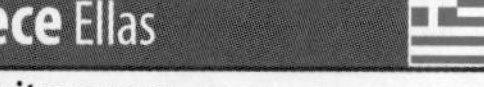

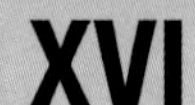

Esztergom

Medieval capital of Hungary set in scenic landscape. Sights: Hungary's largest basilica (completed 1856); royal palace ruins. **112 B2**

Pécs

Attractive old town with Europe's fifth oldest university (founded 1367). Famous for Turkish architecture (Mosque of Gazi Kasim Pasha, Jakovali Hassan Mosque). www.iranypecs.hu/en/index.html **125 A4**

Sopron

Beautiful walled town with many Gothic and Renaissance houses. Nearby: Fertöd with the marvellous Eszergázy Palace. **111 B3** http://portal.sopron.hu/Sopron/portal/english

Ireland
www.ireland.com/en-gb

Aran Islands

Islands with spectacular cliffs and notable pre-Christian and Christian sights, especially on Inishmore. www.aranislands.com **26 B2**

Cashel

Town dominated by the Rock of Cashel (61m) topped by ecclesiastical ruins including 13c cathedral; 15c Halls of the Vicars; beautiful Romanesque 12c Cormac's Chapel (fine carvings). www.cashel.ie **29 B4**

Connemara

Beautiful wild landscape of mountains, lakes, peninsulas and beaches. Clifden is the capital. www.connemara.ie/en **28 A1**

Cork

Pleasant city with its centre along St Patrick's Street and Grand Parade lined with fine 18c buildings. Churches: Georgian St Anne's Shandon (bell tower); 19c cathedral. www.corkcity.ie/traveltourism **29 C3**

County Donegal

Rich scenic landscape of mystical lakes and glens and seascape of cliffs (Slieve League cliffs are the highest in Europe). The town of Donegal has a finely preserved Jacobean castle. www.govisitdonegal.com **26 B2**

Dublin

Capital of Ireland. City of elegant 18c neoclassical and Georgian architecture with gardens and parks (St Stephen's Green, Merrion Square with Leinster House – now seat of Irish parliament). City's main landmark, Trinity College (founded 1591), houses in its Old Library fine Irish manuscripts (7c Book of Durrow, 8c Book of Kells). Two Norman cathedrals: Christ Church; St Patrick's. Other buildings: originally medieval Dublin Castle with State Apartments; James Gandon's masterpieces: Custom House; Four Courts. Museums: National Museum (archaeology, decorative arts, natural history); National Gallery (old masters, Impressionists); Museum of Modern Art; Dublin Writers' Museum. www.visitdublin.com **30 A2**

Glendalough

Impressive ruins of an important early Celtic (6c) monastery with 9c cathedral, 12c St Kevin's Cross, oratory of St Kevin's Church. www.glendalough.ie **30 A2**

Kilkenny

Charming medieval town, with narrow streets dominated by 12c castle (restored 19c). The 13c Gothic cathedral has notable tomb monuments. www.visitkilkenny.ie **30 B1**

Newgrange

Part of a complex that also includes the sites of Knowth, Dowth, Fourknocks, Loughcrew and Tara, Newgrange is one of the best passage graves in Europe, the massive 4500-year-old tomb has stones richly decorated with patterns. www.knowth.com/newgrange.htm **30 A2**

Ring of Kerry

Route around the Iveragh peninsula with beautiful lakes (Lough Leane), peaks overlooking the coastline and islands (Valencia Island, Skelling). Also: Killarney; ruins of 15c Muckross Abbey. www.ringofkerrytourism.com **29 B2**

Italy Italia
www.italia.it

Northern Italy

Alps

Wonderful stretch of the Alps running from the Swiss and French borders to Austria. The region of Valle d'Aosta is one of the most popular ski regions, bordered by the highest peaks of the Alps. **108–109 & 119–120**

Arezzo

Beautiful old town set on a hill dominated by 13c cathedral. Piazza Grande is surrounded by medieval and Renaissance palaces. Main sight: Piero della Francesca's frescoes in the choir of San Francesco. **135 B4**

Assisi

Hill-top town that attracts crowds of pilgrims to the shrine of St Francis of Assisi at the Basilica di San Francesco, comprising two churches, Lower and Upper, with superb frescoes. www.assisi-info.com **136 B1**

Bologna

Elegant city with oldest university in Italy. Historical centre around Piazza Maggiore and Piazza del Nettuno with the Town Hall, Palazzo del Podestà, Basilica di San Petronio. Other churches: San Domenico; San Giacomo Maggiore. The two towers (one incomplete) are symbols of the city. Good collection in the National Gallery (Bolognese). www.bolognawelcome.com **135 A4**

Dolomites Dolomiti

Part of the Alps, this mountain range spreads over the region of Trentino-Alto Adige, with the most picturesque scenery between Bolzano and Cortina d'Ampezzo. www.dolomiti.it **121 A4**

Ferrara

Old town centre around Romanesque-Gothic cathedral and Palazzo Communale. Also: Castello Estense; Palazzo Schifanoia (frescoes); Palazzo dei Diamanti housing Pinacoteca Nazionale. www.ferraraterraeacqua.it/en **121 C4**

Florence Firenze

City with exceptionally rich medieval and Renaissance heritage. Piazza del Duomo has:13–15c cathedral (first dome since antiquity); 14c campanile; 11c baptistry (bronze doors). Piazza della Signoria has: 14c Palazzo Vecchio (frescoes); Loggia della Signoria (sculpture); 16c Uffizi Gallery with one of the world's greatest collections (13–18c). Other great paintings: Museo di San Marco; Palatine Gallery in 15–16c Pitti Palace surrounded by Boboli Gardens. Sculpture: Cathedral Works Museum; Bargello Museum; Academy Gallery (Michelangelo's *David*).

Among many other Renaissance palaces: Medici-Riccardi; Rucellai; Strozzi. The 15c church of San Lorenzo has Michelangelo's tombs of the Medici. Many churches have richly frescoed chapels: Santa Maria Novella, Santa Croce, Santa Maria del Carmine. The 13c Ponte Vecchio is one of the most famous sights. www.visitflorence.com **135 B4**

Italian Lakes

Beautiful district at the foot of the Alps, most of the lakes with holiday resorts. Many lakes are surrounded by aristocratic villas (Maggiore, Como, Garda). **120–121**

Mantua Mántova

Attractive city surrounded by three lakes. Two exceptional palaces: Palazzo Ducale (Sala del Pisanello; Camera degli Sposi, Castello San Giorgio); luxurious Palazzo Tè (brilliant frescoes). Also: 15c Church of Sant'Andrea; 13c law courts. www.turismo.mantova.it **121 B3**

Milan Milano

Modern city, Italy's fashion and design capital (Corso and Galleria Vittoro Emmanuelle II). Churches include: Gothic cathedral (1386–1813), the world's largest (4c baptistry); Romanesque St Ambrose; 15c San Satiro; Santa Maria delle Grazie with Leonardo da Vinci's *Last Supper* in the convent refectory. Great art collections, Brera Gallery, Ambrosian Library, Museum of Modern Art. Castello Sforzesco (15c, 19c) also has a gallery. The famous La Scala opera house opened in 1778. Nearby: monastery at Pavia. www.turismo.milano.it/wps/portal/tur/en **120 B2**

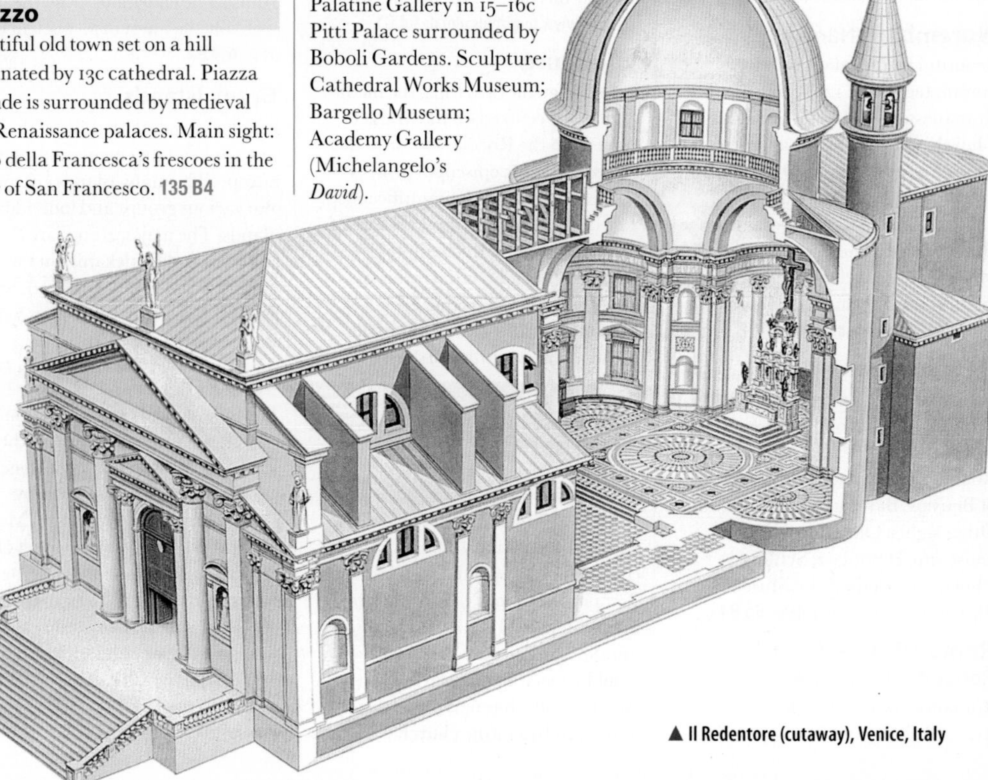

▲ Il Redentore (cutaway), Venice, Italy

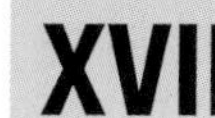

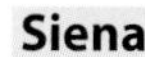

Padua Pádova
Pleasant old town with arcaded streets. Basilica del Santo is a place of pilgrimage to the tomb of St Anthony. Giotto's frescoes in the Scrovegni chapel are exceptional. Also: Piazza dei Signori with Palazzo del Capitano; vast Palazzo della Ragione; church of the Eremitani (frescoes). www.turismopadova.it **121 B4**

Parma
Attractive city centre, famous for Correggio's frescoes in the Romanesque cathedral and church of St John the Evangelist, and Parmigianino's frescoes in the church of Madonna della Steccata. Their works are also in the National Gallery. www.turismo.comune.parma.it **120 C3**

Perúgia
Hill-top town centred around Piazza Quattro Novembre with the cathedral, Fontana Maggiore and Palazzo dei Priori. Also: Collegio di Cambio (frescoes); National Gallery of Umbria; many churches. www.perugiaonline.com **136 B1**

Pisa
Medieval town centred on the Piazza dei Miracoli. Sights: famous Romanesque Leaning Tower, Romanesque cathedral (excellent façade, Gothic pulpit); 12–13c Baptistry; 13c Camposanto cloistered cemetery (fascinating 14c frescoes). www.turismo.pisa.it/en **134 B3**

Ravenna
Ancient town with exceptionally well-preserved Byzantine mosaics. The finest are in 5c Mausoleo di Galla Placidia and 6c Basilica di San Vitale. Good mosaics also in the basilicas of Sant'Apollinare in Classe and Sant'Apollinare Nuovo. www.turismo.ra.it/eng **135 A5**

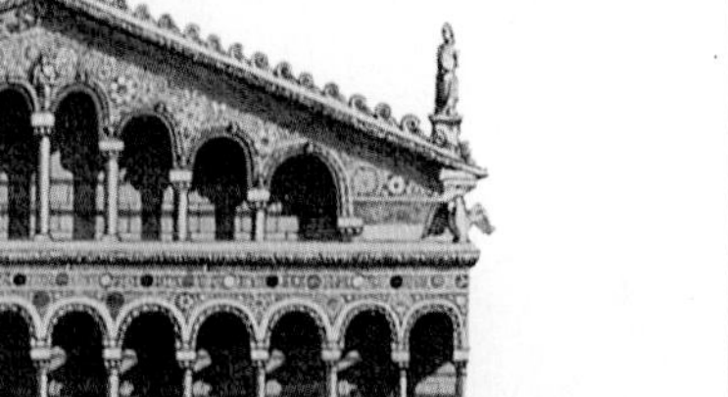

▼ Romanesque cathedral, Pisa, Italy

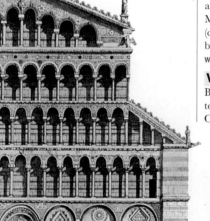

Siena
Outstanding 13–14c medieval town centred on beautiful Piazza del Campo with Gothic Palazzo Publico (frescoes of secular life). Delightful Romanesque-Gothic Duomo (Libreria Piccolomini, baptistry, art works). Many other richly decorated churches. Fine Sienese painting in Pinacoteca Nazionale and Museo dell'Opera del Duomo. www.sienaonline.com **135 B4**

Turin Torino
City centre has 17-18c Baroque layout dominated by twin Baroque churches. Also: 15c cathedral (holds Turin Shroud); Palazzo Reale; 18c Superga Basilica; Academy of Science with rich Egyptian Museum. www.turismotorino.org **119 B4**

Urbino
Set in beautiful hilly landscape, Urbino's heritage is mainly due to the 15c court of Federico da Montefeltro at the magnificent Ducal Palace (notable Studiolo), now also a gallery. www.turismo.pesarourbino.it **136 B1**

Venice Venezia
Stunning old city built on islands in a lagoon, with some 150 canals. The Grand Canal is crossed by the famous 16c Rialto Bridge and is lined with elegant palaces (Gothic Ca'd'Oro and Ca'Foscari, Renaissance Palazzo Grimani, Baroque Rezzonico). The district of San Marco has the core of the best known sights and is centred on Piazza San Marco with 11c Basilica di San Marco (bronze horses, 13c mosaics); Campanile (exceptional views) and Ducal Palace (connected with the prison by the famous Bridge of Sighs). Many churches (Santa Maria Gloriosa dei Frari, Santa Maria della Salute, Redentore, San Giorgio Maggiore, San Giovanni e Paolo) and scuole (Scuola di San Rocco, Scuola di San Giorgio degli Schiavoni) have excellent works of art. The Gallery of the Academy houses superb 14–18c Venetian art. The Guggenheim Museum holds 20c art. http://en.turismovenezia.it **122 B1**

Verona
Old town with remains of 1c Roman Arena and medieval sights including the Palazzo degli Scaligeri; Arche Scaligere; Romanesque Santa Maria Antica; Castelvecchio; Ponte Scaliger. The famous 14c House of Juliet has associations with *Romeo and Juliet*. Many churches with fine art works (cathedral; Sant'Anastasia; basilica di San Zeno Maggiore). www.tourism.verona.it/en **121 B4**

Vicenza
Beautiful town, famous for the architecture of Palladio, including the Olympic Theatre (extraordinary stage), Corso Palladio with many of his palaces, and Palazzo Chiericati. Nearby: Villa Rotonda, the most influential of all Palladian buildings. www.vicenzae.org **121 B4**

Southern Italy

Naples Napoli
Historical centre around Gothic cathedral (crypt). Spaccanapoli area has numerous churches (bizarre Cappella Sansevero, Gesù Nuovo, Gothic Santa Chiara with fabulous tombs). Buildings: 13c Castello Nuovo; 13c Castel dell'Ovo; 15c Palazzo Cuomo.

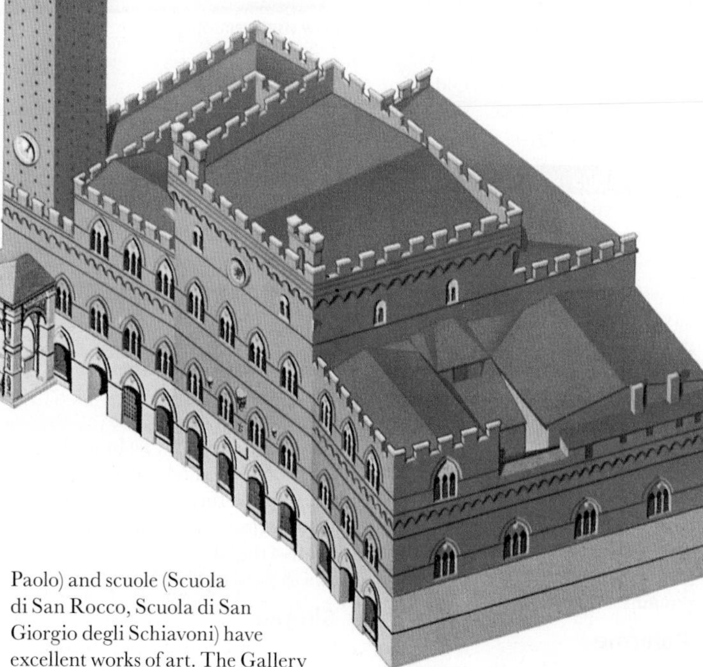

▼ Palazzo Publico, Siena, Italy

Museums: National Archeological Museum (artefacts from Pompeii and Herculaneum); National Museum of Capodimonte (Renaissance painting). Nearby: spectacular coast around Amalfi; Pompeii; Herculaneum. www.inaples.it **170 C2**

Orvieto
Medieval hill-top town with a number of monuments including the Romanesque-Gothic cathedral (façade, frescoes). www.orvietoviva.com/en **168 A2**

Rome Roma
Capital of Italy, exceptionally rich in sights from many eras. Ancient sights: Colosseum; Arch of Constantine; Trajan's Column; Roman and Imperial fora; hills of Palatino and Campidoglio (Capitoline Museum shows antiquities); Pantheon; Castel Sant' Angelo; Baths of Caracalla). Early Christian sights: catacombs (San Calisto, San Sebastiano, Domitilla); basilicas (San Giovanni in Laterano, Santa Maria Maggiore, San Paolo Fuori le Mura). Rome is known for richly decorated Baroque churches: il Gesù, Sant'Ignazio, Santa Maria della Vittoria, Chiesa Nuova. Other churches, often with art treasures: Romanesque Santa Maria in Cosmedin, Gothic Santa Maria Sopra Minerva, Renaissance Santa Maria del Popolo, San Pietro in Vincoli. Several Renaissance and Baroque palaces and villas house superb art collections (Palazzo Barberini, Palazzo Doria Pamphilj, Palazzo Spada, Palazzo Corsini, Villa Giulia, Galleria Borghese) and are beautifully frescoed (Villa Farnesina). Fine Baroque public spaces with fountains: Piazza Navona; Piazza di Spagna with the Spanish Steps; also Trevi Fountain. Nearby: Tivoli; Villa Adriana. Rome also contains the Vatican City (Città del Vaticano). www.turismoroma.it **168 B2**

Volcanic Region

Region from Naples to Sicily. Mount Etna is one of the most famous European volcanoes. Vesuvius dominates the Bay of Naples and has at its foot two of Italy's finest Roman sites, Pompeii and Herculaneum, both destroyed by its eruption in 79AD. Stromboli is one of the beautiful Aeolian Islands.

Sardinia Sardegna

Sardinia has some of the most beautiful beaches in Italy (Alghero). Unique are the nuraghi, some 7000 stone constructions (Su Nuraxi, Serra Orios), the remains of an old civilization (1500–400 BC). Old towns include Cagliari and Sássari. www.sardi.it 178–179

Sicily Sicilia

Surrounded by beautiful beaches and full of monuments of many periods, Sicily is the largest island in the Mediterranean. Taormina with its Greek theatre has one of the most spectacular beaches, lying under the mildly active volcano Mount Etna. Also: Agrigento; Palermo, Siracusa. www.sicilytourism.com 176–177

Agrigento

Set on a hill above the sea and famed for the Valley of the Temples. The nine originally 5c BC Doric temples are Sicily's best-preserved Greek remains. www.agrigento-sicilia.it 176 B2

Palermo

City with Moorish, Norman and Baroque architecture, especially around the main squares (Quattro Canti, Piazza Pretoria, Piazza Bellini). Sights: remains of Norman palace (12c Palatine Chapel); Norman cathedral; Regional Gallery (medieval); some 8000 preserved bodies in the catacombs of the Cappuchin Convent. Nearby: 12c Norman Duomo di Monreale. www.palermotourism.com 176 A2

Syracuse Siracusa

Built on an island connected to the mainland by a bridge, the old town has a 7c cathedral, ruins of the Temple of Apollo; Fountain of Arethusa; archaeological museum. On the mainland: 5c BC Greek theatre with seats cut out of rock; Greek fortress of Euralus; 2c Roman amphitheatre; 5–6c Catacombs of St John. 177 B4

Latvia Latvija

www.latvia.travel/en

Riga

Well-preserved medieval town centre around the cathedral. Sights: Riga Castle; medieval Hanseatic houses; Great Guild Hall; Gothic Church of St Peter; Art Nouveau buildings in the New Town. Nearby: Baroque Rundale Castle. www.latvia.travel/en/riga 8 D4

Lithuania Lietuva

www.lithuania.travel/en-gb

Vilnius

Baroque old town with fine architecture including: cathedral; Gediminas Tower; university complex; Archbishop's Palace; Church of St Anne. Also: remains of Jewish life; Vilnius Picture Gallery (16–19c regional); Lithuanian National Museum. http://vilnius.com 13 A6

Luxembourg

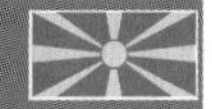

www.visitluxembourg.com/en

Luxembourg

Capital of Luxembourg, built on a rock with fine views. Old town is around the Place d'Armes. Buildings: Grand Ducal Palace; fortifications of Rocher du Bock; cathedral. Museum of History and Art holds an excellent regional collection. 92 B2

Macedonia Makedonija

www.exploringmacedonia.com

Ohrid

Old town, beautifully set by a lake, with houses of wood and brick, remains of a Turkish citadel, many churches (two cathedrals; St Naum south of the lake). www.ohrid.com.mk 182 B2

Skopje

Historic town with Turkish citadel, fine 15c mosques, oriental bazaar, ancient bridge. Superb Byzantine churches nearby. 182 A3

Malta

www.visitmalta.com

Valletta

Capital of Malta. Historic walled city, founded in 16c by the Maltese Knights, with 16c Grand Master's Palace and a richly decorated cathedral. 175 C3

Monaco

www.visitmonaco.com

Monaco

Major resort area in a beautiful location. Sights include: Monte Carlo casino, Prince's Palace at Monaco-Ville; 19c cathedral; oceanographic museum. 133 B3

Netherlands Nederland

http://holland.com

Amsterdam

Capital of the Netherlands. Old centre has picturesque canals lined with distinctive elegant 17–18c merchants' houses. Dam Square has 15c New Church and Royal Palace. Other churches include Westerkerk. The Museumplein has three world-famous museums: the newly restored Rijksmuseum (several art collections including 15–17c painting); Van Gogh Museum; Municipal Museum (art from 1850 on). Other museums: Anne Frank House; Jewish Historical Museum; Rembrandt House; Hermitage Museum (exhibitions). 70 B1

Delft

Well-preserved old Dutch town with gabled red-roofed houses along canals. Gothic churches: New Church; Old Church. Famous for Delftware (two museums). www.delft.nl 70 B1

Haarlem

Many medieval gabled houses centred on the Great Market with 14c Town Hall and 15c Church of St Bavon. Museums: Frans Hals Museum; Teylers Museum. www.haarlemmarketing.co.uk 70 B1

The Hague Den Haag

Seat of Government and of the royal house of the Netherlands. The 17c Mauritshuis houses the Royal Picture Gallery (excellent 15–18c Flemish and Dutch). Other museums: Escher Museum; Meermanno Museum (books); Municipal Museum. 70 B1

Het Loo

Former royal palace and gardens set in a vast landscape (commissioned by future the future King and Queen of England, William and Mary). www.paleishetloo.nl 70 B2

Keukenhof

In spring, landscaped gardens, planted with bulbs of many varieties, are the largest flower gardens in the world. www.keukenhof.nl 70 B1

Leiden

University town of beautiful gabled houses set along canals. The

▼ Westerkerk, Amsterdam, Netherlands

Rijksmuseum Van Oudheden is Holland's most important home to archaeological artefacts from the Antiquity. The 16c Hortus Botanicus is one of the oldest botanical gardens in Europe. The Cloth Hall with van Leyden's Last Judgement. http://leidenholland.com 70 B1

Rotterdam

The largest port in the world. The Boymans-van Beuningen Museum has a huge and excellent decorative and fine art collection (old and modern). Nearby: 18c Kinderdijk with 19 windmills. https://en.rotterdam.info 79 A4

Utrecht

Delightful old town centre along canals with the Netherlands' oldest university and Gothic cathedral. Good art collections: Central Museum; National Museum. www.utrecht.nl 70 B2

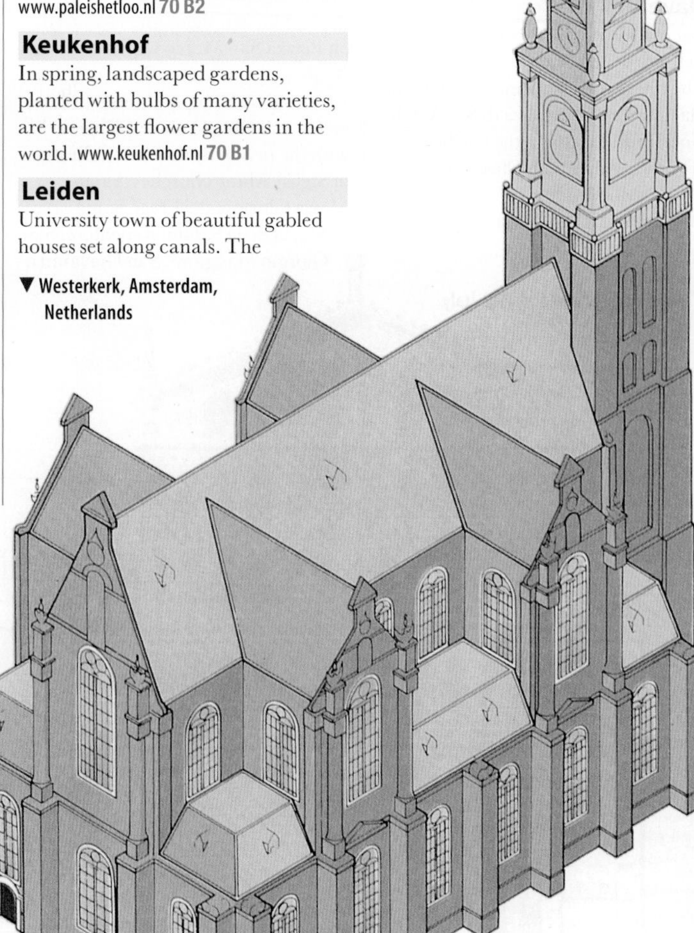

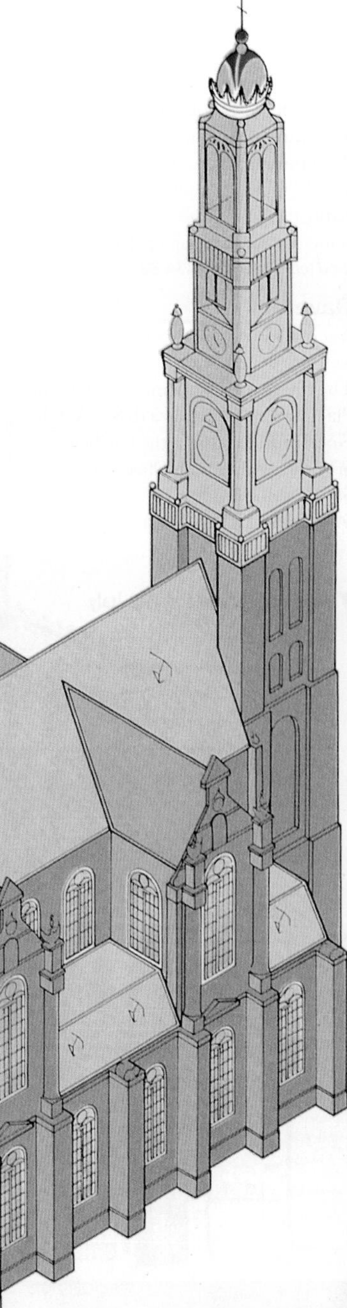

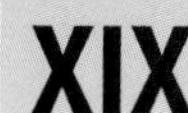

Norway Norge

www.visitnorway.com

Bergen
Norway's second city in a scenic setting. The Quay has many painted wooden medieval buildings. Sights: 12c Romanesque St Mary's Church; Bergenhus fortress with 13c Haakon's Hall; Rosenkrantz Tower; Grieghallen; Bergen Art Museum (Norwegian art); Bryggens Museum. https://en.visitbergen.com **46 B2**

Lappland (Norwegian)
Vast land of Finnmark is home to the Sámi. Nordkapp is the northern point of Europe. Also Finland, Sweden. **192–193**

Norwegian Fjords
Beautiful and majestic landscape of deep glacial valleys filled by the sea. The most thrilling fjords are between Bergen and Ålesund. www.fjords.com **46 & 198**

Oslo
Capital of Norway with a modern centre. Buildings: 17c cathedral; 19c city hall, 19c royal palace; 19c Stortinget (housing parliament); 19c University; 13c Akershus (castle); 12c Akerskirke (church). Museums: National Gallery; Munch Museum; Viking Ship Museum; Folk Museum (reconstructed buildings). www.visitoslo.com **48 C2**

Stavkirker
Wooden medieval stave churches of bizarre pyramidal structure, carved with images from Nordic mythology. Best preserved in southern Norway.

Tromsø
Main arctic city of Norway with a university and two cathedrals. www.visittromso.no/en **192 C3**

Trondheim
Set on the edge of a fjord, a modern city with the superb Nidaros cathedral (rebuilt 19c). Also: Stiftsgaard (royal residence); Applied Arts Museum. www.trondheim.com **199 B7**

Poland Polska
www.poland.travel/en-gb

Częstochowa
Centre of Polish Catholicism, with the 14c monastery of Jasna Góra a pilgrimage site to the icon of the Black Madonna for six centuries. www.jasnagora.pl **86 B3**

Gdańsk
Medieval centre with: 14c Town Hall (state rooms); Gothic brick St Mary's Church, Poland's largest; Long Market has fine buildings (Artus Court); National Museum. www.gdansk.pl/en **69 A3**

Kraków
Old university city, rich in architecture, centred on superb 16c Marketplace with Gothic-Renaissance Cloth Hall containing the Art Gallery (19c Polish), Clock Tower, Gothic red-brick St Mary's Church (altarpiece). Czartoryski Palace has city's finest art collection. Wawel Hill has the Gothic cathedral and splendid Renaissance Royal Palace. The former Jewish ghetto in Kazimierz district has 16c Old Synagogue, now a museum. www.krakow.pl/english **99 A3**

Poznań
Town centred on the Old Square with Renaissance Town Hall and Baroque mansions. Also: medieval castle; Gothic cathedral; National Museum (European masters). **76 B1**

Tatry
One of Europe's most delightful mountain ranges with many beautiful ski resorts (Zakopane). Also in Slovakia. **99 B3**

Warsaw Warszawa
Capital of Poland, with many historic monuments in the Old Town with the Royal Castle (museum) and Old Town Square surrounded by reconstructed 17–18c merchants' houses. Several churches including: Gothic cathedral; Baroque Church of the Nuns of Visitation. Richly decorated royal palaces and gardens: Neoclassical Łazienki Palace; Baroque palace in Wilanów. The National Museum has Polish and European art. www.warsawtour.pl/en **77 C6**

Wrocław
Historic town centred on the Market Square with 15c Town Hall and mansions. Churches: Baroque cathedral; St Elizabeth; St Adalbert. National Museum displays fine art. Vast painting of Battle of Racławice is specially housed. http://visitwroclaw.eu/en **85 A5**

Portugal

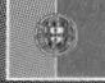

www.visitportugal.com

Alcobaça
Monastery of Santa Maria, one of the best examples of a Cistercian abbey, founded in 1147 (exterior 17–18c). The church is Portugal's largest (14c tombs). www.mosteiroalcobaca.pt/en **154 A1**

Algarve
Modern seaside resorts among picturesque sandy beaches and rocky coves (Praia da Rocha). Old towns: Lagos; Faro. **160 B1** www.visitalgarve.pt/index.php?IDIOMA=vEN

Batalha
Abbey is one of the masterpieces of French Gothic and Manueline architecture (tombs, English Perpendicular chapel, unfinished pantheon). www.mosteirobatalha.pt/en **154 A2**

Braga
Historic town with cathedral and large Archbishop's Palace. **148 A1**

Coimbra
Old town with narrow streets set on a hill. The Romanesque cathedral is particularly fine (portal). The university (founded 1290) has a fascinating Baroque library. Also: Museum of Machado de Castro; many monasteries and convents. **148 B1**

Évora
Centre of the town, surrounded by walls, has narrow streets of Moorish character and medieval and Renaissance architecture. Churches: 12–13c Gothic cathedral; São Francisco with a chapel decorated with bones of some 5000 monks; 15c Convent of Dos Lóis. The Jesuit university was founded in 1559. Museum of Évora holds fine art (particularly Flemish and Portugese). http://www.evora-portugal.com **154 C3**

Guimarães
Old town with a castle with seven towers on a vast keep. Churches: Romanesque chapel of São Miguel; São Francisco. Alberto Sampaio Museum and Martins Sarmento Museum are excellent. www.visitportugal.com/en/node/73742 **148 A1**

Lisbon Lisboa
Capital of Portugal. Baixa is the Neoclassical heart of Lisbon with the Praça do Comércio and Rossío squares. São Jorge castle (Visigothic, Moorish, Romanesque) is surrounded by the medieval quarters. Bairro Alto is famous for *fado* (songs). Monastery of Jerónimos is exceptional. Churches: 12c cathedral; São Vicente de Fora; São Roque (tiled chapels); Torre de Belém; Convento da Madre de Deus. Museums: Gulbenkian Museum (ancient, oriental, European), National Museum of Ancient Art; Design Museum; Modern Art Centre; Azulego Museum (decorative tiles). Nearby: palatial monastic complex Mafra; royal resort Sintra. www.visitlisboa.com **154 B1**

Porto
Historic centre with narrow streets. Views from Clérigos Tower. Churches: São Francisco; cathedral. Soares dos Reis Museum holds fine and decorative arts (18–19c). The suburb of Vila Nova de Gaia is the centre for port wine. www.visitporto.travel **148 A1**

Tomar
Attractive town with the Convento de Cristo, founded in 1162 as the headquarters of the Knights Templar (Charola temple, chapter house, Renaissance cloisters). **154 A2**

Romania

www.romaniatourism.com

Bucovina
Beautiful region in northern Romanian Moldova renowned for a number of 15–16c monasteries and their fresco cycles. Of particular note are Moldovita, Voroneţ and Suceviţa. **17 B6**

Bucharest Bucureşti
Capital of Romania with the majority of sites along the Calea Victoriei and centring on Piaţa Revoluţei with 19c Romanian Athenaeum and 1930s Royal Palace housing the National Art Gallery. The infamous 1980s Civic Centre with People's Palace is a symbol of dictatorial aggrandisement. **17 C7**

Carpathian Mountains Carpaţii
The beautiful Carpathian Mountains have several ski resorts (Sinaia) and peaks noted for first-rate mountaineering (Făgă raşuiui, Rodnei). Danube Delta Europe's largest marshland, a spectacular nature reserve. Travel in the area is by boat, with Tulcea the starting point for visitors. The Romanian Black Sea Coast has a stretch of resorts (Mamaia, Eforie) between Constantaţ and the border, and well-preserved Roman remains in Histria. **17 B6**

Transylvania Transilvania
Beautiful and fascinating scenic region of medieval citadels (Timişoara, Sibiu) provides a setting for the haunting image of the legendary Dracula (Sighişoara, Braşov, Bran Castle). Cluj-Napoca is the main town. **17 B5**

Russia Rossiya
www.visitrussia.org.uk

Moscow Moskva
Capital of Russia, with many monuments. Within the Kremlin's red walls are: 15c Cathedral of the Dormition; 16c Cathedral of the Archangel; Cathedral of the Annunciation (icons), Armour Palace. Outside the walls, Red Square has the Lenin Mausoleum and 16c St Basil's Cathedral. There are a number of monasteries (16c Novodevichi). Two superb museums: Tretiakov Art Gallery (Russian); Pushkin Museum of Fine Art (European); also State Historical Museum. Kolomenskoe, once a royal summer retreat, has the Church of the Ascension. **9 E10**

Novgorod
One of Russia's oldest towns, centred on 15c Kremlin with St Sophia Cathedral (iconostasis, west door). Two other cathedrals: St Nicholas; St George. Museum of History, Architecture and Art has notable icons and other artefacts. http://visitnovgorod.com **9 C7**

Peterhof (Petrovdorets)
Also known as Petrovdorets, Peterhof is a grand palace with numerous pavilions (Monplaisir) set in beautiful parkland interwoven by a system of fountains, cascades and waterways connected to the sea. http://en.peterhofmuseum.ru **9 C6**

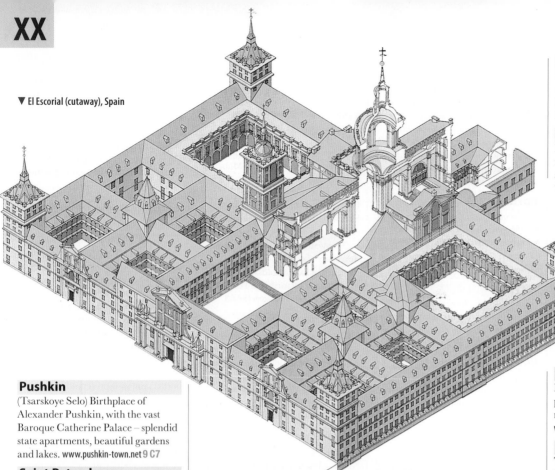
▼ El Escorial (cutaway), Spain

Burgos
Medieval town with Gothic cathedral, Moorish-Gothic Royal Monastery and Charterhouse of Miraflores. **143 B3**

Cáceres
Medieval town surrounded by originally Moorish walls and with several aristocratic palaces with solars. **155 A4**

Córdoba

Capital of Moorish Spain with a labyrinth of streets and houses with tile-decorated patios. The 8–10c Mezquita is the finest mosque in Spain. A 16c cathedral was added at the centre of the building and a 17c tower replaced the minaret. The old Jewish quarter has 14c synagogue http://english.turismodecordoba.org **156 C3**

El Escorial
Immense Renaissance complex of palatial and monastic buildings and mausoleum of the Spanish monarchs. www.patrimonionacional.es **151 B3**

Granada
The Alhambra was hill-top palace-fortress of the rulers of the last Moorish kingdom and is the most splendid example of Moorish art and architecture in Spain. The complex has three principal parts: Alcazaba fortress (11c); Casa Real palace (14c, with later Palace of Carlos V); Generalife gardens. Also: Moorish quarter; gypsy quarter; Royal Chapel with good art in the sacristy. www.turgranada.es **163 A4**

León
Gothic cathedral has notable stained glass. Royal Pantheon commemorates early kings of Castile and León. **142 B1**

Madrid
Capital of Spain, a mainly modern city with 17–19c architecture at its centre around Plaza Mayor. Sights: Royal Palace with lavish apartments; Descalzas Reales Convent (tapestries and other works); Royal Armoury museum. Spain's three leading galleries: Prado (15–18c); Queen Sofia Centre (20c Spanish, Picasso's *Guernica*); Thyssen-Bornemisza Museum (medieval to modern). http://turismomadrid.es/en/ **151 B4**

Oviedo
Gothic cathedral with 12c sanctuary. Three Visigoth (9c) churches: Santullano, Santa María del Naranco, San Miguel de Lillo. **141 A5**

Palma
Situated on Mallorca, the largest and most beautiful of the Balearic islands, with an impressive Gothic cathedral. www.palma.com **166 B2**

Picos de Europa
Mountain range with river gorges and peaks topped by Visigothic and Romanesque churches. **142 A2**

Pushkin
(Tsarskoye Selo) Birthplace of Alexander Pushkin, with the vast Baroque Catherine Palace – splendid state apartments, beautiful gardens and lakes. www.pushkin-town.net **9 C7**

Saint Petersburg
Sankt Peterburg
Founded in 1703 with the SS Peter and Paul Fortress and its cathedral by Peter the Great, and functioning as seat of court and government until 1918. Many of the most famous sights are around elegant Nevski Prospekt. The Hermitage, one of the world's largest and finest art collections is housed in several buildings including the Baroque Winter and Summer palaces. The Mikhailovsky Palace houses the Russian Museum (Russian art). Other sights: neoclassical Admiralty; 19c St Isaac's Cathedral and St Kazan Cathedral; Vasilievsky Island with 18c Menshikov Palace; Alexander Nevsky Monastery; 18c Smolny Convent. www.saint-petersburg.com **9 C7**

Sergiev Posad
(Zagorsk) Trinity St Sergius monastery with 15c cathedral. **9 D11**

Serbia Srbija
www.serbia.travel

Belgrade Beograd
Capital of Serbia. The largely modern city is set between the Danube and Sava rivers. The National Museum holds European art. To the south there are numerous fascinating medieval monasteries, richly embellished with frescoes. www.tob.rs **127 C2**

Slovakia Slovenska Republika
http://slovakia.travel/en

Bratislava
Capital of Slovakia, dominated by the castle (Slovak National Museum, good views). Old Town centred on the Main Square with Old Town Hall and Jesuit Church. Many 18–19c palaces (Mirbach Palace, Pálffy Palace, Primate's Palace), churches (Gothic cathedral, Corpus Christi Chapel) and museums (Slovak National Gallery). www.visitbratislava.com **111 A4**

Košice
Charming old town with many Baroque and neoclassical buildings and Gothic cathedral. **12 D4**

Spišské Podhradie
Region, east of the Tatry, full of picturesque medieval towns (Levoča, Kežmarok, Prešov) and architectural monuments (Spišský Castle). **99 B4**

Tatry
Beautiful mountain region. Poprad is an old town with 19c villas. Starý Smokovec is a popular ski resort. See also Poland. **99 B3**

Slovenia Slovenija
www.slovenia.info/en

Istria Istra
Two town centres, Koper and Piran, with medieval and Renaissance squares and Baroque palaces. See also Croatia. **122 B2**

Julian Alps Julijske Alpe
Wonderfully scenic section of the Alps with lakes (Bled, Bohinj), deep valleys (Planica, Vrata) and ski resorts (Kranjska Gora, Bohinjska Bistrica). **122 A2**

Karst Caves
Numerous caves with huge galleries, extraordinary stalactites and stalagmites, and underground rivers. The most spectacular are Postojna (the most famous, with Predjamski Castle nearby) and Škocjan. www.postojnska-jama.eu/en **123 B3**

Ljubljana
Capital of Slovenia. The old town, dominated by the castle (good views), is principally between Prešeren Square and Town Hall (15c, 18c), with the Three Bridges and colonnaded market. Many Baroque churches (cathedral, St Jacob, St Francis, Ursuline) and palaces (Bishop's Palace, Seminary, Gruber Palace). Also: 17c Križanke church and monastery complex; National Gallery and Modern Gallery show Slovene art. www.visitljubljana.com/en/visitors **123 A3**

Spain España
www.spain.info

Ávila
Medieval town with 2km-long 11c walls. Pilgrimage site to shrines to St Teresa of Ávila (Convent of Santa Teresa, Convent of the Incarnation). www.avila.com/avila_tourism **150 B3**

Barcelona
Showcase of Gothic ('Barri Gòtic': cathedral; Santa María del Mar; mansions on Carrer de Montcada) and *modernista* architecture ('Eixample' area with Manzana de la Discòrdia; Sagrada Familia, Güell Park, La Pedrera). Many elegant boulevards (La Rambla, Passeig de Gràcia). Museums: Modern Catalan Art, Catalan Archaeology, Picasso Museum, Miró Museum, Tàpies Museum. Nearby: monastery of Montserrat (Madonna); Figueres (Dali Museum). www.barcelonaturisme.com/wv3/en **147 C3**

Pyrenees

Unspoiled mountain range with beautiful landscape and vilages full of Romanesque architecture (cathedral of Jaca). The Ordesa National Park has many waterfalls and canyons. **144–145**

Salamanca

Delightful old city with some uniquely Spanish architecture: Renaissance Plateresque is famously seen on 16c portal of the university (founded 1215); Baroque Churrigueresque on 18c Plaza Mayor; both styles at the Convent of San Esteban. Also: Romanesque Old Cathedral; Gothic-Plateresque New Cathedral; House of Shells. www.salamanca.es/en **150 B2**

Santiago di Compostela

Medieval city with many churches and religious institutions. The famous pilgrimage to the shrine of St James the Apostle ends here in the magnificent cathedral, originally Romanesque with many later elements (18c Baroque façade). www.santiagoturismo.com **140 B2**

Segovia

Old town set on a rock with a 1c Roman aqueduct. Also: 16c Gothic cathedral; Alcázar (14–15c, rebuilt 19c); 12-sided 13c Templar church of Vera Cruz. **151 B3**

Seville Sevilla

City noted for festivals and flamenco. The world's largest Gothic cathedral (15c) retains the Orange Court and minaret of a mosque. The Alcazar is a fine example of Moorish architecture. The massive 18c tobacco factory, now part of the university, was the setting for Bizet's *Carmen*. Barrio de Santa Cruz is the old Jewish quarter with narrow streets and white houses. Casa de Pilatos (15–16c) has a fine domestic patio. The Museum of Fine Arts is in a former convent. Nearby: Roman Italica with amphitheatre. **162 A2**

Tarragona

The city and its surroundings have some of the best-preserved Roman heritage in Spain. Also: Gothic cathedral (cloister); Archaeological Museum. www.tarragonaturisme.cat **147 C2**

Toledo

Historic city with Moorish, Jewish and Christian sights. The small 11c mosque of El Cristo de la Luz is one of the earliest in Spain. Two synagogues have been preserved: Santa María la Blanca; El Tránsito. Churches: San Juan de los Reyes; Gothic cathedral (good artworks). El Greco's *Burial of the Count of Orgaz* is in the Church of Santo Tomé. More of his works are in the El Greco house and, with other art, in Hospital de Santa Cruz. **151 C3**

Valencia

The old town has houses and palaces with elaborate façades. Also: Gothic cathedral and Lonja de la Seda church. www.visitvalencia.com **159 B3**

Zaragoza

Town notable for Moorish architecture (11c Aljafería Palace). The Basilica de Nuestra Señora del Pilar, one of two cathedrals, is highly venerated. www.zaragoza.es/turismo **153 A3**

Sweden Sverige 🇸🇪

https://visitsweden.com

Abisko

Popular resort in the Swedish part of Lapland set in an inspiring landscape of lakes and mountains. www.visitabisko.com **194 B9**

Gothenburg Göteborg

Largest port in Sweden, the historic centre has 17–18c Dutch architectural character (Kronhuset). The Art Museum has interesting Swedish works. www.goteborg.com/en **60 B1**

Gotland

Island with Sweden's most popular beach resorts (Ljugarn) and unspoiled countryside with churches in Baltic Gothic style (Dahlem, Bunge). Visby is a pleasant walled medieval town. http://gotland.com/en **57 C4**

Lappland (Swedish)

Swedish part of Lappland with 18c Arvidsjaur the oldest preserved Sámi village. Jokkmokk is a Sámi cultural centre, Abisko a popular resort in fine scenery. Also Finland, Norway. www.kirunalapland.se **192–193**

Lund

Charming university city with medieval centre and a fine 12c Romanesque cathedral (14c astronomical clock, carved tombs). www.visitlund.se/en **61 D3**

Malmö

Old town centre set among canals and parks dominated by a red-brick castle (museums) and a vast market square with Town Hall and Gothic Church of St Peter. www.malmotown.com/en **61 D3**

Mora

Delightful village on the shores of Siljan Lake in the heart of the Dalarna region, home to folklore and traditional crafts. **50 A1**

Stockholm

Capital of Sweden built on a number of islands. The Old Town is largely on three islands with 17–18c houses, Baroque Royal Castle (apartments and museums), Gothic cathedral, parliament. Riddarholms church has tombs of the monarchy. Museums include: National Museum; Modern Museum (one of world's best modern collections); Nordiska Museet (cultural history); open-air Skansen (Swedish houses). Baroque Drottningholm Castle is the residence of the monarchy. www.visitstockholm.com **57 A4**

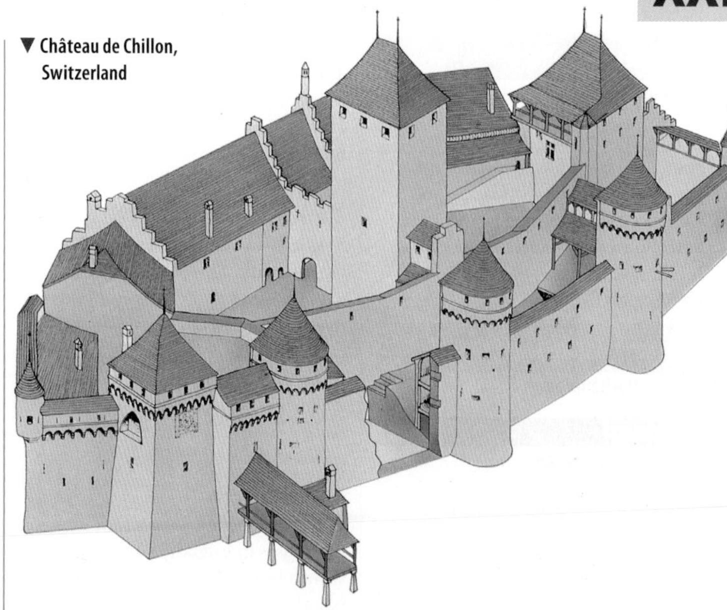

▼ Château de Chillon, Switzerland

Swedish Lakes

Beautiful region around the Vättern and Vänern Lakes. Siljan Lake is in the Dalarna region where folklore and crafts are preserved (Leksand, Mora, Rättvik). **55 B4**

Uppsala

Appealing university town with a medieval centre around the massive Gothic cathedral. www.destinationuppsala.se/en **51 C4**

Switzerland Schweiz ➕

www.myswitzerland.com

Alps

The most popular Alpine region is the Berner Oberland with the town of Interlaken a starting point for exploring the large number of picturesque peaks (Jungfrau). The valleys of the Graubünden have famous ski resorts (Davos, St Moritz). Zermatt lies below the most recognizable Swiss peak, the Matterhorn. **119 A4**

Basle Basel

Medieval university town with Romanesque-Gothic cathedral (tomb of Erasmus). Superb collections: Art Museum; Museum of Contemporary Art. www.basel.com/en **106 B2**

Bern

Capital of Switzerland. Medieval centre has fountains, characteristic streets (Spitalgasse) and tower-gates. The Bärengraben is famed for its bears. Also: Gothic cathedral; good Fine Arts Museum. www.bern.com/en **106 C2**

Geneva Genève

The historic area is centred on the Romanesque cathedral and Place du Bourg du Four. Excellent collections: Art and History Museum; new Museum of Modern and Contemporary Art. On the lake shore: splendid medieval Château de Chillon. www.geneve.com **118 A3**

Interlaken

Starting point for excursions to the most delightful part of the Swiss Alps, the Bernese Oberland, with Grindelwald and Lauterbrunnen – one of the most thrilling valleys leading up to the ski resort of Wengen with views on the Jungfrau. www.interlaken.ch **106 C2**

Lucerne Luzern

On the beautiful shores of Vierwaldstättersee, a charming medieval town of white houses on narrow streets and of wooden bridges (Kapellbrücke, Spreuerbrücke). It is centred on the Kornmarkt with the Renaissance Old Town Hall and Am Rhyn-Haus (Picasso collection). www.luzern.com/en **106 C1**

Zürich

Set on Zürichsee, the old quarter is around Niederdorf with 15c cathedral. Gothic Fraumünster has stained glass by Chagall. Museums: Swiss National Museum (history); Art Museum (old and modern masters); Rietberg Museum (non-European cultures). www.zuerich.com/en **107 B3**

Turkey Türkiye ☪

www.tourismturkey.org

Istanbul

Divided by the spectcular Bosphorus, the stretch of water that separates Europe from Asia, the historic district is surrounded by the Golden Horn, Sea of Marmara and the 5c wall of Theodosius. Major sights: 6c Byzantine church of St Sophia (converted first to a mosque in 1453 and then to a museum in 1934); 15c Topkapi Palace; treasury and Archaeological Museum; 17c Blue Mosque; 19c Bazaar; 16c Süleymaniye Mosque; 12c Kariye Camii; European district with Galata Tower and 19c Dolmabahçe Palace. http://en.istanbul.com **186 A3**

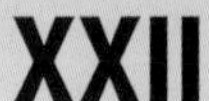

Ukraine Ukraina

www.ukraine.com

Kiev Kyїv
Capital of Ukraine, known for its cathedral (11c, 17c) with Byzantine frescoes and mosaics. The Monastery of the Caves has churches, monastic buildings and catacombs.
www.kiev.info **13 C9**

United Kingdom

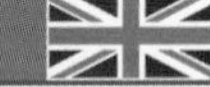

www.visitbritain.com

England
www.visitengland.com

Bath
Elegant spa town with notable 18c architecture: Circus, Royal Crescent, Pulteney Bridge, Assembly Rooms; Pump Room. Also: well-preserved Roman baths; superb Perpendicular Gothic Bath Abbey. Nearby: Elizabethan Longleat House; exceptional 18c landscaped gardens at Stourhead. https://visitbath.co.uk **43 A4**

Brighton
Resort with a sea-front of Georgian, Regency and Victorian buildings, Palace Pier, i360 observation tower, and old town of narrow lanes. The main sight is the Oriental-style Royal Pavilion. Nearby: South Downs National Park.
www.visitbrighton.com **44 C3**

Bristol
Old port city with the fascinating Floating Harbour. Major sights include Gothic 13–14c Church of St Mary Redcliffe, SS Great Britain and 19c Clifton Suspension Bridge.
http://visitbristol.co.uk **43 A4**

Cambridge
City with university founded in the early 13c. Peterhouse (1284) is the oldest college. Most famous colleges were founded in 14–16c: Queen's, King's (with the superb Perpendicular Gothic 15–16c King's College Chapel), St John's (with famous 19c Bridge of Sighs), Trinity, Clare, Gonville and Caius, Magdalene. Museums: excellent Fitzwilliam Museum (classical, medieval, old masters). Kettle's Yard (20c British). www.visitcambridge.org **45 A4**

Canterbury
Medieval city and old centre of Christianity. The Norman-Gothic cathedral has many sights and was a major medieval pilgrimage site (as related in Chaucer's *Canterbury Tales*). St Augustine, sent to convert the English in 597, founded St Augustine's Abbey, now in ruins.
www.canterbury.co.uk **45 B5**

Chatsworth
One of the richest aristocratic country houses in England (largely 17c) set in a large landscaped park. The palatial interior has some 175 richly furnished rooms and a major art collection. www.chatsworth.org **40 B2**

Chester
Charming medieval city with complete walls. The Norman-Gothic cathedral has several abbey buildings. www.visitchester.com **38 A4**

Cornish Coast
Scenic landscape of cliffs and sandy beaches with picturesque villages (Fowey, Mevagissey). St Ives has the Tate Gallery with work of the St Ives Group. St Michael's Mount is reached by causeway at low tide.
www.visitcornwall.com **42 B1**

Dartmoor
Beautiful wilderness area in Devon with tors and its own breed of wild pony as well as free-ranging cattle and sheep. www.dartmoor.gov.uk **42 B3**

Durham
Historic city with England's finest Norman cathedral and a castle, both placed majestically on a rock above the river. www.thisisdurham.com **37 B5**

Eden Project
Centre showing the diversity of plant life on the planet, built in a disused clay pit. Two biomes, one with Mediterranean and Southern African focus and the larger featuring a waterfall, river and tropical trees plants and flowers. Outdoors also features plantations including bamboo and tea. www.edenproject.com **42 B2**

Hadrian's Wall
Built to protect the northernmost border of the Roman Empire in the 2c AD, the walls originally extended some 120km with castles every mile and 16 forts. Best-preserved walls around Hexam; forts at Housesteads and Chesters.
http://hadrianswallcountry.co.uk **37 A4**

Lake District
Beautiful landscape of lakes (Windermere, Coniston) and England's high peaks (Scafell Pike, Skiddaw, Old Man), famous for its poets, particularly Wordsworth.
www.lakedistrict.gov.uk **36 B3**

Leeds Castle
One of the oldest and most romantic English castles, standing in the middle of a lake. Most of the present appearance dates from 19c.
www.leeds-castle.com **45 B4**

Lincoln
Old city perched on a hill with narrow streets, majestically dominated by the Norman-Gothic cathedral and castle.
www.visitlincolnshire.com **40 B3**

Liverpool
City on site of port founded in 1207 and focused around 1846 Albert Dock, now a heritage attraction. Croxteth Hall and Country Park; Speke Hall; Sudley House; Royal Liver Building; Liverpool Cathedral; Walker Art Gallery; Tate Liverpool; University of Liverpool Art Gallery.
www.visitliverpool.com **38 A4**

London
Capital of UK and Europe's largest city. To the east of the medieval heart of the city – now the largely modern financial district and known as the City of London – is the Tower of London (11c White Tower, Crown Jewels) and 1880s Tower Bridge. The popular heart of the city and its entertainment is the West End, around Piccadilly Circus, Leicester Square and Trafalgar Square (Nelson's Column). Many sights of political and royal power: Whitehall (Banqueting House, 10 Downing Street, Horse Guards); Neo-Gothic Palace of Westminster (Houses of Parliament) with Big Ben; The Mall leading to Buckingham Palace (royal residence, famous ceremony of the Changing of the Guard). Numerous churches include: 13–16c Gothic Westminster Abbey (many tombs, Henry VII's Chapel); Wren's Baroque St Paul's Cathedral, St Mary-le-Bow, spire of St Bride's, St Stephen Walbrook. Museums of world fame: British Museum (prehistory, oriental and classical antiquity, medieval); Victoria and Albert Museum (decorative arts); National Gallery (old masters to 19c); National Portrait Gallery (historic and current British portraiture); Tate – Britain and Modern; Science Museum; Natural History Museum. Madame Tussaud's waxworks museum is hugely popular. Other sights include: London Eye, Kensington Palace; Greenwich with Old Royal Observatory (Greenwich meridian), Baroque Royal Naval College, Palladian Queen's House; Tudor Hampton Court Palace; Syon House. Nearby: Windsor Castle (art collection, St George's Chapel).
www.visitlondon.com **44 B3**

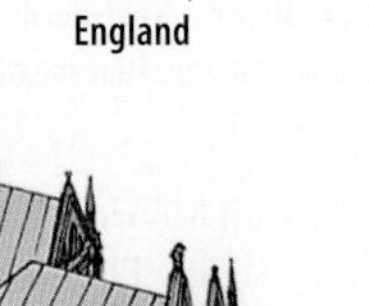

◄ Salisbury Cathedral, England

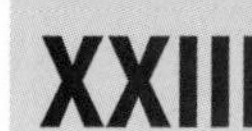

Longleat

One of the earliest and finest Elizabethan palaces in England. The palace is richly decorated. Some of the grounds have been turned into a pleasure park, with the Safari Park, the first of its kind outside Africa. www.longleat.co.uk **43 A4**

Manchester

Founded on a Roman settlement of 79AD and a main player in the Industrial Revolution. Victorian Gothic Town Hall; Royal Exchange; Cathedral. Many museums including Imperial War Museum North, Lowry Centre and Manchester Art Gallery. www.visitmanchester.com **40 B1**

Newcastle upon Tyne

A key player in the Industrial Revolution with 12th century cathedral and many museums as well as strong railway heritage. www.newcastlegateshead.com **37 B5**

Norwich

Medieval quarter has half-timbered houses. 15c castle keep houses a museum and gallery. Many medieval churches include the Norman-Gothic cathedral. www.visitnorwich.co.uk **41 C5**

Oxford

Old university city. Earliest colleges date from 13c: University College; Balliol; Merton. 14–16c colleges include: New College; Magdalen; Christ Church (perhaps the finest). Other buildings: Bodleian Library; Radcliffe Camera; Sheldonian Theatre; cathedral. Good museums: Ashmolean Museum (antiquity to 20c); Museum of the History of Science; Museum of Modern Art; Christ Church Picture Gallery (14–17c). Nearby: outstanding 18c Blenheim Palace. http://experienceoxfordshire.org **44 B2**

Petworth

House (17c) with one of the finest country-house art collections (old masters), set in a huge landscaped park. www.nationaltrust.org.uk **44 C3**

Salisbury

Pleasant old city with a magnificent 13c cathedral built in an unusually unified Gothic style. Nearby: Wilton House. www.visitwiltshire.co.uk **44 B2**

Stonehenge

Some 4000 years old, one of the most famous and haunting Neolithic monuments in Europe. Many other Neolithic sites are nearby. www.english-heritage.org.uk **44 B2**

Stourhead

Early 18c palace famous for its grounds, one of the finest examples of neoclassical landscaped gardening, consisting of a lake surrounded by numerous temples. www.nationaltrust.org.uk **43 A4**

Stratford-upon-Avon

Old town of Tudor and Jacobean half-timbered houses, famed as the birth and burial place of William Shakespeare and home of the Royal Shakespeare Company. www.shakespeare-country.co.uk **44 A2**

Wells

Charming city with beautiful 12–16c cathedral (west facade, scissor arches, chapter house, medieval clock). Also Bishop's Palace; Vicar's Close. www.wellssomerset.com **43 A4**

Winchester

Historic city with 11–16c cathedral. Also: 13c Great Hall, Winchester College, St Cross almshouses. Western gateway to the South Downs National Park. www.visitwinchester.co.uk **44 B2**

York

Attractive medieval city surrounded by well-preserved walls with magnificent Gothic 13–15c Minster. Museums: York City Art Gallery (14–19c); Jorvik Viking Centre. Nearby: Castle Howard. www.visityork.org **40 B2**

Northern Ireland
www.discovernorthernireland.com

Antrim Coast

Spectacular coast with diverse scenery of glens (Glenarm, Glenariff), cliffs (Murlough Bay) and the famous Giant's Causeway, consisting of some 40,000 basalt columns. Carrickefergus Castle is the largest and best-preserved Norman castle in Ireland. http://antrimcoastandglensaonb.ccght.org http://causewaycoastaonb.ccght.org **27 A4**

Belfast

Capital of Northern Ireland. Sights: Donegall Square with 18c Town Hall; neo-Romanesque Protestant cathedral; University Square; Ulster Museum (European painting). http://visit-belfast.com **27 B5**

Giant's Causeway

Spectacular and unique rock formations in the North Antrim coast, formed by volcanic activity 50–60 million years ago. World Heritage Site. www.nationaltrust.org.uk **27 A4**

Scotland
www.visitscotland.com

Edinburgh

Capital of Scotland, built on volcanic hills. The medieval Old Town is dominated by the castle set high on a volcanic rock (Norman St Margaret's Chapel, state apartments, Crown Room). Holyrood House (15c and 17c) has lavishly decorated state apartments and the ruins of Holyrood Abbey (remains of Scottish monarchs). The 15c cathedral has the Crown Spire and Thistle Chapel. The New Town has good Georgian architecture (Charlotte Square, Georgian House). Excellent museums: Scottish National Portrait Gallery, National Gallery of Scotland; Scottish National Gallery of Modern Art. **35 C4**

Glamis Castle

In beautiful, almost flat landscaped grounds, 14c fortress, rebuilt 17c, gives a fairy-tale impression. www.glamis-castle.co.uk **35 B5**

Glasgow

Scotland's largest city, with centre around George Square and 13–15c Gothic cathedral. The Glasgow School of Art is the masterpiece of Charles Rennie Mackintosh. Fine art collections: Glasgow Museum and Art Gallery; Hunterian Gallery; Burrell Collection; Kelvingrove Art Gallery and Museum. **35 C3**

Loch Ness

In the heart of the Highlands, the lake forms part of the scenic Great Glen running from Inverness to Fort William. Famous as home of the fabled Loch Ness Monster (exhibition at Drumnadrochit). Nearby: ruins of 14–16c Urquhart Castle. www.lochness.com **32 D2**

Wales
www.visitwales.com

Caernarfon

Town dominated by a magnificent 13c castle, one of a series built by Edward I in Wales (others include Harlech, Conwy, Beaumaris, Caerphilly). www.caernarfononline.co.uk **38 A2**

Cardiff

Capital of Wales, most famous for its medieval castle, restored 19c in Greek, Gothic and Oriental styles. Also: National Museum and Gallery. www.visitcardiff.com **39 C3**

Vatican City
Città del Vaticano
www.vatican.va

Vatican City Città del Vaticano

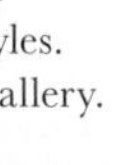

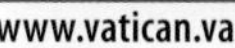

Independent state within Rome. On Piazza San Pietro is the 15–16c Renaissance-Baroque Basilica San Pietro (Michelangelo's dome and *Pietà*), the world's most important Roman Catholic church. The Vatican Palace contains the Vatican Museums with many fine art treasures including Michelangelo's frescoes in the Sistine Chapel. www.museivaticani.val **168 B2**

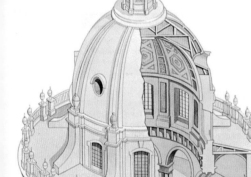

◀ Radcliffe Camera, Oxford, England

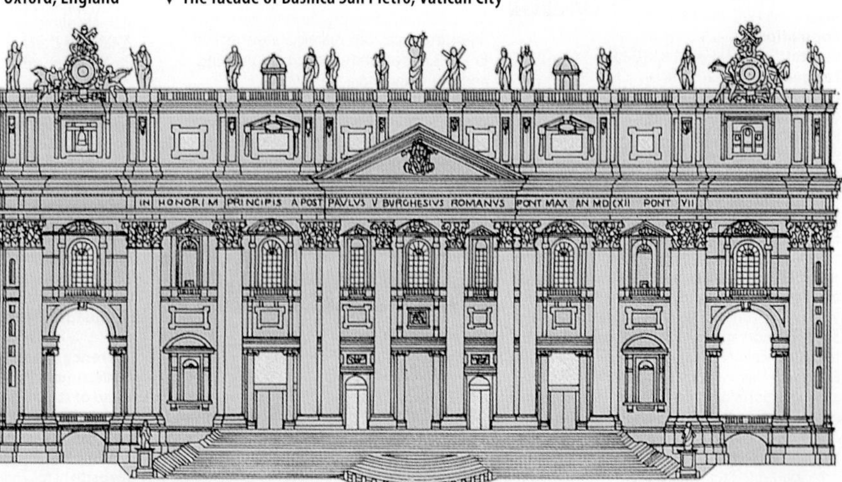

▼ The facade of Basilica San Pietro, Vatican City

European politics and economics

The figures given for capitals' populations are for the whole metropolitan area.

Albania Shqipëria

Area 28,748 km² (11,100 mi²)
Population 2,877,000
Capital Tirana / Tiranë (862,000)
Languages Albanian (official), Greek, Vlach, Romani and Slavic • **GDP** $4,470 (2017)
Currency Lek = 100 Quindars
Government multiparty republic
Head of state President Ilir Meta, 2017
Head of government Prime Minister Edi Rama, Socialist Party, 2013
Website www.kryeministria.al/en

Events In the 2005 general elections, the Democratic Party and its allies won a decisive victory on pledges of reducing crime and corruption, promoting economic growth and decreasing the size of government. The party retained power by a narrow margin in 2009, amid disputes over electoral procedure. After three years of talks, a Stabilisation and Association Agreement was signed with the EU in June 2006, and the country formally applied for membership in April 2009, the same month as it became a member of NATO. Protests at alleged official corruption and vote-rigging led to violent clashes in 2011. The Socialist Party won 53% of the vote in 2013 elections. Albania became an EU candidate member in June 2014.

Economy Although economic growth has begun, Albania is still one of the poorest countries in Europe. 56% of the workforce are engaged in agriculture. Private ownership of land has been encouraged since 1991 and foreign investment is encouraged. Public debt stands at over 70%.

Andorra Principat d'Andorra

Area 468 km² (181 mi²) • **Population** 85,000
Capital Andorra la Vella (44,000)
Languages Catalan (official), French, Castilian and Portuguese • **GDP** $45,000 (2014)
Currency Euro = 100 cents
Government independent state and co-principality
Head of state co-princes: Joan Enric Vives i Sicilia, Bishop of Urgell, 2003 and Emmanuel Macron (see France), 2017
Head of government Chief Executive Antoni Martí Petit, Democrats for Andorra, 2011
Website http://visitandorra.com

Events In 1993 a new democratic constitution was adopted that reduced the roles of the President of France and the Bishop of Urgell to constitutional figureheads. In 2010, the OECD removed Andorra from its list of uncooperative tax havens. Personal income tax was introduced in 2015 and in 2016 Parliament voted to end secrecy of bank accounts held by EU residents.

Economy About 80% of the work force are employed in the services sector, but tourism accounts for about 80% of GDP with an estimated 9 million visiting annually, attracted by its duty-free status and its summer and winter resorts. Agricultural production is limited (2% of the land is arable) and most food has to be imported. The principal livestock activity is sheep rearing. Manufacturing output consists mainly of cigarettes, cigars and furniture.

Austria Österreich

Area 83,859 km² (32,377 mi²)
Population 8,794,000
Capital Vienna / Wien (1,868,000)
Languages German (official)
GDP $44,561 (2016) • **Currency** Euro = 100 cents
Government federal republic
Head of state President Alexander Van der Bellen, Austrian Green Party, 2016
Head of government Federal Chancellor Christian Kern, Social Democratic Party, 2016
Website www.bka.gv.at

Events Since 1999, the far right Freedom Party has made gains, but Alexander Van der Bellen unexpectedly beat its candidate in presidential elections in 2016, a result confirmed when the vote was re-run. Successive poor results for the Social Democrats led to the resignation of long-term Chancellor Heinz Fischer.

Economy Has a well-developed market economy and high standard of living. The economy grew slightly in 2016. The leading economic activities are the manufacture of metals and tourism. Dairy and livestock farming are the principal agricultural activities.

Belarus

Area 207,600 km² (80,154 mi²)
Population 9,499,000
Capital Minsk (2,101,000)
Languages Belarusian, Russian (both official)
GDP $5,787 (2017)
Currency Belarussian ruble = 100 kopek
Government Republic
Head of state President Alexander Lukashenko, 1994
Head of government Andrei Kobyakov, independent, 2014
Website www.belarus.by/en/government

Events Belarus attained its independence in 1991. As a result of a referendum in 1996 the president increased his power at the expense of parliament. In 1997, Belarus signed a Union Treaty committing it to political and economic integration with Russia. Since his election in July 1994 as the country's first president, Alexander Lukashenko, has steadily consolidated his power through authoritarian means. Government restrictions on freedom of speech, the press and religion continue and in early 2005, the US listed Belarus as an outpost of tyranny. Belarus joined the EU's Eastern Partnership in 2009. In 2010, it signed a customs union with Russia and Kazakhstan. Lukashenko won a fifth term as president in October 2015, in elections seen - like those that preceded them - as corrupt. European sanctions imposed in response to earlier political clamp-downs and human-rights breaches remain.

Economy Belarus has faced problems in the transition to a free-market economy. After relaxation of currency rules in early 2011, the value of the ruble dropped sharply and the country's large foreign debts and lack of hard currency led to negotiations with Russia over substantial loans. Agriculture, especially meat and dairy farming, is important. In 2011, the country was forced to apply to the IMF for funds and for a Russian-led bailout.

Belgium Belgique

Area 30,528 km² (11,786 mi²)
Population 11,251,000
Capital Brussels/Bruxelles (1,175,000)
Languages Dutch, French, German (all official)
GDP $41,491 (2016)
Currency Euro = 100 cents
Government federal constitutional monarchy
Head of state King Philippe I, 2013
Head of government Prime Minister Charles Michel, Reformist Movement, 2014
Website www.belgium.be/en

Events In 1993 Belgium adopted a federal system of government. Elections in June 2007 led to the Christian Democrats gaining almost 30% of the vote in Flanders. An uneasy coalition was eventually formed in March 2008, but negotiations for constitutional reform stalled. Former PM Leterme replaced Herman van Rompuy when the latter became President of the European Council. The coalition collapsed in April 2010. Elections in June resulted in gains for the pro-separatist New Flemish Alliance and the Socialist Party in Wallonia. After elections in May 2014, a coalition was formed, led by Charles Michel of the Francophone Reformist Movement. In March 2016, Islamic State attacked Brussels Airport and a metro station killing 35 and wounding more than 300.

Economy Belgium is a major trading nation with a modern, private-enterprise economy, which grew slightly in 2016. The leading activity is manufacturing i.e. steel and chemicals. With few natural resources, it imports substantial quantities of raw materials and export a large volume of manufactures.

Bosnia-Herzegovina Bosna i Hercegovina

Area 51,197 km² (19,767 mi²)
Population 3,872,000
Capital Sarajevo (643,000)
Languages Bosnian/Croatian/Serbian
GDP $4,230 (2016)
Currency Convertible Marka = 100 convertible pfenniga
Government federal republic
Head of state Chairman of the Presidency – rotates between Presidency members Bakir Izetbegović (Party of Democratic Action), Mladen Ivanić (Party of Democratic Progress) and Dragan Čović (Croatian Democratic Union of Bosnia and Herzegovina)
Head of government Prime Minister Denis Zvizdić, Party of Democratic Action, 2015
Website www.fbihvlada.gov.ba/english/index.php

Events In 1992 a referendum approved independence from the Yugoslav federation. The Bosnian Serb population was against independence and in the resulting war occupied over two-thirds of the land. Croat forces seized other parts of the area. The 1995 Dayton Peace Accord ended the war and set up the Bosnian Muslim/Croat Federation and the Bosnian Serb Republic, each with their own president, government, parliament, military and police. There is also a central Bosnian government and rotating presidency. The office of High Representative has the power to impose decisions where the authorities are unable to agree or where political or economic interests are affected; the current incumbent, Valentin Inzko took charge in 2009. EUFOR troops took over from the NATO-led force in 2004. In 2005, agreement was reached to set up state-wide police, defence and security forces, a state court and state taxation system. In 2006, Bosnia joined NATO's Partnership for Peace programme and received its membership action plan in 2010. In 2007, the EU initiated its Stabilisation and Association Agreement with Bosnia, which was eventually signed in March 2015. In February 2016, Bosnia formally applied to join the EU.

Economy Excluding Macedonia, Bosnia was the least developed of the former republics of Yugoslavia. Currently receiving substantial aid, though this will be reduced. The country attracts considerable foreign direct investment and the Convertible Marka is Euro-pegged. The economy grew slightly in 2016.

Bulgaria Bulgariya

Area 110,912 km² (42,822 mi²)
Population 7,102,000
Capital Sofia (1,682,000)
Languages Bulgarian (official), Turkish
GDP $7,369 (2016)
Currency Lev = 100 stotinki
Government multiparty republic
Head of state President Rumen Radev, Independent, 2017
Head of government Prime Minister Boiko Borisov, Citizens for European Development of Bulgaria (GERB), 2014.
Website www.government.bg

Events In 1990 the first non-communist president for 40 years, Zhelyu Zhelev, was elected. A new constitution in 1991 saw the adoption of free-market reforms. Bulgaria joined NATO in 2004. The president was re-elected in 2006. Bulgaria joined the EU in January 2007, but lack of progress in tackling corruption has led to the delay, then scrapping of a large proportion of EU funding. The GERB-led coalition fell in early 2012 after street protests and was replaced in May 2013 by a technocratic government. After independent Ruman Radev beat the GERB candidate in presidential elections in early 2017, PM Boiko Borisov called snap parliamentary elections, in which he won a third term.

Economy The Lev has been pegged to the Euro since 2002. The economy has begun to attract significant amounts of foreign direct investment. Bulgaria experienced macroeconomic stability and strong growth from 1996 to early 2008, and after a sharp decline in GDP in 2009, the economy returned to slight growth from 2010. Manufacturing is the leading economic activity but has outdated technology. The main products are chemicals, metals, machinery and textiles. The valleys of the Maritsa are ideal for winemaking, plums and tobacco. Tourism is increasing rapidly.

Croatia Hrvatska

Area 56,538 km² (21,829 mi²)
Population 4,191,000
Capital Zagreb (1,113,000)
Languages Croatian
GDP $12,405 (2017)
Currency Kuna = 100 lipa
Government multiparty republic
Head of state President Andrej Plenkovic, Croatian Democratic Union, 2016
Head of government Prime Minister Tihomir Oreskovic, Independent, 2016 (outgoing)
Website https://vlada.gov.hr/en

Events A 1991 referendum voted overwhelmingly in favour of independence from Yugoslavia.Serb-dominated areas took up arms to remain in the federation.Serbia armed Croatian Serbs, war broke out between Serbia and Croatia, and Croatia lost much territory. In 1992 United Nations peacekeeping troops were deployed.Following the Dayton Peace Accord of 1995, Croatia and Yugoslavia established diplomatic relations. An agreement between Croatia and the Croatian Serbs provided for the reintegration of Krajina into Croatia in 1998. Kolida Gravar-Kitarovic beat Ivo Josipopovic in presidential elections of 2014/15. After snap elections in September 2016, Andrej Plenkovic's Croatian Democratic Union formed a coalition with the centre-right MOST. Croatia joined NATO in 2009 and the EU in 2013.

Economy The wars badly disrupted Croatia's economy but it emerged from a mild recession in 2000, with tourism, banking and public investment leading the way. The economy continues to struggle and unemployment is high.

Czechia Česka Republica

Area 78,864 km² (30,449 mi²)
Population 10,554,000
Capital Prague/Praha (2,157,000)
Languages Czech (official), Moravian
GDP $18,534
Currency Czech Koruna = 100 haler
Government multiparty republic
Head of state President Milos Zeman, 2013
Head of government Prime Minister Bohuslav Sobotka, SDP, 2014
Website www.vlada.cz/en/

Events In 1992 the government agreed to the secession of the Slovak Republic, and on 1 January 1993 the Czech Republic was created. The Czech Republic was granted full membership of NATO in 1999 and joined the EU in May 2004. Governments have been characterized by short-lived coalitions. PM Petr Nečas was forced to resign in June 2013 over allegations of corruption. After early parliamentary elections in October, Bohuslav Sobotka of the Social Democrats was appointed head of a coalition government in January 2014. In April 2016, the government announced that it would seek cabinet and UN approval to introduce an official short form of the country's name, Czechia.

Economy The country has deposits of coal, uranium, iron ore, tin and zinc. Industries include chemicals, beer, iron and steel. Private ownership of land is gradually being restored. Agriculture employs 12% of the workforce. Inflation is under control. Intensified restructuring among large enterprises, improvements in the financial sector and effective use of available EU funds served to strengthen output growth until the onset of the worldwide economic downturn, because of reduced exports. Prague is now a major tourist destination.

Denmark Danmark

Area 43,094 km² (16,638 mi²)
Population 5,749,000
Capital Copenhagen / København (2,037,000)
Languages Danish (official)
GDP $53,280 (2016)
Currency Krone = 100 øre
Government parliamentary monarchy
Head of state Queen Margrethe II, 1972
Head of government Prime Minister Lars Lokke Rasmussen, Venstre, 2015
Website www.denmark.dk/en

Events In 1992 Denmark rejected the Maastricht Treaty, but reversed the decision in a 1993 referendum. In 1998 the Amsterdam Treaty was ratified by a further referendum. In 2009 Greenland assumed responsibility for many domestic competencies. Former PM Lars Lokke Rasmussen was returned to power in parliamentary elections in 2015.

Economy Danes enjoy a high standard of living with a thoroughly modern market economy featuring high-tech agriculture, up-to-date small-scale and corporate industry, comfortable living standards and a stable currency, which is pegged to the Euro, but still independent. Economic growth gained momentum in 2004, but slowed in 2007. GDP has continued to grow slightly since 2012. Denmark is self-sufficient in oil and natural gas. Services, including tourism, form the largest sector (63% of GDP). Farming employs only 4% of the workforce but is highly productive. Fishing is also important.

Estonia Eesti

Area 45,100 km² (17,413 mi²)
Population 1,316,000
Capital Tallinn (543,000)
Languages Estonian (official), Russian
GDP $17,891 (2016) · **Currency** Euro = 100 cents
Government multiparty republic
Head of state President Kersti Kaljulaid, 2016
Head of government Prime Minister
Juri Ratas, Centre Party, 2016
Website www.valitsus.ee/en
Events In 1992 Estonia adopted a new constitution and multiparty elections were held. Estonia joined NATO in March 2004 and the EU in May 2004. In 2005 a treaty defining the border with Russia was signed, but Russia refused to ratify it after Estonia introduced a reference to the Russian occupation of Estonia. Since late 2016, long-time opposition Centre Party has led a broad coalition. Estonia joined the OECD in 2010 and adopted the Euro in January 2011. Strict language laws are regarded by Russian-speakers as discriminatory. In early 2017, NATO troops were deployed to the country to counter what the alliance perceives as Russian aggression.
Economy Privatisation and free-trade reforms after independence increased foreign investment and trade. Chief natural resources are oil shale and forests. Manufactures include petrochemicals, fertilisers and textiles. Estonia has led the way among new EU states with a strong electronics and communications sector. Since the country emerged from the global financial crisis in 2010, the economy has grown erratically.

Finland Suomi

Area 338,145 km² (130,557 mi²)
Population 5,506,000
Capital Helsinki (1,442,000)
Languages Finnish, Swedish (both official)
GDP $42,611 (2016) · **Currency** Euro = 100 cents
Government multiparty republic
Head of state President Sauli Niinistö,
National Coalition Party, 2012
Head of government Prime Minister
Juha Sipilä, Centre Party, 2015
Website http://valtioneuvosto.fi/en/frontpage
Events In 1986 Finland became a member of EFTA and in 1995 joined the EU. A new constitution was established in March 2000. The Finnish Parliament voted for the EU constitution in 2006. Successive governments have been in the form of multi-party coalitions. In the presidential election of 2012, Sauli Niinistö defeated Pekka-Haavisto of the Green Party.
Economy Forests are Finland's most valuable resource, with wood and paper products accounting for 35% of exports. Engineering, shipbuilding and textile industries have grown. Finland excels in high-tech exports and is a leading light in the telecoms industry. Farming employs 9% of the workforce. Unemployment remains high, although the economy returned to growth in 2011.

France

Area 551,500 km² (212,934 mi²)
Population 66,991,000
Capital Paris (12,405,000)
Languages French (official), Breton, Occitan
GDP $37,294 · **Currency** Euro = 100 cents
Government multiparty republic
Head of state President Emmanuel Macron,
En Marche!, 2017
Head of government Prime Minister
Edouard Philippe, Republicans, 2017
Website www.diplomatie.gouv.fr/en/
Events France was a founder member of both the EU and NATO. Its post-war governments have swung between socialist and centrist/right. François Hollande's reform of employment legislation led to widespread industrial action in 2016. Early 2015 saw multiple attacks by Islamic State, which it claimed to be in retaliation for French bombing raids in Syria. Further attacks followed in 2016 and 2017. Centrist Emmanuel Macron defeated Marine Le Pen of the far right National Front in the 2017 presidential elections.
Economy France is a leading industrial nation. Industries include chemicals and steel. It is the leading producer of farm products in western Europe. Livestock and dairy farming are vital sectors. Despite a degree of recovery, unemployment remains high. It is the world's second largest producer of cheese and wine. Tourism is a major industry.

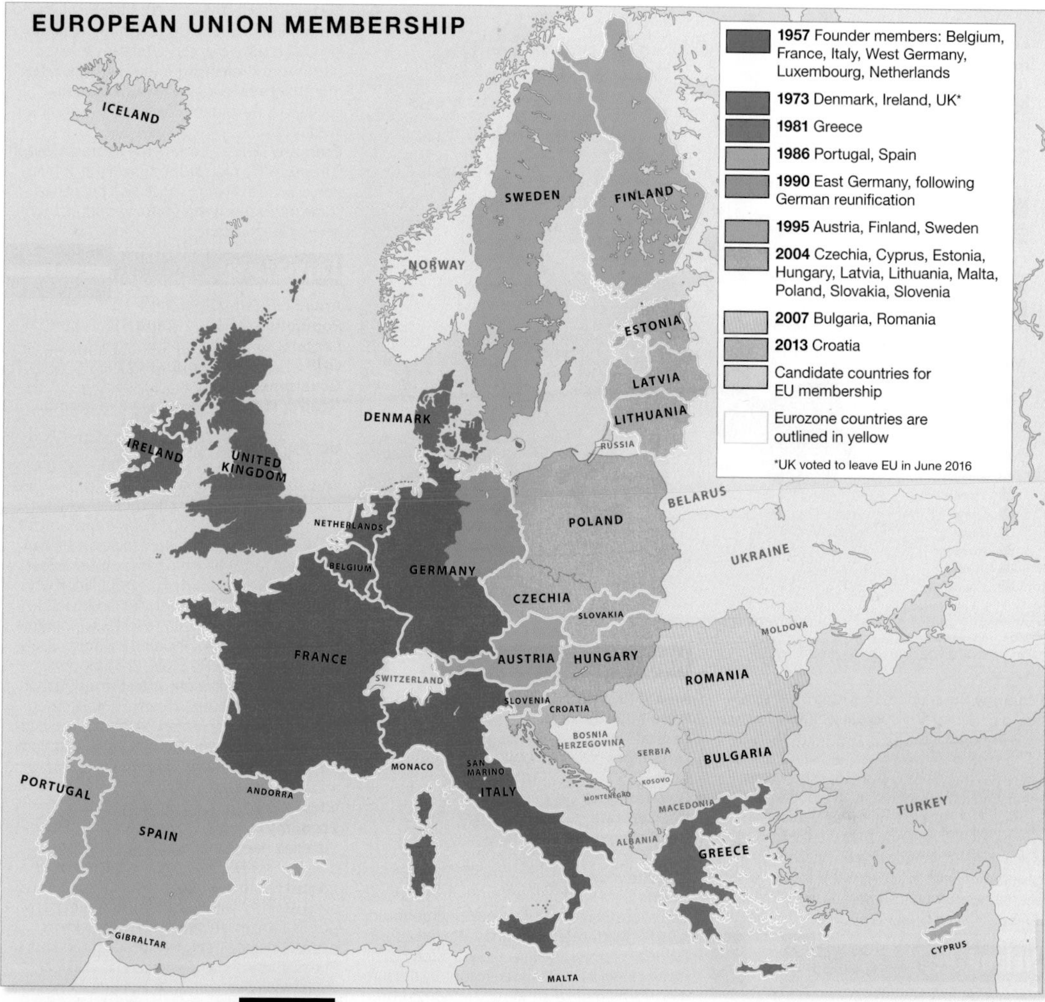

EUROPEAN UNION MEMBERSHIP

1957 Founder members: Belgium, France, Italy, West Germany, Luxembourg, Netherlands

1973 Denmark, Ireland, UK*

1981 Greece

1986 Portugal, Spain

1990 East Germany, following German reunification

1995 Austria, Finland, Sweden

2004 Czechia, Cyprus, Estonia, Hungary, Latvia, Lithuania, Malta, Poland, Slovakia, Slovenia

2007 Bulgaria, Romania

2013 Croatia

Candidate countries for EU membership

Eurozone countries are outlined in yellow

*UK voted to leave EU in June 2016

Germany Deutschland

Area 357,022 km² (137,846 mi²)
Population 82,176,000
Capital Berlin (6,005,000)
Languages German (official)
GDP $41,902 (2016) · **Currency** Euro = 100 cents
Government federal multiparty republic
Head of state President Frank-Walter
Steinmeier, Social Democrat, 2017
Head of government Chancellor Angela Merkel, Christian Democratic Union, 2005
Website www.bundesregierung.de
Events Germany is a major supporter of the European Union, and former chancellor Helmut Köhl was the driving force behind the creation of the Euro. The grand coalition government formed in 2005 between the CDU, CSU and Social Democrats was replaced by one of the CDU, CSU and FDP after elections in 2009. Repeated calls upon German funds in support of weaker Eurozone economies have caused widespread anger. Angela Merkel's CDU only narrowly missed winning an outright majority in 2013 elections. In late 2016, a Tunisian migrant killed 12 by driving a hijacked lorry into a crowd in Berlin. Former Foreign Minister Frank-Walter Steinmeier was elected president in early 2017.
Economy Germany has long been one of the world's greatest economic powers. The economy returned to growth in 2014. Services form the largest economic sector. Machinery and transport equipment account for 50% of exports. It is the world's third-largest car producer. Other major products include ships, iron, steel, petroleum and tyres. It has the world's second-largest lignite mining industry. Other minerals are copper, potash, lead, salt, zinc and aluminium. Germany is the world's second-largest producer of hops and beer, and fifth-largest of wine. Other products are cheese and milk, barley, rye and pork.

Greece Ellas

Area 131,957 km² (50,948 mi²)
Population 10,955,000 · **Capital** Athens/Athina
(4,174,000) · **Languages** Greek (official)
GDP $17,901 (2016) · **Currency** Euro = 100 cents
Government multiparty republic
Head of state President Prokopis Pavlopoulos,
New Democracy, 2015
Head of government Prime Minister
Alexis Tsipras, Syriza, 2015
Website www.primeminister.gr/english
Events In 1981 Greece joined the EU, and Andreas Papandreou became Greece's first Socialist prime minister. The coalition led by Antonis Samaras fell in early 2015 because of continued discontent over the economy. The left-wing Syriza, under Alexis Tsipras, came to power on a ticket of rejecting the international donors' austerity measures. Months of negotiations over extra loans or deferment of repayments failed to reach a compromise, culminating in the Greek PM opting for a referendum on the donor's proposals, with the result being an overwhelming rejection of the EU's terms. Further bailout funds and repayment extensions were agreed in May 2016. By this time more than 50,000 migrants from Syria, Nigeria and elsewhere were being housed in the country.
Economy Greece is one of the poorest members of the European Union. Manufacturing is important. Products: textiles, cement, chemicals, metallurgy. Minerals: lignite, bauxite, chromite. Farmland covers 33% of Greece, grazing land 40%. Major crops: tobacco, olives, grapes, cotton, wheat. Livestock are raised. Tourism provides 15% of GDP. In receipt of multiple loans from Eurozone funds and the IMF, Greece has repeatedly been in danger of defaulting on debt repayments, with the possible result that it would be forced to give up the currency. Austerity measures imposed by the international community have depressed economic activity. Unemployment remains at over 25% and over one-third of the population is below the poverty line.

Hungary Magyarország

Area 93,032 km² (35,919 mi²)
Population 9,798,000
Capital Budapest (3,304,000)
Languages Hungarian (official)
GDP $12,767
Currency Forint = 100 filler
Government multiparty republic
Head of state President János Áder,
Fidesz, 2012.
Head of government Prime Minister
Viktor Orban, Fidesz, 2010
Website www.kormany.hu/en

Events In 1990 multiparty elections were held for the first time. In 1999 Hungary joined NATO and in 2004 it acceded to the EU. In 2012 attempts to change the electoral system led to widespread protests, as have austerity measures imposed by successive governments. Relations with the EU bodies and IMF remain fractious because of the effect of terms imposed for Euro accession and financial bailouts.
Economy Since the early 1990s, Hungary has adopted market reforms and partial privatisation programmes. High levels of public debt meant that Hungary had to appeal for repeated loans from the IMF and EU to prevent economic collapse when the world economic crisis struck. The manufacture of machinery and transport is the most valuable sector. Hungary's resources include bauxite, coal and natural gas. Major crops include grapes for wine-making, maize, potatoes, sugar beet and wheat. Tourism is a growing sector.

Iceland Ísland

Area 103,000 km² (39,768 mi²)
Population 333,000
Capital Reykjavik (210,000)
Languages Icelandic
GDP $57,570 (2017)
Currency Krona = 100 aurar
Government multiparty republic
Head of state President Guðni Thorlacius
Jóhannesson, independent, 2016
Head of government Prime Minister Bjarni
Benediktsson, Independence Party, 2017
Website www.government.is/
Events In 1944, a referendum decisively voted to sever links with Denmark, and Iceland became a fully independent republic. In 1946 it joined NATO. In 1970 Iceland joined the European Free Trade Association. The last post-war US military personnel left in September 2006, the same year that the government voted to resume commercial whaling. There are concerns among environmentalists about the impact of major new industrial complexes powered by Iceland's abundant thermal energy. Even though Sigurdardottir's Social Democratic Alliance had returned some stability to the economy,the Social Democrats were defeated in 2013 parliamentary elections. Parliamentary elections in 2016 were inconclusive and the

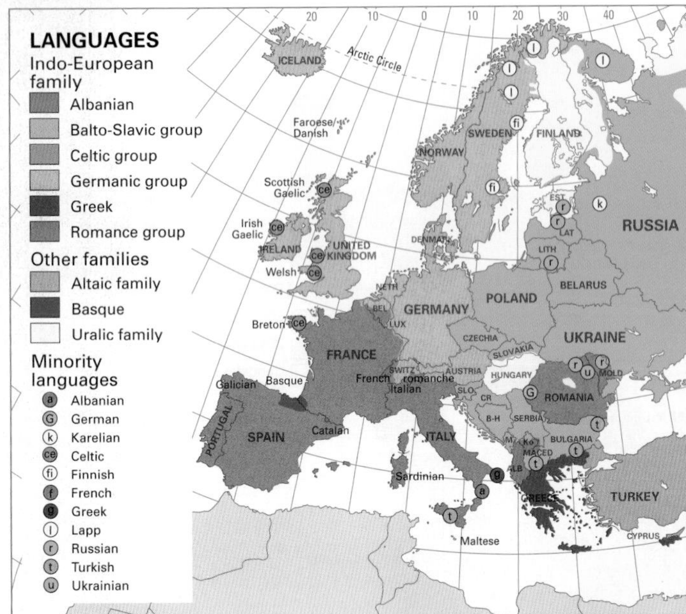

LANGUAGES

Indo-European family
- Albanian
- Balto-Slavic group
- Celtic group
- Germanic group
- Greek
- Romance group

Other families
- Altaic family
- Basque
- Uralic family

Minority languages
- ⓐ Albanian
- ⓖ German
- ⓚ Karelian
- ⓒⓔ Celtic
- ⓕⓘ Finnish
- ⓕ French
- ⓗ Greek
- ⓘ Lapp
- ⓡ Russian
- ⓣ Turkish
- ⓤ Ukrainian

formation of a coalition government took several months.

Economy The economy has long been sensitive to declining fish stocks as well as to fluctuations in world prices for its main exports: fish and fish products, aluminum and ferrosilicon. There has traditionally been low unemployment, and remarkably even distribution of income. Risky levels of investment in overseas companies left Iceland's banks with high debts when the global credit crunch hit, and the government had to apply for IMF funding. The economy returned to its pre-crash size in early 2015.

Ireland Eire

Area 70,273 km² (27,132 mi²)
Population 4,762,000
Capital Dublin (1,905,000)
Languages Irish, English (both official)
GDP $62,085 (2017)
Currency Euro = 100 cents
Government multiparty republic
Head of state President Michael Higgins, Independent (formerly Labour Party), 2011
Head of government Taoiseach Leo Varadkar, Fine Gael, 2017
Website www.gov.ie/en/
Events In 1948 Ireland withdrew from the British Commonwealth and joined the European Community in 1973. The Anglo-Irish Agreement (1985) gave Ireland a consultative role in the affairs of Northern Ireland. Following a 1995 referendum, divorce was legalised. Abortion remains a contentious political issue. In the Good Friday Agreement of 1998 the Irish Republic gave up its constitutional claim to Northern Ireland and a North-South Ministerial Council was established. Sinn Fein got its first seats in the European elections of June 2004. Parliamentary elections of early 2016 led to deadlock, until the two main parties reached an agreement allowing Fine Gael to become a minority government.

Economy Ireland benefited greatly from its membership of the European Union. It joined in circulating the Euro in 2002. Grants have enabled the modernisation of farming, which employs 14% of the workforce. Major products include cereals, cattle and dairy products, sheep, sugar beet and potatoes. Fishing is important. Traditional sectors, such as brewing, distilling and textiles, have been supplemented by high-tech industries, such as electronics. Tourism is the most important component of the service industry. The economy also benefited from a rise in consumer spending, construction and business investment, but growth slowed in 2007 and the country went into recession in 2008, and the joint banking and debt crisis eventually led to the government of Brian Cowen requesting a bailout from the EU and IMF. In 2013, Ireland was the first country to exit from its EU bailout programme and the economy has continued to grow since 2014.

Italy Italia

Area 301,318 km² (116,338 mi²)
Population 60,600,000
Capital Rome / Roma (4,356,000)
Languages Italian (official)
GDP $30,507 (2016) · **Currency** Euro = 100 cents
Government social democracy
Head of state President Sergio Mattarella, 2015
Head of government Prime Minister Paolo Gentiloni, Democratic Party, 2016
Website www.italia.it
Events Since World War II Italy has had a succession of unstable, short-lived governements. In 2016 PM Matteo Renzi resigned after his constitutional reforms were rejected in a referendum. He was replaced by Paolo Gentiloni. By the summer of 2017, more than 500,000 refugees from North Africa and beyond had arrived in Italy.
Economy Italy's main industrial region is the north-western triangle of Milan, Turin and Genoa. It is the world's eighth-largest car and steel producer. Machinery and transport equipment account for 37% of exports. Agricultural production is important. Italy is the world's largest producer of wine. Tourism is a vital economic sector. Italy emerged from a two-year recession at the end of 2013, but unemployment remains high.

Kosovo (Republika e Kosoves/Republika Kosovo)

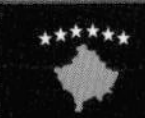

Area 10,887 km² (4203 mi²)
Population 1,908,000
Capital Pristina (504,000)
Languages Albanian, Serbian (both official), Bosnian, Turkish, Roma
GDP $4,472 (2016)
Currency Euro (Serbian dinar in Serb enclaves)
Government Multiparty republic
Head of state President Hashim Thaçi, Independent, 2016
Head of government Prime Minister Isa Mustafa, Democratic League of Kosovo, 2014
Website www.kryeministri-ks.net/?page=2,1
Events An autonomous province with a mainly ethnic Albanian Muslim popluation, Kosovo first declared independence from Serbia in 1990, leading to years of increased ethnic tension and violence. In 1998 conflict between Serb police and the Kosovo Liberation Army led to a violent crackdown by Serbia, which ceased only after more than two months' aerial bombardment by Nato in 1999, during which hundreds of thousands of Kosovo Albanians were massacred or expelled before Serbia agreed to withdraw and a UN peacekeeping force and administration were sent in, which remained in place until 2008. Talks on the status of the province took place in 2003 and 2006. In 2008, independence was declared again and a new constitution was adopted that transferred power from the UN to the ethnic Albanian government, a move that was rejected by Serbia and Russia but recognised by the US and major European countries. The UN referred Kosovo's declaration of independence to the International Court of Justice, which declared in 2010 that it was not illegal. In March 2011, direct talks between Ser-

bia and Kosovo began. In 2013, the EU brokered an agreement on policing for the Serb minority. PM Thaçi claimed victory after early results of parliamentary elections in June 2014, but after months of wrangling Isa Mustafa formed a coalition government. Thaçi became president in early 2016.
Economy Kosovo is one of the poorest areas of Europe, with a high proportion of the population classed as living in poverty. It possesses some mineral resources but the chief economic activity is agriculture.

Latvia Latvija

Area 64,589 km² (24,942 mi²)
Population 1,953,000 · **Capital** Riga (1,018,000)
Languages Latvian (official), Russian
GDP $14,187 (2017) · **Currency** Euro = 100 cents
Government multiparty republic
Head of state President Raimonds Vejonis, Green Party, 2015
Head of government Prime Minister Maris Kucinskis, Liepaja Party, 2016
Website www.mk.gov.lv/en
Events Latvia became a member of NATO and the EU in spring 2004. People applying for citizenship are now required to pass a Latvian language test, which has caused much upset amongst the one third of the population who are Russian speakers. After Ivars Godmanis resigned in February 2009 over his handling of the economic crisis, including having to apply for aid from the IMF, a 6-party coalition was approved by parliament. After the resignation of Valdis Dombrovskis in early 2014, Laimdota Straujuma was appointed PM, and the governing coalition increased its majority in elections in October. Straujuma resigned in December and was replaced by Maris Kucinskis. Latvia adopted the Euro on 1 January 2014.
Economy Latvia has to import many of the materials needed for manufacturing. It produces only 10% of the electricity it needs, and the rest has to be imported from Belarus, Russia and Ukraine. Manufactures include electronic goods, farm machinery and fertiliser. Farm exports include beef, dairy products and pork. The majority of companies, banks, and real estate have been privatised. Unemployment remains very high.

Liechtenstein

Area 157 km² (61 mi²) · **Population** 37,000
Capital Vaduz (5,400) · **GDP** $134,617 (2012)
Languages German (official)
Currency Swiss franc = 100 centimes
Government independent principality
Head of state Prince Hans Adam II (1989)
Head of government Prime Minister Adrian Hasler, Progressive Citizens Party, 2013
Website www.liechtenstein.li
Events Women finally got the vote in 1984. The principality joined the UN in 1990. In 2003 the people voted in a referendum to give Prince Hans Adam II new political powers, rendering the country Europe's only absolute monarchy with the prince having power of veto over the government. Its status as a tax haven has been criticised as it has been alleged that many billions are laundered there each year. The law has been reformed to ensure that anonymity is no longer permitted when opening a bank account. In August 2004 Prince Hans Adam II transferred the day-to-day running of the country to his son Prince Alois, though he did not abdicate and remains titular head of state. The OECD removed Liechtenstein from its list of uncooperative tax havens in 2010. In 2013, the Progressive Citizens Party came first in parliamentary elections.
Economy Liechtenstein is the fourth-smallest country in the world and one of the richest per capita. Since 1945 it has rapidly developed a specialised manufacturing base. It imports more than 90% of its energy requirements. The economy is widely diversified with a large number of small businesses. Tourism is increasingly important.

Lithuania Lietuva

Area 65,200 km² (25,173 mi²)
Population 2,822,000 · **Capital** Vilnius (805,000)
Languages Lithuanian (official), Russian, Polish
GDP $15,090 (2017) · **Currency** Euro = 100 cents
Government multiparty republic
Head of state President Dalia Grybauskaite, 2009
Head of government Prime Minister Saulius Skvernelis, Peasant and Green Union, 2016
Website http://lrvk.lrv.lt/en

Events The Soviet Union recognised Lithuania's independence in September 1991. Lithuania joined NATO in March 2004 and the EU that May. Elections in autumn 2016 led to a change in the make-up of the ruling coalition. Lithuania adopted the Euro on 1 January 2015.
Economy Lithuania is dependent on Russian raw materials. Manufacturing is the most valuable export sector and major products include chemicals, electronic goods and machine tools. Dairy and meat farming and fishing are also important activities. More than 80% of enterprises have been privatised. The economy was badly hit by the 2008 global economic crisis.

Luxembourg

Area 2,586 km² (998 mi²)
Population 576,000
Capital Luxembourg (107,000)
Languages Luxembourgian / Letzeburgish (official), French, German
GDP $101,715 (2017) · **Currency** Euro = 100 cents
Government constitutional monarchy (or grand duchy)
Head of state Grand Duke Henri, 2000
Head of government Prime Minister Xavier Bettel, Democratic Party, 2013
Website www.luxembourg.public.lu/en/
Events Governments have mostly been coalitions led by the Christian Social People's Party under Jean-Claude Juncker. In July 2013, the Social Workers Party withdrew from the latest coalition, provoking early elections. These resulted in a coalition between the Social Democrats, Socialists and Greens.
Economy It has a stable, high-income economy, benefiting from its proximity to France, Germany and Belgium. The city of Luxembourg is a major centre of European administration and finance. In 2009, it implemented stricter laws on transparency in the banking sector. There are rich deposits of iron ore, and is a major producer of iron and steel. Other industries include chemicals, textiles, tourism, banking and electronics.

Macedonia Makedonija

Area 25,713 km² (9,927 mi²)
Population 2,074,000
Capital Skopje (507,000)
Languages Macedonian (official), Albanian
GDP $5,012 (2016) · **Currency** Denar = 100 deni
Government multiparty republic
Head of state President Gjorge Ivanov, VMRO-DPMNE, 2009
Head of government Prime Minister Zoran Zaev, Social Democratic Union, 2017
Events In 1993 the UN accepted the new republic as a member. It formally retains the FYR prefix because of Greek fears that the name implies territorial ambitions towards the Greek region named Macedonia. In August 2004, proposed expansion of rights and local autonomy for Albanians provoked riots by Macedonian nationalists, but the measures went through. In December 2005, EU leaders agreed that Macedonia should become a candidate for membership, if corruption was stamped out, but in February 2007 expressed alarm at political developments during 2006 and continuing problems about rights for ethnic Albanians. In 2008 Greece vetoed NATO's invitation of membership to Macedonia, in a move ruled illegal by the International Court of Justice in 2011. In 2014, Gruevski's VMRO-DPMNE won a fourth term, but he was forced to resign in early 2016 over a wire-tapping scandal. Elections held in December resulted in a coalition government led by Social Democrat Zoran Zaev.
Economy Macedonia is a developing country. The poorest of the six former republics of Yugoslavia, its economy was devastated by UN trade sanctions against Yugoslavia and by the Greek embargo. Economic growth remains erratic. Manufactures, especially metals, dominate exports. Agriculture employs 17% of the workforce. Major crops include cotton, fruits, maize, tobacco and wheat.

Malta

Area 316 km² (122 mi²)
Population 445,000 · **Capital** Valetta (394,000)
Languages Maltese, English (both official)
GDP $25,623 (2017) · **Currency** Euro = 100 cents
Government multiparty republic
Head of state President Marie Louise Coleiro Preca, Labour Party, 2014
Head of government Prime Minister Joseph Muscat, Labour Party, 2013
Website www.gov.mt

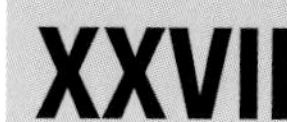

Events In 1990 Malta applied to join the EU. In 1997 the newly elected Malta Labour Party pledged to rescind the application. The Christian Democratic Nationalist Party, led by the pro-European Edward Fenech Adami, regained power in 1998 elections and won again by a narrow margin in March 2008. Malta joined the EU in May 2004 and adopted the Euro on 1 January 2008. In 2013, the Labour Party defeated Lawrence Gonzi's Nationalists to return to power for the first time in 15 years.
Economy Malta produces only about 20% of its food needs, has limited fresh water supplies and has few domestic energy sources. Machinery and transport equipment account for more than 50% of exports. Malta's historic naval dockyards are now used for commercial shipbuilding and repair. Manufactures include chemicals, electronic equipment and textiles. The largest sector is services, especially tourism.

Moldova

Area 33,851 km² (13,069 mi²)
Population 299,000 **Capital** Chisinau (736,000)
Languages Moldovan / Romanian (official)
GDP $2,089 (2017) • **Currency** Leu = 100 bani
Government multiparty republic
Head of state President Igor Dodon, Socialist Party, 2016.
Head of government Prime Minister Pavel Filip, Democratic Party of Moldova, 2016
Website www.moldova.md
Events In 1994 a referendum rejected reunification with Romania and Parliament voted to join the CIS. A new constitution established a presidential parliamentary republic. The Transnistria region mainly inhabited by Russian and Ukrainian speakers declared independence in 1990. This independence has never been recognised and a regional referendum in Transnistria in 2006 that supported eventual union of the region with Russia is similarly being ignored. Relations between Chisinau and Moscow remain strained. Moldova joined the EU's Eastern Partnership in 2009 and signed its Association Agreement in June 2014. Elections in November resulted in pro-European parties remaining in power, although the pro-Russian Socialist Party made major gains. New PM Chiril Gaburici resigned after a few weeks and was followed by several interim replacements before Pavel Filip was appointed in January 2016.
Economy There is a favourable climate and good farmland but no major mineral deposits. Agriculture is important and major products include fruits and grapes for wine-making. Farmers also raise livestock, including dairy cattle and pigs. Moldova has to import materials and fuels for its industries. Exports include food, wine, tobacco and textiles. The economy remains vulnerable to high fuel prices and poor agricultural weather. The economy stagnated in 2014 and then began to contract.

Monaco

Area 1.5 km² (0.6 mi²)
Population 38,000 • **Capital** Monaco-Ville (975)
Languages French (official), Italian, Monegasque • **Currency** Euro = 100 cents
GDP $187,650 • **Government** principality
Head of state Prince Albert II, 2005
Head of government Minister of State Serge Tell, independent, 2016
Website www.gouv.mc
Events Monaco has been ruled by the Grimaldi family since the end of the 13th century and been under the protection of France since 1860.
Economy The chief source of income is tourism. The state retains monopolies in tobacco, the telephone network and the postal service. There is some light industry, including printing, textiles and postage stamps. Also a major banking centre, residents live tax free. In 2010, the OECD removed Monaco from its list of uncooperative tax havens and in 2016 Monaco and the EU signed a tax transparency agreement, due to come into force in 2018.

Montenegro Crna Gora

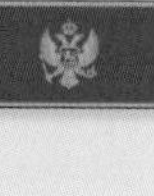

Area 13,812 km² (5,333 mi²)
Population 679,000
Capital Podgorica (187,000)
Languages Serbian (of the Ijekavian dialect)
GDP $6,783 (2016) • **Currency** Euro = 100 cents
Government federal republic
Head of state President Filip Vujanovic, 2003
Head of government Prime Minister Dusko Markovic, Democratic Party of Socialists, 2016
Website www.gov.me/en/homepage
Events In 1992 Montenegro went into federation with Serbia, first as Federal Republic of Yugoslavia, then as a looser State Union of Serbia and Montenegro. Montenegro formed its own economic policy and adopted the Deutschmark as its currency in 1999. It currently uses the Euro, though it is not formally part of the Eurozone. In 2002, Serbia and Montenegro came to a new agreement regarding continued cooperation. On 21 May 2006, the status of the union was decided as 55.54% of voters voted for independence of Montenegro, narrowly passing the 55% threshold needed to validate the referendum under rules set by the EU. On 3 June 2006 the Parliament of Montenegro declared independence. Montenegro was rapidly admitted to the UN, the World Bank and the IMF, joined NATO's Partnership for Peace and applied for EU membership. It was formally named as an EU candidate country in 2010 and accession negotiations started in 2012, just after it joined the WTO. Montenegro became a member of NATO in 2017.
Economy A rapid period of urbanisation and industrialisation was created within the communism era of Montenegro. During 1993, two thirds of the Montenegrin population lived below the poverty line. Financial losses under the effects of the UN sanctions on the economy of Montenegro are estimated to be $6.39 billion. Today there is faster and more efficient privatisation, introduction of VAT and usage of the Euro.

The Netherlands Nederland

Area 41,526 km² (16,033 mi²)
Population 17,000,000
Capital Amsterdam (2,431,000); administrative capital 's-Gravenhage (The Hague) (1,051,000)
Languages Dutch (official), Frisian
GDP $44,654 (2017) • **Currency** Euro = 100 cents
Government constitutional monarchy
Head of state King Willem-Alexander, 2013
Head of government Prime Minister Mark Rutte, People's Party for Freedom and Democracy, 2010
Website www.government.nl
Events A founding member of NATO and the EU. Jan Peter Balkenende's coalition cabinet with the Labour Party and the Christian Union collapsed in early 2010 after Labour refused to sanction continued military deployment in Afghanistan. In 2010 the former junior coalition partner, the Party for Freedom and Democracy, took power, winning again in 2012 and 2017. In 2013, Queen Beatrix abdicated.
Economy The Netherlands has prospered through its close European ties. Private enterprise has successfully combined with progressive social policies. It is highly industrialised. Products include aircraft, chemicals, electronics and machinery. Agriculture is intensive and mechanised, employing only 5% of the workforce. Dairy farming is the leading agricultural activity. It continues to be one of the leading European nations for attracting foreign direct investment.

Norway Norge

Area 323,877 km² (125,049 mi²)
Population 5,267,000 • **Capital** Oslo (1,718,000)
Languages Norwegian (official), Lappish, Finnish
GDP $73,450 • **Currency** Krone = 100 øre
Government constitutional monarchy
Head of state King Harald V, 1991
Head of government Prime Minister Erna Solberg, Conservative Party, 2013
Website www.norway.no/en/uk
Events In referenda in 1972 and 1994 Norway rejected joining the EU. A centre-left coalition, the Labour-led 'Red-Green Alliance' won closely contested elections in September 2005, and retained power in 2009. It was ousted by a Conservative-led minority government in 2013.
Economy Norway has one of the world's highest standards of living. Discovery of oil and gas in adjacent waters in the late 1960s boosted its economic fortunes, with its chief exports now oil and natural gas. Per capita, it is the world's largest producer of hydroelectricity. It is possible oil and gas will begin to run out in Norway in the next two decades but it has been saving its oil budget surpluses and is invested abroad in a fund, valued at more than $250 billion at its height, although this fell rapidly as a result of the global financial crisis. Major manufactures include petroleum products, chemicals, aluminium, wood pulp and paper.

Poland Polska

Area 323,250 km² (124,807 mi²)
Population 38,634,000
Capital Warsaw / Warszawa (metropolitan 3,101,000)
Languages Polish (official)
GDP $12,722 (2017)
Currency Zloty = 100 groszy
Government multiparty republic
Head of state President Andrzej Duda, Law and Justice, 2015
Head of government President Beata Szydlo, Law and Justice, 2015
Website www.premier.gov.pl/en.html
Events Poland joined the OECD in 1996, NATO in 1999 and the EU in 2004. Andrzej Duda narrowly beat Bronislaw Komorowski in presidential elections in May 2015 and Law and Justice were returned to power under Beata Szydio in parliamentary polls six months later. Widespread protests in 2017 led President Duda to veto legislation that would have given Parliament control over the judiciary.
Economy Of the workforce, 27% is employed in agriculture and 37% in industry. Poland is the world's fifth-largest producer of lignite and ships. Copper ore is also a vital resource. Manufacturing accounts for 24% of exports. Agriculture remains important. Economic growth began to speed up in 2013.

Portugal

Area 88,797 km² (34,284 mi²)
Population 10,310,000
Capital Lisbon / Lisboa (2,822,000)
Languages Portuguese (official)
GDP $19,707
Currency Euro = 100 cents
Government multiparty republic
Head of state President Marcelo Rebelo de Sousa, Independent, 2016
Head of government Antonio Costa, Socialist Party, 2015
Website www.portugal.gov.pt/en.aspx
Events In 1986 Portugal joined the EU. In 2002 the Social Democrat Party won the election and formed a coalition government with the Popular Party. The opposition Socialist Party were clear victors in European elections of June 2004, a result attributed in part to the ruling party's support for the war in Iraq. After the collapse of the Socialist government in 2011, the Social Democrat-led coalition introduced strict austerity measures. Inconclusive election results in late 2015 saw the return to power of the Socialists.
Economy Portugal was badly hit by the economic downturn and in April 2011 requested a financial bailout from the IMF and Eurozone funds. Despite budget cuts, public debt remained high, but Portugal exited its bailout in May 2014. Manufacturing accounts for 33% of exports. Textiles, footwear and clothing are major exports. Portugal is the world's fifth-largest producer of tungsten and eighth-largest producer of wine. Olives, potatoes and wheat are also grown. Tourism is very important.

Romania

Area 238,391 km² (92,042 mi²)
Population 19,511,000
Capital Bucharest / Bucuresti (2,403,000)
Languages Romanian (official), Hungarian
GDP $10,097
Currency Romanian leu = 100 bani
Government multiparty republic
Head of state President Klaus Iohannis, National Liberal Party, 2014
Head of government Prime Minister Mihai Tudose, Social Democratic Party, 2017
Website www.gov.ro
Events A new constitution was introduced in 1991. Ion Iliescu, a former communist official, was re-elected in 2000, but barred from standing again in 2004, when he was replaced by Traian Basescu. After losing a vote of no confidence after just 10 months as PM, Boc was reappointed in December 2009. Romania joined NATO in 2004 and joined the EU in January 2007 after making progress towards tackling corruption, although because of this issue France and Germany blocked its Schengen area accession in December 2010. Protests in 2012 led to PM Emil Boc's resignation. Klaus Iohannis beat PM Victor Ponta in presidential elections in late 2014. The latter was forced to resign in June 2015 after investigators questioned him about tax evasion, money laundering and fraud. Adoption of the Euro has been postponed until at least 2022.
Economy The currency was re-valued in 2005. Despite a period of strong economic growth, Romania's large public debt led to the need for substantial IMF loans in 2009, necessitating severe cuts in public services.

Russia Rossiya

Area 17,075,000 km² (6,592,800 mi²)
Population 144,463,000
Capital Moscow / Moskva (17,100,000)
Languages Russian (official), and many others
GDP $10,885 (2017)
Currency Russian ruble = 100 kopeks
Government federal multiparty republic
Head of state President Vladimir Putin 2012
Head of government Prime Minister Dimitry Medvedev, 2012
Website http://government.ru/en/
Events In 1992 the Russian Federation became a co-founder of the CIS (Commonwealth of Independent States). A new Federal Treaty was signed between the central government and the autonomous republics within the Russian Federation, Chechnya refused to sign and declared independence. In December 1993 a new democratic constitution was adopted. From 1994 to 1996, Russia fought a civil war in Chechnya which flared up again in 1999. Putin's chosen successor, Medvedev, was elected by a landslide in elections that were criticised by outside observers for biased media coverage. In 2011 Putin was re-elected as President, after the law that prevented serving a third term was revoked. He appointed former president Medvedev as PM. Critics allege that freedom of speech and dissent are being repressed amid crackdowns on NGOs and opponents of the ruling party. Russia joined the WTO in 2012. In 2014, Russia annexed the Crimean Peninsula and Sevastopol leading to international condemnation and sanctions. Relations with the West worsened in succeeding years.
Economy In 1993 mass privatisation began. By 1996, 80% of the Russian economy was in private hands. A major problem remains the size of Russia's foreign debt. It is reliant on world oil prices to keep its economy from crashing and the sudden fall in oil prices in the second half of 2008 forced it to devalue the ruble several times. The drop in oil prices from 2014 and international sanctions caused the ruble to plummet in value against other currencies. Industry employs 46% of the workforce and contributes 48% of GDP. Mining is the most valuable activity. Russia is the world's leading producer of natural gas and nickel, the second largest producer of aluminium and phosphates, and the third-largest of crude oil, lignite and brown coal. Most farmland is still government-owned or run as collectives, with important products barley, oats, rye, potatoes, beef and veal. In 2006, the ruble became a convertible currency.

San Marino

Area 61 km² (24 mi²)
Population 33,000
Capital San Marino (4,100)
Languages Italian (official)
GDP $44,947 (2017)
Currency Euro = 100 cents
Government multiparty republic
Head of state co-Chiefs of State: Mimma Zavoli and Vanessa D'Ambrosio
Head of government Secretary of State for Foreign and Political Affairs and Economic Planning Nicola Renzi, 2016
Website www.visitsanmarino.com
Events World's smallest republic and perhaps Europe's oldest state, San Marino's links with Italy led to the adoption of the Euro. Its 60-member Great and General Council is elected every five years and headed by two captains regent, who are elected by the council every six months. In 2013 a narrow majority of recorded votes were in favour of joining the EU, but the low turnout invalidated the result.
Economy The economy is largely agricultural. Tourism is vital to the state's income, contributing over 50% of GDP. The economy is generally stable.

Serbia Srbija

Area 77,474 km² (29,913 mi²), including Kosovo
Population 7,058,000
Capital Belgrade / Beograd (metropolitan 1,167,000) • **Languages** Serbian
GDP $5,397 • **Currency** Dinar = 100 paras
Government federal republic
Head of state President Alexander Vucic, Progressive Party, 2017
Head of government Prime Minister Ana Brnabic, independent, 2017
Website www.srbija.gov.rs
Events Serbian attempts to control the Yugoslav federation led to the secession of Slovenia and Croatia in 1991 and to Bosnia-Herzegovina's declaration of independence in 1992 and the three-year war that ended only with the signing of the Dayton Peace Accord. Slobodan Milosovic became president of Yugoslavia in 1997. Kostunica won the elections of September 2000: Milosevic refused to hand over power, but was ousted after a week. From 2003 to 2006, Serbia was part of the State Union of Serbia and Montenegro, After a referendum in May 2006, the Parliament of Montenegro declared Montenegro independent. Serbia assumed the State Union's UN membership. In 2006 Serbia joined the NATO Partnership for Peace programme and in 2008 signed a Stability and Association Agreement with the EU, to which it applied formally for membership in December 2009. Serbia became a candidate member of the EU in 2012 and accession talks began in early 2014. In May of the latter year, the pro-EU Progressive Party scored a landslide victory in parliamentary elections.
Economy The lower-middle income economy was devastated by war and economic sanctions. Industrial production collapsed. Natural resources include bauxite, coal and copper. There is some oil and natural gas. Manufacturing includes aluminium, cars, machinery, plastics, steel and textiles. Agriculture is important. In 2008 Serbia and Russia signed an energy deal, and in October 2009 the latter granted the former a 1 billion Euro loan to ease its budgetary problems. Growth remains erratic.

Slovakia Slovenska Republika

Area 49,012 km² (18,923 mi²)
Population 5,435,000
Capital Bratislava (660,000)
Languages Slovak (official), Hungarian
GDP $16,412 (2017) • **Currency** Euro = 100 cents
Government multiparty republic
Head of state President Andrej Kiska, independent, 2014
Head of government Prime Minister Robert Fico, Direction - Social Democracy (Smer), 2012.
Website http://www.vlada.gov.sk
Events In 1993 the Slovak Republic became a sovereign state, breaking peaceably from the Czech Republic, with whom it maintains close relations. In 1996 the Slovak Republic and Hungary ratified a treaty confirming their borders and stipulating basic rights for the 560,000 Hungarians in the country. The Slovak Republic joined NATO in March 2004 and the EU two months later. There is still a problem with the Romany population. The country adopted the Euro in January 2009. In elections in 2012 Smer returned with a parliamentary majority. Former businessman and philanthropist Andrej Kiska won the presidential election against PM Fico in 2014. SMER lost its majority in 2016.
Economy The transition from communism to private ownership was initially painful with industrial output falling, unemployment and inflation rising, but the economy has become more stable. Manufacturing employs 33% of the workforce. Bratislava and Košice are the chief industrial cities. Major products include ceramics, machinery and steel. Farming employs 12% of the workforce. Crops include barley and grapes. Tourism is growing.

Slovenia Slovenija

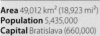

Area 20,256 km² (7,820 mi²)
Population 2,066,000
Capital Ljubljana (280,000)
Languages Slovene
GDP $21,061 (2017) • **Currency** Euro = 100 cents
Government multiparty republic
Head of state President Borut Pahor, Social Democratic Party, 2012
Head of government Prime Minister Miro Cerar, Modern Centre Party, 2014
Website www.vlada.si/en/
Events In 1990 Slovenia declared itself independent, which led to brief fighting between Slovenes and the federal army. In 1992 the EU recognised Slovenia's independence. Janez Drnovsek was elected president in December 2002. Slovenia joined NATO in March 2004 and the EU two months later. In June 2004 the value of the Tolar was fixed against the Euro, which it joined in 2007. The 2008 general election resulted in a coalition government led by the Social Democratic Party. A referendum in June 2010 narrowly approved the settlement of the border dispute with Croatia. After two years of political instability, Ivan Janša was appointed PM in February 2012, leading a centre-right coalition, but his government fell the following year. The succeeding administration fell in May 2014 leading to early elections, which led to a coalition government headed by the newly founded Modern Centre Party led by lawyer Miro Cerar.
Economy The transformation of a centrally planned economy and the fighting in other parts of former Yugoslavia caused problems for Slovenia but the economy eventually experienced strong growth in per capita GDP until this was badly hit by the gobal financial crisis. Manufacturing is the leading activity. Major manufactures include chemicals, machinery, transport equipment, metal goods and textiles. Major crops include maize, fruit, potatoes and wheat.

Spain España

Area 497,548 km² (192,103 mi²)
Population 46,468,000
Capital Madrid (metropolitan 6,530,000)
Languages Castilian Spanish (official), Catalan, Galician, Basque
GDP $26,463 (2017)
Currency Euro = 100 cents
Government constitutional monarchy
Head of state King Felipe VI, 2014
Head of government Prime Minister Mariano Rajoy, Spanish People's Party, 2011 (caretaker)
Website www.lamoncloa.gob.es/lang/en
Events From 1959-98 the militant Basque organisation ETA waged a campaign of terror. Its first ceasefire was broken in 2000 and a second - declared in 2006 - with a bomb attack on Madrid airport at the end of the year. A third ceasefire was declared in September 2010. In March 2004 Al qaeda-related bombers killed 191 people in Madrid, resulting in an election win for the opposition Socialist Party. In the 2008 elections, the socialists increased their numbers in Parliament, but did not gain a majority. Austerity measures brought in to tackle public debt, and as condition of the country's financial bailout, changes to pensions and benefits and rising unemployment led to widespread protests in 2010 and 2011. Local and regional elections in May 2011 resulted in heavy losses for the socialists and the Popular Party won a sweeping majority in general elections in November. After inconclusive elections in 2015, Popular Party PM stayed on as caretaker and gained most seats in new elections in June 2016. A terrorist attack on Barcelona in 2017 killed 16 and injured 120.
Economy Spain's transformation from a largely poor, agrarian society to a prosperous nation came to an end with the economic downturn of 2008. The country's debt burden became untenable and financial bailouts from the international community in 2010 and the Eurozone in 2012 were necessary. Unemployment is more than double the European average. Agriculture now employs only 10% of the workforce and the sector is shrinking further because of recurrent droughts. Spain is the world's third-largest wine producer. Other crops include citrus fruits, tomatoes and olives. Industries: cars, ships, chemicals, electronics, metal goods, steel and textiles.

Sweden Sverige

Area 449,964 km² (173,731 mi²)
Population 10,053,000
Capital Stockholm (2,227,000)
Languages Swedish (official), Finnish
GDP $51,603
Currency Swedish krona = 100 ore
Government constitutional monarchy
Head of state King Carl Gustaf XVI, 1973
Head of government Prime Minister Stefan Löfvén, Social Democrats, 2014
Website www.sweden.gov.se
Events In 1995 Sweden joined the European Union. The cost of maintaining Sweden's extensive welfare services has become a major political issue. In 2003 Sweden rejected adoption of the Euro. Parliamentary elections in October 2014 led to a fragile minority government being formed by the Social Democrats.
Economy Sweden is a highly developed industrial country. It has rich iron ore deposits. Privately owned firms account for about 90% of industrial output. Steel is a major product, used to manufacture aircraft, cars, machinery and ships. Forestry and fishing are important. Agriculture accounts for 2% of GDP and jobs. The Swedish central bank focuses on price stability with its inflation target of 2%.

Switzerland Schweiz

Area 41,284 km² (15,939 mi²)
Population 8,401,000
Capital Bern (407,000)
Languages French, German, Italian, Romansch (all official)
GDP $78,245 (2016)
Currency Swiss Franc = 100 centimes / rappen
Government federal republic
Head of state President of the Swiss Confederation Doris Leuthard, PDC/CVP, 2017
Website www.admin.ch
Events Priding themselves on their neutrality, Swiss voters rejected membership of the UN in 1986 and the EU in 1992 and 2001. However, Switzerland finally became a partner country of NATO in 1997 and joined the organisation in 2002, when it also joined the UN. The federal council is made up of seven federal ministers from whom the president is chosen on an annual basis. A 2005 referendum backed membership of EU Schengen and Dublin agreements, bringing Switzerland into the European passport-free zone and increasing co-operation on crime and asylum seekers. Immigration is becoming an increasingly divisive issue.
Economy Switzerland is a wealthy and stable modern market economy with low unemployment, and per capita GDP grew strongly in 2014. Manufactures include chemicals, electrical equipment, machinery, precision instruments, watches and textiles. Livestock, notably dairy farming, is the chief agricultural activity. Tourism is important, and Swiss banks remain a safe haven for investors. In early 2015, the rapid fall of the value of the Euro on international markets led the Swiss National Bank to reverse the decision of 2011 to peg the Franc to the Euro.

Turkey Türkiye

Area 774,815 km² (299,156 mi²)
Population 79,815,000
Capital Ankara (5,271,000)
Languages Turkish (official), Kurdish
GDP $11,014
Currency New Turkish lira = 100 kurus
Government multiparty republic
Head of state Recep Tayyip Erdogan, Justice and Development Party (AK), 2014
Head of government Binali Yildirim, Justice and Development Party (AK), 2016
Website www.mfa.gov.tr/default.en.mfa
Events The Kurdistan Workers Party (PKK) carried out terrorist activities throughout the 1980s and 1990s, but declared a ceasefire in 1999, changed their name to Congress for Freedom and Democracy in Kurdistan (KADEK) and said they wanted to campaign peacefully for Kurdish rights. In September 2003 they ended a 4-year ceasefire, but declared another in 2006, although this did not hold. In October 2005, the EU opened accession negotiations with Ankara. Membership of the EU is an aim but human rights, the Cyprus issue and the hostility of successive French and Austrian governments are barriers, but it was announced in October that talks would recommence the following month. The PM and President are both former Islamists, although they say they are committed to secularism. The escalating civil war in Syria has caused a refugee crisis on the border. In 2014 elections, PM Erdogan won the first direct presidential election. In 2015's parliamentary elections, the AK lost its majority, and Davutoğlu resigned in May 2016. Conflict in Syria over-spilled into the country, causing a resumption of hostilities between Kurdish and government forces. An attempted military coup in June 2016 was swiftly defeated and thousands were arrested in the ensuing crackdown.
Economy Turkey is an upper-middle-income country, as classified by the World Bank. Agriculture employs 47% of the workforce, but is becoming less important to the economy. Turkey is a leading producer of citrus fruits, barley, cotton, wheat, tobacco and tea. It is a major producer of chromium and phosphate fertilisers. Tourism is a vital source of foreign exchange. In January 2005, the New Turkish lira was introduced at a rate of 1 to 1,000,000 old Turkish lira. As a result of terrorist attacks, tourist numbers had dropped by half by mid-2016, causing serious damage to the economy.

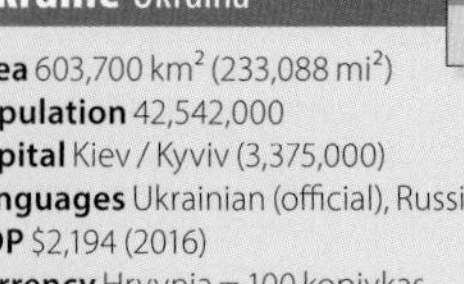

Ukraine Ukraina

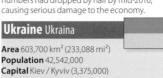

Area 603,700 km² (233,088 mi²)
Population 42,542,000
Capital Kiev / Kyviv (3,375,000)
Languages Ukrainian (official), Russian
GDP $2,194 (2016)
Currency Hryvnia = 100 kopiykas
Government multiparty republic
Head of state Petro Poroshenko, independent, 2014
Head of government Vlodymyr Groysman, Petro Poroshenko Bloc, 2016
Website www.kmu.gov.ua/control/en
Events The Chernobyl disaster of 1986 contaminated large areas of Ukraine. Independence was achieved in 1991 with the dissolution of the USSR. Leonid Kuchma was elected president in 1994. He continued the policy of establishing closer ties with the West and sped up the pace of privatisation. In 2010, the coalition governent of Yulia Tymoshenko fell, and the Party of the Regions formed a coalition with the Communists and the centrist Lytvyn Bloc. Former PM Victor Yanukovic beat Tymoshenko in the presidential elections. Ukraine joined the EU's Eastern Partnership in 2009, but has abandoned plans to join NATO. President Yanukovich's decision to abandon plans for closer ties with the EU led to riots from late 2013, followed by his escape to Russia in February 2014. The following month, Russia sent forces into the Crimean Peninsula to assist separatists. A few days later, after a partially boycotted referendum, the administrations of Crimea and Sevastopol asked Russia for the right to accede, which Russia granted and annexed the region and city. Parliamentary elections in late 2014 resulted in a resounding win for pro-Western parties. Fighting continues in the east despite a fragile ceasefire brokered by France and Germany in February 2015. In July 2017, Ukraine's Association Agreement with the European Union was ratified.
Economy Ukraine is a lower-middle-income economy. Agriculture is important. It is the world's leading producer of sugar beet, the second-largest producer of barley, and a major producer of wheat. Ukraine has extensive raw materials, including coal (though many mines are exhausted), iron ore and manganese ore. Ukraine is reliant on oil and natural gas imports.The economy's dependence on steel exports made it vulnerable to the 2008 global economic downturn and it was offered a massive loan by the IMF. Economic growth remains fragile.

United Kingdom

Area 241,857 km² (93,381 mi²)
Population 65,648,000
Capital London (13,880,000)
Languages English (official), Welsh (also official in Wales), Gaelic
GDP $40,096
Currency Sterling (pound) = 100 pence
Government constitutional monarchy
Head of state Queen Elizabeth II, 1952
Head of government Prime Minister Theresa May, Conservative Party, 2016
Website www.gov.uk
Events The United Kingdom of Great Britain and Northern Ireland is a union of four countries – England, Northern Ireland, Scotland and Wales. Since 1997, Scotland and Wales have had their own legislative assemblies. In 2005 the IRA anounced a permanent cessation of hostilities and the Northern Ireland Assembly was finally reinstated in early 2007. Scotland voted against independence from the UK in September 2014. The Conservative Party won a majority in the parliamentary elections of 2015. In June 2016, voters narrowly chose to leave the EU. Snap elections called in 2017 resulted in the Conservatives losing their parliamentary majority.
Economy The UK is a major industrial and trading nation. A producer of oil, petroleum products, natural gas, potash, salt and lead. Financial services and tourism are the leading service industries. The economic downturn of 2008 led to the government effectively nationalising several banks and bailing out others with huge loans. Economic growth continues to improve.

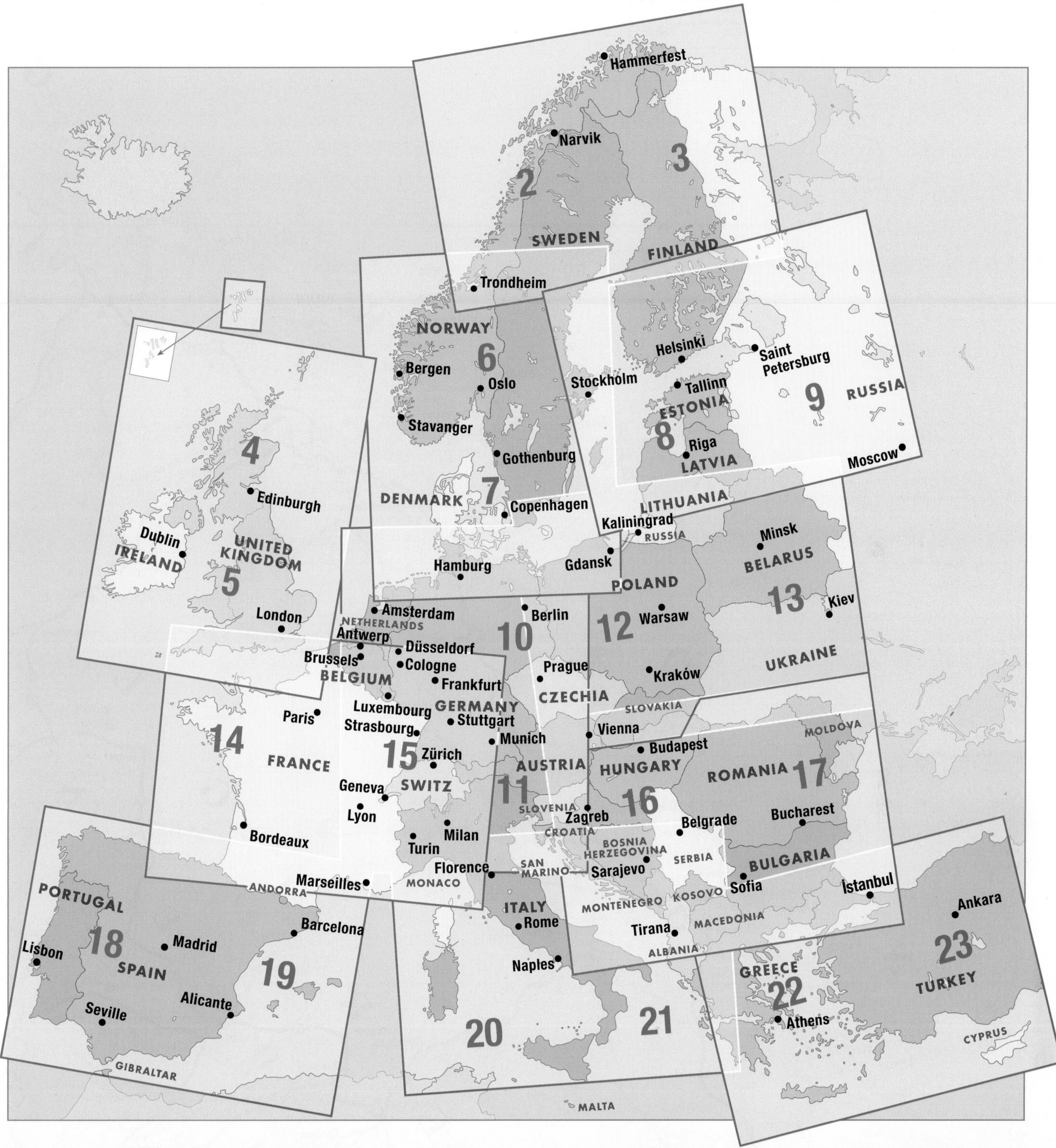

Motorway vignettes

Some countries require you to purchase (and in some cases display) a vignette before using motorways.

In Austria you will need to purchase and display a vignette on the inside of your windscreen. Vignettes are available for purchase at border crossings and petrol stations. More details from www.asfinag.at/toll/toll-sticker

In Belarus all vehicles over 3.5 tonnes and cars and vans under 3.5 tonnes registered outside the Eurasion Economic Union are required to have a BelToll unit installed. This device exchanges data with roadside gantries, enabling motorway tolls to be automatically deducted from the driver's account. http://beltoll.by/index.php/en/

In Czechia, you can buy a vignette at the border and also at petrol stations. Make sure you write your vehicle registration number on the vignette before displaying it. The roads without toll are indicated by a traffic sign saying "Bez poplatku". More details from www.motorway.cz

In Hungary a new e-vignette system was introduced in 2008. It is therefore no longer necessary to display the vignette, though you should make doubly sure the information you give on your vehicle is accurate. Vignettes are sold at petrol stations throughout the country. Buy online at http://toll-charge.hu/

In Slovakia, an electronic vignette must purchased before using the motorways. Vignettes may be purchased online, via a mobile app or at Slovak border crossings and petrol stations displaying the 'eznamka' logo. More details from https://eznamka.sk/selfcare/home/

In Switzerland, you will need to purchase and display a vignette before you drive on the motorway. Bear in mind you will need a separate vignette if you are towing a caravan. www.ezv.admin.ch/ezv/en/home/information-individuals/documents-for-travellers-and-road-taxes/motorway-charge-sticker--vignette-.html

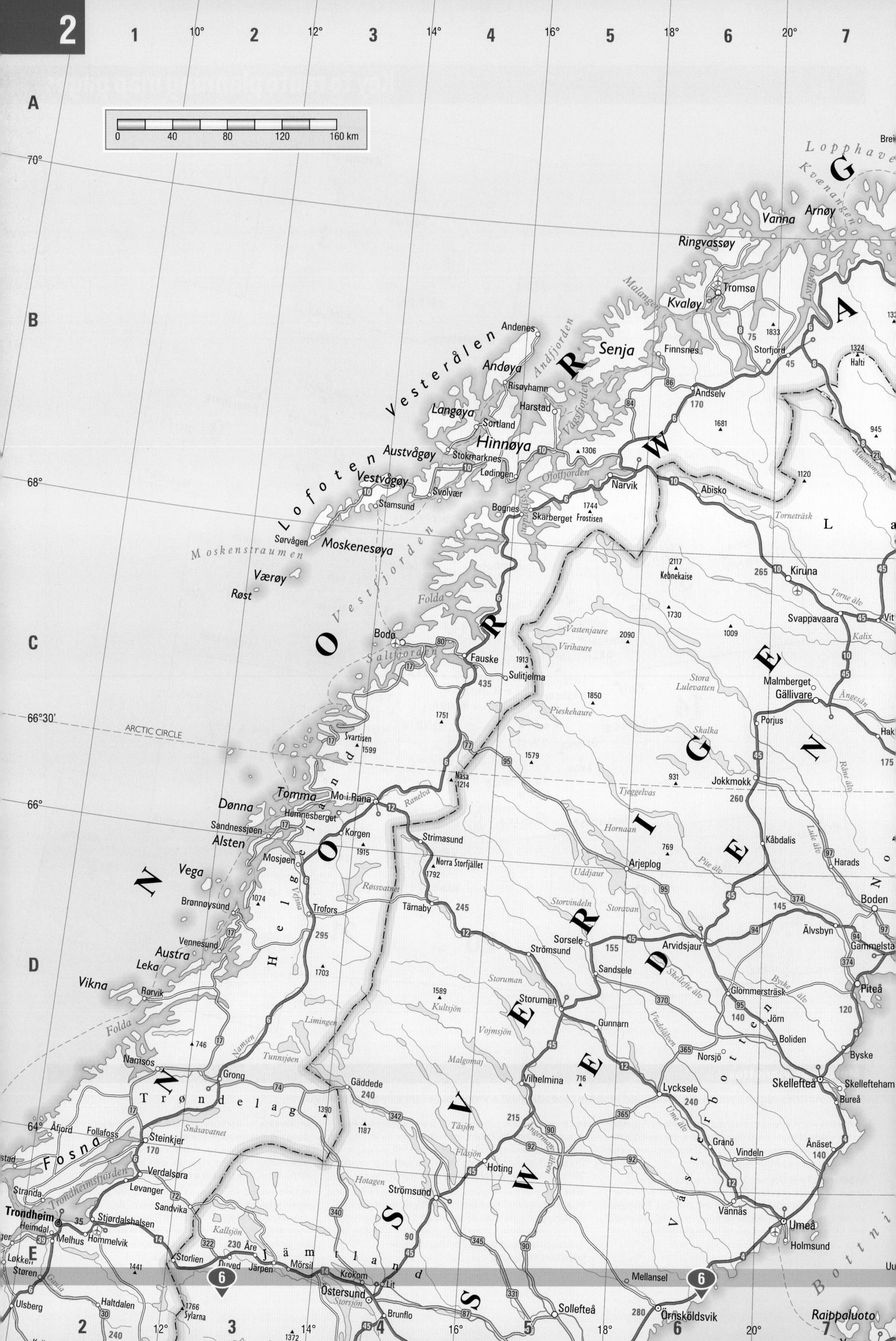
1
2
3
4
5
6
7
10°
12°
14°
16°
18°
20°
A
B
C
D
E
0
40
80
120
160 km
70°
68°
66°30'
66°
64°
ARCTIC CIRCLE
NORWAY
SWEDEN
Lopphavet
Kvænangen
Vanna
Arnøy
Ringvassøy
Kvaløy
Tromsø
Malangen
Lyngen
Senja
Finnsnes
Storfjord
Halti
Andenes
Andfjorden
Vesterålen
Andøya
Risøyhamn
Harstad
Vågsfjorden
Langøya
Sortland
Hinnøya
Austvågøy
Stokmarknes
Lødingen
Lofoten
Vestvågøy
Svolvær
Stamsund
Ofotfjorden
Narvik
Andselv
Abisko
Torneträsk
Bognes
Tysfjorden
Skarberget
Frostisen
Sørvågen
Moskenesøya
Moskenstraumen
Værøy
Røst
Vestfjorden
Folda
Kebnekaise
Kiruna
Torne älv
Svappavaara
Kalix
Bodø
Saltfjorden
Fauske
Sulitjelma
Vastenjaure
Virihaure
Stora Lulevatten
Malmberget
Gällivare
Ångesån
Pieskehaure
Skalka
Porjus
Svartisen
Nasa
Rånealv
Jokkmokk
Råne älv
Tjeggelvas
Tomma
Mo i Rana
Dønna
Hemnesberget
Sandnessjøen
Alsten
Korgen
Strimasund
Hornavan
Kåbdalis
Lule älv
Helgeland
Vega
Mosjøen
Vefsna
Norra Storfjället
Røssvatnet
Uddjaur
Arjeplog
Pite älv
Harads
Brønnøysund
Trofors
Tärnaby
Storvindeln
Storavan
Boden
Vennesund
Austra
Leka
Vikna
Rørvik
Folda
Sorsele
Strömsund
Arvidsjaur
Älvsbyn
Gammelstad
Sandsele
Skellefte älv
Byske älv
Storuman
Kultsjön
Limingen
Vojmsjön
Glommersträsk
Piteå
Gunnarn
Jörn
Boliden
Vindelälven
Namsen
Namsos
Grong
Tunnsjøen
Malgomaj
Norsjö
Byske
Västerbotten
Gäddede
Vilhelmina
Lycksele
Skellefteå
Skelleftehamn
Bureå
Trøndelag
Snåsavatnet
Tåsjön
Ume älv
Ångermanälven
Fosna
Åfjord
Follafoss
Steinkjer
Verdalsøra
Flåsjön
Hoting
Vindeln
Ånäset
Trondheimsfjorden
Stranda
Levanger
Sandvika
Hotagen
Strömsund
Vännäs
Trondheim
Heimdal
Melhus
Stjørdalshalsen
Hommelvik
Kallsjön
Åre
Jämtland
Umeå
Holmsund
Løkken
Støren
Storlien
Duved
Järpen
Mörsil
Krokom
Lit
Mellansel
Gaula
Ulsberg
Haltdalen
Sylarna
Östersund
Storsjön
Brunflo
Sollefteå
Örnsköldsvik
Raippaluoto
Bottnia

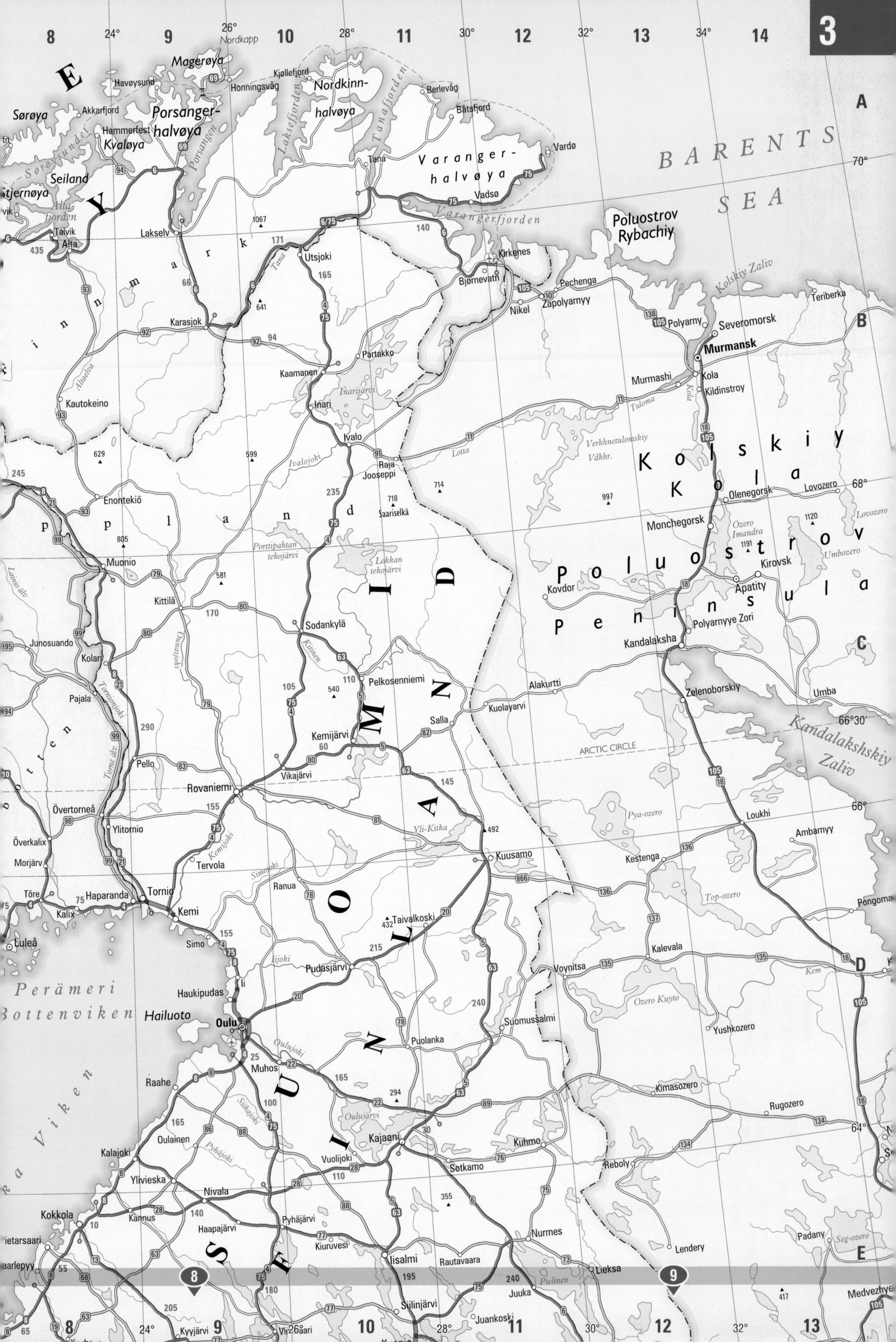
BARENTS SEA
Nordkapp
Magerøya
Honningsvåg
Havøysund
Kjøllefjord
Nordkinn-halvøya
Berlevåg
Båtsfjord
Sørøya
Akkarfjord
Porsanger-halvøya
Hammerfest
Kvaløya
Varanger-halvøya
Vardø
Tana
Vadsø
Varangerfjorden
Seiland
Lakselv
Talvik
Alta
Utsjoki
Kirkenes
Bjørnevatn
Poluostrov Rybachiy
Kolskiy Zaliv
Pechenga
Nikel
Zapolyarnyy
Teriberka
Polyarny
Severomorsk
Murmansk
Kola
Kildinstroy
Murmashi
Tuloma
Karasjok
Partakko
Kaamanen
Inarijärvi
Inari
Kautokeino
Ivalo
Raja Jooseppi
Lotta
Verkhnetulomskiy Vdkhr.
Kolskiy Poluostrov
Kola Peninsula
Olenegorsk
Lovozero
Monchegorsk
Ozero Imandra
Umbozero
Kirovsk
Apatity
Kovdor
Polyarnyye Zori
Kandalaksha
Enontekiö
Saariselkä
Porttipahtan tekojärvi
Lokkan tekojärvi
Muonio
Kittilä
Sodankylä
Junosuando
Kolari
Pajala
Pelkosenniemi
Alakurtti
Kuolayarvi
Salla
Kemijärvi
Zelenoborskiy
Umba
Kandalakshskiy Zaliv
ARCTIC CIRCLE
Pello
Vikajärvi
Rovaniemi
Övertorneå
Ylitornio
Överkalix
Morjärv
Tervola
Yli-Kitka
Kuusamo
Pya-ozero
Loukhi
Ambarnyy
Kestenga
Top-ozero
Töre
Haparanda
Tornio
Kalix
Kemi
Ranua
Taivalkoski
Pongoma
Luleå
Simo
Pudasjärvi
Ii
Kalevala
Voynitsa
Kem
Perämeri
Bottenviken
Haukipudas
Hailuoto
Oulu
Ozero Kuyto
Suomussalmi
Yushkozero
Muhos
Puolanka
Raahe
Kimasozero
Rugozero
Oulujärvi
Oulainen
Kajaani
Kuhmo
Kalajoki
Vuolijoki
Sotkamo
Reboly
Ylivieska
Nivala
Kokkola
Kannus
Haapajärvi
Pyhäjärvi
Kiuruvesi
Nurmes
Padany
Seg-ozero
Lendery
Iisalmi
Rautavaara
Lieksa
Pielinen
Juuka
Siilinjärvi
Juankoski
Kyyjärvi
Medvezhye
FINLAND
SUOMI
NORWAY
Finnmark
Lappland
Norrbotten

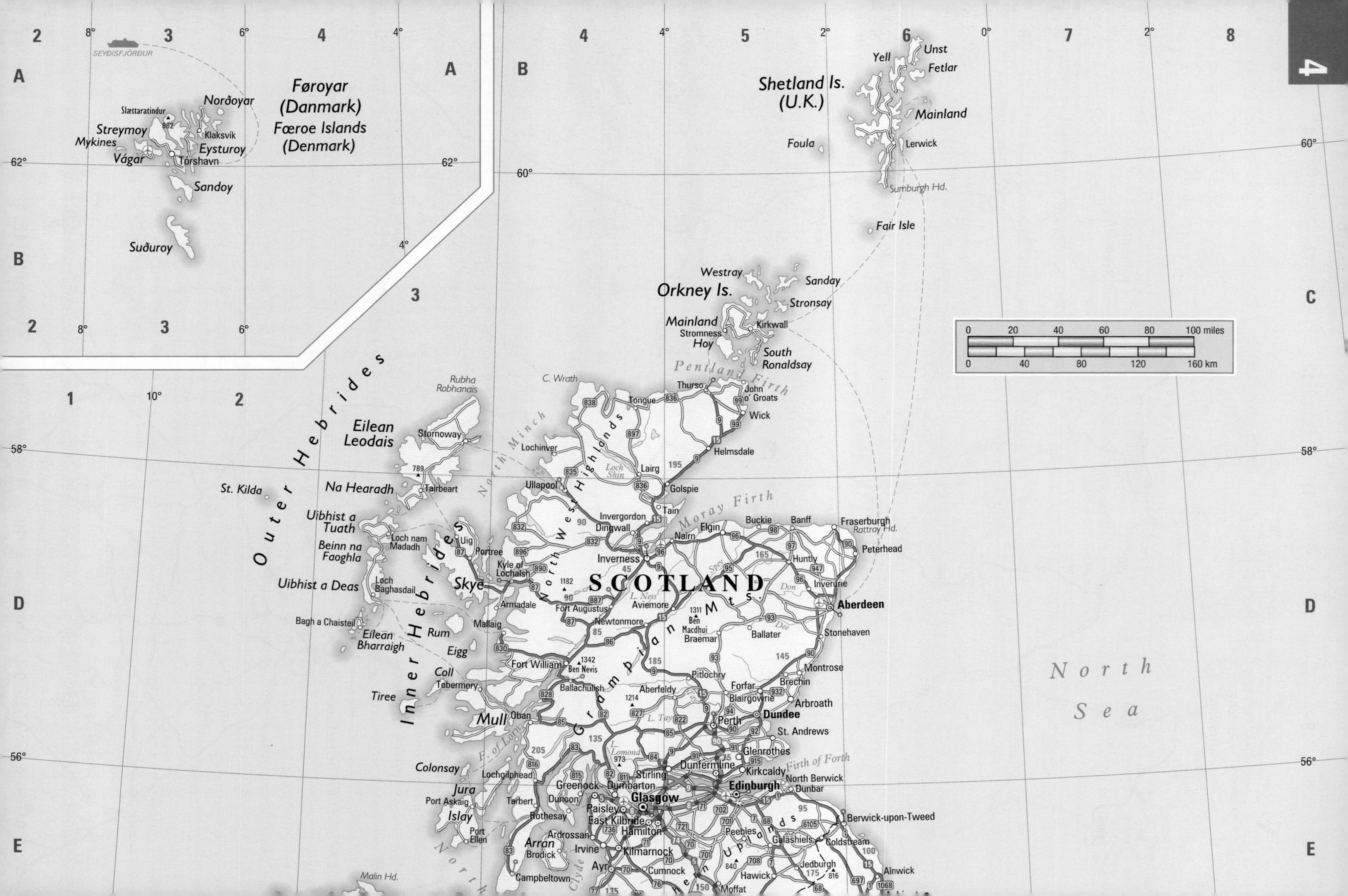

4

A B C D E

8 7 6 5 4 3 2 1

2° 0° 2° 4° 6°

**Shetland Is.
(U.K.)**

Unst
Fetlar
Yell
Mainland
Lerwick
Sumburgh Hd.

Fair Isle

Foula

100 miles
80
60
40
20
0

160 km
120
80
40
0

Westray
Sanday
Stronsay
Orkney Is.
Mainland
Stromness
Kirkwall
Hoy
South
Ronaldsay

Pentland Firth

Thurso
O Groats
John
Wick

Helmsdale

Golspie

Lairg
836

Tongue
897

836

N o r t h   S e a

Fraserburgh
Rattray Hd.
Peterhead
Inverurie
Aberdeen
Stonehaven

Banff
Buckie
Huntly
Elgin
Nairn
Forres
Montrose
Brechin
Arbroath
Dundee
St. Andrews
Glenrothes
Kirkcaldy
North Berwick
Dunbar

Firth of Forth

Berwick-upon-Tweed
Coldstream
Goldstream
Alnwick

Invergordon
Dingwall
Inverness
Aviemore
Newtonmore
Pitlochry
Blairgowrie
Forfar
Perth
Edinburgh
Dunfermline
Stirling

L. Ness

Ben
Madhui
Braemar
Ballater
Aberfeldy

S C O T L A N D

Galashiels
Peebles
Hawick
Jedburgh
Moffat

C. Wrath

Lochinver
Ullapool

North West Highlands

Kyle of
Lochalsh
Armadale

Fort Augustus
Ben Nevis
Fort William
Ballachulish

G r a m p i a n   M t s.

Newtonmore

Dunbarton
Glasgow
Paisley
East Kilbride
Hamilton
Kilmarnock
Cumnock

North Minch

Rubha
Robhanais

Stornoway

Tairbeart

Uig
Portree
Skye

Mallaig

Tobermory
Mull

Oban
L. of Lorne

Loch
joblephead
Dunoon
Rothesay
Brodick
Arran
Ardrossan
Irvine
Ayr

Firth of Clyde

**Eilean
Leodais**

Na Hearadh

Uibhist a
Tuath
Beinn na
Faoghla
Uibhist a Deas

Loch nam
Madadh
Loch
Baghasdail

Eilean
Bharraigh

Bagh a Chaisteil

I n n e r   H e b r i d e s

Rum
Eigg
Coll

Tiree

Colonsay
Jura
Port Askaig
Islay
Port
Ellen
Tarbert
Campbeltown

Malin Hd.

St. Kilda

O u t e r   H e b r i d e s

N o r t h

3

2

4

62°
60°
58°
56°

A
B
C
D
E

8°
6°
4°
2°

**Føroyar
(Danmark)
Fœroe Islands
(Denmark)**

Skattaratindur
882
Streymoy
Mykines
Vágar
Klaksvík
Eysturoy
Tórshavn
Sandoy

Suðuroy

Norðoyar

SEYÐISFJÖRÐUR

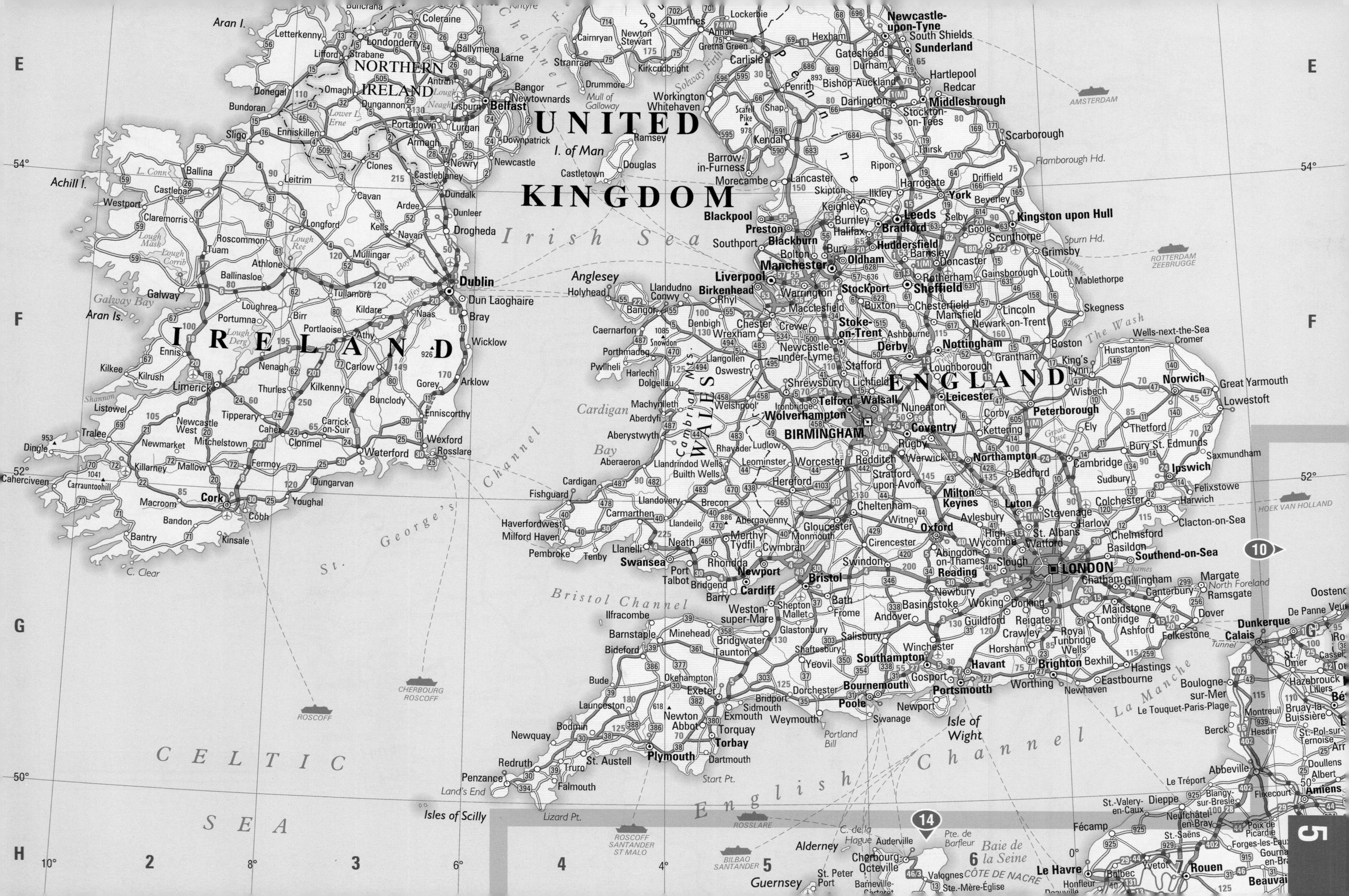

UNITED
KINGDOM
IRELAND
NORTHERN
IRELAND
ENGLAND
WALES
Irish Sea
St. George's Channel
Bristol Channel
English Channel
La Manche
CELTIC
SEA
Cardigan Bay
Galway Bay
The Wash
I. of Man
Isle of Wight
Anglesey
Isles of Scilly
Aran Is.
Achill I.
Alderney
Guernsey
Baie de la Seine
CÔTE DE NACRE
Dublin
Belfast
LONDON
BIRMINGHAM
Manchester
Liverpool
Birkenhead
Leeds
Bradford
Sheffield
Huddersfield
Oldham
Stockport
Blackpool
Preston
Blackburn
Newcastle-upon-Tyne
Sunderland
Middlesbrough
York
Kingston upon Hull
Stoke-on-Trent
Derby
Nottingham
Leicester
Coventry
Wolverhampton
Walsall
Telford
Northampton
Milton Keynes
Luton
Peterborough
Norwich
Ipswich
Oxford
Reading
Southend-on-Sea
Cardiff
Newport
Swansea
Bristol
Southampton
Bournemouth
Poole
Portsmouth
Havant
Brighton
Plymouth
Torbay
Cork
Limerick
Galway
Waterford
Dunkerque
Calais
Le Havre
Rouen
Amiens
AMSTERDAM
ROTTERDAM ZEEBRUGGE
HOEK VAN HOLLAND
ROSCOFF
CHERBOURG ROSCOFF
ROSCOFF SANTANDER ST MALO
ROSSLARE
BILBAO SANTANDER
10
14
E
F
G
H
2
3
4
5
6
7
10°
8°
6°
4°
0°
54°
52°
50°
5

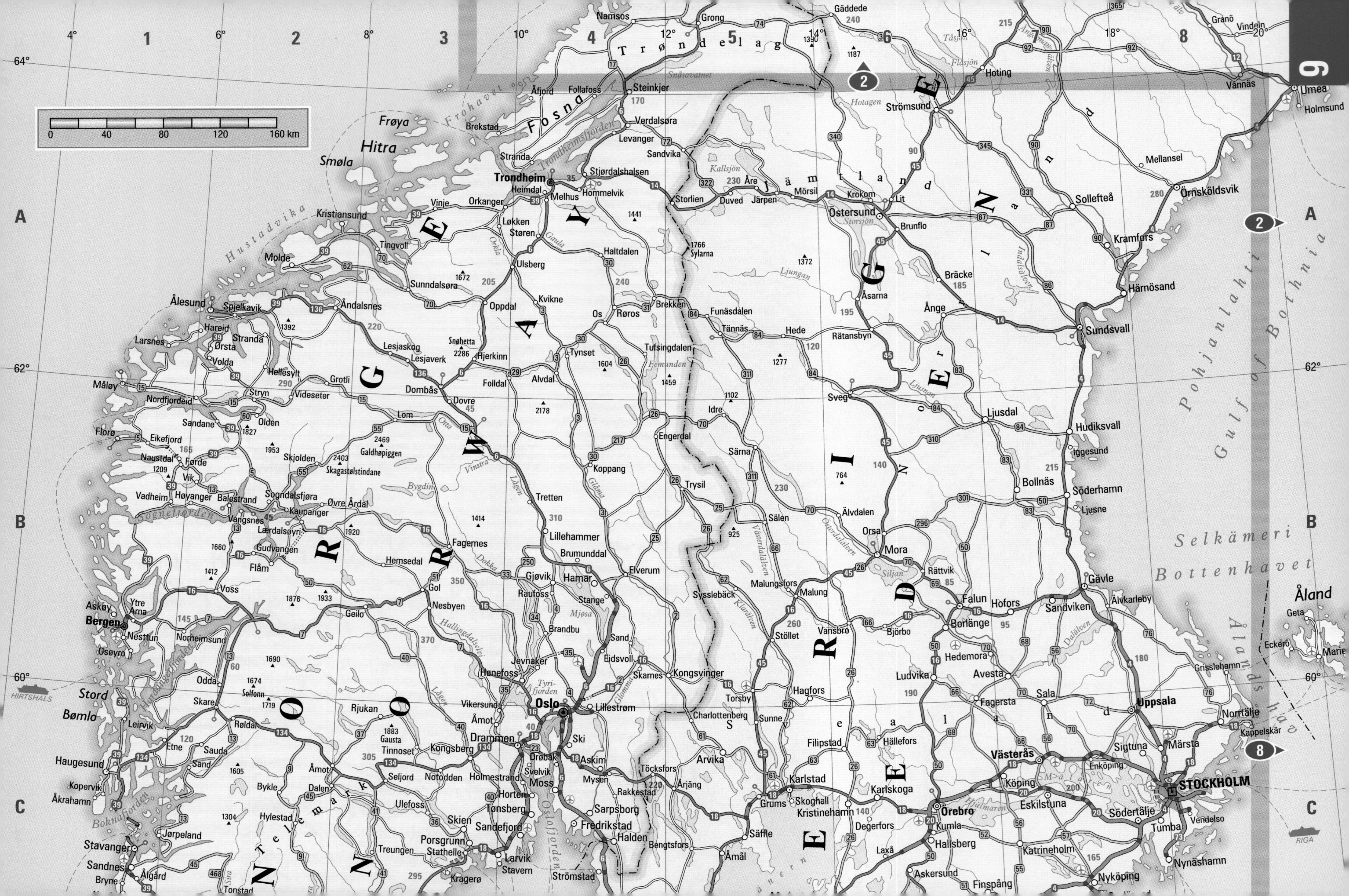

6
NORWAY
SWEDEN
NORGE
SVERIGE
Trøndelag
Jämtland
Dalarna
Värmland
Telemark
Gulf of Bothnia
Pohjanlahti
Selkämeri
Bottenhavet
Ålands hav
Åland
Oslofjorden
Sognefjorden
Hardangerfjorden
Boknafjorden
Trondheimsfjorden
Hustadvika
Frohavet
Fosna
Hitra
Frøya
Smøla
Stord
Bømlo
STOCKHOLM
Oslo
Bergen
Trondheim
Uppsala
Västerås
Örebro
Karlstad
Gävle
Sundsvall
Östersund
Umeå
Härnösand
Örnsköldsvik
Hudiksvall
Söderhamn
Falun
Borlänge
Mora
Sala
Eskilstuna
Södertälje
Norrtälje
Nyköping
Katrineholm
Drammen
Lillehammer
Hamar
Gjøvik
Kongsvinger
Elverum
Røros
Molde
Kristiansund
Ålesund
Åndalsnes
Stavanger
Haugesund
Sandnes
Skien
Porsgrunn
Larvik
Tønsberg
Fredrikstad
Sarpsborg
Halden
Moss
Kongsberg
Voss
Lærdalsøyri
Steinkjer
Namsos
Levanger
Oppdal
Dombås
Sunndalsøra
Førde
Florø
Måløy
Odda
HIRTSHALS
RIGA
0
40
80
120
160 km

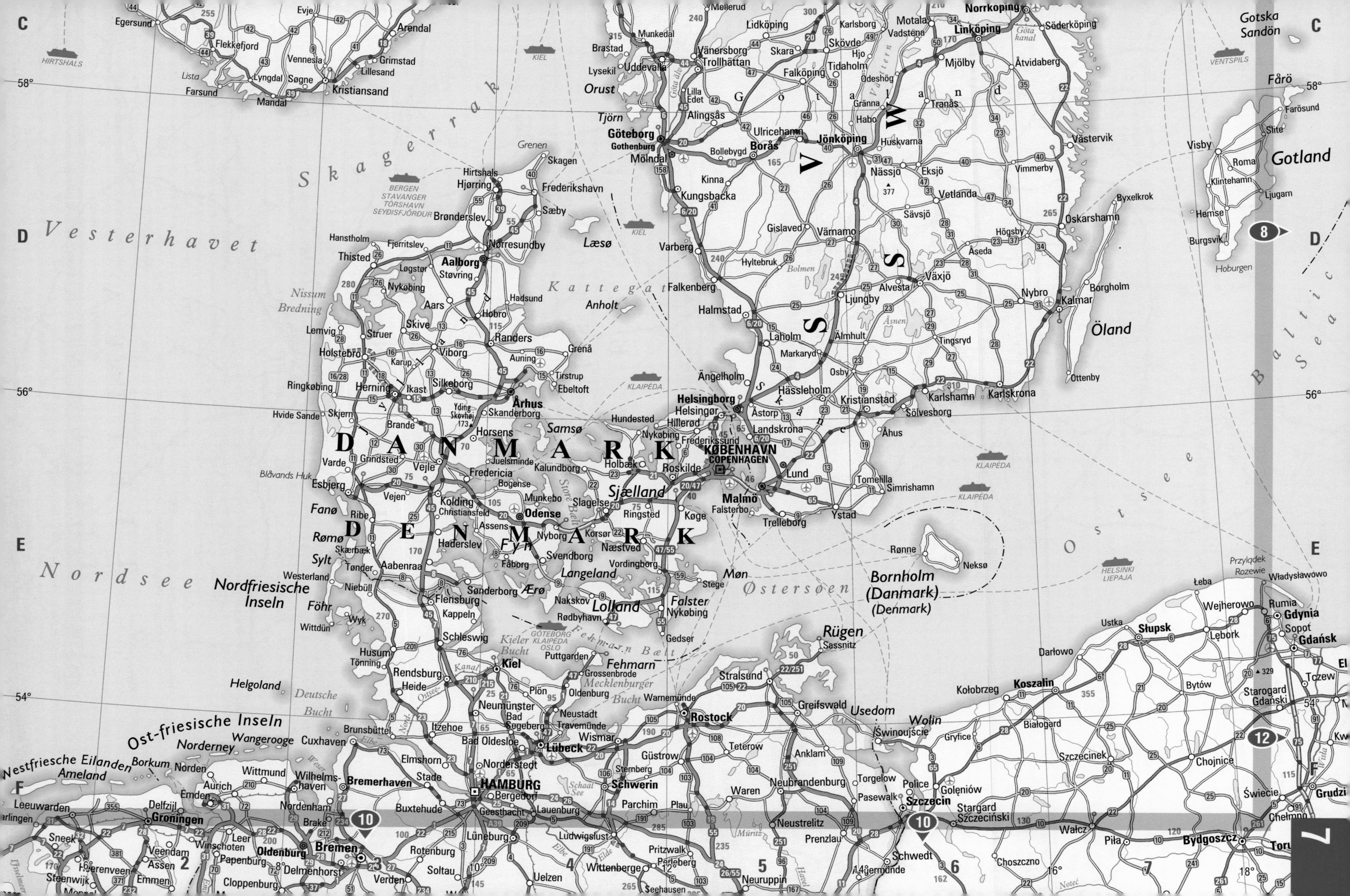
7
Vesterhavet
Skagerrak
Kattegat
Nordsee
Østersøen
Ostsee
Baltic Sea
DANMARK
DENMARK
SVERIGE
Gotland
Öland
Bornholm (Danmark)
(Denmark)
Sjælland
Fyn
Lolland
Falster
Møn
Langeland
Ærø
Samsø
Anholt
Læsø
Rügen
Usedom
Wolin
Fehmarn
Nordfriesische Inseln
Ost-friesische Inseln
Westfriesche Eilanden
Helgoland
Deutsche Bucht
Kieler Bucht
Mecklenburger Bucht
Fehmarn Bælt
Store Bælt
Nissum Bredning
Sylt
Føhr
Rømø
Fanø
Norderney
Wangerooge
Borkum
Ameland
Orust
Tjörn
Gotska Sandön
Fårö
KØBENHAVN
COPENHAGEN
Göteborg
Gothenburg
Malmö
Helsingborg
Helsingør
Århus
Aalborg
Odense
Esbjerg
Kolding
Vejle
Fredericia
Horsens
Randers
Viborg
Silkeborg
Herning
Holstebro
Skive
Frederikshavn
Skagen
Hjørring
Hirtshals
Roskilde
Køge
Næstved
Slagelse
Svendborg
Nyborg
Korsør
Haderslev
Aabenraa
Sønderborg
Tønder
Ribe
Lund
Ystad
Trelleborg
Kristianstad
Karlskrona
Kalmar
Växjö
Jönköping
Linköping
Norrköping
Borås
Halmstad
Varberg
Falkenberg
Visby
Rønne
Neksø
Kristiansand
Arendal
Mandal
Farsund
Egersund
Flekkefjord
HAMBURG
Bremen
Bremerhaven
Kiel
Lübeck
Rostock
Stralsund
Schwerin
Wismar
Flensburg
Schleswig
Rendsburg
Husum
Cuxhaven
Oldenburg
Groningen
Szczecin
Koszalin
Słupsk
Gdynia
Gdańsk
Bydgoszcz
KLAIPĖDA
KIEL
HIRTSHALS
VENTSPILS
HELSINKI
LIEPAJA
BERGEN
STAVANGER
TÓRSHAVN
SEYÐISFJÖRÐUR
GÖTEBORG
OSLO
C
D
E
F
2
3
4
5
6
7
8
10
12
54°
56°
58°
10°
12°
16°
18°

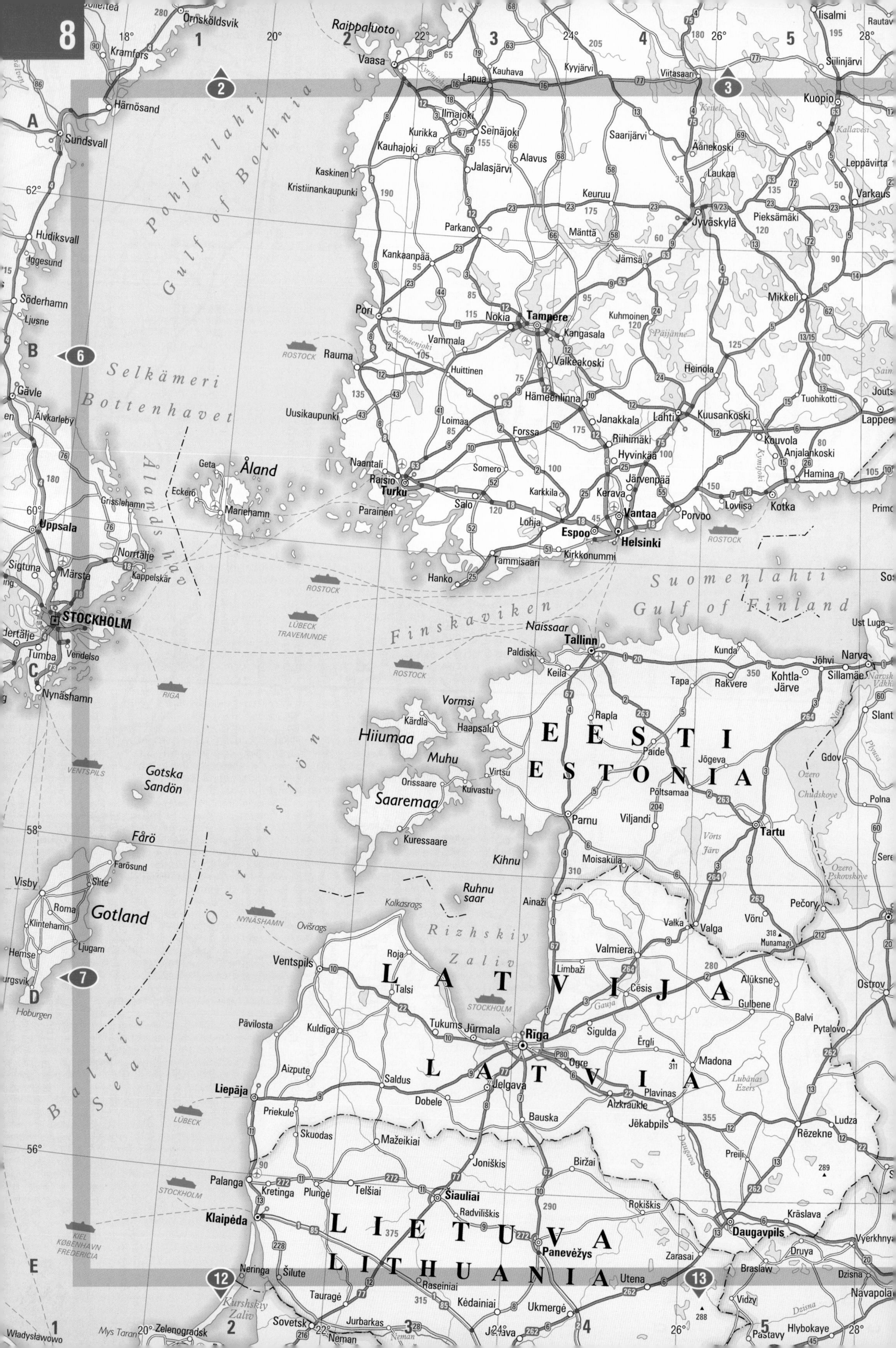
Pohjanlahti
Gulf of Bothnia
Selkämeri
Bottenhavet
Ålands hav
Åland
Finskaviken
Suomenlahti
Gulf of Finland
Östersjön
Baltic Sea
Rizhskiy Zaliv
Hiiumaa
Saaremaa
Vormsi
Muhu
Gotska Sandön
Gotland
Fårö
EESTI
ESTONIA
LATVIJA
LATVIA
LIETUVA
LITHUANIA
STOCKHOLM
Helsinki
Tallinn
Rīga
Turku
Tampere
Vaasa
Uppsala
Vantaa
Espoo
Tartu
Parnu
Liepāja
Ventspils
Klaipėda
Šiauliai
Panevėžys
Daugavpils
Jyväskylä
Kuopio
Mikkeli
Lahti
Pori
Rauma
Mariehamn
Visby
Sundsvall
Härnösand
Hudiksvall
Gävle
Kotka
Porvoo
Narva
Hämeenlinna
Jelgava
Jūrmala
Sigulda
Valmiera
Cēsis
Palanga
Rēzekne
ROSTOCK
LÜBECK TRAVEMÜNDE
RIGA
VENTSPILS
NYNÄSHAMN
STOCKHOLM
KIEL KØBENHAVN FREDERICIA

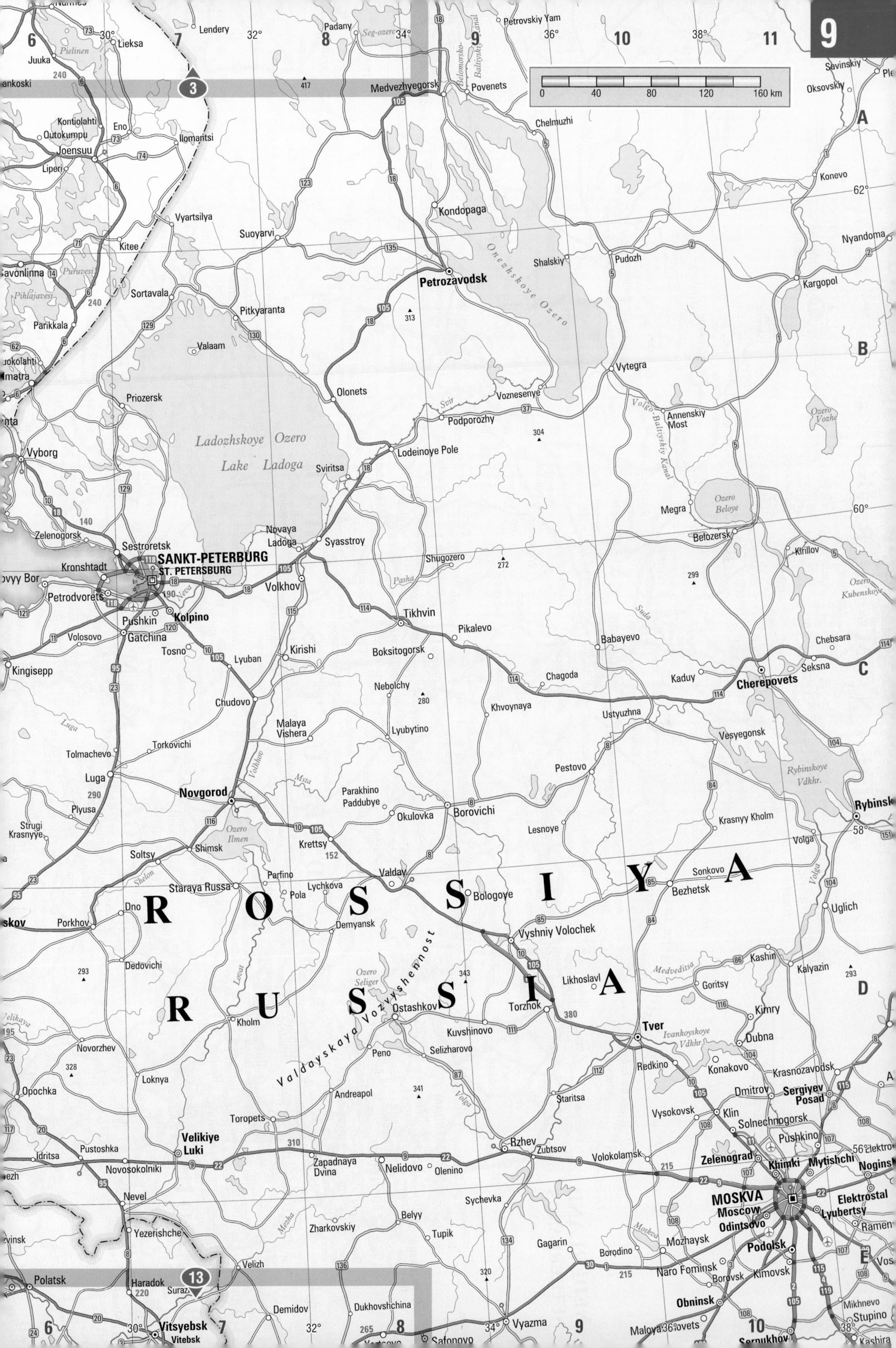

0
40
80
120
160 km
6
7
8
9
10
11
30°
32°
34°
36°
38°
56°
58°
60°
62°
A
B
C
D
E
3
13
ROSSIYA
RUSSIA
Lendery
Lieksa
Juuka
Pielinen
Padany
Seg-ozero
Petrovskiy Yam
Savinskiy
Oksovskiy
Medvezhyegorsk
Povenets
Belomorsko-Baltiyskiy Kanal
417
Kontiolahti
Outokumpu
Eno
Joensuu
Liperi
Ilomantsi
Chelmuzhi
Konevo
Kondopaga
Vyartsilya
Suoyarvi
Kitee
Savonlinna
Puruvesi
Pihlajavesi
Sortavala
Parikkala
Onezhskoye Ozero
Shalskiy
Pudozh
Nyandoma
Kargopol
Petrozavodsk
313
Pitkyaranta
Valaam
Imatra
Priozersk
Olonets
Vytegra
Voznesenye
Svir
Podporozhy
Annenskiy Most
Volgo-Baltiyskiy Kanal
Ozero Vozhe
304
Ladozhskoye Ozero
Lake Ladoga
Vyborg
Lodeinoye Pole
Sviritsa
Megra
Ozero Beloye
Zelenogorsk
Sestroretsk
Novaya Ladoga
Syasstroy
Belozersk
Kirillov
SANKT-PETERBURG
ST. PETERSBURG
Kronshtadt
Shugozero
272
299
Ozero Kubenskoye
Petrodvorets
Neva
Volkhov
Pasha
Suda
Pushkin
Kolpino
Tikhvin
Pikalevo
Gatchina
Volosovo
Kingisepp
Tosno
Kirishi
Boksitogorsk
Babayevo
Chebsara
Seksna
Lyuban
Cherepovets
Kaduy
Chagoda
Nebolchy
280
Chudovo
Khvoynaya
Ustyuzhna
Malaya Vishera
Lyubytino
Vesyegonsk
Luga
Torkovichi
Tolmachevo
Volkhov
Msta
Pestovo
Rybinskoye Vdkhr.
Rybinsk
Novgorod
Parakhino Paddubye
Okulovka
Borovichi
Plyusa
Strugi Krasnyye
Ozero Ilmen
Krettsy
Lesnoye
Krasnyy Kholm
Volga
Soltsy
Shimsk
Valday
Sonkovo
Bezhetsk
Parfino
Staraya Russa
Pola
Lychkova
Bologoye
Uglich
Shelon
Dno
Porkhov
Demyansk
Vyshniy Volochek
Kashin
Dedovichi
293
Lovat
Ozero Seliger
343
Likhoslavl
Medveditsa
Goritsy
Kalyazin
Valdayskaya Vozvyshennost
Torzhok
Kimry
Kholm
Ostashkov
Kuvshinovo
Tver
Ivankovskoye Vdkhr.
Dubna
Novorzhev
Peno
Selizharovo
Redkino
Konakovo
328
Loknya
Krasnozavodsk
Opochka
Andreapol
341
Staritsa
Dmitrov
Sergiyev Posad
Vysokovsk
Klin
Toropets
Solnechnogorsk
Velikiye Luki
Pustoshka
Rzhev
Zubtsov
Pushkino
Idritsa
Novosokolniki
Zapadnaya Dvina
Nelidovo
Olenino
Volokolamsk
Zelenograd
Khimki
Mytishchi
Elektro
Noginsk
Nevel
Sychevka
MOSKVA
Moscow
Elektrostal
Lyubertsy
Odintsovo
Ramen
Mezha
Zharkovskiy
Belyy
Tupik
Moskva
Mozhaysk
Yezerishche
Gagarin
Borodino
Podolsk
Polatsk
Haradok
Surazh
Velizh
320
Naro Fominsk
Borovsk
Klimovsk
Obninsk
Demidov
Dukhovshchina
Mikhnevo
Stupino
Vitsyebsk
Vitebsk
Yartsevo
Safonovo
Vyazma
Maloyaroslavets
Serpukhov
Kashira
Pskov
Novyy Bor
240
140
290
152
310
380
215
220
265

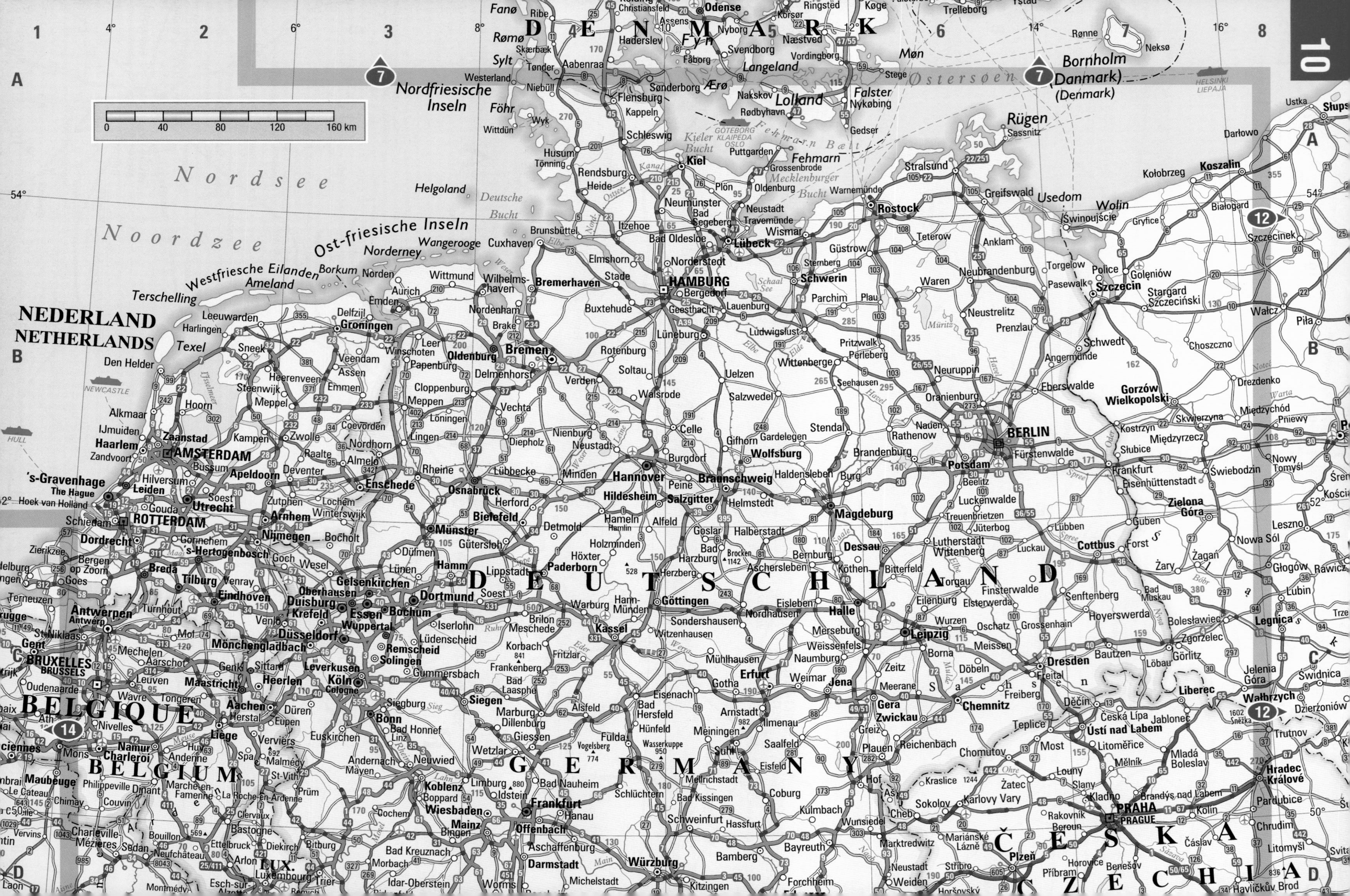
DENMARK
DEUTSCHLAND
GERMANY
NEDERLAND
NETHERLANDS
BELGIQUE
BELGIUM
LUX.
ČESKÁ
CZECHIA
Nordsee
Noordzee
Østersøen
Nordfriesische Inseln
Ost-friesische Inseln
Westfriesche Eilanden
Bornholm (Danmark) (Denmark)
Rügen
Fehmarn
Fehmarn Bælt
Lolland
Falster
Langeland
Fyn
Møn
Helgoland
Deutsche Bucht
Kieler Bucht
Mecklenburger Bucht
Usedom
Wolin
Terschelling
Ameland
Texel
Borkum
Norderney
Wangerooge
Sylt
Föhr
Rømø
Fanø
BERLIN
HAMBURG
AMSTERDAM
ROTTERDAM
PRAHA
PRAGUE
BRUXELLES
BRUSSELS
Odense
Kiel
Lübeck
Rostock
Schwerin
Bremen
Bremerhaven
Hannover
Braunschweig
Magdeburg
Potsdam
Leipzig
Dresden
Chemnitz
Halle
Erfurt
Jena
Kassel
Göttingen
Dortmund
Essen
Duisburg
Düsseldorf
Köln
Cologne
Bonn
Frankfurt
Wiesbaden
Mainz
Würzburg
Münster
Osnabrück
Bielefeld
Szczecin
Gorzów Wielkopolski
Zielona Góra
Koszalin
Legnica
Wałbrzych
Liberec
Ústí nad Labem
Hradec Králové
Plzeň
Groningen
Utrecht
Arnhem
Nijmegen
Eindhoven
Antwerpen
Antwerp
Liège
Namur
Charleroi
Maastricht
Aachen
's-Gravenhage
The Hague
Haarlem
Enschede
Apeldoorn
Zwolle
0 40 80 120 160 km
54°
50°
HELSINKI LIEPAJA
GÖTEBORG KLAIPEDA OSLO
NEWCASTLE
HULL

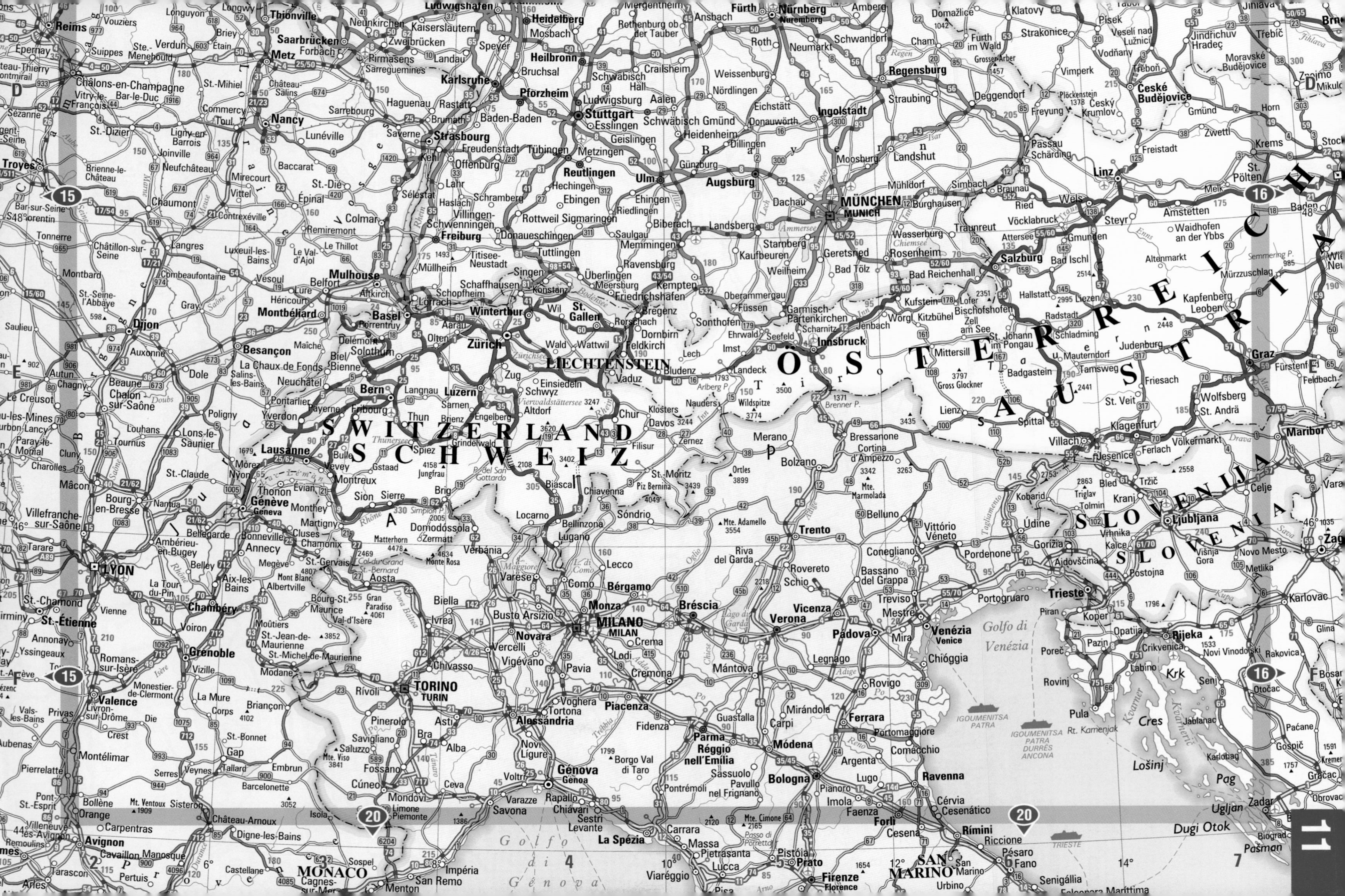

SWITZERLAND
SCHWEIZ
ÖSTERREICH
AUSTRIA
SLOVENIJA
SLOVENIA
LIECHTENSTEIN
MONACO
SAN MARINO
Reims
Metz
Nancy
Strasbourg
Mulhouse
Dijon
Besançon
Lyon
Genève
Grenoble
Valence
Avignon
St.-Étienne
Chambéry
Heidelberg
Karlsruhe
Stuttgart
Ulm
Augsburg
München
Munich
Nürnberg
Regensburg
Ingolstadt
Salzburg
Linz
Innsbruck
Graz
Klagenfurt
Ljubljana
Trieste
Basel
Zürich
Bern
Luzern
Lausanne
Torino
Turin
Milano
Milan
Genova
Verona
Venézia
Venice
Pádova
Bologna
Firenze
Florence
Rimini
Golfo di Venézia
Golfo di Génova
15
16
20

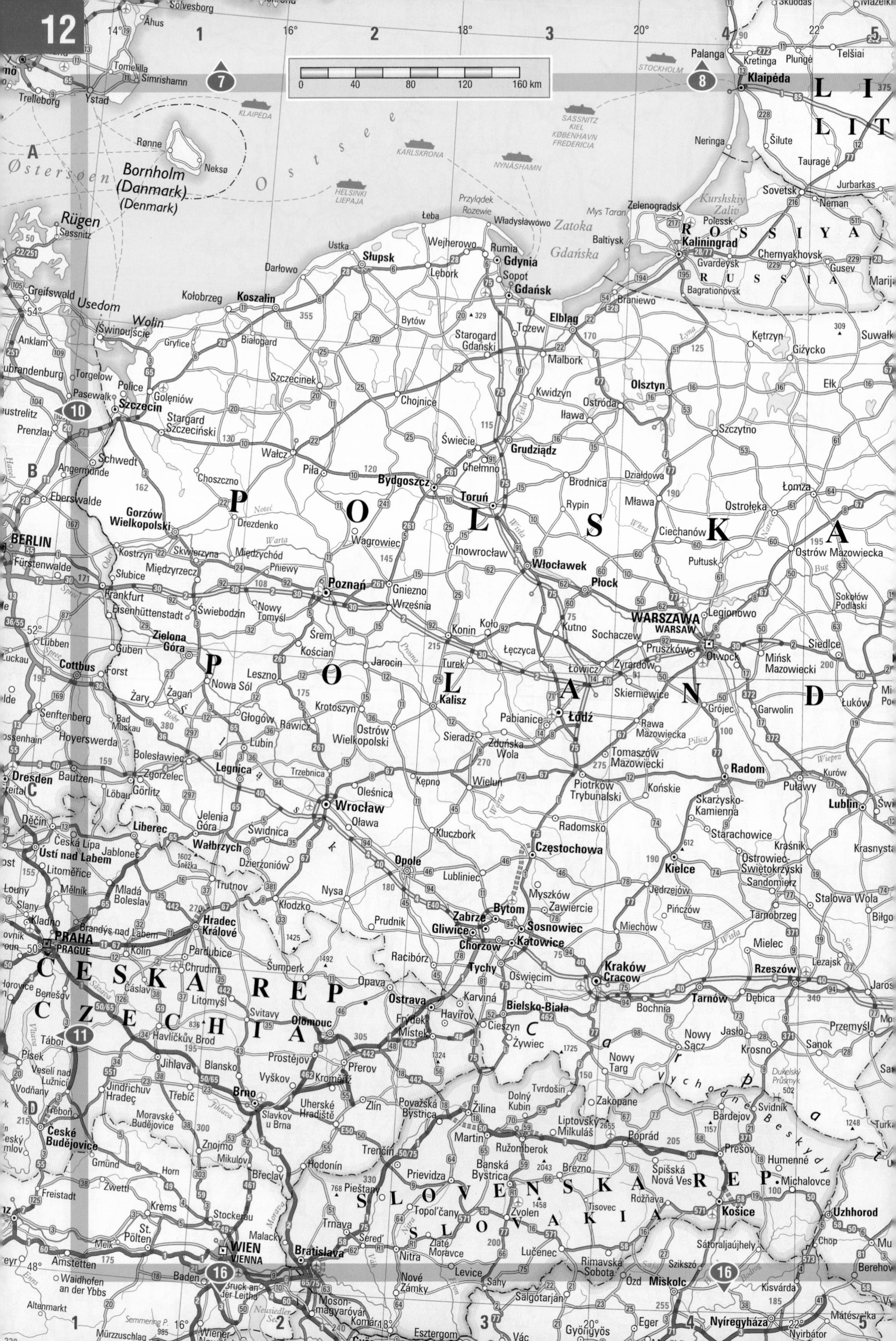

1
2
3
4
5
A
B
C
D
16°
18°
20°
22°
0
40
80
120
160 km
7
8
10
11
16
Sölvesborg
Åhus
Tomelilla
Simrishamn
Trelleborg
Ystad
KLAIPĖDA
Rønne
Bornholm
(Danmark)
(Denmark)
Neksø
Østersøen
Ostsee
KARLSKRONA
HELSINKI
LIEPAJA
NYNÄSHAMN
SASSNITZ
KIEL
KØBENHAVN
FREDERICIA
STOCKHOLM
Palanga
Kretinga
Plungė
Telšiai
Klaipėda
LIT
Neringa
Šilute
Tauragė
Jurbarkas
Sovetsk
Neman
Kurshskiy Zaliv
Zelenogradsk
Polessk
Mys Taran
ROSSIYA
RUSSIA
Baltiysk
Kaliningrad
Gvardeysk
Chernyakhovsk
Gusev
Bagrationovsk
Marij
Rügen
Sassnitz
Greifswald
Usedom
Wolin
Świnoujście
Anklam
Gryfice
Białogard
Kołobrzeg
Koszalin
Darłowo
Ustka
Słupsk
Łeba
Lębork
Wejherowo
Przylądek Rozewie
Władysławowo
Zatoka Gdańska
Rumia
Gdynia
Sopot
Gdańsk
Braniewo
Elbląg
Tczew
Malbork
Starogard Gdański
Bytów
Kętrzyn
Giżycko
Suwałk
Ełk
Olsztyn
Ostróda
Iława
Kwidzyn
Szczytno
Torgelow
Police
Pasewalk
Szczecin
Goleniów
Stargard Szczeciński
Szczecinek
Chojnice
Świecie
Grudziądz
Chełmno
Prenzlau
Schwedt
Angermünde
Wałcz
Piła
Bydgoszcz
Toruń
Brodnica
Działdowo
Mława
Rypin
Łomża
Ostrołęka
Eberswalde
Choszczno
Gorzów Wielkopolski
Drezdenko
Noteć
POLSKA
POLAND
Wągrowiec
Inowrocław
Włocławek
Płock
Ciechanów
Pułtusk
Ostrów Mazowiecka
BERLIN
Kostrzyn
Skwierzyna
Międzychód
Pniewy
Gniezno
Września
Poznań
Fürstenwalde
Słubice
Międzyrzecz
Frankfurt
Eisenhüttenstadt
Świebodzin
Nowy Tomyśl
Konin
Koło
Kutno
Sochaczew
WARSZAWA
WARSAW
Legionowo
Sokołów Podlaski
Lübben
Zielona Góra
Śrem
Kościan
Łęczyca
Pruszków
Otwock
Siedlce
Mińsk Mazowiecki
Guben
Cottbus
Forst
Leszno
Jarocin
Turek
Łowicz
Żyrardów
Skierniewice
Łuków
Nowa Sól
Żary
Żagań
Krotoszyn
Kalisz
Pabianice
Łódź
Grójec
Garwolin
Senftenberg
Bad Muskau
Głogów
Rawicz
Ostrów Wielkopolski
Sieradz
Zduńska Wola
Rawa Mazowiecka
Tomaszów Mazowiecki
Hoyerswerda
Lubin
Bolesławiec
Legnica
Trzebnica
Kępno
Wieluń
Piotrków Trybunalski
Końskie
Radom
Kurów
Puławy
Dresden
Bautzen
Zgorzelec
Görlitz
Löbau
Oleśnica
Wrocław
Oława
Skarżysko-Kamienna
Lublin
Děčín
Liberec
Jelenia Góra
Świdnica
Radomsko
Starachowice
Kraśnik
Česká Lípa
Jablonec
Ústí nad Labem
Wałbrzych
Dzierżoniów
Kluczbork
Częstochowa
Kielce
Ostrowiec Świętokrzyski
Krasnystaw
Litoměřice
Sněžka
Opole
Lubliniec
Sandomierz
Louny
Mělník
Mladá Boleslav
Trutnov
Nysa
Myszków
Zawiercie
Jędrzejów
Pińczów
Stalowa Wola
Slaný
Kladno
Hradec Králové
Kłodzko
Prudnik
Bytom
Zabrze
Gliwice
Sosnowiec
Katowice
Chorzów
Miechów
Tarnobrzeg
Biłgo
PRAHA
PRAGUE
Brandýs nad Labem
Kolín
Pardubice
Racibórz
Tychy
Oświęcim
Kraków
Cracow
Mielec
Rzeszów
Leżajsk
Chrudim
Šumperk
Opava
Ostrava
Karviná
Bielsko-Biała
Bochnia
Tarnów
Dębica
Jarosł
ČESKÁ REP.
CZECHIA
Benešov
Čáslav
Litomyšl
Svitavy
Olomouc
Frýdek-Místek
Havířov
Cieszyn
Żywiec
Nowy Sącz
Jasło
Krosno
Przemyśl
Sanok
Tábor
Havlíčkův Brod
Jihlava
Blansko
Prostějov
Přerov
Kroměříž
Nowy Targ
Dukelský Průsmyk
Písek
Veselí nad Lužnicí
Vodňany
Jindřichův Hradec
Třebíč
Brno
Vyškov
Zlín
Uherské Hradiště
Slavkov u Brna
Považská Bystrica
Žilina
Dolný Kubín
Tvrdošín
Zakopane
Bardejov
Svidník
Vychodné Beskydy
Karpaty
Třeboň
České Budějovice
Moravské Budějovice
Znojmo
Mikulov
Břeclav
Hodonín
Trenčín
Martin
Ružomberok
Liptovský Mikuláš
Poprad
Prešov
Humenné
Michalovce
Gmünd
Horn
Zwettl
Freistadt
Krems
Prievidza
Piešťany
Banská Bystrica
Brezno
Spišská Nová Ves
Rožňava
Košice
Uzhhorod
SLOVENSKÁ REP.
SLOVAKIA
Topoľčany
Zvolen
Tisovec
St. Pölten
Stockerau
Trnava
Sereď
Zlaté Moravce
Malacky
WIEN
VIENNA
Bratislava
Nitra
Lučenec
Rimavská Sobota
Sátoraljaújhely
Chop
Melk
Amstetten
Waidhofen an der Ybbs
Baden
Bruck an der Leitha
Levice
Nové Zámky
Šahy
Ózd
Miskolc
Szikszó
Kisvárda
Berehov
Altenmarkt
Mosonmagyaróvár
Komárom
Salgótarján
Eger
Nyíregyháza
Mátészalka
Mürzzuschlag
Wiener-
Esztergom
Vác
Gyöngyös
Nyírbátor

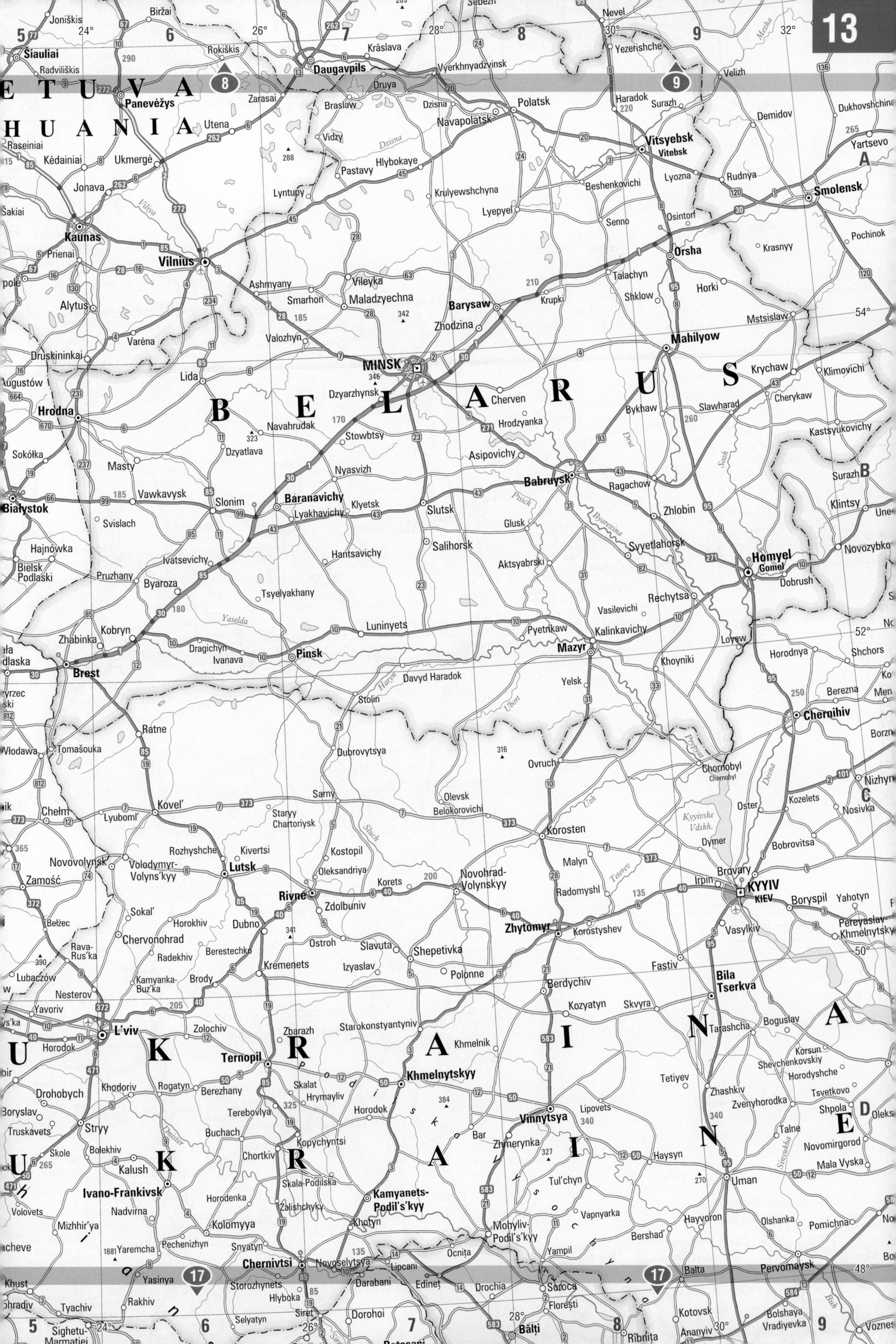
LITHUANIA
BELARUS
UKRAINE
Šiauliai
Joniškis
Biržai
Rokiškis
Daugavpils
Krāslava
Radviliškis
Panevėžys
Zarasai
Utena
Raseiniai
Kėdainiai
Ukmergė
Jonava
Kaunas
Prienai
Vilnius
Alytus
Varėna
Druskininkai
Augustów
Sebezh
Nevel
Yezerishche
Vyerkhnyadzvinsk
Druya
Braslaw
Dzisna
Polatsk
Navapolatsk
Vidzy
Pastavy
Hlybokaye
Lyntupy
Krulyewshchyna
Lyepyel
Haradok
Surazh
Velizh
Dukhovshchina
Demidov
Vitsyebsk
Vitebsk
Yartsevo
Beshenkovichi
Lyozna
Rudnya
Smolensk
Senno
Osintorf
Orsha
Krasnyy
Pochinok
Ashmyany
Smarhon
Vileyka
Maladzyechna
Barysaw
Zhodzina
Krupki
Talachyn
Shklow
Horki
Valozhyn
MINSK
Mahilyow
Mstsislaw
Lida
Hrodna
Dzyarzhynsk
Cherven
Krychaw
Klimovichi
Navahrudak
Stowbtsy
Hrodzyanka
Bykhaw
Slawharad
Cherykaw
Kastsyukovichy
Sokółka
Masty
Dzyatlava
Asipovichy
Babruysk
Ragachow
Surazh
Białystok
Vawkavysk
Slonim
Baranavichy
Lyakhavichy
Klyetsk
Slutsk
Zhlobin
Klintsy
Svislach
Glusk
Svyetlahorsk
Novozybkov
Hajnówka
Bielsk Podlaski
Ivatsevichy
Hantsavichy
Salihorsk
Aktsyabrski
Homyel
Gomel
Dobrush
Pruzhany
Byaroza
Tsyelyakhany
Rechytsa
Vasilevichi
Kobryn
Zhabinka
Luninyets
Pyetrikaw
Kalinkavichy
Brest
Dragichyn
Ivanava
Pinsk
Mazyr
Loyew
Horodnya
Shchors
Khoyniki
Davyd Haradok
Stolin
Yelsk
Berezna
Chernihiv
Włodawa
Tomašouka
Ratne
Dubrovytsya
Ovruch
Chornobyl
Chernobyl
Nizhyn
Chełm
Lyuboml'
Kovel'
Sarny
Olevsk
Belokorovichi
Staryy Chartoriysk
Oster
Kozelets
Nosivka
Korosten
Kyyivske Vdskh.
Dymer
Bobrovitsa
Rozhyshche
Kivertsi
Kostopil
Malyn
Novovolynsk
Volodymyr-Volyns'kyy
Lutsk
Oleksandriya
Korets
Novohrad-Volynskyy
Radomyshl
Brovary
Irpin
KYYIV
KIEV
Boryspil
Yahotyn
Zamość
Rivne
Zdolbuniv
Zhytomyr
Korostyshev
Vasylkiv
Pereyaslav-Khmelnytskyy
Sokal'
Horokhiv
Dubno
Bełżec
Chervonohrad
Ostroh
Slavuta
Shepetivka
Rava-Rus'ka
Radekhiv
Berestechko
Kremenets
Izyaslav
Polonne
Fastiv
Lubaczów
Kamyanka-Buz'ka
Brody
Berdychiv
Bila Tserkva
Nesterov
Yavoriv
Kozyatyn
Skvyra
L'viv
Zolochiv
Zbarazh
Starokonstyantyniv
Tarashcha
Boguslav
Horodok
Ternopil
Khmelnik
Korsun-Shevchenkovskiy
Horodyshche
Drohobych
Khodoriv
Rogatyn
Berezhany
Skalat
Hrymayliv
Khmelnytskyy
Tetiyev
Zhashkiv
Zvenyhorodka
Tsvetkovo
Boryslav
Truskavets'
Stryy
Terebovlya
Horodok
Vinnytsya
Lipovets
Shpola
Buchach
Bar
Zhmerynka
Talne
Skole
Bolekhiv
Kalush
Chortkiv
Kopychyntsi
Haysyn
Novomirgorod
Mala Vyska
Ivano-Frankivsk
Skala-Podilska
Kamyanets-Podil's'kyy
Tul'chyn
Uman
Volovets
Nadvirna
Horodenka
Zalishchyky
Vapnyarka
Mizhhir'ya
Kolomyya
Khotyn
Mohyliv-Podil's'kyy
Hayvoron
Olshanka
Pomichna
Yaremcha
Pechenizhyn
Snyatyn
Bershad'
Chernivtsi
Novoselytsya
Lipcani
Ocnița
Yampil
Pervomaysk
Khust
Yasinya
Storozhynets
Darabani
Edineț
Drochia
Soroca
Balta
Tyachiv
Rakhiv
Hlyboka
Florești
Kotovsk
Bolshaya Vradiyevka
Sighetu-Marmatiei
Selyatyn
Siret
Dorohoi
Bălți
Rîbnița
Ananyiv
Voznesensk
Podil'ska Vysochyna
Dzisna
Viliya
Yaselda
Drut
Sozh
Ptsich
Byarezina
Horyn
Ubort
Prypyat
Desna
Uzh
Sluch
Teterev
Dniester
Southern Buh
Sinyukha
24°
26°
28°
30°
32°
54°
52°
50°
48°
5
6
7
8
9
A
B
C
D
8
9
17
17

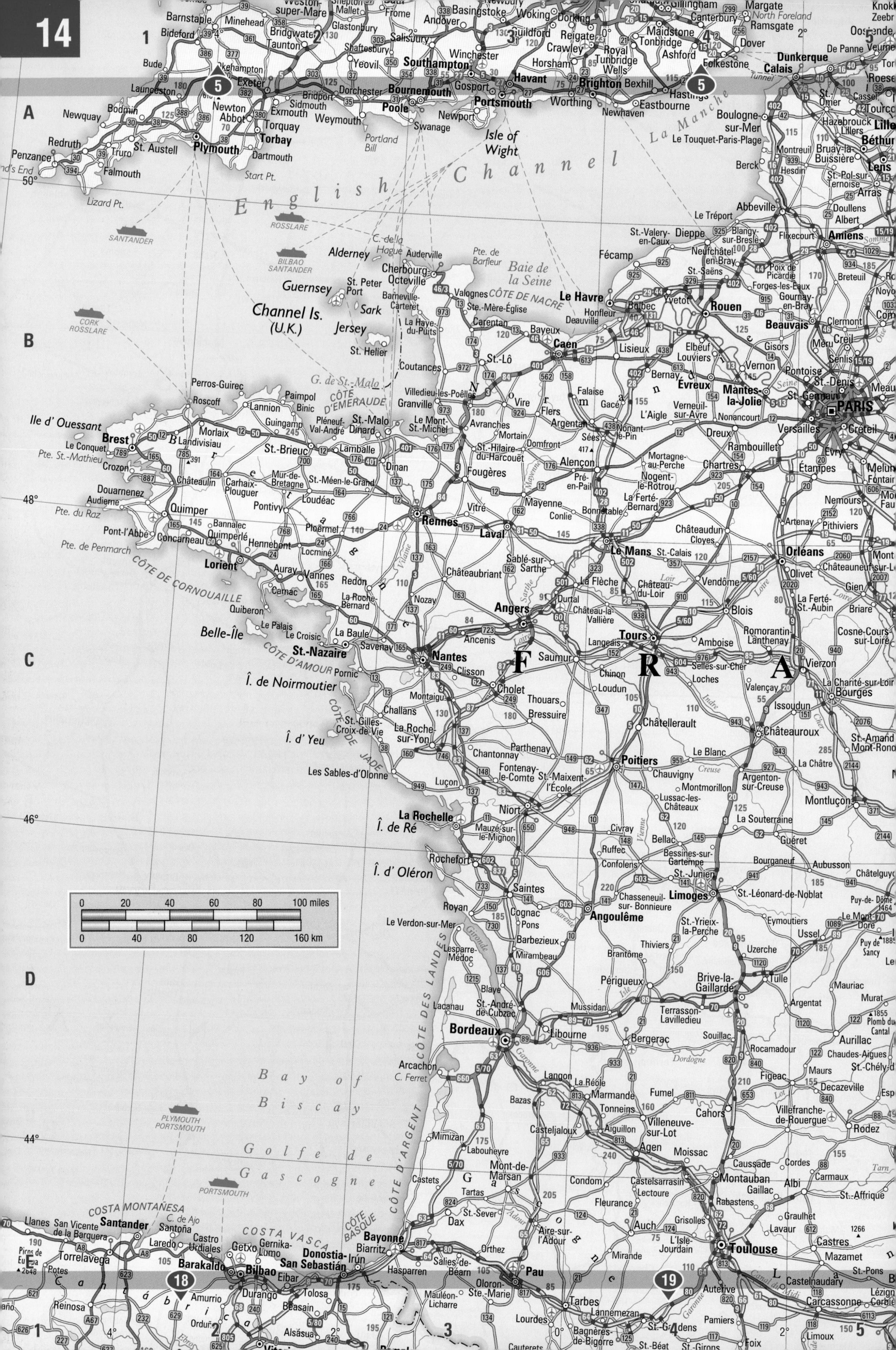
English Channel
La Manche
Isle of Wight
Channel Is. (U.K.)
Alderney
Guernsey
Sark
Jersey
St. Peter Port
St. Helier
Bay of Biscay
Golfe de Gascogne
Baie de la Seine
CÔTE DE NACRE
CÔTE D'EMERAUDE
CÔTE DE CORNOUAILLE
CÔTE D'AMOUR
CÔTE DE JADE
CÔTE DES LANDES
CÔTE D'ARGENT
CÔTE BASQUE
COSTA VASCA
COSTA MONTAÑESA
FRANCE
Bretagne
Normandie
Gascogne
Cantabria
Barnstaple
Minehead
Bridgwater
Taunton
Bideford
Bude
Okehampton
Exeter
Launceston
Bodmin
Newquay
Newton Abbot
Exmouth
Torquay
Torbay
Plymouth
Dartmouth
St. Austell
Truro
Redruth
Penzance
Falmouth
Lizard Pt.
Start Pt.
Weston-super-Mare
Glastonbury
Shaftesbury
Yeovil
Frome
Andover
Basingstoke
Salisbury
Winchester
Southampton
Bournemouth
Poole
Swanage
Portland Bill
Dorchester
Bridport
Sidmouth
Weymouth
Gosport
Portsmouth
Havant
Newport
Woking
Dorking
Guildford
Reigate
Crawley
Horsham
Worthing
Brighton
Royal Tunbridge Wells
Tonbridge
Maidstone
Gillingham
Canterbury
Margate
Ramsgate
Ashford
Dover
Folkestone
Hastings
Bexhill
Eastbourne
Newhaven
North Foreland
Dunkerque
Calais
Boulogne-sur-Mer
Le Touquet-Paris-Plage
St.-Omer
Hazebrouck
Lille
Béthune
Lens
Arras
Montreuil
Hesdin
Berck
Doullens
Albert
Abbeville
Amiens
Le Tréport
St.-Valery-en-Caux
Dieppe
Fécamp
Le Havre
Honfleur
Deauville
Bolbec
Yvetot
Rouen
Elbeuf
Louviers
Vernon
Évreux
Beauvais
Gisors
Creil
Senlis
Pontoise
St.-Denis
PARIS
Versailles
Créteil
Évry
Étampes
Melun
Mantes-la-Jolie
Dreux
Rambouillet
Chartres
Nogent-le-Rotrou
Cherbourg-Octeville
Valognes
Ste.-Mère-Église
Carentan
Bayeux
Caen
Lisieux
Bernay
L'Aigle
St.-Lô
Coutances
Granville
Villedieu-les-Poêles
Vire
Flers
Argentan
Falaise
Alençon
Mortagne-au-Perche
Avranches
Le Mont-St.-Michel
St.-Malo
Dinard
Dinan
Lamballe
St.-Brieuc
Guingamp
Paimpol
Lannion
Perros-Guirec
Roscoff
Morlaix
Landivisiau
Brest
Le Conquet
Ile d' Ouessant
Crozon
Châteaulin
Douarnenez
Audierne
Pte. du Raz
Quimper
Pont-l'Abbé
Pte. de Penmarch
Concarneau
Quimperlé
Lorient
Hennebont
Pontivy
Loudéac
Ploërmel
Rennes
Fougères
Vitré
Laval
Mayenne
Auray
Vannes
Carnac
Quiberon
Belle-Île
Le Palais
Redon
La Baule
Le Croisic
St.-Nazaire
Savenay
Nantes
Ancenis
Châteaubriant
Angers
Saumur
Sablé-sur-Sarthe
La Flèche
Le Mans
Mamers
Châteaudun
Orléans
Blois
Vendôme
Tours
Amboise
Chinon
Loudun
Loches
Romorantin-Lanthenay
Vierzon
Bourges
Issoudun
Châteauroux
Cholet
Clisson
Pornic
Î. de Noirmoutier
St.-Gilles-Croix-de-Vie
Î. d' Yeu
La Roche-sur-Yon
Les Sables-d'Olonne
Luçon
Fontenay-le-Comte
Niort
Parthenay
Bressuire
Thouars
Poitiers
Châtellerault
Chauvigny
Montmorillon
Le Blanc
La Rochelle
Î. de Ré
Rochefort
Î. d' Oléron
Saintes
Royan
Cognac
Angoulême
Confolens
Limoges
Guéret
Montluçon
Le Verdon-sur-Mer
Lesparre-Médoc
Blaye
Barbezieux
Périgueux
Brive-la-Gaillarde
Tulle
Uzerche
Lacanau
Bordeaux
Libourne
Bergerac
Arcachon
C. Ferret
Langon
Marmande
Bazas
Agen
Villeneuve-sur-Lot
Cahors
Figeac
Aurillac
Rodez
Mimizan
Mont-de-Marsan
Dax
Bayonne
Biarritz
Orthez
Pau
Tarbes
Lourdes
Auch
Montauban
Albi
Castres
Toulouse
Carcassonne
Castelnaudary
Santander
Torrelavega
Laredo
Castro Urdiales
Bilbao
Barakaldo
Getxo
Donostia-San Sebastián
Irún
Eibar
Tolosa

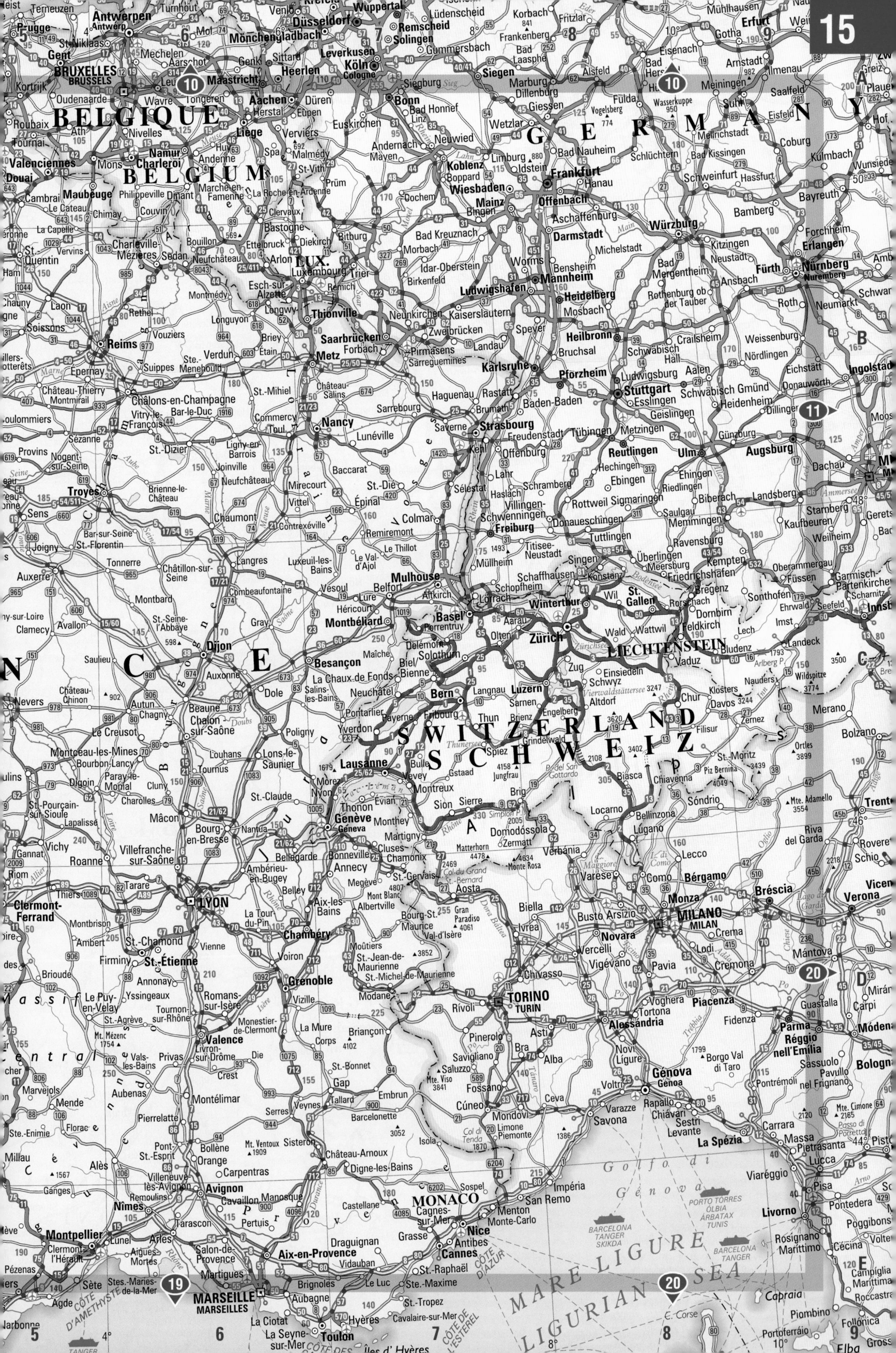
BELGIQUE
BELGIUM
GERMANY
SWITZERLAND
SCHWEIZ
LIECHTENSTEIN
LUX.
MONACO
MARE LIGURE
LIGURIAN SEA
Golfo di Génova
CÔTE D'AMETHYSTE
CÔTE D'AZUR
CÔTE DE L'ESTEREL
Antwerpen
Antwerp
Brugge
Gent
St-Niklaas
Mechelen
BRUXELLES
BRUSSELS
Kortrijk
Oudenaarde
Aarschot
Leuven
Turnhout
Genk
Sittard
Maastricht
Heerlen
Aachen
Tongeren
Wavre
Roubaix
Tournai
Ath
Nivelles
Herstal
Eupen
Liège
Verviers
Namur
Charleroi
Andenne
Huy
Spa
Malmédy
St-Vith
Valenciennes
Mons
Douai
Cambrai
Maubeuge
Philippeville
Dinant
Marche-en-Famenne
La Roche-en-Ardenne
Le Cateau
Chimay
Couvin
La Capelle
Vervins
Charleville-Mézières
Sedan
Bouillon
Neufchâteau
Bastogne
Clervaux
Ettelbruck
Diekirch
Arlon
Luxembourg
Esch-sur-Alzette
Longwy
Thionville
St.-Quentin
Ham
Chauny
Laon
Soissons
Rethel
Reims
Vouziers
Montmédy
Longuyon
Briey
Verdun
Étain
Metz
Épernay
Château-Thierry
Montmirail
Châlons-en-Champagne
Suippes
Ste.-Menehould
St.-Mihiel
Bar-le-Duc
Vitry-le-François
Commercy
Toul
Nancy
Lunéville
Sézanne
Provins
Nogent-sur-Seine
St.-Dizier
Ligny-en-Barrois
Joinville
Troyes
Brienne-le-Château
Neufchâteau
Mirecourt
Vittel
Épinal
St.-Dié
Baccarat
Sens
Bar-sur-Seine
Chaumont
Contrexéville
Remiremont
Colmar
Joigny
St.-Florentin
Tonnerre
Auxerre
Châtillon-sur-Seine
Langres
Luxeuil-les-Bains
Le Val-d'Ajol
Le Thillot
Mulhouse
Belfort
Vesoul
Lure
Héricourt
Montbéliard
Avallon
Clamecy
Montbard
St.-Seine-l'Abbaye
Gray
Combeaufontaine
Dijon
Auxonne
Dole
Besançon
Saulieu
Nevers
Château-Chinon
Autun
Beaune
Chagny
Chalon-sur-Saône
Le Creusot
Montceau-les-Mines
Bourbon-Lancy
Digoin
Paray-le-Monial
Charolles
Cluny
Tournus
Louhans
Lons-le-Saunier
Poligny
Pontarlier
Mâcon
Bourg-en-Bresse
St.-Claude
Nantua
Villefranche-sur-Saône
Roanne
Vichy
Gannat
Riom
Thiers
Tarare
Clermont-Ferrand
Ambérieu-en-Bugey
Bellegarde
LYON
Montbrison
Ambert
St.-Chamond
St.-Étienne
Vienne
La Tour-du-Pin
Chambéry
Aix-les-Bains
Annecy
Belley
Voiron
Grenoble
Firminy
Brioude
Annonay
Le Puy-en-Velay
Yssingeaux
Romans-sur-Isère
Tournon-sur-Rhône
St.-Agrève
Valence
Livron-sur-Drôme
Privas
Die
Crest
Vals-les-Bains
Aubenas
Montélimar
Pierrelatte
Marvejols
Mende
Florac
Ste.-Enimie
Millau
Alès
Pont-St.-Esprit
Bollène
Orange
Carpentras
Villeneuve-lès-Avignon
Avignon
Remoulins
Nîmes
Ganges
Cavaillon
Manosque
Pertuis
Tarascon
Arles
Lunel
Montpellier
Clermont-l'Hérault
Pézenas
Sète
Agde
Aigues-Mortes
Salon-de-Provence
Aix-en-Provence
Martigues
Stes.-Maries-de-la-Mer
MARSEILLE
MARSEILLES
Aubagne
La Ciotat
La Seyne-sur-Mer
Toulon
Hyères
Brignoles
Le Luc
Draguignan
Vidauban
Ste.-Maxime
St.-Tropez
Cavalaire-sur-Mer
St.-Raphaël
Cannes
Grasse
Antibes
Nice
Cagnes-sur-Mer
Menton
Monte-Carlo
San Remo
Impéria
Castellane
Digne-les-Bains
Château-Arnoux
Sisteron
Gap
Tallard
Embrun
Barcelonette
Briançon
La Mure
Corps
St.-Bonnet
Serres
Veynes
Modane
St.-Michel-de-Maurienne
St.-Jean-de-Maurienne
Moûtiers
Bourg-St.-Maurice
Val-d'Isère
Albertville
Megève
Chamonix
Cluses
Bonneville
St.-Gervais
Genève
Geneva
Thonon
Évian
Montreux
Vevey
Lausanne
Morez
Nyon
Yverdon
Neuchâtel
La Chaux-de-Fonds
Bulle
Fribourg
Payerne
Bern
Biel/Bienne
Solothurn
Delémont
Porrentruy
Basel
Lörrach
Altkirch
Olten
Aarau
Zürich
Winterthur
Schaffhausen
Konstanz
St. Gallen
Wil
Wattwil
Wald
Rorschach
Bregenz
Dornbirn
Feldkirch
Vaduz
Bludenz
Landeck
Zug
Luzern
Langnau
Sarnen
Thun
Brienz
Interlaken
Spiez
Gstaad
Einsiedeln
Schwyz
Altdorf
Engelberg
Grindelwald
Jungfrau
Chur
Davos
Klosters
Filisur
Zernez
St.-Moritz
Chiavenna
Sondrio
Biasca
Bellinzona
Locarno
Lugano
Brig
Sion
Sierre
Martigny
Monthey
Zermatt
Matterhorn
Monte Rosa
Domodóssola
Verbania
Aosta
Col du Grand St.-Bernard
Gran Paradiso
Mont Blanc
Biella
Ivrea
Vercelli
Novara
Busto Arsizio
Varese
Como
Lecco
Bérgamo
Monza
MILANO
MILAN
Brescia
Verona
Vicenza
Crema
Lodi
Cremona
Mantova
Pavia
Vigévano
Chivasso
TORINO
TURIN
Rívoli
Pinerolo
Savigliano
Saluzzo
Fossano
Cúneo
Mondovì
Bra
Asti
Alba
Alessandria
Tortona
Voghera
Piacenza
Fidenza
Parma
Réggio nell'Emília
Módena
Carpi
Guastalla
Sassuolo
Bologna
Novi Lígure
Génova
Genoa
Voltri
Savona
Varazze
Rapallo
Chiávari
Sestri Levante
La Spézia
Carrara
Massa
Pietrasanta
Lucca
Pisa
Viaréggio
Livorno
Pontedera
Poggibonsi
Rosignano Marittimo
Cécina
Piombino
Follónica
Portoferráio
Elba
Capraia
C. Corse
Borgo Val di Taro
Pontrémoli
Pavullo nel Frignano
Limone Piemonte
Col di Tenda
Ceva
Isola
Sospel
Lago Maggiore
Lago di Como
Lago di Garda
Lac Léman
Bodensee
Zürichsee
Thunersee
Vierwaldstättersee
Ammersee
Wuppertal
Düsseldorf
Mönchengladbach
Remscheid
Solingen
Lüdenscheid
Gummersbach
Leverkusen
Köln
Cologne
Siegburg
Bonn
Bad Honnef
Düren
Euskirchen
Linz
Neuwied
Andernach
Mayen
Koblenz
Boppard
Limburg
Idstein
Wiesbaden
Mainz
Bingen
Frankfurt
Hanau
Offenbach
Aschaffenburg
Darmstadt
Michelstadt
Bensheim
Worms
Mannheim
Ludwigshafen
Heidelberg
Mosbach
Speyer
Heilbronn
Bruchsal
Karlsruhe
Pforzheim
Stuttgart
Ludwigsburg
Esslingen
Rastatt
Baden-Baden
Brumath
Haguenau
Strasbourg
Kehl
Offenburg
Freudenstadt
Tübingen
Reutlingen
Metzingen
Hechingen
Ebingen
Lahr
Sélestat
Haslach
Schramberg
Rottweil
Sigmaringen
Villingen-Schwenningen
Donaueschingen
Tuttlingen
Freiburg
Titisee-Neustadt
Müllheim
Schopfheim
Singen
Überlingen
Meersburg
Friedrichshafen
Ravensburg
Kempten
Saulgau
Memmingen
Biberach
Riedlingen
Ehingen
Ulm
Günzburg
Augsburg
Dachau
Landsberg
Kaufbeuren
Starnberg
Weilheim
Oberammergau
Füssen
Garmisch-Partenkirchen
Sonthofen
Ehrwald
Seefeld
Innsbruck
Imst
Lech
Nauders
Wildspitze
Merano
Bolzano
Ortles
Mte. Adamello
Riva del Garda
Rovereto
Trento
Geislingen
Heidenheim
Aalen
Schwäbisch Gmünd
Schwäbisch Hall
Crailsheim
Nördlingen
Donauwörth
Dillingen
Eichstätt
Ingolstadt
Weissenburg
Roth
Neumarkt
Ansbach
Fürth
Nürnberg
Nuremberg
Erlangen
Forchheim
Bamberg
Bayreuth
Kulmbach
Coburg
Rothenburg ob der Tauber
Bad Mergentheim
Neustadt
Kitzingen
Würzburg
Schweinfurt
Hassfurt
Bad Kissingen
Mellrichstadt
Schlüchtern
Fulda
Wasserkuppe
Bad Hersfeld
Eisenach
Gotha
Erfurt
Arnstadt
Ilmenau
Suhl
Meiningen
Eisfeld
Saalfeld
Plauen
Hof
Mühlhausen
Alsfeld
Vogelsberg
Giessen
Bad Nauheim
Wetzlar
Marburg
Dillenburg
Siegen
Bad Laasphe
Frankenberg
Korbach
Fritzlar
Neunkirchen
Kaiserslautern
Zweibrücken
Pirmasens
Landau
Saarbrücken
Forbach
Sarreguemines
Château-Salins
Sarrebourg
Saverne
Bad Kreuznach
Idar-Oberstein
Birkenfeld
Morbach
Trier
Bitburg
Prüm
Cochem
Remich
Tanger
Barcelona
Porto Torres
Ólbia
Arbatax
Tunis
Skikda
Massif Central
Bourgogne
Lorraine
Vosges
Provence
Cévennes
Jura
Alpi
10
11
19
20

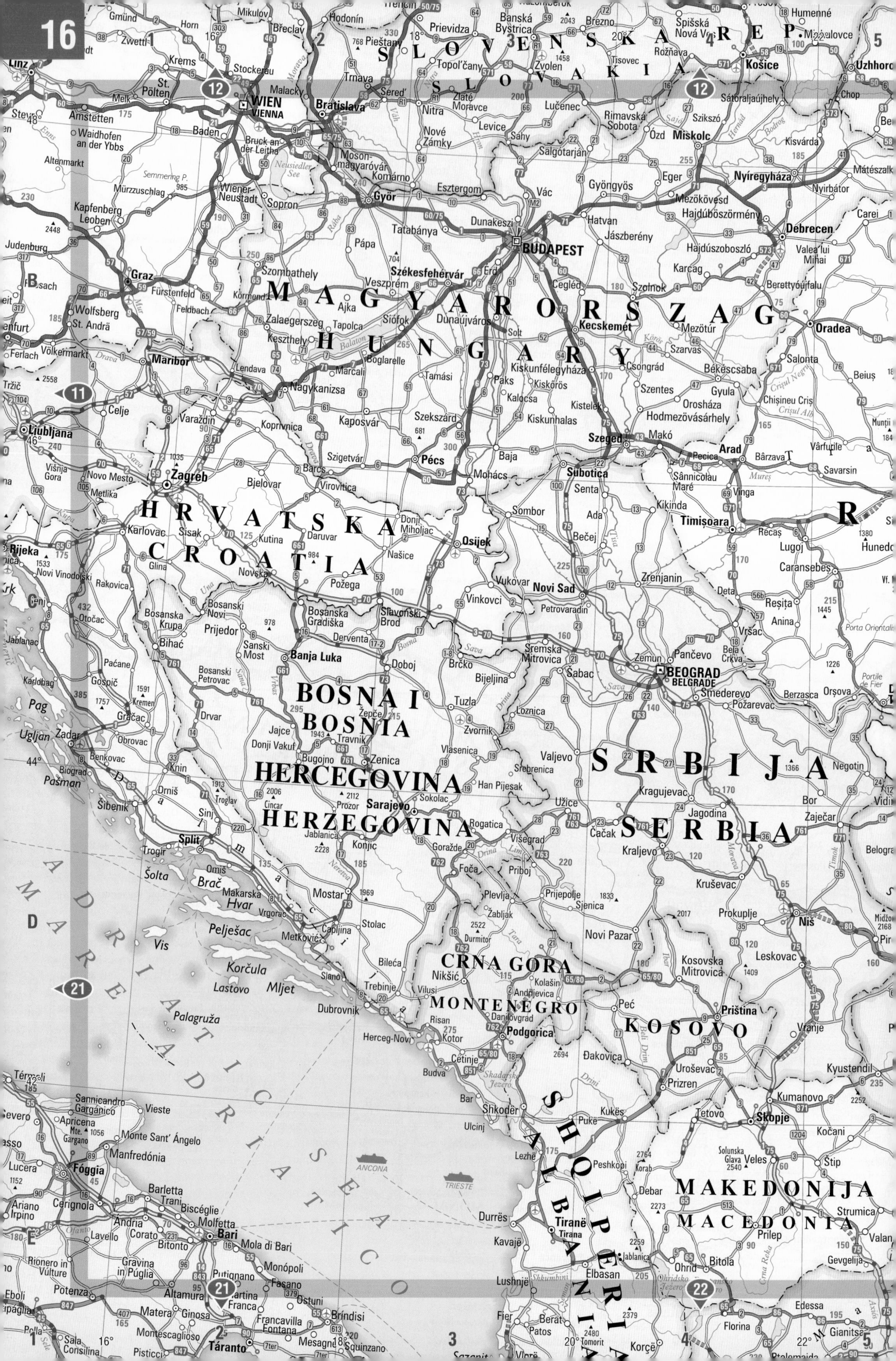
SLOVENSKÁ REP.
SLOVAKIA
MAGYARORSZÁG
HUNGARY
HRVATSKA
CROATIA
BOSNA I HERCEGOVINA
BOSNIA HERZEGOVINA
SRBIJA
SERBIA
CRNA GORA
MONTENEGRO
KOSOVO
SHQIPERIA
ALBANIA
MAKEDONIJA
MACEDONIA
MARE ADRIATICO
ADRIATIC SEA
WIEN
VIENNA
BUDAPEST
BEOGRAD
BELGRADE
Zagreb
Ljubljana
Sarajevo
Podgorica
Tiranë
Skopje
Priština
Bratislava

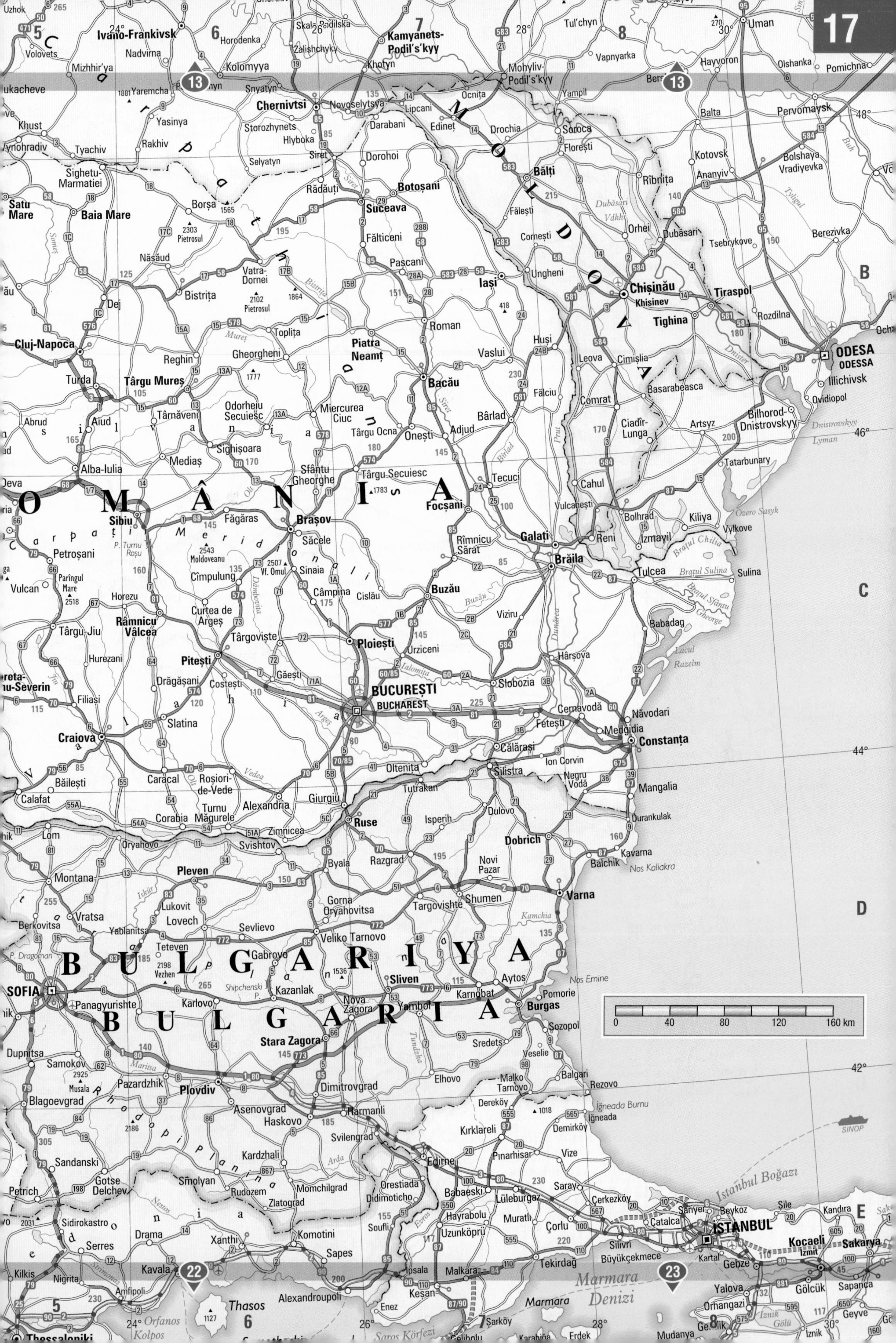
ROMÂNIA
BULGARIYA
BULGARIA
MOLDOVA
Carpathian
Carpaţi Meridionali
Rhodopi Planina
Ivano-Frankivsk
Kamyanets-Podil's'kyy
Uman
Chernivtsi
Mohyliv-Podil's'kyy
Suceava
Botoşani
Bălţi
Chişinău
Khisinev
Tiraspol
Tighina
ODESA
ODESSA
Iaşi
Piatra Neamţ
Bacău
Cluj-Napoca
Târgu Mureş
Braşov
Sibiu
Galaţi
Brăila
Tulcea
Constanţa
Ploieşti
BUCUREŞTI
BUCHAREST
Piteşti
Craiova
Ruse
Varna
Burgas
Pleven
Veliko Tarnovo
Shumen
Stara Zagora
Plovdiv
SOFIA
Edirne
Kırklareli
ISTANBUL
Kocaeli
Sakarya
Tekirdağ
Thasos
Marmara Denizi
İstanbul Boğazı
SINOP
0
40
80
120
160 km
13
22
23

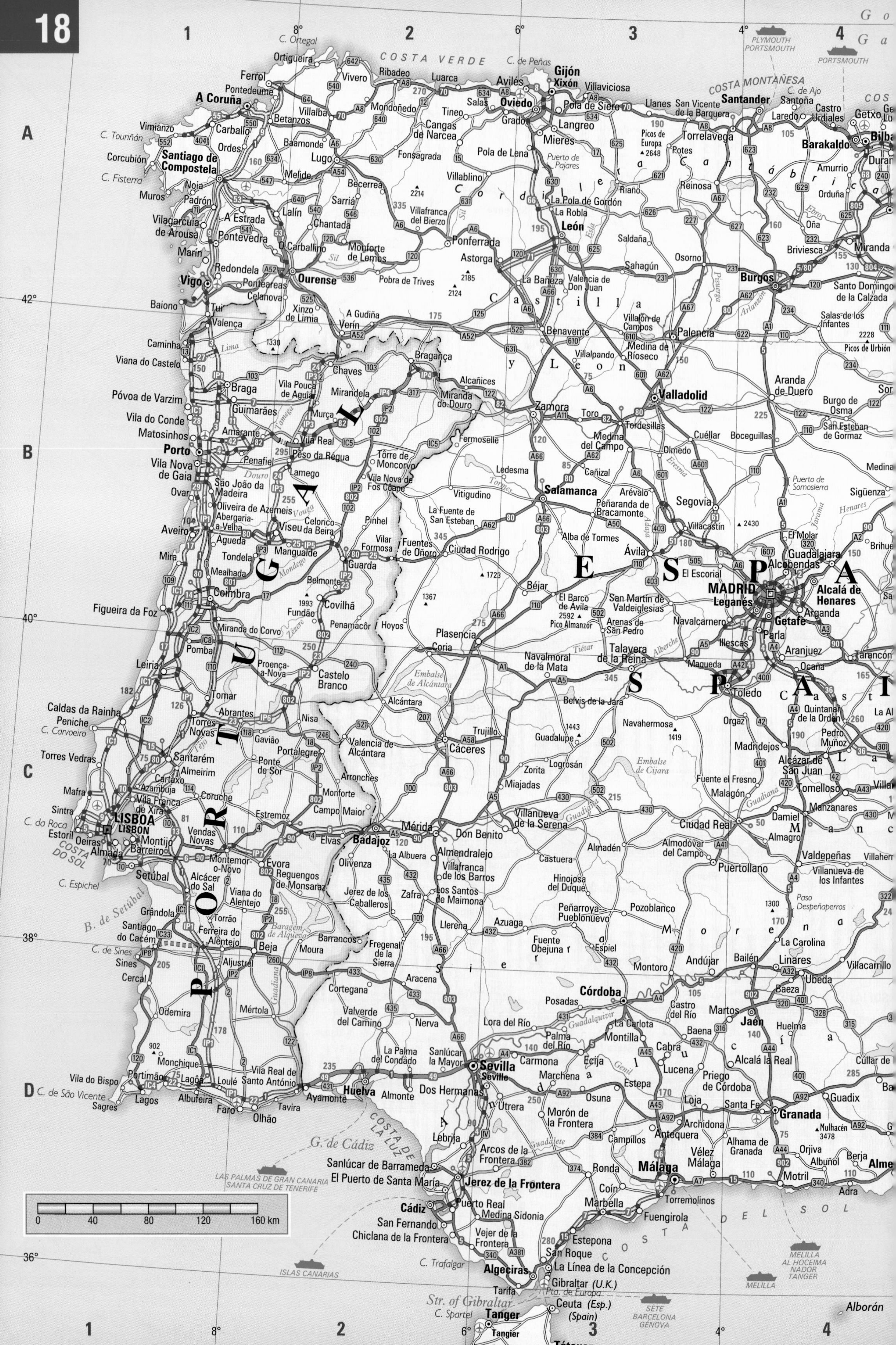

COSTA VERDE
C. Ortegal
Ortigueira
Ferrol
Pontedeume
A Coruña
Betanzos
Vivero
Ribadeo
Luarca
Avilés
Gijón
Xixón
Villaviciosa
C. de Peñas
Oviedo
Grado
Langreo
Mieres
Pola de Siero
Pola de Lena
Llanes
San Vicente de la Barquera
Santander
Santoña
Laredo
Castro Urdiales
Getxo
Bilbao
Barakaldo
COSTA MONTAÑESA
C. de Ajo
Torrelavega
Picos de Europa
2648
Potes
Reinosa
Cordillera Cantábrica
PLYMOUTH
PORTSMOUTH
Vimianzo
C. Touriñán
Carballo
Corcubión
C. Fisterra
Santiago de Compostela
Ordes
Noia
Muros
Padrón
Vilagarcía de Arousa
A Estrada
Pontevedra
Marín
Vigo
Redondela
Ponteareas
Baiona
Lalín
Chantada
O Carballiño
Ourense
Lugo
Melide
Sarria
Becerreá
Monforte de Lemos
Mondoñedo
Villalba
Baamonde
Fonsagrada
Cangas de Narcea
Tineo
Salas
Villablino
Villafranca del Bierzo
Ponferrada
Astorga
La Bañeza
Valencia de Don Juan
León
La Robla
La Pola de Gordón
Riaño
Puerto de Pajares
Saldaña
Sahagún
Osorno
Burgos
Briviesca
Miranda
Oña
Orduña
Amurrio
Santo Domingo de la Calzada
Salas de los Infantes
Picos de Urbión
2228
Pobra de Trives
Celanova
Xinzo de Limia
Verín
A Gudiña
Tui
Valença
Caminha
Viana do Castelo
Póvoa de Varzim
Vila do Conde
Matosinhos
Porto
Vila Nova de Gaia
Braga
Guimarães
Amarante
Penafiel
Peso da Régua
Vila Real
Murça
Mirandela
Chaves
Vila Pouca de Aguiar
Bragança
Miranda do Douro
Alcañices
Zamora
Toro
Benavente
Medina de Ríoseco
Villalpando
Valladolid
Tordesillas
Medina del Campo
Palencia
Villalón de Campos
Aranda de Duero
Burgo de Osma
San Esteban de Gormaz
Castilla y León
Fermoselle
Lamego
Torre de Moncorvo
Vila Nova de Foz Côa
Ovar
São João da Madeira
Oliveira de Azemeis
Aveiro
Águeda
Viseu
Celorico da Beira
Pinhel
Guarda
Mangualde
Tondela
Mealhada
Coimbra
Figueira da Foz
Mira
Belmonte
Covilhã
Fundão
Penamacor
Ledesma
Salamanca
Vitigudino
La Fuente de San Esteban
Ciudad Rodrigo
Fuentes de Oñoro
Vilar Formosa
Alba de Tormes
Peñaranda de Bracamonte
Arévalo
Cañizal
Olmedo
Cuéllar
Boceguillas
Segovia
Villacastín
Puerto de Somosierra
Sigüenza
El Molar
Guadalajara
Alcobendas
Alcalá de Henares
MADRID
Leganés
Getafe
Arganda
Parla
Aranjuez
El Escorial
Ávila
Béjar
El Barco de Ávila
Pico Almanzor
2592
San Martín de Valdeiglesias
Arenas de San Pedro
Navalcarnero
Illescas
ESPAÑA
PORTUGAL
Miranda do Corvo
Pombal
Leiria
Proença-a-Nova
Castelo Branco
Hoyos
Plasencia
Coria
Navalmoral de la Mata
Talavera de la Reina
Maqueda
Toledo
Ocaña
Tarancón
Embalse de Alcántara
Alcántara
Tomar
Abrantes
Torres Novas
Caldas da Rainha
Peniche
C. Carvoeiro
Torres Vedras
Santarém
Almeirim
Cartaxo
Azambuja
Vila Franca de Xira
Mafra
Sintra
C. da Roca
Estoril
Oeiras
LISBOA
LISBON
Almada
Barreiro
Montijo
COSTA DO SOL
Setúbal
C. Espichel
B. de Setúbal
Gavião
Nisa
Portalegre
Ponte de Sor
Coruche
Arronches
Monforte
Campo Maior
Estremoz
Elvas
Badajoz
Valencia de Alcántara
Cáceres
Trujillo
Guadalupe
Logrosán
Zorita
Miajadas
Mérida
Don Benito
Villanueva de la Serena
Belvís de la Jara
Navahermosa
Orgaz
Madridejos
Quintanar de la Orden
Pedro Muñoz
Alcázar de San Juan
Tomelloso
Manzanares
Embalse de Cijara
Fuente el Fresno
Malagón
Ciudad Real
Daniel
Almagro
Valdepeñas
Villanueva de los Infantes
Almodóvar del Campo
Puertollano
Almadén
Castuera
Hinojosa del Duque
Vendas Novas
Montemor-o-Novo
Évora
Reguengos de Monsaraz
Alcácer do Sal
Viana do Alentejo
Grândola
Santiago do Cacém
C. de Sines
Sines
Torrão
Ferreira do Alentejo
Beja
Moura
Barrancos
Aljustrel
Cercal
Odemira
Mértola
Olivenza
La Albuera
Almendralejo
Villafranca de los Barros
Los Santos de Maimona
Zafra
Jerez de los Caballeros
Llerena
Azuaga
Fregenal de la Sierra
Peñarroya-Pueblonuevo
Pozoblanco
Fuente Obejuna
Espiel
Sierra Morena
Paso Despeñaperros
La Carolina
Linares
Bailén
Úbeda
Baeza
Villacarrillo
Andújar
Montoro
Córdoba
Posadas
Aracena
Cortegana
Valverde del Camino
Nerva
Lora del Río
Palma del Río
La Carlota
Montilla
Castro del Río
Baena
Martos
Jaén
Huelma
Alcalá la Real
Cabra
Lucena
Priego de Córdoba
Monchique
Portimão
Lagoa
Loulé
Albufeira
Faro
Olhão
Tavira
Vila Real de Santo António
Vila do Bispo
C. de São Vicente
Sagres
Lagos
Ayamonte
Huelva
Almonte
La Palma del Condado
Sanlúcar la Mayor
Sevilla
Seville
Carmona
Écija
Marchena
Estepa
Osuna
Dos Hermanas
Utrera
Morón de la Frontera
Lebrija
Arcos de la Frontera
Campillos
Antequera
Archidona
Loja
Santa Fe
Granada
Guadix
Alhama de Granada
Mulhacén
3478
Vélez Málaga
Málaga
Torremolinos
Fuengirola
Marbella
Coín
Ronda
Orjiva
Albuñol
Berja
Motril
Adra
COSTA DE LA LUZ
G. de Cádiz
Sanlúcar de Barrameda
El Puerto de Santa María
Jerez de la Frontera
Cádiz
Puerto Real
Medina Sidonia
San Fernando
Chiclana de la Frontera
Vejer de la Frontera
C. Trafalgar
Algeciras
Tarifa
San Roque
La Línea de la Concepción
Gibraltar (U.K.)
Estepona
COSTA DEL SOL
Pta. de Europa
Str. of Gibraltar
C. Spartel
Tanger
Tangier
Ceuta (Esp.)
(Spain)
Tétouan
Alborán
LAS PALMAS DE GRAN CANARIA
SANTA CRUZ DE TENERIFE
ISLAS CANARIAS
MELILLA
AL HOCEIMA
NADOR
TANGER
SETE
BARCELONA
GÉNOVA
0
40
80
120
160 km
42°
40°
38°
36°
8°
6°
4°

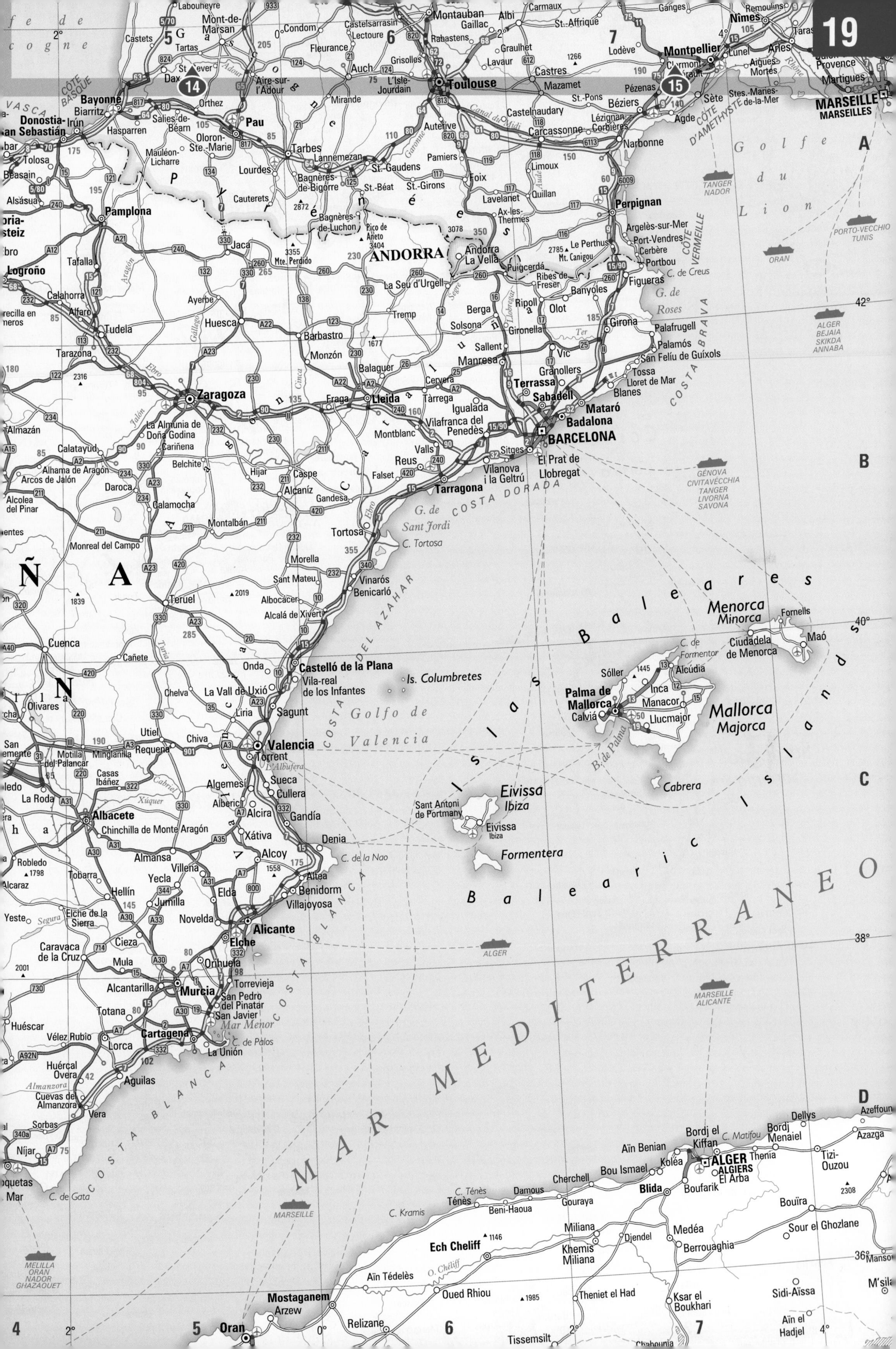

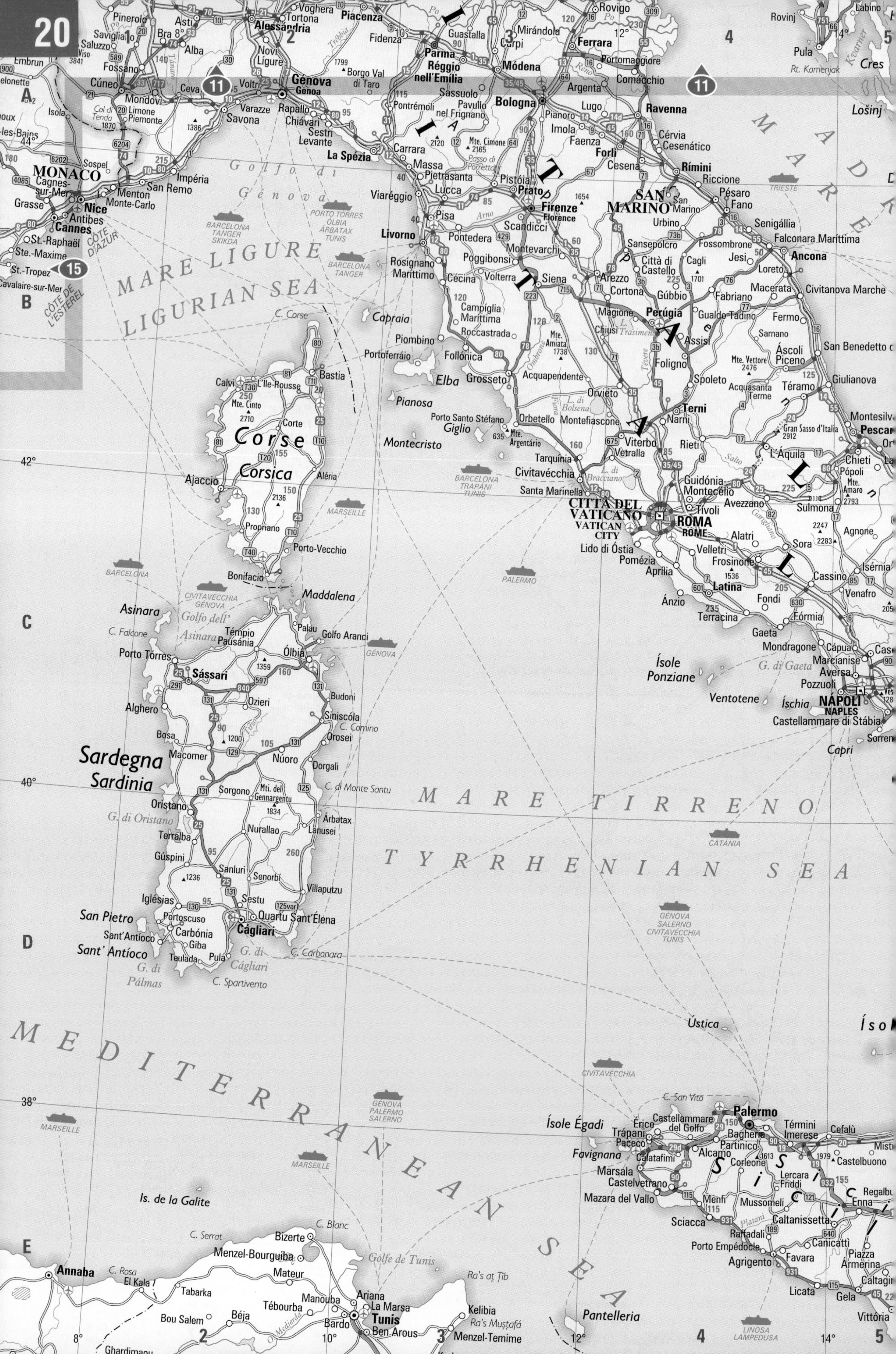
ITALIA
MARE LIGURE
LIGURIAN SEA
Golfo di Génova
Corse
Corsica
Sardegna
Sardinia
MARE TIRRENO
TYRRHENIAN SEA
MEDITERRANEAN SEA
SICILIA
MARE ADRIATICO
MONACO
SAN MARINO
CITTÀ DEL VATICANO
VATICAN CITY
ROMA
ROME
NÁPOLI
NAPLES
Palermo
Tunis
Génova
Genoa
Firenze
Florence
Bologna
Cágliari
Ajaccio
Bastia
Nice
Cannes
Livorno
Ancona
Perúgia
Elba
Capri
Ústica
Pantelleria
Ísole Égadi

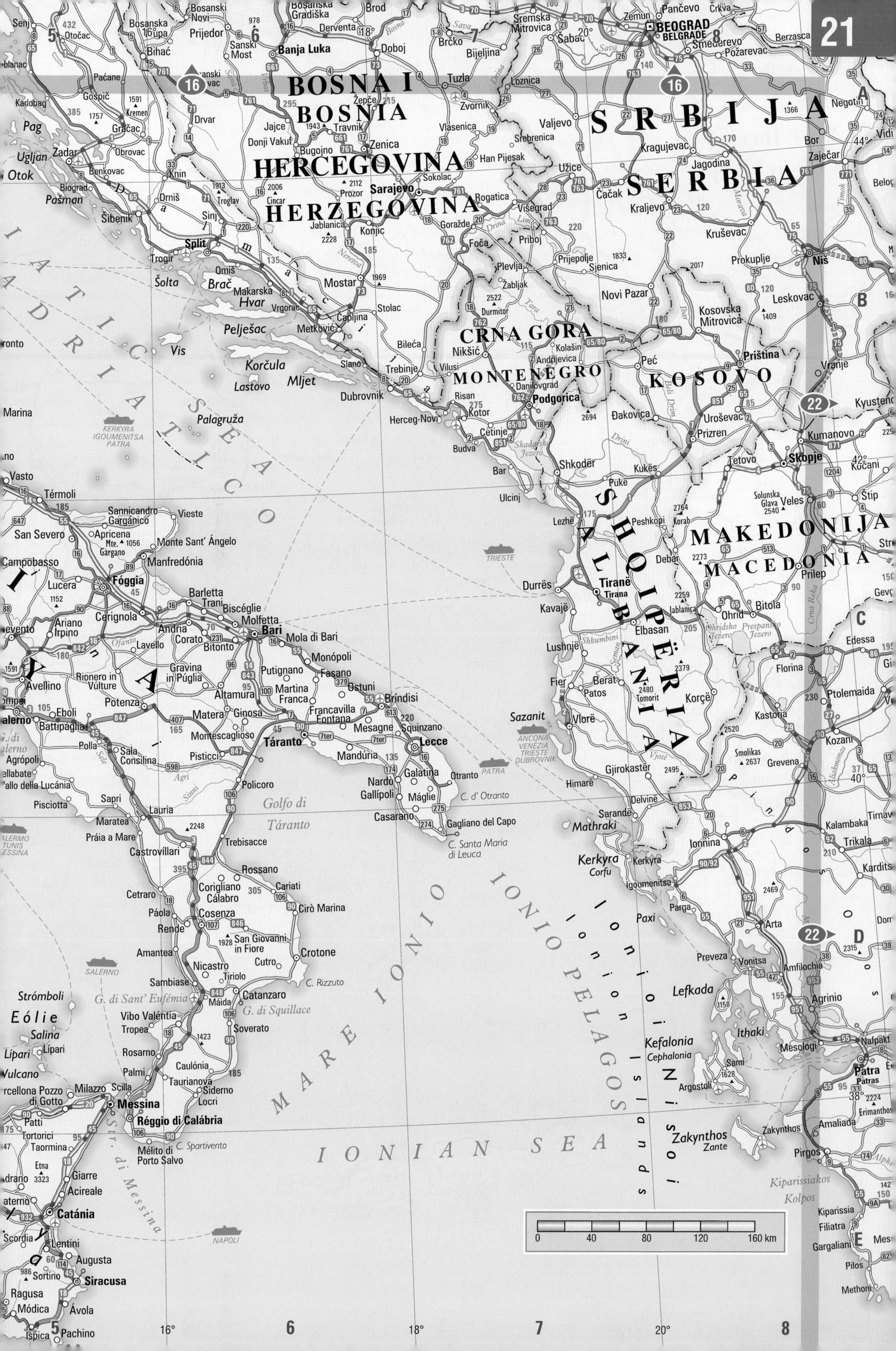
BOSNA I HERCEGOVINA
BOSNIA HERZEGOVINA
SRBIJA
SERBIA
CRNA GORA
MONTENEGRO
KOSOVO
SHQIPËRIA
ALBANIA
MAKEDONIJA
MACEDONIA
ADRIATICO
ADRIATIC SEA
MARE IONIO
IONIO PELAGOS
IONIAN SEA
Ionioi Nisoi
Ionian Islands
Golfo di Táranto
G. di Sant' Eufémia
G. di Squillace
Str. di Messina
Kiparissiakos Kolpos
Eólie
BEOGRAD
BELGRADE
Sarajevo
Podgorica
Priština
Skopje
Tiranë
Tirana
Split
Zadar
Šibenik
Dubrovnik
Mostar
Banja Luka
Tuzla
Zenica
Niš
Kragujevac
Novi Pazar
Kotor
Bar
Shkodër
Durrës
Vlorë
Gjirokastër
Ohrid
Bitola
Korçë
Elbasan
Ioannina
Igoumenitsa
Kerkyra
Corfu
Arta
Preveza
Lefkada
Kefalonia
Cephalonia
Zakynthos
Zante
Patra
Patras
Bari
Fóggia
Táranto
Lecce
Brindisi
Otranto
Gallípoli
Potenza
Matera
Cosenza
Crotone
Catanzaro
Messina
Réggio di Calábria
Catánia
Siracusa
Ragusa
Stromboli
Lípari
Vulcano
Hvar
Brač
Korčula
Mljet
Vis
Lastovo
Pelješac
Pag
Palagruža
C. d' Otranto
C. Santa Maria di Leuca
C. Rizzuto
C. Spartivento
16°
18°
20°
42°
40°
38°
44°
5
6
7
8
A
B
C
D
E
0
40
80
120
160 km

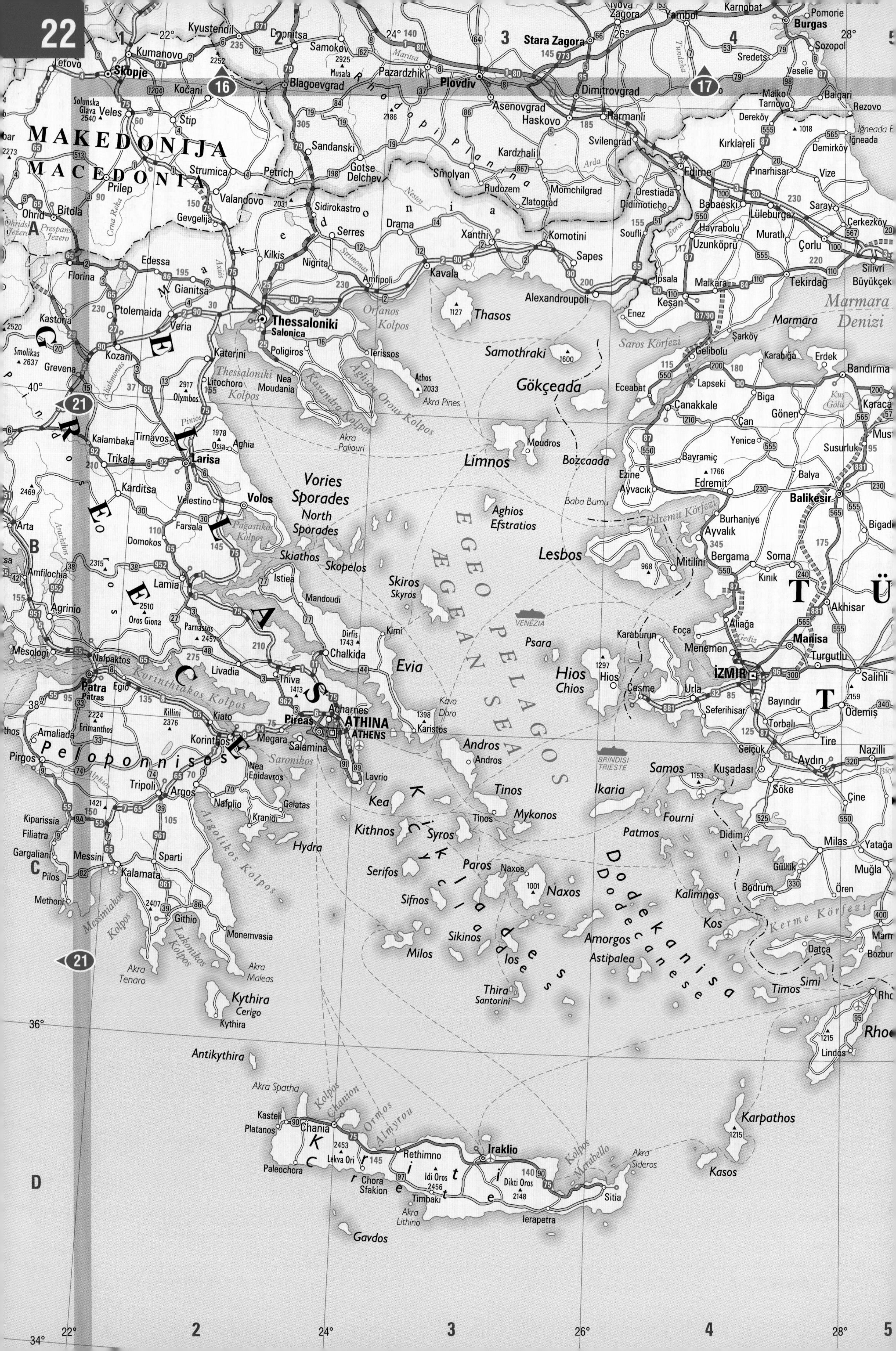
MAKEDONIJA
MACEDONIA
GREECE
ELLAS
TÜ
Skopje
Kumanovo
Kyustendil
Samokov
Stara Zagora
Yambol
Karnobat
Burgas
Pomorie
Sozopol
Sredets
Veselie
Tetovo
Kočani
Blagoevgrad
Pazardzhik
Plovdiv
Dimitrovgrad
Malko Tarnovo
Balgari
Rezovo
Veles
Štip
Asenovgrad
Haskovo
Harmanli
Dereköy
İğneada
Sandanski
Kardzhali
Svilengrad
Kırklareli
Demirköy
Strumica
Petrich
Gotse Delchev
Smolyan
Rudozem
Momchilgrad
Edirne
Pınarhisar
Vize
Prilep
Bitola
Ohrid
Valandovo
Gevgelija
Sidirokastro
Zlatograd
Orestiada
Didimoticho
Babaeski
Lüleburgaz
Saray
Çerkezköy
Serres
Drama
Xanthi
Komotini
Soufli
Hayrabolu
Muratlı
Çorlu
Uzunköprü
Edessa
Florina
Kilkis
Nigrita
Amfipoli
Kavala
Sapes
Silivri
Büyükçek
Gianitsa
Alexandroupoli
Ipsala
Malkara
Keşan
Tekirdağ
Kastoria
Ptolemaida
Veria
Thessaloniki
Salonica
Orfanos Kolpos
Thasos
Enez
Marmara Denizi
Marmara
Smolikas
Grevena
Kozani
Katerini
Poligiros
Ierissos
Samothraki
Saros Körfezi
Şarköy
Gelibolu
Karabiğa
Erdek
Bandırma
Litochoro
Olymbos
Thessaloniki Kolpos
Nea Moudania
Kasandra Kolpos
Aghiou Orous Kolpos
Athos
Akra Pines
Gökçeada
Eceabat
Lapseki
Biga
Gönen
Karacal
Çanakkale
Çan
Kalambaka
Tirnavos
Ossa
Aghia
Larisa
Trikala
Akra Paliouri
Moudros
Limnos
Bozcaada
Yenice
Bayramiç
Susurluk
Ezine
Edremit
Balya
Karditsa
Velestino
Volos
Vories Sporades
North Sporades
Ayvacık
Baba Burnu
Balıkesir
Arta
Farsala
Pagastikos Kolpos
Domokos
Aghios Efstratios
Edremit Körfezi
Burhaniye
Ayvalık
EGEO PELAGOS
AEGEAN SEA
Skiathos
Skopelos
Lesbos
Mitilini
Bergama
Soma
Amfilochia
Lamia
Istiea
Skiros
Skyros
Kınık
Akhisar
Agrinio
Oros Giona
Mandoudi
Parnassos
Dirfis
Kimi
Karaburun
Foça
Aliağa
Manisa
Mesologi
Nafpaktos
Livadia
Chalkida
Evia
Psara
Menemen
Turgutlu
Patra
Patras
Egio
Korinthiakos Kolpos
Thiva
Hios
Chios
Çeşme
Urla
İZMIR
Salihli
Killini
Kiato
Acharnes
Kavo Doro
Seferihisar
Bayındır
Ödemiş
Amaliada
Erimanthos
Korinthos
Megara
Pireas
ATHINA
ATHENS
Salamina
Karistos
Torbalı
Tire
Pirgos
Peloponnisos
Saronikos
Andros
Selçuk
Nazilli
Aydın
Nea Epidavros
Tinos
Ikaria
Samos
Kuşadası
Tripoli
Argos
Nafplio
Lavrio
Kea
Galatas
Söke
Çine
Kiparissia
Filiatra
Kranidi
Kithnos
Mykonos
Fourni
Patmos
Didim
Milas
Yatağa
Gargaliani
Messini
Sparti
Argolikos Kolpos
Hydra
Syros
Pilos
Kalamata
Serifos
Paros
Naxos
Dodekanisa
Dodecanese
Güllük
Muğla
Methoni
Sifnos
Kikladhes
Kalimnos
Bodrum
Ören
Messiniakos Kolpos
Githio
Monemvasia
Kos
Kerme Körfezi
Lakonikos Kolpos
Milos
Sikinos
Amorgos
Datça
Bozburun
Akra Tenaro
Akra Maleas
Ios
Astipalea
Kythira
Cerigo
Thira
Santorini
Timos
Simi
Rhodes
Lindos
Antikythira
Akra Spatha
Kolpos Chanion
Ormos Almyrou
Kasteli
Platanos
Chania
Rethimno
Iraklio
Kolpos Merabello
Akra Sideros
Karpathos
Lefka Ori
Paleochora
Idi Oros
Dikti Oros
Sitia
Kasos
Chora Sfakion
Timbaki
Ierapetra
Akra Lithino
Kriti
Gavdos

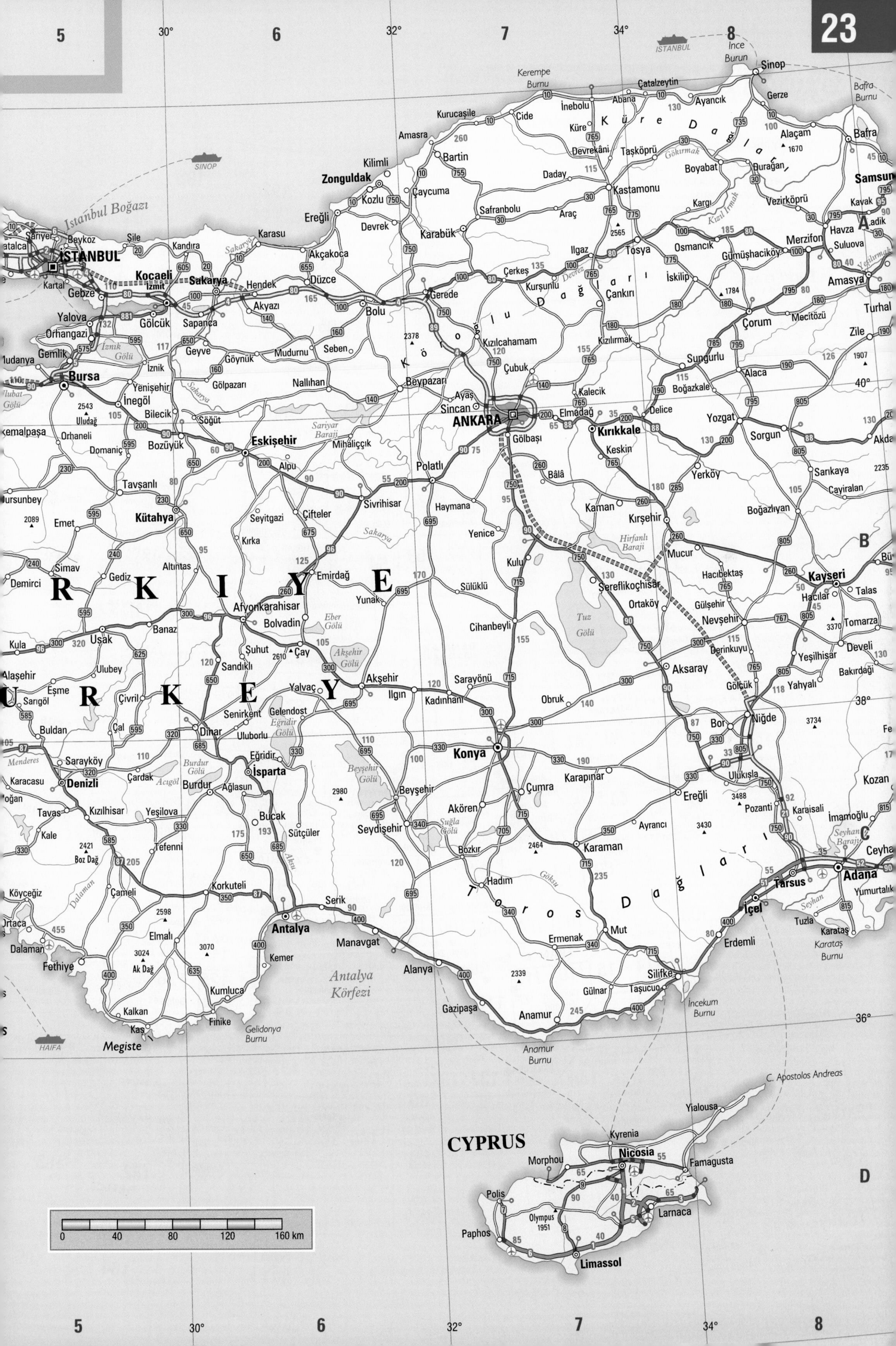
5
6
7
8
30°
32°
34°
İstanbul Boğazı
ISTANBUL
SINOP
HAIFA
Sarıyer
Beykoz
Şile
Kandıra
Karasu
Kartal
Gebze
Kocaeli
İzmit
Sakarya
Hendek
Düzce
Akçakoca
Ereğli
Zonguldak
Kilimli
Kozlu
Çaycuma
Devrek
Amasra
Bartin
Karabük
Safranbolu
Kurucaşile
Cide
Kerempe Burnu
İnebolu
Abana
Çatalzeytin
Ayancık
İnce Burun
Sinop
Gerze
Bafra Burnu
Bafra
Alaçam
Küre
Küre Dağları
Devrekâni
Taşköprü
Gökırmak
Boyabat
Durağan
Daday
Kastamonu
Araç
Ilgaz
Tosya
Kargı
Kızıl Irmak
Osmancık
Gümüşhacıköy
Merzifon
Vezirköprü
Havza
Samsun
Kavak
Suluova
Yeşilırmak
Amasya
Turhal
Zile
Mecitözü
Çorum
İskilip
Çankırı
Kurşunlu
Çerkeş
Ilgaz Dağları
Köroğlu Dağları
Gerede
Bolu
Akyazı
Sapanca
Gölcük
Yalova
Orhangazi
İznik Gölü
İznik
Gemlik
Mudanya
Bursa
Uluabat Gölü
Uludağ
İnegöl
Yenişehir
Bilecik
Söğüt
Gölpazarı
Göynük
Mudurnu
Seben
Nallıhan
Geyve
Kızılcahamam
Çubuk
Beypazarı
Ayaş
Sincan
ANKARA
Elmadağ
Kalecik
Kızılırmak
Sungurlu
Alaca
Boğazkale
Delice
Kırıkkale
Yozgat
Sorgun
Akdağmadeni
Keskin
Yerköy
Sarıkaya
Çayıralan
Boğazlıyan
Gölbaşı
Bâlâ
Kaman
Kırşehir
Hirfanlı Barajı
Mucur
Hacıbektaş
Kayseri
Talas
Hacılar
Tomarza
Develi
Yeşilhisar
Bakırdağı
Yahyalı
Kemalpaşa
Orhaneli
Domaniç
Bozüyük
Eskişehir
Sarıyar Barajı
Mihalıççık
Alpu
Polatlı
Haymana
Sivrihisar
Tavşanlı
Dursunbey
Kütahya
Emet
Seyitgazi
Çifteler
Kırka
Sakarya
Yenice
Kulu
Şereflikoçhisar
Tuz Gölü
Ortaköy
Gülşehir
Nevşehir
Derinkuyu
Aksaray
Gölçük
Niğde
Bor
Ulukışla
Pozantı
Karaisali
Kozan
İmamoğlu
Seyhan Barajı
Ceyhan
Adana
Tarsus
Yumurtalık
Seyhan
Tuzla
Karataş Burnu
İçel
Erdemli
Simav
Demirci
Gediz
Altıntaş
Emirdağ
Yunak
Sülüklü
Cihanbeyli
Afyonkarahisar
Bolvadin
Eber Gölü
Akşehir Gölü
Şuhut
Çay
Sandıklı
Banaz
Uşak
Kula
Ulubey
Alaşehir
Eşme
Sarıgöl
Buldan
Çivril
Çal
Senirkent
Gelendost
Eğirdir Gölü
Uluborlu
Dinar
Yalvaç
Akşehir
Ilgın
Kadınhanı
Sarayönü
Obruk
Konya
Karapınar
Ereğli
Ayrancı
Çumra
Akören
Karaman
Bozkır
Hadım
Toros Dağları
Mut
Ermenek
Silifke
Taşucu
Gülnar
İncekum Burnu
Anamur
Anamur Burnu
Gazipaşa
Alanya
Antalya Körfezi
Manavgat
Serik
Antalya
Kemer
Beyşehir
Beyşehir Gölü
Seydişehir
Suğla Gölü
Eğirdir
Isparta
Burdur
Burdur Gölü
Ağlasun
Bucak
Sütçüler
Acıgöl
Çardak
Denizli
Sarayköy
Menderes
Karacasu
Tavas
Kale
Kızılhisar
Yeşilova
Tefenni
Boz Dağ
Çameli
Dalaman
Köyceğiz
Fethiye
Elmalı
Korkuteli
Ak Dağ
Kumluca
Finike
Kalkan
Kaş
Megiste
Gelidonya Burnu
TÜRKIYE
CYPRUS
C. Apostolos Andreas
Yialousa
Kyrenia
Nicosia
Famagusta
Morphou
Polis
Olympus 1951
Paphos
Larnaca
Limassol
B
C
D
36°
38°
40°
0
40
80
120
160 km

Key to road map pages

Florence **City plan**
Firenze

İstanbul **City approach map**

Milan **City plan and approach map**
Milano See pages 201–228 for city plans and approach maps

97 Map pages at 1:750000

182 Map pages at 1:1 500000

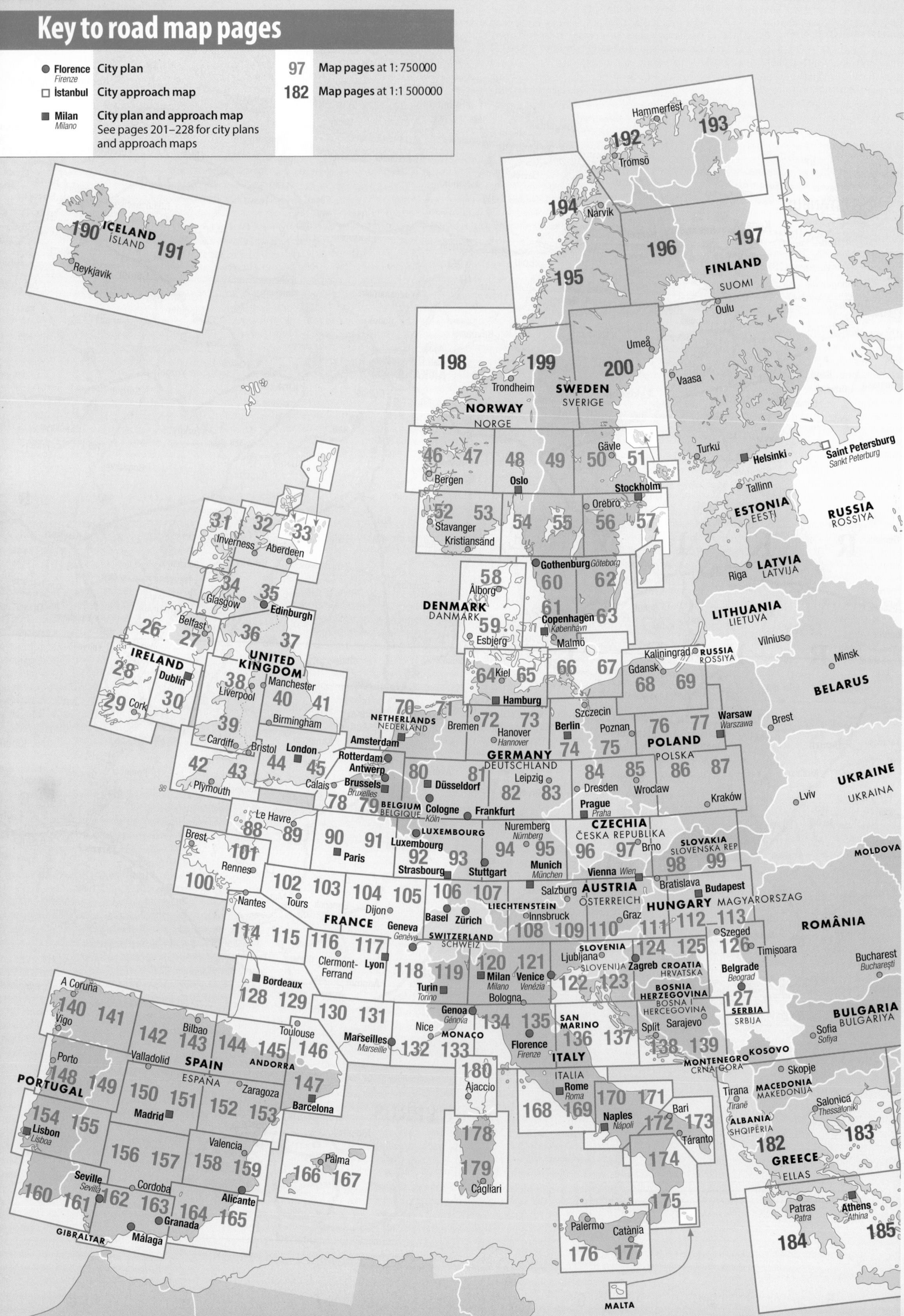

Distance table

Dublin ▶ Göteborg = 477 km

548	Dublin
726	346	Edinburgh
575	1123	1301	Frankfurt
1342	477	176	1067	Göteborg
760	477	1486	485	582	Hamburg

Distances shown in blue involve at least one ferry journey

Amsterdam
2945 **Athina**
1505 3192 **Barcelona**
1484 3742 2803 **Bergen**
650 2412 1863 1309 **Berlin**
197 2895 1308 1586 764 **Bruxelles**
2245 1219 2644 3037 1707 2181 **Bucuresti**
1420 1530 1999 2212 882 1358 852 **Budapest**
367 3100 1269 1783 956 215 2398 1573 **Calais**
533 3630 1817 270 1504 763 3021 2196 548 **Dublin**
1093 3826 1995 176 1696 941 3124 2299 726 346 **Edinburgh**
441 2499 1313 1508 550 383 1804 979 575 1123 1301 **Frankfurt**
1029 3080 2362 819 668 1145 1734 1550 1342 477 176 1067 **Göteborg**
447 2719 1780 1023 286 563 2014 1189 760 477 1486 485 582 **Hamburg**
1560 2539 2338 1063 475 1239 1834 1009 1431 1318 1236 1598 505 1113 **Helsinki**
2756 1145 2990 3653 2223 2706 690 1341 2911 3537 3657 2314 2891 2530 2350 **İstanbul**
965 2782 2090 1103 370 1081 2077 1252 1278 752 479 795 284 518 803 2593 **København**
256 2684 1376 1427 566 198 1983 1158 390 938 1116 180 986 404 1517 2499 714 **Köln**
2331 4460 1268 3723 2869 3141 3917 3222 2069 2617 2795 2400 3282 2700 3817 4342 3014 2339 **Lisboa**
480 3200 1387 458 1074 333 2591 1766 118 430 608 693 122 878 1991 3107 1188 508 2187 **London**
406 2661 1190 1613 749 209 2052 1227 424 972 1150 240 1172 590 1703 2472 900 186 2160 542 **Luxembourg**
1790 3809 617 3183 2364 1600 3262 2622 1528 1634 2254 1930 2742 2160 3276 3589 2473 1798 651 1646 1628 **Madrid**
1210 2683 509 2435 1541 1030 2154 1505 1063 1588 1789 1023 1994 1412 2525 2479 1722 1006 1777 1182 822 1126 **Marseille**
1085 2182 1038 2141 1060 890 1668 992 1072 1620 1798 683 1700 1118 1535 1993 1428 868 2315 1190 679 1655 538 **Milano**
2457 2930 3655 2223 1821 2585 1761 2099 2800 3348 3526 2312 1665 2115 1160 2605 2325 2387 4875 2918 2852 4224 3270 3027 **Moskva**
839 2106 1340 1788 594 789 1497 672 994 1524 1720 398 1347 765 1069 1907 969 580 2545 1094 555 2010 1011 473 2305 **München**
1347 3372 2680 503 960 1463 2667 1842 1660 773 729 1385 316 900 697 3089 590 1304 3604 1778 1490 3063 2312 2018 1823 1559 **Oslo**
510 2917 988 1922 1051 320 2307 1482 281 829 1007 591 1481 899 2012 2727 1209 495 1821 399 351 1280 782 857 2903 810 1799 **Paris**
950 2067 1750 1675 345 888 1362 537 1097 1635 1816 512 1013 652 770 1878 715 690 2870 1205 753 2329 1399 853 1853 388 1305 1061 **Praha**
1691 1140 1385 2706 1502 1520 1904 1263 1678 2226 2404 1289 2265 1683 1977 2237 1993 1474 2653 1796 1285 2002 876 606 3362 918 2583 1389 1309 **Roma**
2347 4223 1031 3736 2894 2150 3709 3010 2078 2626 2804 2344 3295 2713 3826 4034 3023 2318 401 2196 2178 550 1540 2078 4774 2371 3613 1830 2781 2446 **Sevilla**
2206 828 2453 3103 1673 2156 391 790 2361 2891 3087 1764 2341 1980 1800 550 2043 1949 3706 2461 1922 3037 1929 1443 2252 1367 2632 2177 1328 1687 3484 **Sofia**
1393 3418 2726 1063 1006 1509 2713 1888 1673 2254 1069 1431 505 946 167 3185 590 1350 3650 1824 1536 3109 2358 2064 1228 1600 530 1845 1351 2629 3659 2679 **Stockholm**
1256 2128 2366 1909 606 1350 1473 648 1542 2110 2268 1136 1274 886 361 1989 956 1152 3480 1680 1345 2960 2015 1469 1245 996 1506 1677 616 1853 3397 1439 1612 **Warszawa**
1168 1772 1856 1970 640 1114 1067 242 1308 1954 2034 731 1308 947 1088 1583 1010 916 3100 1524 993 2473 1353 818 2137 430 1600 1240 295 1126 2876 1033 1646 727 **Wien**
816 2426 1030 1938 863 619 1810 985 804 1352 1530 464 1497 915 2164 2323 1433 589 2296 922 410 1647 699 292 2552 303 1815 592 691 898 2061 1173 1861 1307 743 **Zürich**

km

RUSSIA
ROSSIYA

Moscow
Moskva

Kiev
Kyyiv

UKRAINE
UKRAINA

MOLDOVA

İstanbul

Ankara

186 187

TURKEY
TÜRKIYE

İzmir

Antalya

188 189

181
Nicosia CYPRUS
KYPROS

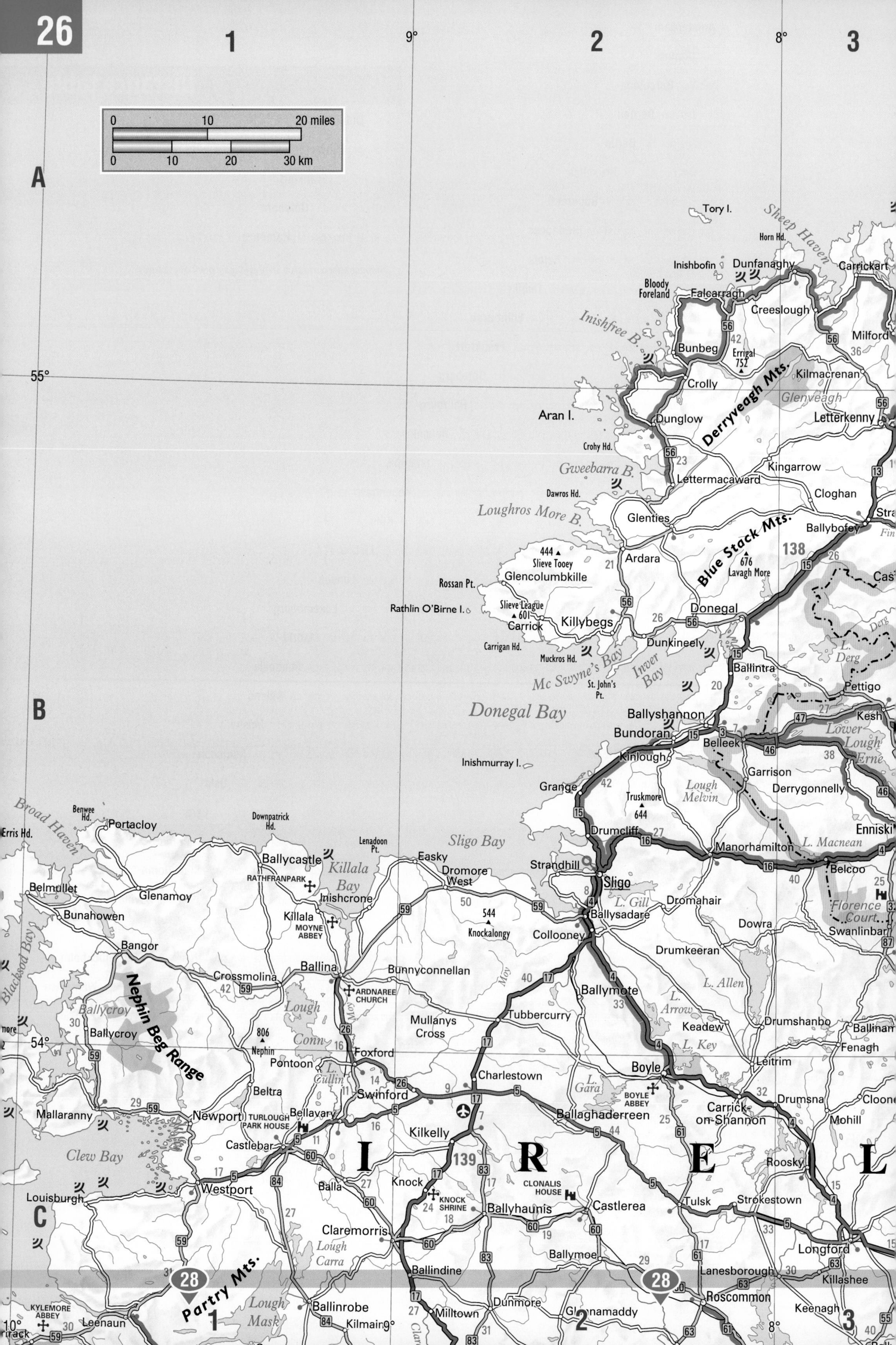

1   9°   2   8°   3

A

0   10   20 miles
0   10   20   30 km

55°

B

54°

C

Tory I.
Horn Hd.
Sheep Haven
Inishbofin   **Dunfanaghy**   Carrickart
Bloody
Foreland   Falcarragh   Creeslough
Bunbeg   56   42   Milford
Inishfree B.   Errigal   56   36
752
Crolly   *Glenveagh*
Kilmacrenan
Aran I.   Dunglow   **Derryveagh Mts.**   Letterkenny   56
Crohy Hd.   56   23   Kingarrow   13
Lettermacaward   Cloghan
Gweebarra B.   Stra
Dawros Hd.   Glenties   **Blue Stack Mts.**   Ballybofey   Fin
Loughros More B.   Ardara   676   15   138   26
444   Lavagh More   Cas
Slieve Tooey   21
Glencolumbkille
Rossan Pt.   56   **Donegal**   *L. Derg*
Rathlin O'Birne I.   26   56
Slieve League   15   Ballintra   Pettigo
601   **Carrick**   Killybegs   Dunkineely   20   27   Kesh
Carrigan Hd.   *Inver Bay*   Ballyshannon   *Lower Lough Erne*   46
Muckros Hd.   *Mc Swyne's Bay*   Bundoran   15   Belleek   38
St. John's   Kinlough   46   Garrison   Derrygonnelly   46
Pt.   Enniski
Inishmurray I.   Grange   42   *Lough Melvin*
Donegal Bay   Truskmore   644
15   Drumcliff   27   Manorhamilton   *L. Macnean*
Sligo Bay   16   16   Belcoo   4
Broad Haven   Easky   Strandhill   26   40   25
Erris Hd.   Benwee   Portacloy   Lenadoon   Dromore   **Sligo**   *Florence*   87
Hd.   Pt.   West   8   L. Gill   Dromahair   *Court.*
Downpatrick   50   59   Ballysadare   Swanlinbar
Belmullet   Hd.   Ballycastle   *Killala*   59   544   4   Dowra
Glenamoy   RATHFRANPARK   *Bay*   Inishcrone   Knockalongy   Colloony   Drumkeeran
Bunahowen   Killala   **Ballymote**   *L. Allen*
Bangor   MOYNE   Bunnyconnellan   *May*   40   17   33   Keadew   Drumshanbo
ABBEY   Ballina   Tubbercurry   Ballinan
Nephin Beg Range   Crossmolina   ARDNAREE   *L. Arrow*   4   Fenagh
42   59   CHURCH   Mullanys   17   **Boyle**   *L. Key*   Leitrim
Ballycroy   *Lough*   Cross   Charlestown   *L.*   4   Drumsna
30   806   *Conn*   16   Foxford   9   Gara   **Boyle**   Cloon
Ballycroy   Nephin   17   5   **Carrick-   Mohill
59   Pontoon   14   26   Charlestown   855   BOYLE   on-Shannon**   Roosky
L.   Beltra   11   ABBEY
Mallaranny   59   *Cullin*   Swinford   7   **Ballaghaderreen**   32
29   Newport   TURLOUGH   Bellavary   Kilkelly   44   Drumsna
PARK HOUSE   5   5   6   17   7   **I   R   E   L**
Castlebar   16   139   Tulsk   Roosky
60   Kilkelly   83   17   CLONALIS   15
Westport   84   Balla   27   Knock   HOUSE   Castlerea   Strokestown
Clew Bay   60   60   24   18   Ballyhaunis   Tulsk   83
Louisburgh   Claremorris   KNOCK   19   Ballymoe   17   Longford
27   SHRINE   83   60   63   Killashee
59   *Lough*   Ballindine   Castlerea   Lanesborough   30
Carra   17   Dunmore   Glanamaddy   63   61   40
28   *Partry Mts.*   Ballinrobe   Milltown   **28**   Roscommon   Keenagh
KYLEMORE   *Lough*   31   27   83
ABBEY   Mask   Kilmaine   2   63   Ball
Leenaun   59   **1**   8°   **3**
track
10°

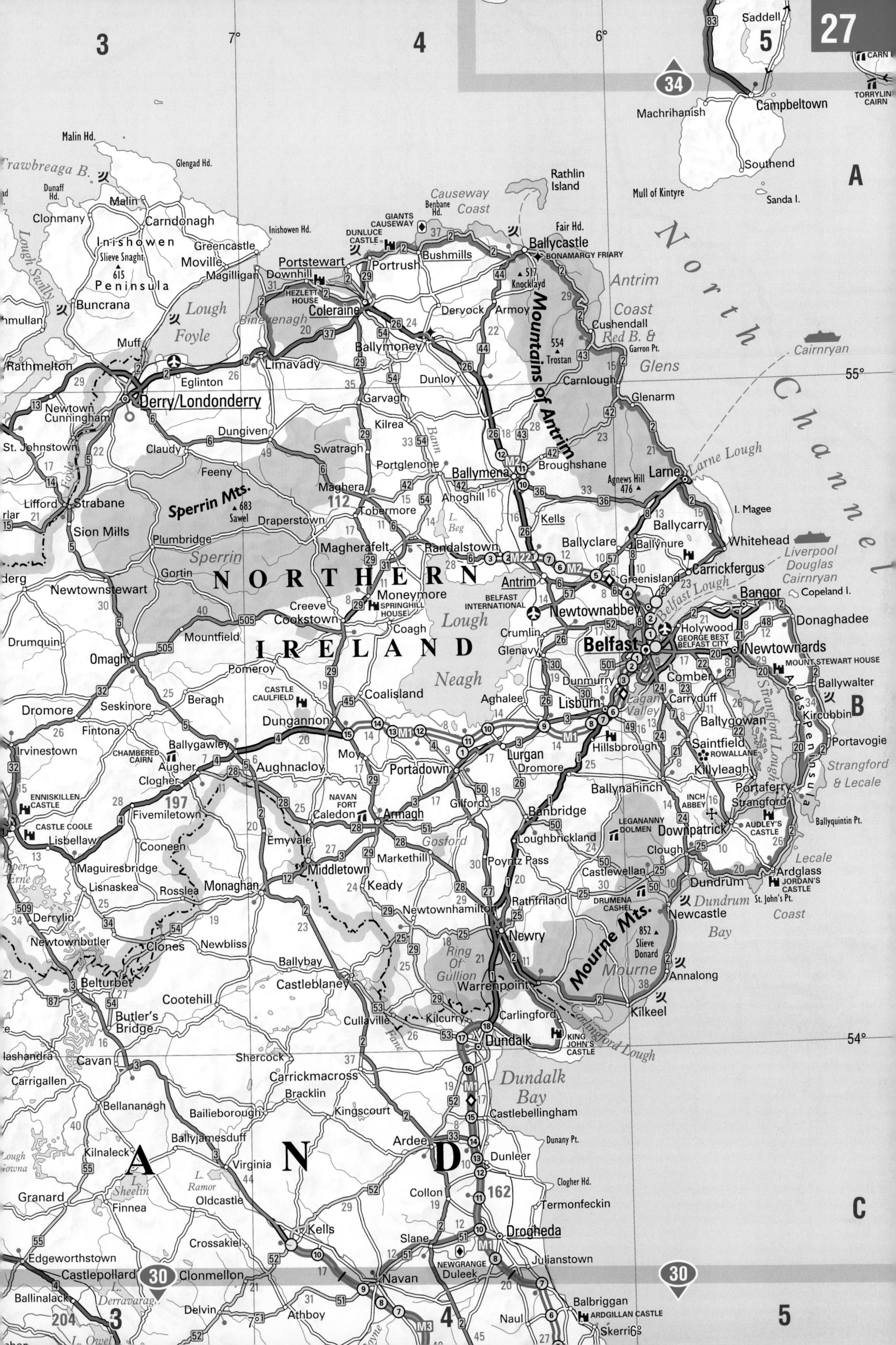

NORTHERN IRELAND
North Channel
Belfast
Derry/Londonderry
Coleraine
Portstewart
Portrush
Bushmills
Ballycastle
Rathlin Island
Causeway Coast
GIANTS CAUSEWAY
DUNLUCE CASTLE
Mountains of Antrim
Antrim Coast
Glens
Larne
Ballymena
Antrim
Lough Neagh
Sperrin Mts.
Omagh
Strabane
Dungannon
Cookstown
Magherafelt
Armagh
Portadown
Lurgan
Lisburn
Newtownabbey
Carrickfergus
Bangor
Newtownards
Donaghadee
Strangford Lough
Downpatrick
Newcastle
Mourne Mts.
Slieve Donard
Newry
Warrenpoint
Carlingford
Dundalk
Dundalk Bay
Drogheda
Navan
Kells
Cavan
Monaghan
Enniskillen Castle
Lough Foyle
Lough Swilly
Inishowen Peninsula
Malin Hd.
Buncrana
Lifford
Campbeltown
Mull of Kintyre
Machrihanish
Southend
Saddell
Sanda I.
Belfast Lough
Larne Lough
Copeland I.
I. Magee
Ards Peninsula
Portaferry
Ardglass
Kilkeel
Annalong
Dundrum Bay
Carlingford Lough
Castleblaney
Carrickmacross
Ardee
Virginia
Bailieborough
Kingscourt
Castlebellingham
Dunleer
Termonfeckin
Julianstown
Balbriggan
Skerries
ARDGILLAN CASTLE
NEWGRANGE
Duleek
Slane
Collon
Athboy
Delvin
Clonmellon
Castlepollard
Edgeworthstown
Granard
Finnea
Oldcastle
Crossakiel
Kilnaleck
Ballyjamesduff
Bellananagh
Belturbet
Butler's Bridge
Clones
Newtownbutler
Lisnaskea
Maguiresbridge
Fivemiletown
Aughnacloy
Caledon
Keady
Middletown
Markethill
Newtownhamilton
Banbridge
Rathfriland
Castlewellan
Ballynahinch
Saintfield
Comber
Holywood
GEORGE BEST BELFAST CITY
BELFAST INTERNATIONAL
Crumlin
Glenavy
Dunmurry
Hillsborough
Dromore
Gilford
Poyntz Pass
Loughbrickland
Ballyclare
Whitehead
Ballycarry
Cushendall
Carnlough
Glenarm
Broughshane
Dervock
Armoy
Ballymoney
Limavady
Eglinton
Dungiven
Claudy
Feeny
Draperstown
Maghera
Tobermore
Kilrea
Garvagh
Swatragh
Portglenone
Ahoghill
Randalstown
Toome
Moneymore
Coagh
Coalisland
Pomeroy
Beragh
Seskinore
Fintona
Dromore
Irvinestown
Ballygawley
Augher
Clogher
Newtownstewart
Gortin
Plumbridge
Sion Mills
Mountfield
Drumquin
Moville
Greencastle
Carndonagh
Malin
Clonmany
Muff
Newtown Cunningham
St. Johnstown
Rathmelton
Emyvale
Rosslea
Newbliss
Ballybay
Cootehill
Shercock
Bracklin
Carrigallen
Cullaville
Kilcurry
Ring Of Gullion
Gosford
Moy
Mourne
Ballywalter
Kircubbin
Portavogie
Killyleagh
Strangford
Clough
Dundrum
Ballygowan
Carryduff
Greenisland
Ballynure
Lecale Coast
Strangford & Lecale
Liverpool
Douglas
Cairnryan
54°
55°
6°
7°

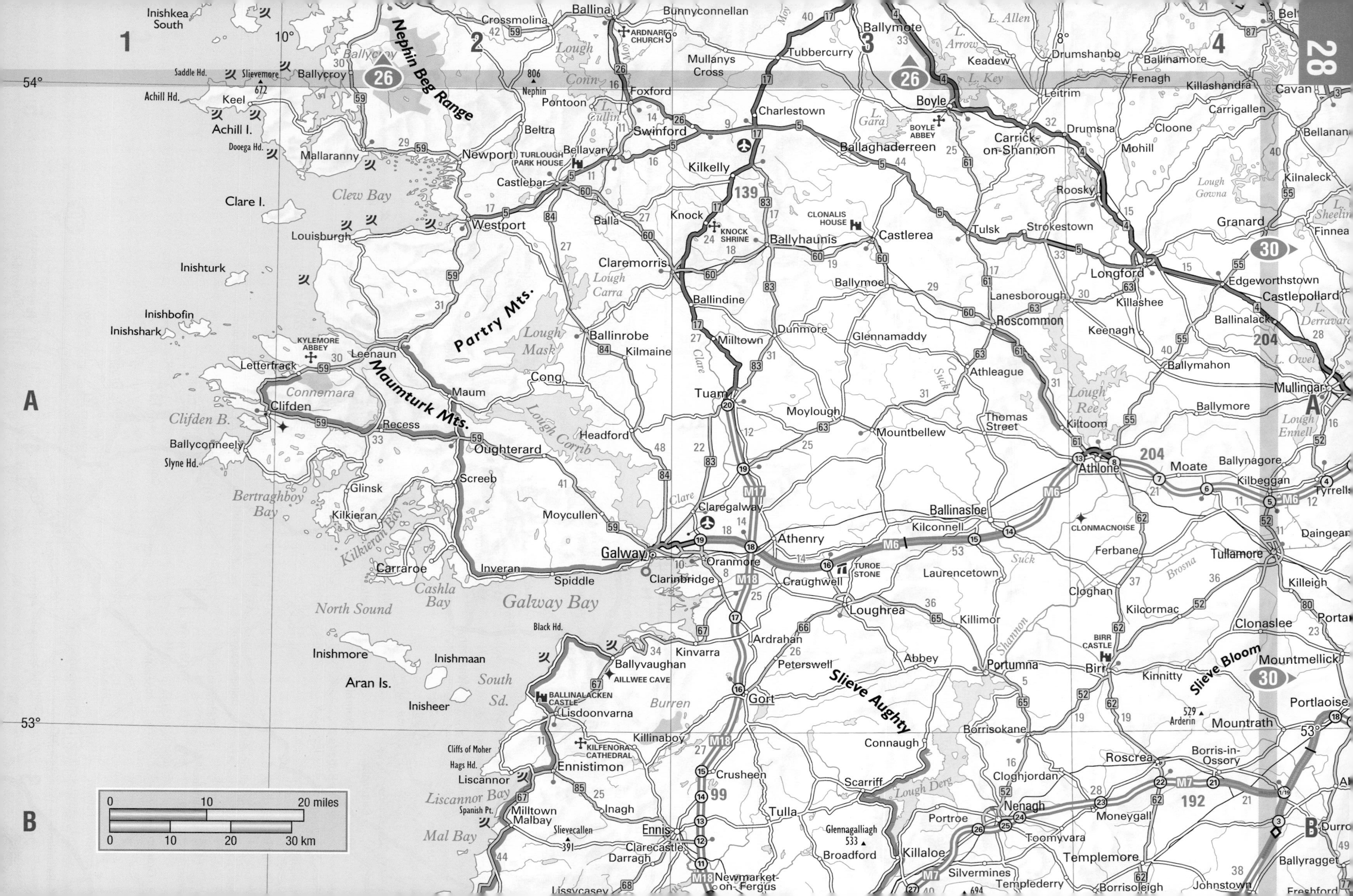

Nephin Beg Range
Partry Mts.
Maumturk Mts.
Slieve Aughty
Slieve Bloom
Inishkea South
Saddle Hd.
Slievemore
Achill Hd.
Keel
Achill I.
Dooega Hd.
Ballycroy
Mallaranny
Clare I.
Clew Bay
Louisburgh
Inishturk
Inishbofin
Inishshark
Kylemore Abbey
Letterfrack
Leenaun
Connemara
Clifden
Clifden B.
Ballyconneely
Slyne Hd.
Bertraghboy Bay
Recess
Glinsk
Kilkieran
Kilkieran Bay
Carraroe
Cashla Bay
North Sound
Inishmore
Inishmaan
Aran Is.
Inisheer
South Sd.
Galway Bay
Black Hd.
Crossmolina
Ballina
Bunnyconnellan
Ardnaree Church
Nephin
Pontoon
Lough Conn
L. Cullin
Foxford
Beltra
Newport
Turlough Park House
Bellavary
Castlebar
Westport
Swinford
Mullanys Cross
Tubbercurry
Charlestown
Kilkelly
Knock
Knock Shrine
Balla
Claremorris
Lough Carra
Lough Mask
Ballinrobe
Kilmaine
Cong
Maum
Oughterard
Lough Corrib
Headford
Screeb
Moycullen
Inveran
Spiddle
Galway
Claregalway
Clarinbridge
Oranmore
Athenry
Ballindine
Milltown
Tuam
Dunmore
Ballyhaunis
Clonalis House
Castlerea
Ballaghaderreen
Ballymote
Boyle
Boyle Abbey
L. Gara
L. Key
Keadew
L. Arrow
L. Allen
Drumshanbo
Leitrim
Carrick-on-Shannon
Drumsna
Mohill
Cloone
Fenagh
Ballinamore
Killashandra
Carrigallen
Cavan
Bellanan
Kilnaleck
Lough Gowna
Granard
Finnea
Rooskey
Tulsk
Strokestown
Longford
Killashee
Lanesborough
Roscommon
Keenagh
Edgeworthstown
Castlepollard
Ballinalack
L. Derravaragh
L. Owel
Mullingar
Lough Ennell
Ballymahon
Ballymore
Glennamaddy
Ballymoe
Athleague
Lough Ree
Kiltoom
Thomas Street
Moylough
Mountbellew
Athlone
Moate
Ballynagore
Kilbeggan
Tyrrellspass
Ballinasloe
Kilconnell
Clonmacnoise
Ferbane
Tullamore
Daingean
Killeigh
Turoe Stone
Craughwell
Laurencetown
Loughrea
Cloghan
Kilcormac
Clonaslee
Mountmellick
Ardrahan
Kinvarra
Peterswell
Abbey
Killimor
Portumna
Birr
Birr Castle
Kinnitty
Arderin
Mountrath
Portlaoise
Ballyvaughan
Aillwee Cave
Burren
Ballinalacken Castle
Lisdoonvarna
Kilfenora Cathedral
Cliffs of Moher
Hags Hd.
Liscannor
Liscannor Bay
Spanish Pt.
Milltown Malbay
Mal Bay
Ennistimon
Slievecallen
Inagh
Killinaboy
Gort
Crusheen
Ennis
Clarecastle
Darragh
Newmarket-on-Fergus
Lissycasey
Tulla
Connaugh
Scarriff
Lough Derg
Glennagalliagh
Broadford
Killaloe
Borrisokane
Cloghjordan
Portroe
Nenagh
Toomyvara
Silvermines
Templederry
Templemore
Moneygall
Roscrea
Borris-in-Ossory
Borrisoleigh
Johnstown
Ballyragget
Freshford
Durrow
Suck
Shannon
Brosna
Moy
Clare
0 10 20 miles
0 10 20 30 km
54°
53°
10°
8°

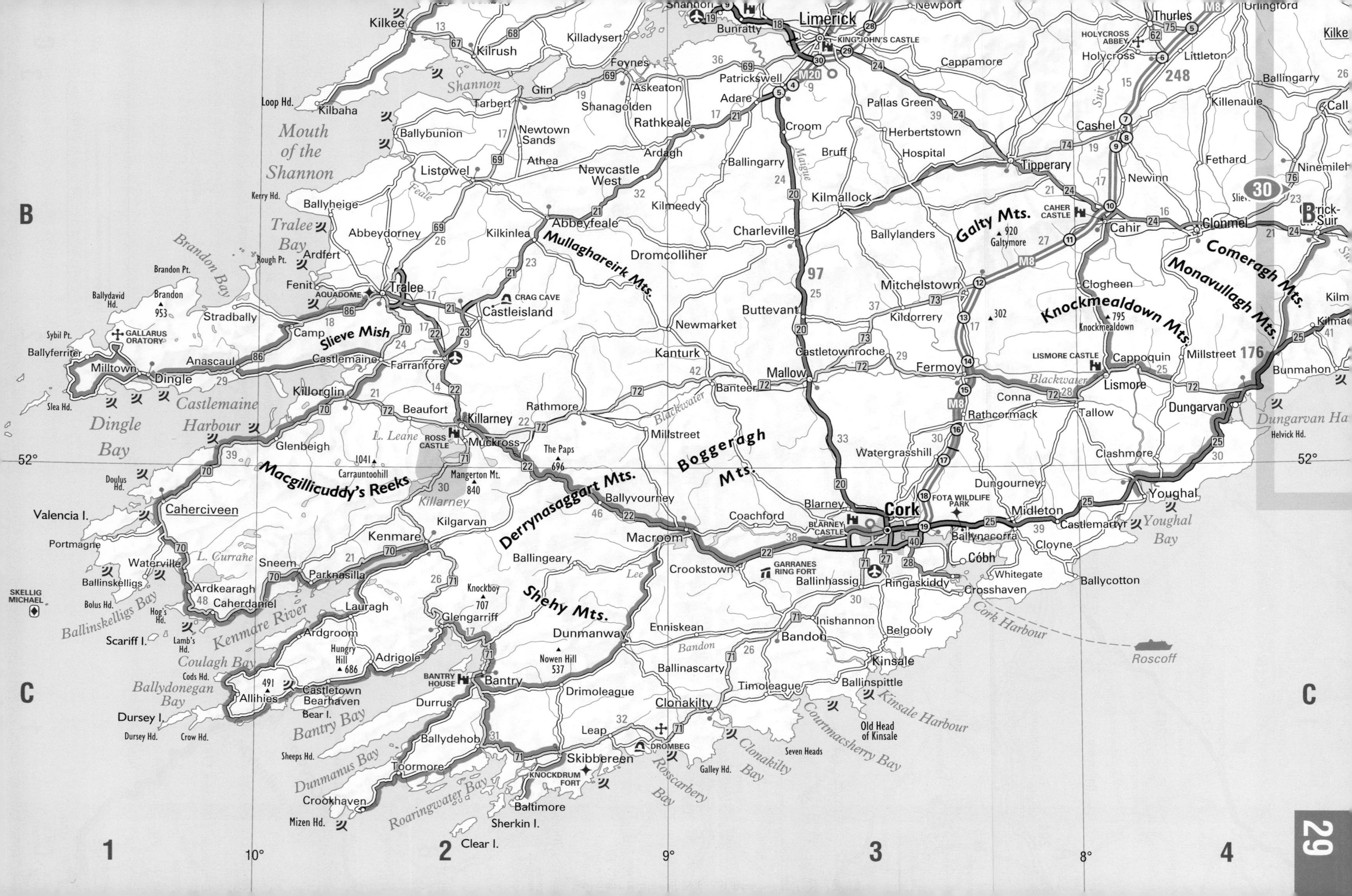
Limerick
Cork
Tralee
Killarney
Kilkee
Kilrush
Killadysert
Foynes
Askeaton
Glin
Tarbert
Shanagolden
Rathkeale
Adare
Patrickswell
Bunratty
Shannon
Newport
Thurles
Holycross
HOLYCROSS ABBEY
Littleton
Cappamore
KING JOHN'S CASTLE
Pallas Green
Herbertstown
Hospital
Tipperary
Cashel
Killenaule
Ballingarry
Fethard
Ninemilehouse
Newinn
Cahir
CAHER CASTLE
Clonmel
Carrick-on-Suir
Kilbaha
Loop Hd.
Mouth of the Shannon
Ballybunion
Newtown Sands
Athea
Listowel
Newcastle West
Ardagh
Ballingarry
Croom
Bruff
Kilmallock
Kilmeedy
Charleville
Dromcolliher
Ballylanders
Galty Mts.
Galtymore
Mitchelstown
Kildorrery
Clogheen
Knockmealdown Mts.
Knockmealdown
Comeragh Mts.
Monavullagh Mts.
Millstreet
Cappoquin
LISMORE CASTLE
Lismore
Bunmahon
Dungarvan
Dungarvan Harbour
Helvick Hd.
Kerry Hd.
Ballyheige
Tralee Bay
Brandon Bay
Brandon Pt.
Brandon
Rough Pt.
Ardfert
Abbeydorney
Fenit
AQUADOME
Kilkinlea
Abbeyfeale
Mullaghareirk Mts.
CRAG CAVE
Castleisland
Newmarket
Buttevant
Kanturk
Mallow
Castletownroche
Fermoy
Conna
Tallow
Rathcormack
Blackwater
Clashmore
Ballydavid Hd.
GALLARUS ORATORY
Sybil Pt.
Ballyferriter
Milltown
Slea Hd.
Dingle
Anascaul
Stradbally
Camp
Slieve Mish
Castlemaine
Farranfore
Killorglin
Castlemaine Harbour
Dingle Bay
Beaufort
Rathmore
Banteer
Millstreet
Boggeragh Mts.
Watergrasshill
Dungourney
Youghal
Youghal Bay
L. Leane
ROSS CASTLE
Muckross
Glenbeigh
Carrauntoohill
Macgillicuddy's Reeks
Mangerton Mt.
The Paps
Killarney
Derrynasaggart Mts.
Ballyvourney
Blarney
BLARNEY CASTLE
Coachford
FOTA WILDLIFE PARK
Midleton
Castlemartyr
Cloyne
Ballynacorra
Cóbh
Whitegate
Crosshaven
Ballycotton
Cork Harbour
Roscoff
Doulus Hd.
Valencia I.
Caherciveen
Portmagne
Waterville
L. Currane
Sneem
Parknasilla
Kenmare
Kilgarvan
Macroom
Ballingeary
Crookstown
GARRANES RING FORT
Ballinhassig
Ringaskiddy
SKELLIG MICHAEL
Ballinskelligs
Ballinskelligs Bay
Bolus Hd.
Hog's Hd.
Ardkearagh
Caherdaniel
Kenmare River
Lauragh
Knockboy
Glengarriff
Shehy Mts.
Dunmanway
Enniskean
Bandon
Inishannon
Belgooly
Kinsale
Scariff I.
Lamb's Hd.
Ardgroom
Coulagh Bay
Hungry Hill
Adrigole
Nowen Hill
Ballinascarty
Cods Hd.
Allihies
Castletown Bearhaven
Ballydonegan Bay
Dursey I.
Dursey Hd.
Crow Hd.
Bear I.
Bantry Bay
BANTRY HOUSE
Bantry
Durrus
Drimoleague
Clonakilty
Timoleague
Ballinspittle
Kinsale Harbour
Old Head of Kinsale
Courtmacsherry Bay
Seven Heads
Sheeps Hd.
Ballydehob
Leap
DROMBEG
Clonakilty Bay
Galley Hd.
Dunmanus Bay
Toormore
Skibbereen
KNOCKDRUM FORT
Rosscarbery Bay
Crookhaven
Roaringwater Bay
Baltimore
Sherkin I.
Mizen Hd.
Clear I.
B
C
1
2
3
4
10°
9°
8°
52°

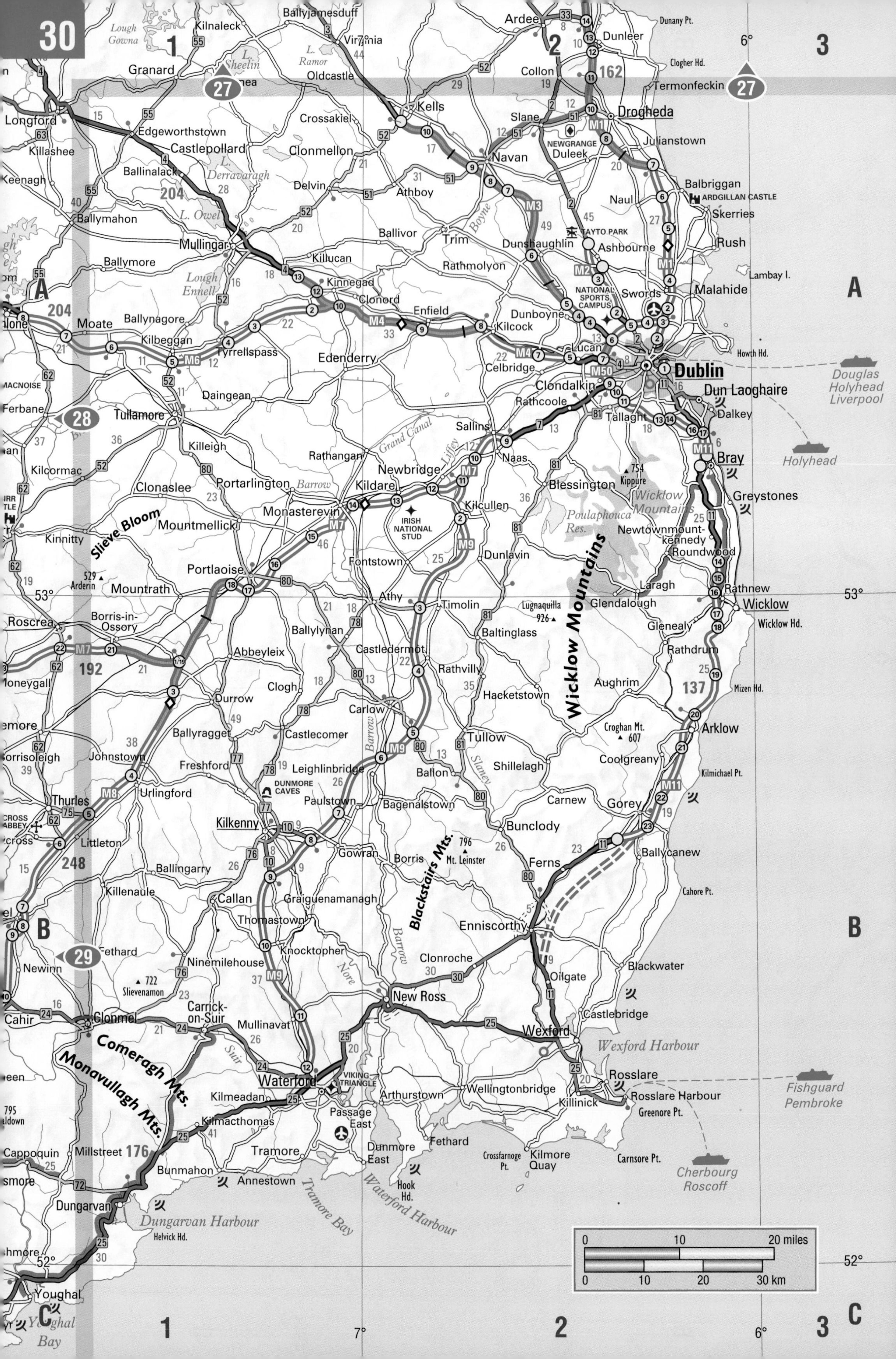
Lough Gowna
Kilnaleck
Ballyjamesduff
Virginia
L. Ramor
Oldcastle
L. Sheelin
Granard
27
Ardee
Dunleer
Dunany Pt.
6°
Clogher Hd.
Collon
Termonfeckin
Longford
Edgeworthstown
Crossakiel
Kells
Slane
Drogheda
Killashee
Castlepollard
L. Derravaragh
Clonmellon
NEWGRANGE
Duleek
Julianstown
Keenagh
Ballinalack
Delvin
Athboy
Navan
Balbriggan
ARDGILLAN CASTLE
L. Owel
Naul
Skerries
Ballymahon
Ballivor
Trim
Boyne
TAYTO PARK
Mullingar
Dunshaughlin
Ashbourne
Rush
Ballymore
Killucan
Rathmolyon
Lambay I.
Lough Ennell
Kinnegad
NATIONAL SPORTS CAMPUS
Swords
Malahide
Clonard
Enfield
Dunboyne
Moate
Ballynagore
Kilbeggan
Kilcock
Tyrrellspass
Edenderry
Celbridge
Lucan
Howth Hd.
Dublin
Douglas
Holyhead
Liverpool
Clondalkin
Dun Laoghaire
Daingean
Rathcoole
Dalkey
Ferbane
28
Tullamore
Tallaght
Sallins
Grand Canal
Rathangan
Killeigh
Liffey
Naas
Bray
Holyhead
Kilcormac
Newbridge
Kippure
Portarlington
Barrow
Kildare
Blessington
Clonaslee
Wicklow Mountains
Greystones
Kilcullen
Monasterevin
Slieve Bloom
Mountmellick
IRISH NATIONAL STUD
Poulaphouca Res.
Newtownmount-kennedy
Kinnitty
Roundwood
Dunlavin
Fontstown
Portlaoise
Arderin
Wicklow Mountains
Mountrath
Laragh
Rathnew
53°
Athy
Glendalough
Timolin
Lugnaquilla
Wicklow
Roscrea
Borris-in-Ossory
Wicklow Hd.
Ballylynan
Glenealy
Baltinglass
Castledermot
Rathdrum
Abbeyleix
Rathvilly
Moneygall
Aughrim
Mizen Hd.
Clogh
Durrow
Hacketstown
Carlow
Arklow
Croghan Mt.
Castlecomer
Tullow
Ballyragget
Johnstown
Coolgreany
Freshford
Leighlinbridge
Shillelagh
Slaney
Kilmichael Pt.
Ballon
DUNMORE CAVES
Thurles
Urlingford
Paulstown
Carnew
Gorey
Bagenalstown
Kilkenny
Bunclody
Littleton
Blackstairs Mts.
Gowran
Mt. Leinster
Ballycanew
Borris
Ballingarry
Ferns
Cahore Pt.
Killenaule
Callan
Graiguenamanagh
Thomastown
Enniscorthy
B
Fethard
Knocktopher
29
Nore
Clonroche
Newinn
Ninemilehouse
Blackwater
Slievenamon
Oilgate
Carrick-on-Suir
New Ross
Cahir
Clonmel
Mullinavat
Castlebridge
Comeragh Mts.
Wexford
Wexford Harbour
Suir
Monavullagh Mts.
Waterford
VIKING TRIANGLE
Rosslare
Fishguard
Pembroke
Kilmeadan
Arthurstown
Wellingtonbridge
Rosslare Harbour
Kilmacthomas
Passage East
Killinick
Greenore Pt.
Cappoquin
Millstreet
Tramore
Dunmore East
Fethard
Crossfarnoge Pt.
Kilmore Quay
Carnsore Pt.
Bunmahon
Annestown
Cherbourg
Roscoff
Tramore Bay
Waterford Harbour
Hook Hd.
Dungarvan
Dungarvan Harbour
Helvick Hd.
0
10
20 miles
0
10
20
30 km
52°
Youghal
Youghal Bay
1
7°
2
3
C

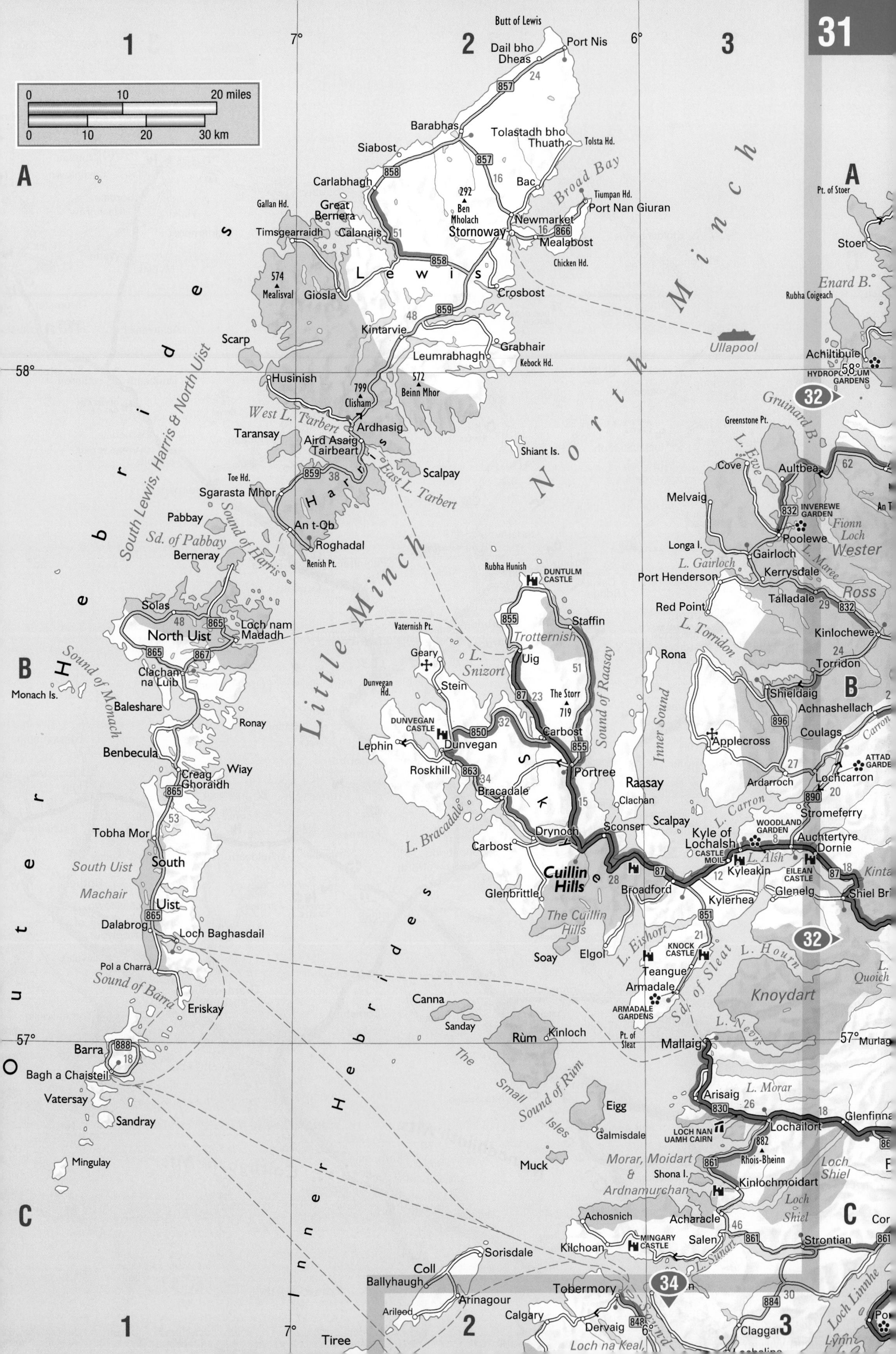
0 10 20 miles
0 10 20 30 km
Butt of Lewis
Port Nis
Dail bho Dheas
Barabhas
Tolastadh bho Thuath
Tolsta Hd.
Siabost
Carlabhagh
Bac
Broad Bay
Tiumpan Hd.
Port Nan Giuran
Gallan Hd.
Great Bernera
Ben Mholach
Newmarket
Stornoway
Timsgearraidh
Calanais
Mealabost
Chicken Hd.
Lewis
Mealisval
Giosla
Crosbost
Kintarvie
Scarp
Grabhair
Leumrabhagh
Kebock Hd.
Husinish
Beinn Mhor
Clisham
West L. Tarbert
Ardhasig
Taransay
Aird Asaig
Tairbeart
Harris
East L. Tarbert
Scalpay
Shiant Is.
Toe Hd.
Sgarasta Mhor
Pabbay
Sound of Harris
Sd. of Pabbay
An t-Ob
Roghadal
Renish Pt.
Berneray
South Lewis, Harris & North Uist
Outer Hebrides
Little Minch
North Minch
Ullapool
Stoer
Pt. of Stoer
Enard B.
Rubha Coigeach
Achiltibuie
HYDROPONICUM GARDENS
Gruinard B.
Greenstone Pt.
L. Ewe
Cove
Aultbea
Melvaig
INVEREWE GARDEN
Poolewe
Fionn Loch
Longa I.
Gairloch
L. Gairloch
L. Maree
Wester Ross
Kerrysdale
Port Henderson
Red Point
Talladale
L. Torridon
Kinlochewe
Torridon
Rona
Shieldaig
Achnashellach
Coulags
Applecross
ATTADALE GARDENS
Lochcarron
Ardarroch
Stromeferry
L. Carron
WOODLAND GARDEN
Auchtertyre
Dornie
Kyle of Lochalsh
CASTLE MOIL
Kyleakin
L. Alsh
EILEAN CASTLE
Shiel Bridge
Glenelg
Kylerhea
Rubha Hunish
DUNTULM CASTLE
Staffin
Solas
North Uist
Loch nam Madadh
Vaternish Pt.
Trotternish
Geary
L. Snizort
Uig
Sound of Monach
Clachan na Luib
Monach Is.
Dunvegan Hd.
Stein
The Storr
Baleshare
Ronay
DUNVEGAN CASTLE
Dunvegan
Carbost
Sound of Raasay
Inner Sound
Benbecula
Lephin
Wiay
Roskhill
Portree
Raasay
Creag Ghoraidh
Bracadale
Clachan
Skye
Scalpay
L. Bracadale
Tobha Mor
Drynoch
Sconser
Carbost
South Uist
South Uist Machair
Cuillin Hills
Broadford
Glenbrittle
The Cuillin Hills
Dalabrog
Loch Baghasdail
L. Eishort
KNOCK CASTLE
L. Hourn
Soay
Elgol
Teangue
Knoydart
Quoich
Pol a Charra
Sound of Barra
Armadale
Sd. of Sleat
ARMADALE GARDENS
Eriskay
Canna
Sanday
Pt. of Sleat
L. Nevis
Barra
Rùm
Kinloch
Mallaig
Murlaggan
Bagh a Chaisteil
The Small Isles
Sound of Rùm
L. Morar
Vatersay
Arisaig
Glenfinnan
Sandray
Eigg
LOCH NAN UAMH CAIRN
Lochailort
Galmisdale
Rhois-Bheinn
Mingulay
Muck
Morar, Moidart & Ardnamurchan
Loch Shiel
Shona I.
Kinlochmoidart
Inner Hebrides
Achosnich
Acharacle
Kilchoan
MINGARY CASTLE
Salen
L. Sunart
Strontian
Coll
Sorisdale
Loch Linnhe
Ballyhaugh
Arinagour
Tobermory
Arileod
Calgary
Dervaig
Claggan
Tiree
Loch na Keal
1 2 3 A B C
7° 6° 58° 57°
32 34

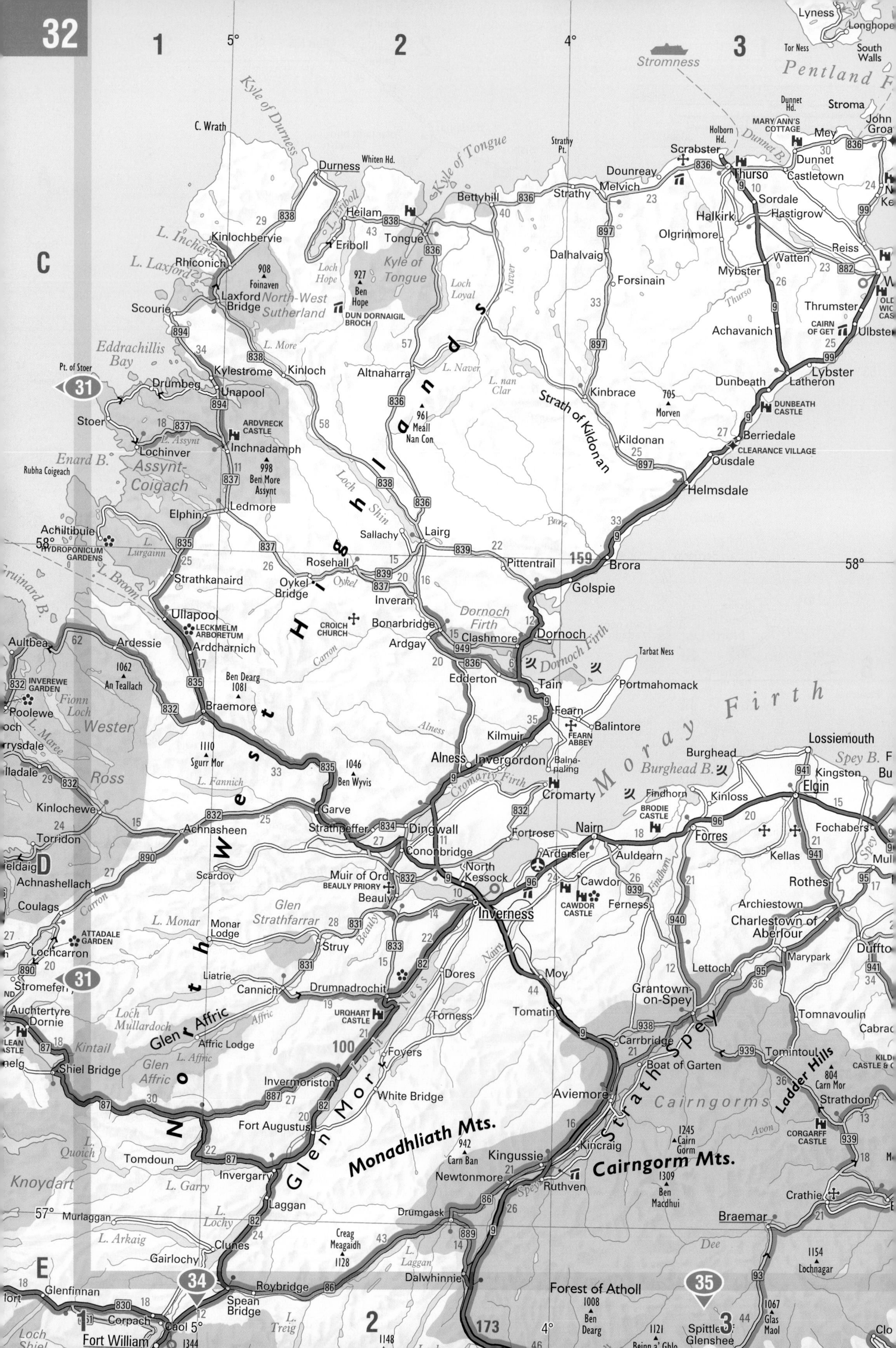

Lyness
Longhope
Tor Ness
South Walls
Stromness
Pentland F
Dunnet Hd.
Stroma
MARY ANN'S COTTAGE
Mey
John o' Groats
Holborn Hd.
Dunnet B.
Scrabster
Thurso
Dunnet
Castletown
Strathy Pt.
Dounreay
Melvich
Strathy
Bettyhill
Sordale
Halkirk
Hastigrow
Olgrinmore
Reiss
Watten
Mybster
Dalhalvaig
Forsinain
Thurso
Thrumster
CAIRN OF GET
Ulbster
Achavanich
Lybster
Latheron
Dunbeath
DUNBEATH CASTLE
Kinbrace
705 Morven
Strath of Kildonan
Kildonan
Berriedale
CLEARANCE VILLAGE
Ousdale
Helmsdale
Brora
Golspie
Pittentrail
Lairg
Sallachy
Rosehall
Oykel Bridge
Inveran
Bonarbridge
Ardgay
CROICH CHURCH
Dornoch Firth
Clashmore
Dornoch
Tarbat Ness
Portmahomack
Edderton
Tain
Fearn
Balintore
FEARN ABBEY
Kilmuir
Alness
Invergordon
Balnapaling
Cromarty Firth
Cromarty
Moray Firth
Burghead
Burghead B.
Findhorn
Kinloss
Lossiemouth
Spey B.
Kingston
Elgin
BRODIE CASTLE
Nairn
Forres
Fochabers
Kellas
Rothes
Auldearn
Ardersier
Cawdor
CAWDOR CASTLE
Ferness
Archiestown
Charlestown of Aberlour
Marypark
Lettoch
Grantown-on-Spey
Tomnavoulin
Tomintoul
Ladder Hills
804 Carn Mor
Strathdon
CORGARFF CASTLE
Cairngorms
Strath Spey
Carrbridge
Boat of Garten
Aviemore
Kincraig
1245 Cairn Gorm
Cairngorm Mts.
1309 Ben Macdhui
Crathie
Braemar
Dee
1154 Lochnagar
1067 Glas Maol
Spittle of Glenshee
1121 Beinn a' Ghlo
Forest of Atholl
1008 Ben Dearg
Dalwhinnie
L. Laggan
Drumgask
Kingussie
Newtonmore
Ruthven
942 Carn Ban
Monadhliath Mts.
Glen Mor
Loch Ness
Tomatin
Moy
Inverness
North Kessock
Dores
Torness
Foyers
White Bridge
Fort Augustus
Invermoriston
URQHART CASTLE
Drumnadrochit
Cannich
Liatrie
Struy
Beauly
BEAULY PRIORY
Muir of Ord
Conon Bridge
Dingwall
Strathpeffer
Garve
Achnasheen
Scardoy
Glen Strathfarrar
Monar Lodge
L. Monar
L. Fannich
1046 Ben Wyvis
1110 Sgurr Mor
Braemore
Ben Dearg 1081
North West Highlands
Ullapool
LECKMELM ARBORETUM
Ardcharnich
Ardessie
1062 An Teallach
Aultbea
INVEREWE GARDEN
Poolewe
Fionn Loch
Wester Ross
L. Maree
Kinlochewe
Torridon
Achnashellach
Coulags
ATTADALE GARDEN
Lochcarron
Stromeferry
Auchtertyre
Dornie
Kintail
Shiel Bridge
Glen Affric
Affric Lodge
Loch Mullardoch
L. Affric
Tomdoun
Invergarry
L. Garry
L. Quoich
Knoydart
Laggan
L. Lochy
Murlaggan
L. Arkaig
Clunes
Gairlochy
Creag Meagaidh 1128
Roybridge
Spean Bridge
Glenfinnan
Corpach
Caol
Fort William
1344
L. Treig
1148
Strathkanaird
L. Broom
Gruinard B.
Achiltibuie
HYDROPONICUM GARDENS
L. Lurgainn
Elphin
Ledmore
Assynt-Coigach
Rubha Coigeach
Enard B.
Lochinver
L. Assynt
Inchnadamph
ARDVRECK CASTLE
998 Ben More Assynt
Stoer
Pt. of Stoer
Drumbeg
Unapool
Kylestrome
Eddrachillis Bay
Kinloch
Scourie
Laxford Bridge
North-West Sutherland
908 Foinaven
Rhiconich
L. Laxford
L. Inchard
Kinlochbervie
C. Wrath
Kyle of Durness
Durness
Whiten Hd.
L. Eriboll
Heilam
Eriboll
Loch Hope
927 Ben Hope
DUN DORNAIGIL BROCH
Kyle of Tongue
Tongue
Loch Loyal
Naver
L. Naver
Altnaharra
961 Meall Nan Con
Loch Shin
L. nan Clar
Oykel
Carron
Alness
Brora

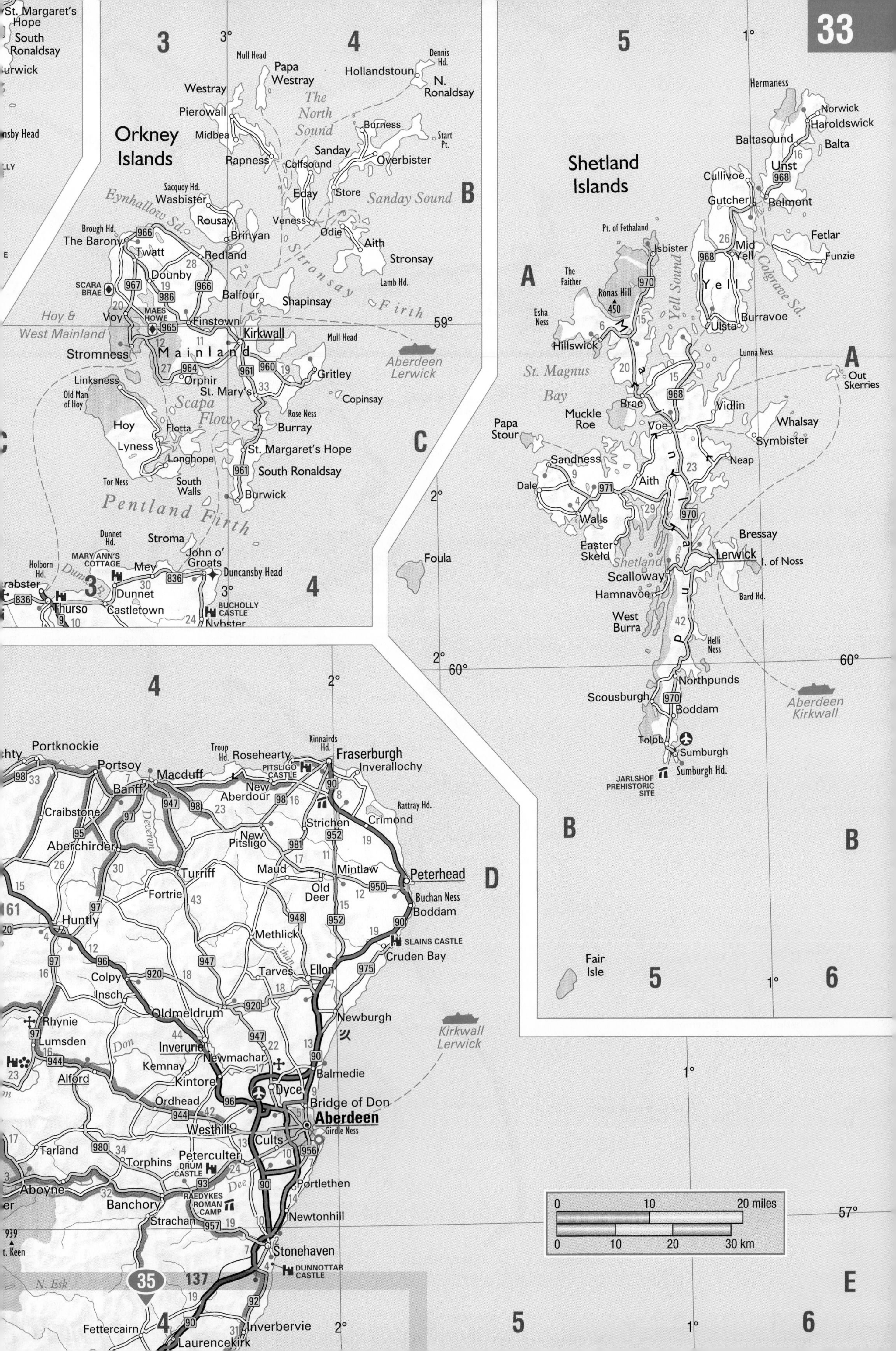

Orkney Islands

St. Margaret's Hope
South Ronaldsay
urwick

3 3° 4 5 1°

Mull Head
Westray
Papa Westray
Hollandstoun
Dennis Hd.
N. Ronaldsay
Pierowall
Midbea
The North Sound
Burness
Sanday
Start Pt.
Rapness
Calfsound
Overbister
Eday
Store
B
Sanday Sound
Sacquoy Hd.
Wasbister
Rousay
Brinyan
Veness
Odie
Aith
Brough Hd.
The Barony
966
Twatt
Redland
Stronsay
Lamb Hd.
Dounby
SCARA BRAE
967 986 28
19
965
MAES HOWE
Voy
Finstown
Balfour
Shapinsay
Kirkwall
Mull Head
59°
Hoy & West Mainland
Stromness
Mainland
964 961 960 19
27
Orphir
Gritley
Linksness
Old Man of Hoy
Scapa Flow
33
St. Mary's
Copinsay
Hoy
Flotta
Burray
Rose Ness
Lyness
Longhope
St. Margaret's Hope
961 South Ronaldsay
Tor Ness
South Walls
Burwick

Eynhallow Sd.
Stronsay Firth
Sanday Sound

Aberdeen Lerwick

Shetland Islands

Hermaness
Norwick
Haroldswick
Baltasound
Balta
Cullivoe
Unst
968
Gutcher
Belmont
Fetlar
Pt. of Fethaland
968 26 Mid Yell
Funzie
The Faither
Isbister
Yell
Esha Ness
Ronas Hill
970 450
6 15
Burravoe
Hillswick
Ulsta
Lunna Ness
20
15
A
Out Skerries
St. Magnus Bay
968
Brae
Vidlin
Papa Stour
Muckle Roe
Voe
Whalsay
Sandness
23
Symbister
Dale
971
Aith
Neap
9
Walls
970
Bressay
4
29
Lerwick
Easter Skeld
6
I. of Noss
Scalloway
Hamnavoe
Bard Hd.
West Burra
42
Helli Ness
60°

Foula
60° 2°
Scousburgh
Northpunds
970
Boddam
Aberdeen Kirkwall
Tolob
Sumburgh
JARLSHOF PREHISTORIC SITE
Sumburgh Hd.

Pentland Firth
Stroma
Holborn Hd.
MARY ANN'S COTTAGE
Mey
John o' Groats
836
rabster
Dunnet Hd.
30 836
Duncansby Head
Thurso
Dunnet
3° 3 4
9 Castletown
BUCHOLLY CASTLE
10
24 Nybster

4 2° 2° 5 1° 6

Portknockie
Portsoy
Macduff
Troup Hd.
Rosehearty
Kinnairds Hd.
Fraserburgh
98 33
7
Banff
New Aberdour
PITSLIGO CASTLE
Inverallochy
98
947
98
90
Craibstone
97
23
Strichen
8
Crimond
95
New Pitsligo
981 952
Rattray Hd.
Aberchirder
Deveron
17
11
19
26
30
Turriff
Maud
Mintlaw
Peterhead
15
Fortrie
43
Old Deer
12
950
Buchan Ness
161
Huntly
948
Boddam
97
97 Methlick
952
19
90
4
Colpy
920
947
SLAINS CASTLE
12
18
Tarves
Cruden Bay
16
97
Insch
18
975
Oldmeldrum
920
Ellon
Rhynie
97
947
Newburgh
Lumsden
44
Inverurie
22
16
944
Newmachar
13
Alford
Kemnay
17
90
23
Balmedie
Kintore
Kirkwall Lerwick
Ordhead
96
Dyce
9
Bridge of Don
944
42
Aberdeen
Westhill
Cults
Girdle Ness
Tarland
980
34
956
Torphins
Peterculter
13
DRUM CASTLE
10
Aboyne
93
24
Portlethen
939
32
RAEDYKES ROMAN CAMP
Dee
90
Newtonhill
Banchory
Strachan
957
19
10
Stonehaven
N. Esk
35 137
DUNNOTTAR CASTLE
7
4
19
92
Fettercairn
4 90
31
Inverbervie
2°
Laurencekirk
57°
E
5 1° 6

Fair Isle
B

0   10   20 miles
0   10   20   30 km

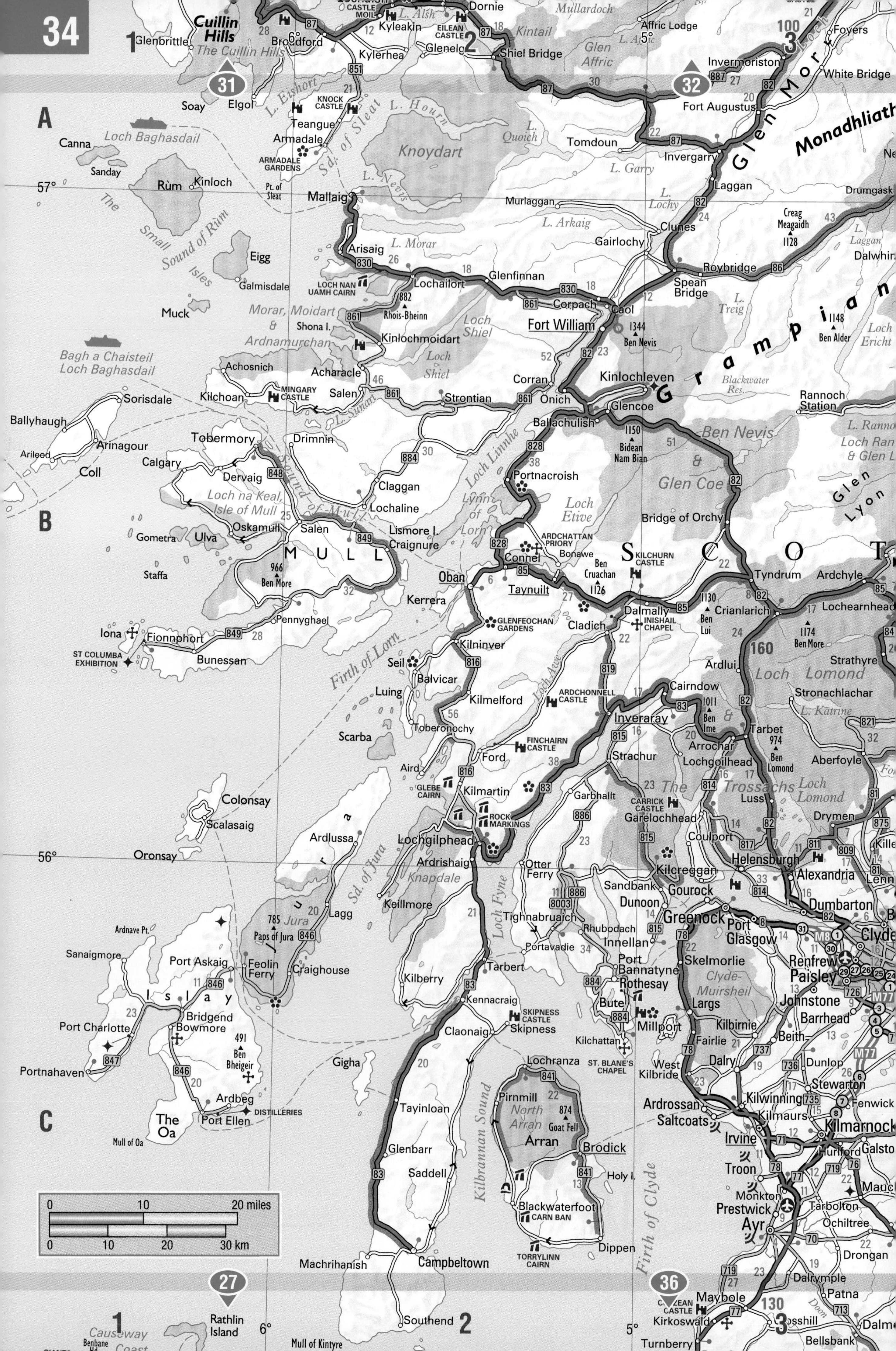
Cuillin Hills
The Cuillin Hills
Glenbrittle
Broadford
Kyleakin
Kylerhea
Dornie
EILEAN CASTLE
Glenelg
Shiel Bridge
Kintail
Mullardoch
Glen Affric
Affric Lodge
Foyers
Invermoriston
White Bridge
Fort Augustus
Glen Mor
Monadhliath
Soay
Elgol
L. Eishort
KNOCK CASTLE
Teangue
Armadale
ARMADALE GARDENS
Sd. of Sleat
L. Hourn
Knoydart
L. Quoich
Tomdoun
Invergarry
L. Garry
Laggan
Drumgask
Canna
Loch Baghasdail
Sanday
Rùm
Kinloch
57°
The Small Isles
Pt. of Sleat
Mallaig
L. Nevis
Murlaggan
L. Arkaig
L. Lochy
Clunes
Gairlochy
Creag Meagaidh
1128
L. Laggan
Dalwhinnie
Sound of Rùm
Eigg
Arisaig
L. Morar
Glenfinnan
Roybridge
Spean Bridge
Galmisdale
LOCH NAN UAMH CAIRN
Lochailort
882
Rhois-Bheinn
Corpach
Caol
Muck
Morar, Moidart & Ardnamurchan
Shona I.
Kinlochmoidart
Loch Shiel
Fort William
1344
Ben Nevis
L. Treig
1148
Ben Alder
Loch Ericht
Grampian
Bagh a Chaisteil
Loch Baghasdail
Achosnich
Acharacle
Corran
Kinlochleven
Blackwater Res.
Rannoch Station
Kilchoan
MINGARY CASTLE
Salen
Strontian
Onich
Glencoe
Sorisdale
Ballyhaugh
Arinagour
Arileod
Coll
L. Sunart
Ballachulish
1150
Bidean Nam Bian
Ben Nevis & Glen Coe
L. Rannoch
Loch Rannoch & Glen Lyon
Tobermory
Drimnin
Loch Linnhe
Calgary
Dervaig
Sound of Mull
Portnacroish
Loch na Keal, Isle of Mull
Claggan
Lochaline
Lynn of Lorn
Loch Etive
Bridge of Orchy
Glen Lyon
Oskamull
Salen
Lismore I.
Gometra
Ulva
Craignure
ARDCHATTAN PRIORY
MULL
Connel
Bonawe
Ben Cruachan
KILCHURN CASTLE
SCOTLAND
Staffa
966
Ben More
Oban
Taynuilt
1126
Tyndrum
Ardchyle
Kerrera
Dalmally
1130
Crianlarich
Lochearnhead
Iona
Fionnphort
Pennyghael
GLENFEOCHAN GARDENS
Cladich
INISHAIL CHAPEL
Ben Lui
1174
Ben More
ST COLUMBA EXHIBITION
Bunessan
Kilninver
Firth of Lorn
Seil
Balvicar
Ardlui
Loch Lomond
Strathyre
Luing
Kilmelford
Loch Awe
ARDCHONNELL CASTLE
Cairndow
Stronachlachar
1011
Ben Ime
L. Katrine
Toberonochy
Inveraray
Tarbet
Scarba
FINCHAIRN CASTLE
Arrochar
974
Ben Lomond
Aird
Ford
Strachur
Lochgoilhead
Aberfoyle
GLEBE CAIRN
Kilmartin
The Trossachs
Loch Lomond
Luss
Colonsay
Garbhallt
CARRICK CASTLE
Garelochhead
Drymen
Jura
Scalasaig
ROCK MARKINGS
Ardlussa
Lochgilphead
Coulport
Helensburgh
Alexandria
56°
Oronsay
Ardrishaig
Knapdale
Otter Ferry
Kilcreggan
Sandbank
Gourock
Sd. of Jura
Dumbarton
Keillmore
Dunoon
Greenock
Port Glasgow
Clyde
785
Jura
Paps of Jura
Lagg
Loch Fyne
Tighnabruaich
Ardnave Pt.
Rhubodach
Innellan
Renfrew
Paisley
Sanaigmore
Port Askaig
Feolin Ferry
Craighouse
Portavadie
Port Bannatyne
Skelmorlie
Clyde-Muirsheil
Rothesay
Johnstone
Islay
Tarbert
Kilberry
Bute
Largs
Barrhead
Bridgend
Bowmore
Kennacraig
SKIPNESS CASTLE
Skipness
Millport
Kilbirnie
Port Charlotte
491
Ben Bheigeir
Claonaig
Kilchattan
Fairlie
Beith
Gigha
Lochranza
ST. BLANE'S CHAPEL
West Kilbride
Dalry
Dunlop
Portnahaven
Stewarton
Ardbeg
Pirnmill
874
Goat Fell
North Arran
Kilwinning
Fenwick
The Oa
Port Ellen
DISTILLERIES
Tayinloan
Ardrossan
Saltcoats
Kilmaurs
Kilmarnock
Mull of Oa
Arran
Brodick
Irvine
Hurlford
Galston
Glenbarr
Kilbrannan Sound
Troon
Saddell
Holy I.
Firth of Clyde
Monkton
Tarbolton
Mauchline
Prestwick
Blackwaterfoot
CARN BAN
Ayr
Ochiltree
0 10 20 miles
0 10 20 30 km
Dippen
Drongan
Machrihanish
Campbeltown
TORRYLINN CAIRN
Dalrymple
Patna
Maybole
CULZEAN CASTLE
Kirkoswald
Dalmellington
Rathlin Island
Southend
Causeway Coast
Benbane
6°
5°
Mull of Kintyre
Turnberry
Bellsbank
Doon

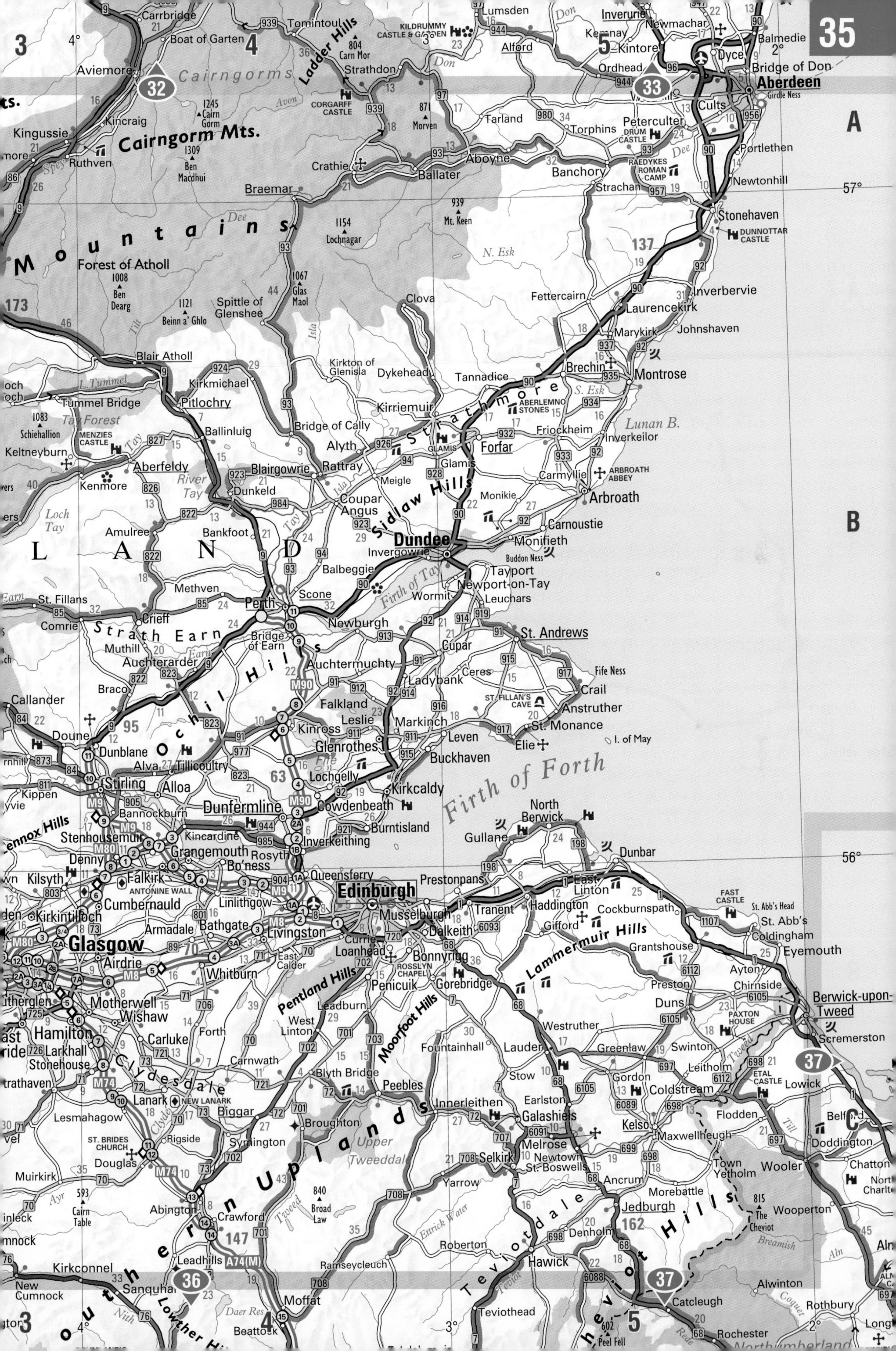
Cairngorms
Cairngorm Mts.
Mountains
Forest of Atholl
Ladder Hills
Carrbridge
Boat of Garten
Tomintoul
Aviemore
Kincraig
Kingussie
Ruthven
1245 Cairn Gorm
1309 Ben Macdhui
804 Carn Mor
Strathdon
KILDRUMMY CASTLE & GARDEN
CORGARFF CASTLE
871 Morven
Lumsden
Alford
Inverurie
Kemnay
Kintore
Newmachar
Dyce
Balmedie
Bridge of Don
Aberdeen
Girdle Ness
Ordhead
Westhill
Cults
Peterculter
DRUM CASTLE
Tarland
Torphins
Crathie
Ballater
Aboyne
Banchory
RAEDYKES ROMAN CAMP
Portlethen
Newtonhill
Strachan
Braemar
1154 Lochnagar
939 Mt. Keen
Stonehaven
DUNNOTTAR CASTLE
N. Esk
1008 Ben Dearg
1121 Beinn a' Ghlo
Spittal of Glenshee
1067 Glas Maol
Clova
Fettercairn
Inverbervie
Laurencekirk
Marykirk
Johnshaven
Blair Atholl
Kirkton of Glenisla
Dykehead
Tannadice
Brechin
Montrose
Kirkmichael
Pitlochry
L. Tummel
Tummel Bridge
1083 Schiehallion
Tay Forest
MENZIES CASTLE
Ballinluig
Kirriemuir
Strathmore
ABERLEMNO STONES
Friockheim
Inverkeilor
Lunan B.
Bridge of Cally
Alyth
GLAMIS
Glamis
Forfar
Keltneyburn
Aberfeldy
Kenmore
River Tay
Loch Tay
Dunkeld
Blairgowrie
Rattray
Meigle
Coupar Angus
Sidlaw Hills
Carmyllie
ARBROATH ABBEY
Arbroath
Monikie
Carnoustie
Monifieth
Buddon Ness
Amulree
Bankfoot
HIGHLAND
Dundee
Invergowrie
Balbeggie
Tayport
Newport-on-Tay
Wormit
Leuchars
Firth of Tay
Methven
Scone
Perth
St. Fillans
Comrie
Crieff
Strath Earn
Bridge of Earn
Newburgh
St. Andrews
Muthill
Auchterarder
Auchtermuchty
Cupar
Ceres
Fife Ness
Crail
Ochil Hills
Braco
Ladybank
Falkland
ST. FILLAN'S CAVE
Anstruther
St. Monance
Elie
I. of May
Callander
Doune
Dunblane
Kinross
Leslie
Markinch
Leven
Glenrothes
Buckhaven
Alva
Tillicoultry
Stirling
Alloa
Lochgelly
Kirkcaldy
Firth of Forth
Kippen
Bannockburn
Dunfermline
Cowdenbeath
Burntisland
Lennox Hills
Stenhousemuir
Kincardine
Inverkeithing
North Berwick
Gullane
Dunbar
Denny
Grangemouth
Rosyth
Bo'ness
Kilsyth
Falkirk
ANTONINE WALL
Queensferry
Prestonpans
Edinburgh
East Linton
Cumbernauld
Linlithgow
Tranent
Haddington
Cockburnspath
FAST CASTLE
St. Abb's Head
St. Abb's
Kirkintilloch
Armadale
Bathgate
Livingston
Musselburgh
Dalkeith
Gifford
Lammermuir Hills
Coldingham
Eyemouth
Glasgow
Airdrie
East Calder
Currie
Loanhead
Bonnyrigg
ROSSLYN CHAPEL
Grantshouse
Ayton
Whitburn
Penicuik
Gorebridge
Preston
Chirnside
Pentland Hills
Berwick-upon-Tweed
Rutherglen
Motherwell
Wishaw
Leadburn
Moorfoot Hills
Duns
PAXTON HOUSE
Scremerston
Hamilton
Carluke
Forth
West Linton
Westruther
Fountainhall
Lauder
Greenlaw
Swinton
Larkhall
Stonehouse
Clydesdale
Carnwath
Blyth Bridge
Peebles
Gordon
Leitholm
Coldstream
ETAL CASTLE
Lowick
Strathaven
Lanark
NEW LANARK
Biggar
Innerleithen
Stow
Earlston
Galashiels
Kelso
Flodden
Belford
Lesmahagow
Broughton
Southern Uplands
Melrose
Newtown St. Boswells
Maxwellheugh
Doddington
ST. BRIDES CHURCH
Douglas
Rigside
Symington
Upper Tweeddale
Selkirk
Town Yetholm
Wooler
Chatton
Muirkirk
Yarrow
Ancrum
Morebattle
593 Cairn Table
840 Broad Law
Abington
Crawford
Jedburgh
Cheviot Hills
815 The Cheviot
Wooperton
Tweed
Ettrick Water
Teviotdale
Roberton
Denholm
Breamish
Kirkconnel
Leadhills
Ramseycleuch
Hawick
Alnwick
New Cumnock
Sanquhar
Lowther Hills
Moffat
Teviothead
Catcleugh
Alwinton
Rothbury
Coquet
Daer Res.
Nith
Beattock
Peel Fell
Rochester
Northumberland
Ayr
Alwinton
A
B
C
57°
56°
4°
3°
2°

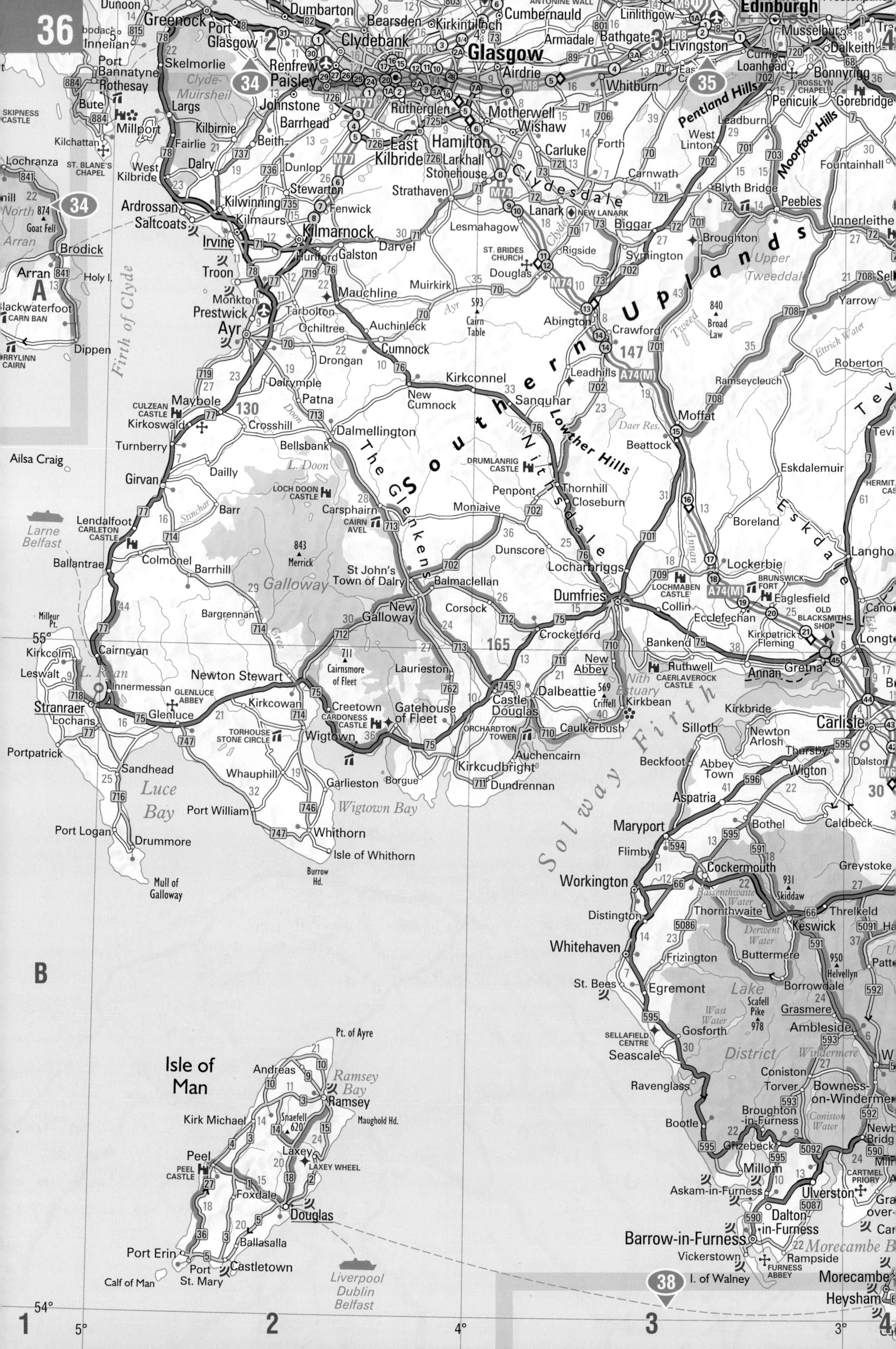
Dunoon
Greenock
Port Glasgow
Dumbarton
Bearsden
Kirkintilloch
Cumbernauld
ANTONINE WALL
Linlithgow
Edinburgh
Clydebank
Glasgow
Armadale
Bathgate
Livingston
Musselburgh
Dalkeith
Skelmorlie
Renfrew
Paisley
Airdrie
Whitburn
Currie
Loanhead
Bonnyrigg
Port Bannatyne
Rothesay
Clyde-Muirsheil
Johnstone
Barrhead
Rutherglen
Motherwell
Wishaw
Pentland Hills
Penicuik
ROSSLYN CHAPEL
Gorebridge
Bute
SKIPNESS CASTLE
Largs
Millport
Kilbirnie
East Kilbride
Hamilton
Leadburn
Moorfoot Hills
Kilchattan
Fairlie
Beith
Carluke
Forth
West Linton
Lochranza
ST. BLANE'S CHAPEL
West Kilbride
Dalry
Dunlop
Larkhall
Stonehouse
Fountainhall
Stewarton
Strathaven
Carnwath
Blyth Bridge
North Arran
Goat Fell
Ardrossan
Saltcoats
Kilwinning
Kilmaurs
Fenwick
Clydesdale
Lanark
NEW LANARK
Peebles
Innerleithen
Arran
Brodick
Kilmarnock
Irvine
Darvel
Lesmahagow
Biggar
Broughton
Troon
Hurlford
Galston
ST. BRIDES CHURCH
Rigside
Symington
Upper Tweeddale
Holy I.
Monkton
Prestwick
Mauchline
Muirkirk
Douglas
Selkirk
Blackwaterfoot
CARN BAN
Tarbolton
Ayr
Ochiltree
Auchinleck
Cairn Table
Abington
Crawford
Broad Law
Yarrow
Southern Uplands
Firth of Clyde
Dippen
Drongan
Cumnock
Tweed
Ettrick Water
Roberton
Dalrymple
Kirkconnel
Leadhills
Ramseycleuch
Maybole
CULZEAN CASTLE
Kirkoswald
Patna
Doon
New Cumnock
Sanquhar
Lowther Hills
Moffat
Crosshill
Dalmellington
Daer Res.
Turnberry
Bellsbank
Beattock
Ailsa Craig
Girvan
Dailly
L. Doon
LOCH DOON CASTLE
DRUMLANRIG CASTLE
The Glenkens
Nithsdale
Penpont
Thornhill
Closeburn
Eskdalemuir
HERMITAGE CASTLE
Lendalfoot
CARLETON CASTLE
Larne Belfast
Barr
Stinchar
Carsphairn
CAIRN AVEL
Moniaive
Boreland
Eskdale
Annan
Ballantrae
Colmonel
Barrhill
Merrick
St John's Town of Dalry
Dunscore
Locharbriggs
Langholm
Galloway
Balmaclellan
LOCHMABEN CASTLE
BRUNSWICK FORT
Lockerbie
Eaglesfield
Milleur Pt.
Bargrennan
New Galloway
Corsock
Dumfries
Collin
Ecclefechan
OLD BLACKSMITHS SHOP
Canonbie
Kirkcolm
Cairnryan
Cairnsmore of Fleet
Crocketford
New Abbey
Bankend
Kirkpatrick Fleming
Longtown
Leswalt
L. Ryan
Innermessan
Newton Stewart
Laurieston
Criffell
Ruthwell
CAERLAVEROCK CASTLE
Annan
Gretna
Nith Estuary
Stranraer
GLENLUCE ABBEY
Glenluce
Kirkcowan
Creetown
CARDONESS CASTLE
Gatehouse of Fleet
Castle Douglas
Dalbeattie
Kirkbean
Kirkbride
Carlisle
Lochans
TORHOUSE STONE CIRCLE
Wigtown
ORCHARDTON TOWER
Caulkerbush
Silloth
Newton Arlosh
Solway Firth
Portpatrick
Auchencairn
Kirkcudbright
Beckfoot
Abbey Town
Thursby
Dalston
Sandhead
Whauphill
Garlieston
Borgue
Dundrennan
Wigton
Luce Bay
Port William
Wigtown Bay
Aspatria
Port Logan
Drummore
Whithorn
Isle of Whithorn
Maryport
Bothel
Caldbeck
Flimby
Burrow Hd.
Cockermouth
Greystoke
Mull of Galloway
Workington
Bassenthwaite Water
Skiddaw
Thornthwaite
Threlkeld
Distington
Keswick
Derwent Water
Whitehaven
Frizington
Buttermere
Helvellyn
B
St. Bees
Egremont
Lake District
Scafell Pike
Borrowdale
Grasmere
Wast Water
SELLAFIELD CENTRE
Gosforth
Ambleside
Pt. of Ayre
Seascale
Windermere
Isle of Man
Andreas
Ramsey Bay
Ramsey
Ravenglass
Coniston
Torver
Bowness-on-Windermere
Kirk Michael
Snaefell
Maughold Hd.
Broughton-in-Furness
Coniston Water
Bootle
Newby Bridge
Laxey
LAXEY WHEEL
Peel
PEEL CASTLE
Grizebeck
Millom
CARTMEL PRIORY
Foxdale
Askam-in-Furness
Ulverston
Grange-over-Sands
Douglas
Dalton-in-Furness
Barrow-in-Furness
Morecambe Bay
Ballasalla
Port Erin
Castletown
Port St. Mary
Calf of Man
Liverpool Dublin Belfast
Vickerstown
Rampside
FURNESS ABBEY
I. of Walney
Morecambe
Heysham
34
35
38
A
1
2
3
4
5°
4°
3°
55°
54°

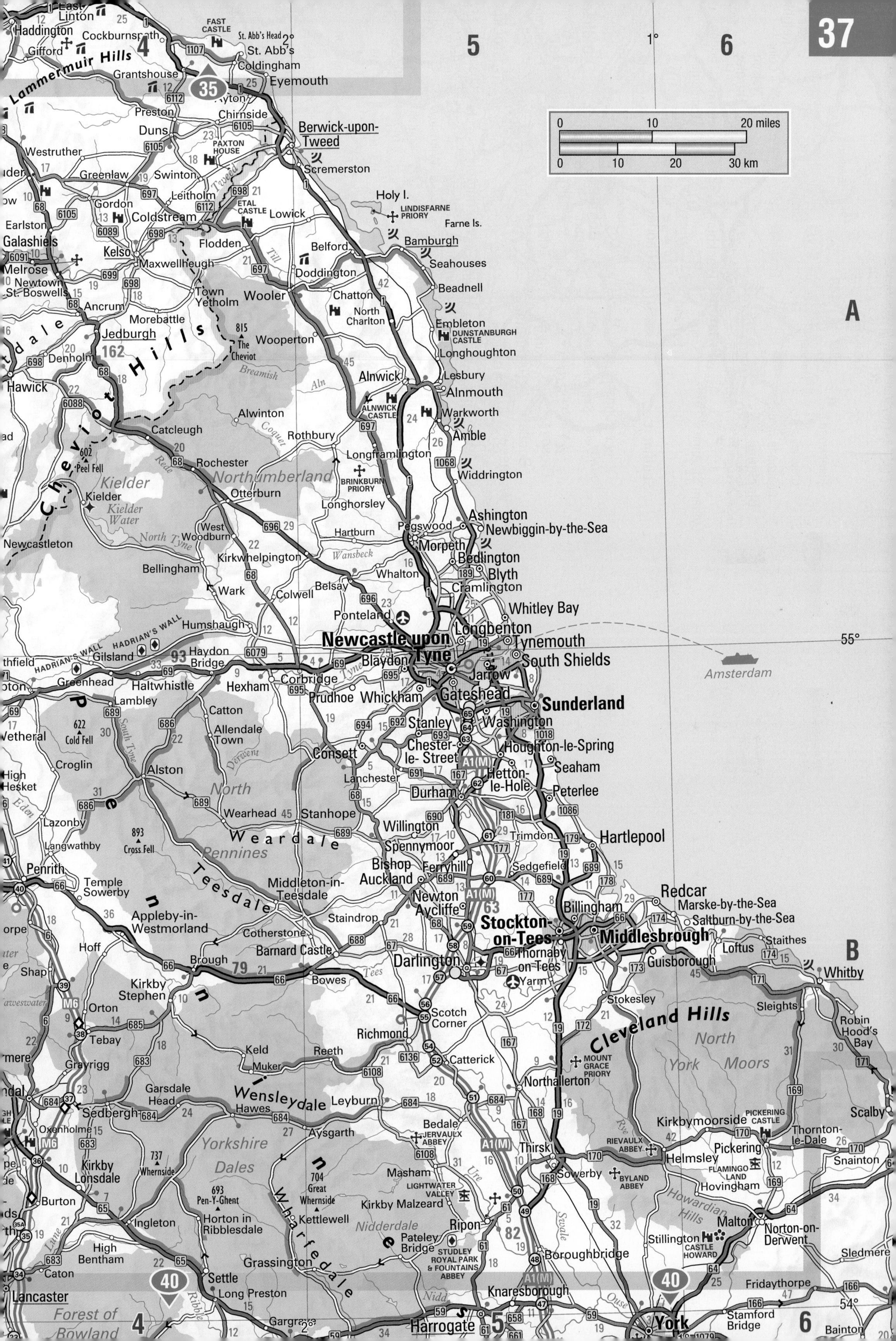
0 10 20 miles
0 10 20 30 km
Berwick-upon-Tweed
Holy I.
Lindisfarne Priory
Farne Is.
Bamburgh
Seahouses
Alnwick
Amble
Morpeth
Newcastle upon Tyne
Tynemouth
South Shields
Gateshead
Sunderland
Durham
Hartlepool
Redcar
Middlesbrough
Stockton-on-Tees
Darlington
Whitby
Cleveland Hills
North York Moors
Northallerton
Thirsk
Ripon
Harrogate
Knaresborough
York
Malton
Pickering
Scarborough
Lancaster
Kendal
Penrith
Hexham
Cheviot Hills
Kielder Water
Northumberland
Wensleydale
Yorkshire Dales
Amsterdam
55°
54°

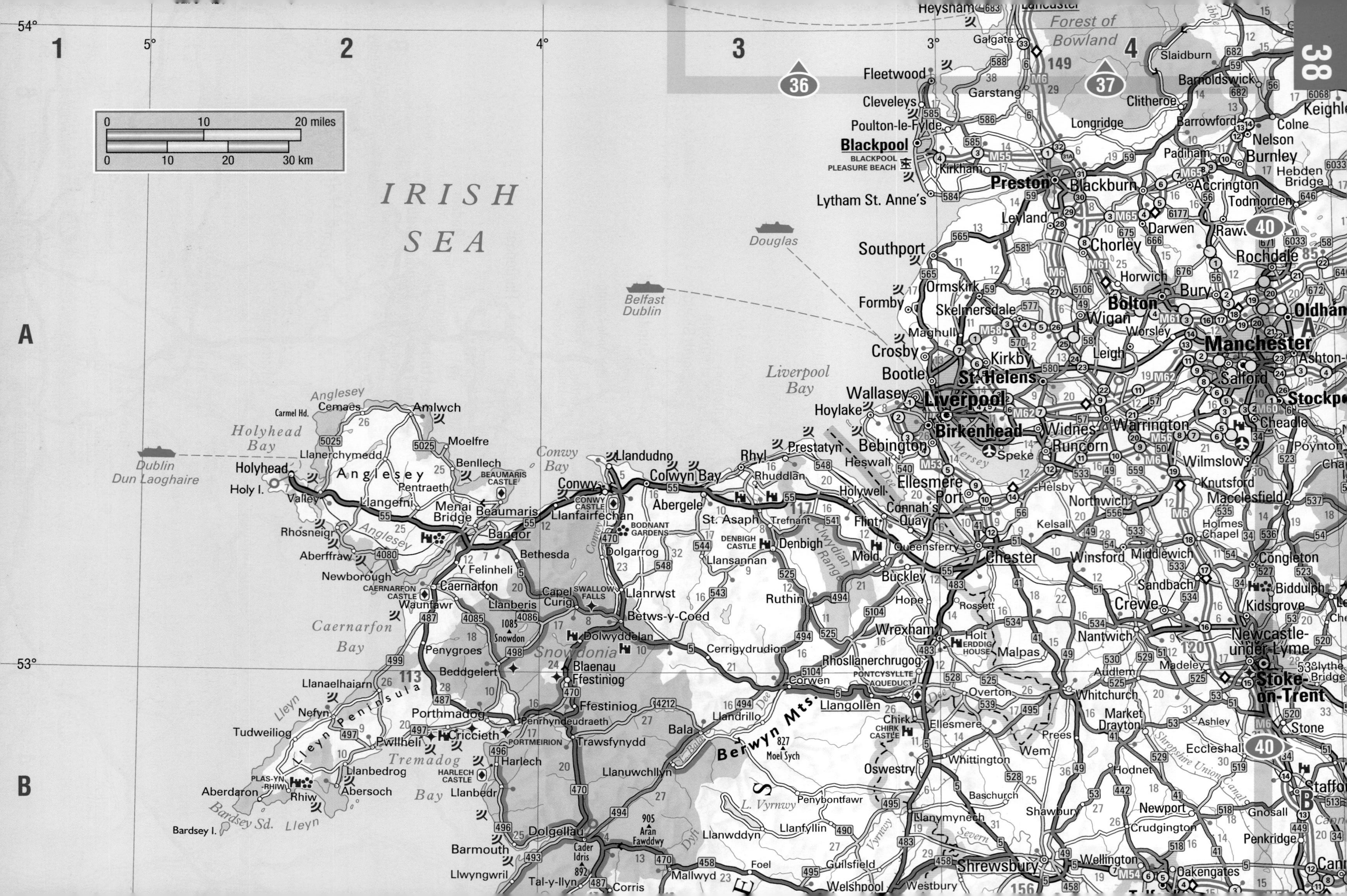

38
IRISH SEA
Liverpool Bay
Holyhead Bay
Conwy Bay
Caernarfon Bay
Tremadog Bay
Bardsey Sd.
Forest of Bowland
0 10 20 miles
0 10 20 30 km
Douglas
Belfast Dublin
Dublin Dun Laoghaire
Anglesey
Lleyn Peninsula
Snowdonia
Snowdon
Berwyn Mts.
Clwydian Range
Mersey
Dee
Severn
Holyhead
Holy I.
Valley
Rhosneigr
Aberffraw
Newborough
Cemaes
Amlwch
Moelfre
Benllech
Llanerchymedd
Llangefni
Pentraeth
Menai Bridge
Beaumaris
Bangor
Caernarfon
Y Felinheli
Bethesda
Llanberis
Capel Curig
Penygroes
Beddgelert
Porthmadog
Criccieth
Pwllheli
Nefyn
Tudweiliog
Llanaelhaearn
Llanbedrog
Abersoch
Aberdaron
Rhiw
Bardsey I.
Harlech
Llanbedr
Barmouth
Dolgellau
Cader Idris
Tal-y-llyn
Llwyngwril
Corris
Mallwyd
Bala
Blaenau Ffestiniog
Ffestiniog
Trawsfynydd
Llanuwchllyn
Betws-y-Coed
Dolwyddelan
Llanrwst
Dolgarrog
Conwy
Llandudno
Llanfairfechan
Colwyn Bay
Abergele
Rhyl
Prestatyn
Rhuddlan
St. Asaph
Denbigh
Trefnant
Llansannan
Ruthin
Cerrigydrudion
Corwen
Llandrillo
Llangollen
Mold
Flint
Holywell
Buckley
Hope
Wrexham
Rhosllanerchrugog
Chirk
Oswestry
Llanfyllin
Penybontfawr
Llanwddyn
Welshpool
Guilsfield
Llanymynech
Shrewsbury
Wellington
Newport
Market Drayton
Whitchurch
Wem
Ellesmere
Overton
Malpas
Holt
Chester
Queensferry
Connah's Quay
Ellesmere Port
Heswall
Hoylake
Wallasey
Birkenhead
Bebington
Liverpool
Bootle
Crosby
Formby
Southport
Ormskirk
Skelmersdale
Maghull
Kirkby
St. Helens
Wigan
Leigh
Widnes
Runcorn
Speke
Warrington
Helsby
Northwich
Winsford
Middlewich
Sandbach
Crewe
Nantwich
Audlem
Kelsall
Knutsford
Wilmslow
Macclesfield
Congleton
Biddulph
Kidsgrove
Newcastle-under-Lyme
Stoke-on-Trent
Madeley
Stone
Eccleshall
Gnosall
Penkridge
Oakengates
Manchester
Salford
Stockport
Cheadle
Oldham
Rochdale
Bury
Bolton
Horwich
Chorley
Darwen
Blackburn
Accrington
Burnley
Nelson
Colne
Todmorden
Preston
Leyland
Lytham St. Anne's
Blackpool
Kirkham
Poulton-le-Fylde
Cleveleys
Fleetwood
Garstang
Galgate
Heysham
Longridge
Clitheroe
Slaidburn
Barnoldswick
Barrowford
Padiham
Hebden Bridge
Keighley

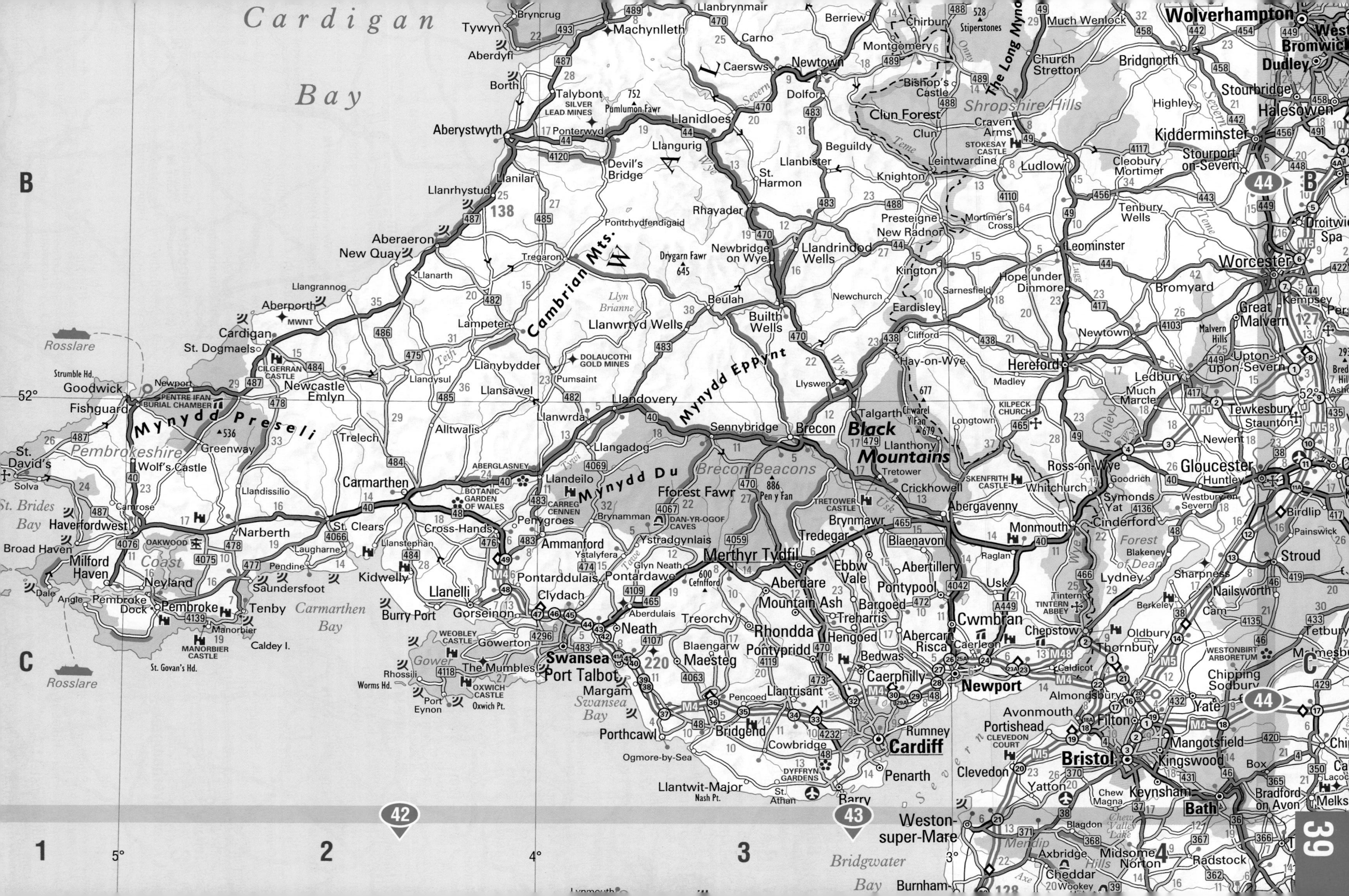

Cardigan Bay
Carmarthen Bay
Swansea Bay
Bridgwater Bay
St. Brides Bay
Cambrian Mts.
Mynydd Preseli
Mynydd Eppynt
Mynydd Du
Black Mountains
Brecon Beacons
Shropshire Hills
Clun Forest
Forest of Dean
Pembrokeshire Coast
Gower
Mendip Hills
Aberystwyth
Cardigan
Carmarthen
Swansea
Cardiff
Newport
Bristol
Bath
Hereford
Gloucester
Worcester
Wolverhampton
Kidderminster
Merthyr Tydfil
Brecon
Llandovery
Lampeter
Haverfordwest
Milford Haven
Pembroke
Tenby
Fishguard
Llanelli
Neath
Port Talbot
Bridgend
Rhondda
Pontypridd
Caerphilly
Cwmbran
Abergavenny
Monmouth
Ross-on-Wye
Chepstow
Leominster
Ludlow
Llandrindod Wells
Builth Wells
Rhayader
Llanidloes
Newtown
Machynlleth
Weston-super-Mare
Rosslare
B
C
1
2
3
4
5°
4°
3°
52°
42
43
44
138
39

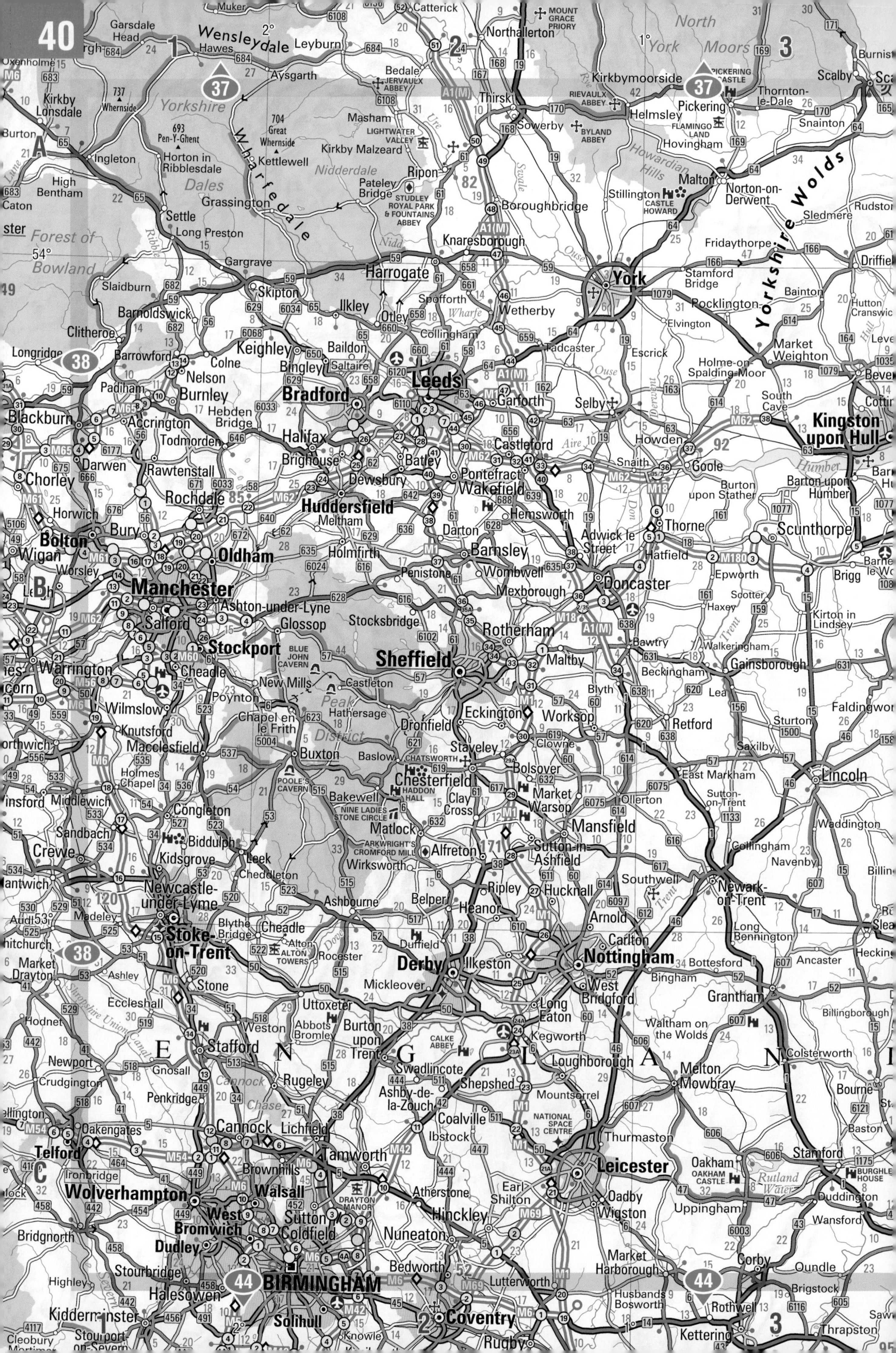
Wensleydale
Hawes
Leyburn
Catterick
Northallerton
MOUNT GRACE PRIORY
North York Moors
Garsdale Head
Oxenholme
Aysgarth
Bedale
JERVAULX ABBEY
Thirsk
RIEVAULX ABBEY
Kirkbymoorside
Helmsley
PICKERING CASTLE
Pickering
Thornton-le-Dale
Scalby
Snainton
Kirkby Lonsdale
Whernside
Yorkshire
Masham
LIGHTWATER VALLEY
Sowerby
BYLAND ABBEY
FLAMINGO LAND
Hovingham
Burton
Pen-Y-Ghent
Great Whernside
Horton in Ribblesdale
Kettlewell
Kirkby Malzeard
Wharfedale
Ingleton
Nidderdale
Ripon
Howardian Hills
High Bentham
Dales
Pateley Bridge
STUDLEY ROYAL PARK & FOUNTAINS ABBEY
Boroughbridge
Stillington
CASTLE HOWARD
Malton
Norton-on-Derwent
Yorkshire Wolds
Caton
Grassington
Settle
Long Preston
Sledmere
Rudston
Forest of Bowland
Knaresborough
Fridaythorpe
Driffield
Gargrave
Harrogate
York
Stamford Bridge
Slaidburn
Skipton
Spofforth
Wetherby
Bainton
Pocklington
Hutton Cranswick
Barnoldswick
Ilkley
Otley
Collingham
Elvington
Clitheroe
Keighley
Baildon
Tadcaster
Escrick
Market Weighton
Longridge
Barrowford
Colne
Bingley
Saltaire
Leeds
Holme-on-Spalding-Moor
Nelson
Padiham
Burnley
Bradford
Garforth
Selby
South Cave
Blackburn
Accrington
Hebden Bridge
Halifax
Castleford
Howden
Kingston upon Hull
Todmorden
Brighouse
Batley
Pontefract
Snaith
Goole
Humber
Darwen
Rawtenstall
Dewsbury
Wakefield
Burton upon Stather
Barton upon Humber
Chorley
Rochdale
Huddersfield
Hemsworth
Thorne
Scunthorpe
Horwich
Meltham
Darton
Adwick le Street
Bury
Barnsley
Hatfield
Bolton
Wigan
Oldham
Holmfirth
Epworth
Brigg
Worsley
Penistone
Wombwell
Doncaster
Manchester
Mexborough
Scotter
Haxey
Kirton in Lindsey
Salford
Ashton-under-Lyne
Glossop
Stocksbridge
Rotherham
Bawtry
Stockport
BLUE JOHN CAVERN
Sheffield
Maltby
Walkeringham
Warrington
Cheadle
Beckingham
Gainsborough
New Mills
Castleton
Blyth
Poynton
Wilmslow
Hathersage
Peak District
Eckington
Worksop
Lea
Retford
Knutsford
Chapel en le Frith
Dronfield
Sturton
Faldingworth
Macclesfield
Buxton
Baslow
Staveley
Clowne
Saxilby
CHATSWORTH
Bolsover
East Markham
Lincoln
Holmes Chapel
Chesterfield
POOLE'S CAVERN
HADDON HALL
Bakewell
Market Warsop
Ollerton
Sutton-on-Trent
Middlewich
Clay Cross
Congleton
NINE LADIES STONE CIRCLE
Matlock
Mansfield
Waddington
Sandbach
Biddulph
Sutton-in-Ashfield
Collingham
Crewe
Kidsgrove
ARKWRIGHT'S CROMFORD MILL
Alfreton
Navenby
Leek
Wirksworth
Southwell
Nantwich
Cheddleton
Ripley
Hucknall
Newark-on-Trent
Newcastle-under-Lyme
Ashbourne
Belper
Heanor
Arnold
Madeley
Blythe Bridge
Cheadle
Carlton
Long Bennington
Stoke-on-Trent
Alton
ALTON TOWERS
Rocester
Duffield
Nottingham
Bottesford
Ancaster
Market Drayton
Ashley
Derby
Ilkeston
Bingham
Stone
Mickleover
West Bridgford
Grantham
Eccleshall
Uttoxeter
Long Eaton
Billingborough
Hodnet
Weston
Abbots Bromley
Burton upon Trent
CALKE ABBEY
Kegworth
Waltham on the Wolds
Stafford
Newport
Gnosall
Swadlincote
Loughborough
Melton Mowbray
Colsterworth
Crudgington
Rugeley
Ashby-de-la-Zouch
Shepshed
Bourne
Penkridge
Cannock Chase
Mountsorrel
Coalville
NATIONAL SPACE CENTRE
Thurmaston
Baston
Oakengates
Cannock
Lichfield
Ibstock
Telford
Tamworth
Leicester
Oakham
OAKHAM CASTLE
Stamford
BURGHLEY HOUSE
Ironbridge
Brownhills
Rutland Water
Wolverhampton
Walsall
DRAYTON MANOR
Atherstone
Earl Shilton
Oadby
Duddington
West Bromwich
Sutton Coldfield
Hinckley
Wigston
Uppingham
Wansford
Bridgnorth
Dudley
Nuneaton
Stourbridge
BIRMINGHAM
Bedworth
Lutterworth
Market Harborough
Corby
Oundle
Highley
Halesowen
Husbands Bosworth
Brigstock
Rothwell
Kidderminster
Solihull
Coventry
Kettering
Thrapston
Cleobury Mortimer
Stourport-on-Severn
Knowle
Rugby
E
N
G
L
A
N
D

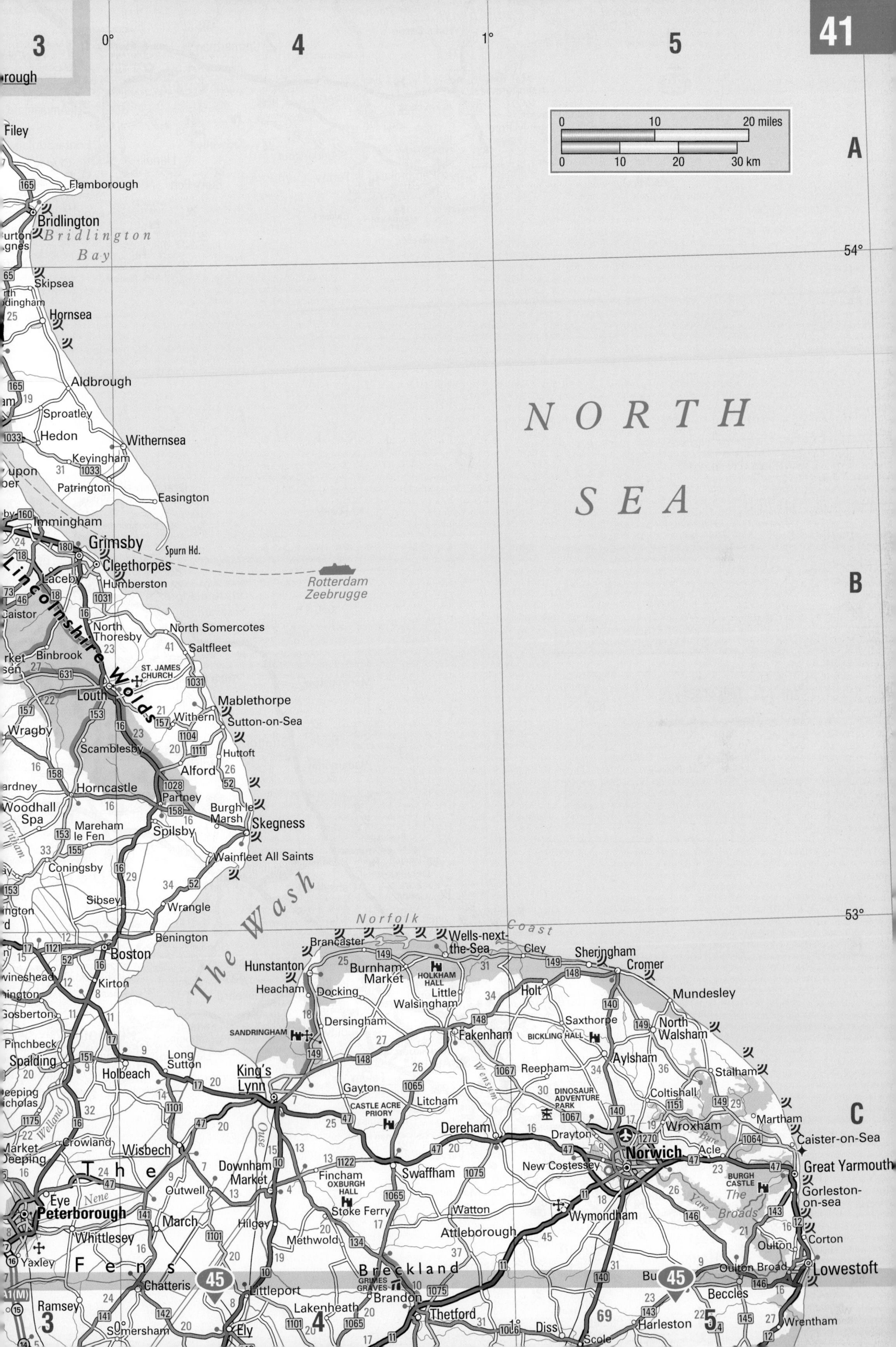

3   0°   4   1°   5

A

54°

B

N O R T H

S E A

Filey

165 Flamborough
Bridlington
Bridlington Bay
rough
rton gnes
65 Skipsea
rth dingham
25 Hornsea
165 Aldbrough
am 19
Sproatley
Hedon
1033 Keyingham
Withernsea
31 1033
upon Patrington
ber
Easington
by 160
Immingham
24 180 Grimsby   Spurn Hd.
18   Cleethorpes
Laceby
73 46   Humberston
Caistor   1031
Rotterdam
Zeebrugge
North   North Somercotes
Thoresby   Saltfleet
rket Binbrook   23
sen   27   ST. JAMES CHURCH
631   1031
157   Louth   21   Mablethorpe
Wragby   153   157   Withern   Sutton-on-Sea
16   23   1104
Scamblesby   20   111   Huttoft
16   158   Alford   26
ardney   Horncastle   1028   52
Woodhall   16   Partney
Spa   153   158   Burgh le
Mareham   16   Spilsby   Marsh   Skegness
le Fen   16
33   155
Coningsby   16   29   Wainfleet All Saints
153
ngton   12   34   52
d   Sibsey   Wrangle
ay   17   Benington
17   1121   Boston
15   52   16
wineshead   12   Kirton
12   8
ngton
Gosberton
Pinchbeck   17   9   Long
Spalding   151   Sutton
20   9   Holbeach
14   17
eping   1101   47   20
icholas   32
1175   Crowland   47
22   The
Market   Wisbech
eeping   16   24
Eye   Nene
Peterborough   141   March
Whittlesey   16
16   Yaxley   F e n s
3   Ramsey   141   142
15   S   omersham

53°

Norfolk   Coast
Brancaster   Wells-next-   Cley
149   the-Sea   Sheringham
Hunstanton   25 Burnham   148   Cromer
Heacham   Market   31   HOLKHAM
Docking   HALL   Mundesley
Little   34   Holt
18   Walsingham   140
Dersingham   148   Saxthorpe   North
SANDRINGHAM   27   Fakenham   BICKLING HALL   149   Walsham
149   Reepham   Aylsham
King's   148   26   1067   30   Coltishall
Long   Lynn   1065   DINOSAUR   140   151
Sutton   7   Gayton   Litcham   ADVENTURE   34   149   29
25   PARK   Wroxham   Martham
20   CASTLE ACRE   1067   19   The
PRIORY   Dereham   16   Drayton   47   Acle   Broads   Caister-on-Sea
13   47   New Costessey   23   BURGH   47   Great Yarmouth
Downham   1122   Swaffham   1075   Norwich   CASTLE   Gorleston-
Market   OXBURGH   1065   146   on-sea
Outwell   HALL   Watton   Wymondham   143   Corton
13   Stoke Ferry   45   21   Oulton
Hilgay   20   37   31   140   Oulton Broad   Lowestoft
Methwold   1065   Attleborough   11   146
134   11   18   Bu
Breckland   140
45   GRIMES   10   1075   45
Chatteris   GRAVES   69   Beccles
Littleport   Brandon   23   145
4   Lakenheath   20   Thetford   31   143   Harleston   27   Wrentham
Ely   1101   1065   11   106   Diss   4   12
17   Scole   5

Wismal

The Wash

Norfolk   Coast

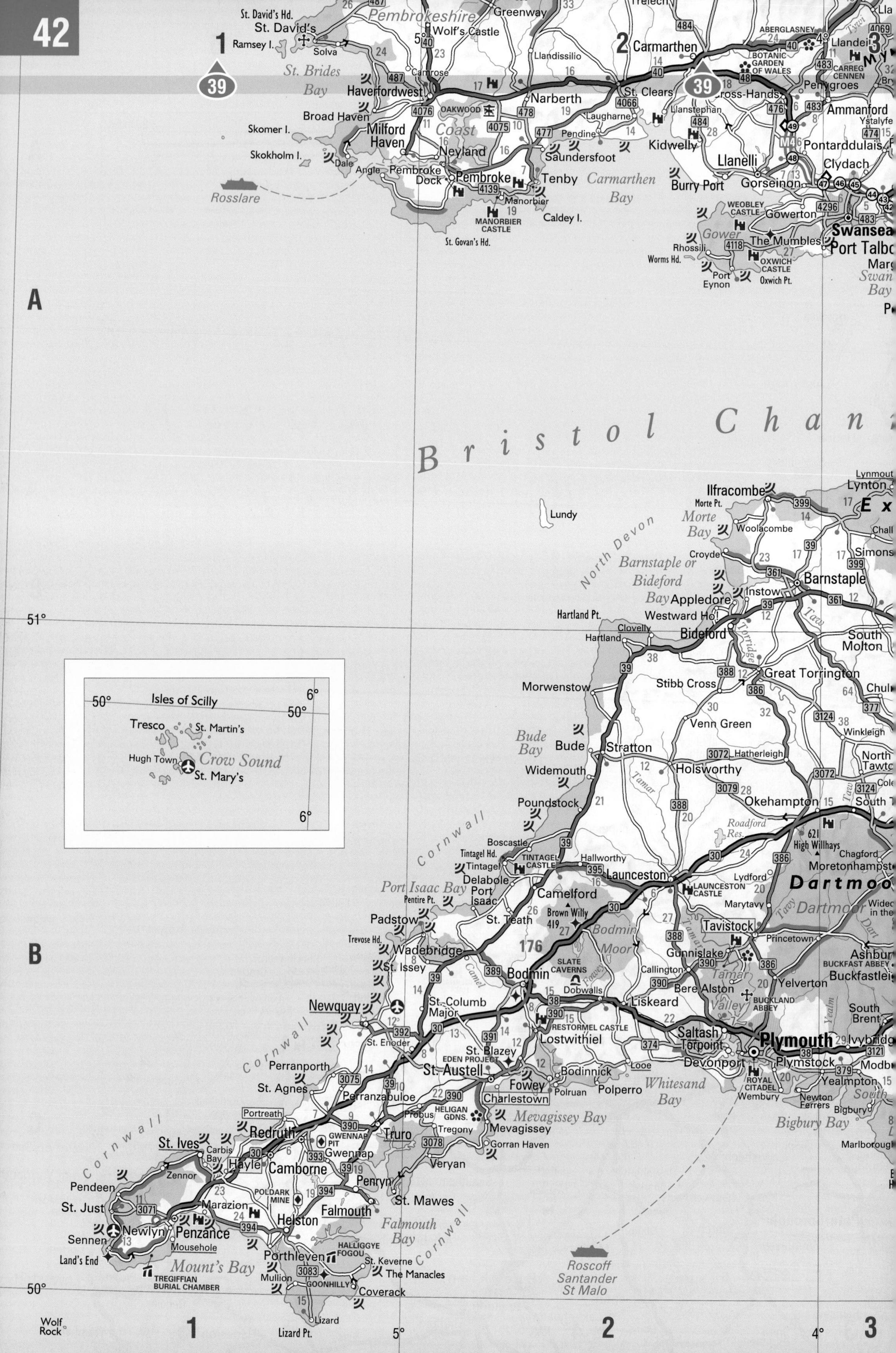
1
2
3
A
B
St. David's Hd.
St. David's
Ramsey I.
Solva
Pembrokeshire
Greenway
Wolf's Castle
Llandissilio
Carmarthen
Aberglasney
Llandeilo
Botanic Garden of Wales
Carreg Cennen
Penygroes
Ammanford
St. Brides Bay
Camrose
Haverfordwest
Narberth
St. Clears
Cross-Hands
Broad Haven
Oakwood
Coast
Laugharne
Llanstephan
Skomer I.
Milford Haven
Pendine
Kidwelly
Pontarddulais
Skokholm I.
Dale
Neyland
Saundersfoot
Llanelli
Clydach
Angle
Pembroke Dock
Pembroke
Tenby
Carmarthen Bay
Burry Port
Gorseinon
Rosslare
Manorbier
Manorbier Castle
Caldey I.
Weobley Castle
Gowerton
Swansea
St. Govan's Hd.
Gower
The Mumbles
Port Talbot
Rhossili
Oxwich Castle
Worms Hd.
Port Eynon
Oxwich Pt.
Swansea Bay
Bristol Channel
Lynmouth
Lynton
Ilfracombe
Morte Pt.
Exmoor
Lundy
Morte Bay
Woolacombe
North Devon
Croyde
Barnstaple or Bideford Bay
Instow
Barnstaple
Appledore
Hartland Pt.
Westward Ho!
Clovelly
Hartland
Bideford
Torridge
South Molton
Great Torrington
Stibb Cross
Morwenstow
Venn Green
Winkleigh
Bude Bay
Bude
Stratton
Hatherleigh
North Tawton
Widemouth
Holsworthy
Tamar
Okehampton
Poundstock
Roadford Res.
Cornwall
Boscastle
High Willhays
Chagford
Tintagel Hd.
Tintagel
Tintagel Castle
Hallworthy
Launceston
Moretonhampstead
Delabole
Port Isaac Bay
Port Isaac
Camelford
Lydford
Launceston Castle
Dartmoor
Pentire Pt.
Marytavy
Brown Willy 419
St. Teath
Tavistock
Padstow
Bodmin Moor
Princetown
Trevose Hd.
Wadebridge
Gunnislake
Ashburton
St. Issey
Slate Caverns
Callington
Buckfast Abbey
Buckfastleigh
Camel
Bodmin
Fowey
Bere Alston
Yelverton
Dobwalls
Tamar Valley
Buckland Abbey
Newquay
St. Columb Major
Liskeard
South Brent
Restormel Castle
Saltash
Lostwithiel
Torpoint
Plymouth
Ivybridge
St. Enoder
Eden Project
St. Blazey
Devonport
Plymstock
Perranporth
St. Austell
Bodinnick
Looe
Royal Citadel
Yealmpton
St. Agnes
Fowey
Polperro
Whitesand Bay
Wembury
Newton Ferrers
Perranzabuloe
Polruan
Charlestown
Bigbury
Portreath
Probus
Heligan Gdns.
Mevagissey Bay
Redruth
Truro
Tregony
Mevagissey
Bigbury Bay
St. Ives
Carbis Bay
Gwennap Pit
Gwennap
Gorran Haven
Marlborough
Hayle
Camborne
Veryan
Zennor
Penryn
Pendeen
Poldark Mine
St. Mawes
St. Just
Marazion
Falmouth
Newlyn
Penzance
Helston
Falmouth Bay
Sennen
Mousehole
Halliggye Fogou
Land's End
Mount's Bay
Porthleven
St. Keverne
Tregiffian Burial Chamber
Mullion
The Manacles
Goonhilly
Coverack
Roscoff
Santander
St Malo
Wolf Rock
Lizard
Lizard Pt.
Isles of Scilly
Tresco
St. Martin's
Hugh Town
Crow Sound
St. Mary's
51°
50°
6°
5°
4°

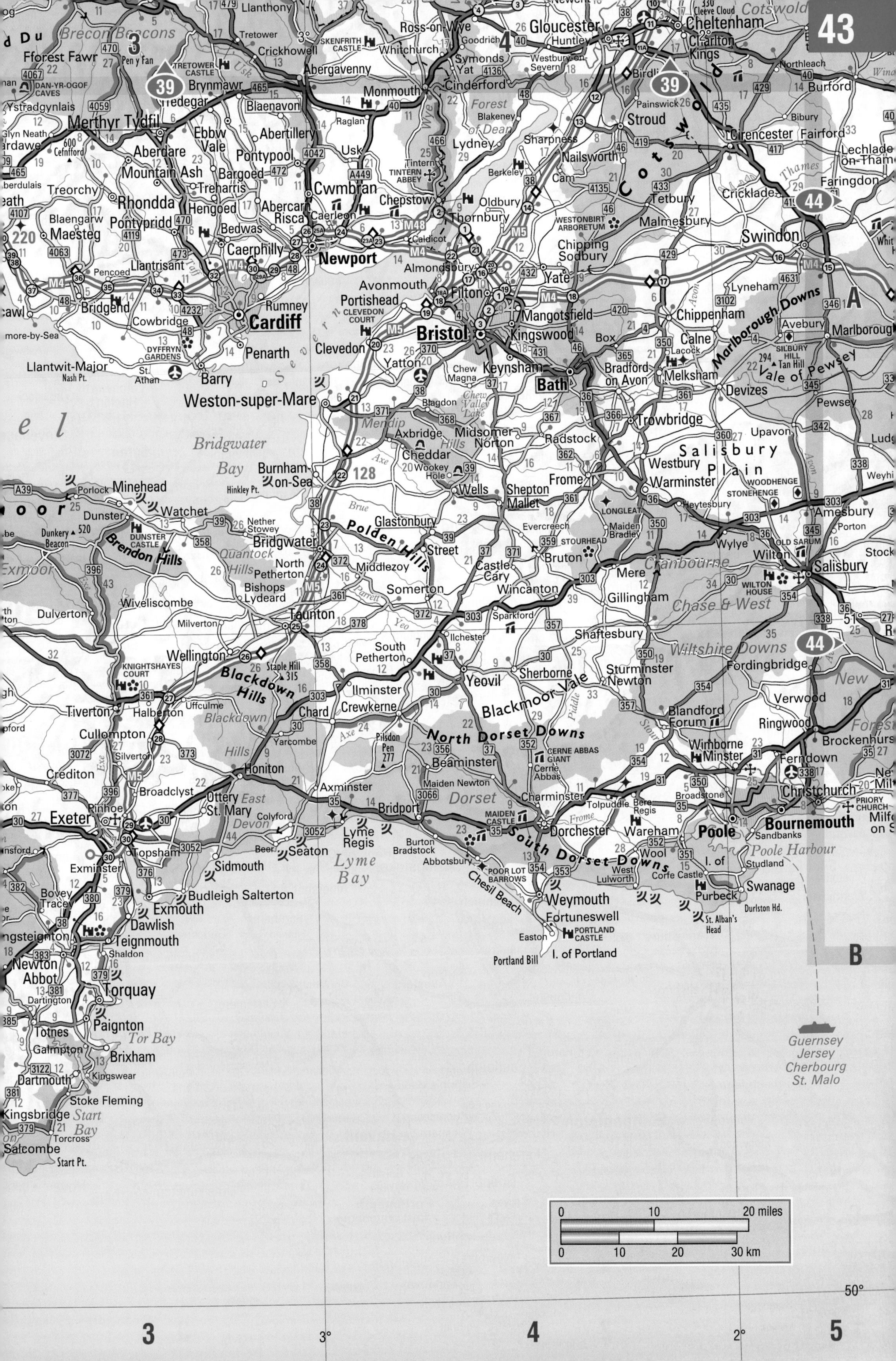
Brecon Beacons
Fforest Fawr
Pen y Fan
DAN-YR-OGOF CAVES
Ystradgynlais
Merthyr Tydfil
Tredegar
Brynmawr
Blaenavon
Abergavenny
Crickhowell
Llanthony
Tretower
TRETOWER CASTLE
Glyn Neath
Aberdare
Mountain Ash
Ebbw Vale
Abertillery
Pontypool
Bargoed
Treharris
Treorchy
Rhondda
Pontypridd
Hengoed
Abercarn
Risca
Bedwas
Caerphilly
Maesteg
Blaengarw
Llantrisant
Pencoed
Bridgend
Cowbridge
Cardiff
Penarth
Barry
Rumney
Newport
Caerleon
Cwmbran
Usk
Raglan
Monmouth
Chepstow
Tintern
TINTERN ABBEY
SKENFRITH CASTLE
Whitchurch
Ross-on-Wye
Goodrich
Symonds Yat
Cinderford
Forest of Dean
Blakeney
Lydney
Gloucester
Huntley
Westbury-on-Severn
Cheltenham
Charlton Kings
Cleeve Cloud
Cotswold
Northleach
Burford
Birdlip
Painswick
Stroud
Bibury
Cirencester
Fairford
Lechlade-on-Thames
Thames
Faringdon
Cricklade
Tetbury
Malmesbury
Swindon
Sharpness
Nailsworth
Berkeley
Cam
Oldbury
Thornbury
WESTONBIRT ARBORETUM
Chipping Sodbury
Yate
Caldicot
Almondsbury
Avonmouth
Portishead
Filton
CLEVEDON COURT
Clevedon
Bristol
Mangotsfield
Kingswood
Keynsham
Bath
Yatton
Chew Magna
Chew Valley Lake
Blagdon
Weston-super-Mare
Lyneham
Chippenham
Marlborough Downs
Avebury
Marlborough
SILBURY HILL
Tan Hill
Vale of Pewsey
Calne
Lacock
Box
Bradford on Avon
Melksham
Devizes
Pewsey
Trowbridge
Upavon
Ludgershall
Radstock
Midsomer Norton
Mendip Hills
Axbridge
Cheddar
Wookey Hole
Wells
Shepton Mallet
Frome
Westbury
Warminster
Salisbury Plain
WOODHENGE
STONEHENGE
Heytesbury
LONGLEAT
Maiden Bradley
Amesbury
Porton
OLD SARUM
Wilton
WILTON HOUSE
Salisbury
Wylye
Stourhead
Bruton
Evercreech
Castle Cary
Wincanton
Mere
Gillingham
Cranborne Chase & West Wiltshire Downs
Shaftesbury
Fordingbridge
New Forest
Verwood
Ringwood
Bridgwater Bay
Burnham-on-Sea
Hinkley Pt.
Minehead
Porlock
Dunster
DUNSTER CASTLE
Watchet
Dunkery Beacon
Exmoor
Brendon Hills
Nether Stowey
Quantock Hills
Bridgwater
North Petherton
Bishops Lydeard
Wiveliscombe
Dulverton
Milverton
Taunton
Glastonbury
Polden Hills
Street
Middlezoy
Somerton
Sparkford
Ilchester
South Petherton
Wellington
Staple Hill
Blackdown Hills
KNIGHTSHAYES COURT
Tiverton
Halberton
Uffculme
Cullompton
Silverton
Crediton
Ilminster
Chard
Crewkerne
Yeovil
Sherborne
Sturminster Newton
Blackmoor Vale
Blandford Forum
Yarcombe
Pilsdon Pen
North Dorset Downs
Beaminster
Maiden Newton
CERNE ABBAS GIANT
Cerne Abbas
Wimborne Minster
Ferndown
Brockenhurst
Christchurch
PRIORY CHURCH
Milford on Sea
Bournemouth
Poole
Poole Harbour
Sandbanks
Studland
Broadstone
Honiton
Axminster
Ottery St. Mary
East Devon
Colyford
Broadclyst
Pinhoe
Exeter
Topsham
Exminster
Sidmouth
Seaton
Beer
Lyme Regis
Lyme Bay
Bridport
Dorset
Burton Bradstock
Abbotsbury
MAIDEN CASTLE
Charminster
Dorchester
Tolpuddle
Bere Regis
Wareham
Wool
POOR LOT BARROWS
South Dorset Downs
Chesil Beach
Weymouth
West Lulworth
Corfe Castle
I. of Purbeck
Swanage
Durlston Hd.
St. Alban's Head
Fortuneswell
PORTLAND CASTLE
Easton
Portland Bill
I. of Portland
Budleigh Salterton
Exmouth
Bovey Tracey
Dawlish
Teignmouth
Shaldon
Kingsteignton
Newton Abbot
Torquay
Dartington
Paignton
Tor Bay
Totnes
Galmpton
Brixham
Kingswear
Dartmouth
Stoke Fleming
Kingsbridge
Start Bay
Torcross
Salcombe
Start Pt.
Llantwit-Major
Nash Pt.
St. Athan
DYFFRYN GARDENS
Guernsey
Jersey
Cherbourg
St. Malo
0
10
20 miles
0
10
20
30 km
50°
3°
2°
3
4
5
A
B
39
44

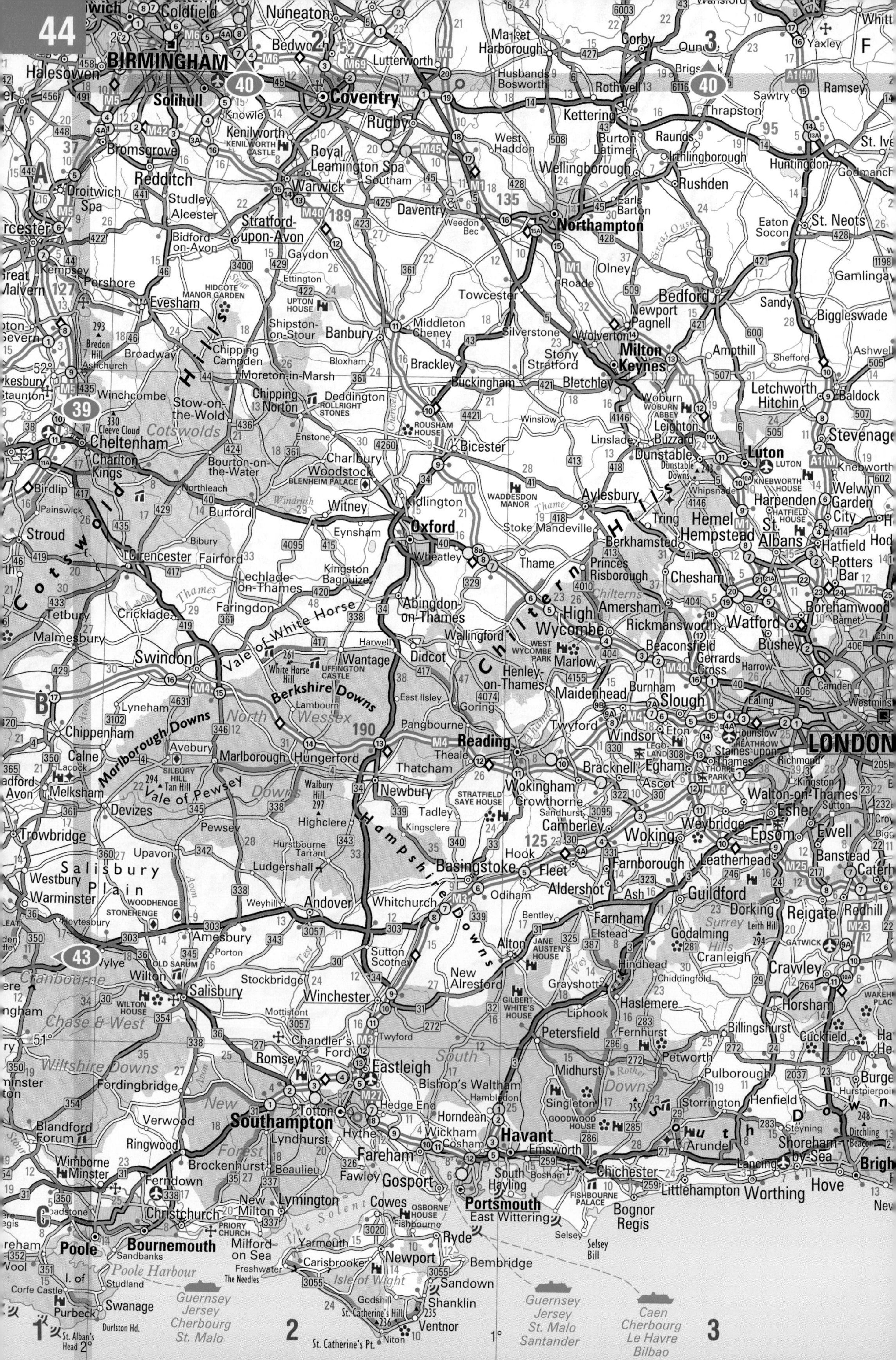
BIRMINGHAM
Solihull
Halesowen
Coventry
Nuneaton
Bedworth
Lutterworth
Market Harborough
Husbands Bosworth
Corby
Oundle
Yaxley
Ramsey
Sawtry
Kettering
Rothwell
Thrapston
Rugby
Kenilworth
Kenilworth Castle
Royal Leamington Spa
Southam
Warwick
Bromsgrove
Redditch
Droitwich Spa
Studley
Alcester
Stratford-upon-Avon
Bidford-on-Avon
Daventry
Weedon Bec
West Haddon
Wellingborough
Burton Latimer
Raunds
Irthlingborough
Rushden
Huntingdon
St. Neots
Eaton Socon
Northampton
Earls Barton
Olney
Gaydon
Evesham
Pershore
Great Malvern
Kempsey
Hidcote Manor Garden
Ettington
Upton House
Shipston-on-Stour
Banbury
Middleton Cheney
Towcester
Roade
Bedford
Newport Pagnell
Sandy
Biggleswade
Gamlingay
Broadway
Chipping Campden
Bredon Hill
Ashchurch
Tewkesbury
Winchcombe
Stow-on-the-Wold
Moreton-in-Marsh
Bloxham
Brackley
Silverstone
Stony Stratford
Wolverton
Milton Keynes
Ampthill
Shefford
Chipping Norton
Rollright Stones
Deddington
Buckingham
Bletchley
Woburn
Woburn Abbey
Letchworth
Hitchin
Baldock
Cheltenham
Cleeve Cloud
Cotswolds
Rousham House
Winslow
Leighton Buzzard
Linslade
Stevenage
Charlton Kings
Bourton-on-the-Water
Enstone
Charlbury
Bicester
Dunstable
Dunstable Downs
Luton
Knebworth House
Birdlip
Northleach
Woodstock
Blenheim Palace
Waddesdon Manor
Aylesbury
Whipsnade
Harpenden
Welwyn Garden City
Painswick
Stroud
Burford
Windrush
Witney
Kidlington
Oxford
Thame
Stoke Mandeville
Tring
Hemel Hempstead
St. Albans
Hatfield House
Hatfield
Cotswold
Bibury
Cirencester
Fairford
Eynsham
Wheatley
Berkhamsted
Chesham
Potters Bar
Lechlade-on-Thames
Kingston Bagpuize
Princes Risborough
Chilterns
Amersham
Borehamwood
Barnet
Tetbury
Cricklade
Faringdon
Abingdon-on-Thames
High Wycombe
Rickmansworth
Watford
Malmesbury
Vale of White Horse
Harwell
Wallingford
Chiltern Hills
Beaconsfield
Bushey
Swindon
White Horse Hill
Uffington Castle
Wantage
Didcot
West Wycombe Park
Marlow
Henley-on-Thames
Gerrards Cross
Harrow
Camden
Berkshire Downs
Lambourn
East Ilsley
Goring
Maidenhead
Burnham
Slough
Ealing
Westminster
Lyneham
Chippenham
North Wessex
Pangbourne
Reading
Twyford
Windsor
Eton
Hounslow
Heathrow
LONDON
Marlborough Downs
Avebury
Calne
Lacock
Marlborough
Hungerford
Thatcham
Theale
Lego Land
Egham
Staines-upon-Thames
Richmond
Silbury Hill
Tan Hill
Melksham
Vale of Pewsey
Devizes
Walbury Hill
Newbury
Wokingham
Bracknell
Ascot
Thorpe Park
Kingston
Walton-on-Thames
Esher
Sutton
Crowthorne
Stratfield Saye House
Sandhurst
Camberley
Tadley
Kingsclere
Highclere
Pewsey
Hampshire Downs
Woking
Weybridge
Epsom
Ewell
Trowbridge
Upavon
Hurstbourne Tarrant
Ludgershall
Basingstoke
Hook
Fleet
Farnborough
Leatherhead
Banstead
Caterham
Salisbury Plain
Westbury
Warminster
Heytesbury
Woodhenge
Stonehenge
Andover
Weyhill
Whitchurch
Odiham
Aldershot
Ash
Guildford
Dorking
Reigate
Redhill
Amesbury
Porton
Bentley
Farnham
Elstead
Godalming
Surrey Hills
Leith Hill
Gatwick
Alton
Jane Austen's House
Cranleigh
Crawley
Old Sarum
Wilton
Wylye
Sutton Scotney
Hindhead
Chiddingfold
Stockbridge
Cranborne Chase & West
Salisbury
Wilton House
New Alresford
Grayshott
Horsham
Wakehurst Place
Winchester
Haslemere
Liphook
Gilbert White's House
Mottisfont
Twyford
Chandler's Ford
Petersfield
Fernhurst
Billingshurst
Cuckfield
Wiltshire Downs
Romsey
Eastleigh
South Downs
Bishop's Waltham
Midhurst
Petworth
Pulborough
Fordingbridge
Hambledon
Henfield
Hurstpierpoint
Blandford Forum
Verwood
New Forest
Southampton
Totton
Hedge End
Horndean
Singleton
Goodwood House
Storrington
Steyning
Ditchling Beacon
Ringwood
Lyndhurst
Hythe
Wickham
Cosham
Havant
Emsworth
Arundel
Shoreham-by-Sea
Wimborne Minster
Brockenhurst
Beaulieu
Fareham
Fawley
Gosport
Chichester
Bosham
Lancing
Worthing
Hove
Ferndown
New Milton
Lymington
Cowes
Osborne House
Portsmouth
South Hayling
Fishbourne Palace
Littlehampton
Bognor Regis
Christchurch
Priory Church
Fishbourne
East Wittering
Selsey
Selsey Bill
Poole
Bournemouth
Milford on Sea
Yarmouth
Ryde
The Solent
Sandbanks
Poole Harbour
Freshwater
The Needles
Carisbrooke
Newport
Bembridge
Isle of Wight
Sandown
Studland
Corfe Castle
Purbeck
Swanage
Godshill
Shanklin
St. Catherine's Hill
Ventnor
Durlston Hd.
St. Alban's Head
Niton
St. Catherine's Pt.
Guernsey
Jersey
Cherbourg
St. Malo
Santander
Caen
Le Havre
Bilbao
A
B
C
D
F
1
2
3
M1
M3
M4
M5
M6
M25
M27
M40
M42
M45
M69
A1(M)
M23

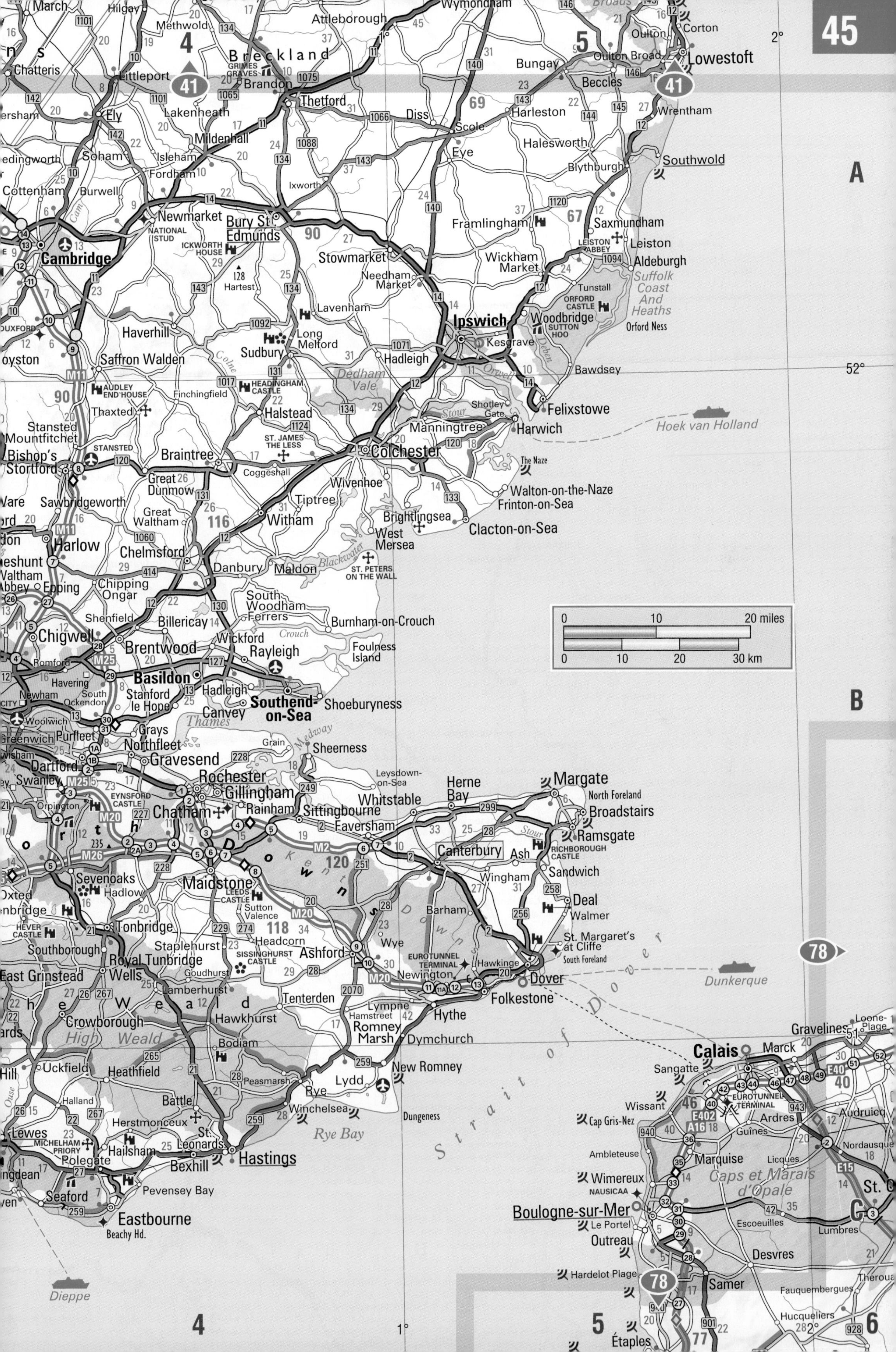
Cambridge
Ipswich
Colchester
Chelmsford
Southend-on-Sea
Basildon
Maidstone
Canterbury
Dover
Folkestone
Hastings
Eastbourne
Lowestoft
Felixstowe
Harwich
Calais
Boulogne-sur-Mer
Strait of Dover
Rye Bay
Hoek van Holland
Dunkerque
Dieppe
0 10 20 miles
0 10 20 30 km
52°
1°
2°
A
B
C
4
5
6
41
78
77

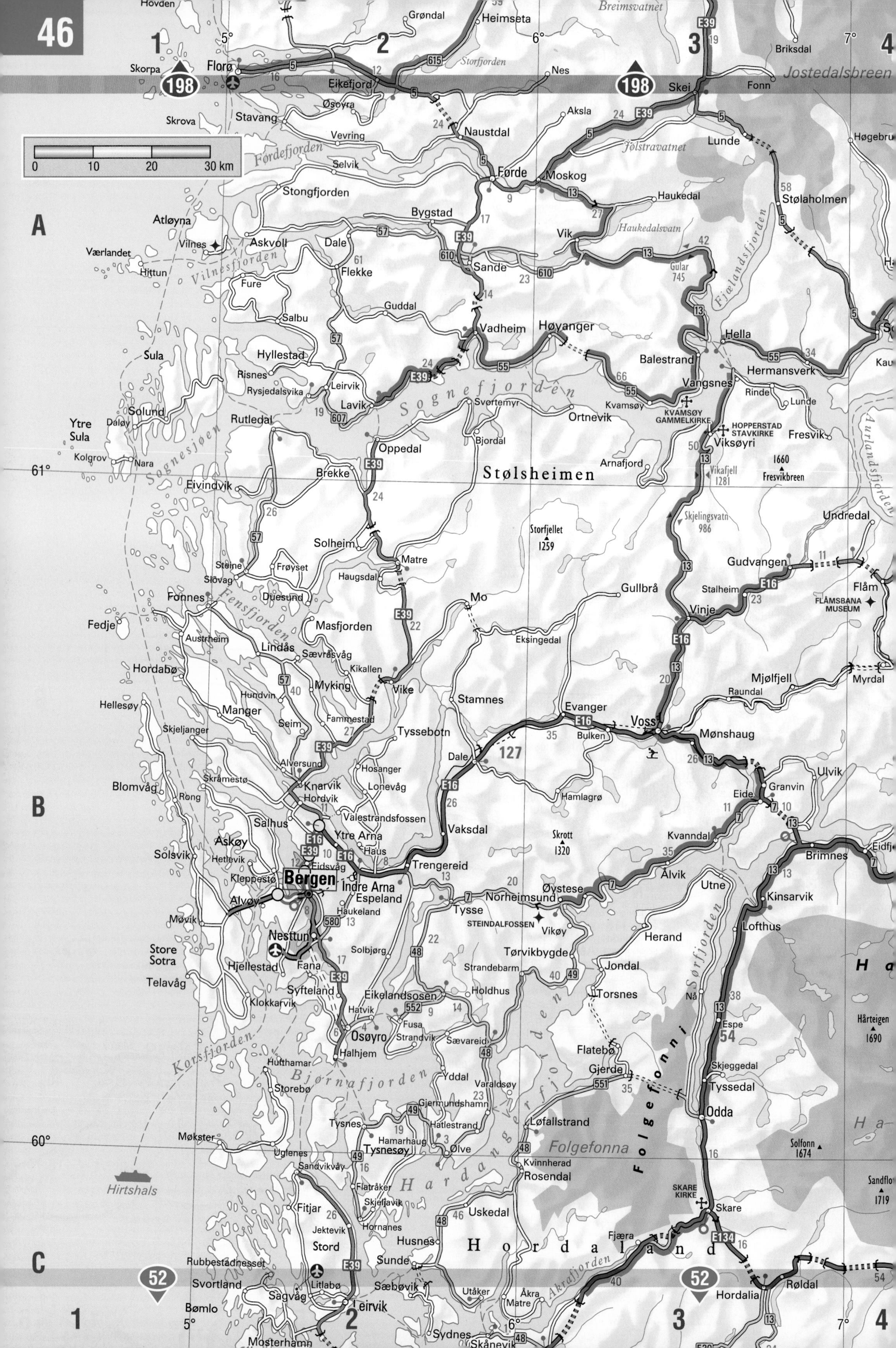

Hovden
Grøndal
Heimseta
Breimsvatnet
Briksdal
Jostedalsbreen
Florø
Skorpa
198
Eikefjord
Storfjorden
Nes
Skei
Fonn
Øsoyra
Stavang
Skrova
Naustdal
Aksla
Lunde
Høgebru
Vevring
Førdefjorden
Jølstravatnet
0
10
20
30 km
Selvik
Førde
Moskog
Stongfjorden
Haukedal
Stølaholmen
Atløyna
Bygstad
Haukedalsvatn
Vik
Fjælandsfjorden
Værlandet
Vilnes
Askvoll
Dale
Sande
Gular
745
Hittun
Vilnesfjorden
Flekke
Fure
Guddal
Salbu
Vadheim
Høyanger
Sula
Hella
Hyllestad
Balestrand
Hermansverk
Risnes
Rysjedalsvika
Leirvik
Vangsnes
Rinde
Lunde
Solund
Lavik
Sognefjorden
Svortemyr
Kvamsøy
Ortnevik
Kvamsøy Gammelkirke
Hopperstad Stavkirke
Viksøyri
Fresvik
Aurlandsfjorden
Ytre Sula
Daløy
Rutledal
Bjordal
Kolgrov
Nara
Oppedal
Arnafjord
1660
Fresvikbreen
61°
Sognesjøen
Brekke
Stølsheimen
Vikafjell
1281
Eivindvik
Skjelingsvatn
986
Undredal
Storfjellet
1259
Solheim
Gudvangen
Steine
Frøyset
Matre
Slovåg
Haugsdal
Stalheim
Flåm
Fonnes
Duesund
Mo
Gullbrå
Flåmsbana Museum
Fensfjorden
Vinje
Fedje
Masfjorden
Austrheim
Eksingedal
Lindås
Sævråsvåg
Kikallen
Hordabø
Myking
Vike
Mjølfjell
Myrdal
Hundvin
Raundal
Hellesøy
Manger
Stamnes
Evanger
Seim
Fammestad
Voss
Skjeljanger
Tyssebotn
Bulken
Mønshaug
127
Alversund
Dale
Hosanger
Skråmestø
Knarvik
Lonevåg
Ulvik
Blomvåg
Rong
Hordvik
Granvin
Eide
Valestrandsfossen
Hamlagrø
Salhus
Ytre Arna
Vaksdal
Askøy
Haus
Kvanndal
Brimnes
Eidfj
Solsvik
Hetlevik
Skrott
1320
Eidsvåg
Trengereid
Ålvik
Kleppestø
Bergen
Indre Arna
Utne
Espeland
Norheimsund
Øystese
Kinsarvik
Alvøy
Tysse
Haukeland
Møvik
Steindalfossen
Vikøy
Lofthus
Herand
Nesttun
Sørfjorden
Store Sotra
Solbjørg
Tørvikbygde
Hjellestad
Fana
Strandebarm
Jondal
Telavåg
Syfteland
Holdhus
Torsnes
Eikelandsosen
Klokkarvik
Hatvik
Fusa
Nå
Espe
Hårteigen
1690
Osøyro
Strandvik
Sævareid
Korsfjorden
Halhjem
Flatebø
Hutthamar
Bjørnafjorden
Yddal
Gjerde
Skjeggedal
Varaldsøy
Storebø
Tyssedal
Gjermundshamn
Folgefonni
Hatlestrand
Odda
Tysnes
Løfallstrand
Møkster
Hamarhaug
Tysnesøy
Ølve
Folgefonna
Solfonn
1674
60°
Uglenes
Kvinnherad
Rosendal
Sandvikvåg
Hardangerfjorden
Hirtshals
Flatråker
Sandflo
1719
Skjelfavik
Skare Kirke
Skare
Fitjar
Uskedal
Jektevik
Hornanes
Stord
Husnes
Fjæra
Hordaland
Rubbestadneset
Sunde
Akrafjorden
52
Svortland
Litlabø
Sæbøvik
Utåker
Hordalia
Røldal
Bømlo
Sagvåg
Leirvik
Åkra
Matre
Mosterhamn
Sydnes
Skånevik
1
2
3
4
A
B
C
5°
6°
7°

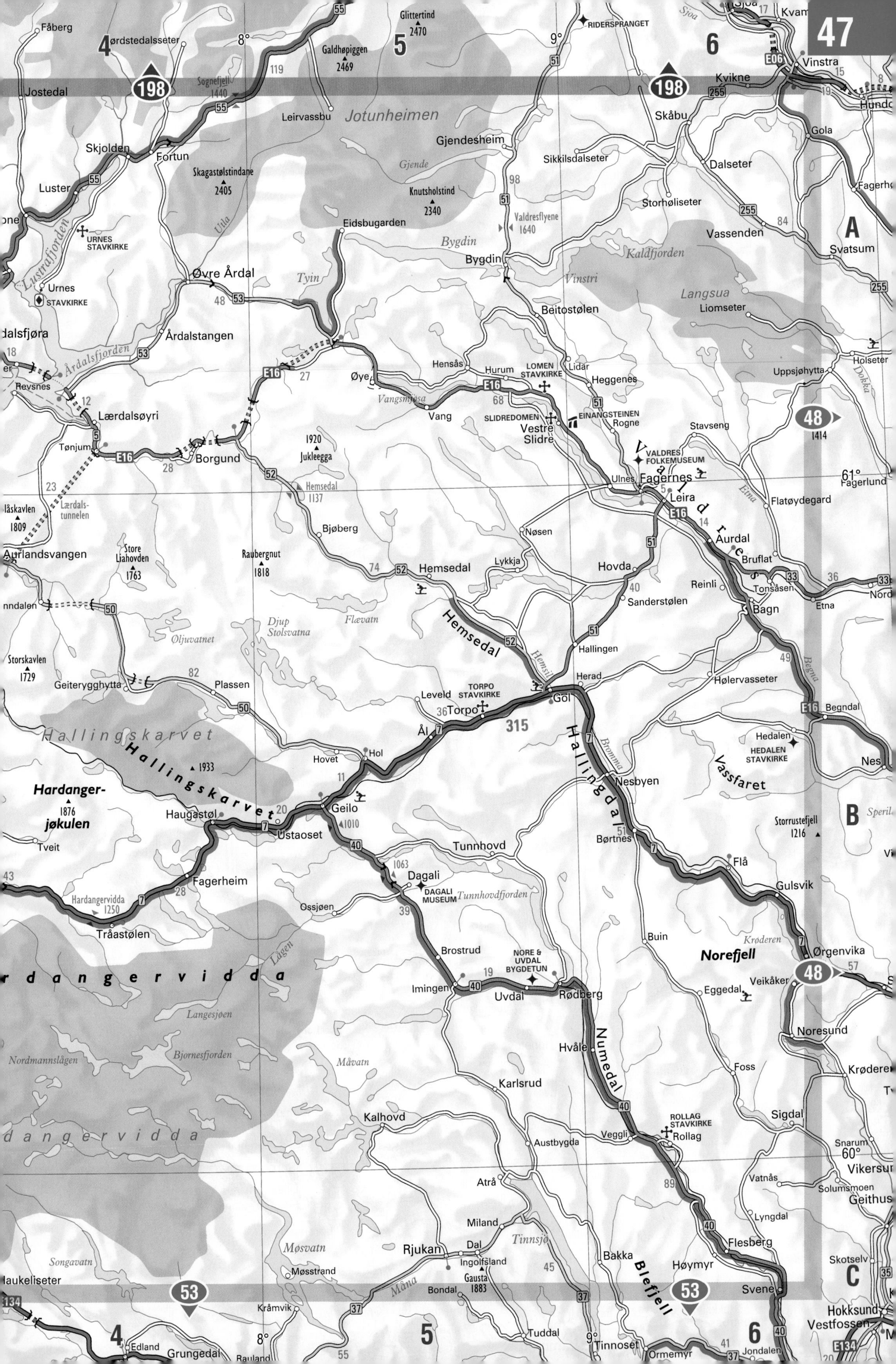
Fåberg
Jostedal
Skjolden
Fortun
Luster
Sognefjell 1440
Galdhøpiggen 2469
Glittertind 2470
Leirvassbu
Jotunheimen
Gjendesheim
Gjende
Skagastølstindane 2405
Knutsholstind 2340
Eidsbugarden
Bygdin
Valdresflyene 1640
URNES STAVKIRKE
Lustrafjorden
Urnes
Øvre Årdal
Tyin
Årdalstangen
Årdalsfjorden
Revsnes
Lærdalsøyri
Tønjum
Borgund
Hemsedal 1137
Jukleegga 1920
Øye
Vangsmjøsa
Vang
Hensås
Hurum
LOMEN STAVKIRKE
SLIDREDOMEN
EINANGSTEINEN
Vestre Slidre
Rogne
Lidar
Heggenes
Beitostølen
Vinstri
Kaldfjorden
Langsua
Liomseter
Sikkilsdalseter
Skåbu
Storhøliseter
Dalseter
Vassenden
Svatsum
Gola
Kvikne
Vinstra
Kvam
Sjoa
RIDERSPRANGET
Holseter
Uppsjøhytta
Dokka
Stavseng
VALDRES FOLKEMUSEUM
Valdres
Ulnes
Fagernes
Leira
Aurdal
Bruflat
Flatøydegard
Fagerlund
Etna
Tonsåsen
Reinli
Bagn
Begna
Begndal
Nes
Hedalen
HEDALEN STAVKIRKE
Vassfaret
Lærdalstunnelen
Store Liahovden 1763
Raubergnut 1818
Aurlandsvangen
Bjøberg
Hemsedal
Lykkja
Nøsen
Hovda
Sanderstølen
Hallingen
Djup Stolsvatna
Flævatn
Øljuvatnet
Storskavlen 1729
Geiterygghytta
Plassen
Hallingskarvet
Herad
Hølervasseter
Leveld
TORPO STAVKIRKE
Torpo
Gol
Ål
Hol
Hovet
Hallingdal
Bromma
Nesbyen
Hardangerjøkulen 1876
Haugastøl
Geilo
Ustaoset
Tunnhovd
Tveit
Fagerheim
Hardangervidda 1250
Tråastølen
Dagali
DAGALI MUSEUM
Tunnhovdfjorden
Ossjøen
Børtnes
Flå
Gulsvik
Storrustefjell 1216
Krøderen
Norefjell
Ørgenvika
Veikåker
Eggedal
Buin
Brostrud
NORE & UVDAL BYGDETUN
Imingen
Uvdal
Rødberg
Hardangervidda
Langesjøen
Nordmannslågen
Bjornesfjorden
Måvatn
Hvåle
Numedal
Karlsrud
Noresund
Foss
Krøderen
Sigdal
Kalhovd
ROLLAG STAVKIRKE
Rollag
Veggli
Austbygda
Snarum
Vikersund
Atrå
Vatnås
Solumsmoen
Geithus
Lyngdal
Miland
Møsvatn
Rjukan
Dal
Tinnsjø
Bakka
Flesberg
Høymyr
Blefjell
Songavatn
Møsstrand
Ingolfsland
Gausta 1883
Haukeliseter
Bondal
Måna
Svene
Skotselv
Hokksund
Vestfossen
Kråmvik
Edland
Grungedal
Rauland
Tuddal
Tinnoset
Ormemyr
Jondalen
198
48
53

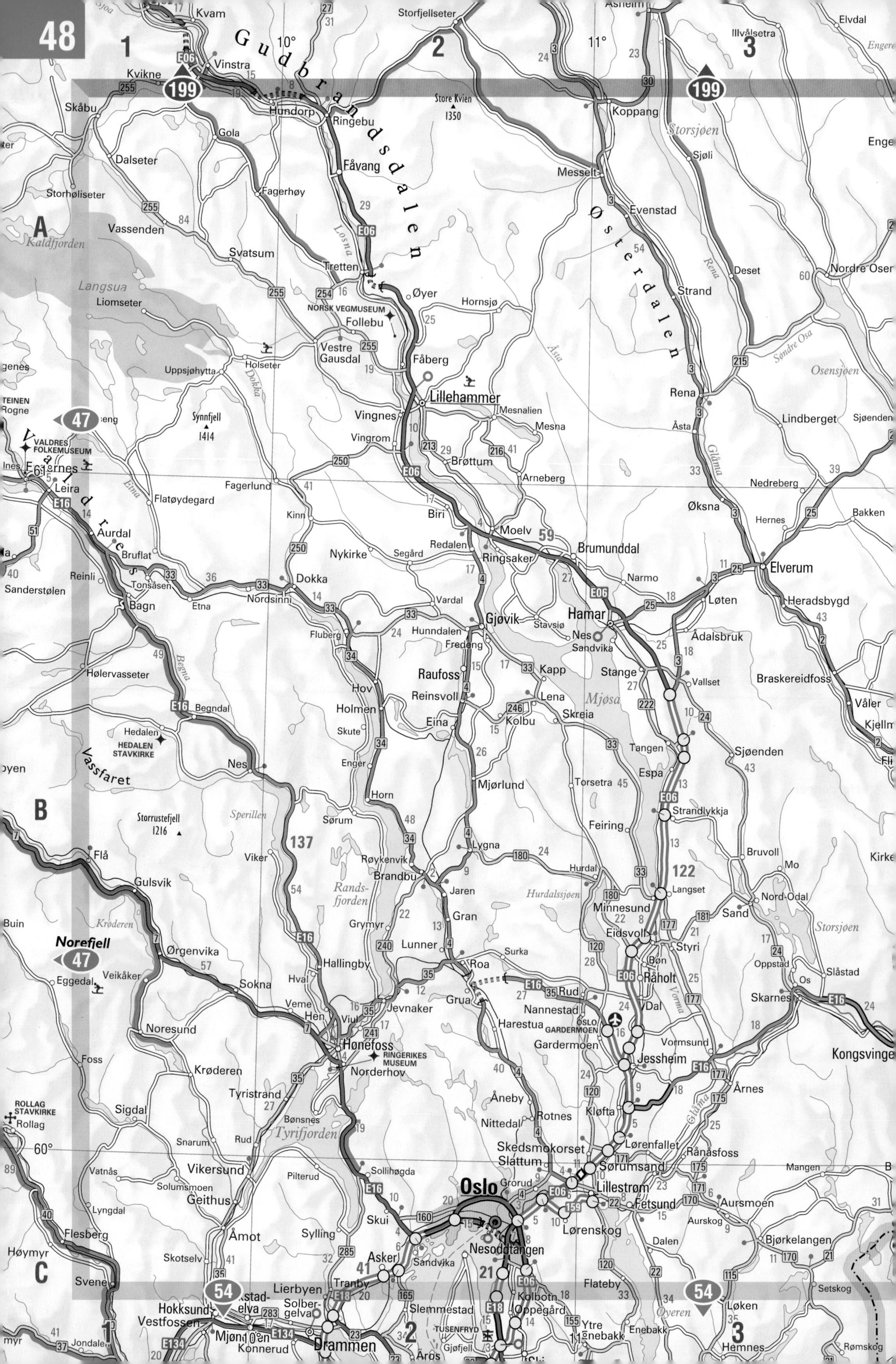

48
Gudbrandsdalen
Østerdalen
Valdres
Vassfaret
Kvam
Vinstra
Kvikne
Skåbu
Hundorp
Ringebu
Storfjellseter
Store Kvien
1350
Koppang
Storsjøen
Sjøli
Ilvålsetra
Elvdal
Gola
Dalseter
Fåvang
Messelt
Evenstad
Storhøliseter
Fagerhøy
Vassenden
Kaldfjorden
Svatsum
Losna
Tretten
Langsua
Liomseter
Øyer
Hornsjø
NORSK VEGMUSEUM
Follebu
Vestre Gausdal
Holseter
Uppsjøhytta
Dokka
Fåberg
Lillehammer
Synnfjell
1414
Vingnes
Vingrom
Mesnalien
Mesna
Brøttum
Arneberg
VALDRES FOLKEMUSEUM
Fagernes
Leira
Flatøydegard
Fagerlund
Kinn
Biri
Moelv
Brumunddal
Aurdal
Bruflat
Nykirke
Segård
Redalen
Ringsaker
Reinli
Tonsåsen
Sanderstølen
Bagn
Etna
Nordsinni
Vardal
Gjøvik
Hamar
Stavsjø
Nes
Sandvika
Fluberg
Hunndalen
Fredeng
Raufoss
Reinsvoll
Kapp
Lena
Skreia
Mjøsa
Stange
Hølervasseter
Begna
Begndal
Hedalen
HEDALEN STAVKIRKE
Hov
Holmen
Skute
Eina
Kolbu
Enger
Mjørlund
Torsetra
Tangen
Espa
Horn
Sørum
Sperillen
Storrustefjell
1216
Feiring
Strandlykkja
Viker
Røykenvik
Brandbu
Lygna
Hurdal
Randsfjorden
Jaren
Gran
Hurdalssjøen
Minnesund
Langset
Eidsvoll
Grymyr
Lunner
Flå
Gulsvik
Krøderen
Norefjell
Ørgenvika
Eggedal
Veikåker
Sokna
Hallingby
Hval
Roa
Surka
Grua
Rud
Nannestad
Harestua
Jevnaker
Veme
Hen
Viul
Hønefoss
RINGERIKES MUSEUM
Norderhov
Noresund
Foss
Krøderen
OSLO GARDERMOEN
Gardermoen
Jessheim
Råholt
Bøn
Dal
Vorma
Vormsund
Styri
Tyristrand
Sigdal
ROLLAG STAVKIRKE
Rollag
Bønsnes
Tyrifjorden
Snarum
Aneby
Nittedal
Rotnes
Kløfta
Skedsmokorset
Slattum
Lørenfallet
Sørumsand
Vikersund
Vatnås
Solumsmoen
Geithus
Pilterud
Sollihøgda
Oslo
Grorud
Lillestrøm
Fetsund
Lørenskog
Skui
Sylling
Lyngdal
Flesberg
Høymyr
Åmot
Skotselv
Svene
Asker
Sandvika
Nesoddtangen
Lierbyen
Tranby
Solbergelva
Hokksund
Vestfossen
Mjøndalen
Konnerud
Drammen
Stad-elva
Slemmestad
TUSENFRYD
Gjøfjell
Kolbotn
Oppegård
Ytre Enebakk
Enebakk
Flateby
Øyeren
Dalen
Aurskog
Aursmoen
Bjørkelangen
Setskog
Løken
Hemnes
Rømskog
Mangen
Rånåsfoss
Årnes
Glåma
Kongsvinger
Skarnes
Slåstad
Os
Oppstad
Storsjøen
Sand
Nord-Odal
Mo
Bruvoll
Kirkenær
Sjøenden
Våler
Kjellmyra
Braskereidfoss
Vallset
Ådalsbruk
Løten
Heradsbygd
Elverum
Narmo
Hernes
Bakken
Øksna
Nedreberg
Åsta
Rena
Lindberget
Sjøenden
Osensjøen
Søndre Osa
Strand
Deset
Nordre Osen
Åsta
Enge

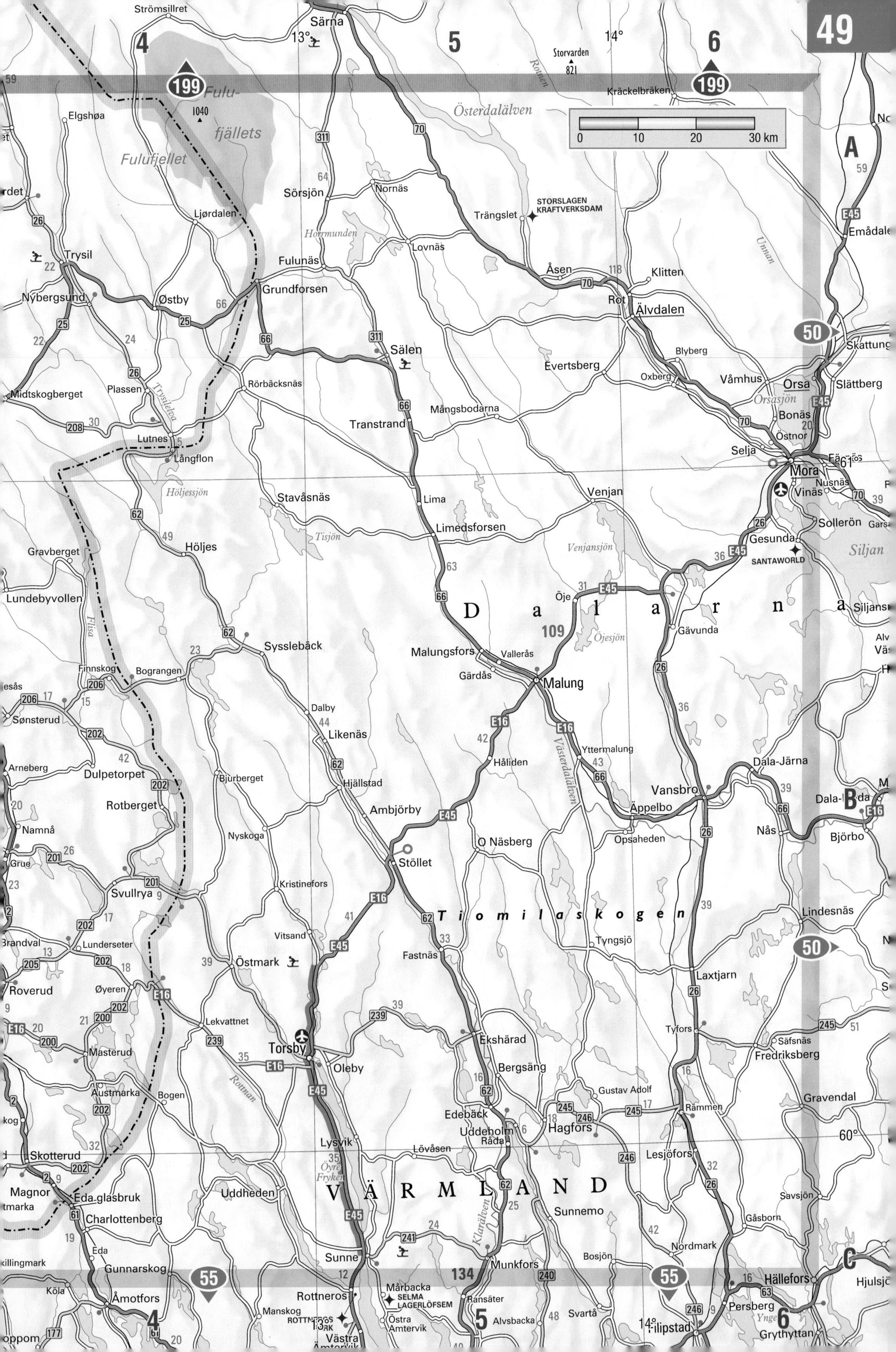
4
5
6
A
B
C
199
50
55
0 10 20 30 km
13°
14°
60°
Strömsillret
Särna
Storvarden 821
Fulu-fjällets
Fulufjellet
1040
Elgshøa
Kräckelbräken
Österdalälven
Rotnen
Nc
59
Emådale
E45
Unnan
Sörsjön
Nornäs
Hormunden
Ljørdalen
Trängslet
STORSLAGEN KRAFTVERKSDAM
Trysil
Fulunäs
Lovnäs
Åsen
Klitten
Nybergsund
Østby
Grundforsen
Rot
Älvdalen
Skattung
Sälen
Blyberg
Evertsberg
Oxberg
Våmhus
Orsa
Slättberg
Midtskogberget
Plassen
Rörbäcksnäs
Trysilelva
Orsasjön
Bonäs
Mångsbodarna
Transtrand
Östnor
Lutnes
Selja
Långflon
Mora
Höljessjön
Nusnäs
Vinäs
Stavåsnäs
Lima
Venjan
Sollerön
Gesunda
Limedsforsen
Tisjön
Venjansjön
SANTAWORLD
Siljan
Gravberget
Höljes
Lundebyvollen
Öje
Dalarna
Siljansn
109
Gävunda
Öjesjön
Flisa
Sysslebäck
Malungsfors
Vallerås
Finnskog
Bograngen
Gärdås
Malung
Sønsterud
Dalby
Likenäs
Västerdalälven
Yttermalung
Håliden
Arneberg
Dulpetorpet
Bjurberget
Hjällstad
Dala-Järna
Vansbro
Rotberget
Ambjörby
Äppelbo
Dala-Floda
Namnå
Nyskoga
Näsberg
Opsaheden
Nås
Björbo
Grue
Stöllet
Svullrya
Kristinefors
Tiomilaskogen
Lindesnäs
Brandval
Lunderseter
Vitsand
Fastnäs
Tyngsjö
Roverud
Östmark
Øyeren
Laxtjarn
Lekvattnet
Tyfors
Säfsnäs
Masterud
Torsby
Ekshärad
Fredriksberg
Oleby
Rottnan
Bergsäng
Austmarka
Bogen
Gustav Adolf
Gravendal
Edebäck
Rämmen
Uddeholm
Hagfors
Råda
Lysvik
Lövåsen
Lesjöfors
Skotterud
Övre Fryken
Magnor
Eda glasbruk
Uddheden
VÄRMLAND
Savsjön
Charlottenberg
Sunnemo
Klarälven
Gåsborn
Eda
Nordmark
Sunne
Bosjön
Gunnarskog
Munkfors
Hällefors
Hjulsjö
Köla
Åmotfors
Rottneros
Mårbacka
SELMA LAGERLÖFSEM
Ransäter
Persberg
Manskog
ROTTNEROS PARK
Östra Åmtervik
Alvsbacka
Svartå
Filipstad
Yngen
Grythyttan
Västra Åmtervik
Eppom
Skillingmark

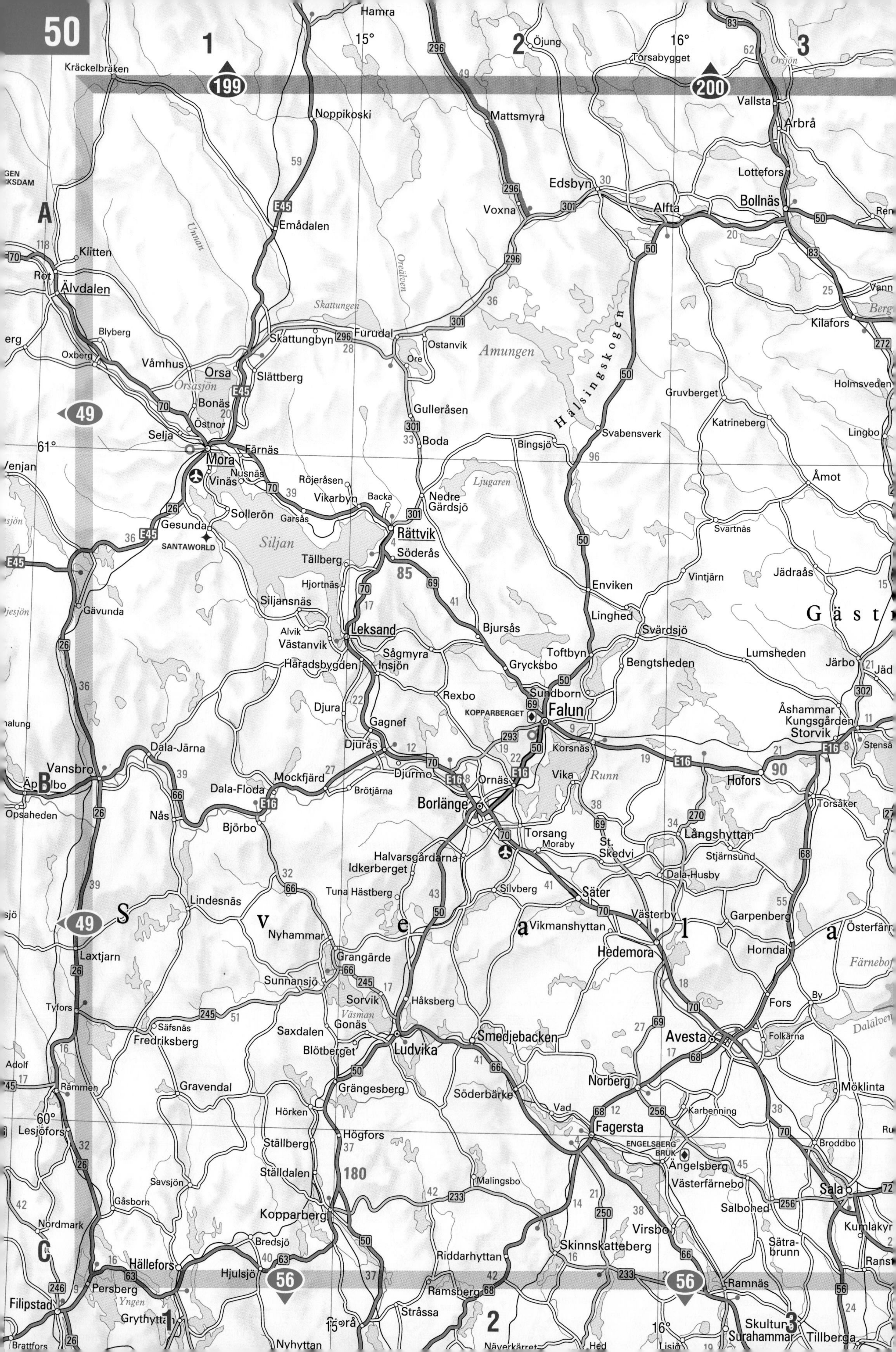
Hamra
15°
1
2
16°
3
Öjung
Torsabygget
Orsjön
199
200
Kräckelbräken
Noppikoski
Mattsmyra
Vallsta
Arbrå
Edsbyn
Voxna
Lottefors
Alfta
Bollnäs
Emådalen
Klitten
Rot
Älvdalen
Skattungen
Amungen
Hälsingskogen
Kilafors
Blyberg
Oxberg
Skattungbyn
Furudal
Ostanvik
Ore
Våmhus
Orsa
Orsasjön
Slättberg
Bonäs
Östnor
Gulleråsen
Gruvberget
Holmsveden
Katrineberg
Lingbo
Selja
61°
Mora
Färnäs
Boda
Bingsjö
Svabensverk
Nusnäs
Vinäs
Röjeråsen
Ljugaren
Vikarbyn
Backa
Nedre Gärdsjö
Åmot
Sollerön
Garsås
Gesunda
SANTAWORLD
Siljan
Rättvik
Svartnäs
Tällberg
Söderås
Hjortnäs
Vintjärn
Jädraås
Gävunda
Siljansnäs
Enviken
Linghed
Gäst
Alvik
Västanvik
Leksand
Bjursås
Svärdsjö
Sågmyra
Toftbyn
Lumsheden
Järbo
Häradsbygden
Insjön
Grycksbo
Bengtsheden
Rexbo
Sundborn
Djura
KOPPARBERGET
Falun
Åshammar
Kungsgården
Storvik
Gagnef
Djurås
Korsnäs
Dala-Järna
Vansbro
Äppelbo
Opsaheden
Dala-Floda
Mockfjärd
Djurmo
Brötjärna
Ornäs
Vika
Runn
Hofors
Torsåker
Nås
Björbo
Borlänge
Torsang
Moraby
St. Skedvi
Långshyttan
Stjärnsund
Halvarsgårdarna
Idkerberget
Dala-Husby
Tuna Hästberg
Silvberg
Säter
Lindesnäs
Svealand
Nyhammar
Vikmanshyttan
Västerby
Garpenberg
Österfärnebo
Hedemora
Laxtjarn
Grangärde
Horndal
Färnebofjärden
Sunnansjö
Sorvik
Håksberg
Fors
By
Tyfors
Säfsnäs
Fredriksberg
Väsman
Saxdalen
Gonäs
Blötberget
Ludvika
Smedjebacken
Avesta
Folkärna
Dalälven
Adolf
Rämmen
Gravendal
Grängesberg
Söderbärke
Norrberg
Möklinta
60°
Lesjöfors
Hörken
Högfors
Vad
Karbenning
Fagersta
Ställberg
ENGELSBERG BRUK
Ängelsberg
Broddbo
Savsjön
Ställdalen
180
Malingsbo
Västerfärnebo
Sala
Gåsborn
Salbohed
Nordmark
Kopparberg
Virsbo
Kumla
Sätra-brunn
Bredsjö
Skinnskatteberg
Hällefors
Riddarhyttan
Ransta
Hjulsjö
56
Ramsberg
Ramnäs
Persberg
Yngen
Filipstad
Grythyttan
Ljusnarsberg
Stråssa
Skultuna
Surahammar
Tillberga
Brattfors
Nyhyttan
Näverkärret
Hed
Lisjö
Unnan
Oreälven
E45
E16
296
301
50
83
70
26
66
245
233
68
256
250
63
246
293
69
270
302
272
49
85
90

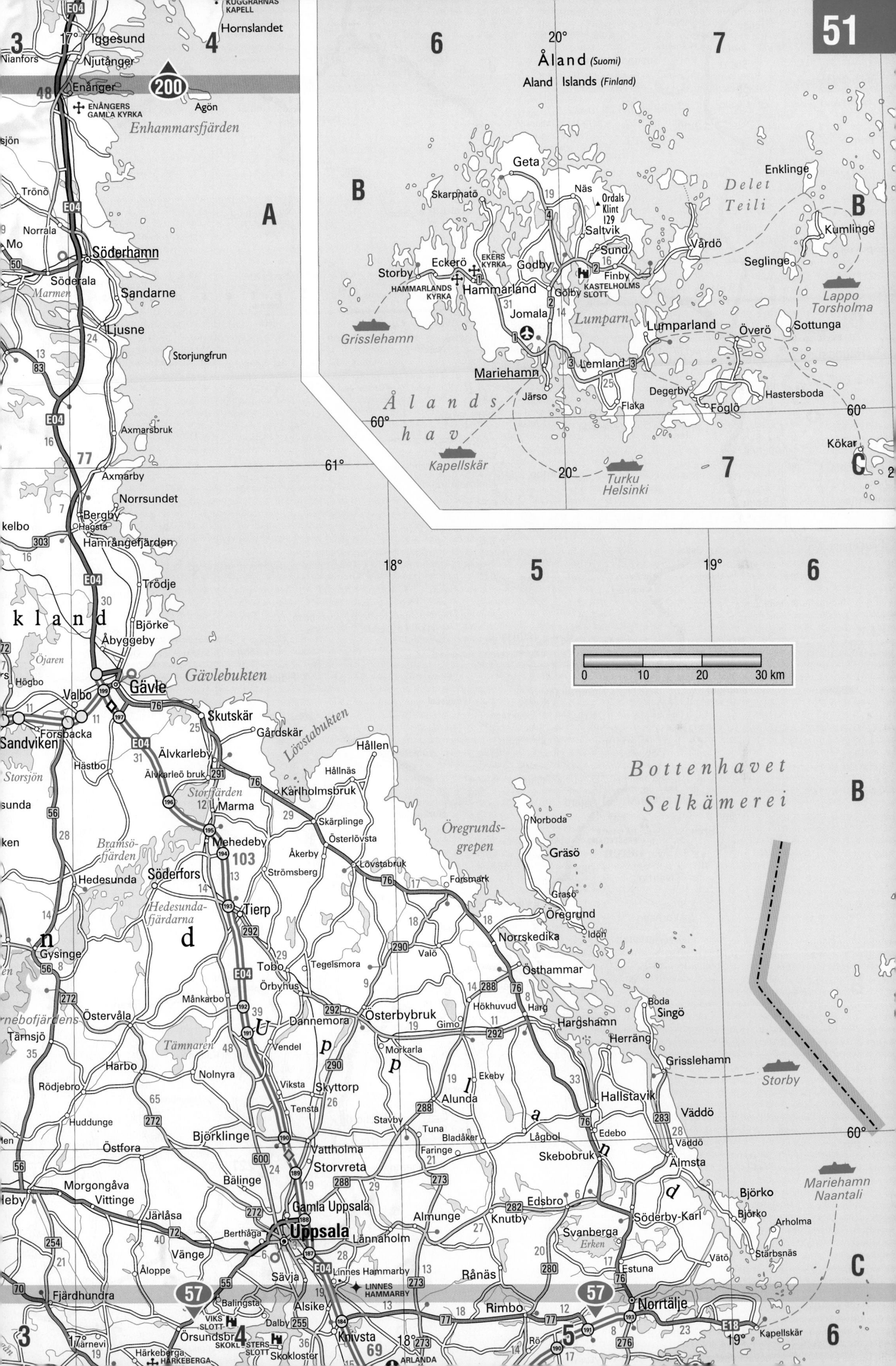
Åland (Suomi)
Aland Islands (Finland)
Geta
Skarpnäto
Näs
Ordals Klint 129
Saltvik
Delet
Teili
Enklinge
Kumlinge
Vårdö
Sund
Seglinge
Storby
Eckerö
EKERS KYRKA
Godby
Finby
KASTELHOLMS SLOTT
HAMMARLANDS KYRKA
Hammarland
Gölby
Lappo
Torsholma
Grisslehamn
Jomala
Lumparn
Lumparland
Överö
Sottunga
Lemland
Mariehamn
Degerby
Hastersboda
Järso
Flaka
Föglö
Ålands hav
Kapellskär
Turku
Helsinki
Kökar
Iggesund
Hornslandet
Nianfors
Njutånger
Enånger
ENÅNGERS GAMLA KYRKA
Agön
Enhammarsfjärden
Trönö
Norrala
Mo
Söderhamn
Söderala
Marmen
Sandarne
Ljusne
Storjungfrun
Axmarsbruk
Axmarby
Norrsundet
Bergby
Hagsta
Hamrångefjärden
Trödje
Björke
Åbyggeby
Öjaren
Högbo
Valbo
Gävle
Gävlebukten
Sandviken
Forsbacka
Skutskär
Gårdskär
Lövstabukten
Hållen
Hållnäs
Älvkarleby
Älvkarleö bruk
Hästbo
Storsjön
Storfjärden
Marma
Karlholmsbruk
Skärplinge
Österlövsta
Mehedeby
Bramsöfjärden
Åkerby
Lövstabruk
Strömsberg
Hedesunda
Söderfors
Hedesundafjärdarna
Tierp
Forsmark
Öregrundsgrepen
Norboda
Gräsö
Öregrund
Norrskedika
Idön
Gysinge
Tobo
Tegelsmora
Valö
Östhammar
Örbyhus
Månkarbo
Östervåla
Dannemora
Österbybruk
Hökhuvud
Harg
Hargshamn
Boda
Singö
Tärnsjö
Tämnaren
Vendel
Morkarla
Gimo
Herräng
Grisslehamn
Storby
Harbo
Nolnyra
Ekeby
Rödjebro
Viksta
Skyttorp
Alunda
Hallstavik
Tensta
Väddö
Huddunge
Stavby
Tuna
Bladåker
Edebo
Lågbol
Björklinge
Vattholma
Faringe
Östfora
Storvreta
Skebobruk
Älmsta
Mariehamn
Naantali
Morgongåva
Bälinge
Vittinge
Gamla Uppsala
Edsbro
Björko
Järlåsa
Almunge
Knutby
Söderby-Karl
Arholma
Berthåga
Uppsala
Lännaholm
Svanberga
Erken
Vänge
Stärbsnäs
Vätö
Åloppe
Linnes Hammarby
Rånäs
Estuna
Sävja
LINNES HAMMARBY
Fjärdhundra
Balingsta
Alsike
Rimbo
Norrtälje
VIKS SLOTT
Dalby
Örsundsbro
SKOKLOSTERS SLOTT
Knivsta
Rö
Kapellskär
Järnevi
Härkeberga
HÄRKEBERGA
Skokloster
ARLANDA
Bottenhavet
Selkämerei
0 10 20 30 km

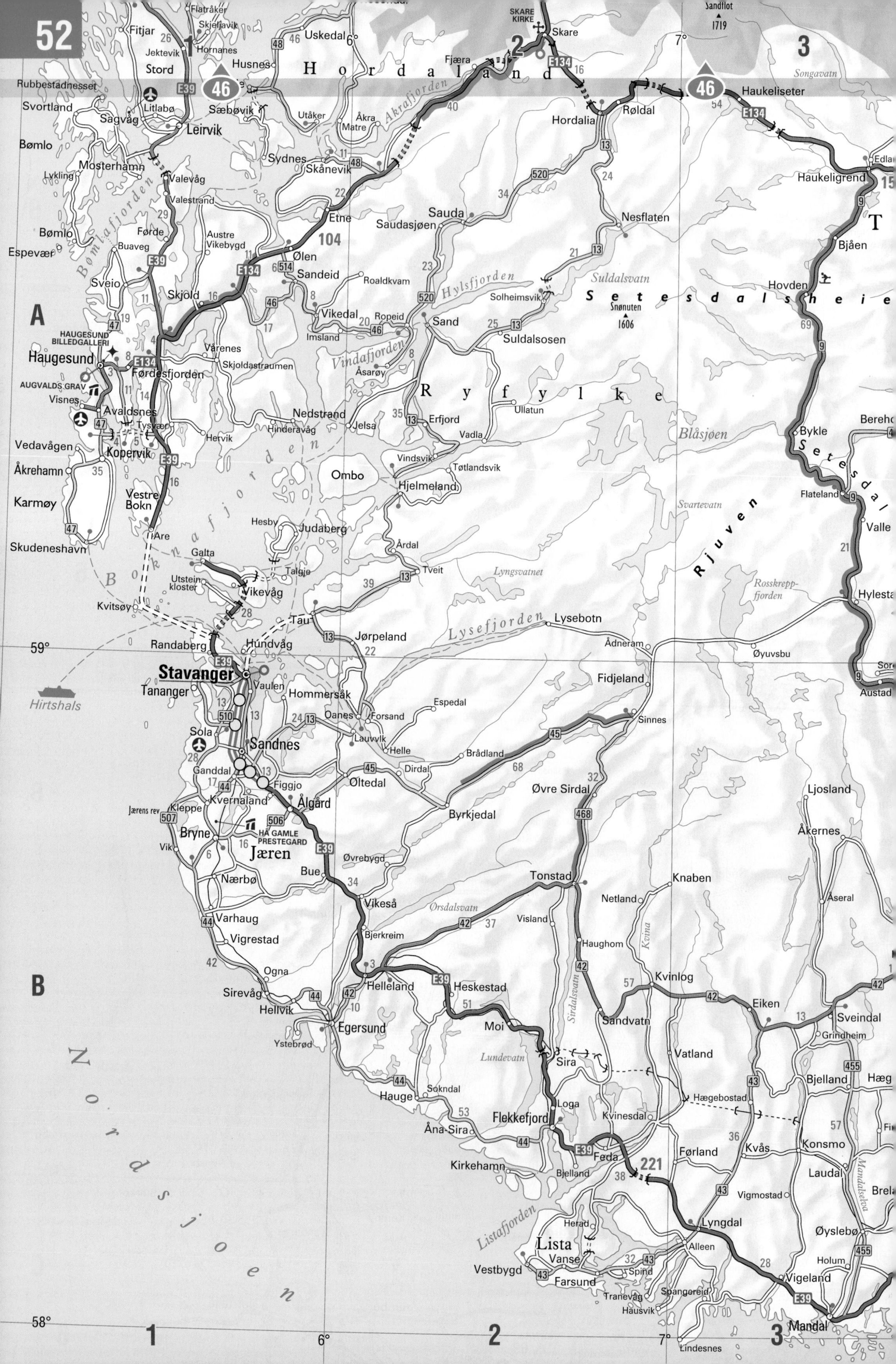
Hordaland
Fitjar
Stord
Husnes
Uskedal
Skare
Fjæra
Akrafjorden
Haukeliseter
Røldal
Hordalia
Bømlo
Svortland
Sagvåg
Leirvik
Sæbøvik
Utåker
Åkra
Matre
Mosterhamn
Valevåg
Sydnes
Skånevik
Etne
Sauda
Saudasjøen
Nesflaten
Haukeligrend
Bjåen
Hovden
Ølen
Sandeid
Roaldkvam
Hylsfjorden
Suldalsvatn
Setesdalsheie
Solheimsvik
Snønuten
1606
Bømlafjorden
Sveio
Skjold
Vikedal
Ropeid
Sand
Suldalsosen
Haugesund
Haugesund Billedgalleri
Augvalds grav
Førdesfjorden
Vårenes
Skjoldastraumen
Vindafjorden
Imsland
Visnes
Avaldsnes
Tysvær
Nedstrand
Jelsa
Hinderåvåg
Hervik
Ryfylke
Ullatun
Erfjord
Vadla
Blåsjøen
Bykle
Setesdal
Vedavågen
Kopervik
Åkrehamn
Karmøy
Vestre Bokn
Skudeneshavn
Ombo
Vindsvik
Tøtlandsvik
Hjelmeland
Flateland
Svartevatn
Rjuven
Valle
Judaberg
Hesby
Boknafjorden
Årdal
Tveit
Lyngsvatnet
Galta
Talgje
Utstein kloster
Vikevåg
Kvitsøy
Rosskreppfjorden
Hylestad
Tau
Jørpeland
Lysefjorden
Lysebotn
Ådneram
Øyuvsbu
Randaberg
Hundvåg
Stavanger
Tananger
Vaulen
Fidjeland
Hirtshals
Hommersåk
Espedal
Oanes
Forsand
Sinnes
Sola
Lauvvik
Helle
Sandnes
Brådland
Ganddal
Dirdal
Øltedal
Figgjo
Øvre Sirdal
Ljosland
Kvernaland
Kleppe
Jærens rev
Ålgård
Byrkjedal
Bryne
Hå gamle prestegard
Jæren
Vik
Åkernes
Øvrebygd
Bue
Nærbø
Tonstad
Knaben
Netland
Åseral
Vikeså
Varhaug
Ørsdalsvatn
Visland
Bjerkreim
Vigrestad
Haughom
Ogna
Kvinlog
Helleland
Heskestad
Sirevåg
Hellvik
Sandvatn
Eiken
Sveindal
Egersund
Moi
Ystebrød
Lundevatn
Sira
Vatland
Sirdalsvatn
Nordsjøen
Hauge
Sokndal
Loga
Hægebostad
Bjelland
Åna-Sira
Flekkefjord
Kvinesdal
Kvås
Konsmo
Feda
Førland
Laudal
Kirkehamn
Vigmostad
Lyngdal
Herad
Listafjorden
Lista
Alleen
Øyslebø
Vanse
Vestbygd
Farsund
Spind
Holum
Vigeland
Tranevåg
Spangereid
Hausvik
Mandal
Lindesnes
Mandalselva
Kvina
59°
58°
6°
7°

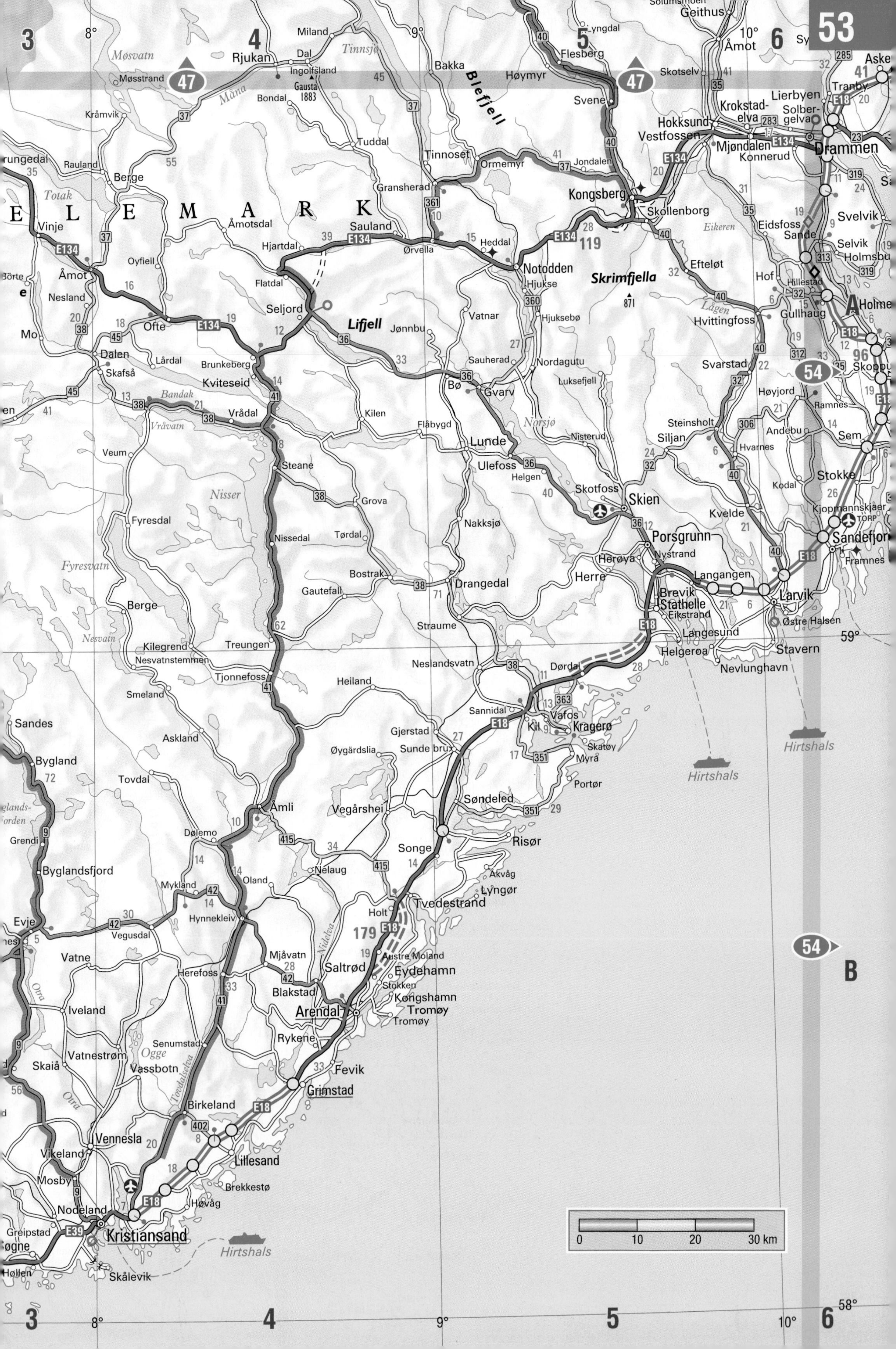
3
4
5
6
Møsvatn
Møsstrand
Rjukan
Miland
Dal
Ingolfsland
Tinnsjø
Gausta 1883
Bondal
Kråmvik
Måna
Bakka
Blefjell
Høymyr
Flesberg
Lyngdal
Geithus
Åmot
Svene
Skotselv
Tuddal
Tinnoset
Ormemyr
Jondalen
Kongsberg
Hokksund
Vestfossen
Krokstad-elva
Mjøndalen
Lierbyen
Solbergelva
Drammen
Konnerud
Tranby
Asker
rungedal
Rauland
Berge
Totak
T E L E M A R K
Vinje
Gransherad
Åmotsdal
Sauland
Hjartdal
Ørvella
Heddal
Notodden
Skollenborg
Eikeren
Eidsfoss
Sande
Svelvik
Selvik
Holmsbu
Oyfiell
Åmot
Nesland
Flatdal
Seljord
Lifjell
Hjukse
Hjuksebø
Skrimfjella
871
Efteløt
Hof
Hillestad
Gullhaug
Holmestrand
Lågen
Hvittingfoss
Ofte
Dalen
Skafså
Lårdal
Brunkeberg
Kviteseid
Jønnbu
Vatnar
Sauherad
Nordagutu
Bø
Gvarv
Luksefjell
Svarstad
Høyjord
Ramnes
Bandak
Vrådal
Vråvatn
Kilen
Flåbygd
Lunde
Norsjø
Nisterud
Steinsholt
Siljan
Andebu
Hvarnes
Sem
Veum
Steane
Ulefoss
Helgen
Skotfoss
Skien
Kodal
Stokke
Nisser
Grova
Kvelde
Kjopmannskjær
Torp
Sandefjord
Fyresdal
Nissedal
Tørdal
Nakksjø
Porsgrunn
Nystrand
Herøya
Fyresvatn
Bostrak
Drangedal
Herre
Langangen
Gautefall
Brevik
Stathelle
Eikstrand
Larvik
Framnes
Berge
Straume
Langesund
Østre Halsen
Nesvatn
Kilegrend
Nesvatnstemmen
Treungen
Helgerøa
Stavern
Nevlunghavn
59°
Neslandsvatn
Dørdal
Tjonnefoss
Smeland
Heiland
Sannidal
Vafos
Kil
Kragerø
Skatøy
Myra
Sandes
Askland
Gjerstad
Sunde bru
Øygärdslia
Hirtshals
Bygland
Tovdal
Portør
Byglandsfjorden
Grendi
Åmli
Vegårshei
Søndeled
Dølemo
Songe
Risør
Byglandsfjord
Nelaug
Åkvåg
Oland
Mykland
Lyngør
Holt
Tvedestrand
Evje
Hynnekleiv
Vegusdal
Vatne
Herefoss
Mjåvatn
Nidelva
Austre Moland
Saltrød
Eydehamn
Stokken
Kongshamn
Blakstad
Arendal
Tromøy
Otra
Iveland
Senumstad
Ogge
Rykene
Vatnestrøm
Skaiå
Vassbotn
Fevik
Tovdalselva
Grimstad
Birkeland
Vennesla
Vikeland
Lillesand
Mosby
Brekkestø
Høvåg
Nodeland
Greipstad
Kristiansand
Søgne
Høllen
Skålevik
0 10 20 30 km
8°
9°
10°
58°
A
B
47
54

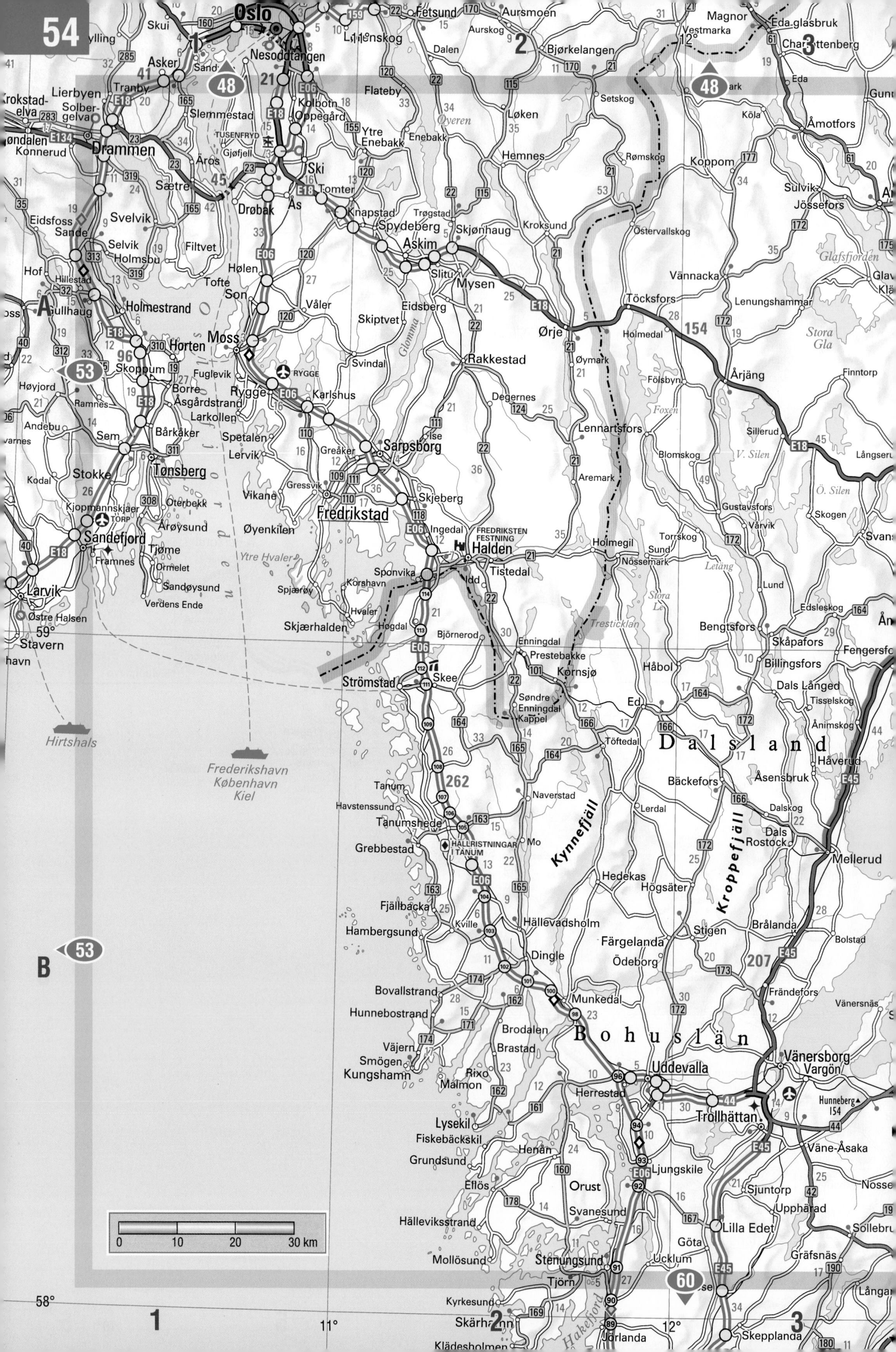
Oslo
Fetsund
Aursmoen
Magnor
Eda glasbruk
Vestmarka
Charlottenberg
Skui
Lillestrøm
Aurskog
Bjørkelangen
Eda
Asker
Sand
Nesoddtangen
Flateby
Setskog
Lierbyen
Tranby
Kolbotn
Oppegård
Løken
Køla
Åmotfors
Krokstad-elva
Solbergelva
Slemmestad
Ytre Enebakk
Enebakk
Øyeren
Drammen
Konnerud
Tusenfryd
Gjøfjell
Åros
Ski
Hemnes
Rømskog
Koppom
Sætre
Tomter
Sulvik
Jössefors
Eidsfoss
Sande
Svelvik
Drøbak
Ås
Knapstad
Trøgstad
Spydeberg
Skjønhaug
Kroksund
Østervallskog
Selvik
Holmsbu
Filtvet
Askim
Glafsfjorden
Hof
Hillestad
Hølen
Tofte
Son
Slitu
Mysen
Vännacka
Holmestrand
Gullhaug
Våler
Eidsberg
Töcksfors
Lenungshammar
Skiptvet
Glomma
Ørje
Holmedal
Moss
Horten
Rakkestad
Øymark
Stora Gla
Skoppum
Svindal
Fuglevik
Rygge
Borre
Åsgårdstrand
Karlshus
Årjäng
Finntorp
Højyord
Ramnes
Larkollen
Degernes
Lennartsfors
Foxen
Andebu
Sem
Bårkåker
Spetalen
Lervik
Ise
Sarpsborg
Greåker
Sillerud
Blomskog
V. Silen
Långserud
Kodal
Stokke
Tønsberg
Aremark
Gressvik
Vikane
Fredrikstad
Skjeberg
Ö. Silen
Kjopmannskjær
Torp
Oterbekk
Årøysund
Øyenkilen
Ingedal
Fredriksten Festning
Halden
Holmegil
Torrskog
Gustavsfors
Vårvik
Skogen
Sandefjord
Tjøme
Framnes
Ormelet
Sandøysund
Verdens Ende
Ytre Hvaler
Sponvika
Tistedal
Sund
Nössemark
Letång
Larvik
Korshavn
Spjærøy
Hvaler
Idd
Stora Le
Lund
Edsleskog
Østre Halsen
Stavern
Skjærhalden
Hogdal
Björnerod
Tresticklan
Bengtsfors
Skåpafors
Fengersfors
Enningdal
Prestebakke
Kornsjø
Håbol
Billingsfors
Strömstad
Skee
Dals Långed
Tisselskog
Söndre Enningdal Kappel
Ed
Ånimskog
Hirtshals
Töftedal
Dalsland
Håverud
Frederikshavn
København
Kiel
Tanum
Bäckefors
Åsensbruk
Naverstad
Havstenssund
Lerdal
Tanumshede
Dalskog
Dals Rostock
Hällristningar i Tanum
Mo
Grebbestad
Kynnefjäll
Mellerud
Kroppefjäll
Hedekas
Högsäter
Fjällbacka
Kville
Hällevadsholm
Brålanda
Hambergsund
Stigen
Färgelanda
Bolstad
Dingle
Ödeborg
Bovallstrand
Frändefors
Vänersnäs
Munkedal
Hunnebostrand
Brodalen
Bohuslän
Väjern
Brastad
Smögen
Kungshamn
Rixo
Malmön
Uddevalla
Vänersborg
Vargön
Herrestad
Hunneberg
Lysekil
Trollhättan
Fiskebäckskil
Väne-Åsaka
Grundsund
Henån
Ljungskile
Ellös
Orust
Sjuntorp
Nossebro
Upphärad
Hälleviksstrand
Svanesund
Lilla Edet
Sollebrunn
Göta
Mollösund
Stenungsund
Ucklum
Gräfsnäs
Tjörn
Långared
Kyrkesund
Skärhamn
Hakefjord
Jörlanda
Skepplanda
Klädesholmen
59°
58°
11°
12°
0
10
20
30 km
1
2
3
A
B
48
53
60
E18
E6
E134
E45

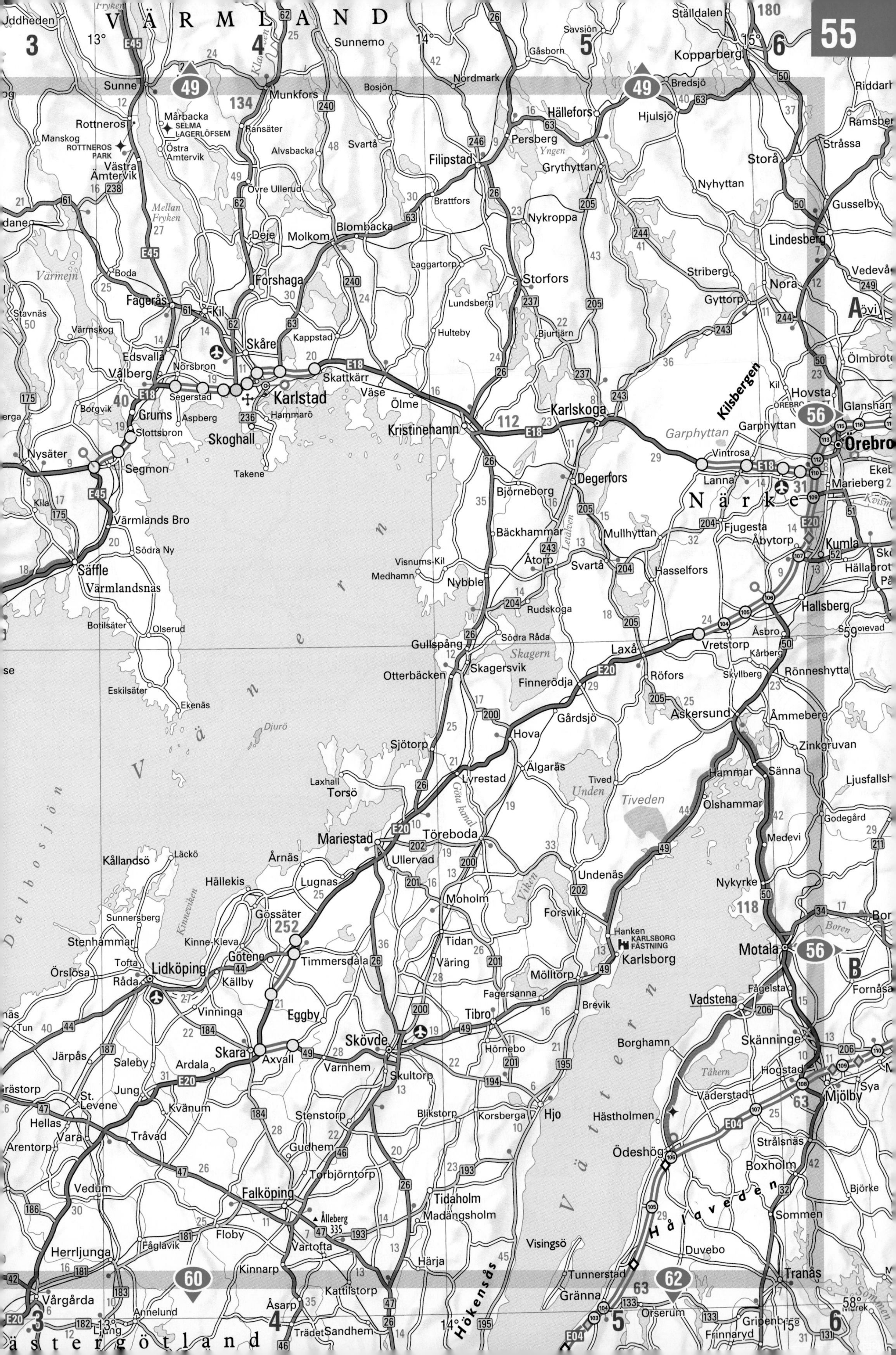

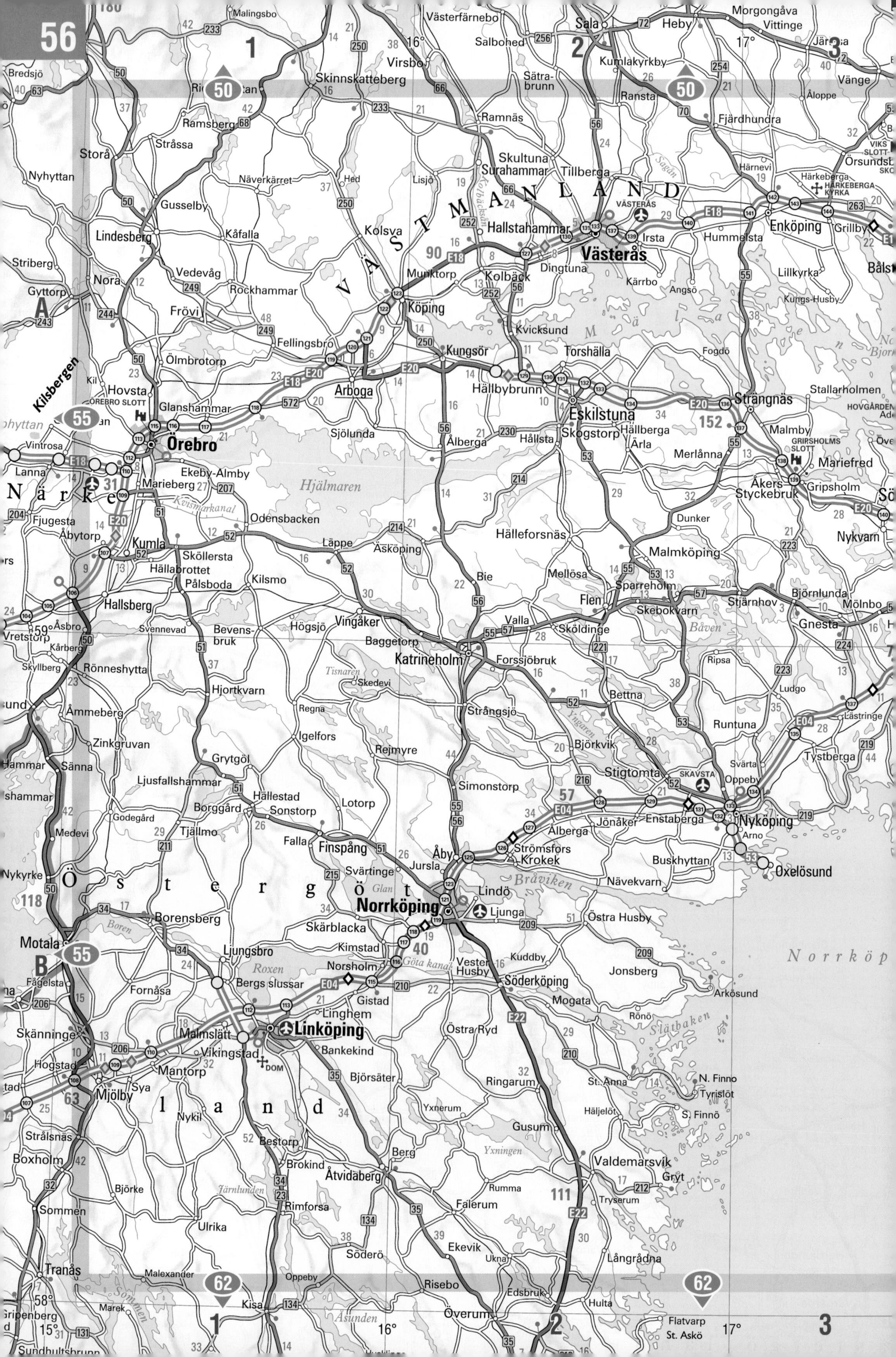
Västmanland
Närke
Östergötland
Mälaren
Hjälmaren
Bråviken
Roxen
Boren
Sommen
Yngaren
Båven
Slätbaken
Norrköp
Malingsbo
Västerfärnebo
Sala
Heby
Morgongåva
Vittinge
Salbohed
Kumlakyrkby
Virsbo
Skinnskatteberg
Sätrabrunn
Ransta
Fjärdhundra
Vänge
Åloppe
Ramsberg
Ramnäs
Stråssa
Storå
Nyhyttan
Skultuna
Surahammar
Tillberga
Härnevi
Örsundsbro
Härkeberga
Härkeberga kyrka
Viks slott
Näverkärret
Hed
Lisjö
Gusselby
Hallstahammar
Västerås
Irsta
Hummelsta
Enköping
Grillby
Lindesberg
Kåfalla
Kolsva
Dingtuna
Kärrbo
Angsö
Lillkyrka
Bålsta
Striberg
Nora
Vedevåg
Munktorp
Kolbäck
Rockhammar
Köping
Kungs-Husby
Gyttorp
Frövi
Kvicksund
Fellingsbro
Kungsör
Torshälla
Fogdö
Ölmbrotorp
Arboga
Hällbybrunn
Eskilstuna
Strängnäs
Stallarholmen
Kilsbergen
Kil
Hovsta
Örebro slott
Glanshammar
Sjölunda
Skogstorp
Hällberga
Ärla
Malmby
Gripsholms slott
Mariefred
Vintrosa
Örebro
Ekeby-Almby
Ålberga
Hållsta
Merlånna
Åkers Styckebruk
Gripsholm
Lanna
Marieberg
Kvismarkanal
Fjugesta
Odensbacken
Dunker
Nykvarn
Åbytorp
Kumla
Sköllersta
Läppe
Äsköping
Hälleforsnäs
Malmköping
Hällabrottet
Pålsboda
Kilsmo
Bie
Mellösa
Sparreholm
Hallsberg
Vingåker
Högsjö
Flen
Skebokvarn
Stjärnhov
Björnlunda
Gnesta
Mölnbo
Åsbro
Vretstorp
Svennevad
Bevensbruk
Baggetorp
Valla
Sköldinge
Kårberg
Skyllberg
Katrineholm
Forssjöbruk
Ripsa
Rönneshytta
Tisnaren
Skedevi
Hjortkvarn
Regna
Bettna
Ludgo
Åmmeberg
Strångsjö
Runtuna
Lästringe
Zinkgruvan
Igelfors
Rejmyre
Björkvik
Tystberga
Grytgöl
Svärta
Hammar
Sänna
Ljusfallshammar
Simonstorp
Stigtomta
Skavsta
Oppeby
Hällestad
Borggård
Sonstorp
Lotorp
Jönåker
Enstaberga
Nyköping
Godegård
Tjällmo
Falla
Finspång
Strömsfors
Krokek
Arno
Medevi
Åby
Jursla
Buskhyttan
Oxelösund
Nykyrke
Svärtinge
Lindö
Nävekvarn
Glan
Norrköping
Ljunga
Östra Husby
Borensberg
Skärblacka
Motala
Kimstad
Kuddby
Ljungsbro
Vester Husby
Jonsberg
Norsholm
Göta kanal
Fågelsta
Fornåsa
Bergs slussar
Söderköping
Arkösund
Gistad
Mogata
Linghem
Rönö
Skänninge
Malmslätt
Linköping
Östra Ryd
Hogstad
Vikingstad
Bankekind
Dom
Mantorp
Björsäter
Ringarum
St. Anna
N. Finno
Tyrislöt
Mjölby
Sya
Yxnerum
Häljelöt
S. Finnö
Nykil
Strålsnäs
Gusum
Bestorp
Yxningen
Boxholm
Berg
Valdemarsvik
Brokind
Åtvidaberg
Gryt
Björke
Järnlunden
Rumma
Tryserum
Sommen
Rimforsa
Falerum
Ulrika
Ekevik
Söderö
Ukna
Långrådna
Tranås
Malexander
Oppeby
Risebo
Edsbruk
Marek
Kisa
Hulta
Gripenberg
Åsunden
Överum
Flatvarp
St. Askö
Sundhultsbrunn
15°
16°
17°
58°
1
2
3
A
B
E4
E18
E20
E22
50
55
62
63
90
111
118
152

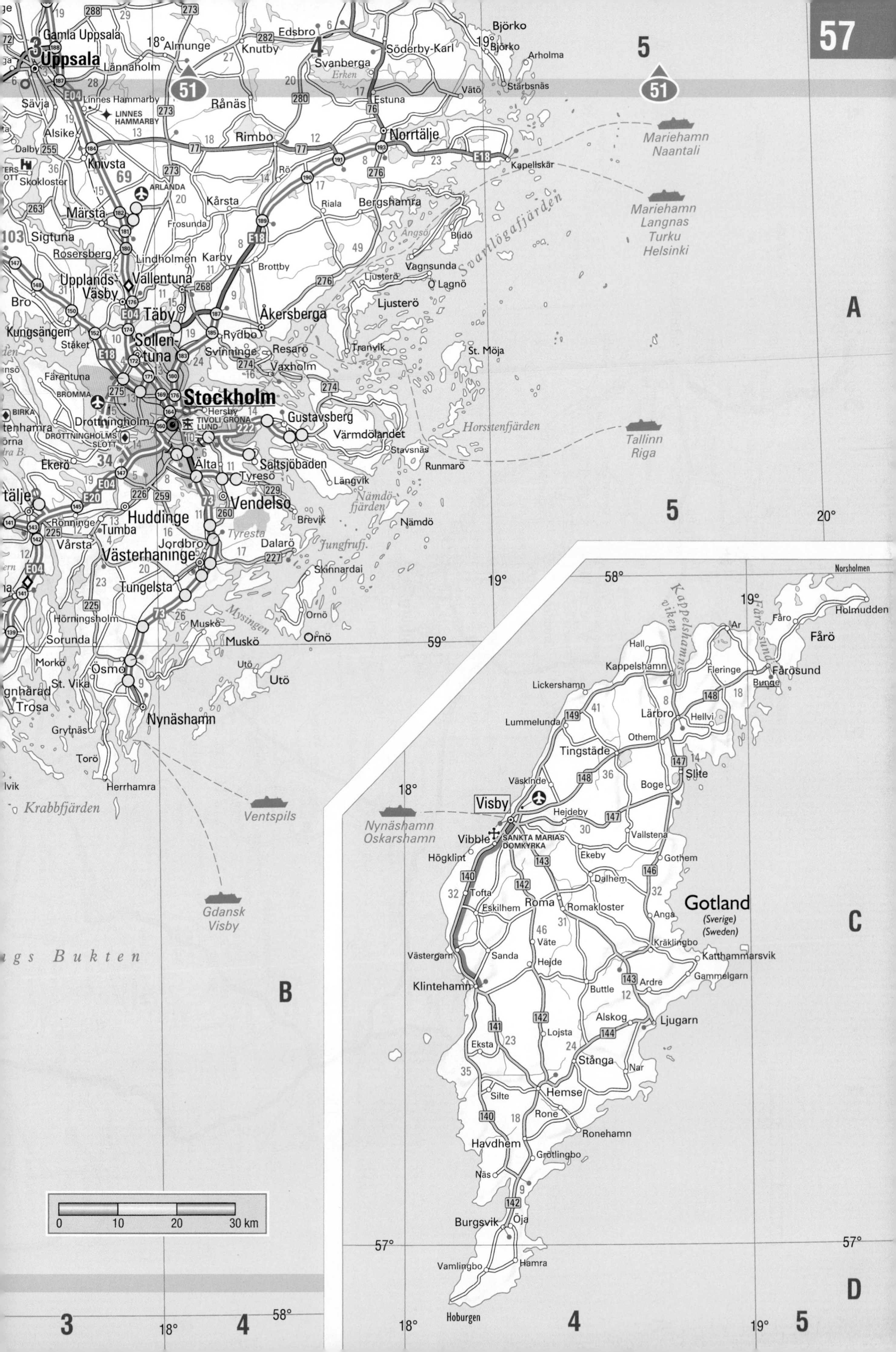
Uppsala
Gamla Uppsala
Almunge
Knutby
Edsbro
Söderby-Karl
Björko
Arholma
Svanberga
Erken
Lännaholm
Estuna
Vätö
Stärbsnäs
Sävja
Linnes Hammarby
LINNES HAMMARBY
Rånäs
Rimbo
Norrtälje
Alsike
Dalby
Knivsta
Kapellskär
Mariehamn
Naantali
Skokloster
ARLANDA
Kårsta
Riala
Bergshamra
Mariehamn
Langnas
Turku
Helsinki
Märsta
Frosunda
Sigtuna
Rosersberg
Lindholmen
Karby
Brottby
Blidö
Ängsö
Svartlögafjärden
Upplands-Väsby
Vallentuna
Vagnsunda
Ljusterö
Lagnö
Bro
Täby
Åkersberga
Kungsängen
Stäket
Sollentuna
Rydbo
Svinninge
Resarö
Tranvik
St. Möja
Vaxholm
Färentuna
BROMMA
Stockholm
Hersby
TIVOLI GRÖNA LUND
Gustavsberg
BIRKA
Drottningholm
DROTTNINGHOLMS SLOTT
Värmdölandet
Horsstenfjärden
Tallinn
Riga
Stavsnäs
Runmarö
Ekerö
Älta
Saltsjöbaden
Tyresö
Längvik
Nämdöfjärden
Södertälje
Vendelsö
Huddinge
Rönninge
Tumba
Vårsta
Brevik
Nämdö
Jordbro
Tyresta
Dalarö
Jungfrufj.
Västerhaninge
Skinnardai
Tungelsta
Hörningsholm
Mysingen
Muskö
Ornö
Sorunda
Utö
Mörkö
Ösmo
St. Vika
Trosa
Nynäshamn
Grytnäs
Torö
Herrhamra
Krabbfjärden
Ventspils
Gdansk
Visby
Bukten
Norsholmen
Kappelshamnsviken
Fårösund
Holmudden
Fårö
Ar
Hall
Kappelshamn
Fleringe
Fårösund
Bunge
Lickershamn
Lärbro
Hellvi
Lummelunda
Othem
Tingstäde
Slite
Väskinde
Boge
Visby
Hejdeby
Nynäshamn
Oskarshamn
Vibble
SANKTA MARIAS DOMKYRKA
Vallstena
Högklint
Ekeby
Gothem
Dalhem
Tofta
Roma
Romakloster
Eskilhem
Gotland
(Sverige)
(Sweden)
Anga
Väte
Kräklingbo
Västergarn
Sanda
Katthammarsvik
Hejde
Gammelgarn
Klintehamn
Buttle
Ardre
Alskog
Ljugarn
Lojsta
Eksta
Stånga
Närs
Hemse
Silte
Rone
Ronehamn
Havdhem
Grötlingbo
Näs
Burgsvik
Öja
Vamlingbo
Hamra
Hoburgen
0 10 20 30 km
A
B
C
D
3
4
5

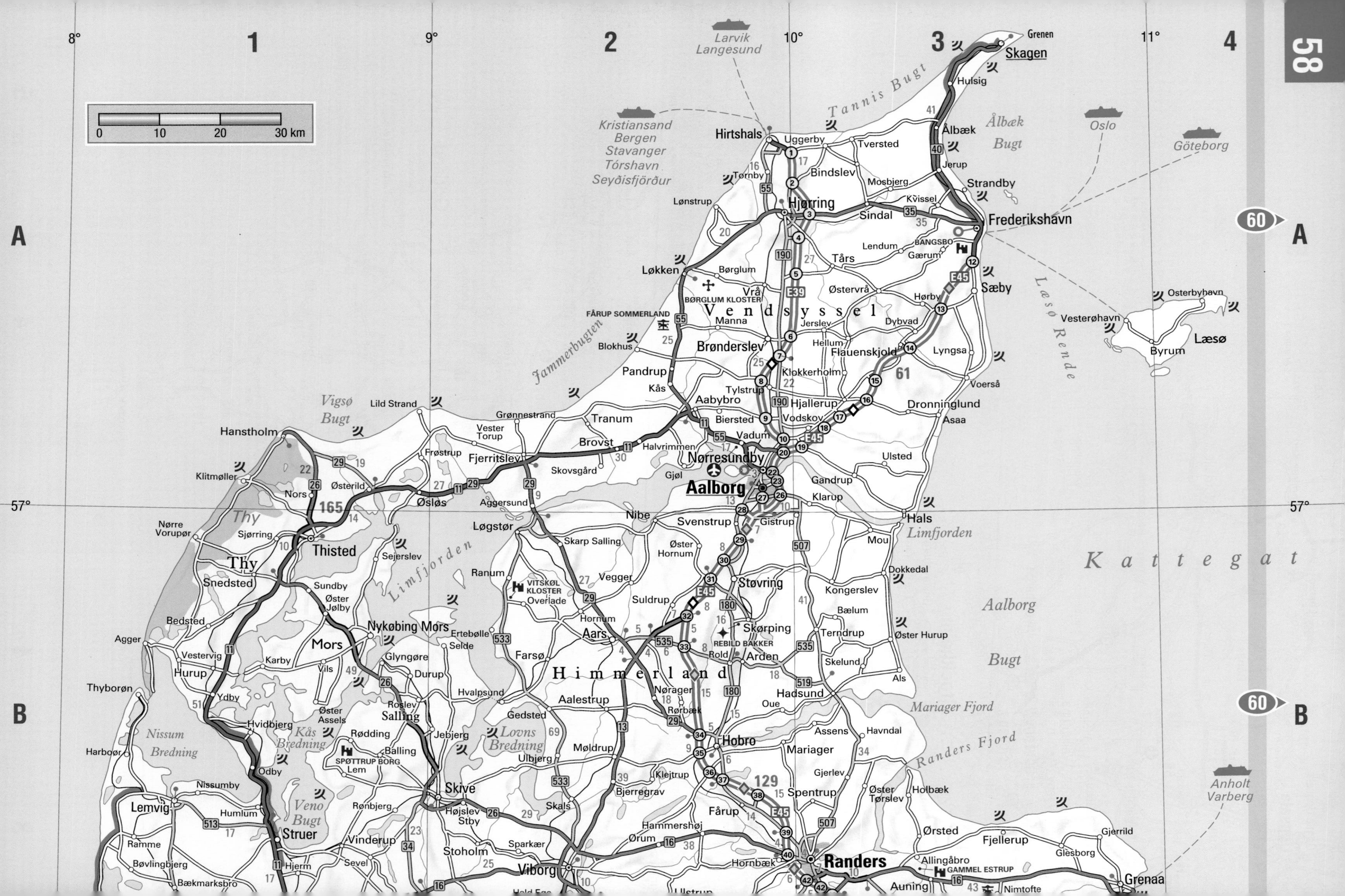
Skagen
Grenen
Frederikshavn
Hjørring
Hirtshals
Læsø
Vendsyssel
Aalborg
Nørresundby
Himmerland
Kattegat
Aalborg Bugt
Tannis Bugt
Ålbæk Bugt
Jammerbugten
Vigsø Bugt
Limfjorden
Læsø Rende
Mariager Fjord
Randers Fjord
Thisted
Thy
Mors
Nykøbing Mors
Skive
Viborg
Randers
Hobro
Struer
Lemvig
Grenaa
Brønderslev
Løkken
Sæby
Kristiansand
Bergen
Stavanger
Tórshavn
Seyðisfjörður
Larvik
Langesund
Oslo
Göteborg
Anholt
Varberg
0
10
20
30 km
8°
9°
10°
11°
57°
1
2
3
4
A
B
60

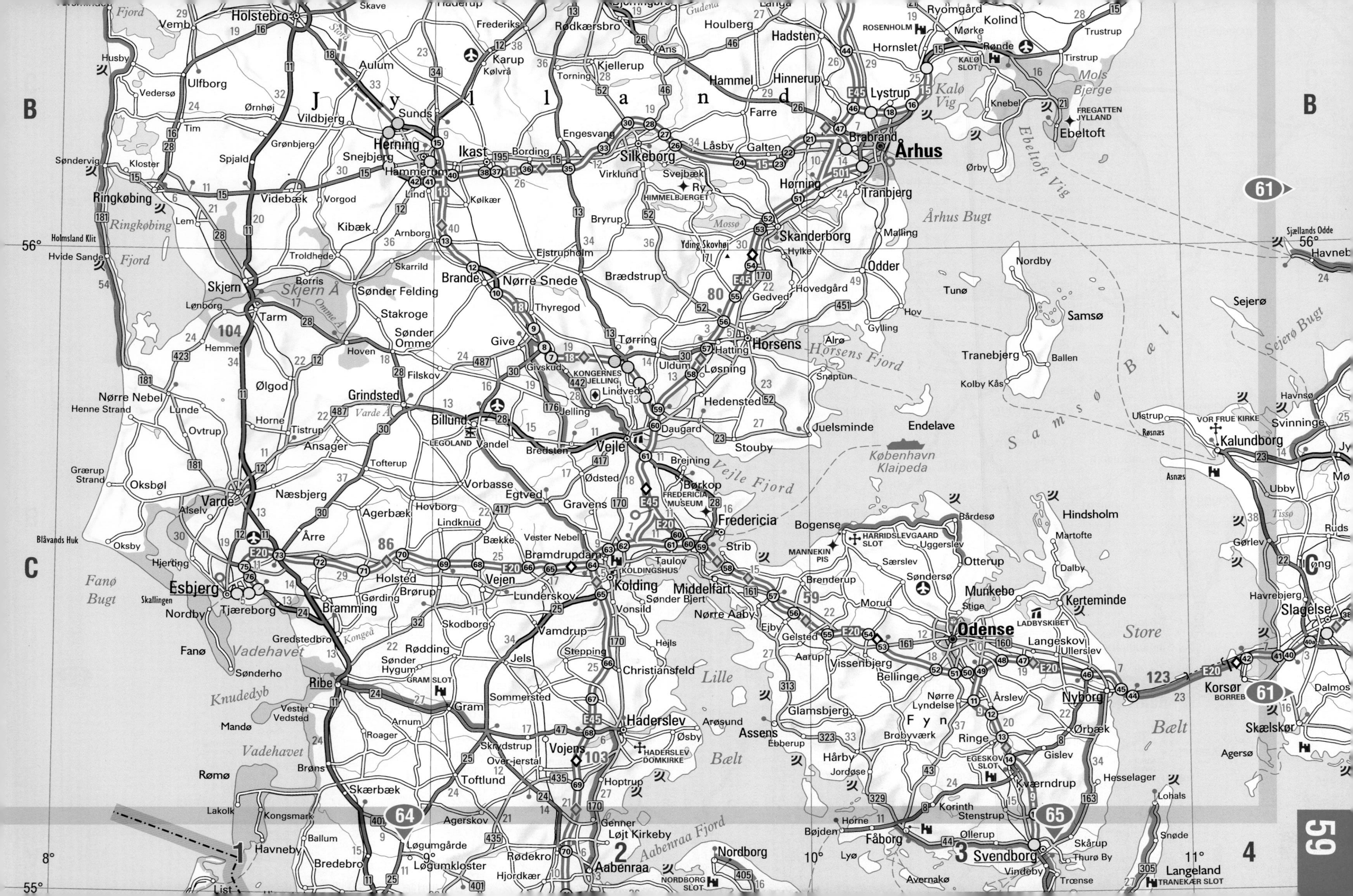
Jylland
Fyn
Holstebro
Herning
Ikast
Silkeborg
Århus
Randers
Horsens
Skanderborg
Vejle
Fredericia
Kolding
Middelfart
Odense
Nyborg
Svendborg
Fåborg
Assens
Haderslev
Aabenraa
Ribe
Esbjerg
Varde
Skjern
Ringkøbing
Billund
Grindsted
Brande
Nørre Snede
Hadsten
Hammel
Ebeltoft
Kalundborg
Korsør
Slagelse
Samsø
Tunø
Endelave
Sejerø
Fanø
Rømø
Langeland
Nordborg
Århus Bugt
Ebeltoft Vig
Horsens Fjord
Vejle Fjord
Samsø Bælt
Lille Bælt
Store Bælt
Vadehavet
Fanø Bugt
Ringkøbing Fjord
København Klaipeda
LEGOLAND
KONGERNES JELLING
FREDERICIA MUSEUM
HARRIDSLEVGAARD SLOT
EGESKOV SLOT
GRAM SLOT
HADERSLEV DOMKIRKE
NORDBORG SLOT
ROSENHOLM
KALØ SLOT
FREGATTEN JYLLAND
VOR FRUE KIRKE
LADBYSKIBET
HIMMELBJERGET
TRANEKÆR SLOT
KOLDINGSHUS
MANNEKIN PIS
56°
55°
8°
9°
10°
11°
B
C
1
2
3
4

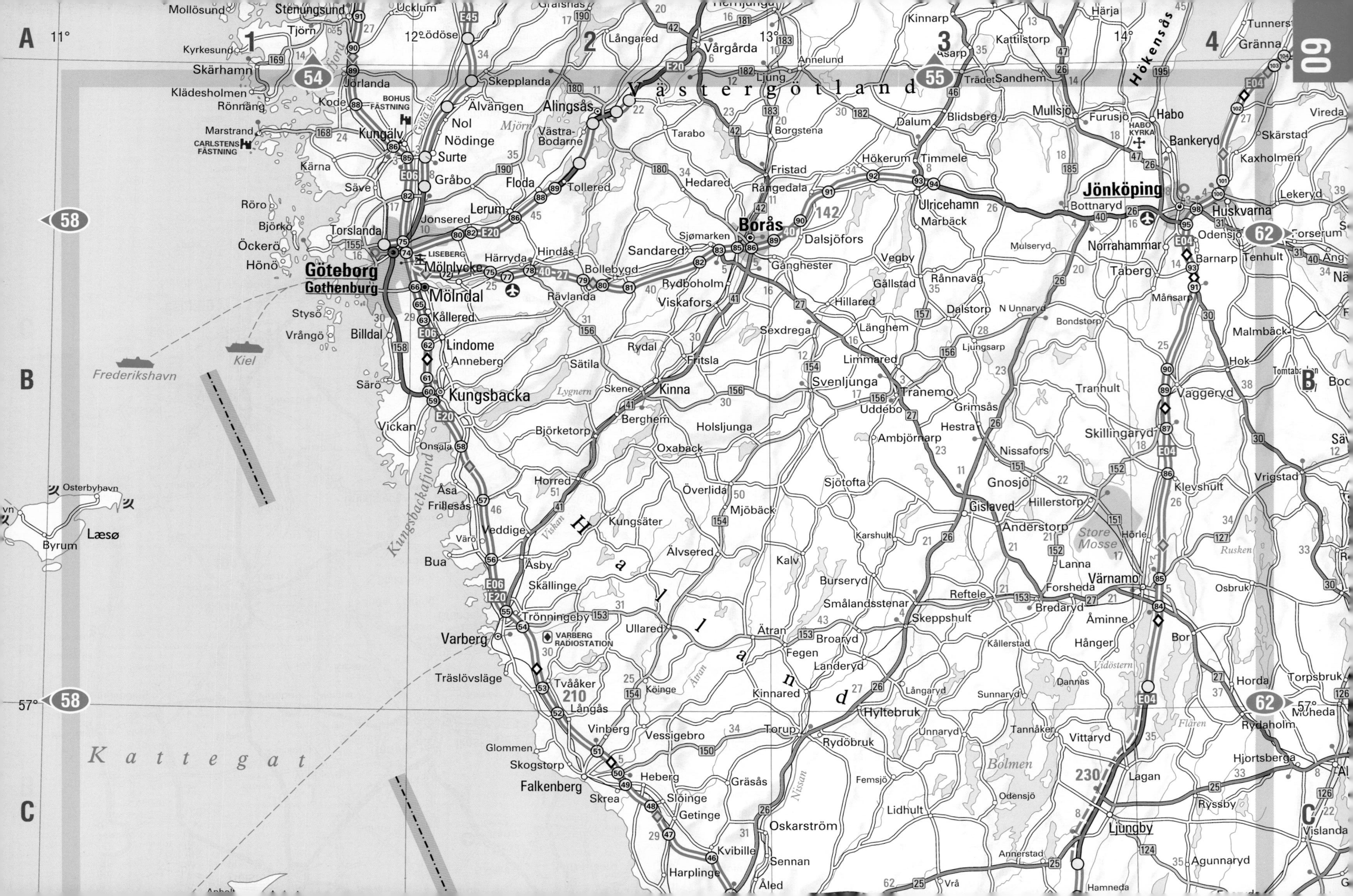
Västergötland
Halland
Kattegat
Göteborg
Gothenburg
Borås
Jönköping
Alingsås
Kungsbacka
Mölndal
Varberg
Falkenberg
Kungälv
Huskvarna
Värnamo
Ljungby
Gislaved
Ulricehamn
Kinna
Svenljunga
Tranemo
Hyltebruk
Vaggeryd
Skillingaryd
Mollösund
Stenungsund
Tjörn
Kyrkesund
Skärhamn
Klädesholmen
Rönnäng
Marstrand
CARLSTENS FÄSTNING
BOHUS FÄSTNING
Kode
Jörlanda
Skepplanda
Älvängen
Nol
Nödinge
Surte
Gråbo
Kärna
Säve
Torslanda
Röro
Björkö
Öckerö
Hönö
Styrsö
Vrångö
Billdal
Särö
Vickan
Onsala
Åsa
Frillesås
Värö
Bua
Veddige
Lindome
Anneberg
Kållered
Mölnlycke
LISEBERG
Härryda
Hindås
Jonsered
Lerum
Floda
Tollered
Västra-Bodarne
Mjörn
Göta älv
Lödöse
Långared
Vårgårda
Annelund
Ljung
Borgstena
Tarabo
Fristad
Hedared
Rångedala
Sjømarken
Sandared
Bollebygd
Rävlanda
Rydboholm
Viskafors
Gånghester
Dalsjöfors
Sätila
Rydal
Fritsla
Skene
Lygnern
Berghem
Björketorp
Horred
Holsljunga
Oxaback
Överlida
Mjöbäck
Kungsäter
Älvsered
Åsby
Skällinge
Trönningeby
VARBERG RADIOSTATION
Träslövsläge
Tvååker
Långås
Vinberg
Vessigebro
Glommen
Skogstorp
Skrea
Heberg
Slöinge
Getinge
Kvibille
Harplinge
Gräsås
Sennan
Åled
Oskarström
Torup
Rydöbruk
Kinnared
Fegen
Ätran
Ullared
Köinge
Kalv
Burseryd
Smålandsstenar
Skeppshult
Broaryd
Landeryd
Långaryd
Sexdrega
Hillared
Länghem
Limmared
Uddebo
Ambjörnarp
Sjötofta
Karshult
Dalstorp
Ljungsarp
Gällstad
Vegby
Rånnaväg
Marbäck
Hökerum
Timmele
Dalum
Blidsberg
Kinnarp
Asarp
Trädet
Sandhem
Kattilstorp
Mullsjö
Härja
Furusjö
Habo
HABO KYRKA
Bankeryd
Bottnaryd
Mulseryd
N Unnaryd
Bondstorp
Norrahammar
Taberg
Månsarp
Barnarp
Tenhult
Odensjö
Hökensås
Gränna
Tunnerstad
Skärstad
Kaxholmen
Vireda
Lekeryd
Forserum
Malmbäck
Hok
Tranhult
Grimsås
Hestra
Nissafors
Gnosjö
Hillerstorp
Anderstorp
Store Mosse
Hörle
Klevshult
Lanna
Forsheda
Reftele
Bredaryd
Åminne
Hånger
Kållerstad
Vidöstern
Bor
Dannäs
Sunnaryd
Unnaryd
Tannåker
Vittaryd
Bolmen
Flåren
Femsjö
Lidhult
Odensjö
Annerstad
Agunnaryd
Ryssby
Lagan
Hjortsberga
Rydaholm
Horda
Torpsbruk
Moheda
Vislanda
Vrigstad
Osbruk
Rusken
Nissan
Viskan
Ätran
Kungsbackafjord
Frederikshavn
Kiel
Læsø
Østerbyhavn
Byrum
11°
12°
13°
14°
57°
A
B
C
1
2
3
4
54
55
58
62

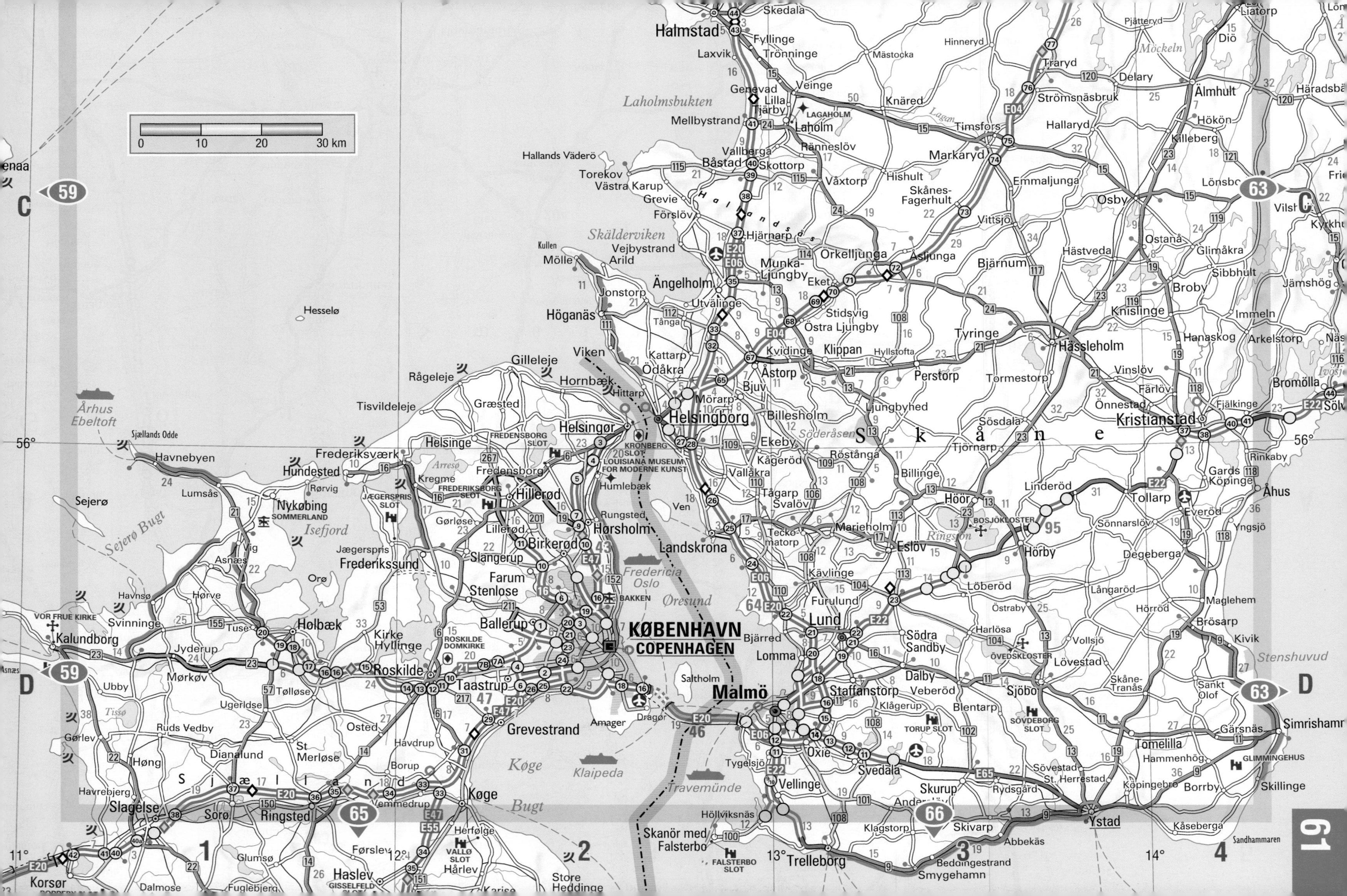
Halmstad
Laholmsbukten
Laholm
Båstad
Torekov
Skälderviken
Hallands Väderö
Kullen
Mölle
Ängelholm
Höganäs
Helsingborg
Helsingør
Hillerød
Hørsholm
Landskrona
Lund
Malmö
KØBENHAVN
COPENHAGEN
Øresund
Saltholm
Amager
Dragør
Køge
Køge Bugt
Roskilde
Holbæk
Kalundborg
Slagelse
Sorø
Ringsted
Korsør
Frederikssund
Frederiksværk
Hundested
Nykøbing
Isefjord
Sejerø
Sejerø Bugt
Hesselø
Sjællands Odde
Gilleleje
Trelleborg
Ystad
Skanör med Falsterbo
Simrishamn
Kristianstad
Hässleholm
Markaryd
Osby
Älmhult
Klippan
Eslöv
Hörby
Tomelilla
Sjöbo
Skurup
Svedala
Vellinge
Skåne
Själland
Hallandsås
Söderåsen
Ringsjön
Stenshuvud
Århus
Ebeltoft
Fredericia
Oslo
Klaipeda
Travemünde
56°
11°
12°
13°
14°
0
10
20
30 km
C
D
1
2
3
4
59
63
65
66

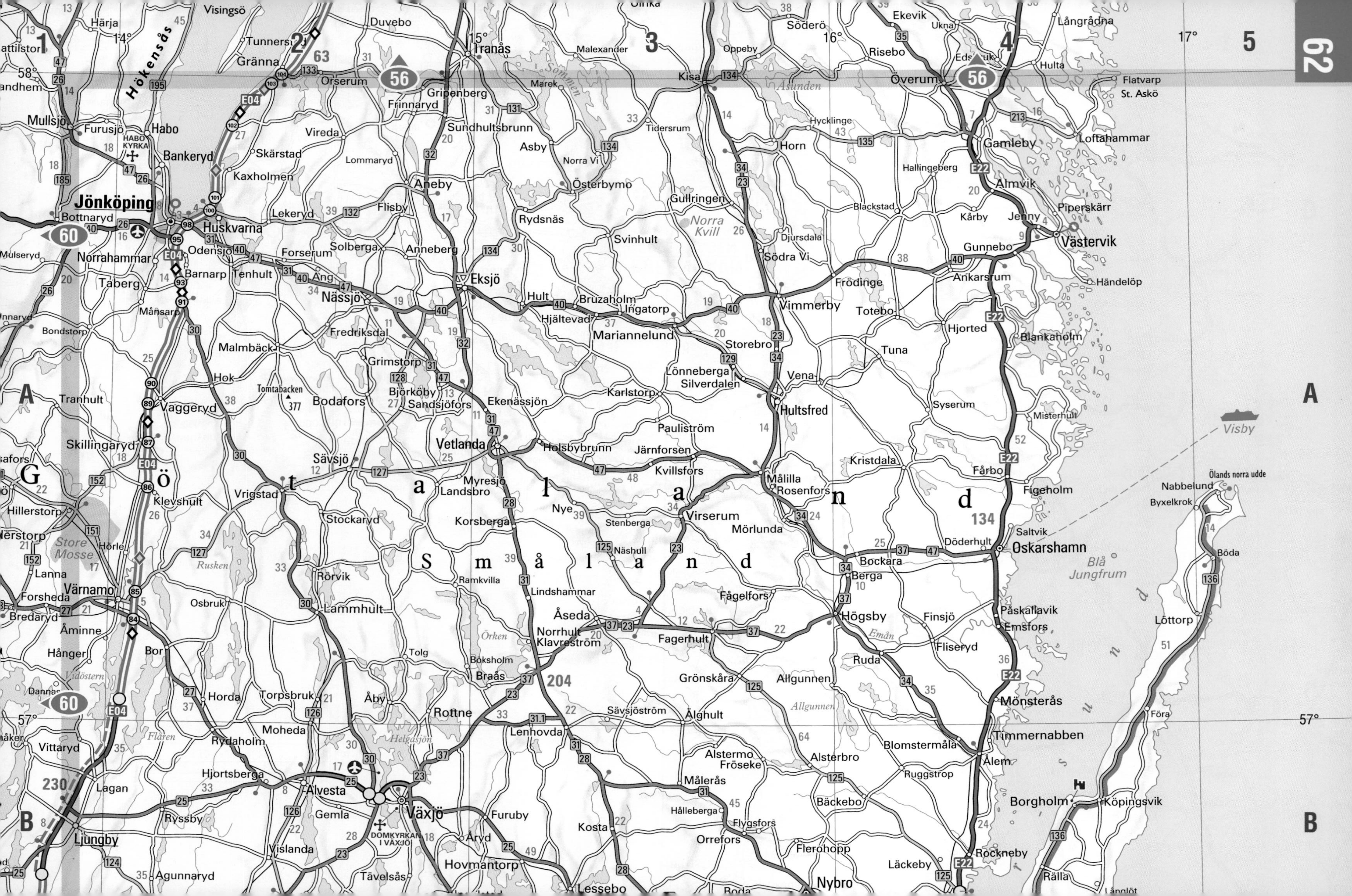
Småland
Götaland
Jönköping
Huskvarna
Tranås
Eksjö
Nässjö
Vetlanda
Värnamo
Växjö
Ljungby
Alvesta
Västervik
Oskarshamn
Hultsfred
Vimmerby
Mönsterås
Borgholm
Nybro
Kisa
Gränna
Habo
Mullsjö
Sävsjö
Vaggeryd
Skillingaryd
Aneby
Eksjö
Högsby
Virserum
Mariannelund
Gamleby
Överum
Åseda
Lessebo
Kosta
Orrefors
Hovmantorp
Rockneby
Köpingsvik
Böda
Löttorp
Visby
Ölands norra udde
Blå Jungfrum
Sommen
Norra Kvill
Store Mosse
Helgasjön
Åsunden
Vidöstern
Hökensås
DOMKYRKAN I VÄXJÖ
HABO KYRKA
Tomtabacken 377
57°
58°
14°
15°
16°
17°
A
B
1
2
3
4
5
E4
E22
56
60
63
134
204
230

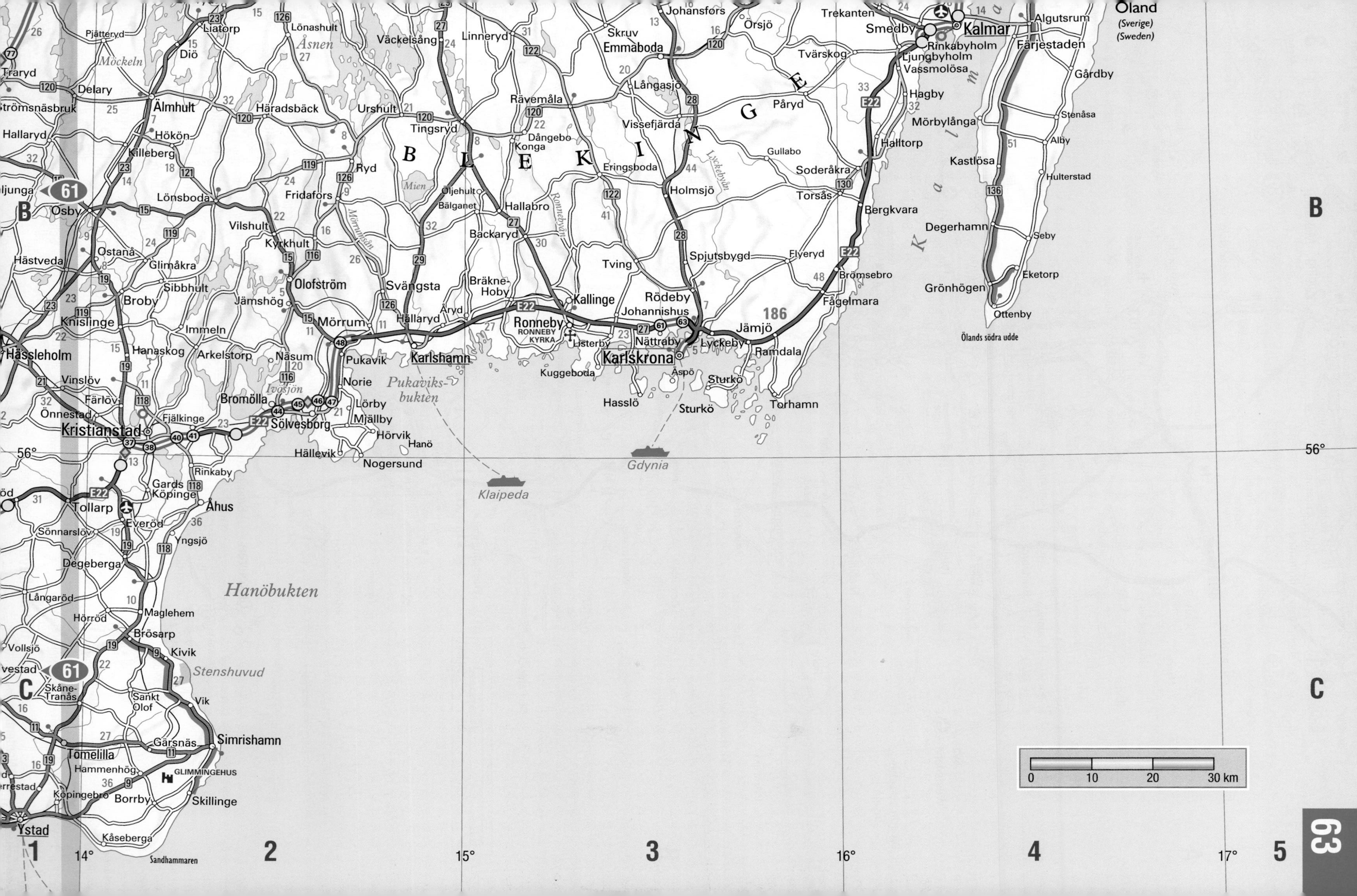

Öland
(Sverige)
(Sweden)

Algutsrum
Färjestaden
Gårdby
Stenåsa
Alby
Hulterstad
Hagby
Mörbylånga
Vassmolösa
Ljungbyholm
Rinkabyholm
Seby
Eketorp
Ottenby
Ölands södra udde

Kalmar
Smedby
Trekanten
Tvärskog
Halltorp
Bergkvara
E22
Brömsebro
Fågelmara
Söderåkra
130
Torsås
Flyeryd
48
Johansfors
Örsjö
Påryd
Gullabo
Holmsjö
Spjutsbygd
Jämjö
Ramdala
186
Torhamn
Skruv
Emmaboda
Långasjö
Visseljärda
Eringsboda
Rödeby
Johannishus
Nättraby
Karlskrona
Sturkö
Aspö
Hasslö
Lyckeby
Listerby
Kallinge
Tving
Ronneby
RONNEBY
KYRKA
Kuggeboda
Råvemåla
Dångebo
Konga
Hallabro
Bäckaryd
Bräkne-Hoby
Linneryd
122
Tingsryd
Öjehult
Bälganet
Hällaryd
Karlshamn
Väckelsäng
Ryd
Svängsta
Pukavik
Norje
Hörvik
Hanö
Nogersund
Urshult
Mörrumsån
Mörrum
Lörby
Mjällby
Hällevik
Olofström
Näsum
Sölvesborg
Vilshult
Jämshög
Bromölla
Åhus
Åsnen
Liatorp
Delary
Diö
Hökön
Killeberg
Immeln
Arkelstorp
Fjälkinge
Gards
Köpinge
Rinkaby
Gärsnäs
Almhult
Lönsboda
Glimåkra
Sibbhult
Hanaskog
Broby
Kristianstad
Tollarp
Everöd
Degeberga
Maglehem
Brösarp
Kivik
Vik
Simrishamn
GLIMMINGEHUS
Sankt
Olof
Vollsjö
Skåne-
Tranås
Tomelilla
Hammenhög
Borrby
Skillinge
Kåseberga
Sandhammaren
Hässleholm
Vinslöv
Önnestad
Sönnarslöv
Hörröd
Långaröd
Ystad

Gdynia

Klaipeda

Pukaviks-bukten

Hanöbukten

Stenshuvud

Lyckebyån

Ronnebyån

Mörrumsån

Mückeln

Hästveda

0   10   20   30 km

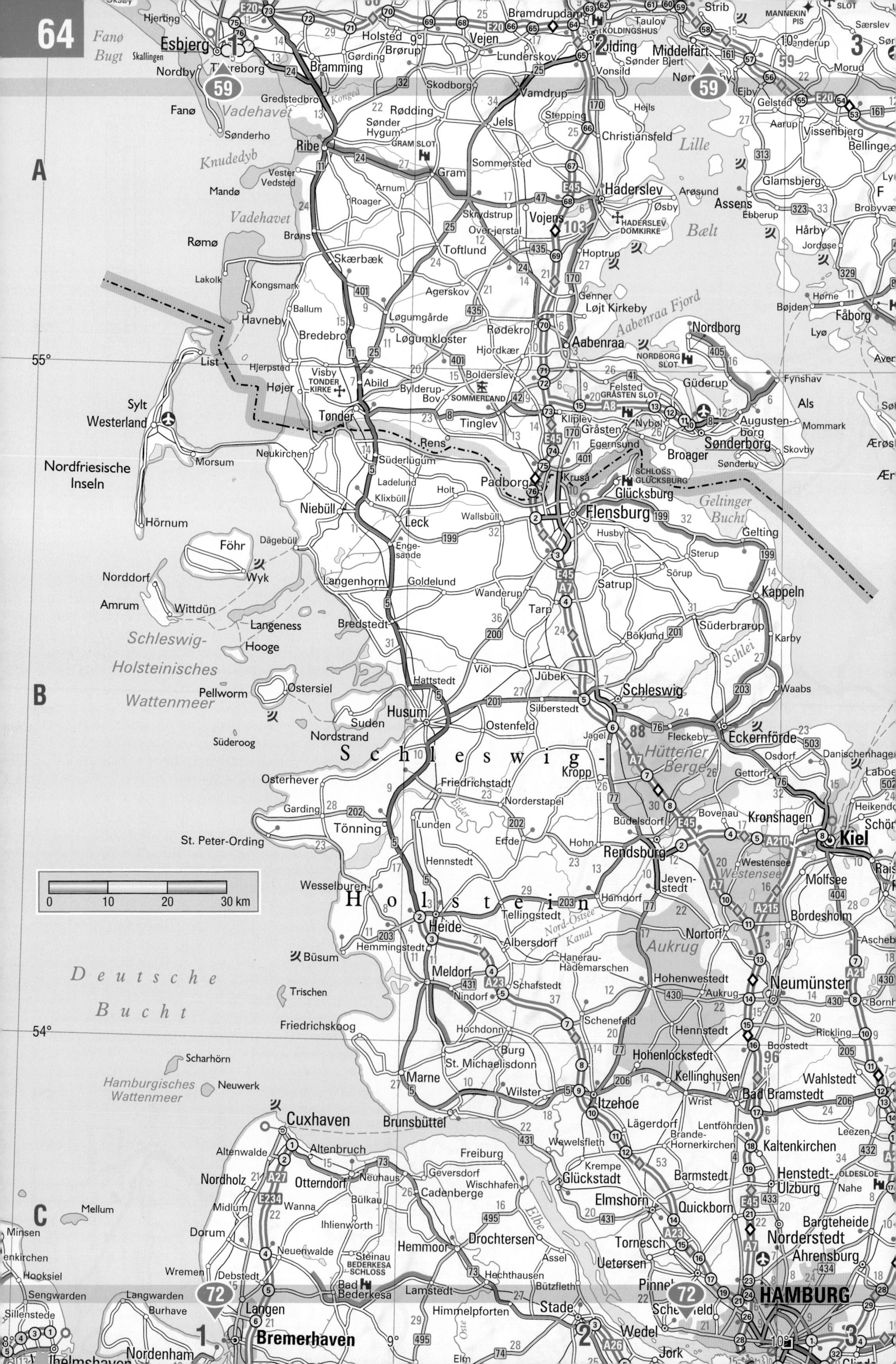
Fanø Bugt
Skallingen
Esbjerg
Hjerting
Nordby
Tjæreborg
Fanø
Sønderho
Vadehavet
Knudedyb
Mandø
Vester Vedsted
Rømø
Lakolk
Kongsmark
Havneby
List
Sylt
Westerland
Morsum
Hörnum
Nordfriesische Inseln
Föhr
Dägebüll
Wyk
Norddorf
Amrum
Wittdün
Langeness
Hooge
Schleswig-Holsteinisches Wattenmeer
Pellworm
Ostersiel
Süderoog
Nordstrand
Suden
Husum
Holsted
Gørding
Bramming
Brørup
Vejen
Gredstedbro
Kongeå
Ribe
Rødding
Sønder Hygum
GRAM SLOT
Gram
Arnum
Roager
Brøns
Skærbæk
Ballum
Bredebro
Løgumgårde
Løgumkloster
Hjerpsted
Højer
Visby
TØNDER KIRKE
Abild
Tønder
Bylderup-Bov
SOMMERLAND
Bolderslev
Tinglev
Rens
Süderlügum
Neukirchen
Ladelund
Klixbüll
Holt
Niebüll
Leck
Engesande
Wallsbüll
Langenhorn
Goldelund
Wanderup
Bredstedt
Viöl
Hattstedt
Jübek
Tarp
Bramdrupdam
KOLDINGHUS
Kolding
Taulov
Strib
Middelfart
Sønder Bjert
Lunderskov
Vonsild
Skodborg
Vamdrup
Jels
Stepping
Hejls
Christiansfeld
Sommersted
Haderslev
HADERSLEV DOMKIRKE
Arøsund
Øsby
Skrydstrup
Vojens
Over-Jerstal
Toftlund
Agerskov
Hoptrup
Genner
Løjt Kirkeby
Aabenraa Fjord
Rødekro
Hjordkær
Aabenraa
Kliplev
Felsted
GRÅSTEN SLOT
Gråsten
Nybøl
Egernsund
Kruså
Padborg
Nordborg
NORDBORG SLOT
Güderup
Fynshav
Als
Augustenborg
Sønderborg
Mommark
Broager
Sønderby
Skovby
SCHLOSS GLÜCKSBURG
Glücksburg
Flensburg
Geltinger Bucht
Gelting
Husby
Sterup
Sörup
Satrup
Kappeln
Süderbrarup
Böklund
Karby
Schlei
Schleswig
Waabs
Silberstedt
Ostenfeld
Jagel
Fleckeby
Eckernförde
Hüttener Berge
Kropp
Gettorf
Osdorf
Danischenhagen
Kronshagen
Kiel
Bovenau
Büdelsdorf
Rendsburg
Westensee
Molfsee
Bordesholm
Jevenstedt
Hamdorf
Nortorf
Aukrug
Hohenwestedt
Neumünster
Hennstedt
Boostedt
Rickling
Schenefeld
Hohenlockstedt
Kellinghusen
Wahlstedt
Bad Bramstedt
Wrist
Lentföhrden
Kaltenkirchen
Henstedt-Ulzburg
Nahe
Bargteheide
Norderstedt
Ahrensburg
HAMBURG
Schleswig-Holstein
Friedrichstadt
Eider
Norderstapel
Osterhever
Garding
Tönning
St. Peter-Ording
Lunden
Erfde
Hohn
Hennstedt
Wesselburen
Tellingstedt
Nord-Ostsee Kanal
Heide
Hemmingstedt
Albersdorf
Hanerau-Hademarschen
Büsum
Meldorf
Nindorf
Schafstedt
Trischen
Deutsche Bucht
Friedrichskoog
Hochdonn
Burg
St. Michaelisdonn
Marne
Wilster
Itzehoe
Scharhörn
Neuwerk
Hamburgisches Wattenmeer
Cuxhaven
Brunsbüttel
Lägerdorf
Brande-Hornerkirchen
Wewelsfleth
Krempe
Glückstadt
Barmstedt
Elmshorn
Quickborn
Tornesch
Uetersen
Pinneberg
Schenefeld
Altenwalde
Altenbruch
Nordholz
Otterndorf
Neuhaus
Geversdorf
Wischhafen
Freiburg
Cadenberge
Bülkau
Wanna
Midlum
Ihlienworth
Elbe
Drochtersen
Mellum
Dorum
Neuenwalde
Steinau
BEDERKESA SCHLOSS
Hemmoor
Assel
Wremen
Debstedt
Bad Bederkesa
Lamstedt
Hechthausen
Bützfleth
Stade
Himmelpforten
Langen
Bremerhaven
Nordenham
Wedel
Jork
Langwarden
Burhave
Sengwarden
Hooksiel
Sillenstede
Minsen
Lille Bælt
Assens
Ebberup
Hårby
Jordløse
Bøjden
Horne
Fåborg
Lyø
Glamsbjerg
Vissenbjerg
Bellinge
Aarup
Gelsted
Ejby
Brobyværk
Særslev
MANNEKIN PIS
Morud
55°
54°
0 10 20 30 km

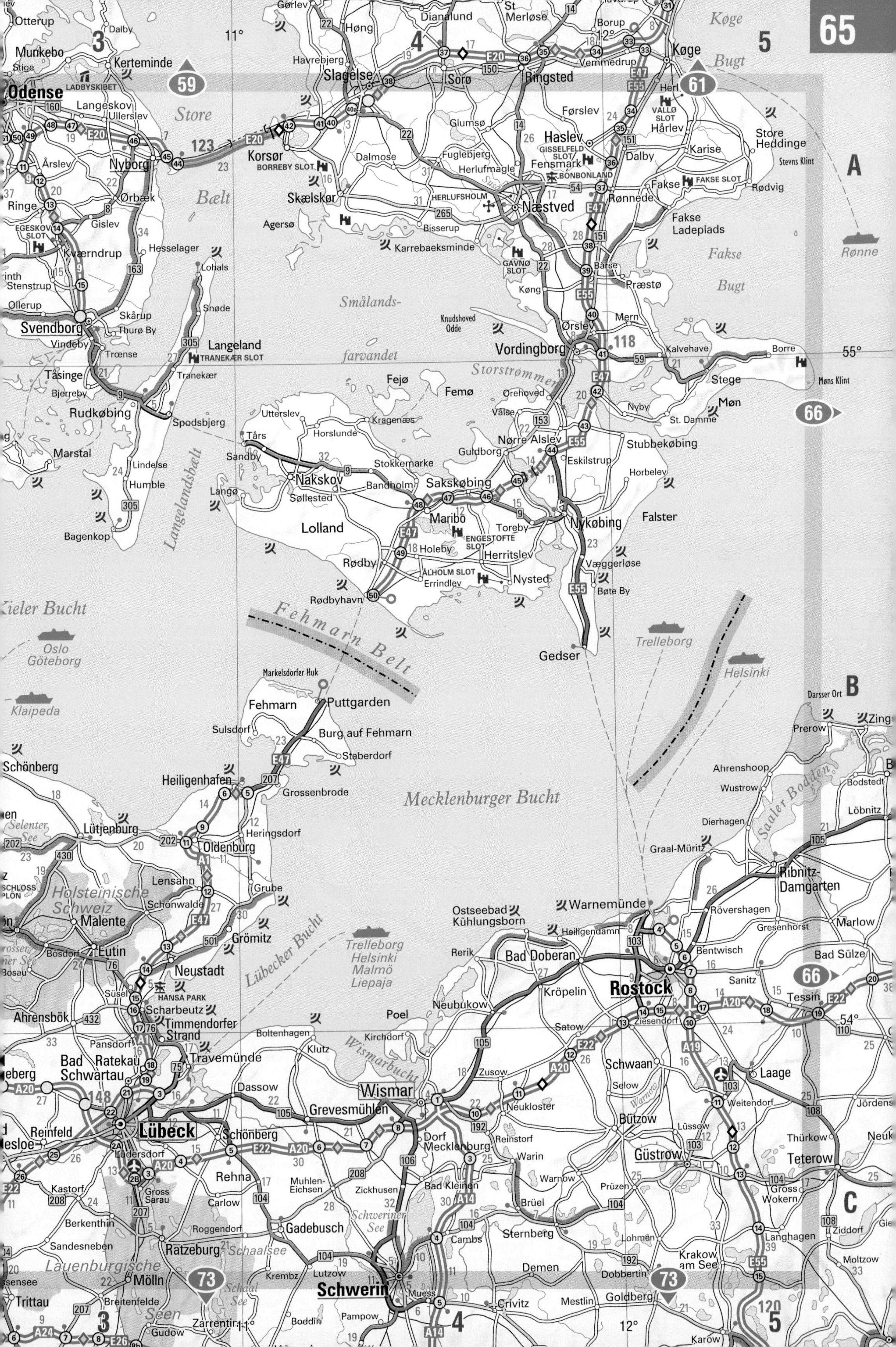
Odense
Svendborg
Langeland
Rudkøbing
Nyborg
Korsør
Slagelse
Sorø
Ringsted
Køge
Haslev
Næstved
Vordingborg
Nakskov
Sakskøbing
Maribo
Lolland
Nykøbing
Falster
Gedser
Stege
Møn
Store Bælt
Smålands-farvandet
Storstrømmen
Fakse Bugt
Køge Bugt
Langelandsbælt
Kieler Bucht
Fehmarn Belt
Fehmarn
Puttgarden
Burg auf Fehmarn
Heiligenhafen
Oldenburg
Mecklenburger Bucht
Lübecker Bucht
Wismarbucht
Neustadt
Eutin
Malente
Holsteinische Schweiz
Lübeck
Travemünde
Wismar
Schwerin
Rostock
Warnemünde
Bad Doberan
Güstrow
Ribnitz-Damgarten
Teterow
Ratzeburg
Mölln
Gadebusch
Saaler Bodden
Trelleborg
Helsinki
Oslo
Göteborg
Klaipeda
Rønne
Trelleborg Helsinki Malmö Liepaja
59
61
66
73
A
B
C
3
4
5
11°
12°
54°
55°

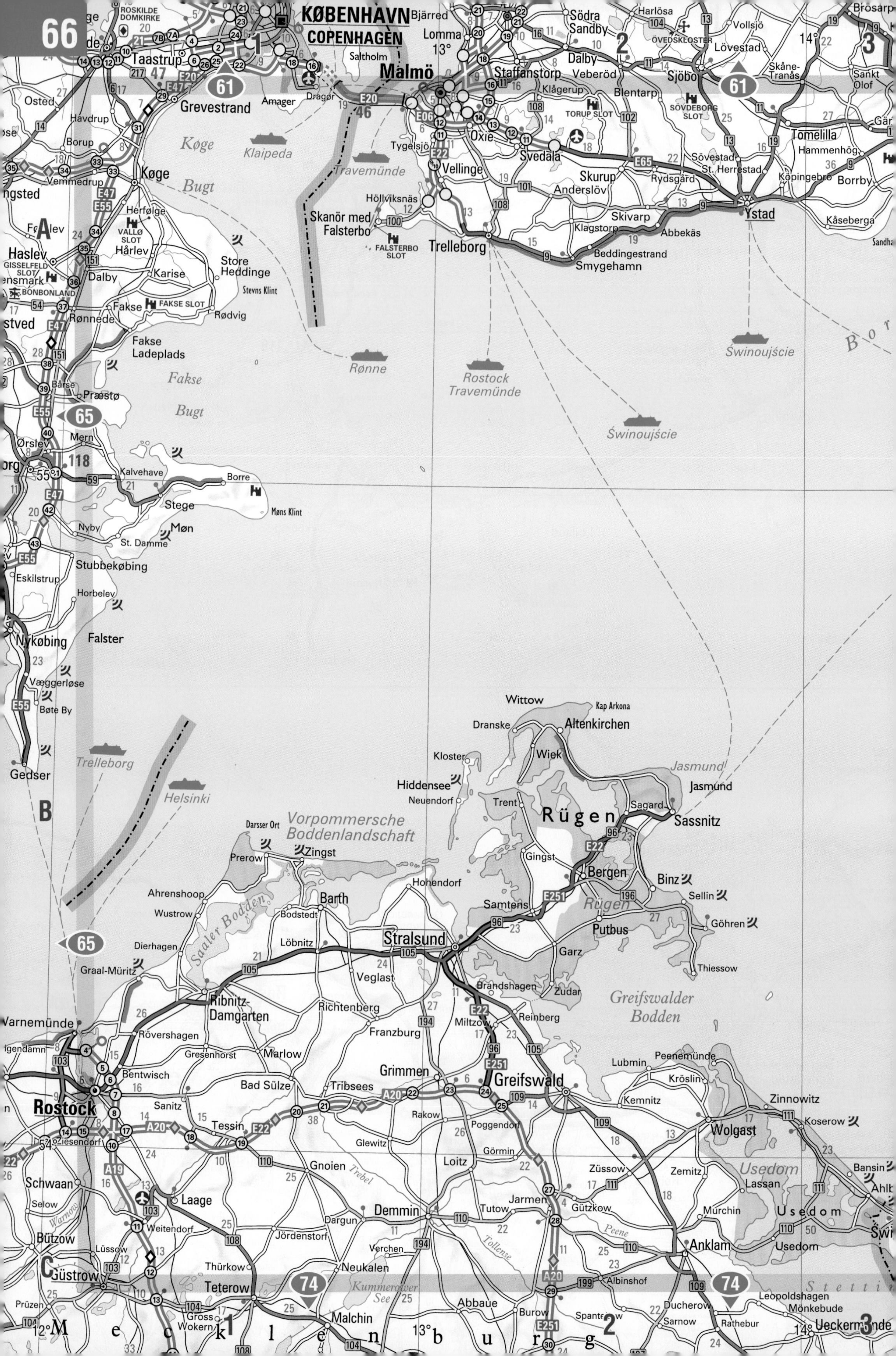
København
Copenhagen
Roskilde Domkirke
Taastrup
Grevestrand
Amager
Dragør
Saltholm
Bjärred
Lomma
Malmö
Södra Sandby
Harlösa
Övedskloster
Vollsjö
Lövestad
Brösarp
Dalby
Veberöd
Staffanstorp
Klågerup
Blentarp
Sjöbo
Skåne-Tranås
Sankt Olof
Sövdeborg Slot
Torup Slot
Tomelilla
Hammenhög
Oxie
Tygelsjö
Svedala
Sövestad
St. Herrestad
Köpingebro
Borrby
Vellinge
Skurup
Rydsgård
Anderslöv
Ystad
Höllviksnäs
Skanör med Falsterbo
Falsterbo Slot
Trelleborg
Skivarp
Klagstorp
Abbekäs
Kåseberga
Beddingestrand
Smygehamn
Osted
Havdrup
Borup
Køge
Køge Bugt
Klaipeda
Travemünde
Vemmedrup
Herfølge
Vallø Slot
Hårlev
Haslev
Gisselfeld Slot
Bonbonland
Karise
Store Heddinge
Stevns Klint
Dalby
Fakse
Fakse Slot
Rødvig
Rønnede
Fakse Ladeplads
Fakse Bugt
Rønne
Rostock
Travemünde
Świnoujście
Bårse
Præstø
Ørslev
Mern
Kalvehave
Borre
Stege
Møns Klint
Møn
Nyby
St. Damme
Stubbekøbing
Eskilstrup
Horbelev
Nykøbing
Falster
Væggerløse
Bøte By
Gedser
Trelleborg
Helsinki
Wittow
Kap Arkona
Dranske
Altenkirchen
Wiek
Kloster
Hiddensee
Neuendorf
Jasmund
Trent
Rügen
Sagard
Sassnitz
Gingst
Bergen
Binz
Sellin
Göhren
Samtens
Putbus
Garz
Thiessow
Zudar
Brandshagen
Greifswalder Bodden
Vorpommersche Boddenlandschaft
Darsser Ort
Prerow
Zingst
Hohendorf
Barth
Ahrenshoop
Wustrow
Saaler Bodden
Bodstedt
Löbnitz
Stralsund
Dierhagen
Graal-Müritz
Veglast
Ribnitz-Damgarten
Richtenberg
Reinberg
Miltzow
Franzburg
Warnemünde
Rövershagen
Gresenhorst
Marlow
Grimmen
Lubmin
Peenemünde
Kröslin
Bentwisch
Bad Sülze
Tribsees
Greifswald
Kemnitz
Zinnowitz
Rostock
Sanitz
Rakow
Koserow
Tessin
Poggendorf
Wolgast
Ziesendorf
Glewitz
Görmin
Usedom
Gnoien
Trebel
Loitz
Züssow
Zemitz
Bansin
Lassan
Schwaan
Laage
Demmin
Tutow
Jarmen
Gützkow
Murchin
Selow
Warnow
Weitendorf
Dargun
Jördenstorf
Peene
Bützow
Lüssow
Verchen
Tollense
Anklam
Thürkow
Neukalen
Albinshof
Güstrow
Teterow
Kummerower See
Prüzen
Gross Wokern
Malchin
Abbaue
Burow
Spantekow
Ducherow
Sarnow
Rathebur
Leopoldshagen
Mönkebude
Ueckermünde
Mecklenburg
Stettin

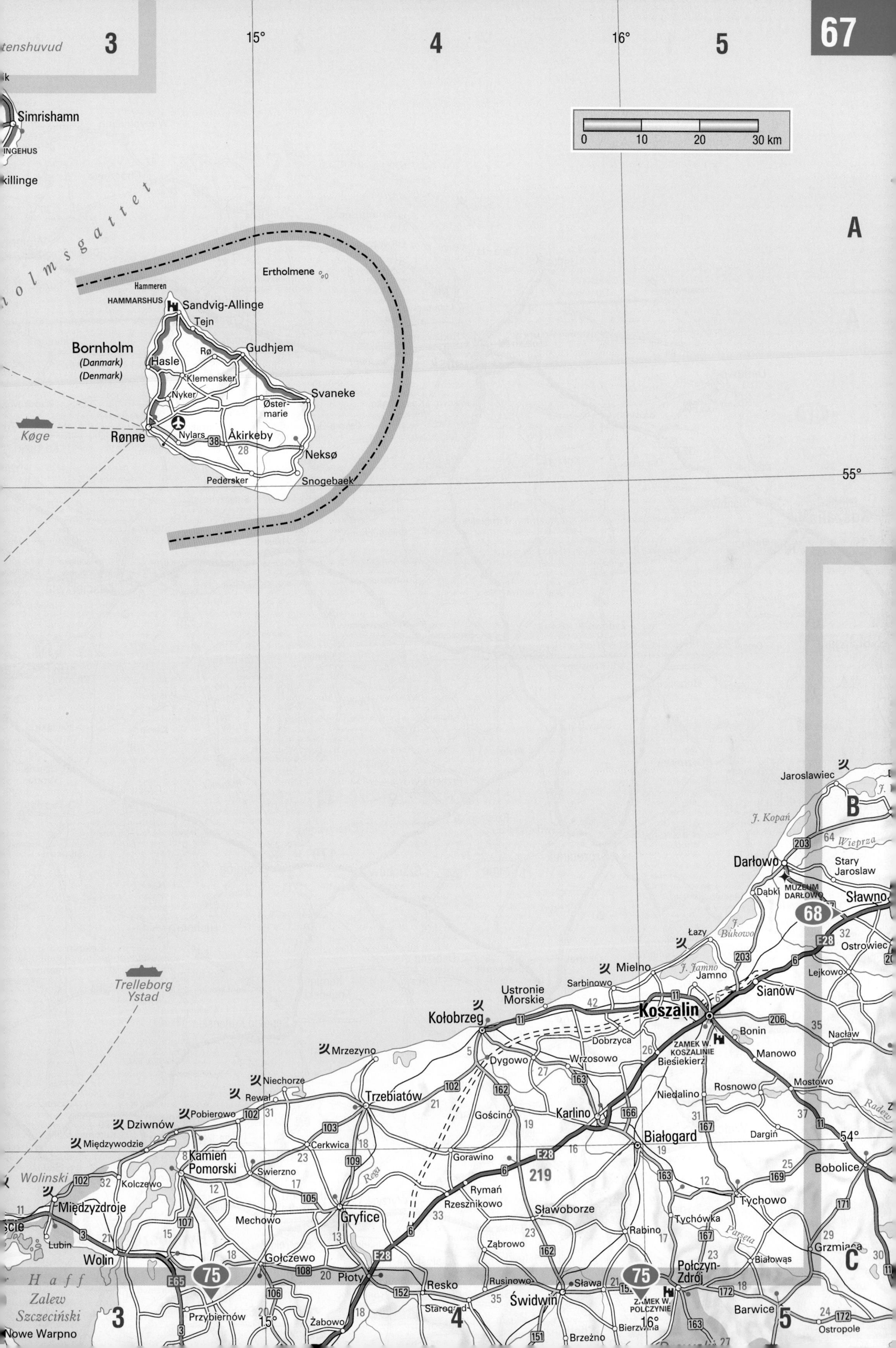

tenshuvud

3 15° 4 16° 5

0 10 20 30 km

A

Simrishamn

INGEHUS

killinge

holmsgattet

Ertholmene ‰

Hammeren

HAMMARSHUS Sandvig-Allinge

Tejn

Bornholm Rø Gudhjem

(Danmark) Hasle Klemensker

(Denmark) Nyker

Øster- Svaneke

marie

Køge Rønne Nylars 38 Åkirkeby 28

Neksø

Pedersker Snogebaek

55°

B

Jaroslawiec

J. Kopań J.

203 64 Wieprza

Darłowo Stary
Jaroslaw

Dąbki MUZEUM
DARŁOWO Sławno

68

Łazy J. E28 32
Bukowo Ostrowiec

203 6

Mielno J. Jamno

Sarbinowo Jamno Lejkowo

Trelleborg Ustronie 42 Sianow
Ystad Morskie

Kołobrzeg 11 Koszalin 206 35 Nacław

11 6 Bonin

Mrzezyno 5 Dobrzyca 26 ZAMEK W. Manowo
Dygowo KOSZALINIE
Niechorze Wrzosowo Biesiekierz Rosnowo Mostowo

Rewal 102 162 163 Niedalino 31 37 Radew

Pobierowo 102 31 Trzebiatów 21 163 11 54°

Dziwnów 103 Gościno 19 Karlino 166 Dargiń 25 Bobolice

Cerkwica 18 6 Ryman E28 16 Białogard 169

Międzywodzie Kamień 23 Gorawino 219 19 163 12 Tychowo 171

Wolinski 102 Pomorski 109 Rzesznikowo 6 Rabino Tychówka Grzmiąca

32 Kolczewo Swierzno 17 Sławoborze 17 167 29

Międzyzdroje 12 105 Mechowo Gryfice 33 Zabrowo 162 Białowąs Barwice

11 107 15 13 E28 Sława Połczyn- 172 30
Zdrój

ście Lubin 3 Gołczewo 108 20 Płoty Rusinowo 75 ZAMEK W. 18

Wolin E65 75 106 Resko 152 Świdwin POŁCZYNIE 163 Barwice

Haff 18 Przybiernów 20 35 16° Ostropole

Zalew Żabowo 18 Staro gard Brzeżno Bierzwnia 151 172

Szczeciński 3 15° 4 5

Nowe Warpno

C

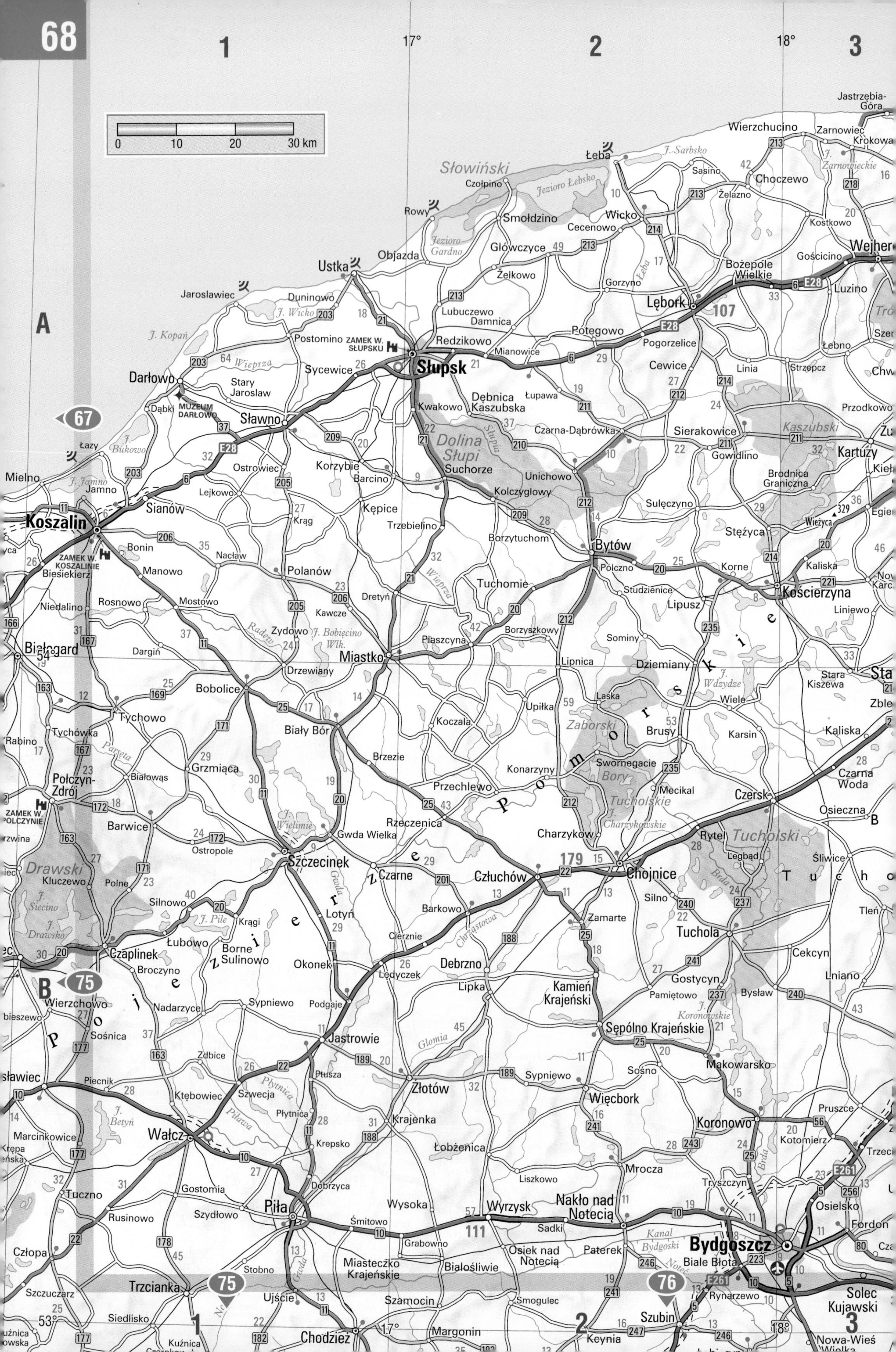
1
2
3
17°
18°
A
B
0 10 20 30 km
Koszalin
Słupsk
Lębork
Bytów
Kościerzyna
Chojnice
Człuchów
Szczecinek
Miastko
Białogard
Połczyn-Zdrój
Wałcz
Piła
Złotów
Bydgoszcz
Tuchola
Czersk
Darłowo
Sławno
Ustka
Łeba
Kartuzy
Wejherowo
Nakło nad Notecią
Sępólno Krajeńskie
Więcbork
Koronowo
Jastrowie
Bobolice
Biały Bór
Czaplinek
Borne Sulinowo
Trzcianka
Chodzież
Szubin
Solec Kujawski
Słowiński
Dolina Słupi
Kaszubski
Zaborski
Bory Tucholskie
Tucholski
Drawski
Pojezierze
Pomorskie
ZAMEK W. SŁUPSKU
ZAMEK W. KOSZALINIE
ZAMEK W. POŁCZYNIE
MUZEUM DARŁOWO
E28
E261
67
75
76
107
111
179

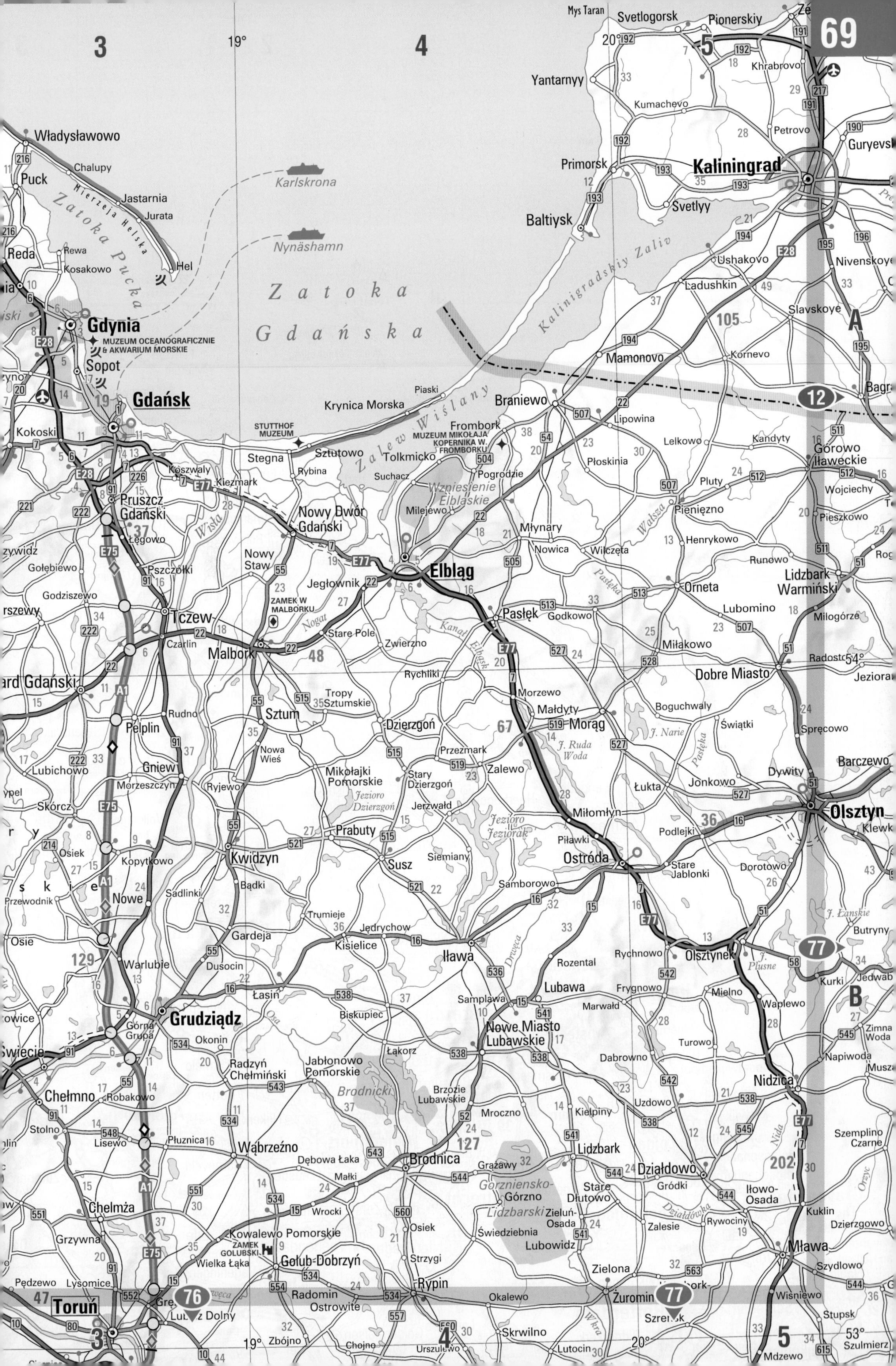
3
4
5
19°
20°
Mys Taran
Svetlogorsk
Pionerskiy
Yantarnyy
Khrabrovo
Kumachevo
Petrovo
Guryevsk
Primorsk
Kaliningrad
Svetlyy
Baltiysk
Kaliningradskiy Zaliv
Ushakovo
Nivenskoye
Ladushkin
Slavskoye
Mamonovo
Kornevo
Bagra
Władysławowo
Chalupy
Puck
Mierzeja Helska
Jastarnia
Jurata
Zatoka Pucka
Hel
Karlskrona
Nynäshamn
Zatoka Gdańska
Reda
Rewa
Kosakowo
Gdynia
MUZEUM OCEANOGRAFICZNIE & AKWARIUM MORSKIE
Sopot
Gdańsk
Kokoski
Krynica Morska
Piaski
STUTTHOF MUZEUM
Zalew Wiślany
Frombork
MUZEUM MIKOŁAJA KOPERNIKA W. FROMBORKU
Braniewo
Lipowina
Lelkowo
Kandyty
Górowo Iławeckie
Stegna
Sztutowo
Tolkmicko
Rybina
Suchacz
Pogrodzie
Płoskinia
Pluty
Wojciechy
Koszwały
Kiezmark
Pruszcz Gdański
Łęgowo
Wzniesienie Elbląskie
Milejewo
Pieniężno
Pieszkowo
Nowy Dwór Gdański
Młynary
Nowica
Wilczęta
Henrykowo
Runowo
Nowy Staw
Elbląg
Pszczółki
Gołębiewo
Godziszewo
Jegłownik
ZAMEK W MALBORKU
Lidzbark Warmiński
Orneta
Pasłęk
Godkowo
Lubomino
Milogórze
Tczew
Czarlin
Malbork
Stare Pole
Zwierzno
Kanał Elbląski
Miłakowo
Radostowo
Jeziorany
Starogard Gdański
Rychliki
Dobre Miasto
Tropy Sztumskie
Sztum
Morzewo
Małdyty
Boguchwały
Pelplin
Rudno
Dzierzgoń
Morąg
Świątki
Sprecowo
J. Narie
Nowa Wieś
Przezmark
J. Ruda Woda
Barczewo
Lubichowo
Gniew
Mikołajki Pomorskie
Stary Dzierzgoń
Zalewo
Dywity
Morzeszczyn
Ryjewo
Łukta
Jonkowo
Skórcz
Jezioro Dzierzgoń
Jerzwałd
Jezioro Jeziorak
Miłomłyn
Olsztyn
Klewki
Prabuty
Podlejki
Osiek
Kopytkowo
Kwidzyn
Susz
Siemiany
Piławki
Ostróda
Stare Jabłonki
Dorotowo
Przewodnik
Nowe
Bądki
Sadlinki
Samborowo
Trumieje
J. Łańskie
Butryny
Jędrychowo
Kisielice
Osie
Gardeja
Iława
Rozental
Rychnowo
Olsztynek
J. Plusne
Warlubie
Dusocin
Kurki
Jedwabno
Łasin
Lubawa
Frygnowo
Mielno
Samplawa
Marwałd
Waplewo
Grudziądz
Górna Grupa
Biskupiec
Nowe Miasto Lubawskie
Świecie
Okonin
Łąkorz
Turowo
Zimna Woda
Radzyń Chełmiński
Jabłonowo Pomorskie
Dabrowno
Napiwoda
Chełmno
Robakowo
Brodnicki
Brzozie Lubawskie
Nidzica
Uzdowo
Stolno
Mroczno
Kiełpiny
Szemplino Czarne
Lisewo
Płużnica
Wąbrzeźno
Dębowa Łaka
Brodnica
Grażawy
Lidzbark
Działdowo
Małki
Gorznieńsko-Lidzbarski
Górzno
Stare Dłutowo
Gródki
Iłowo-Osada
Chełmża
Wrocki
Zieluń-Osada
Zalesie
Rywociny
Kuklin
Grzywna
Kowalewo Pomorskie
Osiek
Świedziebnia
Dzierzgowo
ZAMEK GOLUBSKI
Golub-Dobrzyń
Lubowidz
Mława
Wielka Łąka
Strzygi
Zielona
Szydłowo
Pędzewo
Lysomice
Rypin
Okalewo
Żuromin
Wiśniewo
Toruń
Radomin
Ostrowite
Lubicz Dolny
Szreńsk
Stupsk
Zbójno
Chojno
Urszulewo
Skrwilno
Lutocin
Mdzewo
Szulmierz
53°
54°
A
B
12
76
77
202
127
129
105
36
37
47
48
67
E28
E75
E77
A1

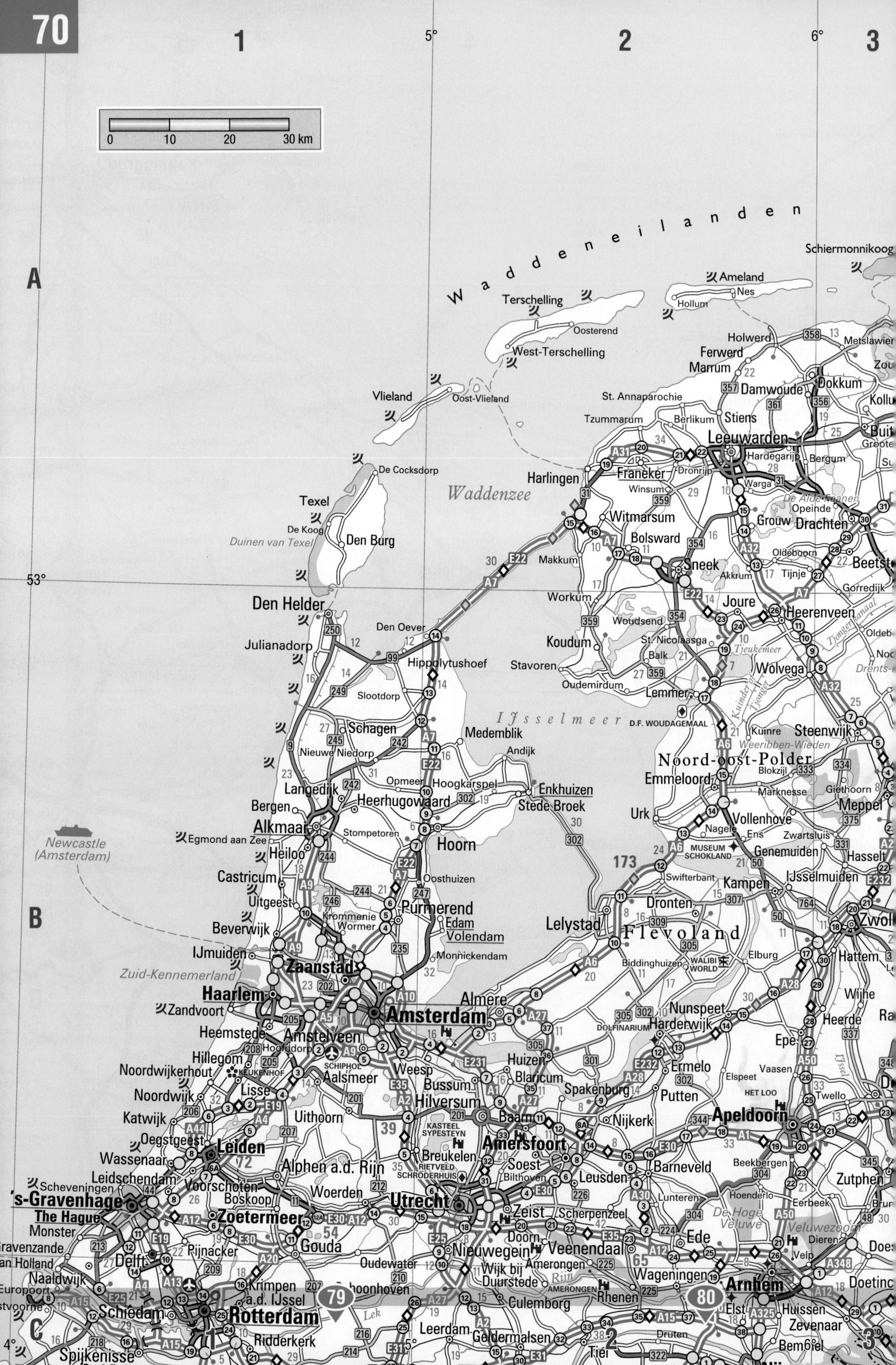
1
2
3
A
B
C
5°
6°
53°
4°
0
10
20
30 km
Waddeneilanden
Schiermonnikoog
Ameland
Nes
Hollum
Terschelling
Oosterend
West-Terschelling
Vlieland
Oost-Vlieland
Holwerd
Ferwerd
Marrum
Metslawier
Dokkum
Damwoude
St. Annaparochie
Tzummarum
Berlikum
Stiens
Leeuwarden
Hardegarijp
Bergum
Harlingen
Franeker
Dronrijp
Winsum
Warga
De Alde Feanen
Opeinde
Witmarsum
Grouw
Drachten
Bolsward
Oldeboorn
Makkum
Sneek
Akkrum
Tijnje
Beetsterzwaag
Gorredijk
Workum
Joure
Heerenveen
Woudsend
Koudum
St. Nicolaasga
Balk
Tjeukemeer
Stavoren
Wolvega
Oudemirdum
Lemmer
Drents-Friese Wold
Waddenzee
De Cocksdorp
Texel
De Koog
Den Burg
Duinen van Texel
Den Helder
Den Oever
Julianadorp
Hippolytushoef
Slootdorp
IJsselmeer
D.F. WOUDAGEMAAL
Schagen
Medemblik
Andijk
Nieuwe Niedorp
Kuinre
Steenwijk
Weerribben-Wieden
Noord-oost-Polder
Emmeloord
Blokzijl
Marknesse
Giethoorn
Meppel
Langedijk
Opmeer
Hoogkarspel
Enkhuizen
Stede Broek
Bergen
Heerhugowaard
Alkmaar
Stompetoren
Hoorn
Urk
Vollenhove
Nagele
Ens
Zwartsluis
Egmond aan Zee
Heiloo
Newcastle (Amsterdam)
MUSEUM SCHOKLAND
Genemuiden
Hasselt
Castricum
Uitgeest
Oosthuizen
Swifterbant
Kampen
IJsselmuiden
Purmerend
Krommenie
Wormer
Edam
Volendam
Dronten
Lelystad
Flevoland
Zwolle
Beverwijk
IJmuiden
Monnickendam
Hattem
Zaanstad
Biddinghuizen
WALIBI WORLD
Elburg
Zuid-Kennemerland
Haarlem
Almere
Nunspeet
Wijhe
Zandvoort
Amsterdam
Heemstede
Amstelveen
DOLFINARIUM
Harderwijk
Heerde
Hoofddorp
Epe
Hillegom
SCHIPHOL
Huizen
Vaassen
Noordwijkerhout
KEUKENHOF
Aalsmeer
Weesp
Blaricum
Ermelo
Elspeet
Lisse
Bussum
Spakenburg
Putten
HET LOO
Twello
Noordwijk
Hilversum
Katwijk
Uithoorn
Baarn
Nijkerk
Apeldoorn
KASTEEL SYPESTEYN
Oegstgeest
Amersfoort
Wassenaar
Leiden
Breukelen
Barneveld
Beekbergen
Leidschendam
Alphen a.d. Rijn
RIETVELD SCHRÖDERHUIS
Soest
Bilthoven
Leusden
Scheveningen
Voorschoten
Woerden
Zutphen
's-Gravenhage
The Hague
Boskoop
Utrecht
Lunteren
Hoenderlo
Eerbeek
Zoetermeer
Zeist
Scherpenzeel
De Hoge Veluwe
Monster
Veluwezoom
Doorn
Ede
Dieren
Gouda
Nieuwegein
Veenendaal
Naaldwijk
Delft
Pijnacker
Oudewater
Wijk bij Duurstede
Amerongen
Wageningen
Velp
Europoort
Krimpen a.d. IJssel
Schoonhoven
AMERONGEN
Rhenen
Arnhem
Doetinchem
Schiedam
Rotterdam
Culemborg
Elst
Huissen
Lek
Zevenaar
Spijkenisse
Ridderkerk
Leerdam
Geldermalsen
Druten
Tiel
Bemmel
79
80
173

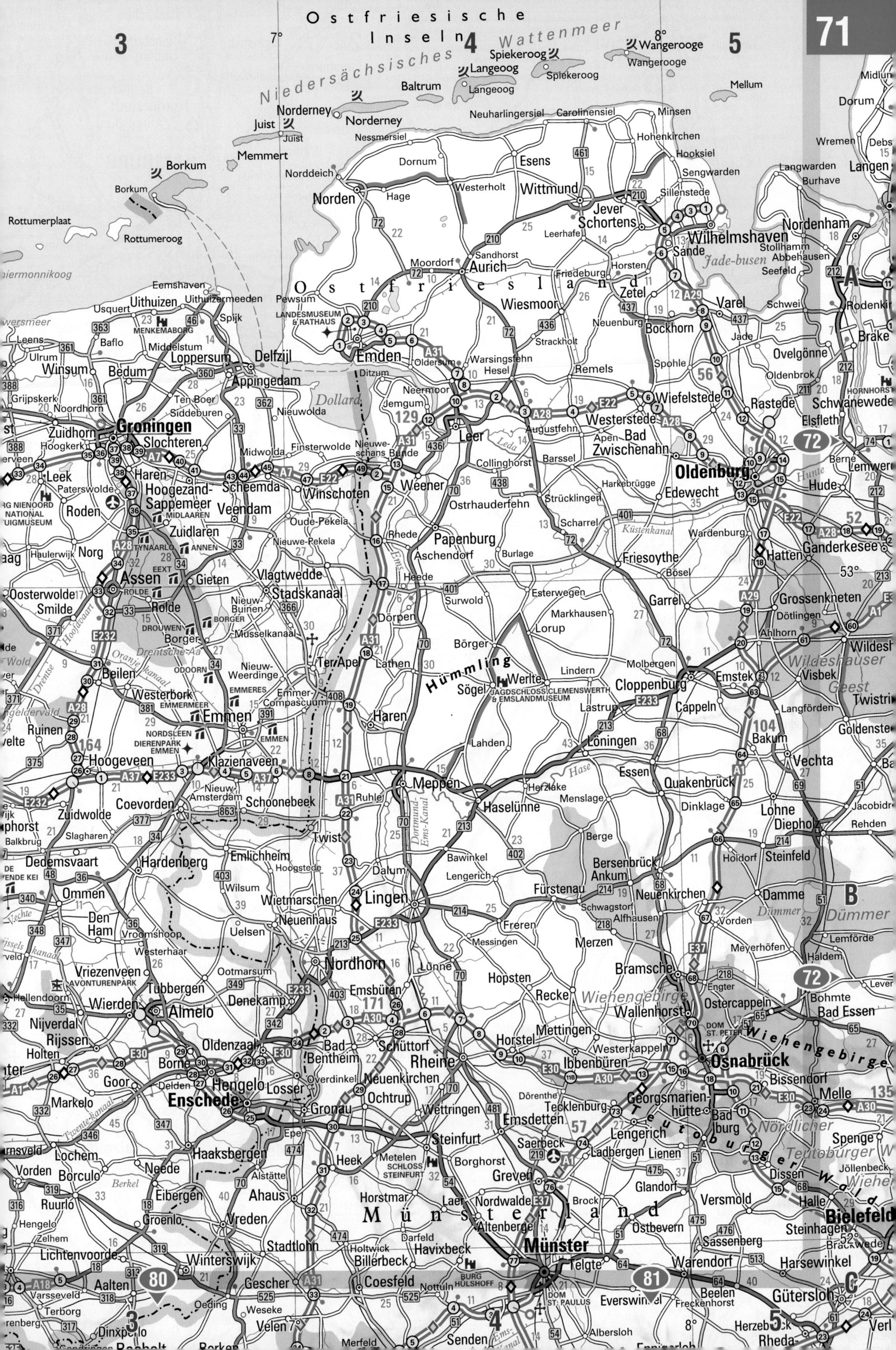
Ostfriesische Inseln
Niedersächsisches Wattenmeer
Wangerooge
Spiekeroog
Langeoog
Baltrum
Norderney
Juist
Memmert
Borkum
Rottumerplaat
Rottumeroog
Mellum
Ostfriesland
Neuharlingersiel
Carolinensiel
Minsen
Hohenkirchen
Hooksiel
Sengwarden
Nessmersiel
Dornum
Esens
Norddeich
Norden
Hage
Westerholt
Wittmund
Jever
Schortens
Wilhelmshaven
Sande
Jade-busen
Leerhafe
Sandhorst
Moordorf
Aurich
Friedeburg
Horsten
Zetel
Varel
Pewsum
Landesmuseum & Rathaus
Emden
Oldersum
Wiesmoor
Neuenburg
Bockhorn
Strackholt
Warsingsfehn
Hesel
Remels
Spohle
Jade
Rastede
Ditzum
Dollard
Neermoor
Jemgum
Leer
Augustfehn
Westerstede
Wiefelstede
Apen
Bad Zwischenahn
Oldenburg
Hunte
Edewecht
Harkebrügge
Collinghorst
Barssel
Strücklingen
Nieuwe-schans
Bunde
Weener
Ostrhauderfehn
Scharrel
Küstenkanal
Wardenburg
Rhede
Papenburg
Aschendorf
Burlage
Friesoythe
Bösel
Hatten
Ganderkesee
Heede
Surwold
Esterwegen
Garrel
Grossenkneten
Dötlingen
Markhausen
Lorup
Ahlhorn
Wildeshausen
Wildeshauser Geest
Dörpen
Börger
Hümmling
Lindern
Molbergen
Cloppenburg
Emstek
Visbek
Lathen
Sögel
Werlte
Jagdschloss Clemenswerth & Emslandmuseum
Lastrup
Cappeln
Langförden
Haren
Lahden
Löningen
Bakum
Vechta
Goldenstedt
Meppen
Essen
Quakenbrück
Hase
Herzlake
Menslage
Haselünne
Dinklage
Lohne
Diepholz
Rehden
Ruhle
Twist
Dortmund-Ems-Kanal
Berge
Holdorf
Steinfeld
Bawinkel
Lengerich
Bersenbrück
Ankum
Neuenkirchen
Damme
Dümmer
Emlichheim
Hoogstede
Dalum
Fürstenau
Schwagstorf
Alfhausen
Vorden
Lemförde
Haldem
Wietmarschen
Lingen
Freren
Messingen
Merzen
Meyerhöfen
Neuenhaus
Uelsen
Nordhorn
Lünne
Hopsten
Bramsche
Engter
Recke
Wiehengebirge
Wallenhorst
Ostercappeln
Bohmte
Bad Essen
Emsbüren
Schüttorf
Mettingen
Westerkappeln
Dom St. Peter
Osnabrück
Bad Bentheim
Rheine
Horstel
Ibbenbüren
Bissendorf
Melle
Neuenkirchen
Ochtrup
Dörenthe
Tecklenburg
Georgsmarienhütte
Bad Iburg
Teutoburger Wald
Nördlicher Teutoburger Wald
Wettringen
Emsdetten
Lengerich
Spenge
Jöllenbeck
Steinfurt
Saerbeck
Ladbergen
Lienen
Metelen
Schloss Steinfurt
Borghorst
Greven
Glandorf
Dissen
Halle
Bielefeld
Horstmar
Laer
Nordwalde
Brock
Versmold
Münsterland
Altenberge
Ostbevern
Steinhagen
Brackwede
Darfeld
Havixbeck
Sassenberg
Harsewinkel
Billerbeck
Holtwick
Burg Hülshoff
Münster
Telgte
Warendorf
Coesfeld
Nottuln
Dom St. Paulus
Everswinkel
Beelen
Freckenhorst
Gütersloh
Herzebrock
Rheda
Senden
Albersloh
Merfeld
Velen
Eemshaven
Uithuizen
Uithuizermeeden
Usquert
Menkemaborg
Spijk
Baflo
Middelstum
Delfzijl
Leens
Ulrum
Winsum
Bedum
Loppersum
Appingedam
Grijpskerk
Noordhorn
Ten Boer
Siddeburen
Nieuwolda
Zuidhorn
Groningen
Slochteren
Hoogkerk
Midwolda
Finsterwolde
Leek
Haren
Paterswolde
Hoogezand-Sappemeer
Scheemda
Winschoten
Roden
Midlaaren
Veendam
Oude-Pekela
Nieuwe-Pekela
Zuidlaren
Tynaarlo
Annen
Haulerwijk
Norg
Eext
Assen
Gieten
Vlagtwedde
Rolde
Stadskanaal
Oosterwolde
Smilde
Nieuw-Buinen
Borger
Drouwen
Musselkanaal
Drentsche Aa
Beilen
Odoorn
Nieuw-Weerdinge
Ter Apel
Westerbork
Emmeres
Emmermeer
Emmer-Compascuum
Emmen
Ruinen
Nordsleen
Dierenpark Emmen
Hoogeveen
Klazienaveen
Nieuw-Amsterdam
Zuidwolde
Coevorden
Schoonebeek
Slagharen
Dedemsvaart
Hardenberg
Ommen
Wilsum
Den Ham
Vroomshoop
Westerhaar
Vriezenveen
Avonturenpark
Hellendoorn
Ootmarsum
Tubbergen
Denekamp
Wierden
Almelo
Nijverdal
Rijssen
Holten
Oldenzaal
Borne
Hengelo
Losser
Goor
Delden
Overdinkel
Markelo
Enschede
Gronau
Epe
Haaksbergen
Lochem
Neede
Vorden
Borculo
Berkel
Alstätte
Ahaus
Eibergen
Ruurlo
Groenlo
Vreden
Zelhem
Lichtenvoorde
Stadtlohn
Winterswijk
Aalten
Gescher
Varsseveld
Terborg
Oeding
Weseke
Dinxperlo
Midlum
Dorum
Wremen
Langwarden
Burhave
Nordenham
Stollhamm
Abbehausen
Seefeld
Schwei
Rodenkirchen
Brake
Ovelgönne
Oldenbrok
Hornhorst
Schwanewede
Elsfleth
Berne
Lemwerder
Hude
53°
7°
8°
3
4
5
A
B
C
56
52
57
104
129
164
171
72
80
81

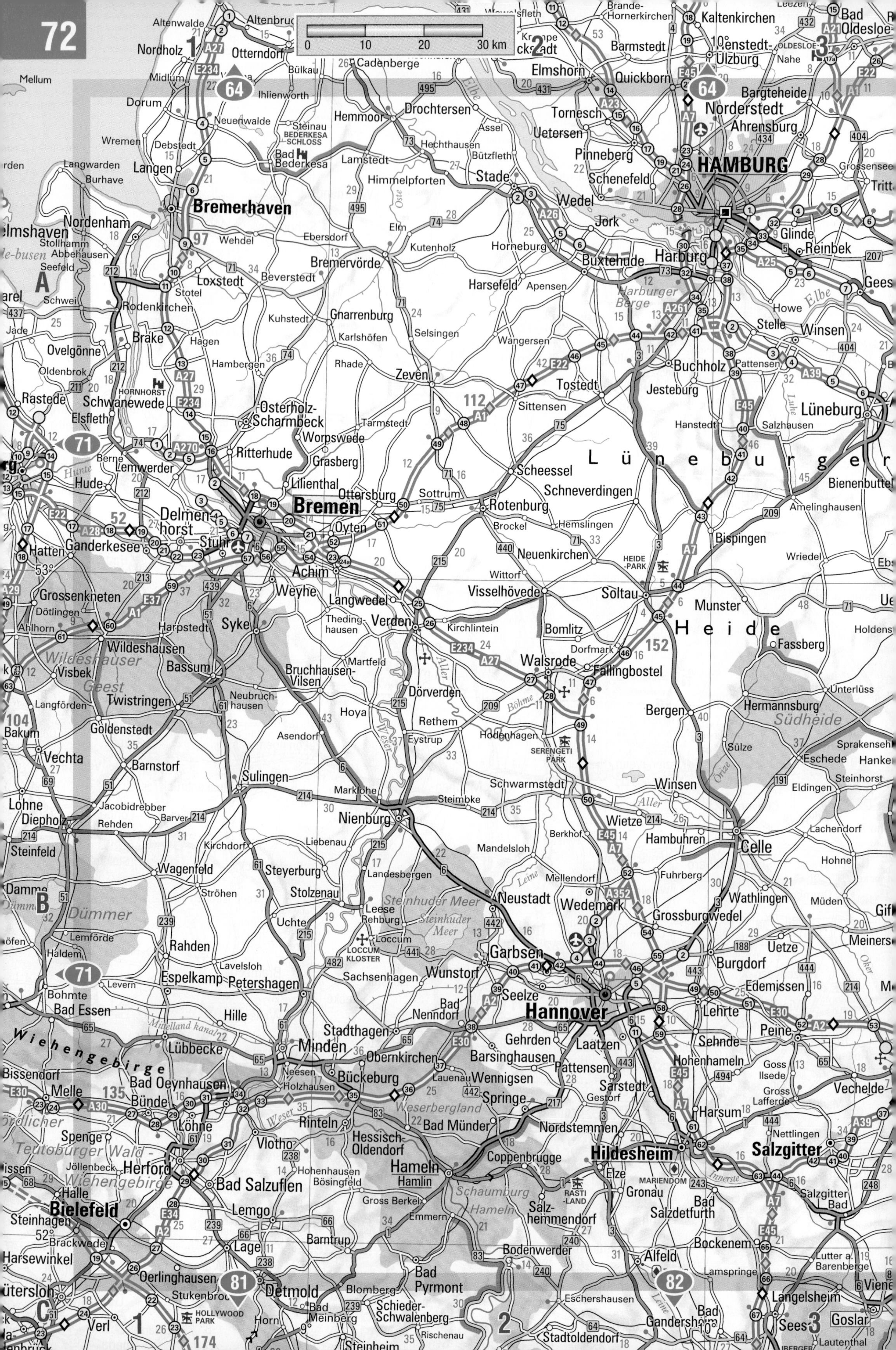
0
10
20
30 km
Altenwalde
Altenbruch
Nordholz
Otterndorf
Cadenberge
Wewelsfleth
Brande-Hornerkirchen
Kaltenkirchen
Bad Oldesloe
Barmstedt
Henstedt-Ulzburg
Glückstadt
Mellum
Midlum
Bülkau
Ihlienworth
Elmshorn
Quickborn
Bargteheide
Dorum
Neuenwalde
Hemmoor
Drochtersen
Tornesch
Norderstedt
Ahrensburg
Wremen
Debstedt
Steinau
BEDERKESA SCHLOSS
Bad Bederkesa
Hechthausen
Assel
Uetersen
Pinneberg
Langwarden
Burhave
Langen
Lamstedt
Bützfleth
Schenefeld
HAMBURG
Grossensee
Trittau
Himmelpforten
Stade
Wedel
Bremerhaven
Nordenham
Stollhamm
Abbehausen
Seefeld
Ebersdorf
Elm
Jork
Glinde
Reinbek
Wehdel
Kutenholz
Horneburg
Harburg
Bremervörde
Buxtehude
Loxstedt
Stotel
Beverstedt
Harsefeld
Apensen
Harburger Berge
Geesthacht
Schwei
Rodenkirchen
Kuhstedt
Gnarrenburg
Selsingen
Howe
Stelle
Winsen
Jade
Brake
Karlshöfen
Wangersen
Ovelgönne
Hagen
Hambergen
Rhade
Zeven
Tostedt
Buchholz
Pattensen
Oldenbrok
HORNHORST
Jesteburg
Lüneburg
Rastede
Schwanewede
Osterholz-Scharmbeck
Sittensen
Elsfleth
Tarmstedt
Worpswede
Hanstedt
Salzhausen
Berne
Lemwerder
Ritterhude
Grasberg
Lüneburger Heide
Hude
Lilienthal
Ottersburg
Sottrum
Scheessel
Schneverdingen
Bienenbüttel
Bremen
Rotenburg
Amelinghausen
Delmenhorst
Oyten
Brockel
Hemslingen
Bispingen
Hatten
Ganderkesee
Stuhr
Neuenkirchen
HEIDE-PARK
Wriedel
Achim
Wittorf
Grossenkneten
Weyhe
Langwedel
Visselhövede
Soltau
Munster
Dötlingen
Thedinghausen
Verden
Kirchlinteln
Bomlitz
Ahlhorn
Harpstedt
Syke
Dorfmark
Fassberg
Wildeshausen
Wildeshauser Geest
Visbek
Bassum
Martfeld
Bruchhausen-Vilsen
Walsrode
Fallingbostel
Twistringen
Neubruchhausen
Dörverden
Unterlüss
Langförden
Bakum
Goldenstedt
Hoya
Rethem
Bergen
Hermannsburg
Südheide
Asendorf
Eystrup
Hodenhagen
SERENGETI PARK
Vechta
Barnstorf
Sulze
Sprakensehl
Eschede
Hankensbüttel
Sulingen
Schwarmstedt
Winsen
Steinhorst
Lohne
Jacobidrebber
Marklohe
Steimbke
Eldingen
Diepholz
Rehden
Barver
Nienburg
Wietze
Lachendorf
Steinfeld
Kirchdorf
Liebenau
Berkhof
Hambühren
Celle
Wagenfeld
Mandelsloh
Hohne
Steyerburg
Landesbergen
Mellendorf
Fuhrberg
Damme
Ströhen
Stolzenau
Steinhuder Meer
Neustadt
Wedemark
Wathlingen
Müden
Dümmer
Uchte
Leese
Rehburg
Grossburgwedel
Gifhorn
Lemförde
Rahden
Loccum
LOCCUM KLOSTER
Garbsen
Uetze
Meinersen
Haldem
Lavelsloh
Burgdorf
Levern
Espelkamp
Petershagen
Sachsenhagen
Wunstorf
Edemissen
Bohmte
Seelze
Bad Nenndorf
Hannover
Lehrte
Bad Essen
Hille
Mittelland kanal
Stadthagen
Gehrden
Peine
Wiehengebirge
Lübbecke
Minden
Obernkirchen
Barsinghausen
Laatzen
Sehnde
Bissendorf
Bad Oeynhausen
Neesen
Bückeburg
Lauenau
Wennigsen
Pattensen
Hohenhameln
Ilsede
Gross Lafferde
Vechelde
Melle
Bünde
Holzhausen
Sarstedt
Gestorf
Löhne
Weserbergland
Springe
Harsum
Spenge
Rinteln
Bad Münder
Nordstemmen
Nettlingen
Salzgitter
Teutoburger Wald
Vlotho
Hessisch-Oldendorf
Hildesheim
Jöllenbeck
Herford
Hameln
Hamlin
Coppenbrügge
Elze
MARIENDOM
Halle
Bad Salzuflen
Hohenhausen
Bösingfeld
Schaumburg
RASTI-LAND
Gronau
Bad Salzdetfurth
Salzgitter-Bad
Bielefeld
Gross Berkel
Salzhemmendorf
Steinhagen
Lemgo
Emmern
Brackwede
Barntrup
Harsewinkel
Lage
Bodenwerder
Alfeld
Bockenem
Lutter a. Barenberge
Oerlinghausen
Bad Pyrmont
Lamspringe
Gütersloh
Stukenbrock
Detmold
Blomberg
Eschershausen
Langelsheim
Verl
HOLLYWOOD PARK
Horn
Bad Meinberg
Schieder-Schwalenberg
Bad Gandersheim
Seesen
Goslar
Rischenau
Steinheim
Stadtoldendorf
Lautenthal

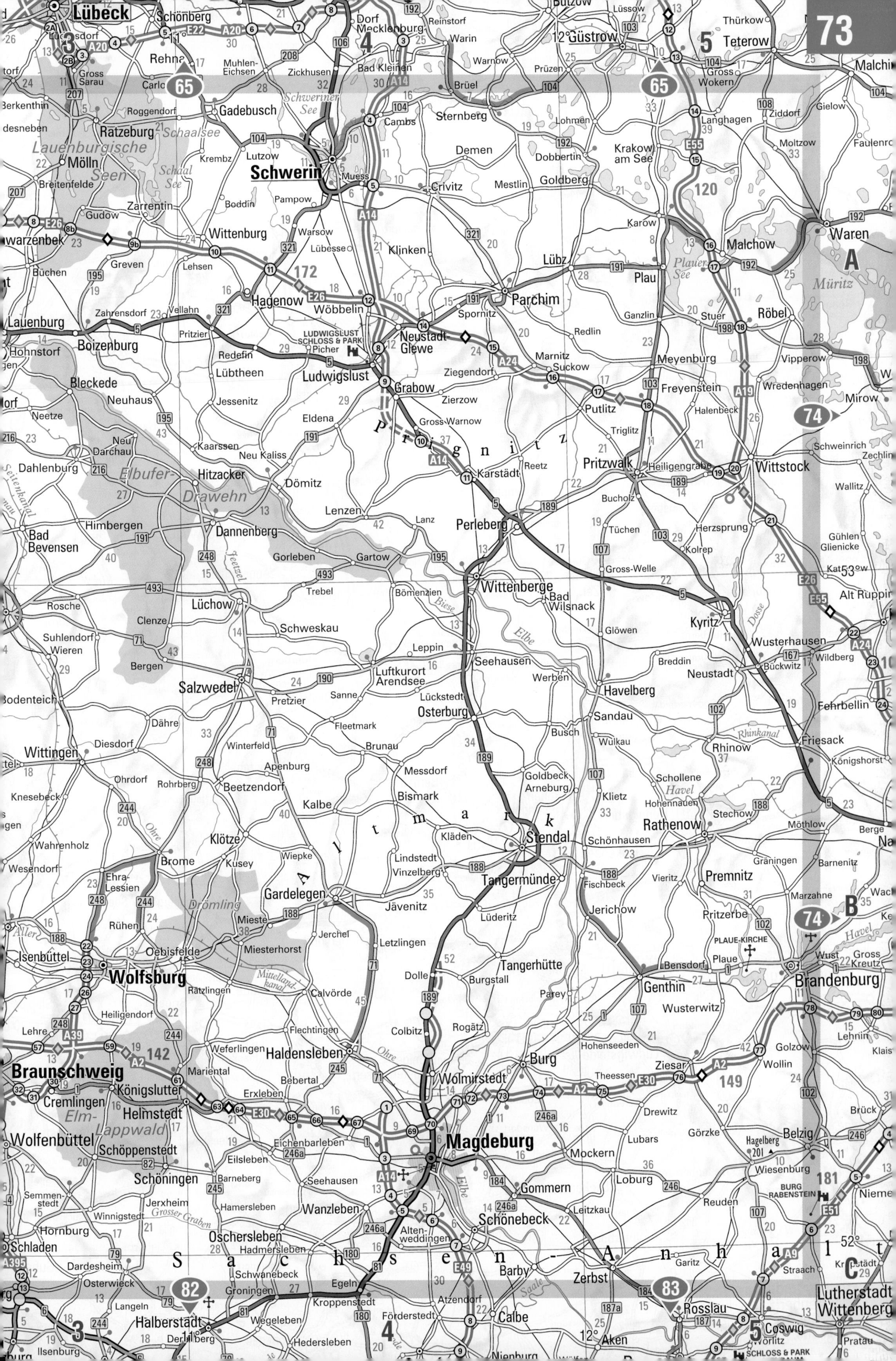
Lübeck
Schönberg
Dorf Mecklenburg
Bützow
Lüssow
Thürkow
Güstrow
Teterow
Reinstorf
Warin
Rehna
Muhlen-Eichsen
Zickhusen
Bad Kleinen
Warnow
Prüzen
Gross Wokern
Malchin
Gross Sarau
Carlow
Brüel
Berkenthin
Roggendorf
Gadebusch
Schweriner See
Cambs
Sternberg
Lohmen
Langhagen
Ziddorf
Gielow
Ratzeburg
Schaalsee
Demen
Dobbertin
Krakow am See
Moltzow
Faulenrost
Lauenburgische Seen
Mölln
Krembz
Lutzow
Schwerin
Mueß
Crivitz
Mestlin
Goldberg
Breitenfelde
Zarrentin
Boddin
Pampow
Gudow
Warsow
Karow
Malchow
Waren
Wittenburg
Lübesse
Klinken
Greven
Lehsen
Lübz
Plau
Plauer See
Müritz
Büchen
Hagenow
Wöbbelin
Parchim
Ganzlin
Stuer
Röbel
Zahrensdorf
Vellahn
Spornitz
Redlin
Lauenburg
Pritzier
Neustadt-Glewe
Boizenburg
Hohnstorf
Redefin
Ludwigslust Schloss & Park
Picher
Marnitz
Suckow
Meyenburg
Vipperow
Lübtheen
Ludwigslust
Ziegendorf
Freyenstein
Wredenhagen
Bleckede
Grabow
Zierzow
Mirow
Neuhaus
Jessenitz
Putlitz
Halenbeck
Eldena
Neetze
Gross Warnow
Neu Darchau
Prignitz
Triglitz
Schweinrich
Karssen
Neu Kaliss
Pritzwalk
Heiligengrabe
Wittstock
Dahlenburg
Karstädt
Reetz
Elbufer-Drawehn
Hitzacker
Dömitz
Bucholz
Lenzen
Lanz
Perleberg
Tüchen
Herzsprung
Himbergen
Dannenberg
Kolrep
Gühlen Glienicke
Bad Bevensen
Gorleben
Gartow
Gross-Welle
Trebel
Bömenzien
Wittenberge
Bad Wilsnack
Kyritz
Alt Ruppin
Rosche
Lüchow
Clenze
Schweskau
Glöwen
Suhlendorf
Wieren
Leppin
Wusterhausen
Wildberg
Bergen
Seehausen
Breddin
Neustadt
Salzwedel
Luftkurort Arendsee
Werben
Havelberg
Bodenteich
Pretzier
Sanne
Lückstedt
Osterburg
Sandau
Fehrbellin
Dähre
Fleetmark
Busch
Wulkau
Rhinkanal
Friesack
Diesdorf
Wittingen
Winterfeld
Brunau
Rhinow
Königshorst
Apenburg
Messdorf
Goldbeck
Arneburg
Schollene
Ohrdorf
Rohrberg
Beetzendorf
Klietz
Havel
Knesebeck
Bismark
Hohennauen
Stechow
Kalbe
Altmark
Rathenow
Möthlow
Wahrenholz
Klötze
Kläden
Stendal
Schönhausen
Brome
Kusey
Wiepke
Lindstedt
Vinzelberg
Tangermünde
Premnitz
Gräningen
Barnewitz
Wesendorf
Ehra-Lessien
Drömling
Gardelegen
Jävenitz
Fischbeck
Vieritz
Marzahne
Jerichow
Pritzerbe
Rühen
Mieste
Lüderitz
Jerchel
Plaue-Kirche
Isenbüttel
Oebisfelde
Miesterhorst
Letzlingen
Plaue
Brandenburg
Wolfsburg
Tangerhütte
Bensdorf
Wust
Gross Kreutz
Mittellandkanal
Dolle
Burgstall
Genthin
Rätzlingen
Calvörde
Parey
Wusterwitz
Heiligendorf
Lehre
Flechtingen
Colbitz
Rogätz
Golzow
Lehnin
Klaistow
Weferlingen
Haldensleben
Hohenseeden
Braunschweig
Mariental
Burg
Ziesar
Wollin
Königslutter
Bebertal
Wolmirstedt
Theessen
Cremlingen
Erxleben
Elm-Lappwald
Helmstedt
Drewitz
Brück
Wolfenbüttel
Schöppenstedt
Eichenbarleben
Magdeburg
Lubars
Görzke
Hagelberg 201
Belzig
Eilsleben
Möckern
Wiesenburg
Schöningen
Barneberg
Seehausen
Loburg
Burg Rabenstein
Niemegk
Semmenstedt
Jerxheim
Gommern
Reuden
Winnigstedt
Grosser Graben
Hamersleben
Wanzleben
Schönebeck
Leitzkau
Hornburg
Oschersleben
Alten-weddingen
Schladen
Hadmersleben
Sachsen-Anhalt
Garitz
Dardesheim
Straach
Kropstädt
Schwanebeck
Barby
Zerbst
Osterwieck
Gröningen
Egeln
Atzendorf
Lutherstadt Wittenberg
Langeln
Kroppenstedt
Förderstedt
Calbe
Rosslau
Halberstadt
Wegeleben
Coswig
Derenburg
Hedersleben
Aken
Wörlitz Schloss & Park
Pratau
Ilsenburg
Nienburg

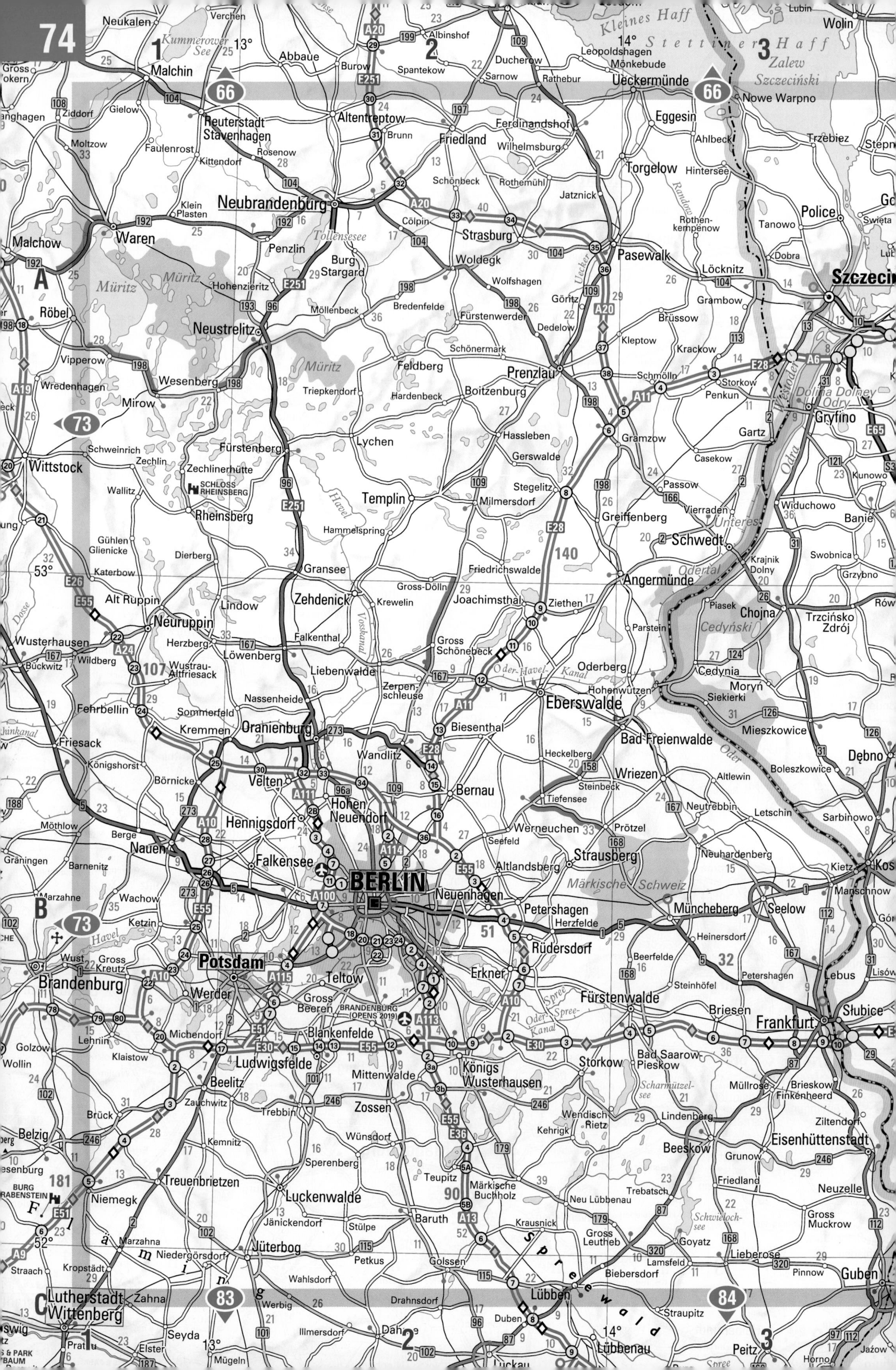
Kleines Haff
Stettiner Haff
Zalew Szczeciński
Kummerower See
Malchin
Neukalen
Verchen
Abbaue
Burow
Albinshof
Spantekow
Ducherow
Sarnow
Rathebur
Leopoldshagen
Mönkebude
Ueckermünde
Nowe Warpno
Lubin
Wolin
Reuterstadt Stavenhagen
Altentreptow
Friedland
Ferdinandshof
Eggesin
Wilhelmsburg
Ahlbeck
Trzebież
Torgelow
Hintersee
Neubrandenburg
Rothemühl
Jatznick
Police
Waren
Malchow
Penzlin
Burg Stargard
Cölpin
Strasburg
Woldegk
Pasewalk
Löcknitz
Szczecin
Müritz
Röbel
Neustrelitz
Wesenberg
Mirow
Feldberg
Prenzlau
Boitzenburg
Gryfino
Wittstock
Fürstenberg
Lychen
Templin
Rheinsberg
Schloss Rheinsberg
Gramzow
Gartz
Schwedt
Gransee
Zehdenick
Joachimsthal
Angermünde
Chojna
Neuruppin
Lindow
Oranienburg
Eberswalde
Bad Freienwalde
Cedynia
Mieszkowice
Dębno
Velten
Hennigsdorf
Bernau
Wriezen
Nauen
Falkensee
BERLIN
Strausberg
Märkische Schweiz
Müncheberg
Seelow
Kostrzyn
Potsdam
Brandenburg
Werder
Teltow
Erkner
Fürstenwalde
Frankfurt
Słubice
Ludwigsfelde
Königs Wusterhausen
Storkow
Beelitz
Zossen
Beeskow
Eisenhüttenstadt
Belzig
Treuenbrietzen
Luckenwalde
Baruth
Jüterbog
Lübben
Lübbenau
Spreewald
Guben
Lutherstadt Wittenberg
Peitz
Fläming
Oder
Odra
Havel
Spree

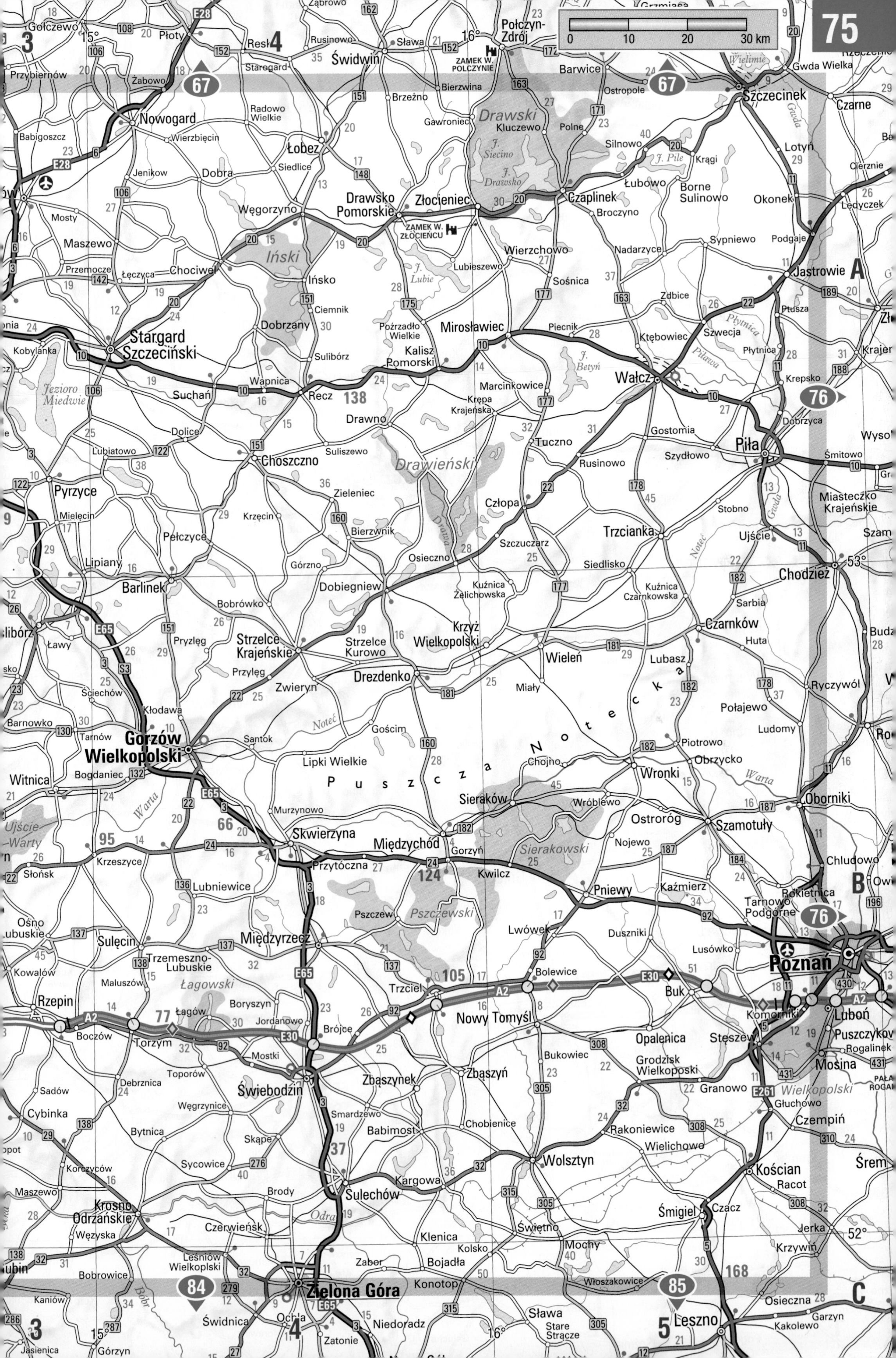

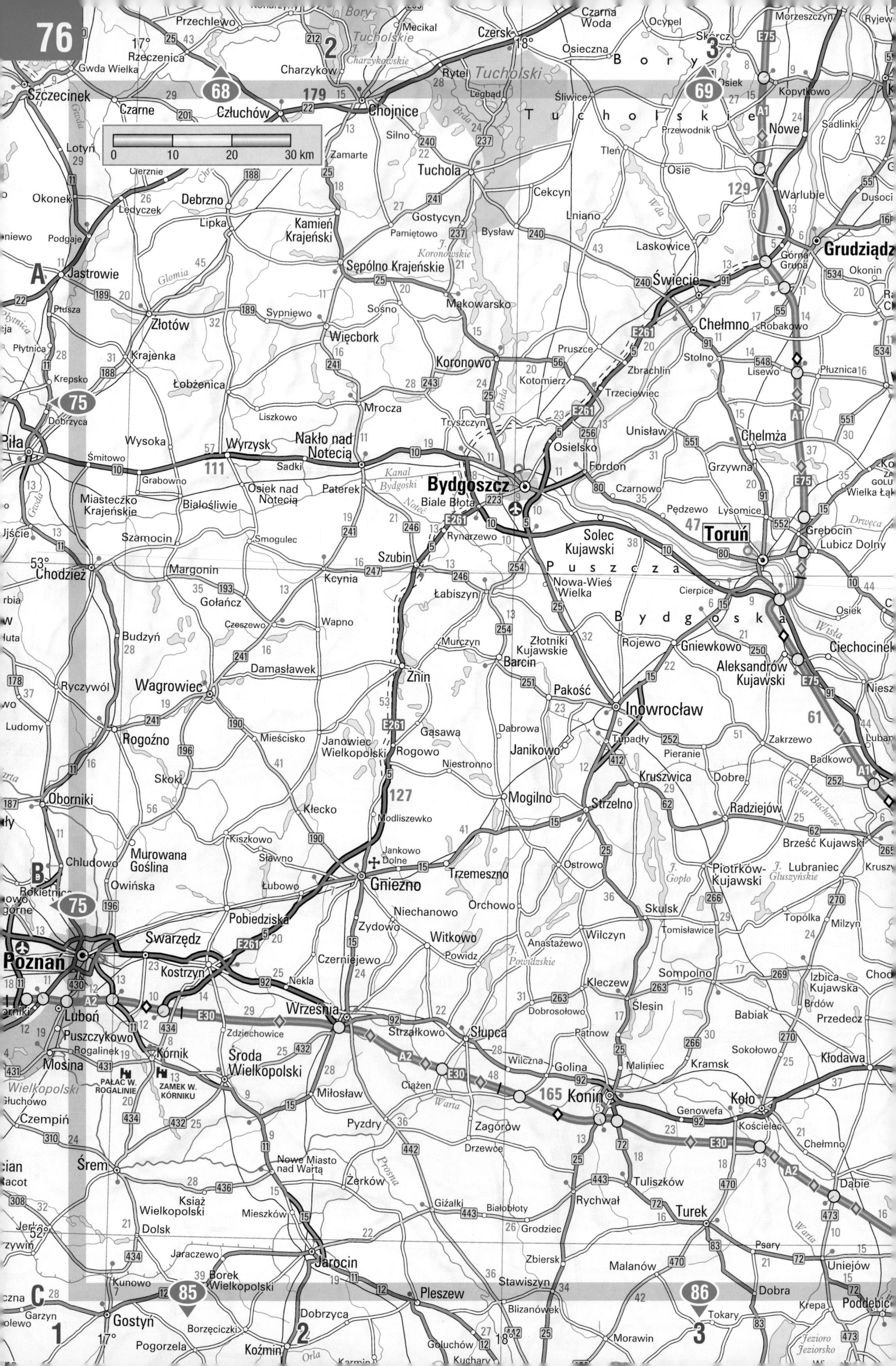

Przechlewo
Bory
Tucholskie
Mecikal
Czersk
Czarna Woda
Ocypel
Skórcz
Morzeszczyn
17°
Rzeczenica
Gwda Wielka
J. Charzykowskie
Charzykowy
Rytel
Tucholski
18°
Osieczna
Bory
Szczecinek
68
179
Chojnice
Legbąd
Śliwice
Osiek
69
Kopytkowo
Czarne
Człuchów
Tucholskie
Nowe
Sadlinki
Lotyń
0 10 20 30 km
Silno
Zamarte
Przewodnik
Tleń
Cierznie
Tuchola
Osie
Okonek
Lędyczek
Debrzno
Lipka
Cekcyn
Warlubie
Dusoci
Kamień Krajeński
Gostycyn
Lniano
Wda
Pamiętowo
J. Koronowskie
Bysław
Laskowice
Grudziądz
Podgaje
Górna Grupa
Okonin
Jastrowie
Glomia
Sępólno Krajeńskie
Świecie
Makowarsko
Chełmno
Robakowo
Ptusza
Sypniewo
Sośno
Złotów
Więcbork
Pruszce
Płytnica
Krajenka
Koronowo
Zbrachlin
Stolno
Lisewo
Płużnica
Krepsko
Łobżenica
Kotomierz
Trzeciewiec
75
Dobrzyca
Liszkowo
Mrocza
Tryszczyn
Brda
Unisław
Chełmża
Piła
Wysoka
Wyrzysk
Nakło nad Notecią
Osielsko
Śmitowo
Sadki
Fordon
Grzywna
Grabowno
Kanał Bydgoski
Bydgoszcz
Czarnowo
Wielka Łąka
Miasteczko Krajeńskie
Białośliwie
Osiek nad Notecią
Paterek
Noteć
Białe Błota
Pędzewo
Lysomice
Drwęca
Grębocin
Ujście
Szamocin
Smogulec
Rynarzewo
Solec Kujawski
Toruń
Lubicz Dolny
53°
Chodzież
Margonin
Kcynia
Szubin
Puszcza
Gołańcz
Łabiszyn
Nowa-Wieś Wielka
Cierpice
Osiek
Czeszewo
Wapno
Bydgoska
Budzyń
Murczyn
Złotniki Kujawskie
Rojewo
Gniewkowo
Ciechocinek
Wisła
Damasławek
Żnin
Barcin
Aleksandrów Kujawski
Ryczywół
Wągrowiec
Pakość
Inowrocław
Ludomy
Gąsawa
Dąbrowa
Tupadły
Zakrzewo
Rogoźno
Mieścisko
Janowiec Wielkopolski
Rogowo
Janikowo
Pieranie
Badkowo
Niestronno
Kruszwica
Dobre
Kanał Bachorze
Skoki
Mogilno
Strzelno
Radziejów
Oborniki
Kłecko
Modliszewko
Brześć Kujawski
Kiszkowo
Murowana Goślina
Jankowo Dolne
Trzemeszno
Ostrowo
Piotrków-Kujawski
Lubraniec
J. Gopło
J. Głuszyńskie
Chludowo
Sławno
Owińska
Łubowo
Gniezno
Rokietnica
Orchowo
Skulsk
Topólka
Milżyn
Niechanowo
Tomisławice
Pobiedziska
Zydowo
Wilczyn
Witkowo
Anastażewo
Swarzędz
Czerniejewo
Powidz
J. Powidzkie
Sompolno
Izbica Kujawska
Poznań
Kostrzyn
Nekla
Kleczew
Brdów
Ślesin
Lubon
Września
Dobrosołowo
Babiak
Przedecz
Puszczykowo
Zdziechowice
Strzałkowo
Słupca
Pątnów
Rogalinek
Kórnik
Środa Wielkopolska
Sokołowo
Kłodawa
Mosina
Wilczna
Golina
Maliniec
Kramsk
Pałac W. Rogalinie
Zamek w Kórniku
Miłosław
Ciążeń
Warta
Konin
Koło
Wielkopolski
Łuchowo
Genowefa
Czempiń
Pyzdry
Zagórów
Kościelec
Chełmno
Drzewce
Śrem
Nowe Miasto nad Wartą
Prosna
Tuliszków
Dąbie
Żerków
Rychwał
Książ Wielkopolski
Mieszków
Giżałki
Białobłoty
Turek
Dolsk
Grodziec
52°
Psary
Jaraczewo
Jarocin
Zbiersk
Malanów
Uniejów
Borek Wielkopolski
Kunowo
Stawiszyn
85
86
Pleszew
Dobra
Krępa
Poddębice
Garzyn
Gostyń
Dobrzyca
Blizanówek
Tokary
Borzęciczki
Pogorzela
Koźmin
Orla
Gołuchów
Kuchary
Morawin
Jezioro Jeziorsko
A
B
C
1
2
3
E75
E261
E30
A1
A2

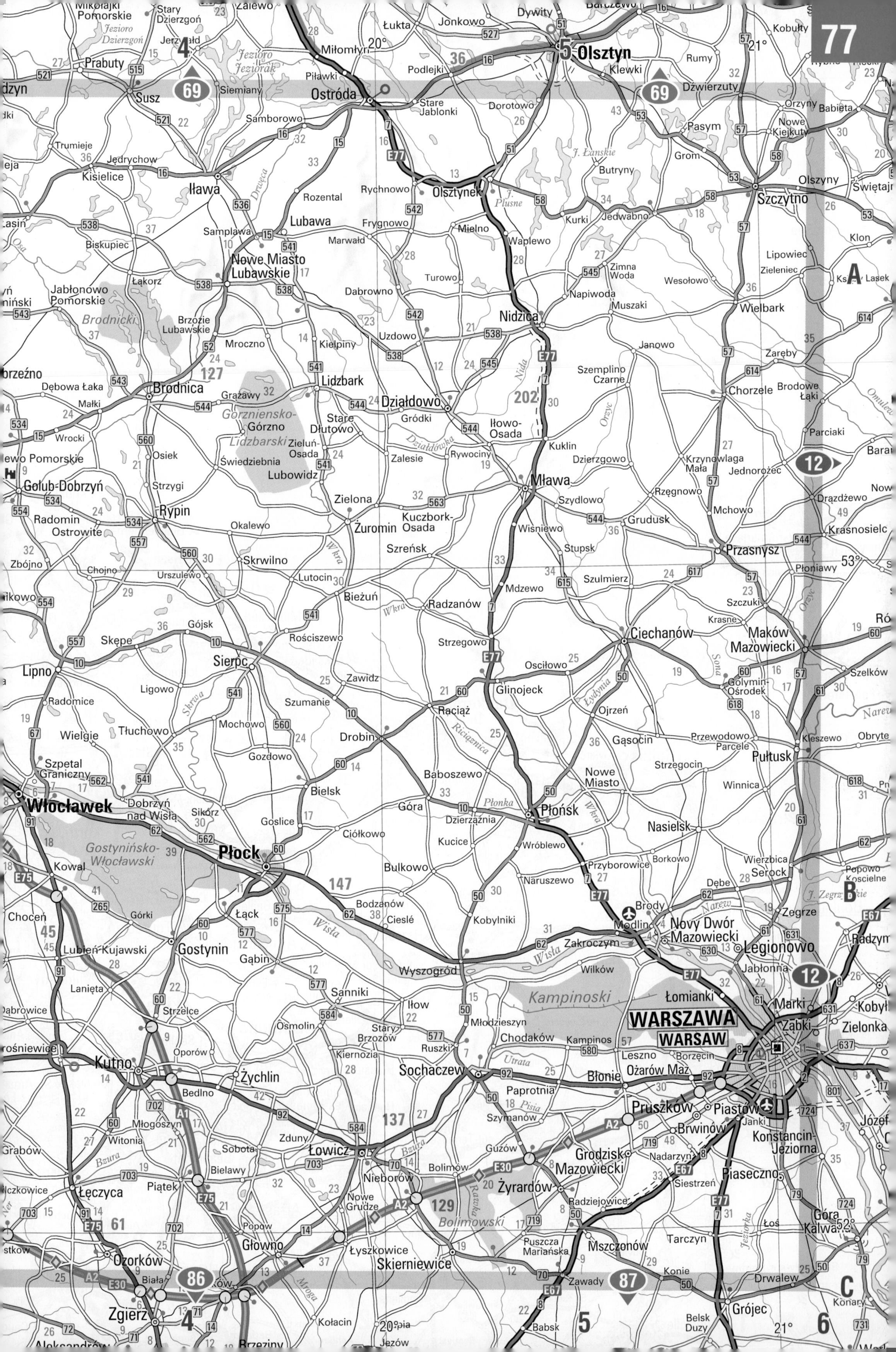

Olsztyn
Ostróda
Iława
Prabuty
Susz
Kisielice
Lubawa
Nowe Miasto Lubawskie
Olsztynek
Nidzica
Szczytno
Pasym
Dźwierzuty
Wielbark
Chorzele
Brodnica
Brodnicki
Lidzbark
Działdowo
Iłowo-Osada
Mława
Rypin
Golub-Dobrzyń
Żuromin
Przasnysz
Maków Mazowiecki
Ciechanów
Sierpc
Lipno
Bieżuń
Radzanów
Glinojeck
Raciąż
Drobin
Pułtusk
Płońsk
Nasielsk
Włocławek
Płock
Gostyniński-Włocławski
Gostynin
Kowal
Wyszogród
Zakroczym
Nowy Dwór Mazowiecki
Modlin
Legionowo
Serock
Zegrze
Kampinoski
Łomianki
WARSZAWA
WARSAW
Marki
Ząbki
Zielonka
Kutno
Żychlin
Sochaczew
Błonie
Ożarów Maz.
Pruszków
Piastów
Łowicz
Nieborów
Bolimowski
Żyrardów
Grodzisk Mazowiecki
Konstancin-Jeziorna
Piaseczno
Góra Kalwaria
Łęczyca
Ozorków
Głowno
Skierniewice
Mszczonów
Grójec
Zgierz
Wisła
E77
E75
E67
E30
A1
A2
12
69
86
87
A
B
C
4
5
6

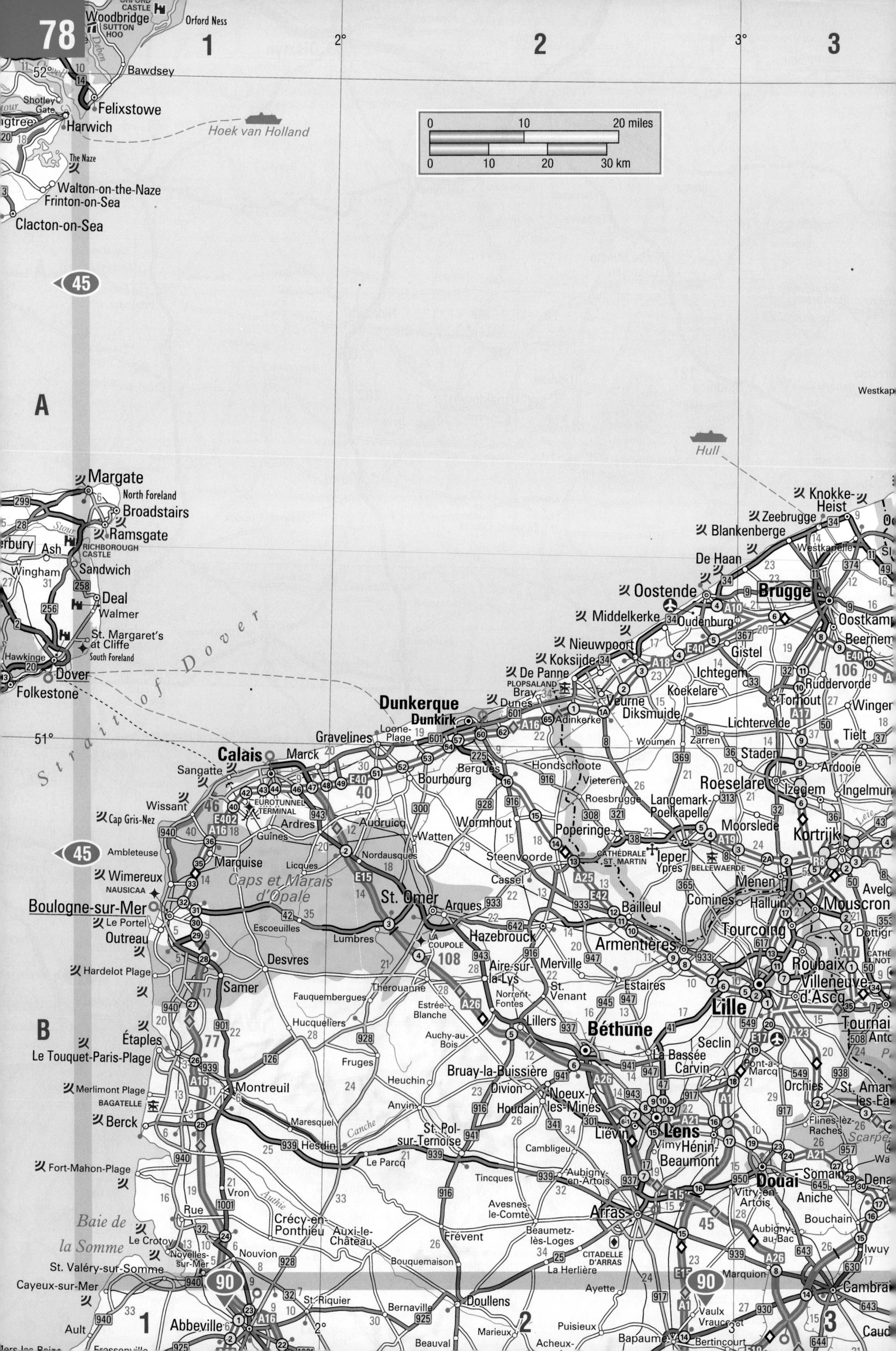
Woodbridge
SUTTON HOO
Orford Ness
Bawdsey
Felixstowe
Shotley Gate
Harwich
Hoek van Holland
The Naze
Walton-on-the-Naze
Frinton-on-Sea
Clacton-on-Sea
0 10 20 miles
0 10 20 30 km
Margate
North Foreland
Broadstairs
Ramsgate
RICHBOROUGH CASTLE
Ash
Wingham
Sandwich
Deal
Walmer
St. Margaret's at Cliffe
South Foreland
Hawkinge
Dover
Folkestone
Strait of Dover
Hull
Westkapelle
Knokke-Heist
Zeebrugge
Blankenberge
De Haan
Oostende
Brugge
Middelkerke
Oudenburg
Oostkamp
Beernem
Nieuwpoort
Gistel
Koksijde
De Panne
PLOPSALAND
Ichtegem
Ruddervoorde
Koekelare
Torhout
Wingene
Veurne
Diksmuide
Adinkerke
Lichtervelde
Tielt
Dunkerque
Dunkirk
Bray-Dunes
Gravelines
Loone-Plage
Woumen
Zarren
Staden
Ardooie
Calais
Marck
Sangatte
Bergues
Hondschoote
Vleteren
Roeselare
Izegem
Ingelmunster
Bourbourg
Roesbrugge
Langemark-Poelkapelle
Wissant
EUROTUNNEL TERMINAL
Cap Gris-Nez
Ardres
Audruicq
Wormhout
Poperinge
Moorslede
Kortrijk
Guînes
Watten
Ambleteuse
Marquise
Licques
Nordausques
Steenvoorde
CATHÉDRALE ST. MARTIN
Ieper
Ypres
BELLEWAERDE
Menen
Wimereux
NAUSICAA
Caps et Marais d'Opale
Cassel
Comines
Halluin
Mouscron
Boulogne-sur-Mer
Le Portel
St. Omer
Arques
Bailleul
Avelgem
Outreau
Escoeuilles
Lumbres
LA COUPOLE
Hazebrouck
Armentières
Tourcoing
Dottignies
Hardelot Plage
Desvres
Merville
Roubaix
Samer
Thérouanne
Aire-sur-la-Lys
St. Venant
Estaires
Villeneuve-d'Ascq
Fauquembergues
Norrent-Fontes
Lille
Tournai
Estrée-Blanche
Lillers
Béthune
Étaples
Hucqueliers
Auchy-au-Bois
Seclin
Le Touquet-Paris-Plage
Fruges
La Bassée
Carvin
Pont-à-Marcq
Orchies
St. Amand-les-Eaux
Bruay-la-Buissière
Heuchin
Divion
Merlimont Plage
BAGATELLE
Montreuil
Houdain
Noeux-les-Mines
Berck
Anvin
Maresquel
Canche
Liévin
Lens
Flines-lez-Raches
Scarpe
St. Pol-sur-Ternoise
Hesdin
Vimy
Hénin-Beaumont
Cambligneu
Le Parcq
Fort-Mahon-Plage
Tincques
Aubigny-en-Artois
Douai
Somain
Denain
Vron
Authie
Vitry-en-Artois
Aniche
Rue
Crécy-en-Ponthieu
Avesnes-le-Comte
Arras
Bouchain
Baie de la Somme
Le Crotoy
Auxi-le-Château
Frévent
Beaumetz-lès-Loges
Aubigny-au-Bac
Iwuy
Noyelles-sur-Mer
Nouvion
Bouquemaison
CITADELLE D'ARRAS
St. Valéry-sur-Somme
La Herlière
Marquion
Cayeux-sur-Mer
Ayette
Cambrai
St. Riquier
Doullens
Bernaville
Vaulx Vraucourt
Ault
Abbeville
Marieux
Puisieux
Bapaume
Bertincourt
Beauval
Acheux
Caudry
A
B
1
2
3
2°
3°
51°
52°

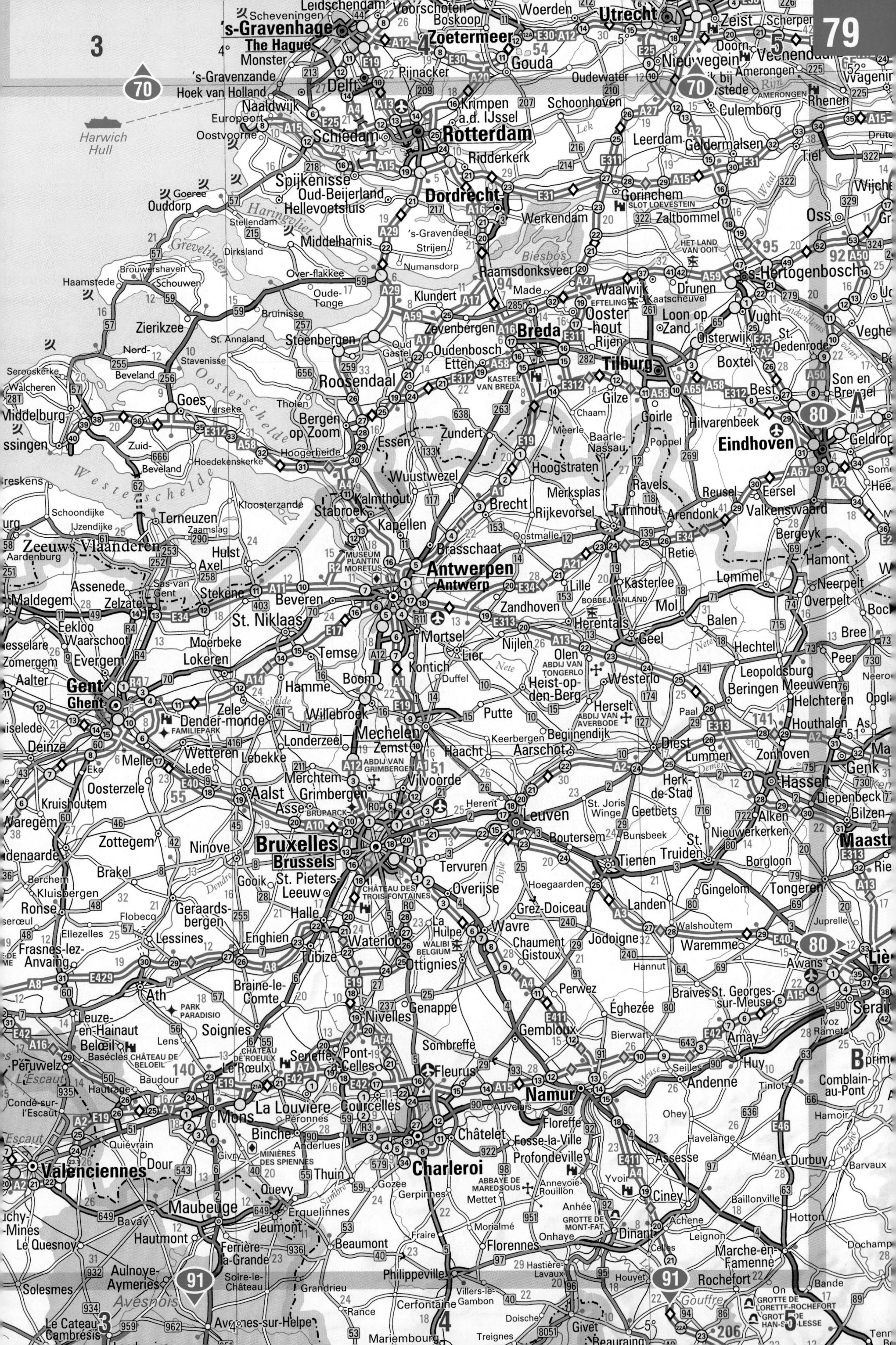

3
4
5
Scheveningen
Leidschendam
Voorschoten
Boskoop
Woerden
Utrecht
Zeist
's-Gravenhage
The Hague
Zoetermeer
Gouda
Monster
Nieuwegein
Veenendaal
Wageningen
's-Gravenzande
Pijnacker
Oudewater
Amerongen
70
Hoek van Holland
Delft
Schoonhoven
Rhenen
Naaldwijk
Krimpen a.d. IJssel
Culemborg
Harwich
Hull
Europoort
Oostvoorne
Schiedam
Rotterdam
Leerdam
Geldermalsen
Tiel
Ridderkerk
Spijkenisse
Oud-Beijerland
Hellevoetsluis
Dordrecht
Gorinchem
SLOT LOEVESTEIN
Zaltbommel
Oss
Goeree
Ouddorp
Haringvliet
Stellendam
Werkendam
's-Gravendeel
Strijen
Middelharnis
Dirksland
Grevelingen
Biesbos
HET LAND VAN OOIT
Brouwershaven
Schouwen
Numansdorp
Over-flakkee
Raamsdonksveer
Waalwijk
Drunen
's-Hertogenbosch
Haamstede
Oude-Tonge
Made
Kaatsheuvel
Klundert
EFTELING
Bruinisse
Zevenbergen
Oosterhout
Loon op Zand
Vught
Zierikzee
St. Annaland
Steenbergen
Breda
Rijen
Oisterwijk
St. Oedenrode
Nord-Beveland
Stavenisse
Oud Gastel
Oudenbosch
Etten
Tilburg
Boxtel
Son en Breugel
Serooskerke
Walcheren
Oosterschelde
Roosendaal
KASTEEL VAN BREDA
Gilze
Best
Middelburg
Goes
Yerseke
Tholen
Bergen op Zoom
Chaam
Goirle
Hilvarenbeek
Eindhoven
Vlissingen
Zuid-Beveland
Essen
Zundert
Meerle
Baarle-Nassau
Poppel
Geldrop
Hoedekenskerke
Hoogerheide
Hoogstraten
Westerschelde
Wuustwezel
Merksplas
Ravels
Reusel
Eersel
Breskens
Kalmthout
Brecht
Rijkevorsel
Turnhout
Arendonk
Valkenswaard
Schoondijke
Kloosterzande
Stabroek
Kapellen
IJzendijke
Terneuzen
Zaamslag
Oostmalle
Bergeyk
Zeeuws Vlaanderen
Aardenburg
Hulst
MUSEUM PLANTIN MORETUS
Brasschaat
Retie
Hamont
Axel
Antwerpen
Antwerp
Lille
Kasterlee
Lommel
Neerpelt
Overpelt
Assenede
Sas-van Gent
Maldegem
Zelzate
Stekene
Beveren
Zandhoven
BOBBEJAANLAND
Mol
Eekloo
Waarschoot
St. Niklaas
Herentals
Balen
Bree
Moerbeke
Mortsel
Nijlen
Geel
Hechtel
Eesselare
Zomergem
Evergem
Lokeren
Temse
Lier
Olen
ABDIJ VAN TONGERLO
Leopoldsburg
Peer
Aalter
Gent
Ghent
Hamme
Boom
Kontich
Duffel
Heist-op-den-Berg
Westerlo
Beringen
Meeuwen
Helchteren
Zele
Dendermonde
FAMILIEPARK
Willebroek
Putte
Herselt
ABDIJ VAN AVERBODE
Paal
Houthalen
Deinze
Melle
Wetteren
Lebekke
Londerzeel
Mechelen
Zemst
Keerbergen
Begijnendijk
Haacht
Aarschot
Diest
Lummen
Zonhoven
Genk
Eke
Lede
Merchtem
ABDIJ VAN GRIMBERGEN
Vilvoorde
Herk-de-Stad
Hasselt
Maastricht
Oosterzele
Kruishoutem
Aalst
Grimbergen
Asse
BRUPARCK
Herent
Leuven
St. Joris Winge
Geetbets
Alken
Diepenbeek
Bilzen
Waregem
Zottegem
Ninove
Bruxelles
Brussels
Boutersem
Bunsbeek
Nieuwerkerken
Oudenaarde
Tervuren
Tienen
St. Truiden
Borgloon
Brakel
Gooik
St. Pieters-Leeuw
Overijse
Hoegaarden
Berchem
Kluisbergen
CHÂTEAU DES TROIS-FONTAINES
Gingelom
Tongeren
Ronse
Flobecq
Geraardsbergen
Halle
Grez-Doiceau
Landen
Ellezelles
Lessines
Enghien
Waterloo
La Hulpe
Wavre
Walshoutem
Jodoigne
Waremme
Frasnes-lez-Anvaing
Tubize
WALIBI BELGIUM
Chaumont Gistoux
Hannut
Awans
Liège
Ottignies
Ath
Braine-le-Comte
Perwez
Braives
St. Georges-sur-Meuse
Seraing
PARK PARADISIO
Leuze-en-Hainaut
Nivelles
Genappe
Éghezée
Ivoz Ramet
Beloeil
Basècles
CHÂTEAU DE BELOEIL
Soignies
Lens
CHÂTEAU DE ROEULX
Gembloux
Bierwart
Amay
Péruwelz
L'Escaut
Seneffe
Pont-à-Celles
Sombreffe
Huy
Le Roeulx
Fleurus
Seilles
Andenne
Comblain-au-Pont
Baudour
Hautrage
Namur
Tinlot
Condé-sur-l'Escaut
Mons
La Louvière
Courcelles
Auvelais
Ohey
Hamoir
Péronnes
Floreffe
Binche
Anderlues
Châtelet
Fosse-la-Ville
Havelange
Quiévrain
Profondeville
Assesse
Méan
Durbuy
Barvaux
Valenciennes
Dour
Givry
MINIÈRES DES SPIENNES
Thuin
Charleroi
Yvoir
ABBAYE DE MAREDSOUS
Annevoie-Rouillon
Ciney
Quevy
Gozee
Gerpinnes
Mettet
Baillonville
Maubeuge
Erquelinnes
Sambre
Anhée
GROTTE DE MONT-FAT
Achene
Hotton
Valenciennes
Bavay
Jeumont
Morialmé
Onhaye
Dinant
Leignon
Le Quesnoy
Hautmont
Ferrière-la-Grande
Beaumont
Fraire
Florennes
Celles
Marche-en-Famenne
Aulnoye-Aymeries
Solre-le-Château
Philippeville
Hastière-Lavaux
Houyet
91
Rochefort
Solesmes
Avesnois
Grandrieu
Villers-le-Gambon
GROTTE DE LORETTE-ROCHEFORT
GROTTE DE HAN-SUR-LESSE
Bande
Le Cateau Cambrésis
Avesnes-sur-Helpe
Rance
Cerfontaine
Doische
Givet
Gouffre
Mariembourg
Treignes
Beauraing
80
A
B

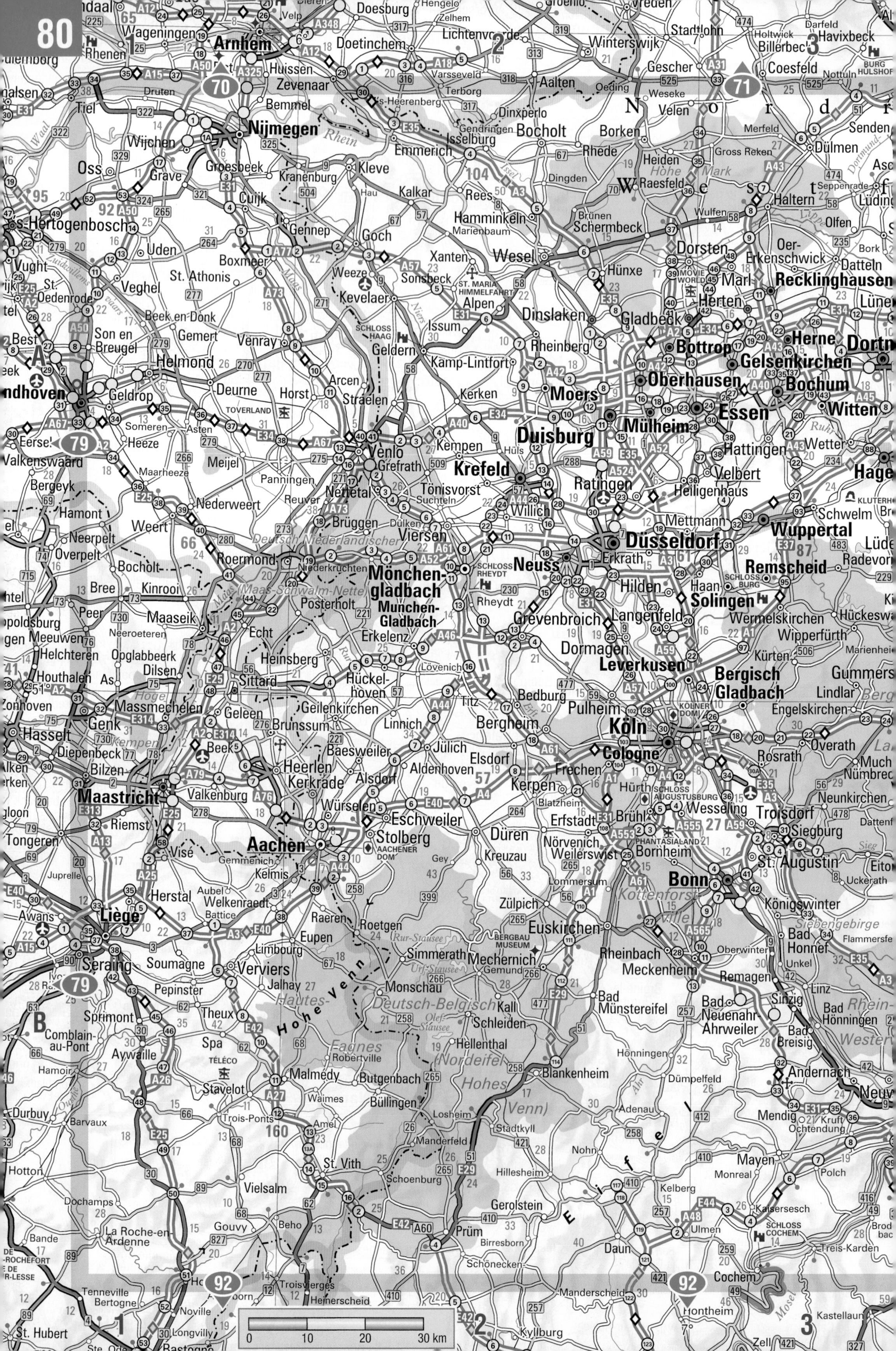
Wageningen
Arnhem
Rhenen
Doesburg
Doetinchem
Lichtenvoorde
Winterswijk
Stadtlohn
Vreden
Gescher
Coesfeld
Billerbeck
Havixbeck
Darfeld
Holtwick
Huissen
Zevenaar
Varsseveld
Terborg
Aalten
Oeding
Weseke
Velen
Tiel
Druten
Bemmel
's-Heerenberg
Dinxperlo
Bocholt
Borken
Merfeld
Senden
Dülmen
Wijchen
Nijmegen
Rhein
Emmerich
Isselburg
Rhede
Heiden
Gross Reken
Oss
Groesbeek
Kranenburg
Kleve
Dingden
Raesfeld
Hohe Mark
Haltern
Seppenrade
Lüdinghausen
Grave
Cuijk
Kalkar
Rees
Hamminkeln
Brünen
Schermbeck
Wulfen
Olfen
's-Hertogenbosch
Gennep
Goch
Marienbaum
Xanten
Wesel
Dorsten
Oer-Erkenschwick
Datteln
Vught
Uden
Boxmeer
St. Athonis
Weeze
Sonsbeck
Hünxe
Marl
Recklinghausen
Veghel
Kevelaer
Alpen
Dinslaken
Herten
Lünen
St. Oedenrode
Beek en Donk
Gemert
Issum
Gladbeck
Herne
Dortmund
Best
Son en Breugel
Venray
Geldern
Kamp-Lintfort
Rheinberg
Bottrop
Gelsenkirchen
Eindhoven
Helmond
Geldrop
Deurne
Horst
Arcen
Straelen
Moers
Oberhausen
Bochum
Essen
Witten
Mülheim
Eersel
Someren
Heeze
Asten
Venlo
Kempen
Kerken
Duisburg
Hattingen
Wetter
Valkenswaard
Maarheeze
Meijel
Panningen
Grefrath
Krefeld
Hüls
Ratingen
Velbert
Heiligenhaus
Hagen
Bergeyk
Nettetal
Tönisvorst
Willich
Mettmann
Wuppertal
Schwelm
Hamont
Nederweert
Weert
Reuver
Brüggen
Dülken
Viersen
Düsseldorf
Erkrath
Neerpelt
Overpelt
Bocholt
Roermond
Niederkrüchten
Mönchengladbach
Munchen-Gladbach
Neuss
Hilden
Haan
Remscheid
Radevormwald
Kinrooi
Bree
Peer
Maaseik
Posterholt
Rheydt
Grevenbroich
Langenfeld
Solingen
Wermelskirchen
Hückeswagen
Leopoldsburg
Meeuwen
Neeroeteren
Echt
Erkelenz
Wipperfürth
Helchteren
Opglabbeek
Dilsen
Heinsberg
Dormagen
Leverkusen
Kürten
Houthalen
As
Sittard
Hückelhoven
Lövenich
Bergisch Gladbach
Gummersbach
Zonhoven
Genk
Massmechelen
Geleen
Brunssum
Geilenkirchen
Linnich
Titz
Bedburg
Pulheim
Lindlar
Engelskirchen
Hasselt
Beek
Baesweiler
Jülich
Bergheim
Köln
Cologne
Overath
Diepenbeck
Bilzen
Heerlen
Kerkrade
Alsdorf
Aldenhoven
Elsdorf
Frechen
Rösrath
Much
Nümbrecht
Maastricht
Valkenburg
Würselen
Eschweiler
Kerpen
Hürth
Wesseling
Troisdorf
Neunkirchen
Tongeren
Riemst
Aachen
Stolberg
Düren
Erfstadt
Brühl
Siegburg
Visé
Kelmis
Kreuzau
Nörvenich
Weilerswist
Bornheim
St. Augustin
Herstal
Welkenraedt
Bonn
Eitorf
Liège
Awans
Eupen
Roetgen
Zülpich
Euskirchen
Königswinter
Seraing
Soumagne
Limbourg
Simmerath
Mechernich
Rheinbach
Bad Honnef
Verviers
Monschau
Kall
Meckenheim
Remagen
Linz
Pepinster
Jalhay
Bad Münstereifel
Bad Neuenahr-Ahrweiler
Sinzig
Bad Hönningen
Sprimont
Theux
Schleiden
Bad Breisig
Comblain-au-Pont
Spa
Hellenthal
Aywaille
Malmedy
Bütgenbach
Blankenheim
Andernach
Neuwied
Stavelot
Waimes
Büllingen
Dümpelfeld
Durbuy
Trois-Ponts
Losheim
Adenau
Mendig
Ochtendung
Amel
Stadtkyll
Manderfeld
Nohn
Mayen
St. Vith
Schoenburg
Hillesheim
Polch
Hotton
Vielsalm
Gerolstein
Kelberg
Kaisersesch
Gouvy
Beho
Prüm
Ulmen
La Roche-en-Ardenne
Birresborn
Daun
Treis-Karden
Schönecken
Cochem
Tenneville
Bertogne
Troisvierges
Hemerscheid
Manderscheid
Hontheim
Noville
Longvilly
Bastogne
Kyllburg
Zell
Kastellaun
St. Hubert
Eifel
Hohe Venn
Hautes-Fagnes
Nordeifel
Kottenforst
Siebengebirge
Deutsch-Belgisch
Deutsch-Niederländischer
Maas-Schwalm-Nette
Rur-Stausee
Urft-Stausee
Olef-Stausee
Kempen
Mosel
Maas
Waal
Niers
Ruhr
Sieg
Ahr
Lippe
Nord
West
Toverland
Schloss Haag
St. Maria Himmelfahrt
Movie World
Schloss Burg
Schloss Rheydt
Kölner Dom
Schloss Augustusburg
Phantasialand
Aachener Dom
Bergbau Museum
Téléco
Schloss Cochem
Burg Hülshoff
Kluterhöhle
0
10
20
30 km

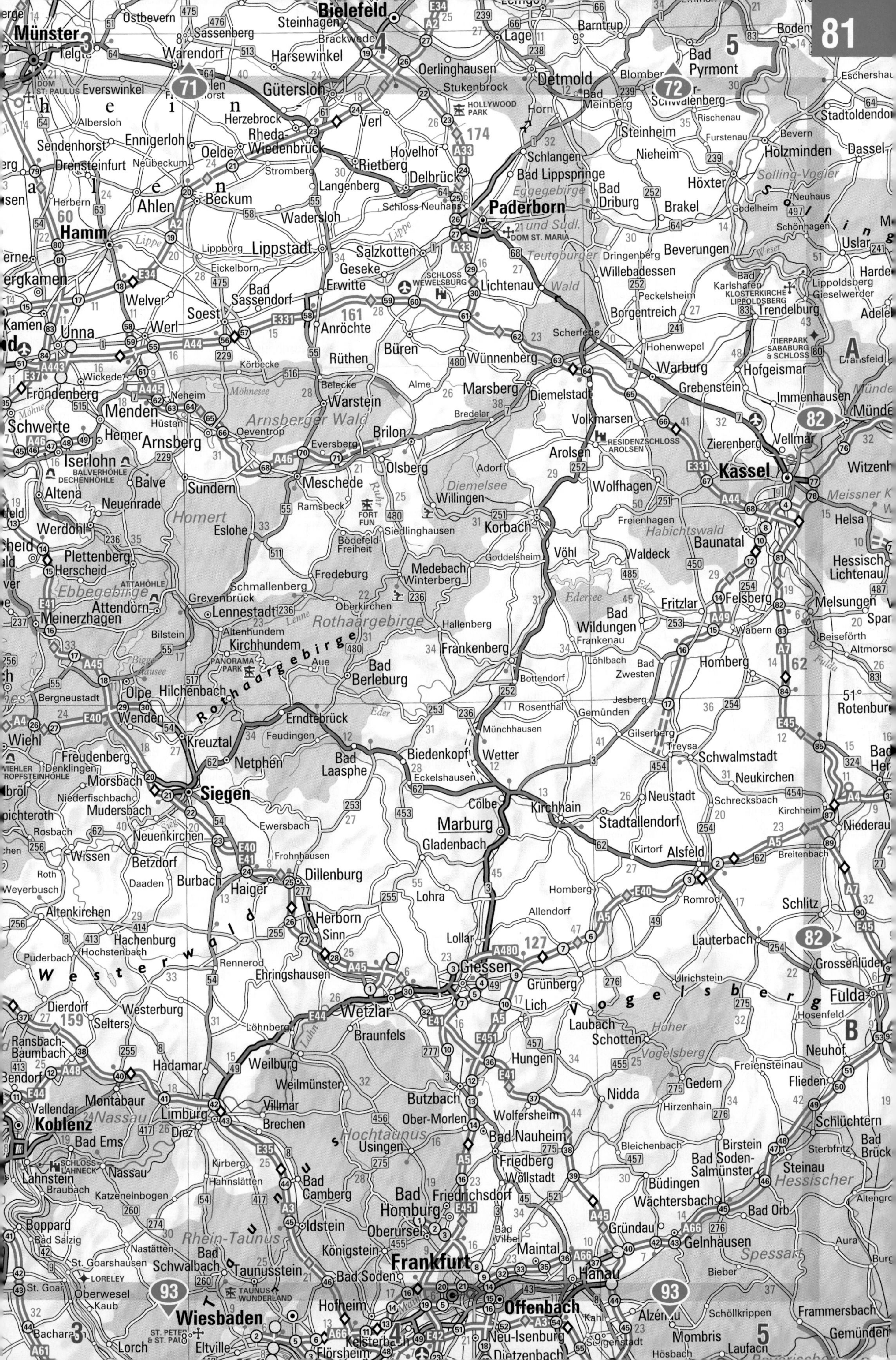

81
Münster
Telgte
Ostbevern
Sassenberg
Warendorf
Everswinkel
Albersloh
Sendenhorst
Ennigerloh
Drensteinfurt
Neubeckum
Oelde
Ahlen
Beckum
Herbern
Hamm
Bielefeld
Steinhagen
Brackwede
Harsewinkel
Gütersloh
Herzebrock
Rheda-Wiedenbrück
Verl
Oerlinghausen
Stukenbrock
Hövelhof
Rietberg
Delbrück
Langenberg
Stromberg
Wadersloh
Schloss Neuhaus
Lage
Barntrup
Detmold
Bad Meinberg
Horn
Blomberg
Bad Pyrmont
Schwalenberg
Steinheim
Nieheim
Schlangen
Bad Lippspringe
Eggegebirge
Paderborn
Bad Driburg
Brakel
Höxter
Holzminden
Bevern
Dassel
Solling-Vogler
Neuhaus
Stadtoldendorf
Eschershausen
Bodenwerder
Fürstenau
Rischenau
Godelheim
Schönhagen
Uslar
Hardegsen
Beverungen
Dringenberg
Willebadessen
Teutoburger Wald
Dom St. Maria
Lippborg
Lippstadt
Salzkotten
Geseke
Erwitte
Eickelborn
Bad Sassendorf
Soest
Werl
Welver
Unna
Kamen
Bergkamen
Anröchte
Rüthen
Büren
Lichtenau
Schloss Wewelsburg
Wünnenberg
Scherfede
Borgentreich
Peckelsheim
Bad Karlshafen
Klosterkirche Lippoldsberg
Lippoldsberg
Gieselwerder
Trendelburg
Hohenwepel
Warburg
Hofgeismar
Tierpark Sababurg & Schloss
Grebenstein
Immenhausen
Hann. Münden
Vellmar
Kassel
Zierenberg
Wolfhagen
Arolsen
Residenzschloss Arolsen
Volkmarsen
Diemelstadt
Marsberg
Bredelar
Alme
Körbecke
Möhnesee
Belecke
Warstein
Wickede
Fröndenberg
Menden
Neheim
Hüsten
Arnsberg
Oeventrop
Arnsberger Wald
Brilon
Eversberg
Olsberg
Meschede
Schwerte
Hemer
Iserlohn
Balverhöhle
Dechenhöhle
Balve
Altena
Sundern
Neuenrade
Homert
Eslohe
Ramsbeck
Fort Fun
Willingen
Diemelsee
Adorf
Korbach
Siedlinghausen
Bödefeld-Freiheit
Werdohl
Plettenberg
Herscheid
Ebbegebirge
Attahöhle
Attendorn
Meinerzhagen
Grevenbrück
Lennestadt
Schmallenberg
Fredeburg
Medebach
Winterberg
Oberkirchen
Rothaargebirge
Hallenberg
Goddelsheim
Vöhl
Waldeck
Edersee
Bad Wildungen
Frankenau
Fritzlar
Felsberg
Melsungen
Baunatal
Habichtswald
Freienhagen
Helsa
Hessisch Lichtenau
Meissner
Bilstein
Altenhundem
Kirchhundem
Panorama Park
Biggesee
Olpe
Hilchenbach
Aue
Bad Berleburg
Frankenberg
Löhlbach
Bad Zwesten
Homberg
Wabern
Beiseförth
Altmorschen
Rotenburg
Bergneustadt
Wenden
Erndtebrück
Feudingen
Bottendorf
Rosenthal
Gemünden
Jesberg
Wiehl
Kreuztal
Netphen
Bad Laasphe
Biedenkopf
Wetter
Münchhausen
Gilserberg
Treysa
Schwalmstadt
Neukirchen
Schrecksbach
Freudenberg
Wiehler Tropfsteinhöhle
Denklingen
Morsbach
Siegen
Niederfischbach
Mudersbach
Eckelshausen
Cölbe
Marburg
Kirchhain
Neustadt
Stadtallendorf
Kirchheim
Niederaula
Bad Hersfeld
Rosbach
Wissen
Neuenkirchen
Betzdorf
Eversbach
Gladenbach
Kirtorf
Alsfeld
Breitenbach
Roth
Daaden
Burbach
Frohnhausen
Dillenburg
Haiger
Lohra
Homberg
Romrod
Schlitz
Weyerbusch
Altenkirchen
Herborn
Sinn
Allendorf
Lollar
Lauterbach
Hachenburg
Hochstenbach
Puderbach
Rennerod
Ehringshausen
Giessen
Grünberg
Grossenlüder
Westerwald
Dierdorf
Westerburg
Selters
Wetzlar
Lich
Laubach
Vogelsberg
Fulda
Hosenfeld
Ransbach-Baumbach
Hadamar
Löhnberg
Braunfels
Hungen
Schotten
Hoher Vogelsberg
Neuhof
Weilburg
Weilmünster
Nidda
Gedern
Freiensteinau
Flieden
Vallendar
Montabaur
Koblenz
Nassau
Limburg
Diez
Villmar
Brechen
Butzbach
Ober-Morlen
Wölfersheim
Hirzenhain
Schlüchtern
Bad Ems
Schloss Lahneck
Lahnstein
Braubach
Hochtaunus
Usingen
Bad Nauheim
Friedberg
Wöllstadt
Bleichenbach
Birstein
Bad Soden-Salmünster
Steinau
Sterbfritz
Bad Brückenau
Hessischer Spessart
Kirberg
Hahnstätten
Katzenelnbogen
Bad Camberg
Idstein
Bad Homburg
Oberursel
Friedrichsdorf
Büdingen
Wächtersbach
Bad Orb
Boppard
Bad Salzig
Nastätten
Rhein-Taunus
Bad Schwalbach
Königstein
Bad Vilbel
Maintal
Gründau
Gelnhausen
Aura
St. Goarshausen
Loreley
St. Goar
Oberwesel
Kaub
Taunusstein
Taunus Wunderland
Bad Soden
Frankfurt
Hanau
Spessart
Bieber
Frammersbach
Wiesbaden
St. Peter & St. Paul
Hofheim
Offenbach
Alzenau
Schöllkrippen
Bacharach
Lorch
Eltville
Flörsheim
Kelsterbach
Neu-Isenburg
Dietzenbach
Seligenstadt
Mombris
Hösbach
Laufach
Gemünden
Taunus

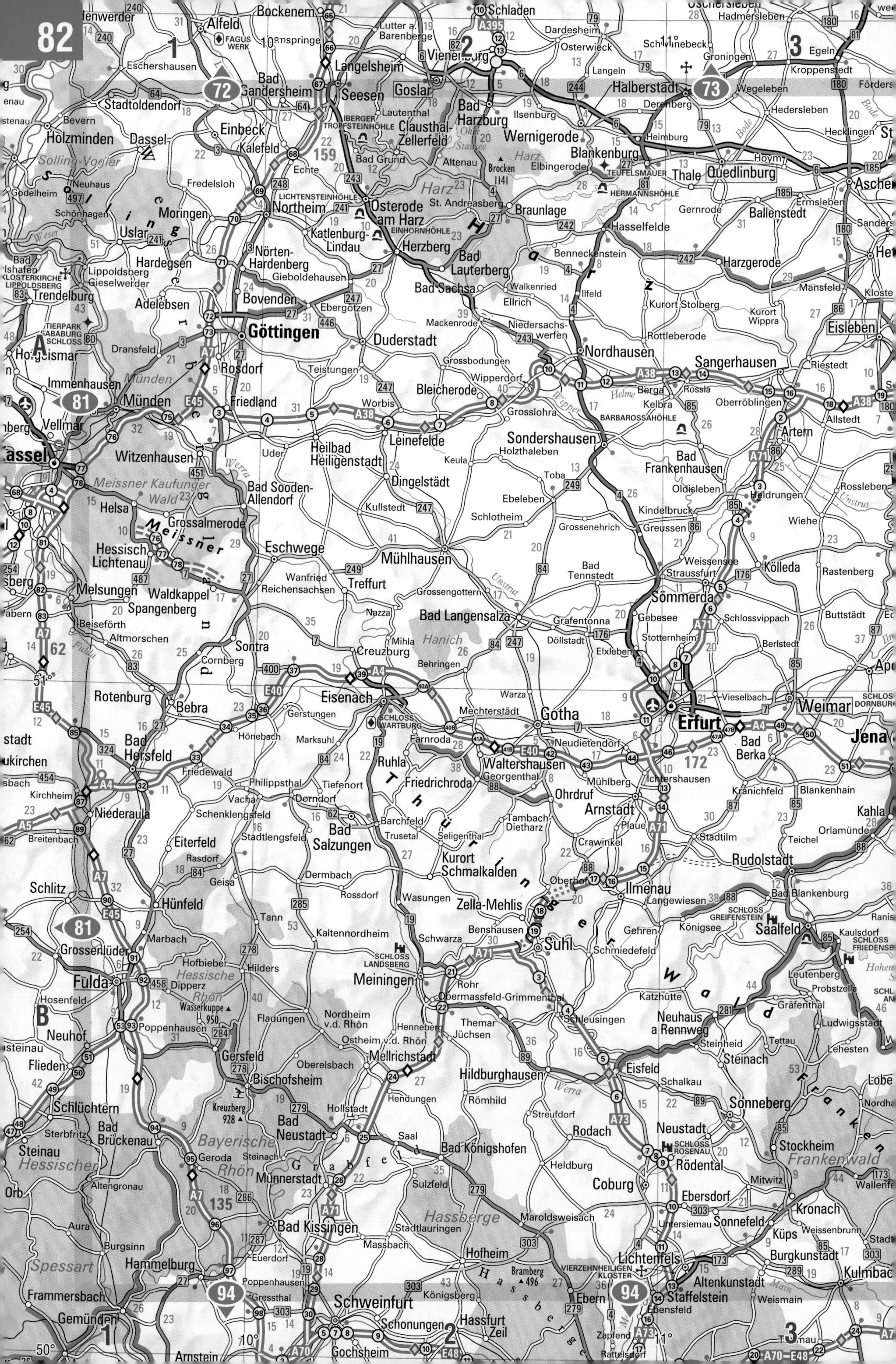
Alfeld
Bockenem
Schladen
Dardesheim
Osterwieck
Schwanebeck
Groningen
Egeln
Kroppenstedt
Hadmersleben
Langelsheim
Vienenburg
Lutter a. Barenberge
Eschershausen
Bad Gandersheim
Seesen
Goslar
Halberstadt
Wegeleben
Stadtoldendorf
Lautenthal
Bad Harzburg
Ilsenburg
Derenberg
Hedersleben
Bevern
Holzminden
Dassel
Einbeck
Kalefeld
Clausthal-Zellerfeld
Wernigerode
Blankenburg
Heimburg
Hecklingen
Solling-Vogler
Echte
Bad Grund
Altenau
Brocken
Harz
Elbingerode
Teufelsmauer
Thale
Quedlinburg
Hoym
Neuhaus
Fredelsloh
Lichtensteinhöhle
Osterode am Harz
St. Andreasberg
Braunlage
Hermannshöhle
Gernrode
Ballenstedt
Ermsleben
Godelheim
Schönhagen
Moringen
Northeim
Katlenburg-Lindau
Einhornhöhle
Hasselfelde
Uslar
Nörten-Hardenberg
Herzberg
Bad Lauterberg
Benneckenstein
Harzgerode
Bad Karlshafen
Klosterkirche Lippoldsberg
Lippoldsberg
Gieselwerder
Hardegsen
Gieboldehausen
Bad Sachsa
Walkenried
Mansfeld
Trendelburg
Adelebsen
Bovenden
Ellrich
Ilfeld
Kurort Stolberg
Kurort Wippra
Tierpark Sababurg
Schloss Sababurg
Ebergötzen
Mackenrode
Niedersachswerfen
Eisleben
Hofgeismar
Dransfeld
Göttingen
Duderstadt
Rottleberode
Nordhausen
Rosdorf
Teistungen
Grossbodungen
Sangerhausen
Riestedt
Immenhausen
Münden
Wipperdorf
Berga
Rossla
Kelbra
Oberröblingen
Allstedt
Vellmar
Friedland
Worbis
Bleicherode
Grosslohra
Barbarossahöhle
Artern
Kassel
Witzenhausen
Heilbad Heiligenstadt
Leinefelde
Sondershausen
Holzthaleben
Bad Frankenhausen
Keula
Uder
Dingelstädt
Toba
Oldisleben
Heldrungen
Rossleben
Meissner Kaufunger Wald
Helsa
Bad Sooden-Allendorf
Kullstedt
Ebeleben
Kindelbruck
Grossalmerode
Schlotheim
Grossenehrich
Greussen
Wiehe
Hessisch Lichtenau
Meissner
Eschwege
Mühlhausen
Weissensee
Kölleda
Rastenberg
Melsungen
Waldkappel
Wanfried
Reichensachsen
Treffurt
Bad Tennstedt
Straussfurt
Spangenberg
Grossengottern
Sömmerda
Gebesee
Schlossvippach
Buttstädt
Beiseförth
Nazza
Bad Langensalza
Grafentonna
Altmorschen
Sontra
Mihla
Hanich
Döllstadt
Stotternheim
Berlstedt
Creuzburg
Elxleben
Cornberg
Behringen
Eisenach
Rotenburg
Bebra
Warza
Vieselbach
Weimar
Gerstungen
Mechterstädt
Gotha
Erfurt
Schloss Wartburg
Hönebach
Marksuhl
Farnroda
Neudietendorf
Bad Berka
Jena
Bad Hersfeld
Ruhla
Waltershausen
Friedewald
Georgenthal
Ichtershausen
Mühlberg
Kirchheim
Philippsthal
Tiefenort
Friedrichroda
Ohrdruf
Arnstadt
Kranichfeld
Blankenhain
Niederaula
Vacha
Dorndorf
Schenklengsfeld
Tambach-Dietharz
Plaue
Kahla
Orlamünde
Breitenbach
Stadtlengsfeld
Bad Salzungen
Barchfeld
Trusetal
Seligenthal
Crawinkel
Stadtilm
Teichel
Eiterfeld
Rasdorf
Kurort Schmalkalden
Rudolstadt
Dermbach
Geisa
Oberhof
Ilmenau
Schlitz
Rossdorf
Wasungen
Zella-Mehlis
Langewiesen
Bad Blankenburg
Hünfeld
Tann
Thüringer Wald
Schloss Greifenstein
Königsee
Saalfeld
Kaltennordheim
Benshausen
Gehren
Kaulsdorf
Schloss Friedensburg
Marbach
Schwarza
Grossenlüder
Schloss Landsberg
Suhl
Schmiedefeld
Hofbieber
Hilders
Fulda
Dipperz
Hessische Rhön
Meiningen
Rohr
Leutenberg
Probstzella
Wasserkuppe
Obermassfeld-Grimmenthal
Katzhütte
Hosenfeld
Fladungen
Nordheim v.d. Rhön
Themar
Schleusingen
Neuhaus a Rennweg
Gräfenthal
Ludwigsstadt
Neuhof
Poppenhausen
Henneberg
Jüchsen
Ostheim v.d. Rhön
Steinheid
Tettau
Lehesten
Gersfeld
Mellrichstadt
Steinach
Flieden
Oberelsbach
Hildburghausen
Eisfeld
Bischofsheim
Kreuzberg
Hendungen
Schalkau
Schlüchtern
Hollstadt
Römhild
Sonneberg
Sterbfritz
Bad Brückenau
Bad Neustadt
Streufdorf
Rodach
Neustadt
Steinau
Saal
Schloss Rosenau
Stockheim
Frankenwald
Hessischer
Geroda
Bayerische Rhön
Grabfeld
Bad Königshofen
Rödental
Altengronau
Münnerstadt
Sulzfeld
Heldburg
Coburg
Mitwitz
Wallenfels
Ebersdorf
Kronach
Hassberge
Maroldsweisach
Untersiemau
Sonnefeld
Küps
Weissenbrunn
Aura
Bad Kissingen
Stadtlauringen
Burgsinn
Massbach
Hofheim
Lichtenfels
Burgkunstadt
Spessart
Hammelburg
Euerdorf
Bramberg
Vierzehnheiligen Kloster
Altenkunstadt
Kulmbach
Poppenhausen
Frammersbach
Gressthal
Königsberg
Ebern
Staffelstein
Weismain
Schweinfurt
Ebensfeld
Gemünden
Schonungen
Hassfurt
Zeil
Zapfendorf
Thurnau
Arnstein
Gochsheim
Rattelsdorf
Weser
Werra
Fulda
Unstrut
Wipper
Helme
Bode
Main
Oker Stausee
Fagus Werk
Iberger Tropfsteinhöhle
A7
A38
A4
A71
A73
A395
A5
A70
E45
E40
E48

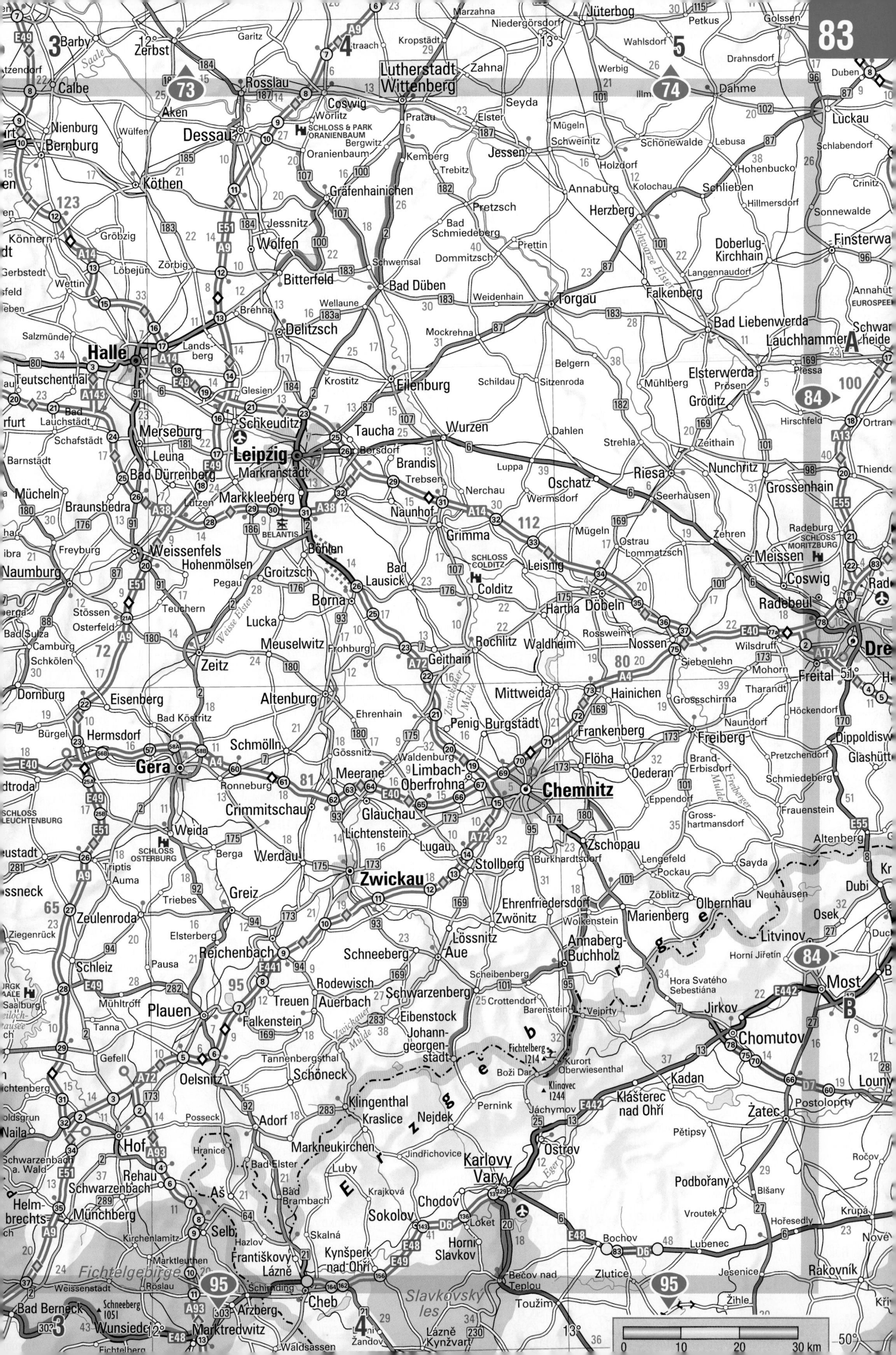
73
74
Barby
Zerbst
Jüterbog
Lutherstadt Wittenberg
Rosslau
Coswig
Calbe
Dessau
Nienburg
Bernburg
Köthen
SCHLOSS & PARK ORANIENBAUM
Oranienbaum
Gräfenhainichen
Kemberg
Jessen
Seyda
Dahme
Luckau
Schönewalde
Annaburg
Herzberg
Schlieben
Finsterwalde
Doberlug-Kirchhain
Könnern
Wolfen
Bitterfeld
Bad Düben
Torgau
Falkenberg
Bad Liebenwerda
Lauchhammer
Halle
Delitzsch
Eilenburg
Elsterwerda
Gröditz
84
Teutschenthal
Merseburg
Schkeuditz
Leipzig
Taucha
Wurzen
Riesa
Leuna
Bad Dürrenberg
Markranstädt
Brandis
Oschatz
Nünchritz
Grossenhain
Markkleeberg
Naunhof
Grimma
Meissen
Coswig
Radebeul
Weissenfels
Naumburg
Hohenmölsen
Groitzsch
Böhlen
Borna
Bad Lausick
Colditz
Leisnig
Döbeln
Hartha
Lucka
Meuselwitz
Zeitz
Rochlitz
Waldheim
Nossen
Dresden
Freital
Eisenberg
Altenburg
Geithain
Mittweida
Hainichen
Hermsdorf
Gera
Schmölln
Penig
Burgstädt
Frankenberg
Freiberg
Dippoldiswalde
Meerane
Limbach-Oberfrohna
Flöha
Oederan
Glauchau
Crimmitschau
Chemnitz
Weida
Werdau
Zwickau
Stollberg
Zschopau
Greiz
Zeulenroda
Marienberg
Olbernhau
Reichenbach
Schneeberg
Aue
Annaberg-Buchholz
Schleiz
Plauen
Rodewisch
Auerbach
Schwarzenberg
Most
Jirkov
Chomutov
Oelsnitz
Falkenstein
Eibenstock
Klingenthal
Kadan
Hof
Adorf
Markneukirchen
Ostrov
Karlovy Vary
Žatec
Rehau
Münchberg
Aš
Selb
Chodov
Sokolov
Podbořany
Erzgebirge
Fichtelgebirge
Cheb
Marktredwitz
Wunsiedel
Bad Berneck
Rakovník
95
0 10 20 30 km

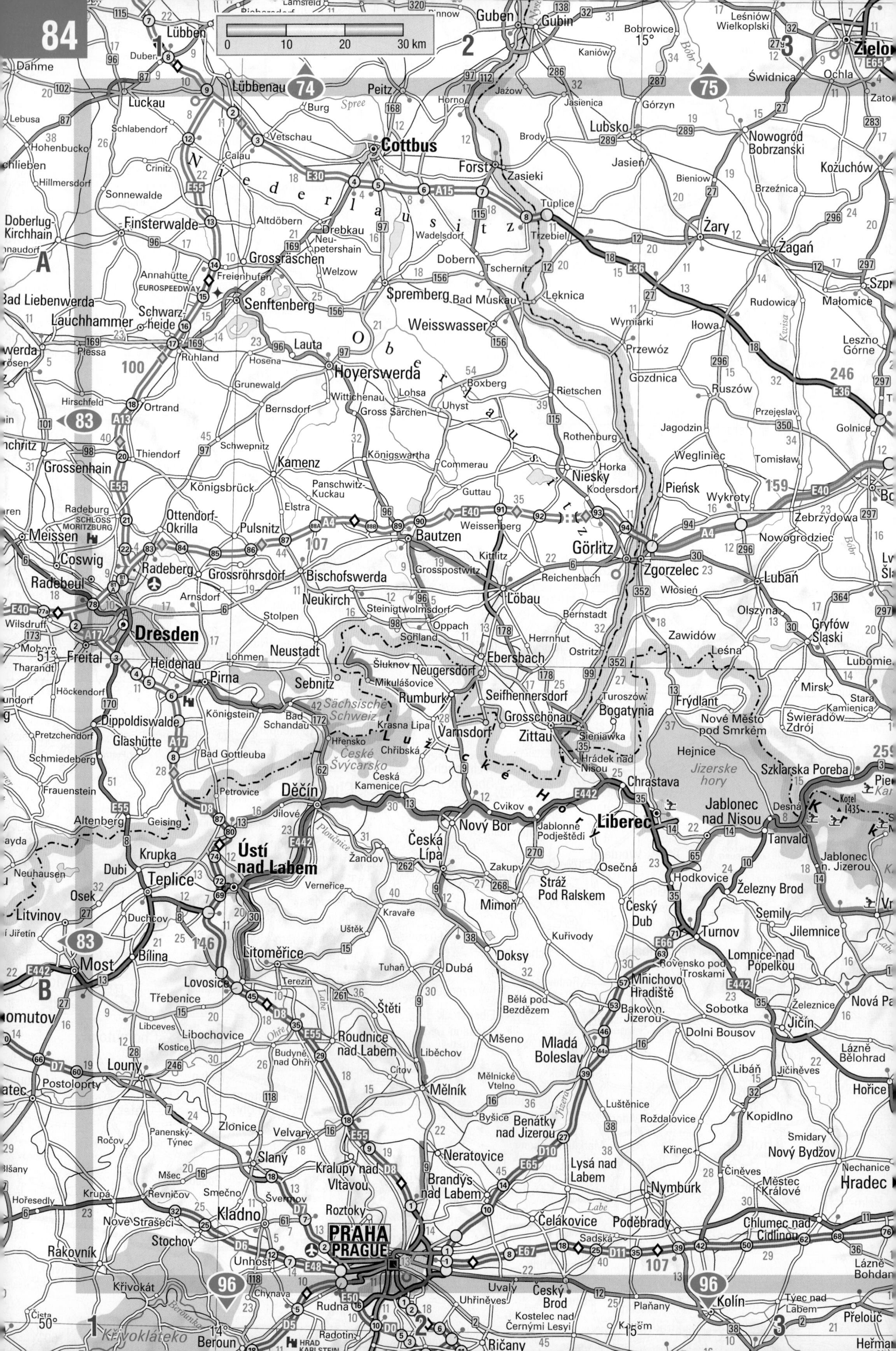
0 10 20 30 km
74
75
83
96
107
Lübben
Lübbenau
Luckau
Dahme
Lebusa
Schlabendorf
Hohenbucko
Hillmersdorf
Sonnewalde
Crinitz
Calau
Vetschau
Burg
Spree
Peitz
Cottbus
Guben
Gubin
Bobrowice
Kaniów
Jasienica
Górzyn
Lubsko
Brody
Forst
Zasieki
Jasień
Bieniow
Nowogród Bobrzański
Brzeźnica
Kożuchów
Świdnica
Ochla
Leśniów Wielkopolski
Niederlausitz
Doberlug-Kirchhain
Finsterwalde
Altdöbern
Drebkau
Neu-petershain
Welzow
Grossräschen
Annahütte
EUROSPEEDWAY
Freienhufen
Senftenberg
Spremberg
Dobern
Tschernitz
Wadelsdorf
Bad Muskau
Tuplice
Trzebiel
Łęknica
Żary
Żagań
Rudowica
Małomice
Bad Liebenwerda
Lauchhammer
Schwarzheide
Ruhland
Plessa
Hosena
Lauta
Hoyerswerda
Oberlausitz
Weisswasser
Boxberg
Lohsa
Wittichenau
Gross Särchen
Uhyst
Rietschen
Wymiarki
Przewóz
Gozdnica
Iłowa
Ruszów
Leszno Górne
Przejęslav
Golnice
Jagodzin
Tomisław
Hirschfeld
Ortrand
Grunewald
Bernsdorf
Schwepnitz
Thiendorf
Grossenhain
Kamenz
Königsbrück
Königswartha
Commerau
Panschwitz-Kuckau
Guttau
Rothenburg
Niesky
Horka
Kodersdorf
Węgliniec
Pieńsk
Wykroty
Radeburg
SCHLOSS MORITZBURG
Ottendorf-Okrilla
Pulsnitz
Elstra
Bautzen
Weissenberg
Görlitz
Zgorzelec
Żebrzydowa
Nowogrodziec
Meissen
Coswig
Radebeul
Radeberg
Grossröhrsdorf
Bischofswerda
Kittlitz
Grosspostwitz
Reichenbach
Löbau
Lubań
Włosień
Wilsdruff
Dresden
Arnsdorf
Neukirch
Steinigtwolmsdorf
Oppach
Bernstadt
Herrnhut
Olszyna
Gryfów Śląski
Freital
Tharandt
Heidenau
Pirna
Lohmen
Stolpen
Neustadt
Sohland
Ebersbach
Ostritz
Zawidów
Leśna
Lubomierz
Höckendorf
Dippoldiswalde
Glashütte
Sebnitz
Šluknov
Neugersdorf
Mikulášovice
Rumburk
Seifhennersdorf
Turoszów
Bogatynia
Frýdlant
Mirsk
Königstein
Bad Schandau
Sächsische Schweiz
Krasna Lipa
Varnsdorf
Grossschönau
Zittau
Sieniawka
Nové Město pod Smrkem
Świeradów Zdrój
Pretzschendorf
Schmiedeberg
Bad Gottleuba
Hřensko
České Švýcarsko
Chřibská
Lužické Hory
Hrádek nad Nisou
Hejnice
Jizerske hory
Szklarska Poreba
Frauenstein
Petrovice
Děčín
Česká Kamenice
Chrastava
Altenberg
Geising
Jílové
Cvikov
Nový Bor
Jablonné Podještědi
Liberec
Jablonec nad Nisou
Desná
Tanvald
Kotel 1435
Krupka
Teplice
Ústí nad Labem
Neuhausen
Dubi
Osek
Litvinov
Duchcov
Bílina
Most
Česká Lípa
Žandov
Verneřice
Zakupy
Stráž Pod Ralskem
Osečná
Hodkovice
Železny Brod
Jablonec n. Jizerou
Mimoň
Český Dub
Kravaře
Úštěk
Semily
Jilemnice
Litoměřice
Lovosice
Třebenice
Terezín
Tuhaň
Dubá
Doksy
Kuřivody
Turnov
Rovensko pod Troskami
Lomnice nad Popelkou
Mnichovo Hradiště
Bakov n. Jizerou
Sobotka
Jičín
Železnice
Nová Paka
Štětí
Bělá pod Bezdězem
Libceves
Libochovice
Kostice
Roudnice nad Labem
Budyně nad Ohří
Liběchov
Mšeno
Mladá Boleslav
Dolni Bousov
Lázně Bělohrad
Louny
Postoloprty
Žatec
Chomutov
Citov
Mělník
Mělnické Vtelno
Luštěnice
Libáň
Jičiněves
Hořice
Kopidlno
Rožďalovice
Byšice
Benátky nad Jizerou
Zlonice
Panenský-Týnec
Ročov
Velvary
Slaný
Kralupy nad Vltavou
Neratovice
Brandýs nad Labem
Lysá nad Labem
Křinec
Smidary
Nový Bydžov
Činěves
Městec Králové
Nechanice
Hradec
Mšec
Hořesedly
Krupá
Revničov
Smečno
Švermov
Nymburk
Kladno
Nové Strašecí
Roztoky
PRAHA
PRAGUE
Stochov
Čelákovice
Poděbrady
Chlumec nad Cidlinou
Rakovník
Unhošť
Sadská
Lázně Bohdaneč
Křivoklát
Chynava
Rudna
Uvaly
Úhřiněves
Český Brod
Plaňany
Kolín
Týec nad Labem
Přelouč
Čistá
Beroun
Křivokláteko
Radotín
HRAD KARLŠTEJN
Říčany
Kostelec nad Černými Lesy
Kouřim
Heřman
Labe
Ohře
Bóbr
Kwisa
Ploučnice
Jizera
Berounka
A
B
1
2
3
50°
15°

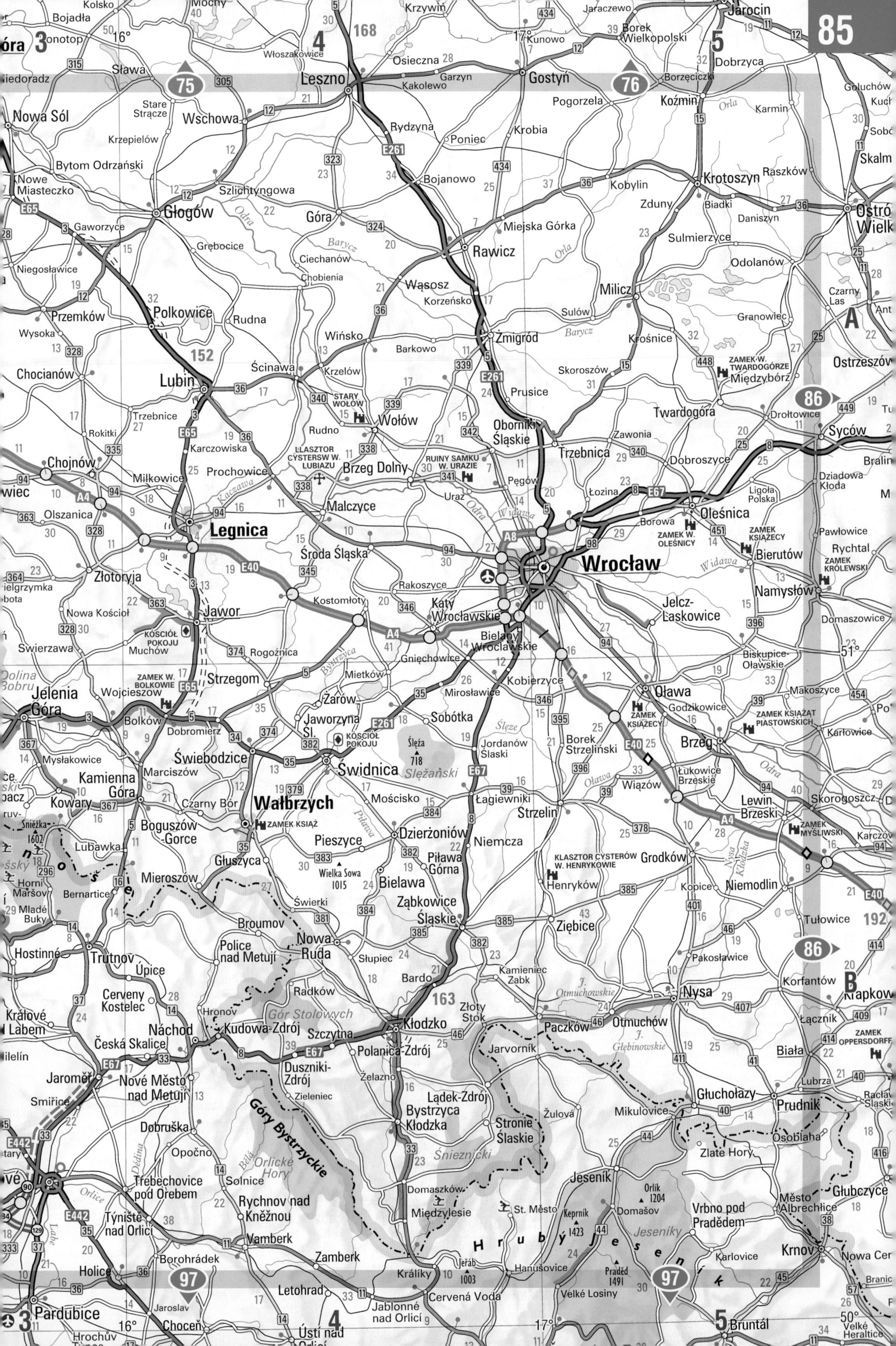
Kolsko
Bojadła
Jaraczewo
Jarocin
Borek Wielkopolski
Kunowo
Krzywiń
Osieczna
Włoszakowice
Leszno
Kakolewo
Garzyn
Gostyń
Borzęciczki
Dobrzyca
Sława
Niedoradz
Nowa Sól
Stare Strącze
Wschowa
Pogorzela
Koźmin
Karmin
Gołuchów
Krzepielów
Rydzyna
Poniec
Krobia
Bytom Odrzański
Nowe Miasteczko
Bojanowo
Szlichtyngowa
Kobylin
Krotoszyn
Raszków
Zduny
Biadki
Głogów
Gaworzyce
Góra
Miejska Górka
Daniszyn
Sulmierzyce
Grębocice
Rawicz
Niegosławice
Ciechanów
Chobienia
Odolanów
Wąsosz
Korzeńsko
Milicz
Przemków
Polkowice
Rudna
Sulów
Wysoka
Żmigród
Krośnice
Granowiec
Wińsko
Barkowo
Chocianów
Ścinawa
Krzelów
Skoroszów
Zamek w. Twardogórze
Międzybórz
Ostrzeszów
Lubin
Stary Wołów
Wołów
Prusice
Trzebnice
Rokitki
Rudno
Oborniki Śląskie
Twardogóra
Drołtowice
Syców
Chojnów
Karczowiska
Zawonia
Trzebnica
Dobroszyce
Bralin
Klasztor Cystersw w. Lubiazu
Ruiny Samku w. Urazie
Prochowice
Brzeg Dolny
Miłkowice
Pęgów
Dziadowa Kłoda
Ligota Polska
Łozina
Uraz
Olszanica
Malczyce
Oleśnica
Borowa
Zamek w. Oleśnicy
Zamek Książęcy
Pawłowice
Legnica
Bierutów
Rychtal
Środa Śląska
Wrocław
Zamek Królewski
Złotoryja
Pielgrzymka
Rakoszyce
Namysłów
Kostomłoty
Kąty Wrocławskie
Jelcz-Laskowice
Nowa Kościoł
Jawor
Bielany Wrocławskie
Domaszowice
Kościół Pokoju
Muchów
Rogoźnica
Swierzawa
Gniechowice
Biskupice-Oławskie
Zamek w. Bolkowie
Strzegom
Mietków
Kobierzyce
Jelenia Góra
Wojcieszów
Żarów
Mirosławice
Oława
Makoszyce
Dolina Bobru
Jaworzyna Śl.
Sobótka
Godzikowice
Bolków
Dobromierz
Zamek Książąt Piastowskich
Karłowice
Mysłakowice
Świebodzice
Ślęża 718
Jordanów Śląski
Borek Strzeliński
Brzeg
Kamienna Góra
Marciszów
Świdnica
Ślężański
Łukowice Brzeskie
Kowary
Czarny Bór
Wałbrzych
Mościsko
Łagiewniki
Wiązów
Lewin Brzeski
Skorogoszcz
Śnieżka 1602
Boguszów-Gorce
Zamek Książ
Strzelin
Lubawka
Dzierżoniów
Niemcza
Zamek Myśliwski
Karczów
Pieszyce
Piława Górna
Klasztor Cysterów w. Henrykowie
Grodków
Horní Maršov
Mieroszów
Głuszyca
Wielka Sowa 1015
Bielawa
Henryków
Kopice
Niemodlin
Bernartice
Mladé Buky
Świerki
Ząbkowice Śląskie
Ziębice
Tułowice
Broumov
Nowa Ruda
Hostinné
Trutnov
Police nad Metují
Słupiec
Pakosławice
Úpice
Kamieniec Ząbk.
J. Otmuchowskie
Korfantów
Krapkowice
Bardo
Radków
Nysa
Cerveny Kostelec
Hronov
Gór Stołowych
Złoty Stok
Łącznik
Králové nad Labem
Náchod
Kudowa-Zdrój
Szczytna
Kłodzko
Paczków
Otmuchów
Zamek Oppersdorff
Česká Skalice
Polanica-Zdrój
Javorník
J. Głębinowskie
Biała
Jaroměř
Nové Město nad Metují
Duszniki-Zdrój
Żelazno
Lubrza
Smiřice
Zieleniec
Lądek-Zdrój
Głuchołazy
Prudnik
Bystrzyca Kłodzka
Mikulovice
Racław. Śląskie
Dobruška
Góry Bystrzyckie
Žulová
Stronie Śląskie
Osoblaha
Opočno
Śnieżnicki
Zlaté Hory
Třebechovice pod Orebem
Orlické Hory
Solnice
Jeseník
Orlík 1204
Głubczyce
Rychnov nad Kněžnou
Domaszków
Międzylesie
St. Město
Kepník 1423
Domašov
Vrbno pod Pradědem
Město Albrechtice
Týniště nad Orlicí
Hrubý Jeseník
Jeseníky
Vamberk
Borohrádek
Zamberk
Karlovice
Krnov
Nowa Cerekwia
Holice
Králíky
Jeřáb 1003
Hanušovice
Praděd 1491
Branice
Letohrad
Červená Voda
Velké Losiny
Pardubice
Jaroslav
Choceň
Jablonné nad Orlicí
Ústí nad Orlicí
Bruntál
Hrochův Týnec
Velké Heraltice
Odra
Barycz
Orla
Widawa
Oława
Bystrzyca
Piława
Ślęza
Kaczawa
Nysa Kłodzka
Orlice
Labe
Dědina
E65
E40
A4
A8
E67
E261
E442
75
76
86
97
152
163
168
192
16°
17°
50°
51°
3
4
5
A
B

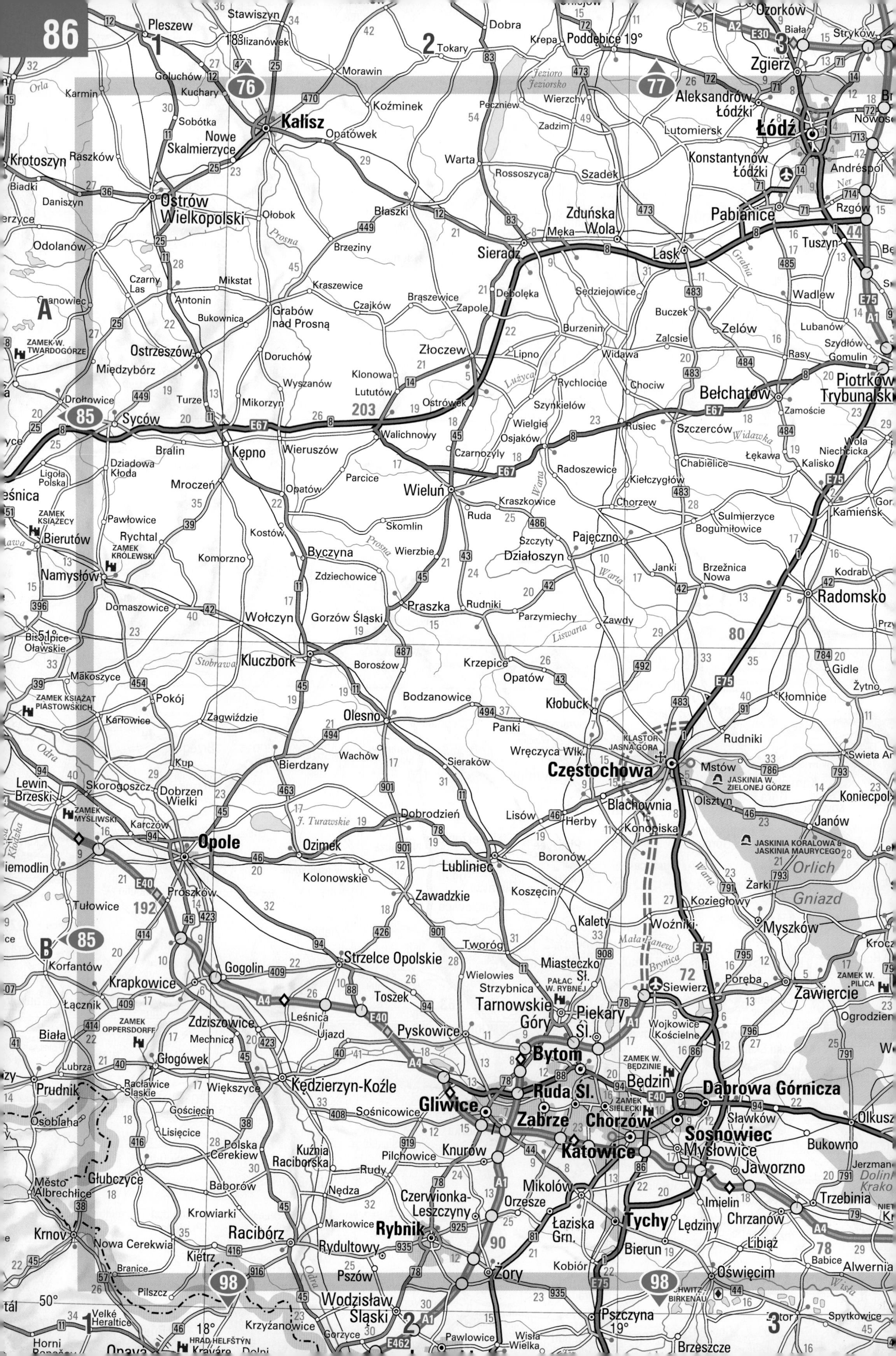
Pleszew
Stawiszyn
Blizanówek
Dobra
Tokary
Krępa
Poddębice 19°
Ozorków
Biała
Stryków
Zgierz
Gołuchów
Morawin
Kuchary
76
Jezioro Jeziorsko
77
Aleksandrów Łódzki
Łódź
Orla
Karmin
Koźminek
Pęczniew
Wierzchy
Zadzim
Lutomiersk
Nowosolna
Sobótka
Nowe Skalmierzyce
Kalisz
Opatówek
Krotoszyn
Raszków
Warta
Rossoszyca
Szadek
Konstantynów Łódzki
Andrespol
Biadki
Daniszyn
Ostrów Wielkopolski
Ołobok
Błaszki
Zduńska Wola
Pabianice
Rzgów
Odolanów
Prosna
Brzeziny
Sieradz
Męka
Łask
Tuszyn
Grabia
Czarny Las
Mikstat
Kraszewice
Dębołęka
Sędziejowice
Wadlew
Granowiec
Antonin
Czajków
Brąszewice
Zapole
Buczek
A
Bukownica
Grabów nad Prosną
Burzenin
Zelów
Lubanów
Zamek w. Twardogórze
Ostrzeszów
Złoczew
Lipno
Widawa
Zalcsie
Rasy
Szydłów
Gomulin
Międzybórz
Doruchów
Rychlocice
Chociw
Piotrków Trybunalski
Klonowa
Lututów
Wyszanów
Drołtowice
Turze
Mikorzyn
Ostrówek
Bełchatów
Zamoście
85
Syców
203
Szynkielów
Wielgie
Osjaków
Rusiec
Szczerców
Widawka
Wola Niechcicka
Walichnowy
Bralin
Kępno
Wieruszów
Czarnożyły
Łękawa
Kalisko
Dziadowa Kłoda
Ligota Polska
Chabielice
Parcice
Radoszewice
Kiełczygłów
Oleśnica
Mroczeń
Opatów
Wieluń
Kraszkowice
Ruda
Chorzew
Sulmierzyce
Bogumiłowice
Kamieńsk
Zamek Książecy
Pawłowice
Rychtal
Kostów
Skomlin
Szczyty
Działoszyn
Pajęczno
Bierutów
Zamek Królewski
Komorzno
Byczyna
Wierzbie
Warta
Janki
Brzeźnica Nowa
Kodrab
Namysłów
Zdziechowice
Radomsko
Domaszowice
Wołczyn
Gorzów Śląski
Praszka
Rudniki
Parzymiechy
Zawdy
Bierutów-Oławskie
Stobrawa
Kluczbork
Boroszów
Liswarta
Krzepice
80
Gidle
Żytno
Mąkoszyce
Zamek Książąt Piastowskich
Pokój
Karłowice
Zagwiździe
Olesno
Bodzanowice
Opatów
Kłobuck
Kłomnice
Panki
Odra
Kup
Wachów
Bierdzany
Sieraków
Wręczyca Wlk.
Klasztor Jasna Góra
Częstochowa
Rudniki
Mstów
Jaskinia w. Zielonej Górze
Święta Anna
Lewin Brzeski
Skorogoszcz
Dobrzeń Wielki
Zamek Myśliwski
Karczów
J. Turawskie
Dobrodzień
Lisów
Herby
Blachownia
Konopiska
Olsztyn
Janów
Koniecpol
Opole
Ozimek
Lubliniec
Boronów
Jaskinia Koralowa & Jaskinia Maurycego
Orlich
Gniazd
Niemodlin
Kolonowskie
Koszęcin
Żarki
Prószków
Tułowice
Zawadzkie
Koziegłowy
192
Kalety
Woźniki
Myszków
B
85
Korfantów
Tworóg
Mała Panew
Brynica
Gogolin
Strzelce Opolskie
Wielowies
Miasteczko Śl.
72
Poręba
Zawiercie
Zamek w. Pilica
Krapkowice
Strzybnica
Pałac w. Rybnej
Siewierz
Łącznik
Toszek
Tarnowskie Góry
Piekary Śl.
Ogrodzieniec
Zamek Oppersdorff
Zdzieszowice
Leśnica
Ujazd
Wojkowice Kościelne
Biała
Mechnica
Pyskowice
Bytom
Głogówek
Zamek w. Będzinie
Będzin
Lubrza
Prudnik
Racławice Śląskie
Większyce
Kędzierzyn-Koźle
Dąbrowa Górnicza
Ruda Śl.
Zamek Sielecki
Gliwice
Zabrze
Chorzów
Sosnowiec
Sławków
Olkusz
Osoblaha
Gościęcin
Sośnicowice
Lisięcice
Polska Cerekiew
Kuźnia Raciborska
Pilchowice
Knurów
Katowice
Mysłowice
Bukowno
Jaworzno
Město Albrechtice
Głubczyce
Rudy
Mikołów
Jerzmanowice
Dolina Krakowska
Baborów
Nędza
Czerwionka-Leszczyny
Orzesze
Imielin
Trzebinia
Krowiarki
Markowice
Rybnik
Łaziska Grn.
Tychy
Lędziny
Chrzanów
Krnov
Nowa Cerekwia
Racibórz
Rydułtowy
90
Bieruń
Libiąż
Kietrz
Branice
Odra
Pszów
Żory
Kobiór
Babice
Alwernia
Oświęcim
Pilszcz
98
Wodzisław Śląski
98
Auschwitz-Birkenau
Wisła
50°
Velké Heraltice
18°
Krzyżanowice
Gorzyce
Pawłowice
Wisła Wielka
Pszczyna 19°
Brzeszcze
Spytkowice
Horní Benešov
Hrad Hradec nad Moravicí
Opava
Kravaře
Dolní

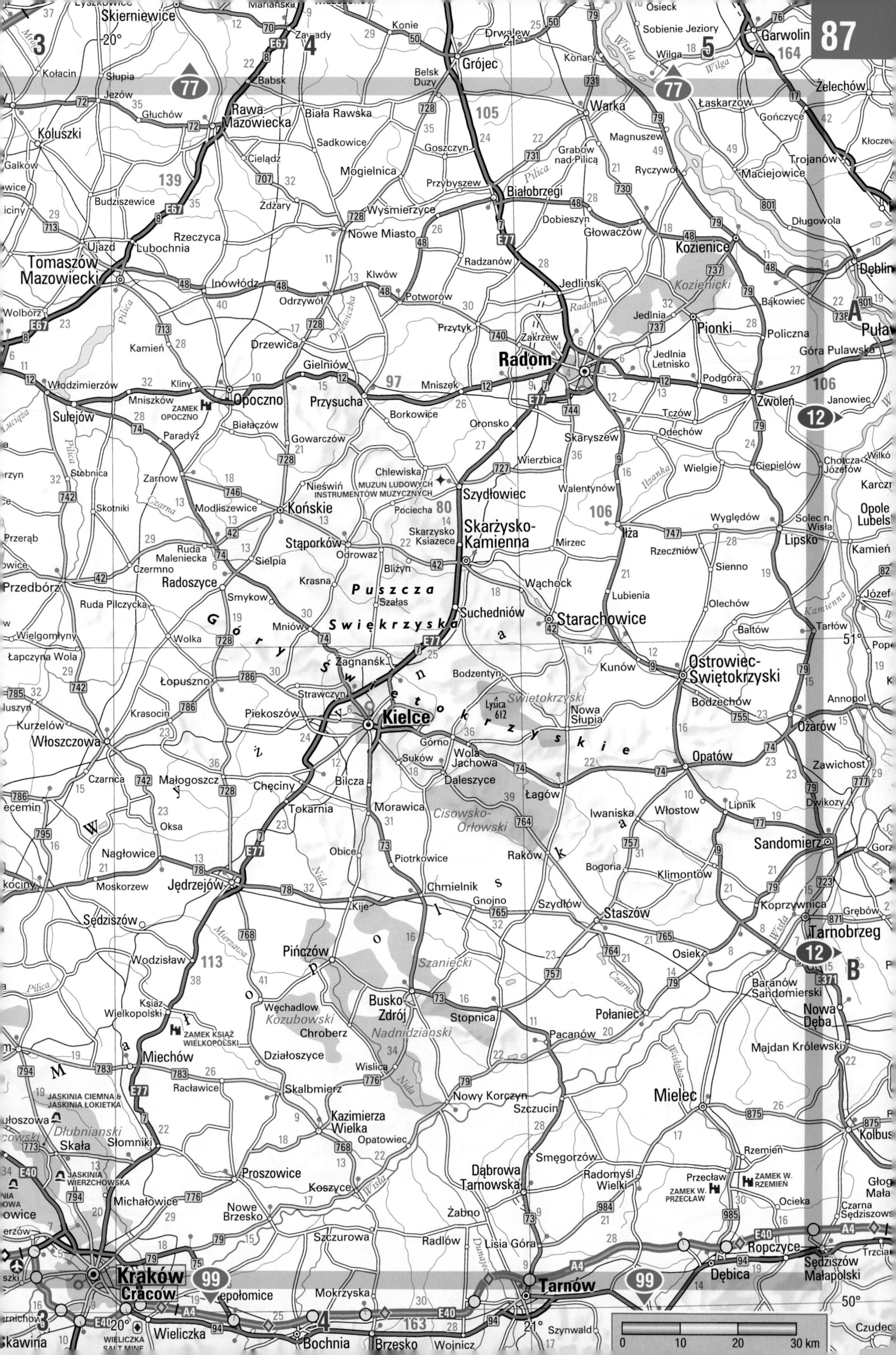
Skierniewice
Konie
Drwalew
Osieck
Sobienie Jeziory
Garwolin
Grójec
Konary
Wilga
Kołacin
Słupia
Babsk
Belsk Duży
Żelechów
Jeżów
Głuchów
Rawa Mazowiecka
Biała Rawska
Warka
Łaskarzów
Gończyce
Koluszki
Sadkowice
Goszczyn
Magnuszew
Kłoczew
Cielądz
Grabów nad Pilicą
Trojanów
Galków
Mogielnica
Ryczywół
Maciejowice
Przybyszew
Białobrzegi
Budziszewice
Żdżary
Wyśmierzyce
Dobieszyn
Nowe Miasto
Głowaczów
Długowola
Rzeczyca
Ujazd
Lubochnia
Kozienice
Tomaszów Mazowiecki
Radzanów
Inowłódz
Klwów
Jedlińsk
Dęblin
Odrzywół
Potworów
Kozienicki
Bąkowiec
Wolbórz
Jedlnia
Pionki
Przytyk
Policzna
Puławy
Zakrzew
Drzewica
Kamień
Radom
Jedlnia Letnisko
Góra Puławska
Gielniów
Podgóra
Włodzimierzów
Kliny
Mniszek
Zwoleń
Janowiec
Mniszków
Opoczno
Przysucha
Zamek Opoczno
Sulejów
Borkowice
Tczów
Oronsko
Odechów
Paradyż
Białaczów
Gowarczów
Skaryszew
Wierzbica
Wielgie
Ciepielów
Chotcza
Józefów
Stobnica
Chlewiska
Muzeum Ludowych Instrumentów Muzycznych
Nieświń
Walentynów
Żarnów
Szydłowiec
Modliszewice
Końskie
Pociecha
Skotniki
Opole Lubelskie
Skarżysko-Kamienna
Skarżysko Ksiazece
Wygledów
Iłża
Solec n. Wisłą
Lipsko
Przeraąb
Stąporków
Odrowąż
Mirzec
Rzeczniów
Ruda Maleniecka
Sielpia
Czermno
Bliżyn
Sienno
Przedbórz
Radoszyce
Krasna
Wąchock
Smykow
Puszcza Świętokrzyska
Szałas
Lubienia
Ruda Pilczycka
Olechów
Starachowice
Suchedniów
Wielgomłyny
Mniów
Tarłów
Wolka
Bałtów
Łapczyna Wola
Zagnańsk
Kunów
Bodzentyn
Ostrowiec-Świętokrzyski
Łopuszno
Strawczyn
Łysica 612
Świętokrzyski
Nowa Słupia
Bodzechów
Annopol
Krasocin
Piekoszów
Kielce
Kurzelów
Włoszczowa
Górno
Ożarów
Góry Świętokrzyskie
Wola Jachowa
Zawichost
Suków
Opatów
Czarnca
Małogoszcz
Chęciny
Bilcza
Daleszyce
Łagów
Dwikozy
Iwaniska
Tokarnia
Morawica
Włostów
Lipnik
Cisowsko-Orłowski
Oksa
Sandomierz
Nagłowice
Obice
Piotrkowice
Raków
Bogoria
Klimontów
Moskorzew
Jędrzejów
Chmielnik
Gnojno
Szydłów
Staszów
Koprzywnica
Sędziszów
Kije
Grębów
Tarnobrzeg
Pińczów
Osiek
Wodzisław
Szaniecki
Baranów Sandomierski
Książ Wielkopolski
Wchadlow
Kozubowski
Busko-Zdrój
Stopnica
Połaniec
Nowa Dęba
Zamek Książ Wielkopolski
Chroberz
Nadnidziański
Pacanów
Majdan Królewski
Miechów
Działoszyce
Wiślica
Racławice
Skalbmierz
Nowy Korczyn
Szczucin
Mielec
Jaskinia Ciemna & Jaskinia Łokietka
Kazimierza Wielka
Ojców
Dłubniański
Skała
Słomniki
Opatowiec
Smęgorzów
Rzemień
Kolbuszowa
Jaskinia Wierzchowska
Proszowice
Dąbrowa Tarnowska
Radomyśl Wielki
Przecław
Zamek W. Przecław
Zamek W. Rzemień
Michałowice
Koszyce
Nowe Brzesko
Żabno
Ocieka
Czarna Sędziszowska
Szczurowa
Radłów
Lisia Góra
Ropczyce
Sędziszów Małopolski
Kraków
Cracow
Tarnów
Dębica
Trzciana
Niepołomice
Mokrzyska
Wieliczka
Wieliczka Salt Mine
Bochnia
Brzesko
Wojnicz
Szynwałd
Czudec
Skawina
Pilica
Wisła
Nida
Czarna
Kamienna
Radomka
Iłżanka
Drzewiczka
Mierzawa
Wisłoka
Dunajec
20°
21°
51°
50°
0
10
20
30 km

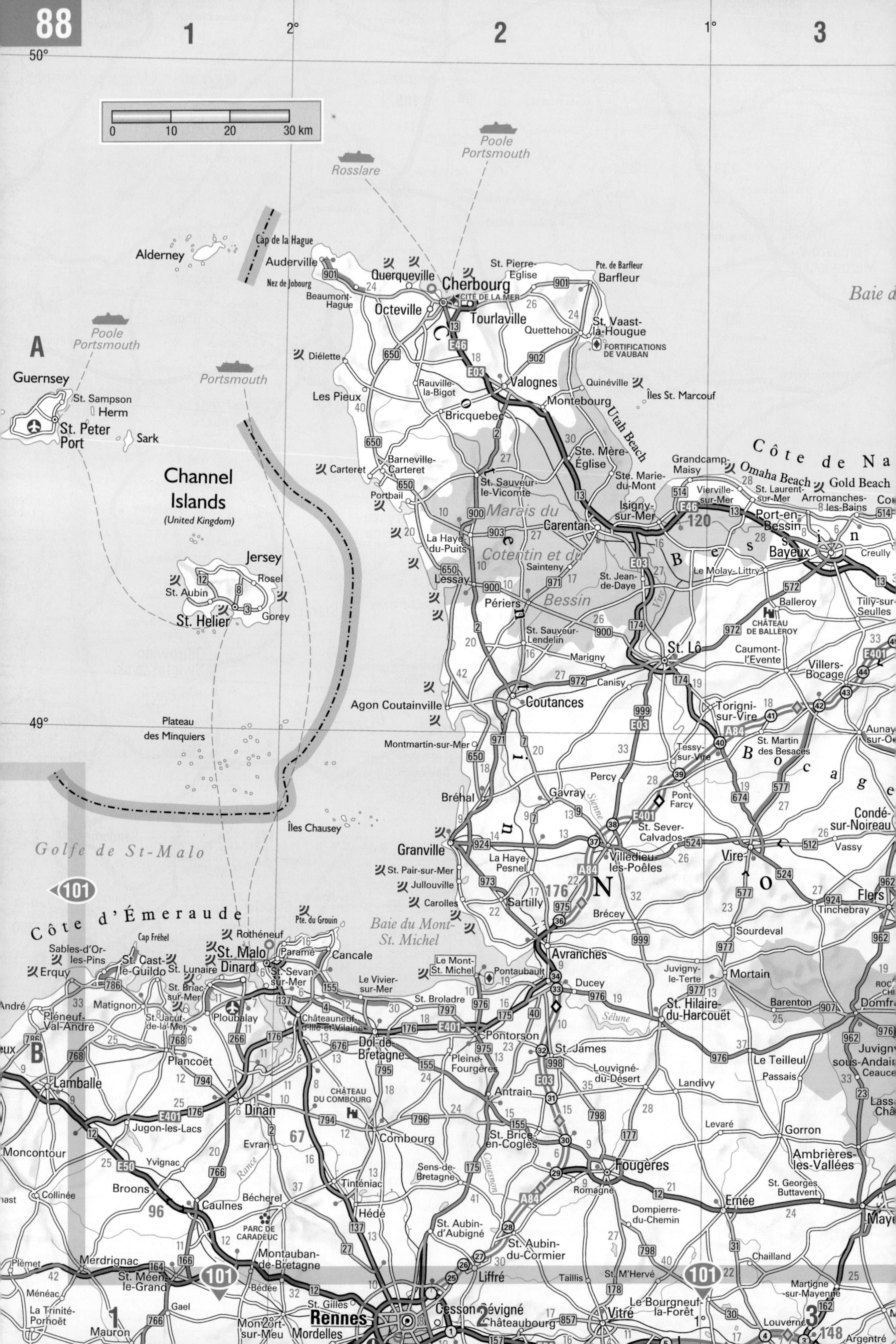
1
2
3
2°
1°
50°
49°
A
B
0 10 20 30 km
Poole
Portsmouth
Rosslare
Portsmouth
Alderney
Cap de la Hague
Auderville
Nez de Jobourg
Beaumont-Hague
Querqueville
Cherbourg
Cité de la Mer
Octeville
Tourlaville
St. Pierre-Eglise
Pte. de Barfleur
Barfleur
Quettehou
St. Vaast-la-Hougue
Fortifications de Vauban
Diélette
Valognes
Quinéville
Îles St. Marcouf
Rauville-la-Bigot
Les Pieux
Bricquebec
Montebourg
Utah Beach
Guernsey
St. Sampson
Herm
St. Peter Port
Sark
Channel Islands
(United Kingdom)
Carteret
Barneville-Carteret
Ste. Mère-Église
Côte de Na
Grandcamp-Maisy
Omaha Beach
Gold Beach
Vierville-sur-Mer
St. Laurent-sur-Mer
Arromanches-les-Bains
Portbail
St. Sauveur-le-Vicomte
Ste. Marie-du-Mont
Isigny-sur-Mer
Port-en-Bessin
Bayeux
Creully
Marais du Cotentin et du Bessin
Carentan
La Haye du-Puits
Jersey
Rosel
St. Aubin
St. Helier
Gorey
Sainteny
Lessay
St. Jean-de-Daye
Le Molay-Littry
Balleroy
Château de Balleroy
Tilly-sur-Seulles
Périers
St. Sauveur-Lendelin
St. Lô
Caumont-l'Evente
Villers-Bocage
Marigny
Canisy
Agon Coutainville
Coutances
Torigni-sur-Vire
Aunay-sur-O
Plateau des Minquiers
Montmartin-sur-Mer
Tessy-sur-Vire
St. Martin des Besaces
Percy
Pont Farcy
Bréhal
Gavray
Condé-sur-Noireau
St. Sever-Calvados
Îles Chausey
Granville
Villedieu-les-Poêles
Vire
Vassy
Golfe de St-Malo
La Haye-Pesnel
St. Pair-sur-Mer
Jullouville
Carolles
Sartilly
Flers
Tinchebray
Côte d'Émeraude
Pte. du Grouin
Baie du Mont-St. Michel
Brécey
Sourdeval
Cap Fréhel
Rothéneuf
Sables-d'Or-les-Pins
St. Cast-le-Guildo
Erquy
St. Malo
Paramé
Cancale
Dinard
St. Lunaire
Le Mont-St. Michel
Pontaubault
Avranches
Juvigny-le-Terte
Mortain
St. Briac-sur-Mer
St. Sevan-sur-Mer
Le Vivier-sur-Mer
Ducey
Matignon
Pléneuf-Val-André
St. Jacut-de-la-Mer
Ploubalay
Châteauneuf-d'Ille-et-Vilaine
St. Broladre
St. Hilaire-du-Harcouët
Barenton
Domfr
Sélune
Dol-de-Bretagne
Pontorson
St. James
Lamballe
Plancoët
Pleine-Fougères
Louvigné-du-Désert
Le Teilleul
Passais
Juvign sous-Andai
Ceauce
Château du Combourg
Antrain
Landivy
Dinan
Jugon-les-Lacs
Evran
Combourg
Levaré
Gorron
Moncontour
Yvignac
St. Brice-en-Coglès
Ambrières-les-Vallées
Broons
Rance
Sens-de-Bretagne
Fougères
Couesnon
Tinténiac
Romagné
Collinée
Caulnes
Bécherel
St. Georges Buttavent
Ernée
Parc de Caradeuc
Hédé
Dompierre-du-Chemin
St. Aubin-d'Aubigné
Merdrignac
Montauban-de-Bretagne
St. Aubin-du-Cormier
Chailland
Plémet
St. Méen-le-Grand
Liffré
Taillis
St. M'Hervé
Bédée
Ménéac
Martigné-sur-Mayenne
St. Gilles
Le Bourgneuf-la-Forêt
La Trinité-Porhoët
Gael
Rennes
Cesson Sévigné
Châteaubourg
Vitré
Louverné
Mauron
Montfort-sur-Meu
Mordelles
Argentré
C o t e n t i n
B e s s i n
B o c a g e
N
101
Baie d

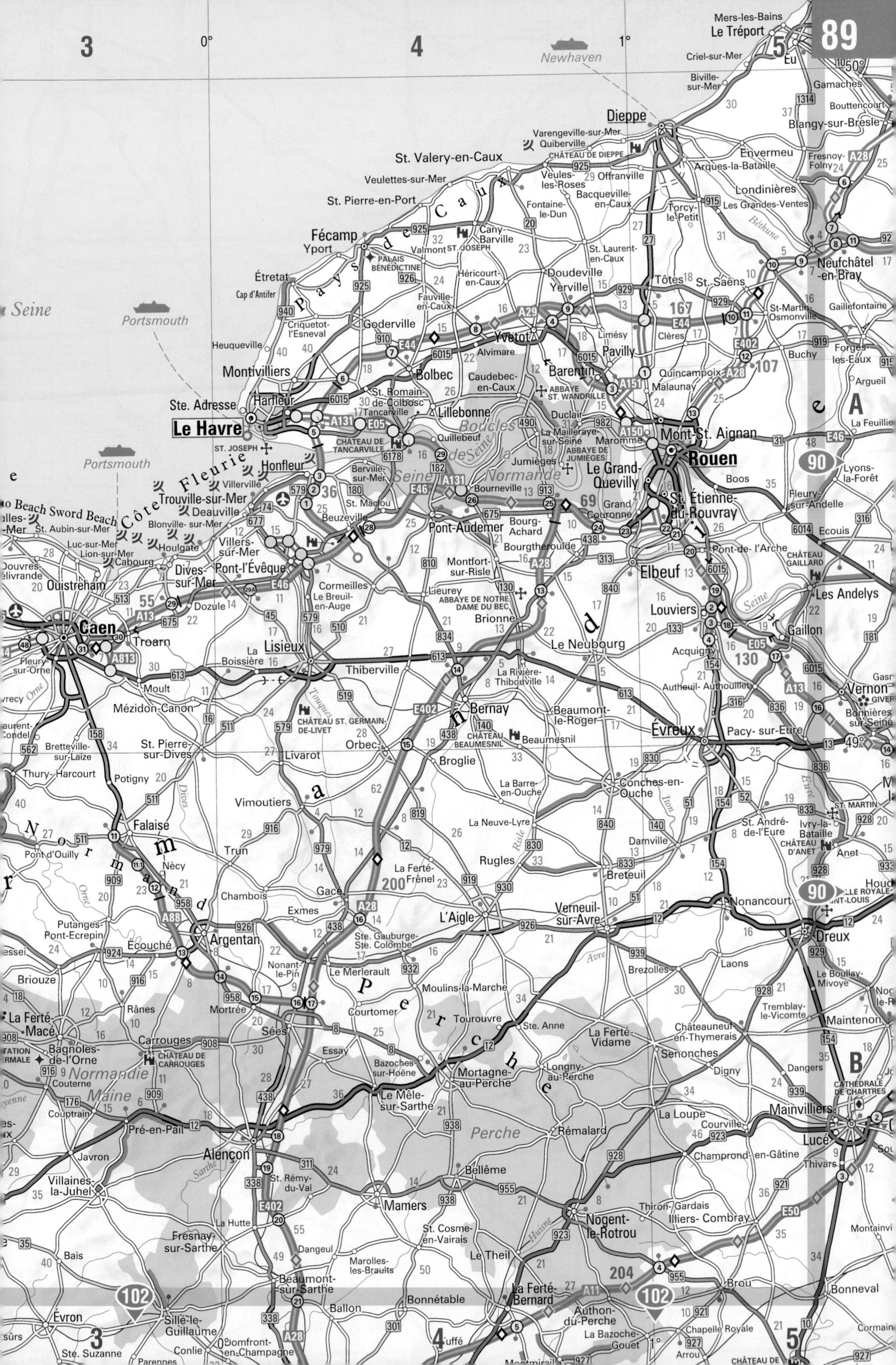
3
0°
4
1°
5
Newhaven
Portsmouth
Mers-les-Bains
Le Tréport
Eu
Criel-sur-Mer
Biville-sur-Mer
Gamaches
Bouttencourt
Blangy-sur-Bresle
Dieppe
Varengeville-sur-Mer
Quiberville
CHÂTEAU DE DIEPPE
St. Valery-en-Caux
Envermeu
Arques-la-Bataille
Fresnoy-Folny
Veulettes-sur-Mer
Veules-les-Roses
Offranville
Londinières
Bacqueville-en-Caux
St. Pierre-en-Port
Fontaine-le-Dun
Torcy-le-Petit
Les Grandes-Ventes
Béthune
Pays de Caux
Fécamp
Yport
Cany-Barville
Valmont
ST. JOSEPH
PALAIS BÉNÉDICTINE
St. Laurent-en-Caux
Neufchâtel-en-Bray
Étretat
Cap d'Antifer
Héricourt-en-Caux
Doudeville
Yerville
Tôtes
St. Saëns
Seine
Fauville-en-Caux
St-Martin-Osmonville
Gaillefontaine
Criquetot-l'Esneval
Goderville
Yvetot
Limésy
Clères
Heuqueville
Alvimare
Pavilly
Forges-les-Eaux
Buchy
Montivilliers
Bolbec
Caudebec-en-Caux
Barentin
Quincampoix
Argueil
Malaunay
Harfleur
St. Romain-de-Colbosc
ABBAYE ST. WANDRILLE
Ste. Adresse
Tancarville
Lillebonne
Le Havre
Boucles de Seine Normande
Duclair
Mont-St. Aignan
La Feuillie
ST. JOSEPH
CHÂTEAU DE TANCARVILLE
Quillebeuf
La Mailleraye-sur-Seine
Maromme
Rouen
Lyons-la-Forêt
Portsmouth
Côte Fleurie
Honfleur
Berville-sur-Mer
ABBAYE DE JUMIÈGES
Jumièges
Le Grand-Quevilly
Boos
Villerville
Trouville-sur-Mer
Bourneville
St. Étienne-du-Rouvray
Fleury-sur-Andelle
Juno Beach
Sword Beach
Deauville
St. Maclou
Grand Couronne
Courseulles-sur-Mer
St. Aubin-sur-Mer
Blonville-sur-Mer
Beuzeville
Pont-Audemer
Bourg-Achard
Ecouis
Luc-sur-Mer
Lion-sur-Mer
Houlgate
Villers-sur-Mer
Bourgtheroulde
Pont-de-l'Arche
CHÂTEAU GAILLARD
Douvres-la-Délivrande
Cabourg
Dives-sur-Mer
Pont-l'Évêque
Montfort-sur-Risle
Elbeuf
Ouistreham
Cormeilles
Le Breuil-en-Auge
Lieurey
ABBAYE DE NOTRE DAME DU BEC
Les Andelys
Dozule
Louviers
Caen
Troarn
Brionne
Gaillon
Fleury-sur-Orne
La Boissière
Lisieux
Le Neubourg
Acquigny
Thiberville
La Rivière-Thibouville
Autheuil-Authouillet
Moult
Vernon
GIVERNY
Mézidon-Canon
Tonques
Bernay
Beaumont-le-Roger
Bonnières-sur-Seine
CHÂTEAU ST. GERMAIN-DE-LIVET
CHÂTEAU BEAUMESNIL
Beaumesnil
Évreux
Pacy-sur-Eure
Bretteville-sur-Laize
St. Pierre-sur-Dives
Livarot
Orbec
Broglie
Thury-Harcourt
Potigny
La Barre-en-Ouche
Conches-en-Ouche
Vimoutiers
Iton
Eure
ST. MARTIN
Ivry-la-Bataille
St. André-de-l'Eure
Falaise
La Neuve-Lyre
Damville
CHÂTEAU D'ANET
Anet
Normandie
Pont d'Ouilly
Trun
Nècy
Rugles
Breteuil
La Ferté-Frênel
Orne
Chambois
Gacé
Risle
Nonancourt
Putanges-Pont-Ecrepin
Exmes
L'Aigle
Verneuil-sur-Avre
Dreux
Argentan
Écouché
Ste. Gauburge-Ste. Colombe
Pays d'Auge
Briouze
Nonant-le-Pin
Le Merlerault
Avre
Brezolles
Laons
Le Boullay-Mivoye
Perche
Moulins-la-Marche
Tremblay-le-Vicomte
Rânes
Mortrée
Courtomer
Tourouvre
Ste. Anne
La Ferté-Vidame
Châteauneuf-en-Thymerais
Maintenon
La Ferté-Macé
Sées
Carrouges
Essay
Senonches
Bagnoles-de-l'Orne
CHÂTEAU DE CARROUGES
Bazoches-sur-Hoëne
Mortagne-au-Perche
Longny-au-Perche
Digny
Dangers
CATHÉDRALE DE CHARTRES
Couterne
Normandie Maine
Le Mêle-sur-Sarthe
La Loupe
Mainvilliers
Courville
Couptrain
Pré-en-Pail
Rémalard
Lucé
Alençon
Champrond-en-Gâtine
Javron
Sarthe
St. Rémy-du-Val
Bellême
Thivars
Villaines-la-Juhel
Mamers
Nogent-le-Rotrou
Thiron-Gardais
Illiers-Combray
La Hutte
St. Cosme-en-Vairais
Huisne
Montainville
Fresnay-sur-Sarthe
Dangeul
Le Theil
Bais
Marolles-les-Braults
Brou
Beaumont-sur-Sarthe
Bonnétable
La Ferté-Bernard
Bonneval
Évron
Sillé-le-Guillaume
Ballon
Authon-du-Perche
Chapelle Royale
Fomfront-en-Champagne
Tuffé
La Bazoche-Gouet
Ste. Suzanne
Conlie
Parennes
Arrou
CHÂTEAU DE ...
A28
A29
A131
A151
A150
A13
A813
A11
E44
E402
E05
E46
E50
90
102

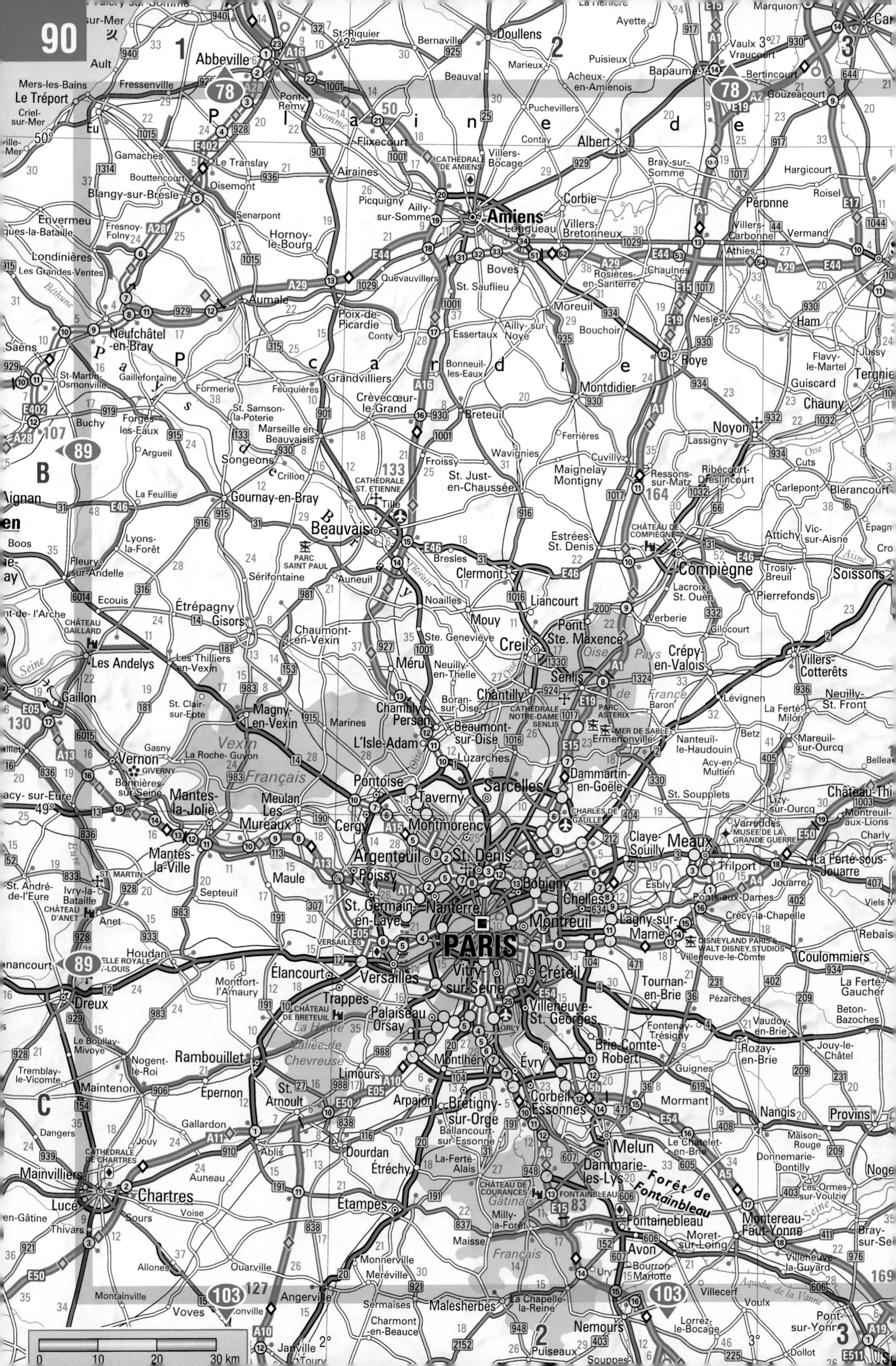

Abbeville
Doullens
Bapaume
Mers-les-Bains
Le Tréport
Criel-sur-Mer
Eu
Fressenville
Ault
St. Riquier
Bernaville
Ayette
Puisieux
Acheux-en-Amiénois
Marieux
Beauval
Pont-Remy
Flixecourt
Gamaches
Le Translay
Oisemont
Bouttencourt
Blangy-sur-Bresle
Airaines
Picquigny
Ailly-sur-Somme
CATHÉDRALE DE AMIENS
Amiens
Villers-Bocage
Contay
Puchevillers
Albert
Bray-sur-Somme
Corbie
Longueau
Villers-Bretonneux
Péronne
Hargicourt
Roisel
Villers-Carbonnel
Vermand
Athies
Gouzeaucourt
Bertincourt
Vaulx Vraucourt
Marquion
Envermeu
Fresnoy-Folny
Senarpont
Hornoy-le-Bourg
Londinières
Les Grandes-Ventes
Quevauvilliers
Boves
St. Saufflieu
Rosières-en-Santerre
Chaulnes
Aumale
Neufchâtel-en-Bray
St-Martin-Osmonville
Gaillefontaine
Poix-de-Picardie
Conty
Essertaux
Ailly-sur-Noye
Moreuil
Bouchoir
Nesle
Ham
Roye
Montdidier
Bonneuil-les-Eaux
Formerie
Feuquières
Grandvilliers
Crèvecœur-le-Grand
Breteuil
Forges-les-Eaux
Buchy
St. Samson-la-Poterie
Marseille en Beauvaisis
Songeons
Crillon
Argueil
Froissy
CATHÉDRALE ST. ETIENNE
Tillé
St. Just-en-Chaussée
Wavignies
Ferrières
Maignelay Montigny
Cuvilly
Ressons-sur-Matz
Lassigny
Noyon
Ribécourt-Dreslincourt
Chauny
Guiscard
Flavy-le-Martel
Tergnier
Jussy
Cuts
Carlepont
Blérancourt
La Feuillie
Gournay-en-Bray
Beauvais
PARC SAINT PAUL
Lyons-la-Forêt
Fleury-sur-Andelle
Sérifontaine
Auneuil
Bresles
Clermont
Estrées-St. Denis
CHÂTEAU DE COMPIÈGNE
Compiègne
Attichy
Vic-sur-Aisne
Trosly-Breuil
Soissons
Pierrefonds
Lacroix-St. Ouen
Ecouis
Étrépagny
Gisors
CHÂTEAU GAILLARD
Les Andelys
Chaumont-en-Vexin
Noailles
Mouy
Liancourt
Pont-Ste. Maxence
Verberie
Gilocourt
Crépy-en-Valois
Villers-Cotterêts
Les Thilliers-en-Vexin
Méru
Ste. Geneviève
Neuilly-en-Thelle
Creil
Senlis
Gaillon
St. Clair-sur-Epte
Magny-en-Vexin
Marines
Chambly
Persan
Boran-sur-Oise
Chantilly
CATHÉDRALE NOTRE-DAME SENLIS
PARC ASTERIX
MER DE SABLE
Ermenonville
Baron
Lévignen
Nanteuil-le-Haudouin
La Ferté-Milon
Neuilly-St. Front
Betz
Mareuil-sur-Ourcq
Acy-en-Multien
Vernon
Gasny
La Roche-Guyon
GIVERNY
Bonnières-sur-Seine
L'Isle-Adam
Beaumont-sur-Oise
Luzarches
Dammartin-en-Goële
Pontoise
Taverny
Sarcelles
CHARLES DE GAULLE
St. Soupplets
Lizy-sur-Ourcq
Château-Thierry
Mantes-la-Jolie
Meulan
Les Mureaux
Cergy
Montmorency
Claye-Souilly
Meaux
Varreddes
MUSÉE DE LA GRANDE GUERRE
Montreuil-aux-Lions
Charly
Mantes-la-Ville
Maule
Argenteuil
St. Denis
Poissy
Bobigny
Chelles
Esbly
Trilport
La Ferté-sous-Jouarre
Jouarre
St. André-de-l'Eure
Ivry-la-Bataille
CHÂTEAU D'ANET
Anet
Septeuil
St. Germain-en-Laye
Nanterre
Montreuil
Lagny-sur-Marne
Ponts-aux-Dames
Crécy-la-Chapelle
Houdan
PARIS
VERSAILLES
DISNEYLAND PARIS & WALT DISNEY STUDIOS
Villeneuve-le-Comte
Coulommiers
Rebais
Dreux
Montfort-l'Amaury
Élancourt
Versailles
Vitry-sur-Seine
Créteil
Tournan-en-Brie
Pézarches
La Ferté-Gaucher
Trappes
CHÂTEAU DE BRETEUIL
Palaiseau
Orsay
Villeneuve-St. Georges
ORLY
Beton-Bazoches
Le Boullay-Mivoye
La Haute Vallée de Chevreuse
Fontenay-Trésigny
Vaudoy-en-Brie
Rozay-en-Brie
Jouy-le-Châtel
Tremblay-le-Vicomte
Nogent-le-Roi
Rambouillet
Limours
Montlhéry
Évry
Brie-Comte-Robert
Guignes
Maintenon
Epernon
St. Arnoult
Arpajon
Brétigny-sur-Orge
Corbeil-Essonnes
Mormant
Nangis
Provins
Dangers
Gallardon
Jouy
Ballancourt-sur-Essonne
Melun
Le Châtelet-en-Brie
Maison-Rouge
CATHÉDRALE DE CHARTRES
Mainvilliers
Ablis
Dourdan
Étréchy
La Ferté-Alais
Dammarie-les-Lys
Donnemarie-Dontilly
Auneau
CHÂTEAU DE COURANCES
FONTAINEBLEAU
Forêt de Fontainebleau
Les Ormes-sur-Voulzie
Nogent
Lucé
Chartres
Sours
Voise
Étampes
Gâtinais
Milly-la-Forêt
Fontainebleau
Montereau-Faut-Yonne
en-Gâtine
Thivars
Maisse
Moret-sur-Loing
Avon
Bray-sur-Seine
Villeneuve-la-Guyard
Allones
Ouarville
Monnerville
Méréville
Ury
Bourron-Marlotte
Villecerf
Montainville
Voves
Angerville
Sermaises
Charmont-en-Beauce
Malesherbes
La Chapelle-la-Reine
Nemours
Voulx
Lorrez-le-Bocage
Pont-sur-Yonne
Janville
Puiseaux
Souppes
Dollot
Plaine de Picardie
Pays de Bray
Vexin Français
Pays de France
Seine
Somme
Oise
Aisne
Eure
Marne
0 10 20 30 km

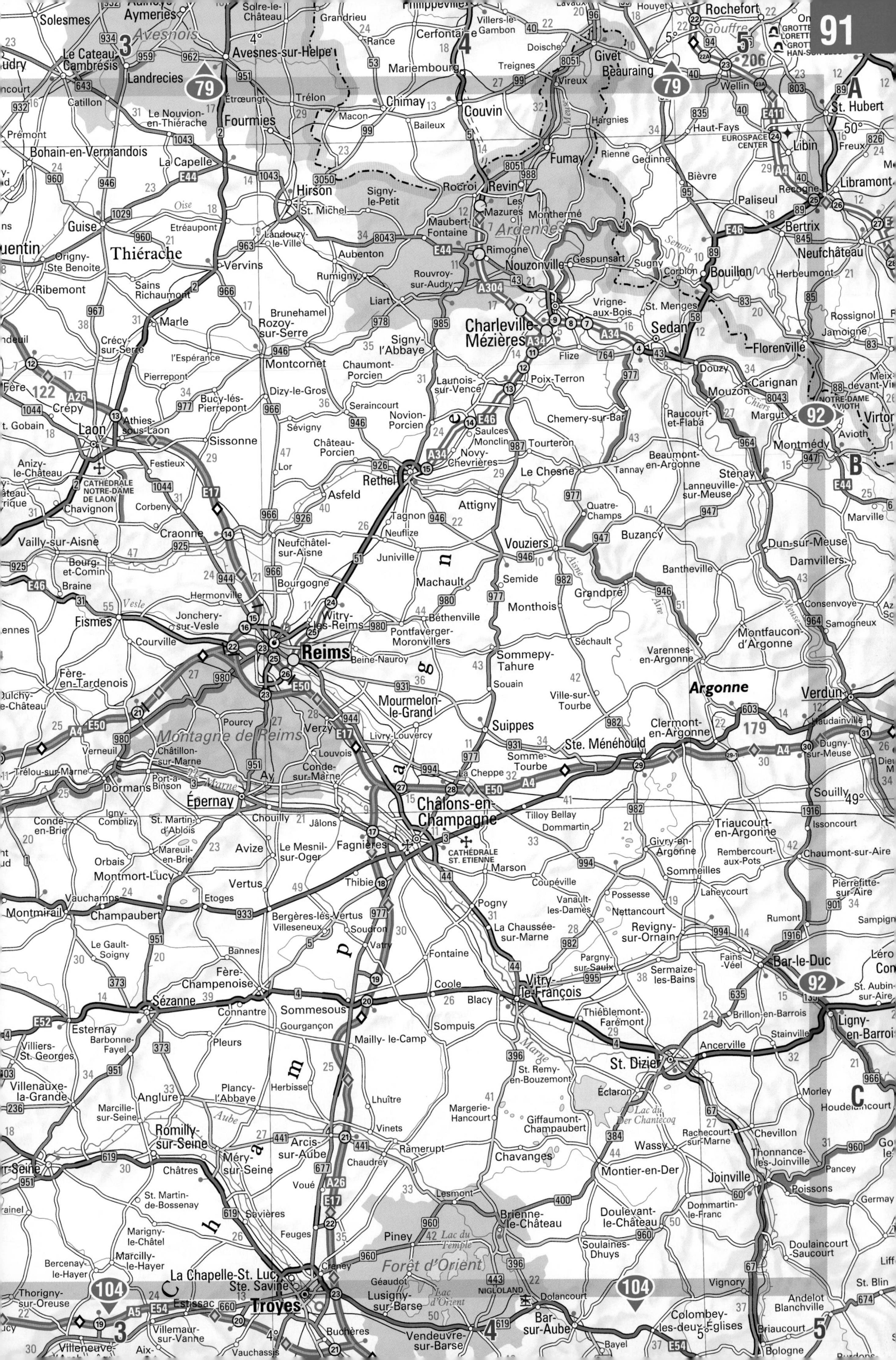

Solesmes
Aymeries
Avesnois
Le Cateau-Cambrésis
Landrecies
Avesnes-sur-Helpe
Solre-le-Château
Grandrieu
Rance
Philippeville
Cerfontaine
Villers-le-Gambon
Mariembourg
Doische
Givet
Beauraing
Houyet
Rochefort
Gouffre
Han-sur-Lesse
Wellin
St. Hubert
Libin
Eurospace Center
Freux
Libramont
Recogne
Catillon
Le Nouvion-en-Thiérache
Étrœungt
Trélon
Fourmies
Chimay
Macon
Baileux
Couvin
Treignes
Vireux
Hargnies
Haut-Fays
Prémont
Bohain-en-Vermandois
La Capelle
Hirson
St. Michel
Signy-le-Petit
Rocroi
Revin
Les Mazures
Fumay
Rienne
Gedinne
Bièvre
Paliseul
Bertrix
Neufchâteau
Herbeumont
Guise
Oise
Étréaupont
Thiérache
Origny-Ste Benoite
Landouzy-la-Ville
Aubenton
Maubert-Fontaine
Ardennes
Monthermé
Rimogne
Nouzonville
Gespunsart
Sugny
Corbion
Bouillon
Semois
Ribemont
Vervins
Sains-Richaumont
Rumigny
Rouvroy-sur-Audry
Liart
Charleville-Mézières
Vrigne-aux-Bois
St. Menges
Sedan
Rossignol
Jamoigne
Florenville
Marle
Brunehamel
Rozoy-sur-Serre
Crécy-sur-Serre
Signy-l'Abbaye
Montcornet
Chaumont-Porcien
Flize
Douzy
Carignan
Mouzon
Chiers
Margut
Notre-Dame d'Avioth
Avioth
Virton
Meix-devant-Virton
l'Espérance
Pierrepont
Dizy-le-Gros
Launois-sur-Vence
Poix-Terron
Fère
Crépy
Bucy-lès-Pierrepont
Serincourt
Novion-Porcien
Chemery-sur-Bar
Raucourt-et-Flaba
Montmédy
St. Gobain
Laon
Athies-sous-Laon
Sissonne
Sévigny
Château-Porcien
Saulces-Monclin
Novy-Chevrières
Tourteron
Beaumont-en-Argonne
Anizy-le-Château
Cathédrale Notre-Dame de Laon
Festieux
Lor
Rethel
Le Chesne
Tannay
Stenay
Lanneuville-sur-Meuse
Chavignon
Corbeny
Asfeld
Attigny
Quatre-Champs
Marville
Craonne
Tagnon
Neuflize
Vouziers
Buzancy
Dun-sur-Meuse
Damvillers
Vailly-sur-Aisne
Bourg-et-Comin
Neufchâtel-sur-Aisne
Juniville
Semide
Grandpré
Bantheville
Braine
Bourgogne
Machault
Monthois
Aire
Consenvoye
Samogneux
Hermonville
Vesle
Fismes
Jonchery-sur-Vesle
Witry-lès-Reims
Bétheniville
Pontfaverger-Moronvilliers
Séchault
Montfaucon-d'Argonne
Meuse
Courville
Reims
Beine-Nauroy
Sommepy-Tahure
Varennes-en-Argonne
Fère-en-Tardenois
Souain
Ville-sur-Tourbe
Argonne
Verdun
Oulchy-le-Château
Mourmelon-le-Grand
Clermont-en-Argonne
Haudainville
Pourcy
Verzy
Livry-Louvercy
Suippes
Dugny-sur-Meuse
Montagne de Reims
Verneuil
Châtillon-sur-Marne
Louvois
Somme-Tourbe
Ste. Ménehould
Trélou-sur-Marne
Port-à-Binson
Marne
Ay
Condé-sur-Marne
La Cheppe
Dormans
Épernay
Châlons-en-Champagne
Souilly
Condé-en-Brie
Igny-Comblizy
St. Martin-d'Ablois
Chouilly
Jâlons
Tilloy Bellay
Dommartin
Triaucourt-en-Argonne
Issoncourt
Mareuil-en-Brie
Avize
Le Mesnil-sur-Oger
Fagnières
Cathédrale St. Etienne
Givry-en-Argonne
Rembercourt-aux-Pots
Chaumont-sur-Aire
Orbais
Montmort-Lucy
Vertus
Thibie
Marson
Coupéville
Sommeilles
Pierrefitte-sur-Aire
Vauchamps
Etoges
Possesse
Laheycourt
Montmirail
Champaubert
Bergères-lès-Vertus
Villeseneux
Soudron
Pogny
Vanault-les-Dames
Nettancourt
La Chaussée-sur-Marne
Revigny-sur-Ornain
Rumont
Sampigny
Le Gault-Soigny
Vatry
Fontaine
Bannes
Pargny-sur-Saulx
Fains-Véel
Bar-le-Duc
Fère-Champenoise
Sermaize-les-Bains
St. Aubin-sur-Aire
Vitry-le-François
Coole
Sézanne
Connantre
Sommesous
Blacy
Thiéblemont-Farémont
Brillon-en-Barrois
Ligny-en-Barrois
Esternay
Gourgançon
Sompuis
Barbonne-Fayel
Pleurs
Mailly-le-Camp
Villiers-St. Georges
Ancerville
Stainville
St. Dizier
St. Remy-en-Bouzemont
Villenauxe-la-Grande
Plancy-l'Abbaye
Herbisse
Éclaron
Lac du Der Chantecoq
Morley
Houdelaincourt
Anglure
Lhuître
Margerie-Hancourt
Giffaumont-Champaubert
Marcille-sur-Seine
Aube
Rachecourt-sur-Marne
Chevillon
Romilly-sur-Seine
Vinets
Arcis-sur-Aube
Ramerupt
Chavanges
Wassy
Thonnance-les-Joinville
Méry-sur-Seine
Châtres
Chaudrey
Montier-en-Der
Joinville
Pancey
Voué
Poissons
St. Martin-de-Bossenay
Lesmont
Germay
Savières
Brienne-le-Château
Doulevant-le-Château
Dommartin-le-Franc
Marigny-le-Châtel
Feuges
Piney
Lac du Temple
Soulaines-Dhuys
Doulaincourt-Saucourt
Marcilly-le-Hayer
Bercenay-le-Hayer
Creney
Forêt d'Orient
La Chapelle-St. Luc
Ste. Savine
Géraudot
Lac d'Orient
Nigloland
Vignory
St. Blin
Thorigny-sur-Oreuse
Estissac
Troyes
Lusigny-sur-Barse
Dolancourt
Andelot Blanchville
Villemaur-sur-Vanne
Bouchères
Vendeuvre-sur-Barse
Bar-sur-Aube
Colombey-les-deux-Églises
Briaucourt
Villeneuve
Aix
Vauchassis
Bayel
Bologne
Champagne

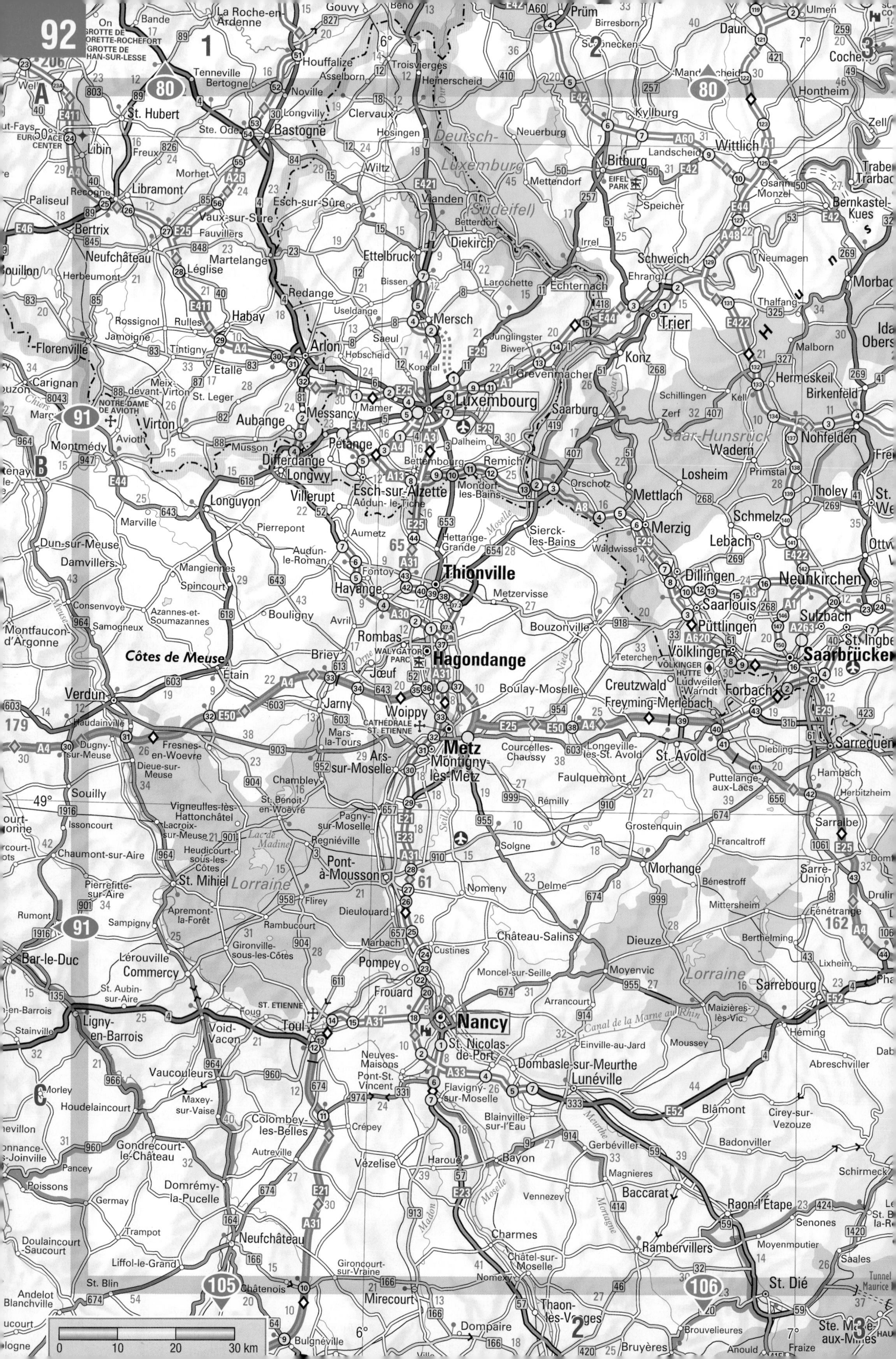

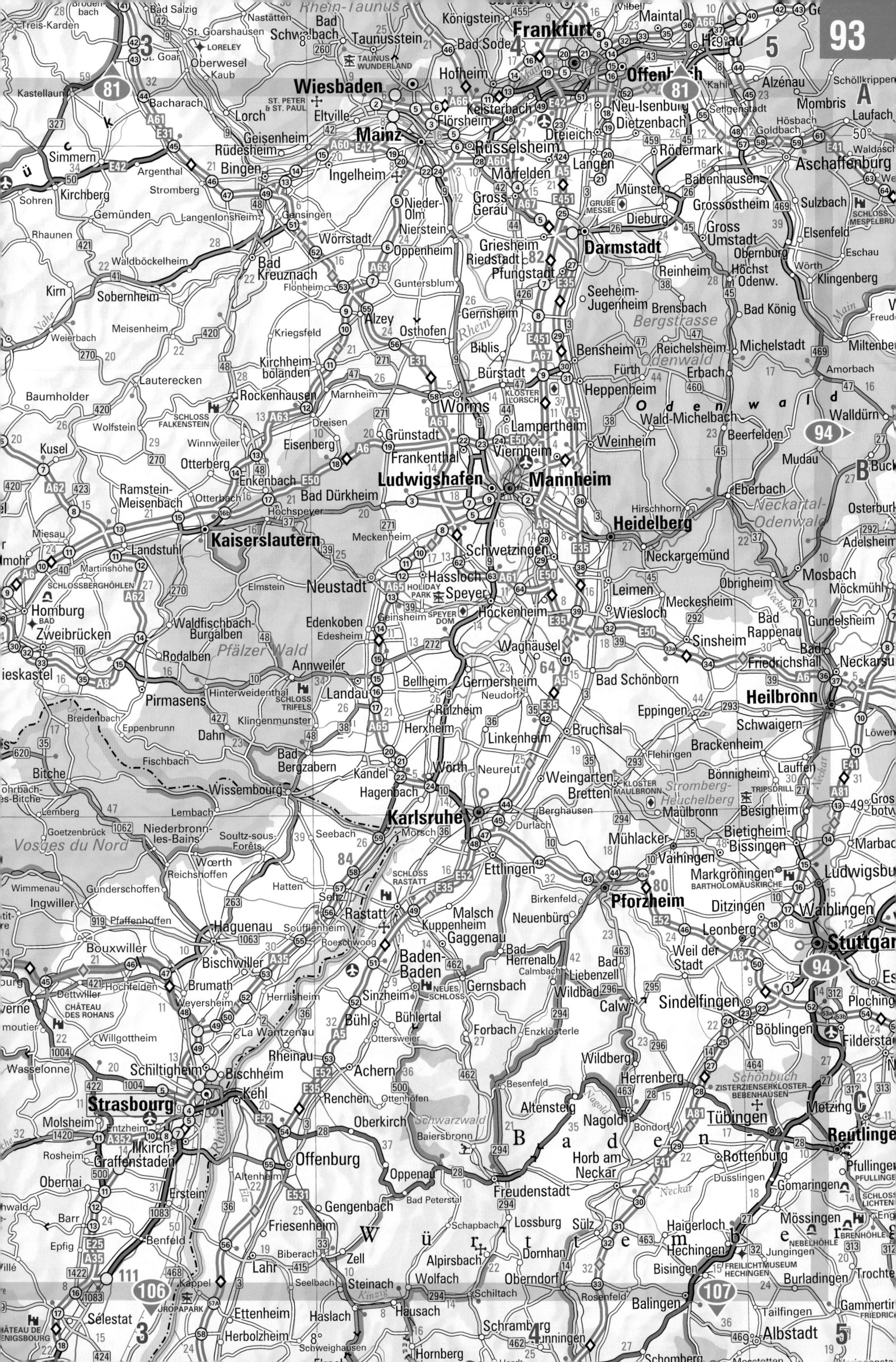
Rhein-Taunus
Treis-Karden
Bad Salzig
Nastätten
Königstein
Frankfurt
Maintal
St. Goarshausen
LORELEY
Oberwesel
Kaub
St. Goar
Bad Schwalbach
Taunusstein
Bad Soden
TAUNUS WUNDERLAND
Offenbach
Hanau
Alzenau
Schöllkrippen
Kastellaun
Wiesbaden
Hofheim
Eltville
Kelsterbach
Neu-Isenburg
Seligenstadt
Mombris
Laufach
Bacharach
Lorch
Mainz
Flörsheim
Dreieich
Dietzenbach
Hösbach
Goldbach
Simmern
Geisenheim
Rüdesheim
Rüsselsheim
Langen
Rödermark
Aschaffenburg
Argenthal
Bingen
Ingelheim
Mörfelden
Babenhausen
Kirchberg
Sohren
Stromberg
Nieder-Olm
Gross-Gerau
Münster
Grossostheim
Sulzbach
Gemünden
Langenlonsheim
Gensingen
GRUBE MESSEL
Dieburg
Rhaunen
Wörrstadt
Nierstein
Darmstadt
Gross Umstadt
Elsenfeld
Oppenheim
Griesheim
Riedstadt
Pfungstadt
Obernburg
Eschau
Waldböckelheim
Bad Kreuznach
Reinheim
Höchst i. Odenw.
Wörth
Klingenberg
Kirn
Sobernheim
Guntersblum
Seeheim-Jugenheim
Brensbach
Bad König
Alzey
Gernsheim
Bergstrasse
Meisenheim
Kriegsfeld
Osthofen
Rhein
Biblis
Bensheim
Reichelsheim
Michelstadt
Miltenberg
Weierbach
Kirchheimbolanden
Odenwald
Amorbach
Bürstadt
Fürth
Erbach
Lauterecken
Baumholder
Marnheim
KLOSTER LORSCH
Heppenheim
Rockenhausen
Worms
Walldürn
SCHLOSS FALKENSTEIN
Dreisen
Lampertheim
Wald-Michelbach
Beerfelden
Wolfstein
Grünstadt
Kusel
Winnweiler
Eisenberg
Frankenthal
Viernheim
Weinheim
Mudau
Otterberg
Enkenbach
Ludwigshafen
Mannheim
Ramstein-Meisenbach
Otterbach
Bad Dürkheim
Eberbach
Neckartal-Odenwald
Hochspeyer
Hirschhorn
Osterburken
Kaiserslautern
Meckenheim
Heidelberg
Adelsheim
Miesau
Landstuhl
Schwetzingen
Neckargemünd
Martinshöhe
Hassloch
Mosbach
SCHLOSSBERGHÖHLEN
Elmstein
Neustadt
HOLIDAY PARK
Speyer
Leimen
Obrigheim
Möckmühl
Homburg
Hockenheim
Meckesheim
BAD Zweibrücken
Waldfischbach-Burgalben
Geinsheim
SPEYER DOM
Wiesloch
Bad Rappenau
Gundelsheim
Edenkoben
Edesheim
Sinsheim
Waghäusel
Rodalben
Pfälzer Wald
Bad Friedrichshall
Neckarsulm
Annweiler
Bad Schönborn
Blieskastel
Bellheim
Germersheim
Pirmasens
Hinterweidenthal
SCHLOSS TRIFELS
Landau
Neudorf
Heilbronn
Breidenbach
Klingenmünster
Rülzheim
Eppingen
Schwaigern
Eppenbrunn
Dahn
Herxheim
Linkenheim
Bruchsal
Brackenheim
Bad Bergzabern
Fischbach
Bitche
Kandel
Wörth
Neureut
Flehingen
Bönnigheim
Lauffen
Wissembourg
Hagenbach
Weingarten
Bretten
KLOSTER MAULBRONN
Stromberg-Heuchelberg
TRIPSDRILL
Lemberg
Lembach
Karlsruhe
Berghausen
Maulbronn
Besigheim
Goetzenbrück
Niederbronn-les-Bains
Soultz-sous-Forêts
Seebach
Mörsch
Durlach
Mühlacker
Bietigheim-Bissingen
Vosges du Nord
Wœrth
Reichshoffen
Ettlingen
Vaihingen
Markgröningen
BARTHOLOMÄUSKIRCHE
Ludwigsburg
Wimmenau
Gunderschoffen
Hatten
SCHLOSS RASTATT
Birkenfeld
Pforzheim
Ditzingen
Ingwiller
Seltz
Rastatt
Malsch
Neuenbürg
Waiblingen
Pfaffenhoffen
Haguenau
Soufflenheim
Kuppenheim
Gaggenau
Leonberg
Stuttgart
Bouxwiller
Roeschwoog
Baden-Baden
Bad Herrenalb
Bad Liebenzell
Weil der Stadt
Bischwiller
Hochfelden
Brumath
Calmbach
Dettwiller
CHÂTEAU DES ROHANS
Weyersheim
Herrlisheim
NEUES SCHLOSS
Gernsbach
Wildbad
Calw
Sindelfingen
Plochingen
Sinzheim
Bühl
Bühlertal
La Wantzenau
Forbach
Enzklösterle
Böblingen
Filderstadt
Willgottheim
Ottersweier
Rheinau
Wildberg
Schönbuch
Wasselonne
Schiltigheim
Bischheim
Achern
Herrenberg
ZISTERZIENSERKLOSTER BEBENHAUSEN
Strasbourg
Kehl
Renchen
Ottenhöfen
Besenfeld
Altensteig
Nagold
Tübingen
Metzingen
Molsheim
Oberkirch
Schwarzwald
Baiersbronn
Bondorf
Reutlingen
Entzheim
Illkirch-Graffenstaden
Offenburg
Rosheim
Baden
Horb am Neckar
Rottenburg
Pfullingen
Obernai
Oppenau
Freudenstadt
Altenheim
Dusslingen
Gomaringen
Erstein
Gengenbach
Bad Peterstal
Neckar
Barr
Friesenheim
Lossburg
Sülz
Haigerloch
Mössingen
Schapbach
Württemberg
Epfig
Benfeld
Lahr
Biberach
Zell
Alpirsbach
Dornhan
Hechingen
Jungingen
NEBELHÖHLE
Bisingen
FREILICHTMUSEUM HECHINGEN
Burladingen
Trochtelfingen
Seelbach
Steinach
Wolfach
Oberndorf
Kappel
EUROPAPARK
Schiltach
Rosenfeld
Balingen
Gammertingen
Ettenheim
Haslach
Hausach
Tailfingen
Sélestat
Herbolzheim
Schramberg
Albstadt
Schweighausen
Hornberg
Schonberg

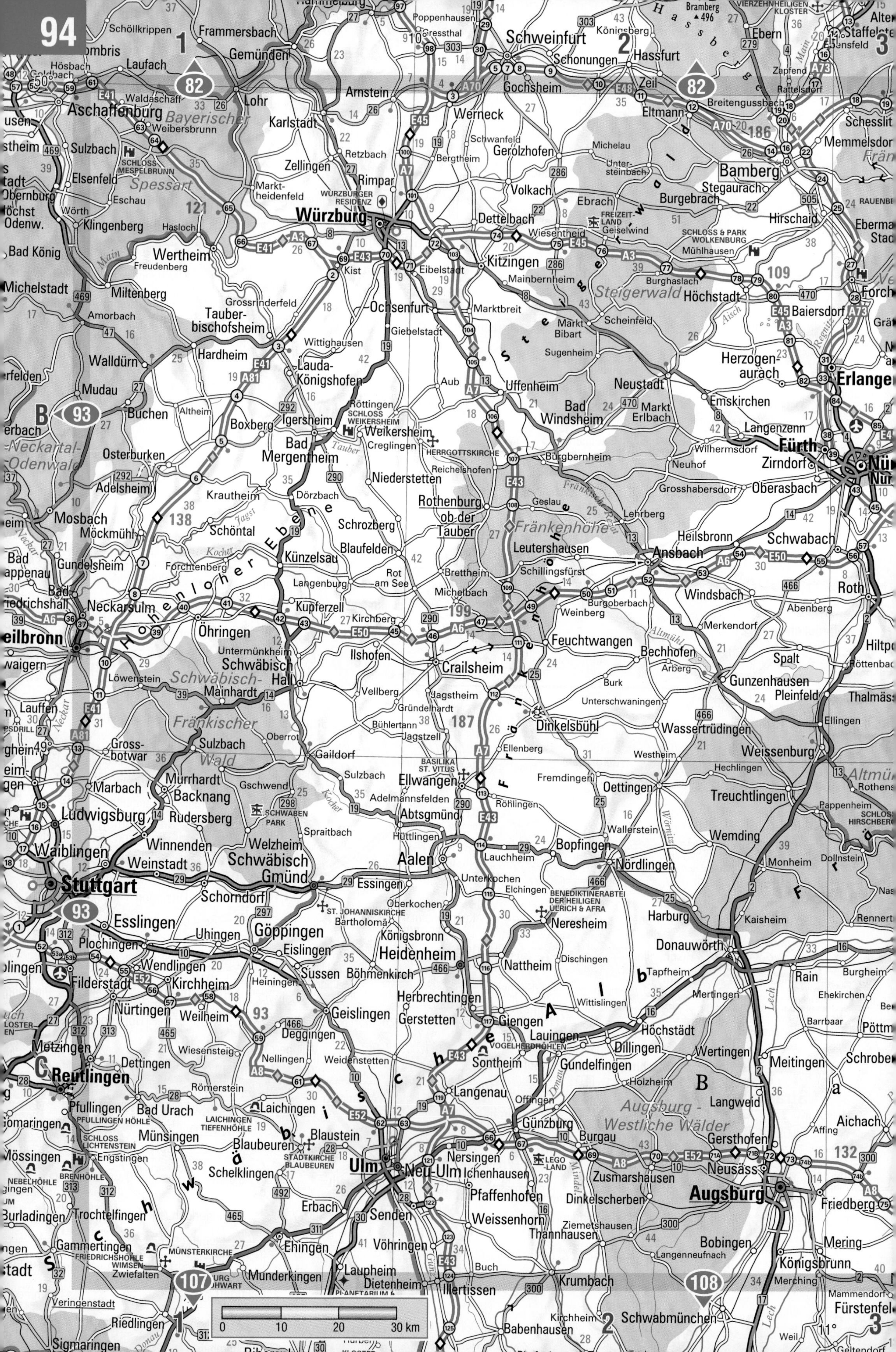
Schöllkrippen
Frammersbach
Gemünden
Laufach
Hösbach
Aschaffenburg
Bayerischer
Spessart
Weibersbrunn
Lohr
Karlstadt
Sulzbach
Elsenfeld
Obernburg
Eschau
Wörth
Klingenberg
Hasloch
Bad König
Wertheim
Freudenberg
Michelstadt
Miltenberg
Amorbach
Walldürn
Mudau
Buchen
Neckartal-Odenwald
Osterburken
Adelsheim
Mosbach
Möckmühl
Gundelsheim
Bad Friedrichshall
Neckarsulm
Heilbronn
Poppenhausen
Schweinfurt
Königsberg
Hassberge
Hassfurt
Schonungen
Gochsheim
Zeil
Eltmann
Ebern
Breitengussbach
Schesslitz
Memmelsdorf
Bamberg
Stegaurach
Burgebrach
Hirschaid
Arnstein
Werneck
Schwanfeld
Gerolzhofen
Bergtheim
Zellingen
Retzbach
Rimpar
Markt-heidenfeld
Würzburg
Würzburger Residenz
Volkach
Michelau
Ebrach
Dettelbach
Wiesentheid
Geiselwind
Freizeit-Land
Schloss & Park Wolkenburg
Mühlhausen
Kitzingen
Eibelstadt
Kist
Mainbernheim
Burghaslach
Höchstadt
Steigerwald
Forchheim
Baiersdorf
Grossrinderfeld
Tauber-bischofsheim
Ochsenfurt
Marktbreit
Giebelstadt
Wittighausen
Markt Bibart
Scheinfeld
Sugenheim
Herzogen-aurach
Erlangen
Hardheim
Lauda-Königshofen
Aub
Uffenheim
Neustadt
Emskirchen
Röttingen
Schloss Weikersheim
Weikersheim
Creglingen
Herrgottskirche
Igersheim
Altheim
Boxberg
Bad Mergentheim
Bad Windsheim
Markt Erlbach
Langenzenn
Fürth
Zirndorf
Wilhermsdorf
Burgbernheim
Reichelshofen
Niederstetten
Neuhof
Grosshabersdorf
Oberasbach
Krautheim
Dörzbach
Rothenburg ob der Tauber
Geslau
Frankenhöhe
Lehrberg
Schöntal
Schrozberg
Hohenloher Ebene
Heilsbronn
Schwabach
Forchtenberg
Künzelsau
Blaufelden
Leutershausen
Ansbach
Schillingsfürst
Brettheim
Langenburg
Rot am See
Michelbach
Kupferzell
Burgoberbach
Windsbach
Roth
Abenberg
Öhringen
Kirchberg
Weinberg
Merkendorf
Feuchtwangen
Untermünkheim
Schwäbisch Hall
Ilshofen
Crailsheim
Bechhofen
Arberg
Spalt
Hiltpoltstein
Löwenstein
Schwäbisch-
Mainhardt
Fränkischer Wald
Vellberg
Jagstheim
Gründelhardt
Bühlertann
Jagstzell
Burk
Unterschwaningen
Gunzenhausen
Pleinfeld
Dinkelsbühl
Wassertrüdingen
Ellingen
Weissenburg
Lauffen
Gross-botwar
Sulzbach
Oberrot
Gaildorf
Ellenberg
Westheim
Hechlingen
Marbach
Murrhardt
Backnang
Gschwend
Basilika St. Vitus
Ellwangen
Fremdingen
Oettingen
Treuchtlingen
Ludwigsburg
Rudersberg
Schwaben Park
Sulzbach
Adelmannsfelden
Abtsgmünd
Röhlingen
Wallerstein
Pappenheim
Waiblingen
Winnenden
Welzheim
Spraitbach
Hüttlingen
Bopfingen
Wemding
Weinstadt
Schwäbisch Gmünd
Aalen
Lauchheim
Nördlingen
Monheim
Stuttgart
Schorndorf
Essingen
Unterkochen
Elchingen
Benediktinerabtei der Heiligen Ulrich & Afra
Neresheim
Harburg
Kaisheim
Esslingen
St. Johanniskirche
Oberkochen
Bartholomä
Königsbronn
Heidenheim
Donauwörth
Plochingen
Uhingen
Göppingen
Eislingen
Wendlingen
Filderstadt
Kirchheim
Süssen
Böhmenkirch
Nattheim
Dischingen
Tapfheim
Rain
Nürtingen
Weilheim
Heiningen
Herbrechtingen
Gerstetten
Mertingen
Geislingen
Deggingen
Giengen
Wittislingen
Höchstädt
Lauingen
Metzingen
Wiesensteig
Dillingen
Wertingen
Meitingen
Dettingen
Nellingen
Weidenstetten
Vogelherdhöhlen
Sontheim
Gundelfingen
Reutlingen
Römerstein
Holzheim
Langenau
Offingen
Pfullingen
Bad Urach
Laichingen
Augsburg - Westliche Wälder
Langweid
Aichach
Schloss Lichtenstein
Münsingen
Laichinger Tiefenhöhle
Blaustein
Günzburg
Burgau
Gersthofen
Mössingen
Engstingen
Blaubeuren
Stadtkirche Blaubeuren
Schelklingen
Ulm
Neu-Ulm
Nersingen
Legoland
Zusmarshausen
Neusäss
Friedberg
Ichenhausen
Pfaffenhofen
Dinkelscherben
Augsburg
Trochtelfingen
Erbach
Senden
Weissenhorn
Ziemetshausen
Thannhausen
Bobingen
Mering
Gammertingen
Friedrichshöhle
Wimsen
Zwiefalten
Münsterkirche
Ehingen
Vöhringen
Langenneufnach
Königsbrunn
Munderkingen
Laupheim
Dietenheim
Illertissen
Buch
Krumbach
Merching
Veringenstadt
Riedlingen
Babenhausen
Kirchheim
Schwabmünchen
Fürstenfeldbruck
Sigmaringen
Schwäbische Alb
0
10
20
30 km

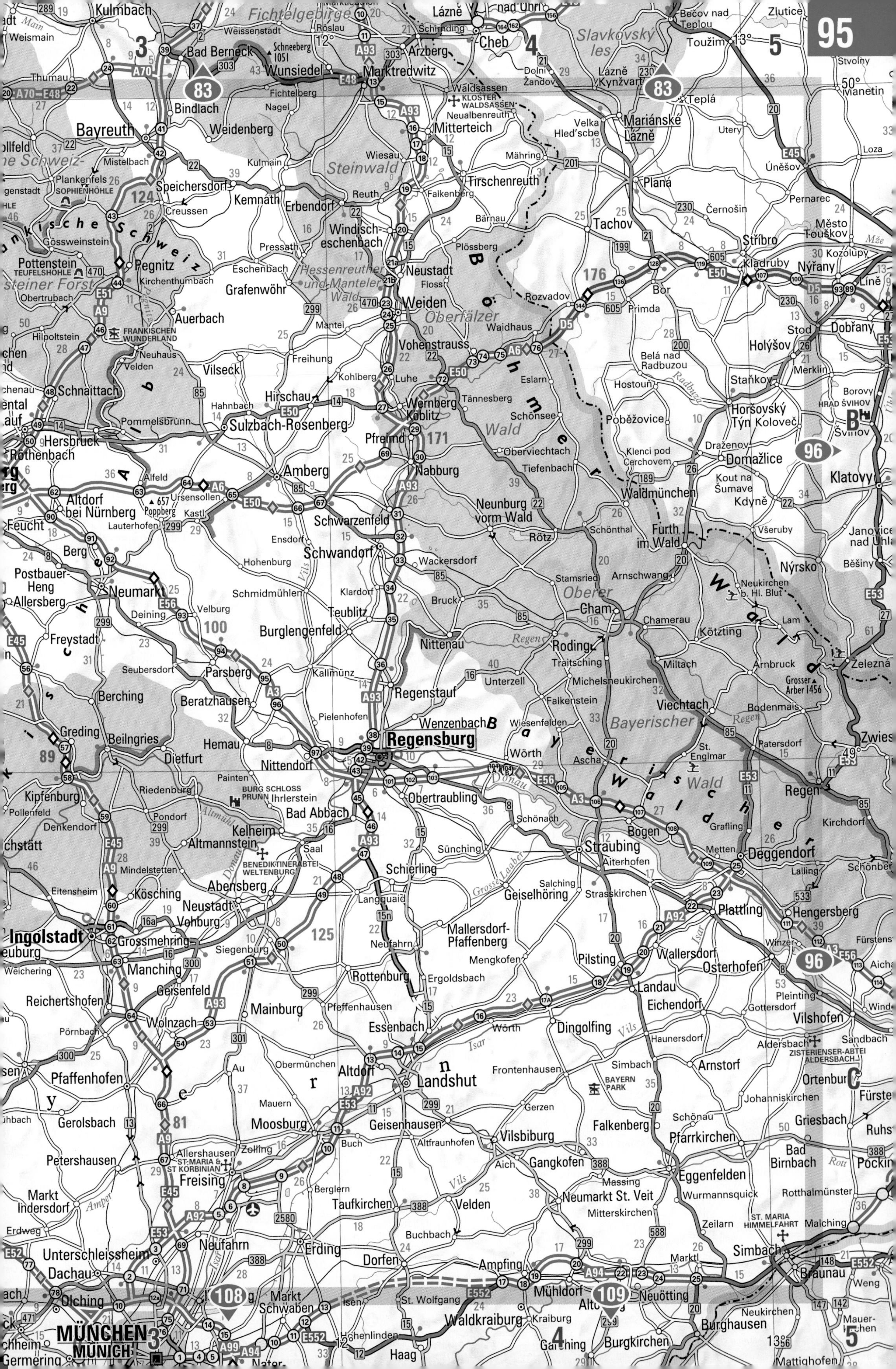
Kulmbach
Bad Berneck
Wunsiedel
Marktredwitz
Arzberg
Cheb
Slavkovský les
Mariánské Lázně
Bayreuth
Weidenberg
Mitterteich
Steinwald
Tirschenreuth
Planá
Speichersdorf
Kemnath
Erbendorf
Tachov
Stříbro
Pegnitz
Grafenwöhr
Neustadt
Weiden
Oberpfälzer Wald
Nýřany
Auerbach
Vohenstrauss
Vilseck
Schnaittach
Hirschau
Wernberg-Köblitz
Sulzbach-Rosenberg
Hersbruck
Pfreimd
Nabburg
Amberg
Domažlice
Klatovy
Altdorf bei Nürnberg
Schwarzenfeld
Neunburg vorm Wald
Waldmünchen
Feucht
Schwandorf
Furth im Wald
Neumarkt
Cham
Burglengenfeld
Nittenau
Roding
Parsberg
Berching
Regenstauf
Viechtach
Regensburg
Beilngries
Hemau
Dietfurt
Bayerischer Wald
Regen
Kelheim
Bad Abbach
Straubing
Deggendorf
Abensberg
Ingolstadt
Plattling
Neustadt
Manching
Mainburg
Rottenburg
Pilsting
Landau
Osterhofen
Vilshofen
Wolnzach
Dingolfing
Pfaffenhofen
Landshut
Moosburg
Vilsbiburg
Freising
Eggenfelden
Pfarrkirchen
Erding
Taufkirchen
Dorfen
Dachau
Mühldorf
Altötting
Simbach
Braunau
Waldkraiburg
Burghausen
MÜNCHEN
MUNICH
Haag
83
96
108
109

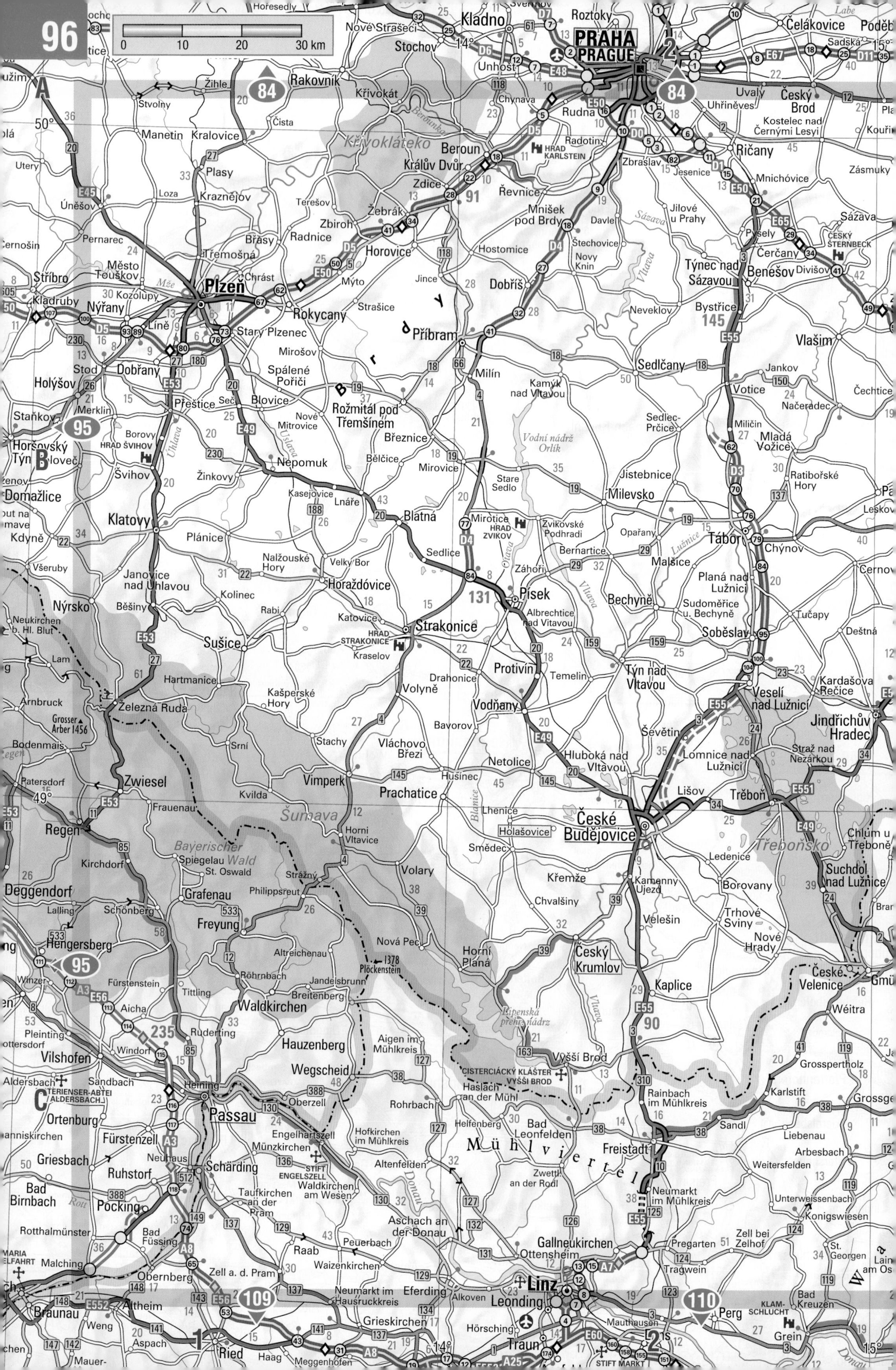
0
10
20
30 km
Kladno
Roztoky
PRAHA
PRAGUE
Čelákovice
Nové Strašecí
Stochov
Unhošť
Rakovník
Křivoklát
Žihle
Stvolny
Čista
Manetin
Kralovice
Plasy
Loza
Kraznějov
Úněšov
Terešov
Křivoklátsko
Beroun
Králův Dvůr
Zdice
Žebrák
Zbiroh
Radnice
Břasy
Třemošná
Pernarec
Město Touškov
Stříbro
Kladruby
Nýřany
Kozolupy
Chrást
Plzeň
Mže
Rokycany
Mýto
Horovice
Hostomice
Jince
Dobříš
Strašice
Brdy
Příbram
Stary Plzenec
Líně
Dobřany
Stod
Holýšov
Staňkov
Merklin
Přeštice
Seč
Blovice
Mirošov
Spálené Poříčí
Rožmitál pod Třemšínem
Nové Mitrovice
Březnice
Bělčice
Mirovice
Nepomuk
Žinkovy
Úhlava
Borovy
HRAD ŠVIHOV
Švihov
Horšovský Týn
Domažlice
Klatovy
Kdyně
Všeruby
Plánice
Kasejovice
Lnáře
Blatná
Sedlice
Nalžouské Hory
Velky Bor
Horaždóvice
Janovice nad Uhlavou
Kolinec
Nýrsko
Běšiny
Rabi
Katovice
HRAD STRAKONICE
Strakonice
Kraselov
Sušice
Hartmanice
Kašperské Hory
Volyně
Drahonice
Protivín
Temelin
Vodňany
Bavorov
Stachy
Vláchovo Březi
Husinec
Netolice
Železná Ruda
Grosser Arber 1456
Arnbruck
Lam
Neukirchen b. Hl. Blut
Bodenmais
Zwiesel
Patersdorf
Frauenau
Regen
Srní
Kvilda
Vimperk
Prachatice
Šumava
Horni Vltavice
Bayerischer Wald
Spiegelau
St. Oswald
Kirchdorf
Deggendorf
Grafenau
Philippsreut
Strážný
Volary
Lalling
Schönberg
Freyung
Hengersberg
Nová Pec
Altreichenau
1378 Plöckenstein
Horní Planá
Winzer
Fürstenstein
Röhrnbach
Jandelsbrunn
Breitenberg
Tittling
Aicha
Waldkirchen
Pleinting
Vilshofen
Windorf
Ruderting
Hauzenberg
Aigen im Mühlkreis
Wegscheid
Aldersbach
Sandbach
TERIENSER-ABTEI ALDERSBACH
Ortenburg
Heining
Passau
Oberzell
Rohrbach
Fürstenzell
Griesbach
Neuhaus
Ruhstorf
Schärding
Engelhartszell
Münzkirchen
STIFT ENGELSZELL
Hofkirchen im Mühlkreis
Altenfelden
Donau
Bad Birnbach
Rott
Pocking
Taufkirchen an der Pram
Waldkirchen am Wesen
Rotthalmünster
Bad Füssing
Raab
Peuerbach
Aschach an der Donau
Malching
Obernberg
Zell a. d. Pram
Waizenkirchen
Eferding
Neumarkt im Hausruckkreis
Alkoven
Braunau
Altheim
Weng
Aspach
Ried
Haag
Grieskirchen
Meggenhofen
Hörsching
Traun
Leonding
Linz
Ottensheim
Gallneukirchen
Mühlviertel
Helfenberg
Bad Leonfelden
Zwettl an der Rodl
Freistadt
Neumarkt im Mühlkreis
Rainbach im Mühlkreis
Pregarten
Tragwein
Zell bei Zelhof
Mauthausen
Perg
KLAM-SCHLUCHT
Grein
STIFT MARKT
Vyšší Brod
CISTERCIÁCKÝ KLÁŠTER VYŠŠÍ BROD
Haslach an der Mühl
Lipenská přehr. nádrž
Český Krumlov
Vltava
Kaplice
Křemže
Chvalšiny
Kamenny Ujezd
Velešin
Smědec
Holašovice
Lhenice
Blanice
České Budějovice
Hluboká nad Vltavou
Lišov
Lomnice nad Lužnicí
Ševětín
Třeboň
Třeboňsko
Borovany
Ledenice
Trhové Sviny
Nové Hrady
České Velenice
Suchdol nad Lužnicí
Chlum u Třeboně
Jindřichův Hradec
Straž nad Nežárkou
Veselí nad Lužnicí
Kardašova Řečice
Týn nad Vltavou
Soběslav
Tučapy
Deštná
Sudoměřice u. Bechyně
Bechyně
Planá nad Lužnicí
Malšice
Tábor
Chýnov
Opařany
Bernartice
Zvíkovské Podhradi
Mirotice
HRAD ZVIKOV
Otava
Záhoří
Písek
Albrechtice nad Vitavou
Stare Sedlo
Milevsko
Jistebnice
Vodní nádrž Orlík
Kamýk nad Vltavou
Milín
Sedlčany
Sedlec-Prčice
Mladá Vožice
Ratibořské Hory
Miličín
Votice
Jankov
Načeradec
Čechtice
Vlašim
Bystřice
Neveklov
Týnec nad Sázavou
Benešov
Divišov
Čerčany
ČESKÝ ŠTERNBECK
Pyšely
Sázava
Mnichóvice
Zásmuky
Jilové u Prahy
Davle
Štechovice
Novy Knin
Mníšek pod Brdy
Řevnice
Radotin
HRAD KARLŠTEJN
Zbraslav
Jesenice
Rudna
Chynava
Říčany
Kostelec nad Černými Lesyí
Uhřiněves
Uvaly
Český Brod
Sadská
Labe
Poděbrady
Kouřim
Liebenau
Arbesbach
Weitersfelden
Unterweissenbach
Konigswiesen
St. Georgen
Bad Kreuzen
Karlstift
Grosspertholz
Weitra
Sandl
Gmünd
Lomnice nad Lužnicí

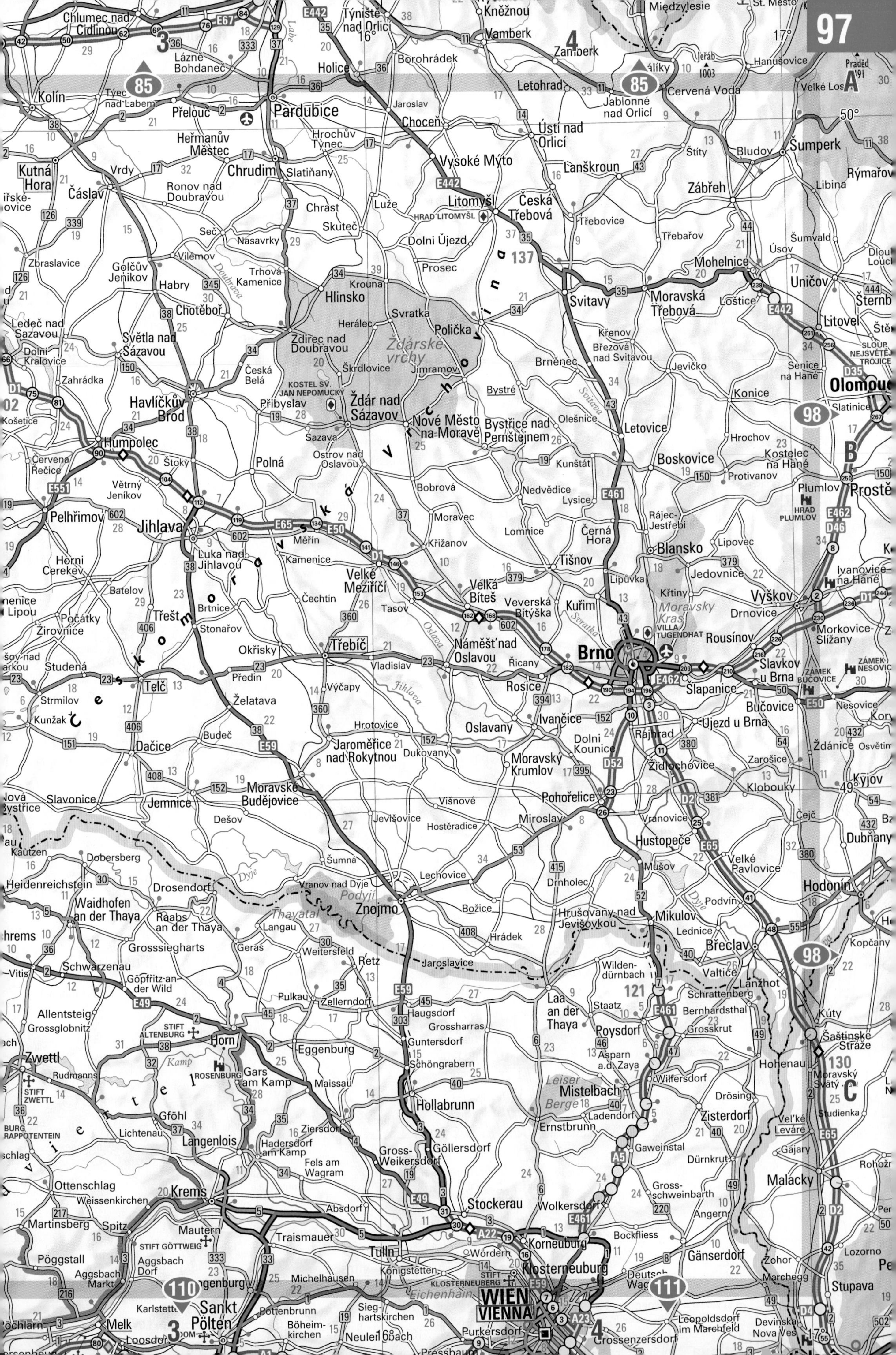

Chlumec nad Cidlinou
Týniště nad Orlicí
Kněžnou
Międzylesie
Vamberk
Žamberk
Lázně Bohdaneč
Holice
Borohrádek
Kolín
Týnec nad Labem
Přelouč
Pardubice
Letohrad
Jablonné nad Orlicí
Červená Voda
Hanušovice
Praděd
Velké Losiny
Heřmanův Městec
Hrochův Týnec
Choceň
Ústí nad Orlicí
Vysoké Mýto
Lanškroun
Štíty
Bludov
Šumperk
Kutná Hora
Čáslav
Vrdy
Chrudim
Slatiňany
Ronov nad Doubravou
Chrast
Luže
Litomyšl
Hrad Litomyšl
Česká Třebová
Zábřeh
Rýmařov
Libina
Skuteč
Seč
Nasavrky
Dolni Újezd
Třebovice
Třebařov
Šumvald
Úsov
Zbraslavice
Vilémov
Golčův Jeníkov
Habry
Trhová Kamenice
Krouna
Prosec
Mohelnice
Uničov
Šternberk
Hlinsko
Svitavy
Moravská Třebová
Loštice
Litovel
Chotěboř
Svratka
Herálec
Polička
Ždírec nad Doubravou
Ledeč nad Sázavou
Světla nad Sázavou
Žďárské vrchy
Křenov
Březová nad Svitavou
Dolni Kralovice
Škrdlovice
Jimramov
Brněnec
Jevíčko
Senice na Hané
Olomouc
Zahrádka
Česká Belá
Kostel sv. Jan Nepomucký
Bystré
Konice
Havlíčkův Brod
Přibyslav
Žďár nad Sázavou
Nové Město na Moravě
Bystřice nad Pernštejnem
Olešnice
Letovice
Slatinice
Humpolec
Sazava
Ostrov nad Oslavou
Hrochov
Červená Řečice
Štoky
Polná
Kunštát
Boskovice
Kostelec na Hané
Protivanov
Bobrová
Nedvědice
Lysice
Plumlov
Hrad Plumlov
Prostějov
Věterný Jeníkov
Pelhřimov
Jihlava
Moravec
Rájec-Jestřebí
Měřín
Lomnice
Černá Hora
Horní Cerekev
Luka nad Jihlavou
Kamenice
Křižanov
Blansko
Lipovec
Velké Meziříčí
Tišnov
Jedovnice
Ivanovice na Hané
Batelov
Lipůvka
Křtiny
Vyškov
Čechtin
Velká Bíteš
Veverská Bítýška
Kuřim
Moravský Kras
Drnovice
Třešť
Brtnice
Tasov
Villa Tugendhat
Počátky
Žirovnice
Stonařov
Náměšť nad Oslavou
Rousínov
Morkovice-Slížany
Okřisky
Třebíč
Brno
Studená
Vladislav
Řicany
Slavkov u Brna
Telč
Předín
Rosice
Šlapanice
Zámek Bučovice
Zámek Nesovice
Strmilov
Výčapy
Želatava
Bučovice
Nesovice
Kunžak
Ivančice
Újezd u Brna
Hrotovice
Oslavany
Rajhrad
Dačice
Budeč
Jaroměřice nad Rokytnou
Dukovany
Dolni Kounice
Ždánice
Moravský Krumlov
Židlochovice
Zarošice
Kyjov
Nová Bystřice
Slavonice
Jemnice
Moravské Budějovice
Višňové
Pohořelice
Klobouky
Dešov
Jevišovice
Hostěradice
Miroslav
Vranovice
Čejč
Hustopeče
Dubňany
Kautzen
Dobersberg
Šumná
Velké Pavlovice
Heidenreichstein
Drosendorf
Vranov nad Dyje
Podyjí
Lechovice
Drnholec
Mušov
Hodonín
Waidhofen an der Thaya
Raabs an der Thaya
Thayatal
Znojmo
Božice
Hrušovany nad Jevišovkou
Mikulov
Podivín
Langau
Lednice
Hrádek
Břeclav
Kopčany
Grosssiegharts
Geras
Weitersfeld
Jaroslavice
Wildendürnbach
Valtice
Schwarzenau
Retz
Lanžhot
Gopfritz an der Wild
Laa an der Thaya
Schrattenberg
Pulkau
Zellerndorf
Staatz
Bernhardsthal
Allentsteig
Grossglobnitz
Haugsdorf
Kúty
Grossharras
Poysdorf
Grosskrut
Šaštínske Stráže
Stift Altenburg
Horn
Eggenburg
Guntersdorf
Asparn a.d. Zaya
Hohenau
Zwettl
Rudmanns
Kamp
Rosenburg
Gars am Kamp
Schöngrabern
Moravský Svätý Ján
Stift Zwettl
Maissau
Leiser Berge
Mistelbach
Wilfersdorf
Drösing
Hollabrunn
Ladendorf
Zisterdorf
Studienka
Gföhl
Ziersdorf
Ernstbrunn
Veľké Leváre
Burg Rappottenstein
Lichtenau
Langenlois
Hadersdorf am Kamp
Göllersdorf
Gaweinstal
Gajary
Fels am Wagram
Gross-Weikersdorf
Dürnkrut
Rohožník
Ottenschlag
Malacky
Weissenkirchen
Krems
Gross-Schweinbarth
Stockerau
Wolkersdorf
Angern
Martinsberg
Spitz
Mautern
Absdorf
Stift Göttweig
Traismauer
Korneuburg
Bockfliess
Pöggstall
Aggsbach Dorf
Tulln
Wördern
Gänserdorf
Lozorno
Aggsbach Markt
Klosterneuburg
Michelhausen
Königstetten
Stift Klosterneuburg
Eichenhain
Deutsch Wagram
Zohor
Marchegg
Stupava
Karlstetten
Wien
Vienna
Sankt Pölten
Pottenbrunn
Sieghartskirchen
Melk
Böheimkirchen
Neulengbach
Leopoldsdorf im Marchfeld
Devínska Nová Ves
Loosdorf
Purkersdorf
Grossenzersdorf
Pressbaum
Lotrinck
Českomoravská vrchovina
Waldviertel

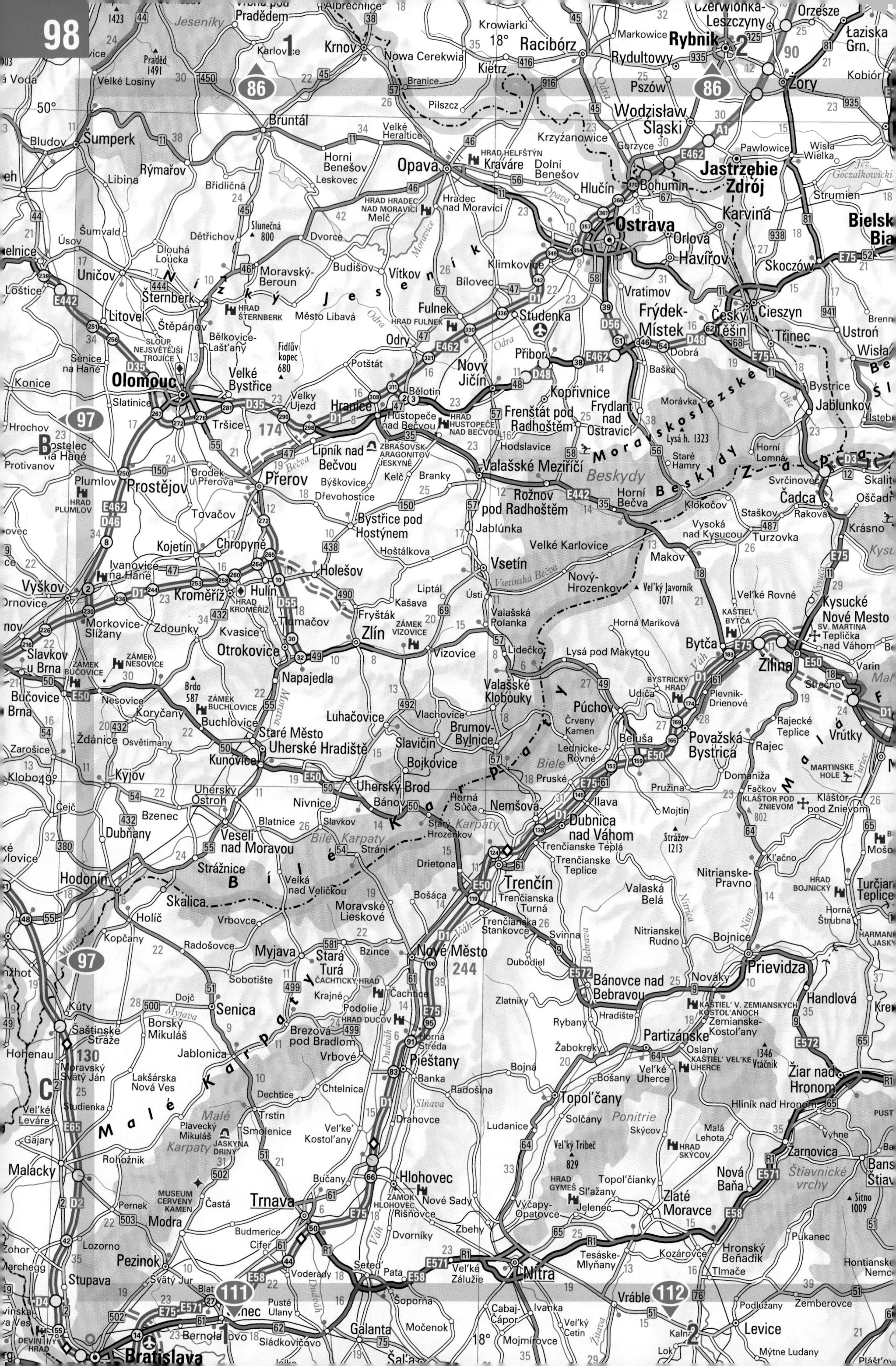

Jeseníky
Praděd 1491
Krnov
Racibórz
Rybnik
Żory
Jastrzębie Zdrój
Wodzisław Śląski
Šumperk
Rýmařov
Bruntál
Opava
Kravaře
Hlučín
Bohumín
Ostrava
Orlová
Havířov
Karviná
Frýdek-Místek
Český Těšín
Cieszyn
Třinec
Uničov
Šternberk
Litovel
Olomouc
Nízký Jeseník
Fulnek
Studénka
Příbor
Kopřivnice
Nový Jičín
Odry
Hranice
Frenštát pod Radhoštěm
Frýdlant nad Ostravicí
Moravskoslezské Beskydy
Lysá h. 1323
Jablunkov
Čadca
Prostějov
Přerov
Lipník nad Bečvou
Valašské Meziříčí
Rožnov pod Radhoštěm
Bystřice pod Hostýnem
Vsetín
Velké Karlovice
Kojetín
Chropyně
Holešov
Kroměříž
Hulín
Vyškov
Zlín
Vizovice
Otrokovice
Napajedla
Kysucké Nové Mesto
Bytča
Žilina
Malá Fatra
Púchov
Považská Bystrica
Bučovice
Slavkov u Brna
Uherské Hradiště
Staré Město
Kunovice
Luhačovice
Uherský Brod
Kyjov
Veselí nad Moravou
Strážnice
Hodonín
Bílé Karpaty
Ilava
Dubnica nad Váhom
Trenčín
Trenčianske Teplice
Prievidza
Bojnice
Handlová
Skalica
Senica
Myjava
Nové Mesto
Piešťany
Bánovce nad Bebravou
Partizánske
Topoľčany
Žiar nad Hronom
Malé Karpaty
Malacky
Hlohovec
Trnava
Zlaté Moravce
Nitra
Pezinok
Modra
Galanta
Sereď
Vráble
Levice
Bratislava
Senec

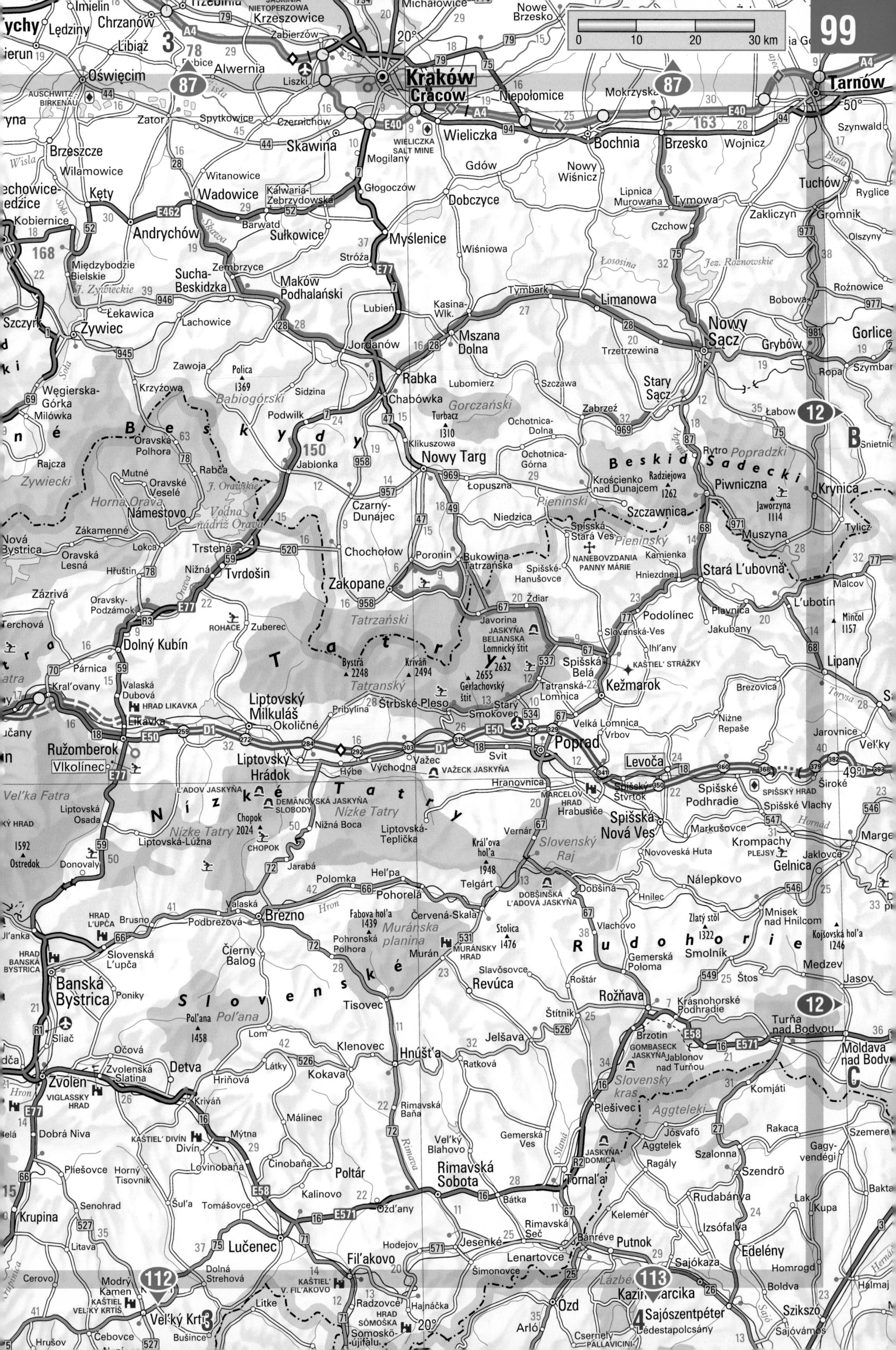

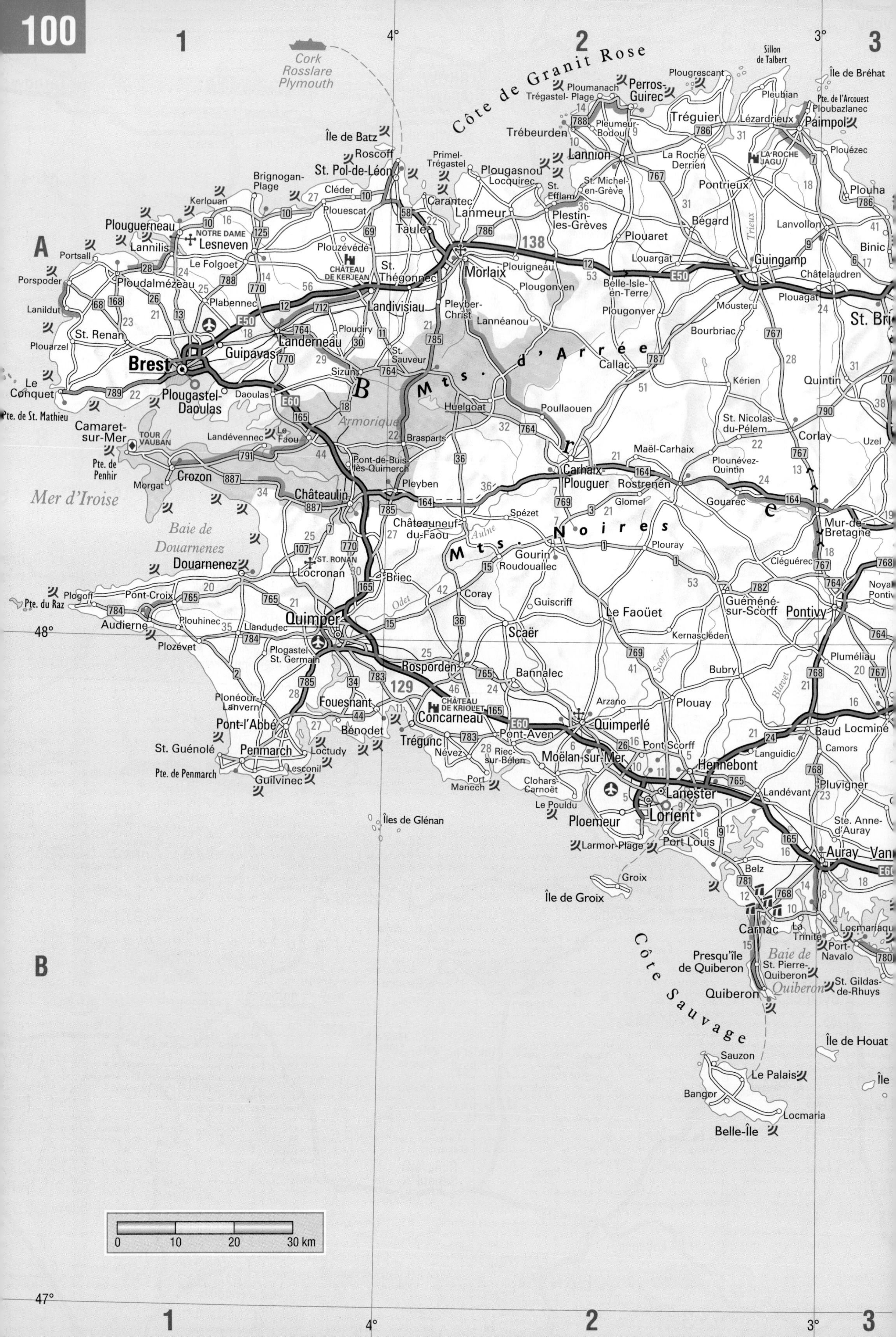
1
2
3
4°
3°
A
B
Cork
Rosslare
Plymouth
Côte de Granit Rose
Sillon de Talbert
Île de Bréhat
Plougrescant
Ploumanach
Perros-Guirec
Trégastel-Plage
Pleubian
Pte. de l'Arcouest
Ploubazlanec
Trébeurden
Pleumeur-Bodou
Tréguier
Lézardrieux
Paimpol
Île de Batz
Roscoff
St. Pol-de-Léon
Primel-Trégastel
Plougasnou
Locquirec
St. Efflam
Lannion
St. Michel-en-Grève
La Roche Derrien
La Roche Jagu
Pontrieux
Plouézec
Plouha
Brignogan-Plage
Kerlouan
Cléder
Plouescat
Carantec
Taulé
Lanmeur
Plestin-les-Grèves
Bégard
Lanvollon
Plouguerneau
Lannilis
Notre Dame
Lesneven
Plouzévédé
Château de Kerjean
St. Thégonnec
Morlaix
Plouigneau
Plouaret
Louargat
Guingamp
Binic
Châtelaudren
Portsall
Porspoder
Le Folgoet
Ploudalmézeau
Plabennec
Landivisiau
Pleyber-Christ
Plougonven
Belle-Isle-en-Terre
Plougonver
Mousteru
Plouagat
St. Brieuc
Lanildut
St. Renan
Ploudiry
Lannéanou
Bourbriac
Plouarzel
Brest
Guipavas
Landerneau
St. Sauveur
Sizun
Mts. d'Arrée
Callac
Kérien
Quintin
Le Conquet
Pte. de St. Mathieu
Plougastel-Daoulas
Daoulas
Huelgoat
Poullaouen
Armorique
St. Nicolas-du-Pélem
Camaret-sur-Mer
Tour Vauban
Landévennec
Le Faou
Brasparts
Corlay
Uzel
Pte. de Penhir
Pont-de-Buis-lès-Quimerch
Maël-Carhaix
Plounévez-Quintin
Morgat
Crozon
Carhaix-Plouguer
Rostrenen
Mer d'Iroise
Pleyben
Châteaulin
Glomel
Gouarec
Baie de Douarnenez
Châteauneuf-du-Faou
Spézet
Aulne
Mts. Noires
Mur-de-Bretagne
Gourin
Plouray
Douarnenez
St. Ronan
Locronan
Briec
Roudouallec
Cléguérec
Pte. du Raz
Plogoff
Pont-Croix
Audierne
Coray
Guiscriff
Guémené-sur-Scorff
Pontivy
Odet
Quimper
Plouhinec
Landudec
Le Faouët
48°
Plozévet
Plogastel St. Germain
Scaër
Kernascléden
Rosporden
Bannalec
Scorff
Bubry
Pluméliau
Blavet
Plonéour-Lanvern
Fouesnant
Château de Kriolet
Concarneau
Arzano
Plouay
Quimperlé
Pont-l'Abbé
Bénodet
Trégunc
Pont-Aven
Pont Scorff
Baud
Locminé
St. Guénolé
Penmarch
Loctudy
Névez
Riec-sur-Bélon
Moëlan-sur-Mer
Hennebont
Languidic
Camors
Pte. de Penmarch
Lesconil
Guilvinec
Port Manech
Clohars-Carnoët
Lanester
Landévant
Pluvigner
Le Pouldu
Lorient
Ploemeur
Îles de Glénan
Ste. Anne-d'Auray
Larmor-Plage
Port Louis
Auray
Vannes
Groix
Île de Groix
Belz
Carnac
La Trinité
Locmariaquer
Port-Navalo
Côte Sauvage
Presqu'île de Quiberon
Baie de Quiberon
St. Pierre-Quiberon
St. Gildas-de-Rhuys
Quiberon
Île de Houat
Sauzon
Le Palais
Bangor
Locmaria
Belle-Île
0
10
20
30 km
47°

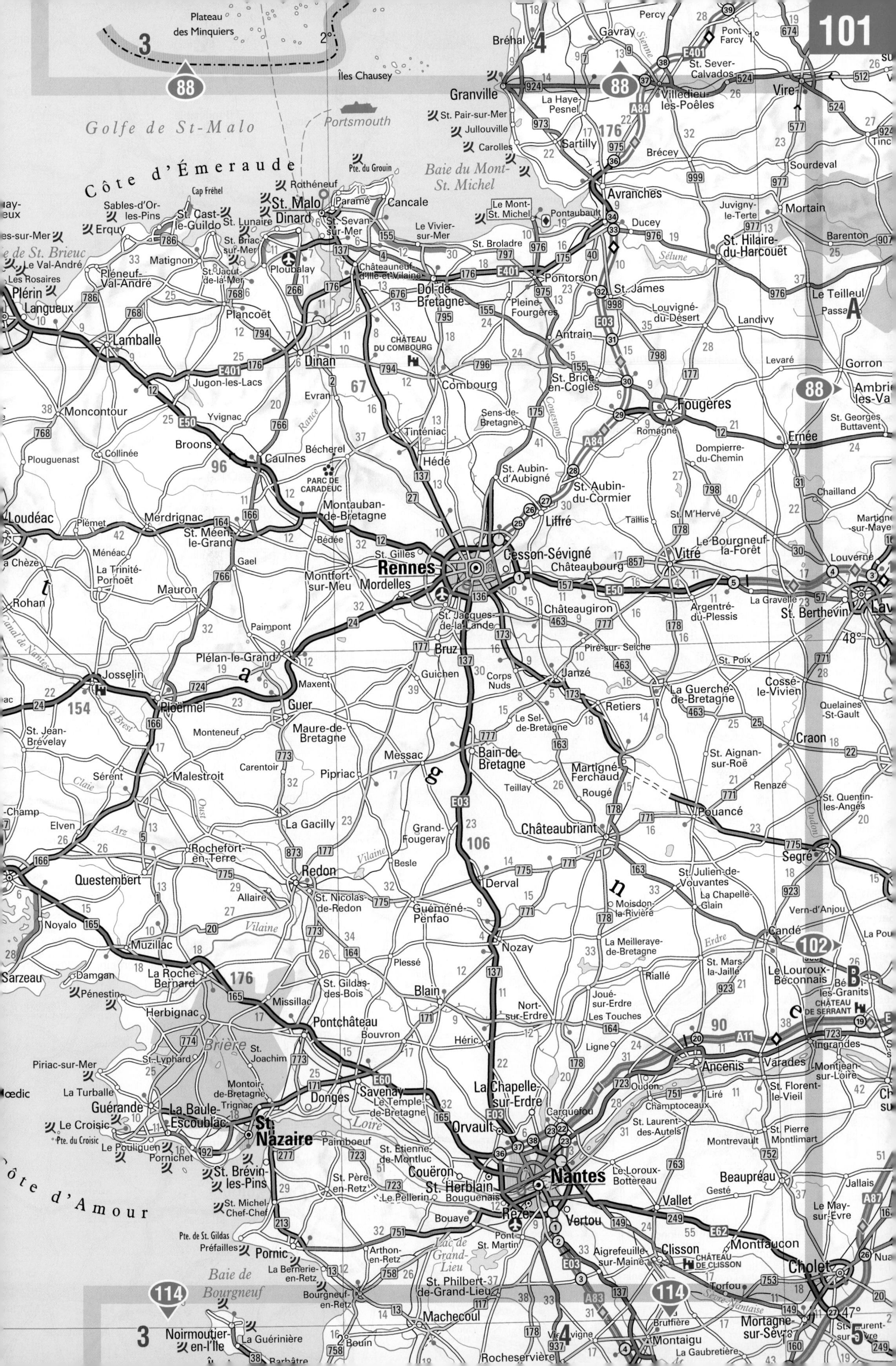

101
Plateau des Minquiers
Îles Chausey
Golfe de St-Malo
Portsmouth
Côte d'Émeraude
Baie du Mont-St. Michel
Granville
Bréhal
Percy
Gavray
Pont Farcy
St. Sever-Calvados
Villedieu-les-Poêles
Vire
St. Pair-sur-Mer
Jullouville
Carolles
La Haye-Pesnel
Sartilly
Brécey
Sourdeval
Pte. du Grouin
Cap Fréhel
Rothéneuf
St. Malo
Paramé
Cancale
Sables-d'Or-les-Pins
St. Cast-le-Guildo
Dinard
St. Lunaire
St. Servan-sur-Mer
Erquy
St. Briac-sur-Mer
Le Vivier-sur-Mer
Le Mont-St. Michel
Pontaubault
Avranches
Ducey
Juvigny-le-Terte
Mortain
St. Hilaire-du-Harcouët
Barenton
Baie de St. Brieuc
Le Val-André
Les Rosaires
Plérin
Matignon
Pléneuf-Val-André
St. Jacut-de-la-Mer
Ploubalay
Châteauneuf-d'Ille-et-Vilaine
Dol-de-Bretagne
St. Broladre
Pontorson
St. James
Pleine-Fougères
Louvigné-du-Désert
Landivy
Le Teilleul
Langueux
Plancoët
Lamballe
Dinan
Château du Combourg
Combourg
Antrain
St. Brice-en-Coglès
Fougères
Levaré
Gorron
Ambrières-les-Vallées
Jugon-les-Lacs
Moncontour
Evran
Yvignac
Broons
Tinténiac
Sens-de-Bretagne
Romagné
St. Georges-Buttavent
Ernée
Plouguenast
Collinée
Caulnes
Bécherel
Hédé
Parc de Caradeuc
St. Aubin-d'Aubigné
St. Aubin-du-Cormier
Dompierre-du-Chemin
Chailland
Loudéac
Plémet
Merdrignac
Montauban-de-Bretagne
Liffré
Taillis
St. M'Hervé
Martigné-sur-Mayenne
St. Méen-le-Grand
Ménéac
La Trinité-Porhoët
La Chèze
Gael
Bédée
St. Gilles
Rennes
Cesson-Sévigné
Châteaubourg
Vitré
Le Bourgneuf-la-Forêt
Louverné
Montfort-sur-Meu
Mordelles
Mauron
Rohan
Châteaugiron
Argentré-du-Plessis
La Gravelle
St. Berthevin
Laval
Paimpont
St. Jacques-de-la-Lande
Bruz
Piré-sur-Seiche
Plélan-le-Grand
Josselin
Guichen
Corps Nuds
Janzé
St. Poix
Cossé-le-Vivien
Ploërmel
Maxent
Guer
Retiers
La Guerche-de-Bretagne
Quelaines-St-Gault
St. Jean-Brévelay
Monteneuf
Maure-de-Bretagne
Le Sel-de-Bretagne
Craon
Sérent
Malestroit
Carentoir
Pipriac
Messac
Bain-de-Bretagne
Martigné-Ferchaud
St. Aignan-sur-Roë
Renazé
Teillay
Rougé
Pouancé
St. Quentin-les-Anges
Elven
La Gacilly
Grand-Fougeray
Châteaubriant
Segré
Rochefort-en-Terre
Redon
Besle
Derval
St. Julien-de-Vouvantes
La Chapelle-Glain
Questembert
Allaire
St. Nicolas-de-Redon
Guémené-Penfao
Moisdon-la-Rivière
Vern-d'Anjou
Noyalo
Muzillac
Nozay
La Meilleraye-de-Bretagne
Candé
Sarzeau
Damgan
La Roche-Bernard
Pénestin
Plessé
St. Gildas-des-Bois
Blain
Rialle
St. Mars-la-Jaille
Le Louroux-Béconnais
Bécon-les-Granits
Château de Serrant
Herbignac
Missillac
Pontchâteau
Bouvron
Nort-sur-Erdre
Joué-sur-Erdre
Les Touches
Brière
St. Lyphard
St. Joachim
Héric
Ligné
Ancenis
Varades
Ingrandes
Piriac-sur-Mer
La Turballe
Guérande
Le Croisic
Pte. du Croisic
La Baule-Escoublac
Montoir-de-Bretagne
Trignac
Donges
Savenay
Le Temple-de-Bretagne
La Chapelle-sur-Erdre
Oudon
Liré
Champtoceaux
Montjean-sur-Loire
St. Florent-le-Vieil
St. Nazaire
Le Pouliguen
Pornichet
Paimboeuf
St. Etienne-de-Montluc
Orvault
Carquefou
St. Laurent-des-Autels
Montrevault
St. Pierre Montlimart
St. Brévin-les-Pins
St. Père-en-Retz
Couëron
St. Herblain
Nantes
Le Loroux-Bottereau
Beaupréau
Jallais
Le Pellerin
Bouguenais
Rezé
Vertou
Vallet
Gesté
Le May-sur-Èvre
St. Michel-Chef-Chef
Bouaye
Pte. de St. Gildas
Préfailles
Pornic
Pont-St. Martin
Aigrefeuille-sur-Maine
Clisson
Château de Clisson
Montfaucon
Cholet
Arthon-en-Retz
Lac de Grand-Lieu
La Bernerie-en-Retz
St. Philbert-de-Grand-Lieu
Torfou
Baie de Bourgneuf
Bourgneuf-en-Retz
Machecoul
Bruffière
Montaigu
Mortagne-sur-Sèvre
St. Laurent-sur-Sèvre
Noirmoutier-en-l'Île
La Guérinière
Barbâtre
Bouin
Rocheservière
Vieillevigne
La Gaubretière
Côte d'Amour
Loire
Vilaine
Rance
Sélune
Couesnon
Erdre
Oust
Arz
Claie
Oudon
Sienne
Sèvre Nantaise
Canal de Nantes à Brest

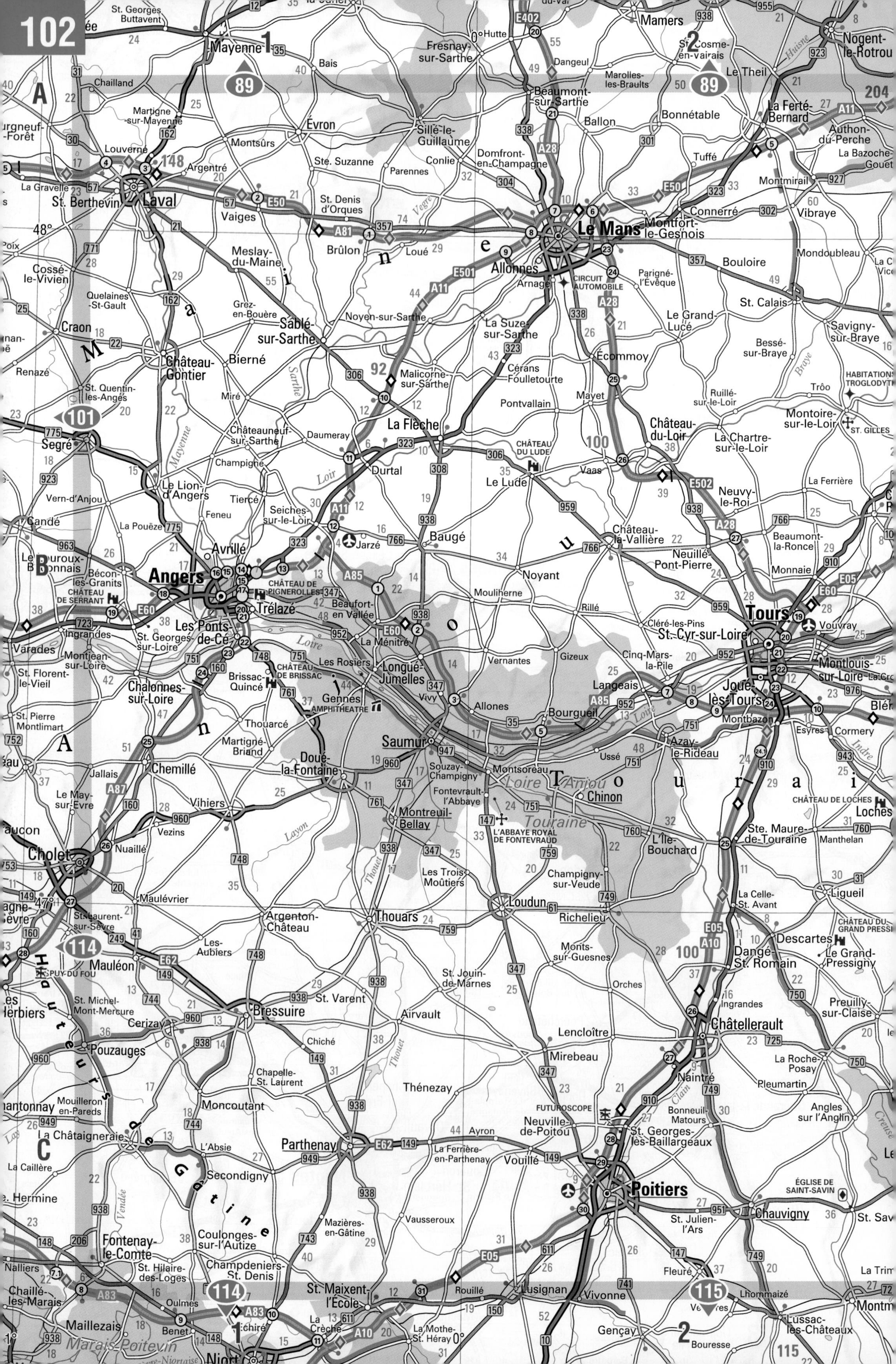
St. Georges Buttavent
Mayenne
Bais
Fresnay-sur-Sarthe
Hutte
Mamers
St. Cosme-en-Vairais
Nogent-le-Rotrou
89
Chailland
Dangeul
Marolles-les-Braults
Le Theil
Beaumont-sur-Sarthe
La Ferté-Bernard
Martigné-sur-Mayenne
Évron
Sillé-le-Guillaume
Ballon
Bonnétable
Authon-du-Perche
Louverné
Montsûrs
Conlie
Domfront-en-Champagne
Tuffé
La Bazoche-Gouet
Argentré
Ste. Suzanne
Parennes
La Gravelle
St. Berthevin
Laval
Vaiges
St. Denis d'Orques
Montmirail
Connerré
Vibraye
Le Mans
Montfort-le-Gesnois
Brûlon
Loué
Meslay-du-Maine
Allonnes
Arnage
CIRCUIT AUTOMOBILE
Parigné-l'Évêque
Bouloire
Mondoubleau
Cossé-le-Vivien
Quelaines-St-Gault
Grez-en-Bouère
Sablé-sur-Sarthe
Noyen-sur-Sarthe
La Suze-sur-Sarthe
Le Grand-Lucé
St. Calais
Savigny-sur-Braye
Craon
Château-Gontier
Bierné
Écommoy
Bessé-sur-Braye
Renazé
Malicorne-sur-Sarthe
Cérans Foulletourte
St. Quentin-les-Anges
Miré
Pontvallain
Mayet
Ruillé-sur-Le-Loir
Trôo
HABITATIONS TROGLODYTES
101
Segré
Châteauneuf-sur-Sarthe
Daumeray
La Flèche
CHÂTEAU DU LUDE
Château-du-Loir
Montoire-sur-le-Loir
ST. GILLES
La Chartre-sur-le-Loir
Champigné
Durtal
Le Lude
Vaas
Le Lion-d'Angers
Vern-d'Anjou
Tiercé
Neuvy-le-Roi
La Ferrière
Candé
La Pouëze
Feneu
Seiches-sur-le-Loir
Jarzé
Baugé
Château-la-Vallière
Beaumont-la-Ronce
Avrillé
Le Louroux-Béconnais
Bécon-les-Granits
CHÂTEAU DE SERRANT
Angers
CHÂTEAU DE PIGNEROLLES
Noyant
Neuillé-Pont-Pierre
Monnaie
Trélazé
Beaufort-en Vallée
Mouliherne
Rillé
Tours
Vouvray
Varades
Ingrandes
Les Ponts-de-Cé
St. Georges-sur-Loire
La Ménitré
Cléré-les-Pins
St. Cyr-sur-Loire
Montjean-sur-Loire
St. Florent-le-Vieil
Les Rosiers
CHÂTEAU DE BRISSAC
Brissac-Quincé
Longué-Jumelles
Vernantes
Gizeux
Cinq-Mars-la-Pile
Montlouis-sur-Loire
Chalonnes-sur-Loire
Gennes
AMPHITHÉATRE
Vivy
Allones
Langeais
Joué-lès-Tours
St. Pierre Montlimart
Thouarcé
Bourgueil
Montbazon
Esvres
Cormery
Martigné-Briand
Saumur
Azay-le-Rideau
Ussé
Doué-la-Fontaine
Souzay-Champigny
Montsoreau
Loire Anjou Touraine
Chinon
Chemillé
Jallais
Le May-sur-Evre
Fontevrault-l'Abbaye
CHÂTEAU DE LOCHES
Loches
Vihiers
Montreuil-Bellay
L'ABBAYE ROYAL DE FONTEVRAUD
L'Île-Bouchard
Ste. Maure-de-Touraine
Manthelan
Vezins
Nuaillé
Cholet
Les Trois-Moûtiers
Champigny-sur-Veude
Maulévrier
Loudun
Richelieu
La Celle-St. Avant
Ligueil
St. Laurent-sur-Sèvre
Argenton-Château
Thouars
CHÂTEAU DU GRAND PRESSIGNY
Descartes
Le Grand-Pressigny
Les Aubiers
Monts-sur-Guesnes
Dangé-St. Romain
114
Mauléon
PUY-DU-FOU
St. Jouin-de-Marnes
Orches
St. Michel-Mont-Mercure
Les Herbiers
St. Varent
Bressuire
Ingrandes
Preuilly-sur-Claise
Cerizay
Airvault
Châtellerault
Lencloître
Pouzauges
Chiché
Mirebeau
La Roche-Posay
Chapelle-St. Laurent
Thénezay
Naintré
Pleumartin
Chantonnay
Mouilleron-en-Pareds
Moncoutant
FUTUROSCOPE
Neuville-de-Poitou
Bonneuil-Matours
Angles sur l'Anglin
La Châtaigneraie
Ayron
St. Georges-lès-Baillargeaux
Hauteurs de Gâtine
Parthenay
L'Absie
La Ferrière-en-Parthenay
Vouillé
La Caillère
Secondigny
Poitiers
ÉGLISE DE SAINT-SAVIN
Ste. Hermine
Vausseroux
St. Julien-l'Ars
Chauvigny
Mazières-en-Gâtine
Fontenay-le-Comte
Coulonges-sur-l'Autize
St. Hilaire-des-Loges
Champdeniers-St. Denis
Nalliers
Chaillé-les-Marais
Oulmes
St. Maixent-l'École
Rouillé
Lusignan
Vivonne
Fleuré
115
Lhommaizé
Maillezais
Benet
Marais Poitevin
Échiré
La Crèche
La Mothe-St. Héray
Gençay
Lussac-les-Châteaux
Bouresse
Niort
Maine
Anjou
Touraine

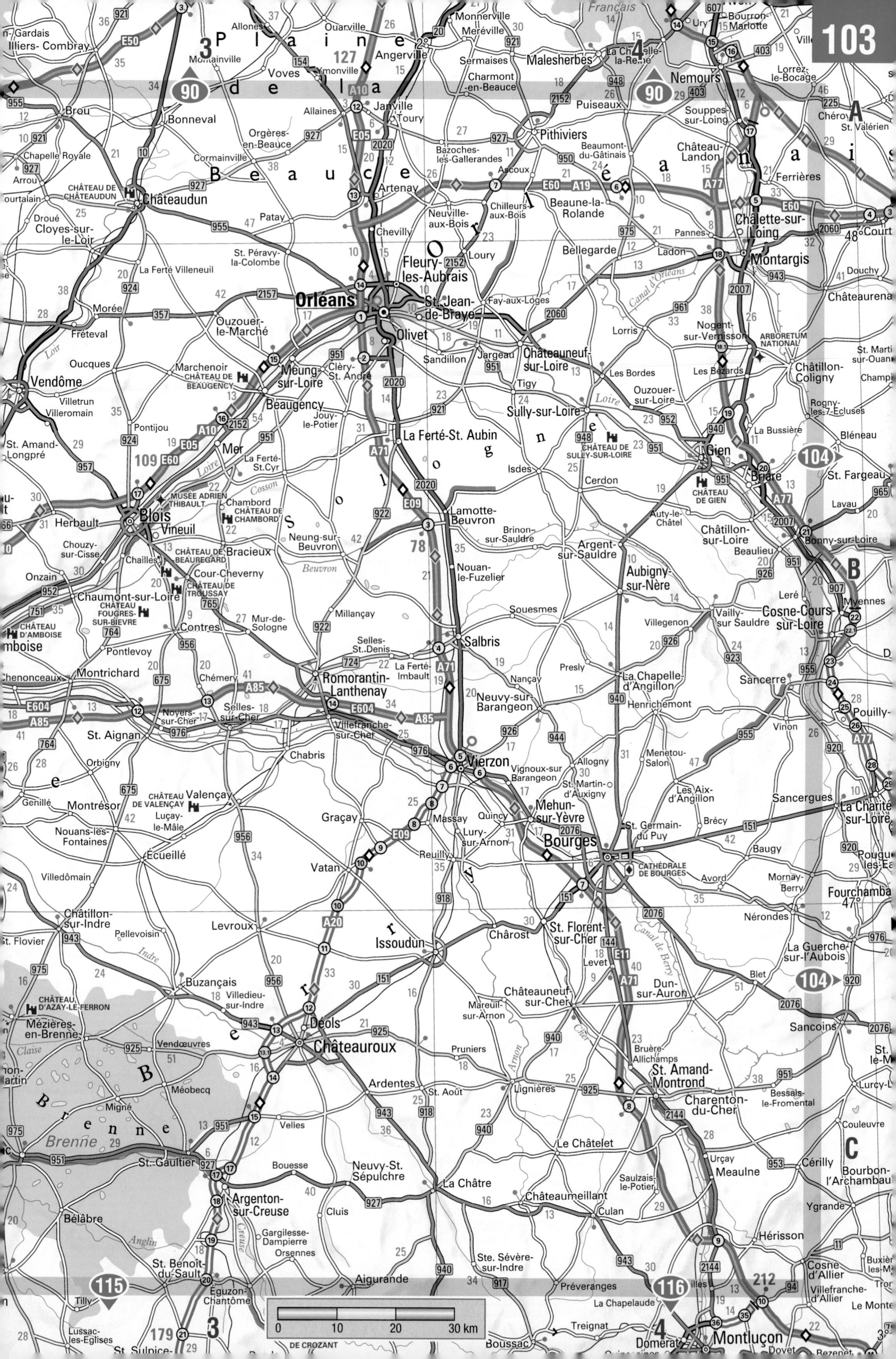

Plaine de la Beauce
Orléans
Fleury-les-Aubrais
St. Jean-de-Braye
Olivet
Pithiviers
Malesherbes
Nemours
Montargis
Châlette-sur-Loing
Châteaudun
Vendôme
Blois
Meung-sur-Loire
Beaugency
Châteauneuf-sur-Loire
Sully-sur-Loire
Gien
Briare
Sologne
La Ferté-St. Aubin
Lamotte-Beuvron
Salbris
Romorantin-Lanthenay
Vierzon
Mehun-sur-Yèvre
Bourges
Issoudun
Châteauroux
Déols
Vatan
Aubigny-sur-Nère
Cosne-Cours-sur-Loire
Sancerre
La Charité-sur-Loire
St. Amand-Montrond
Argenton-sur-Creuse
La Châtre
Montluçon
Brenne
Berry
Chambord
Cheverny
Chaumont-sur-Loire
Contres
Montrichard
St. Aignan
Valençay
Levroux
Buzançais
Châtillon-sur-Indre
Mézières-en-Brenne
St.-Gaultier
St. Benoît-du-Sault
Châteaumeillant
Dun-sur-Auron
Sancoins
Charenton-du-Cher
Lignières
Châteauneuf-sur-Cher
St. Florent-sur-Cher
Henrichemont
Argent-sur-Sauldre
Bellegarde
Lorris
Puiseaux
Janville
Artenay
Châtillon-Coligny
CHÂTEAU DE CHAMBORD
CHÂTEAU DE BEAUGENCY
CHÂTEAU DE CHÂTEAUDUN
CHÂTEAU DE SULLY-SUR-LOIRE
CHÂTEAU DE GIEN
CHÂTEAU DE VALENÇAY
CHÂTEAU D'AZAY-LE-FERRON
CATHÉDRALE DE BOURGES
ARBORETUM NATIONAL
MUSÉE ADRIEN THIBAULT
Loire
Cher
Indre
Creuse
Canal de Berry
Canal d'Orléans
A10
A71
A20
A85
A77
A19
E60
E09
E11
104
90
115
116
0 10 20 30 km

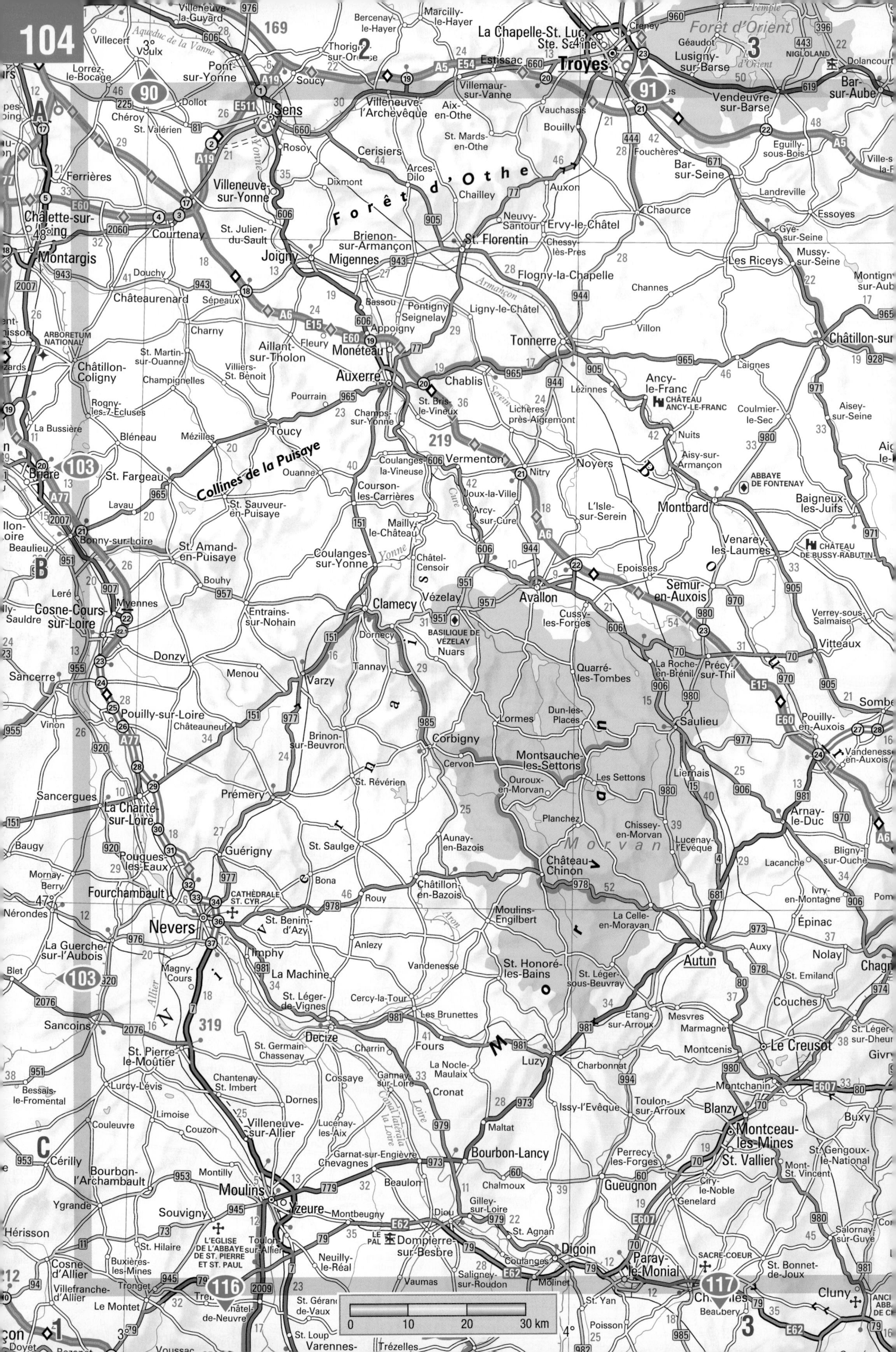
Villeneuve-la-Guyard
Villecerf
Voulx
Aqueduc de la Vanne
Pont-sur-Yonne
Lorrez-le-Bocage
Sens
Chéroy
Dollot
St. Valérien
Rosoy
Soucy
Thorigny-sur-Oreuse
Bercenay-le-Hayer
Marcilly-le-Hayer
La Chapelle-St. Luc
Ste. Savine
Troyes
Creney
Forêt d'Orient
Géaudot
Lusigny-sur-Barse
Lac d'Orient
NIGLOLAND
Dolancourt
Bar-sur-Aube
Vendeuvre-sur-Barse
Estissac
Villemaur-sur-Vanne
Villeneuve-l'Archevêque
Aix-en-Othe
Vauchassis
Bouilly
Fouchères
Bar-sur-Seine
Eguilly-sous-Bois
St. Mards-en-Othe
Cerisiers
Arces-Dilo
Dixmont
Forêt d'Othe
Chailley
Auxon
Villeneuve-sur-Yonne
Ferrières
Châlette-sur-Loing
Montargis
Courtenay
St. Julien-du-Sault
Joigny
Brienon-sur-Armançon
Migennes
Neuvy-Sautour
Ervy-le-Châtel
Chessy-lès-Pres
St. Florentin
Chaource
Landreville
Essoyes
Gyé-sur-Seine
Mussy-sur-Seine
Les Riceys
Flogny-la-Chapelle
Armançon
Douchy
Châteaurenard
Sépeaux
Bassou
Pontigny
Seignelay
Ligny-le-Châtel
Channes
Charny
Appoigny
Villon
Tonnerre
Châtillon-sur-Seine
ARBORETUM NATIONAL
Aillant-sur-Tholon
Fleury
Monéteau
St. Martin-sur-Ouanne
Châtillon-Coligny
Villiers-St. Benoit
Champignelles
Auxerre
Chablis
Ancy-le-Franc
CHÂTEAU ANCY-LE-FRANC
Laignes
Lézinnes
Pourrain
Rogny-les-7-Ecluses
Champs-sur-Yonne
St. Bris-le-Vineux
Serein
Lichères-près-Aigremont
Coulmier-le-Sec
Aisey-sur-Seine
La Bussière
Bléneau
Mézilles
Toucy
Collines de la Puisaye
Nuits
Aisy-sur-Armançon
Briare
Coulanges-la-Vineuse
Vermenton
Nitry
Noyers
ABBAYE DE FONTENAY
St. Fargeau
Ouanne
Courson-les-Carrières
Joux-la-Ville
Montbard
Baigneux-les-Juifs
Lavau
St. Sauveur-en-Puisaye
Arcy-sur-Cure
L'Isle-sur-Serein
Cure
Mailly-le-Château
Bonny-sur-Loire
Beaulieu
St. Amand-en-Puisaye
Coulanges-sur-Yonne
Yonne
Châtel-Censoir
Venarey-les-Laumes
CHÂTEAU DE BUSSY-RABUTIN
Bouhy
Epoisses
Léré
Cosne-Cours-sur-Loire
Myennes
Entrains-sur-Nohain
Clamecy
Vézelay
Avallon
Semur-en-Auxois
Cussy-les-Forges
Verrey-sous-Salmaise
BASILIQUE DE VÉZELAY
Dornecy
Nuars
Vitteaux
Sancerre
Donzy
Menou
Tannay
Quarré-les-Tombes
La Roche-en-Brénil
Précy-sous-Thil
Varzy
Saulieu
Pouilly-sur-Loire
Vinon
Châteauneuf
Brinon-sur-Beuvron
Corbigny
Lormes
Dun-les-Places
Pouilly-en-Auxois
Vandenesse-en-Auxois
Cervon
Montsauche-les-Settons
Les Settons
Liernais
Sancergues
La Charité-sur-Loire
Prémery
St. Révérien
Ouroux-en-Morvan
Planchez
Arnay-le-Duc
Baugy
Guérigny
St. Saulge
Aunay-en-Bazois
Chissey-en-Morvan
Lucenay-l'Evêque
Morvan
Pougues-les-Eaux
Bona
Château-Chinon
Lacanche
Bligny-sur-Ouche
Mornay-Berry
Fourchambault
CATHÉDRALE ST. CYR
Châtillon-en-Bazois
Ivry-en-Montagne
Nérondes
Nevers
St. Benin-d'Azy
Rouy
Moulins-Engilbert
Aron
La Celle-en-Moravan
Épinac
La Guerche-sur-l'Aubois
Imphy
Anlezy
Autun
Auxy
Nolay
Blet
Magny-Cours
La Machine
Vandenesse
St. Honoré-les-Bains
St. Léger-sous-Beuvray
St. Emiland
Allier
St. Léger-des-Vignes
Cercy-la-Tour
Couches
Sancoins
Les Brunettes
Etang-sur-Arroux
Mesvres
Marmagne
St. Léger-sur-Dheune
Decize
St. Pierre-le-Moûtier
St. Germain-Chassenay
Charrin
Fours
Luzy
Montcenis
Le Creusot
La Nocle-Maulaix
Charbonnat
Bessais-le-Fromental
Lurcy-Lévis
Chantenay-St. Imbert
Cossaye
Gannay-sur-Loire
Cronat
Montchanin
Dornes
Issy-l'Evêque
Toulon-sur-Arroux
Blanzy
Buxy
Limoise
Canal latéral à la Loire
Loire
Couleuvre
Couzon
Villeneuve-sur-Allier
Lucenay-les-Aix
Maltat
Montceau-les-Mines
Cérilly
Garnat-sur-Engièvre
Chevagnes
Bourbon-Lancy
Perrecy-les-Forges
St. Vallier
St. Gengoux-le-National
Mont-St. Vincent
Bourbon-l'Archambault
Montilly
Moulins
Beaulon
Chalmoux
Gueugnon
Ciry-le-Noble
Genelard
Ygrande
Yzeure
Souvigny
Montbeugny
Gilley-sur-Loire
Diou
St. Agnan
Salornay-sur-Guye
Hérisson
St. Hilaire
L'EGLISE DE L'ABBAYE DE ST. PIERRE ET ST. PAUL
Toulon-sur-Allier
LE PAL
Dompierre-sur-Besbre
Digoin
Paray-le-Monial
SACRE-COEUR
Cosne-d'Allier
Buxières-les-Mines
Neuilly-le-Réal
Coulanges
Molinet
St. Bonnet-de-Joux
Villefranche-d'Allier
Tronget
Vaumas
Saligney-sur-Roudon
Cluny
Le Montet
Châtel-de-Neuvre
St. Gérand-de-Vaux
Charolles
St. Yan
Beaubery
Poisson
St. Loup
Varennes-
Trézelles
Voussac
0 10 20 30 km
103
90
91
116
117
119
169
219
319

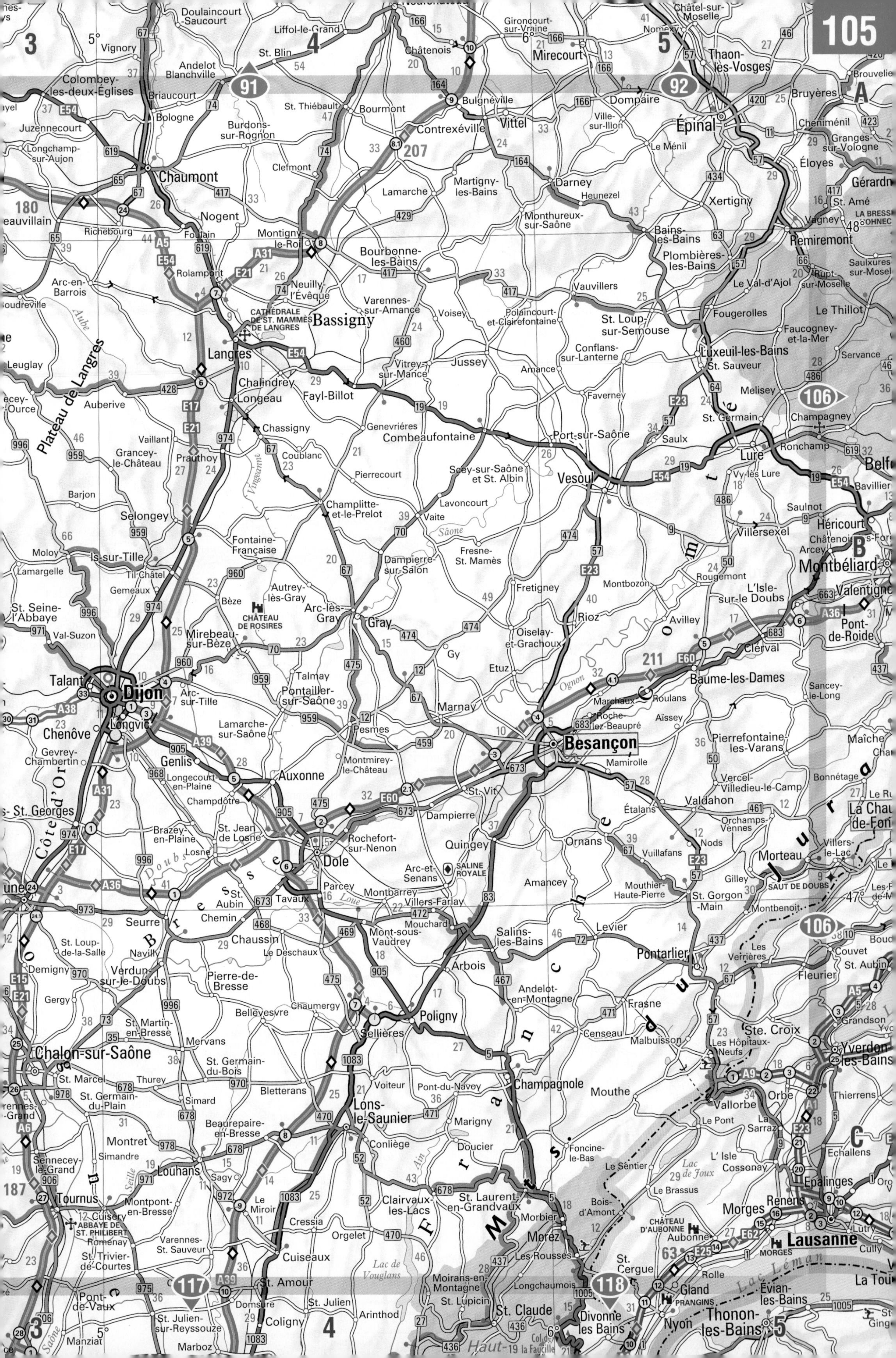
105
Doulaincourt-Saucourt
Liffol-le-Grand
Vignory
Andelot Blanchville
St. Blin
Colombey-les-deux-Églises
Briaucourt
Bologne
Juzennecourt
Longchamp-sur-Aujon
Chaumont
Nogent
Richebourg
Foulain
Rolampont
Arc-en-Barrois
Aube
Langres
Plateau de Langres
Leuglay
Auberive
Chalindrey
Longeau
Vaillant
Grancey-le-Château
Prauthoy
Barjon
Selongey
Moloy
Is-sur-Tille
Lamargelle
Til-Châtel
Gemeaux
St. Seine-l'Abbaye
Val-Suzon
Talant
Dijon
Chenôve
Longvic
Gevrey-Chambertin
Côte d'Or
St. Georges
Genlis
Longecourt-en-Plaine
Champdôtre
Brazey-en-Plaine
St. Jean de Losne
Losne
Seurre
St. Loup-de-la-Salle
Navilly
Verdun-sur-le-Doubs
Demigny
Gergy
Chalon-sur-Saône
St. Marcel
St. Germain-du-Plain
Sennecey-le-Grand
Tournus
Cuisery
ABBAYE DE ST. PHILIBERT
Romenay
St. Trivier-de-Courtes
Pont-de-Vaux
Manziat
Montret
Simandre
Louhans
Sagy
Montpont-en-Bresse
Varennes-St. Sauveur
St. Julien-sur-Reyssouze
Marboz
Domsure
Coligny
St. Amour
St. Julien
Arinthod
Cuiseaux
Cressia
Orgelet
Lac de Vouglans
Moirans-en-Montagne
St. Lupicin
St. Claude
Longchaumois
Les Rousses
Morez
Morbier
St. Laurent-en-Grandvaux
Clairvaux-les-Lacs
Le Miroir
Beaurepaire-en-Bresse
Simard
Thurey
St. Germain-du-Bois
Mervans
St. Martin-en-Bresse
Bellevesvre
Pierre-de-Bresse
Chaussin
Le Deschaux
Chaumergy
Sellières
Poligny
Arbois
Voiteur
Lons-le-Saunier
Conliège
Pont-du-Navoy
Marigny
Doucier
Champagnole
Salins-les-Bains
Mont-sous-Vaudrey
Mouchard
Villers-Farlay
Montbarrey
Parcey
Tavaux
Chemin
St. Aubin
Dole
Rochefort-sur-Nenon
Arc-et-Senans
SALINE ROYALE
Quingey
Dampierre
St. Vit
Auxonne
Montmirey-le-Château
Pesmes
Lamarche-sur-Saône
Pontailler-sur-Saône
Talmay
Mirebeau-sur-Bèze
Arc-sur-Tille
Bèze
CHÂTEAU DE ROSIRES
Autrey-lès-Gray
Fontaine-Française
Arc-lès-Gray
Gray
Gy
Marnay
Etuz
Besançon
Mamirolle
Roche-lez-Beaupré
Marchaux
Oiselay-et-Grachaux
Rioz
Fretigney
Fresne-St. Mamès
Dampierre-sur-Salon
Champlitte-et-le-Prelot
Vaite
Lavoncourt
Scey-sur-Saône et St. Albin
Pierrecourt
Coublanc
Chassigny
Genevriéres
Combeaufontaine
Fayl-Billot
Vitrey-sur-Mance
Jussey
Bassigny
CATHÉDRALE DE ST. MAMMÈS DE LANGRES
Neuilly-l'Évêque
Montigny-le-Roi
Bourbonne-les-Bains
Varennes-sur-Amance
Voisey
Lamarche
Clefmont
Burdons-sur-Rognon
St. Thiébault
Bourmont
Contrexéville
Vittel
Bulgnéville
Châtenois
Gironcourt-sur-Vraine
Mirecourt
Dompaire
Ville-sur-Illon
Châtel-sur-Moselle
Nomexy
Thaon-les-Vosges
Épinal
Le Ménil
Darney
Heunezel
Martigny-les-Bains
Monthureux-sur-Saône
Xertigny
Bains-les-Bains
Plombières-les-Bains
Le Val-d'Ajol
Fougerolles
Vauvillers
Polaincourt-et-Clairefontaine
St. Loup-sur-Semouse
Conflans-sur-Lanterne
Amance
Faverney
Port-sur-Saône
Vesoul
Saône
Luxeuil-les-Bains
St. Sauveur
Saulx
St. Germain
Melisey
Lure
Vy-lès Lure
Villersexel
Saulnot
Héricourt
Montbéliard
Champagney
Ronchamp
Belfort
Remiremont
Éloyes
Bruyères
Cheniménil
Granges-sur-Vologne
Brouvelieures
Gérardmer
St. Amé
Vagney
Rupt-sur-Moselle
Saulxures-sur-Moselotte
Le Thillot
Faucogney-et-la-Mer
Servance
Montbozon
Rougemont
L'Isle-sur-le Doubs
Avilley
Clerval
Baume-les-Dames
Roulans
Aïssey
Ognon
Pierrefontaine-les-Varans
Vercel-Villedieu-le-Camp
Valdahon
Étalans
Orchamps-Vennes
Nods
Ornans
Vuillafans
Amancey
Mouthier-Haute-Pierre
St. Gorgon-Main
Levier
Pontarlier
Andelot-en-Montagne
Frasne
Censeau
Malbuisson
Mouthe
Foncine-le-Bas
Le Sentier
Lac de Joux
Le Brassus
Bois-d'Amont
Vallorbe
Le Pont
La Sarraz
L'Isle
Cossonay
Orbe
Yverdon-les-Bains
Grandson
Ste. Croix
Les Hôpitaux-Neufs
Les Verrières
Fleurier
Couvet
Morteau
SAUT DE DOUBS
Montbenoit
Gilley
Villers-le-Lac
Maîche
Bonnétage
La Chaux-de-Fonds
Le Russey
Sancey-le-Long
Pont-de-Roide
Valentigney
Échallens
Épalinges
Renens
Morges
Lausanne
Lutry
Cully
CHÂTEAU D'AUBONNE
Aubonne
St. Cergue
Rolle
Gland
PRANGINS
Nyon
Divonne les Bains
Lac Léman
Évian-les-Bains
Thonon-les-Bains
Col de la Faucille
Haut-Jura
Jura
Montagnes du Jura
Franche-Comté
Bresse
Doubs
Loue
Ain
Seille
Vingeanne
A5
A31
A38
A39
A36
A6
A9
A1
E17
E21
E15
E54
E60
E62
E23
E25
91
92
106
117
118
180
187
207
211
3
4
5
A
B
C

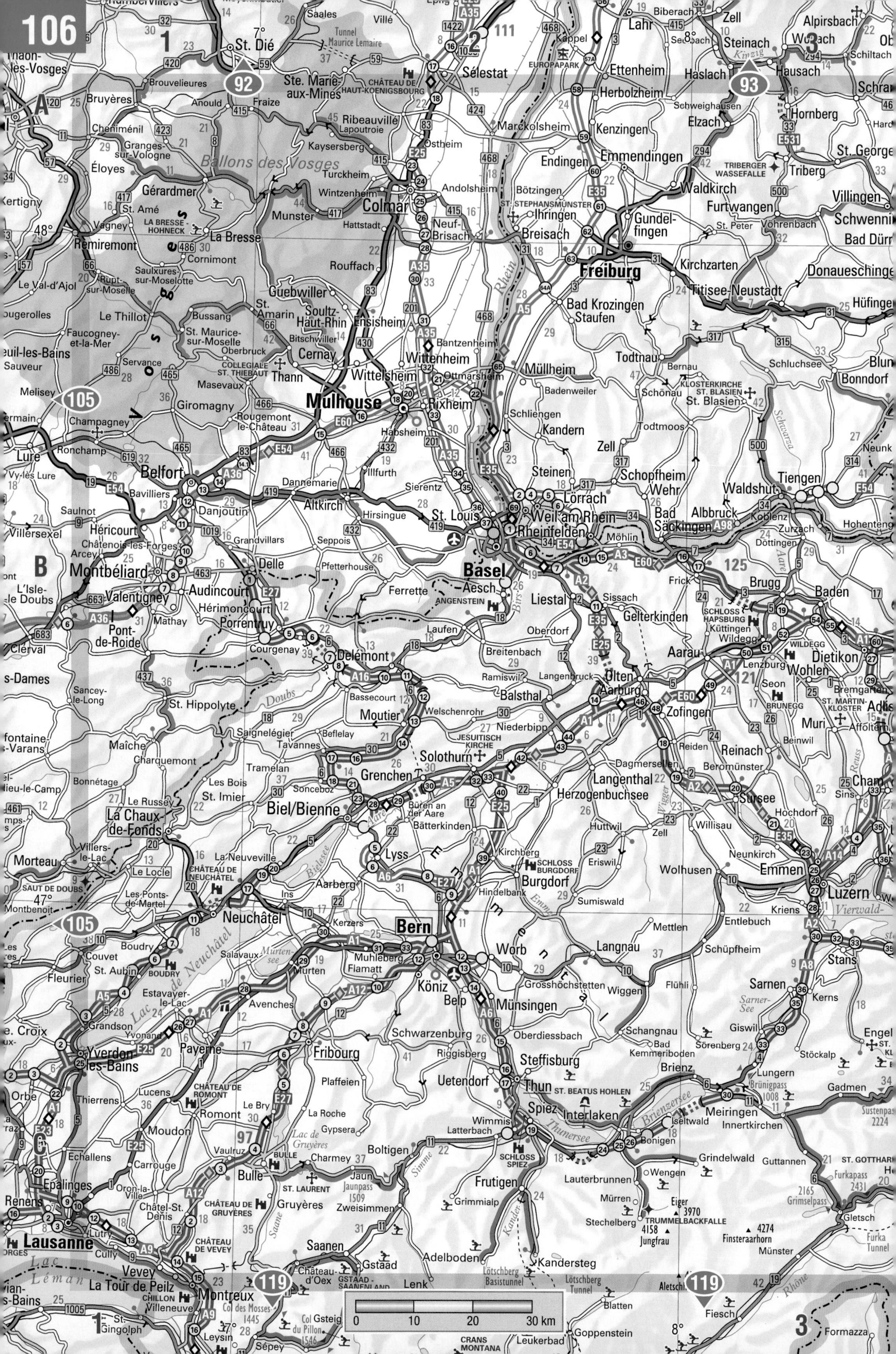
St. Dié
Sélestat
Lahr
Biberach
Zell
Alpirsbach
Steinach
Haslach
Hausach
Schiltach
Ste. Marie-aux-Mines
Château de Haut-Koenigsbourg
Europapark
Ettenheim
Herbolzheim
Kenzingen
Elzach
Hornberg
Bruyères
Fraize
Ribeauvillé
Lapoutroie
Kaysersberg
Marckolsheim
Emmendingen
Endingen
Waldkirch
Triberg
Triberger Wasserfälle
St. Georgen
Ballons des Vosges
Gérardmer
Munster
Turckheim
Colmar
Andolsheim
Bötzingen
Furtwangen
Villingen
Schwenningen
La Bresse
Remiremont
Cornimont
Neuf-Brisach
Breisach
Ihringen
Gundelfingen
St. Peter
Vöhrenbach
Bad Dürrheim
Rouffach
Freiburg
Kirchzarten
Titisee-Neustadt
Donaueschingen
Guebwiller
Soultz-Haut-Rhin
Ensisheim
Bad Krozingen
Staufen
Hüfingen
Le Thillot
Bussang
St. Maurice-sur-Moselle
Cernay
Wittenheim
Todtnau
Schluchsee
Bonndorf
Thann
Wittelsheim
Müllheim
Badenweiler
Schönau
St. Blasien
Giromagny
Mulhouse
Rixheim
Schliengen
Kandern
Todtmoos
Lure
Ronchamp
Belfort
Habsheim
Illfurth
Zell
Steinen
Schopfheim
Wehr
Waldshut
Tiengen
Altkirch
Dannemarie
Sierentz
Lörrach
St. Louis
Weil am Rhein
Rheinfelden
Bad Säckingen
Albbruck
Montbéliard
Héricourt
Delle
Basel
Aesch
Möhlin
Zurzach
Döttingen
Audincourt
Valentigney
Porrentruy
Ferrette
Liestal
Sissach
Frick
Brugg
Baden
Pont-de-Roide
Courgenay
Delémont
Laufen
Breitenbach
Oberdorf
Gelterkinden
Aarau
Lenzburg
Wohlen
Dietikon
Moutier
Balsthal
Olten
Aarburg
Zofingen
St. Hippolyte
Saignelégier
Tavannes
Solothurn
Niederbipp
Reinach
Muri
Grenchen
Langenthal
Herzogenbuchsee
Beromünster
Sursee
Biel/Bienne
St. Imier
La Chaux-de-Fonds
Le Locle
Morteau
Büren an der Aare
Lyss
Huttwil
Willisau
Hochdorf
Burgdorf
Kirchberg
Emmen
Luzern
Neuchâtel
Aarberg
Hindelbank
Sumiswald
Wolhusen
Kriens
Bern
Worb
Langnau
Entlebuch
Schüpfheim
Murten
Köniz
Belp
Münsingen
Stans
Sarnen
Yverdon-les-Bains
Grandson
Payerne
Fribourg
Schwarzenburg
Oberdiessbach
Steffisburg
Thun
Interlaken
Brienz
Meiringen
Innertkirchen
Romont
Le Bry
Spiez
Iseltwald
Bönigen
Moudon
Bulle
Charmey
Jaun
Boltigen
Zweisimmen
Frutigen
Lauterbrunnen
Wengen
Grindelwald
Mürren
Eiger 3970
Jungfrau 4158
Finsteraarhorn 4274
Lausanne
Vevey
Montreux
Villeneuve
Saanen
Gstaad
Adelboden
Kandersteg
Lötschberg Basistunnel
Leukerbad
Fiesch
Gletsch
Münster
Formazza
0 10 20 30 km

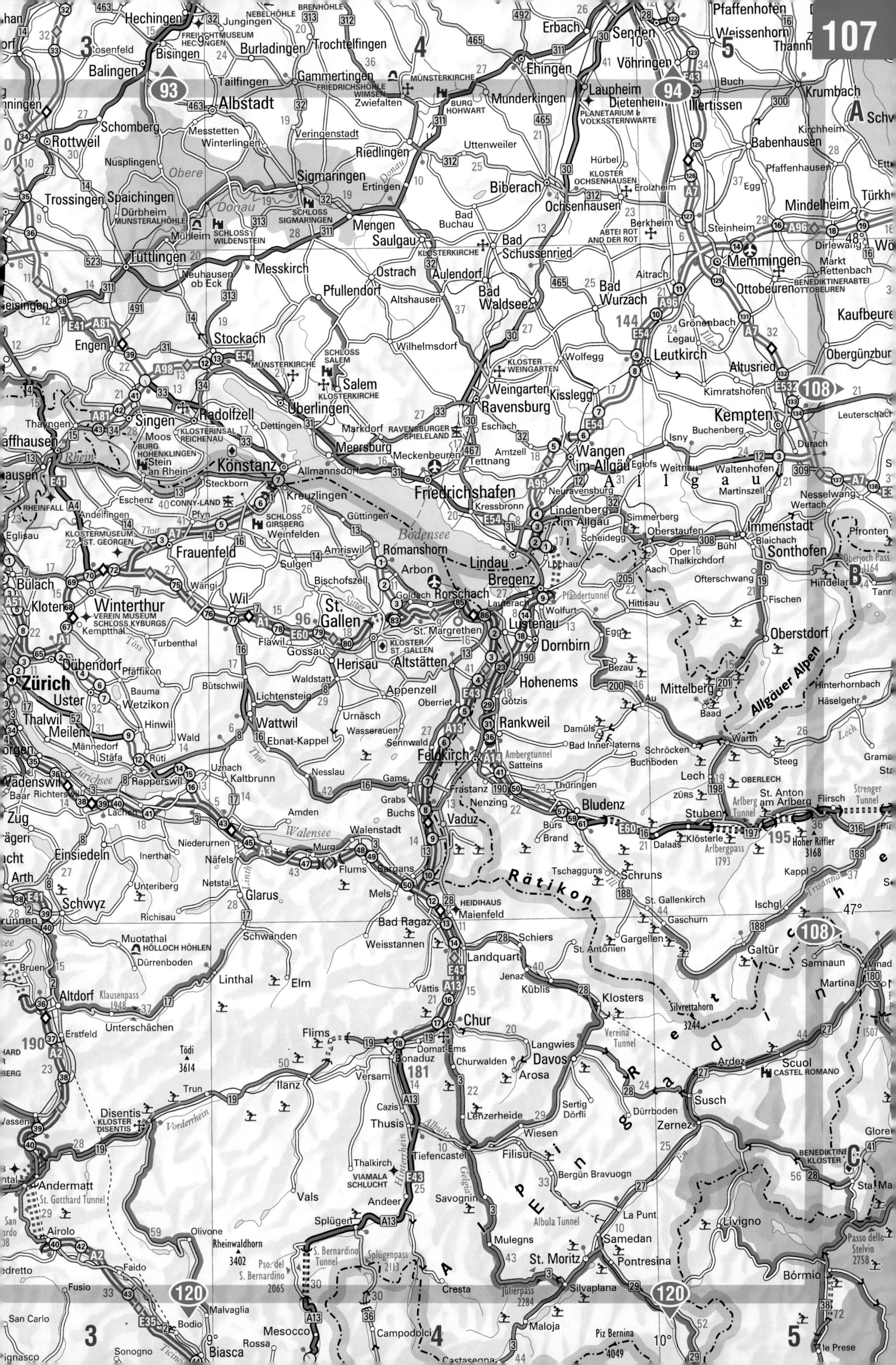
Hechingen
Bisingen
Balingen
Albstadt
Burladingen
Trochtelfingen
Gammertingen
Zwiefalten
Ehingen
Erbach
Senden
Pfaffenhofen
Weissenhorn
Vöhringen
Laupheim
Dietenheim
Illertissen
Krumbach
Munderkingen
Rottweil
Schomberg
Veringenstadt
Riedlingen
Babenhausen
Sigmaringen
Biberach
Ochsenhausen
Trossingen
Spaichingen
Mengen
Saulgau
Bad Schussenried
Memmingen
Mindelheim
Tuttlingen
Messkirch
Ostrach
Aulendorf
Pfullendorf
Bad Waldsee
Bad Wurzach
Ottobeuren
Kaufbeuren
Engen
Stockach
Salem
Leutkirch
Obergünzburg
Singen
Radolfzell
Überlingen
Weingarten
Ravensburg
Kisslegg
Kempten
Meersburg
Markdorf
Wangen im Allgäu
Konstanz
Kreuzlingen
Friedrichshafen
Tettnang
Lindenberg
Immenstadt
Sonthofen
Frauenfeld
Winterthur
Bodensee
Romanshorn
Lindau
Bregenz
Rorschach
St. Gallen
Wil
Herisau
Dornbirn
Oberstdorf
Zürich
Dübendorf
Uster
Appenzell
Altstätten
Hohenems
Mittelberg
Thalwil
Wattwil
Rankweil
Allgäuer Alpen
Meilen
Feldkirch
Rapperswil
Wädenswil
Lech
Zug
Vaduz
Bludenz
St. Anton am Arlberg
Einsiedeln
Walensee
Glarus
Schruns
Schwyz
Bad Ragaz
Rätikon
Landquart
Altdorf
Klosters
Chur
Davos
Arosa
Flims
Ilanz
Scuol
Disentis
Thusis
Zernez
Andermatt
St. Gotthard Tunnel
Airolo
Splügen
Samedan
St. Moritz
Pontresina
Livigno
Bórmio
Biasca
Mesocco
Maloja
Piz Bernina 4049
Alpen
Rhein
Donau
Lustenau
Gossau
Flawil
Kloten
Bülach
Silvaplana
Campodolcino

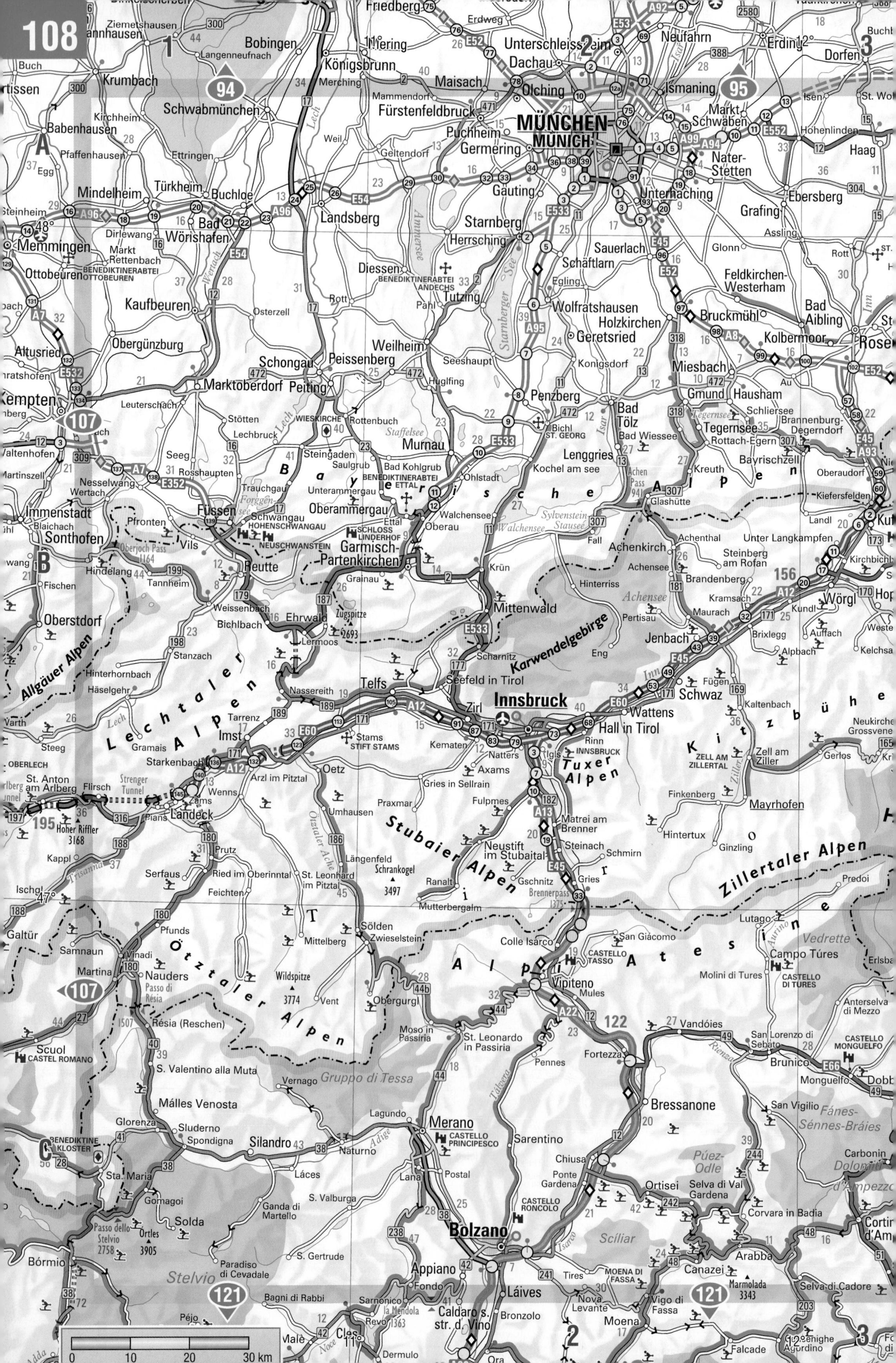
Friedberg
Ziemetshausen
Bobingen
Königsbrunn
Mering
Erdweg
Unterschleissheim
Dachau
Neufahrn
Erding
Dorfen
Krumbach
Langenneufnach
94
Maisach
Olching
Ismaning
95
Schwabmünchen
Fürstenfeldbruck
MÜNCHEN
MUNICH
Markt Schwaben
Babenhausen
Kirchheim
Puchheim
Germering
Hohenlinden
Haag
Pfaffenhausen
Ettringen
Geltendorf
Nater-Stetten
Mindelheim
Türkheim
Buchloe
Landsberg
Gauting
Unterhaching
Ebersberg
Grafing
Memmingen
Bad Wörishofen
Starnberg
Herrsching
Sauerlach
Ottobeuren
BENEDIKTINERABTEI OTTOBEUREN
Markt Rettenbach
Dirlewang
Ammersee
Diessen
BENEDIKTINERABTEI ANDECHS
Schäftlarn
Glonn
Feldkirchen-Westerham
Kaufbeuren
Tutzing
Wolfratshausen
Holzkirchen
Bruckmühl
Bad Aibling
Starnberger See
Geretsried
Kolbermoor
Rosenheim
Obergünzburg
Altusried
Weilheim
Schongau
Peissenberg
Seeshaupt
Miesbach
Kempten
Marktoberdorf
Peiting
Penzberg
Gmund
Hausham
107
Bad Tölz
Tegernsee
Schliersee
Brannenburg-Degerndorf
WIESKIRCHE
Rottenbuch
Staffelsee
Murnau
Bichl
ST. GEORG
Bad Wiessee
Rottach-Egern
Lechbruck
Steingaden
Bad Kohlgrub
Lenggries
Bayrischzell
Nesselwang
Rosshaupten
BENEDIKTINERABTEI ETTAL
Ohlstadt
Kochel am see
Kreuth
Oberaudorf
Immenstadt
Oberammergau
Bayerische Alpen
Achen Pass
Kiefersfelden
Sonthofen
Füssen
Schwangau
HOHENSCHWANGAU
Walchensee
Sylvenstein Stausee
Glashütte
Pfronten
NEUSCHWANSTEIN
SCHLOSS LINDERHOF
Oberau
Fall
Landl
Kufstein
Oberjoch Pass 1164
Vils
Garmisch-Partenkirchen
Achenkirch
Hindelang
Reutte
Tannheim
Grainau
Krün
Steinberg am Rofan
Achensee
Brandenberg
Fischen
Hinterriss
Wörgl
Kundl
Weissenbach
Ehrwald
Zugspitze 2693
Mittenwald
Pertisau
Maurach
Oberstdorf
Bichlbach
Lermoos
Jenbach
Brixlegg
Auffach
Alpbach
Allgäuer Alpen
Stanzach
Karwendelgebirge
Eng
Scharnitz
Hinterhornbach
Seefeld in Tirol
Fügen
Häselgehr
Nassereith
Telfs
Zirl
Innsbruck
Schwaz
Kaltenbach
Kitzbüheler Alpen
Wattens
Hall in Tirol
Lechtaler Alpen
Tarrenz
Imst
Stams
STIFT STAMS
Kematen
Rinn
INNSBRUCK
Steeg
Gramais
Tuxer Alpen
ZELL AM ZILLERTAL
Zell am Ziller
Gerlos
OBERLECH
Starkenbach
Axams
Natters
Igls
St. Anton am Arlberg
Flirsch
Strenger Tunnel
Arzl im Pitztal
Oetz
Gries in Sellrain
Zams
Wenns
Landeck
Fulpmes
Finkenberg
Mayrhofen
Praxmar
Umhausen
Hoher Riffler 3168
Stubaier Alpen
Matrei am Brenner
Hintertux
Steinach
Schmirn
Ginzling
Kappl
Prutz
Neustift im Stubaital
Serfaus
Ried im Oberinntal
Längenfeld
Schrankogel 3497
St. Leonhard im Pitztal
Gschnitz
Gries
Zillertaler Alpen
Predoi
Ischgl
Feichten
Ranalt
Brennerpass 1375
Mutterbergalm
Pfunds
Sölden
Zwieselstein
Mittelberg
Colle Isarco
San Giacomo
Lutago
Vedrette
Galtür
Samnaun
Campo Túres
CASTELLO TASSO
Alpi Atesine
Martina
Vinadi
Nauders
Passo di Résia
Ötztaler Alpen
Wildspitze 3774
Vent
Vipiteno
Mules
Molini di Tures
CASTELLO DI TURES
Obergurgl
Anterselva di Mezzo
Résia (Reschen)
Moso in Passíria
St. Leonardo in Passiria
Vandóies
San Lorenzo di Sebato
CASTELLO MONGUELFO
Scuol
CASTEL ROMANO
Fortezza
Brunico
Pennes
S. Valentino alla Muta
Gruppo di Tessa
Vernago
Monguelfo
Dobbiaco
Málles Venosta
Bressanone
San Vigilio
Fánes-Sénnes-Bráies
Lagundo
Merano
Glorenza
Sluderno
Spondigna
Silandro
Naturno
CASTELLO PRINCIPESCO
Sarentino
BENEDIKTINE KLOSTER
Chiusa
Carbonin
Láces
Púez-Odle
Postal
Lana
Ponte Gardena
Ortisei
Selva di Val Gardena
Dolomiti d'Ampezzo
Sta. Maria
Gomagoi
S. Valburga
CASTELLO RONCOLO
Corvara in Badia
Solda
Ganda di Martello
Cortina d'Ampezzo
Passo dello Stelvio 2758
Ortles 3905
Bolzano
Sciliar
Arabba
Bórmio
S. Gertrude
Paradiso di Cevadale
Appiano
Canazei
Marmolada 3343
Stelvio
121
Fondo
MOENA DI FASSA
Tires
Nova Levante
Vigo di Fassa
Selva di Cadore
Bagni di Rabbi
Sarnonico
Láives
la Mendola 1363
Caldaro s. str. d. Vino
Bronzolo
Moena
Péjo
Revò
Malè
Cles
Dermulo
Ora
Falcade
Cencenighe Agordino
0 10 20 30 km

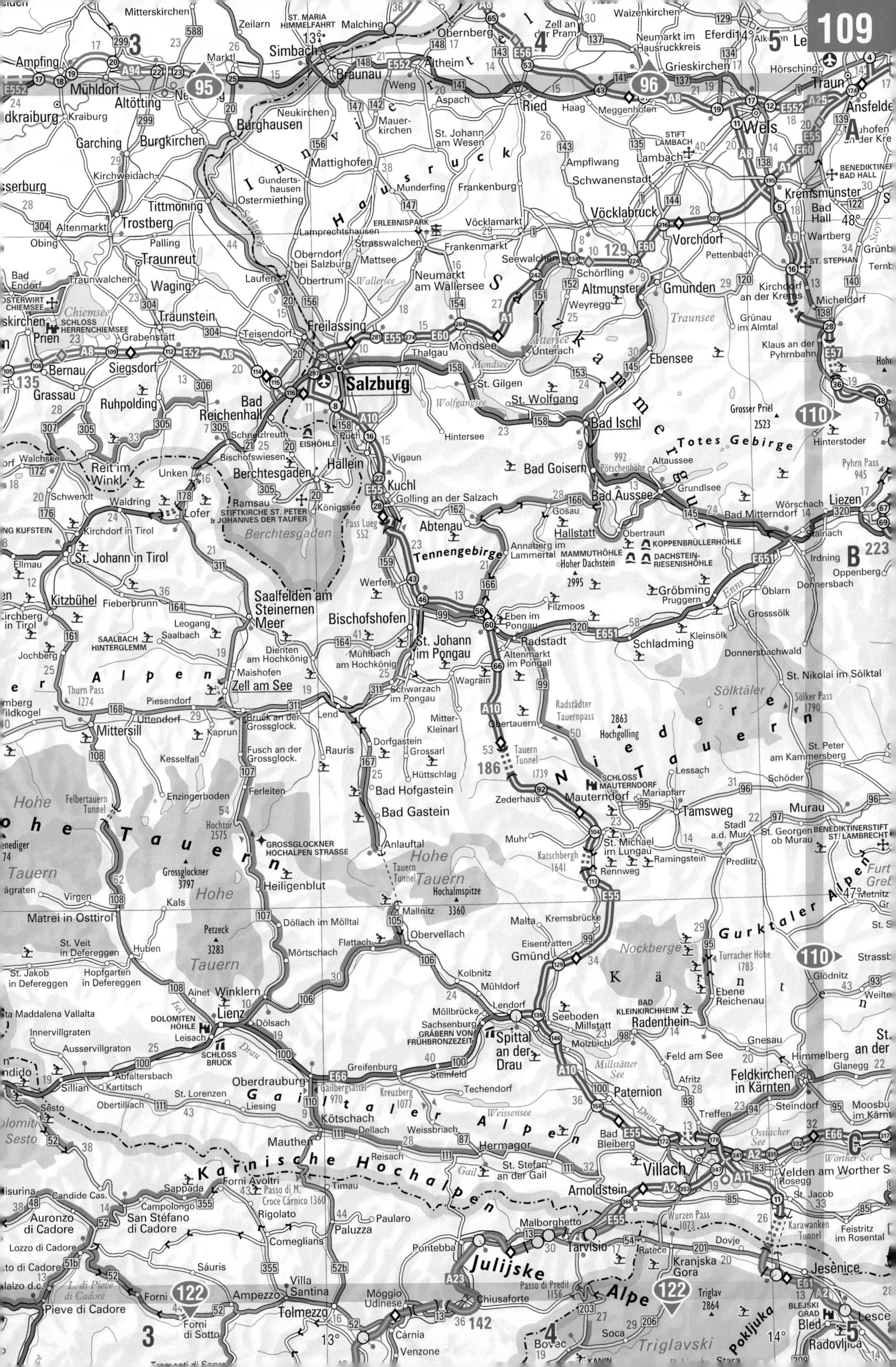
Mitterskirchen
Zeilarn
ST. MARIA HIMMELFAHRT
Malching
Obernberg
Zell an der Pram
Waizenkirchen
Neumarkt im Hausruckkreis
Eferding
Ampfing
Simbach
Braunau
Altheim
Grieskirchen
Hörsching
Traun
Mühldorf
Altötting
Weng
Aspach
Ried
Haag
Meggenhofen
Ansfelden
Kraiburg
Burghausen
Neukirchen
Mauerkirchen
St. Johann am Wesen
Wels
Garching
Burgkirchen
STIFT LAMBACH
Lambach
Mattighofen
Ampflwang
Schwanenstadt
Kirchweidach
Gundertshausen
Ostermiething
Munderfing
Frankenburg
Kremsmünster
BENEDIKTINERSTIFT KREMSMÜNSTER
BAD HALL
Bad Hall
Tittmoning
Trostberg
Altenmarkt
Obing
Palling
ERLEBNISPARK
Lamprechtshausen
Vöcklamarkt
Vöcklabruck
Vorchdorf
Wartberg
Strasswalchen
Frankenmarkt
Traunreut
Oberndorf bei Salzburg
Mattsee
Seewalchen
Schörfling
Pettenbach
Grünburg
ST. STEPHAN
Bad Endorf
Traunwalchen
Waging
Laufen
Obertrum
Wallersee
Neumarkt am Wallersee
Altmunster
Gmunden
Kirchdorf an der Krems
Micheldorf
OSTERWIRT CHIEMSEE
Chiemsee
SCHLOSS HERRENCHIEMSEE
Traunstein
Weyregg
Traunsee
Grünau im Almtal
Prien
Grabenstätt
Teisendorf
Freilassing
Attersee
Unterach
Klaus an der Pyhrnbahn
Thalgau
Mondsee
Bernau
Siegsdorf
Salzburg
Ebensee
St. Gilgen
Grassau
Ruhpolding
Bad Reichenhall
Wolfgangsee
St. Wolfgang
Grosser Priel
Hintersee
Bad Ischl
Totes Gebirge
Hinterstoder
Schneizlreuth
EISHÖHLE
Puch
Walchsee
Reit im Winkl
Unken
Bischofswiesen
Berchtesgaden
Hallein
Vigaun
Bad Goisern
Pötschenhöhe
Altaussee
Pyhrn Pass
Kuchl
Grundlsee
Schwendt
Waldring
Lofer
Ramsau
STIFTKIRCHE ST. PETER & JOHANNES DER TÄUFER
Königssee
Golling an der Salzach
Bad Aussee
Wörschach
Liezen
Kirchdorf in Tirol
Pass Lueg
Abtenau
Gosau
Hallstatt
Obertraun
KOPPENBRÜLLERHÖHLE
Bad Mitterndorf
Stainach
Tennengebirge
Annaberg im Lammertal
MAMMUTHÖHLE
DACHSTEIN-RIESENISHÖHLE
Hoher Dachstein
St. Johann in Tirol
Ellmau
Irdning
Oppenberg
Werfen
Gröbming
Pruggern
Öblarn
Donnersbach
Kitzbühel
Fieberbrunn
Saalfelden am Steinernen Meer
Filzmoos
Enns
Kirchberg in Tirol
Leogang
Saalbach
Bischofshofen
Eben im Pongau
Grosssölk
SAALBACH HINTERGLEMM
Jochberg
Dienten am Hochkönig
Mühlbach am Hochkönig
St. Johann im Pongau
Radstadt
Schladming
Kleinsölk
Donnersbachwald
Maishofen
Altenmarkt im Pongau
St. Nikolai im Sölktal
Alpen
Thurn Pass
Zell am See
Schwarzach im Pongau
Wagrain
Sölktäler
Sölker Pass
Piesendorf
Uttendorf
Bruck an der Grossglock.
Lend
Radstädter Tauernpass
Mittersill
Kaprun
Dorfgastein
Mitter-Kleinarl
Obertauern
Hochgolling
St. Peter am Kammersberg
Kesselfall
Fusch an der Grossglock.
Rauris
Grossarl
Tauern Tunnel
Niedere Tauern
SCHLOSS MAUTERNDORF
Lessach
Hüttschlag
Schöder
Hohe Tauern
Enzingerboden
Ferleiten
Bad Hofgastein
Zederhaus
Mauterndorf
Mariapfarr
Felbertauern Tunnel
Bad Gastein
Tamsweg
Murau
Hochtor
GROSSGLOCKNER HOCHALPEN STRASSE
Anlauftal
Stadl a.d. Mur
St. Georgen ob Murau
BENEDIKTINERSTIFT ST. LAMBRECHT
Muhr
St. Michael im Lungau
Ramingstein
Grossglockner
Katschberghöhe
Rennweg
Predlitz
Heiligenblut
Hochalmspitze
Virgen
Kals
Mallnitz
Matrei in Osttirol
Malta
Kremsbrücke
Gurktaler Alpen
Döllach im Mölltal
Obervellach
Petzeck
Flattach
Eisentratten
Gmünd
Nockberge
Turracher Höhe
St. Veit in Defereggen
Huben
Mörtschach
Glödnitz
St. Jakob in Defereggen
Hopfgarten in Defereggen
Kolbnitz
Mühldorf
Ebene Reichenau
Winklern
Ainet
Kärnten
Sta Maddalena Vallalta
DOLOMITEN HÖHLE
Lienz
Dölsach
Möllbrücke
Lendorf
BAD KLEINKIRCHHEIM
Innervillgraten
Leisach
Sachsenburg
GRÄBERN VON FRÜHBRONZEZEIT
Seeboden
Millstatt
Radenthein
Ausservillgraton
SCHLOSS BRUCK
Spittal an der Drau
Molzbichl
Gnesau
Abfaltersbach
Drau
Greifenburg
Steinfeld
Millstätter See
Feld am See
Himmelberg
Glanegg
Sillian
Kartitsch
Oberdrauburg
Gailbergsattel
Techendorf
Afritz
Feldkirchen in Kärnten
St. Lorenzen
Kreuzberg
Paternion
Obertilliach
Liesing
Gailtaler Alpen
Weissensee
Treffen
Steindorf
Moosburg
Sesto
Kötschach
Dellach
Weissbriach
Bad Bleiberg
Ossiacher See
Mauthen
Hermagor
Reisach
Villach
Wörther See
Velden am Worther See
Karnische Hochalpen
St. Stefan an der Gail
Rosegg
Sappada
Forni Avoltri
Passo di M. Croce Cárnico
Timau
Arnoldstein
St. Jacob
Candide
Campolongo
Rigolato
Auronzo di Cadore
San Stéfano di Cadore
Paularo
Malborghetto
Wurzen Pass
Karawanken Tunnel
Feistritz im Rosental
Lozzo di Cadore
Paluzza
Comeglians
Tarvisio
Ratece
Dovje
Pontebba
Sáuris
Kranjska Gora
Jesenice
Julijske Alpe
L. di Pieve di Cadore
Forni
Villa Santina
Passo di Predil
Triglav
BLEJSKI GRAD
Pieve di Cadore
Ampezzo
Tolmezzo
Móggio Udinese
Chiusaforte
Pokljuka
Bled
Forni di Sotto
Cárnia
Soca
Triglavski
Lesce
Radovljica
Venzone
Bovec

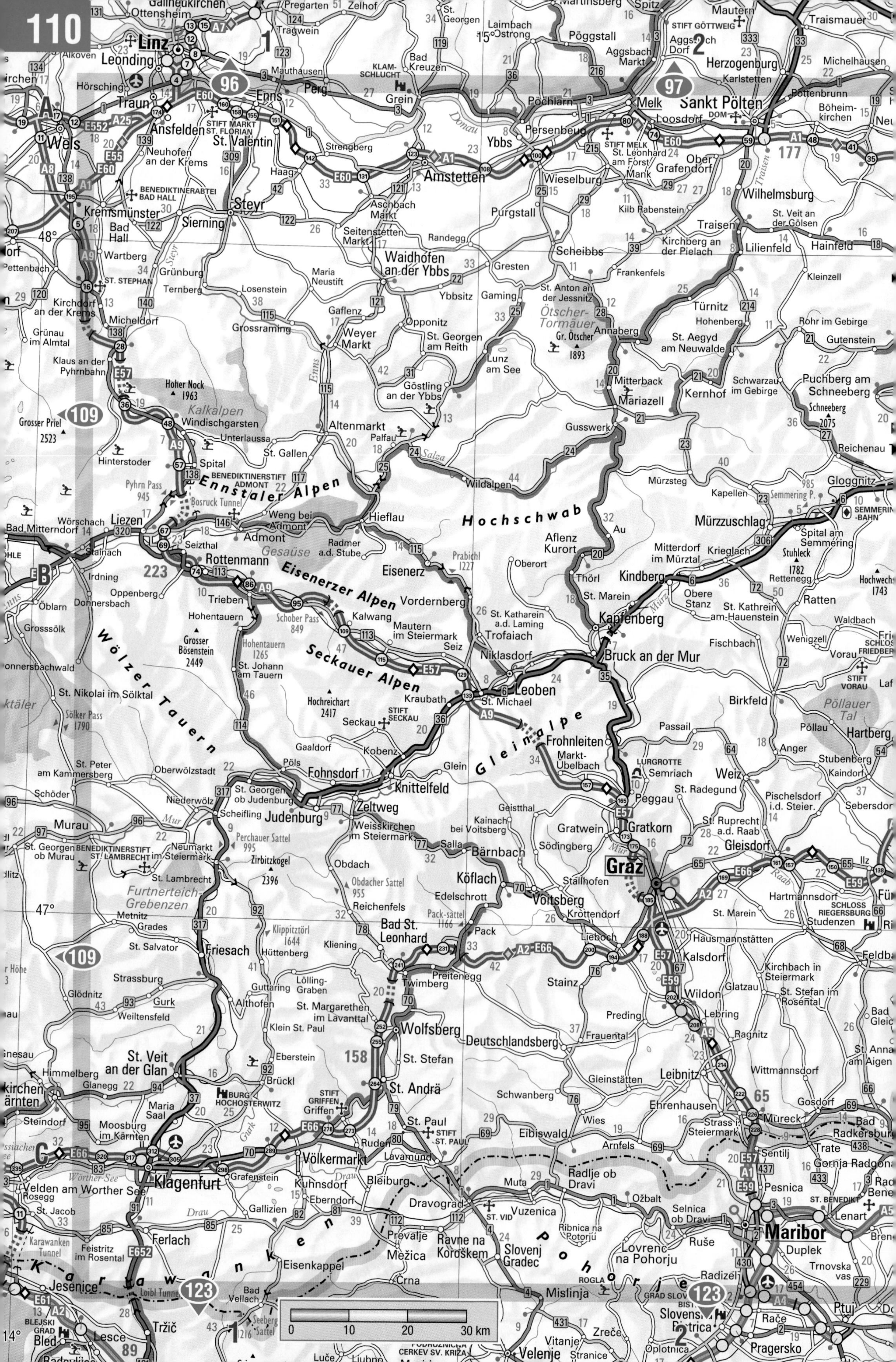
Linz
Leonding
Ottensheim
Pregarten
Zelhof
Tragwein
Mauthausen
Hörsching
Traun
Ansfelden
Enns
Perg
Grein
KLAM-SCHLUCHT
Bad Kreuzen
St. Georgen
Laimbach
Ostrong
Pöggstall
Martinsberg
Spitz
Mautern
STIFT GÖTTWEIG
Traismauer
Aggsbach Dorf
Aggsbach Markt
Herzogenburg
Karlstetten
Michelhausen
Melk
Sankt Pölten
Loosdorf
Pöchlarn
Persenbeug
Ybbs
Donau
Böheimkirchen
Pottenbrunn
Wels
Alkoven
STIFT MARKT ST. FLORIAN
St. Valentin
Neuhofen an der Krems
Strengberg
Haag
Amstetten
Wieselburg
STIFT MELK
St. Leonhard am Forst
Mank
Ober-Grafendorf
Kilb
Rabenstein
Wilhelmsburg
Traisen
St. Veit an der Gölsen
Hainfeld
Lilienfeld
Kirchberg an der Pielach
BENEDIKTINERABTEI BAD HALL
Kremsmünster
Bad Hall
Steyr
Sierning
Aschbach Markt
Seitenstetten Markt
Randegg
Purgstall
Scheibbs
Frankenfels
Wartberg
Grünburg
Ternberg
Losenstein
Maria Neustift
Waidhofen an der Ybbs
Ybbsitz
Gaming
Gresten
St. Anton an der Jessnitz
Ötscher-Tormäuer
Gr. Ötscher 1893
Annaberg
Türnitz
Hohenberg
St. Aegyd am Neuwalde
Kleinzell
Rohr im Gebirge
Gutenstein
ST. STEPHAN
Kirchdorf an der Krems
Micheldorf
Grünau im Almtal
Gaflenz
Weyer Markt
Grossraming
Opponitz
St. Georgen am Reith
Lunz am See
Klaus an der Pyhrnbahn
Hoher Nock 1963
Kalkalpen
Windischgarsten
Grosser Priel 2523
Göstling an der Ybbs
Mitterbach
Mariazell
Kernhof
Schwarzau im Gebirge
Puchberg am Schneeberg
Schneeberg 2075
Altenmarkt
Palfau
Gusswerk
Reichenau
Unterlaussa
Spital
Hinterstoder
St. Gallen
Salza
Wildalpen
Mürzsteg
Kapellen
Semmering P.
Gloggnitz
SEMMERING-BAHN
BENEDIKTINERSTIFT ADMONT
Pyhrn Pass 945
Ennstaler Alpen
Bosruck Tunnel
Hochschwab
Mürzzuschlag
Spital am Semmering
Wörschach
Liezen
Bad Mitterndorf
Weng bei Admont
Admont
Hieflau
Gesäuse
Radmer a.d. Stube
Aflenz Kurort
Mitterdorf im Mürztal
Krieglach
Stuhleck 1782
Rettenegg
Hochwechsel 1743
Stainach
Seizthal
Rottenmann
Irdning
Öblarn
Donnersbach
Oppenberg
Eisenerz
Prabichl 1227
Oberort
Thörl
Kindberg
Obere Stanz
Ratten
Eisenerzer Alpen
Trieben
Vordernberg
St. Marein
Kapfenberg
St. Kathrein am Hauenstein
Waldbach
Grosssölk
Hohentauern
Schober Pass 849
Kalwang
Mautern im Steiermark
St. Katharein a.d. Laming
Trofaiach
Fischbach
Wenigzell
Grosser Bösenstein 2449
Hohentauern 1265
Seiz
Seckauer Alpen
Niklasdorf
Bruck an der Mur
Vorau
STIFT VORAU
Donnersbachwald
St. Johann am Tauern
Leoben
St. Michael
Kraubath
Wölzer Tauern
St. Nikolai im Sölktal
Hochreichart 2417
Seckau
STIFT SECKAU
Birkfeld
Pöllauer Tal
Sölker Pass 1790
Gleinalpe
Frohnleiten
Pöllau
Hartberg
Passail
Gaaldorf
Kobenz
Markt-Übelbach
Anger
Stubenberg
St. Peter am Kammersberg
Oberwölzstadt
Pöls
Fohnsdorf
Glein
LURGROTTE
Semriach
Weiz
Kaindorf
Schöder
St. Georgen ob Judenburg
Niederwölz
Knittelfeld
Peggau
St. Radegund
Pischelsdorf i.d. Steier.
Sebersdorf
Scheifling
Judenburg
Zeltweg
Geistthal
Murau
Weisskirchen im Steiermark
Kainach bei Voitsberg
Gratwein
Gratkorn
St. Ruprecht a.d. Raab
St. Georgen ob Murau
BENEDIKTINERSTIFT ST. LAMBRECHT
Neumarkt im Steiermark
Perchauer Sattel 995
Salla
Bärnbach
Södingberg
Graz
Gleisdorf
Ilz
St. Lambrecht
Zirbitzkogel 2396
Obdach
Köflach
Stallhofen
Hartmannsdorf
Furtnerteich-Grebenzen
Obdacher Sattel 955
Edelschrott
Voitsberg
Krottendorf
St. Marein
SCHLOSS RIEGERSBURG
Studenzen
Metnitz
Grades
Reichenfels
Pack-sattel 1166
Pack
Lieboch
Hausmannstätten
Friesach
Klippitztörl 1644
Bad St. Leonhard
St. Salvator
Hüttenberg
Kliening
Kalsdorf
Feldbach
Strassburg
Lölling-Graben
Twimberg
Preitenegg
Stainz
Kirchbach in Steiermark
Glödnitz
Gurk
Guttaring
Althofen
St. Margarethen im Lavanttal
Wildon
Glatzau
St. Stefan im Rosental
Weitensfeld
Preding
Lebring
Klein St. Paul
Wolfsberg
Deutschlandsberg
Frauental
Ragnitz
Eberstein
St. Stefan
St. Veit an der Glan
Himmelberg
Glanegg
Brückl
St. Andrä
Gleinstätten
Leibnitz
Wittmannsdorf
BURG HOCHOSTERWITZ
Maria Saal
STIFT GRIFFEN
Griffen
Schwanberg
Ehrenhausen
Gosdorf
Steindorf
Moosburg im Kärnten
St. Paul
STIFT ST. PAUL
Eibiswald
Wies
Strass i. Steiermark
Mureck
Bad Radkersburg
Arnfels
Trate
Völkermarkt
Ruden
Lavamünd
Sentilj
Gornja Radgona
Klagenfurt
Grafenstein
Wörther See
Velden am Worther See
Rosegg
Kuhnsdorf
Bleiburg
Drau
Eberndorf
Dravograd
Muta
Radlje ob Dravi
Pesnica
Ožbalt
Selnica ob Dravi
ST. BENEDIKT
Lenart
St. Jacob
Gallizien
ST. VID
Vuzenica
Ribnica na Pohorju
Maribor
Duplek
Karawanken Tunnel
Feistritz im Rosental
Ferlach
Prevalje
Mežica
Ravne na Koroškem
Slovenj Gradec
Pohorje
Lovrenc na Pohorju
Ruše
Trnovska vas
Eisenkappel
Karawanken
Crna
Radizel
Jesenice
Loibl Tunnel
Bad Vellach
Mislinja
ROGLA
GRAD SLOV
Slovenska Bistrica
Ptuj
Rače
Pragersko
Bled
BLEJSKI GRAD
Lesce
Tržič
Seeberg Sattel 1216
Velenje
Vitanje
Stranice
Zreče
Oplotnica
Luče
Ljubno
PODROŽNICA CERKEV SV. KRIŽA
0
10
20
30 km
48°
47°
14°
15°
96
97
109
123
177
223
158
65
89
A
B
C
1
2

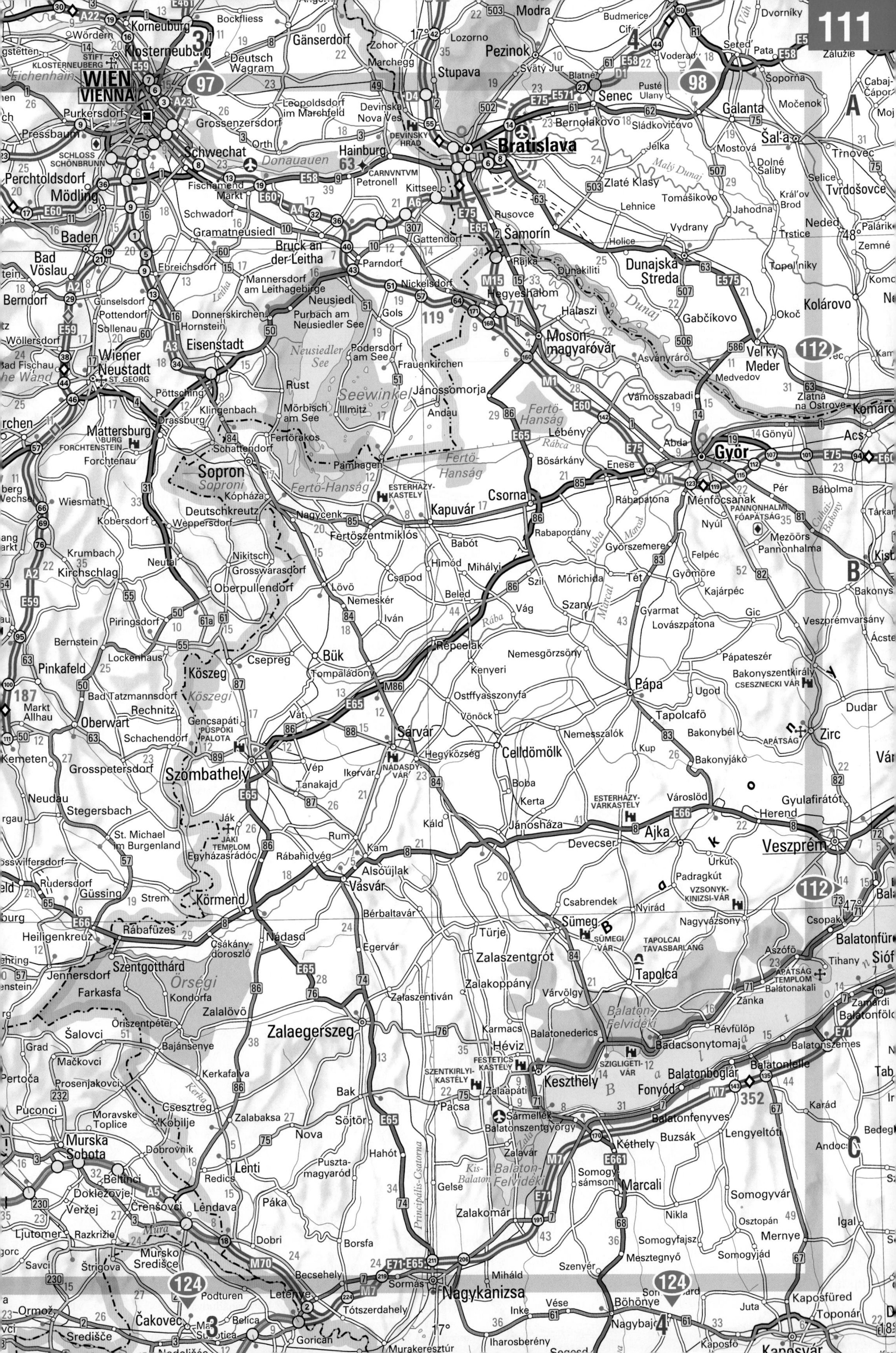
Korneuburg
Klosterneuburg
WIEN
VIENNA
Purkersdorf
Pressbaum
Schwechat
Perchtoldsdorf
Mödling
Baden
Bad Vöslau
Berndorf
Wiener Neustadt
Eisenstadt
Mattersburg
Gänserdorf
Deutsch Wagram
Marchegg
Hainburg
Bruck an der Leitha
Neusiedl
Neusiedler See
Seewinkel
Rust
Sopron
Kapuvár
Csorna
Modra
Pezinok
Stupava
Bratislava
Senec
Galanta
Šaľa
Dunajská Streda
Gabčíkovo
Veľký Meder
Kolárovo
Šamorín
Mosonmagyaróvár
Győr
Pápa
Celldömölk
Sárvár
Szombathely
Kőszeg
Oberwart
Pinkafeld
Güssing
Körmend
Szentgotthárd
Zalaegerszeg
Ajka
Veszprém
Zirc
Sümeg
Tapolca
Keszthely
Hévíz
Fonyód
Balatonboglár
Marcali
Nagykanizsa
Lenti
Murska Sobota
Lendava
Čakovec
Kaposvár
Dunaj
Malý Dunaj
Rába
Marcal
Balaton
Kis-Balaton
Balaton-Felvidéki
Őrségi
Fertő-Hanság
Bakony
97
98
112
124
187
352
119
77
63

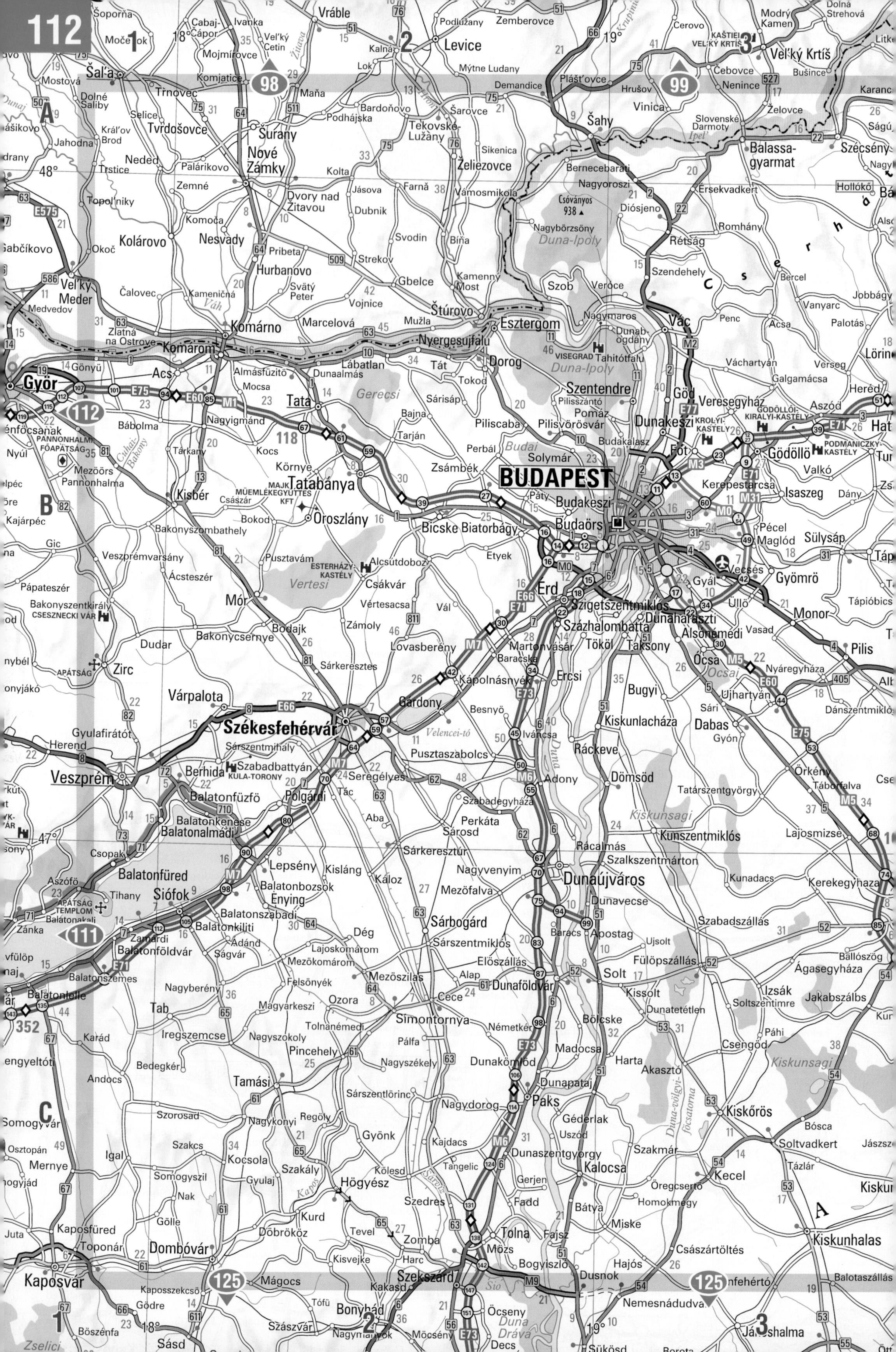
Šoporňa
Močenok
Cabaj-Čápor
Ivanka
Vráble
Podlužany
Zemberovce
Dolná Strehová
Modrý Kameň
Cerovo
Kaštieľ Veľký Krtíš
Veľký Krtíš
Levice
Kalná
Veľký Ceťin
Mojmírovce
Šaľa
Mostová
Komjatice
98
99
Lok
Mýtne Ludany
Demandice
Plášťovce
Hrušov
Čebovce
Bušince
Nenince
Karanc
Dolné Saliby
Trnovec
Maňa
Bardoňovo
Šarovce
Vinica
Želovce
Selice
Tvrdošovce
Šurany
Podhájska
Tekovské Lužany
Šahy
Slovenské Darmoty
Ipeľ
Šášikovo
Kráľov Brod
Jahodná
Drany
Neded
Nové Zámky
Kolta
Sikenica
Želiezovce
Balassagyarmat
Szécsény
Nagy
Trstice
Palárikovo
Bernecebaráti
Zemné
Jasová
Farná
Vámosmikola
Nagyoroszi
Érsekvadkert
Hollókő
Topoľníky
Dvory nad Žitavou
Dubník
Csóványos 938
Diósjenő
Komoča
Nagybörzsöny
Duna-Ipoly
Romhány
Gabčíkovo
Okoč
Kolárovo
Nesvady
Pribeta
Svodin
Biňa
Rétság
Hurbanovo
Strekov
Szendehely
Cserhát
Bercel
Veľký Meder
Čalovec
Kameničná
Svätý Peter
Gbelce
Kamenný Most
Szob
Verőce
Jobbágyi
Medvedov
Váh
Vojnice
Vanyarc
Zlatná na Ostrove
Komárno
Marcelová
Mužla
Štúrovo
Esztergom
Nagymaros
Dunabogdány
Vác
Penc
Acsa
Palotás
Komárom
Nyergesújfalu
Visegrád
Tahitótfalu
Győr
Gönyű
Ács
Almásfüzitő
Lábatlan
Tát
Dorog
Váchartyán
Verseg
Lőrinc
Mocsa
Dunaalmás
Tokod
Galgamácsa
Tata
Gerecsi
Sárisáp
Szentendre
Göd
Veresegyház
Heréd
Bábolma
Nagyigmánd
Bajna
Piliscaba
Pilisvörösvár
Pilisszántó
Pomáz
Dunakeszi
Gödöllői-Királyi-Kastély
Aszód
Pannonhalmi Főapátság
Nyúl
Cuhai-Bakony
Tárkány
Kocs
Tarján
Perbál
Budai
Solymár
Budakalász
Fót
Gödöllő
Podmaniczky-Kastély
Mezőörs
Pannonhalma
Környe
Zsámbék
BUDAPEST
Kerepestarcsa
Valkó
Tatabánya
Kisbér
Majk Műemlékegyüttes Kft
Császár
Páty
Budakeszi
Isaszeg
Dány
Bokod
Oroszlány
Bicske
Biatorbágy
Budaörs
Pécel
Maglód
Sülysáp
Kajárpéc
Bakonyszombathely
Gic
Veszprémvarsány
Pusztavám
Etyek
Alcsútdoboz
Esterházy-Kastély
Vecsés
Gyömrő
Ácsteszér
Vértesi
Csákvár
Érd
Gyál
Üllő
Pápateszér
Bakonyszentkirály
Cseszneki Vár
Mór
Vértesacsa
Vál
Szigetszentmiklós
Dunaharaszti
Tápióbicske
Monor
Bodajk
Zámoly
Százhalombatta
Alsónémedi
Vasad
Dudar
Bakonycsernye
Lovasberény
Martonvásár
Tököl
Taksony
Ócsa
Nyáregyháza
Pilis
Zirc
Apátság
Sárkeresztes
Baracska
Kápolnásnyék
Ercsi
Bugyi
Újhartyán
Várpalota
Gárdony
Besnyő
Sári
Dánszentmiklós
Gyulafirátót
Herend
Székesfehérvár
Velencei-tó
Iváncsa
Kiskunlacháza
Dabas
Gyón
Veszprém
Sárszentmihály
Szabadbattyán
Kula-torony
Berhida
Pusztaszabolcs
Ráckeve
Örkény
Táborfalva
Balatonfűzfő
Polgárdi
Seregélyes
Tác
Adony
Dömsöd
Tatárszentgyörgy
Balatonkenese
Balatonalmádi
Aba
Szabadegyháza
Perkáta
Sárosd
Kiskunsági
Lajosmizse
Csopak
Rácalmás
Kunszentmiklós
Sárkeresztúr
Szalkszentmárton
Balatonfüred
Lepsény
Kisláng
Káloz
Nagyvenyim
Dunaújváros
Kunadacs
Kerekegyháza
Aszófő
Tihany
Apátság Templom
Siófok
Balatonbozsok
Enying
Mezőfalva
Dunavecse
Balatonszabadi
Sárbogárd
Szabadszállás
Zánka
Balatonakali
Balatonkiliti
Zamárdi
Dég
Baracs
Apostag
Ujsolt
Balatonföldvár
Ádánd
Ságvár
Lajoskomárom
Mezőkomárom
Sárszentmiklós
Előszállás
Fülöpszállás
Ballószög
Ágasegyháza
Balatonszemes
Felsőnyék
Mezőszilas
Alap
Dunaföldvár
Solt
Izsák
Nagyberény
Ozora
Cece
Kissolt
Jakabszállás
Balatonlelle
Magyarkeszi
Dunatetétlen
Soltszentimre
Tab
Tolnanémedi
Simontornya
Németkér
Bölcske
Karád
Iregszemcse
Nagyszokoly
Pálfa
Madocsa
Páhi
Csengőd
Pincehely
Kiskunsági
Bedegkér
Nagyszékely
Dunakömlőd
Harta
Akasztó
Andocs
Tamási
Dunapataj
Duna-völgyi-főcsatorna
Sárszentlőrinc
Paks
Kiskőrös
Szorosad
Regöly
Nagydorog
Géderlak
Uszód
Bócsa
Somogyvár
Nagykónyi
Osztopán
Szakcs
Igal
Gyönk
Kajdacs
Szakmár
Soltvadkert
Jászsz
Mernye
Kocsola
Kölesd
Dunaszentgyörgy
Kalocsa
Tázlár
Somogyszil
Szakály
Tengelic
Gerjen
Kecel
Gyulaj
Högyész
Kapos
Sárvíz
Nak
Öregcsertő
Somogyjád
Homokmégy
Gölle
Szedres
Fadd
Bátya
Kaposfüred
Kurd
Tevel
Miske
Juta
Döbrököz
Zomba
Tolna
Fajsz
Kiskunhalas
Toponár
Dombóvár
Kisvejke
Harc
Mözs
Bogyiszló
Császártöltés
Hajós
Kaposvár
Kaposszekcső
Mágocs
Kakasd
Szekszárd
Sió
Dusnok
Balotaszállás
Godre
Tófű
Bonyhád
Őcseny
Nemesnádudvar
Kunfehértó
Duna-Dráva
Böszénfa
Sásd
Szászvár
Nagymányok
Mőcsény
Decs
Sükösd
Jánoshalma
Zselici
125
111
112
352
E575
E75
E60
E66
E71
E77
E73
E60
M1
M0
M2
M3
M5
M6
M7
M9
M31

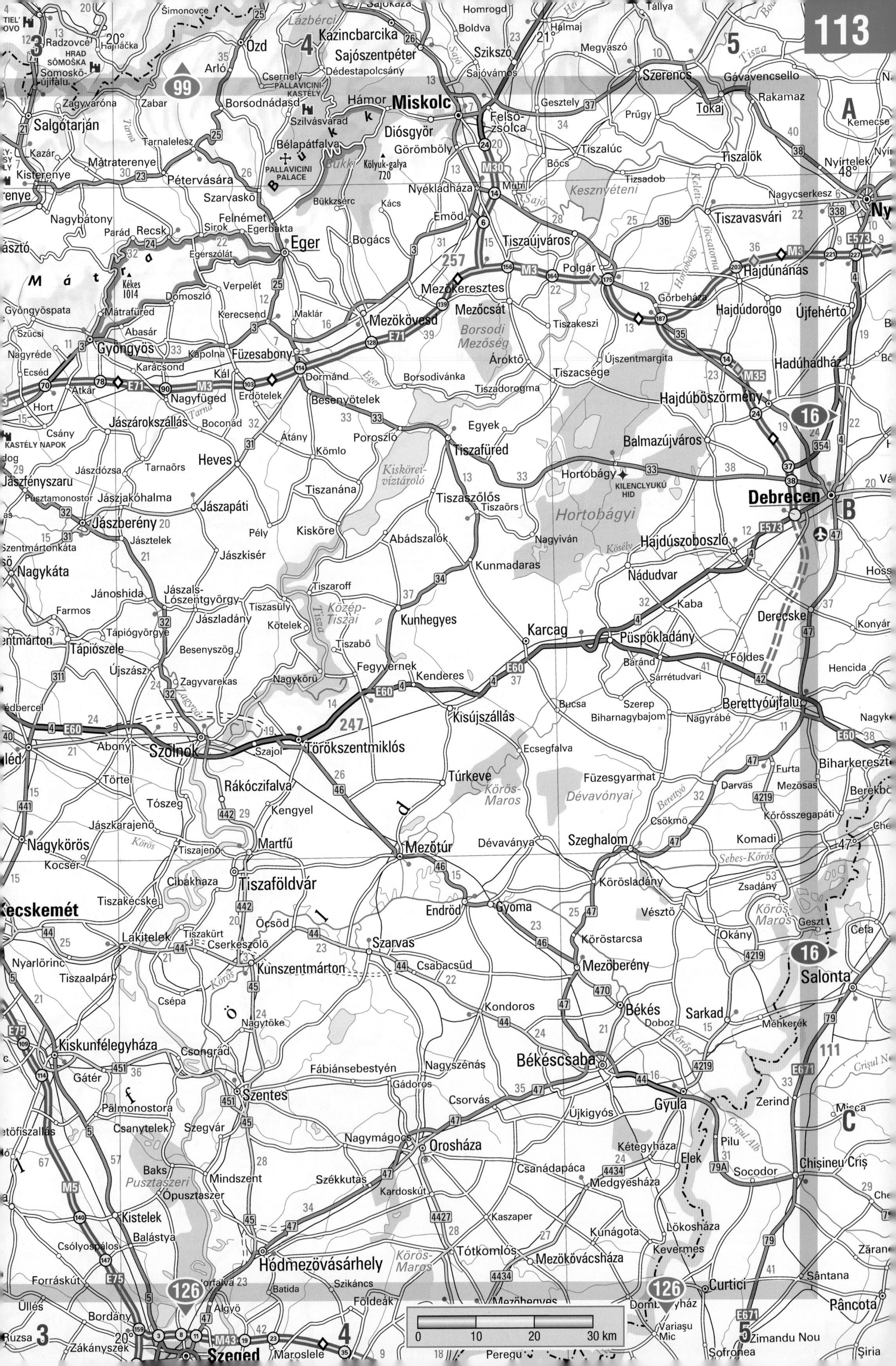

Šimonovce
Sajókaza
Homrogd
Tállya
Boldva
Halmaj
Radzovce
Hajnáčka
Ózd
Kazincbarcika
Szikszó
Megyaszó
HRAD SOMOŠKA
Somoskő-újfalu
Arló
Sajószentpéter
Dédestapolcsány
Sajóvámos
Szerencs
Gávavencsello
Cernely
PALLAVICINI KASTÉLY
Rakamaz
Zagyvaróna
Zabar
Borsodnádasd
Hámor
Miskolc
Felső-zsolca
Gesztely
Tokaj
Salgótarján
Szilvásvárad
Diósgyőr
Prűgy
Kemecse
Tarnalelesz
Bélapátfalva
Görömböly
Tiszalúc
Tiszalök
Kazár
Mátraterenye
Kölyuk-galya 720
Bőcs
Nyírtelek
Kisterenye
Pétervására
PALLAVICINI PALACE
Tiszadob
Keszny‌éteni
Szarvaskő
Nyékládháza
Muhi
Nagycserkesz
Bükkzsérc
Kács
Nagybátony
Felnémet
Emőd
Tiszavasvári
Parád
Recsk
Sirok
Egerbakta
Eger
Bogács
Tiszaújváros
Egerszólát
Polgár
Hajdúnánás
Mátra
Kékes 1014
Verpelét
Mezőkeresztes
Domoszló
Görbeháza
Gyöngyöspata
Mátrafüred
Kerecsend
Maklár
Mezőcsát
Hajdúdorogo
Újfehértó
Szücsi
Abasár
Mezőkövesd
Tiszakeszi
Borsodi Mezőség
Nagyréde
Gyöngyös
Kápolna
Füzesabony
Árokto
Újszentmargita
Hadúhadház
Ecséd
Karácsond
Dormánd
Borsodivánka
Tiszacsege
Kál
Tiszadorogma
Atkár
Nagyfüged
Erdőtelek
Besenyőtelek
Hajdúböszörmény
Hort
Jászárokszállás
Boconád
Egyek
Csány
Átány
Poroszló
Balmazújváros
KASTÉLY NAPOK
Tiszafüred
Heves
Kömlo
Tarnaörs
Jászdózsa
Hortobágy
KILENCLYUKÚ HÍD
Debrecen
Jászfényszaru
Kiskörei-víztároló
Tiszaszőlős
Tiszaörs
Pusztamonostor
Jászjákóhalma
Tiszanána
Jászapáti
Hortobágyi
Jászberény
Pély
Kisköre
Jásztelek
Nagyiván
Abádszalók
Hajdúszoboszló
Szentmártonkáta
Jászkisér
Kösély
Nagykáta
Kunmadaras
Nádudvar
Hoss
Tiszaroff
Jánoshida
Jászals-Lószentgyörgy
Farmos
Tiszasüly
Közép-Tiszai
Kaba
Derecske
Jászladány
Kötelek
Kunhegyes
Konyár
Tápiógyörgye
Karcag
Püspökladány
Tápiószele
Tiszabő
Besenyszög
Fegyvernek
Fődes
Újszász
Kenderes
Báránd
Hencida
Sárrétudvari
Zagyvarekas
Nagykörü
Bucsa
Szerep
Berettyóújfalu
Biharnagybajom
Nagyrábé
Kisújszállás
Abony
Szolnok
Szajol
Törökszentmiklós
Ecsegfalva
Törtel
Furta
Biharkeresztes
Túrkeve
Füzesgyarmat
Darvas
Mezősas
Rákóczifalva
Tószeg
Körös-Maros
Dévavónyai
Berekbo
Kengyel
Kőrösszegapáti
Jászkarajenő
Csökmő
Nagykőrös
Tiszajenő
Martfű
Mezőtúr
Dévaványa
Szeghalom
Komadi
Kocsér
Sebes-Kőrös
Cibakhaza
Körösladány
Zsadány
Tiszaföldvár
Kecskemét
Tiszakécske
Endrőd
Gyoma
Vésztő
Öcsöd
Tiszakürt
Lakitelek
Cserkeszőlő
Szarvas
Köröstarcsa
Okány
Geszt
Cefa
Nyárlőrinc
Csabacsüd
Kunszentmárton
Mezőberény
Salonta
Tiszaalpár
Csépa
Kondoros
Békés
Sarkad
Nagytőke
Doboz
Méhkerék
Kiskunfélegyháza
Csongrád
Békéscsaba
Fábiánsebestyén
Nagyszénás
Gátér
Gádoros
Szentes
Csorvás
Gyula
Zerind
Pálmonostora
Újkígyós
Mișca
Csanytelek
Szegvár
Pilu
Nagymágocs
Orosháza
Kétegyháza
Elek
Baks
Csanádapáca
Socodor
Chișineu Criș
Pusztaszeri
Mindszent
Medgyesháza
Ópusztaszer
Székkutas
Kardoskút
Kistelek
Kaszaper
Balástya
Kunágota
Lőkösháza
Csólyospálos
Tótkomlós
Kevermes
Zărand
Hódmezővásárhely
Mezőkovácsháza
Forráskút
Szikáncs
Sântana
Batida
Curtici
Üllés
Földeák
Dombegyház
Pâncota
Bordány
Algyő
Mezőhegyes
Variașu Mic
Zimandu Nou
Rúzsa
Zákányszék
Szeged
Maroslele
Peregu
Șofronea
Șiria
Crișul Alb
Crișul Negru
Tisza
Sajó
Hernád
Körös
Berettyó
Eger
Tarna
Zagyva
Bükk
M3
M30
M35
M5
M43
E71
E573
E60
E75
E671
0 10 20 30 km
3
4
5
A
B
C
20°
21°
47°
48°
99
126
16
111
257
247

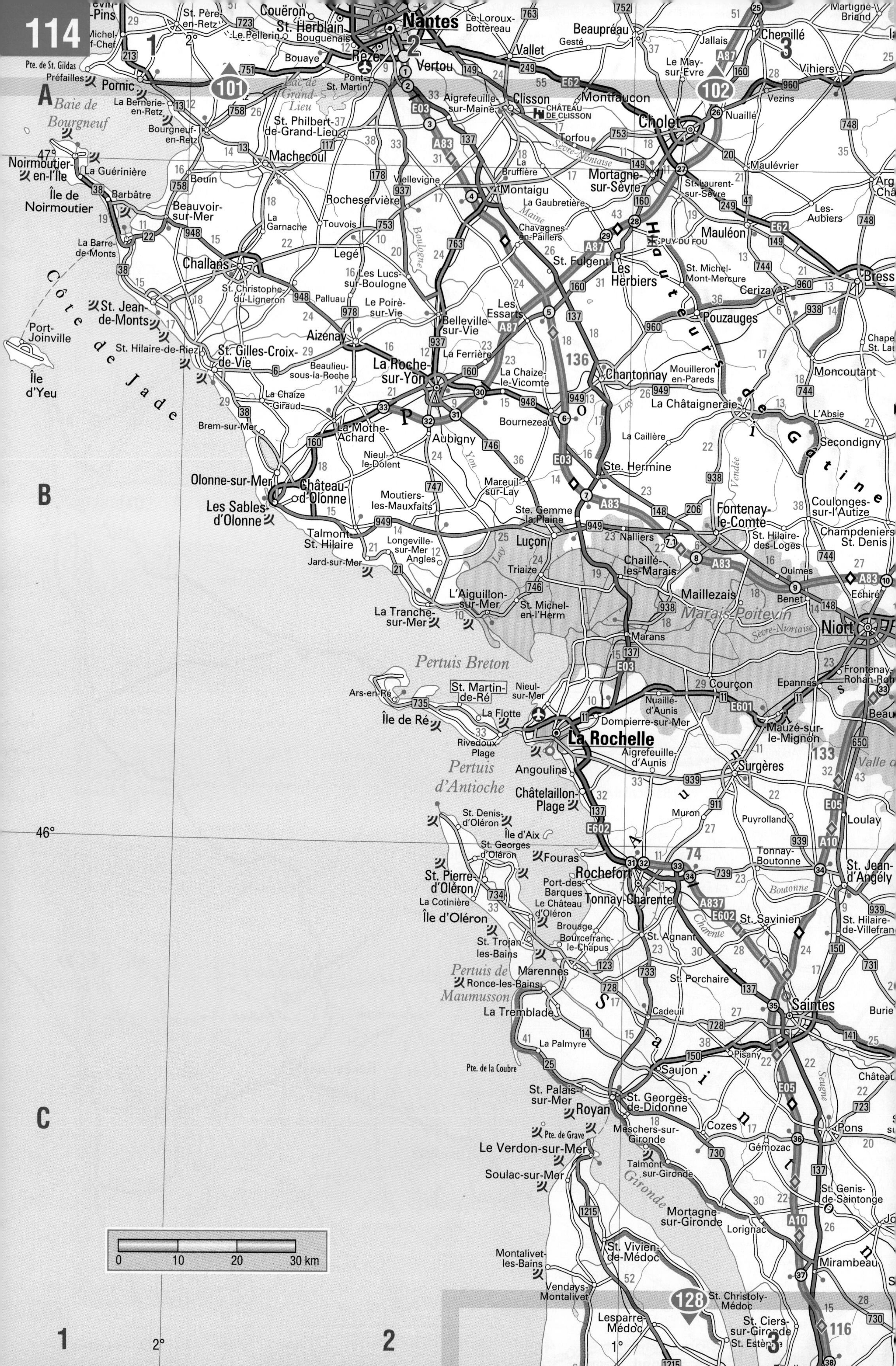
Nantes
St. Herblain
Couëron
St. Père-en-Retz
Le Pellerin
Bouguenais
Rezé
Bouaye
Vertou
Le Loroux-Bottereau
Vallet
Beaupréau
Gesté
Jallais
Chemillé
Le May-sur-Èvre
Vihiers
Pte. de St. Gildas
Préfailles
Pornic
La Bernerie-en-Retz
Baie de Bourgneuf
Bourgneuf-en-Retz
Lac de Grand-Lieu
Pont-St. Martin
Aigrefeuille-sur-Maine
Clisson
CHÂTEAU DE CLISSON
Montfaucon
Cholet
Nuaillé
Vezins
St. Philbert-de-Grand-Lieu
Torfou
Sèvre-Nantaise
Maulévrier
Noirmoutier-en-l'Île
La Guérinière
Machecoul
La Bruffière
Mortagne-sur-Sèvre
St. Laurent-sur-Sèvre
Île de Noirmoutier
Barbâtre
Bouin
Viellevigne
Montaigu
La Gaubretière
Les Aubiers
Beauvoir-sur-Mer
La Garnache
Rocheservière
Touvois
Chavagnes-en-Paillers
PUY-DU FOU
Mauléon
La Barre-de-Monts
Legé
Boulogne
St. Fulgent
Les Herbiers
St. Michel-Mont-Mercure
Challans
Les Lucs-sur-Boulogne
Cerizay
Bressuire
Côte de Jade
St. Christophe-du-Ligneron
Palluau
Le Poiré-sur-Vie
Les Essarts
Pouzauges
St. Jean-de-Monts
Belleville-sur-Vie
Port-Joinville
Aizenay
St. Hilaire-de-Riez
St. Gilles-Croix-de-Vie
La Ferrière
Chapelle-St. Laurent
Beaulieu-sous-la-Roche
La Roche-sur-Yon
La Chaize-le-Vicomte
Chantonnay
Mouilleron-en-Pareds
Moncoutant
Île d'Yeu
La Chaize-Giraud
La Châtaigneraie
L'Absie
Brem-sur-Mer
Bournezeau
Hauteurs de Gâtine
La Mothe-Achard
Aubigny
La Caillère
Secondigny
Nieul-le-Dolent
Yon
Lay
Olonne-sur-Mer
Château-d'Olonne
Ste. Hermine
Vendée
Les Sables-d'Olonne
Moutiers-les-Mauxfaits
Mareuil-sur-Lay
Coulonges-sur-l'Autize
Ste. Gemme-la-Plaine
Fontenay-le-Comte
Talmont-St. Hilaire
Longeville-sur-Mer
Luçon
Nalliers
St. Hilaire-des-Loges
Champdeniers-St. Denis
Angles
Jard-sur-Mer
Triaize
Chaillé-les-Marais
Oulmes
L'Aiguillon-sur-Mer
St. Michel-en-l'Herm
Maillezais
Benet
Échiré
La Tranche-sur-Mer
Marais Poitevin
Sèvre-Niortaise
Marans
Niort
Pertuis Breton
Ars-en-Ré
St. Martin-de-Ré
Nieul-sur-Mer
Courçon
Épannes
Frontenay-Rohan-Rohan
Nuaillé-d'Aunis
La Flotte
Île de Ré
Dompierre-sur-Mer
Mauzé-sur-le-Mignon
Rivedoux-Plage
La Rochelle
Aigrefeuille-d'Aunis
Pertuis d'Antioche
Angoulins
Surgères
Châtelaillon-Plage
Muron
Puyrolland
Loulay
St. Denis-d'Oléron
Île d'Aix
St. Georges-d'Oléron
Fouras
Tonnay-Boutonne
St. Jean-d'Angély
St. Pierre-d'Oléron
Rochefort
Port-des-Barques
Boutonne
La Cotinière
Le Château-d'Oléron
Tonnay-Charente
Île d'Oléron
Brouage
St. Savinien
St. Hilaire-de-Villefranche
Charente
St. Trojan-les-Bains
Bourcefranc-le-Chapus
St. Agnant
Pertuis de Maumusson
Marennes
Ronce-les-Bains
St. Porchaire
La Tremblade
Saintes
Cadeuil
Burie
La Palmyre
Pisany
Pte. de la Coubre
Saujon
Seugne
Château
St. Palais-sur-Mer
Royan
St. Georges-de-Didonne
Pte. de Grave
Meschers-sur-Gironde
Cozes
Pons
Le Verdon-sur-Mer
Gémozac
Talmont-sur-Gironde
Soulac-sur-Mer
Gironde
St. Genis-de-Saintonge
Mortagne-sur-Gironde
Lorignac
Montalivet-les-Bains
St. Vivien-de-Médoc
Mirambeau
Vendays-Montalivet
St. Christoly-Médoc
Lesparre-Médoc
St. Ciers-sur-Gironde
St. Estèphe
Saintonge
Aunis
Poitou
47°
46°
2°
1°
A
B
C
1
2
3
101
102
116
128
133
136
0
10
20
30 km

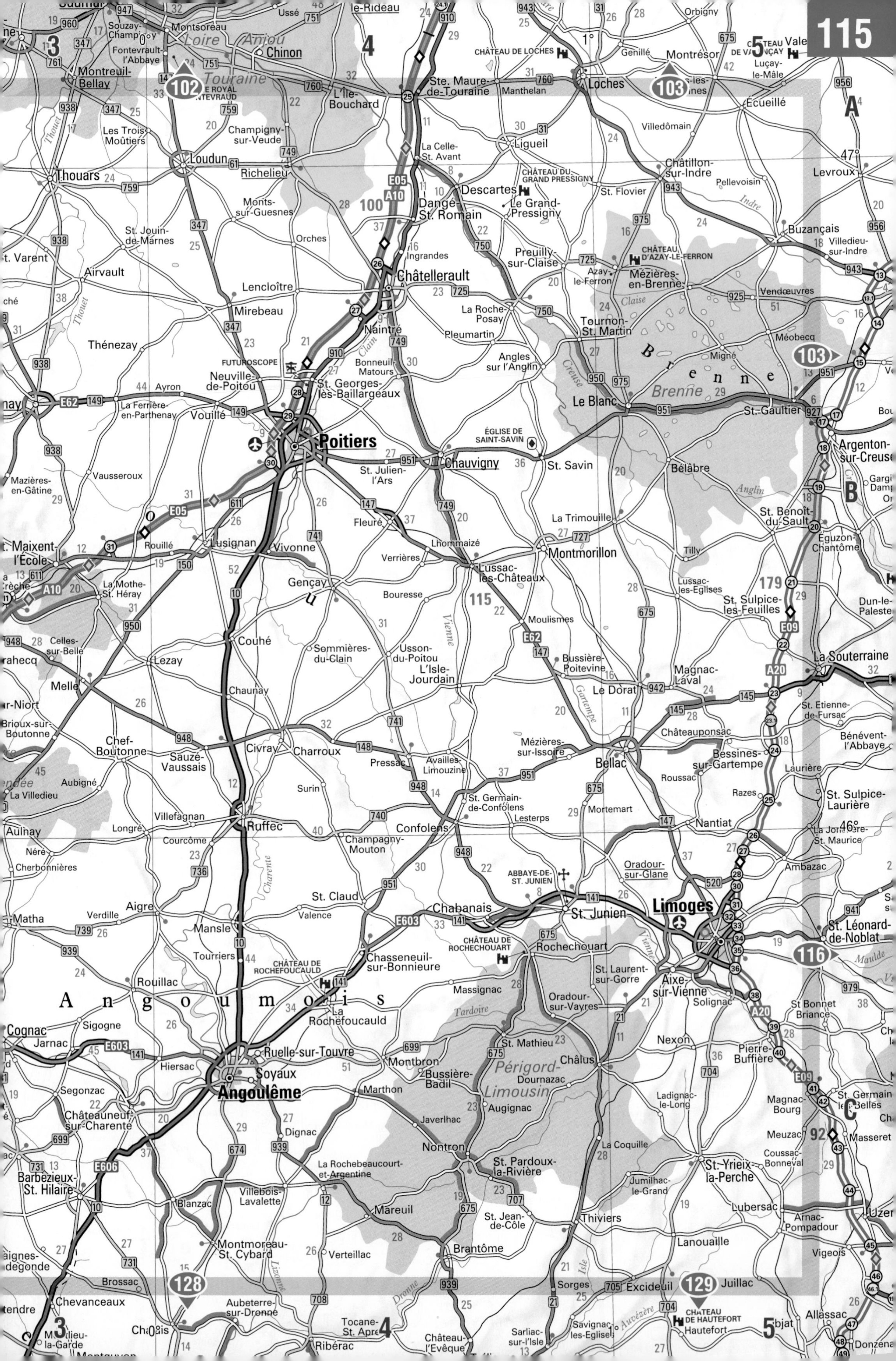
Montsoreau
Souzay-Champigny
Fontevrault-l'Abbaye
Loire Anjou Touraine
Chinon
Ussé
le-Rideau
Montreuil-Bellay
102
L'Ile-Bouchard
Ste. Maure-de-Touraine
Manthelan
Château de Loches
Loches
103
Orbigny
Genillé
Montrésor
Luçay-le-Mâle
Écueillé
Villedômain
Les Trois Moûtiers
Champigny-sur-Veude
Loudun
Richelieu
Thouars
Ligueil
La Celle-St. Avant
Château du Grand Pressigny
Descartes
Le Grand-Pressigny
Châtillon-sur-Indre
Pellevoisin
Levroux
St. Flovier
Monts-sur-Guesnes
Dangé-St. Romain
100
Orches
Ingrandes
St. Jouin-de-Marnes
St. Varent
Airvault
Buzançais
Villedieu-sur-Indre
Preuilly-sur-Claise
Château d'Azay-le-Ferron
Azay-le-Ferron
Mézières-en-Brenne
Châtellerault
Lencloître
Vendœuvres
Mirebeau
La Roche-Posay
Tournon-St. Martin
Naintré
Pleumartin
Méobecq
Thénezay
Futuroscope
Bonneuil-Matours
Angles sur l'Anglin
Migné
Brenne
Neuville-de-Poitou
St. Georges-lès-Baillargeaux
Le Blanc
Ayron
La Ferrière-en-Parthenay
Vouillé
St.-Gaultier
Poitiers
Église de Saint-Savin
Argenton-sur-Creuse
Chauvigny
St. Savin
St. Julien-l'Ars
Bélâbre
Mazières-en-Gâtine
Vausseroux
Anglin
Fleuré
La Trimouille
St. Benoît-du-Sault
Lusignan
Vivonne
Rouillé
St. Maixent-l'École
Lhommaizé
Montmorillon
Éguzon-Chantôme
Verrières
Tilly
Lussac-les-Châteaux
Gençay
La Mothe-St. Héray
Bouresse
Lussac-les-Eglises
179
St. Sulpice-les-Feuilles
Dun-le-Palestel
115
Moulismes
Celles-sur-Belle
Couhé
Sommières-du-Clain
Usson-du-Poitou
L'Isle-Jourdain
Bussière-Poitevine
Magnac-Laval
La Souterraine
Lezay
Melle
Chaunay
Le Dorat
St. Etienne-de-Fursac
Brioux-sur-Boutonne
Châteauponsac
Bénévent-l'Abbaye
Chef-Boutonne
Sauzé-Vaussais
Civray
Charroux
Pressac
Availles-Limouzine
Mézières-sur-Issoire
Bellac
Bessines-sur-Gartempe
Laurière
Aubigné
La Villedieu
Surin
St. Germain-de-Confolens
Mortemart
Roussac
Razes
St. Sulpice-Laurière
Aulnay
Longré
Villefagnan
Ruffec
Confolens
Lesterps
Nantiat
Néré
Courcôme
Champagny-Mouton
La Jonchère-St. Maurice
Cherbonnières
Oradour-sur-Glane
Ambazac
Abbaye-de-St. Junien
Matha
Verdille
Aigre
St. Claud
Valence
Chabanais
St. Junien
Limoges
Mansle
Château de Rochechouart
Rochechouart
St. Léonard-de-Noblat
116
Tourriers
Château de Rochefoucauld
Chasseneuil-sur-Bonnieure
St. Laurent-sur-Gorre
Aixe-sur-Vienne
Rouillac
Massignac
Oradour-sur-Vayres
Solignac
St Bonnet Briance
Angoumois
La Rochefoucauld
Cognac
Sigogne
Jarnac
Hiersac
Ruelle-sur-Touvre
Soyaux
Angoulême
Montbron
Bussière-Badil
St. Mathieu
Périgord-Limousin
Châlus
Dournazac
Nexon
Pierre-Buffière
Segonzac
Marthon
Augignac
Ladignac-le-Long
Magnac-Bourg
St. Germain les Belles
Châteauneuf-sur-Charente
Dignac
Javerlhac
Meuzac
Masseret
Nontron
La Coquille
Coussac-Bonneval
Barbezieux-St. Hilaire
La Rochebeaucourt-et-Argentine
St. Pardoux-la-Rivière
St.-Yrieix-la-Perche
Jumilhac-le-Grand
Villebois-Lavalette
Blanzac
Mareuil
St. Jean-de-Côle
Thiviers
Lubersac
Arnac-Pompadour
Uzerche
Montmoreau-St. Cybard
Verteillac
Brantôme
Lanouaille
Vigeois
Brossac
128
Sorges
Excideuil
129
Juillac
Chevanceaux
Aubeterre-sur-Dronne
Tocane-St. Apre
Château de Hautefort
Hautefort
Allassac
Chalais
Montlieu-la-Garde
Ribérac
Château-l'Evêque
Sarliac-sur-l'Isle
Savignac-les-Eglises
Donzenac
Vienne
Charente
Tardoire
Dronne
Isle
Auvézère
Creuse
Indre
Claise
Gartempe
Clain
Thouet
Maulde

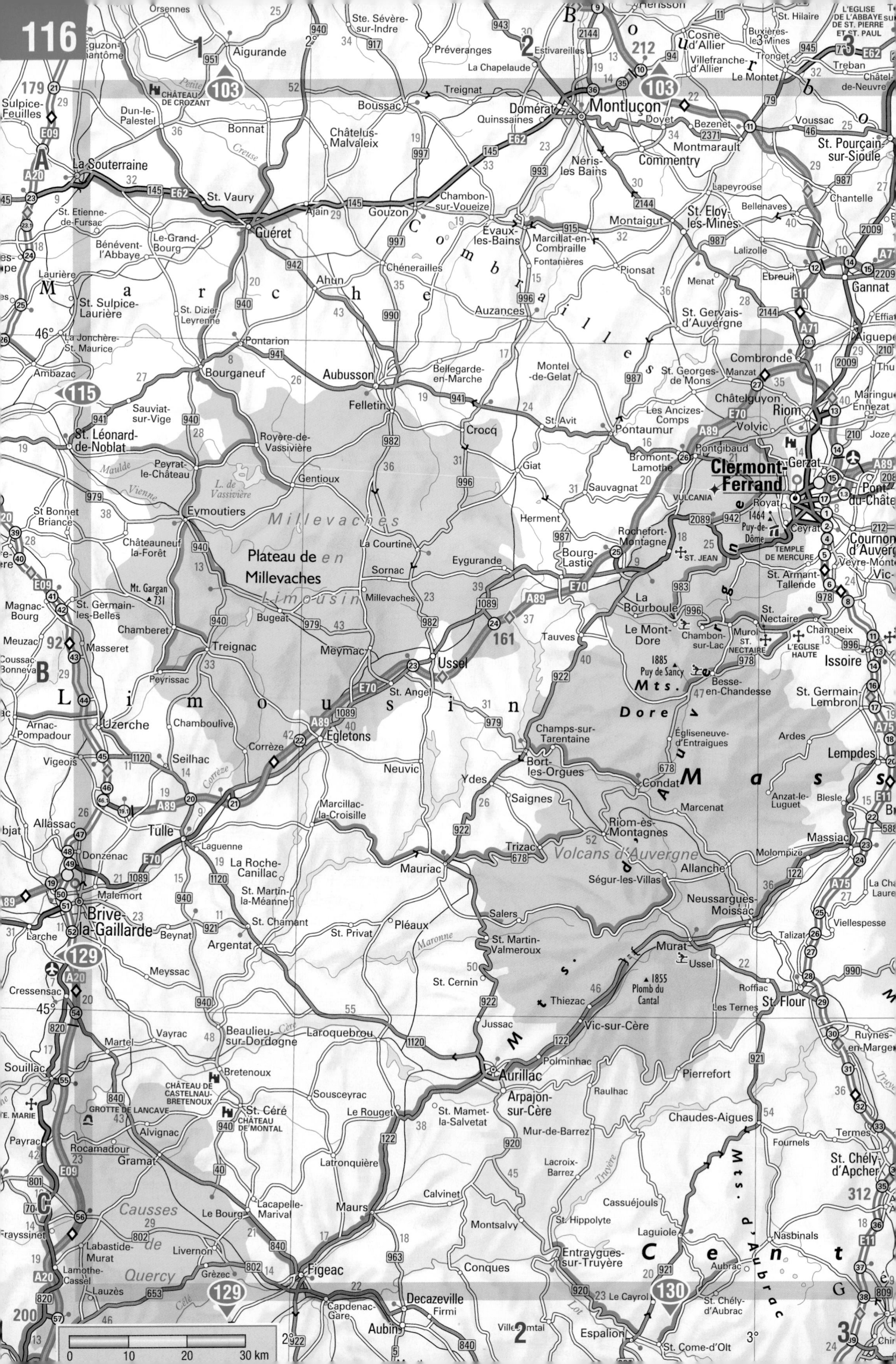

116
Orsennes
Aigurande
Eguzon-Chantôme
Ste. Sévère-sur-Indre
Préveranges
La Chapelaude
Estivareilles
Hérisson
Cosne-d'Allier
Villefranche-d'Allier
Buxières-les-Mines
Tronget
Le Montet
St. Hilaire
L'EGLISE DE L'ABBAYE DE ST. PIERRE ET ST. PAUL
Treban
Châtel-de-Neuvre
Bourbonnais
CHÂTEAU DE CROZANT
Sulpice-les-Feuilles
Dun-le-Palestel
Boussac
Treignat
Domérat
Montluçon
Quinssaines
Doyet
Bezenet
Voussac
St. Pourçain-sur-Sioule
Bonnat
Châtelus-Malvaleix
Néris-les-Bains
Commentry
Montmarault
La Souterraine
St. Vaury
Chambon-sur-Voueize
Lapeyrouse
Chantelle
St. Etienne-de-Fursac
Ajain
Gouzon
Combraille
Evaux-les-Bains
Marcillat-en-Combraille
Montaigut
St. Eloy-les-Mines
Bellenaves
Bénévent-l'Abbaye
Le-Grand-Bourg
Guéret
Fontanières
Lalizolle
Chénerailles
Pionsat
Menat
Ebreuil
Gannat
Laurière
Ahun
Auzances
St. Sulpice-Laurière
St. Dizier-Leyrenne
St. Gervais-d'Auvergne
Effiat
Marche
La Jonchère-St. Maurice
Pontarion
Aigueperse
Ambazac
Bourganeuf
Aubusson
Bellegarde-en-Marche
Montel-de-Gelat
St. Georges-de-Mons
Manzat
Combronde
Châtelguyon
Riom
Maringues
Ennezat
Sauviat-sur-Vige
Felletin
Crocq
St. Avit
Les Ancizes-Comps
Pontaumur
Volvic
St. Léonard-de-Noblat
Royère-de-Vassivière
Pontgibaud
Gerzat
Joze
Peyrat-le-Château
Gentioux
Giat
Bromont-Lamothe
Clermont-Ferrand
L. de Vassivière
Sauvagnat
VULCANIA
Royat
Pont-du-Château
St Bonnet Briance
Eymoutiers
Millevaches
Herment
Rochefort-Montagne
Puy-de-Dôme
Ceyrat
Cournon-d'Auvergne
Châteauneuf-la-Forêt
La Courtine
Bourg-Lastic
ST. JEAN
TEMPLE DE MERCURE
Veyre-Monton
Plateau de Millevaches
Eygurande
Sornac
Mt. Gargan 731
Millevaches
St. Amant-Tallende
Magnac-Bourg
St. Germain-les-Belles
Limousin
Bugeat
La Bourboule
St. Nectaire
Champeix
Meuzac
Chamberet
Masseret
Treignac
Meymac
Le Mont-Dore
Chambon-sur-Lac
Murol
ST. NECTAIRE
L'EGLISE HAUTE
Tauves
Issoire
Coussac-Bonneval
Ussel
1885 Puy de Sancy
Mts. Dore
Besse-en-Chandesse
Peyrissac
St. Angel
St. Germain-Lembron
Limousin
Arnac-Pompadour
Uzerche
Chamboulive
Egletons
Champs-sur-Tarentaine
Églisenenve-d'Entraigues
Ardes
Vigeois
Seilhac
Corrèze
Neuvic
Bort-les-Orgues
Lempdes
Ydes
Condat
Monts d'Auvergne
Saignes
Anzat-le-Luguet
Blesle
Allassac
Tulle
Marcillac-la-Croisille
Marcenat
Riom-ès-Montagnes
Massiac
Laguenne
Trizac
Volcans d'Auvergne
Molompize
Donzenac
La Roche-Canillac
Mauriac
Allanche
Ségur-les-Villas
Malemort
St. Martin-la-Méanne
Neussargues-Moissac
Brive-la-Gaillarde
Salers
Beynat
Argentat
St. Chamant
St. Privat
Pléaux
St. Martin-Valmeroux
Talizat
Viellespesse
Larche
Murat
Ussel
Meyssac
St. Cernin
1855 Plomb du Cantal
Roffiac
Cressensac
Thiezac
Les Ternes
St. Flour
Beaulieu-sur-Dordogne
Laroquebrou
Jussac
Vic-sur-Cère
Ruynes-en-Margeride
Martel
Vayrac
Polminhac
Souillac
Bretenoux
Aurillac
Pierrefort
CHÂTEAU DE CASTELNAU-BRETENOUX
Sousceyrac
Arpajon-sur-Cère
Raulhac
GROTTE DE LANCAVE
St. Céré
CHÂTEAU DE MONTAL
Le Rouget
St. Mamet-la-Salvetat
Chaudes-Aigues
Termes
Alvignac
Mur-de-Barrez
Fournels
Payrac
Rocamadour
Gramat
Latronquière
Lacroix-Barrez
St. Chély-d'Apcher
Causses de Quercy
Le Bourg
Lacapelle-Marival
Maurs
Calvinet
Cassuéjouls
Mts. d'Aubrac
Frayssinet
Labastide-Murat
Livernon
Montsalvy
St. Hippolyte
Laguiole
Nasbinals
Lamothe-Cassel
Figeac
Conques
Entraygues-sur-Truyère
Aubrac
Grèzec
Lauzès
Decazeville
Firmi
Le Cayrol
St. Chély-d'Aubrac
Capdenac-Gare
Aubin
Villecomtal
Espalion
St. Come-d'Olt
Massif Central
0 10 20 30 km

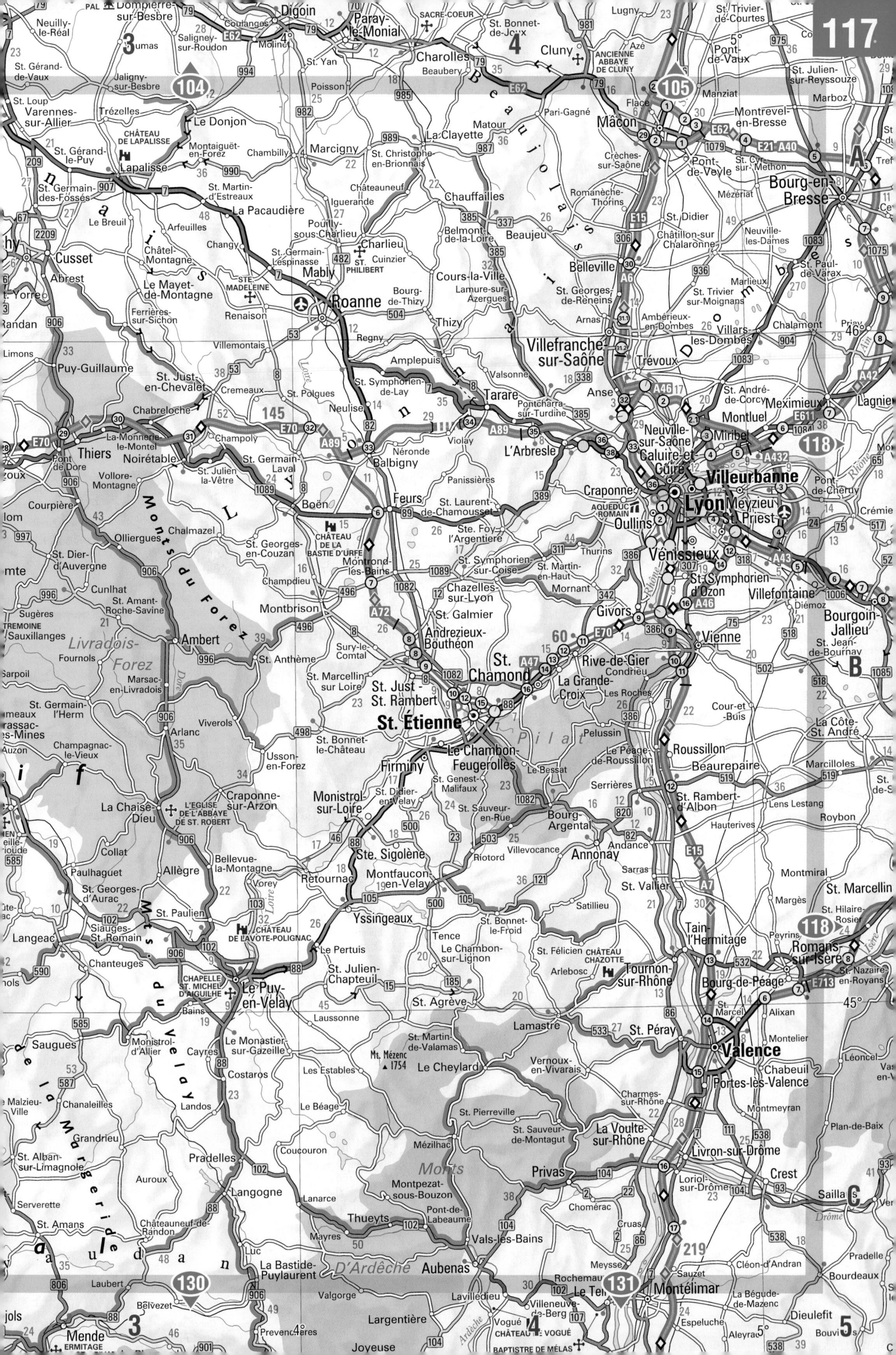

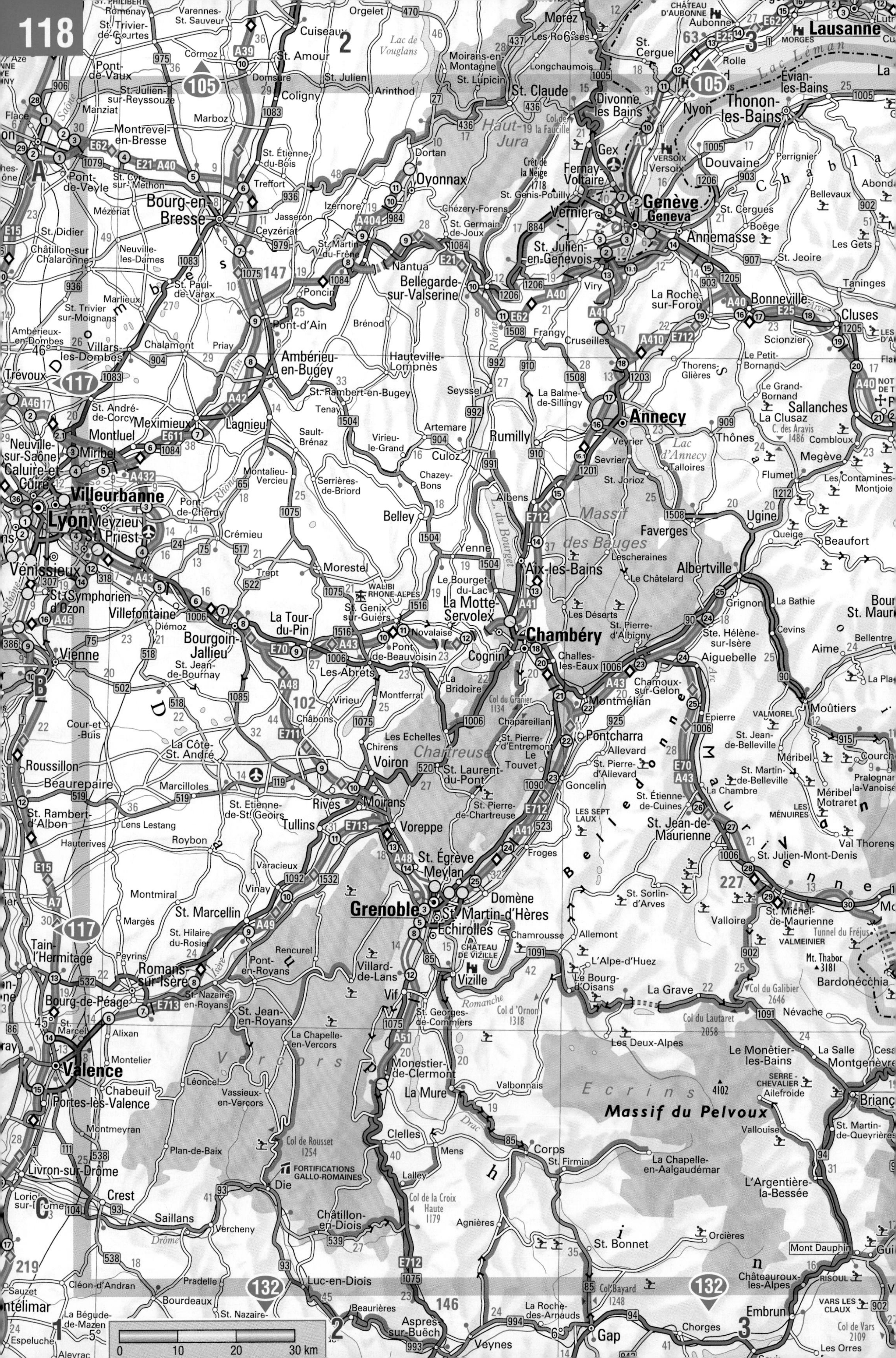
Romenay
Varennes-St. Sauveur
Orgelet
St. Trivier-de-Courtes
Cuiseaux
Lac de Vouglans
Morez
Les Rousses
Château d'Aubonne
Aubonne
Lausanne
Morges
Pont-de-Vaux
Cormoz
St. Amour
Moirans-en-Montagne
Longchaumois
St. Cergue
Rolle
Lac Léman
Domsure
Coligny
St. Julien
Arinthod
St. Lupicin
St. Claude
Divonne-les-Bains
Nyon
Thonon-les-Bains
Évian-les-Bains
St. Julien-sur-Reyssouze
Manziat
Marboz
Haut-Jura
Col de la Faucille
Montrevel-en-Bresse
Dortan
Gex
Versoix
Douvaine
Perrignier
St. Étienne-du-Bois
Oyonnax
Crêt de la Neige 1718
Ferney-Voltaire
Chablais
Pont-de-Veyle
St. Cyr-sur-Menthon
Treffort
Abondance
Bourg-en-Bresse
Izernore
Chézery-Forens
St. Genis-Pouilly
Vernier
Genève
Geneva
Bellevaux
Mézériat
Jasseron
Ceyzériat
St. Germain-de-Joux
St. Cergues
Boëge
St. Didier
St. Martin-du-Frêne
Annemasse
Les Gets
Châtillon-sur-Chalaronne
Neuville-les-Dames
Nantua
St. Julien-en-Genevois
St. Jeoire
Bellegarde-sur-Valserine
Viry
Taninges
St. Paul-de-Varax
Marlieux
Poncin
La Roche-sur-Foron
Bonneville
St. Trivier-sur-Moignans
Cluses
Ambérieux-en-Dombes
Brénod
Frangy
Cruseilles
Scionzier
Villars-les-Dombes
Chalamont
Priay
Pont-d'Ain
Le Petit-Bornand
Trévoux
Ambérieu-en-Bugey
Hauteville-Lompnès
Thorens-Glières
St. Rambert-en-Bugey
Seyssel
La Balme-de-Sillingy
Le Grand-Bornand
St. André-de-Corcy
Meximieux
Lagnieu
Tenay
Annecy
Sallanches
La Clusaz
C. des Aravis 1486
Combloux
Montluel
Sault-Brénaz
Vieu-le-Grand
Artemare
Rumilly
Veyrier
Lac d'Annecy
Thônes
Neuville-sur-Saône
Miribel
Culoz
Sevrier
Talloires
Megève
Caluire-et-Cuire
Montalieu-Vercieu
Serrières-de-Briord
Chazey-Bons
St. Jorioz
Flumet
Les Contamines-Montjoie
Villeurbanne
Pont-de-Chéruy
Albens
L. du Bourget
Massif des Bauges
Faverges
Ugine
Lyon
Meyzieu
St. Priest
Crémieu
Belley
Queige
Beaufort
Vénissieux
Trept
Morestel
Yenne
Lescheraines
Aix-les-Bains
Albertville
Le Châtelard
St. Symphorien-d'Ozon
Walibi Rhône-Alpes
Le Bourget-du-Lac
La Motte-Servolex
Grignon
La Bathie
Bourg-St. Maurice
Villefontaine
Diémoz
La Tour-du-Pin
St. Genix-sur-Guiers
Les Déserts
St. Pierre-d'Albigny
Cevins
Novalaise
Chambéry
Ste. Hélène-sur-Isère
Bellentre
Bourgoin-Jallieu
Vienne
Pont-de-Beauvoisin
Cognin
Challes-les-Eaux
Aiguebelle
Aime
St. Jean-de-Bournay
Les Abrets
La Bridoire
Chamoux-sur-Gelon
La Plagne
Montferrat
Col du Granier 1134
Montmélian
Virieu
Châbons
Chapareillan
Epierre
Moûtiers
Valmorel
Cour-et-Buis
Les Echelles
St. Pierre-d'Entremont
Le Touvet
Pontcharra
Allevard
St. Jean-de-Belleville
La Côte-St. André
Chirens
Chartreuse
Voiron
St. Laurent-du-Pont
St. Pierre-d'Allevard
Méribel
Courchevel
Roussillon
Beaurepaire
Marcilloles
St. Martin-de-Belleville
Pralognan-la-Vanoise
Goncelin
Rives
Moirans
St. Pierre-de-Chartreuse
La Chambre
Méribel Motraret
St. Rambert-d'Albon
Lens Lestang
St. Etienne-de-St. Geoirs
Tullins
Voreppe
Les Sept Laux
St. Étienne-de-Cuines
Les Ménuires
Hauterives
Roybon
St. Égrève
Meylan
Froges
St. Jean-de-Maurienne
Val Thorens
Varacieux
Belledonne
St. Julien-Mont-Denis
Vinay
Montmiral
Domène
St. Sorlin-d'Arves
Maurienne
St. Marcellin
Grenoble
St. Martin-d'Hères
Valloire
St. Michel-de-Maurienne
Margès
Echirolles
Chamrousse
Allemont
Tunnel du Fréjus
Valmeinier
St. Hilaire-du-Rosier
Rencurel
Château de Vizille
Mt. Thabor 3181
Tain-l'Hermitage
Peyrins
Pont-en-Royans
Villard-de-Lans
Vizille
L'Alpe-d'Huez
Romans-sur-Isère
Le Bourg-d'Oisans
La Grave
Bardonècchia
Bourg-de-Péage
St. Nazaire-en-Royans
Vif
Col du Galibier 2646
St. Jean-en-Royans
St. Georges-de-Commiers
Romanche
Col d'Ornon 1318
Névache
St. Marcel
Alixan
La Chapelle-en-Vercors
Col du Lautaret 2058
Vercors
Les Deux-Alpes
Le Monêtier-les-Bains
La Salle
Montgenèvre
Montelier
Monestier-de-Clermont
Valence
Chabeuil
Léoncel
Serre-Chevalier
Portes-les-Valence
Vassieux-en-Vercors
La Mure
Valbonnais
Ecrins
4102
Ailefroide
Briançon
Massif du Pelvoux
Montmeyran
Clelles
Vallouise
St. Martin-de-Queyrières
Plan-de-Baix
Col de Rousset 1254
Mens
Corps
St. Firmin
Drac
Livron-sur-Drôme
Fortifications Gallo-Romaines
La Chapelle-en-Valgaudémar
Die
Lalley
L'Argentière-la-Bessée
Loriol-sur-Drôme
Crest
Col de la Croix Haute 1179
Saillans
Vercheny
Châtillon-en-Diois
Agnières
Orcières
Drôme
St. Bonnet
Mont Dauphin
Guillestre
Pradelle
Luc-en-Diois
Col Bayard 1248
Châteauroux-les-Alpes
Risoul
Sauzet
Cléon-d'Andran
Bourdeaux
Vars les Claux
Montélimar
St. Nazaire-le-Désert
Beaurières
La Roche-des-Arnauds
Embrun
La Bégude-de-Mazenc
Aspres-sur-Buëch
Gap
Chorges
Col de Vars 2109
Espeluche
Veynes
Les Orres
Alevrac
0
10
20
30 km

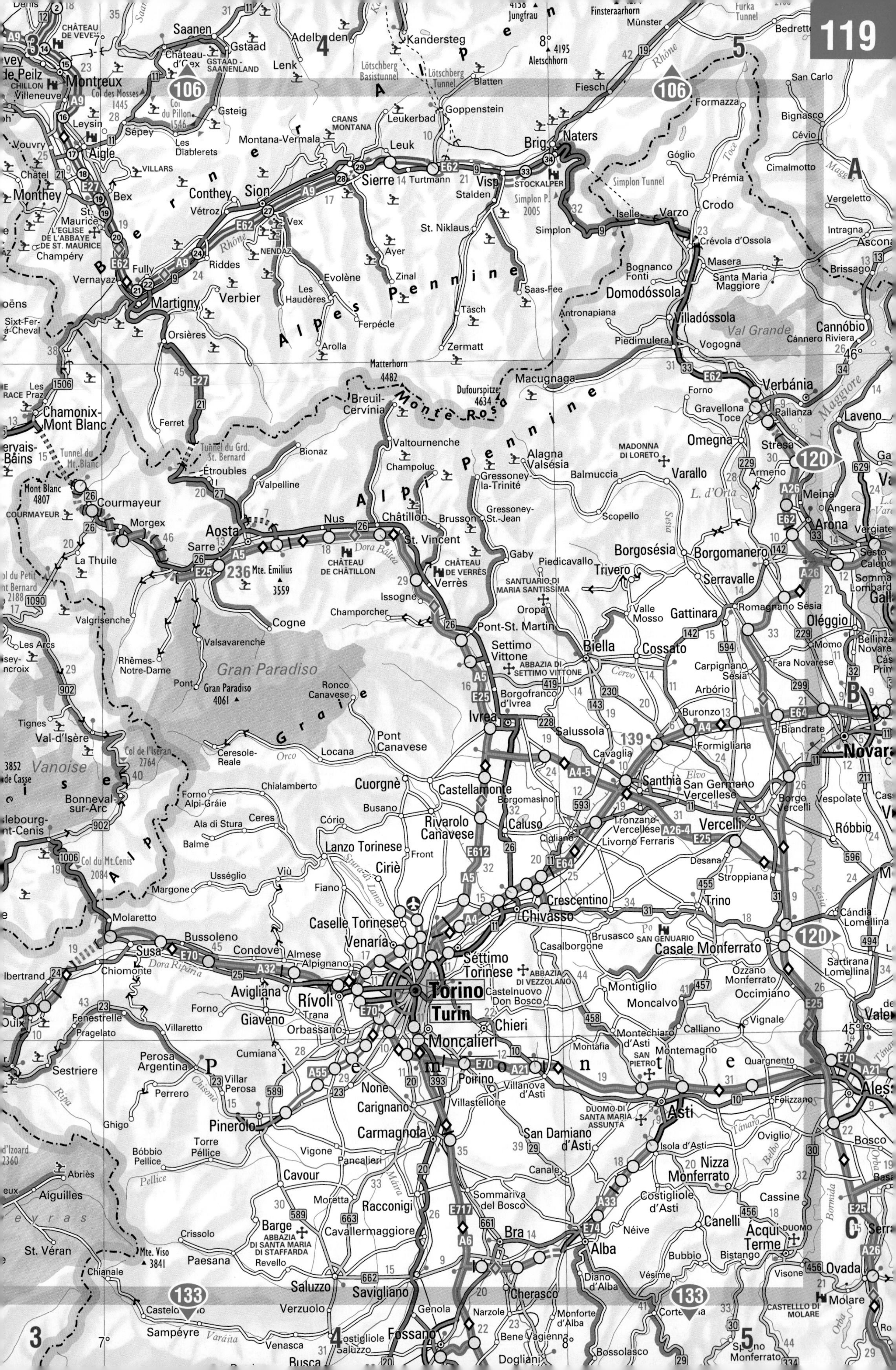
Saanen
Gstaad
Château-d'Œx
GSTAAD - SAANENLAND
Adelboden
Kandersteg
Lenk
Jungfrau
Finsteraarhorn
Münster
Furka Tunnel
Bedretto
Aletschhorn
4195
Montreux
CHILLON
Villeneuve
Col des Mosses
1445
Col du Pillon
1546
Gsteig
Leysin
Sépey
Les Diablerets
Aigle
Vouvry
Châtel
VILLARS
Bex
Monthey
St. Maurice
L'EGLISE DE L'ABBAYE DE ST. MAURICE
Champéry
Lötschberg Basistunnel
Lötschberg Tunnel
Blatten
Goppenstein
Leukerbad
CRANS MONTANA
Montana-Vermala
Leuk
Fiesch
Formazza
San Carlo
Bignasco
Cévio
Brig
Naters
Góglio
Cimalmotto
Sierre
Turtmann
Visp
STOCKALPER
Simplon Tunnel
Prémia
Conthey
Sion
Vétroz
Vex
NENDAZ
Stalden
Simplon P.
2005
Crodo
Vergeletto
Iselle
Varzo
Crévola d'Ossola
Intragna
Ascona
St. Niklaus
Simplon
Masera
Brissago
Riddes
Fully
Vernayaz
Martigny
Verbier
Ayer
Zinal
Evolène
Les Haudères
Ferpècle
Saas-Fee
Bognanco Fonti
Santa Maria Maggiore
Domodóssola
Täsch
Villadóssola
Antronapiana
Val Grande
Cannóbio
Cánnero Riviera
Sixt-Fer-à-Cheval
Orsières
Arolla
Zermatt
Piedimulera
Vogogna
Alpes Pennine
Berner Alpen
Matterhorn
4482
Dufourspitze
4634
Macugnaga
Monte Rosa
Verbánia
Pallanza
Forno
Gravellona Toce
L. Maggiore
Laveno
Les Praz
Chamonix-Mont Blanc
Ferret
Tunnel du Grd. St. Bernard
Étroubles
Bionaz
Breuil-Cervínia
Valtournenche
Champoluc
Alagna Valsésia
MADONNA DI LORETO
Omegna
Stresa
Armeno
Varallo
Balmuccia
L. d'Orta
Tunnel du Mt. Blanc
Mont Blanc
4807
COURMAYEUR
Courmayeur
Valpelline
Gressoney-la-Trinité
Gressoney-St.-Jean
Meina
Angera
Arona
Scopello
Morgex
La Thuile
Aosta
Sarre
Nus
Châtillon
Brusson
St. Vincent
CHÂTEAU DE CHÂTILLON
Dora Báltea
CHÂTEAU DE VERRÈS
Verrès
Mte. Emilius
3559
Gaby
Piedicavallo
Trivero
Borgosésia
Borgomanero
Serravalle
Col du Petit St. Bernard
2188
Alpi Pennine
SANTUARIO DI MARIA SANTISSIMA
Oropa
Valle Mosso
Gattinara
Romagnano Sésia
Oléggio
Valgrisenche
Cogne
Champorcher
Issogne
Pont-St. Martin
Les Arcs
Valsavarenche
Rhêmes-Notre-Dame
Gran Paradiso
4061
Settimo Vittone
ABBAZIA DI SETTIMO VITTONE
Biella
Cossato
Carpignano Sésia
Fara Novarese
Momo
Pont
Ronco Canavese
Borgofranco d'Ivrea
Cervo
Arbório
Ivrea
Buronzo
Biandrate
Novara
Tignes
Val-d'Isère
Alpi Graie
Ceresole-Reale
Orco
Locana
Pont Canavese
Salussola
Cavaglia
Formigliana
Col de l'Iseran
2764
Vanoise
Santhià
Elvo
San Germano Vercellese
Borgo Vercelli
Vespolate
Bonneval-sur-Arc
Chialamberto
Cuorgnè
Castellamonte
Borgomasino
Forno Alpi-Gráie
Ceres
Busano
Caluso
Tronzano-Vercellese
Vercelli
Róbbio
Ala di Stura
Cório
Rivarolo Canavese
Cigliano
Livorno Ferraris
Balme
Lanzo Torinese
Front
Col du Mt.Cenis
2084
Usséglio
Viù
Ciriè
Desana
Stroppiana
Margone
Fiano
Stura di Lanzo
Crescentino
Trino
Molaretto
Caselle Torinese
Chivasso
Cándia Lomellina
Bussoleno
Condove
Venaría
Brusasco
Po
SAN GENUARIO
Casale Monferrato
Susa
Almese
Alpignano
Settimo Torinese
ABBAZIA DI VEZZOLANO
Casalborgone
Dora Ripária
Chiomonte
Ozzano Monferrato
Sartirana Lomellina
Avigliana
Rívoli
Torino
Turin
Castelnuovo Don Bosco
Montiglio
Occimiano
Moncalvo
Forno
Trana
Giaveno
Orbassano
Chieri
Fenestrelle
Villaretto
Pragelato
Moncalieri
Montechiaro d'Asti
Calliano
Vignale
Montafia
Montemagno
Cumiana
SAN PIETRO
Quargnento
Perosa Argentina
Villar Perosa
None
Poirino
Villanova d'Asti
Felizzano
Sestriere
Chisone
Perrero
Piemonte
Carignano
Villastellone
DUOMO DI SANTA MARIA ASSUNTA
Asti
Alessandria
Ghigo
Pinerolo
Carmagnola
San Damiano d'Asti
Isola d'Asti
Nizza Monferrato
Oviglio
Bosco
Torre Péllice
Bóbbio Pellice
Vigone
Pancalieri
Canale
Tánaro
Belbo
Abriès
Aiguilles
Pellice
Cavour
Máira
Moretta
Racconigi
Sommariva del Bosco
Costigliole d'Asti
Cassine
Barge
ABBAZIA DI STAFFARDA
Cavallermaggiore
Bra
Alba
Néive
Canelli
Acqui Terme
DUOMO
Crissolo
St. Véran
Mte. Viso
3841
Paesana
Revello
Bubbio
Bistango
Ovada
Chianale
Saluzzo
Savigliano
Diano d'Alba
Vésime
Visone
Molare
CASTELLO DI MOLARE
Cherasco
Castelo
Verzuolo
Genola
Narzole
Monforte d'Alba
Cortemilia
Sampéyre
Varáita
Costigliole Saluzzo
Fossano
Bene Vagienna
Venasca
Dogliani
Bossolasco
Spigno Monferrato
Busca
Bormida
Orba
106
120
133
139
236
A
B
C
3
4
5
7°
8°
45°
46°

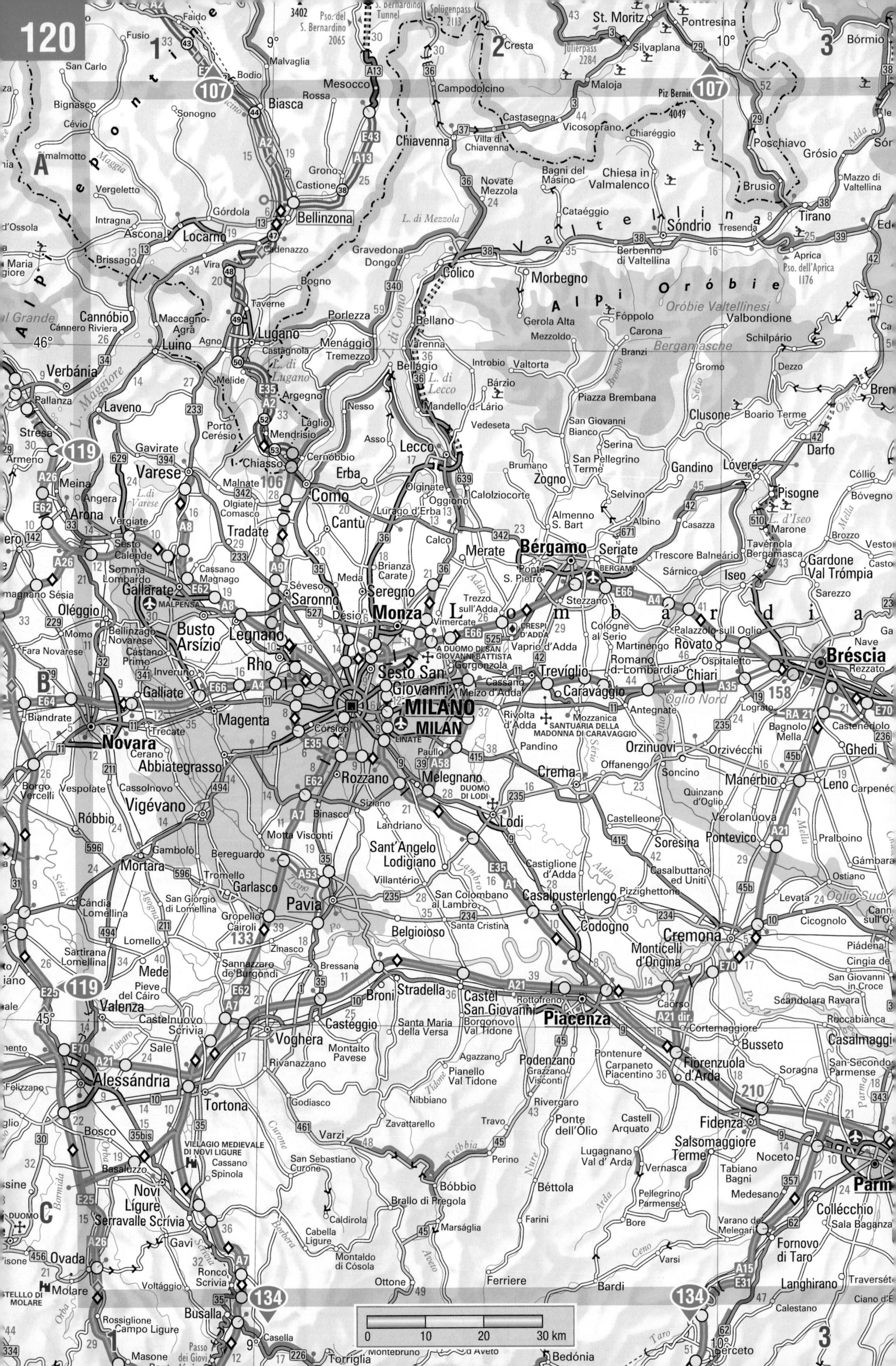

Faido
Fusio
San Bernardino Tunnel
Pso. del S. Bernardino 2065
Splügenpass 2113
Cresta
St. Moritz
Pontresina
Silvaplana
Julierpass 2284
Bórmio
San Carlo
Malvaglia
Bodio
Mesocco
Campodolcino
Maloja
Piz Bernina 4049
Bignasco
Biasca
Rossa
Sonogno
Castasegna
Vicosoprano
Chiaréggio
Poschiavo
Grósio
Cévio
Chiavenna
Villa di Chiavenna
Maggia
Grono
Castione
Bagni del Masino
Chiesa in Valmalenco
Brusio
Mazzo di Valtellina
Vergeletto
Novate Mezzola
Górdola
Bellinzona
Cataéggio
Tirano
Intragna
Ascona
Locarno
L. di Mezzola
Sóndrio
Tresenda
d'Ossola
Cadenazzo
Gravedona
Dongo
Berbenno di Valtellina
Aprica
Pso. dell'Aprica 1176
Brissago
Vira
Colico
Morbegno
Valtellina
Alpi Lepontine
Alpi Oróbie
Oróbie Valtellinesi
Bogno
Taverne
Fóppolo
Valbondione
Cannóbio
Cánnero Riviera
Maccagno-Agra
Porlezza
Bellano
Gerola Alta
Mezzoldo
Carona
Lugano
Castagnola
Menággio
Tremezzo
Varenna
Branzi
Bergamasche
Schilpário
Verbánia
Pallanza
Luino
Agno
Melide
L. di Lugano
Bellágio
L. di Como
Introbio
Valtorta
Gromo
Dezzo
L. Maggiore
Argegno
L. di Lecco
Bárzio
Piazza Brembana
Laveno
Nesso
Mandello d. Lário
Clusone
Boario Terme
Stresa
Porto Cerésio
Mendrísio
Láglio
Vedeseta
San Giovanni Bianco
Armeno
Gavirate
Chiasso
Cernóbbio
Asso
Lecco
Serina
Darfo
Varese
Malnate
Erba
Brumano
San Pellegrino Terme
Gandino
Lóveré
Meina
Angera
L. di Varese
Como
Olginate
Oggiono
Calolziocorte
Zogno
Pisogne
Bóvegno
Arona
Vergiate
Olgiate Comasco
Cantù
Lurago d'Erba
Selvino
Almenno S. Bart
Albino
Casazza
Marone
L. d'Iseo
Tradate
Calco
Merate
Bérgamo
Seriate
Trescore Balneário
Tavérnola Bergamasca
Gardone Val Trómpia
Sesto Calende
Somma Lombardo
Cassano Magnago
Brianza Carate
Ponte S. Pietro
Sárnico
Iseo
Gallarate
Malpensa
Séveso
Saronno
Meda
Seregno
Monza
Trezzo sull'Adda
Stezzano
Sarezzo
Oléggio
Busto Arsízio
Legnano
Désio
Vimercate
Lombardia
Crespi d'Adda
Cologne
Palazzolo sull Oglio
Nave
Momo
Bellinzago Novarese
Castano Primo
Rho
A Duomo di San Giovanni Battista
Vaprio d'Adda
Cologne al Serio
Martinengo
Rovato
Bréscia
Rezzato
Fara Novarese
Inveruno
Sesto San Giovanni
Gorgonzola
Cassano
Treviglio
Romano d. Lombardia
Ospitaletto
Novara
Galliate
Magenta
Melzo
Caravággio
Chiari
Milano
Milan
Linate
Rivolta d'Adda
Mozzanica
Antegnate
Oglio Nord
Lograto
Biandrate
Trecate
Corsico
Santuario della Madonna di Caravaggio
Bagnolo Mella
Castenédolo
Cerano
Abbiategrasso
Paullo
Pandino
Orzinuovi
Orzivécchi
Ghedi
Borgo Vercelli
Vespolate
Cassolnovo
Rozzano
Melegnano
Crema
Offanengo
Soncino
Manérbio
Leno
Carpenedolo
Vigévano
Duomo di Lodi
Lodi
Quinzano d'Oglio
Róbbio
Binasco
Siziano
Landriano
Castelleone
Verolanuova
Pontevico
Motta Visconti
Pralboino
Gambolò
Sant'Angelo Lodigiano
Soresina
Mortara
Bereguardo
Castiglione d'Adda
Casalbuttano ed Uniti
Gámbara
Tromello
Garlasco
Villantério
Ostiano
Cándia Lomellina
San Giorgio di Lomellina
Pavia
San Colombano al Lambro
Casalpusterlengo
Pizzighettone
Levata
Oglio Sud
Gropello Cairoli
Santa Cristina
Codogno
Cremona
Cicognolo
Lomello
Zinasco
Belgioioso
Monticelli d'Ongina
Piádena
Sartirana Lomellina
Bressana
Cingia de
Mede
Sannazzaro de'Burgondi
Broni
Stradella
Castel San Giovanni
Rottofreno
Piacenza
Caorso
San Giovanni in Croce
Pieve del Cáiro
Scandolara Ravara
Valenza
Castelnuovo Scrivia
Castéggio
Santa Maria della Versa
Borgonovo Val Tidone
Cortemaggiore
Roccabianca
Sale
Voghera
Montalto Pavese
Busseto
Casalmaggiore
Alessándria
Rivanazzano
Agazzano
Podenzano
Pontenure
Fiorenzuola d'Arda
San Secondo Parmense
Felizzano
Pianello Val Tidone
Grazzano Visconti
Carpaneto Piacentino
Soragna
Tortona
Nibbiano
Godiasco
Rivergaro
Zavattarello
Travo
Ponte dell'Ólio
Castell Arquato
Fidenza
Bosco
Varzi
Salsomaggiore Terme
Noceto
Villaggio Medievale di Novi Ligure
Cassano Spinola
San Sebastiano Curone
Perino
Lugagnano Val d'Arda
Tabiano Bagni
Parma
Basaluzzo
Vernasca
Novi Lígure
Bóbbio
Béttola
Medesano
Brallo di Pregola
Pellegrino Parmense
Collécchio
Serravalle Scrívia
Caldirola
Farini
Bore
Sala Baganza
Varano de' Melegari
Gavi
Cabella Ligure
Marságlia
Fornovo di Taro
Ovada
Montaldo di Cósola
Varsi
Ronco Scrivia
Voltággio
Ottone
Ferriere
Bardi
Langhirano
Traversét
Molare
Castello di Molare
Ciano d'E
Busalla
Calestano
Rossiglione
Campo Ligure
Casella
Passo dei Giovi
Masone
Torriglia
Montebruno
Bedónia
Berceto
0 10 20 30 km

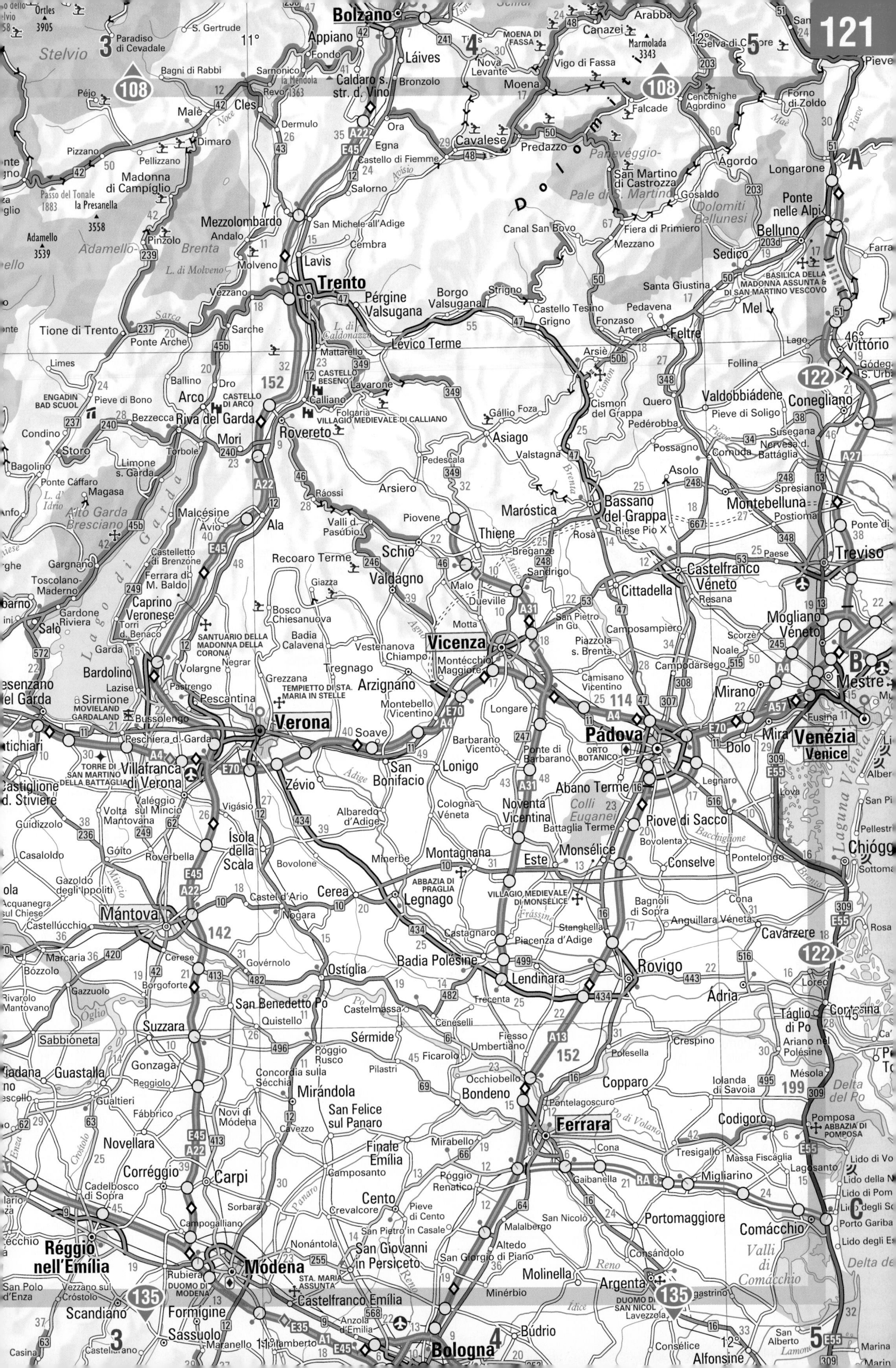
Bolzano
Appiano
Láives
Caldaro s. str. d. Vino
Bronzolo
Ortles
3905
Stelvio
Paradiso di Cevadale
S. Gertrude
Bagni di Rabbi
Sarnonico
Revò
Fondo
Péjo
Malè
Cles
Dermulo
Dimaro
Pizzano
Pellizzano
Madonna di Campíglio
Passo del Tonale 1883
la Presanella 3558
Adamello 3539
Adamello
Brenta
Pinzolo
Ora
Egna
Castello di Fiemme
Salorno
Cavalese
Predazzo
Moena
Nova Levante
Moena di Fassa
Vigo di Fassa
Canazei
Arabba
Marmolada 3343
Selva di Cadore
Falcade
Cencenighe Agordino
Ágordo
Forno di Zoldo
Longarone
Ponte nelle Alpi
Belluno
Sedico
Farra
Dolomiti
Dolomiti Bellunesi
Paneveggio
Pale di S. Martino
San Martino di Castrozza
Gosaldo
Canal San Bovo
Fiera di Primiero
Mezzano
Mezzolombardo
Andalo
San Michele all'Adige
Cembra
Molveno
L. di Molveno
Lavìs
Trento
Vezzano
Pérgine Valsugana
Borgo Valsugana
Strigno
Castello Tesino
Grigno
Pedavena
Fonzaso
Arten
Feltre
Santa Giustina
Mel
Basilica della Madonna Assunta & di San Martino Vescovo
Tione di Trento
Ponte Arche
Sarche
L. di Caldonazzo
Levico Terme
Mattarello
Castello Beseno
Lavarone
Calliano
Folgaria
Villaggio medievale di Calliano
Rovereto
Limes
Ballino
Dro
Arco
Castello di Arco
Riva del Garda
Mori
Torbole
Engadin Bad Scuol
Pieve di Bono
Bezzecca
Condino
Storo
Bagolino
Limone s. Garda
Ponte Cáffaro
Magasa
L. d'Idro
Alto Garda Bresciano
Malcésine
Avio
Ala
Ráossi
Valli d. Pasúbio
Arsiero
Pedescala
Asiago
Gállio
Foza
Valstagna
Arsiè
Cismon del Grappa
Quero
Valdobbiádene
Pieve di Soligo
Conegliano
Vittório
Gódega
Follina
Lago
Pederobba
Possagno
Asolo
Cornuda
Susegana
Nervesa d. Battáglia
Spresiano
Montebelluna
Postioma
Ponte di Piave
Treviso
Bassano del Grappa
Marostica
Riese Pio X
Piovene
Thiene
Schio
Recoaro Terme
Valdagno
Breganze
Sandrigo
Rosà
Castelfranco Véneto
Cittadella
Resana
Paese
Gargnano
Toscolano-Maderno
Castelletto di Brenzone
Ferrara di M. Baldo
Caprino Veronese
Gardone Riviera
Salò
Torri d. Benaco
Garda
Bardolino
Lazise
Santuario della Madonna della Corona
Bosco Chiesanuova
Badia Calavena
Giazza
Malo
Dueville
Motta
Vicenza
Montécchio Maggiore
Vestenanova
Chiampo
Arzignano
Tregnago
Grezzana
Negrar
Volargne
Pastrengo
Pescantina
Tempietto di Sta. Maria in Stelle
Desenzano del Garda
Sirmione
Movieland Gardaland
Bussolengo
Peschiera d. Garda
Verona
Montebello Vicentino
Soave
San Bonifacio
Lonigo
Zévio
Villafranca di Verona
Torre di San Martino della Battaglia
Castiglione d. Stiviere
Valéggio sul Mincio
Volta Mantovana
Vigásio
Ísola della Scala
Guidizzolo
Góito
Roverbella
Casaloldo
Gazoldo degli Ippoliti
Acquanegra sul Chiese
Mántova
Castellùcchio
Marcaria
Bózzolo
Rivarolo Mantovano
Gazzuolo
Sabbioneta
Cerese
Borgoforte
Castel d'Ario
Nogara
Bovolone
Cerea
Legnago
Albaredo d'Adige
Cologna Véneta
Barbarano Vicentino
Ponte di Barbarano
Longare
Noventa Vicentina
Montagnana
Minerbe
Abbazia di Praglia
Este
Monsélice
Villaggio medievale di Monselice
Colli Euganei
Battaglia Terme
Abano Terme
Pádova
Orto Botanico
Camisano Vicentino
San Pietro in Gu
Piazzola s. Brenta
Camposampiero
Campodársego
Scorzè
Noale
Mirano
Mogliano Véneto
Mestre
Venézia Venice
Dolo
Mira
Fusina
Legnaro
Lova
Piove di Sacco
Bovolenta
Conselve
Pontelongo
Chióggia
Sottomarina
Laguna Veneta
Cona
Bagnoli di Sopra
Anguillara Véneta
Cavárzere
Stanghella
Piacenza d'Adige
Frássine
Castagnaro
Badia Polésine
Lendinara
Rovigo
Ádria
Lòreo
Contarina
Táglio di Po
Ariano nel Polésine
Mésola
Delta del Po
Pomposa
Abbazia di Pompósa
Codigoro
Iolanda di Savoia
Copparo
Crespino
Polesella
Fiesso Umbertiano
Occhiobello
Bondeno
Trecenta
Ceneselli
Castelmassa
Ostíglia
Govérnolo
San Benedetto Po
Quistello
Sérmide
Suzzara
Gonzaga
Reggiolo
Guastalla
Viadana
Gualtieri
Fábbrico
Novellara
Corréggio
Carpi
Novi di Módena
Concordia sulla Sécchia
Mirándola
Póggio Rusco
San Felice sul Panaro
Cavezzo
Finale Emília
Ficarolo
Pilastri
Mirabello
Ferrara
Pontelagoscuro
Tresigallo
Massa Fiscáglia
Migliarino
Lagosanto
Lido di Volano
Lido delle Nazioni
Lido di Pomposa
Lido degli Scacchi
Porto Garibaldi
Lido degli Estensi
Comácchio
Valli di Comácchio
Portomaggiore
Consándolo
Argenta
Duomo di San Nicolò
Lavezzola
Gaibanella
San Nicolò
Malalbergo
Altedo
San Giorgio di Piano
Molinella
Minérbio
Búdrio
Bologna
Conselice
Alfonsine
San Alberto
Marina
Póggio Renatico
Cento
Pieve di Cento
Crevalcore
Camposanto
San Pietro in Casale
San Giovanni in Persiceto
Nonántola
Castelfranco Emília
Anzola d'Emília
Sta. Maria Assunta
Módena
Duomo di Modena
Campogalliano
Sorbara
Rubiera
Formigine
Sassuolo
Maranello
Spilamberto
Scandiano
Réggio nell'Emília
Cadelbosco di Sopra
San Polo d'Enza
Vezzano sul Cróstolo
Casina
108
122
135
152
114
142
199
A22
A4
A31
A13
A1
A27
A57
E45
E70
E55
E35
RA 8

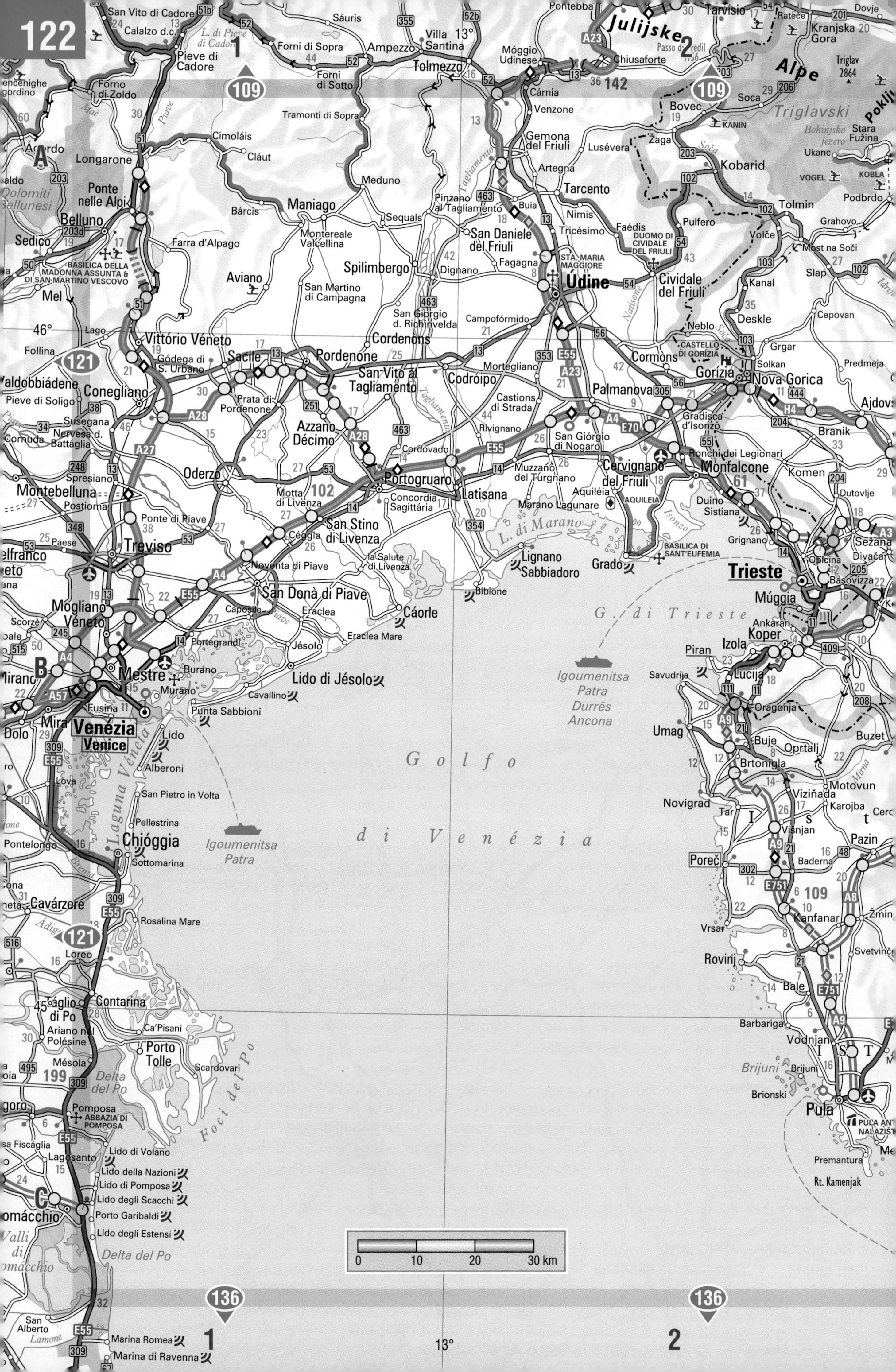

Belluno
Treviso
Venézia
Venice
Mestre
Chióggia
Pordenone
Údine
Gorízia
Nova Gorica
Trieste
Koper
Poreč
Rovinj
Pula
Golfo di Venézia
G. di Trieste
Delta del Po
Laguna Véneta
Julijske Alpe
0 10 20 30 km

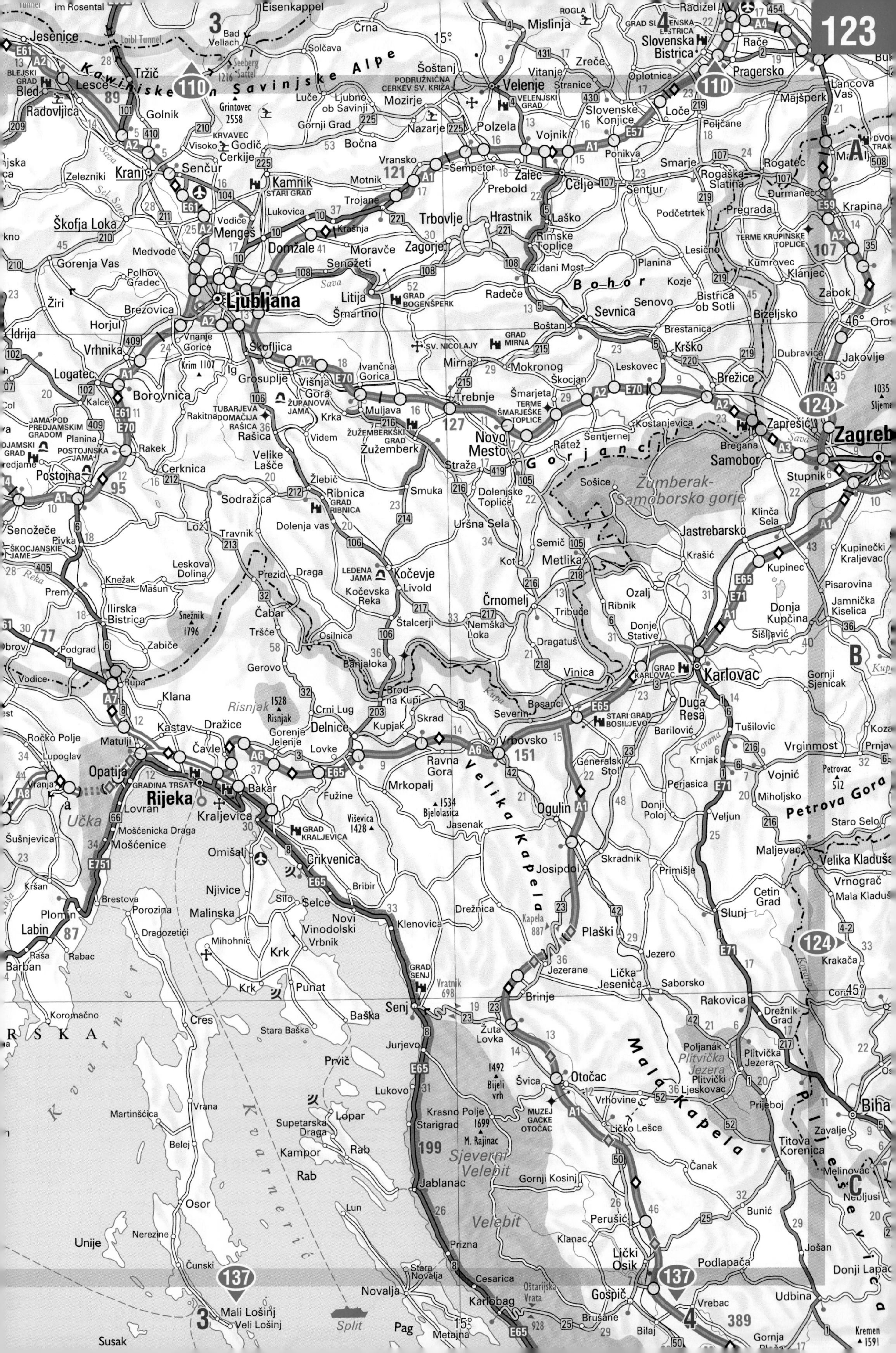

Jesenice
Bled
Radovljica
Lesce
Tržič
Kranj
Sečur
Škofja Loka
Medvode
Kamnik
Menges
Domžale
Ljubljana
Vrhnika
Logatec
Borovnica
Postojna
Idrija
Cerknica
Ribnica
Kočevje
Grosuplje
Litija
Šmartno
Trbovlje
Hrastnik
Zagorje
Celje
Velenje
Žalec
Polzela
Mozirje
Slovenska Bistrica
Slovenske Konjice
Pragersko
Rogaška Slatina
Šentjur
Laško
Sevnica
Krško
Brežice
Trebnje
Novo Mesto
Črnomelj
Metlika
Karlovac
Duga Resa
Zagreb
Zaprešić
Samobor
Jastrebarsko
Krapina
Zabok
Delnice
Rijeka
Opatija
Kraljevica
Crikvenica
Novi Vinodolski
Senj
Krk
Rab
Cres
Mali Lošinj
Veli Lošinj
Novalja
Pag
Karlobag
Gospić
Otočac
Ogulin
Slunj
Plitvička Jezera
Bihać
Udbina
Labin
Plomin
Ilirska Bistrica
Kawinkske Savinjske Alpe
Bohor
Gorjanci
Žumberak-Samoborsko gorje
Velika Kapela
Mala Kapela
Petrova Gora
Sjeverni Velebit
Velebit
Kvarner
Kvarnerić
Učka
Risnjak
Snežnik
Split

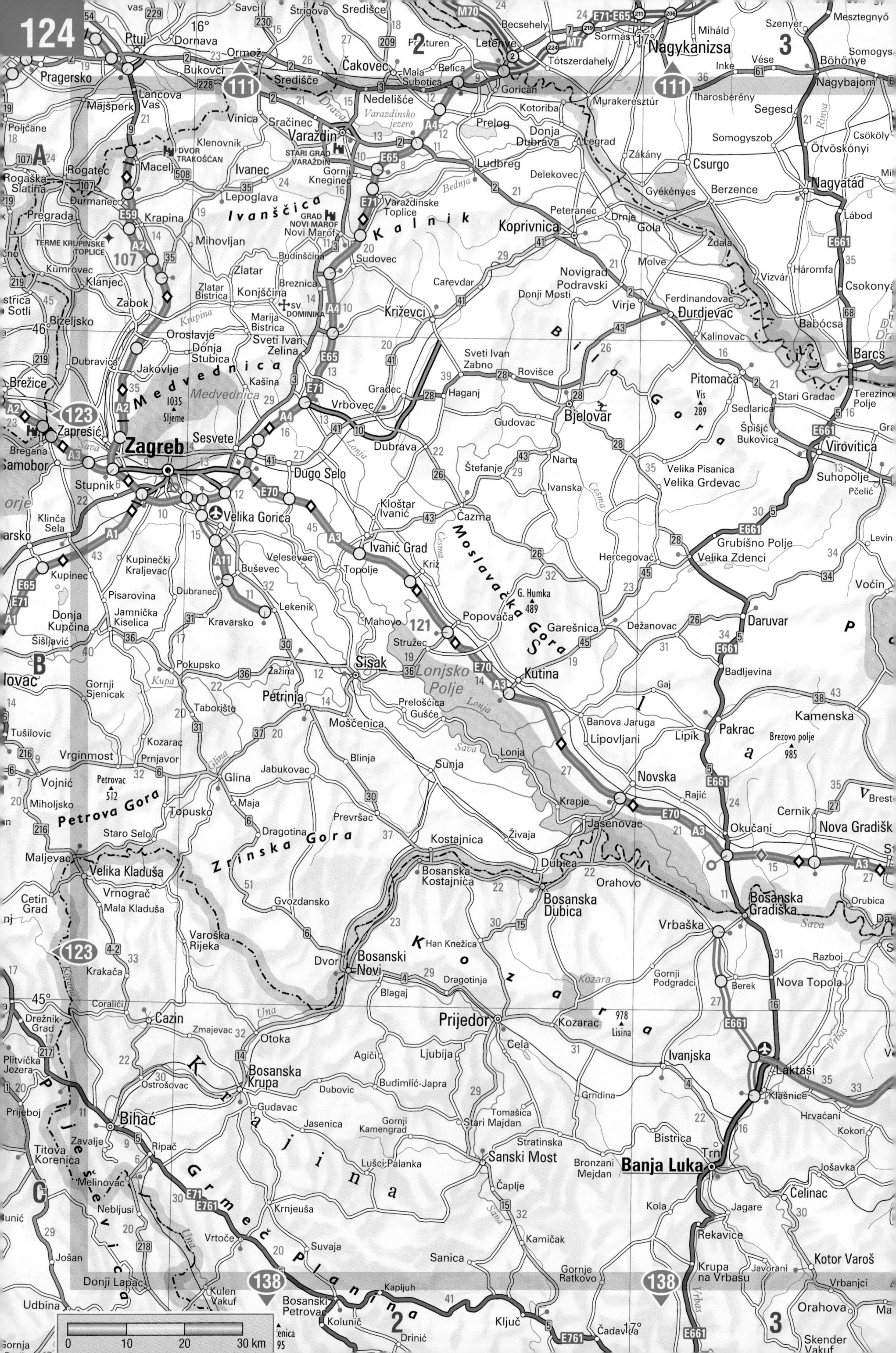
124
Ptuj
Dornava
Ormož
Pragersko
Bukovci
Središče
Čakovec
Nedelišće
Mala Subotica
Belica
Goričan
Letenye
Becsehely
Sormás
Nagykanizsa
Miháld
Szenyér
Mesztegnyő
Böhönye
Vése
Inke
Nagybajom
Iharosberény
Segesd
Somogyszob
Ötvöskónyi
Csököly
Murakeresztúr
Tótszerdahely
Kotoriba
Prelog
Donja Dubrava
Legrad
Zákány
Csurgo
Gyékényes
Berzence
Nagyatád
Lábod
Háromfa
Csokonyavisonta
Vizvár
Babócsa
Barcs
Terezino Polje
Lancova Vas
Majšperk
Poljčane
Vinica
Sračinec
Varaždin
Varaždinsko jezero
STARI GRAD VARAŽDIN
Klenovnik
DVOR TRAKOŠĆAN
Macelj
Rogatec
Rogaška Slatina
Đurmanec
Pregrada
Krapina
Ivanec
Lepoglava
Gornji Kneginec
Ludbreg
Delekovec
Bednja
Varaždinske Toplice
GRAD NOVI MAROF
Novi Marof
Ivanščica
Kalnik
Koprivnica
Peteranec
Drnje
Gola
Ždala
Molve
TERME KRUPINSKE TOPLICE
Mihovljan
Kumrovec
Klanjec
Zlatar
Zlatar Bistrica
Budinšćina
Breznica
Sudovec
Konjščina
SV. DOMINIKA
Carevdar
Križevci
Novigrad Podravski
Donji Mosti
Virje
Ferdinandovac
Đurdjevac
Kalinovac
Zabok
Bizeljsko
Oroslavje
Marija Bistrica
Sveti Ivan Zelina
Donja Stubica
Dubravica
Jakovlje
Brežice
Medvednica
1035 Sljeme
Kašina
Bilo Gora
Sveti Ivan Zabno
Rovišce
Gradec
Haganj
Bjelovar
Pitomača
Vis 289
Stari Gradac
Sedlarica
Špišić Bukovica
Virovitica
Suhopolje
Pčelić
Zaprešić
Bregana
Samobor
Zagreb
Sesvete
Vrbovec
Dubrava
Gudovac
Dugo Selo
Lonja
Štefanje
Narta
Ivanska
Česma
Velika Pisanica
Velika Grdevac
Stupnik
Klinča Sela
Velika Gorica
Kloštar Ivanić
Čazma
Moslavačka Gora
Grubišno Polje
Velika Zdenci
Hercegovac
Levin
Kupinec
Kupinečki Kraljevac
Veleševec
Ivanić Grad
Topolje
Križ
Buševec
Lekenik
G. Humka 489
Voćin
Pisarovina
Dubranec
Jamnička Kiselica
Kravarsko
Donja Kupčina
Šišljavić
Mahovo
Popovača
Garešnica
Dežanovac
Daruvar
Stružec
Lonjsko Polje
Kutina
Badljevina
Pokupsko
Žažina
Sisak
Gaj
Gornji Sjenicak
Kupa
Petrinja
Prelošćica
Gušće
Banova Jaruga
Lipovljani
Lipik
Pakrac
Kamenska
Taborište
Moščenica
Brezovo polje 985
Tušilovic
Kozarac
Vrginmost
Prnjavor
Blinja
Sava
Sunja
Novska
Rajić
Vojnić
Petrovac 512
Glina
Jabukovac
Krapje
Cernik
Nova Gradiška
Miholjsko
Petrova Gora
Topusko
Maja
Jasenovac
Okučani
Staro Selo
Dragotina
Prevršac
Živaja
Kostajnica
Zrinska Gora
Maljevac
Velika Kladuša
Vrnograč
Mala Kladuša
Bosanska Kostajnica
Dubica
Orahovo
Bosanska Dubica
Bosanska Gradiška
Orubica
Cetin Grad
Gvozdansko
Vrbaška
Varoška Rijeka
Han Knežica
Kozara
Razboj
Krakača
Dvor
Bosanski Novi
Dragotinja
Gornji Podgradci
Berek
Nova Topola
Korana
Coralići
Blagaj
Una
Drežnik-Grad
Cazin
Zmajevac
Otoka
Prijedor
Kozarac
978 Lisina
Plitvička Jezera
Agići
Ljubija
Čela
Ivanjska
Laktaši
Vrbas
Ostrošovac
Bosanska Krupa
Budimlić-Japra
Grndina
Klašnice
Prijeboj
Bihać
Gudavac
Dubovic
Jasenica
Gornji Kamengrad
Tomašica
Stari Majdan
Hrvaćani
Kokori
Zavalje
Ripač
Krajina
Stratinska
Bistrica
Titova Korenica
Lušci Palanka
Sanski Most
Bronzani Mejdan
Banja Luka
Jošavka
Melinovac
Grmeč
Čaplje
Čelinac
Nebljusi
Krnjeuša
Kola
Jagare
Sana
Vrtoče
Kamičak
Rekavice
Plješevica
Sanica
Suvaja
Planina
Kotor Varoš
Jošan
Donji Lapac
Kulen Vakuf
Gornje Ratkovo
Krupa na Vrbasu
Javorani
Vrbanjci
Udbina
Bosanski Petrovac
Kolunič
Kapljuh
Drinić
Ključ
Čadavica
Orahova
Skender Vakuf
0 10 20 30 km

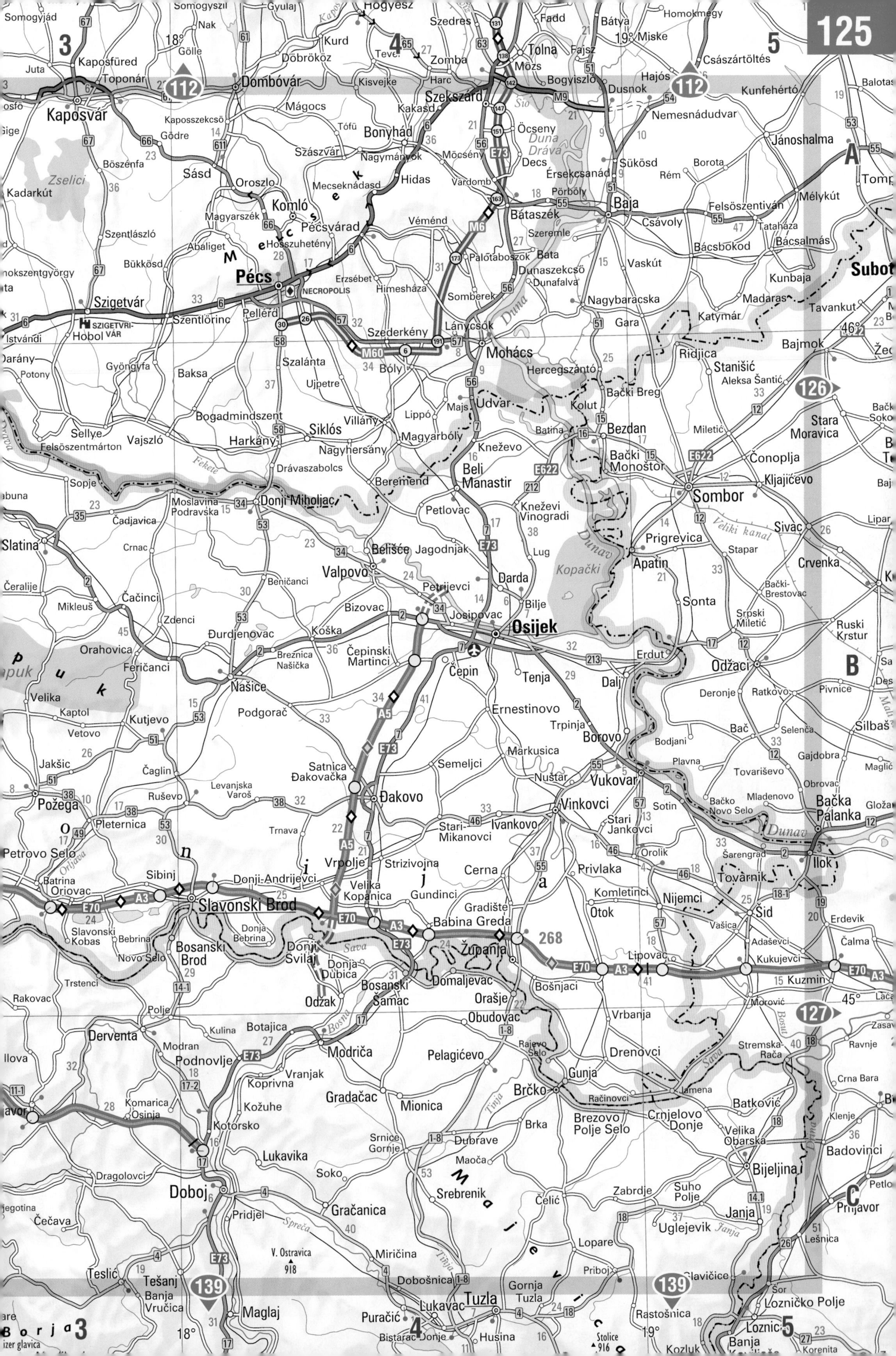

Somogyjád
Somogyszil
Gyulaj
Nak
Hőgyész
Szedres
Fadd
Bátya
Homokmegy
3
4
5
Kaposfüred
Gölle
Kurd
Tolna
Fajsz
Miske
Dőbrököz
Tevel
Zomba
Mözs
Császártöltés
Juta
Toponár
112
Dombóvár
Kisvejke
Harc
Bogyiszló
Dusnok
Hajós
Kunfehértó
Balotas
Kaposvár
Mágocs
Kakasd
Szekszárd
Sió
Nemesnádudvar
Kaposszekcsö
Tófű
Bonyhád
Őcseny
Gödre
Szászvár
Nagymányok
Duna
Dráva
Jánoshalma
Böszénfa
Mőcsény
Decs
Sükösd
Borota
A
Zselici
Sásd
Oroszló
Hidas
Vardomb
Érsekcsanád
Rém
Tomp
Kadarkút
Mecseknádasd
Pörböly
Baja
Mélykút
Komló
Magyarszék
Pécsvárad
Véménd
Bátaszék
Felsőszentiván
Csávoly
Tataháza
Szentlászló
Abaliget
Hosszuhetény
Szeremle
Bácsbokod
Bácsalmás
M
e
c
s
e
k
Palotabozsok
Bata
Bükkösd
Pécs
Erzsébet
Dunaszekcső
Vaskút
Kunbaja
Subot
nokszentgyörgy
Himesháza
NECROPOLIS
Dunafalva
Szigetvár
Pellérd
Somberek
Nagybaracska
Madaras
Tavankut
SZIGETVRI-VÁR
Szentlőrinc
Lánycsók
Gara
Katymár
Hobol
Szederkény
Mohács
Bajmok
Istvándi
M60
Bóly
Hercegszántó
Ridjica
Stanišić
Aleksa Šantić
Darány
Gyöngyfa
Szalánta
Potony
Baksa
Ujpetre
126
Bački Breg
Udvar
Majs
Lippó
Kolut
Bogadmindszent
Villány
Stara Moravica
Sellye
Siklós
Batina
Bezdan
Miletić
Felsőszentmárton
Vajszló
Harkány
Magyarbóly
Kneževo
Bački Monoštor
Nagyharsány
Čonoplja
Beli Manastir
Drávaszabolcs
E622
Fekete
Beremend
Sopje
Kljajićevo
Sombor
abuna
Moslavina Podravska
Donji Miholjac
Petlovac
Kneževi Vinogradi
Čadjavica
Veliki kanal
Sivac
Lipar
Slatina
Crnac
Belišće
Jagodnjak
Prigrevica
Stapar
Lug
Dunav
Crvenka
Kopački
Apatin
Valpovo
Darda
Čeralije
Beničanci
Petrijevci
Bački-Brestovac
Čačinci
Mikleuš
Bizovac
Sonta
Bilje
Zdenci
Josipovac
Srpski Miletić
Ruski Krstur
Osijek
Đurdjenovac
Koška
Orahovica
Breznica Našička
Čepinski Martinci
Erdut
Odžaci
B
puk
Feričanci
Čepin
Tenja
Dalj
Našice
Deronje
Ratkovo
Pivnice
Velika
Ernestinovo
Podgorač
Trpinja
Kaptol
Kutjevo
Borovo
Bač
Selenča
Silbaš
Vetovo
Bodjani
Markusica
Semeljci
Gajdobra
Jakšic
Čaglin
Satnica Đakovačka
Plavna
Tovariševo
Vukovar
Nuštar
Levanjska Varoš
Obrovac
Požega
Ruševo
Đakovo
Vinkovci
Sotin
Bačko Novo Selo
Mladenovo
Bačka Palanka
Gložan
Pleternica
Stari Jankovci
Ivankovo
Trnava
Stari-Mikanovci
Dunav
Orolik
Šarengrad
Ilok
Petrovo Selo
Orljava
Privlaka
Tovarnik
Sibinj
Vrpolje
Strizivojna
Cerna
Batrina
Donji-Andrijevci
Oriovac
Velika Kopanica
Gundinci
Komletinci
Nijemci
Slavonski Brod
Otok
Šid
Erdevik
Gradište
Vašica
Slavonski Kobas
Bebrina
Donja Bebrina
Babina Greda
Adaševci
Čalma
Bosanski Brod
Donji Svilaj
Sava
Županja
268
Lipovac
Kukujevci
Novo Selo
Donja Dubica
E70
A3
Trstenci
Bosanski Šamac
Domaljevac
Bošnjaci
Kuzmin
Rakovac
Odžak
Orašje
Morović
45°
127
Polje
Obudovac
Zasav
Derventa
Kulina
Botajica
Vrbanja
Bosut
Modran
Bosna
Modriča
Rajevo Selo
Stremska-Rača
Ravnje
Ilova
Podnovlje
Pelagićevo
Drenovci
Vranjak
Gunja
Crna Bara
Koprivna
Tinja
Gradačac
Brčko
Račinovci
Jamena
Batković
Komarica
Osinja
Kožuhe
Mionica
Brezovo Polje Selo
Crnjelovo Donje
Klenje
avor
Kotorsko
Brka
Velika Obarska
Badovinci
Srnice Gornje
Dubrave
Drina
Lukavika
Maoča
Bijeljina
Dragolovci
Soko
M
a
j
e
v
i
c
a
Doboj
Srebrenik
Zabrdje
Suho Polje
Petlo
C
Prnjavor
jegotina
Pridjel
Gračanica
Čelić
Janja
Čečava
Spreča
Ugljevik
Lešnica
Lopare
V. Ostravica 918
Miričina
Teslić
Tešanj
Priboj
Slavičice
Šor
Banja Vručica
139
Dobošnica
Gornja Tuzla
Lozničko Polje
Maglaj
Lukavac
Tuzla
Puračić
Rastošnica
Borja
izer glavica
18°
Bistarac Donje
Husina
Stolice 916
19°
Kozluk
Loznica
Banja
Korenita

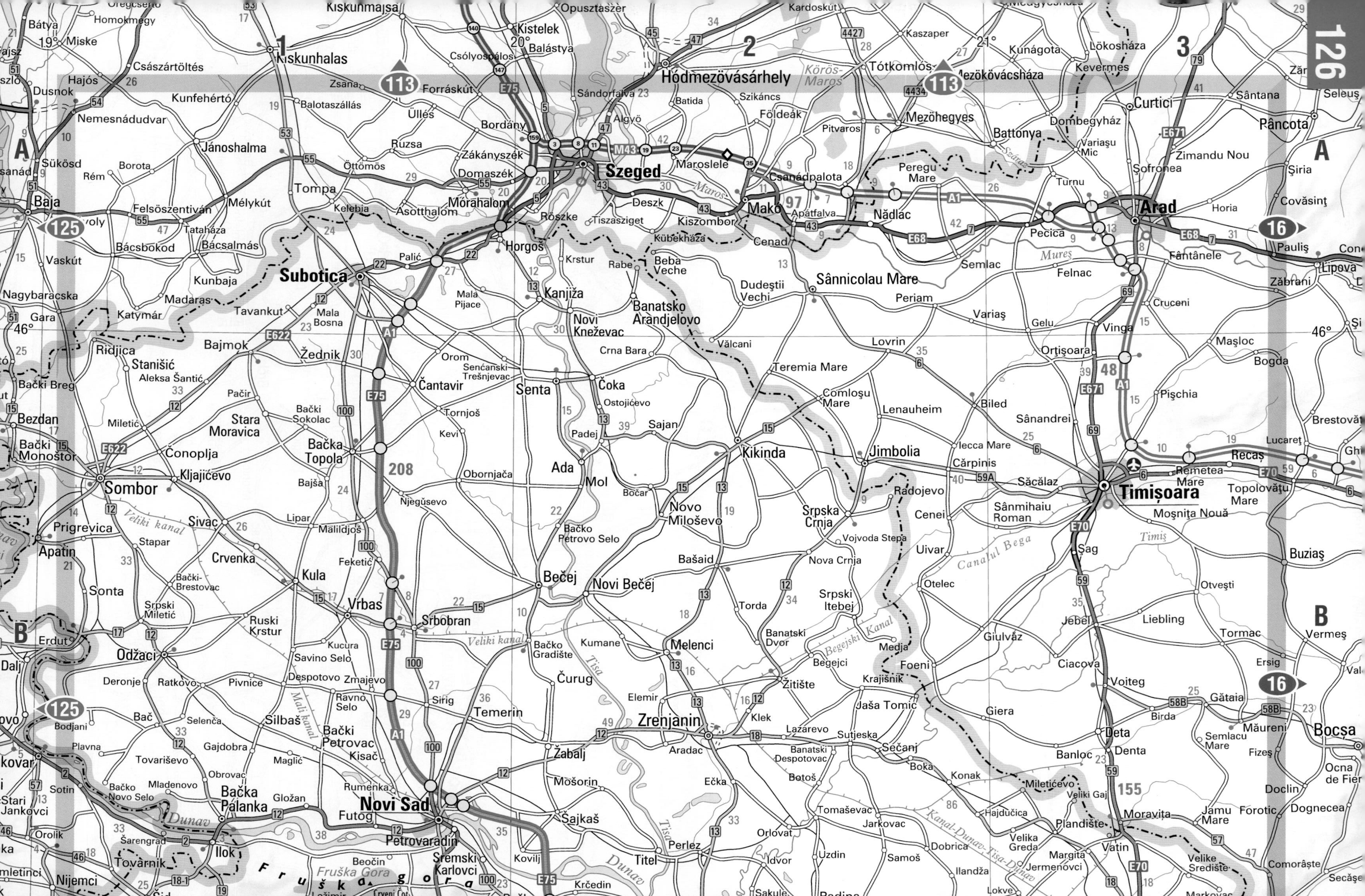
Kiskunhalas
Hódmezővásárhely
Mezőkovácsháza
Kistelek
Szeged
Makó
Nădlac
Arad
Curtici
Pâncota
Lipova
Subotica
Sânnicolau Mare
Kanjiža
Novi Kneževac
Banatsko Arandjelovo
Senta
Čoka
Kikinda
Jimbolia
Timişoara
Recaş
Buziaş
Baja
Sombor
Bačka Topola
Ada
Mol
Novo Miloševo
Srpska Crnja
Apatin
Kula
Vrbas
Srbobran
Bečej
Novi Bečej
Melenci
Odžaci
Zrenjanin
Žitište
Sečanj
Deta
Bocşa
Bačka Palanka
Novi Sad
Petrovaradin
Sremski Karlovci
Titel
Ilok
Šid
Fruška gora
Dunav
Tisa
Mureş
Timiş
Canalul Bega
Veliki kanal
Mali kanal

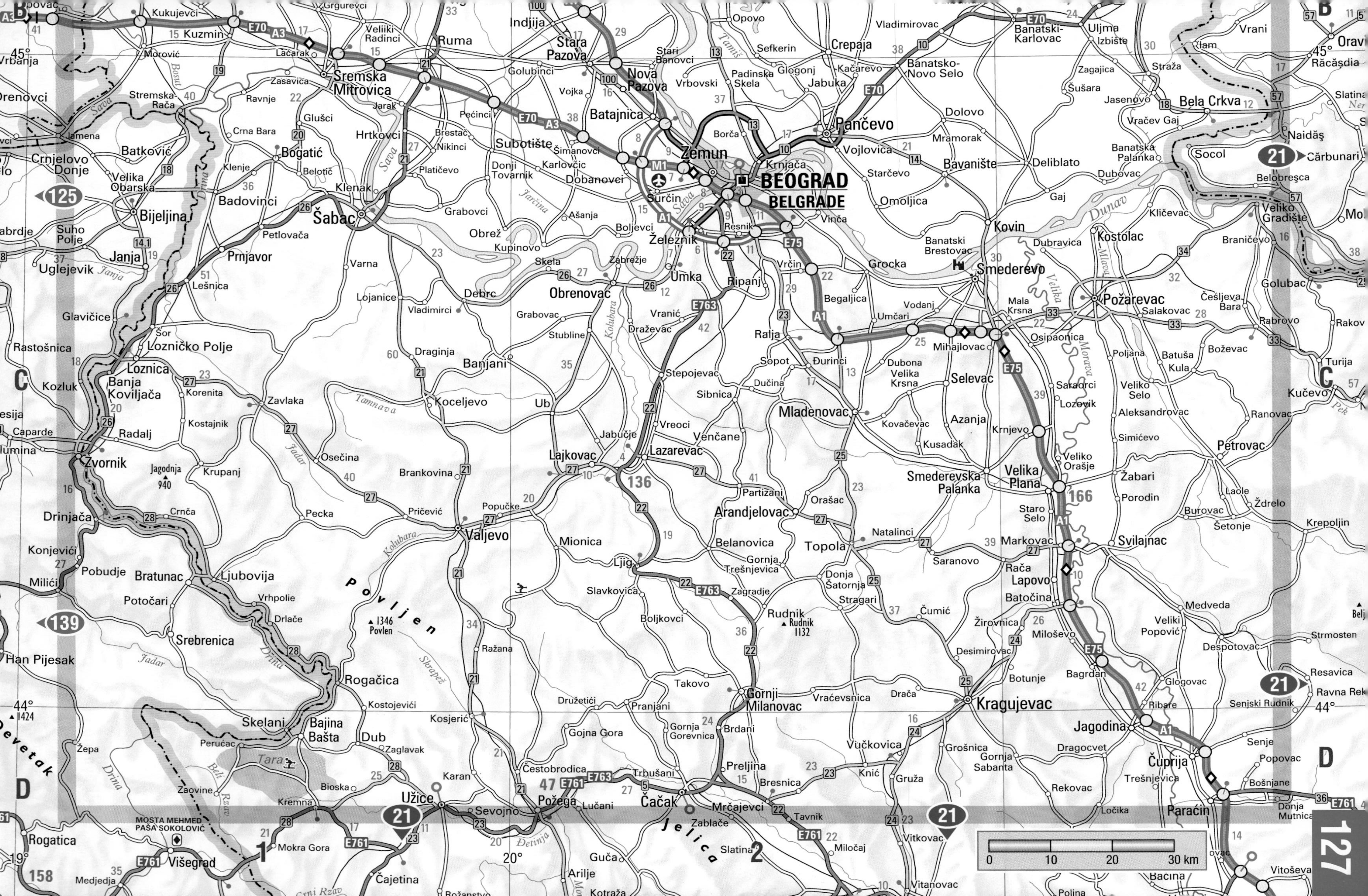
BEOGRAD
BELGRADE
Zemun
Pančevo
Smederevo
Požarevac
Kragujevac
Valjevo
Šabac
Čačak
Užice
Jagodina
Ćuprija
Paraćin
Sremska Mitrovica
Ruma
Obrenovac
Mladenovac
Arandjelovac
Smederevska Palanka
Velika Plana
Kovin
Bela Crkva
Loznica
Zvornik
Bijeljina
Požega
Gornji Milanovac
Lazarevac
Lajkovac
Topola
Svilajnac
Petrovac
Kostolac
Ljubovija
Bajina Bašta
Višegrad
Srebrenica
Bratunac
Rogatica
Povljen
Jelica
Devetak
MOSTA MEHMED PAŠA SOKOLOVIĆ
Dunav
Sava
Drina
Velika Morava
0 10 20 30 km

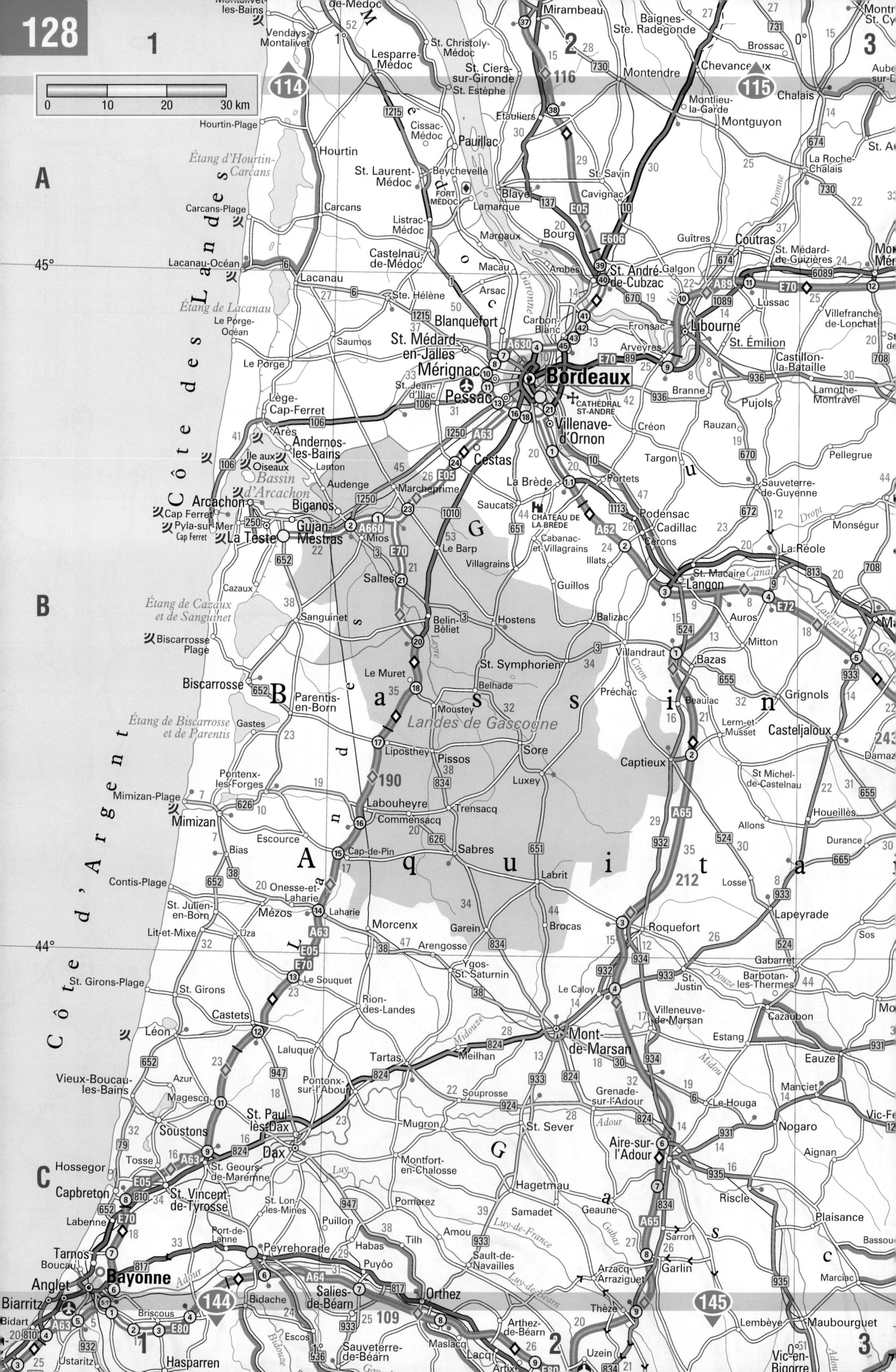

0
10
20
30 km
114
115
116
144
145
190
212
109
Côte des Landes
Côte d'Argent
Landes de Gascogne
Aquitaine
Gascogne
Landes
Médoc
Bordeaux
Mérignac
Pessac
St. Médard-en-Jalles
Blanquefort
Villenave-d'Ornon
Cestas
CATHÉDRAL ST-ANDRÉ
Lesparre-Médoc
Vendays-Montalivet
St. Christoly-Médoc
St. Ciers-sur-Gironde
St. Estèphe
Cissac-Médoc
Pauillac
Hourtin
Hourtin-Plage
Étang d'Hourtin-Carcans
Carcans
Carcans-Plage
St. Laurent-Médoc
Beychevelle
FORT MÉDOC
Lamarque
Listrac-Médoc
Margaux
Castelnau-de-Médoc
Lacanau
Lacanau-Océan
Étang de Lacanau
Le Porge-Océan
Le Porge
Saumos
Ste. Hélène
Arsac
Macau
Ambès
Carbon-Blanc
Blaye
Bourg
Étauliers
Mirambeau
Baignes-Ste. Radegonde
Montendre
Chevanceaux
Brossac
Chalais
Montlieu-la-Garde
Montguyon
La Roche-Chalais
Cavignac
St. Savin
St. André-de-Cubzac
Galgon
Guîtres
Coutras
St. Médard-de-Guizières
Lussac
Libourne
Fronsac
St. Émilion
Arveyres
Castillon-la-Bataille
Villefranche-de-Lonchat
Lamothe-Montravel
Branne
Pujols
Créon
Rauzan
Targon
Pellegrue
Sauveterre-de-Guyenne
Monségur
La Réole
Portets
Podensac
Cadillac
Cérons
La Brède
CHÂTEAU DE LA BRÈDE
Saucats
Cabanac-et-Villagrains
Illats
Lège-Cap-Ferret
Arès
Andernos-les-Bains
Lanton
Île aux Oiseaux
Bassin d'Arcachon
Arcachon
Cap Ferret
Pyla-sur-Mer
La Teste
Gujan-Mestras
Biganos
Audenge
Marcheprime
Mios
Salles
Le Barp
Villagrains
St. Jean-d'Illac
Cazaux
Étang de Cazaux et de Sanguinet
Sanguinet
Biscarrosse-Plage
Biscarrosse
Belin-Béliet
Hostens
Guillos
Balizac
St. Macaire
Langon
Auros
Mitton
Villandraut
Bazas
St. Symphorien
Le Muret
Belhade
Moustey
Préchac
Beaulac
Grignols
Lerm-et-Musset
Casteljaloux
Parentis-en-Born
Étang de Biscarrosse et de Parentis
Gastes
Liposthey
Pissos
Sore
Captieux
Luxey
St Michel-de-Castelnau
Houeillès
Pontenx-les-Forges
Mimizan-Plage
Mimizan
Labouheyre
Commensacq
Trensacq
Escource
Sabres
Cap-de-Pin
Bias
Allons
Durance
Labrit
Losse
Contis-Plage
Onesse-et-Laharie
Laharie
St. Julien-en-Born
Mézos
Uza
Lit-et-Mixe
Morcenx
Garein
Brocas
Roquefort
Lapeyrade
Sos
Arengosse
Ygos-St. Saturnin
Gabarret
Barbotan-les-Thermes
St. Justin
St. Girons-Plage
St. Girons
Le Souquet
Rion-des-Landes
Le Caloy
Castets
Léon
Villeneuve-de-Marsan
Cazaubon
Mont-de-Marsan
Estang
Laluque
Tartas
Meilhan
Eauze
Vieux-Boucau-les-Bains
Azur
Magescq
Pontonx-sur-l'Adour
Souprosse
Grenade-sur-l'Adour
Le Houga
Manciet
Soustons
St. Paul-lès-Dax
Dax
Mugron
St. Sever
Nogaro
Aire-sur-l'Adour
Aignan
Hossegor
Tosse
St. Geours-de-Maremne
Montfort-en-Chalosse
Capbreton
St. Vincent-de-Tyrosse
Hagetmau
Riscle
Labenne
St. Lon-les-Mines
Pomarez
Samadet
Geaune
Plaisance
Tarnos
Boucau
Port-de-Lanne
Puillon
Amou
Sarron
Peyrehorade
Habas
Tilh
Sault-de-Navailles
Garlin
Bayonne
Anglet
Biarritz
Bidart
Puyôo
Arzacq-Arraziguet
Marciac
Salies-de-Béarn
Orthez
Bidache
Briscous
Thèze
Lembeye
Maubourguet
Hasparren
Ustaritz
Escos
Sauveterre-de-Béarn
Maslacq
Lacq
Arthez-de-Béarn
Artix
Uzein
Vic-en-Bigorre
Garonne
Dordogne
Isle
Dronne
Dropt
Leyre
Ciron
Douze
Midouze
Midou
Adour
Luy
Luy-de-France
Luy-de-Béarn
Gabas
Bidouze
45°
44°
A
B
C
1
2
3

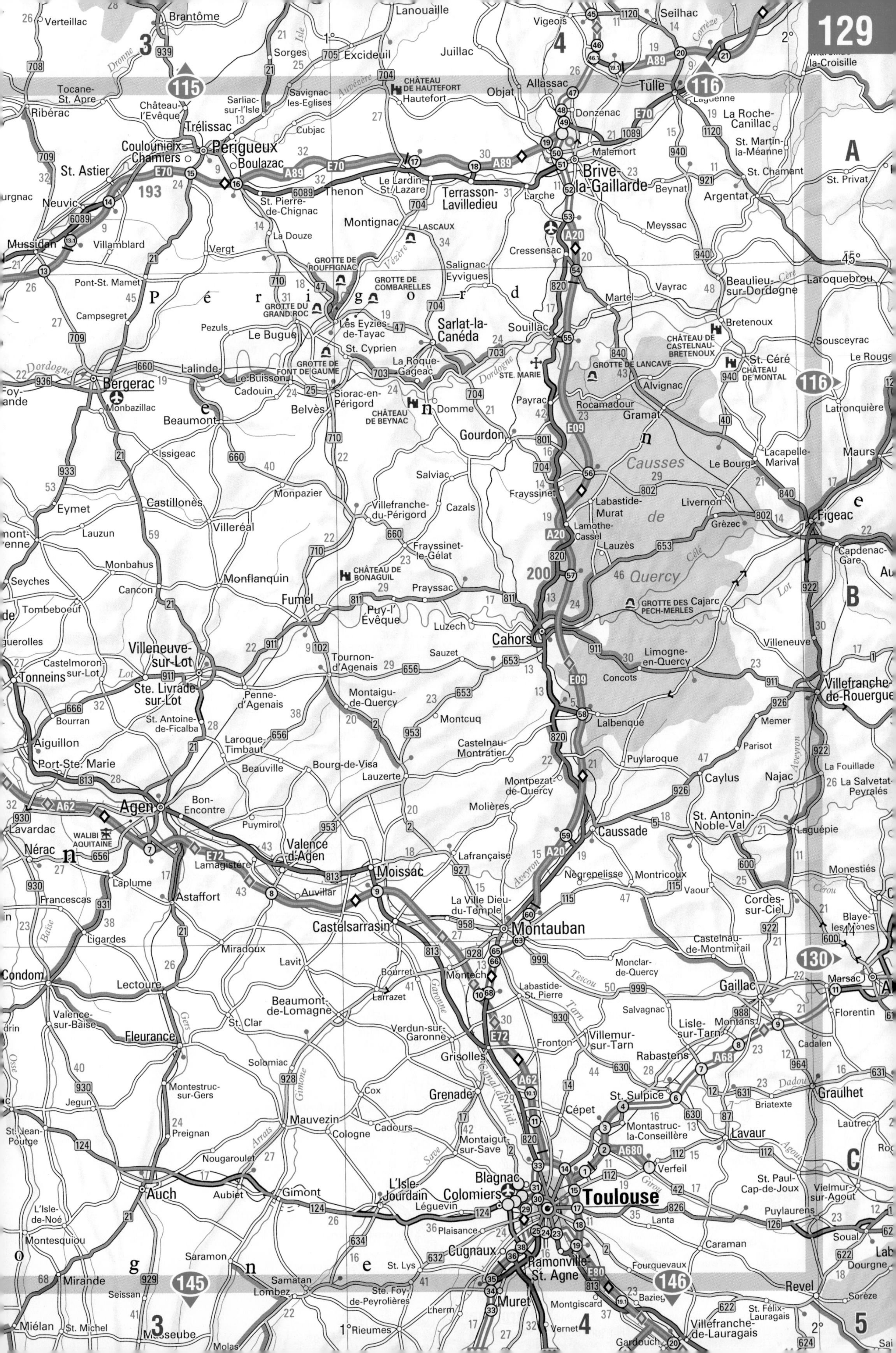

129
Verteillac
Brantôme
Lanouaille
Vigeois
Seilhac
Sorges
Excideuil
Juillac
Ribérac
Tocane-St. Apre
Château-l'Evêque
Sarliac-sur-l'Isle
Savignac-les-Eglises
CHÂTEAU DE HAUTEFORT
Hautefort
Objat
Allassac
Tulle
Laguenne
La Roche-Canillac
Trélissac
Cubjac
Donzenac
Coulounieix-Chamiers
Périgueux
Boulazac
Malemort
St. Martin-la-Méanne
St. Astier
Thenon
Le Lardin-St. Lazare
Terrasson-Lavilledieu
Brive-la-Gaillarde
Beynat
Argentat
St. Chamant
St. Privat
Neuvic
St. Pierre-de-Chignac
Montignac
Larche
Mussidan
Villamblard
La Douze
LASCAUX
Meyssac
Vergt
GROTTE DE ROUFFIGNAC
Cressensac
Salignac-Eyvigues
Pont-St. Mamet
GROTTE DE COMBARELLES
Vayrac
Beaulieu-sur-Dordogne
Laroquebrou
Martel
Périgord
GROTTE DU GRAND ROC
Campsegret
Pezuls
Le Bugue
Les Eyzies-de-Tayac
Sarlat-la-Canéda
Souillac
Bretenoux
St. Cyprien
CHÂTEAU DE CASTELNAU-BRETENOUX
Sousceyrac
Dordogne
Lalinde
Le Buisson
GROTTE DE FONT DE GAUME
La Roque-Gageac
STE. MARIE
GROTTE DE LANCAVE
St. Céré
CHÂTEAU DE MONTAL
Le Rouget
Bergerac
Cadouin
Siorac-en-Périgord
Alvignac
Monbazillac
Belvès
CHÂTEAU DE BEYNAC
Domme
Payrac
Rocamadour
Gramat
Latronquière
Beaumont
Gourdon
Issigeac
Causses
Le Bourg
Lacapelle-Marival
Maurs
Salviac
Eymet
Monpazier
Frayssinet
Castillonès
Villefranche-du-Périgord
Cazals
Labastide-Murat
Livernon
Figeac
Villeréal
Lauzun
Lamothe-Cassel
Grèzec
Frayssinet-le-Gélat
Lauzès
Capdenac-Gare
Monbahus
Quercy
Seyches
Cancon
Monflanquin
CHÂTEAU DE BONAGUIL
Fumel
Prayssac
Tombeboeuf
Puy-l'Évêque
GROTTE DES PECH-MERLES
Cajarc
Luzech
Cahors
Villeneuve
Villeneuve-sur-Lot
Tournon-d'Agenais
Sauzet
Limogne-en-Quercy
Castelmoron-sur-Lot
Tonneins
Ste. Livrade-sur-Lot
Concots
Villefranche-de-Rouergue
Penne-d'Agenais
Montaigu-de-Quercy
Bourran
St. Antoine-de-Ficalba
Montcuq
Lalbenque
Memer
Aiguillon
Laroque-Timbaut
Castelnau-Montratier
Parisot
Port-Ste. Marie
Beauville
Bourg-de-Visa
Lauzerte
Puylaroque
Caylus
Najac
La Fouillade
La Salvetat-Peyralès
Agen
Bon-Encontre
Montpezat-de-Quercy
Lavardac
WALIBI AQUITAINE
Puymirol
Molières
St. Antonin-Noble-Val
Laguépie
Nérac
Valence-d'Agen
Caussade
Lamagistère
Moissac
Lafrançaise
Laplume
Nègrepelisse
Montricoux
Monestiés
Francescas
Astaffort
Auvillar
Vaour
Cordes-sur-Ciel
La Ville Dieu-du-Temple
Castelsarrasin
Montauban
Ligardes
Miradoux
Castelnau-de-Montmiral
Lavit
Monclar-de-Quercy
Condom
Lectoure
Bourret
Montech
Labastide-St. Pierre
Gaillac
Marsac
Larrazet
Florentin
Valence-sur-Baïse
Beaumont-de-Lomagne
Salvagnac
Lisle-sur-Tarn
Montans
Fleurance
St. Clar
Verdun-sur-Garonne
Villemur-sur-Tarn
Fronton
Cadalen
Solomiac
Grisolles
Rabastens
Montestruc-sur-Gers
Cox
Grenade
St. Sulpice
Graulhet
Jegun
Briatexte
Mauvezin
Cépet
Montastruc-la-Conseillère
Lavaur
Lautrec
St. Jean-Poutge
Cologne
Cadours
Preignan
Montaigut-sur-Save
Verfeil
Nougaroulet
L'Isle-Jourdain
Blagnac
St. Paul-Cap-de-Joux
Vielmur-sur-Agout
Auch
Aubiet
Gimont
Colomiers
Toulouse
L'Isle-de-Noé
Léguevin
Puylaurens
Plaisance
Lanta
Montesquiou
Caraman
Soual
Saramon
Cugnaux
Ramonville-St. Agne
Fourquevaux
Dourgne
Mirande
Samatan
Lombez
St. Lys
Seissan
Ste. Foy-de-Peyrolières
Muret
Baziege
Revel
Sorèze
Lherm
Montgiscard
St. Félix-Lauragais
Miélan
St. Michel
Masseube
Rieumes
Vernet
Villefranche-de-Lauragais
Gardouch
Molas

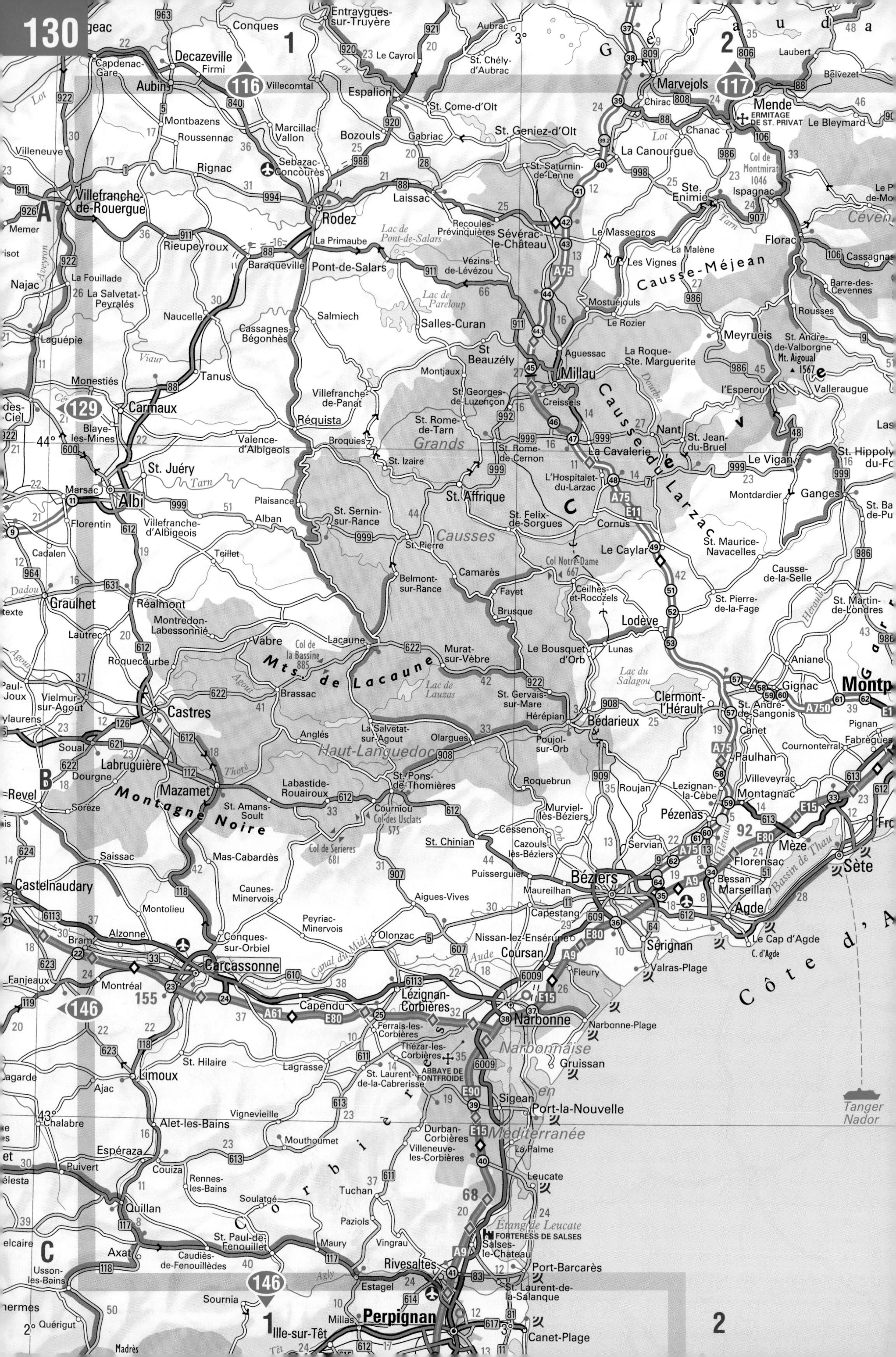
Conques
Entraygues-sur-Truyère
Aubrac
Marvejols
Mende
ERMITAGE DE ST. PRIVAT
Le Bleymard
Laubert
Belvezet
Capdenac-Gare
Decazeville
Firmi
Aubin
Villecomtal
Espalion
Le Cayrol
St. Chély-d'Aubrac
St. Come-d'Olt
Chirac
Chanac
Montbazens
Roussennac
Marcillac-Vallon
Bozouls
Gabriac
St. Geniez-d'Olt
La Canourgue
Col de Montmirat 1046
Villeneuve
Rignac
Sebazac-Concourès
St. Saturnin-de-Lenne
Ste. Enimie
Ispagnac
Villefranche-de-Rouergue
Rodez
Laissac
Recoules-Prévinquières
Sévérac-le-Château
Le Massegros
Florac
Cévennes
Memer
Rieupeyroux
La Primaube
Lac de Pont-de-Salars
Baraqueville
Pont-de-Salars
Vézins-de-Lévézou
La Malène
Les Vignes
Causse-Méjean
Cassagnas
Najac
La Fouillade
La Salvetat-Peyralès
Lac de Pareloup
Mostuéjouls
Barre-des-Cevennes
Naucelle
Salmiech
Salles-Curan
Le Rozier
Rousses
Laguépie
Cassagnes-Bégonhès
Meyrueis
St. Andre-de-Valborgne
Mt. Aigoual 1567
Aguessac
La Roque-Ste. Marguerite
Tanus
Monestiés
Montjaux
St Beauzély
Millau
Carmaux
Villefranche-de-Panat
St. Georges-de-Luzençon
Creissels
L'Esperou
Valleraugue
Blaye-les-Mines
Réquista
St. Rome-de-Tarn
Grands
Nant
St. Jean-du-Bruel
Valence-d'Albigeois
Broquies
St. Rome-de-Cernon
La Cavalerie
Le Vigan
St. Hippoly du-Fo
St. Izaire
St. Juéry
L'Hospitalet-du-Larzac
Montdardier
Ganges
Marsac
Albi
Tarn
Plaisance
St. Affrique
Causse du Larzac
Florentin
Villefranche-d'Albigeois
Alban
St. Sernin-sur-Rance
St. Felix-de-Sorgues
Cornus
Causses
St. Pierre
Le Caylar
St. Maurice-Navacelles
Cadalen
Teillet
Col Notre-Dame 667
Belmont-sur-Rance
Camarès
Causse-de-la-Selle
Fayet
Ceilhes-et-Rocozels
Graulhet
Réalmont
Brusque
St. Pierre-de-la-Fage
St. Martin-de-Londres
Lodève
Montredon-Labessonnié
Lautrec
Vabre
Col de la Bassine 885
Lacaune
Murat-sur-Vèbre
Le Bousquet d'Orb
Lunas
Aniane
Roquecourbe
Mts. de Lacaune
Lac de Lauzas
Lac du Salagou
Gignac
Montp
Vielmur-sur-Agout
Brassac
St. Gervais-sur-Mare
Hérépian
Clermont-l'Hérault
St. André-de-Sangonis
Castres
Bédarieux
Pignan
Anglés
La Salvetat-sur-Agout
Olargues
Poujol-sur-Orb
Canet
Cournonterral
Fabrègues
Soual
Haut-Languedoc
Paulhan
Labruguière
Dourgne
Labastide-Rouairoux
St. Pons-de-Thomières
Roquebrun
Villeveyrac
Revel
Mazamet
Montagne Noire
Montagnac
Sorèze
St. Amans-Soult
Courniou
Col des Usclats 575
Roujan
Lezignan-la-Cèbe
Murviel-lès-Béziers
Pézenas
Cessenon
Mèze
St. Chinian
Cazouls-lès-Béziers
Servian
Saissac
Mas-Cabardès
Col de Serieres 681
Florensac
Bassin de Thau
Sète
Castelnaudary
Puisserguier
Béziers
Bessan
Marseillan
Caunes-Minervois
Maureilhan
Agde
Aigues-Vives
Montolieu
Capestang
Alzonne
Peyriac-Minervois
Nissan-lez-Ensérune
Le Cap d'Agde
C. d'Agde
Bram
Conques-sur-Orbiel
Olonzac
Canal du Midi
Sérignan
Carcassonne
Aude
Coursan
Valras-Plage
Côte d'A
Fanjeaux
Montréal
Fleury
Capendu
Lézignan-Corbières
Narbonne
Narbonne-Plage
Ferrals-les-Corbières
Thézan-les-Corbières
ABBAYE DE FONTFROIDE
Narbonnaise
St. Hilaire
Lagrasse
Gruissan
Limoux
Ajac
St. Laurent-de-la-Cabrerisse
Sigean
Port-la-Nouvelle
Tanger
Nador
Chalabre
Vignevieille
Alet-les-Bains
Durban-Corbières
Méditerranée
Espéraza
Mouthoumet
La Palme
Villeneuve-les-Corbières
Puivert
Couiza
Rennes-les-Bains
Leucate
Tuchan
Corbières
Quillan
Soulatgé
Paziols
Étang de Leucate
FORTERESS DE SALSES
Axat
St. Paul-de-Fenouillet
Caudiès-de-Fenouillèdes
Maury
Vingrau
Salses-le-Chateau
Usson-les-Bains
Rivesaltes
Port-Barcarès
Agly
Estagel
St. Laurent-de-la-Salanque
Sournia
Quérigut
Millas
Perpignan
Ille-sur-Têt
Canet-Plage
Madrès
116
117
129
146
A75
A9
A61
E80
E15
E11
E90
A750

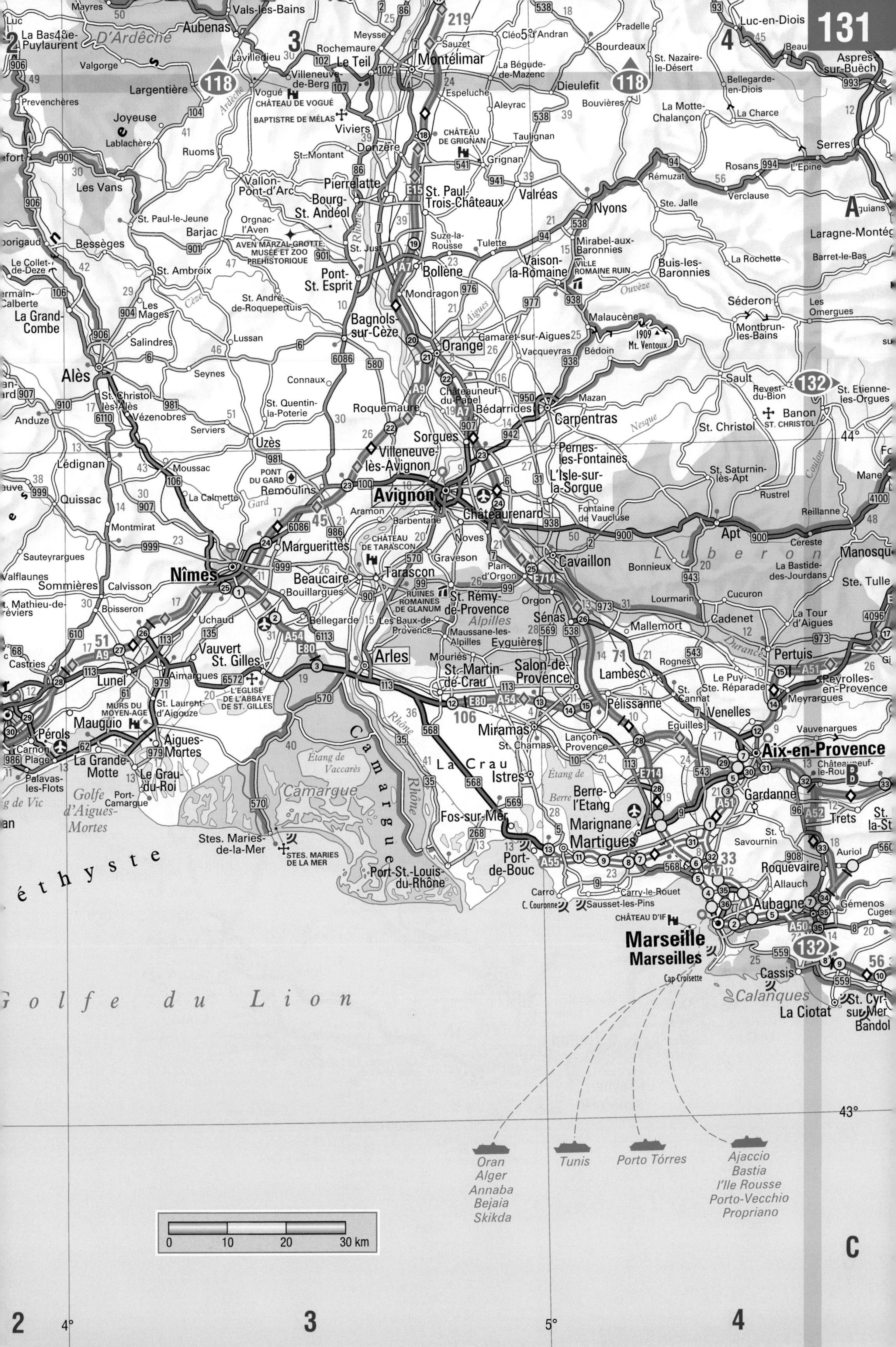

Place names and features

Mayres, Vals-les-Bains, Aubenas, D'Ardèche, La Bas-de-Puylaurent, Valgorge, Largentière, Prevenchères, Joyeuse, Lablachère, Les Vans, Bessèges, St. Ambroix, La Grand-Combe, Salindres, Alès, St. Christol-lès-Alès, Vézenobres, Anduze, Lédignan, Quissac, Montmirat, Sommières, Sauteyrargues, Valflaunes, Calvisson, Boisseron, St. Mathieu-de-Tréviers, Castries, Lunel, Mauguio, Pérols, Carnon Plage, Palavas-les-Flots, La Grande-Motte, Le Grau-du-Roi, Port-Camargue, Aigues-Mortes, St. Laurent-d'Aigouze, Aimargues, Vauvert, St. Gilles, Uchaud, Nîmes, Marguerittes, Beaucaire, Bouillargues, Bellegarde, Tarascon, Arles, St. Martin-de-Crau, Mouriès, St. Rémy-de-Provence, Les Baux-de-Provence, Maussane-les-Alpilles, Eyguières, Salon-de-Provence, Pélissanne, Lambesc, Lançon-Provence, Istres, La Crau, Miramas, St. Chamas, Berre-l'Etang, Fos-sur-Mer, Port-de-Bouc, Martigues, Marignane, Carro, C. Couronne, Carry-le-Rouet, Sausset-les-Pins, Château d'If, Marseille / Marseilles, Cap Croisette, Calanques, Cassis, La Ciotat, St. Cyr-sur-Mer, Bandol, Aubagne, Roquevaire, Allauch, Gémenos, Cuges, Auriol, St. la-St, Trets, Gardanne, Venelles, Aix-en-Provence, Châteauneuf-le-Rou, Meyrargues, Pertuis, La Tour d'Aigues, Cadenet, Cucuron, Lourmarin, Bonnieux, Luberon, Apt, Manosque, Céreste, Reillanne, Rustrel, St. Saturnin-lès-Apt, Fontaine de Vaucluse, L'Isle-sur-la-Sorgue, Pernes-les-Fontaines, Carpentras, Mazan, Bédoin, Mt. Ventoux 1909, Malaucène, Vacqueyras, Gigondas, Beaumes-de-Venise, Sault, Banon, St. Christol, Revest-du-Bion, St. Etienne-les-Orgues, Montbrun-les-Bains, Séderon, Les Omergues, Montmirat.

Rhône, Durance, Gard, Ardèche, Nesque, Ouvèze, Aigues, Coulon

Golfe du Lion, Golfe d'Aigues-Mortes, Golfe de Vic, Étang de Vaccarès, Camargue, Étang de Berre, Alpilles

Montélimar, Le Teil, Rochemaure, Meysse, Sauzet, La Bégude-de-Mazenc, Dieulefit, Bourdeaux, St. Nazaire-le-Désert, Luc-en-Diois, Aspres-sur-Buëch, Serres, L'Epine, Rosans, Verclause, Rémuzat, La Motte-Chalançon, La Charce, Bellegarde-en-Diois, Barret-le-Bas, Laragne-Montégin, La Rochette, Séderon, Nyons, Vaison-la-Romaine, Buis-les-Baronnies, Mirabel-aux-Baronnies, Ste. Jalle, Valréas, Grignan, Taulignan, Suze-la-Rousse, Tulette, Bollène, Mondragon, Orange, Bagnols-sur-Cèze, Pont-St-Esprit, St. Just, Donzère, Pierrelatte, St. Paul-Trois-Châteaux, St. Paul-le-Jeune, Barjac, Vallon-Pont-d'Arc, St. André-de-Roquepertuis, St. Montant, Viviers, Vogüé, Villeneuve-de-Berg, Lavilledieu, Aven Marzal-Grotte Musée et Zoo Préhistorique, Orgnac-l'Aven, Lussan, Connaux, Seynes, St. Quentin-la-Poterie, Uzès, Remoulins, Pont du Gard, Roquemaure, Châteauneuf-du-Pape, Bédarrides, Sorgues, Villeneuve-lès-Avignon, Avignon, Aramon, Barbentane, Châteaurenard, Noves, Graveson, Plan-d'Orgon, Orgon, Sénas, Cavaillon, Mallemort, Rognes, St. Cannat, Eguilles, Vauvenargues, Roquevaire

Oran, Alger, Annaba, Bejaia, Skikda, Tunis, Porto Tórres, Ajaccio, Bastia, l'Ile Rousse, Porto-Vecchio, Propriano

Éthyste

Scale
0   10   20   30 km

Grid references
2   3   4 (top)
2   3   4 (bottom)
A   B   C (right side)
4°   5° (bottom)
44°   43° (right)

Road numbers: 118, 132, 219, 93, 86, 538, 994, 993, 901, 906, 907, 910, 904, 6110, 6086, 580, 977, 976, 938, 950, 942, 941, 940, 999, 981, 986, A7, A9, A54, A51, A52, A50, A55, E15, E80, E714, 113, 568, 570, 543, 569, 973, 900, 4100, 4096, 560

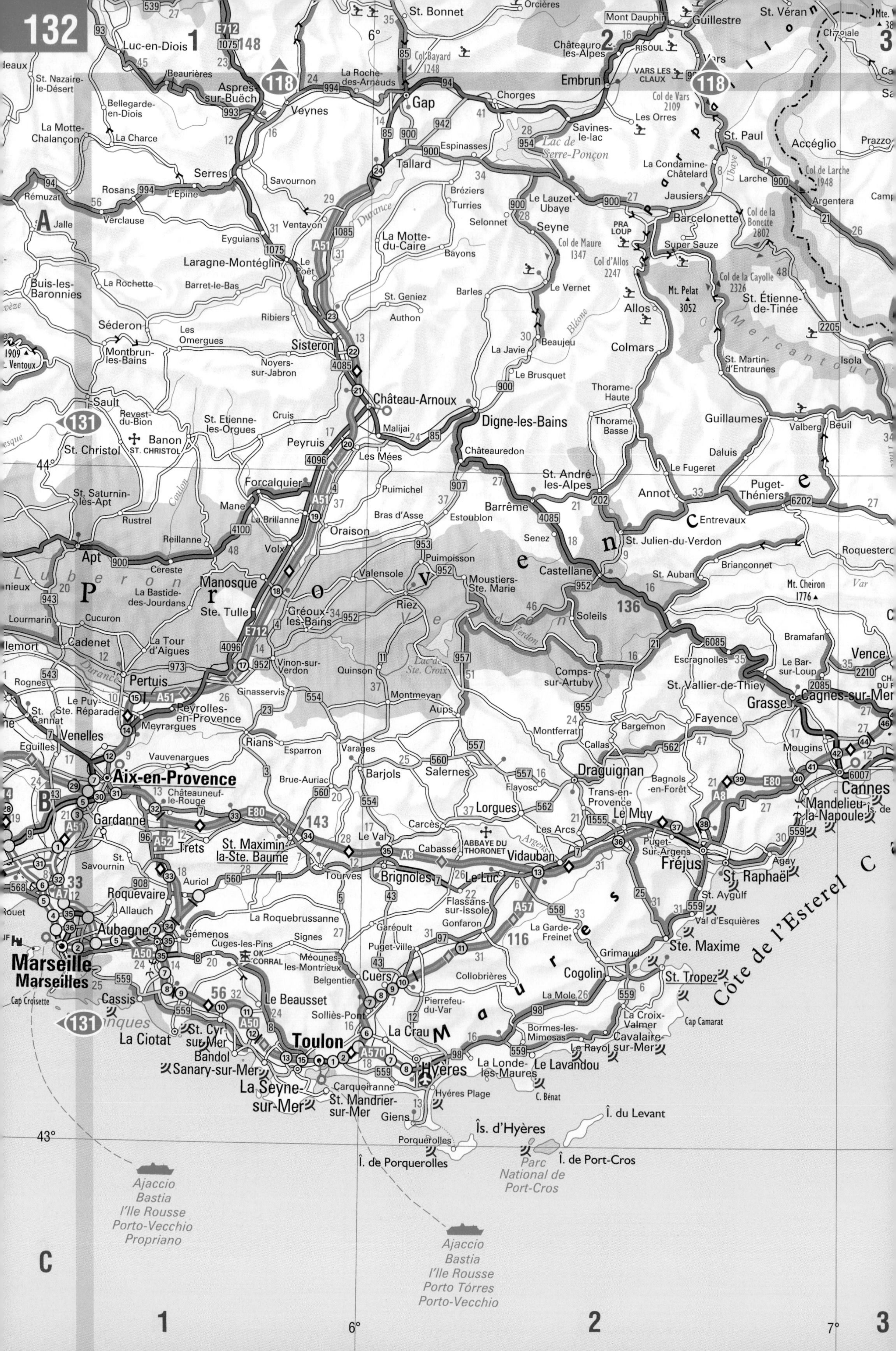

Luc-en-Diois
St. Bonnet
Orcières
Mont Dauphin
Guillestre
St. Véran
Châteauroux-les-Alpes
RISOUL
Vars
St. Nazaire-le-Désert
Beaurières
Aspres-sur-Buëch
La Roche-des-Arnauds
Col Bayard 1248
Embrun
VARS LES CLAUX
Col de Vars 2109
Bellegarde-en-Diois
Veynes
Gap
Chorges
Les Orres
Savines-le-lac
La Motte-Chalançon
La Charce
Espinasses
Lac de Serre-Ponçon
St. Paul
Accéglio
Prazzo
Tallard
La Condamine-Châtelard
Col de Larche 1948
Serres
Rosans
L'Epine
Savournon
Larche
Rémuzat
Bréziers
Turries
Le Lauzet-Ubaye
Jausiers
Argentera
Verclause
Ventavon
Selonnet
Barcelonette
Col de la Bonette 2802
Jalle
Durance
Seyne
PRA LOUP
Eyguians
La Motte-du-Caire
Col de Maure 1347
Super Sauze
Laragne-Montéglin
Le Poët
Bayons
Col d'Allos 2247
Buis-les-Baronnies
La Rochette
Barret-le-Bas
Barles
Le Vernet
Mt. Pelat 3052
Col de la Cayolle 2326
St. Étienne-de-Tinée
St. Geniez
Allos
Ribiers
Authon
Séderon
Les Omergues
Sisteron
Montbrun-les-Bains
Noyers-sur-Jabron
Beaujeu
Colmars
La Javie
Mercantour
Mt. Ventoux
Le Brusquet
St. Martin-d'Entraunes
Isola
Sault
Château-Arnoux
Thorame-Haute
Revest-du-Bion
St. Etienne-les-Orgues
Cruis
Malijai
Digne-les-Bains
Thorame-Basse
Guillaumes
Valberg
Beuil
Banon
ST. CHRISTOL
St. Christol
Peyruis
Les Mées
Châteauredon
Daluis
Forcalquier
St. André-les-Alpes
Le Fugeret
Puget-Théniers
St. Saturnin-lès-Apt
Mane
Puimichel
Barrême
Annot
Entrevaux
Rustrel
La Brillanne
Bras d'Asse
Estoublon
Reillanne
Oraison
Senez
St. Julien-du-Verdon
Apt
Volx
Puimoisson
Castellane
Roquesteron
Céreste
Luberon
Provence
Manosque
Valensole
Moustiers-Ste. Marie
St. Auban
Brianconnet
La Bastide-des-Jourdans
Mt. Cheiron 1776
Lourmarin
Cucuron
Ste. Tulle
Gréoux-les-Bains
Riez
Soleils
Verdon
Cadenet
La Tour d'Aigues
Lac de Ste. Croix
Bramafan
Vence
Pertuis
Vinon-sur-Verdon
Quinson
Escragnolles
Le Bar-sur-Loup
Rognes
Comps-sur-Artuby
St. Vallier-de-Thiey
Le Puy-Ste. Réparade
Ginasservis
Montmeyan
Grasse
Cagnes-sur-Mer
St. Cannat
Peyrolles-en-Provence
Aups
Venelles
Meyrargues
Bargemon
Fayence
Montferrat
Eguilles
Rians
Esparron
Varages
Callas
Mougins
Vauvenargues
Barjols
Salernes
Aix-en-Provence
Brue-Auriac
Draguignan
Bagnols-en-Forêt
Cannes
Châteauneuf-le-Rouge
Flayosc
Trans-en-Provence
Mandelieu-la-Napoule
Gardanne
Lorgues
Le Muy
Carcès
ABBAYE DU THORONET
Les Arcs
Trets
St. Maximin-la-Ste. Baume
Le Val
Cabasse
Puget-sur-Argens
Fréjus
Agay
St. Savournin
Vidauban
Argens
St. Raphaël
Tourves
Brignoles
Le Luc
Auriol
Flassans-sur-Issole
St. Aygulf
Roquevaire
Côte de l'Esterel
Allauch
La Roquebrussanne
Gonfaron
La Garde-Freinet
Val d'Esquières
Aubagne
Gémenos
Signes
Garéoult
Ste. Maxime
Marseille
Marseilles
Cuges-les-Pins
OK CORRAL
Puget-ville
Grimaud
Méounes-les-Montrieux
Collobrières
Cogolin
St. Tropez
Belgentier
Cuers
Maures
Cap Croisette
Cassis
Le Beausset
La Mole
Solliès-Pont
Pierrefeu-du-Var
La Croix-Valmer
Cap Camarat
La Ciotat
St. Cyr-sur-Mer
Bandol
La Crau
Bormes-les-Mimosas
Cavalaire-sur-Mer
Le Rayol
Toulon
Sanary-sur-Mer
La Londe-les-Maures
Le Lavandou
Hyères
Carqueiranne
La Seyne-sur-Mer
St. Mandrier-sur-Mer
Hyères Plage
C. Bénat
Giens
Î. du Levant
Îs. d'Hyères
Porquerolles
Î. de Porquerolles
Î. de Port-Cros
Parc National de Port-Cros
Ajaccio
Bastia
l'Ile Rousse
Porto-Vecchio
Propriano
Ajaccio
Bastia
l'Ile Rousse
Porto Tórres
Porto-Vecchio
44°
43°
6°
7°
A
B
C
1
2
3

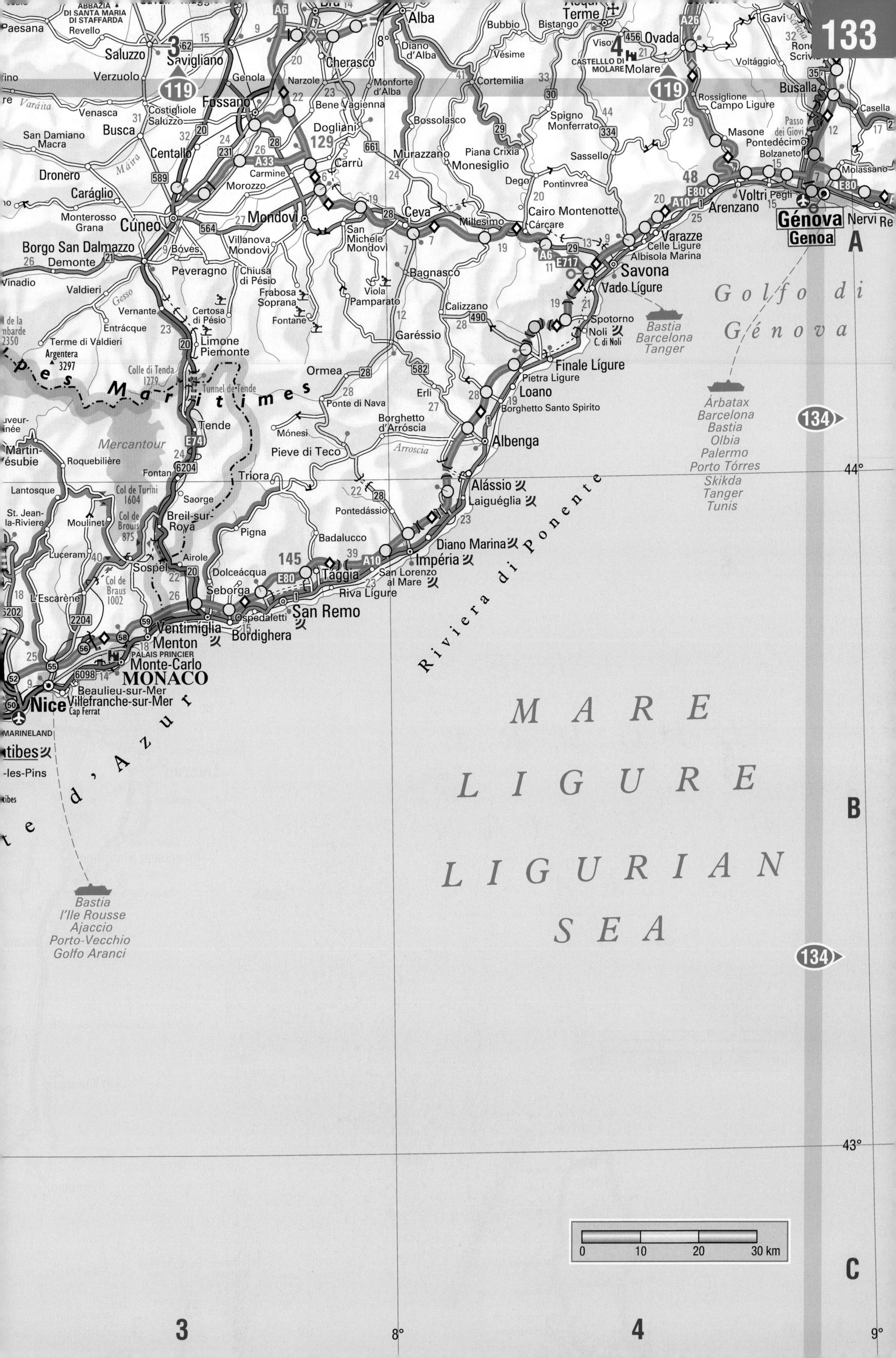

Saluzzo
Savigliano
Fossano
Cúneo
Mondovì
Alba
Cherasco
Ceva
Dogliani
Carrù
Dronero
Caráglio
Borgo San Dalmazzo
Limone Piemonte
Tende
Ormea
Garéssio
Albenga
Alássio
Laiguéglia
Loano
Pietra Ligure
Finale Lígure
Noli
Spotorno
Vado Lígure
Savona
Varazze
Celle Ligure
Albisola Marina
Arenzano
Voltri
Génova
Genoa
Ovada
Molare
Imperia
Diano Marina
San Remo
Bordighera
Ventimiglia
Menton
Monte-Carlo
MONACO
Nice
Beaulieu-sur-Mer
Villefranche-sur-Mer
Cap Ferrat
Golfo di Génova
Riviera di Ponente
MARE LIGURE
LIGURIAN SEA
Alpes Maritimes
Mercantour
Bastia
l'Ile Rousse
Ajaccio
Porto-Vecchio
Golfo Aranci
Árbatax
Barcelona
Olbia
Palermo
Porto Tórres
Skikda
Tanger
Tunis
0 10 20 30 km
44°
43°
8°
9°
A
B
C
3
4
119
134

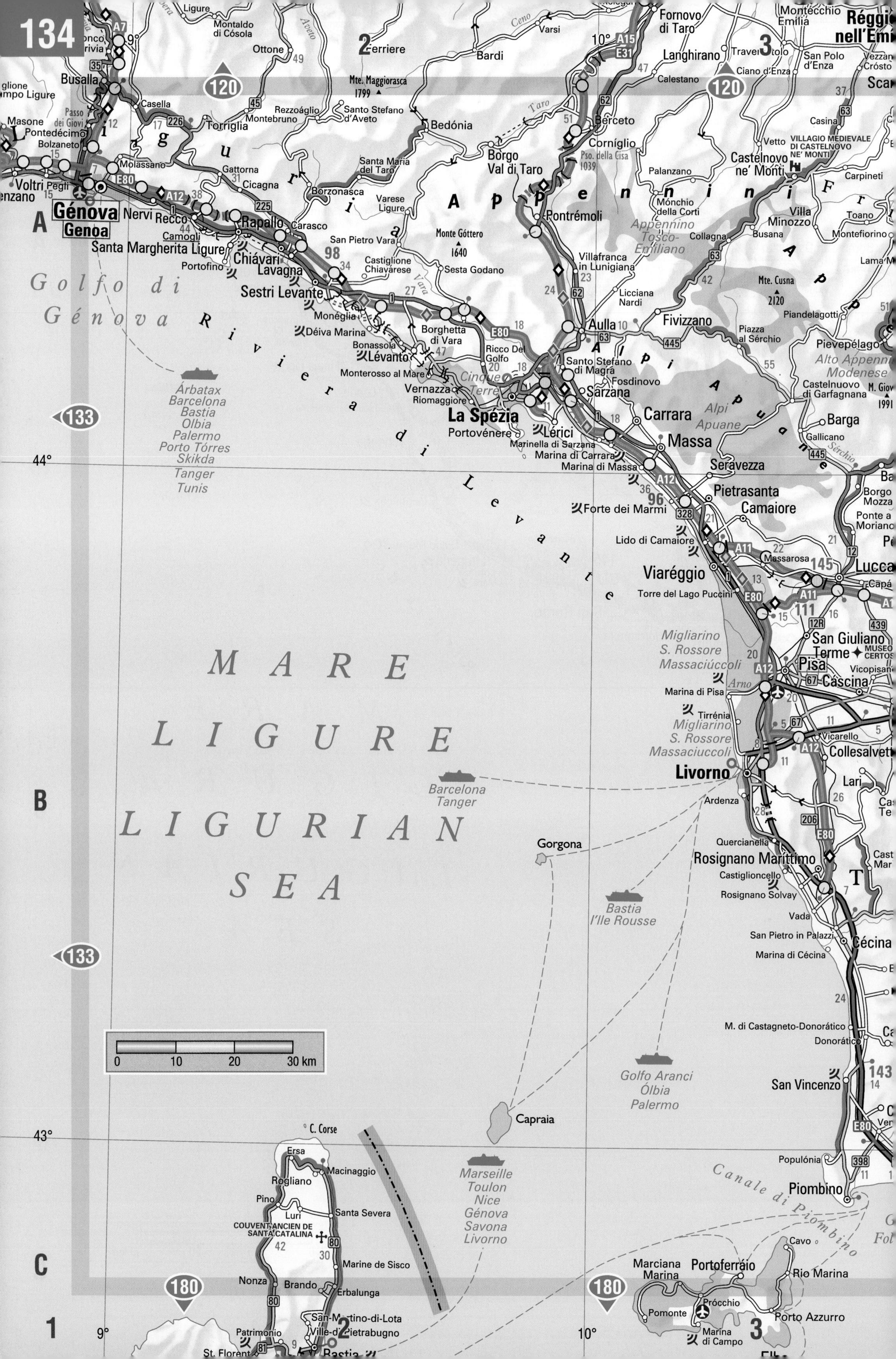

Génova
Genoa
Golfo di Génova
Riviera di Levante
MARE LIGURE
LIGURIAN SEA
La Spézia
Livorno
Pisa
Lucca
Viaréggio
Carrara
Massa
Rapallo
Chiávari
Sestri Levante
Santa Margherita Ligure
Portofino
Cinque Terre
Appennino Tosco-Emiliano
Alpi Apuane
Alto Appennino Modenese
Gorgona
Capraia
Piombino
Canale di Piombino
Portoferraio
Marciana Marina
Bastia
Árbatax Barcelona Bastia Olbia Palermo Porto Tórres Skikda Tanger Tunis
Barcelona Tanger
Bastia l'Ile Rousse
Golfo Aranci Ólbia Palermo
Marseille Toulon Nice Génova Savona Livorno
0 10 20 30 km
120
133
180
44°
43°
9°
10°

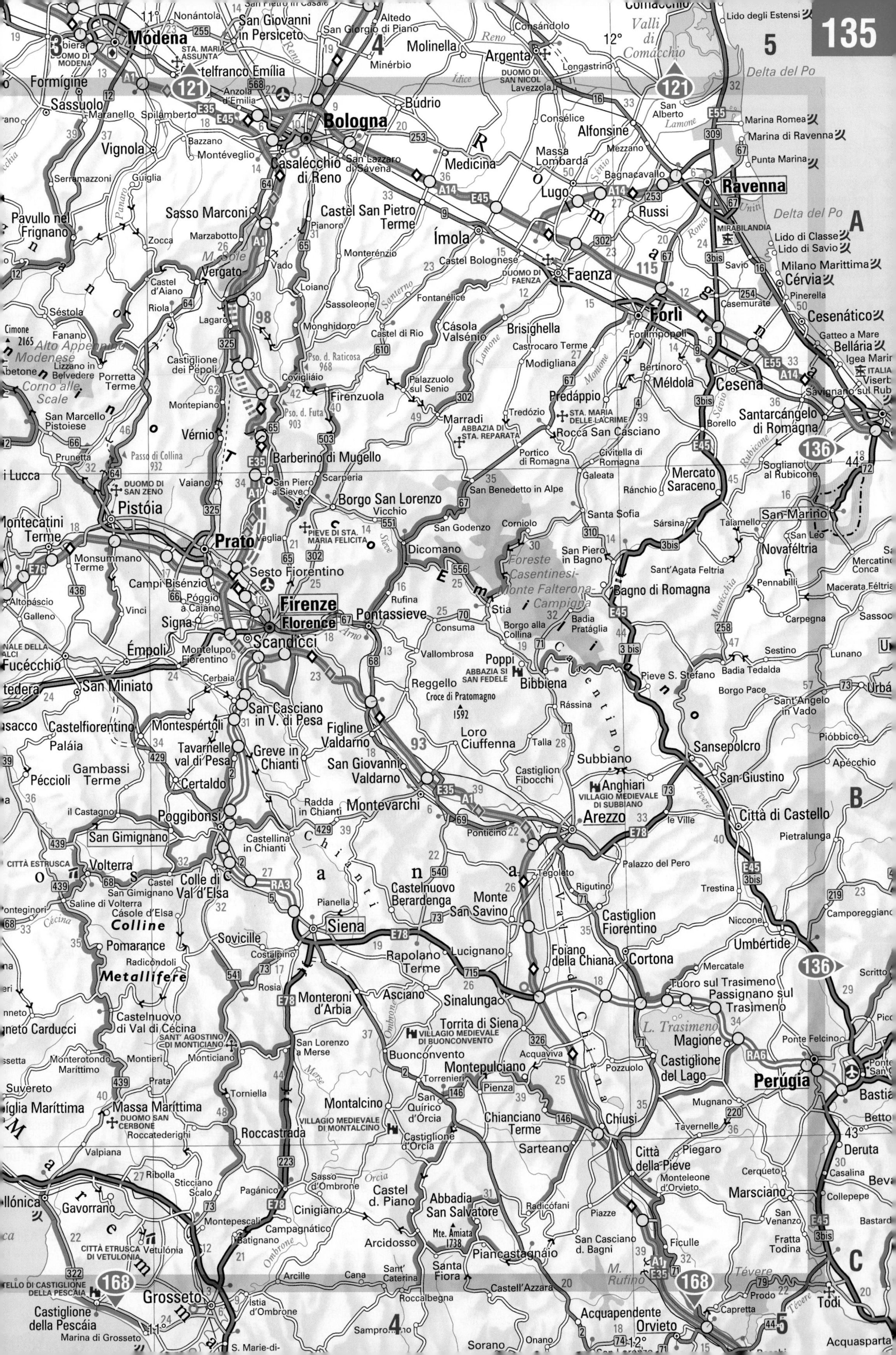
Modena
Nonántola
San Giovanni in Persiceto
San Giorgio di Piano
Altedo
Molinella
Minérbio
Argenta
Consándolo
Longastrino
Valli di Comácchio
Lido degli Estensi
Delta del Po
Formígine
Castelfranco Emília
STA. MARIA ASSUNTA
DUOMO DI MODENA
Anzola d'Emilia
Sassuolo
Maranello
Spilamberto
Bologna
Búdrio
Medicina
Lavezzola
DUOMO DI SAN NICOL
Conselice
Alfonsine
San Alberto
Marina Romea
Marina di Ravenna
Punta Marina
Ravenna
MIRABILANDIA
Vignola
Bazzano
Montéveglio
Casalécchio di Reno
San Lazzaro di Sávena
Massa Lombarda
Lugo
Bagnacavallo
Russi
Serramazzoni
Guiglia
Castel San Pietro Terme
Ímola
Castel Bolognese
Faenza
DUOMO DI FAENZA
Pavullo nel Frignano
Sasso Marconi
Marzabotto
Zocca
Pianoro
Monterénzio
Lido di Classe
Lido di Savio
Milano Marittima
Cérvia
Pinerella
Cesenático
Vergato
M. Sole
Vado
Castel d'Aiano
Riola
Loiano
Sassoleone
Fontanélice
Brisighella
Forlì
Forlimpopoli
Casemurate
Gatteo a Mare
Bellária
Igea Marina
Viserba
Séstola
Fanano
Cimone 2165
Alto Appennino Modenese
Lizzano in Belvedere
Corno alle Scale
Porretta Terme
Lagaro
Castiglione dei Pépoli
Monghidoro
Castel di Rio
Cásola Valsénio
Castrocaro Terme
Modigliana
Bertinoro
Méldola
Cesena
Savignano sul Rubicone
Pso. d. Raticosa 968
Covigliáio
Pso. d. Futa 903
Firenzuola
Palazzuolo sul Senio
Predáppio
Tredózio
STA. MARIA DELLE LACRIME
Rocca San Casciano
Santarcángelo di Romagna
Borello
San Marcello Pistoiese
Montepiano
Vérnio
Marradi
ABBAZIA DI STA. REPARATA
Portico di Romagna
Civitella di Romagna
Galeata
Sogliano al Rubicone
Prunetta
Passo di Collina 932
Barberino di Mugello
Scarperia
San Benedetto in Alpe
Mercato Saraceno
Ránchio
Lucca
Vaiano
San Piero a Sieve
DUOMO DI SAN ZENO
Pistóia
Borgo San Lorenzo
Vicchio
Santa Sofia
Sársina
Talamello
San Marino
Montecatini Terme
Prato
Vaglia
PIEVE DI STA. MARIA FELICITA
San Godenzo
Corniolo
San Piero in Bagno
San Leo
Novafeltria
Monsummano Terme
Sesto Fiorentino
Dicomano
Foreste Casentinesi-Monte Falterona-Campigna
Sant'Agata Feltria
Mercatino Conca
Campi Bisénzio
Pennabilli
Macerata Féltria
Altopáscio
Póggio a Caiano
Vinci
Bagno di Romagna
Galleno
Firenze
Florence
Rufina
Stia
Carpegna
Signa
Pontassieve
Consuma
Borgo alla Collina
Badia Prataglia
Scandicci
Vallombrosa
Poppi
ABBAZIA SI SAN FEDELE
Bibbiena
Sestino
Lunano
Fucécchio
Émpoli
Montelupo Fiorentino
Badia Tedalda
San Miniato
Cerbaia
Reggello
Croce di Pratomagno
Pieve S. Stefano
Borgo Pace
Sant'Angelo in Vado
Urbánia
Castelfiorentino
Montespértoli
San Casciano in V. di Pesa
Figline Valdarno
1592
Rássina
Paláia
Tavarnelle val di Pesa
Greve in Chianti
San Giovanni Valdarno
Loro Ciuffenna
Talla
Sansepolcro
Píobbico
Gambassi Terme
Castiglion Fibocchi
Subbiano
Apécchio
Péccioli
Certaldo
Anghiari
VILLAGIO MEDIEVALE DI SUBBIANO
San Giustino
il Castagno
Poggibonsi
Radda in Chianti
Montevarchi
Ponticino
Arezzo
le Ville
Città di Castello
San Gimignano
Castellina in Chianti
Pietralunga
CITTÀ ESTRUSCA
Volterra
Colle di Val d'Elsa
Castel San Gimignano
Chianti
Castelnuovo Berardenga
Palazzo del Pero
Tegoleto
Rigutino
Trestina
Saline di Volterra
Pianella
Monte San Savino
Castiglion Fiorentino
Cásole d'Elsa
Colline
Siena
Niccone
Camporeggiano
Pomarance
Sovicille
Rapolano Terme
Lucignano
Foiano della Chiana
Cortona
Umbértide
Radicondoli
Costalpino
Metallifere
Rosia
Asciano
Sinalunga
Mercatale
Tuoro sul Trasimeno
Passignano sul Trasimeno
Monteroni d'Arbia
Castelnuovo di Val di Cécina
Torrita di Siena
VILLAGIO MEDIEVALE DI BUONCONVENTO
L. Trasimeno
Magione
Larderello
Giosuè Carducci
SANT' AGOSTINO DI MONTICIANO
San Lorenzo a Merse
Acquaviva
Castiglione del Lago
Ponte Felcino
Monterotondo Maríttimo
Montieri
Monticiano
Buonconvento
Montepulciano
Pozzuolo
Perúgia
Torrenieri
Pienza
Suvereto
Prata
Torniella
Massa Maríttima
DUOMO SAN CERBONE
Roccatederighi
Montalcino
San Quírico d'Órcia
Chianciano Terme
Chiusi
Mugnano
Bastia
VILLAGIO MEDIEVALE DI MONTALCINO
Castiglione d'Órcia
Tavernelle
Roccastrada
Sarteano
Città della Pieve
Piegaro
Deruta
Valpiana
Ribolla
Sticciano
Scalo
Sasso d'Ombrone
Orcia
Castel d. Piano
Radicófani
Monteleone d'Orvieto
Cerqueto
Casalina
Follónica
Gavorrano
Pagánico
Cinigiano
Abbadia San Salvatore
Piazze
Marsciano
Collepepe
Montepescali
Campagnático
Mte. Amiata 1738
San Casciano d. Bagni
San Venanzo
Fratta Todina
CITTÀ ETRUSCA DI VETULONIA
Vetulónia
Batignano
Arcidosso
Piancastagnáio
Ficulle
Arcille
Cana
Sant' Caterina
Santa Fiora
M. Rufino
Castell'Azzara
Tévere
Prodo
Capretta
Todi
CASTELLO DI CASTIGLIONE DELLA PESCAIA
Castiglione della Pescáia
Grosseto
Istia d'Ombrone
Roccalbegna
Acquapendente
Orvieto
Marina di Grosseto
Samprugnano
Sorano
Onano
Acquasparta
S. Marie-di-
Romagna
Appennino
Toscano
Emilia
Casentino
Mugello
Maremma
Val di Chiana
121
136
168

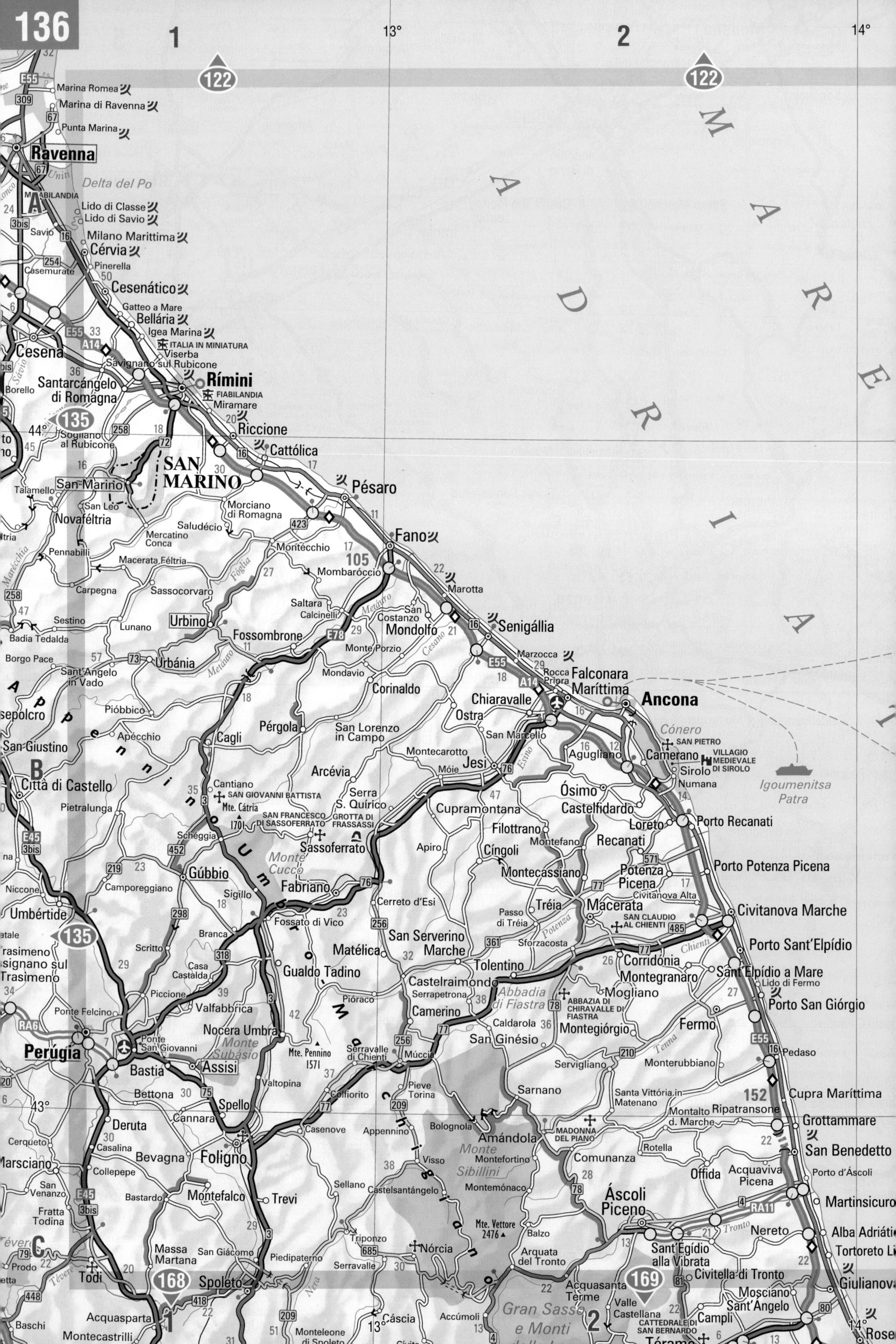

1
13°
2
14°
122
122
MARE ADRIATICO
Marina Romea
Marina di Ravenna
Punta Marina
Ravenna
Delta del Po
MIRABILANDIA
Lido di Classe
Lido di Savio
Savio
Milano Marittima
Cérvia
Pinerella
Casemurate
Cesenático
Gatteo a Mare
Bellária
Igea Marina
ITALIA IN MINIATURA
Viserba
Cesena
Savignano sul Rubicone
Rímini
FIABILANDIA
Miramare
Santarcángelo di Romagna
Borello
135
Sogliano al Rubicone
44°
Riccione
Cattólica
SAN MARINO
San Marino
Talamello
San Leo
Novaféltria
Morciano di Romagna
Saludécio
Pésaro
Mercatino Conca
Pennabilli
Montécchio
Fano
Macerata Féltria
Mombaróccio
Carpegna
Sassocorvaro
Marotta
Saltara
Calcinelli
San Costanzo
Mondolfo
Urbino
Sestino
Lunano
Fossombrone
Senigállia
Badia Tedalda
Monte Porzio
Borgo Pace
Urbánia
Marzocca
Sant'Angelo in Vado
Mondavio
Corinaldo
Rocca Priora
Falconara Maríttima
Ancona
Chiaravalle
Ostra
Piobbico
Pérgola
San Lorenzo in Campo
Cónero
SAN PIETRO
Apécchio
Cagli
San Marcello
Agugliano
Camerano
VILLAGGIO MEDIEVALE DI SIROLO
Sirolo
Numana
Igoumenitsa
Patra
San Giustino
Montecarotto
Móie
Jesi
Arcévia
Città di Castello
Cantiano
SAN GIOVANNI BATTISTA
Serra S. Quírico
Ósimo
Castelfidardo
Cupramontana
Loreto
Porto Recanati
Pietralunga
Mte. Cátria
SAN FRANCESCO DI SASSOFERRATO
GROTTA DI FRASSASSI
Filottrano
Montefano
Recanati
Schéggia
Sassoferrato
Apiro
Cíngoli
Monte Cucco
Porto Potenza Picena
Gúbbio
Montecassiano
Potenza Picena
Niccone
Camporeggiano
Fabriano
Civitanova Alta
Sigillo
Cerreto d'Esi
Tréia
Mácerata
Civitanova Marche
Umbértide
Fossato di Vico
Passo di Tréia
SAN CLAUDIO AL CHIENTI
Porto Sant'Elpídio
Branca
San Severino Marche
Matélica
Sforzacosta
Scritto
Trasimeno
Gualdo Tadino
Tolentino
Corridonia
Sant'Elpídio a Mare
Casa Castalda
Montegranaro
Lido di Fermo
Castelraimondo
Serrapetrona
Abbadia di Fiastra
ABBAZIA DI CHIARAVALLE DI FIASTRA
Mogliano
Piccione
Valfabbrica
Pióraco
Camerino
Caldarola
Porto San Giórgio
Ponte Felcino
Nocera Umbra
Montegiórgio
Fermo
Perúgia
Ponte San Giovanni
Monte Subásio
Mte. Pennino 1571
Serravalle di Chienti
Múccia
San Ginésio
Pedaso
Bastia
Assisi
Servigliano
Monterubbiano
Valtopina
Pieve Torina
Sarnano
Cupra Maríttima
Bettona
Spello
Colfiorito
Santa Vittória in Matenano
152
43°
Cannara
Montalto d. Marche
Ripatransone
Grottammare
Deruta
Casenove
Appennino
Bolognola
MADONNA DEL PIANO
Cerqueto
Casalina
Foligno
Amándola
Rotella
San Benedetto
Bevagna
Monte Sibillini
Montefortino
Visso
Comunanza
Marsciano
Collepepe
Offida
Acquaviva Picena
Porto d'Áscoli
San Venanzo
Bastardo
Montefalco
Sellano
Castelsantángelo
Montemónaco
Áscoli Piceno
Martinsicuro
Fratta Todina
Trevi
Mte. Vettore 2476
Balzo
Nereto
Alba Adriáti
Triponzo
Nórcia
Arquata del Tronto
Sant'Egídio alla Vibrata
Tortoreto Li
Massa Martana
San Giácomo
Piedipaterno
Prodo
Serravalle
Civitella di Tronto
Giulianov
Todi
168
Spoleto
Acquasanta Terme
169
Mosciano Sant'Angelo
Gran Sasso e Monti della Laga
Valle Castellana
Campli
Baschi
Acquasparta
Cáscia
Accúmoli
CATTEDRALE DI SAN BERNARDO
Montecastrilli
Monteleone di Spoleto
Civita
Téramo
Rose
Appennino Umbro-Marchigiano

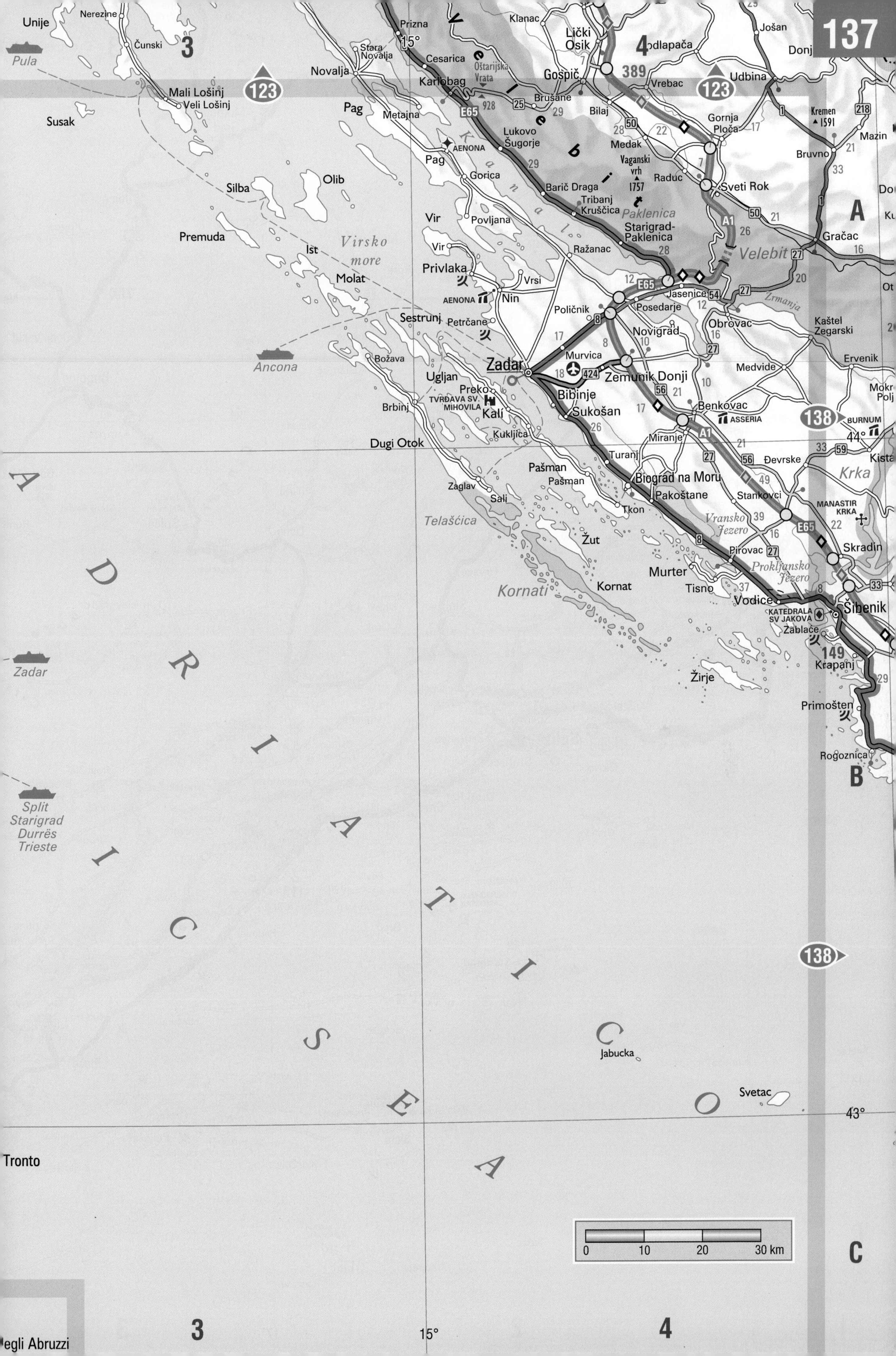

Unije
Nerezine
Pula
Čunski
3
Susak
Mali Lošinj
Veli Lošinj
Silba
Olib
Premuda
Ist
Molat
Virsko more
Ancona

Klanac
Prizna
15°
Stara Novalja
Novalja
Cesarica
Karlobag
E65 928
25
Pag
Metajna
Lukovo Šugorje
AENONA
Gorica
29
Barić Draga
Tribanj
Kruščica
Starigrad-Paklenica
28
Vir
Povljana
Ražanac
Vir
Vrsi
Privlaka
Nin
AENONA
Policnik
8
Zadar
Murvica
424
Bibinje
Zemunik Donji
Sukošan
56
17
Miranje
A1
Turanj
27
56

Lički Osik
Gospić
BruŠane
Bilaj
Medak
Vaganski vrh
1757
Raduc
Paklenica
Velebit
Jasenice 54
Posedarje
12
Novigrad
27
Obrovac
16
Medvide
10
Benkovac
ASSERIA
21
Ðevrske
Stankovci

4
Odlapača
389
Vrebac
Gornja Ploča
22
7
Sveti Rok
A1
26
50
21
20
27
Zrmanja
Kaštel Žegarski
Ervenik
Mokri Polj
BURNUM
44°
Krka
33 59
MANASTIR KRKA
Skradin
33

Jošan
Donj
Udbina
123
Kremen
1591
Bruvno
Mazin
218
21
33
Gračac
16
Ot
Kista
22

Petrčane
Sestrunj
Ugljan
Preko
TVRĐAVA SV. MIHOVILA
Kali
Brbinj
Kukljica
Dugi Otok
Pašman
Pašman
Zaglav
Sali
Žut
Telašćica
Tkon
Biograd na Moru
Pakoštane
Vransko Jezero
39
E65
22
16
Prokljansko Jezero
8
Pirovac
27
Murter
Tisno
37
Vodice
KATEDRALA SV. JAKOVA
Zablaće
149
Krapanj
Šibenik
33
29

Kornati
Kornat
Žirje

A
D
R
I
A
T
I
C
S
E
A

Zadar
Split
Starigrad
Durrës
Trieste

Primošten
Rogoznica
B

Jabucka
Svetac
43°
Tronto

0   10   20   30 km

egli Abruzzi
3
15°
4
C

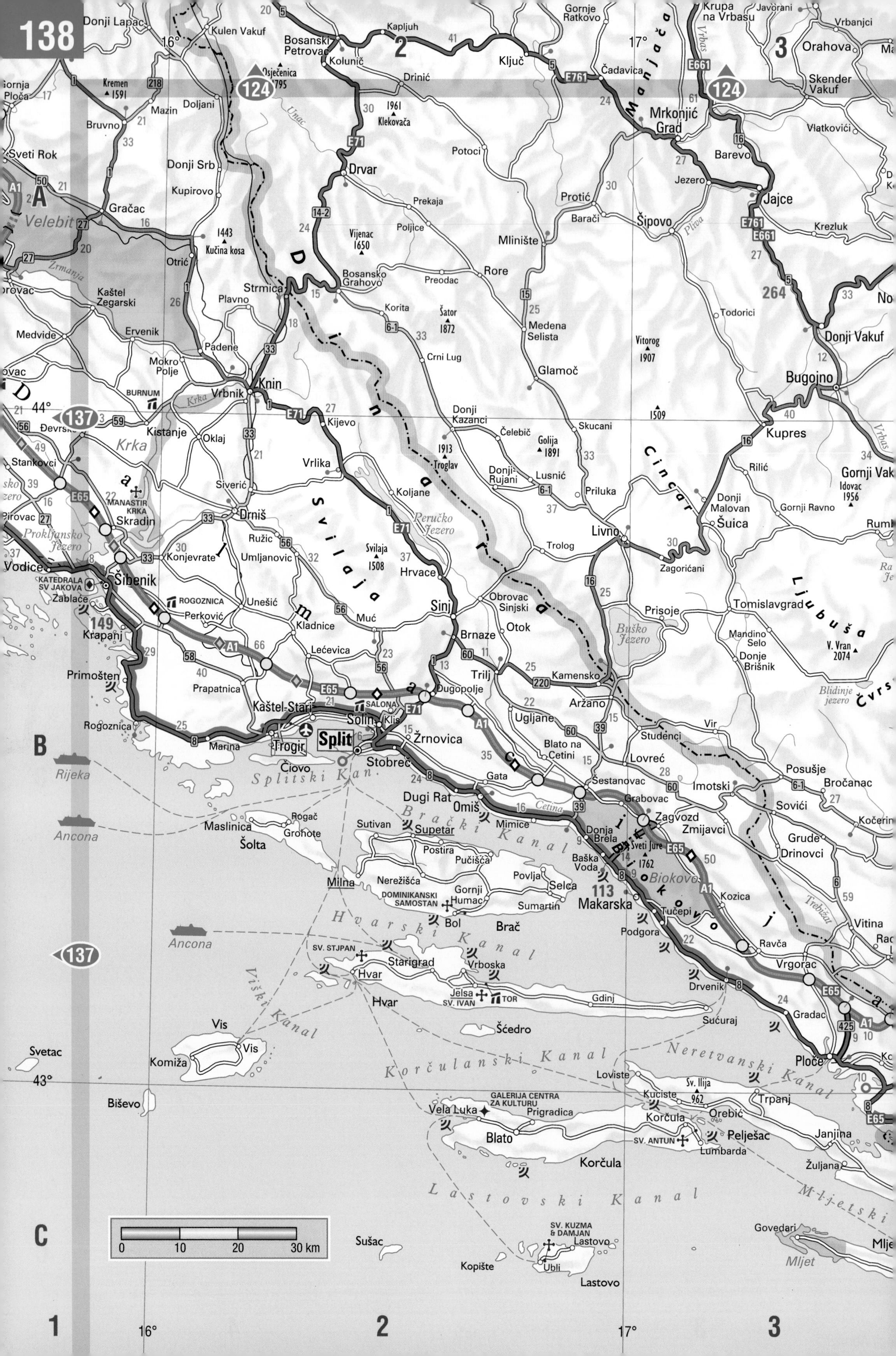
Donji Lapac
Kulen Vakuf
Bosanski Petrovac
Kapljuh
Kolunič
Gornje Ratkovo
Ključ
Krupa na Vrbasu
Javorani
Vrbanjci
Orahova
Kremen 1591
Osječenica 1795
124
Drinić
Čadavica
Mrkonjić Grad
Skender Vakuf
Gornja Ploča
Mazin
Doljani
Bruvno
1961 Klekovača
Potoci
Barevo
Vlatkovići
Sveti Rok
Donji Srb
Kupirovo
Drvar
Jezero
Jajce
Gračac
Velebit
Prekaja
Protić
Barači
Šipovo
Pliva
Vijenac 1650
Poljice
Mliništa
Krezluk
1443 Kučina kosa
Otrić
Zrmanja
Bosansko Grahovo
Preodac
Rore
Kaštel Zegarski
Strmica
Plavno
Korita
Šator 1872
Todorići
Donji Vakuf
Medena Selista
Medvide
Ervenik
Padene
Crni Lug
Vitorog 1907
Mokro Polje
Glamoč
Bugojno
BURNUM
Vrbnik
Knin
Krka
Kijevo
Donji Kazanci
1509
Kupres
137
Đevrske
Kistanje
Oklaj
Čelebič
Golija 1891
Skucani
Cincar
Vrbas
Stankovci
Vrlika
1913 Troglav
Donji Rujani
Lusnić
Rilić
Gornji Vakuf
Idovac 1956
MANASTIR KRKA
Siverić
Koljane
Priluka
Donji Malovan
Gornji Ravno
Skradin
Drniš
Peručko Jezero
Šuica
Pirovac
Prokljansko Jezero
Ružic
Svilaja 1508
Livno
Trolog
Konjevrate
Umljanovic
Hrvace
Zagorićani
Ljubuša
Vodice
KATEDRALA SV JAKOVA
Šibenik
Zablaće
ROGOZNICA
Unešić
Sinj
Obrovac Sinjski
Prisoje
Tomislavgrad
Dinara
Svilaja
Moseć
Perković
Kladnice
Muć
Brnaze
Otok
Buško Jezero
Mandino Selo
Donje Brišnik
V. Vran 2074
Krapanj
Primošten
Lećevica
Trilj
Kamensko
Blidinje jezero
Čvrsnica
Prapatnica
Kaštel-Stari
SALONA
Dugopolje
Klis
Solin
Ugljane
Aržano
Rogoznica
Marina
Trogir
Split
Žrnovica
Vir
Studenci
Blato na Cetini
Lovreć
Posušje
Čiovo
Stobreč
Gata
Šestanovac
Imotski
Bročanac
Rijeka
Splitski Kan.
Dugi Rat
Omiš
Cetina
Grabovac
Zagvozd
Zmijavci
Sovići
Kočerin
Ancona
Maslinica
Rogač
Grohote
Šolta
Sutivan
Supetar
Mimice
Brački Kanal
Donja Brela
Sveti Jure 1762
Grude
Drinovci
Postira
Pučišća
Baška Voda
Biokovo
Milna
Nerežišća
Povlja
Selca
Makarska
Kozica
DOMINIKANSKI SAMOSTAN
Gornji Humac
Sumartin
Tučepi
Bol
Brač
Podgora
Hvarski Kanal
Vitina
Ravča
SV. STJPAN
Starigrad
Vrboska
Vrgorac
Hvar
Jelsa
SV. IVAN
TOR
Gdinj
Drvenik
Viški Kanal
Gradac
Sućuraj
Vis
Šćedro
Svetac
Komiža
Korčulanski Kanal
Neretvanski Kanal
Ploče
Loviste
Biševo
GALERIJA CENTRA ZA KULTURU
Kuciste
Sv. Ilija 962
Trpanj
Vela Luka
Prigradica
Korčula
Orebić
Blato
SV. ANTUN
Pelješac
Lumbarda
Janjina
Žuljana
Lastovski Kanal
Mljetski
Govedari
Mljet
SV. KUZMA & DAMJAN
Lastovo
Sušac
Kopište
Ubli
0 10 20 30 km
A
B
C
1
2
3
16°
17°
44°
43°
A1
E65
E71
E761
E661
8
149
113
264

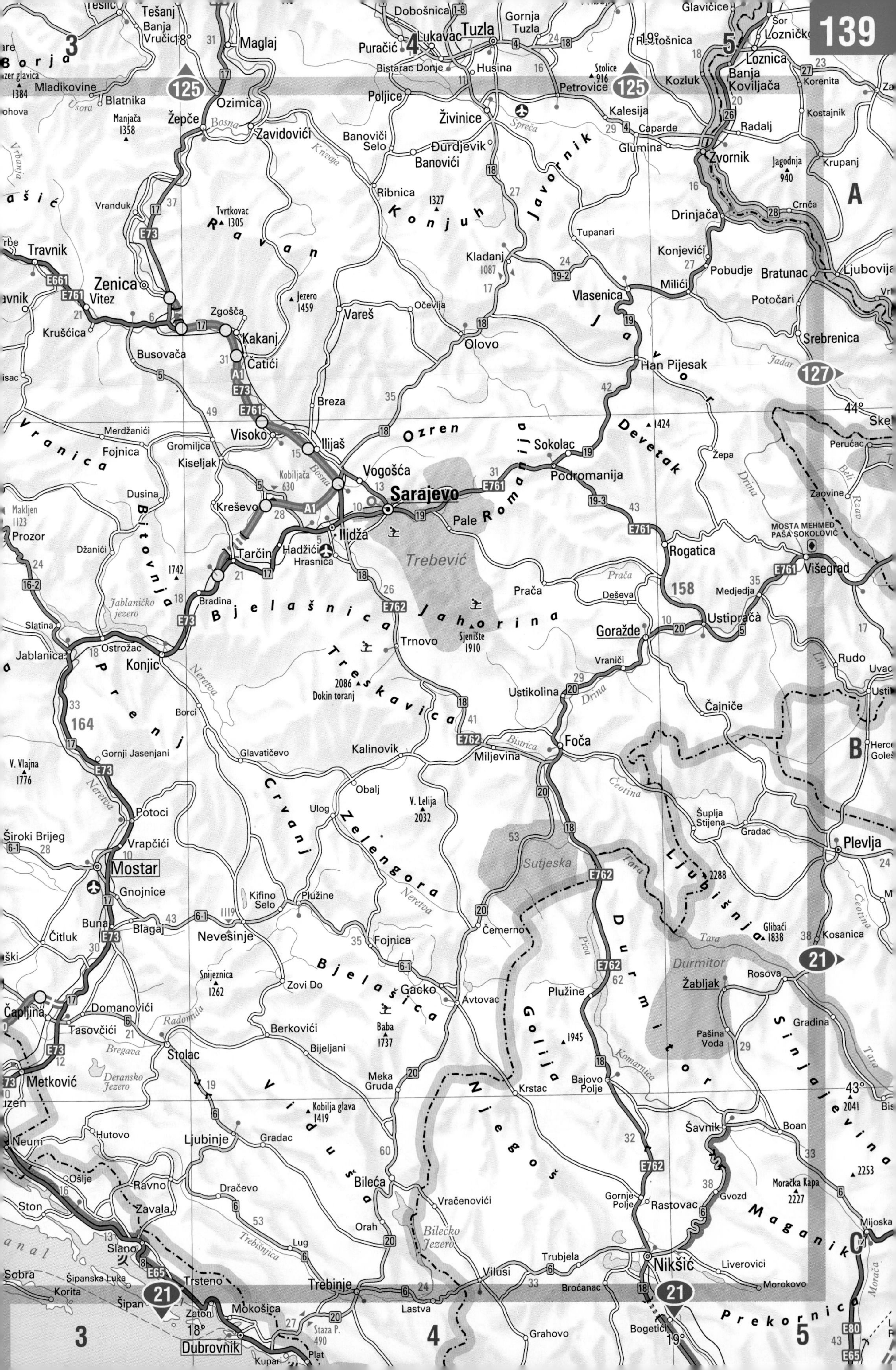

Tešanj
Banja Vručica
Maglaj
Dobošnica
Lukavac
Tuzla
Gornja Tuzla
Puračić
Bistarac Donje
Husina
Glavičice
Šor
Lozničko
Loznica
Banja Koviljača
Korenita
Kozluk
Petrovice
Stolice 916
Mladikovine
Blatnika
Manjača 1358
Žepče
Ozimica
Zavidovići
Poljice
Živinice
Kalesija
Caparde
Glumina
Zvornik
Radalj
Kostajnik
Krupanj
Jagodnja 940
Banovići Selo
Đurđevik
Banovići
Ribnica
Konjuh
Javornik
Drinjača
Crnča
Vranduk
Tvrtkovac 1305
Ravan
Travnik
Zenica
Vitez
Kruščica
Zgošća
Kakanj
Busovača
Čatići
Jezero 1459
Vareš
Očevlja
Kladanj
Tupanari
Konjević
Pobudje
Bratunac
Ljubovija
Vlasenica
Milići
Potočari
Srebrenica
Olovo
Han Pijesak
Jadar
Breza
Visoko
Ilijaš
Merdžanići
Fojnica
Gromiljca
Kiseljak
Kobiljača 630
Vogošća
Sarajevo
Ozren
Sokolac
Podromanija
Devetak
Žepa
Perućac
Vranica
Dusina
Kreševo
Ilidža
Hadžići
Hrasnica
Tarčin
Pale
Romanija
Trebević
Zaovine
Mosta Mehmed Paša Sokolović
Višegrad
Makljen 1123
Prozor
Džanići
Bitovnja 1742
Bradina
Jablaničko jezero
Bjelašnica
Jahorina
Prača
Deševa
Rogatica
Medjedja
Ustiprača
Slatina
Jablanica
Ostrožac
Konjic
Trnovo
Sjenište 1910
Goražde
Vraniči
Rudo
Uvac
Prenj
Treskavica
Dokin toranj 2086
Ustikolina
Drina
Čajniče
Borci
Kalinovik
Miljevina
Bistrica
Foča
Gornji Jasenjani
V. Vlajna 1776
Glavatičevo
Obalj
Čeotina
Potoci
Ulog
V. Lelija 2032
Crvanj
Zelengora
Šupija Stijena
Gradac
Pljevlja
Široki Brijeg
Vrapčići
Mostar
Gnojnice
Sutjeska
Tara
Ljubišnja 2288
Kifino Selo
Plužine
Buna
Čitluk
Blagaj
Nevesinje
Čemerno
Fojnica
Glibaći 1838
Kosanica
Snježnica 1262
Bjelašica
Zovi Do
Gacko
Avtovac
Durmitor
Žabljak
Rosova
Čapljina
Domanovići
Tasovčići
Radomida
Golija
Pivа
Plužine
Sinjajevina
Gradina
Baba 1737
Berkovići
Bijeljani
Stolac
Bregava
Deransko Jezero
Pašina Voda
Komarnica
Metković
Meka Gruda
Krstac
Bajovo Polje
Njegoš
Kobilja glava 1419
Vidusa
Šavnik
Boan
Neum
Hutovo
Ljubinje
Gradac
Oslje
Ravno
Dračevo
Bileća
Vračenovići
Gornje Polje
Rastovac
Gvozd
Moračka Kapa 2227
Maganik
Ston
Zavala
Trebišnjica
Orah
Bilećko Jezero
Mijoska
Slano
Lug
Trubjela
Nikšić
Liverovici
Sobra
Šipanska Luka
Korita
Trsteno
Trebinje
Vilusi
Bročanac
Morokovo
Šipan
Zaton
Mokošica
Lastva
Staza P. 490
Grahovo
Bogetići
Prekornica
Dubrovnik
Plat
Kupari

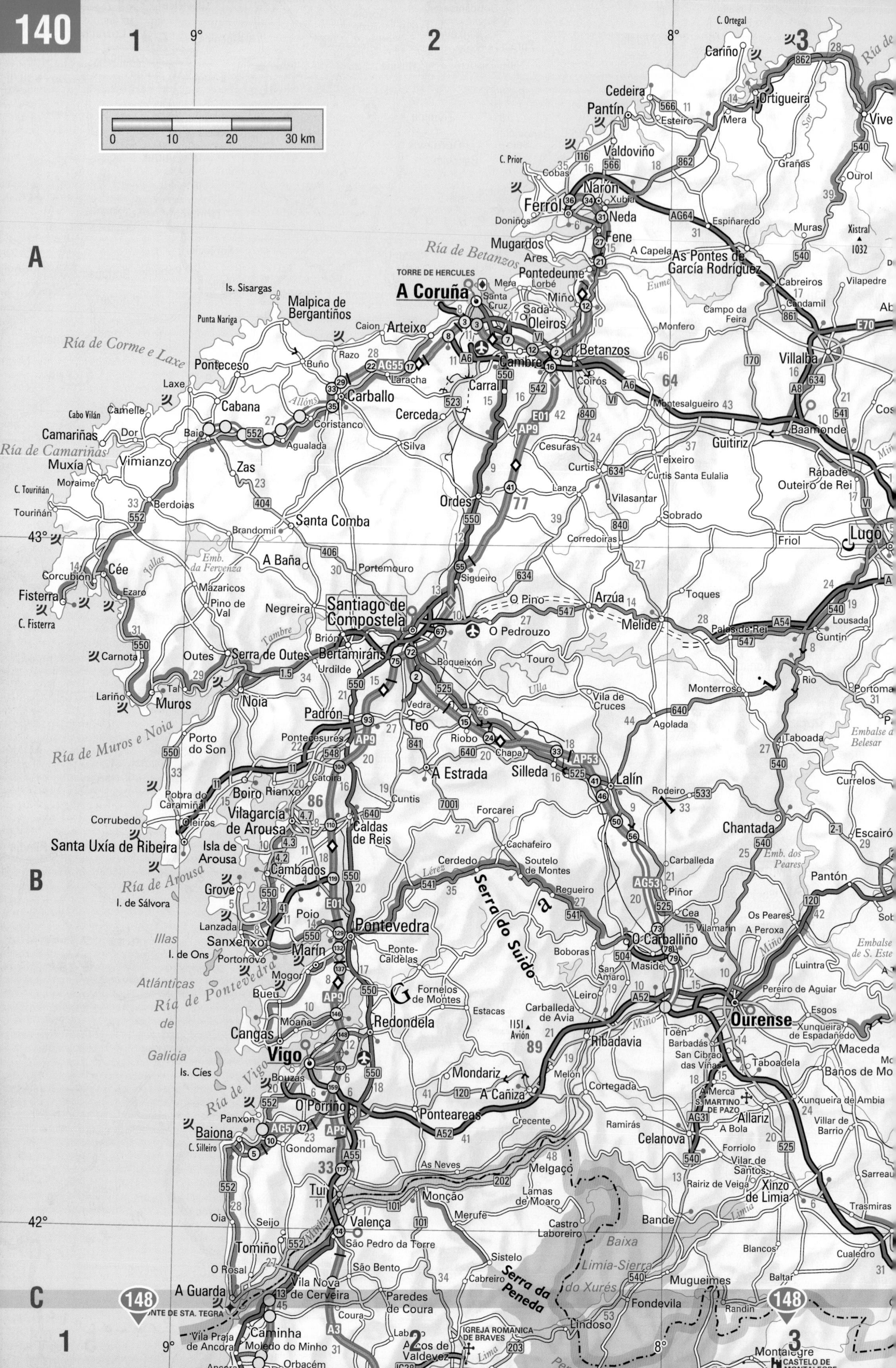

1
2
3
A
B
C
9°
8°
42°
43°
0 10 20 30 km
C. Ortegal
Cariño
Cedeira
Pantín
Ortigueira
Mera
Esteiro
Vive
Valdoviño
C. Prior
Cobas
Grañas
Ourol
Narón
Xubia
Ferrol
Neda
Doniños
Fene
Espiñaredo
Muras
Xistral
1032
Mugardos
Ares
A Capela
As Pontes de García Rodríguez
Ría de Betanzos
Pontedeume
TORRE DE HERCULES
A Coruña
Mera
Lorbé
Santa Cruz
Miño
Cabreiros
Vilapedre
Is. Sisargas
Malpica de Bergantiños
Punta Nariga
Sada
Oleiros
Candamil
Campo da Feira
Caion
Arteixo
Monfero
Ría de Corme e Laxe
Betanzos
Villalba
Ponteceso
Buño
Razo
Cambre
Laracha
Carral
Coirós
Laxe
Carballo
Cabana
Allóns
Montesalgueiro
Cabo Vilán
Camelle
Cerceda
Coristanco
Camariñas
Dor
Baio
Agualada
Baamonde
Ría de Camariñas
Silva
Cesuras
Guitiriz
Muxía
Vimianzo
Teixeiro
Moraime
Zas
Curtis
Curtis Santa Eulalia
Rábade
C. Touriñán
Outeiro de Rei
Lanza
Touriñán
Berdoias
Ordes
Vilasantar
Sobrado
Brandomil
Santa Comba
Corredoiras
Friol
Lugo
Emb. da Fervenza
A Baña
Portemouro
Corcubión
Cée
Sigueiro
Ezaro
Mazaricos
Toques
Fisterra
Pino de Val
O Pino
Arzúa
C. Fisterra
Negreira
Santiago de Compostela
Melide
Palas de Rei
Lousada
O Pedrouzo
Guntín
Carnota
Outes
Serra de Outes
Brión
Bertamiráns
Boqueixón
Touro
Urdilde
Rio
Lariño
Tal
Muros
Noia
Ulla
Vila de Cruces
Monterroso
Portomarín
Vedra
Padrón
Teo
Agolada
Ría de Muros e Noia
Porto do Son
Pontecesures
Riobo
Chapa
Taboada
Embalse de Belesar
Silleda
Lalín
A Estrada
Pobra do Caramiñal
Boiro
Rianxo
Catoira
Rodeiro
Currelos
Cuntis
Corrubedo
Oleiros
Vilagarcía de Arousa
Caldas de Reis
Forcarei
Chantada
Escairó
Santa Uxía de Ribeira
Isla de Arousa
Cachafeiro
Cerdedo
Soutelo de Montes
Carballeda
Emb. dos Peares
Cambados
Ría de Arousa
Grove
Lérez
Regueiro
Piñor
Pantón
I. de Sálvora
Serra do Suido
Poio
Cea
Os Peares
Lanzada
Pontevedra
Vilamarín
A Peroxa
Illas
Sanxenxo
O Carballiño
Embalse de S. Esteban
I. de Ons
Portonovo
Marín
Ponte-Caldelas
Boboras
Maside
Luintra
Mogor
San Amaro
Atlánticas
Ría de Pontevedra
Bueu
Fornelos de Montes
Leiro
Pereiro de Aguiar
Ría de Galicia
Moaña
Redondela
Estacas
Carballeda de Avia
Esgos
Cangas
Avión
Ourense
Xunqueira de Espadanedo
Miño
Toén
Ribadavia
Barbadás
Maceda
Vigo
San Cibrao das Viñas
Taboadela
Is. Cíes
Mondariz
Melón
Baños de Molgas
Bouzas
A Cañiza
Cortegada
A Merca
Ría de Vigo
O Porriño
S. MARTINO DE PAZO
Xunqueira de Ambia
Allariz
Panxón
Ponteareas
Crecente
Ramirás
A Bola
Villar de Barrio
Baiona
Celanova
C. Silleiro
Gondomar
Forriolo
Vilar de Santos
Melgaço
As Neves
Sarreaus
Tui
Monção
Lamas de Moaro
Rairiz de Veiga
Xinzo de Limia
Trasmiras
Oia
Merufe
Seijo
Valença
Castro Laboreiro
Bande
Limia
Baixa Limia-Sierra do Xurés
Tomiño
São Pedro da Torre
Sistelo
Blancos
Cualedro
O Rosal
São Bento
Serra da Peneda
Baltar
Cabreiro
Mugueimes
A Guarda
Vila Nova de Cerveira
Paredes de Coura
Fondevila
148
PONTE DE STA. TEGRA
Randin
Coura
Vila Praia de Ancora
Caminha
Labruja
Arcos de Valdevez
IGREJA ROMANICA DE BRAVES
Lindoso
Lima
Montalegre
CASTELO DE MONTALEGRE
Moledo do Minho
Ancora
Orbacém

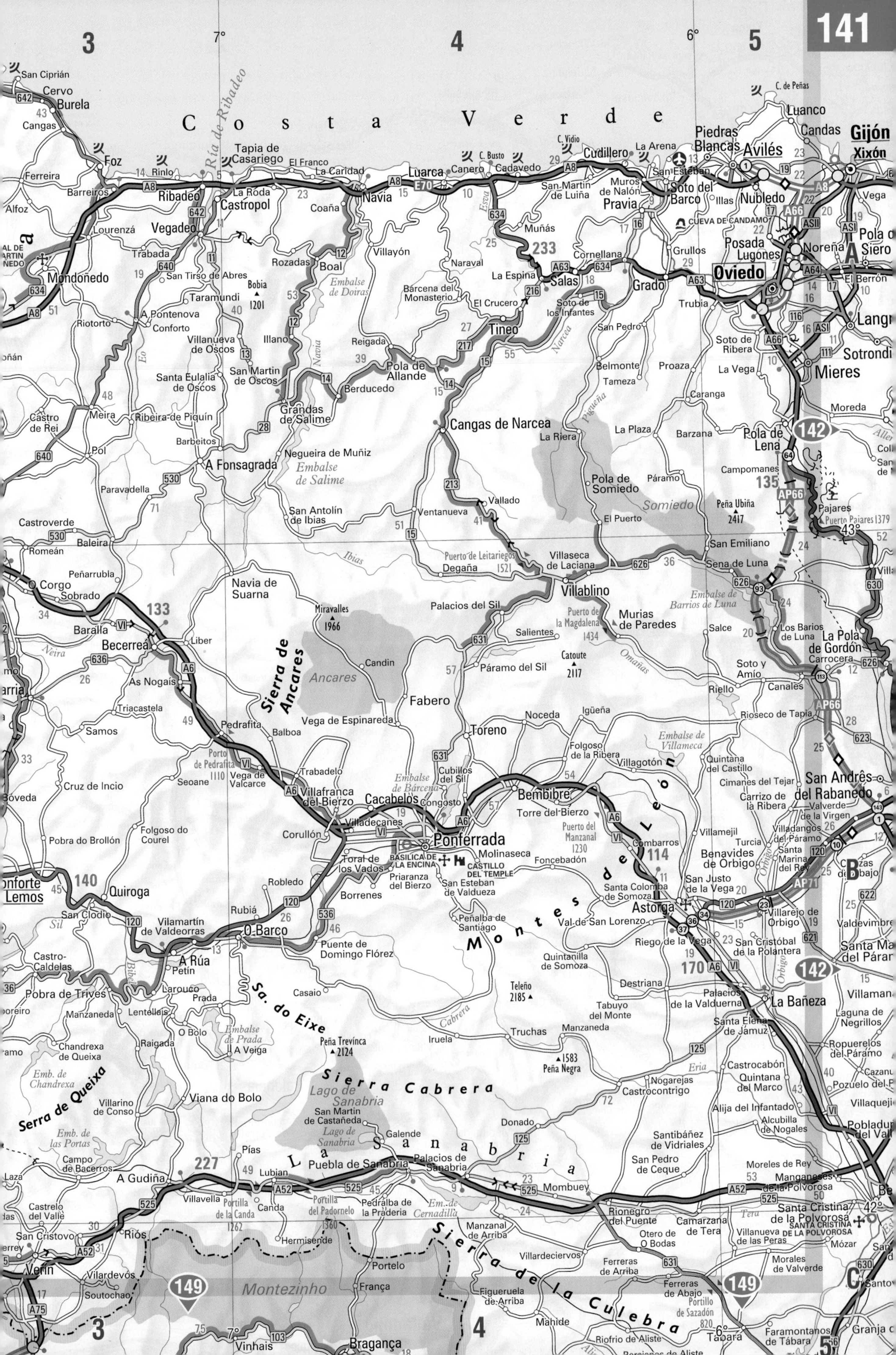

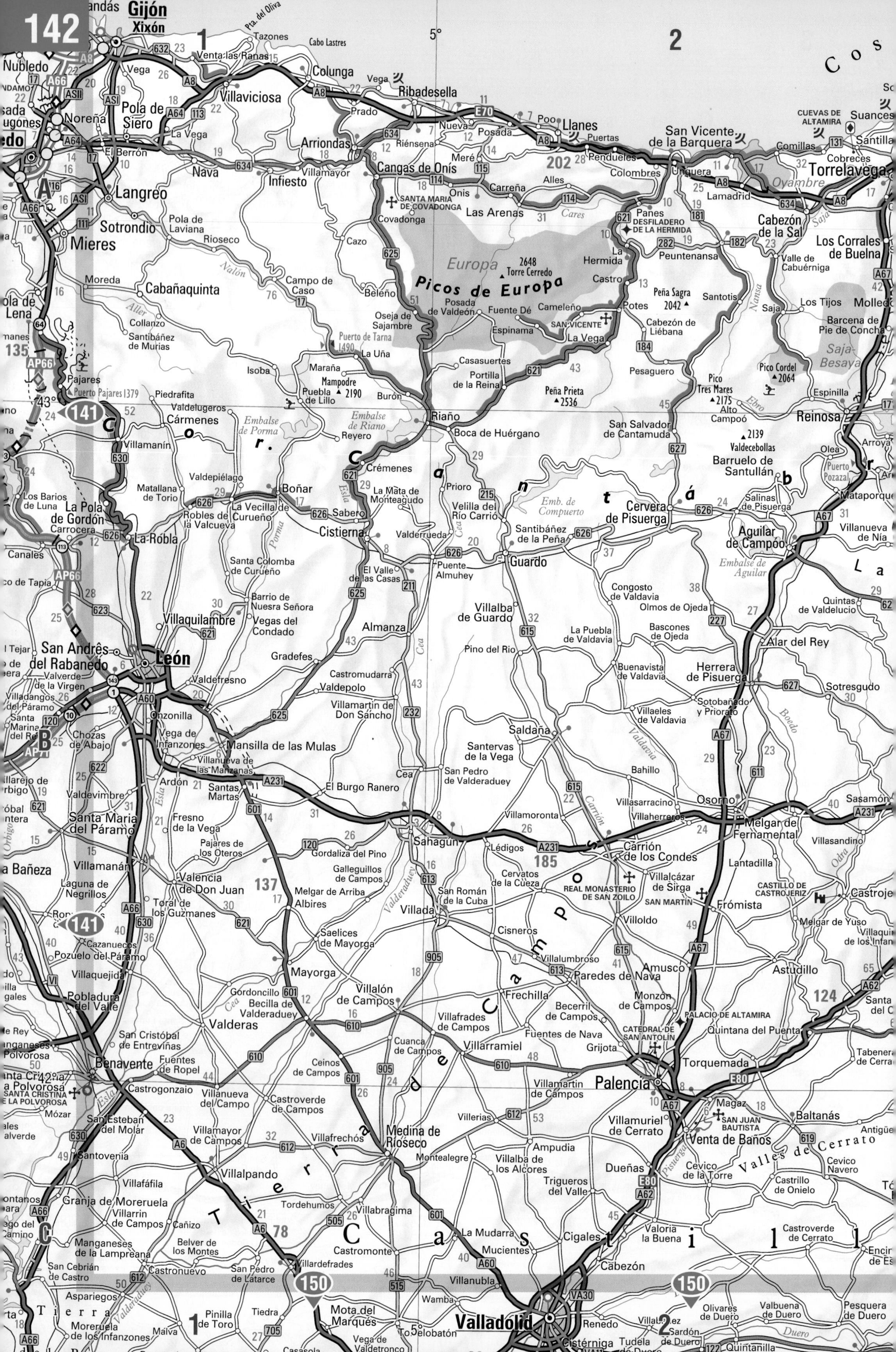
Gijón
Xixón
Picos de Europa
Torre Cerredo
Llanes
San Vicente de la Barquera
Torrelavega
Cangas de Onís
Ribadesella
Villaviciosa
Colunga
Pola de Siero
Langreo
Mieres
Cabezón de la Sal
Los Corrales de Buelna
Reinosa
Riaño
Cervera de Pisuerga
Aguilar de Campóo
Guardo
Cistierna
León
San Andrés del Rabanedo
Mansilla de las Mulas
Sahagún
Saldaña
Carrión de los Condes
Osorno
Herrera de Pisuerga
Frómista
Palencia
Benavente
Medina de Rioseco
Valladolid
Venta de Baños
Dueñas
Villalpando
Mayorga
Valderas
Villalón de Campos
Tierra de Campos
Castilla
Cordillera Cantábrica

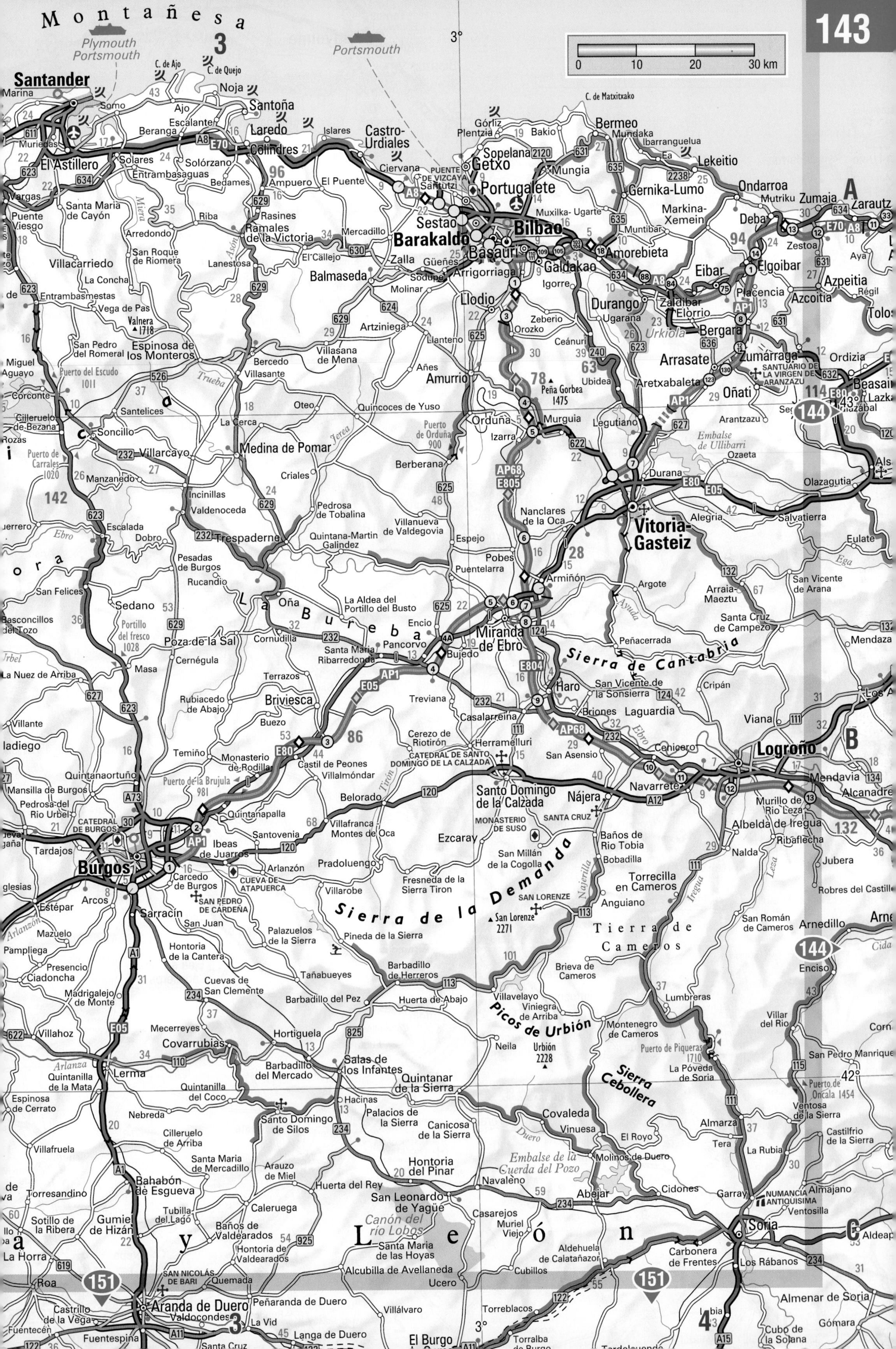
0
10
20
30 km
3°
Montañesa
Plymouth
Portsmouth
C. de Ajo
C. de Quejo
C. de Matxitxako
Santander
El Astillero
Solares
Noja
Santoña
Laredo
Colindres
Castro-Urdiales
Islares
Ajo
Escalante
Beranga
Somo
Muriedas
Solórzano
Entrambasaguas
Bedames
Ampuero
El Puente
Ciervana
Santurtzi
Puente de Vizcaya
Getxo
Portugalete
Sopelana
Plentzia
Górliz
Bakio
Bermeo
Mundaka
Ibarranguelua
Ea
Lekeitio
Mungia
Gernika-Lumo
Ondarroa
Mutriku
Zumaia
Zarautz
Markina-Xemein
Deba
Muxilka-Ugarte
Muntibar
Amorebieta
Zestoa
Aya
Eibar
Elgoibar
Azpeitia
Azcoitia
Régil
Tolosa
Placencia
Zaldibar
Elorrio
Durango
Ugarana
Urkiola
Bergara
Arrasate
Zumárraga
Ordizia
Beasain
Lazkao
Olazábal
Santuario de la Virgen de Aranzazu
Oñati
Aretxabaleta
Arantzazu
Sestao
Barakaldo
Bilbao
Basauri
Galdakao
Arrigorriaga
Igorre
Güeñes
Zalla
Sodupe
Balmaseda
Molinar
Llodio
Zeberio
Orozko
Ceánuri
Ubidea
Artziniega
Llanteno
Villasana de Mena
Añes
Amurrio
Peña Gorbea
1475
Murguia
Legutiano
Orduña
Izarra
Puerto de Orduña
900
Quincoces de Yuso
Berberana
Embalse de Ullibarri
Ozaeta
Durana
Olazagutia
Alsasua
Vitoria-Gasteiz
Nanclares de la Oca
Alegria
Salvatierra
Eulate
Argote
Arraia-Maeztu
San Vicente de Arana
Santa Cruz de Campezo
Peñacerrada
Mendaza
Armiñón
Pobes
Puentelarra
Espejo
Villanueva de Valdegovia
Quintana-Martin Galindez
Pedrosa de Tobalina
Criales
Medina de Pomar
Oteo
La Cerca
Bercedo
Villasante
Espinosa de los Monteros
San Pedro del Romeral
Vega de Pas
Valnera
1718
Entrambasmestas
La Concha
Villacarriedo
San Roque de Riomera
Lanestosa
Arredondo
Riba
Rasines
Ramales de la Victoria
Mercadillo
El Callejo
Santa María de Cayón
Puente Viesgo
Vargas
Miguel Aguayo
Puerto del Escudo
1011
Corconte
Cilleruelo de Bezana
Soncillo
Santelices
Villarcayo
Manzanedo
Puerto de Carrales
1020
Incinillas
Valdenoceda
Trespaderne
Escalada
Dobro
Pesadas de Burgos
Rucandio
San Felices
Sedano
Basconcillos del Tozo
Portillo del fresco
1028
Poza de la Sal
Cernégula
Masa
La Nuez de Arriba
Rubiacedo de Abajo
Villante
La Bureba
Oña
Cornudilla
La Aldea del Portillo del Busto
Encio
Santa María Ribarredonda
Pancorvo
Bujedo
Miranda de Ebro
Terrazos
Briviesca
Buezo
Treviana
Haro
San Vicente de la Sonsierra
Briones
Laguardia
Cripán
Viana
Los Arcos
Sierra de Cantabria
Casalarreina
Cerezo de Riotirón
Herramelluri
Catedral de Santo Domingo de la Calzada
San Asensio
Cenicero
Logroño
Navarrete
Mendavia
Alcanadre
Murillo de Río Leza
Temiño
Monasterio de Rodilla
Castil de Peones
Villalmóndar
Quintanaortuño
Mansilla de Burgos
Pedrosa del Río Urbel
Puerto de la Brujula
981
Quintanapalla
Belorado
Santo Domingo de la Calzada
Nájera
Santa Cruz
Monasterio de Suso
Villafranca-Montes de Oca
Santovenia
Ibeas de Juarros
Ezcaray
Baños de Rio Tobia
Bobadilla
Albelda de Iregua
Ribafrecha
Nalda
Jubera
Catedral de Burgos
Tardajos
Burgos
Arlanzón
Pradoluengo
San Millán de la Cogolla
Torrecilla en Cameros
Robres del Castillo
Carcedo de Burgos
Cueva de Atapuerca
Fresneda de la Sierra Tiron
Villarobe
Anguiano
San Pedro de Cardeña
Sarracín
San Juan
Sierra de la Demanda
San Lorenzo
2271
Tierra de Cameros
San Román de Cameros
Arnedillo
Arnedo
Estépar
Arcos
Mazuelo
Pampliega
Presencio
Ciadoncha
Hontoria de la Cantera
Palazuelos de la Sierra
Pineda de la Sierra
Tañabueyes
Barbadillo de Herreros
Brieva de Cameros
Enciso
Cida
Madrigalejo del Monte
Cuevas de San Clemente
Barbadillo del Pez
Huerta de Abajo
Villavelayo
Viniegra de Arriba
Picos de Urbión
Lumbreras
Villar del Río
Cornago
Villahoz
Mecerreyes
Covarrubias
Hortiguela
Neila
Urbión
2228
Montenegro de Cameros
Puerto de Piqueras
1710
San Pedro Manrique
Arlanza
Quintanilla de la Mata
Lerma
Barbadillo del Mercado
Salas de los Infantes
Quintanar de la Sierra
La Póveda de Soria
Sierra Cebollera
Puerto de Oncala 1454
42°
Espinosa de Cerrato
Quintanilla del Coco
Nebreda
Santo Domingo de Silos
Hacinas
Palacios de la Sierra
Canicosa de la Sierra
Covaleda
Vinuesa
Ventosa de la Sierra
Cilleruelo de Arriba
Villafruela
Duero
Embalse de la Cuerda del Pozo
El Royo
Almarza
Tera
La Rubia
Castilfrío de la Sierra
Santa María de Mercadillo
Arauzo de Miel
Hontoria del Pinar
Molinos de Duero
Bahabón de Esgueva
Torresandino
Huerta del Rey
San Leonardo de Yagüe
Navaleno
Abejar
Cidones
Garray
Numancia Antiquisima
Almajano
Ventosilla
Sotillo de la Ribera
Gumiel de Hizán
Tubilla del Lago
Caleruega
Baños de Valdearados
Hontoria de Valdearados
Cañón del río Lobos
Casarejos
Muriel Viejo
Soria
Aldealpozo
La Horra
Santa María de las Hoyas
Aldehuela de Calatañazor
Carbonera de Frentes
Los Rábanos
León
Roa
San Nicolás de Bari
Quemada
Alcubilla de Avellaneda
Ucero
Cubillos
Almenar de Soria
Castrillo de la Vega
Aranda de Duero
Valdocondes
Peñaranda de Duero
Villálvaro
Torreblacos
Gómara
Cubo de la Solana
Fuentecén
Fuentespina
La Vid
Langa de Duero
El Burgo de Osma
Torralba de Burgo
Santa Cruz
142
144
151

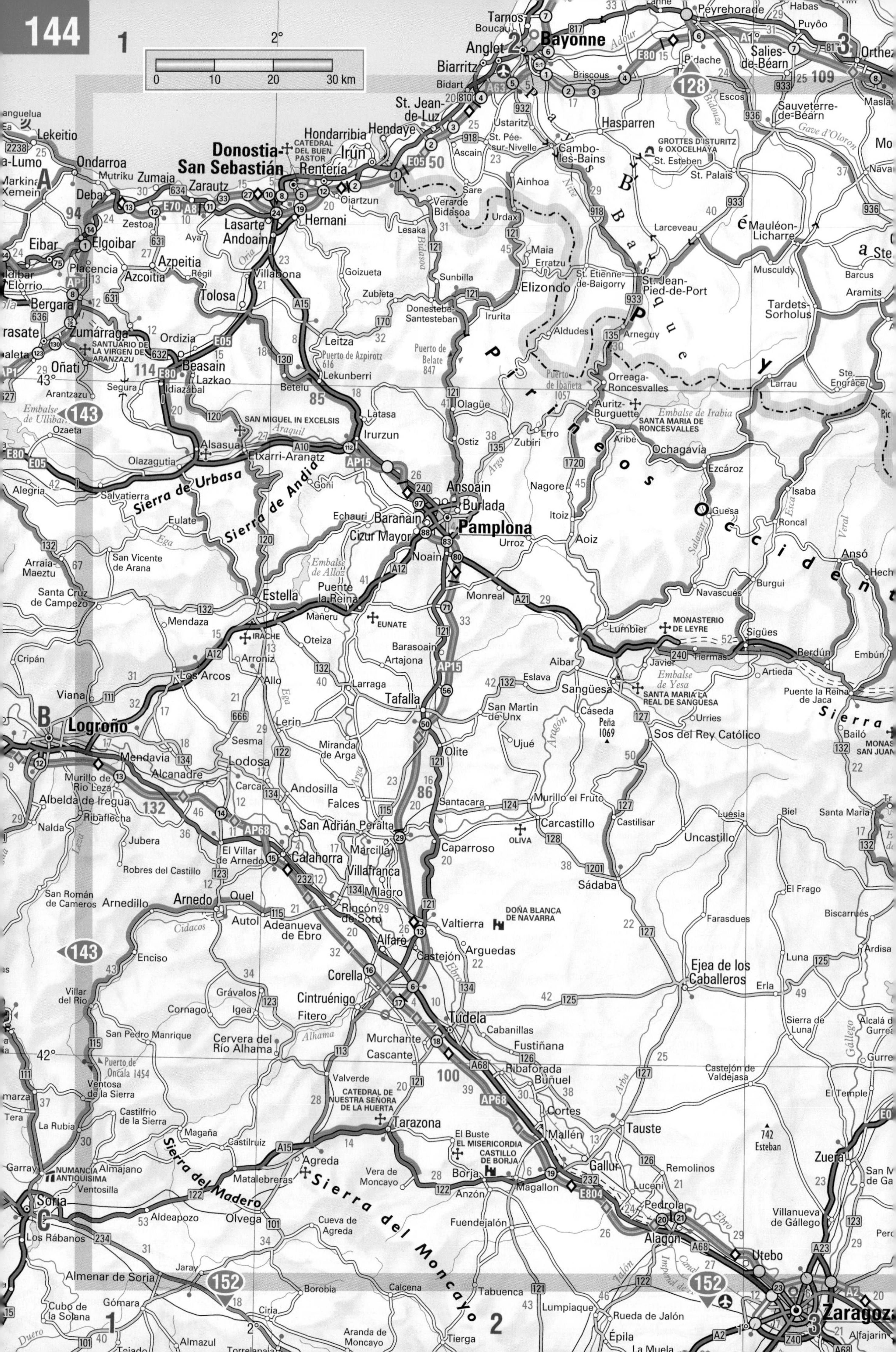
0 10 20 30 km
Bayonne
Anglet
Biarritz
Tarnos
Boucau
Peyrehorade
Habas
Puyôo
Orthez
Salies-de-Béarn
Bidache
Briscous
Bidart
St. Jean-de-Luz
Hendaye
Hondarribia
Irún
Donostia-San Sebastián
CATEDRAL DEL BUEN PASTOR
Rentería
Oiartzun
Hernani
Lasarte
Andoain
Zarautz
Zumaia
Mutriku
Ondarroa
Lekeitio
Deba
Zestoa
Eibar
Elgoibar
Placencia
Azpeitia
Azcoitia
Régil
Tolosa
Villabona
Bergara
Zumárraga
Ordizia
Oñati
SANTUARIO DE LA VIRGEN DE ARANZAZU
Beasain
Lazkao
Idiazábal
Segura
Arantzazu
Embalse de Ullibarri
Ozaeta
Alsasua
Olazagutia
Etxarri-Aranatz
SAN MIGUEL IN EXCELSIS
Sierra de Urbasa
Sierra de Andía
Salvatierra
Alegria
Eulate
Ustaritz
St. Pée-sur-Nivelle
Ascain
Sare
Verarde Bidasoa
Hasparren
GROTTES D'ISTURITZ & OXOCELHAYA
St. Esteben
St. Palais
Cambo-les-Bains
Ainhoa
Urdax
Maia
Erratzu
Elizondo
St. Etienne-de-Baigorry
St. Jean-Pied-de-Port
Larceveau
Mauléon-Licharre
Sauveterre-de-Béarn
Escos
Musculdy
Barcus
Aramits
Tardets-Sorholus
Lesaka
Sunbilla
Goizueta
Zubieta
Donestebe-Santesteban
Irurita
Leitza
Puerto de Azpirotz 616
Lekunberri
Betelu
Puerto de Belate 847
Aldudes
Arneguy
Puerto de Ibañeta 1057
Orreaga-Roncesvalles
Auritz-Burguette
SANTA MARIA DE RONCESVALLES
Embalse de Irabia
Larrau
Ste. Engrâce
Latasa
Irurzun
Olagüe
Ostiz
Zubiri
Erro
Aribe
Ochagavía
Ezcároz
Isaba
Roncal
Ansó
Pirineos Occidentales
Pyrénées
Ansoain
Burlada
Pamplona
Urroz
Nagore
Itoiz
Aoiz
Goñi
Echauri
Barañain
Cizur Mayor
Noain
Embalse de Alloz
Estella
Puente la Reina
Mañeru
EUNATE
Monreal
Guesa
Navascués
Burgui
Lumbier
MONASTERIO DE LEYRE
Sigües
Berdún
Embún
Tiermas
Embalse de Yesa
Javier
Artieda
Puente la Reina de Jaca
Sierra
Arraia-Maeztu
San Vicente de Arana
Santa Cruz de Campezo
Mendaza
IRACHE
Arroniz
Oteiza
Barasoain
Artajona
Larraga
Tafalla
Aibar
Eslava
Sangüesa
SANTA MARIA LA REAL DE SANGUESA
Urries
Cripán
Los Arcos
Allo
Viana
Logroño
Lerin
Sesma
Mendavia
Lodosa
Miranda de Arga
San Martin de Unx
Ujué
Cáseda
Peña 1069
Sos del Rey Católico
Bailó
Olite
Murillo de Rio Leza
Alcanadre
Carcar
Andosilla
Falces
Albelda de Iregua
Ribaflecha
Nalda
Jubera
Santacara
Murillo el Fruto
Carcastillo
Castilisar
Luesia
Biel
Santa Maria
San Adrián
Peralta
OLIVA
Uncastillo
El Villar de Arnedo
Calahorra
Marcilla
Caparroso
Robres del Castillo
Villafranca
Milagro
Sádaba
El Frago
San Román de Cameros
Arnedillo
Arnedo
Quel
Autol
Rincón de Soto
Adeanueva de Ebro
DOÑA BLANCA DE NAVARRA
Valtierra
Farasdues
Biscarrués
Alfaro
Castejón
Arguedas
Enciso
Corella
Ejea de los Caballeros
Luna
Ardisa
Erla
Villar del Río
Grávalos
Igea
Cornago
Cintruénigo
Fitero
Tudela
Cabanillas
Sierra de Luna
San Pedro Manrique
Cervera del Río Alhama
Murchante
Cascante
Fustiñana
Ribaforada
Buñuel
Puerto de Oncala 1454
Ventosa de la Sierra
Valverde
CATEDRAL DE NUESTRA SEÑORA DE LA HUERTA
Castejón de Valdejasa
El Temple
Castilfrio de la Sierra
La Rubia
Tarazona
Cortes
Mallén
Tauste
742 Esteban
Magaña
Castilruiz
El Buste
EL MISERICORDIA
CASTILLO DE BORJA
Garray
NUMANCIA ANTIQUISIMA
Almajano
Agreda
Vera de Moncayo
Borja
Gallur
Remolinos
Zuera
Ventosilla
Matalebreras
Sierra del Madero
Sierra del Moncayo
Magallon
Anzón
Luceni
Pedrola
Soria
Los Rábanos
Aldeapozo
Olvega
Cueva de Agreda
Fuendejalón
Alagón
Villanueva de Gállego
Utebo
Almenar de Soria
Jaray
Borobia
Calcena
Tabuenca
Lumpiaque
Rueda de Jalón
Zaragoza
Cubo de la Solana
Gómara
Ciria
Almazul
Aranda de Moncayo
Tierga
Épila
La Muela
Alfajarín
Duero
Ebro
Aragón
Arga
Ega
Alhama
Cidacos
Jalón
Arba
Gállego
Canal Imperial de Aragón

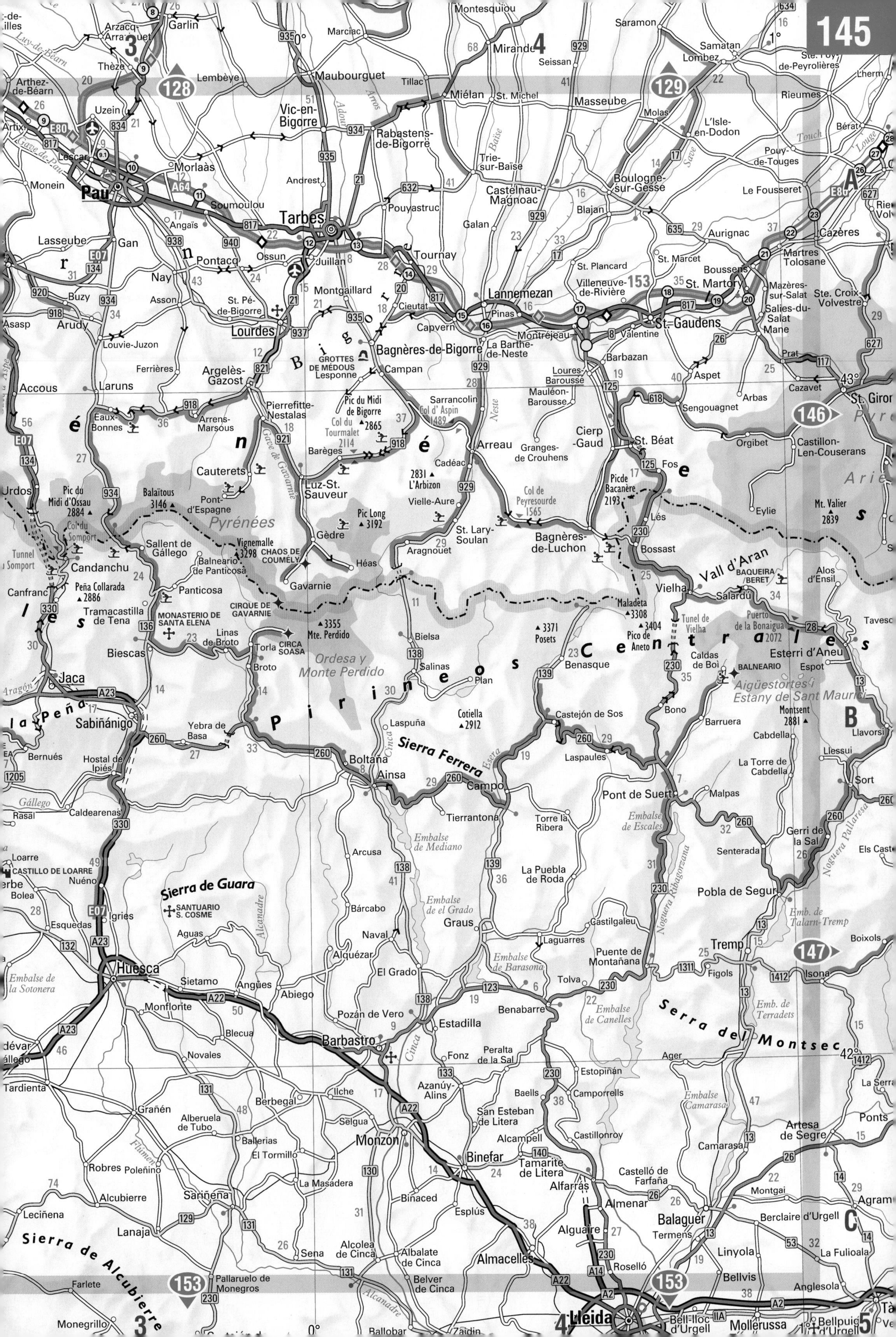

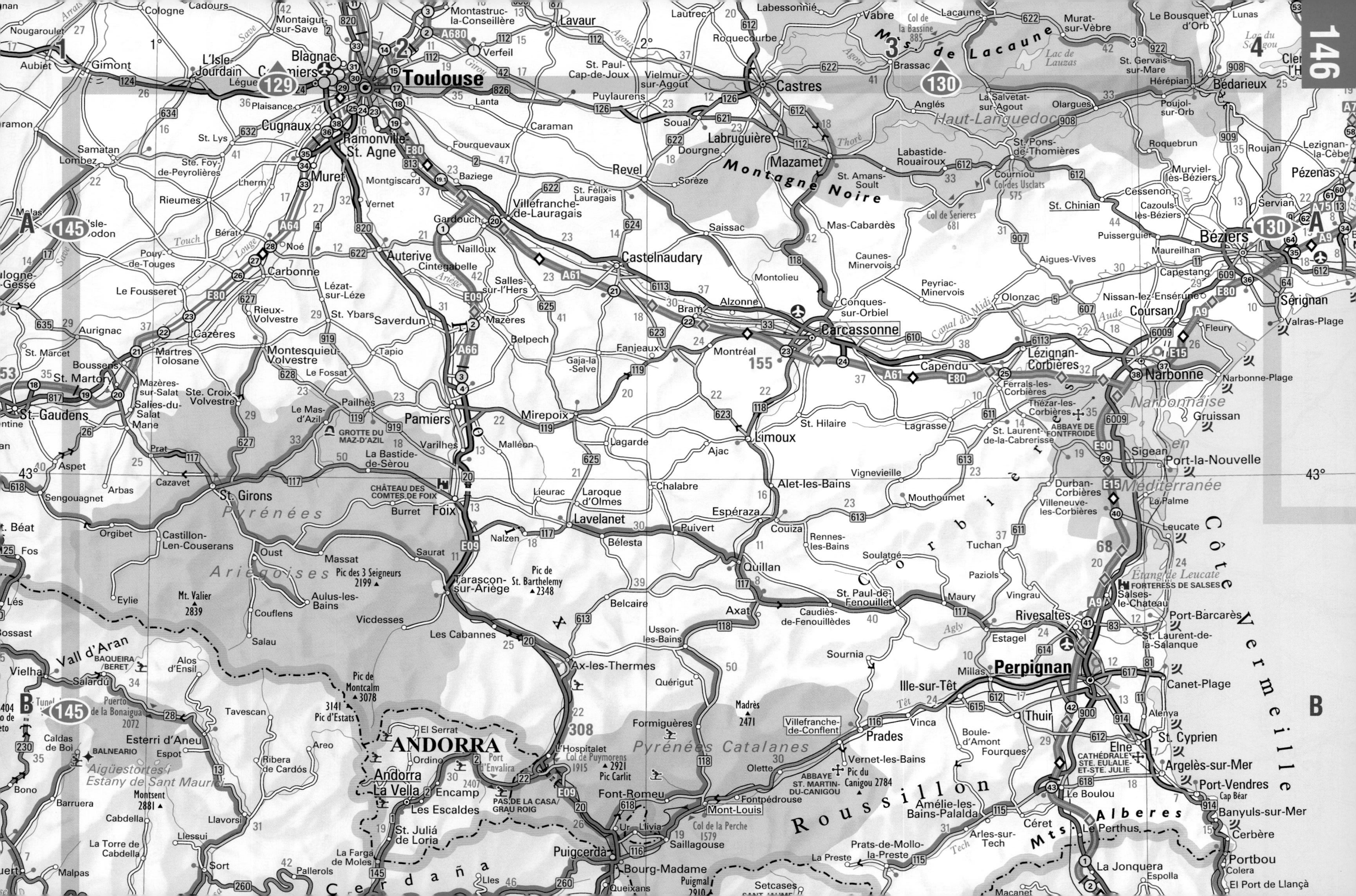

Toulouse
Perpignan
Carcassonne
Narbonne
Béziers
Castres
Castelnaudary
Limoux
Foix
Pamiers
Mirepoix
Muret
St. Gaudens
St. Girons
Lavelanet
Quillan
Prades
Mazamet
Revel
Lavaur
ANDORRA
Andorra La Vella
Puigcerdà
Côte Vermeille
Montagne Noire
Mts. de Lacaune
Roussillon
Pyrénées Catalanes
Méditerranée

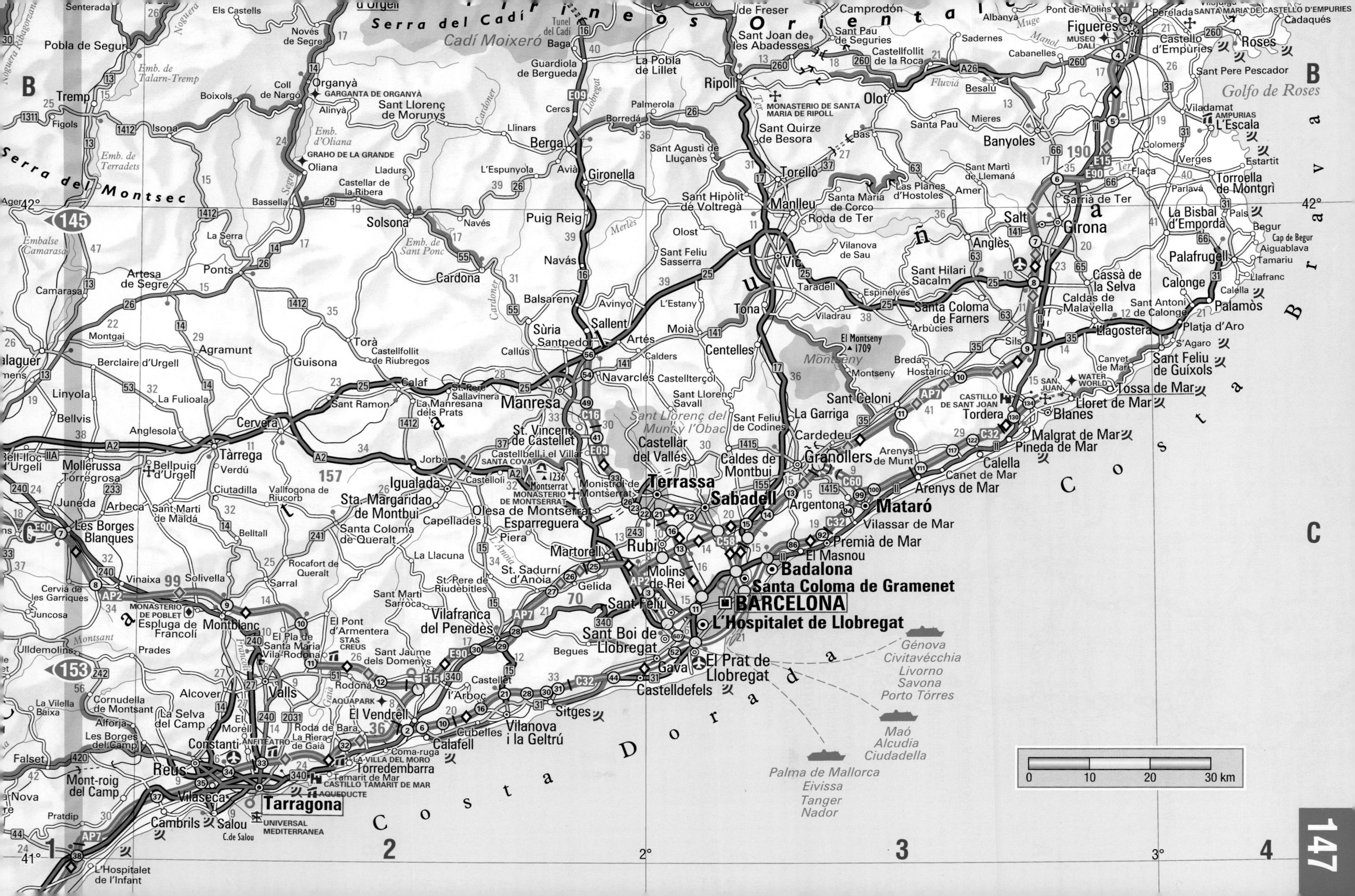
Serra del Cadí
Cadí Moixeró
Serra del Montsec
Costa Brava
Costa Dorada
Golfo de Roses
Figueres
Roses
Cadaqués
L'Escala
Torroella de Montgrì
La Bisbal d'Empordà
Palafrugell
Palamós
Sant Feliu de Guíxols
Tossa de Mar
Lloret de Mar
Blanes
Malgrat de Mar
Pineda de Mar
Calella
Canet de Mar
Arenys de Mar
Mataró
Vilassar de Mar
Premià de Mar
El Masnou
Badalona
Santa Coloma de Gramenet
BARCELONA
L'Hospitalet de Llobregat
El Prat de Llobregat
Castelldefels
Gavà
Sant Boi de Llobregat
Sitges
Vilanova i la Geltrú
Cubelles
Calafell
El Vendrell
Torredembarra
Tarragona
Salou
Cambrils
Reus
Valls
Montblanc
Girona
Salt
Banyoles
Olot
Ripoll
Vic
Manlleu
Torelló
Berga
Solsona
Cardona
Manresa
Terrassa
Sabadell
Granollers
Igualada
Cervera
Tàrrega
Tremp
Organyà
Vilafranca del Penedès
Martorell
Rubí
El Montseny 1709
Génova
Civitavécchia
Livorno
Savona
Porto Tórres
Maó
Alcudia
Ciudadella
Palma de Mallorca
Eivissa
Tanger
Nador
0 10 20 30 km

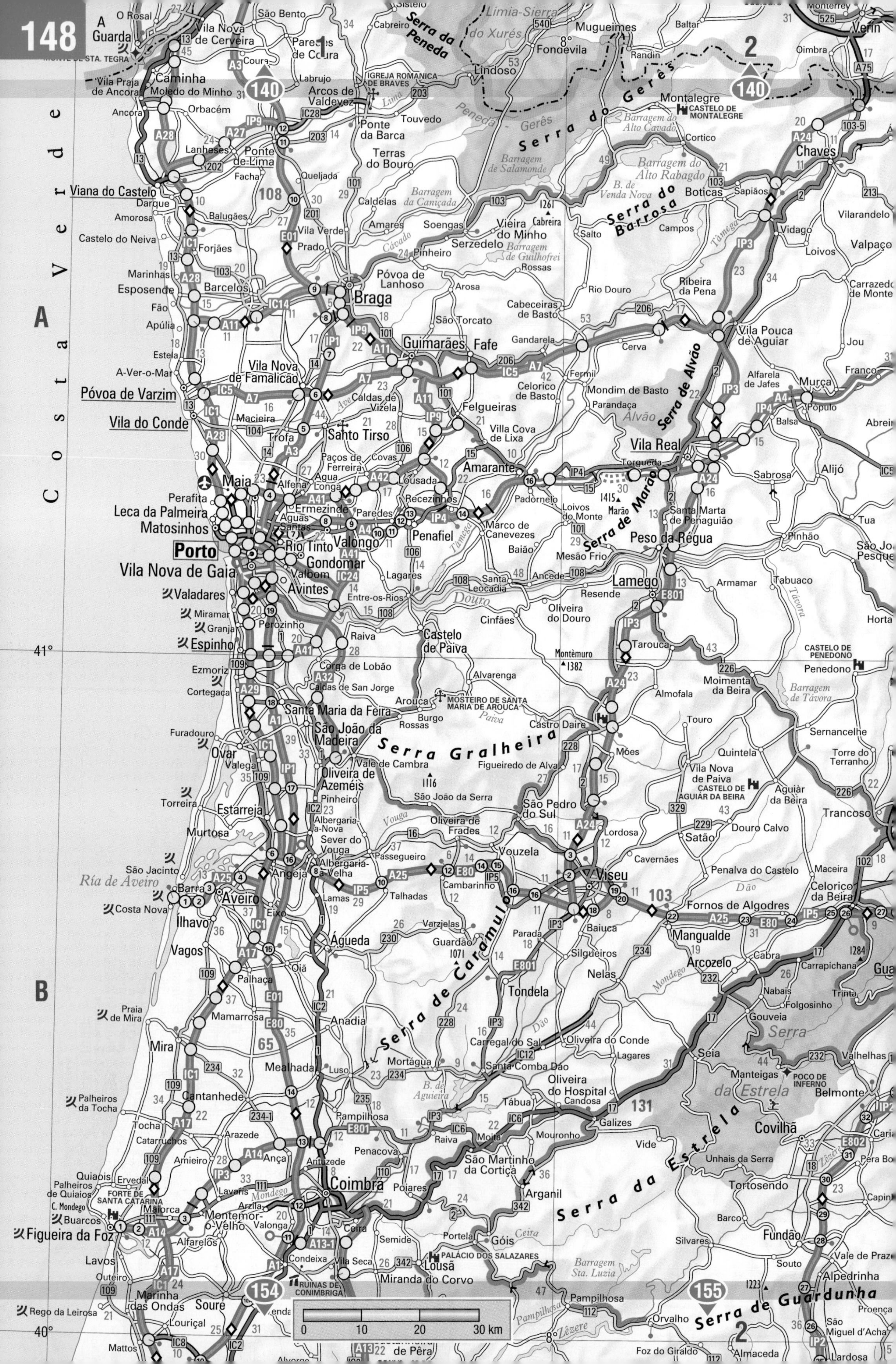
Costa Verde
Serra da Peneda
Limia-Sierra do Xurés
Serra do Gerês
Serra do Barroso
Serra de Alvão
Serra de Marão
Serra Gralheira
Serra de Caramulo
Serra da Estrela
Serra de Guardunha
A Guarda
O Rosal
Vila Nova de Cerveira
Caminha
Moledo do Minho
Vila Praia de Ancora
Ancora
Orbacém
Lanheses
Ponte de Lima
Viana do Castelo
Darque
Amorosa
Castelo do Neiva
Forjães
Marinhas
Esposende
Barcelos
Fão
Apúlia
Estela
A-Ver-o-Mar
Póvoa de Varzim
Vila do Conde
Vila Nova de Famalicão
Trofa
Santo Tirso
Maia
Perafita
Leca da Palmeira
Matosinhos
Porto
Vila Nova de Gaia
Valadares
Miramar
Granja
Espinho
Gondomar
Rio Tinto
Valongo
Avintes
Ermezinde
Paredes
Penafiel
Lousada
Paços de Ferreira
Amarante
Felgueiras
Guimarães
Fafe
Braga
Póvoa de Lanhoso
Vila Verde
Prado
Amares
Ponte da Barca
Arcos de Valdevez
Terras do Bouro
Lindoso
Montalegre
Castelo de Montalegre
Chaves
Verín
Boticas
Vidago
Vila Pouca de Aguiar
Ribeira da Pena
Cabeceiras de Basto
Celorico de Basto
Mondim de Basto
Vila Real
Sabrosa
Alijó
Murça
Peso da Régua
Lamego
Santa Marta de Penaguião
Mesão Frio
Baião
Marco de Canavezes
Cinfães
Castelo de Paiva
Resende
Tarouca
Moimenta da Beira
Penedono
Castelo de Penedono
Sernancelhe
Trancoso
Vila Nova de Paiva
Castelo de Aguiar da Beira
Aguiar da Beira
Castro Daire
São Pedro do Sul
Vouzela
Oliveira de Frades
Viseu
Mangualde
Fornos de Algodres
Celorico da Beira
Penalva do Castelo
Nelas
Tondela
Carregal do Sal
Santa Comba Dão
Oliveira do Hospital
Seia
Gouveia
Manteigas
Poço de Inferno
Covilhã
Belmonte
Tortosendo
Fundão
Unhais da Serra
Arganil
Góis
Lousã
Palácio dos Salazares
Miranda do Corvo
Penacova
Coimbra
Condeixa
Ruinas de Conimbriga
Montemor-o-Velho
Figueira da Foz
Forte de Santa Catarina
Buarcos
Quiaios
Soure
Cantanhede
Mealhada
Anadia
Mortágua
Águeda
Aveiro
Ílhavo
Vagos
Mira
Costa Nova
Barra
Ria de Aveiro
São Jacinto
Murtosa
Estarreja
Torreira
Ovar
Oliveira de Azeméis
São João da Madeira
Santa Maria da Feira
Arouca
Mosteiro de Santa Maria de Arouca
Vale de Cambra
Sever do Vouga
Albergaria-a-Velha
Espinho
Douro
Mondego
Vouga
Dão
Paiva
Tâmega
Lima
Cávado
Zêzere
Barragem de Salamonde
Barragem do Alto Rabagão
Barragem da Caniçada
Barragem Sta. Luzia
0 10 20 30 km
140
154
155
41°
40°
A
B
1
2

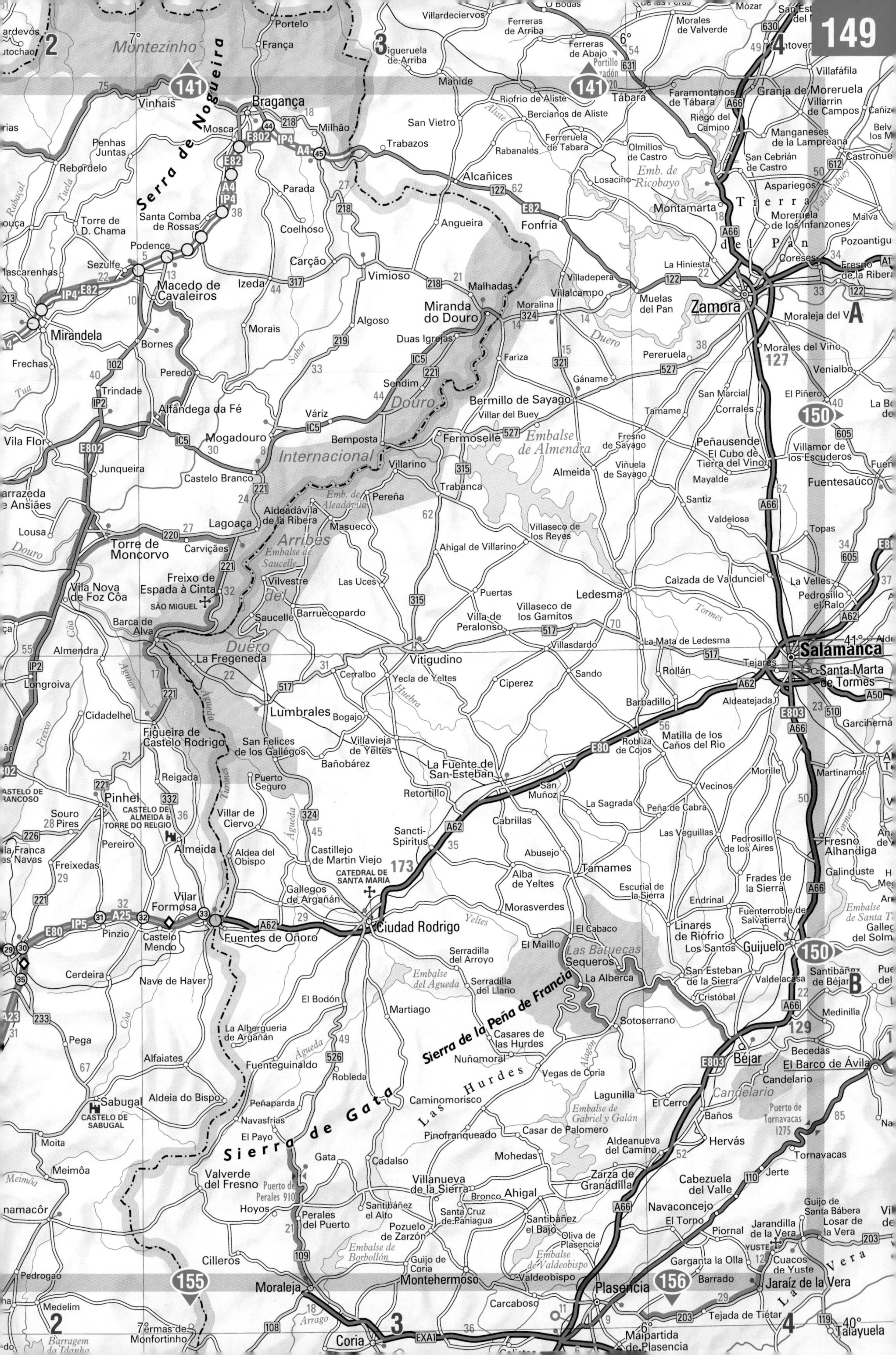
2
3
4
A
B
7°
6°
41°
40°
Montezinho
Portelo
França
Villardeciervos
Ferreras de Arriba
Ferreras de Abajo
Portillo
Mózar
Morales de Valverde
San Esteban del Molar
Santovenia
630
631
Figueruela de Arriba
Mahíde
Riofrío de Aliste
Tábara
Faramontanos de Tábara
Granja de Moreruela
Villafáfila
Villarrín de Campos
Cañizo
Belver de los Montes
141
75
Vinhais
Bragança
Milhão
Mosca
Serra de Nogueira
San Vietro
Bercianos de Aliste
Aliste
Riego del Camino
Manganeses de la Lampreana
Penhas Juntas
Rebordelo
Trabazos
Rabanales
Ferreruela de Tábara
Olmillos de Castro
San Cebrián de Castro
Castronuevo
E802
E82
IP4
A4
218
Alcañices
122
Losacino
Emb. de Ricobayo
Asperiegos
Valderaduey
Tuela
Rabaçal
Parada
Torre de D. Chama
Santa Comba de Rossas
Coelhoso
218
Angueira
Fonfría
Montamarta
Tierra del Pan
Moreruela de los Infanzones
Malva
Pozoantiguo
Coreses
Fresno de la Ribera
Mascarenhas
Podence
Sezulfe
Macedo de Cavaleiros
Izeda
317
Carção
Vimioso
Malhadas
La Hiniesta
Villadepera
Villalcampo
Muelas del Pan
Zamora
Mirandela
Bornes
Morais
Algoso
219
Miranda do Douro
Duas Igrejas
Moralina
324
Duero
Moraleja del Vino
Morales del Vino
127
Frechas
102
Peredo
Sabor
Fariza
321
Pereruela
527
Venialbo
Trindade
IP2
Alfândega da Fé
Sendim
Douro
Gáname
Bermillo de Sayago
San Marcial
Corrales
El Piñero
150
Tua
Vila Flor
IC5
Mogadouro
Váriz
Bemposta
Internacional
Villar del Buey
Fermoselle
Embalse de Almendra
Tamame
Fresno de Sayago
Peñausende
El Cubo de Tierra del Vino
Villamor de los Escuderos
605
Junqueira
Castelo Branco
221
Villarino
Trabanca
315
Almeida
Viñuela de Sayago
Mayalde
Fuentesaúco
Carrazeda de Ansiães
Aldeadávila de la Ribera
Emb. de Aleadávila
Pereña
Masueco
Santiz
A66
Valdelosa
Topas
Lousa
Lagoaça
Torre de Moncorvo
220
Carviçães
Arribes
Embalse de Saucelle
Ahigal de Villarino
Villaseco de los Reyes
Douro
Freixo de Espada à Cinta
SÃO MIGUEL
Vilvestre
Las Uces
Puertas
Ledesma
Calzada de Valdunciel
La Vellés
Pedrosillo el Ralo
Vila Nova de Foz Côa
del
Saucelle
Barruecopardo
Villaseco de los Gamitos
Villa de Peralonso
517
Tormes
A62
Barca de Alva
Côa
Almendra
Duero
La Fregeneda
Vitigudino
Villasdardo
La Mata de Ledesma
Salamanca
Santa Marta de Tormes
Longroiva
Cerralbo
Yecla de Yeltes
Ciperez
Sando
Rollán
Tejares
A50
Cidadelhe
Lumbrales
Bogajo
Huebra
Barbadillo
Aldeatejada
E803
510
Garcihernández
Freixo
Figueira de Castelo Rodrigo
San Felices de los Gallegos
Villavieja de Yeltes
Bañobárez
E80
Robliza de Cojos
Matilla de los Caños del Rio
Águeda
Reigada
Puerto Seguro
La Fuente de San-Esteban
Morille
Martinamor
CASTELO DE RANCOSO
Pinhel
CASTELO DE ALMEIDA & TORRE DO RELGIO
Retortillo
San Muñoz
La Sagrada
Vecinos
Souro Pires
226
Pereiro
Almeida
Villar de Ciervo
324
Sancti-Spíritus
Cabrillas
Peña de Cabra
Las Veguillas
Pedrosillo de los Aires
Fresno Alhándiga
Freixedas
Aldea del Obispo
Castillejo de Martín Viejo
173
CATEDRAL DE SANTA MARIA
Abusejo
Tamames
Frades de la Sierra
Galinduste
Vilar Formosa
Gallegos de Argañán
Alba de Yeltes
Escurial de la Sierra
Endrinal
Fuenterroble de Salvatierra
Embalse de Santa Teresa
Pinzio
Castelo Mendo
IP5
A25
Fuentes de Oñoro
Ciudad Rodrigo
Morasverdes
Yeltes
El Cabaco
Linares de Riofrío
Los Santos
Guijuelo
Cerdeira
Nave de Haver
Serradilla del Arroyo
Embalse del Águeda
Serradilla del Llano
El Maillo
Las Batuecas
Sequeros
La Alberca
San Esteban de la Sierra
Valdelacasa
Santibáñez de Béjar
Cristóbal
233
A23
Pega
Côa
El Bodón
Martiago
Sierra de la Peña de Francia
Sotoserrano
Medinilla
129
La Albergueria de Argañán
Casares de las Hurdes
Béjar
Becedas
El Barco de Ávila
Alfaiates
Fuenteguinaldo
526
Nuñomoral
Alagón
Vegas de Coria
Candelario
Sabugal
CASTELO DE SABUGAL
Aldeia do Bispo
Peñaparda
Robleda
Las Hurdes
Lagunilla
El Cerro
Puerto de Tornavacas
Navasfrías
Caminomorisco
Embalse de Gabriel y Galán
Baños
Moita
El Payo
Sierra de Gata
Pinofranqueado
Casar de Palomero
Hervás
Meimoa
Meimôa
Gata
Cadalso
Mohedas
Aldeanueva del Camino
Tornavacas
Valverde del Fresno
Puerto de Perales 910
Villanueva de la Sierra
Zarza de Granadilla
Cabezuela del Valle
Jerte
110
Penamacôr
Hoyos
Perales del Puerto
Santibáñez el Alto
Bronco
Ahigal
Santa Cruz de Paniagua
Santibáñez el Bajo
Navaconcejo
El Torno
Guijo de Santa Bárbara
Jarandilla de la Vera
Losar de la Vera
203
Pozuelo de Zarzón
Embalse de Borbollón
Oliva de Plasencia
Embalse de Valdeobispo
Piornal
YUSTE
Cuacos de Yuste
La Vera
Pedrogão
Cilleros
109
Guijo de Coria
Valdeobispo
Garganta la Olla
155
Moraleja
Montehermoso
Plasencia
156
Barrado
Jaraíz de la Vera
Medelim
Carcaboso
Tejada de Tiétar
Arrago
108
Termas de Monfortinho
Barragem da Idanha
Coria
EXA1
Malpartida de Plasencia
Talayuela
119

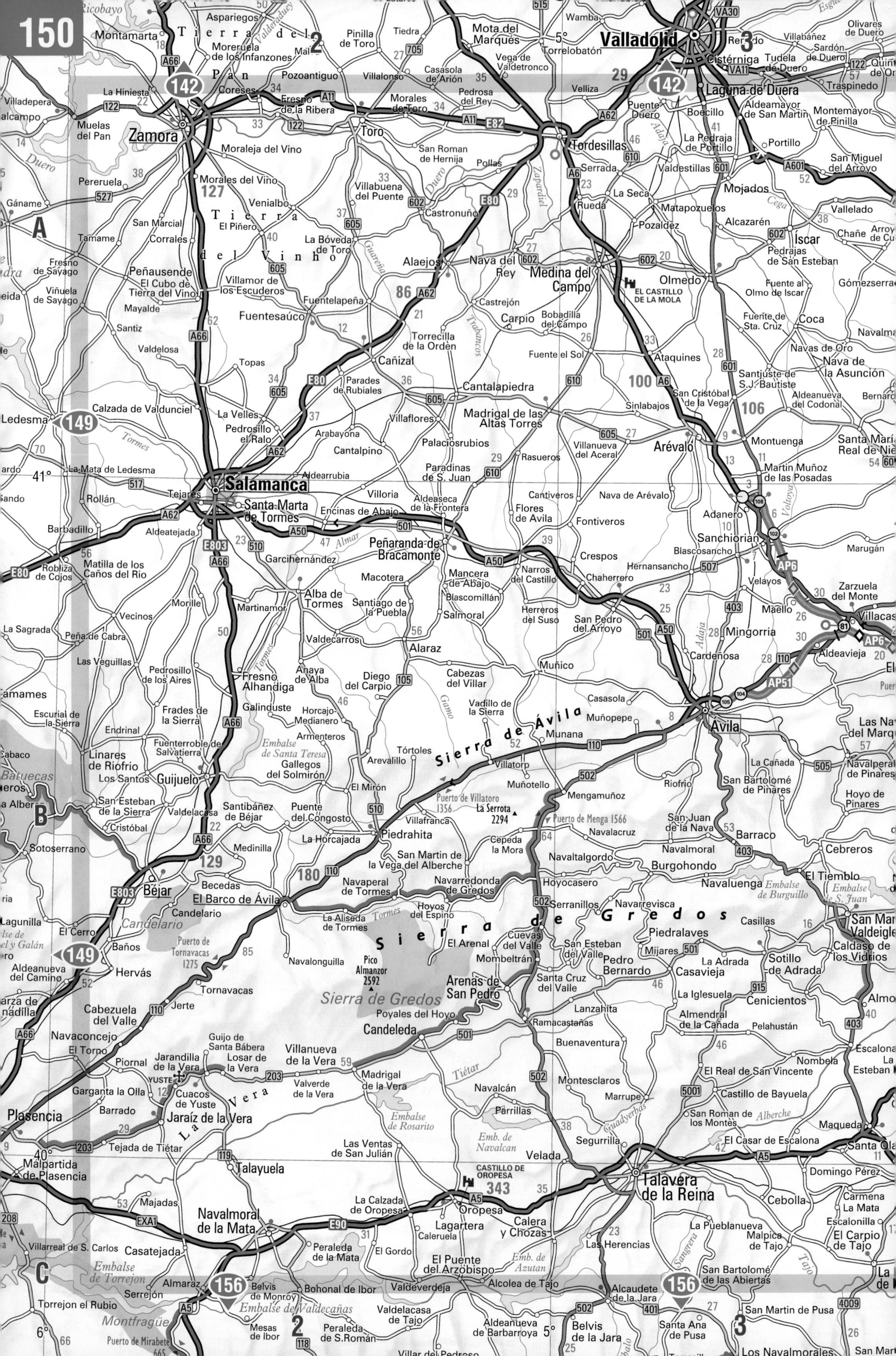
Tierra del Pan
Tierra del Vinho
Zamora
Toro
Tordesillas
Valladolid
Laguna de Duera
Medina del Campo
Olmedo
Íscar
Coca
Arévalo
Salamanca
Santa Marta de Tormes
Peñaranda de Bracamonte
Alba de Tormes
Ledesma
Ávila
Sierra de Ávila
Guijuelo
Béjar
El Barco de Ávila
Piedrahita
Sierra de Gredos
Pico Almanzor 2592
La Serrota 2294
Puerto de Villatoro 1356
Puerto de Menga 1566
Puerto de Tornavacas 1275
Arenas de San Pedro
Candeleda
Hervás
Plasencia
Jaraíz de la Vera
Villanueva de la Vera
La Vera
Navalmoral de la Mata
Oropesa
CASTILLO DE OROPESA
EL CASTILLO DE LA MOLA
Talavera de la Reina
Almaraz
Embalse de Valdecañas
Embalse de Rosarito
Embalse de Santa Teresa
Embalse de Burguillo
Embalse de Torrejon
Montfragüe
Puerto de Mirabete
Tormes
Duero
Tiétar
Alberche
Tajo
Adaja
A
B
C
2
3
41°
40°
5°
6°
142
149
156

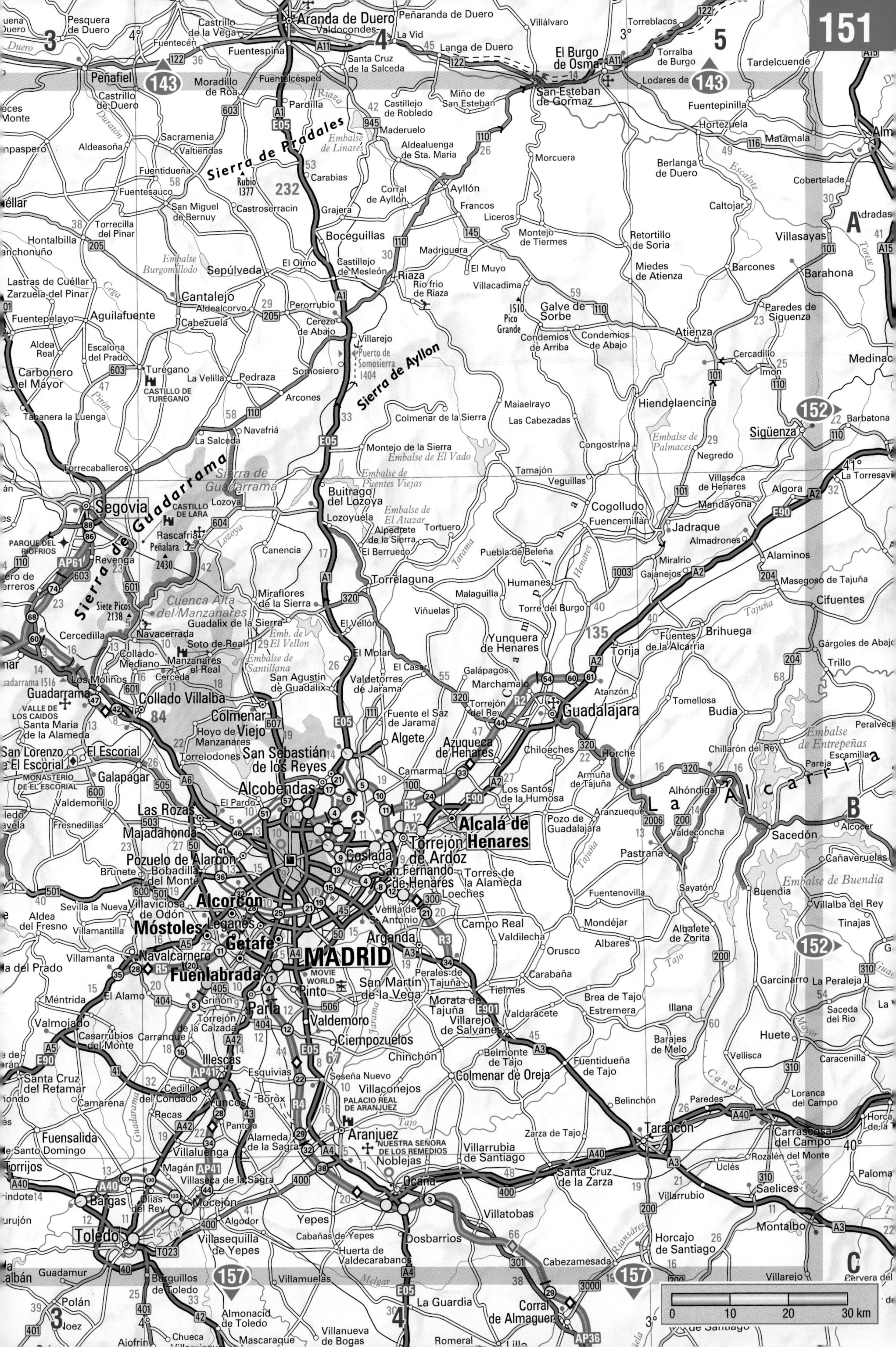
Pesquera de Duero
Castrillo de la Vega
Aranda de Duero
Valdocondes
Peñaranda de Duero
Villálvaro
Torreblacos
Fuentecén
Fuentespina
La Vid
Langa de Duero
El Burgo de Osma
Torralba de Burgo
Tardelcuende
Peñafiel
Moradillo de Roa
Fuentelcésped
Santa Cruz de la Salceda
San Esteban de Gormaz
Lodares de Osma
Castrillo de Duero
Pardilla
Castillejo de Robledo
Miño de San Esteban
Fuentepinilla
Hortezuela
Matamala
Sacramenia
Aldeasoña
Valtiendas
Maderuelo
Embalse de Linares
Aldealuenga de Sta. Maria
Morcuera
Berlanga de Duero
Sierra de Pradales
Fuentidueña
Rubio 1377
Carabias
Corral de Ayllón
Ayllón
Cobertelade
Fuentesaúco
San Miguel de Bernuy
Castroserracín
Grajera
Francos
Liceros
Caltojar
Torrecilla del Pinar
Hontalbilla
Boceguillas
Montejo de Tiermes
Retortillo de Soria
Villasayas
Madriguera
El Muyo
Barcones
Barahona
Embalse Burgomillodo
Sepúlveda
El Olmo
Castillejo de Mesleón
Riaza
Rio frio de Riaza
Miedes de Atienza
Lastras de Cuéllar
Zarzuela del Pinar
Villacadima
Cantalejo
Aldealcorvo
Perorrubio
Galve de Sorbe
Paredes de Siguenza
Fuentepelayo
Aguilafuente
Cabezuela
Cerezo de Abajo
1510 Pico Grande
Condemios de Arriba
Condemios de Abajo
Atienza
Aldea Real
Escalona del Prado
Villarejo
Puerto de Somosierra 1404
Cercadillo
Imón
Medinaceli
Carbonero el Mayor
Turégano
La Velilla
Pedraza
Somosierra
Sierra de Ayllon
Castillo de Turegano
Arcones
Hiendelaencina
Sigüenza
Barbatona
Tabanera la Luenga
Navafría
Colmenar de la Sierra
Maiaelrayo
Las Cabezadas
La Salceda
Montejo de la Sierra
Embalse de El Vado
Congostrina
Embalse de Palmaces
Negredo
Torrecaballeros
Sierra de Guadarrama
Embalse de Puentes Viejas
Tamajón
Veguillas
Villaseca de Henares
La Torresaviñán
Segovia
Castillo de Lara
Lozoya
Buitrago del Lozoya
Embalse de El Atazar
Cogolludo
Mandayona
Algora
Parque del Riofrios
Rascafría
Lozoyuela
Tortuero
Fuencemillán
Jadraque
Almadrones
Peñalara 2430
Revenga
Canencia
Alpedrete de la Sierra
El Berrueco
Puebla de Beleña
Alaminos
Miralrio
Gajanejos
Torrelaguna
Humanes
Masegoso de Tajuña
Cuenca Alta del Manzanares
Miraflores de la Sierra
Malaguilla
Cifuentes
Siete Picos 2138
Viñuelas
Torre del Burgo
Guadalix de la Sierra
Navacerrada
El Vellón
Emb. de El Vellon
Fuentes de la Alcarria
Brihuega
Cercedilla
Soto de Real
Yunquera de Henares
Torija
Gárgoles de Abajo
Collado-Mediano
Manzanares el Real
Embalse de Santillana
El Molar
El Casar
Trillo
Guadarrama 1516
Los Molinos
Cerceda
San Agustin de Guadalix
Galápagos
Marchamalo
Atanzón
Guadarrama
Valdetorres de Jarama
Tomellosa
Valle de los Caidos
Collado Villalba
Torrejón del Rey
Guadalajara
Budia
Santa Maria de la Alameda
Colmenar Viejo
Hoyo de Manzanares
Fuente el Saz de Jarama
Algete
Azuqueca de Henares
Chiloeches
Embalse de Entrepeñas
Peralveche
San Lorenzo de El Escorial
El Escorial
Torrelodones
San Sebastián de los Reyes
Horche
Chillarón del Rey
Pareja
Escamilla
Monasterio de El Escorial
Galapagar
Camarma
Armuña de Tajuña
La Alcarria
Alcobendas
Alhóndiga
Valdemorillo
El Pardo
Los Santos de la Humosa
Aranzueque
Sacedón
Alcocer
Las Rozas
Alcalá de Henares
Pozo de Guadalajara
Valdeconcha
Fresnedillas
Majadahonda
Torrejón de Ardoz
Pastrana
Cañaveruelas
Pozuelo de Alarcón
Coslada
Brunete
Bobadilla del Monte
San Fernando de Henares
Torres de la Alameda
Embalse de Buendía
Loeches
Fuentenovilla
Sayatón
Buendia
Sevilla la Nueva
Villaviciosa de Odón
Alcorcón
Velilla de S. Antonio
Villalba del Rey
Aldea del Fresno
Villamantilla
Móstoles
Leganés
Campo Real
Mondéjar
Albalate de Zorita
Tinajas
Getafe
Valdilecha
Arganda
Albares
Orusco
Villamanta
Navalcarnero
MADRID
Fuenlabrada
Movie World
San Martín de la Vega
Perales de Tajuña
Carabaña
Garcinarro
La Peraleja
Méntrida
El Alamo
Griñón
Pinto
Tielmes
Brea de Tajo
Illana
Saceda del Rio
Valmojado
Torrejón de la Calzada
Parla
Valdemoro
Morata de Tajuña
Villarejo de Salvanés
Valdaracete
Estremera
Casarrubios del Monte
Carranque
Ciempozuelos
Huete
Belmonte de Tajo
Barajes de Melo
Vellisca
Caracenilla
Illescas
Chinchón
Fuentidueña de Tajo
Santa Cruz del Retamar
Esquivias
Seseña Nuevo
Colmenar de Oreja
Cedillo del Condado
Villaconejos
Belinchón
Paredes
Loranca del Campo
Camarena
Borox
Palacio Real de Aranjuez
Recas
Yuncos
Pantoja
Aranjuez
Zarza de Tajo
Tarancón
Carrascosa del Campo
Horcajo de la Sierra
Fuensalida
Alameda de la Sagra
Nuestra Señora de los Remedios
Villarrubia de Santiago
Santo Domingo
Villaluenga
Noblejas
Rozalén del Monte
Torrijos
Magán
Villaseca de la Sagra
Santa Cruz de la Zarza
Uclés
Paloma
Ocaña
Saelices
Bargas
Olías del Rey
Mocejón
Villarrubio
Villatobas
Algodor
Yepes
Montalbo
Toledo
Villasequilla de Yepes
Cabañas de Yepes
Dosbarrios
Horcajo de Santiago
Huerta de Valdecarabanos
Cabezamesada
Guadamur
Burguillos de Toledo
Villamuelas
Villarejo
Cervera del
Polán
La Guardia
Corral de Almaguer
Almonacid de Toledo
Villanueva de Bogas
Chueca
Mascaraque
Romeral
0 10 20 30 km

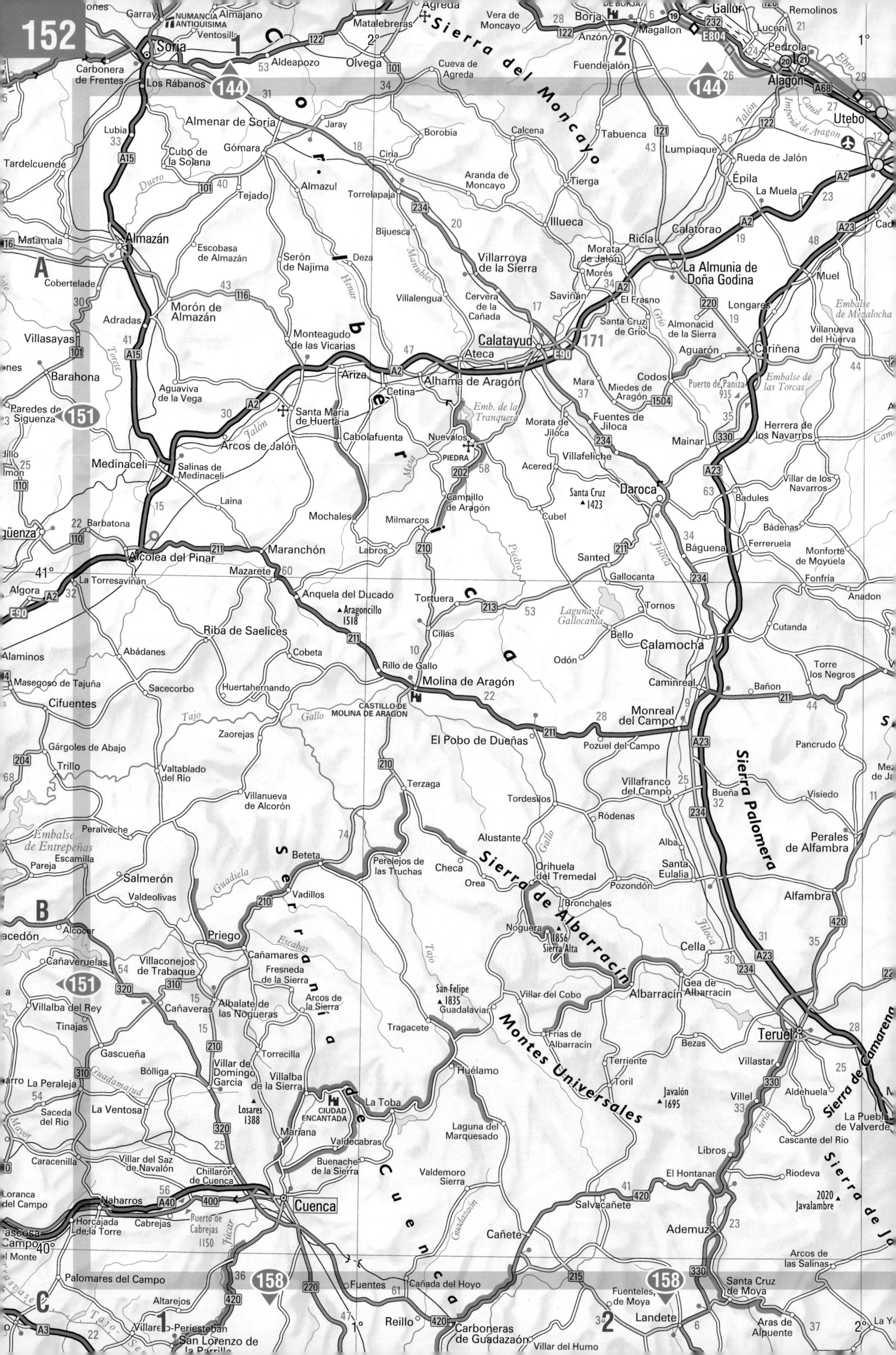
Soria
Garray
Numancia
Almajano
Ventosilla
Carbonera de Frentes
Los Rábanos
Aldeapozo
Olvega
Matalebreras
Ágreda
Vera de Moncayo
Borja
Magallon
Anzón
Fuendejalón
Remolinos
Luceni
Pedrola
Alagón
Utebo
Cueva de Agreda
Sierra del Moncayo
Almenar de Soria
Lubia
Jaray
Borobia
Calcena
Tabuenca
Lumpiaque
Rueda de Jalón
Épila
La Muela
Tardelcuende
Cubo de la Solana
Gómara
Ciria
Aranda de Moncayo
Tierga
Almazul
Torrelapaja
Tejado
Illueca
Ricla
Calatorao
Matamala
Almazán
Escobasa de Almazán
Serón de Najima
Deza
Bijuesca
Villarroya de la Sierra
Morata de Jalón
Morés
La Almunia de Doña Godina
Muel
Cobertelade
Morón de Almazán
Villalengua
Cervera de la Cañada
Saviñán
El Frasno
Santa Cruz de Grío
Almonacid de la Sierra
Longares
Adradas
Villasayas
Monteagudo de las Vicarias
Calatayud
Ateca
Aguarón
Cariñena
Villanueva del Huerva
Barahona
Ariza
Cetina
Alhama de Aragón
Mara
Miedes de Aragón
Codos
Puerto de Paniza
Aguaviva de la Vega
Paredes de Siguenza
Santa María de Huerta
Emb. de la Tranquera
Morata de Jiloca
Fuentes de Jiloca
Herrera de los Navarros
Mainar
Arcos de Jalón
Cabolafuenta
Nuevalos
Piedra
Medinaceli
Salinas de Medinaceli
Campillo de Aragón
Acered
Villafeliche
Daroca
Villar de los Navarros
Santa Cruz
Badules
Laina
Mochales
Milmarcos
Cubel
Bádenas
Barbatona
Sigüenza
Alcolea del Pinar
Maranchón
Labros
Santed
Báguena
Ferreruela
Monforte de Moyuela
Algora
La Torresaviñán
Mazarete
Anquela del Ducado
Aragoncillo
Tortuera
Gallocanta
Tornos
Fonfría
Anadon
Laguna de Gallocanta
Riba de Saelices
Cillas
Bello
Calamocha
Cutanda
Alaminos
Abádanes
Cobeta
Rillo de Gallo
Odón
Torre los Negros
Masegoso de Tajuña
Sacecorbo
Huertahernando
Molina de Aragón
Castillo de Molina de Aragon
Caminreal
Bañon
Cifuentes
Zaorejas
El Pobo de Dueñas
Monreal del Campo
Pozuel del Campo
Pancrudo
Gárgoles de Abajo
Trillo
Valtablado del Rio
Terzaga
Villafranco del Campo
Tordesilos
Bueña
Visiedo
Villanueva de Alcorón
Ródenas
Sierra Palomera
Embalse de Entrepeñas
Peralveche
Alustante
Perales de Alfambra
Pareja
Escamilla
Beteta
Perelejos de las Truchas
Checa
Orea
Alba
Santa Eulalia
Salmerón
Serranía de Cuenca
Sierra de Albarracín
Orihuela del Tremedal
Pozondón
Valdeolivas
Vadillos
Bronchales
Alfambra
Alcocer
Priego
Noguera
Sierra Alta
Cella
Cañaveruelas
Villaconejos de Trabaque
Cañamares
Fresneda de la Sierra
Gea de Albarracin
Albarracín
Villalba del Rey
Cañaveras
Albalate de las Nogueras
Arcos de la Sierra
San Felipe
Guadalaviar
Villar del Cobo
Tinajas
Tragacete
Montes Universales
Frias de Albarracin
Teruel
Bezas
Gascueña
Torrecilla
Terriente
Villastar
Bólliga
Villar de Domingo Garcia
Villalba de la Sierra
Huélamo
Toril
La Peraleja
Javalón
Villel
Aldehuela
Saceda del Rio
La Ventosa
Losares
Ciudad Encantada
La Toba
Sierra de Camarena
Laguna del Marquesado
La Puebla de Valverde
Mariana
Cascante del Rio
Caracenilla
Villar del Saz de Navalón
Valdecabras
Buenache de la Sierra
Libros
Chillarón de Cuenca
Valdemoro Sierra
El Hontanar
Riodeva
Loranca del Campo
Naharros
Cuenca
Salvacañete
Javalambre
Horcajada de la Torre
Cabrejas
Puerto de Cabrejas
Ademuz
Cañete
Sierra de Javalambre
Arcos de las Salinas
Palomares del Campo
Fuentes
Cañada del Hoyo
Santa Cruz de Moya
Altarejos
Fuenteles de Moya
Villarejo-Periesteban
Reillo
Carboneras de Guadazaón
Landete
Aras de Alpuente
San Lorenzo de la Parrilla
Villar del Humo
La Yesa

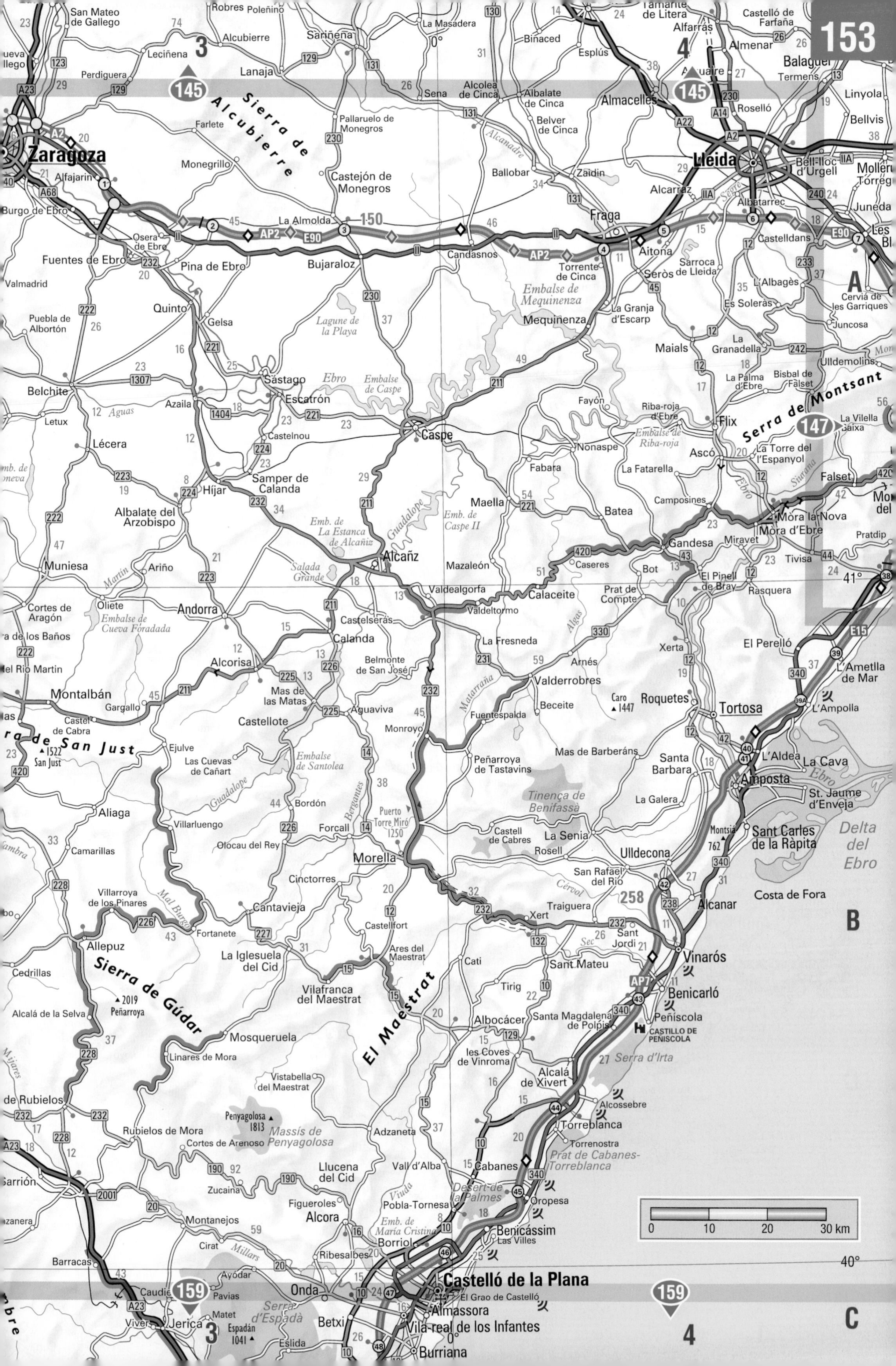

San Mateo de Gallego
Robres
Poleñino
Tamarite de Litera
Castelló de Farfaña
Alfarràs
Almenar
Balaguer
Termens
Linyola
Bellvis
La Masadera
Sariñena
Binaced
Esplús
Alcubierre
Leciñena
Perdiguera
Lanaja
Sierra de Alcubierre
Sena
Alcolea de Cinca
Albalate de Cinca
Belver de Cinca
Almacelles
Roselló
Farlete
Pallaruelo de Monegros
Zaragoza
Alfajarín
Monegrillo
Castejón de Monegros
Ballobar
Zaidín
Lleida
Bell-lloc d'Urgell
Mollerussa
Torregrossa
Alcarràs
Albatàrrec
Juneda
Burgo de Ebro
La Almolda
Fraga
Les Borges Blanques
Osera de Ebro
Candasnos
Aitona
Castelldans
Fuentes de Ebro
Pina de Ebro
Bujaraloz
Torrente de Cinca
Seròs
Sarroca de Lleida
L'Albagès
Valmadrid
Embalse de Mequinenza
Cervià de les Garrigues
Quinto
Gelsa
Lagune de la Playa
Mequinenza
La Granja d'Escarp
Es Soleràs
Puebla de Albortón
Juncosa
Maials
La Granadella
Belchite
Sástago
Ebro
Embalse de Caspe
Escatrón
La Palma d'Ebre
Bisbal de Falset
Ulldemolins
Serra de Montsant
Azaila
Fayón
Riba-roja d'Ebre
Flix
La Vilella Baixa
Letux
Castelnou
Caspe
Embalse de Riba-roja
Nonaspe
Ascó
La Torre del l'Espanyol
Lécera
Fabara
La Fatarella
Falset
Samper de Calanda
Híjar
Maella
Batea
Camposines
Albalate del Arzobispo
Emb. de La Estanca de Alcañiz
Emb. de Caspe II
Guadalope
Gandesa
Móra la Nova
Móra d'Ebre
Miravet
Pratdip
Muniesa
Ariño
Salada Grande
Alcañiz
Mazaleón
Caseres
Bot
El Pinell de Brai
Tivissa
Cortes de Aragón
Oliete
Embalse de Cueva Foradada
Andorra
Valdealgorfa
Valdeltormo
Calaceite
Prat de Comte
Rasquera
Castelserás
Calanda
La Fresneda
Xerta
El Perelló
Alcorisa
Belmonte de San José
Arnés
Valderrobres
L'Ametlla de Mar
Montalbán
Gargallo
Mas de las Matas
Aguaviva
Castellote
Caro 1447
Roquetes
Tortosa
L'Ampolla
Castel de Cabra
Monroyo
Fuentespalda
Beceite
Sierra de San Just
1522 San Just
Ejulve
Las Cuevas de Cañart
Embalse de Santolea
Peñarroya de Tastavins
Mas de Barberáns
Santa Barbara
L'Aldea
La Cava
Amposta
Aliaga
Bordón
Tinença de Benifassà
La Galera
St. Jaume d'Enveja
Villarluengo
Forcall
Puerto Torre Miró 1250
Castell de Cabres
La Senia
Rosell
Montsià 762
Sant Carles de la Ràpita
Delta del Ebro
Camarillas
Olocau del Rey
Morella
Ulldecona
Cinctorres
San Rafael del Río
Alcanar
Costa de Fora
Villarroya de los Pinares
Cantavieja
Traiguera
Fortanete
Castellfort
Xert
Sant Jordi
Vinarós
Allepuz
Sierra de Gúdar
La Iglesuela del Cid
Ares del Maestrat
Cati
Sant Mateu
Cedrillas
Tirig
Benicarló
2019 Peñarroya
Vilafranca del Maestrat
El Maestrat
Peñíscola
Alcalá de la Selva
Albocácer
Santa Magdalena de Polpis
Castillo de Peñíscola
Mosqueruela
les Coves de Vinroma
Serra d'Irta
Linares de Mora
Vistabella del Maestrat
Alcalá de Xivert
Rubielos
Alcossebre
Penyagolosa 1813
Massís de Penyagolosa
Rubielos de Mora
Adzaneta
Torreblanca
Cortes de Arenoso
Torrenostra
Prat de Cabanes-Torreblanca
Llucena del Cid
Vall d'Alba
Cabanes
Sarrión
Zucaina
Desert de les Palmes
Oropesa
Figueroles
Pobla-Tornesa
Montanejos
Alcora
Emb. de María Cristina
Benicàssim
Cirat
Ribesalbes
Borriol
Las Villes
Barracas
Millars
Ayódar
Onda
Castelló de la Plana
El Grao de Castelló
Caudiel
Pavias
Serra d'Espadà
Almassora
Matet
Jérica
Viver
Espadán 1041
Betxi
Vila-real de los Infantes
Eslida
Burriana
0 10 20 30 km
41°
40°
0°
A
B
C
3
4
145
147
150
159
258

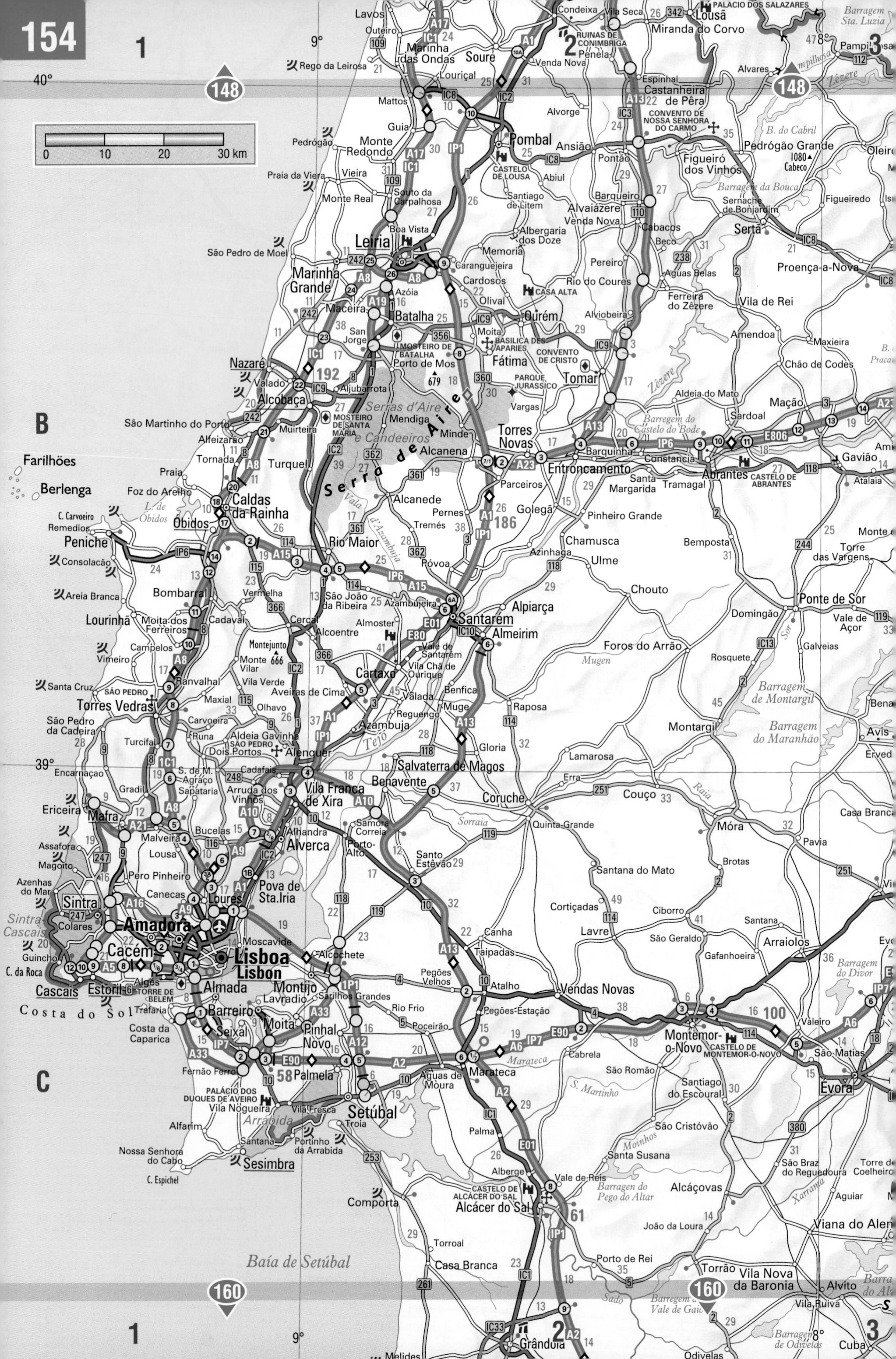

154
1
2
3
B
C
40°
39°
9°
8°
148
160
0 10 20 30 km
Lavos
Condeixa
Vila Seca
Lousã
Miranda do Corvo
PALACIO DOS SALAZARES
Barragem Sta. Luzia
RUINAS DE CONIMBRIGA
Penela
Marinha das Ondas
Soure
Venda Nova
Rego da Leirosa
Louriçal
Espinhal
Castanheira de Pêra
Pampilhosa
Alvares
Zêzere
Mattos
Guia
Alvorge
CONVENTO DE NOSSA SENHORA DO CARMO
B. do Cabril
Pedrógão
Monte Redondo
Pombal
Ansião
Pedrógão Grande
Cabeço
Figueiró dos Vinhos
CASTELO DE LOUSA
Abiul
Praia da Viera
Vieira
Monte Real
Souto da Carpalhosa
Santiago de Litem
Alvaiázere
Venda Nova
Barragem da Bouca
Sernache de Bonjardim
Figueiredo
Boa Vista
Cabacos
Sertã
Leiria
Albergaria dos Doze
São Pedro de Moel
Memoria
Beco
Caranguejeira
Pereiro
Proença-a-Nova
Marinha Grande
Cardosos
Rio do Coures
Aguas Belas
Azóia
CASA ALTA
Ferreira do Zêzere
Vila de Rei
Olival
Alviobeira
Maceira
Batalha
Ourém
San Jorge
MOSTEIRO DE BATALHA
Moita
BASILICA DES APARIES
Amendoa
Maxieira
Porto de Mos
CONVENTO DE CRISTO
Fátima
Chão de Codes
Nazaré
Valado
Tomar
PARQUE JURASSICO
Aljubarrota
Aldeia do Mato
Mação
Alcobaça
Serras d'Aire
Vargas
Mendiga
MOSTEIRO DE SANTA MARIA
Barragem do Castelo do Bode
Sardoal
São Martinho do Porto
Serra de Aire
Minde
Torres Novas
Muirteira
e Candeeiros
Alfeizarão
Alcanena
Barquinha
Constancia
Gavião
Tornada
Turquel
Entroncamento
Abrantes
CASTELO DE ABRANTES
Atalaia
Farilhões
Praia
Parceiros
Santa Margarida
Tramagal
Berlenga
Foz do Arelho
Caldas da Rainha
Alcanede
Golegã
Pinheiro Grande
L. de Óbidos
Pernes
C. Carvoeiro
Remedios
Óbidos
Tremés
Peniche
Rio Maior
Chamusca
Bemposta
Torre das Vargens
Consolacão
Azinhaga
Ulme
Póvoa
Chouto
Bombarral
Vermelha
São João da Ribeira
Azambujeira
Alpiarça
Areia Branca
Ponte de Sor
Lourinhã
Moita dos Ferreiros
Cadaval
Cercal
Almoster
Santarém
Domingão
Vale de Açor
Alcoentre
Almeirim
Campelos
Montejunto
Vale de Santarém
Foros do Arrão
Rosquete
Galveias
Vimeiro
Monte Vilar
Vila Chã de Ourique
Mugen
Ranvalhal
Cartaxo
Santa Cruz
SÃO PEDRO
Vila Verde
Aveiras de Cima
Benfica
Barragem de Montargil
Torres Vedras
Maxial
Valada
Raposa
São Pedro da Cadeira
Carvoeira
Olhavo
Reguengo
Muge
Montargil
Avis
Runa
Aldeia Gavinha
Azambuja
Barragem do Maranhão
Turcifal
SÃO PEDRO
Dois Portos
Alenquer
Tejo
Gloria
Erved
Encarnaçao
S. de M. Agraço
Sapataria
Cadafais
Salvaterra de Magos
Lamarosa
Gradil
Arruda dos Vinhos
Vila Franca de Xira
Benavente
Erra
Couço
Coruche
Raia
Ericeira
Mafra
Samora Correia
Quinta Grande
Sorraia
Móra
Casa Branca
Alhandra
Malveira
Bucelas
Alverca
Porto-Alto
Pavia
Assafora
Lousa
Santo Estêvão
Brotas
Magoito
Pero Pinheiro
Santana do Mato
Azenhas do Mar
Póvoa de Sta. Iria
Canecas
Loures
Corticadas
Sintra
Ciborro
Santana
Sintra-Cascais
Colares
Amadora
Canha
Lavre
São Geraldo
Arraiolos
Moscavide
Taipadas
Gafanhoeira
Barragem do Divor
Guincho
Cacém
Lisboa
Lisbon
Alcochete
C. da Roca
Algés
Pegões Velhos
Atalho
Cascais
Estoril
TORRE DE BELÉM
Almada
Montijo
Vendas Novas
Lavradio
Sarilhos Grandes
Costa do Sol
Trafaria
Barreiro
Rio Frio
Pegões-Estação
Valeiro
Moita
Poceirão
Costa da Caparica
Seixal
Pinhal Novo
Cabrela
Montemor-o-Novo
CASTELO DE MONTEMOR-O-NOVO
São Matias
Marateca
Fernão Ferro
Palmela
Aguas de Moura
São Romão
S. Martinho
Santiago do Escoural
Évora
PALÁCIO DOS DUQUES DE AVEIRO
Vila Nogueira
Vila Fresca
Setúbal
Alfarim
Arrábida
Troia
Palma
São Cristóvão
Santana
Portinho da Arrabida
Moinhos
Nossa Senhora do Cabo
Sesimbra
Santa Susana
São Braz do Regueduoura
Torre de Coelheiros
Xarrama
C. Espichel
Alberge
Vale de Reis
CASTELO DE ALCÁCER DO SAL
Barragen do Pego do Altar
Alcáçovas
Comporta
Alcácer do Sal
Aguiar
João da Loura
Viana do Alentejo
Torroal
Baía de Setúbal
Porto de Rei
Casa Branca
Torrão
Vila Nova da Baronia
Alvito
Sado
Barregem de Vale de Gaio
Vila Ruiva
Barragem de Odivelas
Grândola
Cuba
Melides
Odivelas

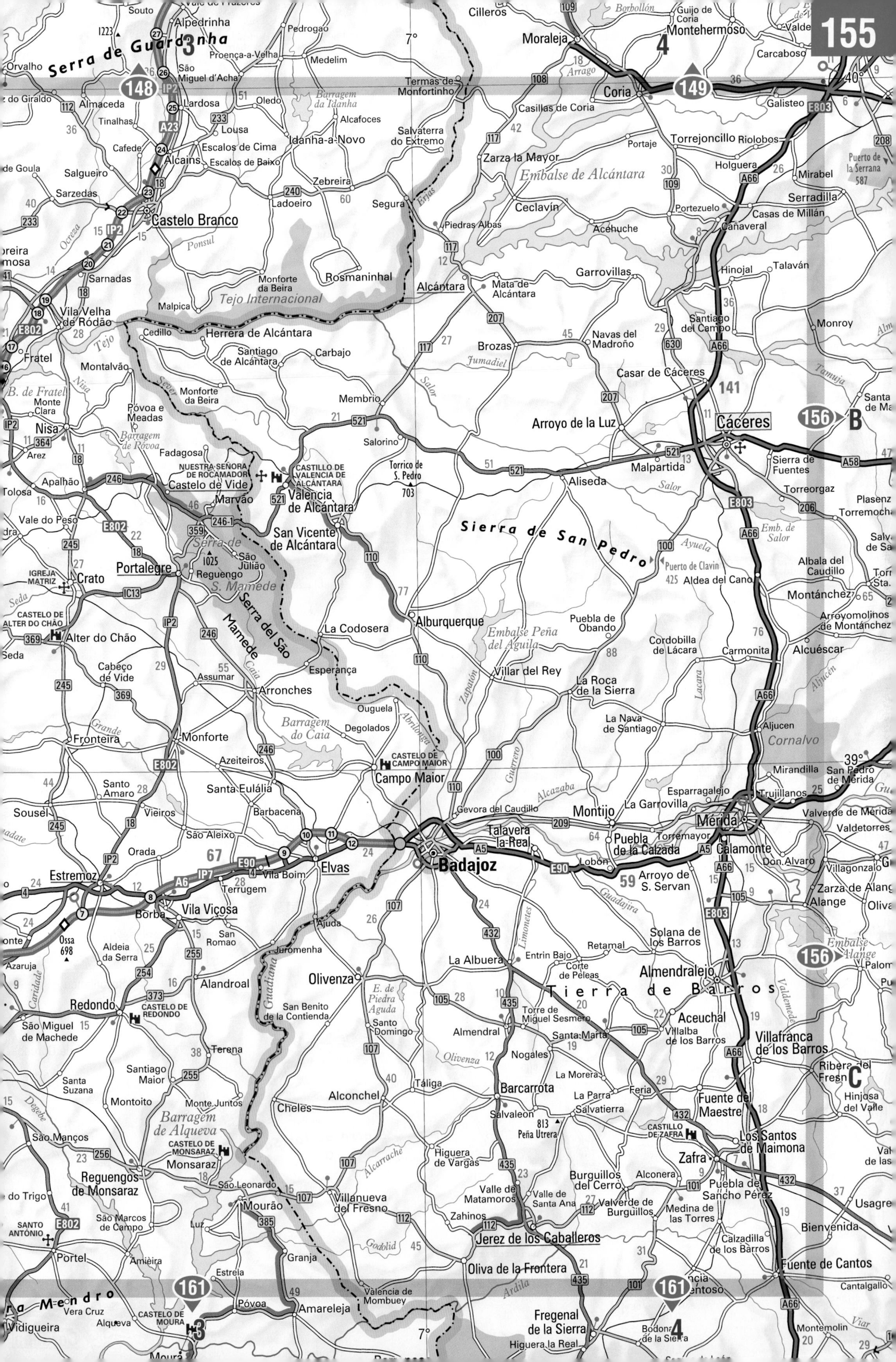
Serra de Guardunha
Souto
Alpedrinha
Pedrogão
Cilleros
Moraleja
Borbollón
Guijo de Coria
Montehermoso
Valdefuentes
Orvalho
São Miguel d'Acha
Proença-a-Velha
Medelim
Termas de Monfortinho
Arrago
Coria
Carcaboso
Galisteo
do Giraldo
Almaceda
Lardosa
Oledo
Barragem da Idanha
Casillas de Coria
Tinalhas
Lousa
Alcafoces
Salvaterra do Extremo
Cafede
Escalos de Cima
Idanha-a-Novo
Zarza la Mayor
Portaje
Torrejoncillo
Riolobos
de Goula
Salgueiro
Alcains
Escalos de Baixo
Embalse de Alcántara
Holguera
Mirabel
Puerto de la Serrana
Sarzedas
Zebreira
Ladoeiro
Segura
Erjas
Ceclavín
Portezuelo
Serradilla
Casas de Millán
Castelo Branco
Ocreza
Piedras Albas
Acehuche
Cañaveral
Ponsul
Rosmaninhal
Garrovillas
Hinojal
Talaván
Sarnadas
Monforte da Beira
Alcántara
Mata de Alcántara
Tejo Internacional
Malpica
Vila Velha de Ródão
Cedillo
Herrera de Alcántara
Brozas
Navas del Madroño
Santiago del Campo
Monroy
Fratel
Tejo
Montalvão
Santiago de Alcántara
Carbajo
Jumadiel
Casar de Cáceres
Tamuja
B. de Fratel
Nisa
Sever
Monforte da Beira
Membrio
Salor
Monte Clara
Póvoa e Meadas
Arroyo de la Luz
Cáceres
Santa Marta de Ma
Nisa
Barragem de Póvoa
Salorino
Arez
Fadagosa
Torrico de S. Pedro
Malpartida
Sierra de Fuentes
Nuestra Señora de Rocamador
Castillo de Valencia de Alcántara
Aliseda
Apalhão
Castelo de Vide
Valencia de Alcántara
Salor
Torreorgaz
Plasenzuela
Tolosa
Marvão
Torremocha
Vale do Peso
San Vicente de Alcántara
Sierra de San Pedro
Emb. de Salor
Salvatierra de Santiago
Serra de São Julião
Reguengo
Ayuela
Puerto de Clavin
Aldea del Cano
Albalá del Caudillo
Igreja Matriz
Crato
Portalegre
S. Mamede
Serra del São Mamede
Montánchez
Seda
Castelo de Alter do Chão
Alburquerque
Puebla de Obando
Arroyomolinos de Montánchez
Alter do Chão
La Codosera
Embalse Peña del Aguila
Cordobilla de Lácara
Carmonita
Alcuéscar
Seda
Cabeço de Vide
Assumar
Caia
Esperança
Villar del Rey
La Roca de la Sierra
Lácara
Aljucén
Arronches
Zapatón
Ouguela
Abrilongo
La Nava de Santiago
Aljucen
Grande
Barragem do Caia
Degolados
Cornalvo
Fronteira
Monforte
Guerrero
Castelo de Campo Maior
Azeiteiros
Campo Maior
Mirandilla
San Pedro de Mérida
Santo Amaro
Santa Eulália
Alcazaba
Esparragalejo
Trujillanos
Sousel
Vieiros
Barbacena
Gevora del Caudillo
Montijo
La Garrovilla
Mérida
Valverde de Mérida
Valdetorres
São Aleixo
Talavera la Real
Puebla de la Calzada
Torremayor
Calamonte
Orada
Badajoz
Elvas
Lobón
Arroyo de S. Servan
Don Alvaro
Estremoz
Vila Boim
Terrugem
Villagonzalo
Guadajira
Zarza de Alange
Alange
Borba
Vila Viçosa
Oliva
Ossa
Ajuda
San Romão
Solana de los Barros
Aldeia da Serra
Juromenha
Retamal
Embalse Alange
Azaruja
Limonetes
La Albuera
Entrín Bajo
Corte de Peleas
Almendralejo
Palomas
Caridade
Alandroal
Olivenza
E. de Piedra Aguda
Tierra de Barros
Redondo
Castelo de Redondo
San Benito de la Contienda
Torre de Miguel Sesmero
Aceuchal
Valdemedel
São Miguel de Machede
Santo Domingo
Almendral
Santa Marta
Villalba de los Barros
Villafranca de los Barros
Terena
Olivenza
Nogales
Santiago Maior
Guadiana
La Morera
Ribera del Fresno
Santa Suzana
Táliga
Barcarrota
Montoito
Monte Juntos
Alconchel
La Parra
Feria
Fuente del Maestre
Hinojosa del Valle
Degebe
Cheles
Salvaleón
Salvatierra
Barragem de Alqueva
Peña Utrera
Castillo de Zafra
Los Santos de Maimona
São Manços
Castelo de Monsaraz
Higuera de Vargas
Zafra
Valencia de las Torres
Monsaraz
Alcarrache
Burguillos del Cerro
Alconera
Reguengos de Monsaraz
São Leonardo
Valle de Matamoros
Valle de Santa Ana
Puebla de Sancho Pérez
Usagre
do Trigo
Mourão
Villanueva del Fresno
Valverde de Burguillos
Medina de las Torres
São Marcos de Campo
Zahínos
Santo António
Luz
Bienvenida
Calzadilla de los Barros
Portel
Amieira
Godolid
Jerez de los Caballeros
Granja
Fuente de Cantos
Estrela
Oliva de la Frontera
Ardila
Valencia de Mombuey
Cantalgallo
Serra de Mendro
Vera Cruz
Castelo de Moura
Póvoa
Amareleja
Fregenal de la Sierra
Bodonal de la Sierra
Vidigueira
Alqueva
Higuera la Real
Montemolín
Viar
Moura

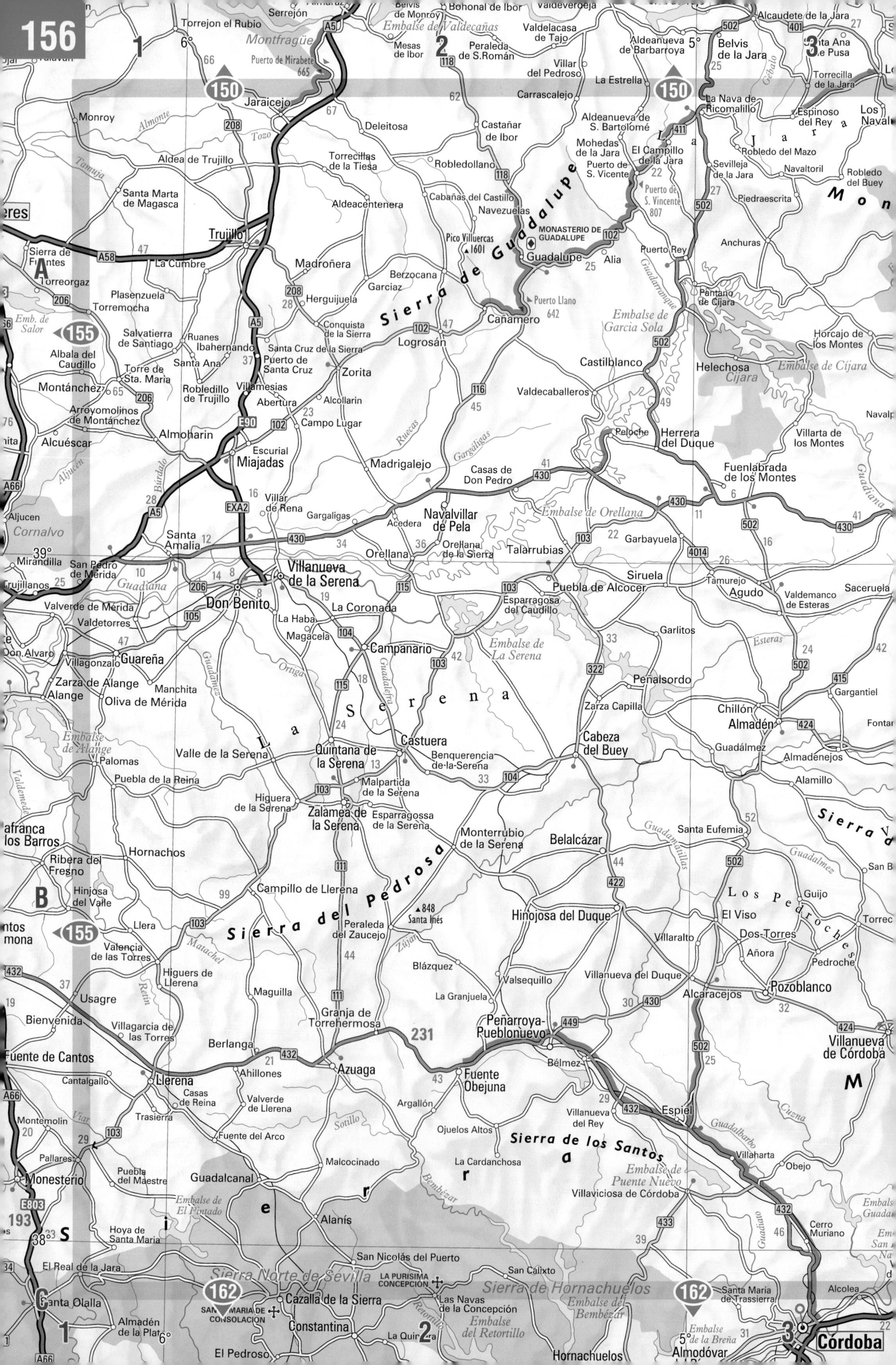

Serrejón
Torrejon el Rubio
Monfragüe
Puerto de Mirabete
665
Bohonal de Ibor
de Monroy
Embalse de Valdecañas
Mesas de Ibor
Peraleda de S.Román
Valdelacasa de Tajo
Villar del Pedroso
Aldeanueva de Barbarroya
La Estrella
Carrascalejo
Alcaudete de la Jara
Belvis de la Jara
Santa Ana de Pusa
Torrecilla de la Jara
La Nava de Ricomalillo
Espinoso del Rey
Los Navalu
150
Jaraicejo
Monroy
Almonte
Tozo
Deleitosa
Castañar de Ibor
Aldeanueva de S. Bartolomé
Mohedas de la Jara
El Campillo de la Jara
Puerto de S. Vicente
Robledo del Mazo
Sevilleja de la Jara
Navaltoril
Robledo del Buey
Tamuja
Aldea de Trujillo
Torrecillas de la Tiesa
Robledollano
Santa Marta de Magasca
Aldeacentenera
Cabañas del Castillo
Navezuelas
Sierra de Guadalupe
Puerto de S. Vincente
807
Piedraescrita
Trujillo
Sierra de Fuentes
La Cumbre
Madroñera
Pico Villuercas
1601
MONASTERIO DE GUADALUPE
Guadalupe
Alia
Puerto Rey
Anchuras
Torreorgaz
Plasenzuela
Torremocha
Berzocana
Garciaz
Herguijuela
Conquista de la Sierra
Puerto Llano
642
Cañamero
Pantano de Cíjara
Emb. de Salor
155
Salvatierra de Santiago
Ruanes
Ibahernando
Santa Cruz de la Sierra
Puerto de Santa Cruz
Logrosán
Embalse de Garcia Sola
Horcajo de los Montes
Albala del Caudillo
Santa Ana
Torre de Sta. María
Montánchez
Robledillo de Trujillo
Villamesias
Zorita
Alcollarin
Castilblanco
Helechosa
Cijara
Embalse de Cíjara
Abertura
Valdecaballeros
Arroyomolinos de Montánchez
Campo Lugar
Almoharin
Alcuéscar
Escurial
Miajadas
Ruecas
Gargáligas
Peloche
Herrera del Duque
Villarta de los Montes
Madrigalejo
Casas de Don Pedro
Fuenlabrada de los Montes
Aljucén
Búrdalo
Villar de Rena
Navalvillar de Pela
Embalse de Orellana
Aljucen
Cornalvo
Gargaligas
Acedera
Garbayuela
Santa Amalia
Orellana
Orellana de la Sierra
Talarrubias
39°
Mirandilla
San Pedro de Mérida
Villanueva de la Serena
Siruela
Tamurejo
Agudo
Valdemanco de Esteras
Saceruela
Trujillanos
Guadiana
Don Benito
Puebla de Alcocer
Esparragosa del Caudillo
Valverde de Mérida
Valdetorres
La Coronada
La Haba
Magacela
Campanario
Embalse de La Serena
Garlitos
Esteras
Don Alvaro
Villagonzalo
Guareña
Ortiga
Guadalefra
Zarza de Alange
Alange
Manchita
Oliva de Mérida
Guadámez
Peñalsordo
Zarza Capilla
Chillón
Almadén
Gargantiel
Fontar
La Serena
Embalse de Alange
Valle de la Serena
Quintana de la Serena
Castuera
Benquerencia de la Serena
Cabeza del Buey
Guadálmez
Almadenejos
Palomas
Puebla de la Reina
Malpartida de la Serena
Alamillo
Higuera de la Serena
Zalamea de la Serena
Esparragossa de la Serena
Monterrubio de la Serena
Belalcázar
Santa Eufemia
Guadamatillas
Sierra de V
Valdemedel
Zafra
Los Barros
Hornachos
Ribera del Fresno
Sierra del Pedrosa
Guadalmez
San B
Hinojosa del Valle
Campillo de Llerena
Los Pedroches
Guijo
848
Santa Inés
Hinojosa del Duque
El Viso
Torrec
Santos de Maimona
Llera
Sierra del Pedrosa
Peraleda del Zaucejo
Zújar
Villaralto
Dos-Torres
Añora
Pedroche
Valencia de las Torres
Matachel
Blázquez
Higuers de Llerena
Retín
Maguilla
Valsequillo
Villanueva del Duque
Alcaracejos
Pozoblanco
Usagre
La Granjuela
Bienvenida
Villagarcia de las Torres
Granja de Torrehermosa
Peñarroya-Pueblonuevo
231
Villanueva de Córdoba
Berlanga
Fuente de Cantos
Ahillones
Azuaga
Bélmez
Llerena
Cantalgallo
Fuente Obejuna
Casas de Reina
Valverde de Llerena
Argallón
Villanueva del Rey
Espiel
Trasierra
Montemolín
Viar
Sotillo
Ojuelos Altos
Sierra de los Santos
Cuzna
Guadalbarbo
Fuente del Arco
Villaharta
Obejo
Pallares
Malcocinado
La Cardanchosa
Embalse de Puente Nuevo
Monesterio
Puebla del Maestre
Guadalcanal
Bembézar
Villaviciosa de Córdoba
Embalse de El Pintado
Alanís
Guadiato
Cerro Muriano
Hoya de Santa Maria
Sierra Morena
El Real de la Jara
San Nicolás del Puerto
San Calixto
Sierra Norte de Sevilla
LA PURISIMA CONCEPCION
Sierra de Hornachuelos
162
Santa Olalla
Cazalla de la Sierra
Las Navas de la Concepción
Embalse del Bembézar
Santa Maria de Trassierra
Alcolea
SAN MARIA DE CONSOLACION
Almadén de la Plata
Constantina
Retortillo
Embalse del Retortillo
La Quintera
Embalse de la Breña
Córdoba
El Pedroso
Hornachuelos
Almodóvar
193

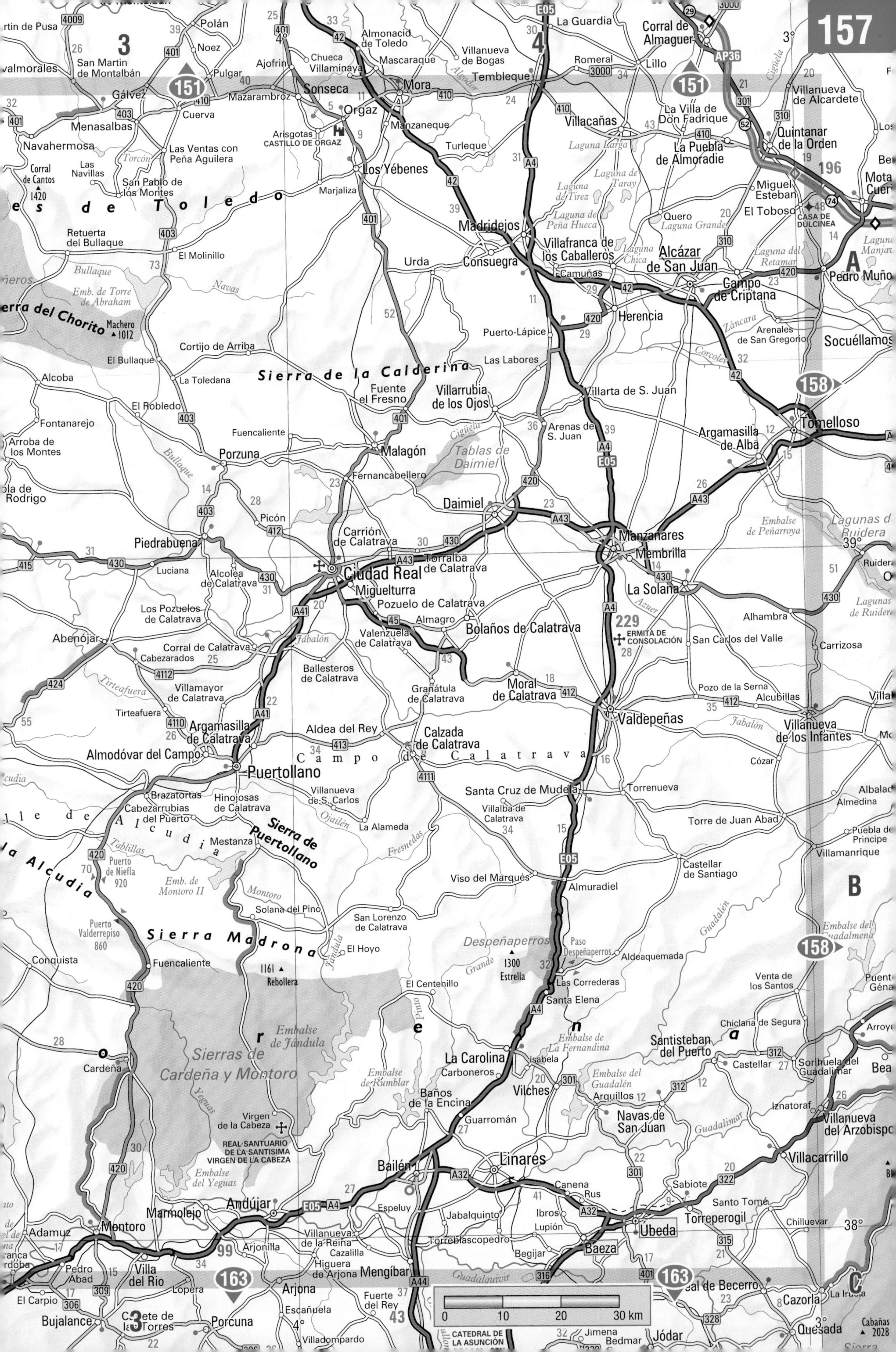
Polán
San Martín de Pusa
San Martín de Montalbán
Noez
Pulgar
Ajofrín
Chueca
Villaminaya
Almonacid de Toledo
Mascaraque
Villanueva de Bogas
La Guardia
Corral de Almaguer
Romeral
Lillo
Tembleque
Gálvez
Menasalbas
Cuerva
Mazarambroz
Sonseca
Orgaz
Mora
Manzaneque
Arisgotas
CASTILLO DE ORGAZ
Villacañas
La Villa de Don Fadrique
Villanueva de Alcardete
Quintanar de la Orden
Navahermosa
Las Ventas con Peña Aguilera
Turleque
Laguna Larga
La Puebla de Almoradie
Corral de Cantos
1420
Las Navillas
San Pablo de los Montes
Los Yébenes
Marjaliza
Montes de Toledo
Laguna de Taray
Laguna de Tirez
Miguel Esteban
El Toboso
CASA DE DULCINEA
Mota del Cuervo
Madridejos
Laguna de Peña Hueca
Quero
Laguna Grande
Retuerta del Bullaque
El Molinillo
Villafranca de los Caballeros
Laguna Chica
Alcázar de San Juan
Laguna del Retamar
Urda
Consuegra
Camuñas
Campo de Criptana
Pedro Muñoz
Bullaque
Emb. de Torre de Abraham
Navas
Sierra del Chorito
Machero
1012
Herencia
Puerto-Lápice
Záncara
Arenales de San Gregorio
Socuéllamos
Cortijo de Arriba
El Bullaque
Las Labores
Corcoles
Alcoba
La Toledana
Sierra de la Calderina
Fuente el Fresno
Villarrubia de los Ojos
Villarta de S. Juan
Tomelloso
El Robledo
Fontanarejo
Fuencaliente
Arenas de S. Juan
Argamasilla de Alba
Arroba de los Montes
Porzuna
Malagón
Cigüela
Tablas de Daimiel
Fernancabellero
Daimiel
Picón
Carrión de Calatrava
Embalse de Peñarroya
Lagunas de Ruidera
Manzanares
Membrilla
Piedrabuena
Luciana
Alcolea de Calatrava
Torralba de Calatrava
Ciudad Real
Miguelturra
La Solana
Ruidera
Los Pozuelos de Calatrava
Pozuelo de Calatrava
Almagro
Bolaños de Calatrava
Azuer
Alhambra
ERMITA DE CONSOLACIÓN
Abenójar
Valenzuela de Calatrava
Jábalón
San Carlos del Valle
Carrizosa
Corral de Calatrava
Cabezarados
Ballesteros de Calatrava
Tirteafuera
Villamayor de Calatrava
Granátula de Calatrava
Moral de Calatrava
Pozo de la Serna
Alcubillas
Valdepeñas
Villanueva de los Infantes
Argamasilla de Calatrava
Aldea del Rey
Calzada de Calatrava
Almodóvar del Campo
Campo de Calatrava
Puertollano
Cózar
Brazatortas
Hinojosas de Calatrava
Villanueva de S. Carlos
Santa Cruz de Mudela
Torrenueva
Cabezarrubias del Puerto
Villalba de Calatrava
Albaladejo
Almedina
Valle de Alcudia
La Alameda
Torre de Juan Abad
Mestanza
Sierra de Puertollano
Fresnedas
Puebla del Príncipe
Puerto de Niefla
920
Emb. de Montoro II
Castellar de Santiago
Villamanrique
Viso del Marqués
Almuradiel
Montoro
Solana del Pino
Puerto Valderrepiso
860
San Lorenzo de Calatrava
Sierra Madrona
El Hoyo
Despeñaperros
Paso Despeñaperros
Aldeaquemada
Embalse del Guadalmena
Conquista
Fuencaliente
1161
Rebollera
1300
Estrella
Grande
El Centenillo
Las Correderas
Venta de los Santos
Santa Elena
Sierra Morena
Embalse de Jándula
Embalse de La Fernandina
Chiclana de Segura
Sierras de Cardeña y Montoro
La Carolina
Carboneros
Isabela
Santisteban del Puerto
Castellar
Sorihuela del Guadalimar
Cardeña
Embalse de Rumblar
Vilches
Embalse del Guadalén
Arquillos
Baños de la Encina
Navas de San Juan
Iznatoraf
Villanueva del Arzobispo
Virgen de la Cabeza
Guarromán
REAL SANTUARIO DE LA SANTÍSIMA VIRGEN DE LA CABEZA
Guadalimar
Villacarrillo
Embalse del Yeguas
Bailén
Linares
Canena
Rus
Sabiote
Santo Tomé
Marmolejo
Andújar
Espeluy
Jabalquinto
Ibros
Torreperogil
Adamuz
Montoro
Villanueva de la Reina
Lupión
Úbeda
Chilluevar
Arjonilla
Cazalilla
Torreblascopedro
Begíjar
Baeza
Pedro Abad
Villa del Río
Higuera de Arjona
Mengíbar
Guadalquivir
Huelma
Real de Becerro
Cazorla
La Iruela
El Carpio
Lopera
Arjona
Fuerte del Rey
Bujalance
Cañete de las Torres
Porcuna
Escañuela
Villardompardo
CATEDRAL DE LA ASUNCIÓN
Jimena
Bedmar
Jódar
Quesada
Cabañas
2028
0 10 20 30 km
151
158
163
196

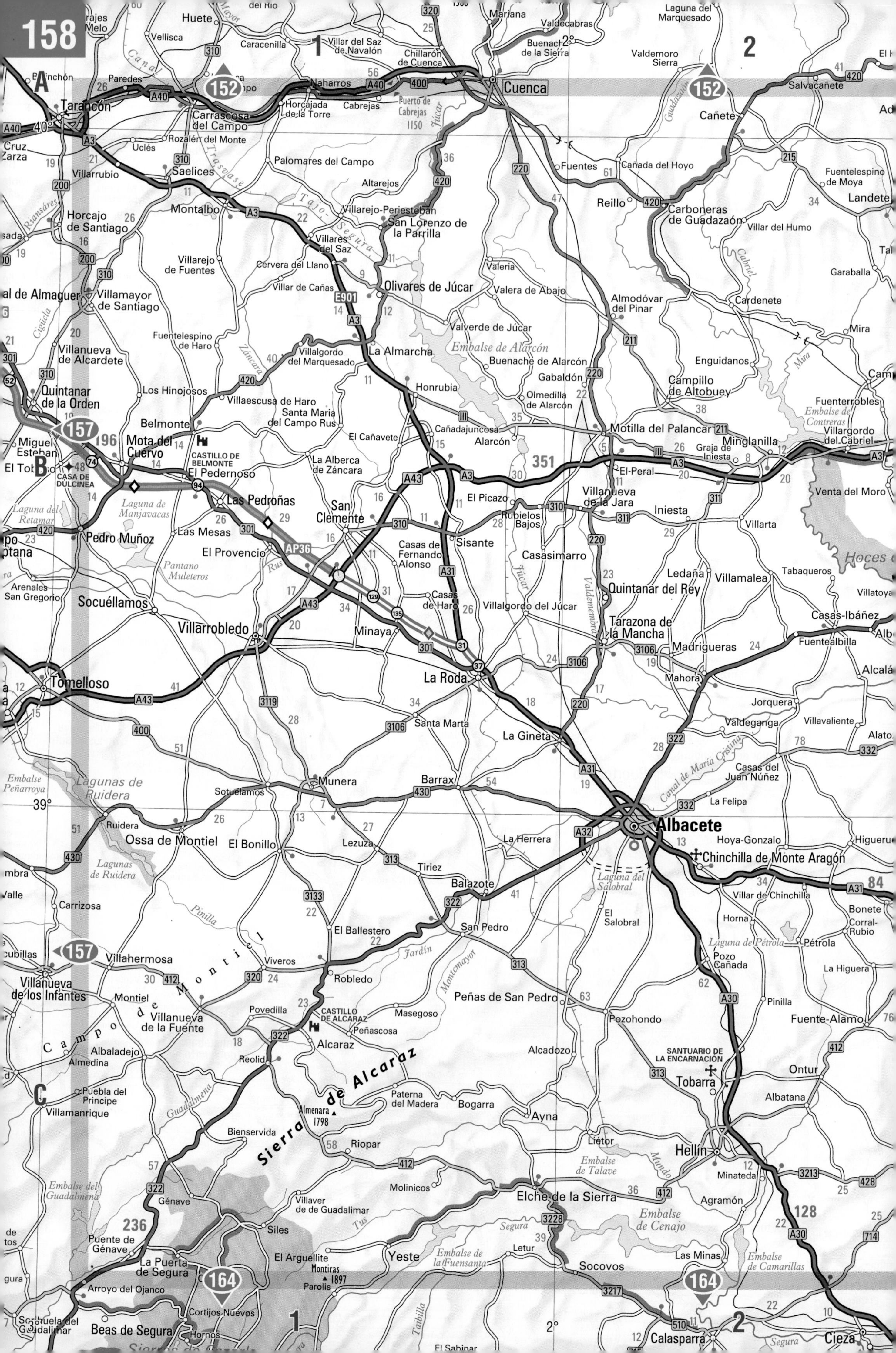
Cuenca
Tarancón
Carrascosa del Campo
Horcajada de la Torre
Cabrejas
Naharros
Villar del Saz de Navalón
Chillarón de Cuenca
Mariana
Valdecabras
Buenache de la Sierra
Laguna del Marquesado
Valdemoro Sierra
Huete
Vellisca
Caracenilla
Paredes
Uclés
Rozalén del Monte
Saelices
Palomares del Campo
Altarejos
Villarrubio
Montalbo
Horcajo de Santiago
Villarejo-Periesteban
San Lorenzo de la Parrilla
Villares del Saz
Villarejo de Fuentes
Cervera del Llano
Villar de Cañas
Olivares de Júcar
Villamayor de Santiago
Fuentelespino de Haro
Villanueva de Alcardete
Quintanar de la Orden
Los Hinojosos
Villaescusa de Haro
Santa María del Campo Rus
Villalgordo del Marquesado
La Almarcha
Honrubia
Belmonte
Mota del Cuervo
Castillo de Belmonte
El Pedernoso
Las Pedroñas
Las Mesas
El Provencio
Pedro Muñoz
Socuéllamos
Villarrobledo
Tomelloso
San Clemente
Casas de Fernando Alonso
Casas de Haro
Minaya
La Roda
Sisante
El Picazo
Rubielos Bajos
Casasimarro
Villalgordo del Júcar
Quintanar del Rey
Tarazona de la Mancha
Madrigueras
Mahora
Villanueva de la Jara
Iniesta
Motilla del Palancar
Alarcón
Cañadajuncosa
El Cañavete
La Alberca de Záncara
Valeria
Valera de Abajo
Valverde de Júcar
Embalse de Alarcón
Buenache de Alarcón
Gabaldón
Olmedilla de Alarcón
Almodóvar del Pinar
Fuentes
Cañada del Hoyo
Reillo
Carboneras de Guadazaón
Villar del Humo
Cañete
Salvacañete
Fuentelespino de Moya
Landete
Garaballa
Cardenete
Enguídanos
Campillo de Altobuey
Mira
Fuenterrobles
Embalse de Contreras
Villargordo del Cabriel
Minglanilla
Graja de Iniesta
El Peral
Venta del Moro
Villarta
Ledaña
Villamalea
Tabaqueros
Casas-Ibáñez
Fuentealbilla
Alcalá
Jorquera
Valdeganga
Villavaliente
Casas del Juan Núñez
La Felipa
Albacete
La Gineta
Barrax
Santa Marta
Munera
Sotuélamos
Lagunas de Ruidera
Embalse Peñarroya
Ruidera
Ossa de Montiel
El Bonillo
Lezuza
Tiriez
Balazote
La Herrera
Laguna del Salobral
El Salobral
Hoya-Gonzalo
Chinchilla de Monte Aragón
Villar de Chinchilla
Bonete
Corral-Rubio
Horna
Pétrola
Laguna del Pétrola
Pozo Cañada
La Higuera
Pinilla
Fuente-Álamo
Ontur
Albatana
Santuario de la Encarnación
Tobarra
Hellín
Minateda
Agramón
Embalse de Camarillas
Las Minas
Cieza
Calasparra
Socovos
Letur
Embalse de la Fuensanta
Yeste
Embalse de Cenajo
Elche de la Sierra
Embalse de Talave
Liétor
Ayna
Bogarra
Molinicos
Riopar
Paterna del Madera
Sierra de Alcaraz
Almenara 1798
Alcaraz
Castillo de Alcaraz
Peñascosa
Masegoso
Povedilla
Reolid
Robledo
Viveros
El Ballestero
San Pedro
Peñas de San Pedro
Pozohondo
Alcadozo
Carrizosa
Villahermosa
Villanueva de los Infantes
Montiel
Villanueva de la Fuente
Campo de Montiel
Albaladejo
Almedina
Puebla del Príncipe
Villamanrique
Bienservida
Embalse del Guadalmena
Génave
Villaverde de Guadalimar
Siles
Puente de Génave
La Puerta de Segura
El Arguellite
Montiras 1897
Parolis
Arroyo del Ojanco
Cortijos Nuevos
Beas de Segura
Hornos
El Sabinar
Embalse de Guadalmena
Casa de Dulcinea
Laguna de Manjavacas
Pantano Muleteros
Arenales San Gregorio
Miguel Esteban
El Toboso
Laguna del Retamar
Villaverde de Guadalimar

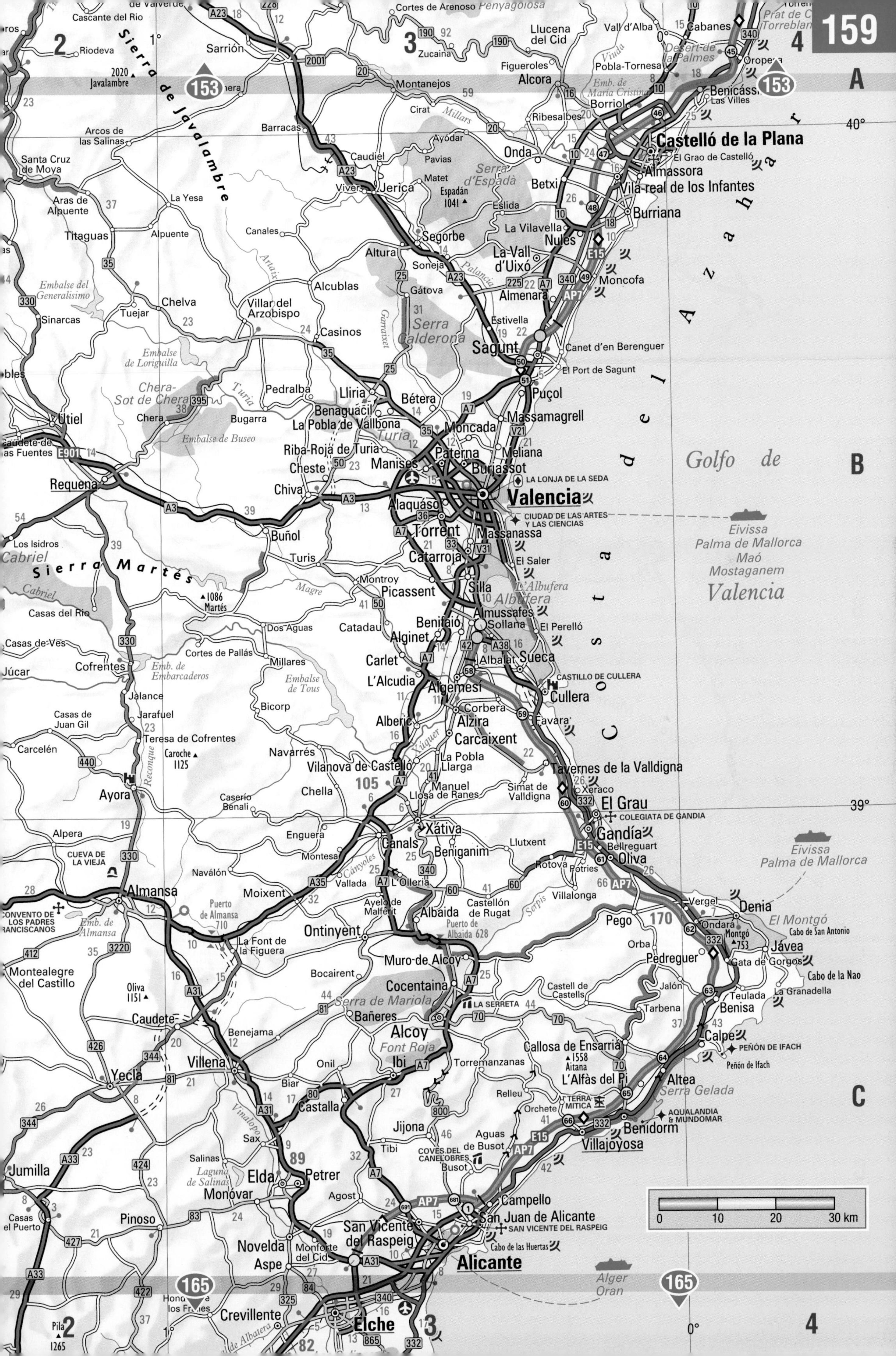

Cascante del Rio
Sierra de Javalambre
Sarrión
Cortes de Arenoso
Penyagolosa
Llucena del Cid
Vall d'Alba
Cabanes
Prat de Cabanes-Torreblanca
Desert de les Palmes
Riodeva
2020 Javalambre
153
Zucaina
Figueroles
Alcora
Pobla-Tornesa
Oropesa
Montanejos
Emb. de María Cristina
Borriol
Benicàssim
Las Villes
A
Cirat
Millars
Ribesalbes
40°
Arcos de las Salinas
Barracas
Ayódar
Castelló de la Plana
El Grao de Castelló
Santa Cruz de Moya
Caudiel
Pavias
Onda
Almassora
Serra d'Espadà
Vila-real de los Infantes
Jerica
Viver
Matet
Espadán 1041
Betxi
Aras de Alpuente
La Yesa
Eslida
Burriana
Titaguas
Alpuente
Canales
Segorbe
La Vilavella
Nules
Altura
La Vall d'Uixó
Soneja
Palancia
Moncofa
Embalse del Generalísimo
Alcublas
Gátova
Almenara
Chelva
Tuejar
Villar del Arzobispo
Serra Calderona
Estivella
Sinarcas
Casinos
Sagunt
Canet d'en Berenguer
Embalse de Loriguilla
El Port de Sagunt
Chera-Sot de Chera
Pedralba
Lliria
Bétera
Puçol
Utiel
Chera
Bugarra
Benaguacil
La Pobla de Vallbona
Moncada
Massamagrell
Turia
Embalse de Buseo
Riba-Roja de Turia
Paterna
Meliana
Caudete de las Fuentes
Cheste
Manises
Burjassot
Golfo de
B
Requena
Chiva
LA LONJA DE LA SEDA
Valencia
Alaquàs
CIUDAD DE LAS ARTES Y LAS CIENCIAS
Torrent
Buñol
Massanassa
Los Isidros
Eivissa
Palma de Mallorca
Maó
Mostaganem
Valencia
Cabriel
Sierra Martés
Turis
Catarroja
El Saler
Montroy
Magre
Picassent
Silla
L'Albufera
1086 Martés
Casas del Rio
Almussafes
Sollana
Dos Aguas
Catadau
Benifaió
El Perelló
Casas de Ves
Alginet
Cortes de Pallás
Sueca
Júcar
Cofrentes
Emb. de Embarcaderos
Millares
Carlet
Albalat
Embalse de Tous
CASTILLO DE CULLERA
L'Alcudia
Algemesí
Cullera
Jalance
Bicorp
Corbera
Casas de Juan Gil
Jarafuel
Alberic
Alzira
Favara
Teresa de Cofrentes
Carcaixent
Carcelén
Caroche 1125
Navarrés
Xúquer
La Pobla Llarga
Tavernes de la Valldigna
Costa del Azahar
Vilanova de Castelló
Manuel
Chella
Llosa de Ranes
Simat de Valldigna
Xeraco
Ayora
Caserío Benali
El Grau
39°
COLEGIATA DE GANDIA
Alpera
Enguera
Xàtiva
Gandía
Canals
Beniganim
Llutxent
Bellreguart
CUEVA DE LA VIEJA
Montesa
Oliva
Navalón
Cànyoles
Rotova
Potries
Almansa
Moixent
Vallada
L'Olleria
Villalonga
Castellón de Rugat
Serpis
Vergel
Dénia
CONVENTO DE LOS PADRES FRANCISCANOS
Puerto de Almansa 710
Ayelo de Malferit
Albaida
Pego
Ondara
El Montgó
Cabo de San Antonio
Emb. de Almansa
Ontinyent
Puerto de Albaida 628
Montgó 753
Jávea
La Font de la Figuera
Orba
Pedreguer
Gata de Gorgos
Montealegre del Castillo
Muro de Alcoy
Cabo de la Nao
Oliva 1151
Bocairent
Castell de Castells
Jalón
Teulada
La Granadella
Cocentaina
Serra de Mariola
LA SERRETA
Benisa
Caudete
Bañeres
Tarbena
Benejama
Alcoy
Calpe
Font Roja
Callosa de Ensarriá
PEÑÓN DE IFACH
Peñón de Ifach
Yecla
Villena
Onil
Ibi
Torremanzanas
1558 Aitana
Altea
L'Alfàs del Pi
Biar
Serra Gelada
Castalla
Relleu
TERRA MITICA
C
Orchete
AQUALANDIA & MUNDOMAR
Jijona
Benidorm
Sax
Aguas de Busot
Villajoyosa
Tibi
COVES DEL CANELOBRES
Jumilla
Salinas
Laguna de Salinas
Busot
Elda
Petrer
Monóvar
Agost
Campello
Casas el Puerto
Pinoso
San Juan de Alicante
San Vicente del Raspeig
SAN VICENTE DEL RASPEIG
Novelda
Monforte del Cid
Cabo de las Huertas
Aspe
Alicante
Alger
Oran
165
Hondón de los Frailes
Crevillente
Elche
Pila 1265
0°
0 10 20 30 km

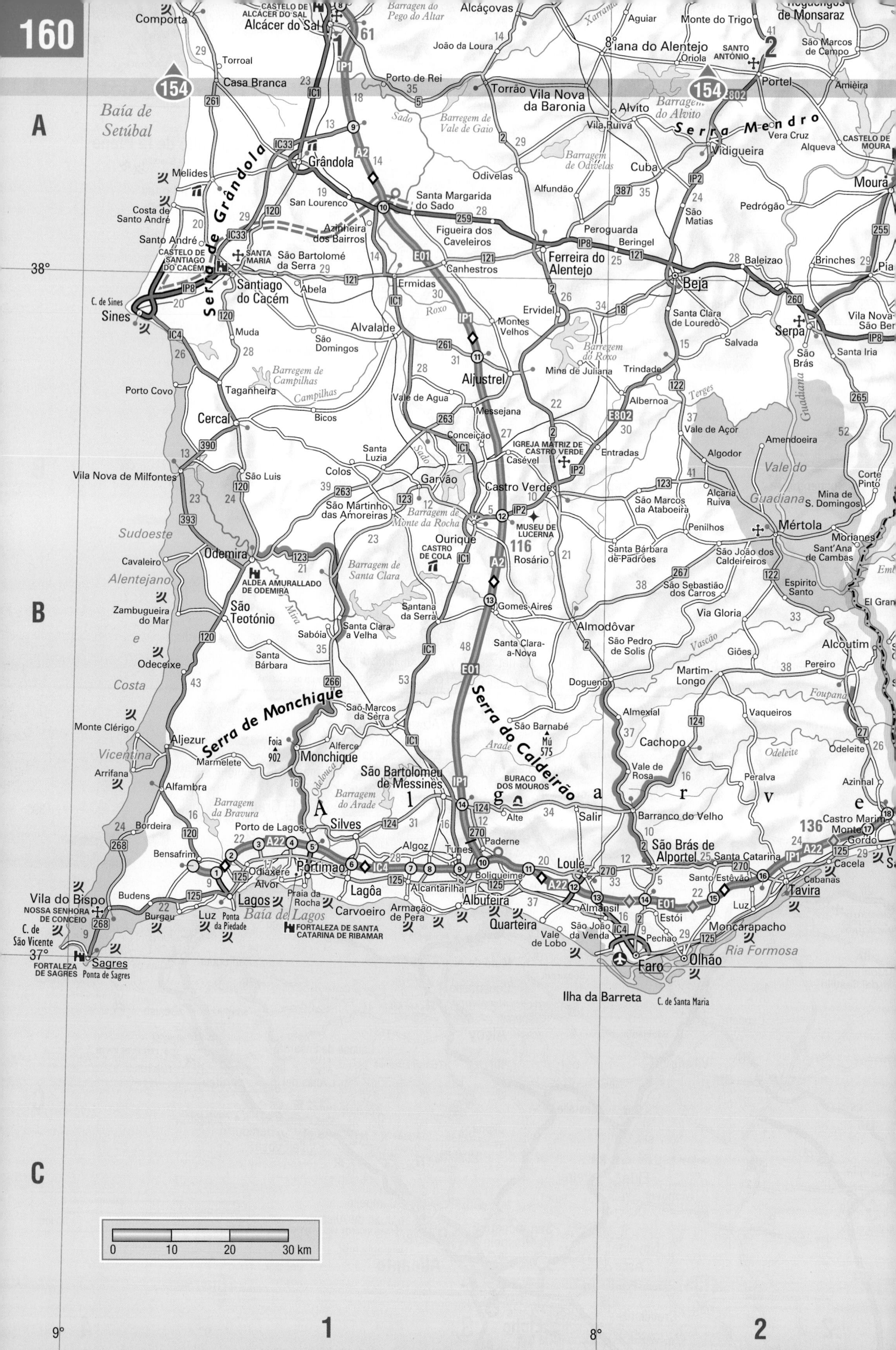

Comporta
Alcácer do Sal
Alcáçovas
Aguiar
Monte do Trigo
de Monsaraz
Torroal
Casa Branca
João da Loura
Viana do Alentejo
Oriola
São Marcos de Campo
Portel
Amieira
Porto de Rei
Torrão
Vila Nova da Baronia
Alvito
Barragem do Alvito
Baía de Setúbal
Barragem de Vale de Gaio
Vila Ruiva
Serra Mendro
Vera Cruz
Alqueva
Castelo de Moura
Vidigueira
Grândola
Barragem de Odivelas
Cuba
Melides
Odivelas
Alfundão
Moura
Serra de Grândola
San Lourenco
Santa Margarida do Sado
Pedrógão
Costa de Santo André
São Matias
Azinheira dos Bairros
Figueira dos Caveleiros
Peroguarda
Santo André
Beringel
Castelo de Santiago do Cacém
Santa Maria
São Bartolomé da Serra
Ferreira do Alentejo
Baleizao
Brinches
Canhestros
Beja
Santiago do Cacém
Abela
Ermidas
C. de Sines
Sines
Ervidel
Santa Clara de Louredo
Vila Nova de São Bento
Serpa
Montes Velhos
Alvalade
Muda
São Domingos
Salvada
Santa Iria
São Brás
Barregem do Roxo
Aljustrel
Mina de Juliana
Trindade
Barregem de Campilhas
Porto Covo
Taganheira
Vale de Agua
Albernoa
Messejana
Cercal
Bicos
Conceição
Vale de Açor
Igreja Matriz de Castro Verde
Entradas
Amendoeira
Santa Luzia
Casével
Algodor
Vila Nova de Milfontes
São Luis
Colos
Garvão
Castro Verde
Vale do Guadiana
Corte Pinto
São Martinho das Amoreiras
Barragem de Monte da Rocha
São Marcos da Ataboeira
Alcaria Ruiva
Mina de S. Domingos
Sudoeste
Ourique
Museu de Lucerna
Penilhos
Mértola
Castro de Cola
Rosário
Santa Bárbara de Padrões
São João dos Caldeireiros
Morianes
Sant'Ana de Cambas
Cavaleiro
Odemira
Aldea Amurallado de Odemira
Barragem de Santa Clara
São Sebastião dos Carros
Espirito Santo
Alentejano
Zambugueira do Mar
São Teotónio
Santana da Serra
Gomes Aires
El Granado
Santa Clara-a Velha
Sabóia
Almodôvar
Via Gloria
São Pedro de Solis
Alcoutim
Odeceixe
Santa Bárbara
Santa Clara-a-Nova
Giões
Pereiro
Martim-Longo
Costa
Serra do Caldeirão
Dogueno
Foupana
Serra de Monchique
São Marcos da Serra
Almexial
Vaqueiros
Monte Clérigo
São Barnabé
Mú 575
Aljezur
Foia 902
Alferce
Cachopo
Odeleite
Vicentina
Marmelete
Monchique
Arade
Arrifana
São Bartolomeu de Messines
Buraco dos Mouros
Vale de Rosa
Alfambra
Peralva
Azinhal
Barragem da Bravura
Barragem do Arade
Algarve
Alte
Salir
Barranco do Velho
Castro Marim
Bordeira
Porto de Lagos
Silves
Paderne
São Brás de Alportel
Monte Gordo
Bensafrim
Odiáxere
Portimão
Algoz
Tunes
Loulé
Santa Catarina
Cacela
Alvor
Boliqueime
Santo Estêvão
Cabanas
Vila do Bispo
Budens
Lagos
Praia da Rocha
Lagôa
Alcantarilha
Albufeira
Almansil
Tavira
Nossa Senhora de Conceio
Burgau
Luz
Ponta da Piedade
Baía de Lagos
Carvoeiro
Armação de Pera
Quarteira
Estói
Luz
C. de São Vicente
Fortaleza de Santa Catarina de Ribamar
Vale de Lobo
São João da Venda
Pechão
Moncarapacho
Fortaleza de Sagres
Sagres
Ponta de Sagres
Faro
Olhão
Ria Formosa
Ilha da Barreta
C. de Santa Maria
A
B
C
1
2
38°
37°
9°
8°
0
10
20
30 km

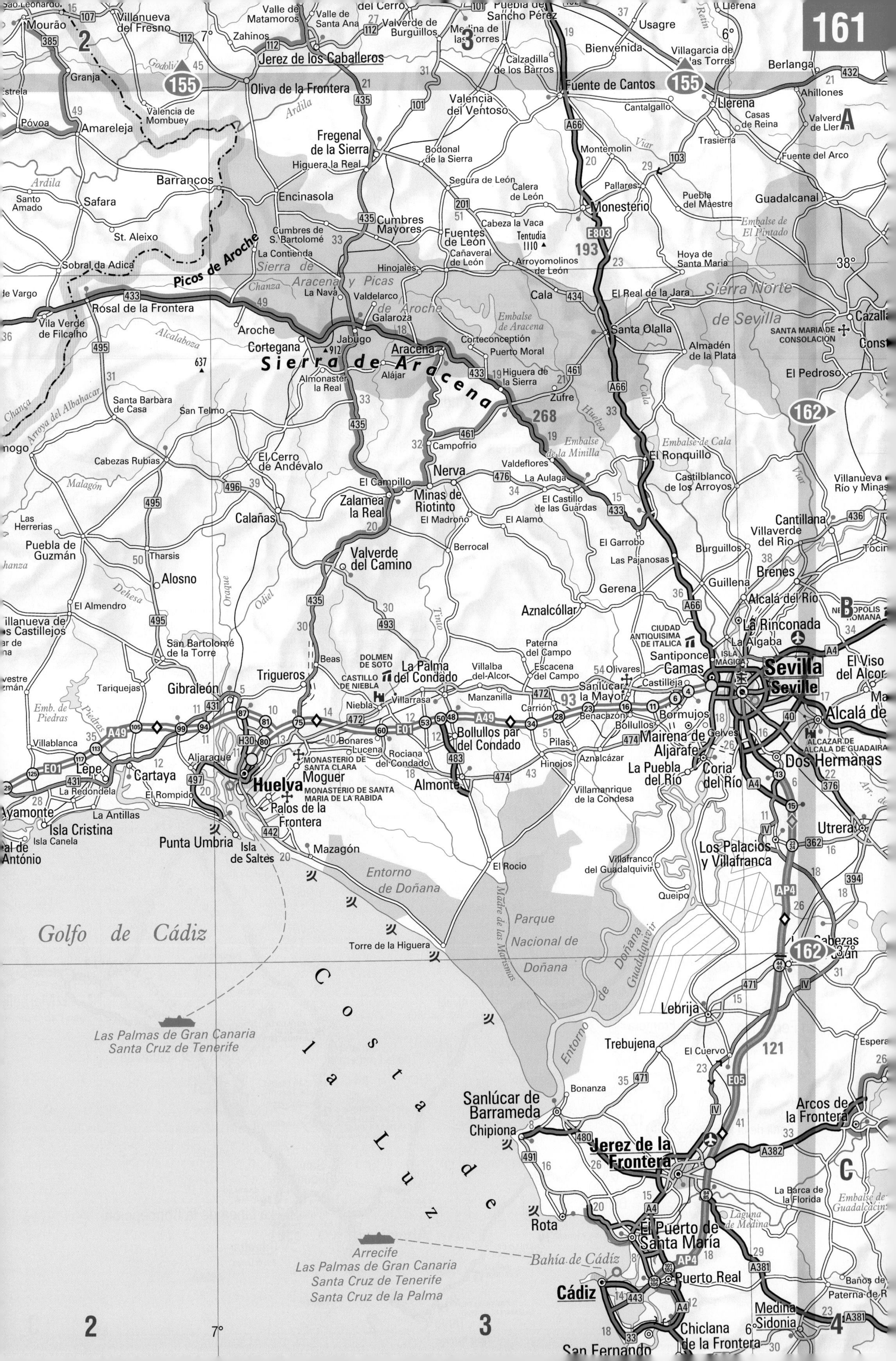
Mourão
Villanueva del Fresno
Valle de Matamoros
Valle de Santa Ana
Valverde de Burguillos
Medina de las Torres
Puebla de Sancho Pérez
Usagre
Llerena
Zahinos
Jerez de los Caballeros
Calzadilla de los Barros
Bienvenida
Villagarcia de las Torres
Berlanga
Granja
Oliva de la Frontera
Valencia del Ventoso
Fuente de Cantos
Cantalgallo
Ahillones
Valencia de Mombuey
Amareleja
Póvoa
Casas de Reina
Valverde de Llerena
Trasierra
Fregenal de la Sierra
Bodonal de la Sierra
Montemolín
Fuente del Arco
Higuera la Real
Barrancos
Segura de León
Calera de León
Pallares
Santo Amado
Safara
Encinasola
Monesterio
Puebla del Maestre
Guadalcanal
Cumbres Mayores
Cumbres de S. Bartolomé
Cabeza la Vaca
Tentudía
Embalse de El Pintado
St. Aleixo
Fuentes de León
Cañaveral de León
La Contienda
Hoya de Santa Maria
Sobral da Adica
Picos de Aroche
Sierra de Aracena y Picas de Aroche
Hinojales
Arroyomolinos de León
La Nava
Valdelarco
Cala
El Real de la Jara
Sierra Norte de Sevilla
Rosal de la Frontera
Vila Verde de Ficalho
Galaroza
Embalse de Aracena
Santa Olalla
Cazalla
Aroche
Jabugo
Corteconcepción
Santa Maria de Consolación
Almadén de la Plata
Cortegana
Aracena
Puerto Moral
Sierra de Aracena
Almonaster la Real
Alájar
Higuera de la Sierra
El Pedroso
Santa Barbara de Casa
San Telmo
Zufre
Campofrío
Embalse de la Minilla
Embalse de Cala
El Ronquillo
Cabezas Rubias
El Cerro de Andévalo
Valdeflores
El Campillo
Nerva
La Aulaga
Castilblanco de los Arroyos
Villanueva del Río y Minas
Zalamea la Real
Minas de Riotinto
El Castillo de las Guardas
Las Herrerias
Calañas
El Madroño
El Alamo
Cantillana
Villaverde del Rio
Puebla de Guzmán
Berrocal
El Garrobo
Burguillos
Tharsis
Valverde del Camino
Las Pajanosas
Brenes
Alosno
Gerena
Guillena
El Almendro
Aznalcóllar
Alcalá del Río
La Rinconada
Ciudad Antiquisima de Italica
San Bartolomé de la Torre
Paterna del Campo
La Algaba
Santiponce
Isla Mágica
Camas
Sevilla
Seville
Dolmen de Soto
Beas
Castillo de Niebla
La Palma del Condado
Villalba del Alcor
Escacena del Campo
Olivares
El Viso del Alcor
Tariquejas
Trigueros
Castilleja
Gibraleón
Villarrasa
Manzanilla
Sanlúcar la Mayor
Niebla
Carrión
Benacazón
Bormujos
Gelves
Alcalá de Guadaira
Bollullos
Emb. de Piedras
Bonares
Lucena
Bollullos par del Condado
Mairena de Aljarafe
Alcazar de Alcala de Guadaira
Villablanca
Rociana del Condado
Pilas
Aznalcázar
Dos Hermanas
Lepe
Cartaya
Aljaraque
Monasterio de Santa Clara
Hinojos
La Puebla del Río
Coria del Río
La Redondela
El Rompido
Huelva
Moguer
Almonte
Villamanrique de la Condesa
Ayamonte
La Antillas
Monasterio de Santa Maria de la Rabida
Palos de la Frontera
Utrera
Isla Cristina
Isla Canela
Punta Umbria
Isla de Saltes
Mazagón
Los Palacios y Villafranca
El Rocio
Villafranco del Guadalquivir
Entorno de Doñana
Queipo
Parque Nacional de Doñana
Golfo de Cádiz
Torre de la Higuera
Cabezas de San Juan
Madre de las Marismas
Lebrija
Las Palmas de Gran Canaria
Santa Cruz de Tenerife
Costa de la Luz
Trebujena
El Cuervo
Bonanza
Arcos de la Frontera
Sanlúcar de Barrameda
Chipiona
Jerez de la Frontera
La Barca de la Florida
Embalse de Guadalcacín
Rota
Laguna de Medina
El Puerto de Santa María
Arrecife
Las Palmas de Gran Canaria
Santa Cruz de Tenerife
Santa Cruz de la Palma
Bahía de Cádiz
Puerto Real
Baños de
Paterna de R
Cádiz
Medina Sidonia
Chiclana de la Frontera
San Fernando
Golfo de Cádiz
A
B
C
2
3
4
155
162
7°
6°
38°
37°

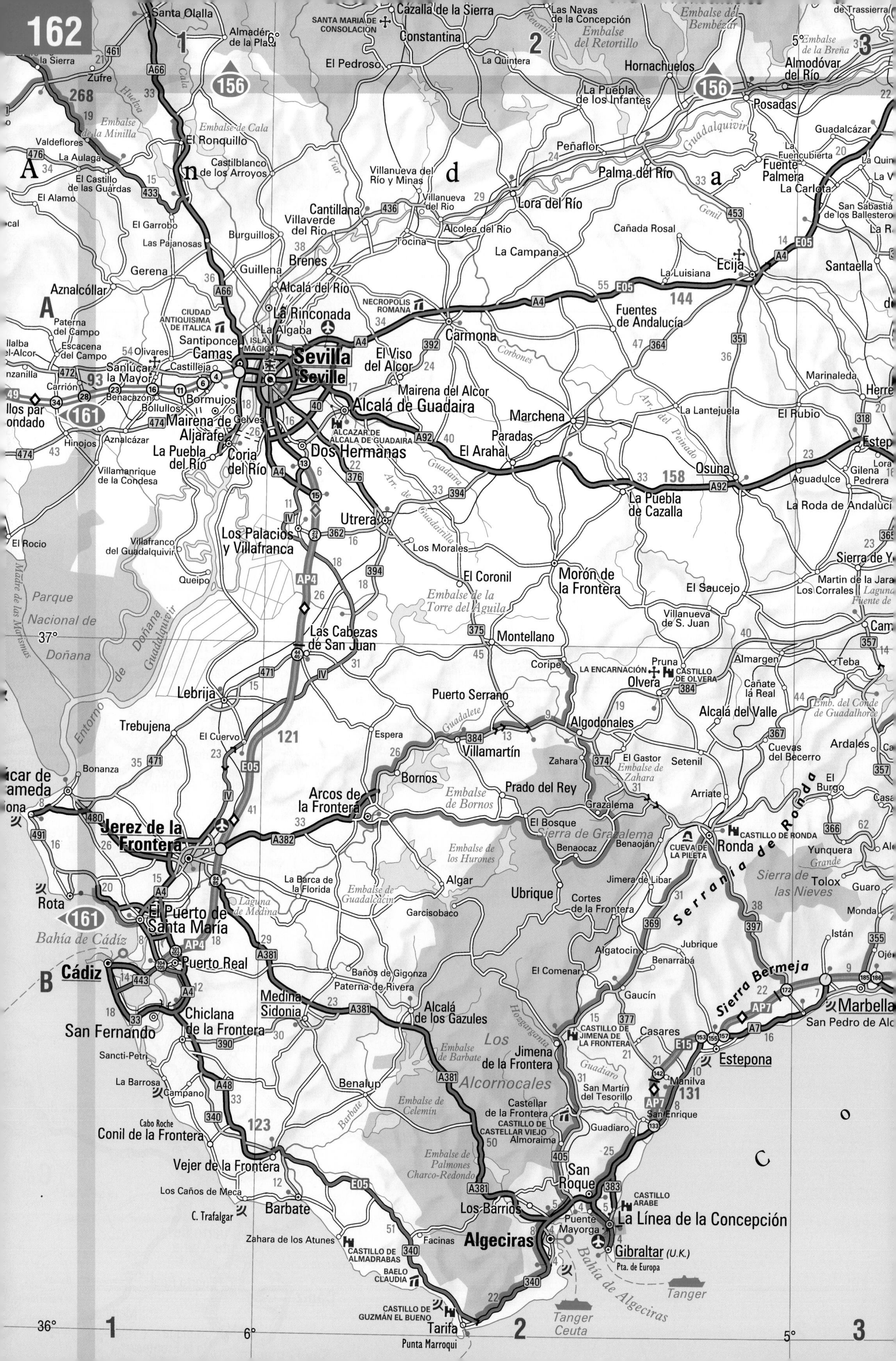

Santa Olalla
Almadén de la Plata
Cazalla de la Sierra
Santa María de Consolación
Constantina
Las Navas de la Concepción
Embalse del Retortillo
Embalse del Bembézar
Embalse de la Breña
Almodóvar del Río
El Pedroso
La Quintera
Hornachuelos
156
La Puebla de los Infantes
Posadas
Zufre
268
Embalse de la Minilla
Embalse de Cala
El Ronquillo
Valdeflores
La Aulaga
El Castillo de las Guardas
Castilblanco de los Arroyos
Villanueva del Río y Minas
Peñaflor
Palma del Río
Guadalcázar
La Fuencubierta
Fuente Palmera
La Carlota
El Alamo
El Garrobo
Las Pajanosas
Burguillos
Cantillana
Villaverde del Río
Villanueva del Río
Lora del Río
Alcolea del Río
Tocina
Cañada Rosal
San Sebastián de los Ballesteros
Gerena
Guillena
Brenes
La Campana
La Luisiana
Ecija
Santaella
Aznalcóllar
Alcalá del Río
Ciudad Antiquísima de Itálica
Necrópolis Romana
La Rinconada
Fuentes de Andalucía
144
Paterna del Campo
Escacena del Campo
Santiponce
La Algaba
Isla Mágica
Carmona
Camas
Sevilla
Seville
Olivares
Castilleja
Sanlúcar la Mayor
El Viso del Alcor
Carrión
Benacazón
93
Bormujos
Mairena del Alcor
Marinaleda
Bollullos
Mairena de Aljarafe
Gelves
Alcalá de Guadaira
Alcázar de Alcalá de Guadaira
Marchena
La Lantejuela
El Rubio
161
Hinojos
Aznalcázar
La Puebla del Río
Coria del Río
Dos Hermanas
El Arahal
Paradas
Osuna
Villamanrique de la Condesa
La Puebla de Cazalla
158
Aguadulce
Gilena
Pedrera
La Roda de Andalucía
Utrera
El Rocío
Villafranco del Guadalquivir
Los Palacios y Villafranca
Los Morales
Queipo
El Coronil
Morón de la Frontera
El Saucejo
Sierra de Yeguas
Martín de la Jara
Los Corrales
Parque Nacional de Doñana
Madre de las Marismas
Embalse de la Torre del Águila
Villanueva de S. Juan
37°
Las Cabezas de San Juan
Montellano
Entorno de Doñana
Coripe
Pruna
La Encarnación
Castillo de Olvera
Olvera
Almargen
Teba
Cañete la Real
Lebrija
Puerto Serrano
Emb. del Conde de Guadalhorce
Alcalá del Valle
Trebujena
Espera
121
Algodonales
El Cuervo
Villamartín
Zahara
El Gastor
Embalse de Zahara
Setenil
Cuevas del Becerro
Ardales
Bonanza
Sanlúcar de Barrameda
Bornos
Prado del Rey
Arcos de la Frontera
Embalse de Bornos
Grazalema
Arriate
El Burgo
Jerez de la Frontera
El Bosque
Sierra de Grazalema
Benaocaz
Benaoján
Cueva de la Pileta
Ronda
Castillo de Ronda
Serranía de Ronda
Yunquera
Embalse de los Hurones
Jimera de Libar
Sierra de las Nieves
Tolox
Guaro
Rota
El Puerto de Santa María
La Barca de la Florida
Algar
Embalse de Guadalcacín
Laguna de Medina
Garcisobaco
Ubrique
Cortes de la Frontera
Monda
Bahía de Cádiz
Puerto Real
Jubrique
Algatocín
Benarrabá
Istán
Cádiz
Baños de Gigonza
Paterna de Rivera
El Comenar
Sierra Bermeja
Chiclana de la Frontera
Medina Sidonia
Alcalá de los Gazules
Gaucín
San Fernando
Marbella
San Pedro de Alcántara
Sancti-Petri
Los Alcornocales
Castillo de Jimena de la Frontera
Casares
Estepona
Embalse de Barbate
Jimena de la Frontera
La Barrosa
Campano
Benalup
Manilva
San Martín del Tesorillo
131
Embalse de Celemín
Cabo Roche
Conil de la Frontera
123
Castellar de la Frontera
Castillo de Castellar Viejo
Almoraima
San Enrique
Guadiaro
Vejer de la Frontera
Embalse de Palmones Charco-Redondo
San Roque
Los Caños de Meca
Barbate
Castillo Árabe
Los Barrios
La Línea de la Concepción
C. Trafalgar
Puente Mayorga
Zahara de los Atunes
Castillo de Almadrabas
Facinas
Algeciras
Gibraltar (U.K.)
Pta. de Europa
Baelo Claudia
Bahía de Algeciras
Tanger
Castillo de Guzmán el Bueno
Tarifa
Tanger Ceuta
Punta Marroquí
36°
6°
5°
1
2
3
A
B
Andalucía

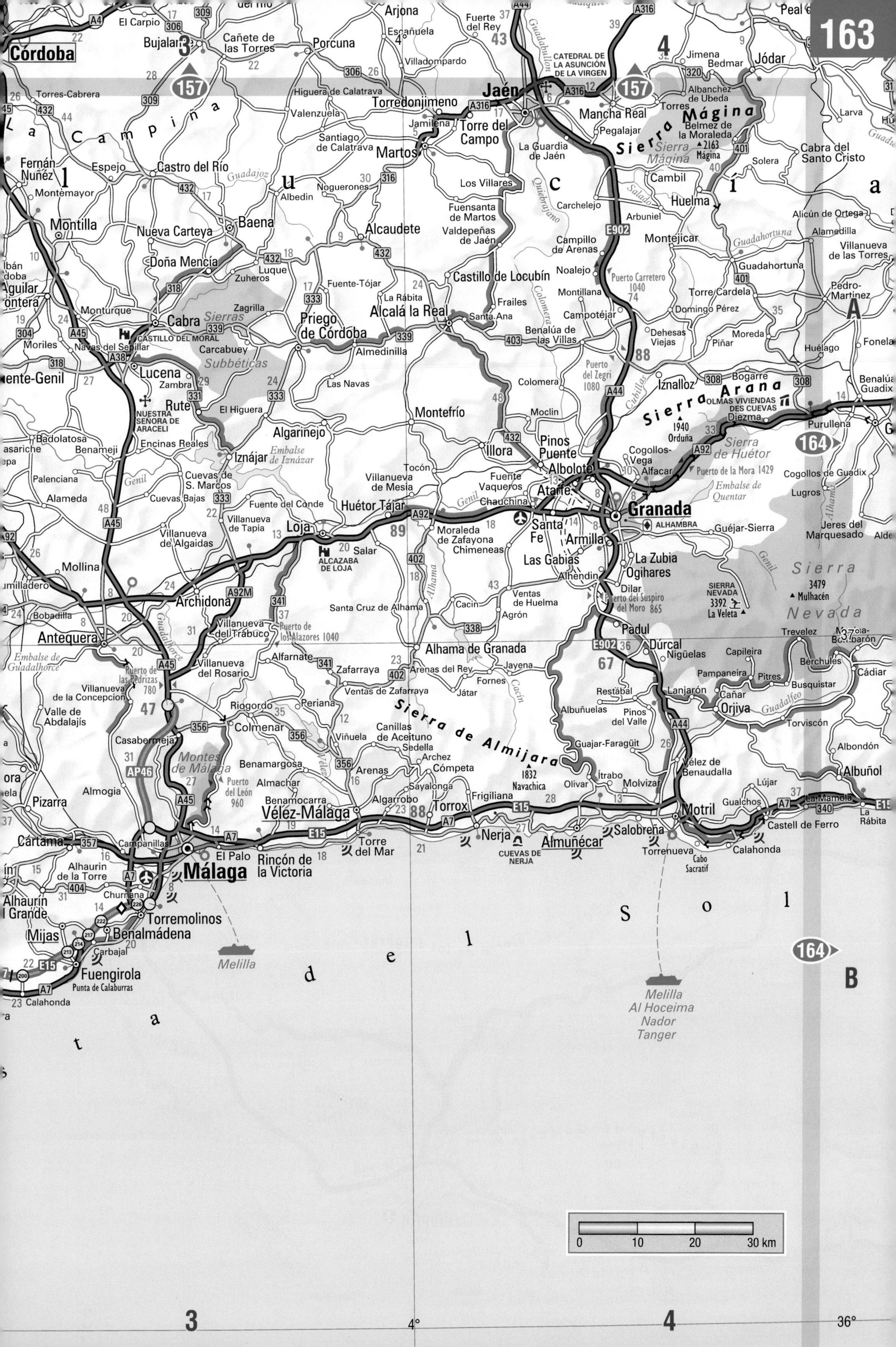
Córdoba
El Carpio
Bujalance
Cañete de las Torres
Porcuna
Arjona
Escañuela
Villadompardo
Fuerte del Rey
Torres-Cabrera
La Campiña
Higuera de Calatrava
Torredonjimeno
Valenzuela
Jaén
CATEDRAL DE LA ASUNCIÓN DE LA VIRGEN
Jamilena
Torre del Campo
Santiago de Calatrava
Martos
Mancha Real
Pegalajar
Jimena
Bedmar
Jódar
Albanchez de Ubeda
Torres
Sierra Mágina
Belmez de la Moraleda
2163 Mágina
Larva
Cabra del Santo Cristo
Solera
Fernán Núñez
Montemayor
Espejo
Castro del Río
Guadajoz
Noguerones
Albedin
Los Villares
La Guardia de Jaén
Cambil
Huelma
Montilla
Nueva Carteya
Baena
Alcaudete
Fuensanta de Martos
Valdepeñas de Jaén
Carchelejo
Arbuniel
Alicún de Ortega
Alamedilla
Villanueva de las Torres
Montejícar
Guadahortuna
Campillo de Arenas
Doña Mencía
Luque
Zuheros
Fuente-Tójar
La Rábita
Castillo de Locubín
Noalejo
Montillana
Puerto Carretero 1040
Torre Cardela
Pedro-Martinez
Aguilar de la Frontera
Monturque
Cabra
Zagrilla
Sierras Subbéticas
Priego de Córdoba
Alcalá la Real
Frailes
Santa Ana
Campotéjar
Domingo Pérez
CASTILLO DEL MORAL
Moriles
Navas del Selpillar
Carcabuey
Almedinilla
Benalúa de las Villas
Dehesas Viejas
Moreda
Piñar
Huélago
Fonelas
Lucena
Zambra
Puente-Genil
Las Navas
Colomera
Puerto del Zegri 1080
Iznalloz
Bogarre
Benalúa de Guadix
Rute
NUESTRA SEÑORA DE ARACELI
El Higuera
Montefrío
Moclín
Sierra Arana
OLMAS VIVIENDAS DES CUEVAS
Diezma
Purullena
Badolatosa
Benamejí
Encinas Reales
Algarinejo
Illora
Pinos Puente
1940 Orduña
Sierra de Huétor
Palenciana
Iznájar
Embalse de Iznázar
Tocón
Cogollos-Vega
Albolote
Alfacar
Puerto de la Mora 1429
Cogollos de Guadix
Cuevas de S. Marcos
Villanueva de Mesía
Fuente Vaqueros
Atarfe
Embalse de Quentar
Lugros
Alameda
Cuevas Bajas
Fuente del Conde
Huétor Tájar
Chauchina
Granada
ALHAMBRA
Guéjar-Sierra
Jeres del Marquesado
Villanueva de Tapia
Villanueva de Algaidas
Loja
Salar
Moraleda de Zafayona
Chimeneas
Santa Fe
Armilla
ALCAZABA DE LOJA
Las Gabias
La Zubia
Ogíhares
Alhendín
Sierra Nevada
3479 Mulhacén
3392 La Veleta
Mollina
Archidona
Ventas de Huelma
Cacín
Agrón
Dílar
Puerto del Suspiro del Moro 865
Bobadilla
Antequera
Villanueva del Trabuco
Puerto de los Alazores 1040
Santa Cruz de Alhama
Padul
Embalse de Guadalhorce
Puerto de las Pedrizas 780
Villanueva del Rosario
Alfarnate
Zafarraya
Alhama de Granada
Dúrcal
Nigüelas
Capileira
Trevelez
Arenas del Rey
Jayena
Fornes
Pampaneira
Pitres
Bérchules
Cádiar
Villanueva de la Concepcion
Valle de Abdalajís
Riogordo
Periana
Ventas de Zafarraya
Játar
Restábal
Lanjarón
Cañar
Busquistar
Casabermeja
Colmenar
Viñuela
Sierra de Almijara
Albuñuelas
Pinos del Valle
Órgiva
Torviscón
Montes de Málaga
Canillas de Aceituno
Sedella
Guajar-Faragüit
Albondón
Benamargosa
Archez
Cómpeta
1832 Navachica
Vélez de Benaudalla
Albuñol
Almogía
Puerto del León 960
Almachar
Arenas
Sayalonga
Frigiliana
Ítrabo
Olivar
Molvizar
Lújar
Pizarra
Benamocarra
Algarrobo
Vélez-Málaga
Torrox
Motril
Gualchos
La Mamola
La Rábita
Cártama
Campanillas
Torre del Mar
Nerja
CUEVAS DE NERJA
Almuñécar
Salobreña
Torrenueva
Cabo Sacratif
Calahonda
Castell de Ferro
El Palo
Rincón de la Victoria
Alhaurín de la Torre
Málaga
Alhaurín el Grande
Churriana
Torremolinos
Benalmádena
Mijas
Carbajal
Fuengirola
Punta de Calaburras
Calahonda
Melilla
Melilla
Al Hoceima
Nador
Tanger
Costa del Sol
Andalucía
157
164
0
10
20
30 km
3
4
4°
36°
A
B

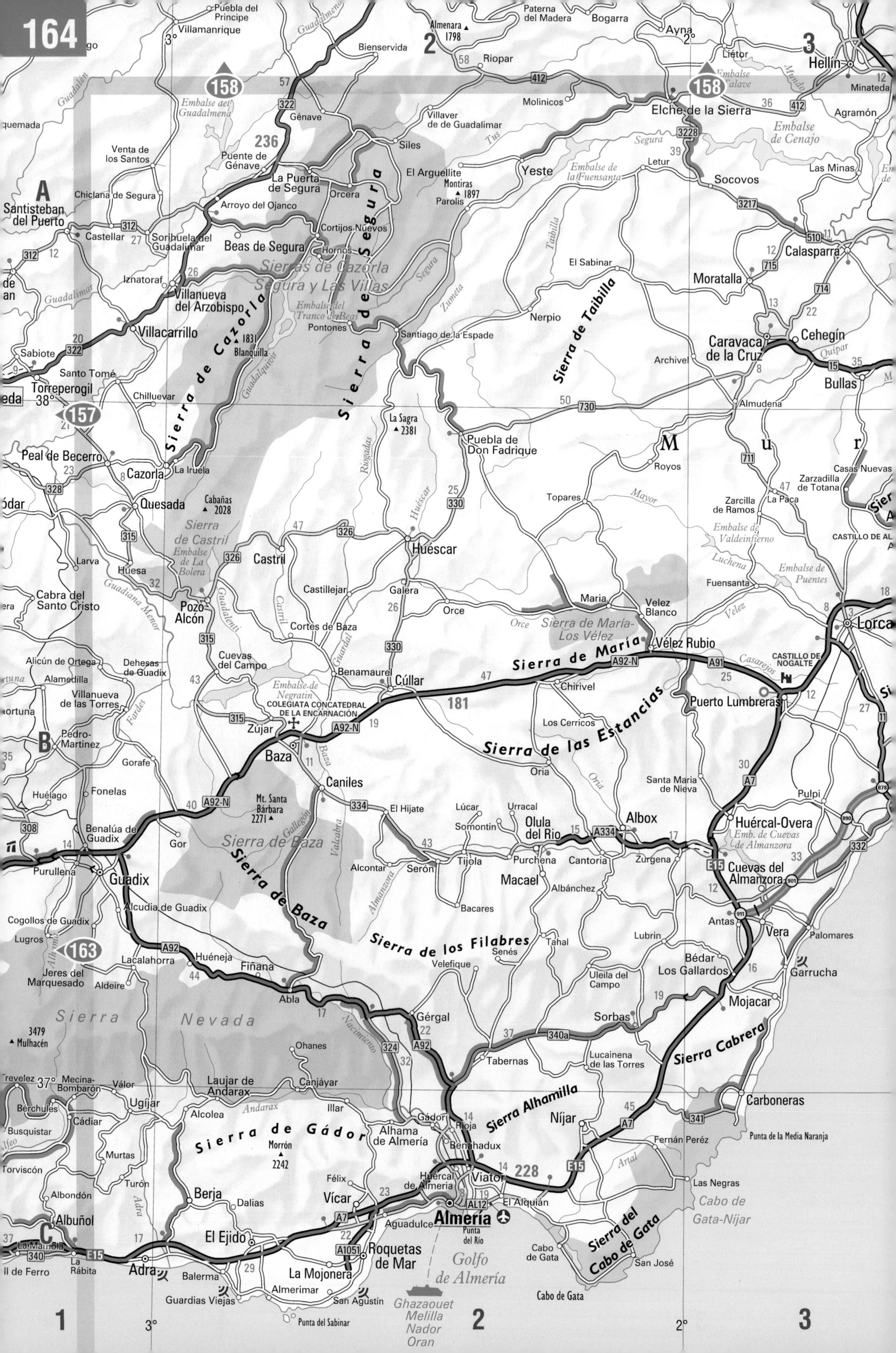
Puebla del Príncipe
Villamanrique
Bienservida
Almenara 1798
Paterna del Madera
Bogarra
Ayna
Liétor
Hellín
Minateda
Riopar
Molinicos
Elche de la Sierra
Agramón
Embalse de Cenajo
Embalse del Guadalmena
Génave
Villaver de de Guadalimar
Siles
Venta de los Santos
Puente de Génave
La Puerta de Segura
El Arguellite
Montiras 1897
Parolis
Yeste
Embalse de la Fuensanta
Letur
Socovos
Las Minas
Chiclana de Segura
Orcera
Arroyo del Ojanco
Santisteban del Puerto
Castellar
Sorihuela del Guadalimar
Beas de Segura
Cortijos Nuevos
Hornos
Sierras de Cazorla Segura y Las Villas
El Sabinar
Calasparra
Moratalla
Iznatoraf
Villanueva del Arzobispo
Embalse del Tranco de Beas
Pontones
Santiago de la Espade
Nerpio
Sierra de Taibilla
Cehegín
Caravaca de la Cruz
Archivel
Bullas
Villacarrillo
Blanquilla 1831
Sabiote
Santo Tomé
Torreperogil
Sierra de Cazorla
Sierra de Segura
Chilluevar
La Sagra 2381
Almudena
Puebla de Don Fadrique
Peal de Becerro
Cazorla
La Iruela
Royos
Casas Nuevas
Zarzadilla de Totana
Quesada
Cabañas 2028
Topares
Zarcilla de Ramos
La Paca
Embalse de Valdeinfierno
CASTILLO DE AL
Sierra de Castril
Embalse de La Bolera
Castril
Huéscar
Larva
Huesa
Castillejar
Galera
Fuensanta
Embalse de Puentes
Cabra del Santo Cristo
Pozo Alcón
Orce
Maria
Velez Blanco
Lorca
Sierra de María-Los Vélez
Cortes de Baza
Vélez Rubio
Alicún de Ortega
Dehesas de Guadix
Alamedilla
Cuevas del Campo
Sierra de María
CASTILLO DE NOGALTE
Villanueva de las Torres
Benamaurel
Cúllar
Chirivel
Embalse de Negratín
COLEGIATA CONCATEDRAL DE LA ENCARNACIÓN
Zújar
Puerto Lumbreras
Pedro-Martinez
Sierra de las Estancias
Los Cerricos
Baza
Gorafe
Oria
Caniles
Santa Maria de Nieva
Huélago
Fonelas
Mt. Santa Bárbara 2271
El Hijate
Lúcar
Urracal
Pulpí
Benalúa de Guadix
Somontin
Olula del Rio
Albox
Huércal-Overa
Emb. de Cuevas de Almanzora
Gor
Sierra de Baza
Purullena
Guadix
Alcontar
Serón
Tíjola
Purchena
Cantoria
Zurgena
Cuevas del Almanzora
Macael
Albánchez
Alcudia de Guadix
Bacares
Antas
Vera
Palomares
Cogollos de Guadix
Lubrin
Lugros
Sierra de los Filabres
Tahal
Senés
Bédar
Los Gallardos
Garrucha
Lacalahorra
Huéneja
Velefique
Jeres del Marquesado
Aldeire
Fiñana
Uleila del Campo
Abla
Mojacar
Sierra Nevada
Gérgal
Sorbas
Sierra Cabrera
3479 Mulhacén
Ohanes
Tabernas
Lucainena de las Torres
Trevelez
Mecina-Bombarón
Válor
Laujar de Andarax
Canjáyar
Ugíjar
Carboneras
Bérchules
Alcolea
Illar
Sierra Alhamilla
Cádiar
Gádor
Níjar
Busquistar
Sierra de Gádor
Alhama de Almería
Rioja
Morrón 2242
Benahadux
Fernán Peréz
Punta de la Media Naranja
Murtas
Torviscón
Turón
Félix
Huércal de Almería
Viator
Las Negras
Albondón
Berja
Vícar
El Alquián
Cabo de Gata-Níjar
Dalias
Albuñol
Aguadulce
Almería
Punta del Río
Sierra del Cabo de Gata
La Mamola
El Ejido
Roquetas de Mar
Golfo de Almería
Cabo de Gata
San José
La Rábita
Adra
Balerma
La Mojonera
Il de Ferro
Almerimar
Guardias Viejas
San Agustín
Ghazaouet Melilla Nador Oran
Punta del Sabinar
Cabo de Gata

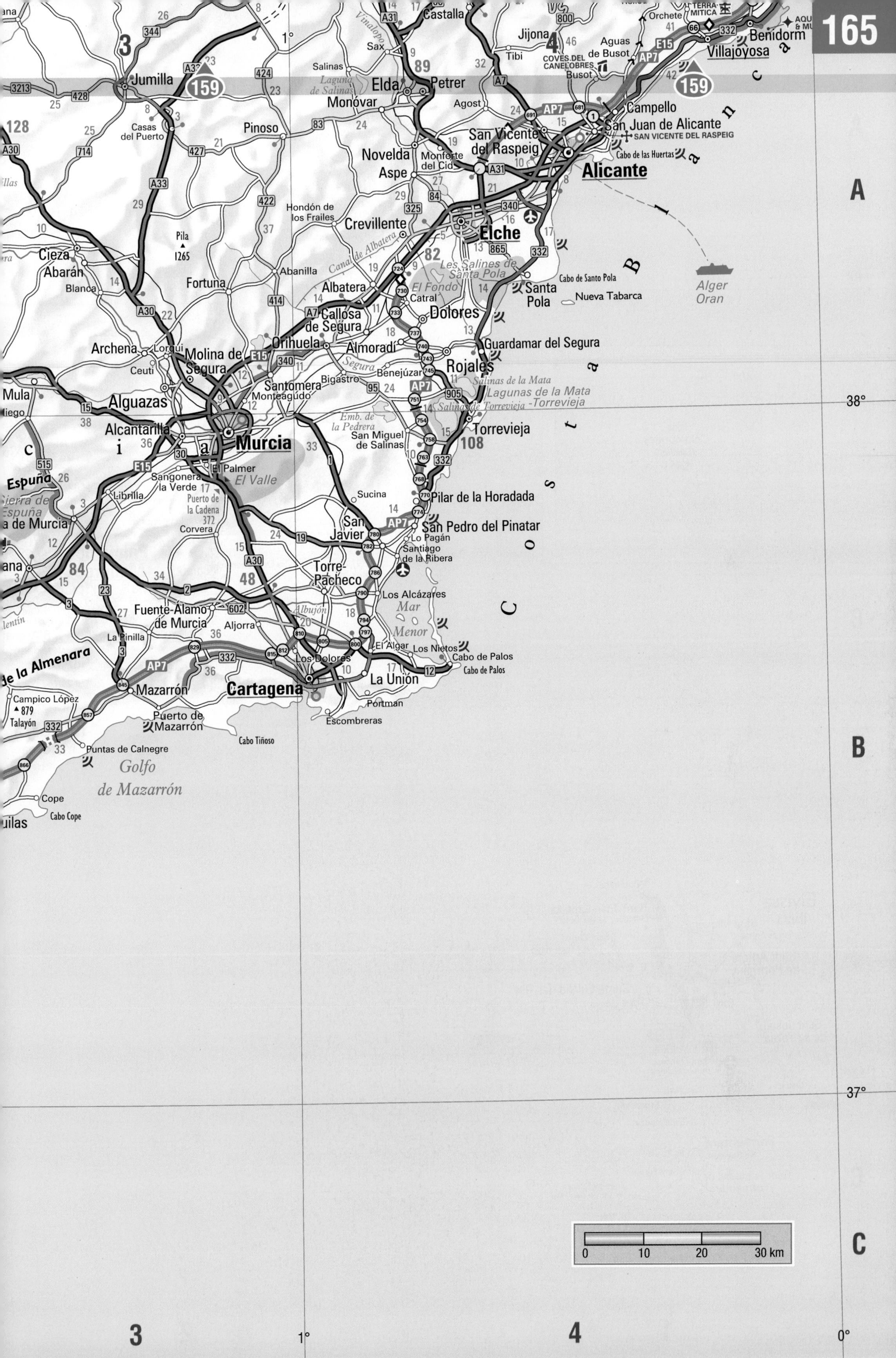
Jumilla
Cieza
Abarán
Blanca
Fortuna
Archena
Molina de Segura
Alguazas
Alcantarilla
Murcia
Mula
Pinoso
Elda
Petrer
Monóvar
Novelda
Aspe
Crevillente
Elche
Alicante
San Vicente del Raspeig
San Juan de Alicante
Campello
Villajoyosa
Benidorm
Jijona
Castalla
Albatera
Callosa de Segura
Orihuela
Almoradí
Dolores
Catral
Santa Pola
Nueva Tabarca
Cabo de Santo Pola
Guardamar del Segura
Rojales
Torrevieja
Pilar de la Horadada
San Pedro del Pinatar
San Javier
Torre-Pacheco
Los Alcázares
Mar Menor
Fuente-Álamo de Murcia
Cartagena
La Unión
Cabo de Palos
Mazarrón
Puerto de Mazarrón
Golfo de Mazarrón
Cabo Tiñoso
Escombreras
Portman
Cope
Cabo Cope
Alger
Oran
Costa Blanca
A
B
C
3
4
1°
0°
38°
37°
0 10 20 30 km

A

1   2°   2

40°

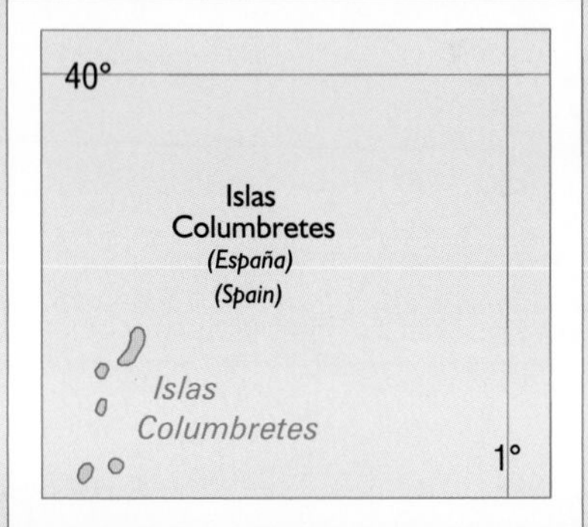

Islas
Columbretes
(España)
(Spain)

40°

*Islas
Columbretes*

1°

ISLAS
BALEARES

BALEARIC
ISLANDS

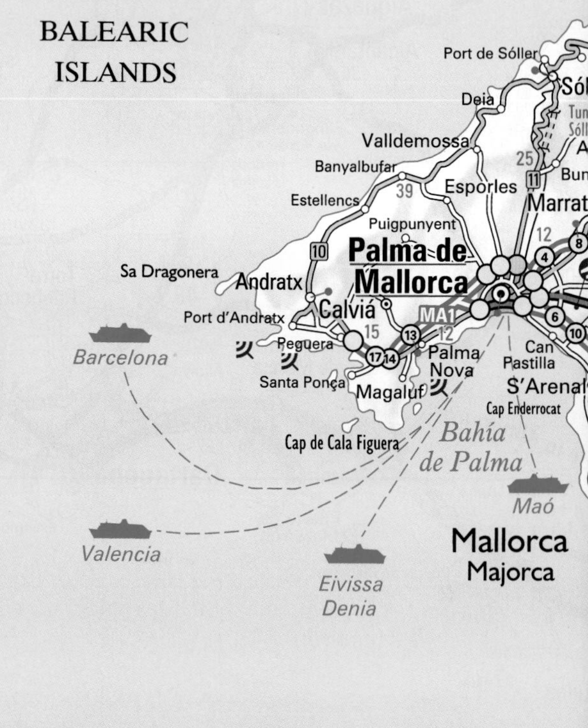

Port de Sóller
Deià   Só
Valldemossa   Tun
Banyalbufar   Sóll
Estellencs   39   Esporles   11   Bun
Puigpunyent   Marrat
25
Sa Dragonera   10   **Palma de**   39
Andratx   **Mallorca**
Port d'Andratx   15   13   12
Calvià   MA1   4
Peguera   12   6   10
17 14   **Palma**   Can
Santa Ponça   **Nova**   Pastilla
Magaluf   S'Arenal
Cap Enderrocat

B

Barcelona

Cap de Cala Figuera   *Bahía
de Palma*

Maó

Valencia   **Mallorca**
                              Majorca
*Eivissa
Denia*

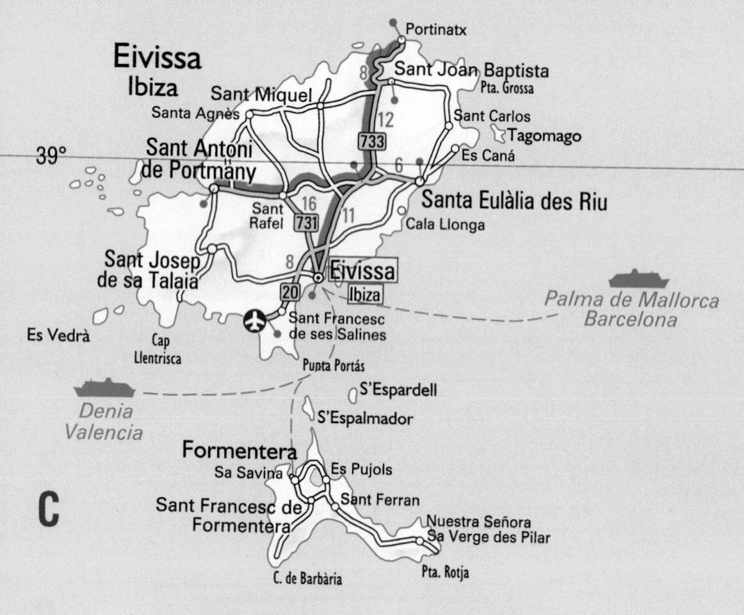

Eivissa
Ibiza   Portinatx
Sant Miquel   Sant Joan Baptista
Santa Agnès   Pta. Grossa
8
12   Sant Carlos
Sant Antoni   733   *Tagomago*
de Portmany   6   Es Caná
39°
16   Sant   **Santa Eulàlia des Riu**
731   Rafel   11
Sant Josep   Cala Llonga
de sa Talaia   8   **Eivissa**
20   Ibiza
Es Vedrà   Sant Francesc
Cap   de ses Salines   *Palma de Mallorca
Llentrisca   Barcelona*
Punta Portás
S'Espardell
*Denia   S'Espalmador
Valencia*
Formentera   Es Pujols
Sa Savina   Sant Ferran
Sant Francesc de   Nuestra Señora
Formentera   Sa Verge des Pilar
C   C. de Barbària   Pta. Rotja

1   2°   2

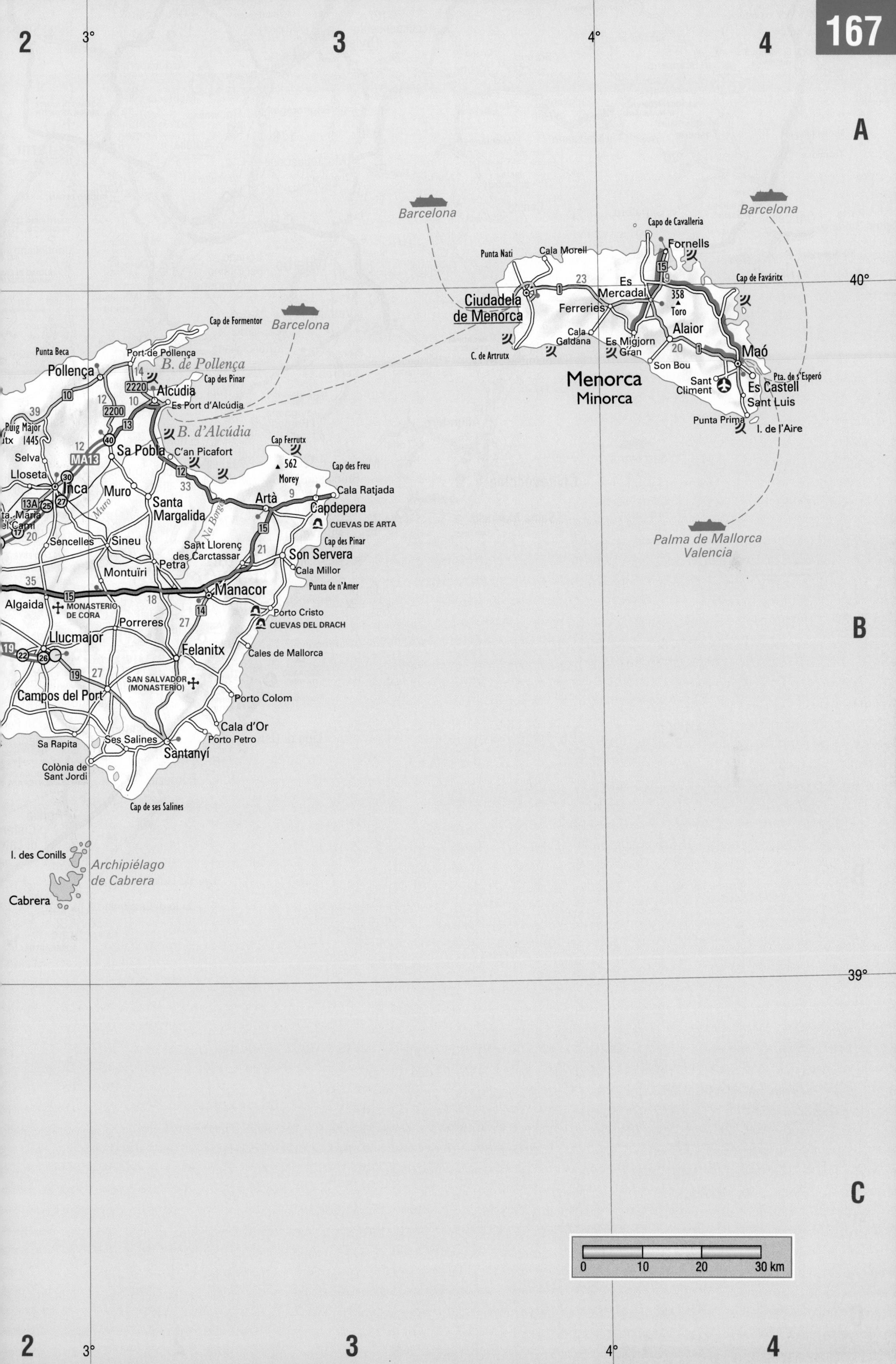

A

Barcelona

Barcelona

Capo de Cavalleria

Punta Nati

Cala Morell

Fornells

15

9

23

Cap de Favàritx

40°

Cap de Formentor

Barcelona

Ciudadela
de Menorca

Es
Mercadal

Ferreries

358
Toro

Alaior

20

1

Maó

Punta Beca

Port de Pollença

Cap des Pinar

B. de Pollença

Pollença

14

2220

Alcúdia

C. de Artrutx

Cala
Galdàna

Es Migjorn
Gran

Son Bou

Sant
Climent

Pta. de s'Esperó

Es Castell
Sant Luis

10

12

10

2200

13

Es Port d'Alcúdia

B. d'Alcúdia

Menorca
Minorca

Punta Prima

I. de l'Aire

39

Puig Major
utx 1445

Selva

12

40

Sa Pobla

C'an Picafort

Cap Ferrutx

▲ 562
Morey

Cap des Freu

MA13

33

Santa
Margalida

12

Artà

9

Cala Ratjada

Lloseta

30

Inca

27

Muro

Capdepera

CUEVAS DE ARTA

Palma de Mallorca
Valencia

B

13A

25

Muro

Sant Llorenç
des Carctassar

15

Cap des Pinar

ta. Maria
el Camí

17

20

Sencelles

Sineu

Petra

21

Son Servera

Cala Millor

Montuïri

Punta de n'Amer

35

15

18

Manacor

Algaida

MONASTERIO
DE CORA

14

Porto Cristo

CUEVAS DEL DRACH

Porreres

27

Llucmajor

19

22

26

Felanitx

Cales de Mallorca

19

27

SAN SALVADOR
(MONASTERIO)

Porto Colom

Campos del Port

Sa Rapita

Ses Salines

Santanyí

Cala d'Or
Porto Petro

Colònia de
Sant Jordi

Cap de ses Salines

I. des Conills

Archipiélago
de Cabrera

Cabrera

39°

B

C

0   10   20   30 km

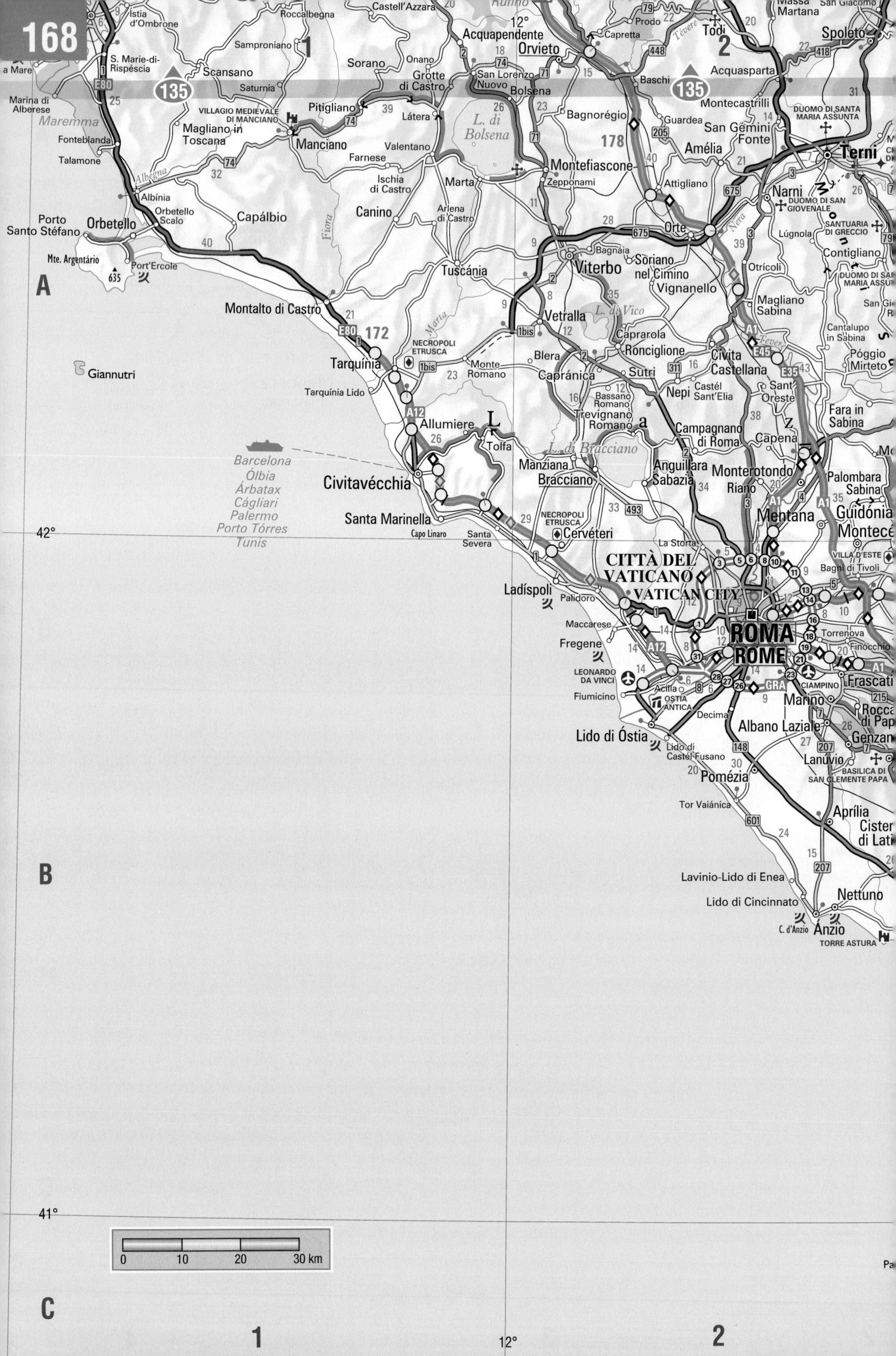
Ístia d'Ombrone
Roccalbegna
Castell'Azzara
Acquapendente
Orvieto
Prodo
Capretta
Todi
Massa Martana
San Giacomo
Spoleto
Sampronìano
S. Marie-di-Rispéscia
Scansano
Sorano
Onano
Grotte di Castro
San Lorenzo Nuovo
Bolsena
Baschi
Acquasparta
Saturnia
Pitigliano
Látera
Montecastrilli
Marina di Alberese
Maremma
VILLAGIO MEDIEVALE DI MANCIANO
Magliano in Toscana
Manciano
Valentano
L. di Bolsena
Bagnorégio
Guardea
San Gémini Fonte
DUOMO DI SANTA MARIA ASSUNTA
Fonteblanda
Talamone
Farnese
Amélia
Terni
Montefiascone
Zepponami
Albegna
Albínia
Ischia di Castro
Marta
Attigliano
Narni
DUOMO DI SAN GIOVENALE
Orbetello Scalo
Arlena di Castro
Porto Santo Stéfano
Orbetello
Capálbio
Canino
Orte
Nera
SANTUARIA DI GRECCIO
Lúgnola
Fiora
Bagnáia
Contigliano
Mte. Argentário
Port'Ercole
Tuscánia
Viterbo
Soriano nel Cimino
Otrícoli
Vignanello
DUOMO DI SAN MARIA ASSUNTA
Montalto di Castro
Vetralla
L. di Vico
Magliano Sabina
Caprarola
Ronciglione
Cantalupo in Sabina
Tarquínia
NECROPOLI ETRUSCA
Monte Romano
Blera
Civita Castellana
Póggio Mirteto
Giannutri
Caprânica
Sutri
Tarquínia Lido
Bassano Romano
Nepi
Castél Sant'Elia
Sant'Oreste
Trevignano Romano
Allumiere
Tolfa
Campagnano di Roma
Capena
Fara in Sabina
L. di Bracciano
Barcelona
Ólbia
Árbatax
Cágliari
Palermo
Porto Tórres
Tunis
Civitavécchia
Manziana
Bracciano
Anguillara Sabazia
Monterotondo
Riano
Palombara Sabina
Santa Marinella
Capo Linaro
Santa Severa
Cervéteri
Mentana
Guidónia
Montecel
La Storta
CITTÀ DEL VATICANO
VATICAN CITY
VILLA D'ESTE
Bagni di Tivoli
Ladíspoli
Palidoro
Maccarese
ROMA
ROME
Torrenova
Fregene
Finócchio
LEONARDO DA VINCI
CIAMPINO
Frascati
Fiumicino
Acilia
OSTIA ANTICA
Marino
Rocca di Papa
Decima
Albano Laziale
Genzano
Lido di Óstia
Lido di Castél Fusano
Lanúvio
BASILICA DI SAN CLEMENTE PAPA
Pomézia
Tor Vaiánica
Aprília
Cisterna di Latina
Lavinio-Lido di Enea
Lido di Cincinnato
Nettuno
C. d'Anzio
Anzio
TORRE ASTURA
12°
42°
41°
A
B
C
1
2
0
10
20
30 km

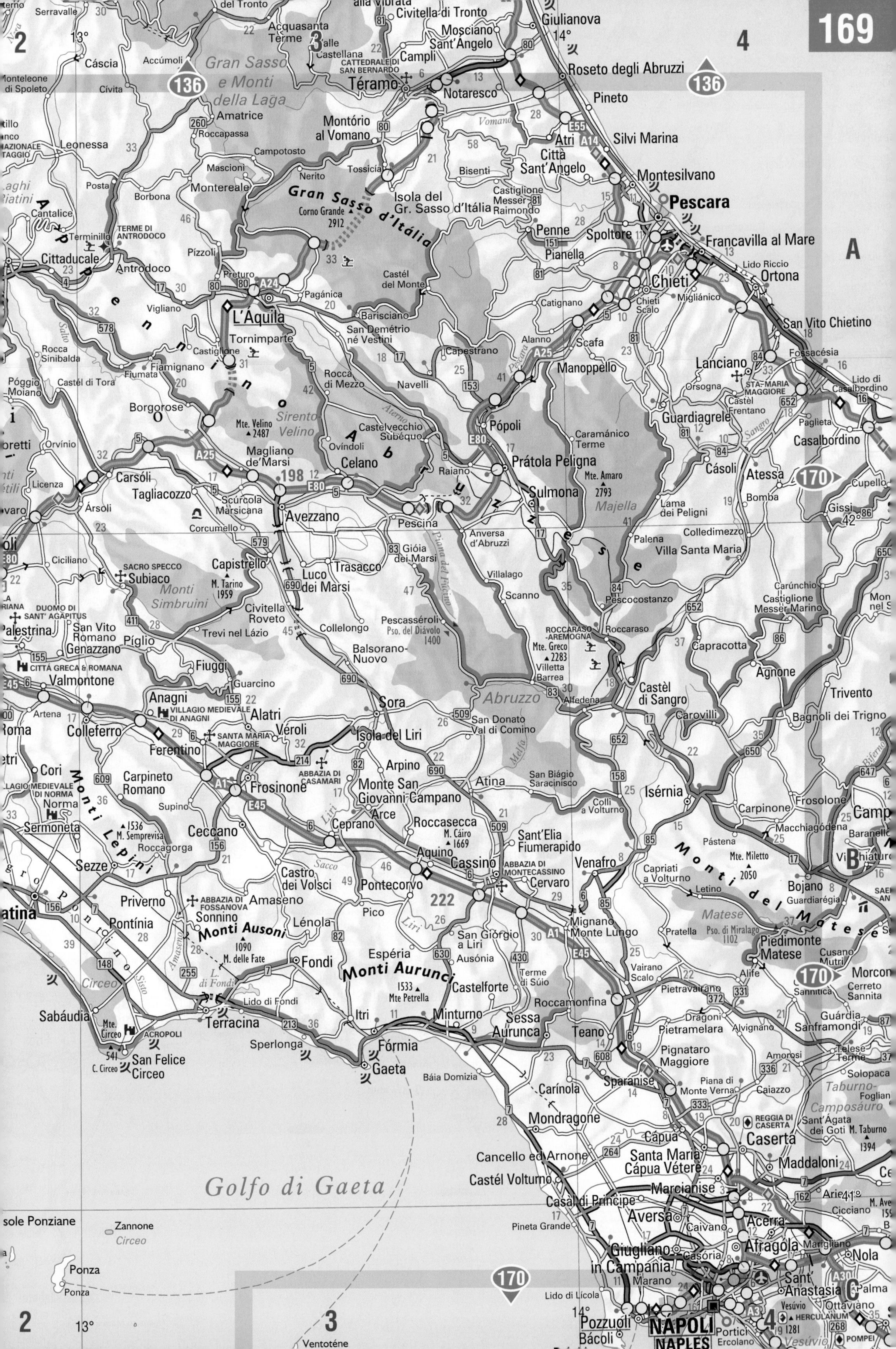
Gran Sasso e Monti della Laga
Gran Sasso d'Itália
Corno Grande 2912
Appennino
Abruzzo
Sirento Velino
Mte. Velino 2487
Monti Simbruini
M. Tarino 1959
Monti Lepini
M. Semprevisa 1536
Monti Ausoni
M. delle Fate 1090
Monti Aurunci
Mte Petrella 1533
M. Cáiro 1669
Majella
Mte. Amaro 2793
Mte. Greco 2283
Monti del Matese
Mte. Miletto 2050
Pso. di Miralago 1102
M. Taburno 1394
Taburno-Camposáuro
Golfo di Gaeta
Piana del Fúcino
Serravalle
Civitella di Tronto
Giulianova
Mosciano Sant'Angelo
Acquasanta Terme
Valle Castellana
Accúmoli
Cáscia
Campli
CATTEDRALE DI SAN BERNARDO
Téramo
Notaresco
Roseto degli Abruzzi
Pineto
Monteleone di Spoleto
Cívita
Amatrice
Roccapassa
Montório al Vomano
Atri
Silvi Marina
Città Sant'Angelo
Montesilvano
Pescara
Leonessa
Campotosto
Mascioni
Nerito
Tossícia
Bisenti
Posta
Borbona
Montereale
Isola del Gr. Sasso d'Itália
Castiglione Messer Raimondo
Cantalice
Terminillo
TERME DI ANTRODOCO
Pízzoli
Penne
Spoltore
Francavilla al Mare
Pianella
Cittaducale
Antrodoco
Preturo
Castél del Monte
Chieti
Chieti Scalo
Lido Riccio
Ortona
Miglianico
Vigliano
L'Áquila
Pagánica
Barisciano
Catignano
San Vito Chietino
Tornimparte
San Demétrio né Vestini
Alanno
Scafa
Rocca Sinibalda
Castiglione
Fiamignano
Fiumata
Capestrano
Manoppello
Lanciano
Fossacésia
Póggio Moiano
Castél di Tora
Rocca di Mezzo
Navelli
Orsogna
STA. MARIA MAGGIORE
Castél Frentano
Lido di Casalbordino
Borgorose
Pópoli
Guardiagrele
Paglieta
Caramánico Terme
Castelvecchio Subéquo
Casalbordino
Orvínio
Magliano de'Marsi
Ovíndoli
Celano
Raiano
Prátola Peligna
Cásoli
Atessa
Cupello
Licenza
Carsóli
Tagliacozzo
Sulmona
Bomba
Gissi
Ársoli
Scúrcola Marsicana
Avezzano
Pescina
Lama dei Peligni
Corcumello
Anversa d'Abruzzi
Palena
Colledimezzo
Villa Santa Maria
Ciciliano
Capistrello
Gióia dei Marsi
Trasacco
Luco dei Marsi
SACRO SPECCO
Subiaco
Villalago
Carúnchio
Castiglione Messer Marino
Scanno
Pescocostanzo
DUOMO DI SANT' AGAPITUS
Palestrina
Civitella Roveto
San Vito Romano
Genazzano
Píglio
Trevi nel Lázio
Collelongo
Pescasséroli
Pso. del Diávolo 1400
ROCCARASO-AREMOGNA
Roccaraso
Capracotta
Balsorano-Nuovo
Villetta Barrea
CITTÁ GRECA & ROMANA
Fiuggi
Agnone
Valmontone
Guarcino
Castèl di Sangro
Trivento
Anagni
VILLAGIO MEDIEVALE DI ANAGNI
Alatri
Sora
Alfedena
Artena
Roma
Colleferro
San Donato Val di Comino
Carovilli
Bagnoli dei Trigno
SANTA MARIA MAGGIORE
Véroli
Isola del Liri
Ferentino
Cori
ABBAZIA DI CASAMARI
Arpino
Carpineto Romano
Frosinone
Monte San Giovanni Campano
Atina
San Biágio Saracinisco
Isérnia
Frosolone
Colli a Volturno
Carpinone
VILLAGIO MEDIEVALE DI NORMA
Norma
Supino
Arce
Ceprano
Roccasecca
Sant'Elia Fiumerapido
Macchiagódena
Sermoneta
Ceccano
Roccagorga
Aquino
Cassino
ABBAZIA DI MONTECASSINO
Venafro
Pástena
Baranello
Sezze
Castro dei Volsci
Pontecorvo
Cervaro
Capriati a Volturno
Letino
Bojano
Guardiarégia
Latina
Priverno
ABBAZIA DI FOSSANOVA
Amaseno
Pico
Sonnino
Pontínia
Lénola
Mignano Monte Lungo
Pratella
Matese
Piedimonte Matese
Cusano Mutri
San Giórgio a Liri
Espéria
Ausónia
Fondi
Terme di Súio
Vairano Scalo
Alife
Morcone
Cerreto Sannita
Circeo
Lido di Fondi
Castelforte
Pietravairano
Terracina
Roccamonfina
Sabáudia
Mte. Circeo 541
ACROPOLI
Itri
Minturno
Sessa Aurunca
Teano
Dragoni
Alvignano
Pietramelara
Guárdia Sanframondi
Sperlonga
Fórmia
Pignataro Maggiore
Telese Terme
Amorosi
San Felice Circeo
C. Circeo
Gaeta
Báia Domízia
Solopaca
Sparanise
Carínola
Piana di Monte Verna
Caiazzo
Mondragone
REGGIA DI CASERTA
Sant'Ágata dei Goti
Cápua
Caserta
Cancello ed Arnone
Santa Maria Cápua Vétere
Maddaloni
Castél Volturno
Marcianise
Casal di Principe
Arienzo
Aversa
Caivano
Acerra
Cicciano
Pineta Grande
Isole Ponziane
Zannone
Giugliano in Campania
Casória
Afragola
Marigliano
Nola
Ponza
Marano
Sant'Anastasia
Palma
Lido di Lícola
Pozzuoli
Bácoli
NÁPOLI NAPLES
Pórtici
Ercolano
Vesúvio 1281
HERCULANEUM
Ottaviano
POMPEI
Ventoténe
Vomano
Aterno
Pescara
Sangro
Liri
Sacco
Melfa
Biferno
Sisto
Salto
A14
A24
A25
A1
A30
A3
E45
E55
E80
136
170
198
222

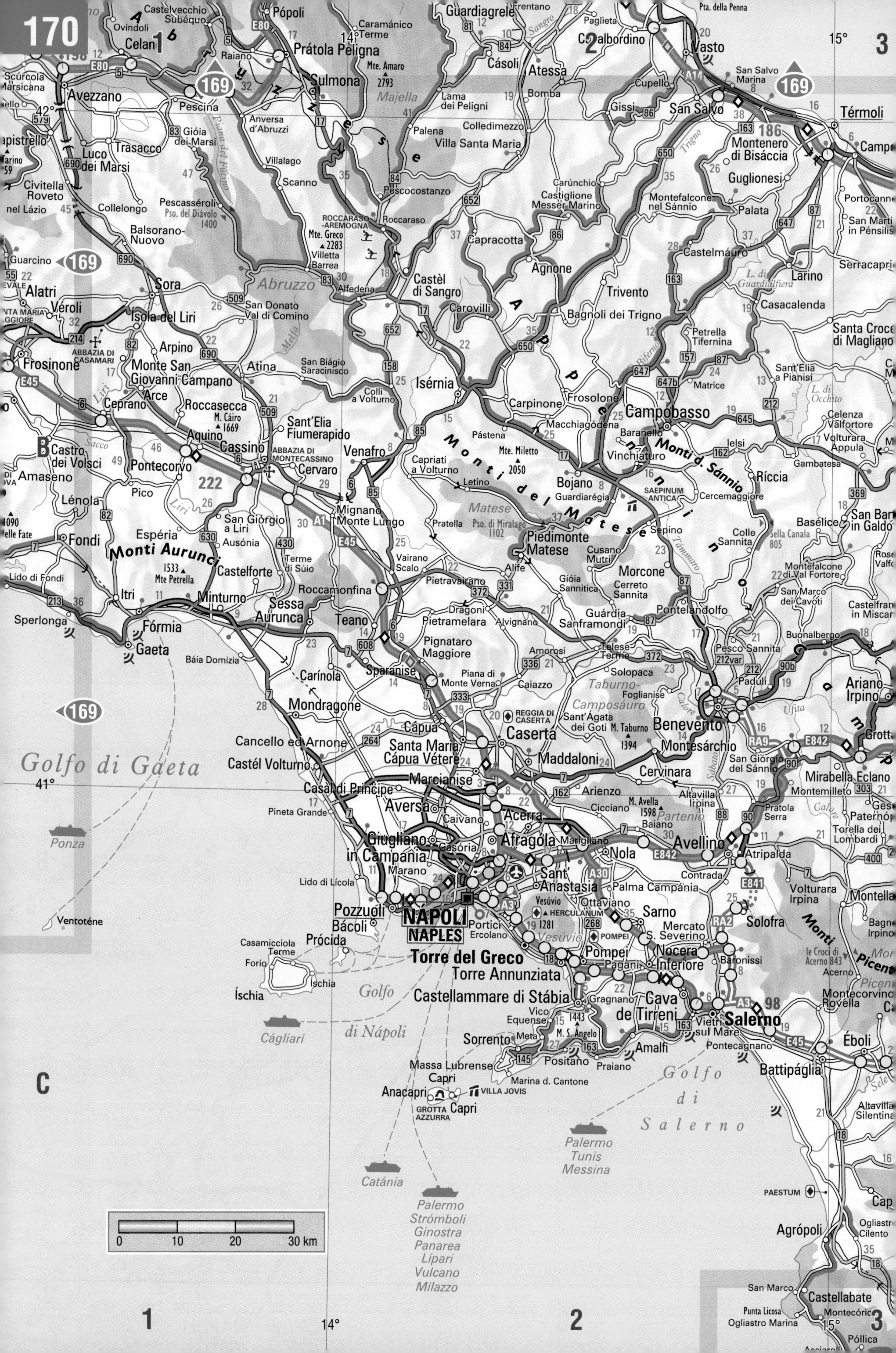
Castelvecchio Subéquo
Ovindoli
Celano
Pópoli
Caramánico Terme
Guardiagrele
Frentano
Paglieta
Casalbordino
Pta. della Penna
Vasto
Prátola Peligna
Cásoli
Atessa
Raiano
Sulmona
Mte. Amaro 2793
Majella
Scúrcola Marsicana
Avezzano
Pescina
Bomba
Cupello
San Salvo Marina
Lama dei Peligni
Gissi
San Salvo
Térmoli
Anversa d'Abruzzi
Palena
Colledimezzo
Villa Santa Maria
Montenero di Bisáccia
Trasacco
Gióia dei Marsi
Luco dei Marsi
Villalago
Guglionesi
Scanno
Civitella Roveto
Pescocostanzo
Carúnchio
Castiglione Messer Marino
Montefalcone nel Sánnio
Palata
Portocannone
Collelongo
Pescasséroli
Pso. del Diávolo 1400
Roccaraso
ROCCARASO -AREMOGNA
San Martino in Pénsilis
Balsorano-Nuovo
Mte. Greco 2283
Capracotta
Villetta Barrea
Castelmáuro
Guarcino
Agnone
Serracapriola
Alatri
Abruzzo
Alfedena
Castèl di Sangro
L. di Guardialfiera
Larino
Sora
Trivento
Véroli
San Donato Val di Comino
Carovilli
Casacalenda
Ísola del Liri
Bagnoli dei Trigno
Santa Croce di Magliano
Petrella Tifernina
ABBAZIA DI CASAMARI
Arpino
Frosinone
Monte San Giovanni Campano
Atina
San Biágio Saracinisco
Sant'Elia a Pianisi
Arce
Isérnia
Matrice
Ceprano
Colli a Volturno
Frosolone
Campobasso
Roccasecca
Carpinone
L. di Occhito
M. Cáiro 1669
Celenza Valfortore
Aquino
Sant'Elia Fiumerapido
Macchiagódena
Baranello
Castro dei Volsci
Cassino
Pástena
Monti d. Sánnio
Volturara Áppula
Pontecorvo
ABBAZIA DI MONTECASSINO
Venafro
Vinchiaturo
Ielsi
Amaseno
Cervaro
Mte. Miletto 2050
Gambatesa
Capriati a Volturno
Ríccia
Pico
Letino
Bojano
Guardiarégia
Lénola
SAEPINUM ANTICA
Cercemaggiore
Mignano Monte Lungo
Matese
San Bartolomeo in Galdo
Pratella
Pso. di Miralago 1102
Basélice
San Giórgio a Liri
Sepino
Fondi
Espéria
Ausónia
Piedimonte Matese
Colle Sannita
Sella Canala 805
Monti Aurunci
Terme di Súio
Cusano Mutri
Vairano Scalo
Alife
1533 Mte Petrella
Castelforte
Morcone
Montefalcone di Val Fortore
Lido di Fondi
Itri
Pietravairano
Gióia Sannitica
Cerreto Sannita
San Marco dei Cavoti
Roccamonfina
Minturno
Sessa Aurunca
Dragoni
Pontelandolfo
Castelfranco in Miscano
Sperlonga
Fórmia
Teano
Pietramelara
Alvignano
Guárdia Sanframondi
Buonalbergo
Gaeta
Pignataro Maggiore
Amorosi
Telese Terme
Pesco Sannita
Báia Domizia
Carínola
Sparanise
Piana di Monte Verna
Caiazzo
Solopaca
Padùli
Ariano Irpino
Taburno-Camposáuro
Foglianise
Mondragone
REGGIA DI CASERTA
Sant'Ágata dei Goti
M. Taburno 1394
Benevento
Cápua
Caserta
Cancello ed Arnone
Santa Maria Cápua Vétere
Montesárchio
San Giórgio del Sánnio
Mirabella Eclano
Golfo di Gaeta
Castél Volturno
Maddaloni
Cervinara
Montemilleto
Marcianise
Casal di Principe
Arienzo
Altavilla Irpina
Pratola Serra
Aversa
Cicciano
M. Avella 1598
Baiano
Partenio
Paternópoli
Pineta Grande
Caivano
Acerra
Torella dei Lombardi
Ponza
Giugliano in Campania
Afragola
Marigliano
Avellino
Casória
Nola
Atripalda
Lido di Lícola
Marano
Sant'Anastasia
Contrada
Palma Campania
Volturara Irpina
Montella
Pozzuoli
Bácoli
NÁPOLI
NAPLES
Portici
Ercolano
Ottaviano
Sarno
Solofra
Monti Picentini
Ventoténe
Vesúvio 1281
HERCULANUM
POMPEI
Mercato S. Severino
Casamicciola Terme
Prócida
Torre del Greco
Pompei
Nocera Inferiore
Baronissi
Le Croci di Acerno 843
Acerno
Forío
Torre Annunziata
Pagani
Íschia
Golfo di Nápoli
Castellammare di Stábia
Gragnano
Cava de' Tirreni
Montecorvino Rovella
Vico Equense
M. S. Angelo 1443
Vietri sul Mare
Salerno
Cágliari
Sorrento
Meta
Positano
Amalfi
Praiano
Pontecagnano
Éboli
Battipáglia
Massa Lubrense
Capri
Anacapri
VILLA JOVIS
Marina d. Cantone
GROTTA AZZURRA
Golfo di Salerno
Altavilla Silentina
Palermo
Tunis
Messina
Catánia
PAESTUM
Strómboli
Ginostra
Panarea
Lípari
Vulcano
Milazzo
Agrópoli
Ogliastro Cilento
0 10 20 30 km
San Marco
Castellabate
Punta Licosa
Ogliastro Marina
Montecórice
Póllica
A B C
1 2 3
14° 15° 41° 42°
169 222 186 98

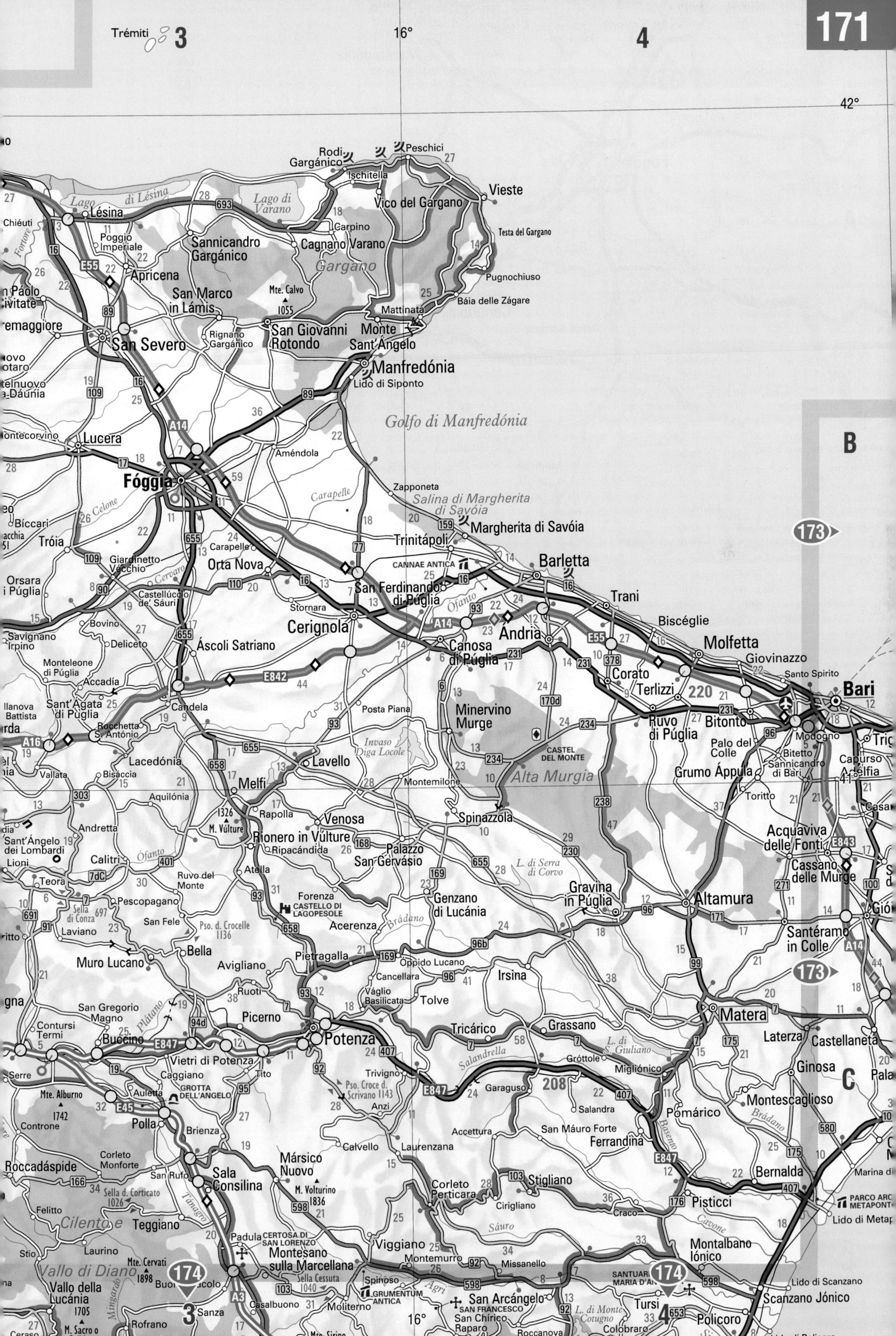

Trémiti
3
16°
4
42°
B
C
173
174
Rodi Gargánico
Peschici
Ischitella
Vieste
Lago di Lésina
Lago di Varano
Lésina
Chiéuti
Vico del Gargano
Carpino
Testa del Gargano
Poggio Imperiale
Sannicandro Gargánico
Cagnano Varano
Gargano
Apricena
Pugnochiuso
San Páolo Civitate
San Marco in Lámis
Mte. Calvo
1055
Báia delle Zágare
Mattinata
San Severo
Rignano Gargánico
San Giovanni Rotondo
Monte Sant'Angelo
Manfredónia
Lido di Siponto
Golfo di Manfredónia
Lucera
Fóggia
Améndola
Zapponeta
Salina di Margherita di Savóia
Carapelle
Celone
Bíccari
Tróia
Margherita di Savóia
Trinitápoli
Carapelle
Giardinetto Vecchio
Orta Nova
Cervaro
CANNAE ANTICA
Barletta
Orsara di Púglia
Castellúccio de' Sáuri
San Ferdinando di Púglia
Ófanto
Trani
Stornara
Bovino
Cerignola
Ándria
Bisceglie
Savignano Irpino
Deliceto
Áscoli Satriano
Canosa di Púglia
Molfetta
Giovinazzo
Monteleone di Púglia
Accadía
Corato
Santo Spirito
Bari
Terlizzi
Sant'Ágata di Púglia
Candela
Posta Piana
Minervino Murge
Ruvo di Púglia
Bitonto
Rocchetta S. António
Invaso Diga Locone
Modugno
Lacedónia
Lavello
CASTEL DEL MONTE
Palo del Colle
Bitetto
Sannicandro di Bari
Capurso
Vallata
Bisáccia
Melfi
Montemilone
Alta Murgia
Grumo Áppula
Aquilónia
Rapolla
Spinazzola
Toritto
1326
M. Vúlture
Sant'Ángelo dei Lombardi
Andretta
Venosa
Acquaviva delle Fonti
Lioni
Rionero in Vúlture
Ripacándida
Palazzo San Gervásio
Calitri
Ófanto
L. di Serra di Corvo
Cassano delle Murge
Teora
Atella
Ruvo del Monte
Gravina in Púglia
Altamura
Sella di Conza 697
Pescopagano
Forenza
CASTELLO DI LAGOPESOLE
Genzano di Lucánia
Laviano
San Fele
Pso. d. Crocelle 1136
Acerenza
Bradano
Santéramo in Colle
Muro Lucano
Bella
Pietragalla
Óppido Lucano
Avigliano
Cancellara
Irsina
Ruoti
Váglio Basilicata
Tolve
San Gregorio Magno
Picerno
Matera
Contursi Termi
Buccino
Plátano
Potenza
Tricárico
Grassano
Laterza
Castellaneta
Vietri di Potenza
L. di S. Giuliano
Serre
Caggiano
Tito
Trivigno
Grottole
Miglionico
Ginosa
Salandrella
GROTTA DELL'ANGELO
Pso. Croce d. Scrivano 1143
Garaguso
Mte. Alburno
1742
Auletta
Anzi
Montescaglioso
Salandra
Pomárico
Controne
Polla
Brienza
Accettura
San Máuro Forte
Ferrandina
Bradano
Basento
Calvello
Laurenzana
Corleto Monforte
Roccadáspide
San Rufo
Mársico Nuovo
Bernalda
Sala Consilina
Stigliano
M. Volturino 1836
Sella d. Corticato 1026
Corleto Perticara
Cirigliano
Pisticci
PARCO ARC METAPONT
Felitto
Cilento e
Teggiano
Craco
Lido di Metap
Tánagro
Cavone
Sáuro
Padula
CERTOSA DI SAN LORENZO
Stio
Laurino
Montesano sulla Marcellana
Viggiano
Montemurro
Montalbano Iónico
Vallo di Diano
Mte. Cervati 1898
Missanello
Vallo della Lucánia
Sella Cessuta 1040
Spinoso
GRUMENTUM ANTICA
Agri
San Arcángelo
SAN FRANCESCO
SANTUARIO MARIA D'A
Lido di Scanzano
Scanzano Jónico
1705
Casalbuono
Sanza
Rofrano
Moliterno
San Chírico Raparo
L. di Monte Cotugno
Tursi
Colobraro
Policoro
Ceraso
M. Sacro o Gelbison
Mingardo
Mte. Sirino
Roccanova
Lido di Policoro
Marina di
A14
A16
A3
E55
E842
E847
E45
E843

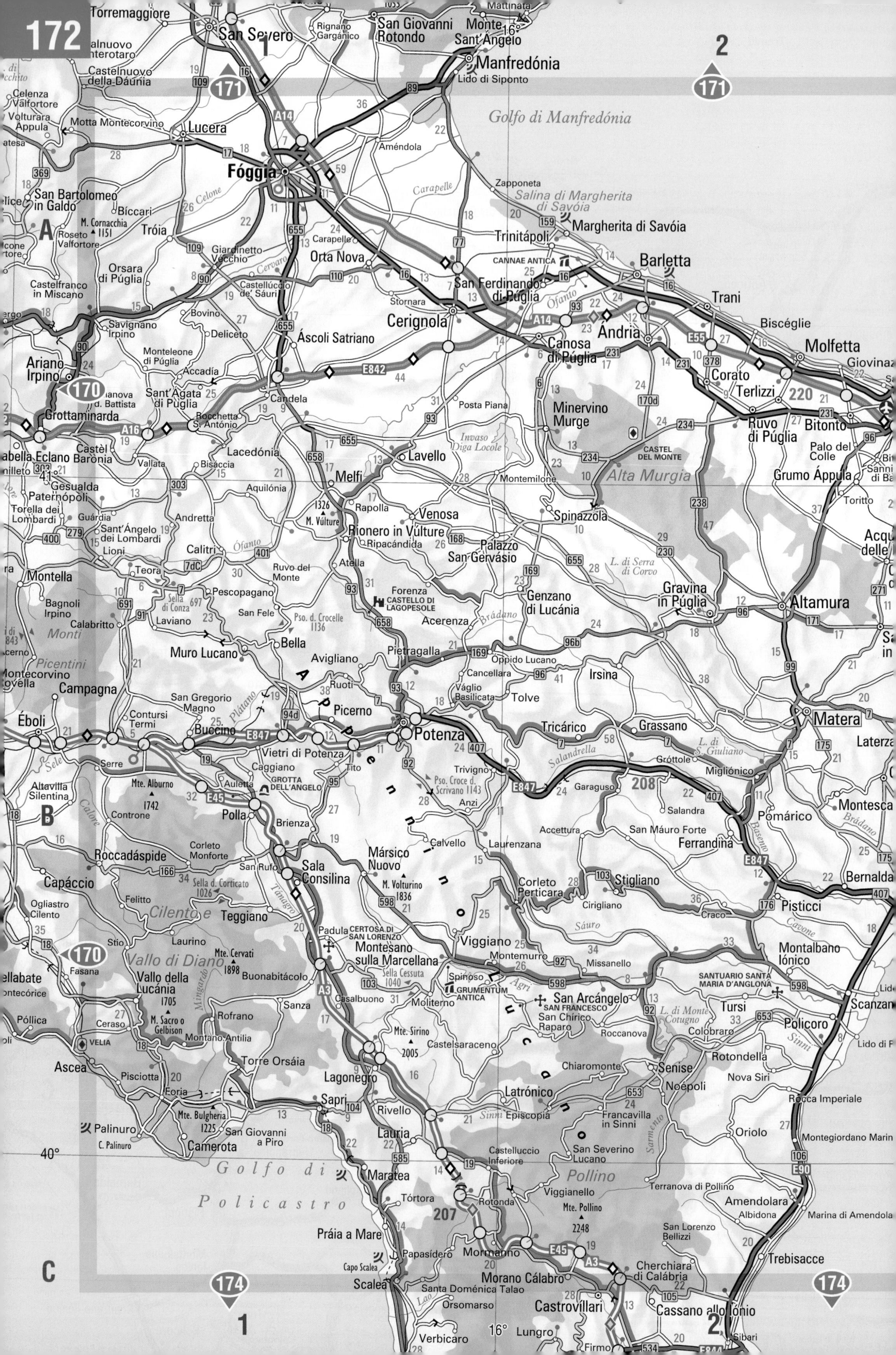

Torremaggiore
San Severo
San Giovanni Rotondo
Monte Sant'Ángelo
Manfredónia
Lido di Siponto
Golfo di Manfredónia
Lucera
Fóggia
Castelnuovo della Dáunia
Motta Montecorvino
San Bartolomeo in Galdo
Bíccari
Tróia
Orsara di Púglia
Castelfranco in Miscano
Amendola
Zapponeta
Salina di Margherita di Savóia
Margherita di Savóia
Trinitápoli
Orta Nova
Carapelle
Stornara
Cerignola
San Ferdinando di Púglia
Barletta
Trani
Bisceglie
Molfetta
Ándria
Canosa di Púglia
Corato
Terlizzi
Ruvo di Púglia
Bitonto
Áscoli Satriano
Ariano Irpino
Grottaminarda
Sant'Agata di Puglia
Candela
Rocchetta S. António
Lacedónia
Minervino Murge
Castel del Monte
Alta Murgia
Lavello
Melfi
Rapolla
Venosa
Rionero in Vúlture
Spinazzola
Palazzo San Gervásio
Genzano di Lucánia
Gravina in Púglia
Altamura
Grumo Áppula
Montella
Calitri
Muro Lucano
Bella
Avigliano
Pietragalla
Oppido Lucano
Irsina
Tolve
Éboli
Campagna
Buccino
Potenza
Tricárico
Grassano
Matera
Laterza
Polla
Sala Consilina
Marsico Nuovo
Montescaglioso
Pomárico
Ferrandina
Stigliano
Pisticci
Bernalda
Capáccio
Roccadáspide
Teggiano
Viggiano
Montemurro
Montalbano Iónico
Scanzano
Policoro
Tursi
San Arcángelo
Senise
Rotondella
Nova Siri
Lagonegro
Lauria
Latrónico
Sapri
Maratea
Palinuro
Camerota
Ascea
Golfo di Policastro
Práia a Mare
Scalea
Mormanno
Rotonda
Castrovillari
Morano Cálabro
Cassano allo Iónio
Trebisacce
Amendolara
Oriolo
Pollino
Mte. Pollino 2248
Vallo di Diano
Cilento e
Appennino Lucano

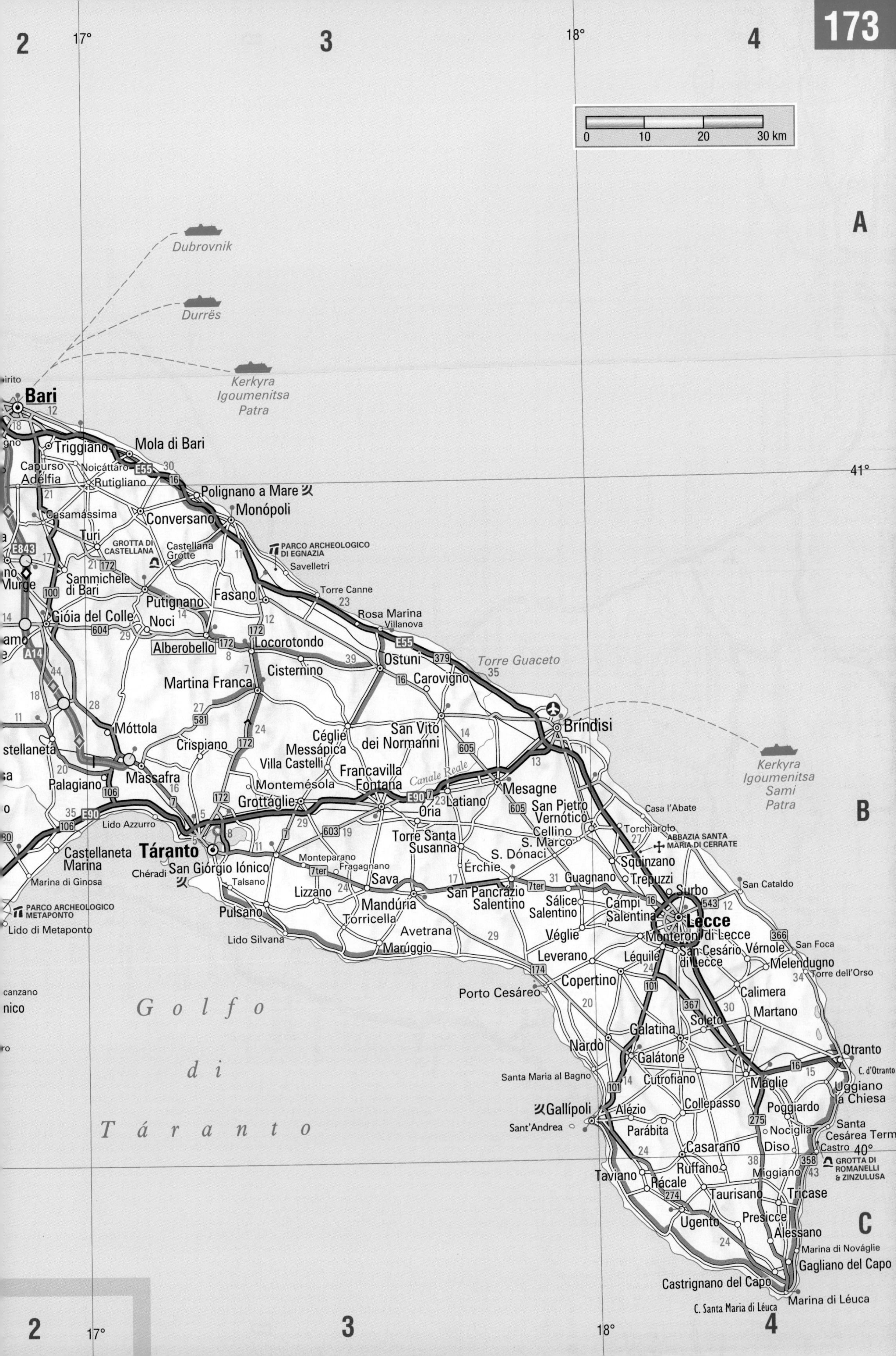

2   17°   3   18°   4

A

0   10   20   30 km

Dubrovnik

Durrës

Kerkyra
Igoumenitsa
Patra

spirito
Bari
12
18
gno   Triggiano   Mola di Bari
Capurso   Noicáttaro   E55   30
Adélfia   Rutigliano   16   41°
21   Polignano a Mare
Casamássima   Conversano   Monópoli
Turi   GROTTA DI   Castellana
CASTELLANA   Grotte   PARCO ARCHEOLOGICO
604   172   11   DI EGNAZIA
Sammichele   Putignano   Savelletri
di Bari   Noci   Fasano   Torre Canne
Gióia del Colle   172   23   Rosa Marina
100   Alberobello   172   Locorotondo   Villanova
14   604   29   8   7   39   Ostuni   379   *Torre Guaceto*
amo   Martina Franca   Cisternino   16   Carovigno   35
14   E55
18   28   27   Céglie   San Vito   14   Brindisi
Móttola   581   Messápica   dei Normanni   605   13   11
11   24   Villa Castelli   Kerkyra
stellaneta   Crispiano   172   Montemésola   Francavilla   Igoumenitsa
20   Palagiano   Massafra   172   Grottáglie   Fontana   *Canale Reale*   Mesagne   Sami   B
106   16   603   19   E90   7   Latiano   San Pietro   Casa l'Abate   Patra
35   E90   7   5   Oria   605   Vernótico   Torchiarolo
106   Lido Azzurro   29   Torre Santa   Cellino   27   ABBAZIA SANTA
30   8   11   Susanna   S. Marco   MARIA DI CERRATE
Táranto   7   Monteparano   Fragagnano   S. Dónaci   Squinzano   San Cataldo
Castellaneta   Chéradi   San Giórgio Iónico   7ter   Érchie   31   Guagnano   Trepuzzi
Marina   Talsano   24   Sava   17   San Pancrázio   7ter   Sálice   Campi   16   Surbo   543   12
Marina di Ginosa   Lizzano   Mandúria   Salentino   Salentino   Salentina   San Cataldo   **Lecce**
PARCO ARCHEOLOGICO   Pulsano   Torricella   Véglie   Léquile   Monteroni di Lecce   366
METAPONTO   Avetrana   29   Leverano   24   San Cesário   Vérnole   San Foca
Lido di Metaponto   Marúggio   Copertino   101   di Lecce   Melendugno
174   367   30   Calimera   34   Torre dell'Orso
canzano   *G o l f o*   Porto Cesáreo   20   101   Soleto   Martano
nico   Nardò   Galatina
ro   *d i*   Santa Maria al Bagno   14   Galátone   Cutrofiano   Otranto
Santa   16   15
T á r a n t o   **Gallípoli**   Alézio   Collepasso   Máglie   C. d'Otranto
Sant'Andrea   Parábita   Poggiardo   Uggiano
275   la Chiesa
24   Nociglia   Santa
Casarano   Cesárea Term
Ruffano   38   Diso   Castro   40°
Taviano   Miggiano   358   GROTTA DI
274   Rácale   43   ROMANELLI
Ugento   Taurisano   Tricase   & ZINZULUSA
Presicce
Alessano   C
24   Marina di Nováglie
Gagliano del Capo
Castrignano del Capo   Marina di Léuca
C. Santa Maria di Léuca

2   17°   3   18°   4

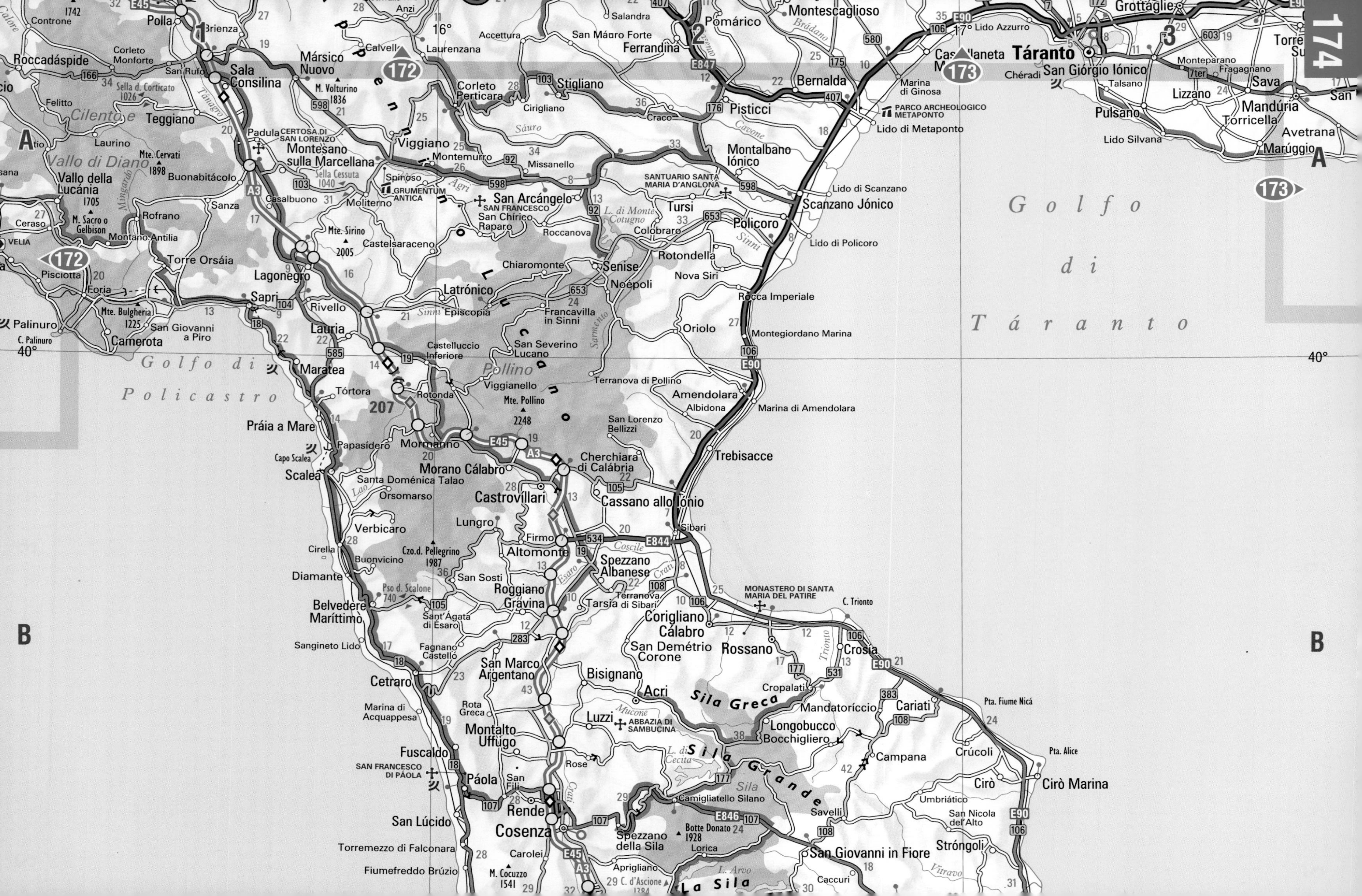

Golfo di Táranto
Golfo di Policastro
Táranto
Grottáglie
San Giórgio Iónico
Chéradi
Lido Azzurro
Castellaneta Marina
Talsano
Pulsano
Lido Silvana
Lizzano
Monteparano
Fragagnano
Sava
Mandúria
Torricella
Avetrana
Marúggio
Montescaglioso
Pomárico
Salandra
San Máuro Forte
Ferrandina
Bernalda
Marina di Ginosa
PARCO ARCHEOLOGICO METAPONTO
Lido di Metaponto
Pisticci
Montalbano Iónico
Lido di Scanzano
Scanzano Jónico
Policoro
Lido di Policoro
Tursi
SANTUARIO SANTA MARIA D'ANGLONA
Colobraro
Rotondella
Nova Siri
Rocca Imperiale
Oriolo
Montegiordano Marina
Amendolara
Albidona
Marina di Amendolara
Trebisacce
Terranova di Pollino
San Lorenzo Bellizzi
Cherchiara di Calábria
Cassano allo Ionio
Sibari
Stigliano
Cirigliano
Craco
Accettura
Corleto Perticara
Laurenzana
Anzi
Calvello
Mársico Nuovo
M. Volturino 1836
Viggiano
Montemurro
Missanello
San Arcángelo
SAN FRANCESCO
San Chírico Raparo
Roccanova
Spinoso
GRUMENTUM ANTICA
Moliterno
Mte. Sirino 2005
Castelsaraceno
Chiaromonte
Senise
Noépoli
L. di Monte Cotugno
Francavilla in Sinni
San Severino Lucano
Latrónico
Episcopia
Castelluccio Inferiore
Viggianello
Pollino
Mte. Pollino 2248
Rotonda
Mormanno
Morano Cálabro
Castrovíllari
Lungro
Firmo
Altomonte
Spezzano Albanese
Terranova
Tarsia di Sibari
Roggiano Grávina
San Sosti
Corigliano Cálabro
Rossano
San Demétrio Corone
MONASTERO DI SANTA MARIA DEL PATIRE
C. Trionto
Crosia
Cropalati
Mandatoríccio
Cariati
Pta. Fiume Nicá
Longobucco
Bocchigliero
Campana
Crúcoli
Pta. Alice
Cirò
Cirò Marina
Umbriático
San Nicola dell'Alto
Stróngoli
Savelli
San Giovanni in Fiore
Caccuri
Sila Greca
Sila Grande
La Sila
Camigliatello Silano
L. di Cecita
Botte Donato 1928
Lorica
Spezzano della Sila
Aprigliano
C. d'Ascione
L. Arvo
Acri
Bisignano
Luzzi
ABBAZIA DI SAMBUCINA
San Marco Argentano
Fagnano Castello
Sant'Ágata di Esaro
Rota Greca
Montalto Uffugo
Rose
San Fili
Rende
Cosenza
Carolei
M. Cocuzzo 1541
Páola
SAN FRANCESCO DI PÁOLA
Fuscaldo
San Lúcido
Torremezzo di Falconara
Fiumefreddo Brúzio
Cetraro
Marina di Acquappesa
Sangineto Lido
Belvedere Maríttimo
Diamante
Cirella
Buonvicino
Pso d. Scalone 740
Czo.d. Pellegrino 1987
Verbicaro
Orsomarso
Santa Doménica Talao
Papasídero
Scalea
Capo Scalea
Práia a Mare
Tórtora
Maratea
Lauria
Rivello
Lagonegro
Sapri
Torre Orsáia
San Giovanni a Piro
Camerota
Mte. Bulgheria 1225
Palinuro
C. Palinuro
Pisciotta
Foria
Ceraso
VELIA
M. Sacro o Gelbison 1705
Montano Antilia
Rofrano
Sanza
Buonabitácolo
Mte. Cervati 1898
Casalbuono
Montesano sulla Marcellana
Sella Cessuta 1040
Padula
CERTOSA DI SAN LORENZO
Sala Consilina
San Rufo
Teggiano
Polla
Brienza
Corleto Monforte
Roccadáspide
Sella d. Corticato 1026
Felitto
Controne
Calore
Cilento
Vallo di Diano
Vallo della Lucánia
Laurino
Apennino Lucano
207
172
173
40°
16°
17°
A
B

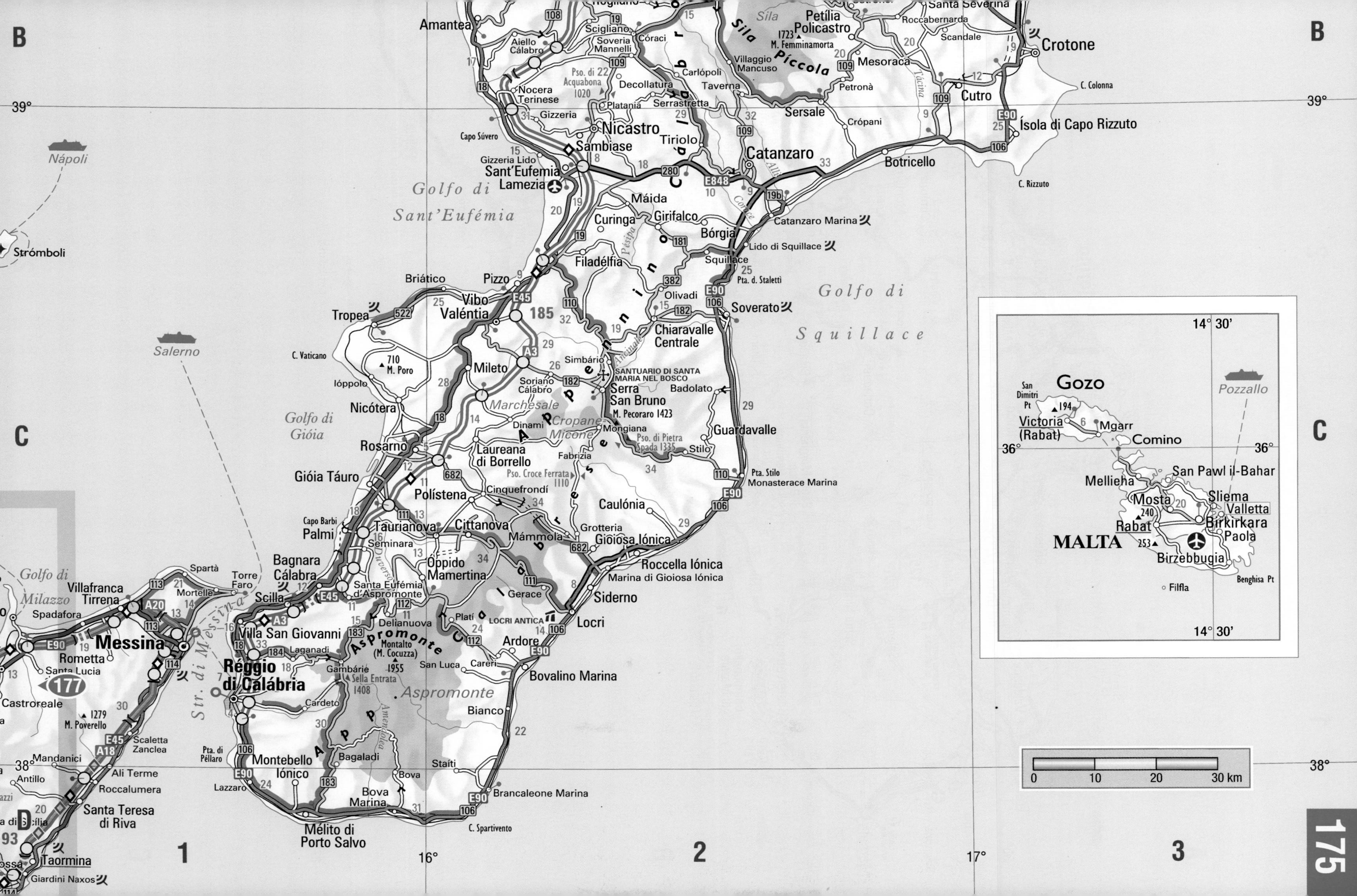

B

C

Inset map: Malta & Gozo

Gozo

San Dimitri Pt

Victoria (Rabat) ▲194

Mgarr 6

Comino

Pozzallo

San Pawl il-Bahar

Mellieha

Mosta 20

MALTA

Rabat ▲253

240

Birzebbugia

San Pawl il-Bahar

Sliema

Valletta

Birkirkara

Paola

Benghisa Pt

Filfla

14° 30'

14° 30'

36°

36°

30 km

20

10

0

Main map (Calabria / Sicily)

Crotone

C. Colonna

Santa Severina

Roccabernarda

Scandale

Isola di Capo Rizzuto

C. Rizzuto

Cutro

Mesoraca

Petilia Policastro

M. Femminamorta 1723

Villaggio Mancuso

Tácina

Petronà

Crópani

Botricello

Sila Piccola

Sila

Catanzaro

Sersale

Carlópoli

Taverna

Serrastretta

Tiriolo

Decollatura

Platania

Soveria Mannelli

Scigliano

Nicastro

Sambiase

Gizzeria

Sant'Eufemia Lamezia

Pso. di Acquabona 1020

Gimigliano

Decollatura

Catanzaro Marina

Lido di Squillace

Borgia

Squillace

Catanzaro Marina

Golfo di Squillace

Girifalco

Maida

Curinga

Filadélfia

Olivadi

Chiaravalle Centrale

Simbário

Serra San Bruno

M. Pecoraro 1423

Santuario di Santa Maria nel Bosco

Badolato

Guardavalle

Pta. Stilo

Monasterace Marina

Stilo

Pso. di Pietra Spada 1133

Roccella Iónica

Marina di Gioiosa Iónica

Gioiosa Iónica

Caulónia

Grotteria

Siderno

Locri

Locri Antica

Ardore

Bovalino Marina

Brancaleone Marina

C. Spartivento

Marchesale

Cropani

Micone

Dinami

Soriano Cálabro

Laureana di Borrello

Cinquefrondi

Fabrizia

Mámmola

Mileto

Vibo Valéntia

Pizzo

Briático

Tropea

C. Vaticano

Nicotera

Rosarno

Gióia Táuro

Capo Barbi

Palmi

Bagnara Cálabra

Scilla

Torre Faro

Villa San Giovanni

Reggio di Calábria

Spartà

Mortelle

Messina

Villafranca Tirrena

Rometta

Spadafora

Castroreale

Polistena

Taurianova

Seminara

Cittanova

Oppido Mamertina

Santa Eufemia d'Aspromonte

Plati

Gerace

Cáreri

San Luca

Aspromonte

M. Cocuzza (M. Montalto) 1955

Gambárie

Sella Entrata

Delianuova

Bagaladi

Bova

Bova Marina

Amendolea

Staiti

Bianco

Montebello Iónico

Cardeto

Melito di Porto Salvo

Lazzaro

Pta. di Pélaro

Str. di Messina

Golfo di Sant'Eufémia

Golfo di Gióia

Ioppolo

M. Poro 710

Strómboli

Golfo di Milazzo

Nápoli

Salerno

Taormina

Giardini Naxos

Santa Teresa di Riva

Alì Terme

Roccalumera

Scaletta Zanclea

Mandanici

M. Poverello 1279

Santa Lucia

Amantea

Aiello Cálabro

Nocera Terinese

Gizzeria Lido

Golfo di Sant'Eufémia

185

A3

B

C

39°

39°

38°

38°

17°

16°

3

2

1

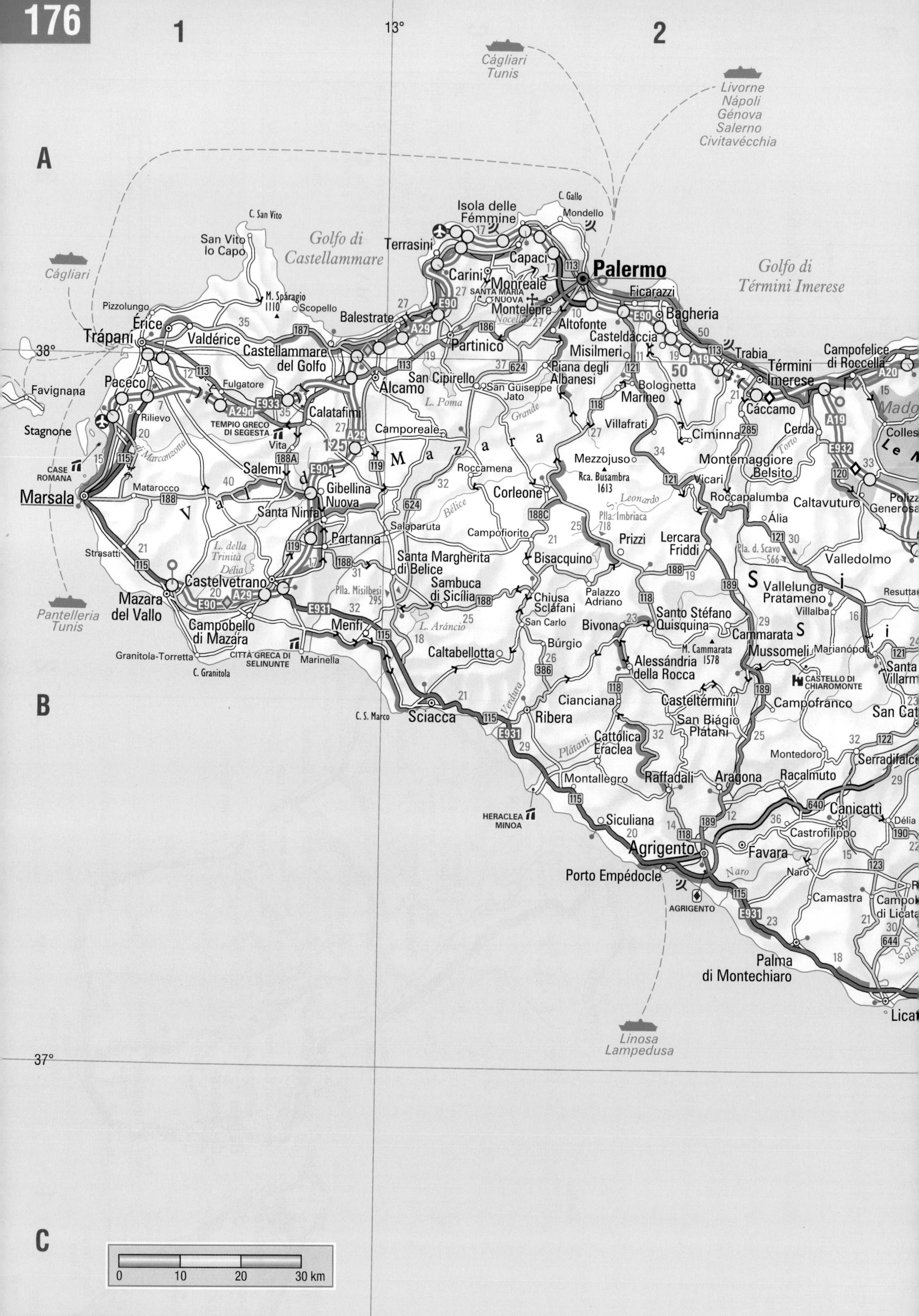
1
13°
2
A
B
C
Cágliari
Tunis
Livorne
Nápoli
Génova
Salerno
Civitavécchia
Cágliari
Pantelleria
Tunis
Linosa
Lampedusa
Golfo di Castellammare
Golfo di Términi Imerese
38°
37°
C. San Vito
San Vito lo Capo
M. Spáragio 1110
Scopello
Isola delle Fémmine
C. Gallo
Mondello
Terrasini
Capaci
Carini
Palermo
Monreale
Ficarazzi
Bagheria
SANTA MARIA NUOVA
Montelepre
Nocella
Altofonte
Casteldáccia
Misilmeri
Trabia
Términi Imerese
Campofelice di Roccella
Balestrate
Partinico
Pizzolungo
Érice
Trápani
Valdérice
Castellammare del Golfo
Favignana
Paceco
Fulgatore
Álcamo
San Cipirello
San Giuseppe Jato
Piana degli Albanesi
Bolognetta
Marineo
Cáccamo
Stagnone
Rilievo
TEMPIO GRECO DI SEGESTA
Calatafimi
Vita
L. Poma
Camporeale
Grande
Villafrati
Ciminna
Cerda
Colles
CASE ROMANA
Marsala
Matarocco
Salemi
Gibellina Nuova
Santa Ninfa
Mazara
Roccamena
Corleone
Mezzojuso
Rca. Busambra 1613
Montemaggiore Belsito
Vicari
Roccapalumba
Caltavuturo
Polizzi Generosa
Bélice
Leonardo
Plla. Imbriaca 718
Prizzi
Lercara Friddi
Ália
Plla. d. Scavo 566
Valledolmo
Strasatti
L. della Trinità
Délia
Partanna
Salaparuta
Campofiorito
Bisacquino
Santa Margherita di Belice
Castelvetrano
Mazara del Vallo
Sambuca di Sicília
Plla. Misilbesi 295
Chiusa Sclafani
Palazzo Adriano
Vallelunga Pratameno
Villalba
Resuttano
Campobello di Mazara
Menfi
L. Aráncio
San Carlo
Bivona
Santo Stéfano Quisquina
Cammarata
M. Cammarata 1578
Mussomeli
Marianópoli
Granitola-Torretta
CITTÀ GRECA DI SELINUNTE
Marinella
C. Granitola
Caltabellotta
Búrgio
Alessándria della Rocca
CASTELLO DI CHIAROMONTE
Santa Caterina Villarmosa
Campofranco
Cianciana
Casteltérmini
San Biágio Plátani
C. S. Marco
Sciacca
Ribera
Verdura
Plátani
Cattólica Eraclea
Montedoro
Serradifalco
Montallegro
Raffadali
Aragona
Racalmuto
HERACLEA MINOA
Canicattì
Siculiana
Castrofilippo
Délia
Agrigento
Favara
Porto Empédocle
Naro
AGRIGENTO
Camastra
Campobello di Licata
Palma di Montechiaro
Licata
Salso
0
10
20
30 km

1 13° 2

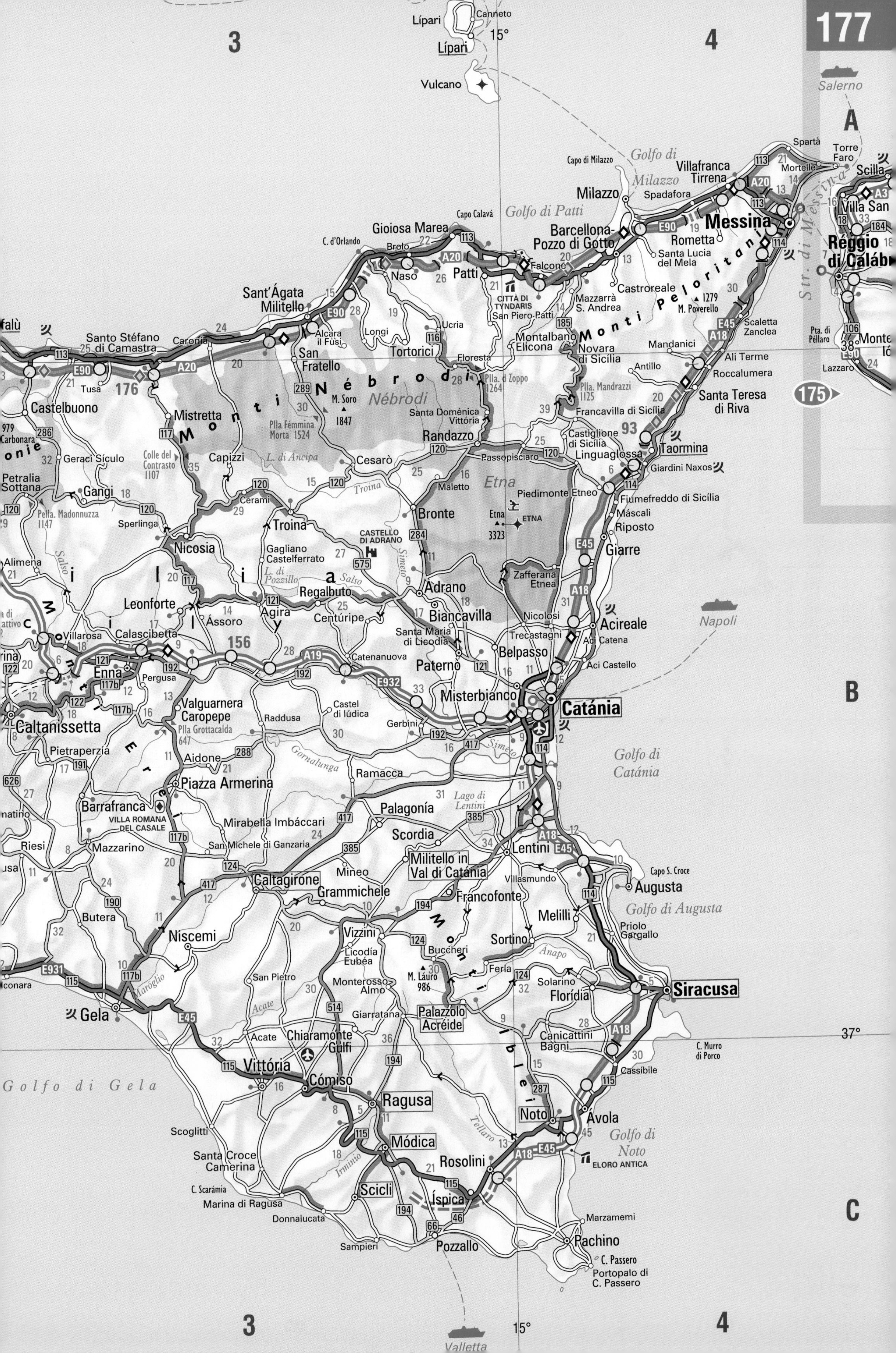
3
4
A
B
C
15°
37°
38°
Lípari
Canneto
Vulcano
Salerno
Napoli
Valletta
Golfo di Milazzo
Capo di Milazzo
Milazzo
Spadafora
Villafranca Tirrena
Spartà
Torre Faro
Mortelle
Scilla
Villa San
Réggio di Calábria
Str. di Messina
Messina
Rometta
Santa Lucia del Mela
Castroreale
Monti Peloritani
M. Poverello 1279
Barcellona-Pozzo di Gotto
Golfo di Patti
Capo Calavá
C. d'Orlando
Gioiosa Marea
Brolo
Patti
Falcone
Naso
CITTÀ DI TYNDARIS
San Piero Patti
Mazzarrà S. Andrea
Montalbano Elicona
Novara di Sicília
Floresta
Plla. d. Zoppo 1264
Plla. Mandrazzi 1125
Scaletta Zanclea
Mandanici
Antillo
Ali Terme
Roccalumera
Pta. di Péllaro
Lazzaro
Monte
Santa Teresa di Riva
Francavilla di Sicília
Castiglione di Sicília
Taormina
Linguaglossa
Giardini Naxos
Sant'Ágata Militello
Alcara li Fusi
Longi
Ucria
Tortorici
San Fratello
Santo Stéfano di Camastra
Caronía
Cefalù
Tusa
Castelbuono
Mistretta
Monti Nébrodi
Nébrodi
M. Soro 1847
Plla Fémmina Morta 1524
Santa Doménica Vittória
Randazzo
Passopisciaro
Etna
Piedimonte Etneo
Fiumefreddo di Sicília
Máscali
Riposto
Giarre
ETNA 3323
Maletto
Bronte
Cesarò
L. di Áncipa
Troina
Capizzi
Colle del Contrasto 1107
Geraci Sículo
Petralia Sottana
Gangi
Pella. Madonnuzza 1147
Sperlinga
Cerami
Nicosia
CASTELLO DI ADRANO
Gagliano Castelferrato
L. di Pozzillo
Salso
Simeto
Alimena
Carbonara
Leonforte
Regalbuto
Adrano
Zafferana Etnea
Biancavilla
Nicolosi
Trecastagni
Acireale
Aci Catena
Aci Castello
Agira
Ássoro
Centúripe
Calascibetta
Villarosa
Enna
Pergusa
Catenanuova
Santa Maria di Licodia
Paternò
Belpasso
Misterbianco
Catánia
Caltanissetta
Valguarnera Caropepe
Plla Grottacalda 647
Raddusa
Castel di Iúdica
Gerbini
Pietraperzia
Aidone
Gornalunga
Ramacca
Golfo di Catánia
Piazza Armerina
Barrafranca
VILLA ROMANA DEL CASALE
Mirabella Imbáccari
Lago di Lentini
Palagonía
Scordia
Riesi
Mazzarino
San Michele di Ganzaria
Lentini
Militello in Val di Catánia
Mineo
Caltagirone
Grammichele
Villasmundo
Francofonte
Capo S. Croce
Augusta
Golfo di Augusta
Melilli
Priolo Gargallo
Butera
Niscemi
Vizzini
Licodía Eubéa
Buccheri
Sortino
Anapo
M. Lauro 986
Ferla
Monterosso Almo
San Pietro
Solarino
Florídia
Siracusa
Gela
Maroglio
Acate
Giarratana
Palazzolo Acréide
Canicattini Bagni
C. Murro di Porco
Cassíbile
Chiaramonte Gulfi
Vittória
Cómiso
Golfo di Gela
Ragusa
Noto
Avola
Golfo di Noto
Monti Iblei
Monti Erei
Tellaro
ELORO ANTICA
Scoglitti
Santa Croce Camerina
Módica
Irminio
Rosolini
C. Scarámia
Marina di Ragusa
Scicli
Íspica
Donnalucata
Sampieri
Pozzallo
Marzamemi
Pachino
C. Passero
Portopalo di C. Passero
E90
E45
E931
E932
A18
A19
A20
113
114
115
117
117b
120
121
122
124
185
190
191
192
194
284
286
287
288
289
385
417
514
575
626
175
176

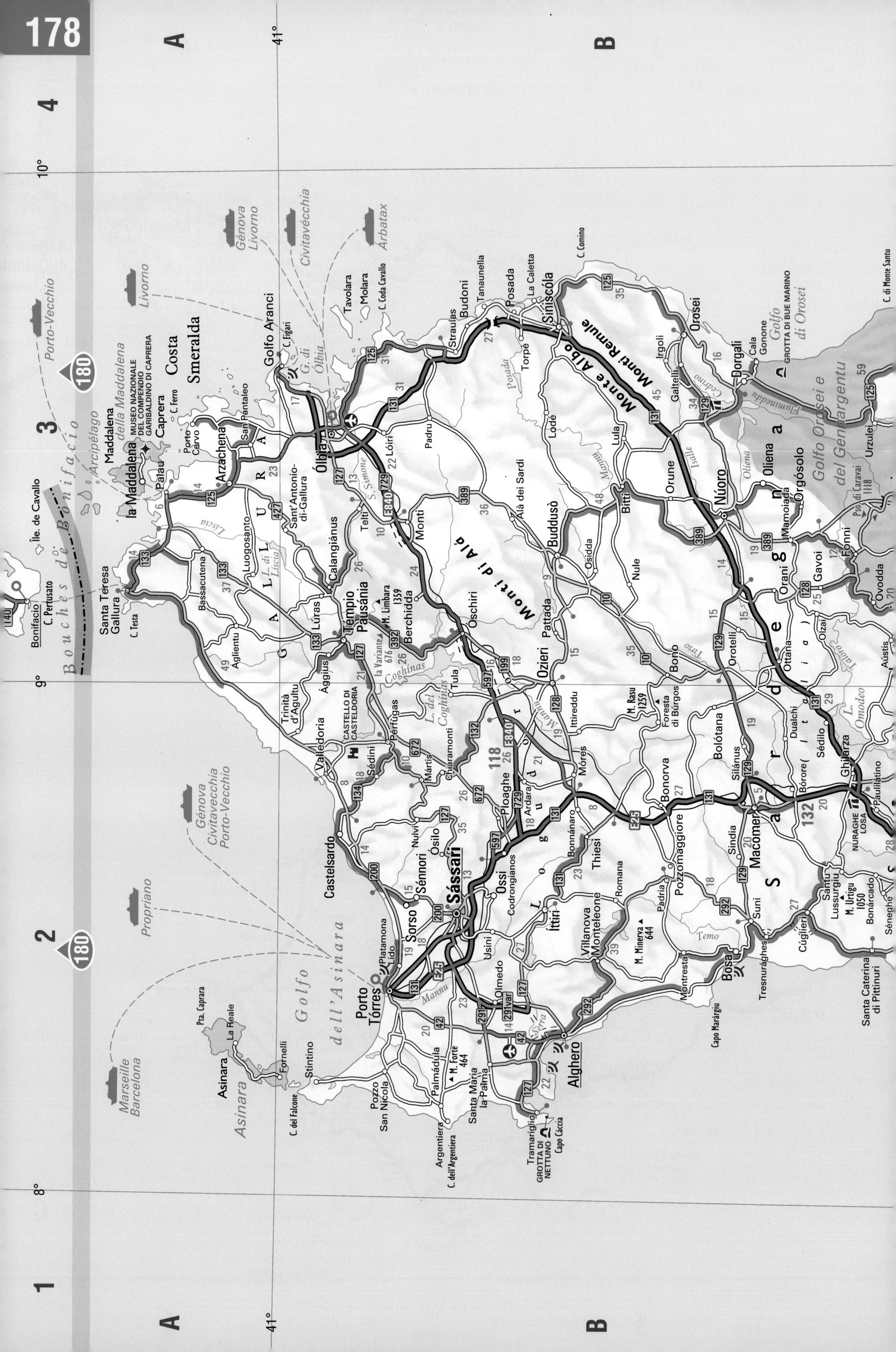

A B

4 3 2 1

41° 10° 9° 8°

Bouches de Bonifacio

Porto-Vecchio
180

Marseille Barcelona
Propriano

Génova Civitavecchia Porto-Vecchio

Bonifacio
C. Pertusato
île de Cavallo
Pta. Capraia
La Reale
Asinara
C. del Falcone
Fornelli
Stintino
Pozzo San Nicola
Argentiera
C. dell'Argentiera
Tramariglio
GROTTA DI NETTUNO
Capo Caccia

Santa Teresa Gallura
C. Testa
Bassacutena
Aglientu
Luogosanto
Trinità d'Agultu
Valledoria
Castelsardo
Sorso
Sénnori
Platamona Lido
Porto Tórres
Santa Maria la Palma
M. Forte 464
Palmadula
Olmedo
Alghero
M. Minerva 644

Maddalena
la Maddalena
Palau
Arzachena
Costa Smeralda
Porto Cervo
San Pantaleo
C. Ferro
Sant'Antonio-di-Gallura
Luras
Tempio Pausania
M. Limbara 1359
Aggius
Calangiánus
Berchidda
Oschiri
Perfugas
Martis
Chiaramonti
Sédini
Nulvi
Ósilo
Sássari
Ossi
Tula
Ploaghe
Codrongianos
Ittiri
Usini
Uri
Villanova Monteleone
Thiesi
Bonnánaro
Mores
Ittireddu
Bonorva
Romana
Padria
Pozzomaggiore
Montresta
Suni
Tresnurághes
Bosa
Cuglieri
Santa Caterina di Pittinuri

Golfo Aranci
Olbia
G. di Olbia
C. Figari
Tavolara
Molara
C. Coda Cavallo
Straulas
Budoni
Tanaunella
Posada
La Caletta
Siniscóla
Orosei
Loiri
Padru
Monti
Telti
Torpè
Lode
Lula
Bitti
Nule
Osidda
Alà dei Sardi
Buddusò
Pattada
Bono
Orune
Oroteli
Foresta di Bùrgos
M. Rasu 1259
Ozieri
Ardara
Bolótana
Silanus
Sindia
Macomer
Bórore
Sédilo
Ghilarza
Paulilátino
Dualchi
Noragugume
NURAGHE LOSA

Nuoro
Oliena
Oliena
Orgòsolo
Dorgali
Cala Gonone
GROTTA DI BUE MARINO
Golfo Oresei e del Gennargentu
Orani
Oniferi
Sarule
Ottana
Gavoi
Ovodda
Fonni
L'Ittiri
C. di Monte Santu

Génova Livorno
Civitavécchia
Arbatax
Livorno

Monte Albo
Monti Remule
Monti di Alà
Gallura
Barbagia
Golfo dell'Asinara
Asinara

40° 40°

Putzu Idu, Tramatza, Busachi, Monti del Gennargentu, Désulo, La Mármora 1834, 42

I. di Mal di Ventre, Riola Sardo, Solarussa, Fordongiánus, (I t a l y), Meana Sardo, Aritzo, Flumendosa, Lotzorai, Árbatax, Cágliari Civitavécchia Génova Ólbia

Cábras, Oristano, Siamanna, Samugheo, Árzana, Tortolì, Lanusei, Bari Sardo

San Giovanni di Sinis, SAN GIOVANNI DI SINIS, Marina di Torre Grande, C. San Marco, THARROS, Asuni, Seúlo, Seúi, Gáiro, Ulássai, Ussássai

Golfo di Oristano, Capo d. Frasca, Arboréa, Marrúbiu, Mte. Arci 812, Áles, Sénis, Usellus, Láconi, Nurallao, Jerzu, Marina di Gáiro

San Antanío di Santadi, Terralba, Uras, Mógoro, SU NARAXI, Turri, Barúmini, Ísili, Nurri, Tertenía, Perdasdefogu, Melisenda

Sitzerri, Lunamatrona, Mándas, L. Mulárgia, Escalaplano, Marina di Árbus, Sardara, Villamar, SACRO FUNTANA COBERTA, Ballao, Goni

Campidano, Arbus, Gúspini, San Gavino Monreale, Sanluri, Guasila, Suelli, Senorbì, San Nicolò Gerrei, NURAGHE FUNTANA, Flumendosa

C, Bau, Gonnosfanádiga, Samassi, Serramanna, Sant'Andrea Frius, San Vito, Villaputzu, PORTO CORALLO, C

Capo Pécora, Mte. Línas 1236, Villacidro, Fluminimaggiore, Monastir, Dolianova, Muravera

Buggerru, GROTTA DI SAN GIOVANNI DI DOMUSNOVAS, Vallermosa, Villasor, Punta Serpeddì 1067, Burcei

Masúa, Domusnóvas, Iglésias, Silíqua, Decimomannu, Sestu, Sínnai, M. dei Sette Fratelli 1023, C. Ferrato

Gonnesa, Assémini, Selárgius, Villamassárgia, Cixerri, Cágliari, Quartu Sant'Elena, Castiádas, Poetto

Portoscuso, Capoterra, CUILI PIRAS COMPLESSO MEGALITICO

San Pietro, Carloforte, Carbónia, Acquacadda, Narcao, M. Carávius, Golfo di Cágliari, Serpentara

La Caletta, Calasetta, San Giovanni Suérgiu, Santadi, Solánas, Villasimíus, C. Carbonara

Sant'Antíoco, Golfo di Pálmas, Giba, P. Sébera 979, Sarroch, Árbatax Civitavécchia

39° Sant'Antíoco, Cannai, Pula, CITTÀ ROMANA 39°

Capo Sperone, Porto Pino, Teulada, Santa Margherita, Nápoli

D, Dómus de María, D

Capo Teulada, Capo Spartivento, Palermo, Trápani

0 10 20 30 km

1 8° 2 9° 3 10° 4

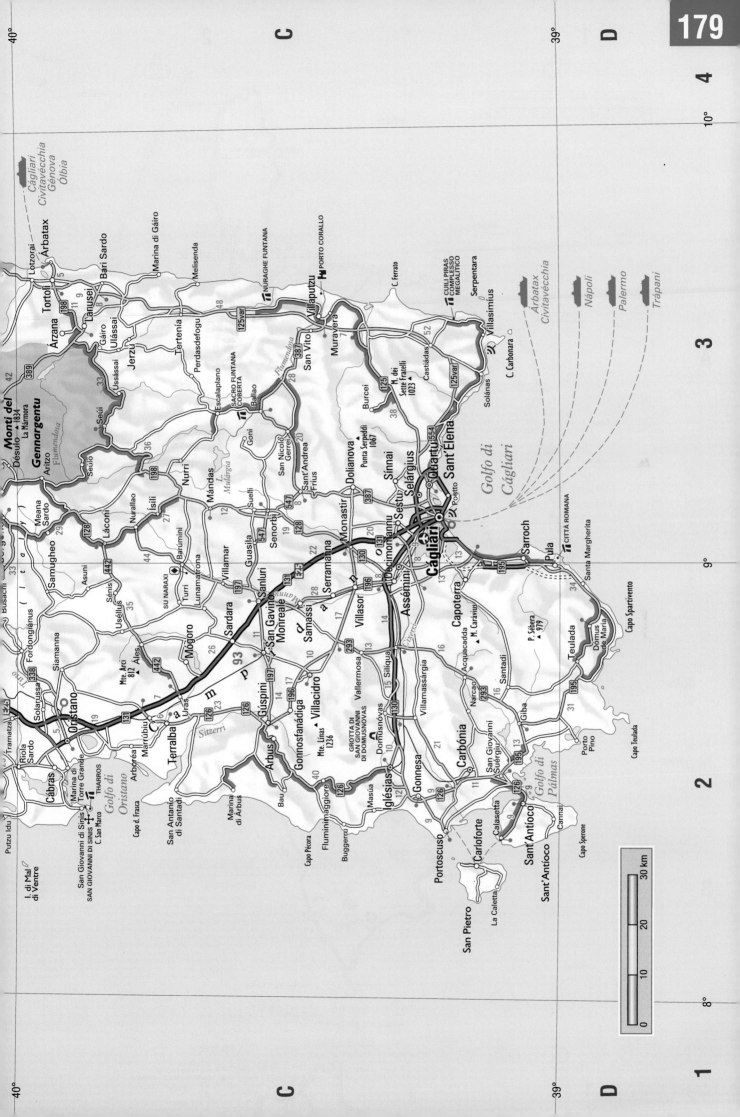

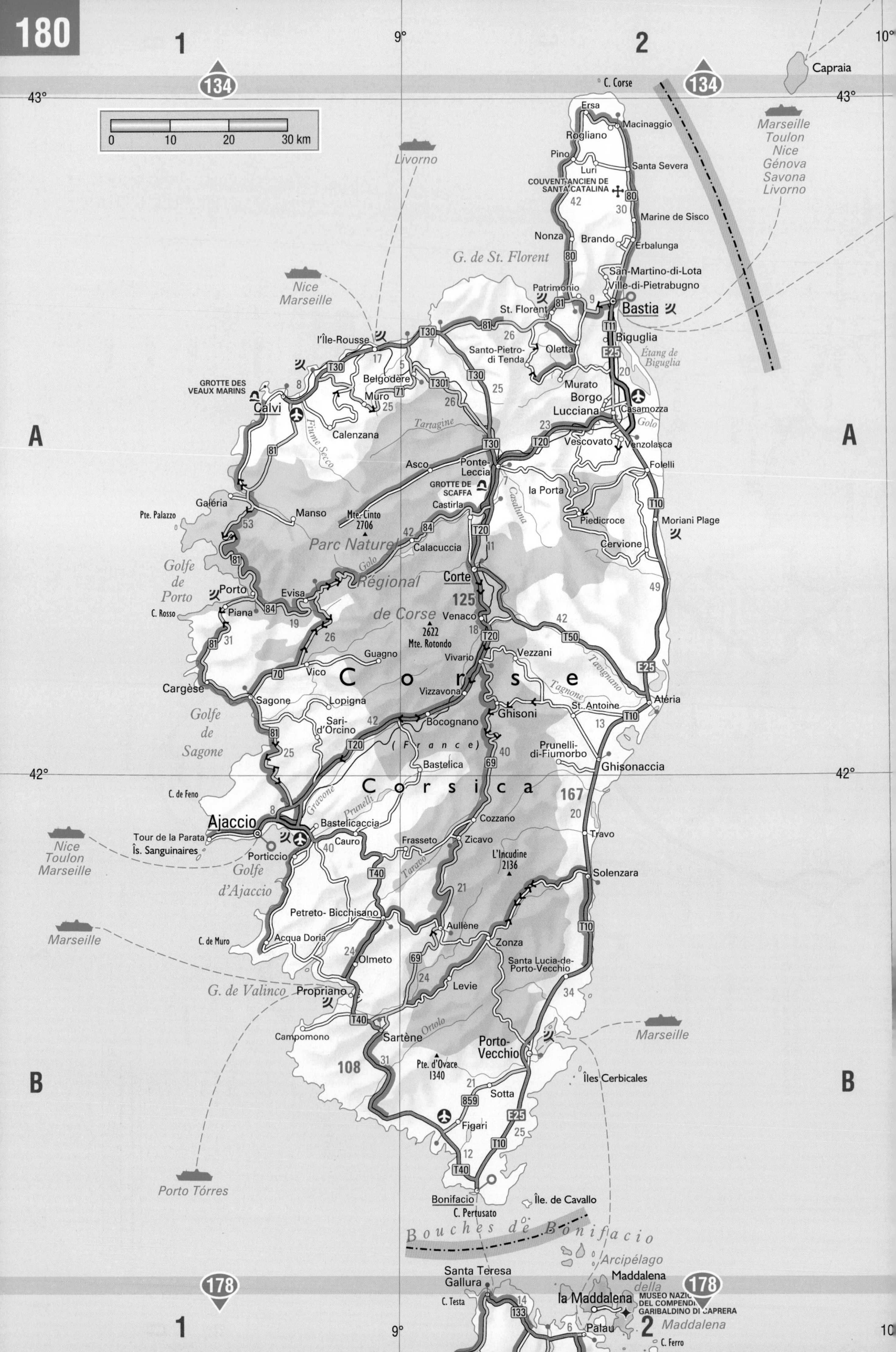

1
2
134
134
C. Corse
Capraia
Marseille
Toulon
Nice
Génova
Savona
Livorno
Livorno
Ersa
Macinaggio
Rogliano
Pino
Luri
Santa Severa
COUVENT ANCIEN DE SANTA CATALINA
Marine de Sisco
Nonza
Brando
Erbalunga
G. de St. Florent
San-Martino-di-Lota
Ville-di-Pietrabugno
Patrimonio
St. Florent
Bastia
Nice
Marseille
Biguglia
Étang de Biguglia
l'Île-Rousse
Santo-Pietro-di Tenda
Oletta
Belgodère
Muro
Murato
Borgo
Lucciana
Casamozza
GROTTE DES VEAUX MARINS
Calvi
Calenzana
Fiume Secco
Tartagine
Golo
Vescovato
Venzolasca
A
A
Asco
Ponte-Leccia
GROTTE DE SCAFFA
Castirla
Folelli
la Porta
Casaluna
Galéria
Pte. Palazzo
Manso
Mte. Cinto 2706
Piedicroce
Moriani Plage
Parc Naturel Régional de Corse
Calacuccia
Cervione
Golfe de Porto
Porto
Evisa
Corte
C. Rosso
Piana
Venaco
2622 Mte. Rotondo
Guagno
Vivario
Vezzani
Tavignano
Tagnone
Cargèse
Vico
Corse
Vizzavona
Aléria
Sagone
Lopigna
St. Antoine
Golfe de Sagone
Sari-d'Orcino
Bocognano
Ghisoni
(France)
Prunelli-di-Fiumorbo
Bastelica
Ghisonaccia
42°
42°
C. de Feno
Corsica
Gravone
Prunelli
Ajaccio
Bastelicaccia
Cozzano
Tour de la Parata
Îs. Sanguinaires
Nice
Toulon
Marseille
Porticcio
Cauro
Frasseto
Zicavo
Travo
Golfe d'Ajaccio
Taravo
L'Incudine 2136
Solenzara
Marseille
Petreto-Bicchisano
Aullène
C. de Muro
Acqua Doria
Zonza
Olmeto
Santa Lucia-de-Porto-Vecchio
Levie
G. de Valinco
Propriano
Ortolo
Marseille
Campomono
Sartène
Porto-Vecchio
Pte. d'Ovace 1340
B
B
Îles Cerbicales
Sotta
Figari
Porto Tórres
Bonifacio
C. Pertusato
Île. de Cavallo
Bouches de Bonifacio
Arcipélago della Maddalena
Santa Teresa Gallura
Maddalena
178
178
C. Testa
la Maddalena
MUSEO NAZIONALE DEL COMPENDIO GARIBALDINO DI CAPRERA
1
2
Palau
C. Ferro
9°
9°
10°
43°
43°
0
10
20
30 km

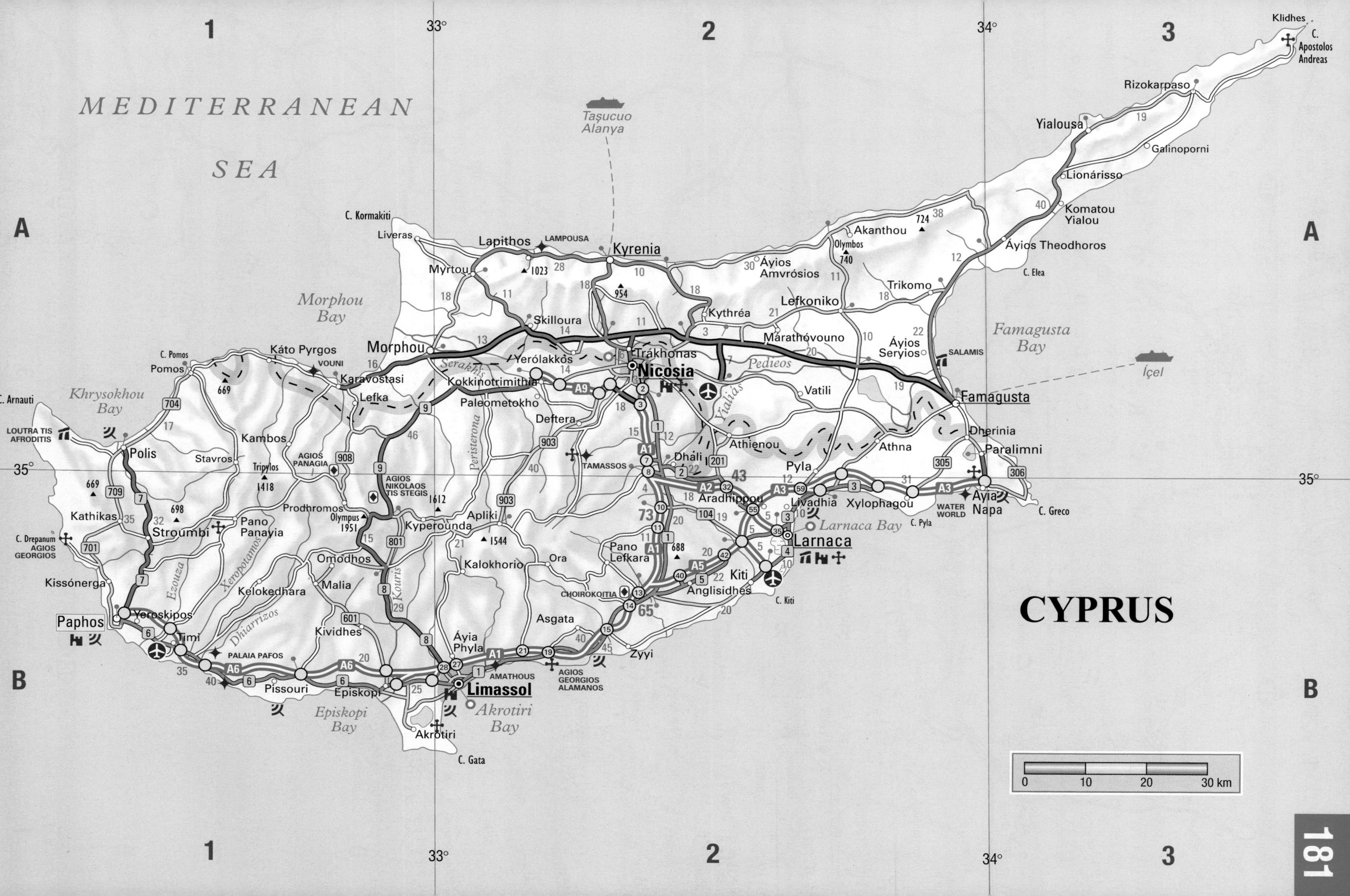
CYPRUS
MEDITERRANEAN SEA
Morphou Bay
Khrysokhou Bay
Famagusta Bay
Larnaca Bay
Akrotiri Bay
Episkopi Bay
Taşucuo Alanya
İçel
Klidhes
C. Apostolos Andreas
Rizokarpaso
Yialousa
Galinoporni
Lionárisso
Komatou Yialou
Áyios Theodhoros
C. Elea
Akanthou
Olymbos
Trikomo
Lefkoniko
Áyios Amvrósios
Kythréa
Marathóvouno
Áyios Seryios
SALAMIS
Famagusta
Dherinia
Paralimni
Ayia Napa
WATER WORLD
C. Greco
C. Pyla
Xylophagou
Athna
Vatili
Athienou
Pyla
Livadhia
Larnaca
Kiti
C. Kiti
Anglisidhes
Aradhippou
Dháli
TAMASSOS
Nicosia
Trákhonas
Kyrenia
Lapithos
LAMPOUSA
Myrtou
Liveras
C. Kormakiti
Skilloura
Yerólakkos
Kokkinotrimithia
Paleometokho
Deftera
Morphou
Karavostasi
Lefka
Káto Pyrgos
VOUNI
Pomos
C. Pomos
C. Arnauti
LOUTRA TIS AFRODITIS
Polis
Kambos
Stavros
Tripylos
AGIOS PANAGIA
AGIOS NIKOLAOS TIS STEGIS
Olympus
Prodhromos
Kyperounda
Apliki
Kalokhorio
Ora
Pano Lefkara
CHOIROKOITIA
Asgata
Zyyi
AGIOS GEORGIOS ALAMANOS
AMATHOUS
Limassol
Áyia Phyla
Akrotiri
C. Gata
Episkopi
Pissouri
PALAIA PAFOS
Kividhes
Malia
Omodhos
Kelokedhara
Pano Panayia
Stroumbi
Kathikas
C. Drepanum
AGIOS GEORGIOS
Kissónerga
Paphos
Yeroskipos
Timi
Pedieos
Yialias
Serakhis
Peristerona
Kouris
Xeropotamos
Dhiarrizos
Ezouza
0 10 20 30 km

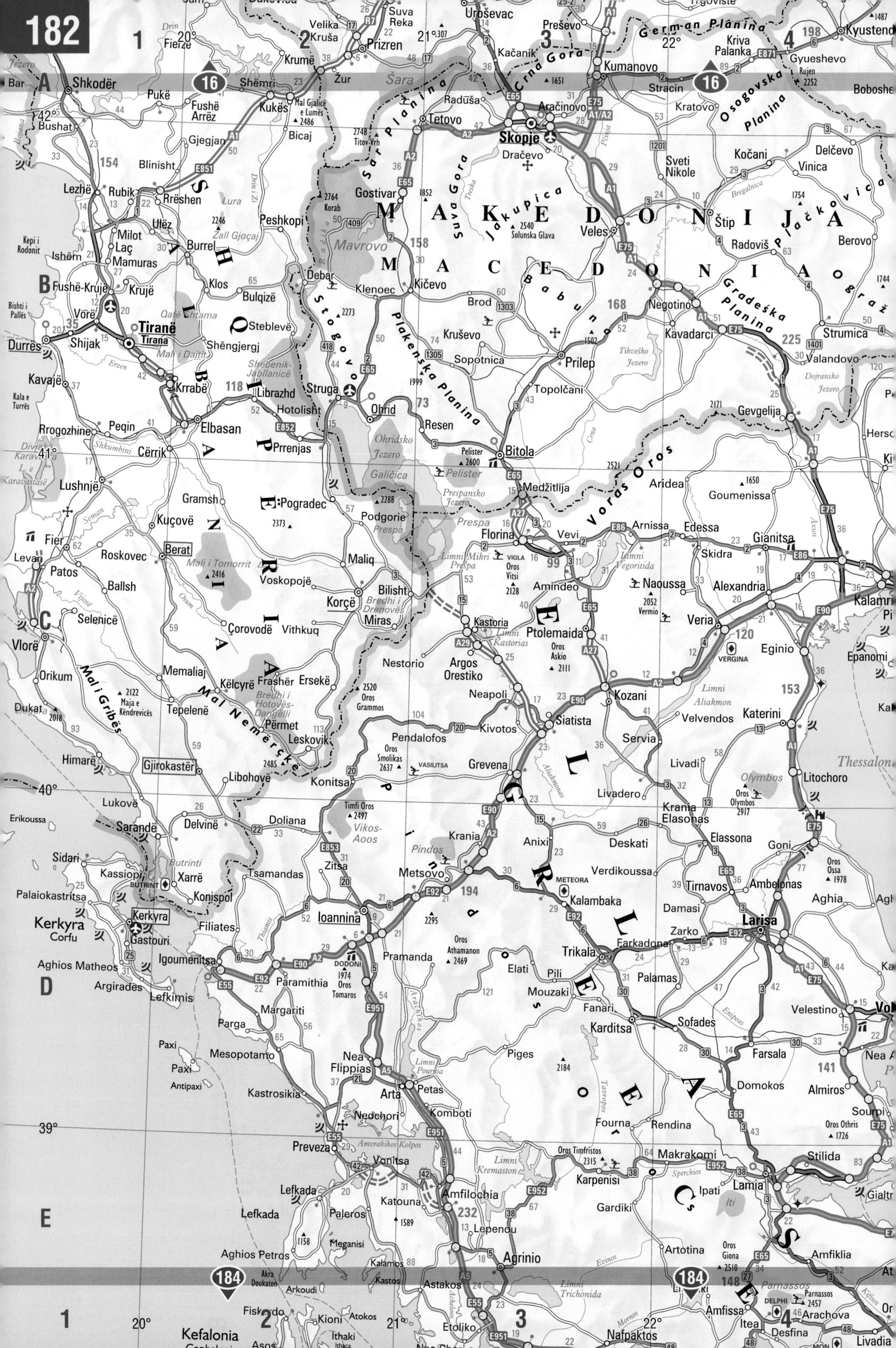
1
2
3
4
A
B
C
D
E
Shkodër
Bar
Bushat
Lezhë
Rubik
Rrëshen
Milot
Laç
Mamuras
Burrel
Peshkopi
Ishëm
Kepi i Rodonit
Fushë-Krujë
Krujë
Vorë
Bishti i Pallës
Durrës
Shijak
Tiranë
Tirana
Kavajë
Kala e Turrës
Krrabë
Elbasan
Librazhd
Hotolisht
Prrenjas
Rrogozhinë
Peqin
Cërrik
Lushnjë
Gramsh
Kuçovë
Fier
Levan
Patos
Roskovec
Berat
Ballsh
Selenicë
Vlorë
Çorovodë
Vithkuq
Orikum
Dukat
Memaliaj
Këlcyrë
Tepelenë
Himarë
Gjirokastër
Libohovë
Përmet
Leskovik
Frashër
Ersekë
Korçë
Bilisht
Maliq
Voskopojë
Pogradec
Podgorie
Mali i Tomorrit
Mal i Gribës
Mal Nemërçkë
Lukovë
Delvinë
Sarandë
Xarrë
Konispol
Butrinti
Erikoussa
Sidari
Kassiopi
Palaiokastritsa
Kerkyra
Corfu
Gastouri
Aghios Matheos
Argirades
Lefkimis
Igoumenitsa
Filiates
Paramithia
Margariti
Parga
Paxi
Antipaxi
Mesopotamo
Kastrosikia
Preveza
Vonitsa
Lefkada
Aghios Petros
Meganisi
Kalamos
Kastos
Arkoudi
Akra Doukaton
Fiskardo
Kefalonia
Kioni
Ithaki
Atokos
Astakos
Etoliko
Nafpaktos
Agrinio
Lepenou
Amfilochia
Katouna
Paleros
Arta
Petas
Komboti
Neochori
Nea Flippias
Ioannina
Pramanda
Dodoni
Tsamandas
Zitsa
Konitsa
Doliana
Metsovo
Krania
Grevena
Pendalofos
Kivotos
Neapoli
Siatista
Kozani
Servia
Velvendos
Nestorio
Argos Orestiko
Kastoria
Ptolemaida
Amindeo
Florina
Vevi
Arnissa
Edessa
Skidra
Naoussa
Veria
Alexandria
Gianitsa
Eginio
Vergina
Katerini
Litochoro
Olymbos
Livadi
Livadero
Deskati
Anixi
Kalambaka
Meteora
Trikala
Elassona
Krania Elasonas
Tirnavos
Ambelonas
Larisa
Farkadona
Damasi
Zarko
Pili
Elati
Mouzaki
Palamas
Karditsa
Fanari
Sofades
Farsala
Domokos
Piges
Velestino
Almiros
Sourpi
Stilida
Lamia
Ipati
Makrakomi
Karpenisi
Gardiki
Rendina
Fourna
Artotina
Amfissa
Itea
Delphi
Arachova
Desfina
Livadia
Amfiklia
Goni
Aghia
Gonies
Thessaloniki
Epanomi
Kalamria
Medžitlija
Bitola
Resen
Ohrid
Struga
Kičevo
Klenoec
Debar
Gostivar
Tetovo
Skopje
Kumanovo
Aračinovo
Dračevo
Veles
Prilep
Topolčani
Kruševo
Sopotnica
Brod
Negotino
Kavadarci
Gevgelija
Valandovo
Strumica
Radoviš
Štip
Sveti Nikole
Kočani
Vinica
Delčevo
Berovo
Kratovo
Stracin
Kriva Palanka
Gyueshevo
Kyustendil
Boboshevo
Uroševac
Kačanik
Preševo
Prizren
Suva Reka
Velika Kruša
Krumë
Kukës
Shëmri
Žur
Fushë Arrëz
Pukë
Gjegjan
Blinisht
Bicaj
Ulëz
Klos
Bulqizë
Steblevë
Shëngjergj
Fierzë
Radusa
MAKEDONIJA
MACEDONIA
SHQIPERIA
ALBANIA
ELLADA
GREECE
Šar Planina
Crna Gora
German Planina
Osogovska Planina
Plačkovica
Gradeška Planina
Babuna
Jakupica
Suva Gora
Stogovo
Plakenska Planina
Voras Oros
Pindos
Mavrovo
Ohridsko Jezero
Prespansko Jezero
Galičica
Pelister
Dojransko Jezero
Limni Vegoritida
Limni Kastorias
Limni Aliakmon
Limni Trichonida
Limni Kremaston
Amvrakikos Kolpos
Oros Smolikas 2637
Oros Grammos 2520
Oros Olymbos 2917
Oros Giona 2510
Parnassos 2457
Oros Timfristos 2315
Oros Athamanon 2469
Oros Vermio 2052
Oros Vitsi 2128
Oros Askio 2111
Oros Ossa 1978
Oros Othris 1726
Timfi Oros 2497
Vikos-Aoos
Korab 2764
Titov Vrh 2748
Solunska Glava 2540
Pelister 2600
Oros Tomaros 1974
Mal Gjalicë e Lumës 2486
Maja e Këndrevicës 2122
Aridea
Goumenissa
Vasilitsa
Vigla
Thessalon
20°
21°
22°
39°
40°
41°
42°
16
184
154
158
168
225
118
120
153
141
194
232
99
148
73
35
A1
A2
E65
E75
E90
E92
E55
E951
E952
E86
E852
E853
E851
E871

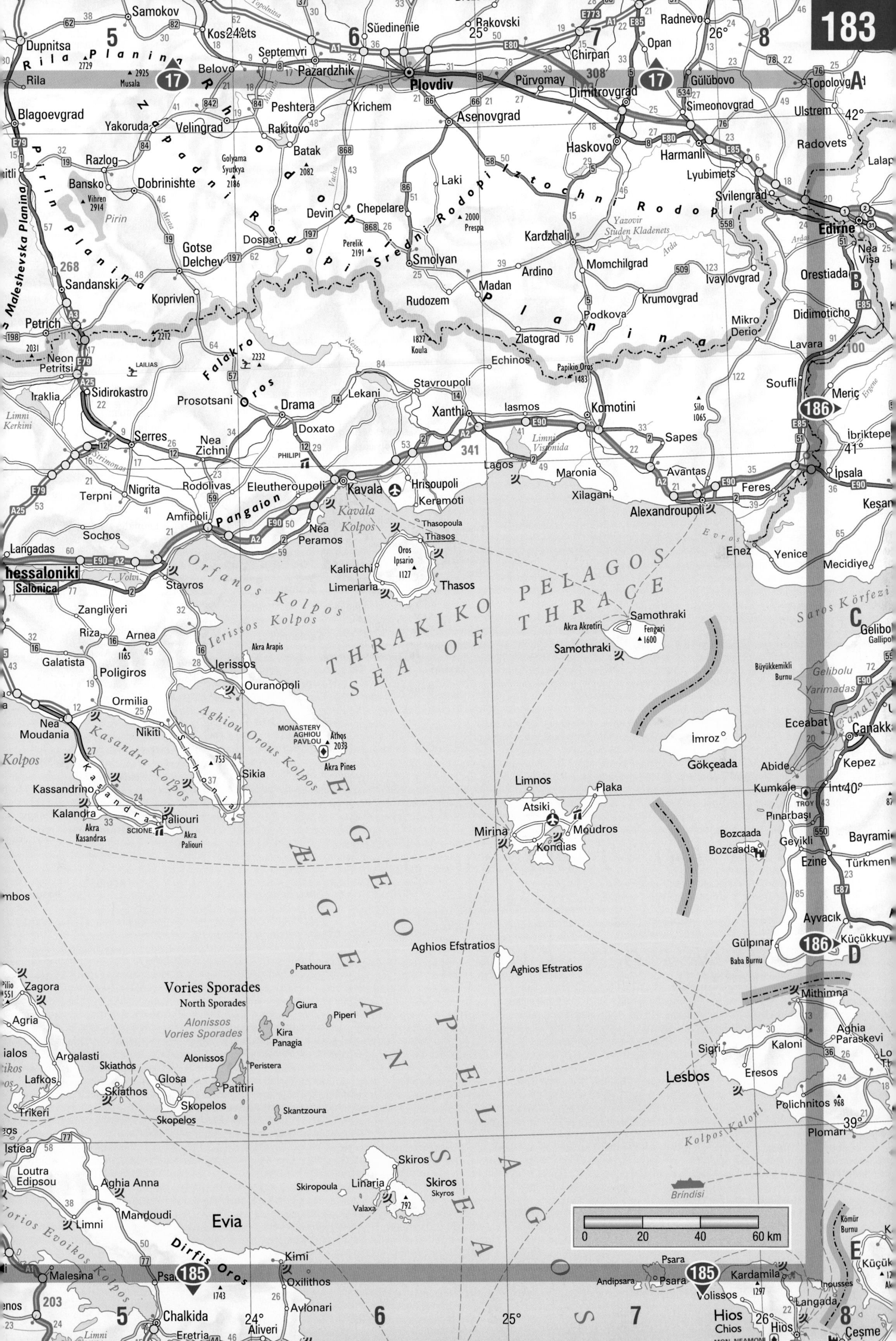

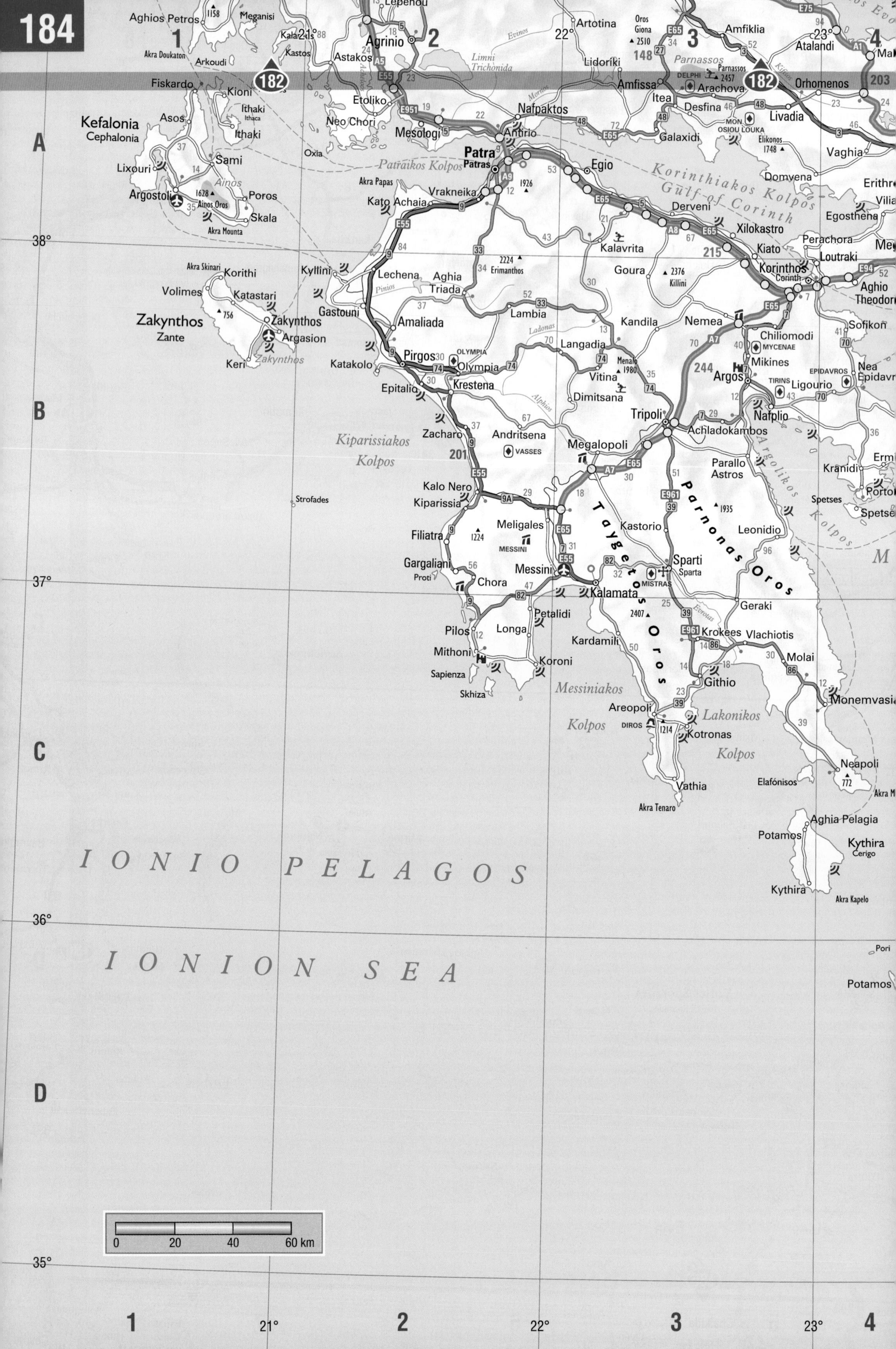

Aghios Petros
Meganisi
Kalamos
Kastos
Akra Doukaton
Arkoudi
Fiskardo
Kioni
Ithaki
Ithaca
Kefalonia
Cephalonia
Asos
Lixouri
Sami
Ainos
Argostoli
Ainos Oros
Poros
Skala
Akra Mounta
Akra Skinari
Korithi
Volimes
Katastari
Zakynthos
Zante
Argasion
Keri
Lepenou
Agrinio
Astakos
Etoliko
Neo Chori
Mesologi
Oxia
Limni Trichonida
Evinos
Artotina
Oros Giona
Lidoriki
Parnassos
Delphi
Arachova
Amfiklia
Atalandi
Amfissa
Itea
Desfina
Livadia
Orhomenos
Galaxidi
Mon. Osiou Louka
Elikonos
Vaghia
Nafpaktos
Antirio
Patra
Patras
Patraikos Kolpos
Egio
Korinthiakos Kolpos
Gulf of Corinth
Domvena
Derveni
Xilokastro
Kiato
Perachora
Loutraki
Korinthos
Corinth
Egosthena
Akra Papas
Vrakneika
Kato Achaia
Kalavrita
Erimanthos
Killini
Goura
Kyllini
Lechena
Aghia Triada
Pinios
Gastouni
Amaliada
Lambia
Ladonas
Kandila
Nemea
Chiliomodi
Mycenae
Mikines
Sofikon
Katakolo
Pirgos
Olympia
Langadia
Menalo
Vitina
Argos
Tirins
Epidavros
Ligourio
Nea Epidavros
Epitalio
Krestena
Dimitsana
Alphios
Tripoli
Achladokambos
Nafplio
Kiparissiakos Kolpos
Zacharo
Andritsena
Vasses
Megalopoli
Parallo Astros
Argolikos Kolpos
Kranidi
Porto Heli
Spetses
Strofades
Kalo Nero
Kiparissia
Meligales
Messini
Kastorio
Parnonas Oros
Taygetos Oros
Leonidio
Filiatra
Gargaliani
Proti
Chora
Messini
Kalamata
Sparti
Sparta
Mistras
Geraki
Evrotas
Petalidi
Pilos
Longa
Kardamili
Krokees
Vlachiotis
Molai
Mithoni
Sapienza
Skhiza
Koroni
Messiniakos Kolpos
Githio
Monemvasia
Areopoli
Diros
Kotronas
Lakonikos Kolpos
Neapoli
Elafónisos
Vathia
Akra Tenaro
Aghia Pelagia
Potamos
Kythira
Cerigo
Akra Kapelo
IONIO PELAGOS
IONION SEA
Pori
0
20
40
60 km
A
B
C
D
1
2
3
4
21°
22°
23°
38°
37°
36°
35°

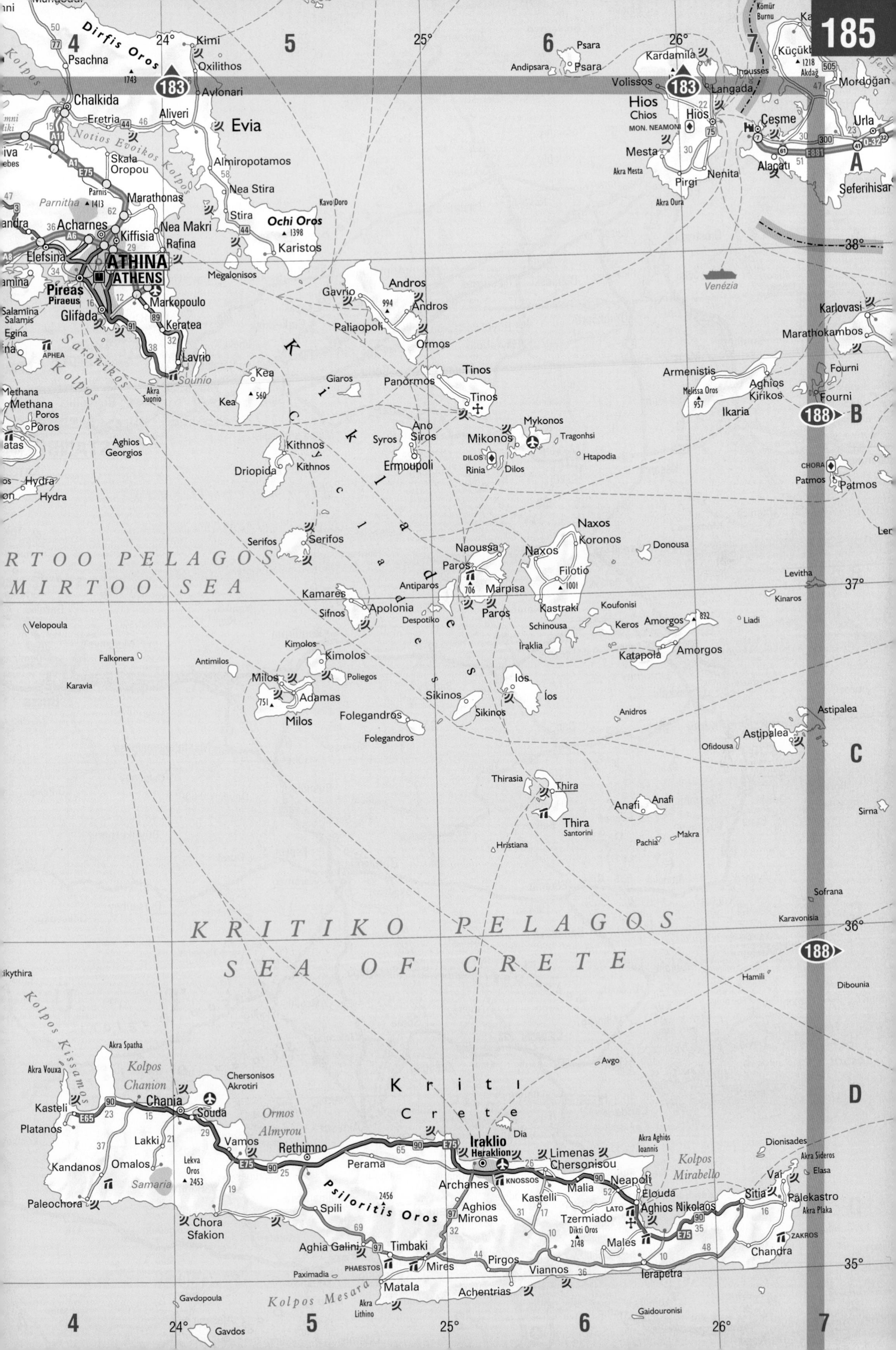

Dirfis Oros
Psachna
Kimi
Oxilithos
Avlonari
Chalkida
Eretria
Aliveri
Evia
Notios Evoikos Kolpos
Skala Oropou
Almiropotamos
Nea Stira
Stira
Ochi Oros
Kavo Doro
Karistos
Parnitha
Parnis
Marathonas
Acharnes
Kiffisia
Nea Makri
Rafina
Elefsina
ATHINA
ATHENS
Megalonisos
Pireas
Piraeus
Glifada
Markopoulo
Keratea
Lavrio
Sounio
Akra Suonio
Salamina
Salamis
Egina
APHEA
Saronikos Kolpos
Methana
Poros
Hydra
Aghios Georgios
Kea
Giaros
Kithnos
Driopida
Serifos
Gavrio
Andros
Paliaopoli
Ormos
Tinos
Panormos
Syros
Ano Siros
Ermoupoli
Mykonos
Mikonos
Tragonhsi
Htapodia
DILOS
Rinia
Dilos
Kiklades
Cyclades
Psara
Andipsara
Kardamila
Volissos
Hios
Chios
MON. NEAMONI
Langada
Mesta
Akra Mesta
Pirgi
Nenita
Akra Oura
Inousses
Kömür Burnu
Küçükbahçe
Akdağ
Mordoğan
Çesme
Urla
Alaçatı
Seferihisar
Venézia
Karlovasi
Marathokambos
Armenistis
Melissa Oros
Aghios Kirikos
Ikaria
Fourni
CHORA
Patmos
MIRTOO PELAGOS
MIRTOO SEA
Velopoula
Falkonera
Karavia
Antimilos
Kimolos
Poliegos
Milos
Adamas
Kamares
Sifnos
Apolonia
Antiparos
Despotiko
Paros
Naoussa
Marpisa
Naxos
Koronos
Filotio
Kastraki
Donousa
Koufonisi
Schinousa
Iraklia
Keros
Amorgos
Katapola
Levitha
Kinaros
Liadi
Ios
Sikinos
Folegandros
Anidros
Astipalea
Ofidousa
Thirasia
Thira
Santorini
Anafi
Pachia
Makra
Hristiana
Sirna
Sofrana
Karavonisia
KRITIKO PELAGOS
SEA OF CRETE
Kithira
Hamili
Dibounia
Kolpos Kissamos
Akra Spatha
Akra Vouxa
Kolpos Chanion
Chersonisos Akrotiri
Kasteli
Chania
Souda
Platanos
Ormos Almyrou
Kriti
Crete
Avgo
Dia
Lakki
Vamos
Rethimno
Kandanos
Omalos
Lekva Oros
Samaria
Paleochora
Chora Sfakion
Psiloritis Oros
Perama
Spili
Iraklio
Heraklion
KNOSSOS
Archanes
Aghios Mironas
Limenas Chersonisou
Malia
Kastelli
Akra Aghios Ioannis
Kolpos Mirabello
Neapoli
Elouda
LATO
Aghios Nikolaos
Tzermiado
Dikti Oros
Dionisades
Akra Sideros
Elasa
Vai
Sitia
Palekastro
Akra Plaka
ZAKROS
Chandra
Aghia Galini
Timbaki
PHAESTOS
Mires
Pirgos
Viannos
Males
Ierapetra
Paximadia
Matala
Kolpos Mesara
Akra Lithino
Achentrias
Gaidouronisi
Gavdopoula
Gavdos

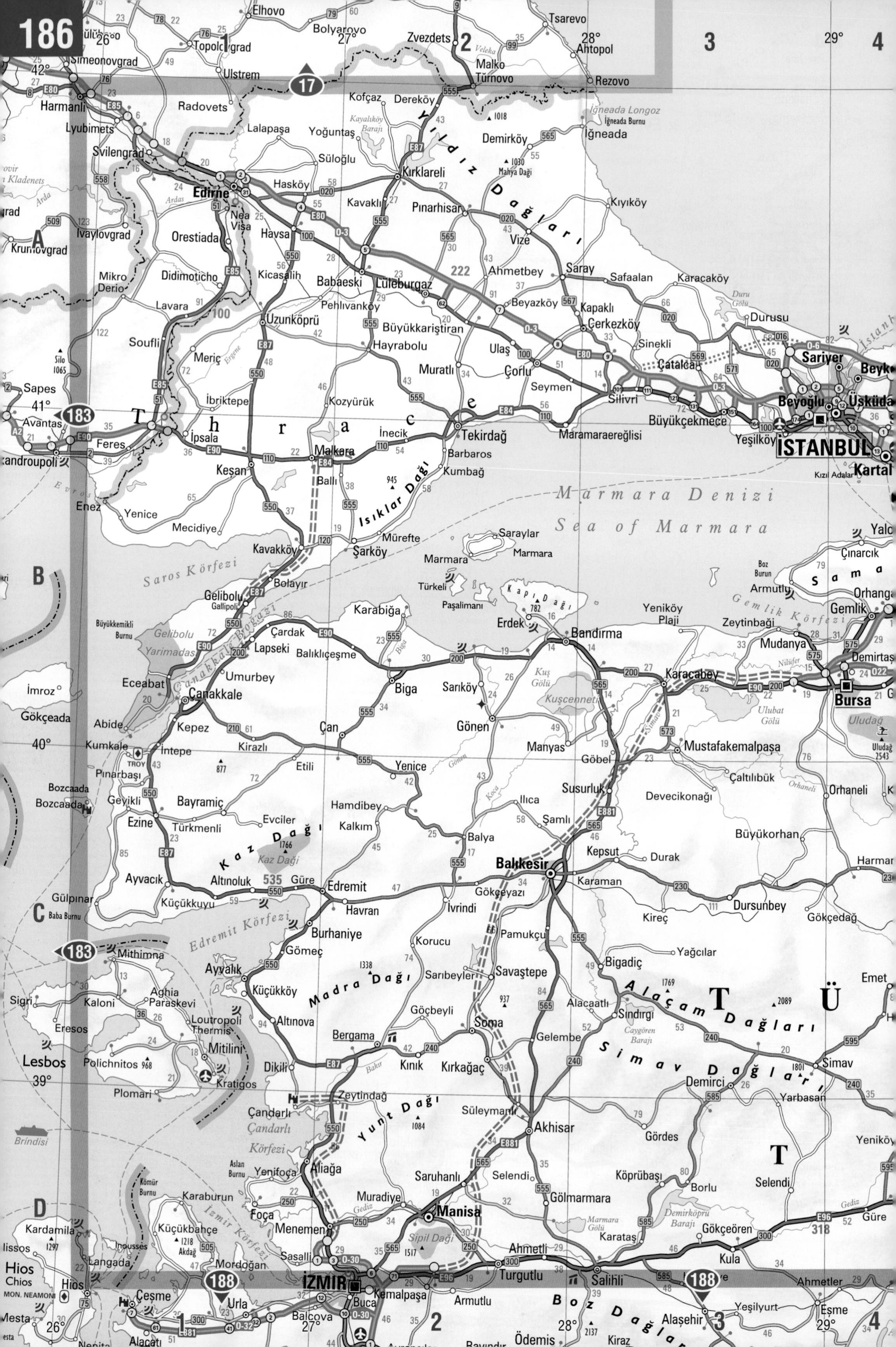
Elhovo
Bolyarovo
Tsarevo
Topolovgrad
Zvezdets
Malko Tŭrnovo
Ahtopol
Simeonovgrad
Ulstrem
Rezovo
Harmanli
Radovets
Kofçaz
Dereköy
Lyubimets
Lalapaşa
Yoğuntaş
Demirköy
İğneada
İğneada Longoz
İğneada Burnu
Svilengrad
Süloğlu
Kırklareli
Mahya Dağı
Yıldız Dağları
Edirne
Hasköy
Kavaklı
Pınarhisar
Kıyıköy
Nea Visa
Ivaylovgrad
Krumovgrad
Orestiada
Havsa
Vize
Didimoticho
Kicasalih
Babaeski
Lüleburgaz
Ahmetbey
Saray
Safaalan
Karacaköy
Mikro Derio
Lavara
Pehlivanköy
Beyazköy
Kapaklı
Durusu
Uzunköprü
Büyükkarıştıran
Çerkezköy
Soufli
Meriç
Hayrabolu
Sinekli
Silo 1065
Muratlı
Ulaş
Çatalca
Sarıyer
Beykoz
Çorlu
Sapes
Seymen
Silivri
Beyoğlu
Üsküdar
Avantas
İbriktepe
Kozyürük
Thrace
Büyükçekmece
İpsala
İnecik
Tekirdağ
Marmaraereğlisi
Yeşilköy
İSTANBUL
Feres
Alexandroupoli
Malkara
Barbaros
Keşan
Kumbağ
Kızıl Adalar
Kartal
Ballı
Işıklar Dağı
Marmara Denizi
Sea of Marmara
Enez
Yenice
Mecidiye
Mürefte
Saraylar
Kavakköy
Şarköy
Marmara
Çınarcık
Saros Körfezi
Boz Burun
Bolayır
Armutlu
Türkeli
Paşalimanı
Kapı Dağı
Gelibolu
Gallipoli
Karabiğa
Erdek
Yeniköy Plajı
Gemlik
Gemlik Körfezi
Orhangazi
Büyükkemikli Burnu
Gelibolu Yarimadası
Çardak
Lapseki
Bandırma
Zeytinbağı
Mudanya
Balıklıçeşme
Çanakkale Boğazı
Demirtaş
Umurbey
Karacabey
İmroz
Eceabat
Biga
Sarıköy
Kuş Gölü
Kuşcenneti
Bursa
Gökçeada
Çanakkale
Abide
Gönen
Ulubat Gölü
Uludağ
Kepez
Çan
Kumkale
İntepe
Kirazlı
Manyas
Mustafakemalpaşa
Uludağ 2543
Troy
Göbel
Pınarbaşı
Etili
Yenice
Çaltılıbük
Bozcaada
Geyikli
Bayramiç
Susurluk
Devecikonağı
Orhaneli
Hamdibey
Ilıca
Ezine
Türkmenli
Evciler
Kalkım
Şamlı
Kaz Dağı
Balya
Büyükorhan
Kepsut
Durak
Ayvacık
Altınoluk
Güre
Balıkesir
Karaman
Gülpınar
Baba Burnu
Küçükkuyu
Edremit
Havran
Gökçeyazı
İvrindi
Dursunbey
Kireç
Gökçedağ
Edremit Körfezi
Burhaniye
Pamukçu
Mithimna
Gömeç
Korucu
Yağcılar
Ayvalık
Madra Dağı
Sarıbeyler
Savaştepe
Bigadiç
Sigri
Kaloni
Aghia Paraskevi
Küçükköy
Alaçam Dağları
Emet
Loutropoli Thermis
Altınova
Göçbeyli
Alacaatlı
Sındırgı
Eresos
Soma
Caygören Barajı
Mitilini
Bergama
Gelembe
Lesbos
Polichnitos
Dikili
Kınık
Kırkağaç
Simav Dağları
Simav
Kratigos
Demirci
Plomari
Zeytindağ
Yarbasan
Yunt Dağı
Süleymanlı
Çandarlı
Çandarlı Körfezi
Akhisar
Gördes
Brindisi
Yeniköy
Aslan Burnu
Yenifoça
Aliağa
Kömür Burnu
Saruhanlı
Selendi
Köprübaşı
Karaburun
Borlu
Muradiye
Gölmarmara
Kardamila
Foça
Manisa
Demirköprü Barajı
Küçükbahçe
Marmara Gölü
Menemen
Gökçeören
Gediz
Güre
Inousses
Akdağ
İzmir Körfezi
Sipil Dağı
Karataş
Langada
Mordoğan
Sasalli
Ahmetli
Kula
Hios
Chios
Mon. Neamoni
Çeşme
İZMİR
Turgutlu
Salihli
Ahmetler
Urla
Kemalpaşa
Buca
Armutlu
Boz Dağlar
Yeşilyurt
Eşme
Mesta
Balçova
Alaşehir
Alaçatı
Ödemiş
Kiraz

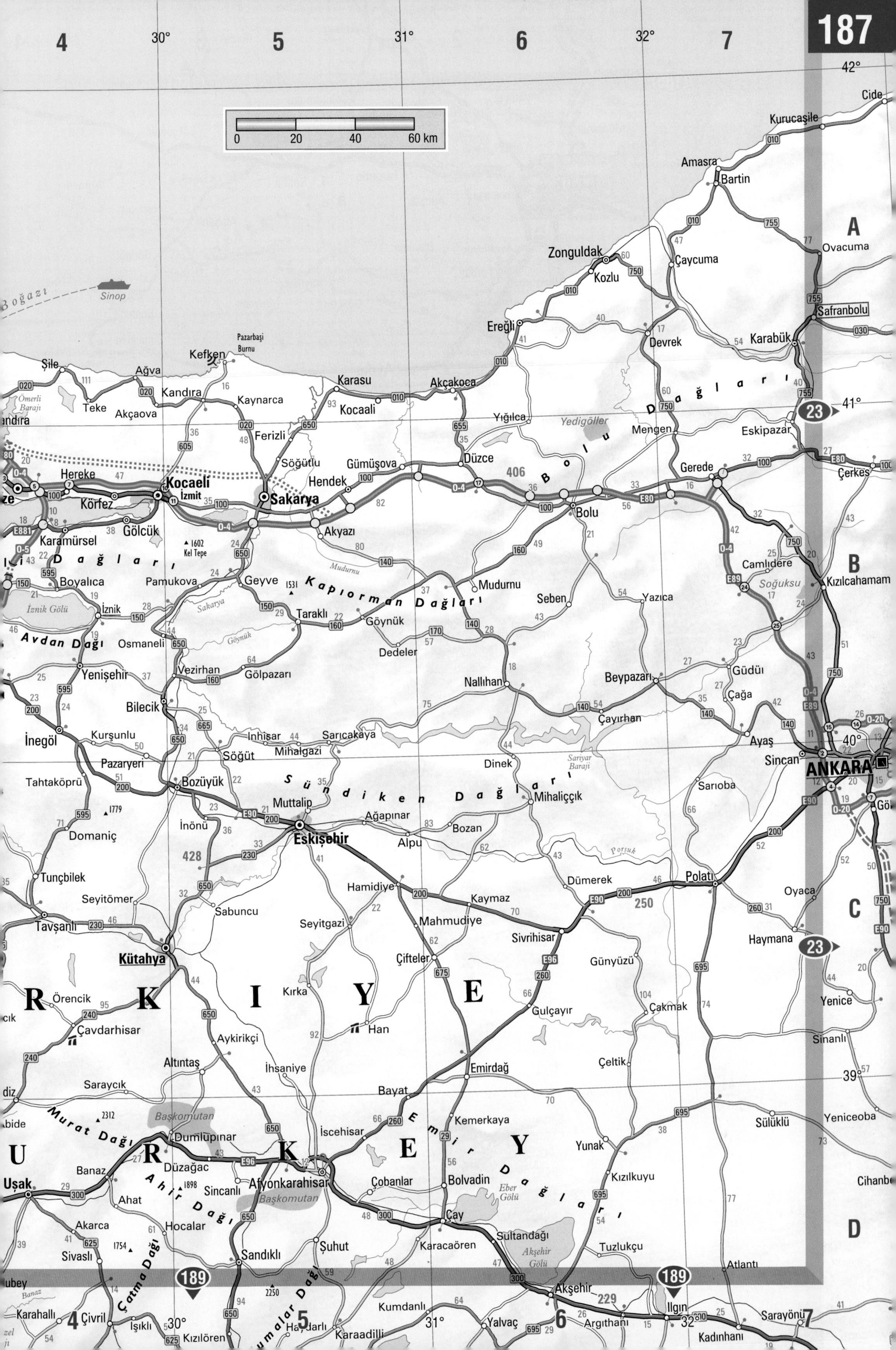
0
20
40
60 km
Sinop
Kefken
Pazarbaşi Burnu
Şile
Ağva
Kandıra
Teke
Akçaova
Kaynarca
Karasu
Kocaali
Akçakoca
Ferizli
Söğütlu
Gümüşova
Hendek
Düzce
Kocaeli
İzmit
Sakarya
Hereke
Körfez
Gölcük
Karamürsel
Akyazı
Kel Tepe
Boyalıca
Pamukova
Geyve
İznik
İznik Gölü
Avdan Dağı
Osmaneli
Taraklı
Göynük
Dedeler
Mudurnu
Kapıorman Dağları
Yenişehir
Vezirhan
Gölpazarı
Bilecik
İnegöl
Kurşunlu
Pazaryeri
Tahtaköprü
Bozüyük
İnhisar
Söğüt
Mihalgazi
Sarıcakaya
Sündiken Dağları
Muttalip
İnönü
Eskişehir
Ağapınar
Alpu
Bozan
Domaniç
Tunçbilek
Seyitömer
Tavşanlı
Sabuncu
Kütahya
Hamidiye
Seyitgazi
Kaymaz
Mahmudiye
Sivrihisar
Çifteler
Örencik
Çavdarhisar
Kırka
Han
Aykirikçi
Altıntaş
İhsaniye
Saraycık
Murat Dağı
Başkomutan
Dumlupınar
Düzağaç
Banaz
Uşak
Ahat
Sincanlı
Afyonkarahisar
Ahir Dağı
Hocalar
Akarca
Sivaslı
Sandıklı
Şuhut
Çatma Dağı
Karahallı
Çivril
Işıklı
Kızılören
Kumdanlı
Karaadilli
Çobanlar
Bolvadin
Çay
Karacaören
Sultandağı
Akşehir Gölü
Eber Gölü
Akşehir
Argıthanı
Yalvaç
Ilgın
Kadınhanı
Sarayönü
Bayat
İscehisar
Kemerkaya
Emir Dağları
Emirdağ
Gulçayır
Çakmak
Çeltik
Yunak
Kızılkuyu
Tuzlukçu
Atlantı
Sülüklü
Yeniceoba
Cihanbeyli
Günyüzü
Dümerek
Polatlı
Haymana
Oyaca
Yenice
Sinanlı
Sarıoba
Sincan
ANKARA
Ayaş
Çağa
Güdül
Beypazarı
Çayırhan
Nallıhan
Dinek
Mihaliççık
Sarıyar Barajı
Seben
Yazıca
Bolu
Bolu Dağları
Yedigöller
Yığılca
Mengen
Gerede
Eskipazar
Çerkeş
Camlıdere
Soğuksu
Kızılcahamam
Zonguldak
Kozlu
Ereğli
Devrek
Çaycuma
Amasra
Bartin
Kurucaşile
Cide
Ovacuma
Safranbolu
Karabük
TÜRKİYE
189
23

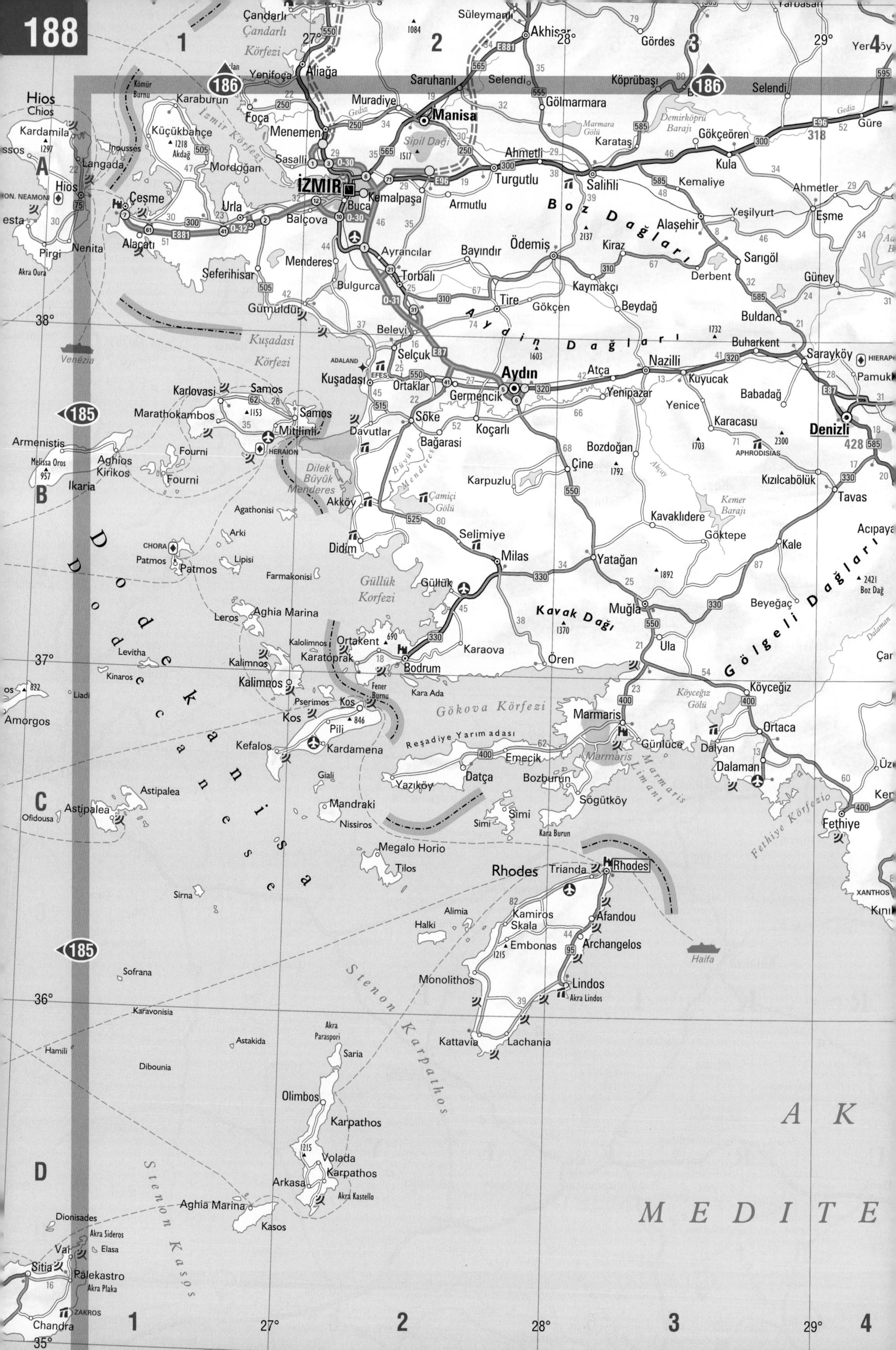

İZMIR
Manisa
Aydın
Denizli
Muğla
Çandarlı
Aliağa
Foça
Menemen
Karaburun
Çeşme
Urla
Alaçatı
Seferihisar
Kemalpaşa
Torbalı
Ödemiş
Tire
Salihli
Turgutlu
Alaşehir
Kula
Eşme
Sarıgöl
Nazilli
Selçuk
Kuşadası
Söke
Didim
Milas
Bodrum
Marmaris
Datça
Fethiye
Dalaman
Köyceğiz
Ortaca
Tavas
Yatağan
Çine
Hios
Chios
Samos
Ikaria
Patmos
Leros
Kalimnos
Kos
Astipalea
Nissiros
Tilos
Halki
Simi
Rhodes
Lindos
Karpathos
Kasos
Sitia
Amorgos
Boz Dağları
Aydın Dağları
Gölgeli Dağları
Kavak Dağı
Dodecanisa
Dodecanese
Stenon Karpathos
Stenon Kasos
Gökova Körfezi
Güllük Korfezi
Kuşadasi Körfezi
İzmir Körfezi
Fethiye Körfezi
Marmaris Limanı
A K
M E D I T E
1
2
3
4
A
B
C
D
27°
28°
29°
38°
37°
36°
35°

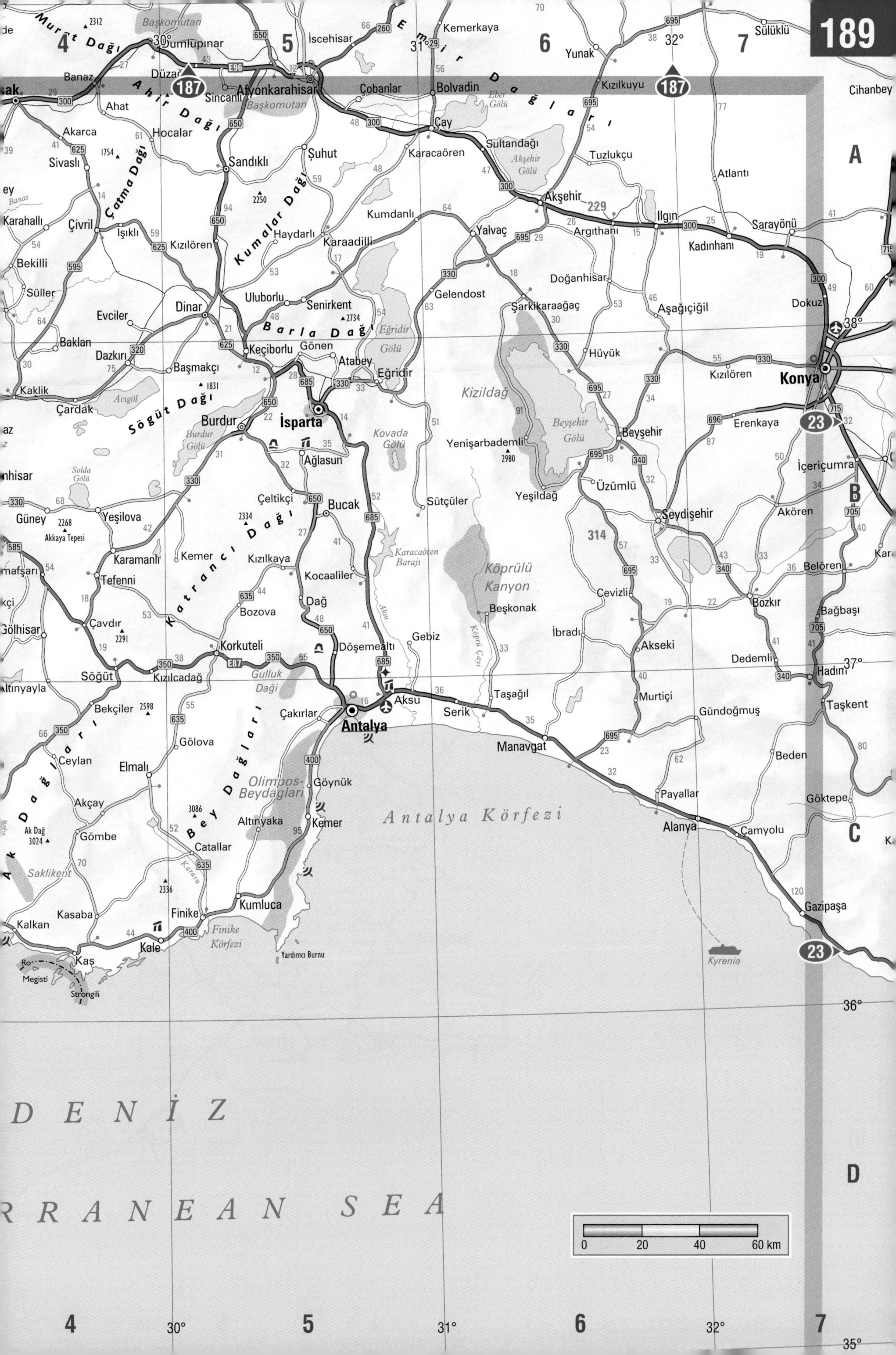
Murat Dağı
Başkomutan
Dumlupınar
İscehisar
Emir Dağları
Kemerkaya
Yunak
Sülüklü
Cihanbey
Banaz
Düzağaç
Ahir Dağı
Sincanlı
Afyonkarahisar
Başkomutan
Çobanlar
Bolvadin
Eber Gölü
Kızılkuyu
Ahat
Akarca
Hocalar
Çay
Sultandağı
Tuzlukçu
Sivaslı
Çatma Dağı
Sandıklı
Şuhut
Karacaören
Akşehir Gölü
Atlantı
Banaz
Karahallı
Çivril
Işıklı
Kumalar Dağı
Kumdanlı
Akşehir
Ilgın
Sarayönü
Argıthanı
Kadınhanı
Bekilli
Kızılören
Haydarlı
Karaadilli
Yalvaç
Süller
Uluborlu
Senirkent
Gelendost
Doğanhisar
Dokuz
Dinar
Evciler
Barla Dağı
Eğridir Gölü
Şarkikaraağaç
Aşağıçiğil
Baklan
Dazkırı
Keçiborlu
Gönen
Atabey
Eğridir
Hüyük
Kızılören
Konya
Başmakçı
Kaklik
Çardak
Acıgöl
Söğüt Dağı
Kizildağ
Beyşehir Gölü
Burdur
Isparta
Erenkaya
Burdur Gölü
Kovada Gölü
Yenişarbademli
Beyşehir
Ağlasun
Salda Gölü
Çeltikçi
Yeşildağ
Üzümlü
İçeriçumra
Bucak
Sütçüler
Güney
Yeşilova
Akkaya Tepesi
Katrancı Dağı
Seydişehir
Akören
Karamanlı
Kemer
Kızılkaya
Karacaören Barajı
Köprülü Kanyon
Belören
Tefenni
Kocaaliler
Cevizli
Bozkır
Bozova
Dağ
Beşkonak
Bağbaşı
Gölhisar
Çavdır
Korkuteli
Gebiz
İbradı
Akseki
Dedemli
Hadım
Söğüt
Kızılcadağ
Gulluk Dağı
Döşemealtı
Taşağıl
Murtiçi
Altınyayla
Bekçiler
Çakırlar
Aksu
Serik
Gündoğmuş
Taşkent
Antalya
Manavgat
Gölova
Ceylan
Elmalı
Beden
Olimpos-Beydağları
Göynük
Payallar
Akçay
Bey Dağları
Göktepe
Altınyaka
Kemer
Antalya Körfezi
Alanya
Camyolu
Ak Dağ
Gömbe
Catallar
Saklikent
Karasu
Kumluca
Finike
Gazipaşa
Kasaba
Kalkan
Finike Körfezi
Kale
Kaş
Yardımcı Burnu
Kyrenia
Ro
Megisti
Strongili
DENİZ
RRANEAN SEA
0 20 40 60 km
30°
31°
32°
35°
36°
37°
38°

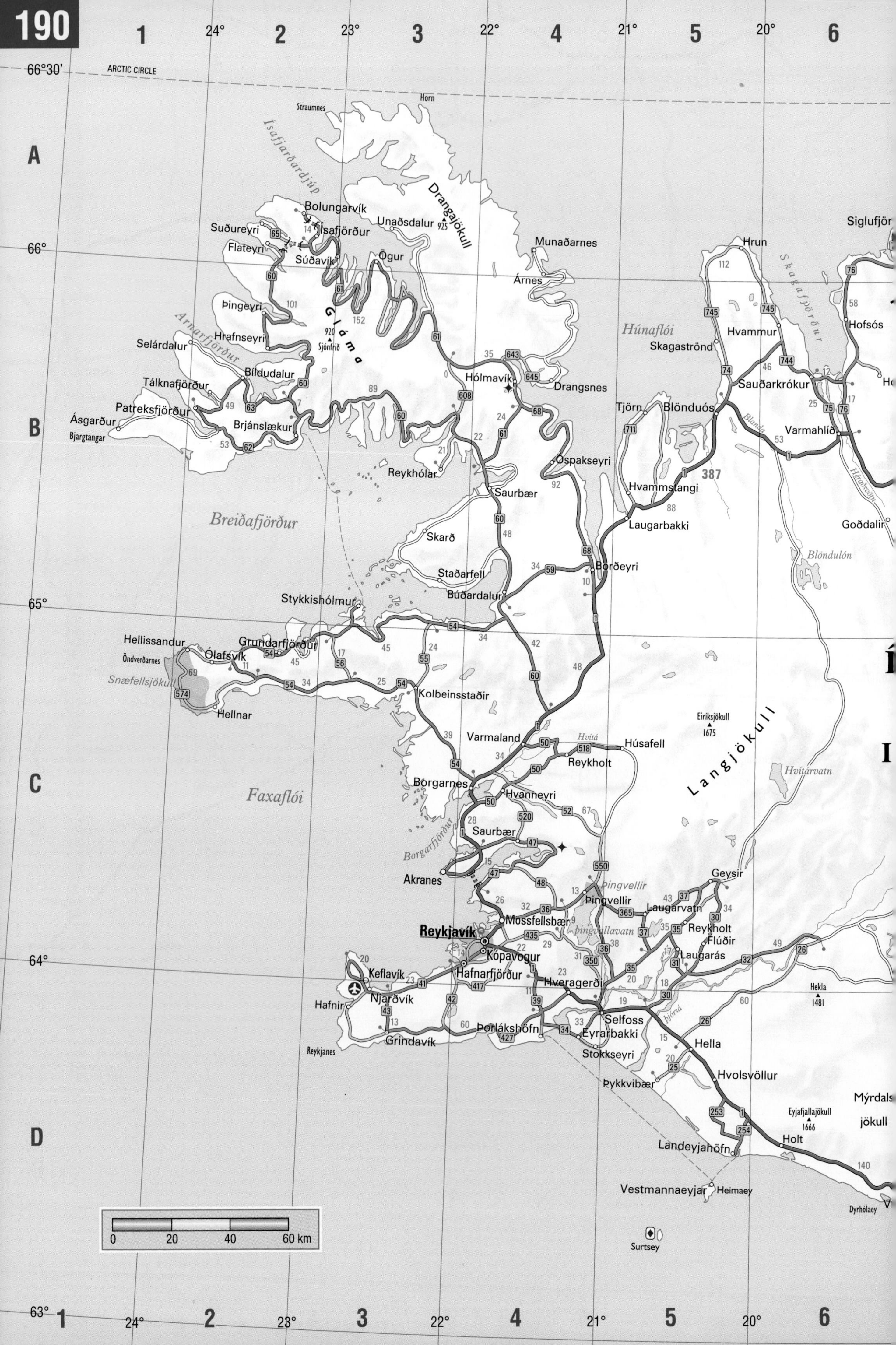
ARCTIC CIRCLE
Horn
Straumnes
Ísafjarðardjúp
Drangajökull
Bolungarvík
Ísafjörður
Unaðsdalur
Suðureyri
Flateyri
Súðavík
Ögur
Munaðarnes
Árnes
Þingeyri
Glámа
Sjónfríð
Arnarfjörður
Hrafnseyri
Selárdalur
Bíldudalur
Tálknafjörður
Patreksfjörður
Ásgarður
Bjargtangar
Brjánslækur
Hólmavík
Drangsnes
Reykhólar
Óspakseyri
Saurbær
Breiðafjörður
Skarð
Staðarfell
Búðardalur
Borðeyri
Stykkishólmur
Hellissandur
Öndverðarnes
Grundarfjörður
Ólafsvík
Snæfellsjökull
Hellnar
Kolbeinsstaðir
Varmaland
Húsafell
Reykholt
Borgarnes
Hvanneyri
Faxaflói
Borgarfjörður
Saurbær
Akranes
Þingvellir
Mossfellsbær
Reykjavík
Kópavogur
Hafnarfjörður
Keflavík
Njarðvík
Hafnir
Reykjanes
Grindavík
Þorlákshöfn
Hveragerði
Þingvallavatn
Selfoss
Eyrarbakki
Stokkseyri
Húnaflói
Skagaströnd
Tjörn
Blönduós
Hvammstangi
Laugarbakki
Hrun
Skagafjörður
Hvammur
Sauðarkrókur
Varmahlíð
Blanda
Siglufjör
Hofsós
Goðdalir
Blöndulón
Eiríksjökull
Langjökull
Hvítá
Hvítárvatn
Geysir
Laugarvatn
Reykholt
Flúðir
Laugarás
Hekla
Þjórsá
Hella
Hvolsvöllur
Þykkvibær
Landeyjahöfn
Holt
Vestmannaeyjar
Heimaey
Surtsey
Mýrdalsjökull
Eyjafjallajökull
Dyrhólaey
0 20 40 60 km

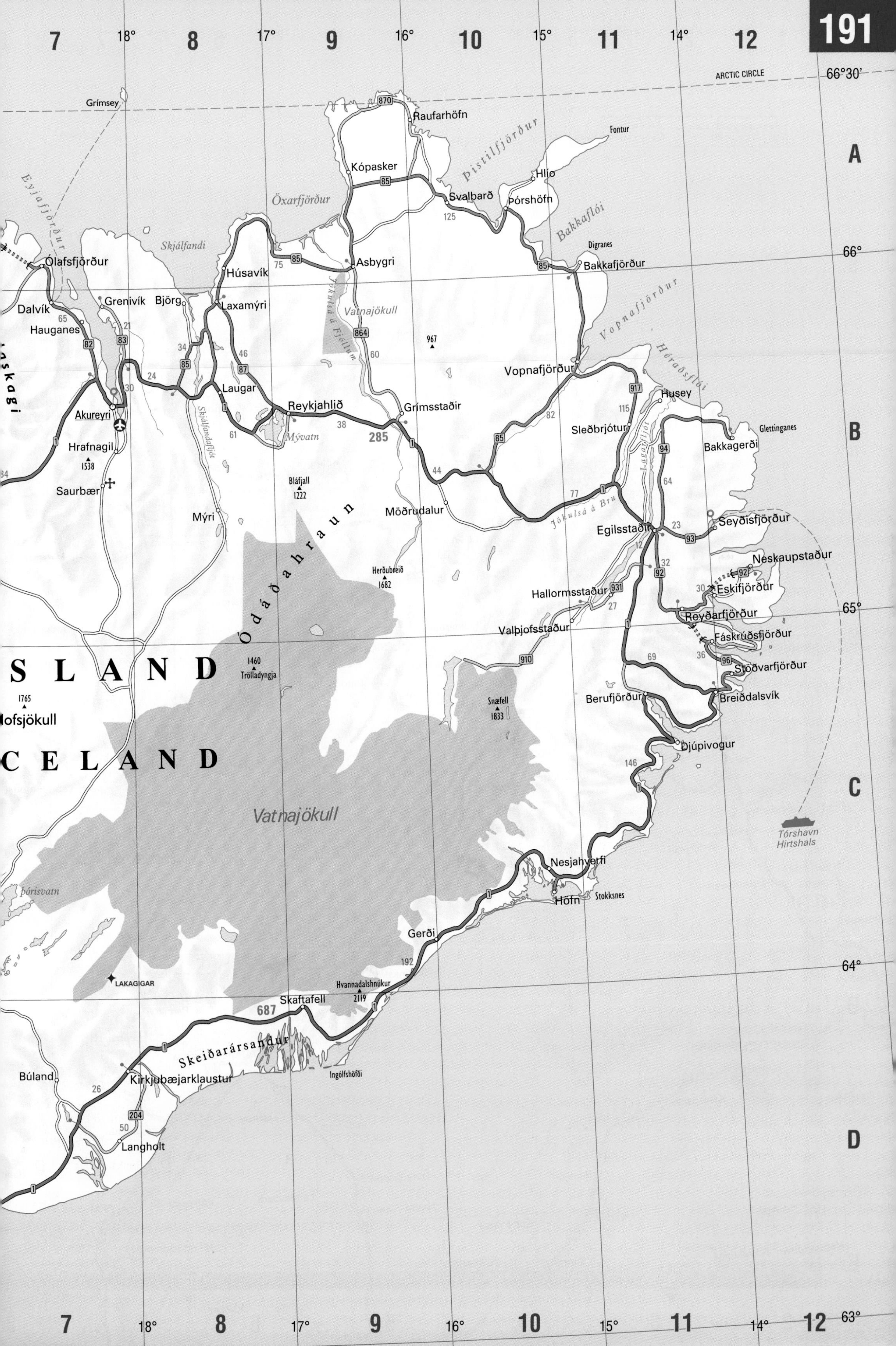

ARCTIC CIRCLE
66°30'

7 18° **8** 17° **9** 16° **10** 15° **11** 14° **12**

Grímsey

Raufarhöfn
870

Kópasker
85

Öxarfjörður
Pistilfjörður
Fontur
Hlio

Svalbarð
Þórshöfn
125
Bakkaflói

A

Ólafsjörður
Húsavík
75
85
Asbygri
Digranes
Bakkafjörður
85

66°

Dalvík
Grenivík Björg
Laxamýri
Vatnajökull
Vopnafjörður
Vopnafjörður
864
Husey
917

Hauganes
65
21
34
46
60
967
85
82
115
Bakkagerði
Glettinganes

82
83
85
87
Reykjahlið
Grímsstaðir
Sleðbrjótur
94

B

24
30
Laugar
38
285
44
285
77
Egilsstaðir
23
Seyðisfjörður

Akureyri
1
61
Mývatn
1
12
93

Hrafnagil
1538
Bláfjall
1222
Möðrudalur
32
92
Neskaupstaður
92

Saurbær
Herðubreið
1682
Hallormsstaður
931
30
Eskifjörður

Mýri
Óðáðahraun
27
Reyðarfjörður
Fáskrúðsfjörður

65°

S L A N D
1460
Trölladyngja
Valþjofsstaður
910
69
36
96
Stöðvarfjörður

1765
Hofsjökull
Snæfell
1833
Berufjörður
Breiðdalsvík

C E L A N D
Vatnajökull
146
Djúpivogur

Þórsvatn
Nesjahverfi
Tórshavn
Hirtshals

C

1
Höfn
Stokksnes

Gerði
192

64°

Búland
Hvannadalshnúkur
2119

Lakagigar
Skaftafell
687

26
Kirkjubæjarklaustur
Ingólfshöfði
Skeiðarársandur

204
50

Langholt

D

1

63°

7 18° **8** 17° **9** 16° **10** 15° **11** 14° **12**

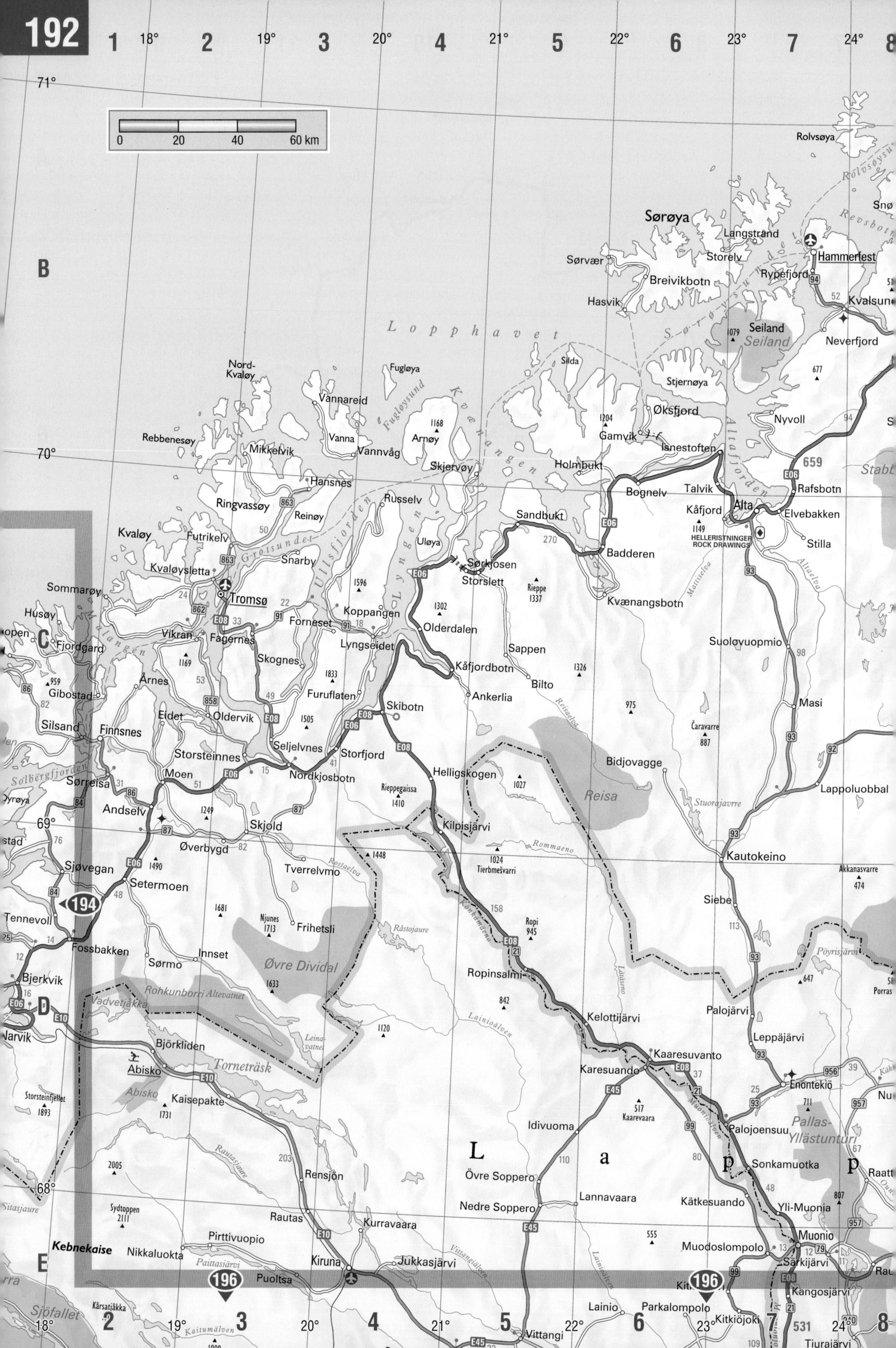
0 20 40 60 km
Rolvsøya
Sørøya
Langstrand
Hammerfest
Sørvær
Storelv
Rypefjord
Breivikbotn
Hasvik
Kvalsund
Seiland
Neverfjord
Lopphávet
Silda
Stjernøya
Nord-Kvaløy
Fugløya
Vannareid
Øksfjord
Nyvoll
Gamvik
Isnestoften
Vanna
Arnøy
Rebbenesøy
Mikkelvik
Vannvåg
Skjervøy
Holmbukt
Hansnes
Bognelv
Talvik
Rafsbotn
Ringvassøy
Russelv
Alta
Reinøy
Kåfjord
Elvebakken
Sandbukt
Kvaløy
Futrikelv
HELLERISTNINGER ROCK DRAWINGS
Uløya
Stilla
Badderen
Snarby
Kvaløysletta
Sørkjosen
Storslett
Sommarøy
Tromsø
Rieppe 1337
Kvænangsbotn
Husøy
Koppangen
Forneset
Olderdalen
Vikran
Fagernes
Lyngseidet
Fjordgard
Sappen
Suolovuopmio
Skognes
Kåfjordbotn
Gibostad
Årnes
Bilto
Furuflaten
Ankerlia
Masi
Eidet
Oldervik
Skibotn
Silsand
Finnsnes
Čaravarre 887
Storsteinnes
Seljelvnes
Storfjord
Bidjovagge
Moen
Helligskogen
Sørreisa
Nordkjosbotn
Reisa
Lappoluobbal
Rieppegaissa 1410
Andselv
Kilpisjärvi
Skjold
Øverbygd
Kautokeino
Sjøvegan
Tverrelvmo
Tierbmešvarri 1024
Akkanasvarre 474
Setermoen
Siebe
194
Tennevoll
Njunes 1713
Frihetsli
Ropi 945
Fossbakken
Innset
Sørmo
Øvre Dividal
Ropinsalmi
Bjerkvik
Palojärvi
Porras
Vadvetjåkka
Rohkunborri
Altevatnet
Kelottijärvi
Narvik
Leppäjärvi
Björkliden
Kaaresuvanto
Abisko
Torneträsk
Karesuando
Enontekiö
Storsteinfjellet 1893
Kaisepakte
517 Kaarevaara
Idivuoma
Palojoensuu
Pallas-Yllästunturi
L a p p
Sonkamuotka
Rensjön
Övre Soppero
Lannavaara
Kätkesuando
Yli-Muonia
Sydtoppen 2111
Rautas
Nedre Soppero
Kurravaara
Pirttivuopio
Muonio
Muodoslompolo
Kebnekaise
Nikkaluokta
Kiruna
Jukkasjärvi
Särkijärvi
Puoltsa
196
Kangosjärvi
Kårsatjåkka
Lainio
Parkalompolo
Kitkiöjoki
Tiurajärvi
Vittangi
Sjöfallet

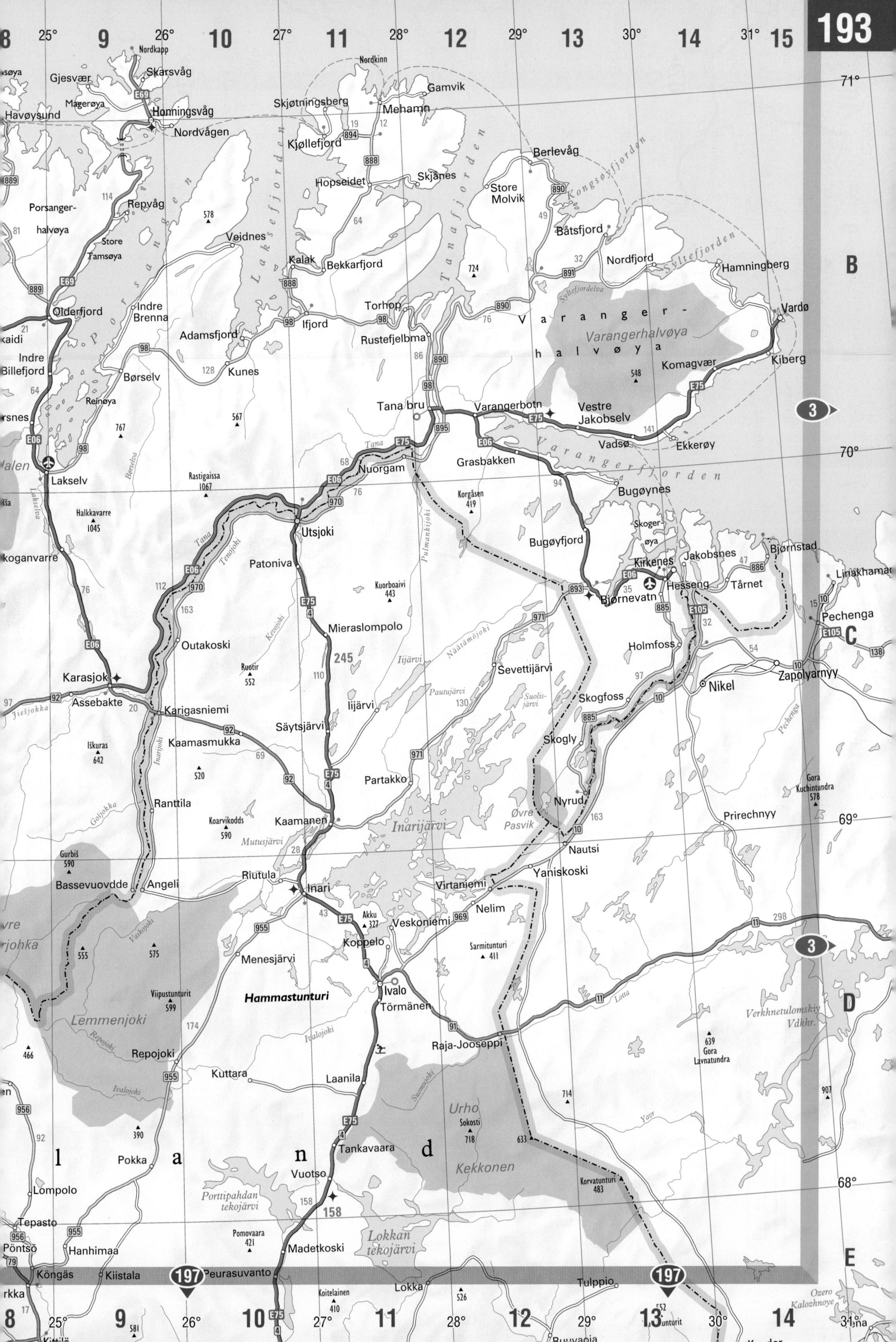

B

C

D

E

25° 9 26° 10 27° 11 28° 12 29° 13 30° 14 31° 15

71°

70°

69°

68°

Nordkapp
Skarsvåg
Gjesvær
Mågerøya
Havøysund
Honningsvåg
E69
Nordvågen
søya
889
Porsanger-
halvøya
81
Store
Tamsøya
Repvåg
114
578
Veidnes
Kalak
Bekkarfjord
E69
889
Olderfjord
Indre
Brenna
Adamsfjord
98
98
Torhop
98
Ifjord
Rustefjelbma
rsnes
E06
64
Reinøya
Børselv
128
Kunes
767
567
Indre
Billefjord
21
kaidi
Indre
Billefjord
64
Lakselv
Halkkavarre
1045
Rastigaissa
1067
koganvarre
76
Tana bru
895
E75
68
Nuorgam
970
76
Utsjoki
E06
112
970
Outakoski
163
E06
Patoniva
E75
4
Mieraslompolo
245
110
Karasjok
Assebakte
20
92
97
92
Karigasniemi
Iškuras
642
92
Kaamasmukka
69
Säytsjärvi
520
92
Ranttila
E75
4
Koarvikodds
590
Partakko
Kaamanen
28
Gurbiš
590
Riutula
Bassevuovdde
Angeli
Inari
43
955
E75
Akku
377
Veskoniemi
969
Koppelo
Menesjärvi
4
Viipustunturit
599
Hammastunturi
Ivalo
Törmänen
Lemmenjoki
174
466
Repojoki
955
Raja-Jooseppi
Kuttara
Laanila
956
Urho
Sokosti
718
92
390
E75
4
Tankavaara
l a n d
Pokka
Vuotso
Lompolo
158
Kekkonen
Tepasto
Pomovaara
421
158
Hanhimaa
Köngäs
Kiistala
197
Peurasuvanto
Madetkoski
Lokkan
tekojärvi
Lokka
rkka
79
17
E75
4
Koitelainen
410
526

Skjøtningsberg
Gamvik
Nordkinn
Mehamn
12
19
Kjøllefjord
894
888
Hopseidet
Skjånes
64
Store
Molvik
Berlevåg
890
Båtsfjord
49
32
891
Nordfjord
Hamningberg
724
Vardø
890
Varanger-
halvøya
548
Komagvær
E75
Kiberg
98
890
Varangerbotn
Vestre
Jakobselv
Grasbakken
E75
Vadsø
141
E06
Ekkerøy
Tana
Korgåsen
419
94
Bugøynes
Bugøyfjord
Skoger-
øya
Kirkenes
Jakobsnes
Bjørnstad
E06
47
886
Hesseng
Tårnet
Liinakhamari
893
35
Bjørnevatn
971
885
E105
15
10
Pechenga
Holmfoss
54
E105
C
Näätämöjoki
Sevettijärvi
97
10
Nikel
Zapolyarnyy
Iijärvi
130
Pautujärvi
Suolis-
järvi
Skogfoss
10
138
Iijärvi
971
Skogly
885
Inarijärvi
Øvre
Pasvik
Nyrud
Prirechnyy
Gora
Kuchintundra
578
10
163
Nautsi
Mutusjärvi
Virtaniemi
Yaniskoski
Nelim
Sarmitunturi
411
11
298
3
Øvre
johka
Vaskojoki
555
575
Verkhnetulomskiy
Vdkhr.
639
Gora
Lavnatundra
714
907
D
633
Korvatunturi
483
197
Tulppio
Ozero
Kalozhnoye
52
unturit

8 17 25° 9 581 26° 10 27° 11 28° 12 29° 13 30° 14 31°a

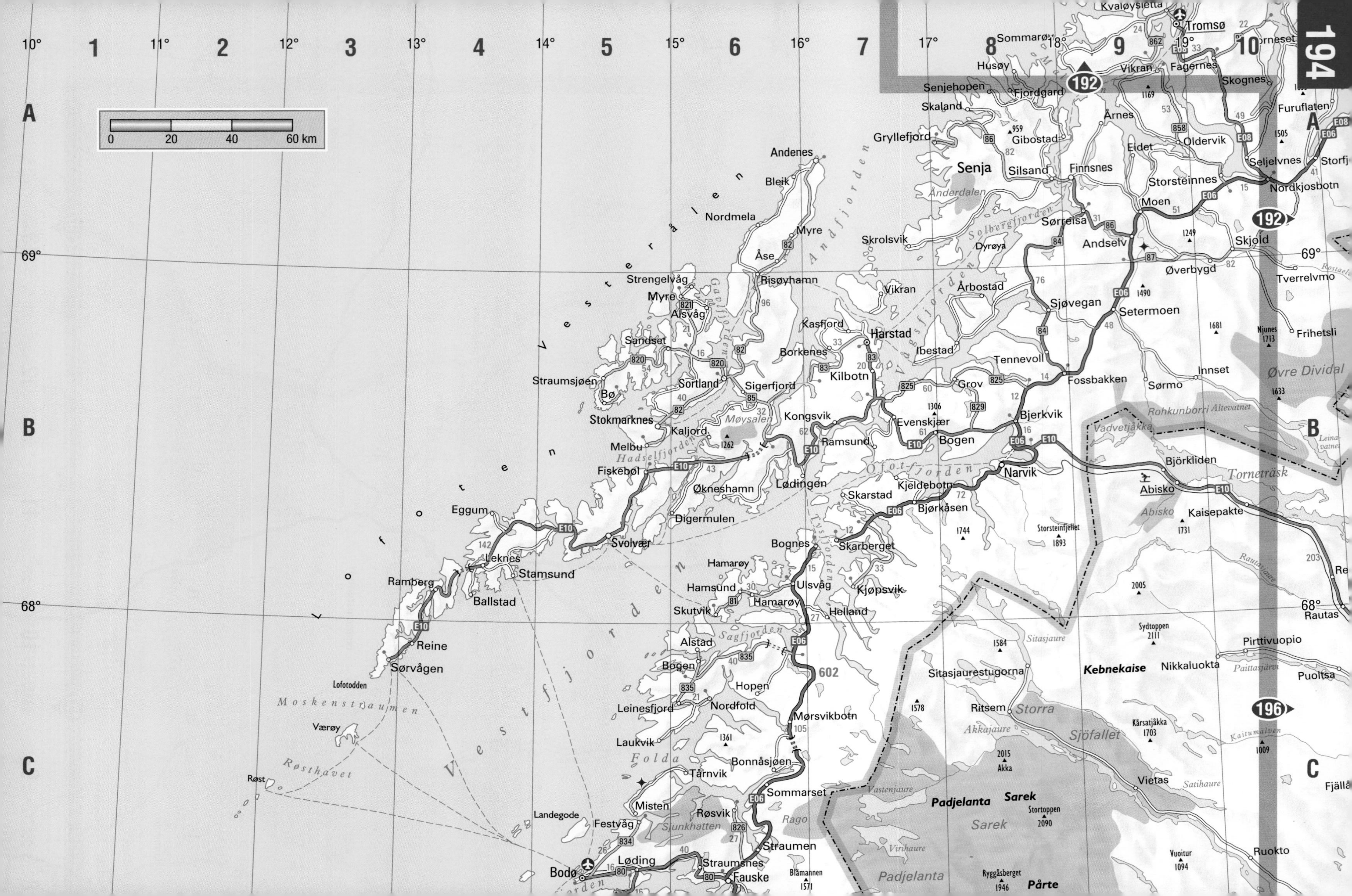
Vesterålen
Lofoten
Vestfjorden
Andfjorden
Senja
Tromsø
Narvik
Harstad
Svolvær
Bodø
Fauske
Sortland
Stokmarknes
Andenes
Finnsnes
Leknes
Reine
Å
Sørvågen
Ramberg
Ballstad
Stamsund
Eggum
Fiskebøl
Melbu
Lødingen
Kebnekaise
Abisko
Björkliden
Torneträsk
Kaisepakte
Nikkaluokta
Ritsem
Storra Sjöfallet
Padjelanta
Sarek
Værøy
Røst
Moskenstraumen
Røsthavet
Lofotodden
Landegode
Øvre Dividal
Setermoen
Bjerkvik
Andselv
Moen
Nordkjosbotn
Skjold
Sjøvegan
Gryllefjord
Skrolsvik
Evenskjær
Bogen
Kjeldebotn
Bjørkåsen
Skarberget
Bognes
Ulsvåg
Hamarøy
Hamsund
Skutvik
Mørsvikbotn
Sommarset
Straumen
Straumsnes
Løding
Misten
Festvåg
Rognan
Kilbotn
Sigerfjord
Myre
Alsvåg
Strengelvåg
Bø
Straumsjøen
Sandset
0 20 40 60 km

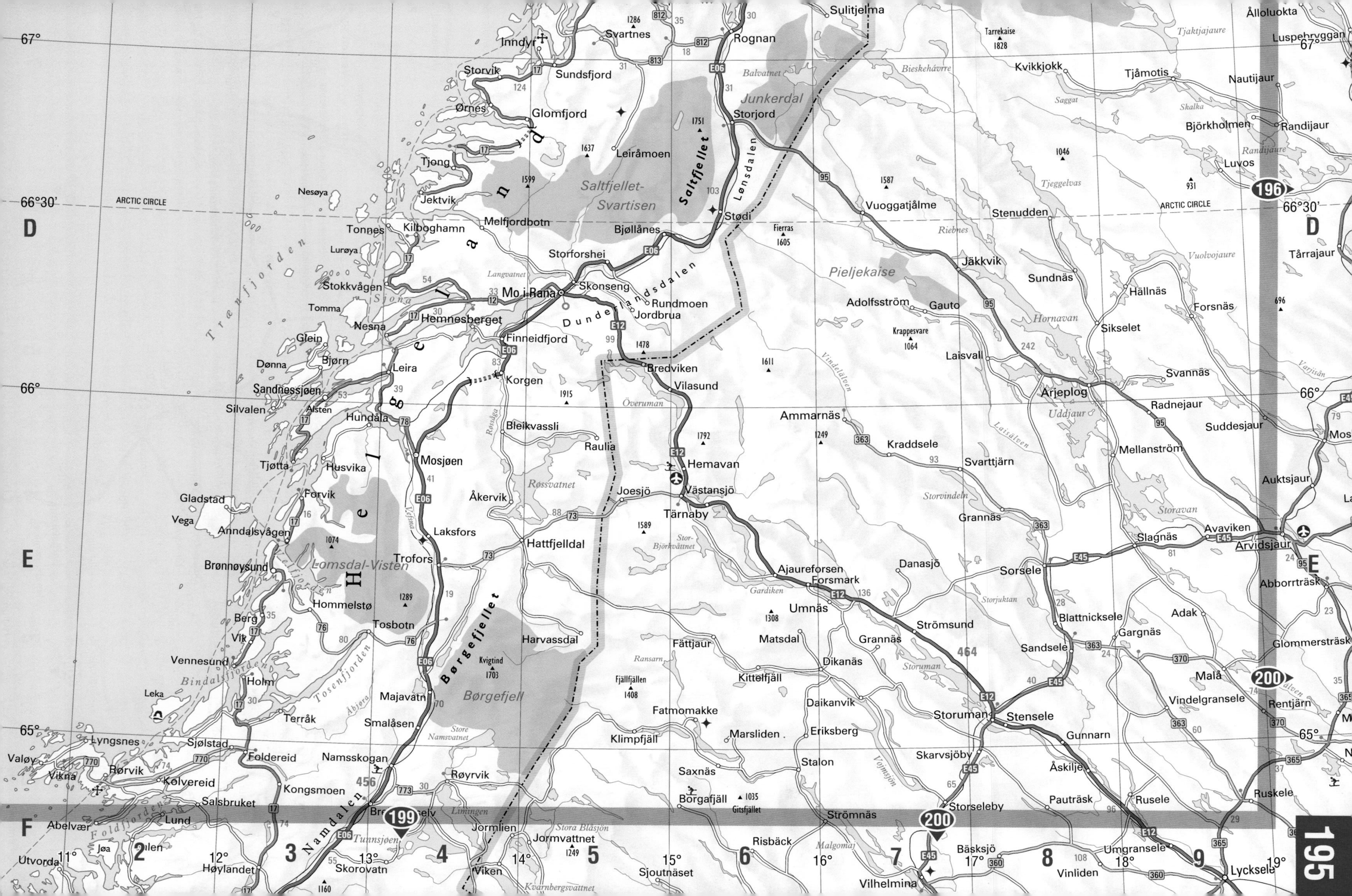
Saltfjellet
Saltfjellet-Svartisen
Junkerdal
Lønsdalen
Dunderlandsdalen
Helgeland
Børgefjellet
Børgefjell
Lomsdal-Visten
Namdalen
Pieljekaise
Trænfjorden
Bindalsfjorden
Tosenfjorden
Foldfjorden
ARCTIC CIRCLE
Mo i Rana
Mosjøen
Sandnessjøen
Brønnøysund
Storuman
Vilhelmina
Lycksele
Arvidsjaur
Arjeplog
Sorsele
Tärnaby
Hemavan
Västansjö
Jäkkvik
Sulitjelma
Rognan
Storjord
Stødi
Bjøllånes
Skonseng
Storforshei
Finneidfjord
Korgen
Hattfjelldal
Trofors
Majavatn
Nesna
Glomfjord
Ørnes
Inndyr
Sundsfjord
Svartnes
Kvikkjokk
Tjåmotis
Nautijaur
Sikselet
Adolfsström
Laisvall
Ammarnäs
Stensele
Malå
Namsskogan
Kongsmoen
Terråk
Abelvær
Vikna
Rørvik
Lund
Høylandet
Foldereid
Salsbruket
Kolvereid
Leka
Vega
Gladstad
Tjøtta
Dønna
Lurøya
Tonnes
Kilboghamn
Jektvik
Tjong
Melfjordbotn
Vindelälven
Laisälven
Storjuktan
Malgomaj
Vojmsjön
Røyrvik
Sjoutnäset
Borgafjäll
Saxnäs
Fatmomakke
Klimpfjäll
Kittelfjäll
Dikanäs
Stalon
Strömnäs
Risbäck
Jormvattnet
Jormlien
Viken
Skorovatn
D
E
F
196
199
200

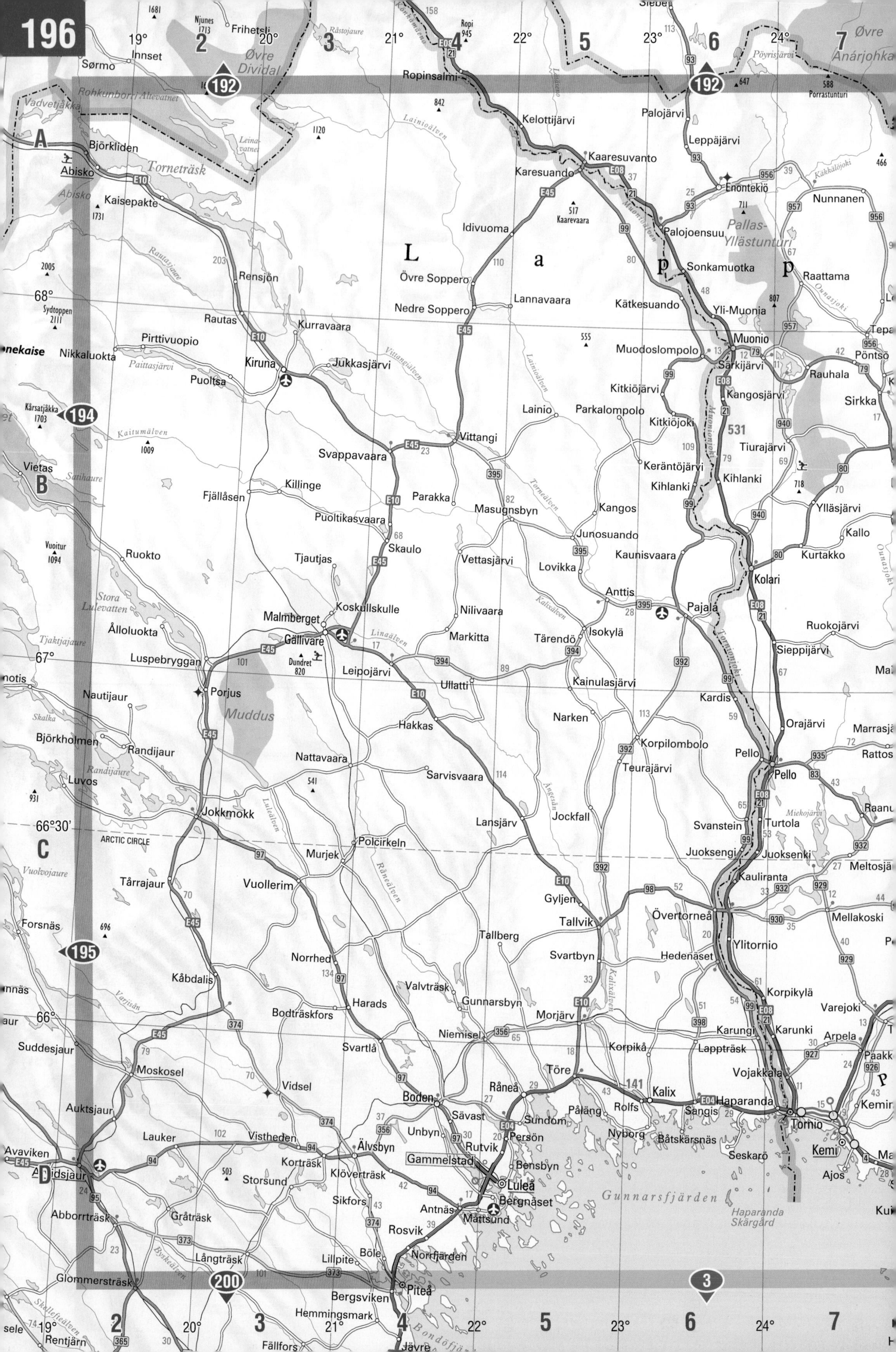
Kiruna
Gällivare
Jokkmokk
Boden
Luleå
Piteå
Kalix
Haparanda
Tornio
Kemi
Pajala
Kolari
Muonio
Enontekiö
Karesuando
Arvidsjaur
Älvsbyn
Övertorneå
Torneträsk
Muddus
ARCTIC CIRCLE
Gunnarsfjärden
Lapp

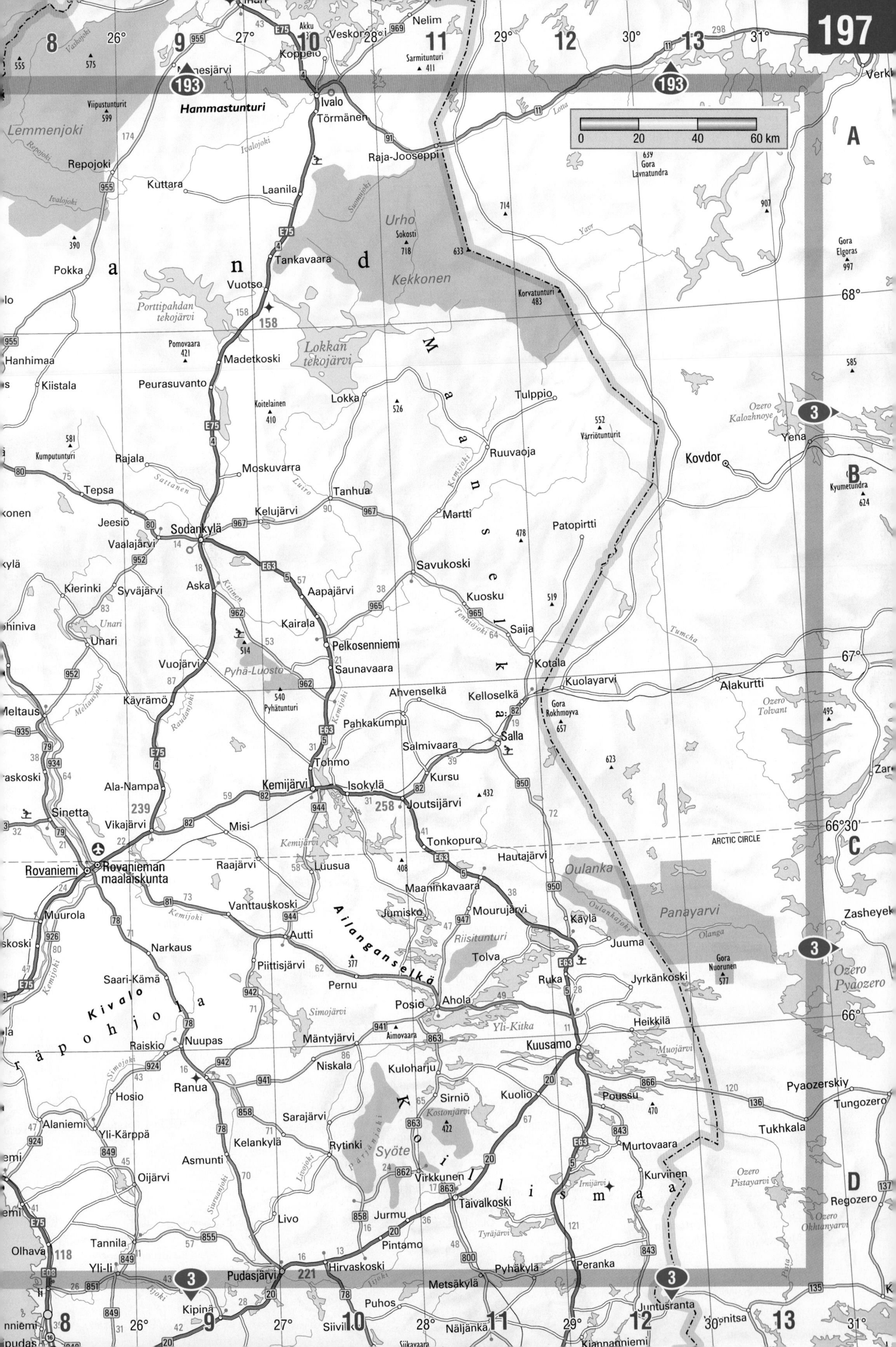

Hammastunturi
Lemmenjoki
Ivalo
Törmänen
Raja-Jooseppi
Urho Kekkonen
Lokkan tekojärvi
Porttipahdan tekojärvi
Sodankylä
Savukoski
Pelkosenniemi
Salla
Kemijärvi
Rovaniemi
Rovaniemen maalaiskunta
Kuusamo
Posio
Taivalkoski
Pudasjärvi
Ranua
Kovdor
Alakurtti
Oulanka
Panayarvi
Ozero Pyaozero
Syöte
Maanselkä
Ailanganselkä
Koillismaa
Kivalo
Peräpohjola
ARCTIC CIRCLE
Korvatunturi
Rokua
0 20 40 60 km

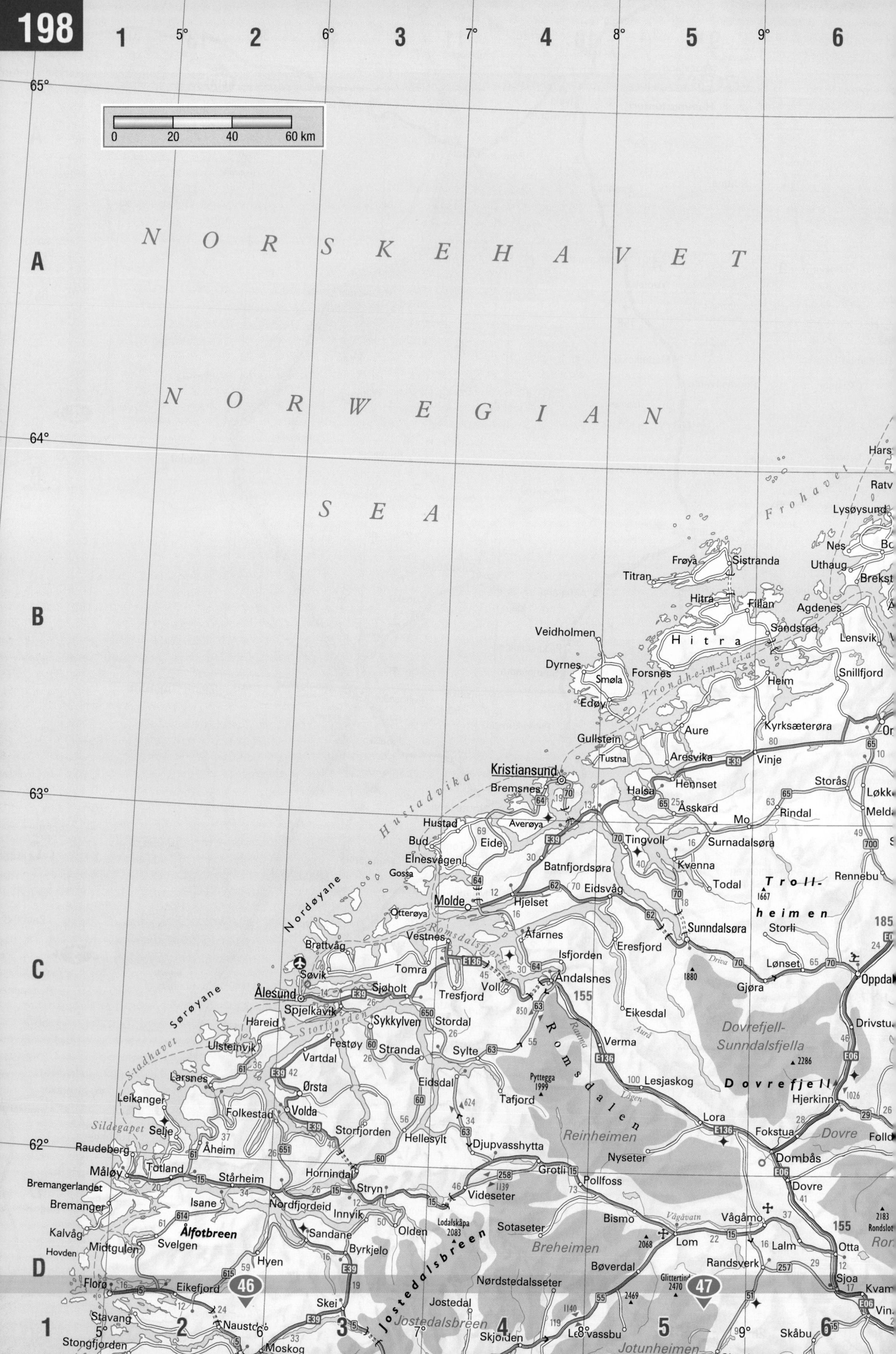
0 20 40 60 km
NORSKEHAVET
NORWEGIAN SEA
Frohavet
Hustadvika
Trondheimsleia
Nordøyane
Sørøyane
Stadhavet
Sildegapet
Romsdalsfjorden
Storfjorden
Titran
Frøya
Sistranda
Hitra
Fillan
Sandstad
Veidholmen
Dyrnes
Smøla
Edøy
Forsnes
Helm
Hars
Ratv
Lysøysund
Nes
Uthaug
Brekst
Agdenes
Lensvik
Snillfjord
Kyrksæterøra
Gullstein
Aure
Tustna
Aresvika
Vinje
Kristiansund
Bremsnes
Averøya
Halsa
Hennset
Åsskard
Storås
Løkk
Meld
Rindal
Mo
Hustad
Bud
Eide
Elnesvågen
Gossa
Tingvoll
Surnadalsøra
Kvenna
Batnfjordsøra
Todal
Rennebu
Eidsvåg
Molde
Hjelset
Trollheimen
Otterøya
Sunndalsøra
Storli
Vestnes
Åfarnes
Brattvåg
Isfjorden
Eresfjord
Søvik
Tomra
Åndalsnes
Lønset
Oppdal
Ålesund
Sjøholt
Voll
Tresfjord
Gjøra
Spjelkavik
Hareid
Sykkylven
Stordal
Eikesdal
Drivstua
Romsdalen
Rauma
Dovrefjell-Sunndalsfjella
Ulsteinvik
Festøy
Vartdal
Stranda
Sylte
Verma
Aura
Driva
Larsnes
Ørsta
Eidsdal
Pyttegga 1999
Lesjaskog
Dovrefjell
Hjerkinn
Leikanger
Volda
Tafjord
Lågen
Folkestad
Selje
Storfjorden
Hellesylt
Reinheimen
Lora
Fokstua
Dovre
Folld
Raudeberg
Åheim
Djupvasshytta
Nyseter
Dombås
Måløy
Totland
Hornindal
Grotli
Pollfoss
Bremangerlandet
Stårheim
Stryn
Videseter
Bremanger
Isane
Nordfjordeid
Innvik
Bismo
Vågåvatn
Vågåmo
Kalvåg
Ålfotbreen
Sandane
Olden
Lodalskåpa 2083
Sotaseter
Lom
Lalm
Rondslot
Otta
Hovden
Midtgulen
Svelgen
Byrkjelo
Breheimen
Ror
Hyen
Jostedalsbreen
Bøverdal
Randsverk
Florø
Eikefjord
Nordstedalsseter
Glittertind 2470
Sjoa
Kvam
Stavang
Skei
Jostedal
Vin
Naustdal
Stongfjorden
Moskog
Jostedalsbreen
Skjolden
Leirvassbu
Jotunheimen
Skåbu
46
47
155
185

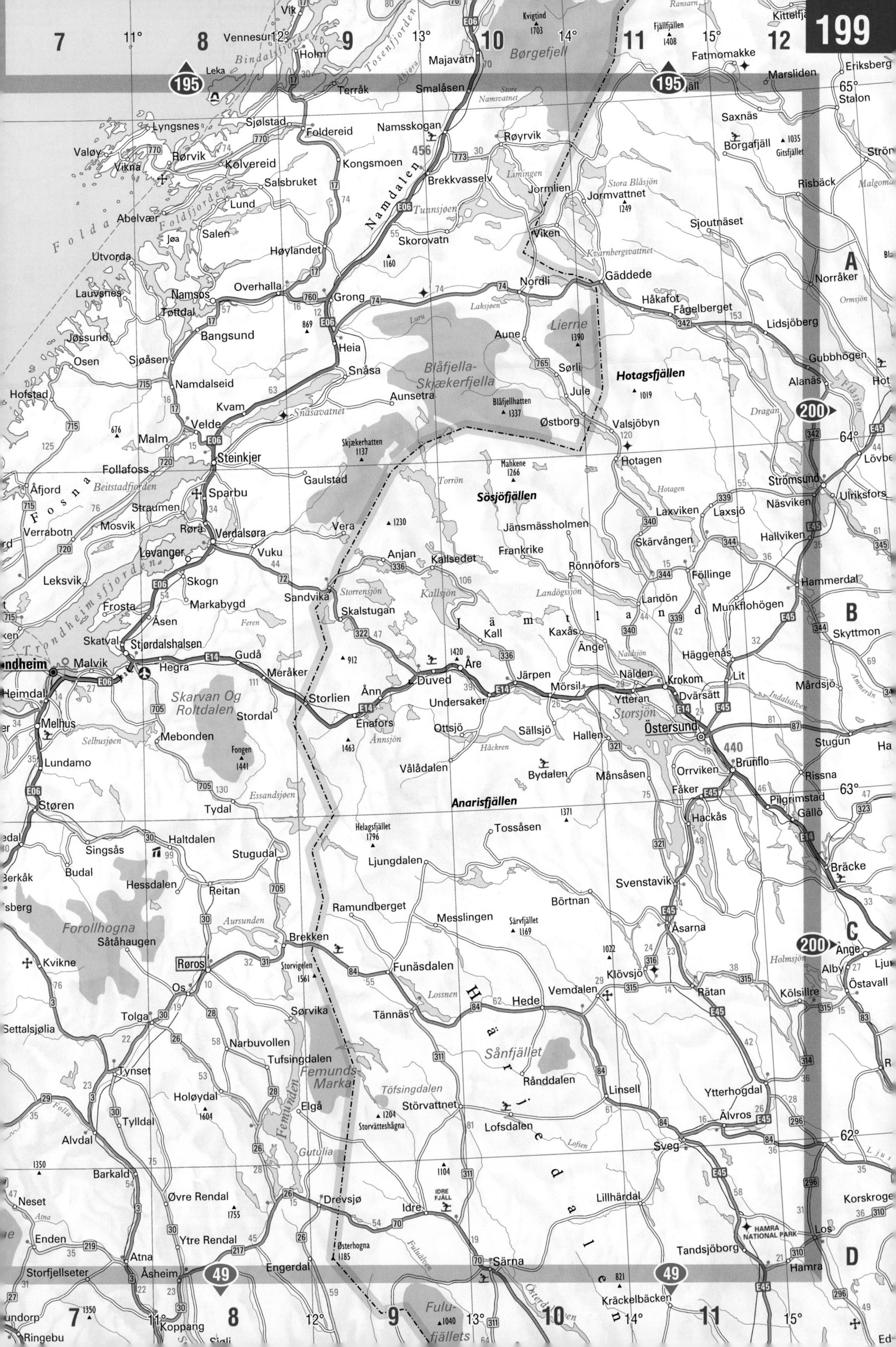
7
8
9
10
11
12
Vennesund
Holm
Vik
Majavatn
Børgefjell
Kvigtind
1703
Fjällfjällen
1408
Fatmomakke
Kittelfjäll
Eriksberg
Marsliden
195
Leka
Bindalsfjorden
Tosenfjorden
Terråk
Smalåsen
Store Namsvatnet
Stalon
Saxnäs
Lyngsnes
Sjølstad
Foldereid
Namsskogan
Røyrvik
Borgafjäll
Gitsfjället
1035
Valøy
Vikna
Rørvik
Kolvereid
Kongsmoen
456
Limingen
Risbäck
Malgomaj
Salsbruket
Brekkvasselv
Namdalen
Jormlien
Jormvattnet
Stora Blåsjön
1249
Lund
Abelvær
Foldfjorden
Folda
Tunnsjøen
Sjoutnäset
Jøa
Salen
Skorovatn
Viken
Utvorda
Høylandet
Kvarnbergsvattnet
1160
A
Nordli
Gäddede
Norråker
Lauvsnes
Namsos
Overhalla
Grong
Laksjøen
Håkafot
Fågelberget
Ormsjön
Tøttdal
Luru
Lierne
Lidsjöberg
869
Jøssund
Bangsund
Aune
1390
Heia
Gubbhögen
Osen
Sjøåsen
Snåsa
Blåfjella-Skjækerfjella
Sørli
Hotagsfjällen
Alanäs
Hofstad
Namdalseid
Jule
1019
Aunsetra
Blåfjellhatten
1337
Dragan
Flåsjön
200
Kvam
Snåsavatnet
Østborg
Valsjöbyn
Velde
676
Malm
64°
Skjækerhatten
1137
Hotagen
Lövberga
Steinkjer
Follafoss
Mahkene
1266
Gaulstad
Torrön
Åfjord
Beitstadfjorden
Sparbu
Hotagen
Strömsund
Ulriksfors
Sösjöfjällen
Fosna
Straumen
Laxviken
Laxsjö
Näsviken
Mosvik
1230
Jänsmässholmen
Verrabotn
Røra
Verdalsøra
Vera
Skärvången
Hallviken
Levanger
Vuku
Anjan
Frankrike
Kallsedet
Rönnöfors
Föllinge
Leksvik
Skogn
Hammerdal
Sandvika
Storrensjön
Kallsjön
Landögssjön
Landön
Munkflohögen
Trondheimsfjorden
Frosta
Markabygd
Skalstugan
Jämtland
B
Åsen
Feren
Kall
Kaxås
Skyttmon
Skatval
Stjørdalshalsen
1420
Änge
Naldsjön
Häggenås
Trondheim
Malvik
Hegra
Gudå
Meråker
912
Åre
Lit
Heimdal
Duved
Järpen
Nälden
Krokom
Mårdsjö
Skarvan Og Roltdalen
Storlien
Ånn
Undersaker
Mörsil
Ytteran
Dvärsätt
Indalsälven
Ammerån
Stordal
Storsjön
Melhus
Enafors
Ottsjö
Sällsjö
Hallen
Östersund
Selbusjøen
Mebonden
Ånnsjön
Håckren
440
Stugun
Fongen
1441
1463
Lundamo
Vålådalen
Bydalen
Månsåsen
Brunflo
Orrviken
Rissna
Essandsjøen
Fåker
Støren
Tydal
Anarisfjällen
Pilgrimstad
63°
Gällö
1371
Helagsfjället
1796
Tossåsen
Hackås
Haltdalen
Singsås
Stugudal
Ljungdalen
Bräcke
Budal
Berkåk
Hessdalen
Reitan
Svenstavik
Börtnan
Ramundberget
Messlingen
Särvfjället
1169
Forollhogna
Aursunden
Åsarna
Såtåhaugen
Brekken
C
1022
Ånge
Holmsjön
Kvikne
Røros
Storvigelen
1561
Funäsdalen
Klövsjö
Alby
Östavall
Os
Vemdalen
Rätan
Kölsillre
Lossnen
Hede
Tolga
Sørvika
Tännäs
Settalsjølia
Härjedalen
Narbuvollen
Sånfjället
Tufsingdalen
Femundsmarka
Tynset
Rånddalen
Töfsingdalen
Linsell
Ytterhogdal
Holøydal
1604
Femunden
Elgå
1204
Storvätteshågna
Störvattnet
Älvros
Tylldal
Lofsdalen
Alvdal
Gutulia
Sveg
62°
1350
Barkald
1104
Lofsen
Ljusnan
Øvre Rendal
1755
Drevsjø
Idre
Idre Fjäll
Lillhärdal
Korskrogen
Neset
Atna
Enden
Ytre Rendal
Fulunäs
Hamra National Park
Tandsjöborg
Los
Atna
Østerhogna
1185
D
Storfjellseter
Åsheim
49
Engerdal
Särna
Hamra
Österdalälven
821
Kräckelbäcken
Fulufjällets
1040
Fundorp
Koppang
Ringebu
Sjoli
11°
12°
13°
14°
15°

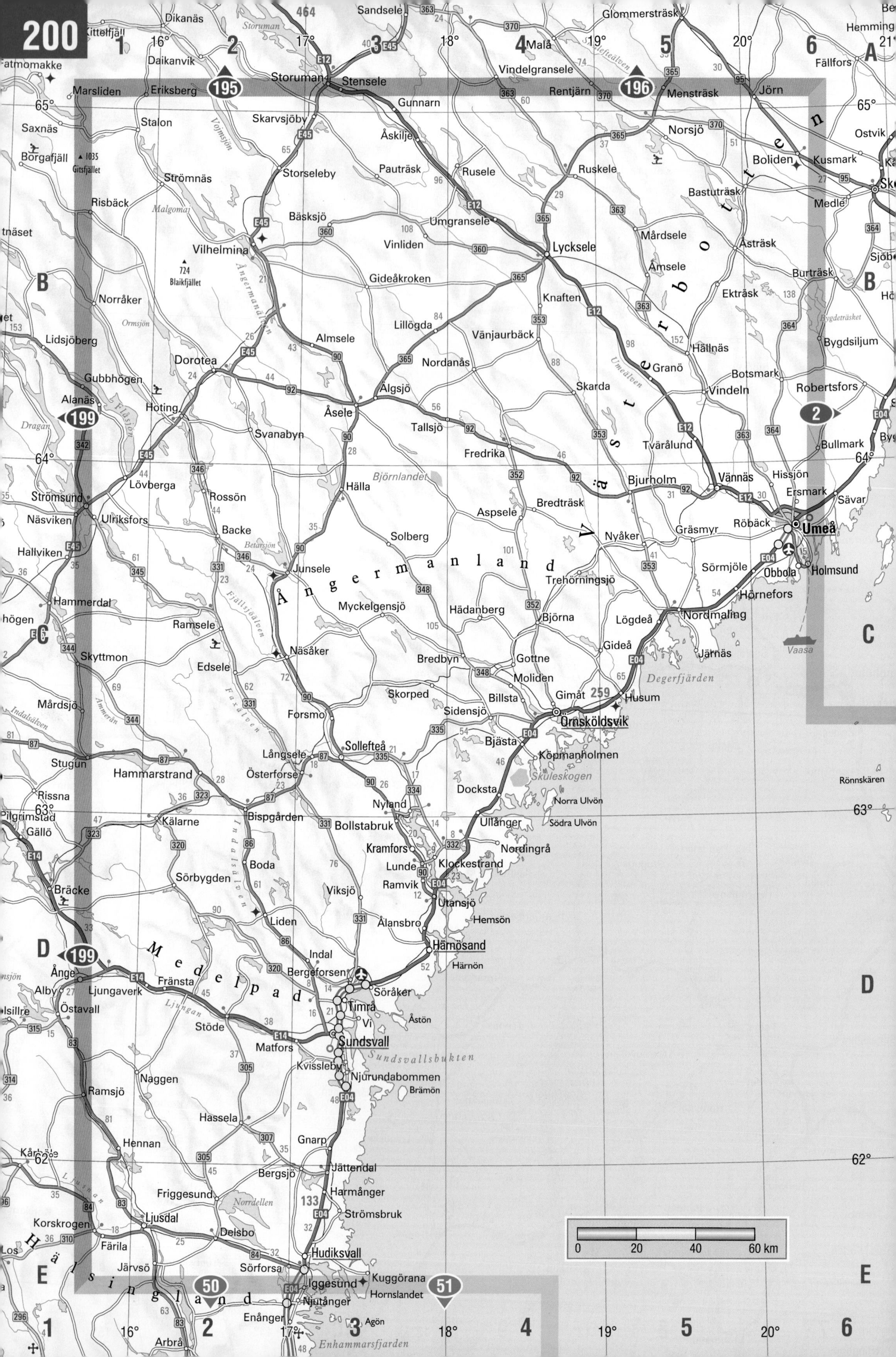
Storuman
Stensele
Vilhelmina
Dorotea
Åsele
Lycksele
Norsjö
Boliden
Skellefteå
Vindeln
Vännäs
Umeå
Holmsund
Robertsfors
Nordmaling
Örnsköldsvik
Husum
Sollefteå
Kramfors
Härnösand
Timrå
Sundsvall
Strömsund
Hammerdal
Bräcke
Ånge
Ljusdal
Hudiksvall
Iggesund
Järvsö
Ångermanland
Västerbotten
Medelpad
Hälsingland
Degerfjärden
Sundsvallsbukten
Enhammarsfjärden
Vaasa
Rönnskären
0 20 40 60 km

City plans · Plans de villes
Stadtpläne · Piante di città

Motorway	Autoroute	Autobahn	Autostrada
Major through route	Route principale majeur	Hauptstrecke	Strada di grande communicazione
Through route	Route principale	Schnellstrasse	Strada d'importanza regionale
Secondary road	Route secondaire		
Dual carriageway	Chaussées séparées	Nebenstrasse	Strada d'interesse locale
Other road	Autre route	Zweispurig Schnellstrasse	Strada a carreggiate doppie
Tunnel	Tunnel	Nebenstrecke	Altra strada
Limited access / pedestrian road	Rue réglementée / rue piétonne	Tunnel	Galleria stradale
One-way street	Sens unique	Beschränkter Zugang / Fussgängerzone	Strada pedonale / a accesso limitato
Parking	Parc de stationnement	Einbahnstrasse	Senso unico
Motorway number A7	Numéro d'autoroute	Parkplatz	Parcheggio
National road number 447	Numéro de route nationale	Autobahnnummer A7	Numero di autostrada
European road number E45	Numéro de route européenne	Nationalstrassen-nummer 447	Numero di strada nazionale
Destination GENT	Destination	Europäische Strassennummer E45	Numero di strada europea
Car ferry	Bac passant les autos	Ziel GENT	Destinazione
Railway	Chemin de fer	Autofähre	Traghetto automobili
Rail / bus station	Gare / gare routière	Eisenbahn	Ferrovia
Underground, metro station	Station de métro	Bahnhof / Busstation	Stazione ferrovia / pullman
Cable car	Téléférique	U-Bahnstation	Metropolitano
Abbey, cathedral	Abbaye, cathédrale	Drahtseilbahn	Funivia
Church of interest	Église intéressante	Abtei, Kloster, Kathedrale	Abbazia, duomo
Synagogue	Synagogue	Interessante Kirche	Chiesa da vedere
Hospital	Hôpital	Synagoge	Sinagoga
Police station	Police	Krankenhaus	Ospedale
Post office	Bureau de poste	Polizeiwache	Polizia
Tourist information	Office de tourisme	Postamt	Ufficio postale
Place of interest	Autre curiosité	Informationsbüro	Ufficio informazioni turistiche
		Sonstige Sehenswürdigkeit	Luogo da vedere

Approach maps · Agglomérations
Carte régionale · Regionalkarte

Toll motorway A10 – with motorway number	Autoroute à péage – avec numéro d'autoroute	Gebührenpflichtige Autobahn A10 – mit Autobahnnummer	Autostrada a pedaggio – con numero
Toll-free motorway E51 – with European road number	Autoroute – avec numéro de route européenne	Gebührenfreie Autobahn E51 – Europäische Strassennummer	Autostrada – con numero di strada europea
Pre-pay motorway – vignette required	Autoroute – 'vignette'	Autobahn – 'vignette'	Autostrada – 'vignette'
Motorway services	Aire de service	Autobahnservice	Area di servizio autostradale
Motorway junction full access, restricted access	Échangeur d'autoroute accès libre, accès reglementé	Autobahnkreuz – voller / begrenzter Zugang	Raccordi autostradali – completo / parziali
Under construction	En construction	Im Bau	In construzione
Tunnel	Tunnel	Tunnel	Galleria stradale
Major route dual carriageway 14 single carriageway 14	Route principale chausées séparées chausée sans séparation	Hauptstrecke – zweispurige 14 Schnellstrasse 14	Strada di grande communicazione carreggiata doppia carreggiata unica
Secondary route dual carriageway 96 single carriageway 96	Route secondaire chausées séparées chausée sans séparation	Nebenstrasse – zweispurige 96 Schnellstrasse 96	Strada d'interesse locale – carreggiata doppia carreggiata unica
Other road	Autre route	Nebenstrecke	Altra strada
Car ferry	Bac passant les autos	Autofähre	Traghetto automobili
Destination GIRONA	Destination	Ziel GIRONA	Destinazione
Railway	Chemin de fer	Eisenbahn	Ferrovia
Railway station Estación Central	Gare	Hauptbahnhof Estación Central	Stazione ferrovia
Height – in metres 234	Altitude – en mètres	Höhe – über dem Meeresspiegel 234	Altezza in metri
Airport	Aéroport principal	Flughafen	Aeroporto
Airfield	Autre aéroport	Flugplatz	Aerodromo / campo d'aviazione
City plan coverage area	Région de plan de ville	Vom Stadtplan abgedecktes Gebiet	Area della pianta della città

Alicante

0 km 0.5

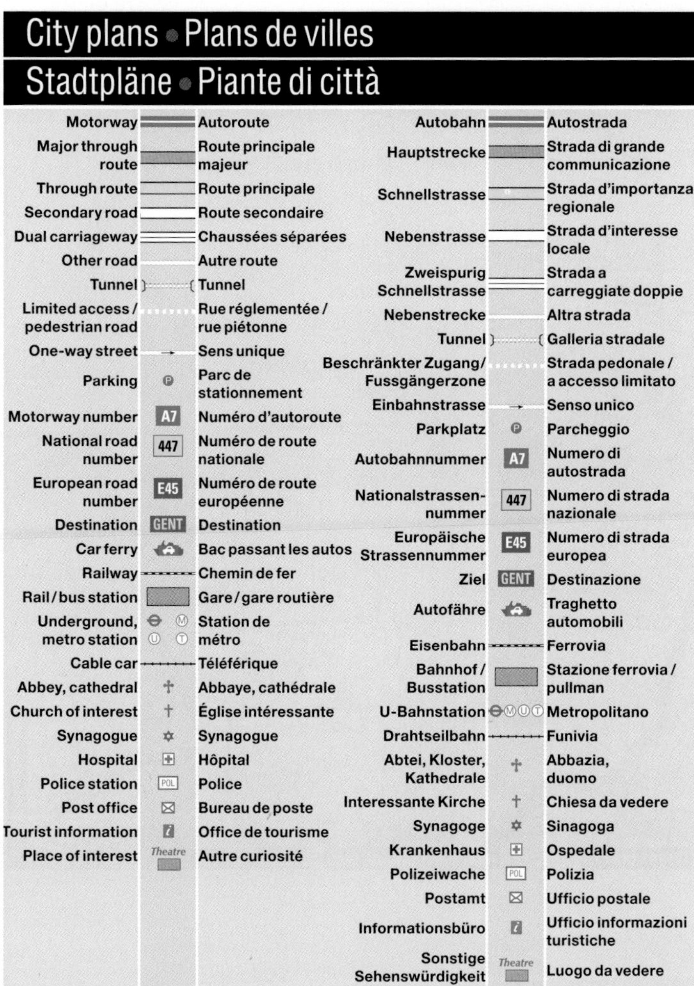

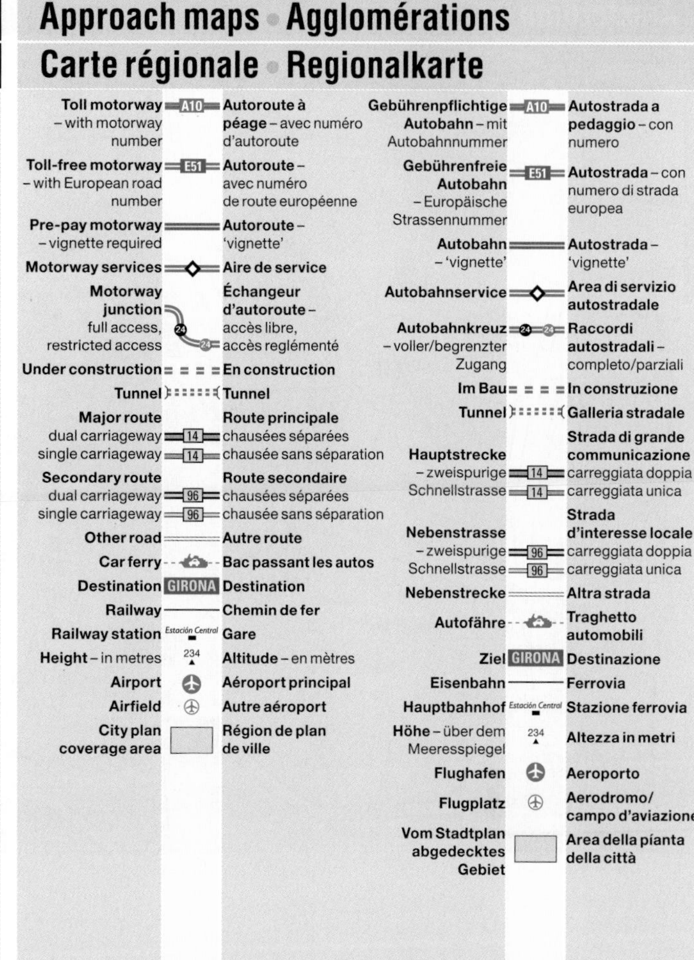

Antwerpen Antwerp

0 km 1

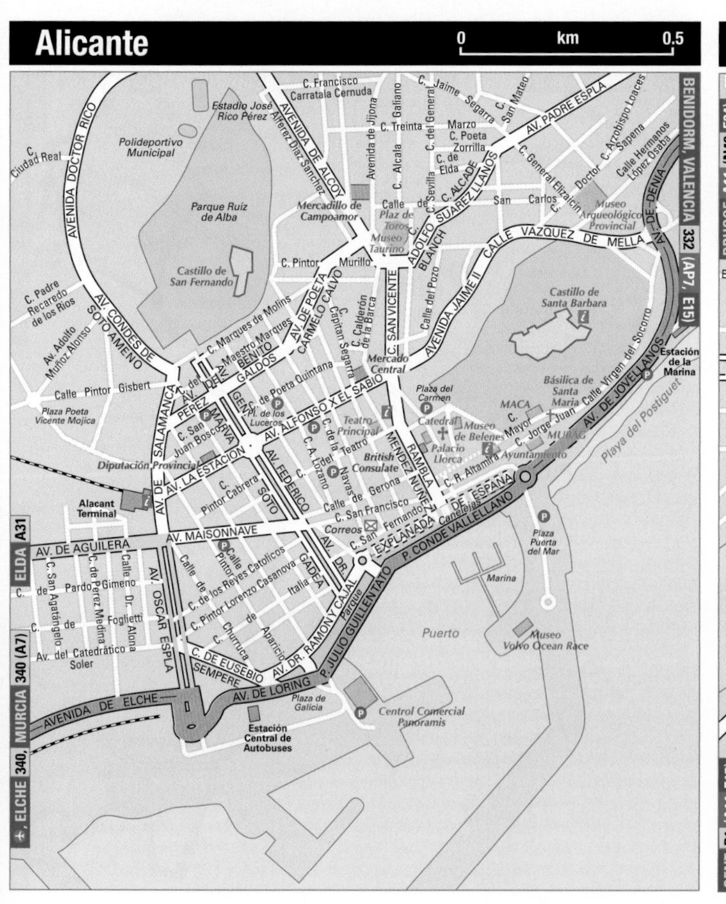

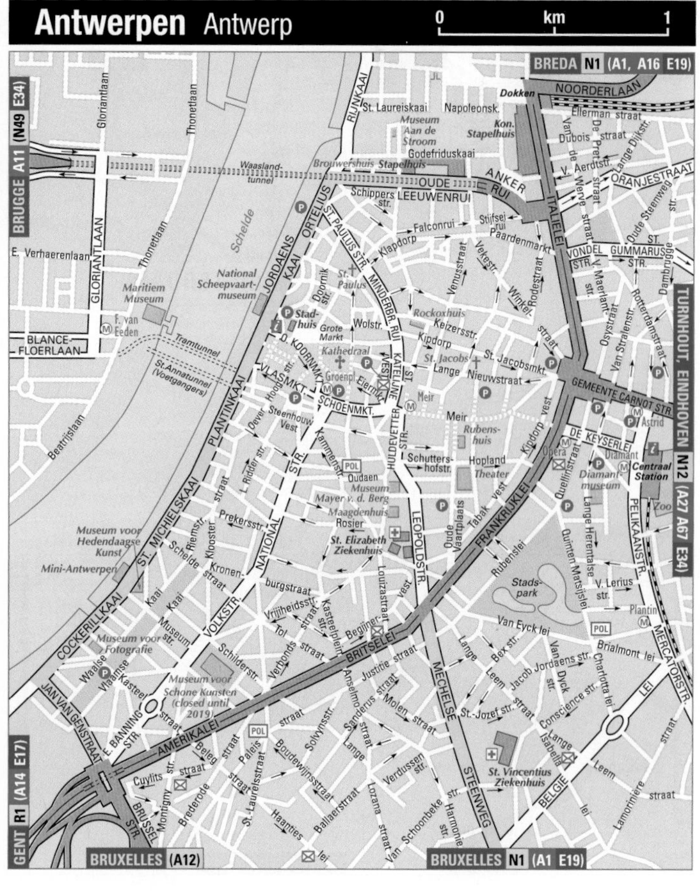

Amsterdam

0 km 2

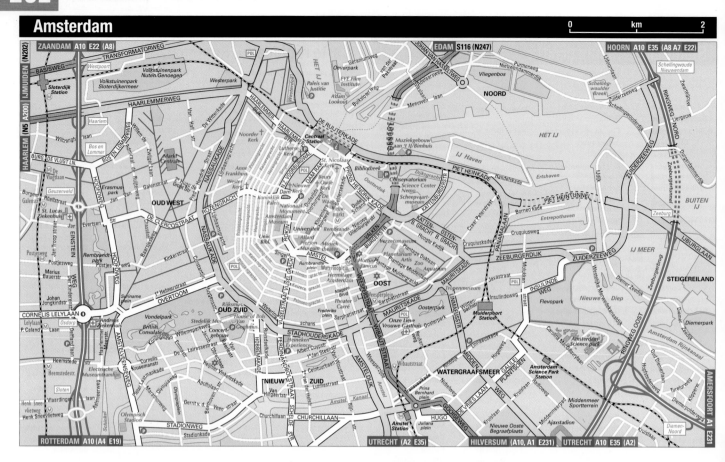

Amsterdam

0 km 5

Athina Athens

0 km 5

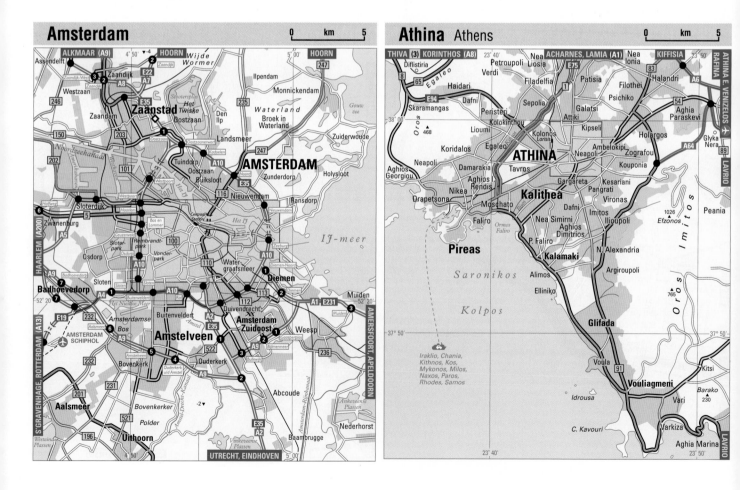

Athina Athens

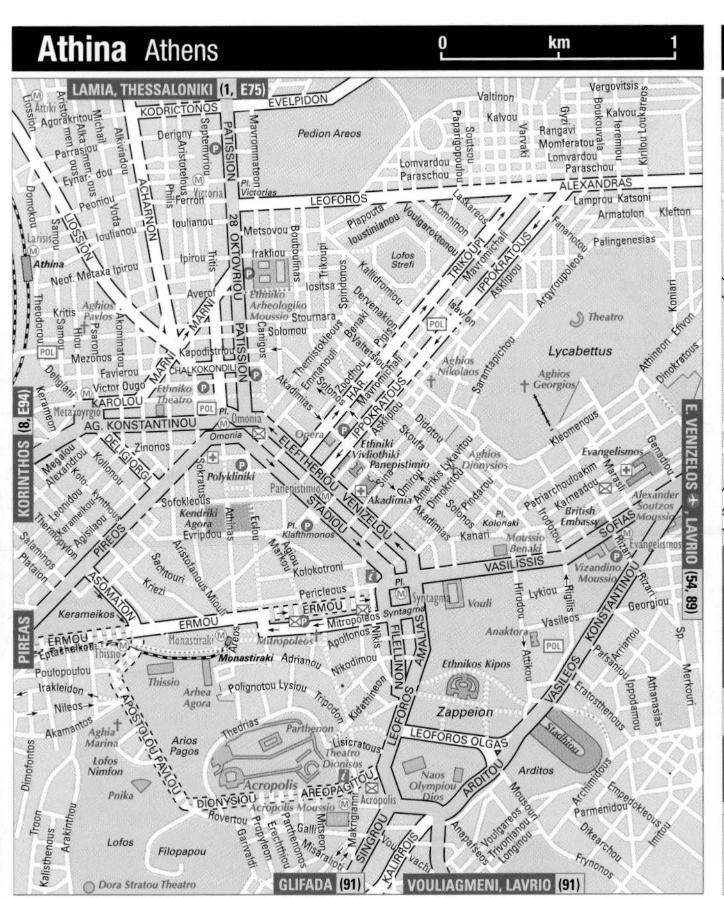
0 km 1
LAMIA, THESSALONIKI (1, E75)
KORINTHOS (8, E94)
PIREAS
E. VENIZELOS ✈ LAVRIO (54, 89)
GLIFADA (91)
VOULIAGMENI, LAVRIO (91)
Athina
Omonia
Syntagma
Monastiraki
Lycabettus
Acropolis
Zappeion
Ethnikos Kipos
Vouli
Pedion Areos
LEOFOROS ALEXANDRAS
VASILISSIS SOFIAS
Filopapou
Dora Stratou Theatro

Basel

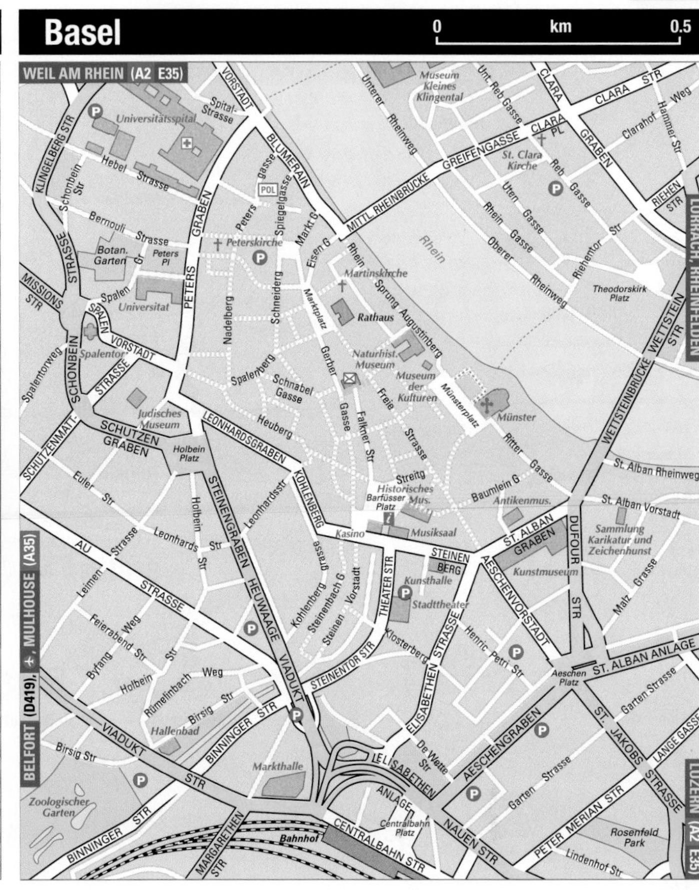
0 km 0.5
WEIL AM RHEIN (A2 E35)
LÖRRACH, RHEINFELDEN
BELFORT (D419), ✈, MULHOUSE (A35)
LUZERN (A2 E35)
Rhein
Münster
Rathaus
Universität
Universitätsspital
Bahnhof
Centralbahn Platz
Markthalle
Zoologischer Garten
Kunstmuseum
Kunsthalle
Stadttheater
Musiksaal
Historisches Museum
Barfüsser Platz
Spalentor
Jüdisches Museum
Holbein Platz
Theodorskirch Platz
St. Alban Rheinweg
Rosenfeld Park
MITTL. RHEINBRÜCKE
WETTSTEINBRÜCKE

Barcelona

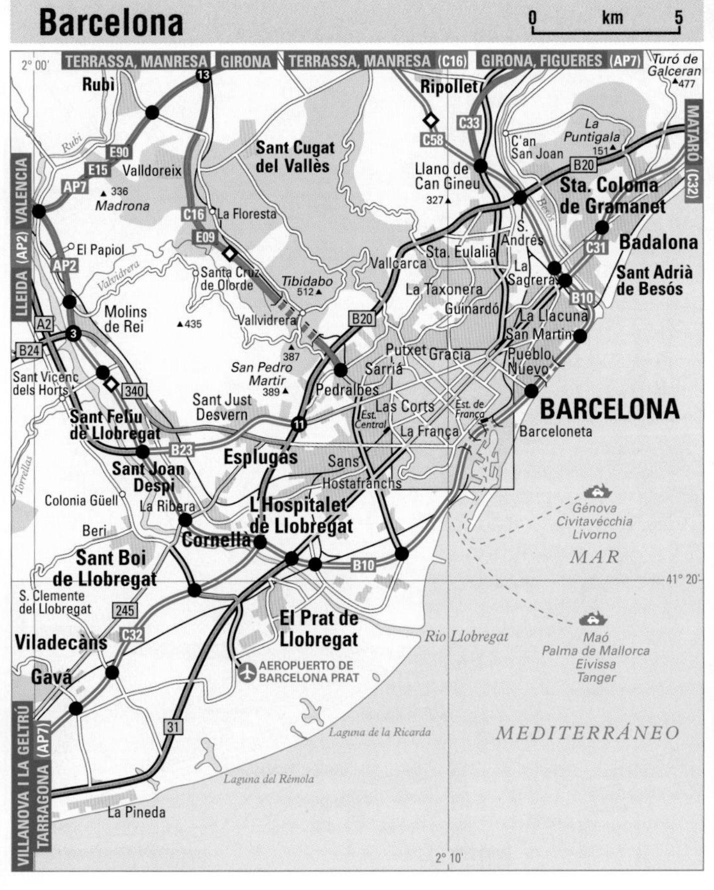
0 km 5
TERRASSA, MANRESA
GIRONA
TERRASSA, MANRESA (C16)
GIRONA, FIGUERES (AP7)
MATARÓ (C32)
LLEIDA (AP2) VALENCIA
VILANOVA I LA GELTRÚ TARRAGONA (AP7)
BARCELONA
Barceloneta
Rubí
Ripollet
Sant Cugat del Vallès
Sta. Coloma de Gramanet
Badalona
Sant Adrià de Besós
Molins de Rei
Sant Feliu de Llobregat
Sant Joan Despí
Esplugas
Cornellà
L'Hospitalet de Llobregat
Sant Boi de Llobregat
El Prat de Llobregat
Viladecans
Gavà
Tibidabo
AEROPUERTO DE BARCELONA PRAT
MAR MEDITERRÁNEO
Génova Civitavécchia Livorno
Maó Palma de Mallorca Eivissa Tanger
Rio Llobregat
La Pineda

Barcelona

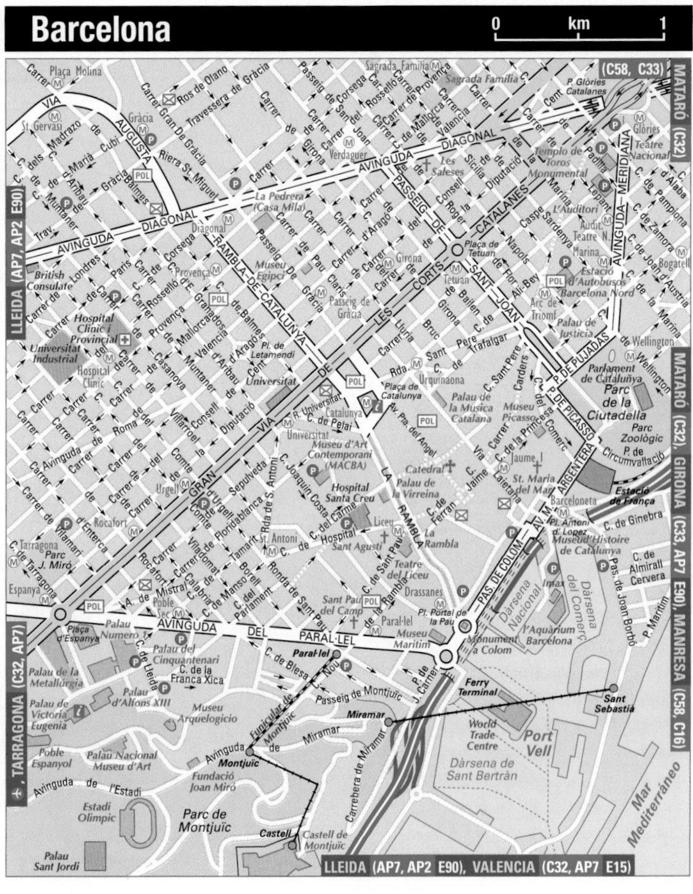
0 km 1
(C58, C33)
MATARÓ (C32)
LLEIDA (AP7, AP2 E90)
MATARÓ (C32), GIRONA (C33, AP7 E90), MANRESA (C58, C16)
✈, TARRAGONA (C32, AP7)
LLEIDA (AP7, AP2 E90), VALENCIA (C32, AP7 E15)
AVINGUDA DIAGONAL
GRAN VIA DE LES CORTS CATALANES
AVINGUDA DEL PARAL·LEL
PASSEIG DE GRÀCIA
RAMBLA DE CATALUNYA
Plaça de Catalunya
Sagrada Família
La Pedrera (Casa Milà)
Parc de la Ciutadella
Parc de Montjuïc
Estadi Olímpic
Palau Sant Jordi
Port Vell
Moll d'Espanya
World Trade Centre
Monument a Colom
Estació de França
Mar Mediterràneo

Berlin

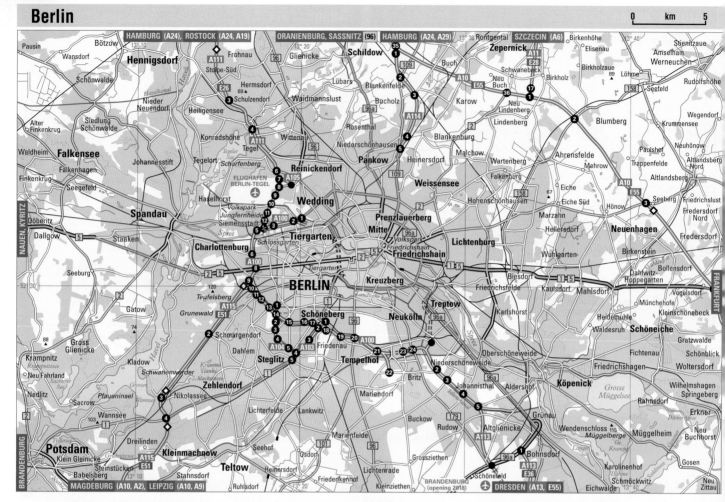

Berlin

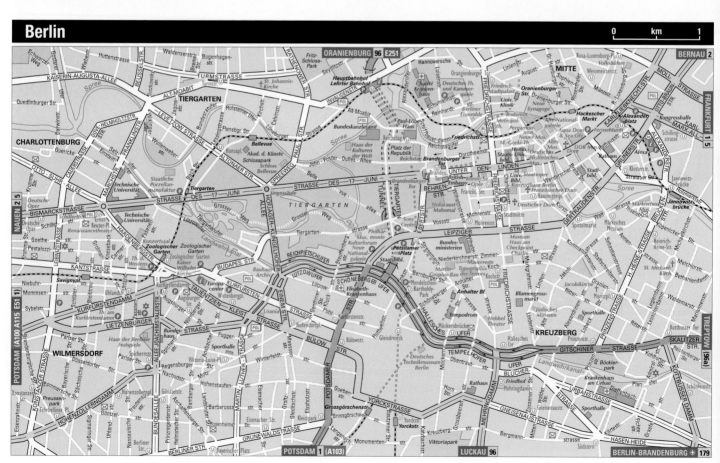

Beograd Belgrade

0 km 1

Bruxelles Brussels

0 km 5

Bordeaux

0 km 5

Bordeaux

0 km 1

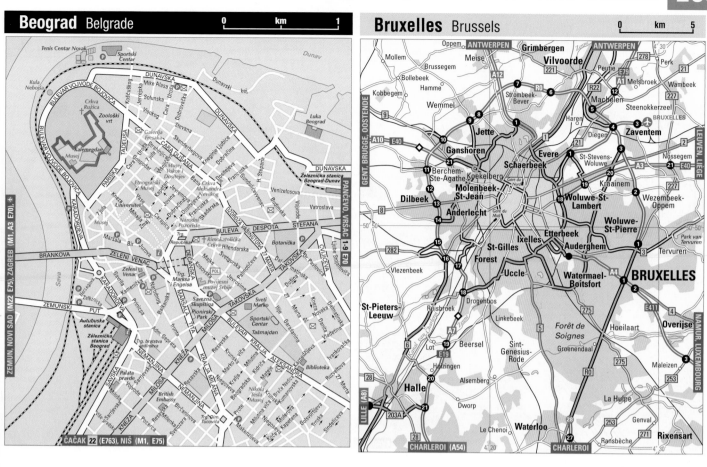

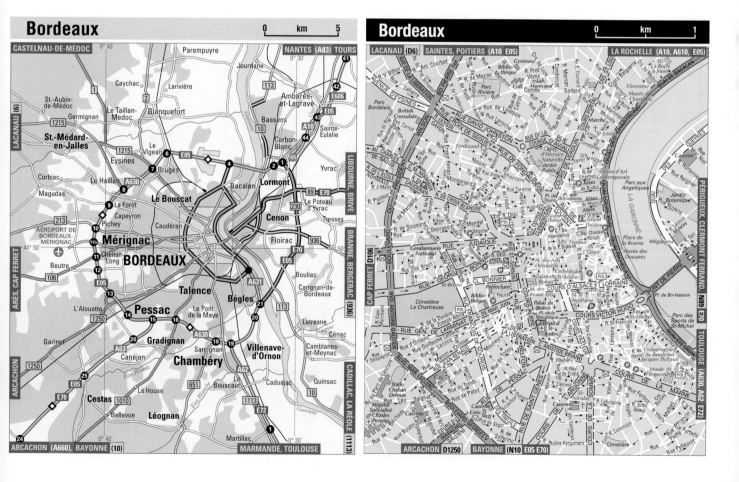

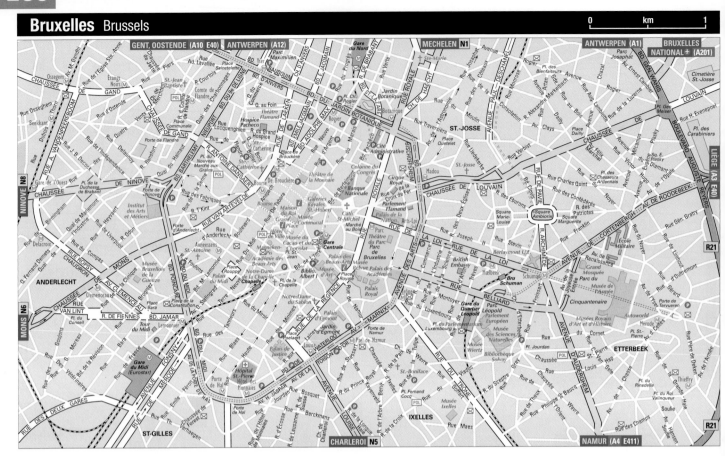

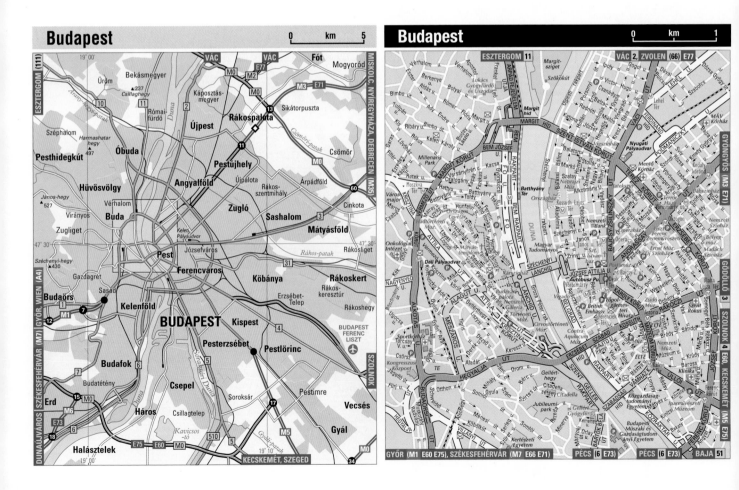

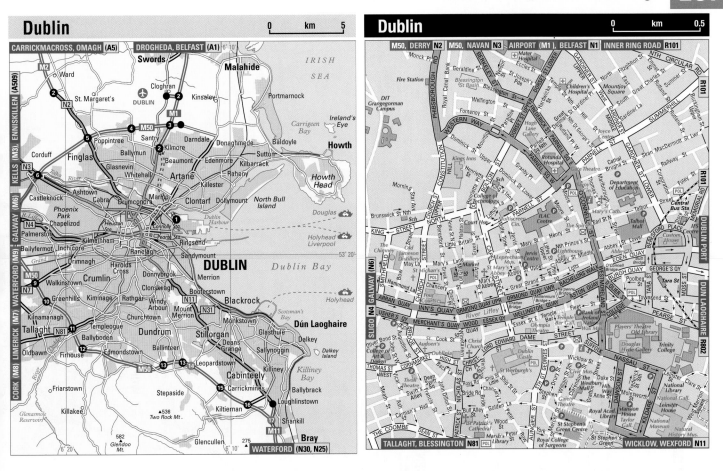

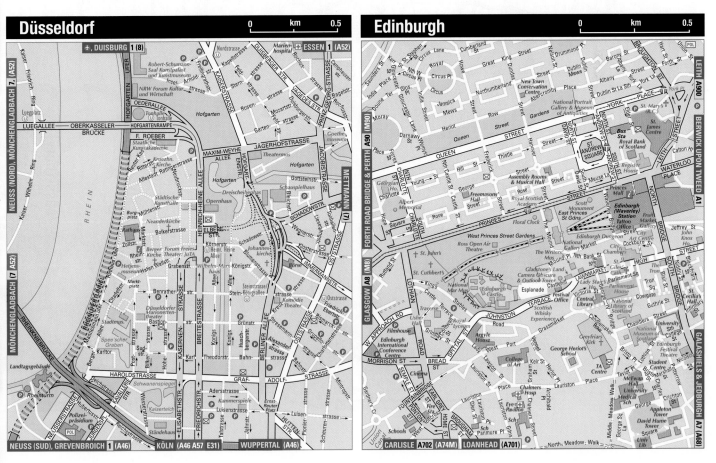

For **Cologne** see page 212
For **Copenhagen** see page 212

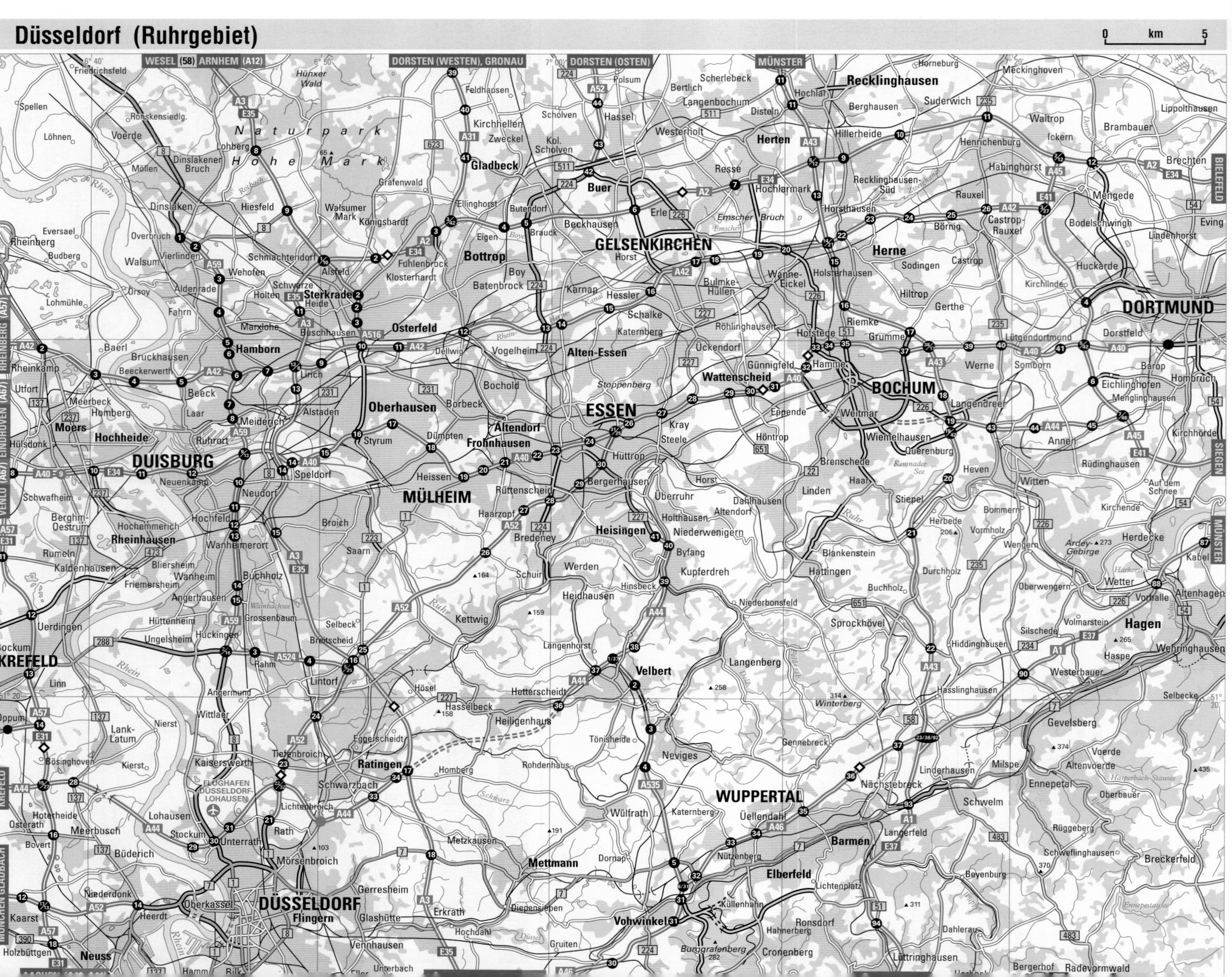
Düsseldorf (Ruhrgebiet)
0 km 5
WESEL (58) ARNHEM (A12)
DORSTEN (WESTEN), GRONAU
DORSTEN (OSTEN)
MÜNSTER
BIELEFELD
SIEGEN
KREFELD
MÖNCHEN GLADBACH
VENLO (A67) EINDHOVEN (A67)
RHEINBERG (A57)
Naturpark Hohe Mark
Recklinghausen
Herten
Gladbeck
Buer
GELSENKIRCHEN
Bottrop
Herne
DORTMUND
BOCHUM
Wattenscheid
ESSEN
Alten-Essen
Oberhausen
Osterfeld
Sterkrade
Hamborn
DUISBURG
Moers
Hochheide
Rheinhausen
MÜLHEIM
Heisingen
Velbert
Hagen
WUPPERTAL
Barmen
Elberfeld
Vohwinkel
Mettmann
Ratingen
DÜSSELDORF
Neuss
KREFELD
FLUGHAFEN DÜSSELDORF-LOHAUSEN

Firenze Florence

0 km 1

SESTO, BOLOGNA (A1 E35)

VIAREGGIO (A11 E76)

PONTASSIEVE (67), ROMA (67 A1 E35)

Frankfurt

0 km 0.5

SIEGEN, DORTMUND 3 (A5 A45 E41)

WIESBADEN (A66), KÖLN (A66 A3)

HANAU, FULDA 8 40 (A66)

OFFENBACH 43

WIESBADEN 44 (A648, A66)

MAINZ 44 (A3 A60), MANNHEIM 44 (A5)

DARMSTADT 3 (A661)

Genève Geneva

0 km 1

LAUSANNE 1 (A1, E25)

ST-GENIS-POUILLY 984

THONON-LES-BAINS (5)

BONNEVILLE (205)

ANNECY 1 (201)

LAC LÉMAN

Génova Genoa

0 km 1

SAVONA 1, MILANO (A7 E62)

LA SPEZIA 1, FIRENZE (A12 E80, A11 E76)

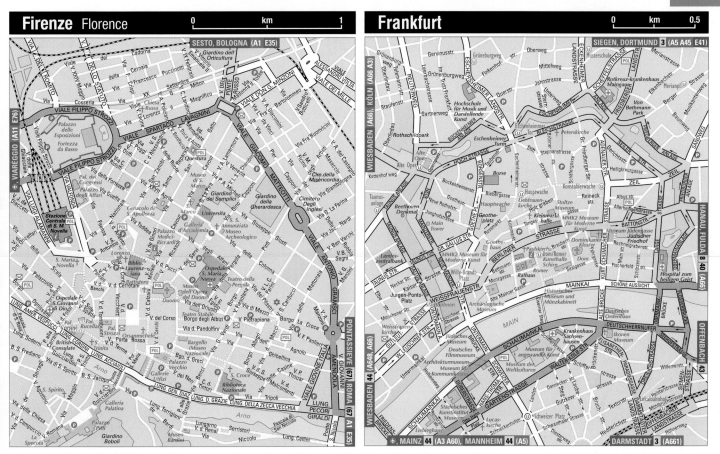

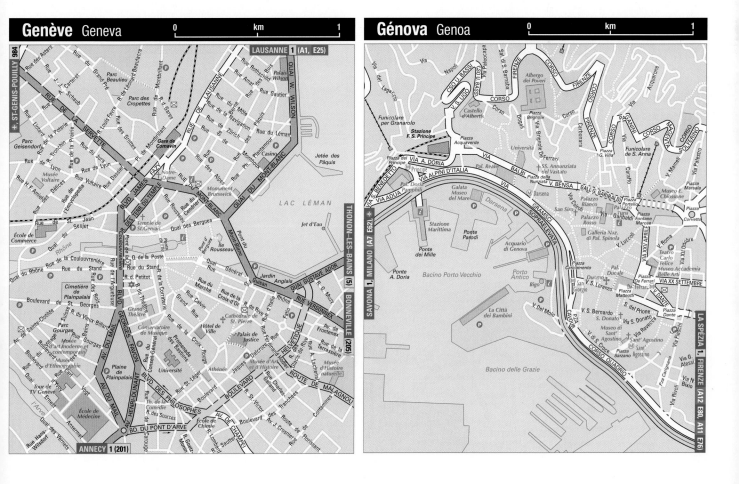

Granada

0 km 0.5

✈, SEVILLA (A92) · JAÉN (A44 E902) · MOTRIL (A44 E902) · MOTRIL (A44 E902) Paseo del Salon

ALBAICAN · ALHAMBRA · Palacio de Carlos V · Palacio Real · Catedral · Palacio Arzobispal · Palacio Madraza · Ayuntamiento · Capitanía General · Diputación · Hospital San Juan de Dios · Jardín Botánico · Torre Bermejas · Puerta de las Granadas · Casa de los Tiros · Campo del Príncipe · Museo de Falla · Museo Arqueológico · Palacio de Zafra · El Bañuelo · Real Cancillería · Puerta de Elvira · Puerta Real · Plaza Nueva · Plaza Santa Ana · Plaza Isabel la Católica · Plaza de Bib-Rambla · Plaza del Campillo · Plaza de Mariana Pineda · Plaza de la Trinidad · Plaza del Triunfo · Plaza de los Lobos · Plaza Universidad · Plaza San Miguel Baja · Plaza Larga · Plaza Aliatar · Plaza Abad · Plaza Sto. Domingo · Fuente de las Batallas

Gran Vía de Colón · Calle Reyes Católicos · Acera del Casino · Acera del Darro · Calle de las Recogidas · C. Angel Ganivet · Calle San Matías · C. de la Pavaneras · C. Santa Escolástica · Calle de Molinos · Cuesta del Caidero · C. Antequeruela Baja · Paseo de la Alhambra · Cuesta de Gomérez · Carrera del Darro · Calle de San Juan de los Reyes · Paseo de Padre Manjón · Cuesta del Chapiz · Cuesta de Alcazaba · Camino Nuevo de San Nicolás · Calle Elvira · Calle de San Jerónimo · Calle Gran Capitán · Calle San Juan de Dios · Calle Mano Hierro · Río Darro · Calle de Santiago · Calle de Alhamar · Callejón Niño del Royo

Göteborg Gothenburg

0 km 1

UDDEVALLA (E06) · TROLLHÄTTAN E45 · ALINGSÅS (E20) · BORÅS (E06, E20, 40) · MÖLNDAL (E06 E20) · VARBERG (158 E06 E20)

GULLBERGSVASS · LUNDBYVASSEN · HEDEN · HAGA · VASASTADEN · LORENSBERG · GÖTA ÄLV · Lundbyhamnen · Frihamnen · Göteborgs Operan · Maritiman · Centralstationen · Nordstaden · Börsen · Rådhuset · Göteborgs Stadsmuseum · British Consulate · Domkyrkan · Stora Teatern · Bussterminal · Gamla Ullevi · Universitet · Vasaparken · Stadsteatern · Göteborgs Konserthus · Götaplatsen · Konstmuseet · Universitetsbiblioteket · Renströms Parken · Trädgårdsföreningens Park · Oscar Fredriks Kyrkan · Skansparken · Skansen Kronan · Folkteatern

Götaälvbron · Lundbyleden · Götaleden · Götatunneln · Mårten Krakowgatan · Odinsgatan · Ullevigatan · Skånegatan · Nya Allén · Parkgatan · Södra Vägen · Linnégatan · Sprängkullsgatan · Aschebergsgatan · Viktoriagatan · Vasagatan · Kungsgatan · Drottninggatan · Östra Hamngatan · Västra Hamngatan · Första Långgatan · Andra Långgatan · Tredje Långgatan · Fjärde Långgatan

Hamburg

0 km 5

NEUMÜNSTER, KIEL (A215) · ITZEHOE, HEIDE · ELMSHORN · BERLIN · LÜBECK · LAUENBURG (5) · HANNOVER, BREMEN (A1) · LÜNEBURG (A250)

HAMBURG · Pinneberg · Halstenbek · Schenefeld · Osdorf · Blankenese · Altona · St. Pauli · Harburg · Wilhelmsburg · Norderstedt · Flughafen Hamburg · Wulfsmühle · Hohenraden · Hasloh · Tangstedt · Winzeldorf · Bönningstedt · Rellingen · Ellerbek · Egenbüttel · Neuegenbüttel · Krupunder · Brande · Friedrichshulde · Eidelstedt · Schnelsen · Niendorf · Garstedt · Glashütte · Moorbek · Lemsahl · Wohldorf Ohlstedt · Ochsenzoll · Mellingstedt · Bergstedt · Langenhorn · Poppenbüttel · Volksdorf · Hummelsbüttel · Sasel · Berne · Meiendorf · Wellingsbüttel · Fuhlsbüttel · Ohlsdorf · Bramfeld · Farmsen · Gross Borstel · Alsterdorf · Steilshoop · Rahlstedt · Lokstedt · Winterhude · Tonndorf · Stellingen · Lurup · Volkspark · Hinschenfelde · Wandsbek · Sülldorf · Iserbrook · Bahrenfeld · Eimsbüttel · Harvestehude · Barmbek · Uhlenhorst · Eilbek · Rotherbaum · Marienthal · Jenfeld · Gross Flottbek · Nienstedten · Othmarschen · Ottensen · Planten un Blomen · Hohenfelde · St. Georg · Hamm · Horn · Hammerbrook · Billstedt · Finkenwerder · Waltershof · Steinwerder · Kl. Grasbrook · Rothenburgsort · Kirchsteinbek · Billbrook · Rosengarten · Neuenfelde · Veddel · Boberg · Nincop · Vierzigstücken · Francop · Altenwerder · Reiherstieg · Georgswerder · Billwerder · Bf. Mittlerer Landweg · Moorfleet · Hobenwisch · Moorburg · Hohe Schaar · Kirchsteinbek · Tatenberg · Allermöhe · Neugraben-Fischbek · Neuwiedenthal · Spadenland · Bostelbek · Moorwerder · Ochsenwerder · Neu Wulmstorf · Hausbruch · Heimfeld · Fünfhausen · Neudorf · Eissendorf · Marschlande · Elbe

9°50' · 10°00' · 53°40' · 53°30'

Hamburg

0 km 1

KIEL 447 (A7, E45 A215) · FLUGHAFEN HAMBURG ✈ 433 · ITZEHOE 4/5 (A23) · LÜBECK 434 (75) · WEDEL 4 (431), BREMEN (A7 A1, E22) · LAUENBURG 4 (5), HANNOVER 4 (A1 A7, E45)

Krankenhaus Jerusalem · Zoologisches Museum · Universität · Mus. für Völkerkunde · Alte Universität · Moorweide · Aussenalster · Binnenalster · Planten un Blomen · Congress-Centrum-Hamburg · Alte Botanischer Garten · Dammtor · Hamburg Messe · Kleine Wallanlagen · Grosse Wallanlagen · Staatsoper Hamburg · Finanzamt · Musikhalle · Museum für Hamburgische Geschichte · Johannes Brahms Mus. · Michel-Park · Michaeliskirche · Rathaus · Börse · Bucerius Kunst Forum · St. Petri · St. Jacobi · Thalia Theater · Ohnsorg Theater · Kunsthalle · Deichtorhallen · Nikolaikirchturm · Katharinen Kirche · Speicherstadtmuseum · Deutsches Zollmuseum · Internationales Maritimes Museum · Museumsschiff Rickmer Rickmers · Museumsschiff Cap San Diego · Landungsbr. · Sternschanze · Sternschanzenpark · Heinrich-Hertz-Turm · Schlump · Feldstrasse · Messehallen · Stadthausbr. · Baumwall · Rödingsmarkt · Jungfernstieg · Gänsemarkt · Hbf.

Schröderstiftstrasse · Rentzelstr. · Grindelallee · Grindelhof · Rothenbaumchaussee · Mittelweg · Harvestehuder Weg · An der Verbindungsbahn · Ed. Siemers Allee · Karolinenstrasse · Marseillerstr. · Alsterglacis · Kennedybrücke · Lombardsbrücke · Esplanade · Gorch Fock Wall · Holsten Wall · Glacischaussee · Kaiser Wilhelm Strasse · Jungfernstieg · Ballindamm · Glockengiesserwall · Mönckebergstrasse · Steinstrasse · Speersort · Ludwig-Erhard-Strasse · Willy-Brandt-Strasse · Ost-West-Strasse · Johannisbollwerk · Vorsetzen · Bei den Mühren · Kehrwieder · Am Sandtorkai · Binnenhafen · Zollkanal · Alsterkreuzfahrt · Atlantic · Elbe

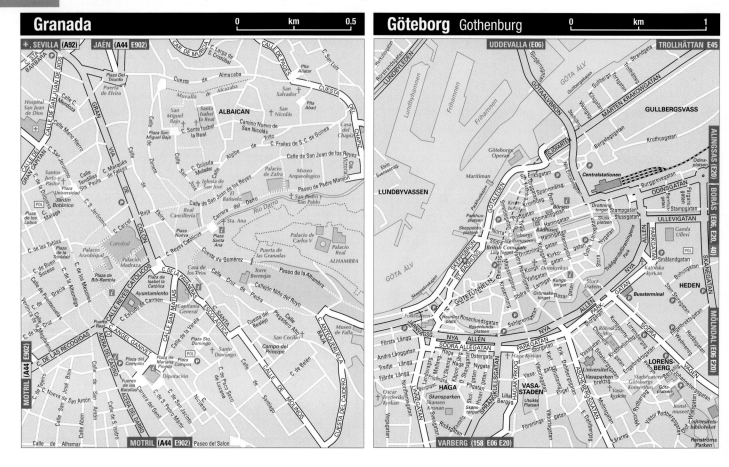

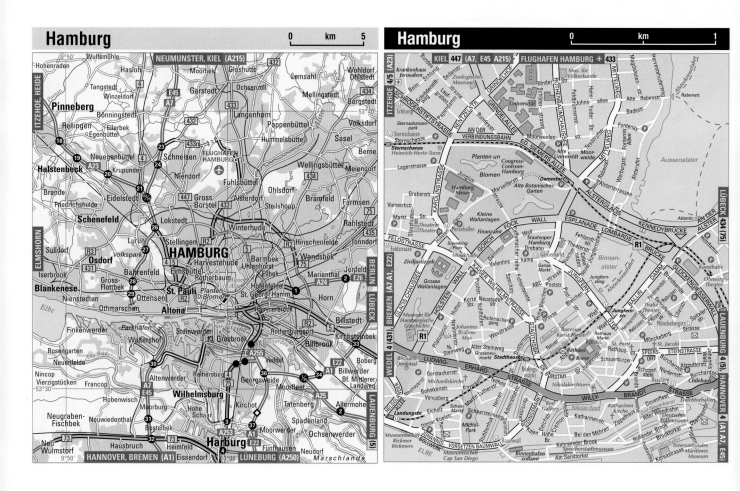

Helsinki

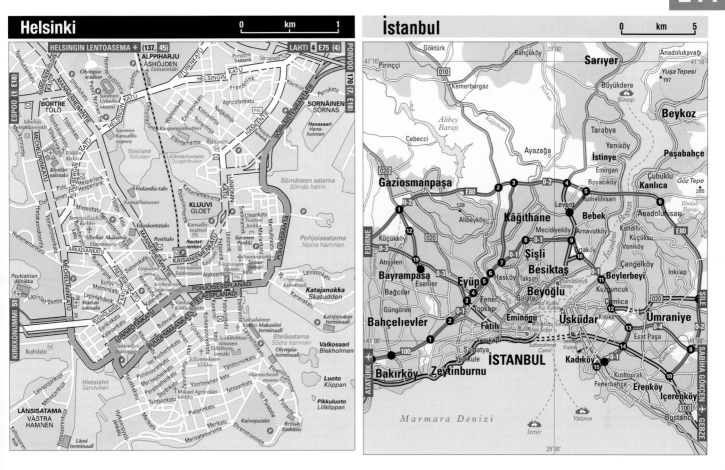

İstanbul

Helsinki

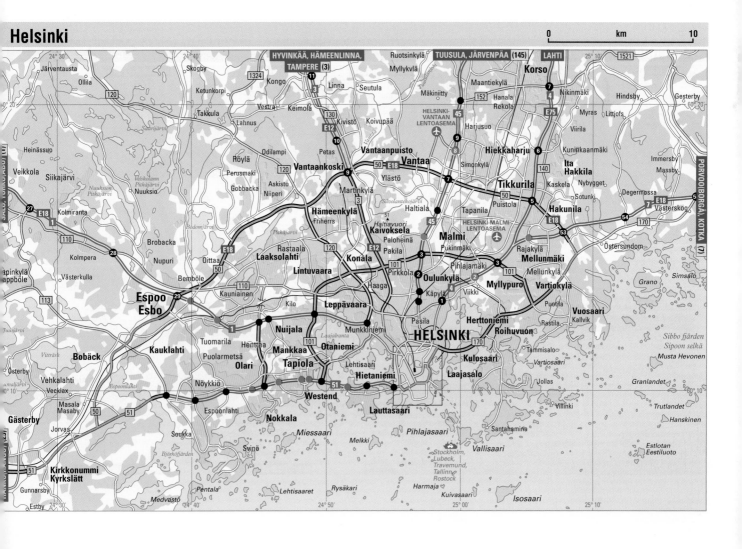

København Copenhagen

Köln Cologne

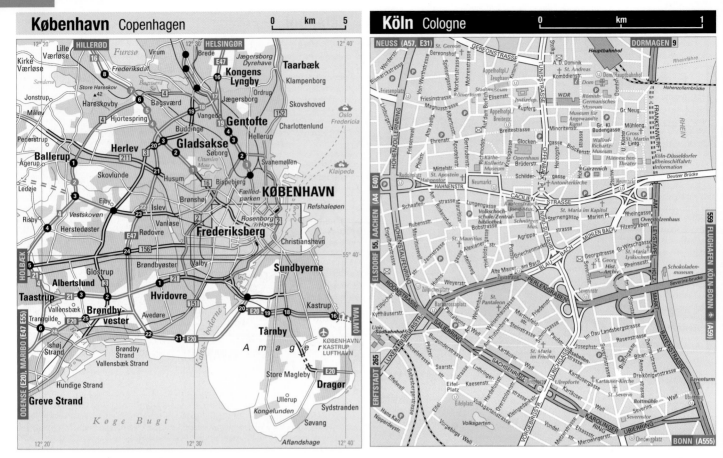

København Copenhagen

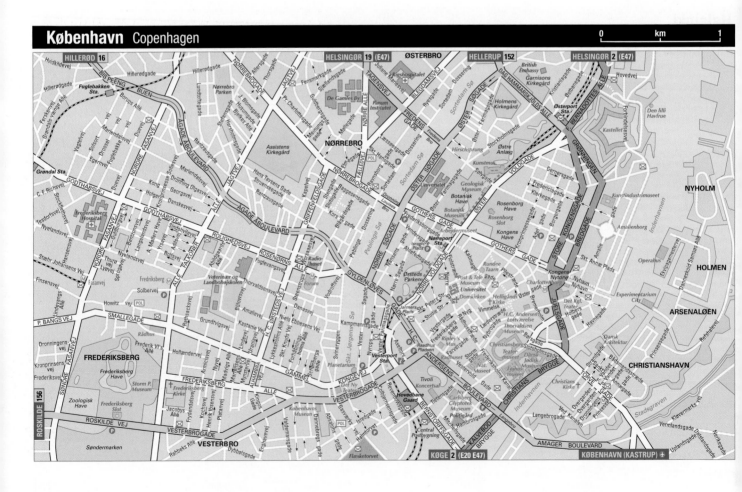

Lisboa Lisbon

0 km 1

Lisboa Lisbon

0 km 5

London

0 km 2

Congestion Charging Zone

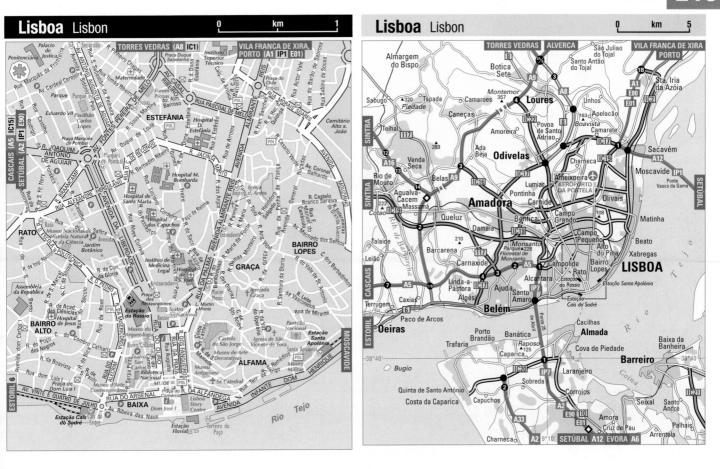

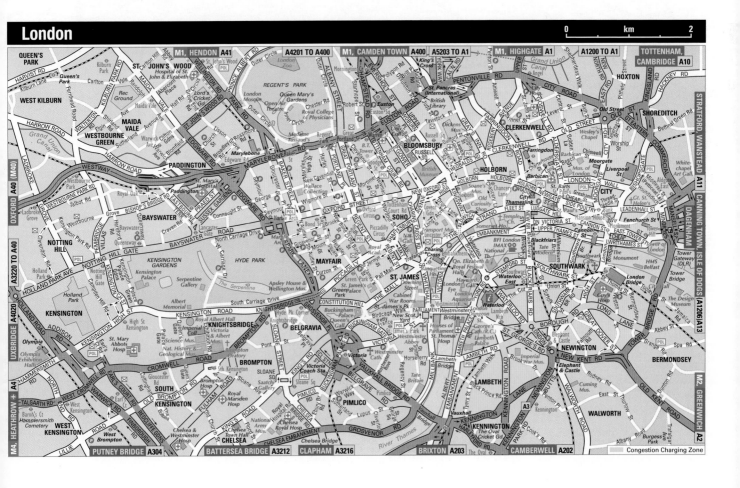

London

0 km 10
LONDON
Westminster
City
Watford
St Albans
Hemel Hempstead
Harlow
Hatfield
Hertford
Enfield
Barnet
Harrow
Ealing
Richmond
Kingston upon Thames
Croydon
Sutton
Bromley
Orpington
Dagenham
Romford
Dartford
Epsom
Woking
Guildford
Dorking
Reigate
Redhill
Crawley
East Grinstead
Sevenoaks
Tonbridge
Staines-upon-Thames
Slough
Uxbridge
Hounslow
Esher
Weybridge
Chertsey
Caterham
Potters Bar
Cheshunt
Waltham Abbey
Hoddesdon
Brentwood
Rickmansworth
Borehamwood

Lyon

0 km 5

MÂCON, DIJON (A31) — MÂCON (A6), DIJON (A6, A31) — GENEVE (A40) & ✈ (A432) — CHAMBÉRY, GRENOBLE (A48) & ✈ (A432) — VIENNE, VALENCE, MARSEILLE — ST. ETIENNE (A47)

Lissieu, Civrieux-d'Azergues, Dommartin, La Tour-de-Salvagny, Dardilly, Limonest, Albigny, Neuville-sur-Saône, Fleurieu-sur-Saône, Couzon-au-Mont-d'Or, Rochetaillée-sur-Saône, Fontaines-St.-Martin, Fontaines-sur-Saône, Cailloux-sur-Fontaines, Sathonay-Village, Sathonay-Camp, Collonges-au-Mont-d'Or, St.-Didier-au-Mont-d'Or, St.-Cyr-Au-Mont-d'Or, Champagne-au-Mont-d'Or, Rillieux-la-Pape, Miribel, Neyron, St.-Maurice-de-Beynost, Beynost, Parc de loisirs de Miribel-Jonage, Caluire-et-Cuire, Marcy-l'Etoile, Charbonnières-les-Bains, Écully, La Croix-Rousse, Villeurbanne, Vaulx-en-Velin, Meyzieu, Ste.-Genis-les-Ollières, Tassin-la-Demi-Lune, Craponne, LYON, Montchat, Monplaisir, Décines-Charpieu, Chassieu, Francheville, Ste.-Foy-lès-Lyon, Bron, Aérodrome Lyon-Bron, Genas, La Mulatière, Oullins, Chaponost, Pierre-Bénite, St.-Genis-Laval, St.-Fons, Vénissieux, St.-Priest, Manissieux, La Fouillouse, Mions, Soucieu-en-Jarrest, Brignais, Irigny, Feyzin, Corbas, Vourles, Orliénas, Vernaison, Charly, Toussieu, Chapotin, St.-Pierre-de-Chandieu, Solaize, St.-Symphorien-d'Ozon, Taluyers, Millery, Montagny, Chaponnay, T.G.V.

Lyon

0 km 1

MÂCON, DIJON (A46, A6 E15) — CHAMBÉRY (A43 E70) & ✈ (A432) — VALENCE, MARSEILLE (A7 E15)

Quai de la Pêcherie, Quai St. Antoine, Quai des Célestins, Quai Jean Moulin, Quai Jules-Courmont, Quai Gailleton, Quai Victor Augagneur, Quai Claude Bernard, Quai Romain Rolland, Quai Fulchiron, Quai Tilsitt, Cours Lafayette, Cours Gambetta, Cours de la Liberté, Pt. Lafayette, Pt. Wilson, Pt. de la Guillotière, Pt. de l'Université, Pt. Bonaparte, Pt. du Maréchal Juin, Rue Grenette, Rue de la République, Rue du Président Édouard Herriot, Place des Terreaux, Hôtel de Ville, Palais des Beaux Arts, Musée de l'imprimerie et de la communication graphique, Palais de la Bourse, Pl. des Cordeliers, St. Bonaventure, Pl. Bellecour, Hôtel Dieu, Pl. des Célestins, Th. des Célestins, Pl. Antonin Poncet, Clocher de la Charité, Musée des Arts Décoratifs, Musée Historique des Tissus, Abbaye d'Ainay, Ampère, Pl. Carnot, Cathédrale St.-Jean, Palais de Justice, Vieux Lyon, Musée Gadagne, Pl. du Change, Gare St.-Paul, Préfecture du Rhône, Rhône, Saône, Piscine

Luxembourg

0 km 0.5

TRIER, KOBLENZ (A1 E44) — MERSCH (7 E421), BITBURG (11 E29) — ARLON (A6) — LONGWY (5 E44) — ESCH (A4), LONGWY (5 E44) — REMICH (2 E29) — THIONVILLE, METZ (A3 E25)

Villa Vauban, Avenue Emile Reuter, Boulevard Royal, Boulevard Grande Duchesse Charlotte, Villa Louvigny, Avenue Monterey, Avenue Marie-Thérèse, British Embassy, Grand Rue, Place d'Armes, Palais Municipal, Hôtel de Ville, Palais Grand Ducal, Chambre des Députés, Théâtre des Capucins, Musées de l'État, Cathédrale Notre Dame, Bibliothèque Nationale, Pl. de la Constitution, Gëlle Fra, Boulevard Roosevelt, Pont Adolphe, Vallée de la Pétrusse, Viaduc, Citadelle St.-Esprit, Bock Casemates, Musée Nat. d'Histoire Naturelle, Plateau du Rham, Archives Nationales, Auberge de la Jeunesse, Palais de Justice, Chapelle St.-Quirin, Arcelor Mittal Former HQ, Place des Martyrs, Clinique Ste-Thérèse, Avenue de la Liberté, Avenue de la Gare, Boulevard d'Avranches, Place de Paris, Place de Strasbourg, Gare Centrale, Banque Int. à Luxembourg, Rue de Hollerisch, St-Pierre et Paul, Stade A. Hammerel, Allée Pierre de Mansfeld

Madrid

0 km 5

COLMENAR VIEJO — BURGOS, SANTANDER (N623) — BILBAO (AP1, AP68) — VALLADOLID (AP6, N601) — A CORUÑA (AP6, A6) — GUADALAJARA, ZARAGOZA — ALBACETE A31, VALENCIA — TALAVERA, BADAJOZ — PARLA, TOLEDO — ARANJUEZ, GRANADA (A44)

El Pardo, El Encinar de los Reyes, Aeropuerto de Madrid-Barajas, Portilleros de las Rozas, Fuencarral, Barajas, Hortaleza, Aravaca, La Estación, Tetuán, Chamartín, Canillas, Ciudad Lineal, Ciudad Fin de Semana, Canillejas, San Cristobal, Pozuelo de Alarcón, Humera, Universidad, Ventas, Chamberí, Salamanca, Pueblo Nuevo, Coslada, Casa de Campo, Estación Príncipe Pío, Estación de Atocha, Retiro, MADRID, Moratalaz, Vicálvaro, Latina, Arganzuela, Campamento, Carabanchel Bajo, Legazpi, Mediodía, Ventorro del Cano, Palomeras, Usera, Cuatro Vientos, Carabanchel Alto, Entrevías, Vallecas, Mercamadrid, Villaverde, La Fortuna, Villaverde Bajo, Canteras de Vallecas, Cumbres de Vallecas, Alcorcón, Leganés, Canal del Manzanares, Salmedina, Getafe, Perales del Río, Fuenlabrada, Manzanares

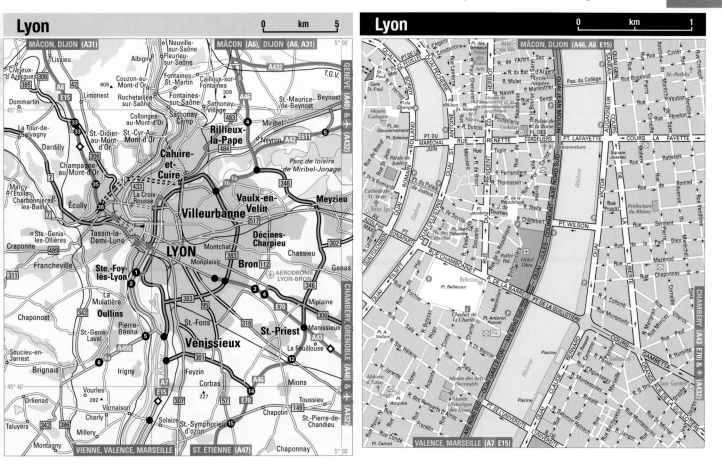

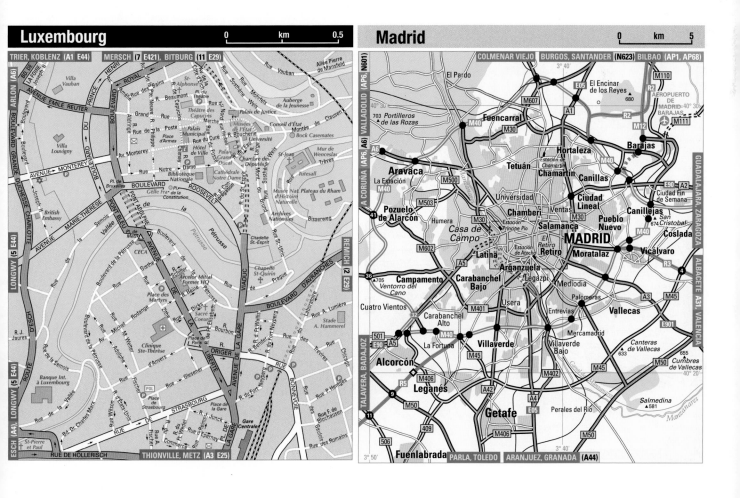

Madrid

0 km 1

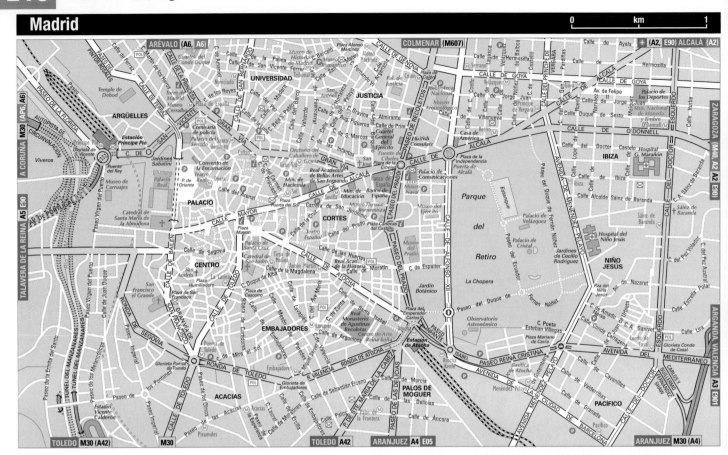

Málaga

0 km 0.5

Marseille / Marseilles

0 km 0.5

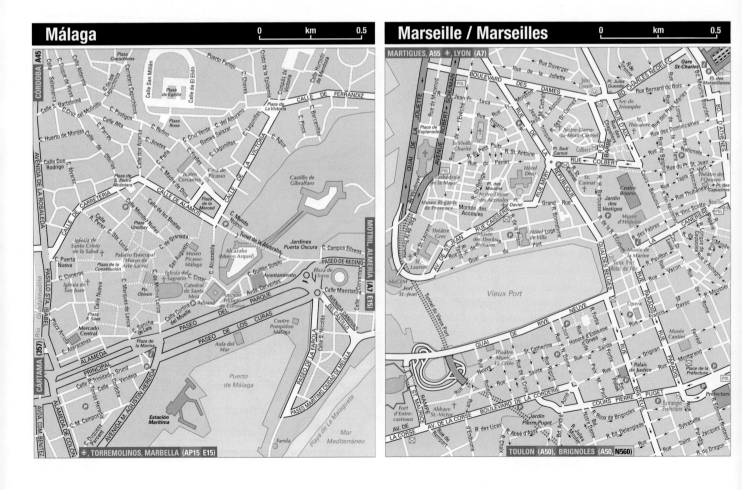

Milano Milan

0 km 5

Milano Milan

0 km 1

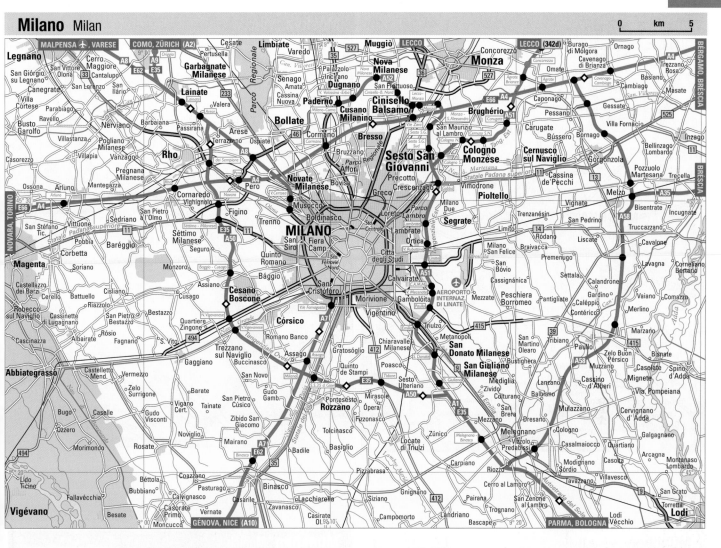

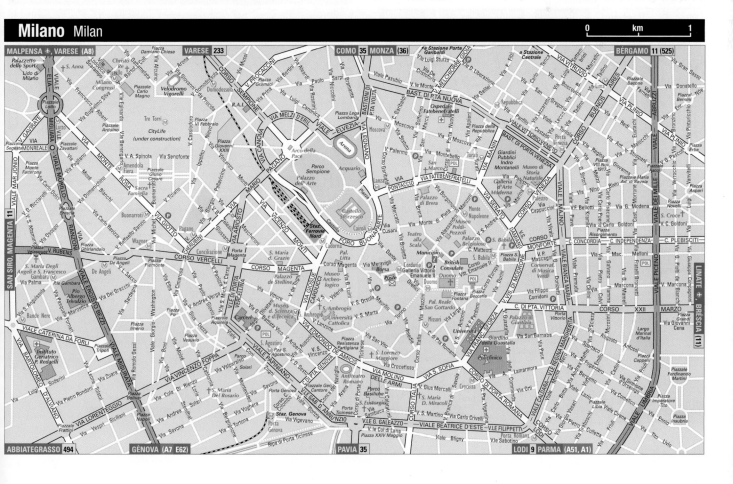

Moskva Moscow

0 km 5

SHEREMETYEVO ✈, SANKT PETERBURG

SERGIYEV POSAD, YAROSLAVL

VLADIMIR, NIZHNIY NOVGOROD

KOLOMNA, RYAZAN

TULA, OREL, KURSK

DOMODEDOVO ✈, NOVOMOSKOVSK

VNUKOVO ✈, OBNINSK

SMOLENSK, MINSK

MOSKVA

Moskva Moscow

0 km 1

YAROSLAVL M8

SHEREMETYEVO ✈ M10 E105

SMOLENSK M1 E30

VLADIMIR (M7), KOLOMNA (M5)

VNUKOVO ✈ (M3), DOMODEDOVO ✈ (M4)

München Munich

0 km 5

✈, LANDSHUT

INGOLSTADT, NÜRNBERG

✈, LANDSHUT

PARSDORF (A94), PASSAU (A94 12)

PARSDORF, PASSAU (12)

PARSDORF (A94), PASSAU (A94 12)

STARNBERG A952

GARMISCH-PARTENKIRCHEN

ROSENHEIM, SALZBURG

LANDSBERG, MEMMINGEN

AUGSBURG

MÜNCHEN

München Munich

0 km 1

INGOLSTADT (A9, E45), MÜNCHEN ✈ (11)

PARSDORF (A94 E552)

PARSDORF (A94 E552)

SALZBURG (A995, A8 E52)

STARNBERG (A95 E533 A952)

GERMERING 2

AUGSBURG (A8 E52)

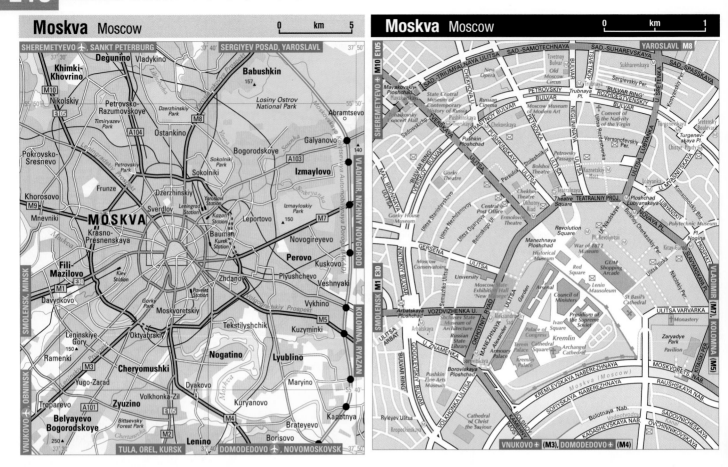

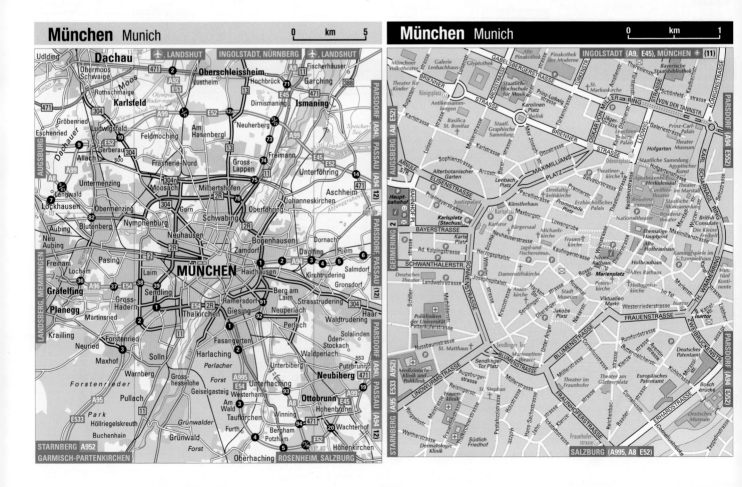

Nápoli Naples

0 km 5

Nápoli Naples

0 km 1

Oslo

0 km 5

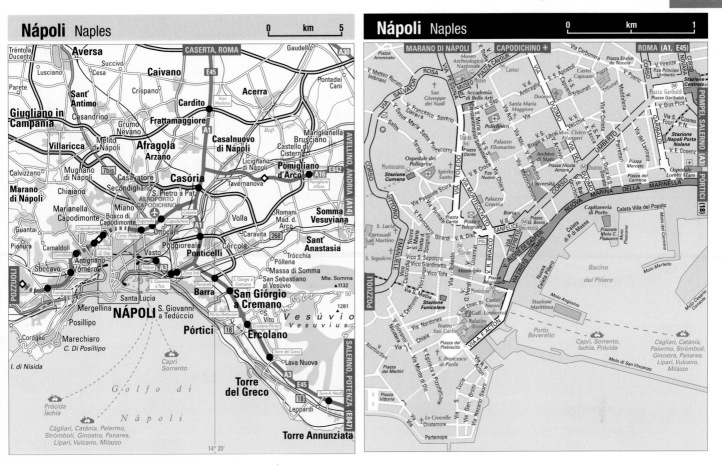

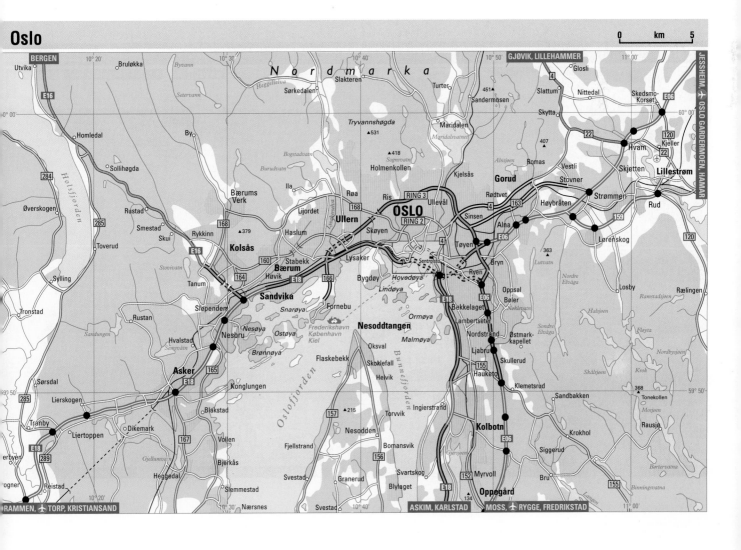

Oslo

0 km 0.5

RING 2
RING 2/3, RØA 168
LILLESTRØM 4 (22)
OSLO ✈ 4 (22, E06)
DRAMMEN, TORP ✈ E18
KARLSTAD E18, RYGGE ✈ E18, FREDRIKSTAD E18 (E06)

Paris

0 km 1

BOULEVARD PÉRIPHÉRIQUE
ARGENTEUIL (909)
ROUEN D14 A15
✈ CHARLES DE GAULLE, LILLE (A1, E15 E19)
MEAUX (N3)
ST-GERMAIN-EN-LAYE N13 (A14)
ROUEN (A13 E05)
NOISY-LE-SEC (A3)
VERSAILLES 910
✈ ORLY (A6), LE MANS (A10 A11 E50)
REIMS (A4 E50)

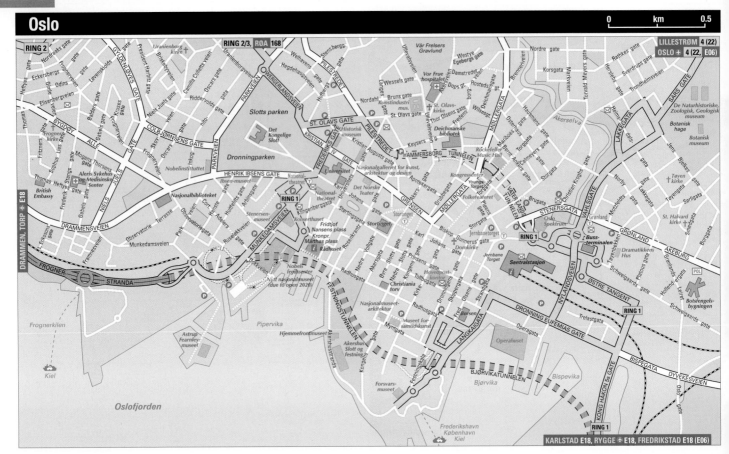

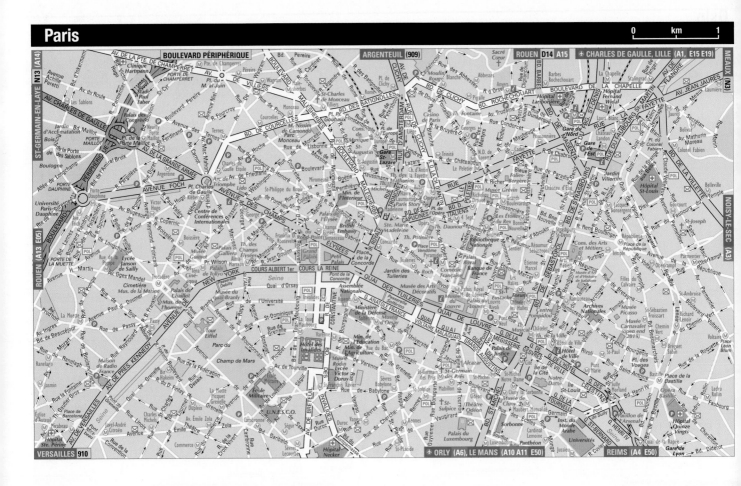

Paris

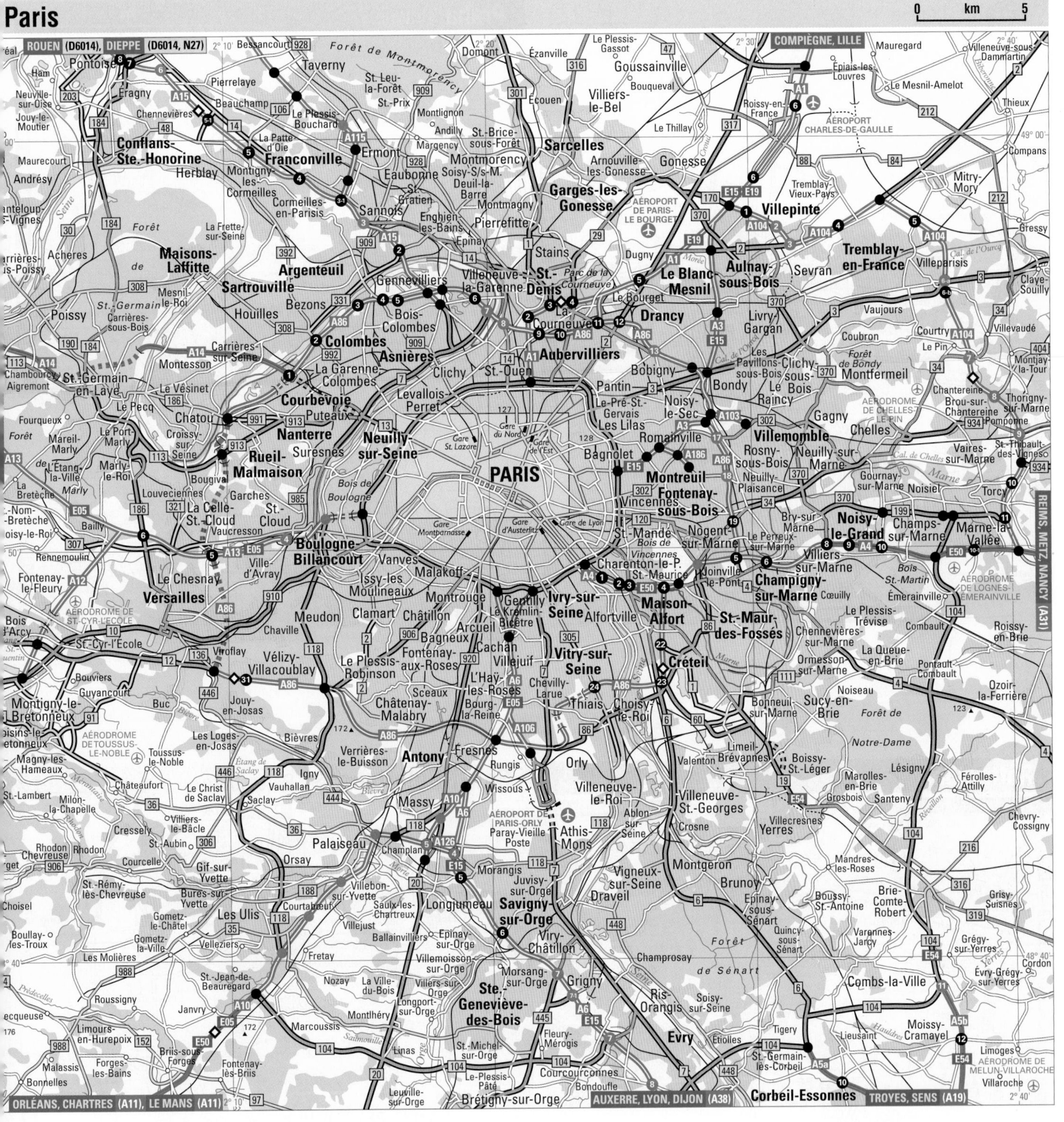
0 km 5
ROUEN (D6014), DIEPPE (D6014, N27)
COMPIÈGNE, LILLE
REIMS, METZ, NANCY (A31)
ORLÉANS, CHARTRES (A11), LE MANS (A11)
AUXERRE, LYON, DIJON (A38)
TROYES, SENS (A19)
PARIS
Pontoise
Taverny
Forêt de Montmorency
Domont
Ézanville
Goussainville
Le Plessis-Gassot
Mauregard
Villeneuve-sous-Dammartin
Épiais-lès-Louvres
Le Mesnil-Amelot
Roissy-en-France
AÉROPORT CHARLES-DE-GAULLE
Villiers-le-Bel
Écouen
Conflans-Ste.-Honorine
Franconville
Herblay
Ermont
Eaubonne
Montmorency
Sarcelles
Gonesse
Garges-lès-Gonesse
AÉROPORT DE PARIS-LE BOURGET
Villepinte
Tremblay-Vieux-Pays
Mitry-Mory
Compans
Tremblay-en-France
Villeparisis
Sevran
Aulnay-sous-Bois
Le Blanc-Mesnil
Drancy
Dugny
Le Bourget
Stains
St.-Denis
La Courneuve
Aubervilliers
Pierrefitte
Épinay
Villeneuve-la-Garenne
Gennevilliers
Argenteuil
Sannois
Cormeilles-en-Parisis
Maisons-Laffitte
Sartrouville
Houilles
Bezons
Colombes
Bois-Colombes
Asnières
Clichy
St.-Ouen
Levallois-Perret
Neuilly-sur-Seine
Courbevoie
La Garenne-Colombes
Puteaux
Nanterre
Suresnes
Rueil-Malmaison
Chatou
Le Vésinet
Le Pecq
St.-Germain-en-Laye
Poissy
Carrières-sous-Poissy
Achères
Montesson
Carrières-sur-Seine
Marly-le-Roi
Louveciennes
Bougival
La Celle-St.-Cloud
Garches
St.-Cloud
Vaucresson
Boulogne-Billancourt
Bois de Boulogne
Versailles
Le Chesnay
Ville-d'Avray
Chaville
Meudon
Vanves
Issy-les-Moulineaux
Malakoff
Montrouge
Clamart
Châtillon
Bagneux
Fontenay-aux-Roses
Le Plessis-Robinson
Vélizy-Villacoublay
Viroflay
Jouy-en-Josas
Buc
Guyancourt
Montigny-le-Bretonneux
St.-Cyr-l'École
Bois-d'Arcy
AÉRODROME DE ST.-CYR-L'ÉCOLE
AÉRODROME DE TOUSSUS-LE-NOBLE
Toussus-le-Noble
Les Loges-en-Josas
Bièvres
Châtenay-Malabry
Sceaux
Bourg-la-Reine
L'Haÿ-les-Roses
Cachan
Arcueil
Gentilly
Le Kremlin-Bicêtre
Villejuif
Ivry-sur-Seine
Vitry-sur-Seine
Chevilly-Larue
Thiais
Choisy-le-Roi
Alfortville
Maisons-Alfort
Créteil
Charenton-le-P.
St.-Maurice
St.-Mandé
Vincennes
Bois de Vincennes
Fontenay-sous-Bois
Montreuil
Bagnolet
Les Lilas
Le Pré-St.-Gervais
Pantin
Bobigny
Noisy-le-Sec
Romainville
Bondy
Les Pavillons-sous-Bois
Livry-Gargan
Clichy-sous-Bois
Le Raincy
Montfermeil
Villemomble
Rosny-sous-Bois
Neuilly-Plaisance
Neuilly-sur-Marne
Gagny
Chelles
Vaires-sur-Marne
Torcy
Noisiel
Champs-sur-Marne
Noisy-le-Grand
Marne-la-Vallée
Villiers-sur-Marne
Bry-sur-Marne
Le Perreux-sur-Marne
Nogent-sur-Marne
Joinville-le-Pont
Champigny-sur-Marne
St.-Maur-des-Fossés
Chennevières-sur-Marne
Ormesson-sur-Marne
La Queue-en-Brie
Le Plessis-Trévise
Pontault-Combault
Roissy-en-Brie
Ozoir-la-Ferrière
Émerainville
AÉRODROME DE LOGNES-ÉMERAINVILLE
Sucy-en-Brie
Bonneuil-sur-Marne
Noiseau
Forêt de Notre-Dame
Boissy-St.-Léger
Limeil-Brévannes
Valenton
Villeneuve-St.-Georges
Villecresnes
Yerres
Brunoy
Montgeron
Crosne
Orly
Rungis
Fresnes
Antony
Wissous
AÉROPORT DE PARIS-ORLY
Paray-Vieille-Poste
Athis-Mons
Villeneuve-le-Roi
Ablon-sur-Seine
Juvisy-sur-Orge
Savigny-sur-Orge
Viry-Châtillon
Vigneux-sur-Seine
Draveil
Massy
Palaiseau
Verrières-le-Buisson
Igny
Orsay
Gif-sur-Yvette
Les Ulis
Longjumeau
Morangis
Champlan
Chilly-Mazarin
Villebon-sur-Yvette
Ste.-Geneviève-des-Bois
Grigny
Ris-Orangis
Évry
Corbeil-Essonnes
Forêt de Sénart
Combs-la-Ville
Moissy-Cramayel
Lieusaint
Brie-Comte-Robert
Brétigny-sur-Orge
Montlhéry
Marcoussis
Limours-en-Hurepoix
Chevreuse
St.-Rémy-lès-Chevreuse
Magny-les-Hameaux
Châteaufort
Saclay
Fontenay-lès-Briis
Briis-sous-Forges

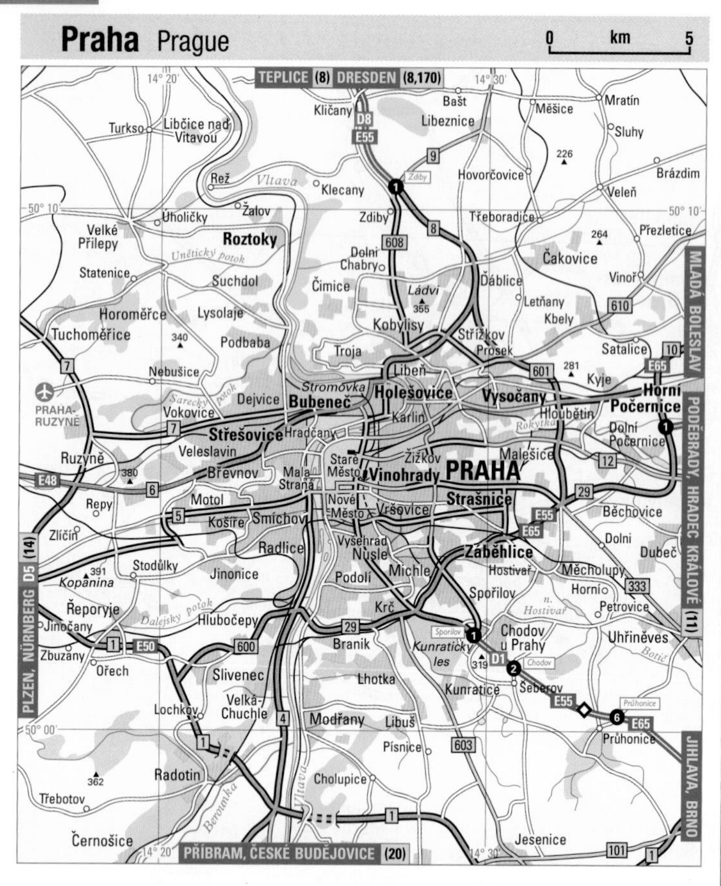
Praha Prague
0 km 5
TEPLICE (8) DRESDEN (8,170)
MLADÁ BOLESLAV
PODĚBRADY, HRADEC KRÁLOVÉ (11)
JIHLAVA, BRNO
PŘÍBRAM, ČESKÉ BUDĚJOVICE (20)
PLZEN, NÜRNBERG D5 (14)
PRAHA
Roztoky
Holešovice
Bubeneč
Vysočany
Střešovice
Vinohrady
Strašnice
Záběhlice
Horní Počernice
PRAHA-RUZYNĚ
Vltava
Libčice nad Vltavou
Turkso
Klíčany
Bašt
Libeznice
Měšice
Mratín
Sluhy
Brázdim
Veleň
Hovorčovice
Řež
Klecany
Žalov
Úholičky
Velké Přílepy
Statenice
Zdiby
Třeboradice
Čakovice
Přezletice
Vinoř
Ďáblice
Letňany
Kbely
Suchdol
Čimice
Dolní Chabry
Horoměřice
Lysolaje
Tuchoměřice
Kobylisy
Střížkov
Prosek
Podbaba
Troja
Satalice
Nebušice
Libeň
Kyje
Vokovice
Dejvice
Hradčany
Karlín
Hloubětín
Dolní Počernice
Ruzyně
Veleslavin
Břevnov
Malá Strana
Staré Město
Žižkov
Malešice
Repy
Motol
Nové Město
Vršovice
Košíře
Smíchov
Běchovice
Zličín
Radlice
Vyšehrad
Nusle
Dolní
Dubeč
Stodůlky
Jinonice
Podolí
Michle
Hostivař
Měcholupy
Kopanina
Spořilov
Horní
Řeporyje
Krč
Petrovice
Jinočany
Hlubočepy
Chodov u Prahy
Uhříněves
Zbuzany
Braník
Kunratický les
Ořech
Slivenec
Lhotka
Kunratice
Šeberov
Velká-Chuchle
Lochkov
Modřany
Libuš
Průhonice
Písnice
Radotín
Třebotov
Cholupice
Černošice
Jesenice

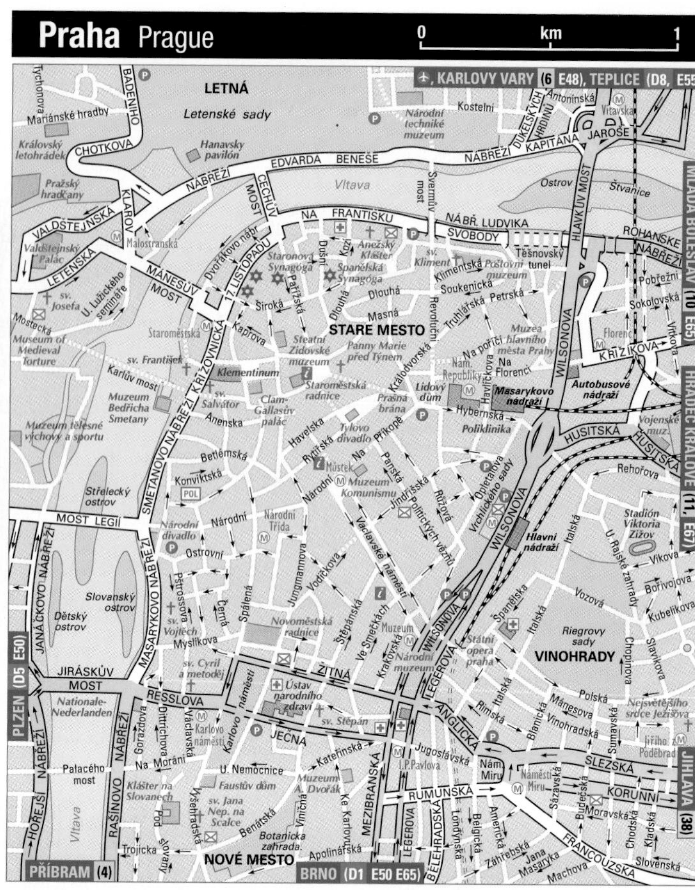
Praha Prague
0 km 1
KARLOVY VARY (6 E48), TEPLICE (D8, E55)
MLADÁ BOLESLAV (10 E65)
HRADEC KRÁLOVÉ (11, E67)
JIHLAVA (38)
BRNO (D1 E50 E65)
PŘÍBRAM (4)
PLZEN (D5 E50)
LETNÁ
Letenské sady
Národní technické muzeum
Hanavský pavilon
Královský letohrádek
Pražský hrad
Vltava
EDVARDA BENEŠE
NÁBŘEŽÍ
STARE MESTO
Staronová Synagoga
Španělská Synagoga
Staroměstská radnice
Klementinum
Karlův most
Muzeum Bedřicha Smetany
Obecní dům
Prašná brána
Masarykovo nádraží
Autobusové nádraží
Hlavní nádraží
Národní muzeum
Státní opera praha
Národní divadlo
Novoměstská radnice
VINOHRADY
Riegrovy sady
Střelecký ostrov
Slovanský ostrov
Dětský ostrov
MOST LEGIÍ
JIRÁSKŮV MOST
Nationale-Nederlanden
Palackého most
Klášter na Slovanech
U. Nemocnice
Faustův dům
Muzeum A. Dvořák
Botanická zahrada
NOVÉ MESTO
WILSONOVA
HUSITSKÁ
KORUNNÍ
SLEZSKÁ
FRANCOUZSKÁ
Štvanice

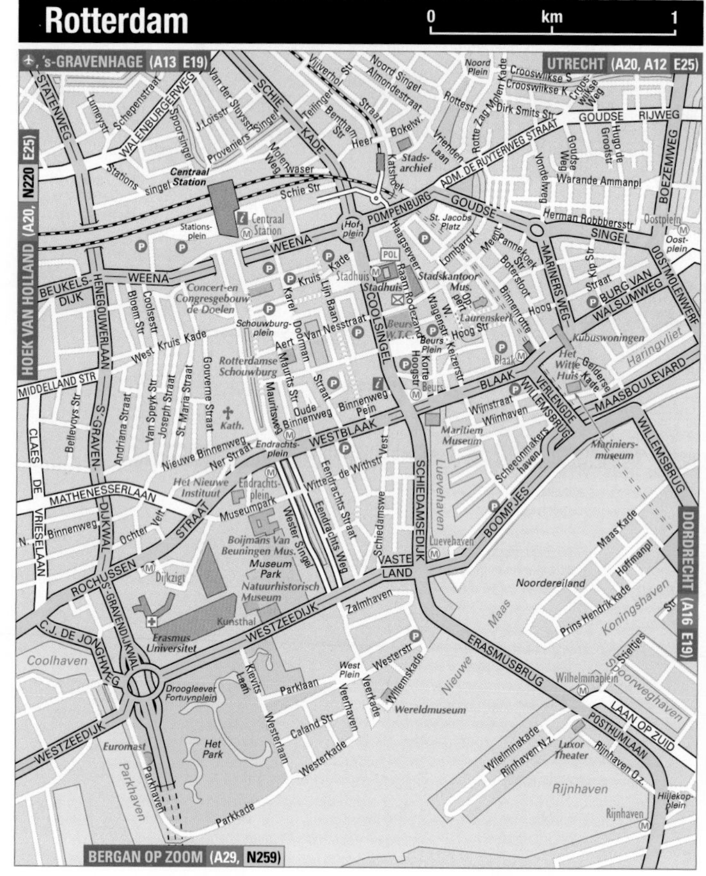
Rotterdam
0 km 1
's-GRAVENHAGE (A13 E19)
UTRECHT (A20, A12 E25)
HOEK VAN HOLLAND (A20, N220 E25)
DORDRECHT (A16 E19)
BERGAN OP ZOOM (A29, N259)
Centraal Station
Stadhuis
Concert-en Congresgebouw de Doelen
Rotterdamse Schouwburg
Museumpark
Boijmans Van Beuningen Mus.
Natuurhistorisch Museum
Kunsthal
Erasmus Universiteit
Maritiem Museum
Euromast
Het Park
Maas
Nieuwe Maas
Noordereiland
Koningshaven
Wereldmuseum
Rijnhaven
Coolhaven
Parkhaven
Luxor Theater
WEENA
COOLSINGEL
BLAAK
BOOMPJES
WESTBLAAK
ERASMUSBRUG
MAASBOULEVARD
WESTZEEDIJK
SCHIEDAMSEDIJK
POMPENBURG
GOUDSE SINGEL

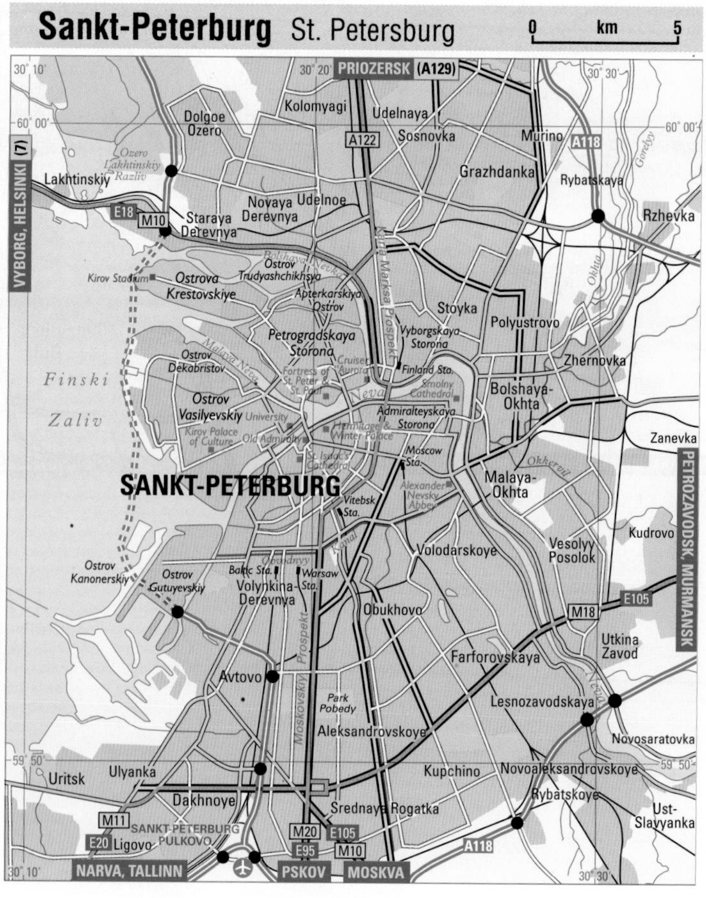
Sankt-Peterburg St. Petersburg
0 km 5
PRIOZERSK (A129)
VYBORG, HELSINKI (7)
PETROZAVODSK, MURMANSK
NARVA, TALLINN
PSKOV
MOSKVA
SANKT-PETERBURG
Finski Zaliv
Kolomyagi
Udelnaya
Dolgoe Ozero
Sosnovka
Murino
Grazhdanka
Lakhtinskiy
Rybatskaya
Rzhevka
Staraya Derevnya
Novaya Derevnya
Udelnoe
Kirov Stadium
Ostrova Krestovskiye
Stoyka
Polyustrovo
Petrogradskaya Storona
Zhernovka
Ostrov Dekabristov
Ostrov Vasilyevskiy
Bolshaya-Okhta
Zanevka
Malaya-Okhta
Kudrovo
Volodarskoye
Vesolyy Posolok
Ostrov Kanonerskiy
Ostrov Gutuyevskiy
Volynkina-Derevnya
Obukhovo
Utkina Zavod
Farforovskaya
Avtovo
Lesnozavodskaya
Park Pobedy
Aleksandrovskoye
Novosaratovka
Uritsk
Ulyanka
Kupchino
Novoaleksandrovskoye
Rybatskoye
Dakhnoye
Srednaya Rogatka
Ust-Slavyanka
SANKT-PETERBURG PULKOVO
Ligovo

Roma Rome

0 km 5

VITERBO
CIVITA CASTELLANA
FIRENZE (A1)
RIETI
Mentana
ORTE, FIRENZE
S. Angelo Romano
415
Montecélio
Ogliata
Via Clàudia
Ost. Nuova
Bracciaese
493
La Riccia
2
Isola Farnese
2 bis
3
Via Flaminia
A1 dir.
4
Via Salaria
Settebagni
Romitório
12° 40'
Santa Maria di Galéria
Tragliatella
La Storta
Via Cássia
Prima Porta
Le Casette
42° 00'
Guidónia
636
Cle. Centrone
Bufalotta
Torre Lupara
A1
E45
San Nicola
La Giustiniana
Le Sprete
Inviolata
Tragliata
Tomba di Nerone
Ottávia
G.R.A.
Boccea
ROMA
Galéria
San Onófrio
AEROPORTO D. URBE
San Basílio
Ponte Lucano
Bagni di Tivoli
Agro Romano
Tor di Quinto
Tufello
Settecamini
Via Tiburtina
L'AQUILA, PESCARA (A25)
Albuccione
Aniene
Tivoli
Torrimpietra
Torrevécchia
Flaminio
Trieste
Monte Sacro
Settecamini
Lunghezza
Torrimpietro
Primavalle
Parioli
Pietralata
Torre Cervara
A24
Salone
E80
Lunghezza
Corcolle
139
Trionfale
Città Del Vaticano
Vatican City
Nomentano
Fiorentini
Torre Cervara
La Bottáccia
Casalotti
Stazione Termini
Tiburtino
Tor Sapienza
Cast. di Passerano
Maccarese -Fregene
Cast. di Guido
La Monachina
Monte spaccato
Aurelio
Trastevere
Portonaccio
Prenestino Labicano
Ost. d. Osa
Tor Pignattara
La Selce
Via Aurélia
Gianicolense
Valcannuta
Centocelle
Pantano Borghese
Maccarese
Malagrotta
Quadraro
Torrenova
Monteverde Nuovo
Garbatella
6
Finócchio
Bonifica di Maccarese
A12
E80
La Pisana
Corviale
Ostiense
7
Cinecittà
Torre Gáia
Laghetto
FROSINONE, NAPOLI (A3)
Cast. Malnome
Via Casilina
Magliana
L'Annunziatella
Roma Torrenova
41° 50'
Autostrada Azzurra
Via Tuscolana
M. Pórzio Catone
Colonna
E.U.R.
A1 dir.
Monte Pórzio Catone
Bonifica di Porto
Ponte Galéria
Casál Morena
215
S. Cesáreo
Via del Mare
216
Cecchignola
St. Torricola
AEROPORTO DI CIAMPINO
Montecómpatri
Fiumicino
Focene
AEROPORTO INTERCONTINENTALE LEONARDO DA VINCI
Tévere
511
Frascati
Camáldoli
G.R.A.
Spinaceto
Ciampino
Rocca Priora
Acília
Vitínia
215
Grottaferrata
Porto
Valleranello
Ostia Malpasso
148
Castél di Leva
Santa Maria della Mole
Marino
8
Colli Albani
Óstia Antica
Via C. Colombo
Frattócchie
Mte. Iano
938
Rocca di Papa
296
Ísola Sacra
Cast. di Décima
Mandriola
Falcognana
7
217
948
Mte. Cavo
956
Lago Albano
Casál Palocco
Cast. Porziano
12° 30'
207
Lido d. Faro
12° 20'
LIDO DI ÓSTIA
LATINA, TERRACINA
APRÍLIA
VELLETRI

Roma Rome

0 km 1

TERNI (3)
VITERBO (2)
FIRENZE 4 (A1 dir, A1 E35)
Galleria Nazionale d'Arte Moderna e Contemporanea
Bioparco
Museo Naz. di Villa Giulia
Viale delle Belle Arti
Ministero Difesa Marina
Villa Borghese
Piazzale Clodio
Circonv. Clodia
Via Sabotino
Piazza G. Mazzini
Mazzini
Via Monte Santo
Via Ostavia
Via Monte Zebio
Via Pòdgora
Via Trionfale
Viale Angelico
Viale Giuseppe
Via L. Settembrini
Lungot. delle Armi
Lung. d. Navi
Fiume
Flaminia
Via Po
Via Adda
Villa Albani
Viale Regina Margherita
Corso Trieste
Via d. Fontanella
Villa Paganini
Via Capodistria
Via Nomentana
Via Alessandro Torlonia
Villa Massimo
Musei di Villa Torlonia
Villa Torlonia
Via Lazzaro Spallanzani
Via Bellunto
Via Fedro
Via Tommaso d'Aquino
Circonv. Trionfale
Viale Trionfale
Via Rodi
Via Graz. Lante
Via della Giuliana
V. S. Pellico
Via Brofferio
Via G. Ferrari
Viale delle Milizie
Lepanto
Cesare
Lungotevere Arnaldo da Brescia
Via Flaminio
Piazza del Popolo
V.le Washington
Viale del Muro Torto
Porta del Popolo
Giardino del Pincio
Galoppatoio
V.le S. Paolo d. Brasile
V.le d. Museo Borghese
Via Pinciana
Corso d'Italia
Museo e Gall. Borghese
Via Tevere
Via Salaria
Via Savoia
Via Nizza
Via Alessandria
MACRO - Museo d'Arte Contemporanea di Roma
Porta Pia
Via Nomentana
Via Bari
Piazza Salerno
Policlinico
Via Belluno
V.le d. Uccelliera
V. P. Raimondi
Viale Medaglie d'Oro
Via V. A. Labriola
Via Savonarola
Via Andrea Doria
Viale Giulio Cesare
Via Barletta
Ottaviano
Fabio Massimo
Via Pompeo Magno
Piazza della Libertà
Via Germanico
Via Cola di Rienzo
Via Cicerone
Via Fed. Cesi
Lungotevere Mellini
Lung. in Augusta
Via di Ripetta
Via del Corso
Via del Babuino
Villa Medici
Spagna
Trinità dei Monti
Via Sistina
Via Ludovisi
Via Vittorio Veneto
Via Sicilia
Via Boncompagni
Via Piemonte
Via Toscana
Min. dei Trasporti
Piazzale di Porta Pia
British Embassy
Via XX Settembre
Via Gaeta
Piazza della Croce Rossa
Viale Castro Pretorio
Castro Pretorio
Biblioteca Nazionale
Policlinico Umberto I
Viale Regina Elena
V. A. Borelli
Piazzale degli Eroi
Via Candia
Viale Leone IV
Via Tunisi
Cipro
Via Cipro
Via Angelo Emo
Via Pirandello
Viale Vaticano
Via degli Ammiragli
Valle Aurelia
Crescenzio
Piazza Adriana
Piazza Cavour
Palazzo di Giustizia
Mausoleo di Augusto
Via Tomacelli
Piazza di Spagna
Min. Industria
Min. Agricoltura e Foreste
Barberini
Via Barberini
Pal. Barberini
Mus. Naz. Romano
S. Maria d. Angeli
Piazza d. Repubblica
Repubblica
Piazza d. Cinquecento
Piazzale di Roma
Central Bus Station
Palestro
Via dei Mille
Viale dell' Università
Sapienza Università di Roma
Via dei Ramni
Musei Vaticani
CITTÀ DEL VATICANO VATICAN CITY
Borgo Vittorio
Castel S. Angelo
Lung. Marzio
Via Tomacelli
Via Font. di Borghese
Posta Centrale
Piazza San Silvestro
Via del Tritone
Giardino del Quirinale
Via d. Quattro Fontane
Min. d. Difesa Esercito
Via Torino
Termini
Stazione Centrale Roma-Termini
Via Marsala
Min. Difesa Aeronautica
Via d. Scienze
S. Pietro in Vaticano
Stazione Vaticana
Piazza San Pietro
Via della Conciliazione
Ospedale S. Spirito
Borgo S. Spirito
L. Vaticano
L. Castello
Lung. Tor di Nona
S. Agostino
C. d. Rinascimento
Piazza Navona
Camera dei Deputati
Piazza Colonna
Fontana di Trevi
Pal. d. Quirinale
Via del Quirinale
Via Nazionale
Teatro d. Opera
Via Cavour
Via Principe Amedeo
Via Giolitti
Viale Pretoriano
Via Tiburtina
Via Aurelia
Campi Sportivi
Via di Porta Cavalleggeri
Pontificia Università Urbaniana
Via dei Coronari
Chiesa Nuova
Pantheon
V. Seminario
Ss. Apostoli
Ministero dell'Interno
Via Milano
V. A. Depretis
S. M. Maggiore
Via Carlo Alberto
Via dei Sabelli
Via dei Reti
S. M. Immacolata
Via dei Sardi
Via del Cottolengo
Via Gregorio VII
Via Innocenzo III
Stazione di S. Pietro
Pontificio Collegio Americano del Nord
V. delle Fornaci
Gianicolo
Ospedale Pediatrico Bambino Gesù
Piazza d. Minerva
Corso Vittorio Emanuele II
Via del Plebiscito
Via IV Novembre
Palazzo Venezia
Col. Traiano
Via Panisperna
Via d. Serpenti
Via Cavour
Vittorio Emanuele
Piazza Vitt. Emanuele II
Via Principe Eugenio
Via di Porta Maggiore
Via G. Giolitti
Piazza di Porta Maggiore
Via Casilina
Via Labicana
Via della Cava Aurelia
Villa Abamelek
Via Nuova delle Fornaci
Mon. a G. Garibaldi
Palazzo Corsini
Orto Botanico
Palazzo Farnese
Campo d. Fiori
Pal. d. Cancelleria
L. d. Sangallo
L. Gianicolense
Lung. della Farnesina
Lung. dei Tebaldi
Via Giulia
Via Arenula
Teatro di Marcello
Via d. Teatro di Marcello
Mon. a Vittorio Emanuele II
Musei Capitolini
Piazza d. Campidoglio
Pal. d. Conservatori
Via dei Fori Imperiali
Foro Romano
Colosseo
Via Annibaldi
V. le d. Monte Oppio
Colle Oppio
Museo d'Arte Orientale
Parco di Traiano
Via Merulana
Via Machiavelli
Via Emanuele Filiberto
Via Manzoni
Viale Manzoni
Via Statilia
Via S. Croce in Gerusalemme
Piazza di S. Croce in Gerus.
Via Tasso
Via Aurelia Antica
Villa Doria Pamphili
S. Pancrazio
Via Garibaldi
S. Pietro in Montorio
Via Lungaretta
S. Maria in Trastevere
V. S. Francesco
Via Nic. Fabrizi
S. Cecilia
V. d. Genovesi
Lung. d. Anguillara
Lung. dei Cenci
I. Tiberina
Via Luciano Manara
V. d. Scala
Via Sonnino
Via Mazzini
Circo Massimo
Via S. Teodoro
Monte Palatino
Arco di Costantino
Via Labicana
Via Domus Aurea
Via Ruggero Bonghi
Via di S. Giovanni in Laterano
Ospedale S. Giovanni
Piazza di S. Giov. in Laterano
Via Claudia
Parco del Celio
Viale Carlo Felice
CIVITAVECCHIA 1 (A12 E80)
FROSINONE 6 (A1 E45)
'LEONARDO DA VINCI' (A12)
LATINA 148
Restricted Zones (ZTL)

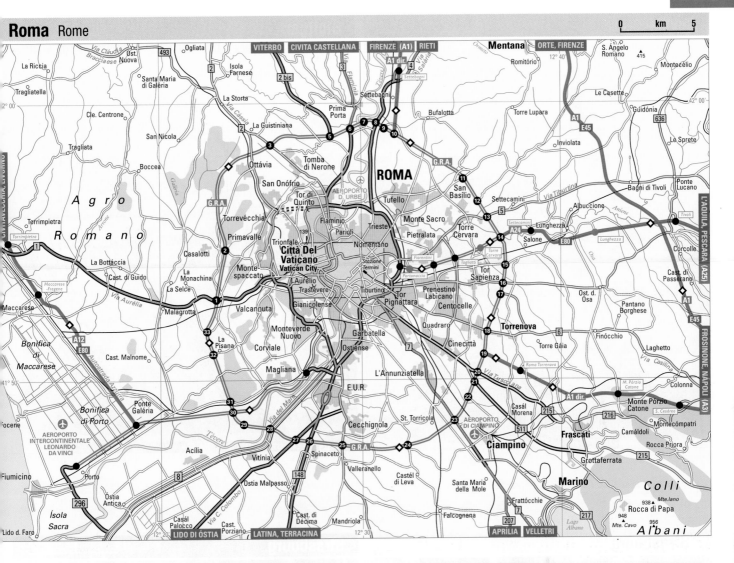

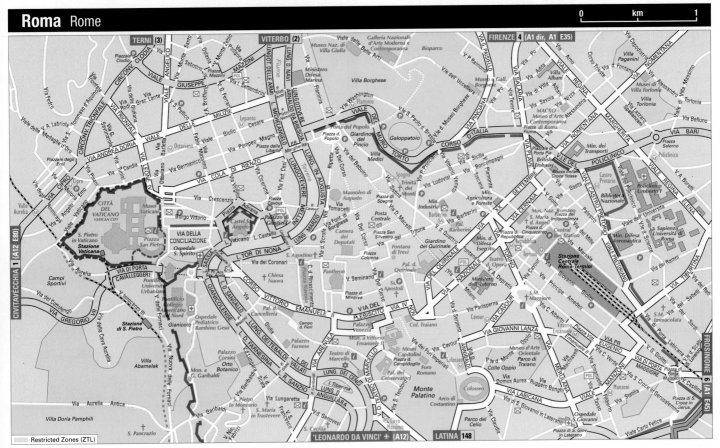

Sevilla Seville

0 km 0.5

CORDOBA (A4 E05)

GRANADA (A92)

CÁDIZ (A4, AP4 E05)

CORIA DEL RÍO (660) HUELVA (A49 E01), MONESTERIO (A66 E803)

Stuttgart

0 km 0.5

HEILBRONN 27, WÜRZBURG (A81 E41)

FELLBACH 14, AALEN (29), ULM (10)

SINGEN 14, (A81 E41), STRASBOURG (A81 28)

TÜBINGEN 27, AUGSBURG (A8 E52)

LEONBERG, KARLSRUHE (A8 E52)

Strasbourg

0 km 5

METZ A35 ACHERN (D2) SELTZ

NANCY (A33)

OBERNAI MOLSHEIM, ST. DIÉ (D1420 A352)

OFFENBURG (33), A5

OFFENBURG (33a), A5

SÉLESTAT

BASEL (A5)

Strasbourg

0 km 0.5

METZ A4 E25

BISCHHEIM A350

SÉLESTAT, MULHOUSE A35

SAVERNE, NANCY (A351 D1004, N4)

MOLSHEIM (A35 A352)

KEHL (28), OFFENBURG (28 A5)

KEHL (28)

ERSTEIN, SÉLESTAT (A35 D1083)

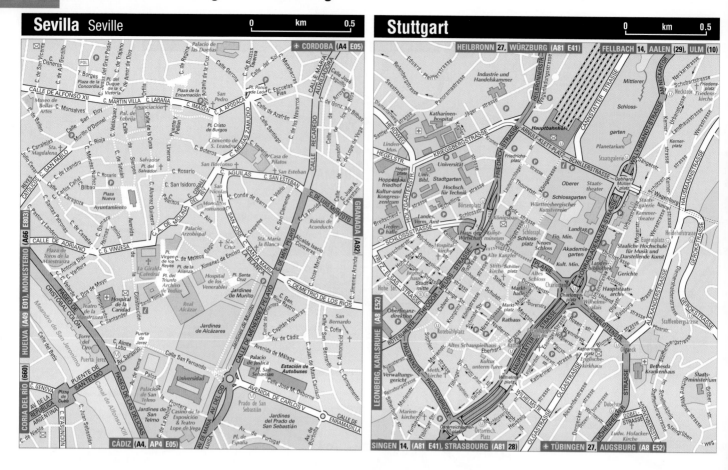

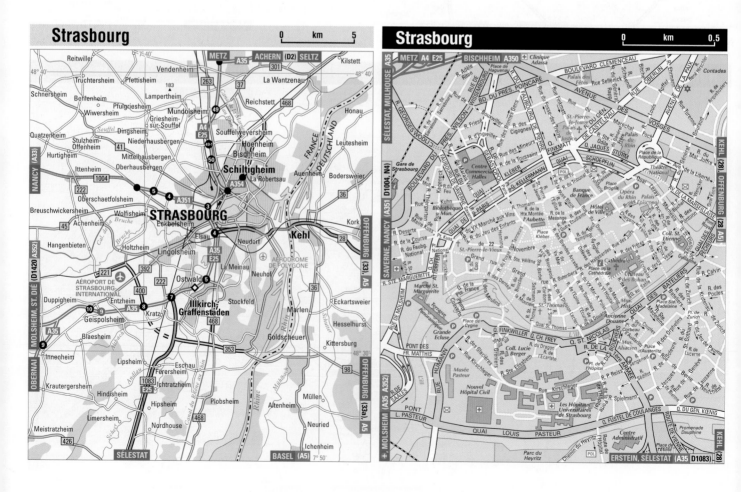

Stockholm

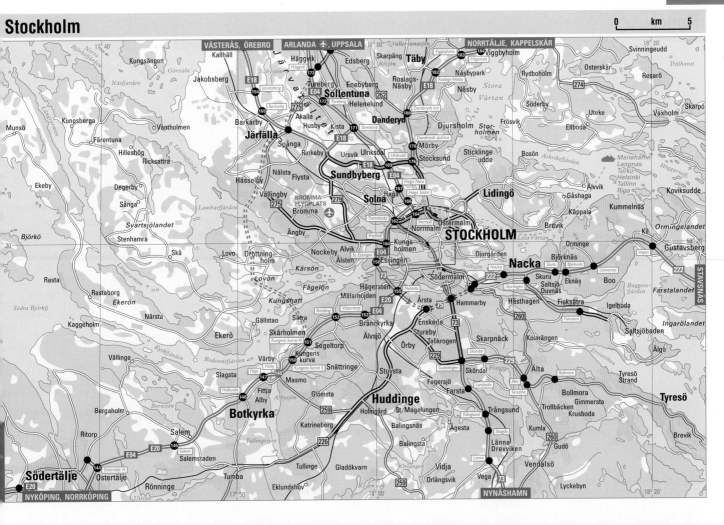

Stockholm

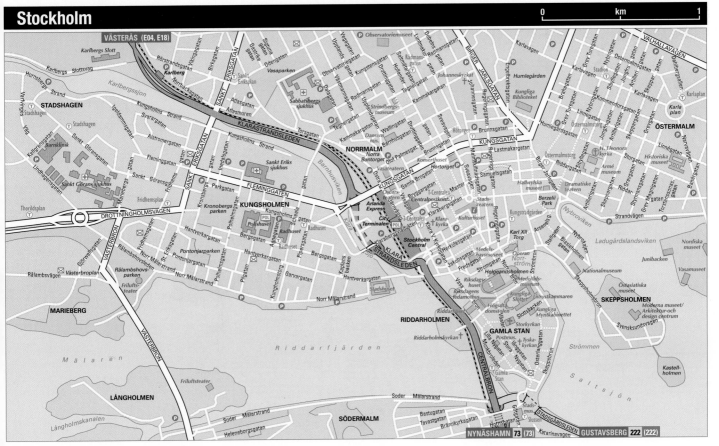

Torino Turin

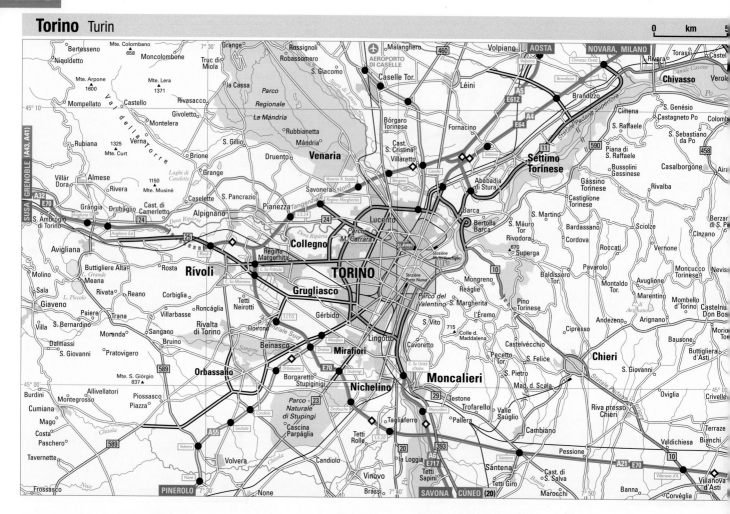

Venézia Venice

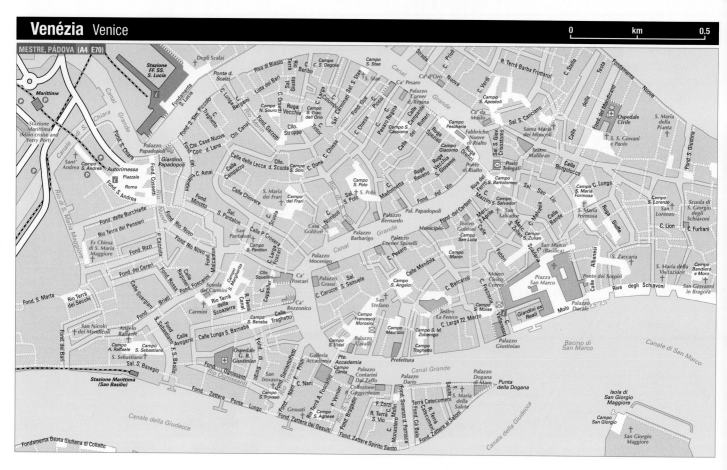

Torino Turin

0 km 1

CASELLE
RIVOLI (25), SUSA (A32 E70)
CHIVASSO (11)
CHIERI (10), ASTI (A21 E70)
PINEROLO (23)
CARIGNANO (20)
MONCALIERI (393), SAVONA (A6 E717)

C. PR. EUGENIO
CORSO REG. MARGHERITA
Via Cottolengo
C. GIULIO CESARE
Piazza della Repubblica
Consolata
Porta Palatina
CORSO XI FEBBRAIO
Corso Lungo D. Firenze
Corso Lungo Dora Savona
Corso Palermo
Via Foggia
Via Messina
Ospedale Maria Adelaide
Corso Lungo Dora Firenze
Corso Lungo Dora Siena
CORSO REGINA MARGHERITA
Via Santo Giulia
Teatro Romano
Palazzo Reale
Giardino Reale
Armeria Reale
Palazio di Città
Piazza Savoia
Piazza Arbarello
Citadella
VIA CERNAJA
Via S. Valfrè
Piazza Castello
Palazzo Madama
VIA PIETRO MICCA
Teatro Regio
Teatro Alfieri
Teatro Carignano
Palazzo Carignano
Università
Mole Antonelliana
Università di Studi
Piazza Solferino
Banca d'Italia
Museo Egizio e Gall. Sabauda
San Filippo Neri
Bibl. Naz.
VIA PO
Piazza S. Carlo
Santa Cristina
VIA ROMA
Piazza Carlo Emanuele II
Ospedale di S. Giovanni Battista
Piazza Vittorio Veneto
Ponte Vittorio Emanuele
Piazza Gran Madre di Dio
Piazza Carlo Felice
Porta Nuova
Stazione Porta Nuova
CORSO VITTORIO EMANUELE II
Piazza Bodoni
Piazza Cavour
Piazza Maria Teresa
Fiume Po
CORSO MONCALIERI
Santa Maria del Monte
Museo Nazionale della Montagna
Chiesa Evangelica Valdese
Tempio Israelitico
Piazza Madama Cristina
C. MASSIMO D'AZEGLIO
Parco del Valentino
Ponte Umberto I
Corso Fiume
Piazza Crimea
CORSO RE UMBERTO
CORSO SACCHI
Marconi
VIA NIZZA
C. G. Marconi

Wien Vienna

0 km 5

STOCKERAU
POYSDORF, BRNO (52)
TULLN
LINZ, SALZBURG (A1)
BRATISLAVA (9), GYŐR (M1)
BADEN
WIENER NEUSTADT, GRAZ
EISENSTADT
BRUCK
BRUNN

Hagenbrunn
Föhrenhain
Kritzendorf
Kierling
Klosterneuburg
Langenzersdorf
Stammersdorf
Kapellerfeld
Helmahof
Gerasdorf bei Wien
Deutsch-Wagram
Weidling
Strebersdorf
Oberlisse
Nordrand-Siedlung
Aderklaa
Parbasdorf
Neusüssenbrunn
Süssenbrunn
Grossjedlersdorf
Grossfeld-Siedlung
Hermannskogel 542
Schwartz-lackenau
Floridsdorf
Jedlesee
Grinzing
Nussdorf
Leopoldau
Salmannsdorf
Sievering
Heiligenstadt
Donaufeld
Breitenlee
Neuessling
Neustift am Walde
Döbling
Kagran
Neukagran
Hirschstetten
Raasdorf
Pötzleinsdorf
Währing
Brigittenau
Donaupark
UNO City
Neuwaldegg
Hernals
Leopoldstadt
Donaustadt
Ottakring
Alsergrund
Messe
Stadlau
Aspern
FLUGPLATZ ASPERN
Am Steinhof
Hütteldorf
WIEN
Essling
Gross-Enzersdorf
Penzing
Baumgarten
Rudolfsheim
Landstrasse
Gross Biberhaufen
Maria
Wieden
Prater
Fünfhaus
Margareten
Freudenau
Sankt Veit
Hietzing
Meidling
Simmering
Simmeringer Heide
Oberhausen
Favoriten
Lainz
Speising
Kaiserebersdorf
Mühlleiten
Hetzendorf
Altmannsdorf
Wienerberg
Albern
Lobau
P. A. Hansson Siedlung
Mauer
Erlaa
Inzersdorf
Oberlaa
Mannswörth
Atzgersdorf
Kledering
Rodaun
Siebenhirten
Rothneusiedl
Unterlaa
Rannersdorf
Schwechat
Perchtoldsdorf
Vösendorf
Neukettenhof
FLUGHAFEN WIEN-SCHWECHAT
Zwölfaxing
Rustenfeld
Donau

Warszawa Warsaw

0 km 5

GDAŃSK, OLSZTYN (51)
OSTROŁĘKA
BIAŁYSTOK
SIEDLCE, BREST
ŁÓDŹ A2
KATOWICE (1)
RADOM, KRAKÓW

Łomianki
Kobyłka
Henryków
Grodzisk
Maciołki
Dąbrowa
Tarchomin
Marcelin
Białołęka Dworska
Marki
Młociński Park
Brzeziny
Wólka Węglowa
Żerań
Zielonka
Laski
Młociny
Drewnica
Lasek Bielański
Pelcowizna
Bródno
Żacisze
Ząbki
Kłaudyn
Wawrzyszew
Bielany
Marymont
Targówek
Bemowo
Żoliborz
Praga Północ
Utrata
Kawęczyn
Rembertów
Lasek Na Kole
Stare Miasto
Praga
Nowe-Babice
Powązki
Grochów
Wygoda
Zielona
Górce
Koło
Muranów
Park Skaryszewski
WARSZAWA
Marysin Wawerski
Blizne
Jelonki
Wola
Powiśle
Saska Kępa
Czyste
Ujazdów
Wawer
Chrzanów
Śródmieście
Anin
Odolany
Park Łazienkowski
Las
Szczęśliwice
Ochota
Sielce
Siekierki
Gołąbki
Włochy
Mokotów
Zerzeń
Międzylesie
Czerniaków
Augustówka
Ursus
Raków
Wierzbno
Radość
Sadyba
Salomea
Okęcie
Służew
Wilanów
Zawady
Opacz
WARSZAWA OKĘCIE
Służewiec
Julianów
Michałowice
Miedzeszyn
Raszyn
Załuski
Wyczółki
Powsinek
Bartyki
Imielin
Błota
Sokołów
Jaworowa
Grabów
Natolin
Falenty
Kabaty
Janki
Dawidy
Pyry
Moczydło
Okrzeszyn
Łady
Las Kabacki
Powsin
Bielawa
Wisła

Warszawa Warsaw

0 km 1

GDAŃSK 7 E77
OSTROŁĘKA 61
BIAŁYSTOK 629 (8 E67)
ŁOWICZ, KONIN 629 (2 E30)
WŁOCŁAWEK 634 (7, 62)
BREST 2 E30
ŁÓDŹ 2 (A2), KRAKÓW 2 (8, 7, E77)
OKĘCIE 634
GÓRA KALWARIA 7 (79)

Dworzec Gdański
ZYGMUNTA SŁOMIŃSKIEGO
Ogród Zoologiczny
Park Praski
Warszawa Wileńska
Ząbkowska
PRAGA
Warszawa Wschodnia
Kościół Św. Jana Bożego
Bonifraterska
Konwiktorska
NOWE MIASTO
STARE MIASTO
Rynek Starego Miasta
WYBRZEŻE GDAŃSKIE
MOST ŚLĄSKO-DĄBROWSKI
AL. SOLIDARNOŚCI
JAGIELLOŃSKA
TARGOWA
WYBRZEŻE HELSKIE
Ogród Krasińskich
Biblioteka Narodowa
Muzeum Archeologiczne (d. Arsenał)
Zamek Królewski
Kościół Św. Anny
Kościół Ewangelicko-Reformowany
Opera Kameralna
Pl. Bankowy
Pl. Teatralny
Teatr Wielki Opery i Baletu
Urząd miasta (City Hall)
ALEJA JANA PAWŁA II
AL. SOLIDARNOŚCI
Ogród Saski
Pl. Piłsudskiego
Uniwersytet
Teatr Polski
Kościół Ewangelicko-Augsburski
Nowy Świat
Pl. Mirowski
Elektoralna
Grzybowska
Pl. Grzybowski
Filharmonia
Muzeum Chopina
Warszawa Powiśle
POWIŚLE
Szpital Dziecięcy
MOST ŚWIĘTOKRZYSKI
MOST ŚREDNICOWY
WYBRZEŻE KOŚCIUSZKOWSKIE
WISŁA
Port Praski
Warszawa Stadion
GROCHOWSKA
Park Skaryszewski
Stadion Narodowy w Warszawie
MOST PONIATOWSKIEGO
AL. J. PONIATOWSKIEGO
WAŁ MIEDZESZYŃSKI
Wałeczynch
Twarda
Świętokrzyska
Pałac Kultury i Nauki
Centrum Warszawa Śródmieście
Rondo ONZ
Szpital Zakaźny
Warszawa Centralna
AL. JEROZOLIMSKIE
Nowogrodzka
Muz. Wojska Polskiego
Muz. Narodowe
Książęca
Kościół Św. Aleksandra
W. Śródm. Wkd
W. Ochota
Teatr Muzyczny Roma
Hoża
Wilcza
ŚRÓDMIEŚCIE
MARSZAŁKOWSKA
CHAŁUBIŃSKIEGO
Pl. Artura Zawiszy
Szpital Kliniczny Akademii Medycznej
Koszykowa
Politechnika Warszawska
Pl. Konstytucji
Pl. Zbawiciela
UJAZDÓW
Park Ujazdowski
Zamek Ujazdowski
AL. ARMII LUDOWEJ
Łazienkowska
Stadion Legia
Miedzyszkolny Park Sportowy
Ogród Botaniczny
Szwoleżerów
British Embassy
Obserwatorium Astronomiczne
Pałac Łazienkowski
Teatr na Wyspie
Park Łazienkowski
Belwederska
Bagatela
Pl. Unii Lubelskiej
RASZYŃSKA
GRÓJECKA
Pl. Narutowicza
Filtry
Filtrowa
Szpital Nowowiejski
Nowowiejska
WAWELSKA
Park im. Józefa Piłsudskiego
Biblioteka Narodowa
Politechnika Warszawska
Stadion "Skra"
Centr. Onkologii
Stefana Banacha
ŻWIRKI I WIGURY
NIEPODLEGŁOŚCI
WARYŃSKIEGO
PUŁAWSKA
Rakowiecka
Pole Mokotowskie
SOLEC
CZERNIAKOWSKA
MOST ŁAZIENKOWSKI
Podchorążych
Bartycka

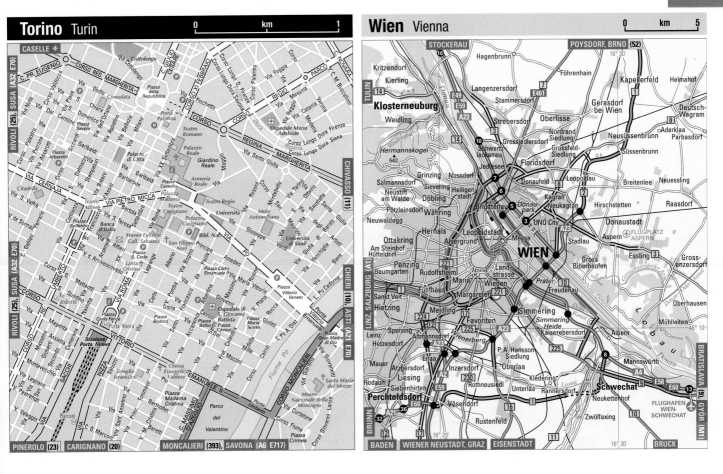

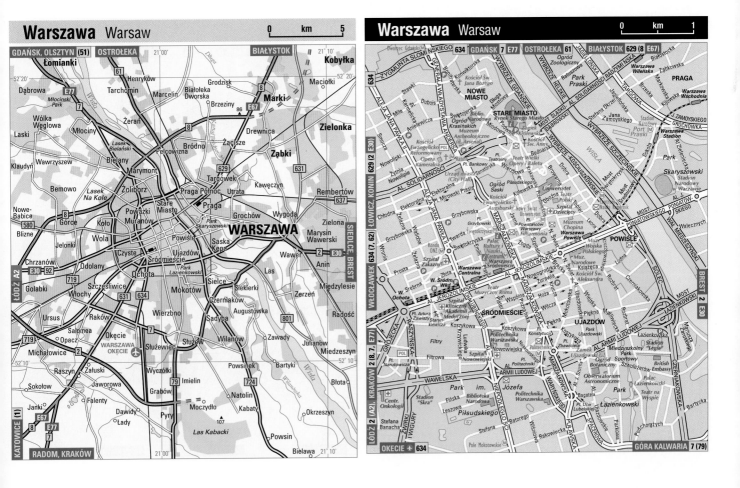

Wien Vienna

0 km 1

STOCKERAU 227 (A22 E49 E59)

DEUTSCH-WAGRAM 8

SCHWECHAT ✈ 227 (A4 E60)

ST. PÖLTEN, LINZ 1 (A1 E60)

WIENER NEUSTADT, GRAZ 17 (A2 E59)

SCHWECHAT 225

Zagreb

0 km 0.5

LJUBLJANA (A3 E70)

KARLOVAC (A1 E65, E71)

SLAVONSKI BROD (A3 E70)

Zürich

0 km 0.5

BASEL (A1, A3 E60)

BÜLACH (A1b)

WINTERTHUR (A1, E60)

UITIKON

BADEN (3)

CHUR (A3 A13)

CHUR (A3 A13)

RAPPERSWIL 17

WATTWIL 52 (8)

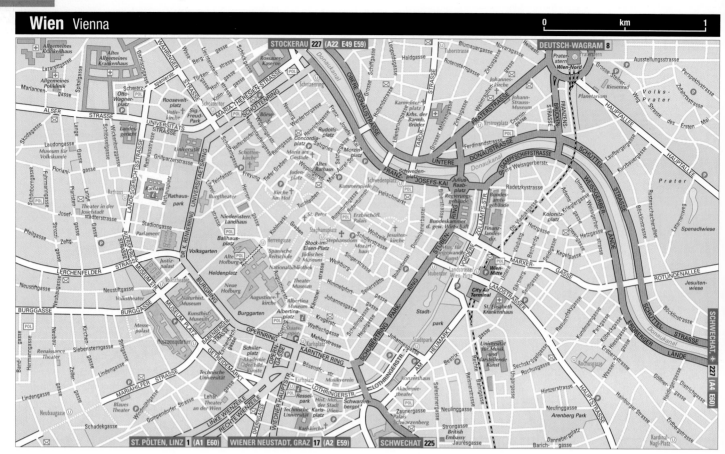

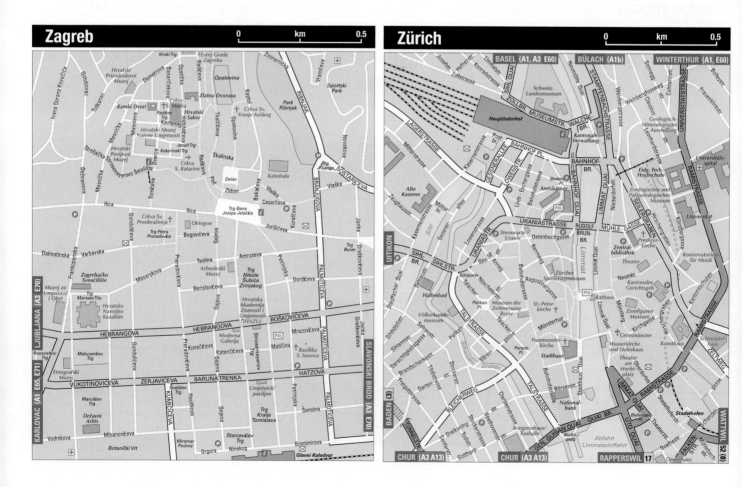

	English	French	German	Italian
(A)	Austria	Autriche	Österreich	Austria
(AL)	Albania	Albanie	Albanien	Albania
(AND)	Andorra	Andorre	Andorra	Andorra
(B)	Belgium	Belgique	Belgien	Belgio
(BG)	Bulgaria	Bulgarie	Bulgarien	Bulgaria
(BIH)	Bosnia-Herzegovin	Bosnie-Herzegovine	Bosnien-Herzegowina	Bosnia-Herzogovina
(BY)	Belarus	Belarus	Weissrussland	Bielorussia
(CH)	Switzerland	Suisse	Schweiz	Svizzera
(CY)	Cyprus	Chypre	Zypern	Cipro
(CZ)	Czechia	République Tchèque	Tschechische Republik	Repubblica Ceca
(D)	Germany	Allemagne	Deutschland	Germania
(DK)	Denmark	Danemark	Dänemark	Danimarca
(E)	Spain	Espagne	Spanien	Spagna
(EST)	Estonia	Estonie	Estland	Estonia
(F)	France	France	Frankreich	Francia
(FIN)	Finland	Finlande	Finnland	Finlandia
(FL)	Liechtenstein	Liechtenstein	Liechtenstein	Liechtenstein
(FO)	Faeroe Islands	Îles Féroé	Färoër-Inseln	Isole Faroe
(GB)	United Kingdom	Royaume Uni	Grossbritannien und Nordirland	Regno Unito
(GBZ)	Gibraltar	Gibraltar	Gibraltar	Gibilterra
(GR)	Greece	Grèce	Greichenland	Grecia
(H)	Hungary	Hongrie	Ungarn	Ungheria
(HR)	Croatia	Croatie	Kroatien	Croazia
(I)	Italy	Italie	Italien	Italia
(IRL)	Ireland	Irlande	Irland	Irlanda
(IS)	Iceland	Islande	Island	Islanda
(KOS)	Kosovo	Kosovo	Kosovo	Kosovo
(L)	Luxembourg	Luxembourg	Luxemburg	Lussemburgo
(LT)	Lithuania	Lituanie	Litauen	Lituania
(LV)	Latvia	Lettonie	Lettland	Lettonia
(M)	Malta	Malte	Malta	Malta
(MC)	Monaco	Monaco	Monaco	Monaco
(MD)	Moldova	Moldavie	Moldawien	Moldavia
(MK)	Macedonia	Macédoine	Makedonien	Macedonia
(MNE)	Montenegro	Monténégro	Montenegro	Montenegro
(N)	Norway	Norvège	Norwegen	Norvegia
(NL)	Netherlands	Pays-Bas	Niederlande	Paesi Bassi
(P)	Portugal	Portugal	Portugal	Portogallo
(PL)	Poland	Pologne	Polen	Polonia
(RO)	Romania	Roumanie	Rumanien	Romania
(RSM)	San Marino	Saint-Marin	San Marino	San Marino
(RUS)	Russia	Russie	Russland	Russia
(S)	Sweden	Suède	Schweden	Svezia
(SK)	Slovakia	République Slovaque	Slowak Republik	Repubblica Slovacca
(SLO)	Slovenia	Slovénie	Slowenien	Slovenia
(SRB)	Serbia	Serbie	Serbien	Serbia
(TR)	Turkey	Turquie	Türkei	Turchia
(UA)	Ukraine	Ukraine	Ukraine	Ucraina

Bae–Bea 233

Baena E 163 A3
Baesweiler D 80 B2
Baeza E 157 C4
Baflo NL 71 A3
Baga E 147 B2
Bagaladi I 175 C1
Bagenkop DK 65 B3
Baggetorp S 56 A2
Bagh a Chaisteil GB 31 C1
Bagheria I 176 A2
Bagn N 47 B6
Bagnacavallo I 135 A4
Bagnáia I 168 A2
Bagnara Cálabra I 175 C1
Bagnasco I 133 A4
Bagnères-de-Bigorre
F 145 A4
Bagnères-de-Luchon
F 145 B4
Bagni del Másino I 120 A2
Bagni di Lucca I 134 A3
Bagni di Rabbi I 121 A3
Bagni di Tivoli I 168 B2
Bagno di Romagna
I 135 B4
Bagnoles-de-l'Orne
F 89 B3
Bagnoli dei Trigno
I 170 B2
Bagnoli di Sopra I 121 B4
Bagnoli Irpino I 170 C3
Bagnolo Mella I 120 B3
Bagnols-en-Forêt
F 132 B2
Bagnols-sur-Cèze
F 131 A3
Bagnorégio I 168 A2
Bagolino I 121 B3
Bagrationovsk RUS 12 A4
Bagrdan SRB 127 C3
Báguena E 152 A2
Bahabón de Esgueva
E 143 C3
Bahillo E 142 B2
Báia delle Zágare
I 171 B4
Báia Domizia I 169 B3
Baia Mare RO 17 B5
Baiano I 170 C2
Baião P 148 A1
Baiersbronn D 93 C4
Baiersdorf D 94 B3
Baignes-Ste Radegonde
F 115 C3
Baigneux-les-Juifs
F 104 B3
Baildon GB 40 B2
Bailén E 157 B4
Băileşti RO 17 C5
Baileux B 91 A4
Bailieborough IRL 27 C4
Bailleul F 78 B2
Baillonville B 79 B5
Bailó E 144 B3
Bain-de-Bretagne
F 101 B4
Bains F 117 B3
Bains-les-Bains F 105 A5
Bainton GB 40 B3
Baio E 140 A2
Baiona E 140 B2
Bais F 89 B3
Baiso I 134 A3
Baiuca P 148 B2
Baja H 125 A4
Bajánsenye H 111 C3
Bajina Bašta SRB 127 D1
Bajmok SRB 126 B1
Bajna H 112 B2
Bajovo Polje MNE 139 B4
Bajša SRB 126 B1
Bak H 111 C3
Bakar HR 123 B3
Bakewell GB 40 B2
Bakio E 143 A4
Bakka N 47 C6
Bakkafjörður IS 191 A11
Bakkagerði IS 191 B12
Bække DK 59 C2
Bakken N 48 B3
Baklan TR 189 B4
Bækmarksbro DK 58 B1
Bakonybél H 111 B4
Bakonycsernye H 112 B2
Bakonyjákó H 111 B4
Bakonyszentkirály
H 111 B4
Bakonyszombathely
H 112 B1
Bakov nad Jizerou
CZ 84 B2
Bąkowiec PL 87 A5
Baks H 113 C4
Baksa H 125 B4
Bakum D 71 B5
Bala GB 38 B3
Bâlâ TR 23 B7
Balaguer E 145 C4
Balassagyarmat H 112 A3
Balástya H 113 C4
Balatonakali H 111 C4
Balatonalmádi H 112 B2
Balatonboglár H 111 C4
Balatonbozsok H 112 C2
Balatonederics H 111 C4
Balatonfenyves H 111 C4
Balatonföldvár H 112 C1
Balatonfüred H 112 C1
Balatonfűzfő H 112 B2
Balatonkenese H 112 B2
Balatonkiliti H 112 C2
Balatonlelle H 111 C4
Balatonszabadi H 112 C2
Balatonszemes H 111 C4
Balatonszentgyörgy
H 111 C4
Balazote E 158 C1
Balbeggie GB 35 B4
Balbigny F 117 B4
Balboa E 141 B4
Balbriggan IRL 30 A2
Balchik BG 17 D8
Balçova TR 188 A2
Baldock GB 44 B3
Bale HR 122 B2
Baleira E 141 A3
Baleizao P 160 A2
Balen B 79 A5
Balerma E 164 C2
Balestrand N 46 A3
Balestrate I 176 A2
Balfour GB 33 B4
Bälganet S 63 B3
Balgari BG 17 D7
Balıkesir TR 186 C2
Balıklıçeşme TR 186 B2
Bälinge S 51 C4
Balingen D 107 A3
Balingsta S 56 A3
Balintore GB 32 D3
Balizac F 128 B2
Balk NL 70 B2
Balkbrug NL 71 B3
Balla IRL 28 A2
Ballachulish GB 34 B2
Ballaghaderreen
IRL 26 C2
Ballancourt-sur-
Essonne F 90 C2
Ballantrae GB 36 A2
Ballao I 179 C3
Ballasalla GB 36 B2
Ballater GB 32 D3
Ballen DK 59 C3
Ballenstedt D 82 A3
Ballerias E 145 C3
Balleroy F 88 A3
Ballerup DK 61 D2
Ballesteros de Calatrava
E 157 B4
Ballı TR 186 B2
Ballina IRL 26 B1
Ballinalack IRL 30 A1
Ballinamore IRL 26 B3
Ballinascarty IRL 29 C3
Ballinasloe IRL 28 A3
Ballindine IRL 28 A3
Balling DK 58 B1
Ballingarry
Limerick IRL 29 B3
Tipperary IRL 30 B1
Ballingeary IRL 29 C2
Ballinhassig IRL 29 C3
Ballinluig GB 35 B4
Ballino I 121 B3
Ballinrobe IRL 28 A2
Ballinskelligs IRL 29 C1
Ballinspittle IRL 29 C3
Ballintra IRL 26 B2
Ballivor IRL 30 A2
Ballobar E 153 A4
Ballon
F 102 A2
IRL 30 B2
Ballószög H 112 C3
Ballsh AL 182 C1
Ballstad N 194 B4
Ballum DK 64 A1
Ballybay IRL 27 B4
Ballybofey IRL 26 B3
Ballybunion IRL 29 B2
Ballycanew IRL 30 B2
Ballycarry GB 27 B5
Ballycastle
GB 27 A4
IRL 26 B1
Ballyclare GB 27 B5
Ballyconneely IRL 28 A1
Ballycotton IRL 29 C3
Ballycroy IRL 26 B1
Ballydehob IRL 29 C2
Ballyferriter IRL 29 B1
Ballygawley GB 27 B3
Ballygowan GB 27 B5
Ballyhaunis IRL 28 A3
Ballyheige IRL 29 B2
Ballyjamesduff IRL 27 C3
Ballylanders IRL 29 B3
Ballylynan IRL 30 B1
Ballymahon IRL 28 A4
Ballymena GB 27 B4
Ballymoe IRL 28 A3
Ballymoney GB 27 A4
Ballymore IRL 28 A4
Ballymote IRL 26 B2
Ballynacorra IRL 29 C3
Ballynagore IRL 30 A1
Ballynahinch GB 27 B5
Ballynure GB 27 B5
Ballyragget IRL 30 B1
Ballysadare IRL 26 B2
Ballyshannon IRL 26 B2
Ballyvaughan IRL 28 A2
Ballyvourney IRL 29 C2
Ballywalter GB 27 B5
Balmaclellan GB 36 A2
Balmaseda E 143 A3
Balmazújváros H 113 B5
Balme I 119 B4
Balmedie GB 33 D4
Balmuccia I 119 B5
Balna-paling GB 32 D2
Balneario de Panticosa
E 145 B3
Balotaszállás H 126 A1
Balsa P 148 A2
Balsareny E 147 C2
Balsorano-Nuovo I 169 B3
Bålsta S 57 A3
Balsthal CH 106 B2
Balta UA 17 A8
Baltanás E 142 C2
Baltar E 140 C3
Baltasound GB 33 A6
Bălţi MD 17 B7
Baltimore IRL 29 C2
Baltinglass IRL 30 B2
Baltiysk RUS 69 A4
Baltów PL 87 A5
Balugães P 148 A1
Bælum DK 58 B3
Balve D 81 A3
Balvi LV 8 D5
Balvicar GB 34 B2
Balya TR 186 C2
Balzo I 136 C2
Bamberg D 94 B2
Bamburgh GB 37 A5
Banatska Palanka
SRB 127 C3
Banatski Brestovac
SRB 127 C2
Banatski Despotovac
SRB 126 B2
Banatski Dvor
SRB 126 B2
Banatski-Karlovac
SRB 127 B3
Banatsko Arandjelovo
SRB 126 A2
Banatsko-Novo Selo
SRB 127 C2
Banaz TR 187 D4
Banbridge GB 27 B4
Banbury GB 44 A2
Banchory GB 33 D4
Bande
B 79 B5
E 140 B3
Bandholm DK 65 B4
Bandırma TR 186 B2
Bandol F 132 B1
Bandon IRL 29 C3
Bañeres E 159 C3
Banff GB 33 D4
Bangor
F 100 B2
Down GB 27 B5
Gwynedd GB 38 A2
IRL 26 B1
Bangsund N 199 A8
Banie PL 74 A3
Banja Koviljača
SRB 127 C1
Banjaloka SLO 123 B3
Banja Luka BIH 124 C3
Banjani SRB 127 C1
Banja Vručica BIH 125 C3
Banka SK 98 C1
Bankekind S 56 B1
Bankend GB 36 A3
Bankeryd S 62 A2
Bankfoot GB 35 B4
Bankso BG 183 B5
Banloc RO 126 B3
Bannalec F 100 B2
Bannes F 91 C3
Bannockburn GB 35 B4
Bañobárez E 149 B3
Bañon E 152 B2
Banon F 132 A1
Baños E 149 B4
Baños de Gigonza
E 162 B2
Baños de la Encina
E 157 B4
Baños de Molgas
E 140 B3
Baños de Rio Tobia
E 143 B4
Baños de Valdearados
E 143 C3
Bánov CZ 98 C1
Banova Jaruga HR 124 B2
Bánovce nad Bebravou
SK 98 C2
Banovići BIH 139 A4
Banovići Selo BIH 139 A4
Bánréve H 99 C4
Bansin D 66 C3
Banská Belá SK 98 C2
Banská Bystrica
SK 99 C3
Banská Štiavnica
SK 98 C2
Bansko BG 183 B5
Banstead GB 44 B3
Banteer IRL 29 B3
Bantheville F 91 B5
Bantry IRL 29 C2
Bantzenheim F 106 B2
Banyalbufar E 166 B2
Banyoles E 147 B3
Banyuls-sur-Mer F 146 B4
Bapaume F 90 A2
Bar
MNE 16 D3
UA 13 D7
Barabhas GB 31 A2
Barači BIH 138 A2
Baracs H 112 C2
Baracska H 112 B2
Barahona E 151 A5
Barajes de Melo E 151 B5
Barakaldo E 143 A4
Baralla E 141 B3
Barañain E 144 B2
Baranavichy BY 13 B7
Báránd H 113 B5
Baranda SRB 127 B2
Baranello I 170 B2
Baranów Sandomierski
PL 87 B5
Baraqueville F 130 A1
Barasoain E 144 B2
Barbacena P 155 C3
Barbadás E 140 B3
Barbadillo E 149 B4
Barbadillo de Herreros
E 143 B3
Barbadillo del Mercado
E 143 B3
Barbadillo del Pez
E 143 B3
Barban HR 123 B3
Barbarano Vicento
I 121 B4
Barbariga HR 122 C2
Barbaros TR 186 B2
Barbastro E 145 B4
Barbate E 162 B2
Barbatona E 152 A1
Barbâtre F 114 B1
Barbazan F 145 A4
Barbeitos E 141 A3
Barbentane F 131 B3
Barberino di Mugello
I 135 A4
Barbezieux-St Hilaire
F 115 C3
Barbonne-Fayel F 91 C3
Barbotan-les-Thermes
F 128 C2
Barby D 73 C4
Bárcabo E 145 B4
Barca de Alva P 149 A3
Barcarrota E 155 C4
Barcellona-Pozzo di
Gotto I 177 A4
Barcelona E 147 C3
Barcelonette F 132 A2
Barcelos P 148 A1
Bárcena del Monasterio
E 141 A4
Barcena de Pie de
Concha E 142 A2
Barchfeld D 82 B2
Barcin PL 76 B2
Barcino PL 68 A1
Bárcis I 122 A1
Barco P 148 B2
Barcones E 151 A5
Barcs H 124 B3
Barcus F 144 A3
Bardejov SK 12 D4
Bårdesø DK 59 C3
Bardi I 120 C2
Bardney GB 40 B3
Bardo PL 85 B4
Bardolino I 121 B3
Bardonécchia I 118 B3
Bardoňovo SK 112 A2
Barèges F 145 B4
Barenstein D 83 B5
Barentin F 89 A4
Barenton F 88 B3
Barevo BIH 138 A3
Barfleur F 88 A2
Barga I 134 A3
Bargas E 151 C3
Barge I 119 C4
Bargemon F 132 B2
Barghe I 120 B3
Bargoed GB 39 C3
Bargrennan GB 36 A2
Bargteheide D 64 C3
Barham GB 45 B5
Bari I 173 A2
Barič Draga HR 137 A4
Barilović HR 123 B4
Bari Sardo I 179 C3
Barisciano I 169 A3
Barjac F 131 A3
Barjols F 132 B1
Barjon F 105 B3
Bårkåker N 54 A1
Barkald N 199 D7
Barkowo
Dolnośląskie PL 85 A4
Pomorskie PL 68 B2
Bârlad RO 17 B7
Bar-le-Duc F 91 C5
Barles F 132 A2
Barletta I 171 B4
Barlinek PL 75 B4
Barmouth GB 38 B2
Barmstedt D 64 C2
Barnard Castle GB 37 B5
Barnarp S 62 A2
Bärnau D 95 B4
Bärnbach A 110 B2
Barneberg D 73 B4
Barnenitz D 74 B1
Barnet GB 44 B3
Barnetby le Wold
GB 40 B3
Barneveld NL 70 B2
Barneville-Carteret
F 88 A2
Barnoldswick GB 40 B1
Barnowko PL 75 B3
Barnsley GB 40 B2
Barnstädt D 83 A3
Barnstaple GB 42 A2
Barnstorf D 72 B1
Barntrup D 72 C2
Baron F 90 B2
Baronissi I 170 C2
Barqueiro P 154 B2
Barquinha P 154 B2
Barr
F 93 C3
GB 36 A2
Barra P 148 B1
Barracas E 159 A3
Barraco E 150 B3
Barrado E 150 B2
Barrafranca I 177 B3
Barranco do Velho
P 160 B2
Barrancos P 161 A3
Barrax E 158 B1
Barrbaar D 94 C2
Barre-des-Cevennes
F 130 A2
Barreiro P 154 C1
Barreiros E 141 A3
Barrême F 132 B2
Barret-le-Bas F 132 A1
Barrhead GB 34 C3
Barrhill GB 36 A2
Barrio de Nuesra
Señora E 142 B1
Barrowford GB 40 B1
Barrow-in-Furness
GB 36 B3
Barrow upon Humber
GB 40 B3
Barruecopardo E 149 A3
Barruelo de Santullán
E 142 B2
Barruera E 145 B4
Barry GB 39 C3
Bårse DK 65 A4
Barsinghausen D 72 B2
Barssel D 71 A4
Bar-sur-Aube F 104 A3
Bar-sur-Seine F 104 A3
Barth D 66 B1
Bartholomä D 94 C1
Bartin TR 187 A7
Barton upon Humber
GB 40 B3
Barúmini I 179 C2
Baruth D 74 B2
Barvaux B 80 B1
Barver D 72 B1
Barwałd PL 99 B3
Barwice PL 68 B1
Barysaw BY 13 A8
Barzana E 141 A5
Bârzava RO 16 B4
Bárzio I 120 B2
Bas E 147 B3
Bašaid SRB 126 B2
Basaluzzo I 120 C1
Basarabeasca MD 17 B8
Basauri E 143 A4
Baschi I 168 A2
Baschurch GB 38 B4
Basconcillos del Tozo
E 143 B3
Bascones de Ojeda
E 142 B2
Basécles B 79 B3
Basel CH 106 B2
Basélice I 170 B2
Basildon GB 45 B4
Basingstoke GB 44 B2
Baška
CZ 98 B2
HR 123 C3
Baška Voda HR 138 B2
Bäsksjö S 200 B3
Baslow GB 40 B2
Başmakçı TR 189 B5
Basovizza I 122 B2
Bassacutena I 178 A3
Bassano del Grappa
I 121 B4
Bassano Romano I 168 A2
Bassecourt CH 106 B2
Bassella E 147 B2
Bassevuovdde N 193 D9
Bassou F 104 B2
Bassoues F 128 C3
Bassum D 72 B1
Båstad S 61 C2
Bastardo I 136 C1
Bastelica F 180 A2
Bastelicaccia F 180 B1
Bastia
F 180 A2
I 136 B1
Bastogne B 92 A1
Baston GB 40 C3
Bastuträsk S 200 B6
Bata H 125 A4
Batajnica SRB 127 C2
Batak BG 183 B6
Batalha P 154 B2
Bátaszék H 125 A4
Batea E 153 A4
Batelov CZ 97 B3
Bath GB 43 A4
Bathgate GB 35 C4
Batida H 126 A2
Batignano I 135 C4
Batina HR 125 B4
Bátka SK 99 C4
Batković BIH 125 C5
Batley GB 40 B2
Batnfjordsøra N 198 C4
Batočina SRB 127 C3
Bátonyterenye H 113 B3
Batrina HR 125 B3
Båtsfjord N 193 B13
Båtskärsnäs S 196 D6
Battaglia Terme I 121 B4
Bätterkinden CH 106 B2
Battice B 80 B1
Battipáglia I 170 C2
Battle GB 45 C4
Battonya H 126 A3
Batuša SRB 127 C3
Bátya H 112 C2
Bau I 179 C2
Baud F 100 B2
Baudour B 79 B3
Baugé F 102 B1
Baugy F 103 B4
Bauma CH 107 B3
Baume-les-Dames
F 105 B5
Baumholder D 93 B3
Baunatal D 81 A5
Baunei I 178 B3
Bauska LV 8 D4
Bautzen D 84 A2
Bavanište SRB 127 C2
Bavay F 79 B3
Bavilliers F 106 B1
Bavorov CZ 96 B2
Bawdsey GB 45 A5
Bawinkel D 71 B4
Bawtry GB 40 B2
Bayat TR 187 D5
Bayel F 105 A3
Bayeux F 88 A3
Bayındır TR 188 A2
Bayon F 92 C2
Bayonne F 128 C1
Bayons F 132 A2
Bayramiç TR 186 C1
Bayreuth D 95 B3
Bayrischzell D 108 B3
Baza E 164 B2
Bazas F 128 B2
Baziege F 146 A2
Bazoches-les-
Gallerandes F 103 A4
Bazoches-sur-Hoëne
F 89 B4
Bazzano I 135 A4
Beaconsfield GB 44 B3
Beade E 140 B2
Beadnell GB 37 A5
Beaminster GB 43 B4
Bearsden GB 34 C3
Beas E 161 B3
Beasain E 144 A1
Beas de Segura E 164 A2
Beattock GB 36 A3
Beaubery F 117 A4
Beaucaire F 131 B3
Beaufort
F 118 B3
IRL 29 B2
Beaufort-en Vallée
F 102 B1
Beaugency F 103 B3
Beaujeu
Alpes-de-Haute-Provence F 132 A2
Rhône F 117 A4
Beaulac F 128 B2
Beaulieu
F 103 B4
GB 44 C2
Beaulieu-sous-la-Roche
F 114 B2
Beaulieu-sur-Dordogne
F 129 B4
Beaulieu-sur-Mer
F 133 B3
Beaulon F 104 C2
Beauly GB 32 D2
Beaumaris GB 38 A2
Beaumesnil F 89 A4
Beaumetz-lès-Loges
F 78 B2
Beaumont
B 79 B4
F 129 B3
Beaumont-de-Lomagne
F 129 C3
Beaumont-du-Gâtinais
F 103 A4
Beaumont-en-Argonne
F 91 B5
Beaumont-Hague F 88 A2
Beaumont-la-Ronce
F 102 B2
Beaumont-le-Roger
F 89 A4

Beaumont-sur-Oise F 90 B2
Beaumont-sur-Sarthe F 102 A2
Beaune F 105 B3
Beaune-la-Rolande F 103 A4
Beaupréau F 101 B5
Beauraing B 91 A4
Beaurepaire F 117 B5
Beaurepaire-en-Bresse F 105 C4
Beaurières F 132 A1
Beauvais F 90 B2
Beauval F 90 A2
Beauville F 129 B3
Beauvoir-sur-Mer F 114 B1
Beauvoir-sur-Niort F 114 B3
Beba Veche RO 126 A2
Bebertal D 73 B4
Bebington GB 38 A3
Bebra D 82 B1
Bebrina HR 125 B3
Beccles GB 45 A5
Becedas E 150 B2
Beceite E 153 B4
Bečej SRB 126 B2
Becerreá E 141 B3
Becerril de Campos E 142 B2
Bécherel F 101 A4
Bechhofen D 94 B2
Bechyně CZ 96 B2
Becilla de Valderaduey E 142 B1
Beckfoot GB 36 B3
Beckingham GB 40 B3
Beckum D 81 A4
Beco P 154 B2
Bécon-les-Granits F 102 B1
Bečov nad Teplou CZ 83 B4
Becsehely H 111 C3
Bedale GB 37 B5
Bedames E 143 A3
Bédar E 164 B3
Bédarieux F 130 B2
Bédarrides F 131 A3
Bedburg D 80 B2
Beddgelert GB 38 A2
Beddingestrand S 66 A2
Bédée F 101 A4
Bedegkér H 112 C2
Beden TR 189 C7
Bedford GB 44 A3
Będków PL 87 A3
Bedlington GB 37 A5
Bedlno PL 77 B4
Bedmar E 163 A4
Bédoin F 131 A4
Bedónia I 134 A2
Bedretto CH 107 C3
Bedsted DK 58 B1
Bedum NL 71 A3
Bedwas GB 39 C3
Bedworth GB 40 C2
Będzin PL 86 B3
Beekbergen NL 70 B2
Beek en Donk NL 80 A1
Beelen D 71 C5
Beelitz D 74 B1
Beer GB 43 B3
Beerfelde D 74 B3
Beerfelden D 93 B4
Beernem B 78 A3
Beeskow D 74 B3
Beetsterzwaag NL 70 A3
Beetzendorf D 73 B4
Beflelay CH 106 B2
Begaljica SRB 127 C2
Bégard F 100 A2
Begejci SRB 126 B2
Begijar E 157 C4
Begijnendijk B 79 A4
Begndal N 48 B1
Begues E 147 C2
Beguildy GB 39 B3
Begur E 147 C4
Beho B 80 B1
Behringen D 82 A2
Beilen NL 71 B3
Beilngries D 95 B3
Beine-Nauroy F 91 B4
Beinwil CH 106 B3
Beiseförth D 82 A1
Beith GB 34 C3
Beitostølen N 47 A5
Beiuş RO 16 B5
Beja P 160 A2
Béjar E 149 B4
Bekçiler TR 189 C4
Békés H 113 C5
Békéscsaba H 113 C5
Bekilli TR 189 A4
Bekkarfjord N 193 B11
Bela SK 98 B2
Bélâbre F 115 B5
Bela Crkva SRB 127 C3
Belalcázar E 156 B2
Belánad Radbuzou CZ 95 B4
Belanovica SRB 127 C2
Bélapátfalva H 113 A4
Bělápod Bezdězem CZ 84 B2
Belcaire F 146 B2
Bełchatów PL 86 A3
Belchite E 153 A3
Bělčice CZ 96 B1
Belcoo GB 26 B3
Belecke D 81 A4
Beled H 111 B4
Belej HR 123 C3
Beleño E 142 A1
Bélesta F 146 B2
Belevi TR 188 A2
Belfast GB 27 B5
Belford GB 37 A5
Belfort F 106 B1
Belgentier F 132 B1
Belgern D 83 A5
Belgioioso I 120 B2
Belgodère F 180 A2
Belgooly IRL 29 C3
Belgrade = Beograd SRB 127 C2
Belhade F 128 B2
Belica HR 124 A2
Beli Manastir HR 125 B4
Belin-Bèliet F 128 B2
Belinchón E 151 B4
Belišće HR 125 B4
Bělkovice-Lašťany CZ 98 B1
Bella I 172 B1
Bellac F 115 B5
Bellágio I 120 B2
Bellananagh IRL 27 C3
Bellano I 120 A2
Bellária I 136 A1
Bellavary IRL 26 C1
Belleau F 90 B3
Belleek GB 26 B2
Bellegarde
Gard F 131 B3
Loiret F 103 B4
Bellegarde-en-Diois F 132 A1
Bellegarde-en-Marche F 116 B2
Bellegarde-sur-Valserine F 118 A2
Belle-Isle-en-Terre F 100 A2
Bellême F 89 B4
Bellenaves F 116 A3
Bellentre F 118 B3
Bellevaux F 118 A3
Bellevesvre F 105 C4
Belleville F 117 A4
Belleville-sur-Vie F 114 B2
Bellevue-la-Montagne F 117 B3
Belley F 118 B2
Bellheim D 93 B4
Bellinge DK 59 C3
Bellingham GB 37 A4
Bellinzago Novarese I 120 B1
Bellinzona CH 120 A2
Bell-lloc d'Urgell E 153 A4
Bello E 152 B2
Bellpuig d'Urgell E 147 C2
Bellreguart E 159 C3
Bellsbank GB 36 A2
Belltall E 147 C2
Belluno I 121 A5
Bellver de Cerdanya E 146 B2
Bellvis E 147 C1
Bélmez E 156 B2
Belmez de la Moraleda E 163 A4
Belmont GB 33 A6
Belmont-de-la-Loire F 117 A4
Belmonte
Asturias E 141 A4
Cuenca E 158 B1
P 148 B2
Belmonte de San José E 153 B3
Belmonte de Tajo E 151 B4
Belmont-sur-Rance F 130 B1
Belmullet IRL 26 B1
Belobreşca RO 127 C3
Beloeil B 79 B3
Belogradchik BG 16 D5
Belokorovichi UA 13 C8
Belorado E 143 B3
Belotič SRB 127 C1
Bělotin CZ 98 B1
Belovo BG 183 A6
Belozersk RUS 9 C10
Belp CH 106 C2
Belpasso I 177 B3
Belpech F 146 A2
Belper GB 40 B2
Belsay GB 37 A5
Belsk Duzy PL 87 A4
Beltinci SLO 111 C3
Beltra IRL 26 C1
Belturbet IRL 27 B3
Beluša SK 98 B2
Belvedere Maríttimo I 174 B1
Belver de Cinca E 153 A4
Belver de los Montes E 142 C1
Belvès F 129 B3
Belvezet F 130 A2
Belvis de la Jara E 150 C3
Belvis de Monroy E 150 C2
Belyy RUS 9 E8
Belz F 100 B2
Bełżec PL 13 C5
Belzig D 73 B5
Bembibre E 141 B4
Bembridge GB 44 C2
Bemmel NL 80 A1
Bemposta
Bragança P 149 A3
Santarém P 154 B2
Benabarre E 145 B4
Benacazón E 161 B3
Benaguacil E 159 B3
Benahadux E 164 C2
Benalmádena E 163 B3
Benalúa de Guadix E 164 B1
Benalúa de las Villas E 163 A4
Benalup E 162 B2
Benamargosa E 163 B3
Benamaurel E 164 B2
Benameji E 163 A3
Benamocarra E 163 B3
Benaocaz E 162 B2
Benaoján E 162 B2
Benarrabá E 162 B2
Benasque E 145 B4
Benátky nad Jizerou CZ 84 B2
Benavente
E 142 B1
P 154 C2
Benavides de Órbigo E 141 B5
Benavila P 154 B3
Bendorf D 81 B3
Benedikt SLO 110 C2
Benejama E 159 C3
Benejúzar E 165 A4
Benešov CZ 96 B2
Bénestroff F 92 C2
Benet F 114 B3
Bene Vagienna I 133 A3
Bénévent-l'Abbaye F 116 A1
Benevento I 170 B2
Benfeld F 93 C3
Benfica P 154 B2
Bengtsfors S 54 A3
Bengtsheden S 50 B2
Beničanci HR 125 B4
Benicarló E 153 B4
Benicássim E 153 B4
Benidorm E 159 C3
Benifaió E 159 B3
Beniganim E 159 C3
Benington GB 41 B4
Benisa E 159 C4
Benkovac HR 137 A4
Benllech GB 38 A2
Benneckenstein D 82 A2
Bénodet F 100 B1
Benquerencia de la Serena E 156 B2
Bensafrim P 160 B1
Bensbyn S 196 D5
Bensdorf D 73 B5
Benshausen D 82 B2
Bensheim D 93 B4
Bentley GB 44 B3
Bentwisch D 65 B5
Beočin SRB 126 B1
Beograd = Belgrade SRB 127 C2
Beragh GB 27 B3
Beranga E 143 A3
Berat AL 182 C1
Bérat F 146 A2
Beratzhausen D 95 B3
Bérbaltavár H 111 B3
Berbegal E 145 C3
Berbenno di Valtellina I 120 A2
Berberana E 143 B3
Bercedo E 143 A3
Bercel H 112 B3
Bercenay-le-Hayer F 91 C3
Berceto I 134 A2
Berchem B 79 B3
Berchidda I 178 B3
Berching D 95 B3
Berchtesgaden D 109 B4
Bérchules E 163 B4
Bercianos de Aliste E 149 A3
Berck F 78 B1
Berclaire d'Urgell E 147 C1
Berdoias E 140 A1
Berducedo E 141 A4
Berdún E 144 B3
Berdychiv UA 13 D8
Bere Alston GB 42 B2
Bereguardo I 120 B2
Berehommen N 53 A3
Berehove UA 16 A5
Berek BIH 124 B3
Beremend H 125 B4
Bere Regis GB 43 B4
Berestechko UA 13 C6
Berettyóújfalu H 113 B5
Berezhany UA 13 D6
Berezivka UA 17 B9
Berezna UA 13 C9
Berg
D 95 B3
N 195 E3
S 56 B2
Berga
Sachsen-Anhalt D 82 A3
Thüringen D 83 B4
E 147 B2
S 62 A4
Bergama TR 186 C2
Bérgamo I 120 B2
Bergara E 143 A4
Bergby S 51 B4
Berge
Brandenburg D 74 B1
Niedersachsen D 71 B4
Telemark N 53 A4
Telemark N 53 A4
Bergeforsen S 200 D3
Bergen
Mecklenburg-Vorpommern D 66 B2
Niedersachsen D 72 B2
Niedersachsen D 73 B3
N 46 B2
NL 70 B1
Bergen op Zoom NL 79 A4
Bergerac F 129 B3
Bergères-lés-Vertus F 91 C4
Bergeyk NL 79 A5
Berghausen D 93 C4
Bergheim D 80 B2
Berghem S 60 B2
Berg im Gau D 95 C3
Bergisch Gladbach D 80 B3
Bergkamen D 81 A3
Bergkvara S 63 B4
Berglern D 95 C3
Bergnäset S 196 D5
Bergneustadt D 81 A3
Bergsäng S 49 B5
Bergshamra S 57 A4
Bergsjö S 200 E3
Bergs slussar S 56 B1
Bergsviken S 196 D4
Bergtheim D 94 B2
Bergues F 78 B2
Bergum NL 70 A2
Bergün Bravuogn CH 107 C4
Bergwitz D 83 A4
Berhida H 112 B2
Beringel P 160 A2
Beringen B 79 A5
Berja E 164 C2
Berkåk N 199 C7
Berkeley GB 43 A4
Berkenthin D 65 C3
Berkhamsted GB 44 B3
Berkheim D 107 A5
Berkhof D 72 B2
Berkovići BIH 139 B4
Berkovitsa BG 17 D5
Berlanga E 156 B2
Berlanga de Duero E 151 A5
Berlevåg N 193 B13
Berlikum NL 70 A2
Berlin D 74 B2
Berlstedt D 82 A3
Bermeo E 143 A4
Bermillo de Sayago E 149 A3
Bern CH 106 C2
Bernalda I 174 A2
Bernardos E 150 A3
Bernartice
Jihočeský CZ 96 B2
Vychodočeský CZ 85 B3
Bernau
Baden-Württemberg D 106 B3
Bayern D 109 B3
Brandenburg D 74 B2
Bernaville F 90 A2
Bernay F 89 A4
Bernburg D 83 A3
Berndorf A 111 B3
Berne D 72 A1
Bernecebarati H 112 A2
Bernhardsthal A 97 C4
Bernkastel-Kues D 92 B3
Bernolakovo SK 111 A4
Bernsdorf D 84 A2
Bernstadt D 84 A2
Bernstein A 111 B3
Bernués E 145 B3
Beromünster CH 106 B3
Beroun CZ 96 B2
Berovo MK 182 B4
Berre-l'Etang F 131 B4
Berriedale GB 32 C3
Berriew GB 39 B3
Berrocal E 161 B3
Bersenbrück D 71 B4
Bershad' UA 13 D8
Bertamiráns E 140 B2
Berthåga S 51 C4
Berthelming F 92 C2
Bertincourt F 90 A2
Bertinoro I 135 A5
Bertogne B 92 A1
Bertrix B 91 B5
Berufjörður IS 191 C11
Berville-sur-Mer F 89 A4
Berwick-upon-Tweed GB 37 A4
Berzasca RO 16 C4
Berzence H 124 A3
Berzocana E 156 A2
Besalú E 147 B3
Besançon F 105 B5
Besenfeld D 93 C4
Besenyötelek H 113 B4
Besenyszög H 113 B4
Beshenkovichi BY 13 A8
Besigheim D 93 C5
Běšiny CZ 96 B1
Beška SRB 126 B2
Beşkonak TR 189 B6
Besle F 101 B4
Besnyö H 112 B2
Bessais-le-Fromental F 103 C4
Bessan F 130 B2
Besse-en-Chandesse F 116 B2
Bessèges F 131 A3
Bessé-sur-Braye F 102 B2
Bessines-sur-Gartempe F 115 B5
Best NL 79 A5
Bestorp S 56 B1
Betanzos E 140 A2
Betelu E 144 A2
Bétera E 159 B3
Beteta E 152 B1
Béthenville F 91 B4
Bethesda GB 38 A2
Béthune F 78 B2
Beton-Bazoches F 90 C3
Bettembourg L 92 B2
Betterdorf L 92 B2
Bettna S 56 B2
Béttola I 120 C2
Bettona I 136 B1
Bettyhill GB 32 C2
Betws-y-Coed GB 38 A3
Betxi E 159 B3
Betz F 90 B2
Betzdorf D 81 B3
Beuil F 132 A2
Beulah GB 39 B3
Beuzeville F 89 A4
Bevagna I 136 C1
Bevens-bruk S 56 A1
Beveren B 79 A4
Beverley GB 40 B3
Bevern D 81 A5
Beverstedt D 72 A1
Beverungen D 81 A5
Beverwijk NL 70 B1
Bex CH 119 A4
Bexhill GB 45 C4
Beyazköy TR 186 A2
Beychevelle F 128 A2
Beydağ TR 188 A3
Beyeğaç TR 188 B3
Beykoz TR 186 A4
Beynat F 129 A4
Beyoğlu TR 186 A4
Beypazarı TR 187 B6
Beyşehir TR 189 B6
Bezas E 152 B2
Bezau A 107 B4
Bezdan SRB 125 B4
Bèze F 105 B4
Bezenet F 116 A2
Bezhetsk RUS 9 D10
Béziers F 130 B2
Bezzecca I 121 B3
Biadki PL 85 A5
Biała
Łódzkie PL 77 C4
Opolskie PL 85 B5
Białaczów PL 87 A4
Biała Podlaska PL 13 B5
Biała Rawska PL 87 A4
Biale Błota PL 76 A2
Białobłoty PL 76 B2
Białobrzegi PL 87 A4
Białogard PL 67 C4
Bialośliwie PL 76 A2
Białowąs PL 68 B1
Biały Bór PL 68 B1
Białystok PL 13 B5
Biancavilla I 177 B3
Bianco I 175 C2
Biandrate I 119 B5
Biar E 159 C3
Biarritz F 144 A2
Bias F 128 B1
Biasca CH 120 A1
Biatorbágy H 112 B2
Bibbiena I 135 B4
Bibbona I 134 B3
Biberach
Baden-Württemberg D 93 C4
Baden-Württemberg D 107 A4
Bibinje HR 137 A4
Bibione I 122 B2
Biblis D 93 B4
Bibury GB 44 B2
Bicaj AL 182 B2
Biccari I 171 B3
Bicester GB 44 B2
Bichl D 108 B2
Bichlbach A 108 B1
Bicorp E 159 B3
Bicos P 160 B1
Bicske H 112 B2
Bidache F 128 C1
Bidart F 144 A2
Biddinghuizen NL 70 B2
Biddulph GB 40 B1
Bideford GB 42 A2
Bidford-on-Avon GB 44 A2
Bidjovagge N 192 C6
Bie S 56 A2
Bieber D 81 B5
Biebersdorf D 74 C2
Biedenkopf D 81 B4
Biel E 144 B3
Bielany Wroclawskie PL 85 A4
Bielawa PL 85 B4
Bielawy PL 77 B4
Biel / Bienne CH 106 B2
Bielefeld D 72 B1
Biella I 119 B5
Bielsa E 145 B4
Bielsk PL 77 B4
Bielsko-Biała PL 99 B3
Bielsk Podlaski PL 13 B5
Bienenbuttel D 72 A3
Bieniow PL 84 A3
Bienservida E 158 C1
Bienvenida E 156 B1
Bierdzany PL 86 B2
Bierné F 102 B1
Biersted DK 58 A2
Bierun PL 86 B3
Bierutów PL 85 A5
Bierwart B 79 B5
Bierzwina PL 75 A4
Bierzwnik PL 75 A4
Biescas E 145 B3
Biesenthal D 74 B2
Biesiekierz PL 67 B5
Bietigheim-Bissingen D 93 C5
Bièvre B 91 B5
Bieżuń PL 77 B4
Biga TR 186 B2
Bigadiç TR 186 C3
Biganos F 128 B2
Bigas P 148 B2
Bigastro E 165 A4
Bigbury GB 42 B3
Biggar GB 36 A3
Biggin Hill GB 45 B4
Biggleswade GB 44 A3
Bignasco CH 119 A5
Biguglia F 180 A2
Bihać BIH 124 C1
Biharnagybajom H 113 B5
Bijeljani BIH 139 B4
Bijeljina BIH 125 C5
Bijuesca E 152 A2
Bilaj HR 137 A4
Bila Tserkva UA 13 D9
Bilbao E 143 A4
Bilcza PL 87 B4
Bildudalur IS 190 B2
Bileća BIH 139 C4
Bilecik TR 187 B4
Biled RO 126 B2
Biłgoraj PL 12 C5
Bilhorod-Dnistrovskyy UA 17 B9
Bílina CZ 84 B1
Bilisht AL 182 C2
Bilje HR 125 B4
Billdal S 60 B1
Billerbeck D 71 C4
Billericay GB 45 B4
Billesholm S 61 C2
Billingborough GB 40 C3
Billinge S 61 D3
Billingham GB 37 B5
Billinghay GB 41 B3
Billingsfors S 54 B3
Billingshurst GB 44 B3
Billom F 116 B3
Billsta S 200 C4
Billund DK 59 C2
Bílovec CZ 98 B2
Bilstein D 81 A4
Bilthoven NL 70 B2
Bilto N 192 C5
Bilzen B 80 B1
Bíňa SK 112 B2
Binaced E 145 C4
Binasco I 120 B2
Binbrook GB 41 B3
Binche B 79 B4
Bindlach D 95 B3
Bindslev DK 58 A3
Binefar E 145 C4
Bingen D 93 B3
Bingham GB 40 C3
Bingley GB 40 B2
Bingsjö S 50 A2
Binic F 100 A3
Binz D 66 B2
Biograd na Moru HR 137 B4
Bionaz I 119 B4
Bioska SRB 127 D1
Birda RO 126 B3
Birdlip GB 44 B1
Biri N 48 B2
Birkeland N 53 B4

Courcelles-Chaussy F 92 B2
Courchevel F 118 B3
Cour-Cheverny F 103 B3
Courcôme F 115 C4
Courçon F 114 B3
Cour-et-Buis F 117 B4
Courgenay CH 106 B2
Courmayeur I 119 B3
Courniou F 130 B1
Cournon-d'Auvergne F 116 B3
Cournonterral F 130 B2
Courpière F 117 B3
Coursan F 130 B2
Courseulles-sur-Mer F 89 A3
Cours-la-Ville F 117 A4
Courson-les-Carrières F 104 B2
Courtalain F 103 A3
Courtenay F 104 A2
Courtomer F 89 B4
Courville
Eure-et-Loire F 89 B5
Marne F 91 B3
Coussac-Bonneval F 115 C5
Coutances F 88 A2
Couterne F 89 B3
Coutras F 128 A2
Couvet CH 106 C1
Couvin B 91 A4
Couzon F 104 C2
Covadonga E 142 A1
Covaleda E 143 C4
Covarrubias E 143 B3
Covas P 148 A1
Cove GB 31 B3
Coventry GB 44 A2
Coverack GB 42 B1
Covigliáio I 135 A4
Covilhã P 148 B2
Cowbridge GB 39 C3
Cowdenbeath GB 35 B4
Cowes GB 44 C2
Cox F 129 C4
Cózar E 157 B4
Cozes F 114 C3
Cozzano F 180 B2
Craco I 174 A2
Cracow = Kraków PL 99 A3
Craibstone GB 33 D4
Craighouse GB 34 C2
Craignure GB 34 B2
Crail GB 35 B5
Crailsheim D 94 B2
Craiova RO 17 C5
Cramlington GB 37 A5
Cranleigh GB 44 B3
Craon F 101 B5
Craonne F 91 B3
Craponne F 117 B4
Craponne-sur-Arzon F 117 B3
Crathie GB 32 D3
Crato P 155 B3
Craughwell IRL 28 A3
Craven Arms GB 39 B4
Crawford GB 36 A3
Crawinkel D 82 B2
Crawley GB 44 B3
Creag Ghoraidh GB 31 B1
Crecente E 140 B2
Crèches-sur-Saône F 117 A4
Crécy-en-Ponthieu F 78 B1
Crécy-la-Chapelle F 90 C2
Crécy-sur-Serre F 91 B3
Crediton GB 43 B3
Creeslough IRL 26 A3
Creetown GB 36 B2
Creeve GB 27 B4
Creglingen D 94 B2
Creil F 90 B2
Creissels F 130 A2
Crema I 120 B2
Cremeaux F 117 B3
Crémenes E 142 B1
Crémieu F 118 B2
Cremlingen D 73 B3
Cremona I 120 B3
Creney F 91 C4
Črenšovci SLO 111 C3
Créon F 128 B2
Crepaja SRB 127 B2
Crépey F 92 C1
Crépy F 91 B3
Crépy-en-Valois F 90 B2
Cres HR 123 C3
Crescentino I 119 B5
Crespino I 121 C4
Crespos E 150 B3
Cressage GB 39 B4
Cressensac F 129 A4
Cressia F 105 C4
Crest F 117 C5
Cresta CH 107 C4
Créteil F 90 C2
Creully F 88 A3
Creussen D 95 B3
Creutzwald F 92 B2
Creuzburg D 82 A2
Crevalcore I 121 C4
Crèvecoeur-le-Grand F 90 B2
Crevillente E 165 A4
Crévola d'Ossola I 119 A5
Crewe GB 38 A4
Crewkerne GB 43 B4
Criales E 143 B3
Crianlarich GB 34 B3
Criccieth GB 38 B2
Crickhowell GB 39 C3
Cricklade GB 44 B2
Crieff GB 35 B4
Criel-sur-Mer F 90 A1
Crikvenica HR 123 B3
Crillon F 90 B1
Crimmitschau D 83 B4
Crimond GB 33 D5
Crinitz D 84 A1
Cripán E 143 B4
Criquetot-l'Esneval F 89 A4
Crispiano I 173 B3
Crissolo I 119 C4
Cristóbal E 149 B4
Crivitz D 73 A4
Črna SLO 110 C1
Crna Bara
Srbija SRB 127 C1
Vojvodina SRB 126 B2
Crnac HR 125 B3
Crnča SRB 127 C1
Crni Lug
BIH 138 A2
HR 123 B3
Črni Vrh SLO 123 B3
Crnjelovo Donje BIH 125 C5
Črnomelj SLO 123 B4
Crocketford GB 36 A3
Crocq F 116 B2
Crodo I 119 A5
Croglin GB 37 B4
Crolly IRL 26 A2
Cromarty GB 32 D2
Cromer GB 41 C5
Cronat F 104 C2
Crookhaven IRL 29 C2
Crookstown IRL 29 C3
Croom IRL 29 B3
Cropalati I 174 B2
Crópani I 175 C2
Crosbost GB 31 A2
Crosby GB 38 A3
Crosía I 174 B2
Crossakiel IRL 27 C3
Cross-Hands GB 39 C2
Crosshaven IRL 29 C3
Crosshill GB 36 A2
Crossmolina IRL 26 B1
Crotone I 175 B3
Crottendorf D 83 B4
Crouy F 90 B3
Crowborough GB 45 B4
Crowland GB 41 C3
Crowthorne GB 44 B3
Croyde GB 42 A2
Croydon GB 44 B3
Crozon F 100 A1
Cruas F 117 C4
Cruceni RO 126 A3
Crúcoli I 174 B3
Cruden Bay GB 33 D5
Crudgington GB 38 B4
Cruis F 132 A1
Crumlin GB 27 B4
Cruseilles F 118 A3
Crusheen IRL 28 B3
Cruz de Incio E 141 B3
Crvenka SRB 126 B1
Črveny Kamen SK 98 B2
Csabacsüd H 113 C4
Csabrendek H 111 B4
Csákánydoroszló H 111 C3
Csákvár H 112 B2
Csanádapáca H 113 C4
Csanádpalota H 126 A2
Csány H 113 B3
Csanytelek H 113 C4
Csapod H 111 B3
Császár H 112 B2
Császártöltés H 112 C3
Csávoly H 125 A5
Csemö H 113 B3
Csengöd H 112 C3
Csépa H 113 C4
Csepreg H 111 B3
Cserkeszölö H 113 C4
Csernely H 113 A4
Csesztreg H 111 C3
Csökmö H 113 B5
Csököly H 124 A3
Csokonyavisonta H 124 A3
Csólyospálos H 113 C3
Csongrád H 113 C4
Csopak H 112 C1
Csorna H 111 B4
Csorvás H 113 C4
Csurgo H 124 A3
Cuacos de Yuste E 150 B2
Cualedro E 140 C3
Cuanca de Campos E 142 B1
Cuba P 160 A2
Cubel E 152 A2
Cubelles E 147 C2
Cubillos E 143 C4
Cubillos del Sil E 141 B4
Cubjac F 129 A3
Cubo de la Solana E 152 A1
Çubuk TR 23 A7
Cuckfield GB 44 B3
Cucuron F 131 B4
Cudillero E 141 A4
Cuéllar E 151 A3
Cuenca E 152 B1
Cuers F 132 B2
Cuerva E 157 A3
Cueva de Agreda E 144 C2
Cuevas Bajas E 163 A3
Cuevas del Almanzora E 164 B3
Cuevas del Becerro E 162 B2
Cuevas del Campo E 164 B2
Cuevas del Valle E 150 B2
Cuevas de San Clemente E 143 B3
Cuevas de San Marcos E 163 A3
Cuges-les-Pins F 132 B1
Cúglieri I 178 B2
Cugnaux F 129 C4
Cuijk NL 80 A1
Cuinzier F 117 A4
Cuiseaux F 105 C4
Cuisery F 105 C4
Culan F 103 C4
Culemborg NL 79 A5
Cúllar E 164 B2
Cullaville GB 27 B4
Cullera E 159 B3
Cullivoe GB 33 A5
Cullompton GB 43 B3
Cully CH 106 C1
Culoz F 118 B2
Cults GB 33 D4
Cumbernauld GB 35 C4
Cumbres de San Bartolomé E 161 A3
Cumbres Mayores E 161 A3
Cumiana I 119 C4
Čumić SRB 127 C2
Cumnock GB 36 A2
Çumra TR 23 C7
Cúneo I 133 A3
Cunlhat F 117 B3
Čunski HR 123 C3
Cuntis E 140 B2
Cuorgnè I 119 B4
Cupar GB 35 B4
Cupello I 170 A2
Cupra Marittima I 136 B2
Cupramontana I 136 B2
Čuprija SRB 127 D3
Curinga I 175 C2
Currelos E 140 B3
Currie GB 35 C4
Curtea de Argeş RO 17 C6
Curtici RO 126 A3
Curtis E 140 A2
Curtis Santa Eulalia E 140 A2
Čurug SRB 126 B2
Cusano Mutri I 170 B2
Cushendall GB 27 A4
Cusset F 117 A3
Cussy-les-Forges F 104 B3
Custines F 92 C2
Cutanda E 152 B2
Cutro I 175 B2
Cutrofiano I 173 B4
Cuts F 90 B3
Cuvilly F 90 B2
Cuxhaven D 64 C1
Cvikov CZ 84 B2
Cwmbran GB 39 C3
Cybinka PL 75 B3
Czacz PL 75 B5
Czajków PL 86 A2
Czaplinek PL 75 A5
Czarlin PL 69 A3
Czarna-Dąbrówka PL 68 A2
Czarna Woda PL 68 B3
Czarnca PL 87 B3
Czarne PL 68 B1
Czarnków PL 75 B5
Czarnowo PL 76 A3
Czarnozyly PL 86 A2
Czarny Bór PL 85 B4
Czarny-Dunajec PL 99 B3
Czarny Las PL 86 A1
Czchow PL 99 B4
Czechowice-Dziedzice PL 98 B2
Czempiń PL 75 B5
Czermno PL 87 A4
Czernichow PL 99 B3
Czerniejewo PL 76 B2
Czernikowo PL 76 B3
Czersk PL 68 B2
Czerwieńsk PL 75 B4
Czerwionka-Leszczyny PL 86 B2
Częstochowa PL 86 B3
Czeszewo PL 76 B2
Człopa PL 75 A5
Człuchów PL 68 B2
Czołpino PL 68 A2

D

Dağ TR 189 B5
Daaden D 81 B3
Dabas H 112 B3
Dąbie PL 76 B3
Dąbki PL 67 B5
Dabo F 92 C3
Dabrowa PL 76 B2
Dąbrowa Górnicza PL 86 B3
Dąbrowa Tarnowska PL 87 B4
Dąbrowice PL 77 B4
Dabrowno PL 77 A5
Dachau D 108 A2
Dačice CZ 97 B3
Daday TR 23 A7
Dagali N 47 B5
Dägebüll D 64 B1
Dagmersellen CH 106 B2
Dahlen D 83 A4
Dahlenburg D 73 A3
Dahme D 83 A5
Dahn D 93 B3
Dähre D 73 B3
Daikanvik S 195 E7
Dail bho Dheas GB 31 A2
Dailly GB 36 A2
Daimiel E 157 A4
Daingean IRL 30 A1
Đakovica KOS 16 D4
Đakovo HR 125 B4
Dal
Akershus N 48 B3
Telemark N 47 C5
Dalaas A 107 B5
Dalabrog GB 31 B1
Dala-Floda S 50 B1
Dala-Husby S 50 B2
Dala-Järna S 50 B1
Dalaman TR 188 C3
Dalarö S 57 A4
Dalbeattie GB 36 B3
Dalby
DK 59 C3
Skåne S 61 D3
Uppsala S 57 A3
Värmland S 49 B4
Dale
Pembrokeshire GB 39 C1
Shetland GB 33 A5
Hordaland N 46 B2
Sogn og Fjordane N 46 A2
Dalen
Akershus N 48 C3
Telemark N 53 A4
Daleszyce PL 87 B4
Dalhalvaig GB 32 C3
Dalheim L 92 B2
Dalhem S 57 C4
Dalias E 164 C2
Dalj HR 125 B4
Dalkeith GB 35 C4
Dalkey IRL 30 A2
Dalmally GB 34 B3
Dalmellington GB 36 A2
Dalmose DK 65 A4
Daløy N 46 A1
Dalry
Dumfries & Galloway GB 34 C3
North Ayrshire GB 36 A2
Dalrymple GB 36 A2
Dalseter N 47 A6
Dalsjöfors S 60 B3
Dalskog S 54 B3
Dals Långed S 54 B3
Dals Rostock S 54 B3
Dalston GB 36 B4
Dalstorp S 60 B3
Dalton-in-Furness GB 36 B3
Daluis F 132 A2
Dalum
D 71 B4
S 60 B3
Dalvík IS 191 B7
Dalwhinnie GB 32 E2
Dalyan TR 188 C3
Damasi GR 182 D4
Damasławek PL 76 B2
Damazan F 129 B3
Damgan F 101 B3
Dammarie-les-Lys F 90 C2
Dammartin-en-Goële F 90 B2
Damme D 71 B5
Damnica PL 68 A2
Dampierre F 105 B4
Dampierre-sur-Salon F 105 B4
Damüls A 107 B4
Damville F 89 B5
Damvillers F 92 B1
Damwoude NL 70 A2
Danasjö S 195 E7
Danbury GB 45 B4
Dångebo S 63 B3
Dangers F 89 B5
Dangé-St Romain F 102 C2
Dangeul F 89 B4
Danilovgrad MNE 16 D3
Danischenhagen D 64 B3
Daniszyn PL 85 A5
Danjoutin F 106 B1
Dannas S 60 B3
Dannemarie F 106 B2
Dannemora S 51 B4
Dannenberg D 73 A4
Dánszentmiklós H 112 B3
Dány H 112 B3
Daoulas F 100 A1
Darabani RO 17 A7
Darány H 125 B3
Darda HR 125 B4
Dardesheim D 73 C3
Darfeld D 71 B4
Darfo I 120 B3
Dargiń PL 68 A1
Dargun D 66 C1
Darlington GB 37 B5
Darłowo PL 68 A1
Darmstadt D 93 B4
Darney F 105 A5
Daroca E 152 A2
Darque P 148 A1
Darragh IRL 28 B2
Dartford GB 45 B4
Dartington GB 43 B3
Dartmouth GB 43 B3
Darton GB 40 B2
Daruvar HR 124 B3
Darvas H 113 B5
Darvel GB 36 A2
Darwen GB 38 A4
Dassel D 82 A1
Dassow D 65 C3
Datça TR 188 C2
Datteln D 80 A3
Dattenfeld D 81 B3
Daugard DK 59 C2
Daugavpils LV 8 E5
Daumeray F 102 B1
Daun D 80 B2
Daventry GB 44 A2
Davle CZ 96 B2
Davor HR 124 B3
Davos CH 107 C4
Davutlar TR 188 B2
Davyd Haradok BY 13 B7
Dawlish GB 43 B3
Dax F 128 C1
Dazkırı TR 189 B4
Deal GB 45 B5
Deauville F 89 A4
Deba E 143 A4
Debar MK 182 B2
Dębe PL 77 B5
Dębica PL 87 B5
Dębnica Kaszubska PL 68 A2
Dębno PL 74 B3
Dębołęka PL 86 A2
Dębowa Łaka PL 69 B4
Debrc SRB 127 C1
Debrecen H 113 B5
Debrznica PL 75 B4
Debrzno PL 68 B2
Debstedt D 72 A1
Decazeville F 130 A1
Dechtice SK 98 C1
Decima I 168 B2
Decimomannu I 179 C2
Děčín CZ 84 B2
Decize F 104 C2
De Cocksdorp NL 70 A1
Decollatura I 175 B2
Decs H 125 A4
Deddington GB 44 B2
Dedeler TR 187 B5
Dedelow D 74 A2
Dedemli TR 189 B7
Dedemsvaart NL 71 B3
Dédestapolcsány H 113 A4
Dedovichi RUS 9 D6
Deeping St Nicholas GB 41 C3
Deftera CY 181 A2
Dég H 112 C2
Degaña E 141 B4
Degeberga S 61 D4
Degerby FIN 51 B7
Degerfors S 55 A5
Degerhamn S 63 B4
Degernes N 54 A2
Deggendorf D 95 C4
Deggingen D 94 C1
Dego I 133 A4
Degolados P 155 B3
De Haan B 78 A3
Dehesas de Guadix E 164 B1
Dehesas Viejas E 163 A4
Deia E 166 B2
Deining D 95 B3
Deinze B 79 B3
Déiva Marina I 134 A2
Dej RO 17 B5
Deje S 55 A4
De Koog NL 70 A1
Delabole GB 42 B2
Delary S 61 C3
Delbrück D 81 A4
Delčevo MK 182 B4
Delden NL 71 B3
Deleitosa E 156 A2
Delekovec HR 124 A2
Delémont CH 106 B2
Delft NL 70 B1
Delfzijl NL 71 A3
Délia I 176 B2
Delianuova I 175 C1
Deliblato SRB 127 C3
Delice TR 23 B7
Deliceto I 171 B3
Delitzsch D 83 A4
Dellach A 109 C4
Delle F 106 B2
Delme F 92 C2
Delmen-horst D 72 A1
Delnice HR 123 B3
Delsbo S 200 E2
Delvin IRL 30 A1
Delvinë AL 182 D2
Demandice SK 112 A2
Demen D 73 A4
Demidov RUS 13 A9
Demigny F 105 C3
Demirci TR 186 C3
Demirköy TR 186 A2
Demirtaş TR 186 B4
Demmin D 66 C2
Demonte I 133 A3
Demyansk RUS 9 D8
Denain F 78 B3
Denbigh GB 38 A3
Den Burg NL 70 A1
Dender-monde B 79 A4
Denekamp NL 71 B4
Den Ham NL 71 B3
Den Helder NL 70 B1
Denholm GB 35 C5
Denia E 159 C4
Denizli TR 188 B4
Denkendorf D 95 C3
Denklingen D 81 B3
Denny GB 35 B4
Den Oever NL 70 B2
Denta RO 126 B3
Déols F 103 C3
De Panne B 78 A2
Derbent TR 188 A3
Derby GB 40 C2
Derecske H 113 B5
Dereköy TR 186 A2
Derenberg D 82 A2
Derinkuyu TR 23 B8
Dermbach D 82 B2
Dermulo I 121 A4
Deronje SRB 125 B5
Derrygonnelly GB 26 B3
Derrylin GB 27 B3
Derry/Londonderry GB 27 B3
Dersingham GB 41 C4
Deruta I 136 C1
Dervaig GB 34 B1
Derval F 101 B4
Derveni GR 184 A3
Derventa BIH 125 C3
Dervock GB 27 A4
Desana I 119 B5
Descartes F 102 C2
Desenzano del Garda I 121 B3
Deset N 48 A3
Deševa BIH 139 B4
Desfina GR 184 A3
Desimirovac SRB 127 C2
Désio I 120 B2
Deskati GR 182 D3
Deskle SLO 122 A2
Desná CZ 84 B3
Dešov CZ 97 C3
Despotovac SRB 127 C3
Despotovo SRB 126 B1
Dessau D 83 A4
Děštná CZ 96 B2
Destriana E 141 B4
Désulo I 179 B3
Desvres F 78 B1
Deszk H 126 A2
Deta RO 126 B3
Detmold D 72 C1
Dětřichov CZ 98 B1
Dettelbach D 94 B2
Dettingen
Baden-Württemberg D 94 C1
Baden-Württemberg D 107 B4
Dettwiller F 93 C3
Detva SK 99 C3
Deurne NL 80 A1
Deutschkreutz A 111 B3
Deutschlandsberg A 110 C2
Deutsch Wagram A 111 A3
Deva RO 16 C5
Dévaványa H 113 B4
Devecikonağı TR 186 C3
Devecser H 111 B4
Develi TR 23 B8
Deventer NL 70 B3
Devil's Bridge GB 39 B3
Devin BG 183 B6
Devinska Nova Ves SK 111 A3
Devizes GB 43 A5
Devonport GB 42 B2
Devrek TR 187 A6
Devrekâni TR 23 A7
Đevrske HR 137 B4
De Wijk NL 71 B3

Gol–Gué 247

Gols A 111 B3
Golspie GB 32 D3
Golssen D 74 C2
Golub-Dobrzyń PL 77 A4
Golubinci SRB 127 C2
Gołuchów PL 86 A1
Golymin-Ośrodek
PL 77 B5
Golzow D 73 B5
Gomagoi I 108 C1
Gómara E 152 A1
Gomaringen D 93 C5
Gömbe TR 189 C4
Gömeç TR 186 C1
Gomel = Homyel BY 13 B9
Gomes Aires P 160 B1
Gómezserracin E 150 A3
Gommern D 73 B4
Gomulin PL 86 A3
Gonäs S 50 B2
Goncelin F 118 B2
Gończyce PL 87 A5
Gondomar
E 140 B2
P 148 A1
Gondrecourt-le-Château
F 92 C1
Gondrin F 128 C3
Gönen
Balıkesir TR 186 B2
Isparta TR 189 B5
Gonfaron F 132 B2
Goñi E 144 B2
Goni
GR 182 D4
I 179 C3
Gonnesa I 179 C2
Gonnosfanádiga I 179 C2
Gönyü H 111 B4
Gonzaga I 121 C3
Goodrich GB 39 C4
Goodwick GB 39 B1
Gooik B 79 B4
Goole GB 40 B3
Goor NL 71 B3
Göpfritz an der Wild
A 97 C3
Goppenstein CH 119 A4
Göppingen D 94 C1
Gor E 164 B2
Góra
Dolnośląskie PL 85 A4
Mazowieckie PL 77 B5
Gorafe E 164 B1
Gorawino PL 67 C4
Goražde BIH 139 B4
Gőrbeháza H 113 B5
Gordaliza del Pino
E 142 B1
Gördes TR 186 D3
Gørding DK 59 C1
Górdola CH 120 A1
Gordon GB 35 C5
Gordoncillo E 142 B1
Gorebridge GB 35 C4
Gorenja Vas SLO 123 A3
Gorenje Jelenje
HR 123 B3
Gorey
GB 88 A1
IRL 30 B2
Gorgonzola I 120 B2
Gorica HR 137 A4
Gorican HR 124 A2
Gorinchem NL 79 A4
Goring GB 44 B2
Goritsy RUS 9 D10
Göritz D 74 A2
Gorízia I 122 B2
Górki PL 77 B4
Gorleben D 73 A4
Gorleston-on-sea
GB 41 C5
Gørlev DK 61 D1
Görlitz D 84 A2
Górliz E 143 A4
Görmin D 66 C2
Górna Grupa PL 69 B3
Gorna Oryahovitsa
BG 17 D6
Gornja Gorevnica
SRB 127 D2
Gornja Ploča HR 137 A4
Gornja Radgona
SLO 110 C2
Gornja Sabanta
SRB 127 D3
Gornja Trešnjevica
SRB 127 C2
Gornja Tuzla BIH 125 C4
Gornje Polje MNE 139 C4
Gornje Ratkovo
BIH 124 C2
Gornji Grad SLO 123 A3
Gornji Humac HR 138 B2
Gornji Jasenjani
BIH 139 B3
Gornji Kamengrad
BIH 124 C2
Gornji Kneginec
HR 124 A2
Gornji Kosinj HR 123 C4
Gornji Milanovac
SRB 127 C2
Gornji Podgradci
BIH 124 B3
Gornji Ravno BIH 138 B3
Gornji Sjenicak HR 124 B1
Gornji Vakuf BIH 138 B3
Górno PL 87 B4
Görömböly H 113 A4
Górowo Iławeckie
PL 69 A5
Gorran Haven GB 42 B2
Gorredijk NL 70 A3
Gorron F 88 B3
Gorseinon GB 39 C2
Gort IRL 28 A3
Gortin GB 27 B3
Görzke D 73 B5
Gorzkowice PL 86 A3
Górzno
Kujawsko-Pomorskie
PL 77 A4
Zachodnio-Pomorskie
PL 75 A4
Gorzów Śląski PL 86 A2
Gorzów Wielkopolski
PL 75 B4
Górzyca PL 74 B3
Gorzyce PL 98 B2
Górzyn PL 84 A2
Gorzyń PL 75 B4
Gorzyno PL 68 A2
Gosaldo I 121 A4
Gosau A 109 B4
Gosberton GB 41 C3
Gościcino PL 68 A3
Gościęcin PL 86 B2
Gościm PL 75 B4
Gościno PL 67 B4
Gosdorf A 110 C2
Gosforth GB 36 B3
Goslar D 82 A2
Goslice PL 77 B4
Gospič HR 137 A4
Gosport GB 44 C2
Gössäter S 55 B4
Gossau CH 107 B4
Goss Ilsede D 72 B3
Gössnitz D 83 B4
Gössweinstein D 95 B3
Gostivar MK 182 B2
Gostkow PL 77 C4
Göstling an der Ybbs
A 110 B1
Gostomia PL 75 A5
Gostycyn PL 76 A2
Gostyń PL 85 A5
Gostynin PL 77 B4
Goszczyn PL 87 A4
Göta S 54 B3
Göteborg = Gothenburg
S 60 B1
Götene S 55 B4
Gotha D 82 B2
Gothem S 57 C4
Gothenburg = Göteborg
S 60 B1
Gotse Delchev BG 183 B5
Gottersdorf D 95 C4
Göttingen D 82 A1
Gottne S 200 C4
Götzis A 107 B4
Gouarec F 100 A2
Gouda NL 70 B1
Goudhurst GB 45 B4
Goumenissa GR 182 C4
Goura GR 184 B3
Gourdon F 129 B4
Gourgançon F 91 C4
Gourin F 100 A2
Gournay-en-Bray F 90 B1
Gourock GB 34 C3
Gouveia P 148 B2
Gouvy B 80 B1
Gouzeacourt F 90 A3
Gouzon F 116 A2
Govedari HR 138 C3
Govérnolo I 121 B3
Gowarczów PL 87 A4
Gowerton GB 39 C2
Gowidlino PL 68 A2
Gowran IRL 30 B1
Goyatz D 74 B3
Göynük
TR 187 B5
Antalya TR 189 C5
Gozdnica PL 84 A3
Gozdowo PL 77 B4
Gozee B 79 B4
Graal-Müritz D 65 B5
Grabenstätt D 109 B3
Grabhair GB 31 A2
Gråbo S 60 B2
Grabovac
HR 138 B2
SRB 127 C2
Grabovci SRB 127 C1
Grabow D 73 A4
Grabów PL 77 B4
Grabow nad Pilicą
PL 87 A5
Grabów nad Prosną
PL 86 A2
Grabowno PL 76 A2
Grabs CH 107 B4
Gračac HR 138 A1
Gračanica BIH 125 C4
Graçay F 103 B3
Grad SLO 111 C3
Gradac
BIH 139 C4
HR 138 B3
MNE 139 B5
Gradačac BIH 125 C4
Gradec HR 124 B2
Gradefes E 142 B1
Grades A 110 C1
Gradil P 154 C1
Gradina
HR 124 B3
MNE 139 B5
Gradisca d'Isonzo
I 122 B2
Gradište HR 125 B4
Grado
E 141 A4
I 122 B2
Grafenau D 96 C1
Gräfenberg D 95 B3
Gräfenhainichen D 83 A4
Grafenschlag A 97 C3
Grafenstein A 110 C1
Gräfenthal D 82 B3
Grafentonna D 82 A2
Grafenwöhr D 95 B3
Grafing D 108 A2
Grafling D 95 C4
Gräfsnäs S 54 B3
Gragnano I 170 C2
Grahovo SLO 122 A2
Graiguenamanagh
IRL 30 B2
Grain GB 45 B4
Grainau D 108 B2
Graja de Iniesta E 158 B2
Grajera E 151 A4
Gram DK 59 C2
Gramais A 108 B1
Gramat F 129 B4
Gramatneusiedl A 111 A3
Grambow D 74 A3
Grammichele I 177 B3
Gramsh AL 182 C2
Gramzow D 74 A3
Gran N 48 B2
Granada E 163 A4
Granard IRL 27 C3
Grañas E 140 A3
Granátula de Calatrava
E 157 B4
Grancey-le-Château
F 105 B4
Grandas de Salime
E 141 A4
Grandcamp-Maisy F 88 A2
Grand-Champ F 100 B3
Grand Couronne F 89 A5
Grand-Fougeray F 101 B4
Grândola P 160 A1
Grandpré F 91 B4
Grandrieu
B 79 B4
F 117 C3
Grandson CH 106 C1
Grandvillars F 106 B1
Grandvilliers F 90 B1
Grañén E 145 C3
Grangärde S 50 B1
Grange IRL 26 B2
Grangemouth GB 35 B4
Grange-over-Sands
GB 36 B4
Grängesberg S 50 B1
Granges-de Crouhens
F 145 B4
Granges-sur-Vologne
F 106 A1
Gräningen D 73 B5
Granitola-Torretta
I 176 B1
Granja
Évora P 155 C3
Porto P 148 A1
Granja de Moreruela
E 142 C1
Granja de Torrehermosa
E 156 B2
Gränna S 55 B5
Grannäs
Västerbotten S 195 E7
Västerbotten S 195 E8
Granö S 200 B5
Granollers E 147 C3
Granowiec PL 85 A5
Granowo PL 75 B5
Gransee D 74 A2
Gransherad N 53 A5
Grantham GB 40 C3
Grantown-on-Spey
GB 32 D3
Grantshouse GB 35 C5
Granville F 88 B2
Granvin N 46 B3
Grærup Strand DK 59 C1
Gräsås S 60 C2
Grasbakken N 193 B12
Grasberg D 72 A2
Grasmere GB 36 B3
Gräsmyr S 200 C5
Grasö S 51 B5
Grassano I 172 B2
Grassau D 109 B3
Grasse F 132 B2
Grassington GB 40 A2
Græsted DK 61 C2
Gråsten DK 64 B2
Grästorp S 54 B3
Gratkorn A 110 B2
Gråträsk S 196 D2
Gratwein A 110 B2
Graulhet F 129 C4
Graus E 145 B4
Grávalos E 144 B2
Gravberget N 49 B4
Grave NL 80 A1
Gravedona I 120 A2
Gravelines F 78 A2
Gravellona Toce I 119 B5
Gravendal S 50 B1
Gravens DK 59 C2
Gravesend GB 45 B4
Graveson F 131 B3
Gravina in Púglia I 172 B2
Gray F 105 B4
Grayrigg GB 37 B4
Grays GB 45 B4
Grayshott GB 44 B3
Graz A 110 B2
Grazalema E 162 B2
Grążawy PL 69 B4
Grazzano Visconti
I 120 C2
Greåker N 54 A2
Great Dunmow GB 45 B4
Great Malvern GB 39 B4
Great Torrington
GB 42 B2
Great Waltham GB 45 B4
Great Yarmouth GB 41 C5
Grebbestad S 54 B2
Grebenstein D 81 A5
Grębocice PL 85 A4
Grębocin PL 76 A3
Greding D 95 B3
Gredstedbro DK 59 C1
Greencastle IRL 27 A3
Greenhead GB 37 B4
Greenisland GB 27 B5
Greenlaw GB 35 C5
Greenock GB 34 C3
Greenway GB 39 C2
Greenwich GB 45 B4
Grefrath D 80 A2
Greifenburg A 109 C4
Greiffenberg D 74 A2
Greifswald D 66 B2
Grein A 110 A1
Greipstad N 53 B3
Greiz D 83 B4
Grenaa DK 58 B3
Grenade F 129 C4
Grenade-sur-l'Adour
F 128 C2
Grenchen CH 106 B2
Grendi N 53 B3
Grenivík IS 191 B7
Grenoble F 118 B2
Gréoux-les-Bains
F 132 B1
Gresenhorst D 66 B1
Gressoney-la-Trinité
I 119 B4
Gressoney-St.-Jean
I 119 B4
Gressthal D 82 B2
Gressvik N 54 A1
Gresten A 110 B2
Gretna GB 36 B3
Greussen D 82 A2
Greve in Chianti I 135 B4
Greven
Mecklenburg-Vorpommern D 73 A3
Nordrhein-Westfalen
D 71 B4
Grevena GR 182 C3
Grevenbroich D 80 A2
Grevenbrück D 81 A4
Grevenmacher L 92 B2
Grevesmühlen D 65 C4
Grevestrand DK 61 D2
Grevie S 61 C2
Greystoke GB 36 B4
Greystones IRL 30 A2
Grez-Doiceau B 79 B4
Grèzec F 129 B4
Grez-en-Bouère F 102 B1
Grezzana I 121 B4
Grgar SLO 122 A2
Grgurevci SRB 127 B1
Gries A 108 B2
Griesbach D 96 C1
Griesheim D 93 B4
Gries in Sellrain A 108 B2
Grieskirchen A 109 A4
Griffen A 110 C1
Grignan F 131 A3
Grignano I 122 B2
Grigno I 121 A4
Grignols F 128 B2
Grignon F 118 B3
Grijota E 142 B2
Grijpskerk NL 71 A3
Grillby S 56 A3
Grimaud F 132 B2
Grimbergen B 79 B4
Grimma D 83 A4
Grimmen D 66 B2
Grimmialp CH 106 C2
Grimsås S 60 B3
Grimsby GB 41 B3
Grimslöv S 62 B2
Grímsstaðir IS 191 B9
Grimstad N 53 B4
Grimstorp S 62 A2
Grindavík IS 190 D3
Grindelwald CH 106 C3
Grindheim N 52 B3
Grindsted DK 59 C1
Griñón E 151 B4
Gripenberg S 62 A2
Gripsholm S 56 A3
Grisolles F 129 C4
Grisslehamn S 51 B5
Gritley GB 33 C4
Grizebeck GB 36 B3
Grndina BIH 124 C2
Gröbming A 109 B4
Gröbzig D 83 A3
Grocka SRB 127 C2
Gröditz D 83 A5
Gródki PL 77 A5
Grodków PL 85 B5
Grodziec PL 76 B3
Grodzisk Mazowiecki
PL 77 B5
Grodzisk Wielkopolski
PL 75 B5
Groenlo NL 71 B3
Groesbeek NL 80 A1
Grohote HR 138 B2
Groitzsch D 83 A4
Groix F 100 B2
Grójec PL 77 C5
Grom PL 77 A5
Gromiljca BIH 139 B4
Grömitz D 65 B3
Gromnik PL 99 B4
Gromo I 120 B2
Gronau
Niedersachsen D 72 B2
Nordrhein-Westfalen
D 71 B4
Grønbjerg DK 59 B1
Grönenbach D 107 B5
Grong N 199 A9
Grönhögen S 63 B4
Groningen
D 73 C4
NL 71 A3
Grønnestrand DK 58 A2
Grono CH 120 A2
Grönskåra S 62 A3
Grootegast NL 71 A3
Gropello Cairoli I 120 B1
Grorud N 48 C2
Grósio I 120 A3
Grošnica SRB 127 D2
Grossalmerode D 82 A1
Grossarl A 109 B4
Gross Beeren D 74 B2
Gross Berkel D 72 B2
Grossbodungen D 82 A2
Gross-botwar D 94 C1
Grossburgwedel D 72 B2
Grosschönau D 84 B2
Gross-Dölln D 74 A2
Grossenbrode D 65 B4
Grossenehrich D 82 A2
Grossengottern D 82 A2
Grossenhain D 83 A5
Grossenkneten D 71 B5
Grossenlüder D 81 B5
Grossensee D 72 A3
Grossenzersdorf A 111 A3
Grosseto I 135 C4
Gross-Gerau D 93 B4
Grossgerungs A 96 C2
Grossglobnitz A 97 C3
Grosshabersdorf D 94 B2
Grossharras A 97 C4
Grosshartmansdorf
D 83 B5
Grosshöchstetten
CH 106 C2
Gross Kreutz D 74 B1
Grosskrut A 97 C4
Gross Lafferde D 72 B3
Gross Leutheb D 74 B3
Grosslohra D 82 A2
Grossmehring D 95 C3
Gross Muckrow D 74 B3
Gross Oesingen D 72 B3
Grossostheim D 93 B5
Grosspertholz A 96 C2
Grosspetersdorf A 111 B3
Grosspostwitz D 84 A2
Grossraming A 110 B1
Grossräschen D 84 A2
Gross Reken D 80 A3
Grossrinderfeld D 94 B1
Grossröhrsdorf D 84 A2
Gross Sarau D 65 C3
Gross Särchen D 84 A2
Grossschirma D 83 B5
Gross Schönebeck
D 74 B2
Grossschweinbarth
A 97 C4
Grosssiegharts A 97 C3
Grosssölk A 109 B4
Gross Umstadt D 93 B4
Grosswarasdorf A 111 B3
Gross Warnow D 73 A4
Gross-Weikersdorf
A 97 C3
Gross-Welle D 73 A5
Grosswilfersdorf A 110 B2
Gross Wokern D 65 C5
Grostenquin F 92 C2
Grosuplje SLO 123 B3
Grotli N 198 C4
Grötlingbo S 57 C4
Grottáglie I 173 B3
Grottaminarda I 170 B3
Grottammare I 136 C2
Grotte di Castro I 168 A1
Grotteria I 175 C2
Gróttole I 172 B2
Grouw NL 70 A2
Grov N 194 B8
Grova N 53 A4
Grove E 140 B2
Grua N 48 B2
Grube D 65 B4
Grubišno Polje HR 124 B3
Grude BIH 138 B3
Grudusk PL 77 A5
Grudziądz PL 69 B3
Grue N 49 B4
Gruissan F 130 B2
Grullos E 141 A4
Grumo Áppula I 171 B4
Grums S 55 A4
Grünau im Almtal
A 109 B4
Grünberg D 81 B4
Grünburg A 110 B1
Grundarfjörður IS 190 C2
Gründau D 81 B5
Gründelhardt D 94 B1
Grundforsen S 49 A4
Grundlsee A 109 B4
Grundsund S 54 B2
Grunewald D 84 A1
Grungedal N 53 A3
Grunow D 74 B3
Grünstadt D 93 B4
Gruvberget S 50 A3
Gruyères CH 106 C2
Gruža SRB 127 D2
Grybów PL 99 B4
Grycksbo S 50 B2
Gryfice PL 67 C4
Gryfino PL 74 A3
Gryfów Śląski PL 84 A3
Gryllefjord N 194 A8
Grymyr N 48 B2
Gryt S 56 B2
Grytgöl S 56 B1
Grythyttan S 55 A5
Grytnäs S 57 B3
Grzmiąca PL 68 B1
Grzybno PL 74 A3
Grzywna PL 76 A3
Gschnitz A 108 B2
Gschwend D 94 C1
Gstaad CH 106 C2
Gsteig CH 119 A4
Guadahortuna E 163 A4
Guadalajara E 151 B4
Guadalaviar E 152 B2
Guadalcanal E 156 B2
Guadalcázar E 162 A3
Guadalix de la Sierra
E 151 B4
Guadálmez E 156 B3
Guadalupe E 156 A2
Guadamur E 151 C3
Guadarrama E 151 B3
Guadiaro E 162 B2
Guadix E 164 B1
Guagnano I 173 B3
Guagno F 180 A1
Guajar-Faragüit E 163 B4
Gualchos E 163 B4
Gualdo Tadino I 136 B1
Gualtieri I 121 C3
Guarcino I 169 B3
Guarda P 149 B2
Guardamar del Segura
E 165 A4
Guardão P 148 B1
Guardavalle I 175 C2
Guardea I 168 A2
Guárdia I 172 B1
Guardiagrele I 169 A4
Guardiarégia I 170 B2
Guárdia Sanframondi
I 170 B2
Guardias Viejas E 164 C2
Guardiola de Bergueda
E 147 B2
Guardo E 142 B2
Guareña E 156 B1
Guaro E 162 B3
Guarromán E 157 B4
Guasila I 179 C3
Guastalla I 121 C3
Gubbhögen S 199 A12
Gúbbio I 136 B1
Guben D 74 C3
Gubin PL 74 C3
Gudå N 199 B8
Gudavac BIH 124 C2
Guddal N 46 A2
Güderup DK 64 B2
Gudhem S 55 B4
Gudhjem DK 67 A3
Gudovac HR 124 B2
Gudow D 73 A3
Güdül TR 187 B7
Gudvangen N 46 B3
Guebwiller F 106 B2
Guéjar-Sierra E 163 A4
Guéméné-Penfao
F 101 B4
Guéméné-sur-Scorff
F 100 A2
Güeñes E 143 A3
Guer F 101 B3
Guérande F 101 B3
Guéret F 116 A1

Hengoed GB 39 C3
Hénin-Beaumont F 78 B2
Henley-on-Thames GB 44 B3
Hennan S 200 D1
Henneberg D 82 B2
Hennebont F 100 B2
Henne Strand DK 59 C1
Hennigsdorf D 74 B2
Hennset N 198 B5
Hennstedt
Schleswig-Holstein D 64 B2
Schleswig-Holstein D 64 B2
Henrichemont F 103 B4
Henryków PL 85 B5
Henrykowo PL 69 A5
Hensås N 47 A5
Henstedt-Ulzburg D 64 C2
Heppenheim D 93 B4
Herad
Buskerud N 47 B6
Vest-Agder N 52 B2
Heradsbygd N 48 B3
Heraklion = Iraklio GR 185 D6
Herálec CZ 97 B4
Herand N 46 B3
Herbault F 103 B3
Herbern D 81 A3
Herbertstown IRL 29 B3
Herbeumont B 91 B5
Herbignac F 101 B3
Herbisse F 91 C4
Herbitzheim F 92 B3
Herbolzheim D 106 A2
Herborn D 81 B4
Herbrechtingen D 94 C2
Herby PL 86 B2
Herceg-Novi MNE 16 D3
Hercegovać HR 124 B3
Hercegszántó H 125 B4
Herchen D 80 B3
Heréd H 112 B3
Hereford GB 39 B4
Herefoss N 53 B4
Hereke TR 187 B4
Herencia E 157 A4
Herend H 111 B4
Herent B 79 B4
Herentals B 79 A4
Hérépian F 130 B2
Herfølge DK 61 D2
Herford D 72 B1
Herguijuela E 156 A2
Héric F 101 B4
Héricourt F 106 B1
Héricourt-en-Caux F 89 A4
Hérimoncourt F 106 B1
Heringsdorf D 65 B4
Herisau CH 107 B4
Hérisson F 103 C4
Herk-de-Stad B 79 B5
Herlufmagle DK 65 A4
Hermagor A 109 C4
Hermannsburg D 72 B3
Hermansverk N 46 A3
Heřmanův Městec CZ 97 B3
Herment F 116 B2
Hermeskeil D 92 B2
Hermisende E 141 C4
Hermonville F 91 B3
Hermsdorf D 83 B3
Hernani E 144 A2
Hernansancho E 150 B3
Herne D 80 A3
Herne Bay GB 45 B5
Hernes N 48 B3
Herning DK 59 B1
Herøya N 53 A5
Herramelluri E 143 B3
Herräng S 51 B5
Herre N 53 A5
Herrenberg D 93 C4
Herrera E 162 A3
Herrera de Alcántara E 155 B3
Herrera del Duque E 156 A2
Herrera de los Navarros E 152 A2
Herrera de Pisuerga E 142 B2
Herreros del Suso E 150 B2
Herrestad S 54 B2
Herrhamra S 57 B3
Herritslev DK 65 B4
Herrlisheim F 93 C3
Herrljunga S 55 B4
Herrnhut D 84 A2
Herrsching D 108 A2
Hersbruck D 95 B3
Hersby S 57 A4
Herscheid D 81 A3
Herselt B 79 A4
Herso GR 182 B4
Herstal B 80 B1
Herstmonceux GB 45 C4
Herten D 80 A3
Hertford GB 44 B3
Hervás E 149 B4
Hervik N 52 A1
Herxheim D 93 B4
Herzberg
Brandenburg D 74 B1
Brandenburg D 83 A5
Niedersachsen D 82 A2
Herzebrock D 81 A4
Herzfelde D 74 B2
Herzlake D 71 B4
Herzogenaurach D 94 B2
Herzogenbuchsee CH 106 B2
Herzogenburg A 110 A2
Herzsprung D 73 A5
Hesby N 52 A1
Hesdin F 78 B2
Hesel D 71 A4
Heskestad N 52 B2
Hessdalen N 199 C8
Hesselager DK 65 A3
Hesseng N 193 C13
Hessisch Lichtenau D 82 A1
Hessisch-Oldendorf D 72 B2
Hestra S 60 B3
Heswall GB 38 A3
Hetlevik N 46 B2
Hettange-Grande F 92 B2
Hetton-le-Hole GB 37 B5
Hettstedt D 82 A3
Heuchin F 78 B2
Heudicourt-sous-les-Côtes F 92 C1
Heunezel F 105 A5
Heuqueville F 89 A4
Heves H 113 B4
Héviz H 111 C4
Hexham GB 37 B4
Heysham GB 36 B4
Heytesbury GB 43 A4
Hidas H 125 A4
Hieflau A 110 B1
Hiendelaencina E 151 A5
Hiersac F 115 C4
High Bentham GB 37 B4
Highclere GB 44 B2
High Hesket GB 37 B4
Highley GB 39 B4
High Wycombe GB 44 B3
Higuera de Arjona E 157 C4
Higuera de Calatrava E 163 A3
Higuera de la Serena E 156 B2
Higuera de la Sierra E 161 B3
Higuera de Vargas E 155 C4
Higuera la Real E 161 A3
Higuers de Llerena E 156 B1
Higueruela E 158 C2
Híjar E 153 A3
Hilchenbach D 81 A4
Hildburghausen D 82 B2
Hilden D 80 A2
Hilders D 82 B1
Hildesheim D 72 B2
Hilgay GB 41 C4
Hillared S 60 B3
Hille D 72 B1
Hillegom NL 70 B1
Hillerød DK 61 D2
Hillerstorp S 60 B3
Hillesheim D 80 B2
Hillestad N 53 A6
Hillmersdorf D 83 A5
Hillsborough GB 27 B4
Hillswick GB 33 A5
Hilpoltstein D 95 B3
Hiltpoltstein D 94 B3
Hilvarenbeek NL 79 A5
Hilversum NL 70 B2
Himarë AL 182 C1
Himbergen D 73 A3
Himesháza H 125 A4
Himmelberg A 109 C5
Himmelpforten D 72 A2
Himód H 111 B4
Hinckley GB 40 C2
Hindås S 60 B2
Hindelang D 108 B1
Hindelbank CH 106 B2
Hinderavåg N 52 A1
Hindhead GB 44 B3
Hinjosa del Valle E 156 B1
Hinnerup DK 59 B3
Hinneryd S 61 C3
Hinojal E 155 B4
Hinojales E 161 B3
Hinojos E 161 B3
Hinojosa del Duque E 156 B2
Hinojosas de Calatrava E 157 B3
Hinterhornbach A 108 B1
Hinterriss A 108 B2
Hintersee
A 109 B4
D 74 A3
Hinterstoder A 110 B1
Hintertux A 108 B2
Hinterweidenthal D 93 B3
Hinwil CH 107 B3
Hios GR 185 A7
Hippolytushoef NL 70 B1
Hirschaid D 94 B2
Hirschau D 95 B3
Hirschfeld D 83 A5
Hirschhorn D 93 B4
Hirsingue F 106 B2
Hirson F 91 B4
Hirtshals DK 58 A2
Hirvaskoski FIN 197 D10
Hirzenhain D 81 B5
Hisarcık TR 186 C4
Hishult S 61 C3
Hissjön S 200 C6
Hitchin GB 44 B3
Hitra N 198 B5
Hittarp S 61 C2
Hittisau A 107 B4
Hittun N 46 A1
Hitzacker D 73 A4
Hjallerup DK 58 A3
Hjällstad S 49 B5
Hjältevad S 62 A3
Hjärnarp S 61 C2
Hjartdal N 53 A4
Hjellestad N 46 B2
Hjelmeland N 52 A2
Hjelset N 198 C4
Hjerkinn N 198 C6
Hjerm DK 58 B1
Hjerpsted DK 64 A1
Hjerting DK 59 C1
Hjo S 55 B5
Hjordkær DK 64 A2
Hjørring DK 58 A2
Hjorted S 62 A4
Hjortkvarn S 56 B1
Hjortnäs S 50 B1
Hjortsberga S 62 B2
Hjukse N 53 A5
Hjuksebø N 53 A5
Hjulsjö S 55 A5
Hliník nad Hronom SK 98 C2
Hlinsko CZ 97 B3
Hlío IS 191 A10
Hlohovec SK 98 C1
Hlubokánad Vltavou CZ 96 B2
Hlučín CZ 98 B2
Hlyboka UA 17 A6
Hlybokaye BY 13 A7
Hniezdne SK 99 B4
Hnilec SK 99 C4
Hnúšťa SK 99 C3
Hobol H 125 A3
Hobro DK 58 B2
Hobscheid L 92 B1
Hocalar TR 189 A4
Hochdonn D 64 B2
Hochdorf CH 106 B3
Hochfelden F 93 C3
Hochspeyer D 93 B3
Höchstadt D 94 B2
Höchstädt D 94 C2
Hochstenbach D 81 B3
Höchst im Odenwald D 93 B5
Höckendorf D 83 B5
Hockenheim D 93 B4
Hoddesdon GB 44 B3
Hodejov SK 99 C3
Hodenhagen D 72 B2
Hodkovice CZ 84 B3
Hódmezővásárhely H 113 C4
Hodnet GB 38 B4
Hodonín CZ 98 C1
Hodslavice CZ 98 B2
Hoedekenskerke NL 79 A3
Hoegaarden B 79 B4
Hoek van Holland NL 79 A4
Hoenderlo NL 70 B2
Hof
D 83 B3
N 53 A6
Hofbieber D 82 B1
Hoff GB 37 B4
Hofgeismar D 81 A5
Hofheim
Bayern D 82 B2
Hessen D 93 A4
Hofkirchen im Mühlkreis A 96 C1
Höfn IS 191 C10
Hofors S 50 B3
Hofsós IS 190 B6
Hofstad N 199 A7
Höganäs S 61 C2
Högbo S 51 B3
Hogdal S 54 A2
Høgebru N 46 A4
Högfors S 50 C2
Högklint S 57 C4
Högsäter S 54 B3
Högsby S 62 A4
Högsjö S 56 A1
Hogstad S 55 B6
Högyész H 112 C2
Hohenau A 97 C4
Hohenberg A 110 B2
Hohenbucko D 83 A5
Hohenburg D 95 B3
Hohendorf D 66 B1
Hohenems A 107 B4
Hohenhameln D 72 B3
Hohenhausen D 72 B1
Hohenkirchen D 71 A4
Hohenlinden D 108 A2
Hohenlockstedt D 64 C2
Hohenmölsen D 83 A4
Hohennauen D 73 B5
Hohen Neuendorf D 74 B2
Hohenseeden D 73 B5
Hohentauern A 110 B1
Hohentengen D 106 B3
Hohenwepel D 81 A5
Hohenwestedt D 64 B2
Hohenwutzen D 74 B3
Hohenzieritz D 74 A2
Hohn D 64 B2
Hohne D 72 B3
Hohnstorf D 73 A3
Højer DK 64 B1
Højslev Stby DK 58 B2
Hok S 62 A2
Hökerum S 60 B3
Hökhuvud S 51 B5
Hokksund N 53 A5
Hökön S 63 B2
Hol N 47 B5
Hólar IS 190 B6
Holašovice CZ 96 C2
Holbæk
Aarhus Amt. DK 58 B3
Vestsjællands Amt. DK 61 D1
Holbeach GB 41 C4
Holdenstedt D 73 B3
Holdhus N 46 B2
Holdorf D 71 B5
Holeby DK 65 B4
Hølen N 54 A1
Hølervasseter N 47 B6
Holešov CZ 98 B1
Holguera E 155 B4
Holíč SK 98 C1
Holice
CZ 97 A3
SK 111 B4
Höljes S 49 B4
Hollabrunn A 97 C4
Hollandstoun GB 33 B4
Høllen N 53 B3
Hollfeld D 95 B3
Hollókő H 112 B3
Hollstadt D 82 B2
Hollum NL 70 A2
Höllviksnäs S 66 A1
Holm N 195 E3
Hólmavík IS 190 B4
Holmbukt N 192 B5
Holmedal S 54 A2
Holmegil N 54 A2
Holmen N 48 B2
Holme-on-Spalding-Moor GB 40 B3
Holmes Chapel GB 38 A4
Holmestrand N 54 A1
Holmfirth GB 40 B2
Holmfoss N 193 C14
Holmsbu N 54 A1
Holmsjö S 63 B3
Holmsund S 200 C6
Holmsveden S 50 A3
Holmudden S 57 C5
Hölö S 57 A3
Holøydal N 199 C8
Holsbybrunn S 62 A3
Holseter N 48 A1
Holsljunga S 60 B2
Holstebro DK 59 B1
Holsted DK 59 C1
Holsworthy GB 42 B2
Holt
D 64 B2
Norfolk GB 41 C5
Wrexham GB 38 A4
IS 190 D6
N 53 B4
Holten NL 71 B3
Holtwick D 71 B4
Holum N 52 B3
Holwerd NL 70 A2
Holycross IRL 29 B4
Holyhead GB 38 A2
Holýšov CZ 95 B5
Holywell GB 38 A3
Holywood GB 27 B5
Holzdorf D 83 A5
Holzhausen D 72 B1
Holzheim D 94 C2
Holzkirchen D 108 B2
Holzminden D 81 A5
Holzthaleben D 82 A2
Homberg
Hessen D 81 A5
Hessen D 81 B5
Homburg D 93 B3
Hommelstø N 195 E3
Hommersåk N 52 B1
Homokmegy H 112 C3
Homokszentgyörgy H 124 A3
Homyel = Gomel BY 13 B9
Honaz TR 188 B4
Hondarribia E 144 A2
Hondón de los Frailes E 165 A4
Hondschoote F 78 B2
Hönebach D 82 B1
Hønefoss N 48 B2
Honfleur F 89 A4
Høng DK 61 D1
Honiton GB 43 B3
Hönningen D 80 B2
Honningsvåg N 193 B9
Hönö S 60 B1
Honrubia E 158 B1
Hontalbilla E 151 A3
Hontheim D 92 A2
Hontianske-Nemce SK 98 C2
Hontoria de la Cantera E 143 B3
Hontoria del Pinar E 143 C3
Hontoria de Valdearados E 143 C3
Hoofddorp NL 70 B1
Hoogerheide NL 79 A4
Hoogeveen NL 71 B3
Hoogezand-Sappemeer NL 71 A3
Hoogkarspel NL 70 B2
Hoogkerk NL 71 A3
Hoogstede D 71 B3
Hoogstraten B 79 A4
Hook GB 44 B3
Hooksiel D 71 A5
Höör S 61 D3
Hoorn NL 70 B2
Hope GB 38 A3
Hopen N 194 C6
Hope under Dinmore GB 39 B4
Hopfgarten A 108 B3
Hopfgarten in Defereggen A 109 C3
Hopseidet N 193 B11
Hopsten D 71 B4
Hoptrup DK 59 C2
Hora Svatého Sebestiána CZ 83 B5
Horaždóvice CZ 96 B1
Horb am Neckar D 93 C4
Horbelev DK 65 B5
Hørby DK 58 A3
Hörby S 61 D3
Horcajada de la Torre E 158 A1
Horcajo de los Montes E 156 A3
Horcajo de Santiago E 151 C4
Horcajo-Medianero E 150 B2
Horche E 151 B4
Horda S 62 A2
Hordabø N 46 B1
Hordalia N 52 A2
Hordvik N 46 B2
Hořesedly CZ 83 B5
Horezu RO 17 C6
Horgen CH 107 B3
Horgoš SRB 126 A1
Horia RO 126 A3
Hořice CZ 84 B3
Horjul SLO 123 A3
Horka D 84 A2
Hörken S 50 B1
Horki BY 13 A9
Hörle S 60 B4
Horn
A 97 C3
D 81 A4
N 48 B2
S 62 A3
Horna E 158 C2
Hornachos E 156 B1
Hornachuelos E 162 A2
Horná Mariková SK 98 B2
Hornanes N 46 C2
Horná Streda SK 98 C1
Horná Štrubna SK 98 C2
Horná Súča SK 98 C1
Hornbæk
Aarhus Amt. DK 58 B2
Frederiksværk DK 61 C2
Hornberg D 106 A3
Hornburg D 73 B3
Horncastle GB 41 B3
Horndal S 50 B3
Horndean GB 44 C2
Horne
Fyns Amt. DK 64 A3
Ribe Amt. DK 59 C1
Hörnebo S 55 B5
Horneburg D 72 A2
Hörnefors S 200 C5
Horní Bečva CZ 98 B2
Horní Benešov CZ 98 B1
Horní Cerekev CZ 97 B3
Horní Jiřetín CZ 83 B5
Horní Lomná CZ 98 B2
Horní Maršov CZ 85 B3
Hornindal N 198 D3
Hørning DK 59 B3
Hörningsholm S 57 A3
Horní Planá CZ 96 C2
Horní Slavkov CZ 83 B4
Horni Vltavice CZ 96 C1
Hornnes N 53 B3
Horno D 84 A2
Hornos E 164 A2
Hornoy-le-Bourg F 90 B1
Hornsea GB 41 B3
Hornsjø N 48 A2
Hornslet DK 59 B3
Hornstein A 111 B3
Hörnum D 64 B1
Hornum DK 58 B2
Horný Tisovník SK 99 C3
Horodenka UA 13 D6
Horodnya UA 13 C9
Horodok
Khmelnytskyy UA 13 D7
Horodok *continued*
Lviv UA 13 D5
Horokhiv UA 13 C6
Horovice CZ 96 B1
Horred S 60 B2
Hörröd S 61 D4
Hörsching A 110 A1
Horsens DK 59 C2
Horsham GB 44 B3
Hørsholm DK 61 D2
Horslunde DK 65 B4
Horšovský Týn CZ 95 B4
Horst NL 80 A2
Horstel D 71 B4
Horsten D 71 A4
Horstmar D 71 B4
Hort H 113 B3
Horta P 148 A2
Horten N 54 A1
Hortezuela E 151 A5
Hortiguela E 143 B3
Hortobágy H 113 B5
Horton in Ribblesdale GB 37 B4
Hørve DK 61 D1
Hörvik S 63 B2
Horwich GB 38 A4
Hosanger N 46 B2
Hösbach D 93 A5
Hosena D 84 A2
Hosenfeld D 81 B5
Hosingen L 92 A2
Hosio FIN 197 D8
Hospental CH 107 C3
Hospital IRL 29 B3
Hossegor F 128 C1
Hosszuhetény H 125 A4
Hostal de Ipiés E 145 B3
Hoštálkova CZ 98 B1
Hostalric E 147 C3
Hostens F 128 B2
Hostěradice CZ 97 C4
Hostinné CZ 85 B3
Hostomice CZ 96 B2
Hostouň CZ 95 B4
Hotagen S 199 B11
Hoting S 200 B2
Hotolisht AL 182 B2
Hotton B 79 B5
Houdain F 78 B2
Houdan F 90 C1
Houdelaincourt F 92 C1
Houeillès F 128 B3
Houffalize B 92 A1
Houghton-le-Spring GB 37 B5
Houlberg DK 59 B2
Houlgate F 89 A3
Hounslow GB 44 B3
Hourtin F 128 A1
Hourtin-Plage F 128 A1
Houthalen B 79 A5
Houyet B 79 B4
Hov
DK 59 C3
N 48 B2
Hova S 55 B5
Høvåg N 53 B4
Hovborg DK 59 C1
Hovda N 47 B6
Hovden N 52 A3
Hove GB 44 C3
Hovedgård DK 59 C2
Hovelhof D 81 A4
Hoven DK 59 C1
Hovet N 47 B5
Hovingham GB 40 A3
Hovmantorp S 62 B3
Hovsta S 56 A1
Howden GB 40 B3
Howe D 72 A3
Höxter D 81 A5
Hoya D 72 B2
Hoya de Santa Maria E 161 B3
Hoya-Gonzalo E 158 C2
Høyanger N 46 A3
Hoyerswerda D 84 A2
Høyjord N 53 A6
Hoylake GB 38 A3
Høylandet N 199 A9
Hoym D 82 A3
Høymyr N 47 C6
Hoyocasero E 150 B3
Hoyo de Manzanares E 151 B4
Hoyo de Pinares E 150 B3
Hoyos E 149 B3
Hoyos del Espino E 150 B2
Hrabusiče SK 99 C4
Hradec Králové CZ 85 B3
Hradec nad Moravicí CZ 98 B1
Hrádek CZ 97 C4
Hrádek nad Nisou CZ 84 B2
Hradište SK 98 C2
Hrafnagil IS 191 B7
Hrafnseyri IS 190 B2
Hranice
Severomoravsky CZ 98 B1
Západočeský CZ 83 B4
Hranovnica SK 99 C4

Jawor PL 85 A4
Jaworzno PL 86 B3
Jaworzyna Śl. PL 85 B4
Jayena E 163 B4
Jażow PL 84 A2
Jebel RO 126 B3
Jebjerg DK 58 B2
Jedburgh GB 35 C5
Jedlinsk PL 87 A5
Jedlnia PL 87 A5
Jedlnia Letnisko PL 87 A5
Jednorożec PL 77 A6
Jedovnice CZ 97 B4
Jędrychow PL 69 B4
Jędrzejów PL 87 B4
Jedwabno PL 77 A5
Jeesiö FIN 197 B9
Jegłownik PL 69 A4
Jegun F 129 C3
Jēkabpils LV 8 D4
Jektevik N 46 C2
Jektvik N 195 D4
Jelcz-Laskowice PL 85 A5
Jelenec SK 98 C2
Jelenia Góra PL 85 B3
Jelgava LV 8 D3
Jelka SK 111 A4
Jelling DK 59 C2
Jels DK 59 C2
Jelsa
HR 138 B2
N 52 A2
Jelšava SK 99 C4
Jemgum D 71 A4
Jemnice CZ 97 B3
Jena D 82 B3
Jenaz CH 107 C4
Jenbach A 108 B2
Jenikow PL 75 A4
Jennersdorf A 111 C3
Jenny S 62 A4
Jerchel D 73 B4
Jeres del Marquesado
E 164 B1
Jerez de la Frontera
E 162 B1
Jerez de los Caballeros
E 155 C4
Jerica E 159 B3
Jerichow D 73 B5
Jerka PL 75 B5
Jermenovci SRB 126 B3
Jerslev DK 58 A3
Jerte E 150 B2
Jerup DK 58 A3
Jerxheim D 73 B3
Jerzmanowice PL 87 B3
Jerzu I 179 C3
Jerzwałd PL 69 B4
Jesberg D 81 B5
Jesenice
Středočeský CZ 83 B5
Středočeský CZ 96 B2
SLO 109 C5
Jeseník CZ 85 B5
Jesenké SK 99 C4
Jesi I 136 B2
Jésolo I 122 B1
Jessen D 83 A4
Jessenitz D 73 A4
Jessheim N 48 B3
Jessnitz D 83 A4
Jesteburg D 72 A2
Jeumont F 79 B4
Jeven-stedt D 64 B2
Jever D 71 A4
Jevičko CZ 97 B4
Jevišovice CZ 97 C3
Jevnaker N 48 B2
Jezerane HR 123 B4
Jezero
BIH 138 A3
HR 123 B4
Jezów PL 87 A3
Jičín CZ 84 B3
Jičiněves CZ 84 B3
Jihlava CZ 97 B3
Jijona E 159 C3
Jilemnice CZ 84 B3
Jilové CZ 84 B2
Jilovéu Prahy CZ 96 B2
Jimbolia RO 126 B2
Jimena E 163 A4
Jimena de la Frontera
E 162 B2
Jimera de Libar E 162 B2
Jimramov CZ 97 B4
Jince CZ 96 B1
Jindřichovice CZ 83 B4
Jindřichův Hradec
CZ 96 B3
Jirkov CZ 83 B5
Jistebnice CZ 96 B2
Joachimsthal D 74 B2
João da Loura P 154 C2
Jobbágyi H 112 B3
Jochberg A 109 B3
Jockfall S 196 C5
Jódar E 163 A4
Jodoigne B 79 B4
Joensuu FIN 9 A6
Joesjö S 195 E5
Joeuf F 92 B1
Jõgeva EST 8 C5
Johanngeorgenstadt
D 83 B4
Johannishus S 63 B3
Johanniskirchen D 95 C4
Johansfors S 63 B3
John o'Groats GB 32 C3
Johnshaven GB 35 B5
Johnstone GB 34 C3
Johnstown IRL 30 B1
Jõhvi EST 8 C5
Joigny F 104 B2
Joinville F 91 C5
Jokkmokk S 196 C2
Jöllenbeck D 72 B1
Jomala FIN 51 B6
Jönåker S 56 B2
Jonava LT 13 A6
Jonchery-sur-Vesle
F 91 B3
Jondal N 46 B3
Jondalen N 53 A5
Joniškis LT 8 D3
Jönköping S 62 A2
Jonkowo PL 69 B5
Jønnbu N 53 A5
Jonsberg S 56 B2
Jonsered S 60 B2
Jonstorp S 61 C2
Jonzac F 114 C3
Jorba E 147 C2
Jordanów PL 99 B3
Jordanowo PL 75 B4
Jordanów Ślaski PL 85 B4
Jordbro S 57 A4
Jordbrua N 195 D5
Jördenstorf D 66 C1
Jordet N 49 A4
Jordøse DK 59 C3
Jork D 72 A2
Jörlanda S 60 B1
Jormlien S 199 A10
Jormvattnet S 199 A11
Jörn S 200 A6
Jørpeland N 52 A2
Jorquera E 158 B2
Jošan HR 123 C4
Jošavka BIH 124 C3
Josipdol HR 123 B4
Josipovac HR 125 B4
Jössefors S 54 A3
Josselin F 101 B3
Jøssund N 199 A7
Jostedal N 47 A4
Jósvafő H 99 C4
Jou P 148 A2
Jouarre F 90 C3
Joué-lès-Tours F 102 B2
Joué-sur-Erdre F 101 B4
Joure NL 70 B2
Joutseno FIN 9 B6
Joutsijärvi FIN 197 C10
Joux-la-Ville F 104 B2
Jouy F 90 C1
Jouy-le-Châtel F 90 C3
Jouy-le-Potier F 103 B3
Joyeuse F 131 A3
Joze F 116 B3
Juankoski FIN 8 A6
Juan-les-Pins F 132 B3
Jübek D 64 B2
Jubera E 144 B1
Jubrique E 162 B2
Jüchsen D 82 B2
Judaberg N 52 A1
Judenburg A 110 B1
Juelsminde DK 59 C3
Jugon-les-Lacs F 101 A3
Juillac F 129 A4
Juillan F 145 A4
Juist D 71 A4
Jukkasjärvi S 196 B3
Jule N 199 A10
Julianadorp NL 70 B1
Julianstown IRL 30 A2
Jülich D 80 B2
Jullouville F 88 B2
Jumeaux F 117 B3
Jumièges F 89 A4
Jumilhac-le-Grand
F 115 C5
Jumilla E 159 C2
Jumisko FIN 197 C11
Juncosa E 153 A4
Juneda E 147 C1
Jung S 55 B4
Jungingen D 93 C5
Junglingster L 92 B2
Juniville F 91 B4
Junosuando S 196 B5
Junqueira P 149 A2
Junsele S 200 C2
Juoksengi S 196 C6
Juoksenki FIN 196 C6
Juprelle B 80 B1
Jurata PL 69 A3
Jurbarkas LT 12 A5
Jurjevo HR 123 C3
Jūrmala LV 8 D3
Jurmu FIN 197 D10
Juromenha P 155 C3
Jursla S 56 B2
Jussac F 116 C2
Jussey F 105 B4
Jussy F 90 B3
Juta H 125 A3
Jüterbog D 74 C2
Juuka FIN 3 E11
Juuma FIN 197 C12
Juvigny-le-Terte F 88 B2
Juvigny-sous-Andaine
F 89 B3
Juzennecourt F 105 A3
Jyderup DK 61 D1
Jyrkänkoski FIN 197 C12
Jyväskylä FIN 8 A4

K

Kaamanen FIN 193 C11
Kaamasmukka
FIN 193 C10
Kaaresuvanto FIN 192 D6
Kaarssen D 73 A4
Kaatscheuvel NL 79 A5
Kaba H 113 B5
Kåbdalis S 196 C3
Kačarevo SRB 127 C2
Kács H 113 B4
Kadan CZ 83 B5
Kadarkút H 125 A3
Kadınhanı TR 189 A7
Kaduy RUS 9 C10
Kåfalla S 56 A1
Kåfjord N 192 C7
Kåfjordbotn N 192 C4
Kågeröd S 61 D3
Kahl D 93 A5
Kahla D 82 B3
Kainach bei Voitsberg
A 110 B2
Kaindorf A 110 B2
Kainulasjärvi S 196 C5
Kairala FIN 197 B10
Kaisepakte S 192 D3
Kaisersesch D 80 B3
Kaiserslautern D 93 B3
Kaisheim D 94 C2
Kajaani FIN 3 D10
Kajárpéc H 111 B4
Kajdacs H 112 C2
Kakanj BIH 139 A4
Kakasd H 125 A4
Kaklik TR 189 B4
Kakolewo PL 85 A4
Kál H 113 B4
Kalajoki FIN 3 D8
Kalak N 193 B11
Kalamata GR 184 B3
Kalambaka GR 182 D3
Kalamria GR 182 C4
Kalandra GR 183 D5
Kälarne S 200 D2
Kalavrita GR 184 A3
Kalbe D 73 B4
Kalce SLO 123 B3
Káld H 111 B4
Kale
Antalya TR 189 C4
Denizli TR 188 B3
Kalecik TR 23 A7
Kalefeld D 82 A2
Kalesija BIH 139 A4
Kalety PL 86 B2
Kalevala RUS 3 D12
Kalhovd N 47 B5
Kalí HR 137 A4
Kalimnos GR 188 C2
Kaliningrad RUS 69 A5
Kalinkavichy BY 13 B8
Kalinovac HR 124 A3
Kalinovik BIH 139 B4
Kalinovo SK 99 C3
Kalirachi GR 183 C6
Kaliska
Pomorskie PL 68 A3
Pomorskie PL 68 B3
Kalisko PL 86 A3
Kalisz PL 86 A2
Kalisz Pomorski PL 75 A4
Kaljord N 194 B6
Kalkan TR 189 C4
Kalkar D 80 A2
Kalkım TR 186 C2
Kall
D 80 B2
S 199 B10
Källby S 55 B4
Kållered S 60 B2
Kållerstad S 60 B3
Kallinge S 63 B3
Kallmünz D 95 B3
Kallo FIN 196 B7
Kallsedet S 199 B9
Källvik S 56 B3
Kalmar S 63 B4
Kalmthout B 79 A4
Kalná SK 112 A2
Kalocsa H 112 C2
Kalokhorio CY 181 B2
Kalo Nero GR 184 B2
Kaloni GR 186 C1
Káloz H 112 C2
Kals A 109 B3
Kalsdorf A 110 C2
Kaltbrunn CH 107 B4
Kaltenbach A 108 B2
Kaltenkirchen D 64 C2
Kaltennordheim D 82 B2
Kalundborg DK 61 D1
Kalush UA 13 D6
Kalv S 60 B3
Kalvåg N 198 D1
Kalvehave DK 65 A5
Kalwang A 110 B1
Kalwaria-Zebrzydowska
PL 99 B3
Kalyazin RUS 9 D10
Kam H 111 B3
Kaman TR 23 B7
Kamares GR 185 C5
Kambos CY 181 A1
Kamen D 81 A3
Kamenice CZ 97 B3
Kamenice nad Lipou
CZ 96 B3
Kameničná SK 112 B2
Kamenný Most SK 112 B2
Kamenny Ujezd CZ 96 C2
Kamenska HR 124 B3
Kamensko HR 138 B2
Kamenz D 84 A2
Kamičak BIH 124 C2
Kamień PL 87 A4
Kamieniec Zabk PL 85 B4
Kamienka SK 99 B4
Kamień Krajeński
PL 76 A2
Kamienna Góra PL 85 B4
Kamień Pomorski
PL 67 C3
Kamieńsk PL 86 A3
Kamiros Skala GR 188 C2
Kamnik SLO 123 A3
Kampen NL 70 B2
Kampinos PL 77 B5
Kamp-Lintfort D 80 A2
Kampor HR 123 C3
Kamyanets-Podil's'kyy
UA 13 D7
Kamyanka-Buz'ka
UA 13 C6
Kamýk nad Vltavou
CZ 96 B2
Kanal SLO 122 A2
Kanalia GR 182 D4
Kandalaksha RUS 3 C13
Kandanos GR 185 D4
Kandel D 93 B4
Kandern D 106 B2
Kandersteg CH 106 C2
Kandila GR 184 B3
Kandıra TR 187 A5
Kandyty PL 69 A5
Kanfanar HR 122 B2
Kangasala FIN 8 B4
Kangos S 196 B5
Kangosjärvi FIN 196 B6
Kaniów PL 75 C3
Kanjiža SRB 126 A2
Kankaanpää FIN 8 B3
Kannus FIN 3 E8
Kanturk IRL 29 B3
Kapaklı TR 186 A2
Kapellen
A 110 B2
B 79 A4
Kapellskär S 57 A5
Kapfenberg A 110 B2
Kapfenstein A 110 C2
Kaplice CZ 96 C2
Kapljuh BIH 124 C2
Kápolna H 113 B4
Kápolnásnyék H 112 B2
Kaposfő H 125 A3
Kaposfüred H 125 A3
Kaposszekcsö H 125 A4
Kaposvár H 125 A3
Kapp N 48 B2
Kappel D 93 C3
Kappeln D 64 B2
Kappelshamn S 57 C4
Kappl A 107 B5
Kappstad S 55 A4
Kaprun A 109 B3
Kaptol HR 125 B3
Kapuvár H 111 B4
Karaadilli TR 189 A5
Karabiğa TR 186 B2
Karabük TR 187 A7
Karaburun TR 186 D1
Karacabey TR 186 B3
Karacaköy TR 186 A3
Karacaören TR 189 A5
Karacasu TR 188 B3
Karácsond H 113 B4
Karád H 112 C1
Karahallı TR 189 A4
Karaisali TR 23 C8
Karaman
Balıkesir TR 186 C3
Karaman TR 23 C7
Karamanlı TR 189 B4
Karamürsel TR 187 B4
Karan SRB 127 D1
Karancslapujto H 113 A3
Karaova TR 188 B2
Karapınar TR 23 C7
Karasjok N 193 C9
Karasu TR 187 A5
Karataş
Adana TR 23 C8
Manisa TR 188 A3
Karatoprak TR 188 B2
Karavostasi CY 181 A1
Karbenning S 50 B3
Kårberg S 55 B5
Kårböle S 199 D12
Karby
D 64 B2
DK 58 B1
Kårby S 62 A4
Karby S 57 A4
Karcag H 113 B4
Karczów PL 86 B1
Karczowiska PL 85 A4
Kardamena GR 188 C2
Kardamila GR 185 A7
Kardamili GR 184 C3
Kardašova Rečice
CZ 96 B2
Kardis S 196 C6
Karditsa GR 182 D3
Kärdla EST 8 C3
Kardoskút H 113 C4
Kardzhali BG 183 B7
Karesuando S 192 D6
Kargı TR 23 A8
Kargopol RUS 9 B11
Kargowa PL 75 B4
Karigasniemi FIN 193 C9
Karise DK 65 A5
Karistos GR 185 A5
Karkkila FIN 8 B4
Karlholmsbruk S 51 B4
Karlino PL 67 B4
Karlobag HR 137 A4
Karlovac HR 123 B4
Karlovasi GR 188 B1
Karlovčic SRB 127 C2
Karlovice CZ 85 B5
Karlovo BG 17 D6
Karlovy Vary CZ 83 B4
Karłowice PL 86 B1
Karlsborg S 55 B5
Karlshamn S 63 B2
Karlshöfen D 72 A2
Karlshus N 54 A1
Karlskoga S 55 A5
Karlskrona S 63 B3
Karlsrud N 47 B5
Karlsruhe D 93 B4
Karlstad S 55 A4
Karlstadt D 94 B1
Karlstetten A 110 A2
Karlstift A 96 C2
Karlstorp S 62 A3
Karmacs H 111 C4
Karmin PL 85 A5
Kärna S 60 B1
Karnobat BG 17 D7
Karojba HR 122 B2
Karow D 73 A5
Karpacz PL 85 B3
Karpathos GR 188 D2
Karpenisi GR 182 E3
Karpuzlu TR 188 B2
Kärrbo S 56 A2
Karrebaeksminde
DK 65 A4
Karshult S 60 B3
Karsin PL 68 B2
Kårsta S 57 A4
Karstädt D 73 A4
Kartal TR 186 B4
Kartitsch A 109 C3
Kartuzy PL 68 A3
Karungi S 196 C6
Karunki FIN 196 C7
Karup DK 59 B2
Karviná CZ 98 B2
Kås DK 58 A2
Kaş TR 189 C4
Kasaba TR 189 C4
Kašava CZ 98 B1
Kåseberga S 66 A3
Kasejovice CZ 96 B1
Kasfjord N 194 B7
Kashin RUS 9 D10
Kašina HR 124 B2
Kasina-Wielka PL 99 B4
Kaskinen FIN 8 A2
Kašperské Hory CZ 96 B1
Kassandrino GR 183 C5
Kassel D 81 A5
Kassiopi GR 182 D1
Kastamonu TR 23 A7
Kastav HR 123 B3
Kasteli GR 185 D4
Kastellaun D 93 A3
Kastelli GR 185 D6
Kaštel-Stari HR 138 B2
Kaštel Zegarski
HR 138 A1
Kasterlee B 79 A4
Kastl D 95 B3
Kastlösa S 63 B4
Kastorf D 65 C3
Kastoria GR 182 C3
Kastorio GR 184 B3
Kastraki GR 185 C6
Kastrosikia GR 182 D2
Kastsyukovichy
BY 13 B10
Kaszaper H 113 C4
Katakolo GR 184 B2
Katapola GR 185 C6
Katastari GR 184 B1
Katerbow D 74 B1
Katerini GR 182 C4
Kathikas CY 181 B1
Kätkesuando S 196 A6
Katlenburg-Lindau
D 82 A2
Kato Achaia GR 184 A2
Káto Pyrgos CY 181 A1
Katouna GR 182 E3
Katovice CZ 96 B1
Katowice PL 86 B3
Katrineberg S 50 A3
Katrineholm S 56 B2
Kattarp S 61 C2
Kattavia GR 188 D2
Katthammarsvik S 57 C4
Kattilstorp S 55 B4
Katwijk NL 70 B1
Katymár H 125 A5
Kąty Wrocławskie
PL 85 A4
Katzenelnbogen D 81 B3
Katzhütte D 82 B3
Kaub D 93 A3
Kaufbeuren D 108 B1
Kauhajoki FIN 8 A3
Kauhava FIN 8 A3
Kaukonen FIN 196 B7
Kauliranta FIN 196 C6
Kaulsdorf D 82 B3
Kaunas LT 13 A5
Kaunisvaara S 196 B6
Kaupanger N 47 A4
Kautokeino N 192 C7
Kautzen A 97 C3
Kavadarci MK 182 B4
Kavajë AL 182 B1
Kavakköy TR 186 B1
Kavaklı TR 186 A2
Kavaklıdere TR 188 B3
Kavala GR 183 C6
Kavarna BG 17 D8
Kävlinge S 61 D3
Kawcze PL 68 A1
Kaxås S 199 B10
Kaxholmen S 62 A2
Käylä FIN 197 C12
Kaymakçı TR 188 A3
Kaymaz TR 187 C6
Kaynarca TR 187 A5
Käyrämö FIN 197 C9
Kayseri TR 23 B8
Kaysersberg F 106 A2
Kazanlak BG 17 D6
Kazár H 113 A3
Kazimierza Wielka
PL 87 B4
Kazincbarcika H 113 A4
Kaźmierz PL 75 B5
Kcynia PL 76 A2
Kdyně CZ 95 B5
Kea GR 185 B5
Keadew IRL 26 B2
Keady GB 27 B4
Kecel H 112 C3
Keçiborlu TR 189 B5
Kecskemét H 113 C3
Kėdainiai LT 13 A5
Kędzierzyn-Koźle
PL 86 B2
Keel IRL 28 A1
Keenagh IRL 28 A4
Keerbergen B 79 A4
Kefalos GR 188 C1
Kefken TR 187 A5
Keflavík IS 190 C3
Kegworth GB 40 C2
Kehl D 93 C3
Kehrigk D 74 B2
Keighley GB 40 B2
Keila EST 8 C4
Keillmore GB 34 C2
Keiss GB 32 C3
Keith GB 33 D4
Kelankylä FIN 197 D10
Kelberg D 80 B2
Kelbra D 82 A3
Kelč CZ 98 B1
Kelchsau A 108 B3
Këlcyrë AL 182 C2
Keld GB 37 B4
Kelebia H 126 A1
Kelekçi TR 188 B4
Kelemér H 99 C4
Keles TR 186 C4
Kelheim D 95 C3
Kell D 92 B2
Kellas GB 32 D3
Kellinghusen D 64 C2
Kelloselkä FIN 197 C11
Kells
GB 27 B4
IRL 27 C4
Kelmis B 80 B2
Kelokedhara CY 181 B1
Kelottijärvi FIN 192 D6
Kelsall GB 38 A4
Kelso GB 35 C5
Kelsterbach D 93 A4
Keltneyburn GB 35 B3
Kelujärvi FIN 197 B10
Kemaliye TR 188 A3
Kemalpaşa TR 188 A2
Kematen A 108 B2
Kemberg D 83 A4
Kemer
Antalya TR 189 C5
Burdur TR 189 B5
Muğla TR 189 C4
Kemerkaya TR 187 D6
Kemeten A 111 B3
Kemi FIN 196 D7
Kemijärvi FIN 197 C10
Keminmaa FIN 196 D7
Kemnath D 95 B3
Kemnay GB 33 D4
Kemnitz
Brandenburg D 74 B1
Mecklenburg-Vorpommern D 66 B2
Kempen D 80 A2
Kempsey GB 39 B4
Kempten D 107 B5

Kemptthal CH 107 B3
Kendal GB 37 B4
Kenderes H 113 B4
Kengyel H 113 B4
Kenilworth GB 44 A2
Kenmare IRL 29 C2
Kenmore GB 35 B4
Kennacraig GB 34 C2
Kenyeri H 111 B4
Kenzingen D 106 A2
Kepez TR 186 B1
Kępice PL 68 A1
Kępno PL 86 A2
Kepsut TR 186 C3
Keramoti GR 183 C6
Keräntöjärvi S 196 B6
Keratea GR 185 B4
Kerava FIN 8 B4
Kerecsend H 113 B4
Kerekegyhaza H 112 C3
Kerepestarcsa H 112 B3
Keri GR 184 B1
Kérien F 100 A2
Kerkafalva H 111 C3
Kerken D 80 A2
Kerkrade NL 80 B2
Kerkyra GR 182 D1
Kerlouan F 100 A1
Kernascléden F 100 A2
Kernhof A 110 B2
Kerns CH 106 C3
Kerpen D 80 B2
Kerrysdale GB 31 B3
Kerta H 111 B4
Kerteminde DK 59 C3
Kerzers CH 106 C2
Keşan TR 186 B1
Kesgrave GB 45 A5
Kesh GB 26 B3
Keskin TR 23 B7
Kesselfall A 109 B3
Kestenga RUS 3 D12
Keswick GB 36 B3
Keszthely H 111 C4
Kétegyháza H 113 C5
Kéthely H 111 C4
Kętrzyn PL 12 A4
Kettering GB 44 A3
Kettlewell GB 40 A1
Kęty PL 99 B3
Ketzin D 74 B1
Keula D 82 A2
Keuruu FIN 8 A4
Kevelaer D 80 A2
Kevermes H 113 C5
Kevi SRB 126 B1
Keyingham GB 41 B3
Keynsham GB 43 A4
Kežmarok SK 99 B4
Khimki RUS 9 E10
Khisinev = Chişinău
MD 17 B8
Khmelnik UA 13 D7
Khmelnytskyy UA 13 D7
Khodoriv UA 13 D6
Kholm RUS 9 D7
Khotyn UA 13 D7
Khoyniki BY 13 C8
Khust UA 17 A5
Khvoynaya RUS 9 C9
Kiato GR 184 A3
Kibæk DK 59 B1
Kiberg N 193 B14
Kicasalih TR 186 A1
Kičevo MK 182 B2
Kidderminster GB 39 B4
Kidlington GB 44 B2
Kidsgrove GB 40 B1
Kidwelly GB 39 C2
Kiefersfelden D 108 B3
Kiel D 64 B3
Kielce PL 87 B4
Kiełczygłów PL 86 A3
Kielder GB 37 A4
Kiełpino PL 68 A3
Kielpiny PL 77 A4
Kierinki FIN 197 B8
Kiernozia PL 77 B4
Kierspe D 81 A3
Kietrz PL 86 B2
Kietz D 74 B3
Kiev = Kyyiv UA 13 C9
Kiezmark PL 69 A3
Kiffisia GR 185 A4
Kifino Selo BIH 139 B4
Kihlanki
FIN 196 B6
S 196 B6
Kiistala FIN 197 B8
Kije PL 87 B4
Kijevo HR 138 B2
Kikallen N 46 B2
Kikinda SRB 126 B2
Kil
N 53 B5
Örebro S 55 A6
Värmland S 55 A4
Kila S 55 A3
Kilafors S 50 A3
Kilbaha IRL 29 B2
Kilbeggan IRL 30 A1
Kilberry GB 34 C2
Kilbirnie GB 34 C3
Kilboghamn N 195 D4
Kilbotn N 194 B7
Kilb Rabenstein A 110 A2
Kilchattan GB 34 C2
Kilchoan GB 34 B1
Kilcock IRL 30 A2
Kilconnell IRL 28 A3
Kilcormac IRL 28 A4
Kilcreggan GB 34 C3
Kilcullen IRL 30 A2
Kilcurry IRL 27 B4
Kildare IRL 30 A2
Kildinstroy RUS 3 B13
Kildonan GB 32 C3
Kildorrery IRL 29 B3
Kilegrend N 53 A4
Kilen N 53 A4
Kilgarvan IRL 29 C2
Kiliya UA 17 C8
Kilkee IRL 29 B2
Kilkeel GB 27 B4
Kilkelly IRL 26 C2
Kilkenny IRL 30 B1
Kilkieran IRL 28 A2
Kilkinlea IRL 29 B2
Kilkis GR 182 B4
Killadysert IRL 29 B2
Killala IRL 26 B1
Killaloe IRL 28 B3
Killarney IRL 29 B2
Killashandra IRL 27 B3
Killashee IRL 28 A4
Killearn GB 34 B3
Killeberg S 61 C4
Killeigh IRL 30 A1
Killenaule IRL 29 B4
Killimor IRL 28 A3
Killin GB 34 B3
Killinaboy IRL 28 B2
Killinge S 196 B3
Killinick IRL 30 B2
Killorglin IRL 29 B2
Killucan IRL 30 A1
Killybegs IRL 26 B2
Killyleagh GB 27 B5
Kilmacrenan IRL 26 A3
Kilmacthomas IRL 30 B1
Kilmaine IRL 28 A2
Kilmallock IRL 29 B3
Kilmarnock GB 36 A2
Kilmartin GB 34 B2
Kilmaurs GB 36 A2
Kilmeadan IRL 30 B1
Kilmeedy IRL 29 B3
Kilmelford GB 34 B2
Kilmore Quay IRL 30 B2
Kilmuir GB 32 D2
Kilnaleck IRL 27 C3
Kilninver GB 34 B2
Kilpisjärvi FIN 192 C4
Kilrea GB 27 B4
Kilrush IRL 29 B2
Kilsmo S 56 A1
Kilsyth GB 35 C3
Kiltoom IRL 28 A3
Kilwinning GB 36 A2
Kimasozero RUS 3 D12
Kimi GR 185 A5
Kimolos GR 185 C5
Kimovsk RUS 9 E10
Kimratshofen D 107 B5
Kimry RUS 9 D10
Kimstad S 56 B1
Kinbrace GB 32 C3
Kincardine GB 35 B4
Kincraig GB 32 D3
Kindberg A 110 B2
Kindelbruck D 82 A3
Kingarrow IRL 26 B2
Kingisepp RUS 9 C6
Kingsbridge GB 43 B3
Kingsclere GB 44 B2
Kingscourt IRL 27 C4
King's Lynn GB 41 C4
Kingsteignton GB 43 B3
Kingston
Greater London
GB 44 B3
Moray GB 32 D3
Kingston Bagpuize
GB 44 B2
Kingston upon Hull
GB 40 B3
Kingswear GB 43 B3
Kingswood GB 43 A4
Kington GB 39 B3
Kingussie GB 32 D2
Kınık
Antalya TR 188 C4
İzmir TR 186 C2
Kinloch
Highland GB 31 B2
Highland GB 32 C2
Kinlochbervie GB 32 C1
Kinlochewe GB 32 D1
Kinlochleven GB 34 B3
Kinlochmoidart GB 34 B2
Kinloch Rannoch
GB 35 B3
Kinloss GB 32 D3
Kinlough IRL 26 B2
Kinn N 48 B2
Kinna S 60 B2
Kinnared S 60 B3
Kinnarp S 55 B4
Kinnegad IRL 30 A1
Kinne-Kleva S 55 B4
Kinnitty IRL 28 A4
Kinrooi B 80 A1
Kinross GB 35 B4
Kinsale IRL 29 C3
Kinsarvik N 46 B3
Kintarvie GB 31 A2
Kintore GB 33 D4
Kinvarra IRL 28 A3
Kioni GR 184 A1
Kiparissia GR 184 B2
Kipfenburg D 95 C3
Kippen GB 35 B3
Kiraz TR 188 A3
Kirazlı TR 186 B1
Kirberg D 81 B4
Kirchbach in Steiermark
A 110 C2
Kirchberg
CH 106 B2
Baden-Württemberg
D 94 B1
Rheinland-Pfalz D 93 B3
Kirchberg am Wechsel
A 110 B2
Kirchberg an der
Pielach A 110 A2
Kirchberg in Tirol
A 109 B3
Kirchbichl A 108 B3
Kirchdorf
Bayern D 96 C1
Mecklenburg-
Vorpommern D 65 C4
Niedersachsen D 72 B1
Kirchdorf an der Krems
A 109 B5
Kirchdorf in Tirol
A 109 B3
Kirchenlamitz D 83 B3
Kirchenthumbach D 95 B3
Kirchhain D 81 B4
Kirchheim
Baden-Württemberg
D 94 C1
Bayern D 108 A1
Hessen D 81 B5
Kirchheimbolanden
D 93 B4
Kirchhundem D 81 A4
Kirchlintein D 72 B2
Kirchschlag A 111 B3
Kirchweidach D 109 A3
Kirchzarten D 106 B2
Kircubbin GB 27 B5
Kireç TR 186 C3
Kırıkkale TR 23 B7
Kirillov RUS 9 C11
Kirishi RUS 9 C8
Kırka TR 187 C5
Kırkağaç TR 186 C2
Kirkbean GB 36 B3
Kirkbride GB 36 B3
Kirkby GB 38 A4
Kirkby Lonsdale GB 37 B4
Kirkby Malzeard GB 40 A2
Kirkbymoorside GB 37 B6
Kirkby Stephen GB 37 B4
Kirkcaldy GB 35 B4
Kirkcolm GB 36 B1
Kirkconnel GB 36 A2
Kirkcowan GB 36 B2
Kirkcudbright GB 36 B2
Kirkehamn N 52 B2
Kirke Hyllinge DK 61 D1
Kirkenær N 49 B4
Kirkenes N 193 C14
Kirkham GB 38 A4
Kirkintilloch GB 35 C3
Kirkjubæjarklaustur
IS 191 D7
Kirkkonummi FIN 8 B4
Kırklareli TR 186 A2
Kirkmichael GB 35 B4
Kirk Michael GB 36 B2
Kirkoswald GB 36 A2
Kirkpatrick Fleming
GB 36 A3
Kirkton of Glenisla
GB 35 B4
Kirkwall GB 33 C4
Kirkwhelpington GB 37 A5
Kirn D 93 B3
Kirovsk RUS 3 C13
Kirriemuir GB 35 B5
Kırşehir TR 23 B8
Kirton GB 41 C3
Kirton in Lindsey
GB 40 B3
Kirtorf D 81 B5
Kiruna S 196 B3
Kisa S 62 A3
Kisač SRB 126 B1
Kisbér H 112 B2
Kiseljak BIH 139 B4
Kisielice PL 69 B4
Kisköre H 113 B4
Kiskőrös H 112 C3
Kiskunfélegyháza
H 113 C3
Kiskunhalas H 112 C3
Kiskunlacháza H 112 B2
Kiskunmajsa H 113 C3
Kisláng H 112 C2
Kisslegg D 107 B4
Kissolt H 112 C3
Kissónerga CY 181 B1
Kist D 94 B1
Kistanje HR 138 B1
Kistelek H 113 C3
Kisterenye H 113 A3
Kisújszállás H 113 B4
Kisvárda H 16 A5
Kisvejke H 112 C2
Kiszkowo PL 76 B2
Kiszombor H 126 A2
Kitee FIN 9 A7
Kithnos GR 185 B5
Kiti CY 181 B2
Kitkiöjärvi S 196 B6
Kitkiöjoki S 196 B6
Kittelfjäll S 195 E6
Kittendorf D 74 A1
Kittilä FIN 196 B7
Kittlitz D 84 A2
Kittsee A 111 A4
Kitzbühel A 109 B3
Kitzingen D 94 B2
Kiuruvesi FIN 3 E10
Kivertsi UA 13 C6
Kividhes CY 181 B1
Kivik S 63 C2
Kivotos GR 182 C3
Kıyıköy TR 186 A3
Kızılcabölük TR 188 B4
Kızılcadağ TR 189 B4
Kızılcahamam TR 23 A7
Kızılırmak TR 23 A7
Kızılkaya TR 189 B5
Kızılkuyu TR 187 D6
Kızılören
Afyon TR 189 A5
Konya TR 189 B7
Kjeldebotn N 194 B7
Kjellerup DK 59 B2
Kjellmyra N 49 B4
Kjøllefjord N 193 B11
Kjopmannskjaer N 54 A1
Kjøpsvik N 194 B7
Kl'ačno SK 98 C2
Kladanj BIH 139 A4
Kläden D 73 B4
Klädesholmen S 60 B1
Kladnice HR 138 B2
Kladno CZ 84 B2
Kladruby CZ 95 B4
Klagenfurt A 110 C1
Klågerup S 61 D3
Klagstorp S 66 A2
Klaipėda LT 8 E2
Klaistow D 74 B1
Klaksvík FO 4 A3
Klana HR 123 B3
Klanac HR 123 C4
Klanjec HR 123 A4
Klardorf D 95 B4
Klarup DK 58 A3
Klašnice BIH 124 C3
Klässbol S 55 A3
Klášterec nad Ohří
CZ 83 B5
Kláštor pod Znievom
SK 98 C2
Klatovy CZ 96 B1
Klaus an der Pyhrnbahn
A 110 B1
Klazienaveen NL 71 B3
Kłecko PL 76 B2
Kleczew PL 76 B3
Klein Plasten D 74 A1
Klein Sankt Paul A 110 C1
Kleinsölk A 109 B4
Kleinzell A 110 B2
Klejtrup DK 58 B2
Klek SRB 126 B2
Klemensker DK 67 A3
Klenak SRB 127 C1
Klenci pod Cerchovem
CZ 95 B4
Klenica PL 75 C4
Klenje SRB 127 C1
Klenoec MK 182 B2
Klenovec SK 99 C3
Klenovica HR 123 B3
Klenovnik HR 124 A2
Kleppe N 52 B1
Kleppestø N 46 B2
Kleptow D 74 A2
Kleszewo PL 77 B6
Kleve D 80 A2
Klevshult S 60 B4
Klewki PL 77 A5
Kličevac SRB 127 C3
Kliening A 110 C1
Klietz D 73 B5
Klikuszowa PL 99 B3
Klimkovice CZ 98 B2
Klimontów PL 87 B5
Klimovichi BY 13 B9
Klimpfjäll S 195 E5
Klin RUS 9 D10
Klinča Sela HR 123 B4
Klingenbach A 111 B3
Klingenberg D 93 B5
Klingenmunster D 93 B4
Klingenthal D 83 B4
Klinken D 73 A4
Klintehamn S 57 C4
Kliny PL 87 A4
Kliplev DK 64 B2
Klippan S 61 C3
Klis HR 138 B2
Klitmøller DK 58 A1
Klitten S 49 A6
Klixbüll D 64 B1
Kljajićevo SRB 126 B1
Ključ BIH 138 A2
Klobouky CZ 97 C4
Kłobuck PL 86 B2
Klockestrand S 200 D3
Kłodawa
Lubuskie PL 75 B4
Wielkopolskie PL 76 B3
Kłodzko PL 85 B4
Kløfta N 48 B3
Klokkarvik N 46 B2
Klokkerholm DK 58 A3
Klokočov SK 98 B2
Kłomnice PL 86 B3
Klonowa PL 86 A2
Kloosterzande NL 79 A4
Kłopot PL 74 B3
Klos AL 182 B2
Kloštar Ivanić HR 124 B2
Kloster
D 66 B2
DK 59 B1
Klösterle A 107 B5
Klostermansfeld D 82 A3
Klosterneuburg A 97 C4
Klosters CH 107 C4
Kloten CH 107 B3
Klötze D 73 B4
Klöverträsk S 196 D4
Klövsjö S 199 C11
Kluczbork PL 86 B2
Kluczewo PL 75 A5
Kluisbergen B 79 B3
Klundert NL 79 A4
Klutz D 65 C4
Klwów PL 87 A4
Klyetsk BY 13 B7
Knaben N 52 B2
Knaften S 200 B4
Knapstad N 54 A2
Knäred S 61 C3
Knaresborough GB 40 A2
Knarvik N 46 B2
Knebel DK 59 B3
Knebworth GB 44 B3
Knesebeck D 73 B3
Knesselare B 78 A3
Knežak SLO 123 B3
Kneževi Vinogradi
HR 125 B4
Kneževo HR 125 B4
Knić SRB 127 D2
Knighton GB 39 B3
Knin HR 138 A2
Knislinge S 61 C4
Knittelfeld A 110 B1
Knivsta S 57 A3
Knock IRL 28 A3
Knocktopher IRL 30 B1
Knokke-Heist B 78 A3
Knowle GB 44 A2
Knurów PL 86 B2
Knutby S 51 C5
Knutsford GB 38 A4
Kobarid SLO 122 A2
København =
Copenhagen DK 61 D2
Kobenz A 110 B1
Kobersdorf A 111 B3
Kobiernice PL 99 B3
Kobierzyce PL 85 B4
Kobilje SLO 111 C3
Kobiór PL 86 B2
Koblenz
CH 106 B3
D 81 B3
Kobryn BY 13 B6
Kobylanka PL 75 A3
Kobylin PL 85 A5
Kobylniki PL 77 B5
Kocaali TR 187 A5
Kocaaliler TR 189 B5
Kocaeli = İzmit TR 187 B4
Kočani MK 182 B4
Koçarlı TR 188 B2
Koceljevo SRB 127 C1
Kočerin BIH 138 B3
Kočevje SLO 123 B3
Kočevska Reka
SLO 123 B3
Kochel am see D 108 B2
Kocs H 112 B2
Kocsér H 113 B3
Kocsola H 112 C2
Koczala PL 68 B2
Kodal N 53 A6
Kode S 60 B1
Kodersdorf D 84 A2
Kodrab PL 86 A3
Koekelare B 78 A2
Kofçaz TR 186 A2
Köflach A 110 B2
Køge DK 61 D2
Kohlberg D 95 B4
Kohtla-Järve EST 8 C5
Köinge S 60 B2
Kojetín CZ 98 B1
Kökar FIN 51 C7
Kokava SK 99 C3
Kokkinotrimithia 181 A2
Kokkola FIN 3 E8
Kokori BIH 124 C3
Kokoski PL 69 A3
Koksijde B 78 A2
Kola
BIH 124 C3
RUS 3 B13
Köla S 54 A3
Kołacin PL 87 A3
Kolari FIN 196 B6
Kolárovo SK 112 B1
Kolašin MNE 16 D3
Kolbäck S 56 A2
Kolbacz PL 75 A3
Kolbeinsstaðir IS 190 C3
Kolbermoor D 108 B3
Kolbnitz A 109 C4
Kolbotn N 54 A1
Kolbu N 48 B2
Kolby Kås DK 59 C3
Kolczewo PL 67 C3
Kolczyglowy PL 68 A2
Kolding DK 59 C2
Kölesd H 112 C2
Kolgrov N 46 A1
Kolín CZ 97 A3
Kolind DK 59 B3
Kolinec CZ 96 B1
Koljane HR 138 B2
Kølkær DK 59 B2
Kölleda D 82 A3
Kollum NL 70 A3
Köln = Cologne D 80 B2
Koło PL 76 B3
Kołobrzeg PL 67 B4
Kolochau D 83 A5
Kolomyya UA 13 D6
Kolonowskie PL 86 B2
Koloveč CZ 95 B5
Kolpino RUS 9 C7
Kolrep D 73 A5
Kölsillre S 199 C12
Kolsko PL 75 C4
Kolsva S 56 A1
Kolta SK 112 A2
Kolunič BIH 138 A2
Koluszki PL 87 A3
Kolut SRB 125 B4
Kolvereid N 199 A8
Kølvrå DK 59 B2
Komadi H 113 B5
Komagvær N 193 B14
Komarica BIH 125 C3
Komárno SK 112 B2
Komárom H 112 B2
Komatou Yialou
CY 181 A3
Komboti GR 182 D3
Komen SLO 122 B2
Komin HR 138 B3
Komiža HR 138 B2
Komjáti H 99 C4
Komjatice SK 112 A2
Komletinci HR 125 B4
Komló H 125 A4
Kömlo H 113 B4
Komoča SK 112 B2
Komorniki PL 75 B5
Komorzno PL 86 A2
Komotini GR 183 B7
Konak SRB 126 B2
Konakovo RUS 9 D10
Konarzyny PL 68 B2
Kondias GR 183 D7
Kondopaga RUS 9 A9
Kondorfa H 111 C3
Kondoros H 113 C4
Konevo RUS 9 A11
Køng DK 65 A4
Konga S 63 B3
Köngäs FIN 196 B7
Kongerslev DK 58 B3
Kongsberg N 53 A5
Kongshamn N 53 B4
Kongsmark DK 64 A1
Kongsmoen N 199 A9
Kongsvik N 194 B7
Kongsvinger N 48 B3
Konice CZ 97 B4
Konie PL 77 C5
Koniecpol PL 86 B3
Königsberg D 82 B2
Königsbronn D 94 C2
Königsbrück D 84 A1
Königsbrunn D 94 C2
Konigsdorf D 108 B2
Königsee D 82 B3
Königshorst D 74 B1
Königslutter D 73 B3
Königssee D 109 B3
Königstein
Hessen D 81 B4
Sachsen D 84 B2
Königstetten A 97 C4
Königswartha D 84 A2
Konigswiesen A 96 C2
Königswinter D 80 B3
Königs Wusterhausen
D 74 B2
Konin PL 76 B3
Konispol AL 182 D2
Konitsa GR 182 C2
Köniz CH 106 C2
Konjevići BIH 139 A5
Konjevrate HR 138 B2
Konjic BIH 139 B3
Konjščina HR 124 A2
Könnern D 83 A3
Konnerud N 53 A6
Konopiska PL 86 B2
Konotop PL 75 C4
Końskie PL 87 A4
Konsmo N 52 B3
Konstancin-Jeziorna
PL 77 B6
Konstantynów Łódzki
PL 86 A3
Konstanz D 107 B4
Kontich B 79 A4
Kontiolahti FIN 9 A6
Konya TR 189 B7

Mau–Mir 259

Maubourguet F 145 A4
Mauchline GB 36 A2
Maud GB 33 D4
Mauer-kirchen A 109 A4
Mauern D 95 C3
Mauguio F 131 B3
Maulbronn D 93 C4
Maule F 90 C1
Mauléon F 114 B3
Mauléon-Barousse
F 145 B4
Mauléon-Licharre
F 144 A3
Maulévrier F 114 A3
Maum IRL 28 A2
Maurach A 108 B2
Maure-de-Bretagne
F 101 B4
Maureilhan F 130 B2
Măureni RO 126 B3
Mauriac F 116 B2
Mauron F 101 A3
Maurs F 116 C2
Maury F 146 B3
Maussane-les-Alpilles
F 131 B3
Mautern A 97 C3
Mauterndorf A 109 B4
Mautern im Steiermark
A 110 B1
Mauthausen A 110 A1
Mauthen A 109 C3
Mauvezin F 129 C3
Mauzé-sur-le-Mignon
F 114 B3
Maxent F 101 B3
Maxey-sur-Vaise F 92 C1
Maxial P 154 B1
Maxieira P 154 B2
Maxwellheugh GB 35 C5
Mayalde E 149 A4
Maybole GB 36 A2
Mayen D 80 B3
Mayenne F 88 B3
Mayet F 102 B2
Mayorga E 142 B1
Mayres F 117 C4
Mayrhofen A 108 B2
Mazagón E 161 B3
Mazaleón E 153 A4
Mazamet F 130 B1
Mazan F 131 A4
Mazara del Vallo I 176 B1
Mazarambroz E 157 A3
Mazarete E 152 B1
Mazaricos E 140 B2
Mazarrón E 165 B3
Mažeikiai LT 8 D3
Mazères F 146 A2
Mazères-sur-Salat
F 145 A4
Mazières-en-Gâtine
F 115 B3
Mazin HR 138 A1
Mazuelo E 143 B3
Mazyr BY 13 B8
Mazzarino I 177 B3
Mazzarrà Sant'Andrea
I 177 A4
Mazzo di Valtellina
I 120 A3
Mdzewo PL 77 B5
Mealabost GB 31 A2
Mealhada P 148 B1
Méan B 79 B5
Meana Sardo I 179 C3
Meaulne F 103 C4
Meaux F 90 C2
Mebonden N 199 B8
Mecerreyes E 143 B3
Mechelen B 79 A4
Mechernich D 80 B2
Mechnica PL 86 B2
Mechowo PL 67 C4
Mechterstädt D 82 B2
Mecidiye TR 186 B1
Mecikal PL 68 B2
Mecina-Bombarón
E 164 C1
Mecitözü TR 23 A8
Meckenbeuren D 107 B4
Meckenheim
Rheinland-Pfalz D 80 B3
Rheinland-Pfalz D 93 B4
Meckesheim D 93 B4
Mecseknádasd H 125 A4
Meda
I 120 B2
P 149 B2
Medak HR 137 A4
Mede I 120 B1
Medebach D 81 A4
Medelim P 155 A3
Medemblik NL 70 B2
Medena Selista
BIH 138 A2
Medesano I 120 C3
Medevi S 55 B5
Medgidia RO 17 C8
Medgyesháza H 113 C5
Medhamn S 55 A4
Mediaş RO 17 B6
Medicina I 135 A4
Medinaceli E 152 A1
Medina de las Torres
E 155 C4
Medina del Campo
E 150 A3
Medina de Pomar
E 143 B3
Medina de Rioseco
E 142 C1
Medina Sidonia E 162 B2
Medinilla E 150 B2
Medja SRB 126 B2
Medjedja BIH 139 B5
Medulin HR 122 C2
Meduno I 122 A1
Medveda SRB 127 C3
Medvedov SK 111 B4
Medvezhyegorsk
RUS 9 A9
Medvide HR 137 A4
Medvode SLO 123 A3
Medzev SK 99 C4
Medžitlija MK 182 C3
Meerane D 83 B4
Meerle B 79 A4
Meersburg D 107 B4
Meeuwen B 79 A5
Megalo Horio GR 188 C2
Megalopoli GR 184 B3
Megara GR 185 A4
Megève F 118 B3
Meggenhofen A 109 A4
Megra RUS 9 B10
Megyaszó H 113 A5
Mehamn N 193 A11
Mehedeby S 51 B4
Méhkerék H 113 C5
Mehun-sur-Yèvre
F 103 B4
Meigle GB 35 B4
Meijel NL 80 A1
Meilen CH 107 B3
Meilhan F 128 C2
Meimôa P 149 B2
Meina I 119 B5
Meine D 73 B3
Meinersen D 72 B3
Meinerzhagen D 81 A3
Meiningen D 82 B2
Meira E 141 A3
Meiringen CH 106 C3
Meisenheim D 93 B3
Meissen D 83 A5
Meitingen D 94 C2
Meix-devant-Virton
B 92 B1
Męka PL 86 A2
Meka Gruda BIH 139 B4
Mel I 121 A5
Melbu N 194 B5
Melč CZ 98 B1
Meldal N 198 B6
Méldola I 135 A5
Meldorf D 64 B2
Melegnano I 120 B2
Melenci SRB 126 B2
Melendugno I 173 B4
Melfi I 172 B1
Melfjordbotn N 195 D4
Melgaço P 140 B2
Melgar de Arriba E 142 B1
Melgar de Fernamental
E 142 B2
Melgar de Yuso E 142 B2
Melhus N 199 B7
Meliana E 159 B3
Melide
CH 120 B1
E 140 B2
Melides P 160 A1
Meligales GR 184 B2
Melilli I 177 B4
Melinovac HR 124 C1
Melisenda I 179 C3
Melisey F 105 B5
Mélito di Porto Salvo
I 175 D1
Melk A 110 A2
Melksham GB 43 A4
Mellakoski FIN 196 C7
Mellanström S 195 E9
Mellbystrand S 61 C2
Melle
B 79 A3
D 71 B5
F 115 B3
Mellendorf D 72 B2
Mellerud S 54 B3
Mellieha M 175 C3
Mellösa S 56 A2
Mellrichstadt D 82 B2
Mělnické Vtelno CZ 84 B2
Mělník CZ 84 B2
Melón E 140 B2
Melrose GB 35 C5
Mels CH 107 B4
Melsungen D 82 A1
Meltaus FIN 197 C8
Meltham GB 40 B2
Melton Mowbray
GB 40 C3
Meltosjärvi FIN 196 C7
Melun F 90 C2
Melvaig GB 31 B3
Melvich GB 32 C3
Mélykút H 126 A1
Melzo I 120 B2
Memaliaj AL 182 C1
Membrilla E 157 B4
Membrio E 155 B3
Memer F 129 B4
Memmelsdorf D 94 B2
Memmingen D 107 B5
Memoria P 154 B2
Menàggio I 120 A2
Menai Bridge GB 38 A2
Menasalbas E 157 A3
Menat F 116 A2
Mendavia E 144 B1
Mendaza E 144 B1
Mende F 130 A2
Menden D 81 A3
Menderes TR 188 A2
Mendig D 80 B3
Mendiga P 154 B2
Mendrisio CH 120 B1
Ménéac F 101 A3
Menemen TR 188 A2
Menen B 78 B3
Menesjärvi FIN 193 D10
Menetou-Salon F 103 B4
Menfi I 176 B1
Ménfőcsanak H 111 B4
Mengamuñoz E 150 B3
Mengen
D 107 A4
TR 187 B7
Mengeš SLO 123 A3
Mengíbar E 157 C4
Mengkofen D 95 C4
Menou F 104 B2
Mens F 118 C2
Menslage D 71 B4
Mensträsk S 200 A5
Mentana I 168 A2
Menton F 133 B3
Méntrida E 151 B3
Méobecq F 115 B5
Méounes-les-Montrieux
F 132 B1
Meppel NL 70 B3
Meppen D 71 B4
Mequinenza E 153 A4
Mer F 103 B3
Mera
Coruña E 140 A2
Coruña E 140 A3
Meråker N 199 B8
Merano I 108 C2
Merate I 120 B2
Mercadillo E 143 A3
Mercatale I 135 B5
Mercatino Conca I 136 B1
Mercato San Severino
I 170 C2
Mercato Saraceno
I 135 B5
Merching D 108 A1
Merchtem B 79 B4
Merdrignac F 101 A3
Merdžanići BIH 139 B3
Meré E 142 A2
Mere GB 43 A4
Meréville F 90 C2
Merfeld D 80 A3
Méribel F 118 B3
Méribel Motraret F 118 B3
Meriç TR 186 A1
Mérida E 155 C4
Mérignac F 128 B2
Měřín CZ 97 B3
Mering D 94 C2
Merkendorf D 94 B2
Merklin CZ 96 B1
Merksplas B 79 A4
Merlånna S 56 A2
Merlimont Plage F 78 B1
Mern DK 65 A5
Mernye H 111 C4
Mersch L 92 B2
Merseburg D 83 A3
Mers-les-Bains F 90 A1
Merthyr Tydfil GB 39 C3
Mertingen D 94 C2
Mértola P 160 B2
Méru F 90 B2
Merufe P 140 B2
Mervans F 105 C4
Merville F 78 B2
Méry-sur-Seine F 91 C3
Merzen D 71 B4
Merzifon TR 23 A8
Merzig D 92 B2
Mesagne I 173 B3
Mesão Frio P 148 A2
Mesas de Ibor E 156 A2
Meschede D 81 A4
Meschers-sur-Gironde
F 114 C3
Meslay-du-Maine F 102 B1
Mesna N 48 A2
Mesnalien N 48 A2
Mesocco CH 120 A2
Mésola I 122 C1
Mesologi GR 184 A2
Mesopotamo GR 182 D2
Mesoraca I 175 B2
Messac F 101 B4
Messancy B 92 B1
Messdorf D 73 B4
Messei F 88 B3
Messejana P 160 B1
Messelt N 48 A3
Messina I 177 A4
Messingen D 71 B4
Messini GR 184 B3
Messkirch D 107 B4
Messlingen S 199 C9
Messtetten D 107 A3
Mesta GR 185 A6
Mestanza E 157 B3
Městec Králové CZ 84 B3
Mestlin D 73 A4
Město Albrechlice
CZ 85 B5
Město Libavá CZ 98 B1
Město Touškov CZ 96 B1
Mestre I 122 B1
Mesvres F 104 C3
Mesztegnyő H 111 C4
Meta I 170 C2
Metajna HR 137 A4
Metelen D 71 B4
Methana GR 185 B4
Methlick GB 33 D4
Methven GB 35 B4
Methwold GB 41 C4
Metković HR 139 B3
Metlika SLO 123 B4
Metnitz A 110 C1
Metsäkylä FIN 197 D11
Metslawier NL 70 A3
Metsovo GR 182 D3
Metten D 95 C4
Mettendorf D 92 B2
Mettet B 79 B4
Mettingen D 71 B4
Mettlach D 92 B2
Mettlen CH 106 C2
Mettmann D 80 A2
Metz F 92 B2
Metzervisse F 92 B2
Metzingen D 94 C1
Meulan F 90 B1
Meung-sur-Loire F 103 B3
Meuselwitz D 83 A4
Meuzac F 115 C5
Mevagissey GB 42 B2
Mexborough GB 40 B2
Meximieux F 118 B2
Mey GB 32 C3
Meyenburg D 73 A5
Meyerhöfen D 71 B5
Meylan F 118 B2
Meymac F 116 B2
Meyrargues F 132 B1
Meyrueis F 130 A2
Meyssac F 129 A4
Meysse F 117 C4
Meyzieu F 117 B4
Mèze F 130 B2
Mézériat F 117 A5
Mežica SLO 110 C1
Mézidon-Canon F 89 A3
Mézières-en-Brenne
F 115 B5
Mézières-sur-Issoire
F 115 B4
Mézilhac F 117 C4
Mézilles F 104 B2
Mézin F 128 B3
Mezőberény H 113 C5
Mezőcsát H 113 B4
Mezőfalva H 112 C2
Mezőhegyes H 126 A2
Mezőkeresztes H 113 B4
Mezőkomárom H 112 C2
Mezőkövácsháza
H 113 C4
Mezőkövesd H 113 B4
Mezőörs H 111 B4
Mézos F 128 B1
Mezőszilas H 112 C2
Mezőtúr H 113 B4
Mezquita de Jarque
E 153 B3
Mezzano
Emilia Romagna
I 135 A5
Trentino Alto Adige
I 121 A4
Mezzojuso I 176 B2
Mezzoldo I 120 A2
Mezzolombardo I 121 A4
Mgarr M 175 C3
Miajadas E 156 A2
Miały PL 75 B5
Mianowice PL 68 A2
Miasteczko Krajeńskie
PL 76 A2
Miasteczko Sł. PL 86 B2
Miastko PL 68 A1
Michalovce SK 12 D4
Michałowice PL 87 B3
Michelau D 94 B2
Michelbach D 94 B2
Micheldorf A 110 B1
Michelhausen A 110 A2
Michelsneukirchen
D 95 B4
Michelstadt D 93 B5
Michendorf D 74 B2
Mickleover GB 40 C2
Midbea GB 33 B4
Middelburg NL 79 A3
Middelfart DK 59 C2
Middelharnis NL 79 A4
Middelkerke B 78 A2
Middelstum NL 71 A3
Middlesbrough GB 37 B5
Middleton Cheney
GB 44 A2
Middleton-in-Teesdale
GB 37 B4
Middletown GB 27 B4
Middlewich GB 38 A4
Middlezoy GB 43 A4
Midhurst GB 44 C3
Midleton IRL 29 C3
Midlum D 64 C1
Midsomer Norton
GB 43 A4
Midtgulen N 198 D2
Midtskogberget N 49 A4
Midwolda NL 71 A4
Mid Yell GB 33 A5
Miechów PL 87 B4
Miedes de Aragón
E 152 A2
Miedes de Atienza
E 151 A4
Międzybodzie Bielskie
PL 99 B3
Międzybórz PL 85 A5
Międzychód PL 75 B4
Międzylesie PL 85 B4
Międzyrzec Podlaski
PL 12 C5
Międzyrzecz PL 75 B4
Międzywodzie PL 67 B3
Międzyzdroje PL 67 C3
Miejska Górka PL 85 A4
Miélan F 145 A4
Mielec PL 87 B5
Mielęcin PL 75 A3
Mielno
Warmińsko-Mazurskie
PL 77 A5
Zachodnio-Pomorskie
PL 67 B5
Miengo E 143 A3
Mieraslompolo
FIN 193 C11
Miercurea Ciuc RO 17 B6
Mieres
Asturias E 141 A5
Girona E 147 B3
Mieroszów PL 85 B4
Mierzyn PL 86 A3
Miesau D 93 B3
Miesbach D 108 B2
Mieścisko PL 76 B2
Mieste D 73 B4
Miesterhorst D 73 B4
Mieszków PL 76 B2
Mieszkowice PL 74 B3
Mietków PL 85 B4
Migennes F 104 B2
Miggiano I 173 C4
Migliánico I 169 A4
Migliarino I 121 C4
Migliónico I 172 B2
Mignano Monte Lungo
I 169 B3
Migné F 115 B5
Miguel Esteban E 157 A4
Miguelturra E 157 B4
Mihajlovac SRB 127 C2
Miháld H 111 C4
Mihalgazi TR 187 B5
Mihalıççık TR 187 C6
Mihályi H 111 B4
Mihla D 82 A2
Mihohnić HR 123 B3
Miholjsko HR 123 B4
Mihovljan HR 124 A1
Mijares E 150 B3
Mijas E 163 B3
Mike H 124 A3
Mikines GR 184 B3
Mikkeli FIN 8 B5
Mikkelvik N 192 B3
Mikleuš HR 125 B3
Mikołajki Pomorskie
PL 69 B4
Mikolów PL 86 B2
Mikonos GR 185 B6
Mikorzyn PL 86 A2
Mikro Derio GR 183 B8
Mikstat PL 86 A1
Mikulášovice CZ 84 B2
Mikulov CZ 97 C4
Mikulovice CZ 85 B5
Milagro E 144 B2
Miłakowo PL 69 A5
Milan = Milano I 120 B2
Miland N 47 C5
Milano = Milan I 120 B2
Milano Marittima I 135 A5
Milas TR 188 B2
Milazzo I 177 A4
Mildenhall GB 45 A4
Milejewo PL 69 A4
Milelín CZ 85 B3
Miletić SRB 125 B5
Miletićevo SRB 126 B3
Mileto I 175 C2
Milevsko CZ 96 B2
Milford IRL 26 A3
Milford Haven GB 39 C1
Milford on Sea GB 44 C2
Milhão P 149 A3
Milići BIH 139 A5
Miličin CZ 96 B2
Milicz PL 85 A5
Milín CZ 96 B2
Militello in Val di
Catánia I 177 B3
Miljevina BIH 139 B4
Milkowice PL 85 A4
Millançay F 103 B3
Millares E 159 B3
Millas F 146 B3
Millau F 130 A2
Millesimo I 133 A4
Millevaches F 116 B2
Millom GB 36 B3
Millport GB 34 C3
Millstatt A 109 C4
Millstreet
Cork IRL 29 B2
Waterford IRL 29 B4
Milltown
Galway IRL 28 A3
Kerry IRL 29 B1
Milltown Malbay IRL 28 B2
Milly-la-Forêt F 90 C2
Milmarcos E 152 A2
Milmersdorf D 74 A2
Milna HR 138 B2
Milnthorpe GB 37 B4
Milogórze PL 69 A5
Miłomłyn PL 69 B4
Milos GR 185 C5
Miloševo SRB 127 C3
Miłosław PL 76 B2
Milot AL 182 B1
Milówka PL 99 B3
Miltach D 95 B4
Miltenberg D 94 B1
Milton Keynes GB 44 A3
Miltzow D 66 B2
Milverton GB 43 A3
Milzyn PL 76 B3
Mimice HR 138 B2
Mimizan F 128 B1
Mimizan-Plage F 128 B1
Mimoň CZ 84 B2
Mina de Juliana P 160 B1
Mina de São Domingos
P 160 B2
Minas de Riotinto
E 161 B3
Minateda E 158 C2
Minaya E 158 B1
Minde P 154 B2
Mindelheim D 108 A1
Mindelstetten D 95 C3
Minden D 72 B1
Mindszent H 113 C4
Minehead GB 43 A3
Mineo I 177 B3
Minerbe I 121 B4
Minérbio I 121 C4
Minervino Murge I 171 B4
Minglanilla E 158 B2
Mingorria E 150 B3
Minnesund N 48 B3
Miño E 140 A2
Miño de San Esteban
E 151 A4
Minsen D 71 A4
Minsk BY 13 B7
Mińsk Mazowiecki
PL 12 B4
Minsterley GB 39 B4
Mintlaw GB 33 D4
Minturno I 169 B3
Mionica
BIH 125 C4
SRB 127 C2
Mios F 128 B2
Mira
E 158 B2
I 121 B5
P 148 B1
Mirabel E 155 B4
Mirabel-aux-Baronnies
F 131 A4
Mirabella Eclano I 170 B3
Mirabella Imbáccari
I 177 B3
Mirabello I 121 C4
Miradoux F 129 B3
Miraflores de la Sierra
E 151 B4
Miralrio E 151 B5
Miramar P 148 A1
Miramare I 136 A1
Miramas F 131 B3
Mirambeau F 114 C3
Miramont-de-Guyenne
F 129 B3
Miranda de Arga E 144 B2
Miranda de Ebro E 143 B4
Miranda do Corvo
P 148 B1
Miranda do Douro
P 149 A3
Mirande F 129 C3
Mirandela P 149 A2
Mirandilla E 155 C4
Mirándola I 121 C4
Miranje HR 137 A4
Mirano I 121 B5
Miras AL 182 C2
Miravet E 153 A4
Miré F 102 B1
Mirebeau F 102 C2
Mirebeau-sur-Bèze
F 105 B4
Mirecourt F 105 A5
Mirepoix F 146 A2
Mires GR 185 D5
Miribel F 117 B4
Miričina BIH 125 C4
Mirina GR 183 D7
Mirna SLO 123 B4
Miroslav CZ 97 C4
Mirosławice PL 85 B4
Mirosławiec PL 75 A5
Mirošov CZ 96 B1

Mirotice CZ 96 B2
Mirovice CZ 96 B2
Mirow D 74 A1
Mirsk PL 84 B3
Mirzec PL 87 A5
Misi FIN 197 C9
Misilmeri I 176 A2
Miske H 112 C3
Miskolc H 113 A4
Mislinja SLO 110 C2
Missanello I 174 A2
Missillac F 101 B3
Mistelbach
A 97 C4
D 95 B3
Misten N 194 C5
Misterbianco I 177 B4
Misterhult S 62 A4
Mistretta I 177 B3
Misurina I 109 C3
Mitchelstown IRL 29 B3
Mithimna GR 186 C1
Mithoni GR 184 C2
Mitilini GR 186 C1
Mitilinii GR 188 B1
Mittelberg
Tirol A 108 C1
Vorarlberg A 107 B5
Mittenwald D 108 B2
Mittenwalde D 74 B2
Mitterback A 110 B2
Mitterdorf im Mürztal
A 110 B2
Mitter-Kleinarl A 109 B4
Mittersheim F 92 C2
Mittersill A 109 B3
Mitterskirchen D 95 C4
Mitterteich D 95 B4
Mitton F 128 B2
Mittweida D 83 B4
Mitwitz D 82 B3
Mizhhir'ya UA 13 D5
Mjällby S 63 B2
Mjåvatn N 53 B4
Mjöbäck S 60 B2
Mjölby S 56 B1
Mjølfjell N 46 B3
Mjøndalen N 53 A6
Mjørlund N 48 B2
Mladá Boleslav CZ 84 B2
Mladá Vožice CZ 96 B2
Mladé Buky CZ 85 B3
Mladenovac SRB 127 C2
Mladenovo SRB 126 B1
Mladikovine BIH 139 A3
Mława PL 77 A5
Mlinište BIH 138 A2
Młodzieszyn PL 77 B5
Młogoszyn PL 77 B4
Młynary PL 69 A4
Mnichóvice CZ 96 B2
Mnichovo Hradiště
CZ 84 B2
Mniów PL 87 A4
Mnisek nad Hnilcom
SK 99 C4
Mníšek pod Brdy
CZ 96 B2
Mniszek PL 87 A4
Mniszków PL 87 A4
Mo
Hedmark N 48 B3
Hordaland N 46 B2
Møre og Romsdal
N 198 C5
Telemark N 53 A3
Gävleborg S 51 A3
Västra Götaland S 54 B2
Moaña E 140 B2
Moate IRL 28 A4
Mocejón E 151 C4
Močenok SK 111 A4
Mochales E 152 A1
Mochowo PL 77 B4
Mochy PL 75 B5
Mockern D 73 B4
Mockfjärd S 50 B1
Möckmühl D 94 B1
Mockrehna D 83 A4
Moclin E 163 A4
Mocsa H 112 B2
Mőcsény H 125 A4
Modane F 118 B3
Modbury GB 42 B3
Módena I 121 C3
Módica I 177 C3
Modigliana I 135 A4
Modlin PL 77 B5
Mödling A 111 A3
Modliszewice PL 87 A4
Modliszewko PL 76 B2
Modogno I 171 B4
Modra SK 98 C1
Modran BIH 125 C3
Modriča BIH 125 C4
Möðrudalur IS 191 B10
Modrý Kamen SK 99 C3
Moëlan-sur-Mer F 100 B2
Moelfre GB 38 A2
Moelv N 48 B2
Moen N 194 A9
Moena I 121 A4
Moerbeke B 79 A3
Moers D 80 A2
Móes P 148 B2
Moffat GB 36 A3
Mogadouro P 149 A3
Mogata S 56 B2
Móggio Udinese I 122 A2
Mogielnica PL 87 A4
Mogilany PL 99 B3
Mogilno PL 76 B2
Mogliano I 136 B2
Mogliano Véneto I 122 B1
Mogor E 140 B2
Mógoro I 179 C2
Moguer E 161 B3
Mohács H 125 B4
Moheda S 62 A2
Mohedas E 149 B3
Mohedas de la Jara
E 156 A2
Mohelnice CZ 97 B4
Mohill IRL 26 C3
Möhlin CH 106 B2
Moholm S 55 B5
Mohorn D 83 A5
Mohyliv-Podil's'kyy
UA 13 D7
Moi N 52 B2
Moià E 147 C3
Móie I 136 B2
Moimenta da Beira
P 148 B2
Mo i Rana N 195 D5
Moirans F 118 B2
Moirans-en-Montagne
F 118 A2
Moisaküla EST 8 C4
Moisdon-la-Rivière
F 101 B4
Moissac F 129 B4
Moita
Coimbra P 148 B1
Guarda P 149 B2
Santarém P 154 B2
Setúbal P 154 C1
Moita dos Ferreiros
P 154 B1
Moixent E 159 C3
Mojacar E 164 B3
Mojados E 150 A3
Mojmírovce SK 112 A2
Mojtin SK 98 C2
Möklinta S 50 B3
Mokošica HR 139 C4
Mokronog SLO 123 B4
Mokro Polje HR 138 A2
Mokrzyska PL 99 A4
Møkster N 46 B2
Mol
B 79 A5
SRB 126 B2
Mola di Bari I 173 A3
Molai GR 184 C3
Molare I 133 A4
Molaretto I 119 B4
Molas F 145 A4
Molassano I 134 A1
Molbergen D 71 B4
Mold GB 38 A3
Molde N 198 C4
Møldrup DK 58 B2
Moledo do Minho
P 148 A1
Molfetta I 171 B4
Molfsee D 64 B3
Moliden S 200 C4
Molières F 129 B4
Molina de Aragón
E 152 B2
Molina de Segura
E 165 A3
Molinar E 143 A3
Molinaseca E 141 B4
Molinella I 121 C4
Molinet F 104 C2
Molinicos E 158 C1
Molini di Tures I 108 C2
Molinos de Duero
E 143 C4
Molins de Rei E 147 C3
Moliterno I 174 A1
Molkom S 55 A4
Möllbrücke A 109 C4
Mölle S 61 C2
Molledo E 142 A2
Möllenbeck D 74 A2
Mollerussa E 147 C1
Mollet de Perelada
E 146 B3
Mollina E 163 A3
Mölln D 73 A3
Molló E 146 B3
Mollösund S 54 B2
Mölltorp S 55 B5
Mölnbo S 56 A3
Mölndal S 60 B2
Mölnlycke S 60 B2
Molompize F 116 B3
Moloy F 105 B3
Molsheim F 93 C3
Moltzow D 73 A5
Molve HR 124 A3
Molveno I 121 A3
Molvizar E 163 B4
Molzbichl A 109 C4
Mombaróccio I 136 B1
Mombeltrán E 150 B2
Mombris D 93 A5
Mombuey E 141 B4
Momchilgrad BG 183 B7
Mommark DK 64 B3
Momo I 119 B5
Monaghan IRL 27 B4
Monar Lodge GB 32 D2
Monasterace Marina
I 175 C2
Monasterevin IRL 30 A1
Monasterio de Rodilla
E 143 B3
Monastir I 179 C3
Monbahus F 129 B3
Monbazillac F 129 B3
Moncada E 159 B3
Moncalieri I 119 B4
Moncalvo I 119 B5
Monção P 140 B2
Moncarapacho P 160 B2
Moncel-sur-Seille F 92 C2
Monchegorsk RUS 3 C13
Mönchengladbach =
Munchen-Gladbach
D 80 A2
Mónchio della Corti
I 134 A3
Monchique P 160 B1
Monclar-de-Quercy
F 129 C4
Moncofa E 159 B3
Moncontour F 101 A3
Moncoutant F 114 B3
Monda E 162 B3
Mondariz E 140 B2
Mondavio I 136 B1
Mondéjar E 151 B4
Mondello I 176 A2
Mondim de Basto
P 148 A2
Mondolfo I 136 B2
Mondoñedo E 141 A3
Mondorf-les-Bains
L 92 B2
Mondoubleau F 102 B2
Mondovì I 133 A3
Mondragon F 131 A3
Mondragone I 170 B1
Mondsee A 109 B4
Monéglia I 134 A2
Monegrillo E 153 A3
Monein F 145 A3
Monemvasia GR 184 C4
Mónesi I 133 A3
Monesiglio I 133 A4
Monesterio E 161 A3
Monestier-de-Clermont
F 118 C2
Monestiés F 130 A1
Monéteau F 104 B2
Moneygall IRL 28 B4
Moneymore GB 27 B4
Monfalcone I 122 B2
Monfero E 140 A2
Monflanquin F 129 B3
Monflorite E 145 B3
Monforte P 155 B3
Monforte da Beira
E 155 B3
P 155 B3
Monforte d'Alba I 133 A3
Monforte del Cid E 165 A4
Monforte de Lemos
E 140 B3
Monforte de Moyuela
E 152 A2
Monghidoro I 135 A4
Mongiana I 175 C2
Monguelfo I 108 C3
Monheim D 94 C2
Moniaive GB 36 A3
Monifieth GB 35 B5
Monikie GB 35 B5
Monistrol-d'Allier
F 117 C3
Monistrol de Montserrat
E 147 C2
Monistrol-sur-Loire
F 117 B4
Mönkebude D 74 A2
Monkton GB 36 A2
Monmouth GB 39 C4
Monnaie F 102 B2
Monnerville F 90 C2
Monnickendam NL 70 B2
Monolithos GR 188 C2
Monópoli I 173 B3
Monor H 112 B3
Monóvar E 159 C3
Monpazier F 129 B3
Monreal
D 80 B3
E 144 B2
Monreal del Campo
E 152 B2
Monreale I 176 A2
Monroy E 155 B4
Monroyo E 153 B3
Mons B 79 B3
Monsaraz P 155 C3
Monschau D 80 B2
Monségur F 128 B3
Monselice I 121 B4
Mønshaug N 46 B3
Monster NL 70 B1
Mönsterås S 62 A4
Monsummano Terme
I 135 B3
Montabaur D 81 B3
Montafia I 119 C5
Montagnac F 130 B2
Montagnana I 121 B4
Montaigu F 114 B2
Montaigu-de-Quercy
F 129 B4
Montaiguët-en-Forez
F 117 A3
Montaigut F 116 A2
Montaigut-sur-Save
F 129 C4
Montainville F 90 C1
Montalbán E 153 B3
Montalbán de Córdoba
E 163 A3
Montalbano Elicona
I 177 A4
Montalbano Iónico
I 174 A2
Montalbo E 158 B1
Montalcino I 135 B4
Montaldo di Cósola
I 120 C2
Montalegre P 148 A2
Montalieu-Vercieu
F 118 B2
Montalivet-les-Bains
F 114 C2
Montallegro I 176 B2
Montalto delle Marche
I 136 C2
Montalto di Castro
I 168 A1
Montalto Pavese I 120 C2
Montalto Uffugo I 174 B2
Montalvão P 155 B3
Montamarta E 149 A4
Montana BG 17 D5
Montana-Vermala
CH 119 A4
Montánchez E 156 A1
Montanejos E 153 B3
Montano Antilia I 172 B1
Montans F 129 C4
Montargil P 154 B2
Montargis F 103 B4
Montastruc-la-
Conseillère F 129 C4
Montauban F 129 B4
Montauban-de-Bretagne
F 101 A3
Montbard F 104 B3
Montbarrey F 105 B4
Montbazens F 130 A1
Montbazon F 102 B2
Montbéliard F 106 B1
Montbenoit F 105 C5
Montbeugny F 104 C2
Montblanc E 147 C2
Montbozon F 105 B5
Montbrison F 117 B4
Montbron F 115 C4
Montbrun-les-Bains
F 131 A4
Montceau-les-Mines
F 104 C3
Montcenis F 104 C3
Montchanin F 104 C3
Montcornet F 91 B4
Montcuq F 129 B4
Montdardier F 130 B2
Mont-de-Marsan F 128 C2
Montdidier F 90 B2
Monteagudo E 165 A3
Monteagudo de las
Vicarias E 152 A1
Montealegre E 142 C2
Montealegre del Castillo
E 159 C2
Montebello Iónico
I 175 D1
Montebello Vicentino
I 121 B4
Montebelluna I 121 B5
Montebourg F 88 A2
Montebruno I 134 A2
Monte-Carlo MC 133 B3
Montecarotto I 136 B2
Montecassiano I 136 B2
Montecastrilli I 168 A2
Montecatini Terme
I 135 B3
Montécchio I 136 B1
Montécchio Emilia
I 121 C3
Montécchio Maggiore
I 121 B4
Montech F 129 C4
Montechiaro d'Asti
I 119 B5
Monte Clara P 155 B3
Monte Clérigo P 160 B1
Montecórice I 170 C2
Montecorvino Rovella
I 170 C2
Monte da Pedra P 155 B3
Monte de Goula P 155 B3
Montederramo E 141 B3
Montedoro I 176 B2
Monte do Trigo P 155 C3
Montefalco I 136 C1
Montefalcone di Val
Fortore I 170 B3
Montefalcone nel
Sánnio I 170 B2
Montefano I 136 B2
Montefiascone I 168 A2
Montefiorino I 134 A3
Montefortino I 136 C2
Montefranco I 168 A2
Montefrío E 163 A4
Montegiordano Marina
I 174 A2
Montegiórgio I 136 B2
Monte Gordo P 160 B2
Montegranaro I 136 B2
Montehermoso E 149 B3
Montejicar E 163 A4
Montejo de la Sierra
E 151 A4
Montejo de Tiermes
E 151 A4
Monte Juntos P 155 C3
Montel-de-Gelat F 116 B2
Monteleone di Púglia
I 171 B3
Monteleone di Spoleto
I 169 A2
Monteleone d'Orvieto
I 135 C5
Montelepre I 176 A2
Montelibretti I 168 A2
Montelier F 117 C5
Montélimar F 131 A3
Montella
E 146 B2
I 170 C3
Montellano E 162 A2
Montelupo Fiorentino
I 135 B4
Montemaggiore Belsito
I 176 B2
Montemagno I 119 C5
Montemayor E 163 A3
Montemayor de Pinilla
E 150 A3
Montemésola I 173 B3
Montemilleto I 170 B2
Montemilone I 172 A1
Montemolin E 161 A3
Montemónaco I 136 C2
Montemor-o-Novo
P 154 C2
Montemor-o-Velho
P 148 B1
Montemurro I 174 A1
Montendre F 128 A2
Montenegro de Cameros
E 143 B4
Montenero di Bisáccia
I 170 B2
Monteneuf F 101 B3
Monteparano I 173 B3
Montepescali I 135 C4
Montepiano I 135 A4
Monte Porzio I 136 B2
Montepulciano I 135 B4
Monte Real P 154 B2
Montereale I 169 A3
Montereale Valcellina
I 122 A1
Montereau-Faut-Yonne
F 90 C2
Monte Redondo P 154 B2
Monterénzio I 135 A4
Monte Romano I 168 A1
Monteroni d'Arbia
I 135 B4
Monteroni di Lecce
I 173 B4
Monterosso al Mare
I 134 A2
Monterosso Almo I 177 B3
Monterosso Grana
I 133 A3
Monterotondo I 168 A2
Monterotondo Maríttimo
I 135 B3
Monterrey E 141 C3
Monterroso E 140 B3
Monterrubio de la
Serena E 156 B2
Monterubbiano I 136 B2
Montesa E 159 C3
Montesalgueiro E 140 A2
Monte San Giovanni
Campano I 169 B3
Montesano sulla
Marcellana I 174 A1
Monte San Savino
I 135 B4
Monte Sant'Ángelo
I 171 B3
Montesárchio I 170 B2
Montescaglioso I 171 C4
Montesclaros E 150 B3
Montesilvano I 169 A4
Montespértoli I 135 B4
Montesquieu-Volvestre
F 146 A2
Montesquiou F 129 C3
Montestruc-sur-Gers
F 129 C3
Montes Velhos P 160 B1
Montevarchi I 135 B4
Montéveglio I 135 A4
Monte Vilar P 154 B1
Montfaucon F 101 B4
Montfaucon-d'Argonne
F 91 B5
Montfaucon-en-Velay
F 117 B4
Montferrat
Isère F 118 B2
Var F 132 B2
Montfort-en-Chalosse
F 128 C2
Montfort-l'Amaury
F 90 C1
Montfort-le-Gesnois
F 102 A2
Montfort-sur-Meu
F 101 A4
Montfort-sur-Risle F 89 A4
Montgai E 147 C1
Montgaillard F 145 A4
Montgenèvre F 118 C3
Montgiscard F 146 A2
Montgomery GB 39 B3
Montguyon F 128 A2
Monthermé F 91 B4
Monthey CH 119 A3
Monthois F 91 B4
Monthureux-sur-Saône
F 105 A4
Monti I 178 B3
Monticelli d'Ongina
I 120 B2
Montichiari I 120 B3
Monticiano I 135 B4
Montiel E 158 C1
Montier-en-Der F 91 C4
Montieri I 135 B4
Montiglio I 119 B5
Montignac F 129 A4
Montigny-le-Roi F 105 B4
Montigny-lès-Metz
F 92 B2
Montigny-sur-Aube
F 105 B3
Montijo
E 155 C4
P 154 C2
Montilla E 163 A3
Montillana E 163 A4
Montilly F 104 C2
Montivilliers F 89 A4
Montjaux F 130 A1
Montjean-sur-Loire
F 102 B1
Montlhéry F 90 C2
Montlieu-la-Garde
F 128 A2
Mont-Louis F 146 B3
Montlouis-sur-Loire
F 102 B2
Montluçon F 116 A2
Montluel F 117 B5
Montmarault F 116 A2
Montmartin-sur-Mer
F 88 B2
Montmédy F 92 B1
Montmélian F 118 B3
Montmeyan F 132 B2
Montmeyran F 117 C4
Montmirail
Marne F 91 C3
Sarthe F 102 A2
Montmiral F 118 B2
Montmirat F 131 B3
Montmirey-le-Château
F 105 B4
Montmoreau-St Cybard
F 115 C4
Montmorency F 90 C2
Montmorillon F 115 B4
Montmort-Lucy F 91 C3
Montoir-de-Bretagne
F 101 B3
Montoire-sur-le-Loir
F 102 B2
Montoito P 155 C3
Montolieu F 146 A3
Montório al Vomano
I 169 A3
Montoro E 157 B3
Montpellier F 131 B2
Montpezat-de-Quercy
F 129 B4
Montpezat-sous-Bouzon
F 117 C4
Montpon-Ménestérol
F 128 A3
Montpont-en-Bresse
F 105 C4
Montréal
Aude F 146 A3
Gers F 128 C3
Montredon-Labessonnié
F 130 B1
Montréjeau F 145 A4
Montrésor F 103 B3
Montresta I 178 B2
Montret F 105 C4
Montreuil
Pas de Calais F 78 B1
Seine St Denis F 90 C2
Montreuil-aux-Lions
F 90 B3
Montreuil-Bellay F 102 B1
Montreux CH 106 C1
Montrevault F 101 B4
Montrevel-en-Bresse
F 118 A2
Montrichard F 103 B3
Montricoux F 129 B4
Mont-roig del Camp
E 147 C1
Montrond-les-Bains
F 117 B4
Montrose GB 35 B5
Montroy E 159 B3
Montsalvy F 116 C2
Montsauche-les-Settons
F 104 B3
Montseny E 147 C3
Montsoreau F 102 B2

Nassenheide D 74 B2
Nassereith A 108 B1
Nässjö S 62 A2
Nastätten D 81 B3
Næstved DK 65 A4
Näsum S 63 B2
Näsviken S 199 B12
Natalinci SRB 127 C2
Naters CH 119 A5
Nater-Stetten D 108 A2
Nattavaara S 196 C3
Natters A 108 B2
Nattheim D 94 C2
Nättraby S 63 B3
Naturno I 108 C1
Naucelle F 130 A1
Nauders A 108 C1
Nauen D 74 B1
Naul IRL 30 A2
Naumburg D 83 A3
Naundorf D 83 B5
Naunhof D 83 A4
Naustdal N 46 A2
Nautijaur S 196 C2
Nautsi RUS 193 D13
Nava E 142 A1
Navacerrada E 151 B3
Navaconcejo E 149 B4
Nava de Arévalo E 150 B3
Nava de la Asunción E 150 A3
Nava del Rey E 150 A2
Navafriá E 151 A4
Navahermosa E 157 A3
Navahrudak BY 13 B6
Naval E 145 B4
Navalacruz E 150 B3
Navalcán E 150 B2
Navalcarnero E 151 B3
Navaleno E 143 C3
Navalmanzano E 151 A3
Navalmoral E 150 B3
Navalmoral de la Mata E 150 C2
Naválón E 159 C3
Navalonguilla E 150 B2
Navalperal de Pinares E 150 B3
Navalpino E 157 A3
Navaltalgordo E 150 B3
Navaltoril E 156 A3
Navaluenga E 150 B3
Navalvillar de Pela E 156 A2
Navan IRL 30 A2
Navaperal de Tormes E 150 B2
Navapolatsk BY 13 A8
Navarclés E 147 C2
Navarredonda de Gredos E 150 B2
Navarrenx F 144 A3
Navarrés E 159 B3
Navarrete E 143 B4
Navarrevisca E 150 B3
Navás E 147 C2
Navascués E 144 B2
Navas del Madroño E 155 B4
Navas del Rey E 151 B3
Navas del Sepillar E 163 A3
Navas de Oro E 150 A3
Navas de San Juan E 157 B4
Navasfrias E 149 B3
Nave I 120 B3
Nave de Haver P 149 B3
Nävekvarn S 56 B2
Navelli I 169 A3
Navenby GB 40 B3
Näverkärret S 56 A1
Naverstad S 54 B2
Navés E 147 C2
Navezuelas E 156 A2
Navia E 141 A4
Navia de Suarna E 141 B4
Navilly F 105 C4
Năvodari RO 17 C8
Naxos GR 185 B6
Nay F 145 A3
Nazaré P 154 B1
Nazarje SLO 123 A3
Nazilli TR 188 B3
Nazza D 82 A2
Nea Anchialos GR 182 D4
Nea Epidavros GR 184 B4
Nea Flippias GR 182 D2
Nea Kalikratia GR 183 C5
Nea Makri GR 185 A4
Nea Moudania GR 183 C5
Neap GB 33 A5
Nea Peramos GR 183 C6
Neapoli
Kozani GR 182 C3
Kriti GR 185 D6
Lakonia GR 184 C4
Nea Stira GR 185 A5
Neath GB 39 C3
Nea Visa GR 186 A1
Nea Zichni GR 183 B5
Nebljusi HR 124 C1
Neblo SLO 122 A2
Nebolchy RUS 9 C8
Nebra D 82 A3
Nebreda E 143 C3
Nechanice CZ 84 B3
Neckargemünd D 93 B4
Neckarsulm D 94 B1
Neda E 140 A2
Neded SK 112 A1
Nedelišće HR 124 A2
Nederweert NL 80 A1
Nedreberg N 48 B3
Nedre Gärdsjö S 50 B2
Nedre Soppero S 196 A4
Nedstrand N 52 A1
Nedvědice CZ 97 B4
Nędza PL 86 B2
Neede NL 71 B3
Needham Market GB 45 A5
Needingworth GB 44 A3
Neermoor D 71 A4
Neeroeteren B 80 A1
Neerpelt B 79 A5
Neesen D 72 B1
Neetze D 73 A3
Nefyn GB 38 B2
Negotin SRB 16 C5
Negotino MK 182 B4
Negrar I 121 B3
Negredo E 151 A5
Negreira E 140 B2
Nègrepelisse F 129 B4
Negru Vodă RO 17 D8
Negueira de Muñiz E 141 A4
Neheim D 81 A3
Neila E 143 B4
Néive I 119 C5
Nejdek CZ 83 B4
Nekla PL 76 B2
Neksø DK 67 A4
Nelas P 148 B2
Nelaug N 53 B4
Nelidovo RUS 9 D8
Nelim FIN 193 D12
Nellingen D 94 C1
Nelson GB 40 B1
Neman RUS 12 A5
Nemea GR 184 B3
Nemesgörzsöny H 111 B4
Nemeskér H 111 B3
Nemesnádudvar H 125 A5
Nemesszalók H 111 B4
Németkér H 112 C2
Nemours F 103 A4
Nemška Loka SLO 123 B4
Nemšová SK 98 C2
Nenagh IRL 28 B3
Nenince SK 112 A3
Nenita GR 185 A7
Nenzing A 107 B4
Neochori GR 182 D3
Neo Chori GR 184 A2
Neon Petritsi GR 183 B5
Nepi I 168 A2
Nepomuk CZ 96 B1
Nérac F 129 B3
Neratovice CZ 84 B2
Nerchau D 83 A4
Néré F 115 C3
Neresheim D 94 C2
Nereto I 136 C2
Nerezine HR 123 C3
Nerežišća HR 138 B2
Neringa LT 12 A4
Néris-les Bains F 116 A2
Nerito I 169 A3
Nerja E 163 B4
Néronde F 117 B4
Nérondes F 103 C4
Nerpio E 164 A2
Nersingen D 94 C2
Nerva E 161 B3
Nervesa della Battáglia I 121 B5
Nervi I 134 A2
Nes
Buskerud N 48 B1
Hedmark N 48 B2
NL 70 A2
Sogn og Fjordane N 46 A3
Sør-Trøndelag N 198 B6
Nesbyen N 47 B6
Neset N 199 D7
Nesflaten N 52 A2
Nesjahverfi IS 191 C10
Neskaupstaður IS 191 B12
Nesland N 53 A3
Neslandsvatn N 53 B5
Nesle F 90 B2
Nesna N 195 D4
Nesoddtangen N 48 C2
Nesovice CZ 98 B1
Nesselwang D 108 B1
Nesslau CH 107 B4
Nessmersiel D 71 A4
Nesso I 120 B2
Nesterov UA 13 C5
Nestorio GR 182 C3
Nesttun N 46 B2
Nesvady SK 112 B2
Nesvatnstemmen N 53 B4
Nether Stowey GB 43 A3
Netland N 52 B2
Netolice CZ 96 B2
Netphen D 81 B4
Netstal CH 107 B4
Nettancourt F 91 C4
Nettetal D 80 A2
Nettlingen D 72 B3
Nettuno I 168 B2
Neualbenreuth D 95 B4
Neubeckum D 81 A4
Neubrandenburg D 74 A2
Neubruchhausen D 72 B1
Neubukow D 65 B4
Neuburg D 94 C3
Neuchâtel CH 106 C1
Neu Darchau D 73 A3
Neudau A 111 B3
Neudietendorf D 82 B2
Neudorf D 93 B4
Neuenbürg D 93 C4
Neuenburg D 71 A4
Neuendorf D 66 B2
Neuenhagen D 74 B2
Neuenhaus D 71 B3
Neuenkirchen
Niedersachsen D 71 B5
Niedersachsen D 72 A2
Nordrhein-Westfalen D 71 B4
Nordrhein-Westfalen D 81 B3
Neuenrade D 81 A3
Neuenwalde D 64 C1
Neuerburg D 92 A2
Neufahrn
Bayern D 95 C3
Bayern D 95 C4
Neuf-Brisach F 106 A2
Neufchâteau
B 92 B1
F 92 C1
Neufchâtel-en-Bray F 90 B1
Neufchâtel-sur-Aisne F 91 B4
Neuflize F 91 B4
Neugersdorf D 84 B2
Neuhardenberg D 74 B3
Neuharlingersiel D 71 A4
Neuhaus
Bayern D 95 B3
Bayern D 96 C1
Niedersachsen D 64 C2
Niedersachsen D 73 A3
Niedersachsen D 81 A5
Neuhaus a Rennweg D 82 B3
Neuhausen
CH 107 B3
D 83 B5
Neuhausen ob Eck D 107 B3
Neuhof
Bayern D 94 B2
Hessen D 82 B1
Neuhofen an der Krems A 110 A1
Neuillé-Pont-Pierre F 102 B2
Neuilly-en-Thelle F 90 B2
Neuilly-le-Réal F 104 C2
Neuilly-l'Évêque F 105 B4
Neuilly-St Front F 90 B3
Neu-Isenburg D 93 A4
Neukalen D 66 C1
Neu Kaliss D 73 A4
Neukirch D 84 A2
Neukirchen
A 109 A4
Hessen D 81 B5
Schleswig-Holstein D 64 B1
Neukirchen am Grossvenediger A 109 B3
Neukirchen bei Heiligen Blut D 95 B4
Neukloster D 65 C4
Neulengbach A 110 A2
Neulise F 117 B4
Neu Lübbenau D 74 B2
Neum BIH 139 C3
Neumagen D 92 B2
Neumarkt D 95 B3
Neumarkt am Wallersee A 109 B4
Neumarkt im Hausruckkreis A 109 A4
Neumarkt im Mühlkreis A 96 C2
Neumarkt im Steiermark A 110 B1
Neumarkt Sankt Veit D 95 C4
Neumünster D 64 B2
Neunburg vorm Wald D 95 B4
Neung-sur-Beuvron F 103 B3
Neunkirch
Luzern CH 106 B3
Schaffhausen CH 107 B3
Neunkirchen
A 111 B3
Nordrhein-Westfalen D 80 B3
Saarland D 92 B3
Neunkirchen am Brand D 94 B3
Neuötting D 95 C4
Neupetershain D 84 A2
Neuravensburg D 107 B4
Neureut D 93 B4
Neuruppin D 74 B1
Neusäss D 94 C2
Neusiedl A 111 B3
Neuss D 80 A2
Neussargues-Moissac F 116 B2
Neustadt
Bayern D 94 B2
Bayern D 95 B4
Bayern D 95 C3
Brandenburg D 73 B5
Hessen D 81 B5
Niedersachsen D 72 B2
Rheinland-Pfalz D 93 B4
Sachsen D 84 A2
Schleswig-Holstein D 65 B3
Thüringen D 82 B3
Thüringen D 83 B3
Neustadt-Glewe D 73 A4
Neustift im Stubaital A 108 B2
Neustrelitz D 74 A2
Neutal A 111 B3
Neutrebbin D 74 B3
Neu-Ulm D 94 C2
Neuves-Maisons F 92 C2
Neuvic
Corrèze F 116 B2
Dordogne F 129 A3
Neuville-aux-Bois F 103 A4
Neuville-de-Poitou F 115 B4
Neuville-les-Dames F 117 A5
Neuville-sur-Saône F 117 B4
Neuvy-le-Roi F 102 B2
Neuvy-Santour F 104 A2
Neuvy-St Sépulchre F 103 C3
Neuvy-sur-Barangeon F 103 B4
Neuwied D 80 B3
Neuzelle D 74 B3
Névache F 118 B3
Neveklov CZ 96 B2
Nevel RUS 9 D6
Neverfjord N 192 B7
Nevers F 104 C2
Nevesinje BIH 139 B4
Névez F 100 B2
Nevlunghavn N 53 B5
Nevşehir TR 23 B8
New Abbey GB 36 B3
New Aberdour GB 33 D4
New Alresford GB 44 B2
Newark-on-Trent GB 40 B3
Newbiggin-by-the-Sea GB 37 A5
Newbliss IRL 27 B3
Newborough GB 38 A2
Newbridge IRL 30 A2
Newbridge on Wye GB 39 B3
Newburgh
Aberdeenshire GB 33 D4
Fife GB 35 B4
Newbury GB 44 B2
Newby Bridge GB 36 B4
Newcastle GB 27 B5
Newcastle Emlyn GB 39 B2
Newcastleton GB 37 A4
Newcastle-under-Lyme GB 40 B1
Newcastle upon Tyne GB 37 B5
Newcastle West IRL 29 B2
Newchurch GB 39 B3
New Costessey GB 41 C5
New Cumnock GB 36 A2
Newent GB 39 C4
New Galloway GB 36 A2
Newham GB 45 B4
Newhaven GB 45 C4
Newington GB 45 B5
Newinn IRL 29 B4
Newlyn GB 42 B1
Newmachar GB 33 D4
Newmarket
Suffolk GB 45 A4
Western Isles GB 31 A2
IRL 29 B3
Newmarket-on-Fergus IRL 28 B3
New Mills GB 40 B2
New Milton GB 44 C2
New Pitsligo GB 33 D4
Newport
Isle of Wight GB 44 C2
Newport GB 39 C4
Pembrokeshire GB 39 B2
Telford & Wrekin GB 38 B4
Mayo IRL 28 A2
Tipperary IRL 29 B3
Newport-on-Tay GB 35 B5
Newport Pagnell GB 44 A3
Newquay GB 42 B1
New Quay GB 39 B2
New Radnor GB 39 B3
New Romney GB 45 C4
New Ross IRL 30 B2
Newry GB 27 B4
New Scone GB 35 B4
Newton Abbot GB 43 B3
Newton Arlosh GB 36 B3
Newton Aycliffe GB 37 B5
Newton Ferrers GB 42 B2
Newtonhill GB 33 D4
Newtonmore GB 32 D2
Newton Stewart GB 36 B2
Newtown
Herefordshire GB 39 B4
Powys GB 39 B3
Newtownabbey GB 27 B5
Newtownards GB 27 B5
Newtownbutler GB 27 B3
Newtown Cunningham IRL 27 B3
Newtownhamilton GB 27 B4
Newtownmountkennedy IRL 30 A2
Newtown St Boswells GB 35 C5
Newtown Sands IRL 29 B2
Newtownstewart GB 27 B3
Nexon F 115 C5
Neyland GB 39 C2
Nibbiano I 120 C2
Nibe DK 58 B2
Nicastro I 175 C2
Niccone I 135 B5
Nice F 133 B3
Nickelsdorf A 111 B4
Nicolosi I 177 B4
Nicosia
CY 181 A2
I 177 B3
Nicótera I 175 C1
Nidda D 81 B5
Niğde TR 23 C8
Nidzica PL 77 A5
Niebla E 161 B3
Nieborów PL 77 B5
Niebüll D 64 B1
Niechanowo PL 76 B2
Niechorze PL 67 B4
Niedalino PL 67 B5
Niederaula D 82 B1
Niederbipp CH 106 B2
Niederbronn-les-Bains F 93 C3
Niederfischbach D 81 B3
Niedergörsdorf D 74 C1
Niederkrüchten D 80 A2
Niederndorf A 108 B3
Nieder-Olm D 93 B4
Niedersachswerfen D 82 A2
Niederstetten D 94 B1
Niederurnen CH 107 B4
Niederwölz A 110 B1
Niedoradz PL 85 A3
Niedzica PL 99 B4
Niegosławice PL 85 A3
Nieheim D 81 A5
Niemcza PL 85 B4
Niemegk D 74 B1
Niemisel S 196 C5
Niemodlin PL 85 B5
Nienburg
Niedersachsen D 72 B2
Sachsen-Anhalt D 83 A3
Niepołomice PL 99 A4
Nierstein D 93 B4
Niesky D 84 A2
Niestronno PL 76 B2
Nieświń PL 87 A4
Nieszawa PL 76 B3
Nieul-le-Dolent F 114 B2
Nieul-sur-Mer F 114 B2
Nieuw-Amsterdam NL 71 B3
Nieuw-Buinen NL 71 B3
Nieuwegein NL 70 B2
Nieuwe Niedorp NL 70 B1
Nieuwe-Pekela NL 71 A3
Nieuwerkerken B 79 B5
Nieuwe-schans NL 71 A4
Nieuwolda NL 71 A3
Nieuwpoort B 78 A2
Nieuw-Weerdinge NL 71 B3
Nigrita GR 183 C5
Nigüelas E 163 B4
Níjar E 164 C2
Nijemci HR 125 B5
Nijkerk NL 70 B2
Nijlen B 79 A4
Nijmegen NL 80 A1
Nijverdal NL 71 B3
Nikel RUS 193 C14
Nikinci SRB 127 C1
Nikiti GR 183 C5
Nikitsch A 111 B3
Nikkaluokta S 196 B2
Nikla H 111 C4
Niklasdorf A 110 B2
Nikšić MNE 139 C4
Nilivaara S 196 B4
Nîmes F 131 B3
Nimis I 122 A2
Nimtofte DK 58 B3
Nin HR 137 A4
Nindorf D 64 B2
Ninemilehouse IRL 30 B1
Ninove B 79 B4
Niort F 114 B3
Niš SRB 16 D4
Nisa P 155 B3
Niscemi I 177 B3
Niskala FIN 197 D10
Nissafors S 60 B3
Nissan-lez-Ensérune F 130 B2
Nissedal N 53 A4
Nissumby DK 58 B1
Nisterud N 53 A5
Niton GB 44 C2
Nitra SK 98 C2
Nitrianske-Pravno SK 98 C2
Nitrianske Rudno SK 98 C2
Nitry F 104 B2
Nittedal N 48 B2
Nittenau D 95 B4
Nittendorf D 95 B3
Nivala FIN 3 E9
Nivelles B 79 B4
Nivnice CZ 98 C1
Nižná SK 99 B3
Nižná Boca SK 99 C3
Nižne Repaše SK 99 B4
Nizza Monferrato I 119 C5
Njarðvík IS 190 D3
Njegůsevo SRB 126 B1
Njivice HR 123 B3
Njurundabommen S 200 D3
Njutånger S 200 E3
Noailles F 90 B2
Noain E 144 B2
Noale I 121 B5
Noalejo E 163 A4
Noblejas E 151 C4
Noceda E 141 B4
Nocera Inferiore I 170 C2
Nocera Terinese I 175 B2
Nocera Umbra I 136 B1
Noceto I 120 C3
Noci I 173 B3
Nociglia I 173 B4
Nodeland N 53 B3
Nödinge S 60 B2
Nods F 105 B5
Noé F 146 A2
Noépoli I 174 A2
Noeux-les-Mines F 78 B2
Noez E 157 A3
Nogales E 155 C4
Nogara I 121 B4
Nogarejas E 141 B4
Nogaro F 128 C2
Nogent F 105 A4
Nogent l'Artaud F 90 C3
Nogent-le-Roi F 90 C1
Nogent-le-Rotrou F 89 B4
Nogent-sur-Seine F 91 C3
Nogent-sur-Vernisson F 103 B4
Nogersund S 63 B2
Noguera E 152 B2
Noguerones E 163 A3
Nohfelden D 92 B3
Nohn D 80 B2
Noia E 140 B2
Noicáttaro I 173 A2
Noirétable F 117 B3
Noirmoutier-en-l'Île F 114 A1
Noja E 143 A3
Nojewo PL 75 B5
Nokia FIN 8 B3
Nol S 60 B2
Nola I 170 C2
Nolay F 104 C3
Noli I 133 A4
Nolnyra S 51 B4
Nombela E 150 B3
Nomeny F 92 C2
Nomexy F 92 C2
Nonancourt F 89 B5
Nonant-le-Pin F 89 B4
Nonántola I 121 C4
Nonaspe E 153 A4
None I 119 C4
Nontron F 115 C4
Nonza F 180 A2
Noordhorn NL 71 A3
Noordwijk NL 70 B1
Noordwijkerhout NL 70 B1
Noordwolde NL 70 B3
Noppikoski S 50 A1
Nora S 55 A6
Nørager DK 58 B2
Norberg S 50 B2
Norboda S 51 B5
Nórcia I 136 C2
Nordagutu N 53 A5
Nordanås S 200 B4
Nordausques F 78 B2
Nordborg DK 64 A2
Nordby
Aarhus Amt. DK 59 C3
Ribe Amt. DK 59 C1
Norddeich D 71 A4
Norddorf D 64 B1
Norden D 71 A4
Nordenham D 72 A1
Norderhov N 48 B2
Norderney D 71 A4
Norderstapel D 64 B2
Norderstedt D 64 C3
Nordfjord N 193 B14
Nordfjordeid N 198 D3
Nordfold N 194 C6

Nordhalben D 82 B3
Nordhausen D 82 A2
Nordheim vor der Rhön D 82 B2
Nordholz D 64 C1
Nordhorn D 71 B4
Nordingrå S 200 D4
Nordkjosbotn N 192 C3
Nordli N 199 A10
Nördlingen D 94 C2
Nordmaling S 200 C5
Nordmark S 49 C6
Nordmela N 194 A6
Nord-Odal N 48 B3
Nordre Osen N 48 A3
Nordsinni N 48 B1
Nørdstedalsseter N 198 D4
Nordstemmen D 72 B2
Nordvågen N 193 B10
Nordwalde D 71 B4
Noreña E 142 A1
Noresund N 48 B1
Norg NL 71 A3
Norheimsund N 46 B3
Norie S 63 B2
Norma I 169 B2
Nornäs S 49 A5
Norrahammar S 62 A2
Norråker S 200 B1
Norrala S 51 A3
Norra Vi S 62 A3
Nørre Aaby DK 59 C2
Nørre Alslev DK 65 B4
Nørre Lyndelse DK 59 C3
Nørre Nebel DK 59 C1
Norrent-Fontes F 78 B2
Nørre Snede DK 59 C2
Nørresundby DK 58 A2
Nørre Vorupør DK 58 B1
Norrfjärden S 196 D4
Norrhed S 196 C3
Norrhult Klavreström S 62 A3
Norrköping S 56 B2
Norrskedika S 51 B5
Norrsundet S 51 B4
Norrtälje S 57 A4
Nors DK 58 A1
Norsbron S 55 A4
Norsholm S 56 B1
Norsjö S 200 B5
Nörten-Hardenberg D 82 A1
Northallerton GB 37 B5
Northampton GB 44 A3
North Berwick GB 35 B5
North Charlton GB 37 A5
Northeim D 82 A2
Northfleet GB 45 B4
North Frodingham GB 40 B3
North Kessock GB 32 D2
Northleach GB 44 B2
North Molton GB 42 A3
North Petherton GB 43 A3
Northpunds GB 33 B5
North Somercotes GB 41 B4
North Tawton GB 42 B3
North Thoresby GB 41 B3
North Walsham GB 41 C5
Northwich GB 38 A4
Norton GB 40 A3
Nortorf D 64 B2
Nort-sur-Erdre F 101 B4
Nörvenich D 80 B2
Norwich GB 41 C5
Norwick GB 33 A6
Nøsen N 47 B5
Nossa Senhora do Cabo P 154 C1
Nossebro S 55 B3
Nössemark S 54 A2
Nossen D 83 A5
Notaresco I 169 A3
Noto I 177 C4
Notodden N 53 A5
Nottingham GB 40 C2
Nottuln D 71 C4
Nouan-le-Fuzelier F 103 B4
Nouans-les-Fontaines F 103 B3
Nougaroulet F 129 C3
Nouvion F 78 B1
Nouzonville F 91 B4
Nova H 111 C3
Nová Baňa SK 98 C2
Nová Bystrica SK 99 B3
Nová Bystřice CZ 97 B3
Nova Crnja SRB 126 B2
Novafeltria I 135 B5
Nova Gorica SLO 122 B2
Nova Gradiška HR 124 B3
Nováky SK 98 C2
Novalaise F 118 B2
Novales E 145 B3
Nova Levante I 108 C2
Novalja HR 137 A3
Nová Paka CZ 84 B3
Nova Pazova SRB 127 C2
Nová Pec CZ 96 C1
Novara I 120 B1
Novara di Sicília I 177 A4
Nova Siri I 174 A2
Novate Mezzola I 120 A2
Nova Topola BIH 124 B3
Novaya Ladoga RUS 9 B8
Nova Zagora BG 17 D6
Nové Hrady CZ 96 C2
Novelda E 165 A4
Novellara I 121 C3
Nové Město SK 98 C1
Nové Město nad Metují CZ 85 B4
Nové Město na Moravě CZ 97 B4
Nové Město pod Smrkem CZ 84 B3
Nové Mitrovice CZ 96 B1
Noventa di Piave I 122 B1
Noventa Vicentina I 121 B4
Novés E 151 B3
Noves F 131 B3
Nové Sady SK 98 C1
Novés de Segre E 147 B2
Nové Strašeci CZ 84 B1
Nové Zámky SK 112 B2
Novgorod RUS 9 C7
Novi Bečej SRB 126 B2
Novi di Módena I 121 C3
Novigrad
Istarska HR 122 B2
Zadarsko-Kninska HR 137 A4
Novigrad Podravski HR 124 A2
Novi Kneževac SRB 126 A2
Novi Ligure I 120 C1
Noville B 92 A1
Novi Marof HR 124 A2
Novion-Porcien F 91 B4
Novi Pazar
BG 17 D7
SRB 16 D4
Novi Sad SRB 126 B1
Novi Slankamen SRB 126 B2
Novi Travnik BIH 139 A3
Novi Vinodolski HR 123 B3
Novohrad-Volynskyy UA 13 C7
Novo Mesto SLO 123 B4
Novo Miloševo SRB 126 B2
Novorzhev RUS 9 D6
Novo Selo BIH 125 B3
Novoselytsya UA 17 A7
Novosokolniki RUS 9 D6
Novoveská Huta SK 99 C4
Novovolynsk UA 13 C6
Novska HR 124 B2
Nový Bor CZ 84 B2
Nový Bydžov CZ 84 B3
Novy-Chevrières F 91 B4
Novy Dwór Mazowiecki PL 77 B5
Nový-Hrozenkov CZ 98 B2
Nový Jičín CZ 98 B2
Novy Knin CZ 96 B2
Nowa Cerekwia PL 86 B1
Nowa Dęba PL 87 B5
Nowa Karczma PL 68 A3
Nowa Kościoł PL 85 A3
Nowa Ruda PL 85 B4
Nowa Słupia PL 87 B5
Nowa Sól PL 85 A3
Nowa Wieś PL 69 B4
Nowa-Wieś Wielka PL 76 B3
Nowe PL 69 B3
Nowe Brzesko PL 87 B4
Nowe Grudze PL 77 B4
Nowe Kiejkuty PL 77 A6
Nowe Miasteczko PL 85 A3
Nowe Miasto
Mazowieckie PL 77 B5
Mazowieckie PL 87 A4
Nowe Miasto Lubawskie PL 69 B4
Nowe Miasto nad Wartą PL 76 B2
Nowe Skalmierzyce PL 86 A2
Nowe Warpno PL 74 A3
Nowica PL 69 A4
Nowogard PL 75 A4
Nowogród Bobrzanski PL 84 A3
Nowogrodziec PL 84 A3
Nowosolna PL 86 A3
Nowy Dwór Gdański PL 69 A4
Nowy Korczyn PL 87 B4
Nowy Sącz PL 99 B4
Nowy Staw PL 69 A4
Nowy Targ PL 99 B4
Nowy Tomyśl PL 75 B5
Nowy Wiśnicz PL 99 B4
Noyalo F 101 B3
Noyal-Pontivy F 100 A3
Noyant F 102 B2
Noyelles-sur-Mer F 78 B1
Noyen-sur-Sarthe F 102 B1
Noyers F 104 B2
Noyers-sur-Cher F 103 B3
Noyers-sur-Jabron F 132 A1
Noyon F 90 B2
Nozay F 101 B4
Nuaillé F 102 B1
Nuaillé-d'Aunis F 114 B3
Nuars F 104 B2
Nubledo E 141 A5
Nuéno E 145 B3
Nuestra Señora Sa Verge des Pilar E 166 C1
Nueva E 142 A2
Nueva Carteya E 163 A3
Nuevalos E 152 A2
Nuits F 104 B3
Nuits-St Georges F 105 B3
Nule I 178 B3
Nules E 159 B3
Nulvi I 178 B2
Numana I 136 B2
Numansdorp NL 79 A4
Nümbrecht D 81 B3
Nunchritz D 83 A5
Nuneaton GB 40 C2
Nunnanen FIN 196 A7
N Unnaryd S 60 B3
Nuñomoral E 149 B3
Nunspeet NL 70 B2
Nuorgam FIN 193 B11
Núoro I 178 B3
Nurallao I 179 C3
Nuremberg = Nürnberg D 94 B3
Nurmes FIN 3 E11
Nürnberg = Nuremberg D 94 B3
Nurri I 179 C3
Nürtingen D 94 C1
Nus I 119 B4
Nusnäs S 50 B1
Nusplingen D 107 A3
Nuštar HR 125 B4
Nuupas FIN 197 C9
Nyåker S 200 C5
Nyáregyháza H 112 B3
Nyarlörinc H 113 C3
Nyasvizh BY 13 B7
Nybble S 55 A5
Nybergsund N 49 A4
Nybøl DK 64 B2
Nyborg
DK 59 C3
S 196 D6
Nybro S 62 B3
Nybster GB 32 C3
Nyby DK 65 B5
Nye S 62 A3
Nyékládháza H 113 B4
Nyergesujfalu H 112 B2
Nyhammar S 50 B1
Nyhyttan S 55 A5
Nyirád H 111 B4
Nyirbátor H 16 B5
Nyíregyháza H 16 B4
Nyker DK 67 A3
Nykil S 56 B1
Nykirke N 48 B2
Nykøbing
Falster DK 65 B4
Vestsjællands Amt. DK 61 D1
Nykøbing Mors DK 58 B1
Nyköping S 56 B3
Nykroppa S 55 A5
Nykvarn S 56 A3
Nykyrke S 55 B5
Nyland S 200 C3
Nylars DK 67 A3
Nymburk CZ 84 B3
Nynäshamn S 57 B3
Nyon CH 118 A3
Nyons F 131 A4
Nýřany CZ 96 B1
Nýrsko CZ 95 B5
Nyrud N 193 C13
Nysa PL 85 B5
Nysäter S 55 A3
Nyseter N 198 C5
Nyskoga S 49 B4
Nysted DK 65 B4
Nystrand N 53 A5
Nyúl H 111 B4
Nyvoll N 192 B7

O

Oadby GB 40 C2
Oakengates GB 38 B4
Oakham GB 40 C3
Oanes N 52 B2
Obalj BIH 139 B4
Oban GB 34 B2
O Barco E 141 B4
Obbola S 200 C6
Obdach A 110 B1
Obejo E 156 B3
Oberammergau D 108 B2
Oberasbach D 94 B2
Oberau D 108 B2
Oberaudorf D 108 B3
Oberbruck F 106 B1
Oberdiessbach CH 106 C2
Oberdorf CH 106 B2
Oberdrauburg A 109 C3
Oberelsbach D 82 B2
Obere Stanz A 110 B2
Ober Grafendorf A 110 A2
Obergünzburg D 108 B1
Obergurgl A 108 C2
Oberhausen D 80 A2
Oberhof D 82 B2
Oberkirch D 93 C4
Oberkirchen D 81 A4
Oberkochen D 94 C2
Obermassfeld-Grimmenthal D 82 B2
Ober-Morlen D 81 B4
Obermünchen D 95 C3
Obernai F 93 C3
Obernberg A 96 C1
Obernburg D 93 B5
Oberndorf D 93 C4
Oberndorf bei Salzburg A 109 B3
Obernkirchen D 72 B2
Oberort A 110 B2
Oberpullendorf A 111 B3
Oberriet CH 107 B4
Oberröblingen D 82 A3
Oberrot D 94 B1
Oberstaufen D 107 B5
Oberstdorf D 107 B5
Obertauern A 109 B4
Obertilliach A 109 C3
Obertraubling D 95 C4
Obertraun A 109 B4
Obertrubach D 95 B3
Obertrum A 109 B4
Oberursel D 81 B4
Obervellach A 109 C4
Oberviechtach D 95 B4
Oberwart A 111 B3
Oberwesel D 93 A3
Oberwinter D 80 B3
Oberwölzstadt A 110 B1
Oberzell D 96 C1
Obice PL 87 B4
Óbidos P 154 B1
Obing D 109 B3
Objat F 129 A4
Objazda PL 68 A2
Öblarn A 109 B5
Obninsk RUS 9 E10
O Bolo E 141 B3
Oborniki PL 75 B5
Oborniki Śląskie PL 85 A4
Obornjača SRB 126 B1
Obrenovac SRB 127 C2
Obrež SRB 127 C1
Obrigheim D 93 B5
Obrov SLO 123 B3
Obrovac
HR 137 A4
SRB 126 B1
Obrovac Sinjski HR 138 B2
Obruk TR 23 B7
Obrzycko PL 75 B5
Obudovac BIH 125 C4
Ocaña E 151 C4
O Carballiño E 140 B2
Occhiobello I 121 C4
Occimiano I 119 B5
Očevlja BIH 139 A4
Ochagavía E 144 B2
Ochiltree GB 36 A2
Ochla PL 84 A3
Ochotnica-Dolna PL 99 B4
Ochotnica-Górna PL 99 B4
Ochsenfurt D 94 B2
Ochsenhausen D 107 A4
Ochtendung D 80 B3
Ochtrup D 71 B4
Ocieka PL 87 B5
Ockelbo S 50 B3
Öckerö S 60 B1
Ocniţa MD 17 A7
O Corgo E 141 B3
Očová SK 99 C3
Ócsa H 112 B3
Öcseny H 125 A4
Öcsöd H 113 C4
Octeville F 88 A2
Ocypel PL 69 B3
Ödåkra S 61 C2
Odby DK 58 B1
Odda N 46 B3
Odder DK 59 C3
Ödeborg S 54 B2
Odeceixe P 160 B1
Odechów PL 87 A5
Odeleite P 160 B2
Odemira P 160 B1
Ödemiş TR 188 A2
Ödensbacken S 56 A1
Odense DK 59 C3
Odensjö
Jönköping S 62 A2
Kronoberg S 60 C3
Oderberg D 74 B3
Oderzo I 122 B1
Odesa = Odessa UA 17 B9
Ödeshög S 55 B5
Odessa = Odesa UA 17 B9
Odiáxere P 160 B1
Odie GB 33 B4
Odiham GB 44 B3
Odintsovo RUS 9 E10
Odivelas P 160 A1
Odolanów PL 85 A5
Odón E 152 B2
Odorheiu Secuiesc RO 17 B6
Odrowaz PL 87 A4
Odry CZ 98 B1
Odrzywół PL 87 A4
Ødsted DK 59 C2
Odžaci SRB 126 B1
Odžak BIH 125 B4
Oebisfelde D 73 B3
Oederan D 83 B5
Oeding D 71 C3
Oegstgeest NL 70 B1
Oelde D 81 A4
Oelsnitz D 83 B4
Oer-Erkenschwick D 80 A3
Oerlinghausen D 72 C1
Oettingen D 94 C2
Oetz A 108 B1
Oeventrop D 81 A4
Offanengo I 120 B2
Offenbach D 81 B4
Offenburg D 93 C3
Offida I 136 C2
Offingen D 94 C2
Offranville F 89 A5
Ofte N 53 A4
Ofterschwang D 107 B5
Oggiono I 120 B2
Ogihares E 163 A4
Ogliastro Cilento I 170 C3
Ogliastro Marina I 170 C2
Ogmore-by-Sea GB 39 C3
Ogna N 52 B1
Ogre LV 8 D4
Ogrodzieniec PL 86 B3
Ogulin HR 123 B4
Ögur IS 190 A3
Ohanes E 164 B2
Ohey B 79 B5
Ohlstadt D 108 B2
Ohrdorf D 73 B3
Ohrdruf D 82 B2
Ohrid MK 182 B2
Öhringen D 94 B1
Oia E 140 B2
Oiã P 148 B1
Oiartzun E 144 A2
Oijärvi FIN 197 D8
Oilgate IRL 30 B2
Oimbra E 148 A2
Oiselay-et-Grachoux F 105 B4
Oisemont F 90 B1
Oisterwijk NL 79 A5
Öja S 57 C4
Öje S 49 B5
Ojén E 162 B3
Ojrzeń PL 77 B5
Ojuelos Altos E 156 B2
Okalewo PL 77 A4
Okány H 113 C5
Okehampton GB 42 B2
Oklaj HR 138 B2
Økneshamn N 194 B6
Okoč SK 111 B4
Okoličné SK 99 B3
Okonek PL 68 B1
Okonin PL 69 B3
Okřisky CZ 97 B3
Oksa PL 87 B4
Oksbøl DK 59 C1
Oksby DK 59 C1
Øksfjord N 192 B6
Øksna N 48 B3
Okučani HR 124 B3
Okulovka RUS 9 C8
Ólafsfjörður IS 191 A7
Ólafsvík IS 190 C2
ÖLagnö S 57 A4
Olagüe E 144 B2
Oland N 53 B4
Olargues F 130 B1
Oława PL 85 B5
Olazagutia E 144 B1
Olbernhau D 83 B5
Ólbia I 178 B3
Olching D 108 A2
Oldbury GB 43 A4
Oldcastle IRL 27 C3
Old Deer GB 33 D4
Oldeberkoop NL 70 B3
Oldeboorn NL 70 A2
Olden N 198 D3
Oldenbrok D 71 A5
Oldenburg
Niedersachsen D 71 A5
Schleswig-Holstein D 65 B3
Oldenzaal NL 71 B3
Olderdalen N 192 C4
Olderfjord N 193 B9
Oldersum D 71 A4
Oldervik N 192 C2
Oldham GB 40 B1
Oldisleben D 82 A3
Oldmeldrum GB 33 D4
Olea E 142 B2
Oleby S 49 B5
Olechów PL 87 A5
Oledo P 155 B3
Olèggio I 120 B1
Oleiros
Coruña E 140 A2
Coruña E 140 B1
P 154 B3
Oleksandriya UA 13 C7
Olen B 79 A4
Ølen N 52 A1
Olenegorsk RUS 3 B13
Olenino RUS 9 D8
Olesa de Montserrat E 147 C2
Oleśnica PL 85 A5
Olešnice CZ 97 B4
Olesno PL 86 B2
Oletta F 180 A2
Olette F 146 B3
Olevsk UA 13 C7
Olfen D 80 A3
Olgiate Comasco I 120 B1
Olginate I 120 B2
Ølgod DK 59 C1
Olgrinmore GB 32 C3
Olhão P 160 B2
Olhava FIN 197 D8
Olhavo P 154 B1
Oliana E 147 B2
Olias del Rey E 151 C4
Oliena I 178 B3
Oliete E 153 B3
Olimbos GR 188 D2
Olite E 144 B2
Oliva E 159 C3
Oliva de la Frontera E 155 C4
Oliva de Mérida E 156 B1
Oliva de Plasencia E 149 B3
Olivadi I 175 C2
Olival P 154 B2
Olivar E 163 B4
Olivares E 161 B3
Olivares de Duero E 142 C2
Olivares de Júcar E 158 B1
Oliveira de Azeméis P 148 B1
Oliveira de Frades P 148 B1
Oliveira do Conde P 148 B2
Oliveira do Douro P 148 A1
Oliveira do Hospital P 148 B2
Olivenza E 155 C3
Olivet F 103 B3
Olivone CH 107 C3
Öljehult S 63 B3
Olkusz PL 86 B3
Ollerton GB 40 B2
Ollerup DK 65 A3
Olliergues F 117 B3
Ölmbrotorp S 56 A1
Ölme S 55 A4
Olmedilla de Alarcón E 158 B1
Olmedillo de Roa E 143 C3
Olmedo
E 150 A3
I 178 B2
Olmeto F 180 B1
Olmillos de Castro E 149 A3
Olmos de Ojeda E 142 B2
Olney GB 44 A3
Ołobok PL 86 A2
Olocau del Rey E 153 B3
Olofström S 63 B2
Olomouc CZ 98 B1
Olonets RUS 9 B8
Olonne-sur-Mer F 114 B2
Olonzac F 130 B1
Oloron-Ste Marie F 145 A3
Olost E 147 C3
Olot E 147 B3
Olovo BIH 139 A4
Olpe D 81 A3
Olsberg D 81 A4
Olsene B 79 B3
Olserud S 55 A4
Olshammar S 55 B5
Olshanka UA 13 D9
Olszanica PL 85 A3
Olsztyn
Śląskie PL 86 B3
Warmińsko-Mazurskie PL 69 B5
Olsztynek PL 77 A5
Olszyna PL 84 A3
Olszyny PL 77 A6
Oltedal N 52 B2
Olten CH 106 B2
Olteniţa RO 17 C7
Olula del Rio E 164 B2
Ølve N 46 B2
Olvega E 144 C2
Olvera E 162 B2
Olympia GR 184 B2
Olzai I 178 B3
Omagh GB 27 B3
Omalos GR 185 D4
Omegna I 119 B5
Omiš HR 138 B2
Omišalj HR 123 B3
Ommen NL 71 B3
Omodhos CY 181 B1
Omoljica SRB 127 C2
On B 79 B5
Oña E 143 B3
Onano I 168 A1
O Näsberg S 49 B5
Oñati E 143 A4

St Jouin-de-Marnes F 102 C1
St Juéry F 130 B1
St Julien F 118 A2
St Julien-Chapteuil F 117 B4
St Julien-de-Vouvantes F 101 B4
St Julien-du-Sault F 104 A2
St Julien-du-Verdon F 132 B2
St Julien-en-Born F 128 B1
St Julien-en-Genevois F 118 A3
St Julien-l'Ars F 115 B4
St Julien la-Vêtre F 117 B3
St Julien-Mont-Denis F 118 B3
St Julien-sur-Reyssouze F 118 A2
St Junien F 115 C4
St Just
F 131 A3
GB 42 B1
St Just-en-Chaussée F 90 B2
St Just-en-Chevalet F 117 B3
St Justin F 128 C2
St Just-St Rambert F 117 B4
St Keverne GB 42 B1
St Lary-Soulan F 145 B4
St Laurent-d'Aigouze F 131 B3
St Laurent-de-Chamousset F 117 B4
St Laurent-de-Condel F 89 A3
St Laurent-de-la-Cabrerisse F 146 A3
St Laurent-de-la-Salanque F 146 B3
St Laurent-des-Autels F 101 B4
St Laurent-du-Pont F 118 B2
St Laurent-en-Caux F 89 A4
St Laurent-en-Grandvaux F 105 C4
St Laurent-Médoc F 128 A2
St Laurent-sur-Gorre F 115 C4
St Laurent-sur-Mer F 88 A3
St Laurent-sur-Sèvre F 114 B3
St Leger B 92 B1
St Léger-de-Vignes F 104 C2
St Léger-sous-Beuvray F 104 C3
St Léger-sur-Dheune F 104 C3
St Léonard-de-Noblat F 116 B1
St Leonards GB 45 C4
St Lô F 88 A2
St Lon-les-Mines F 128 C1
St Louis F 106 B2
St Loup F 117 A3
St Loup-de-la-Salle F 105 C3
St Loup-sur-Semouse F 105 B5
St Lunaire F 101 A3
St Lupicin F 118 A2
St Lyphard F 101 B3
St Lys F 146 A2
St Macaire F 128 B2
St Maclou F 89 A4
St Maixent-l'École F 115 B3
St Malo F 88 B1
St Mamet-la-Salvetat F 116 C2
St Mandrier-sur-Mer F 132 B1
St Marcel
Drôme F 117 C4
Saône-et-Loire F 105 C3
St Marcellin F 118 B2
St Marcellin sur Loire F 117 B4
St Marcet F 145 A4
St Mards-en-Othe F 104 A2
St Margaret's-at-Cliffe GB 45 B5
St Margaret's Hope GB 33 C4
St Mars-la-Jaille F 101 B4
St Martin-d'Ablois F 91 C3
St Martin-d'Auxigny F 103 B4
St Martin-de-Belleville F 118 B3
St Martin-de-Bossenay F 91 C3
St Martin-de-Crau F 131 B3
St Martin-de-Londres F 130 B2
St Martin-d'Entraunes F 132 A2
St Martin-de-Queyrières F 118 C3
St Martin-de-Ré F 114 B2
St Martin des Besaces F 88 A3
St Martin-d'Estreaux F 117 A3
St Martin-de-Valamas F 117 C4
St Martin-d'Hères F 118 B2
St Martin-du-Frêne F 118 A2
St Martin-en-Bresse F 105 C4
St Martin-en-Haut F 117 B4
St Martin-la-Méanne F 116 B1
St Martin-Osmonville F 90 B1
St Martin-sur-Ouanne F 104 B2
St Martin-Valmeroux F 116 B2
St Martin-Vésubie F 133 A3
St Martory F 145 A4
St Mary's GB 33 C4
St Mathieu F 115 C4
St Mathieu-de-Tréviers F 131 B2
St Maurice CH 119 A3
St Maurice-Navacelles F 130 B2
St Maurice-sur-Moselle F 106 B1
St Mawes GB 42 B1
St Maximin-la-Ste Baume F 132 B1
St Méard-de-Gurçon F 128 B3
St Médard-de-Guizières F 128 A2
St Médard-en-Jalles F 128 B2
St Méen-le-Grand F 101 A3
St Menges F 91 B4
St Merløse DK 61 D1
St Město CZ 85 B4
St M'Hervé F 101 A4
St Michel
Aisne F 91 B4
Gers F 145 A4
St Michel-Chef-Chef F 101 B3
St Michel-de-Castelnau F 128 B2
St Michel-de-Maurienne F 118 B3
St Michel-en-Grève F 100 A2
St Michel-enl'Herm F 114 B2
St Michel-Mont-Mercure F 114 B3
St Mihiel F 92 C1
St Monance GB 35 B5
St Montant F 131 A3
St Moritz CH 107 C4
St Nazaire F 101 B3
St Nazaire-en-Royans F 118 B2
St Nazaire-le-Désert F 131 A4
St Nectaire F 116 B2
St Neots GB 44 A3
St Nicolas-de-Port F 92 C2
St Nicolas-de-Redon F 101 B3
St Nicolas-du-Pélem F 100 A2
St Niklaas B 79 A4
St Omer F 78 B2
St Pair-sur-Mer F 88 B2
St Palais F 144 A2
St Palais-sur-Mer F 114 C2
St Pardoux-la-Rivière F 115 C4
St Paul-Cap-de-Joux F 129 C4
St Paul-de-Fenouillet F 146 B3
St Paul-de-Varax F 118 A2
St Paulien F 117 B3
St Paul-le-Jeune F 131 A3
St Paul-lès-Dax F 128 C1
St Paul-Trois-Châteaux F 131 A3
St Pé-de-Bigorre F 145 A3
St Pée-sur-Nivelle F 144 A2
St Péravy-la-Colombe F 103 B3
St Péray F 117 C4
St Père-en-Retz F 101 B3
St Peter Port GB 88 A1
St Petersburg = Sankt-Peterburg RUS 9 C7
St Philbert-de-Grand-Lieu F 114 A2
St Pierre F 130 B1
St Pierre-d'Albigny F 118 B3
St Pierre-d'Allevard F 118 B3
St Pierre-de-Chartreuse F 118 B2
St Pierre-de-Chignac F 129 A3
St Pierre-de-la-Fage F 130 B2
St Pierre-d'Entremont F 118 B2
St Pierre-d'Oléron F 114 C2
St Pierre-Eglise F 88 A2
St Pierre-en-Port F 89 A4
St Pierre-le-Moûtier F 104 C2
St Pierre Montlimart F 101 B4
St Pierre-Quiberon F 100 B2
St Pierre-sur-Dives F 89 A3
St Pierreville F 117 C4
St Pieters-Leeuw B 79 B4
St Plancard F 145 A4
St Poix F 101 B4
St Pol-de-Léon F 100 A2
St Polgues F 117 B3
St Pol-sur-Ternoise F 78 B2
St Pons-de-Thomières F 130 B1
St Porchaire F 114 C3
St Pourçain-sur-Sioule F 116 A3
St Priest F 117 B4
St Privat F 116 B2
St Quay-Portrieux F 100 A3
St Quentin F 90 B3
St Quentin-la-Poterie F 131 A3
St Quentin-les-Anges F 102 B1
St Rambert-d'Albon F 117 B4
St Rambert-en-Bugey F 118 B2
St Raphaël F 132 B2
St Rémy-de-Provence F 131 B3
St Rémy-du-Val F 89 B4
St Remy-en-Bouzemont F 91 C4
St Renan F 100 A1
St Révérien F 104 B2
St Riquier F 90 A1
St Romain-de-Colbosc F 89 A4
St Rome-de-Cernon F 130 A1
St Rome-de-Tarn F 130 A1
St Sadurní-d'Anoia E 147 C2
St Saëns F 89 A5
St Sampson GB 88 A1
St Samson-la-Poterie F 90 B1
St Saturnin-de-Lenne F 130 A2
St Saturnin-lès-Apt F 131 B4
St Sauflieu F 90 B2
St Saulge F 104 B2
St Sauveur
Finistère F 100 A2
Haute-Saône F 105 B5
St Sauveur-de-Montagut F 117 C4
St Sauveur-en-Puisaye F 104 B2
St Sauveur-en-Rue F 117 B4
St Sauveur-Lendelin F 88 A2
St Sauveur-le-Vicomte F 88 A2
St Sauveur-sur-Tinée F 132 A3
St Savin
Gironde F 128 A2
Vienne F 115 B4
St Savinien F 114 C3
St Savournin F 131 B4
St Seine-l'Abbaye F 105 B3
St Sernin-sur-Rance F 130 B1
St Sevan-sur-Mer F 88 B1
St Sever F 128 C2
St Sever-Calvados F 88 B2
St Sorlin-d'Arves F 118 B3
St Soupplets F 90 B2
St Sulpice F 129 C4
St Sulpice-Laurière F 116 A1
St Sulpice-les-Feuilles F 115 B5
St Symphorien F 128 B2
St Symphoriende-Lay F 117 B4
St Symphorien d'Ozon F 117 B4
St Symphoriensur-Coise F 117 B4
St Teath GB 42 B2
St Thégonnec F 100 A2
St Thiébault F 105 A4
St Trivier-de-Courtes F 118 A2
St Trivier sur-Moignans F 117 A4
St Trojan-les-Bains F 114 C2
St Tropez F 132 B2
St Truiden B 79 B5
St Vaast-la-Hougue F 88 A2
St Valérien F 104 A2
St Valery-en-Caux F 89 A4
St Valéry-sur-Somme F 78 B1
St Vallier
Drôme F 117 B4
Saône-et-Loire F 104 C3
St Vallier-de-Thiey F 132 B2
St Varent F 102 C1
St Vaury F 116 A1
St Venant F 78 B2
St Véran F 119 C3
St Vincent I 119 B4
St Vincent-de-Tyrosse F 128 C1
St Vit F 105 B4
St Vith B 80 B2
St Vivien-de-Médoc F 114 C2
St Yan F 117 A4
St Ybars F 146 A2
St Yorre F 117 A3
St Yrieix-la-Perche F 115 C5
Saissac F 146 A3
Saja E 142 A2
Sajan SRB 126 B2
Šajkaš SRB 126 B2
Sajókaza H 99 C4
Sajószentpéter H 113 A4
Sajóvámos H 113 A4
Sakarya TR 187 B5
Šakiai LT 13 A5
Sakskøbing DK 65 B4
Sakule SRB 126 B2
Sala S 50 C3
Šal'a SK 111 A4
Sala Baganza I 120 C3
Sala Consilina I 172 B1
Salakovac SRB 127 C3
Salamanca E 150 B2
Salamina GR 185 B4
Salandra I 172 B2
Salaparuta I 176 B1
Salar E 163 A3
Salardú E 145 B4
Salas E 141 A4
Salas de los Infantes E 143 B3
Salau F 146 B2
Salavaux CH 106 C2
Salbertrand I 119 B3
Salbohed S 50 C3
Salbris F 103 B4
Salbu N 46 A2
Salce E 141 B4
Salching D 95 C4
Salcombe GB 43 B3
Saldaña E 142 B2
Saldus LV 8 D3
Sale I 120 C1
Saleby S 55 B4
Salem D 107 B4
Salemi I 176 B1
Salen
Argyll & Bute GB 34 B2
Highland GB 34 B2
N 199 A8
Sälen S 49 A5
Salernes F 132 B2
Salerno I 170 C2
Salers F 116 B2
Salford GB 40 B1
Salgótarján H 113 A3
Salgueiro P 155 B3
Salhus N 46 B2
Sali HR 137 B4
Sálice Salentino I 173 B3
Salientes E 141 B4
Salies-de-Béarn F 144 A3
Salies-du-Salat F 145 A4
Salignac-Eyvigues F 129 B4
Saligney-sur-Roudon F 104 C2
Salihli TR 188 A3
Salihorsk BY 13 B7
Salinas
Alicante E 159 C3
Huesca E 145 B4
Salinas de Medinaceli E 152 A1
Salinas de Pisuerga E 142 B2
Salindres F 131 A3
Saline di Volterra I 135 B3
Salins-les-Bains F 105 C4
Salir P 160 B1
Salisbury GB 44 B2
Salla
A 110 B1
FIN 197 C11
Sallachy GB 32 C2
Sallanches F 118 B3
Sallent E 147 C2
Sallent de Gállego E 145 B3
Salles F 128 B2
Salles-Curan F 130 A1
Salles-sur-l'Hers F 146 A2
Sallins IRL 30 A2
Sällsjö S 199 B10
Salmerón E 152 B1
Salmiech F 130 A1
Salmivaara FIN 197 C11
Salmoral E 150 B2
Salo FIN 8 B3
Salò I 121 B3
Salobreña E 163 B4
Salon-de-Provence F 131 B4
Salonica = Thessaloniki GR 182 C4
Salonta RO 16 B4
Salorino E 155 B3
Salornay-sur-Guye F 104 C3
Salorno I 121 A4
Salou E 147 C2
Šalovci SLO 111 C3
Salsbruket N 199 A8
Salses-le-Chateau F 146 B3
Salsomaggiore Terme I 120 C2
Salt E 147 C3
Saltaire GB 40 B2
Saltara I 136 B1
Saltash GB 42 B2
Saltburn-by-the-Sea GB 37 B6
Saltcoats GB 34 C3
Saltfleet GB 41 B4
Salto P 148 A2
Saltrød N 53 B4
Saltsjöbaden S 57 A4
Saltvik
FIN 51 B7
S 62 A4
Saludécio I 136 B1
Salussola I 119 B5
Saluzzo I 119 C4
Salvacañete E 152 B2
Salvada P 160 B2
Salvagnac F 129 C4
Salvaleon E 155 C4
Salvaterra de Magos P 154 B2
Salvaterra do Extremo P 155 B4
Salvatierra
Avila E 143 B4
Badajoz E 155 C4
Salvatierra de Santiago E 156 A1
Salviac F 129 B4
Salzburg A 109 B4
Salzgitter D 72 B3
Salzgitter Bad D 72 B3
Salzhausen D 72 A3
Salzhemmendorf D 72 B2
Salzkotten D 81 A4
Salzmünde D 83 A3
Salzwedel D 73 B4
Samadet F 128 C2
Samandıra TR 186 B4
Samassi I 179 C2
Samatan F 146 A1
Sambiase I 175 C2
Sambir UA 13 D5
Samborowo PL 69 B4
Sambuca di Sicília I 176 B2
Samedan CH 107 C4
Samer F 78 B1
Sami GR 184 A1
Şamlı TR 186 C2
Sammichele di Bari I 173 B2
Samnaun CH 107 C5
Samobor HR 123 B4
Samoëns F 118 A3
Samogneux F 92 B1
Samokov BG 17 D5
Samora Correia P 154 C2
Šamorín SK 111 A4
Samos
E 141 B3
GR 188 B1
Samoš SRB 126 B2
Samothraki GR 183 C7
Samper de Calanda E 153 A3
Sampéyre I 133 A3
Sampieri I 177 C3
Sampigny F 92 C1
Samplawa PL 69 B4
Samproniano I 168 A1
Samtens D 66 B2
Samugheo I 179 C2
San Adrián E 144 B2
San Agustín E 164 C2
San Agustin de Guadalix E 151 B4
Sanaigmore GB 34 C1
San Alberto I 135 A5
San Amaro E 140 B2
Sânandrei RO 126 B3
San Andrês del Rabanedo E 142 B1
San Antanio di Santadi I 179 C2
San Antolín de Ibias E 141 A4
San Arcángelo I 174 A2
Sanary-sur-Mer F 132 B1
San Asensio E 143 B4
San Bartoloméde las Abiertas E 150 C3
San Bartoloméde la Torre E 161 B2
San Bartoloméde Pinares E 150 B3
San Bartolomeo in Galdo I 170 B3
San Benedetto del Tronto I 136 C2
San Benedetto in Alpe I 135 B4
San Benedetto Po I 121 B3
San Benito E 156 B3
San Benito de la Contienda E 155 C3
San Biágio Plátani I 176 B2
San Biágio Saracinisco I 169 B3
San Bonifacio I 121 B4
San Calixto E 156 C2
San Cándido I 109 C3
San Carlo
CH 119 A5
I 176 B2
San Carlos del Valle E 157 B4
San Casciano dei Bagni I 135 C4
San Casciano in Val di Pesa I 135 B4
San Cataldo
Puglia I 173 B4
Sicilia I 176 B2
San Cebrián de Castro E 149 A4
Sancergues F 104 B1
Sancerre F 103 B4
San Cesário di Lecce I 173 B4
Sancey-le-Long F 105 B5
Sanchiorian E 150 B3
San Chírico Raparo I 174 A2
Sanchonuño E 151 A3
San Cibrao das Viñas E 140 B3
San Cipirello I 176 B2
San Ciprián E 141 A3
San Clemente E 158 B1
San Clodio E 141 B3
Sancoins F 104 C1
San Colombano al Lambro I 120 B2
San Costanzo I 136 B2
San Crisóbal de Entreviñas E 142 B1
San Cristóbal de la Polantera E 141 B5
San Cristóbal de la Vega E 150 A3
San Cristovo E 141 C3
Sancti-Petri E 162 B1
Sancti-Spiritus E 149 B3
Sand
Hedmark N 48 B3
Rogaland N 52 A2
Sanda S 57 C4
San Damiano d'Asti I 119 C5
San Damiano Macra I 133 A3
Sandane N 198 D3
San Daniele del Friuli I 122 A2
Sandanski BG 183 B5
Sandared S 60 B2
Sandarne S 51 A4
Sandau D 73 B5
Sandbach
D 96 C1
GB 38 A4
Sandbank GB 34 C3
Sandbanks GB 43 B5
Sandbukt N 192 C5
Sandby DK 65 B4
Sande
D 71 A5
Sogn og Fjordane N 46 A2
Vestfold N 54 A1
Sandefjord N 54 A1
Sandeid N 52 A1
San Demétrio Corone I 174 B2
San Demétrio né Vestini I 169 A3
Sandersleben D 82 A3
Sanderstølen N 47 B6
Sandes N 53 B3
Sandesneben D 65 C3
Sandhead GB 36 B2
Sandhem S 60 B3
Sandhorst D 71 A4
Sandhurst GB 44 B3
Sandıklı TR 189 A5
Sandillon F 103 B4
Sandl A 96 C2

Sjøli N 48 A3
Sjølstad N 199 A9
Sjölunda S 56 A1
Sjømarken S 60 B2
Sjørring DK 58 B1
Sjötofta S 60 B3
Sjötorp S 55 B4
Sjoutnäset S 199 A11
Sjøvegan N 194 B8
Sjuntorp S 54 B3
Skåbu N 47 A6
Skafså N 53 A4
Skaftafell IS 191 D9
Skagaströnd IS 190 B5
Skagen DK 58 A3
Skagersvik S 55 B5
Skaiå N 53 B3
Skaidi N 193 B8
Skala GR 184 A1
Skała PL 87 B3
Skaland N 194 A8
Skala Oropou GR 185 A4
Skala-Podilska UA 13 D7
Skalat UA 13 D6
Skalbmierz PL 87 B4
Skålevik N 53 B4
Skalica SK 98 C1
Skalité SK 98 B2
Skällinge S 60 B2
Skalná CZ 83 B4
Skals DK 58 B2
Skælskør DK 65 A4
Skalstugan S 199 B9
Skanderborg DK 59 B2
Skånes-Fagerhult S 61 C3
Skåne-Tranås S 61 D3
Skånevik N 52 A1
Skänninge S 55 B6
Skanör med Falsterbo S 66 A1
Skåpafors S 54 A3
Skąpe PL 75 B4
Skara S 55 B4
Skærbæk DK 64 A1
Skarberget N 194 B7
Skärblacka S 56 B1
Skarð IS 190 B3
Skarda S 200 B4
Skare N 46 C3
Skåre S 55 A4
Skärhamn S 60 B1
Skarnes N 48 B3
Skärplinge S 51 B4
Skarpnatö FIN 51 B6
Skarp Salling DK 58 B2
Skarrild DK 59 C1
Skarstad N 194 B7
Skärstad S 62 A2
Skarsvåg N 193 A9
Skarszewy PL 69 A3
Skårup DK 65 A3
Skärvången S 199 B11
Skarvsjöby S 195 F8
Skaryszew PL 87 A5
Skarżysko-Kamienna PL 87 A4
Skarzysko Ksiazece PL 87 A4
Skatøy N 53 B5
Skattkärr S 55 A4
Skattungbyn S 50 A1
Skatval N 199 B7
Skaulo S 196 B4
Skave DK 59 B1
Skawina PL 99 B3
Skebobruk S 51 C5
Skebokvarn S 56 A2
Skedala S 61 C2
Skedevi S 56 B1
Skedsmokorset N 48 B3
Skee S 54 B2
Skegness GB 41 B4
Skei N 46 A3
Skela SRB 127 C2
Skelani BIH 127 D1
Skellefteå S 2 D7
Skelleftehamn S 2 D7
Skelmersdale GB 38 A4
Skelmorlie GB 34 C3
Skelund DK 58 B3
Skender Vakuf BIH 138 A3
Skene S 60 B2
Skępe PL 77 B4
Skepplanda S 60 B2
Skeppshult S 60 B3
Skerries IRL 30 A2
Ski N 54 A1
Skiathos GR 183 D5
Skibbereen IRL 29 C2
Skibotn N 192 C4
Skidra GR 182 C4
Skien N 53 A5
Skierniewice PL 77 C5
Skillingaryd S 60 B4
Skillinge S 63 C2
Skillingmark S 49 C4
Skilloura CY 181 A2
Skinnardai S 57 A4
Skinnskatteberg S 50 C2
Skipmannvik N 195 C6
Skipness GB 34 C2
Skipsea GB 41 B3
Skipton GB 40 B1
Skiptvet N 54 A2
Skiros GR 183 E6
Skivarp S 66 A2
Skive DK 58 B2
Skjånes N 193 B12
Skjærhalden N 54 A2
Skjeberg N 54 A2
Skjeggedal N 46 B3
Skjeljanger N 46 B1
Skjeljavik N 46 C2
Skjern DK 59 C1
Skjervøy N 192 B4
Skjold
Rogaland N 52 A1
Troms N 192 C3
Skjoldastraumen N 52 A1
Skjolden N 47 A4
Skjønhaug N 54 A2
Skjøtningsberg N 193 A11
Škocjan SLO 123 B4
Skoczów PL 98 B2
Skodborg DK 59 C2
Škofja Loka SLO 123 A3
Škofljica SLO 123 B3
Skog S 51 A3
Skoganvarre N 193 C9
Skogen S 54 A3
Skogfoss N 193 C13
Skoghall S 55 A4
Skogly N 193 C13
Skogn N 199 B8
Skognes N 192 C3
Skogstorp
Halland S 60 C2
Södermanland S 56 A2
Skoki PL 76 B2
Skokloster S 57 A3
Sköldinge S 56 A2
Skole UA 13 D5
Skollenborg N 53 A5
Sköllersta S 56 A1
Skomlin PL 86 A2
Skonseng N 195 D5
Skopelos GR 183 D5
Skopje MK 182 A3
Skoppum N 54 A1
Skórcz PL 69 B3
Skorogoszcz PL 86 B1
Skoroszów PL 85 A5
Skorovatn N 199 A10
Skorped S 200 C3
Skørping DK 58 B2
Skotfoss N 53 A5
Skotniki PL 87 A3
Skotselv N 48 C1
Skotterud N 49 C4
Skottorp S 61 C2
Skovby DK 64 B2
Skövde S 55 B4
Skovsgård DK 58 A2
Skrad HR 123 B3
Skradin HR 138 B1
Skradnik HR 123 B4
Skråmestø N 46 B1
Škrdlovice CZ 97 B3
Skrea S 60 C2
Skreia N 48 B2
Skrolsvik N 194 A7
Skruv S 63 B3
Skrwilno PL 77 A4
Skrydstrup DK 59 C2
Skucani BIH 138 B2
Skudeneshavn N 52 A1
Skui N 48 C2
Skulsk PL 76 B3
Skultorp S 55 B4
Skultuna S 56 A2
Skuodas LT 8 D2
Skurup S 66 A2
Skute N 48 B2
Skuteč CZ 97 B3
Skutskär S 51 B4
Skutvik N 194 B6
Skvyra UA 13 D8
Skwierzyna PL 75 B4
Skýcov SK 98 C2
Skyllberg S 55 B5
Skyttmon S 200 C1
Skyttorp S 51 B4
Sládkovičovo SK 111 A4
Slagelse DK 61 D1
Slagharen NL 71 B3
Slagnäs S 195 E9
Slaidburn GB 40 B1
Slane IRL 30 A2
Slangerup DK 61 D2
Slano HR 139 C3
Slantsy RUS 8 C6
Slaný CZ 84 B2
Slap SLO 122 A2
Šlapanice CZ 97 B4
Slåstad N 48 B3
Slatina
BIH 139 B3
HR 125 B3
RO 17 C6
Slatiňany CZ 97 B3
Slatinice CZ 98 B1
Slättberg S 50 A1
Slattum N 48 C2
Slavičin CZ 98 B1
Slavkov CZ 98 C1
Slavkovica SRB 127 C2
Slavkov u Brna CZ 97 B4
Slavonice CZ 97 C3
Slavonski Brod HR 125 B4
Slavonski Kobas HR 125 B3
Slavŏsovce SK 99 C4
Slavskoye RUS 69 A5
Slavuta UA 13 C7
Sława
Lubuskie PL 85 A4
Sława *continued*
Zachodnio-Pomorskie PL 67 C4
Slawharad BY 13 B9
Sławków PL 86 B3
Sławno
Wielkopolskie PL 76 B2
Zachodnio-Pomorskie PL 68 A1
Sławoborze PL 67 C4
Sl'ažany SK 98 C2
Sleaford GB 40 C3
Sleðbrjótur IS 191 B11
Sledmere GB 40 A3
Sleights GB 37 B6
Slemmestad N 54 A1
Ślesin PL 76 B3
Sliač SK 99 C3
Sliema M 175 C3
Sligo IRL 26 B2
Slite S 57 C4
Slitu N 54 A2
Sliven BG 17 D7
Śliwice PL 68 B3
Slobozia RO 17 C7
Slochteren NL 71 A3
Slöinge S 60 C2
Słomniki PL 87 B4
Slonim BY 13 B6
Słońsk PL 75 B3
Slootdorp NL 70 B1
Slottsbron S 55 A4
Slough GB 44 B3
Slövag N 46 B2
Slovenj Gradec SLO 110 C2
Slovenska Bistrica SLO 123 A4
Slovenská L'upča SK 99 C3
Slovenská-Ves SK 99 B4
Slovenské Darmoty SK 112 A3
Slovenske Konjice SLO 123 A4
Słubice PL 74 B3
Sluderno I 108 C1
Sluis NL 78 A3
Šluknov CZ 84 A2
Slunj HR 123 B4
Słupca PL 76 B2
Słupia PL 87 A3
Słupiec PL 85 B4
Słupsk PL 68 A2
Slutsk BY 13 B7
Smålandsstenar S 60 B3
Smalåsen N 195 E4
Smardzewo PL 75 B4
Smarhon BY 13 A7
Smarje SLO 123 A4
Šmarjeta SLO 123 B4
Šmartno SLO 123 A3
Smečno CZ 84 B2
Smedby S 63 B4
Smědec CZ 96 C2
Smederevo SRB 127 C2
Smederevska Palanka SRB 127 C2
Smedjebacken S 50 B2
Smęgorzów PL 87 B5
Smeland N 53 B4
Smidary CZ 84 B3
Śmigiel PL 75 B5
Smilde NL 71 B3
Smiřice CZ 85 B3
Smithfield GB 36 B4
Śmitowo PL 75 A5
Smögen S 54 B2
Smogulec PL 76 A2
Smołdzino PL 68 A2
Smolenice SK 98 C1
Smolensk RUS 13 A10
Smolník SK 99 C4
Smolyan BG 183 B6
Smuka SLO 123 B3
Smygehamn S 66 A2
Smykow PL 87 A4
Snainton GB 40 A3
Snaith GB 40 B2
Snaptun DK 59 C3
Snarby N 192 C3
Snarum N 48 B1
Snåsa N 199 A9
Snedsted DK 58 B1
Sneek NL 70 A2
Sneem IRL 29 C2
Snejbjerg DK 59 B1
Snillfjord N 198 B6
Šnjegotina BIH 125 C3
Snøde DK 65 A3
Snøfjord N 193 B8
Snogebaek DK 67 A4
Snyatyn UA 13 D6
Soave I 121 B4
Sober E 140 B3
Sobernheim D 93 B3
Soběslav CZ 96 B2
Sobota
Dolnośląskie PL 85 A3
Łódzkie PL 77 B4
Sobotište SK 98 C1
Sobotka CZ 84 B3
Sobótka
Dolnośląskie PL 85 B4
Wielkopolskie PL 86 A1
Sobra HR 139 C3
Sobrado
Coruña E 140 A2
Sobrado *continued*
Lugo E 141 B3
Sobral da Adica P 161 A2
Sobral de Monte Agraço P 154 C1
Sobreira Formosa P 154 B3
Søby DK 64 B3
Soca SLO 122 A2
Sochaczew PL 77 B5
Sochos GR 183 C5
Socodor RO 113 C5
Socol RO 127 C3
Socovos E 164 A3
Socuéllamos E 158 B1
Sodankylä FIN 197 B9
Soderåkra S 63 B4
Söderala S 51 A3
Söderås S 50 B2
Söderbärke S 50 B2
Söderby-Karl S 51 C5
Söderfors S 51 B4
Söderhamn S 51 A4
Söderköping S 56 B2
Söderö S 56 B1
Södertälje S 57 A3
Södingberg A 110 B2
Södra Finnö S 56 B2
Södra Ny S 55 A4
Södra Råda S 55 A5
Södra Sandby S 61 D3
Södra Vi S 62 A3
Sodražica SLO 123 B3
Sodupe E 143 A3
Soengas P 148 A1
Soest
D 81 A4
NL 70 B2
Sofades GR 182 D4
Sofia BG 17 D5
Sofikon GR 184 B4
Şofronea RO 126 A3
Sögel D 71 B4
Sogliano al Rubicone I 135 A5
Sogndalsfjøra N 46 A4
Søgne N 53 B3
Sögütköy TR 188 C3
Soham GB 45 A4
Sohland D 84 A2
Sohren D 93 B3
Soignies B 79 B4
Soissons F 90 B3
Söjtör H 111 C3
Sokal' UA 13 C6
Söke TR 188 B2
Sokna N 48 B1
Sokndal N 52 B2
Soknedal N 199 C7
Soko BIH 125 C4
Sokolac BIH 139 B4
Sokółka PL 13 B5
Sokolov CZ 83 B4
Sokołowo PL 76 B3
Sokołów Podlaski PL 12 B5
Sola N 52 B1
Solana de los Barros E 155 C4
Solana del Pino E 157 B3
Solánas I 179 C3
Solares E 143 A3
Solarino I 177 B4
Solarussa I 179 C2
Solas GB 31 B1
Solberg S 200 C3
Solberga S 62 A2
Solber-gelva N 53 A6
Solbjørg N 46 B2
Solčany SK 98 C2
Solčava SLO 123 A3
Solda I 108 C1
Sölden A 108 C2
Solec Kujawski PL 76 A3
Soleils F 132 B2
Solenzara F 180 B2
Solera E 163 A4
Solesmes F 79 B3
Soleto I 173 B4
Solgne F 92 C2
Solheim N 46 B2
Solheimsvik N 52 A2
Solignac F 115 C5
Solihull GB 44 A2
Solin HR 138 B2
Solingen D 80 A3
Solivella E 147 C2
Solkan SLO 122 B2
Söll A 108 B3
Sollana E 159 B3
Sollebrunn S 54 B3
Sollefteå S 200 C3
Sollenau A 111 B3
Sollen-tuna S 57 A3
Sóller E 166 B2
Sollerön S 50 B1
Søllested DK 65 B4
Solliès-Pont F 132 B2
Sollihøgda N 48 C2
Solnechnogorsk RUS 9 D10
Solnice CZ 85 B4
Solofra I 170 C2
Solomiac F 129 C3
Solopaca I 170 B2
Solórzano E 143 A3
Solothurn CH 106 B2
Solre-le-Château F 79 B4
Solsona E 147 C2
Solsvik N 46 B1
Solt H 112 C3
Soltau D 72 B2
Soltsy RUS 9 C7
Soltszentimre H 112 C3
Soltvadkert H 112 C3
Solumsmoen N 48 C1
Solund N 46 A1
Solva GB 39 C1
Sölvesborg S 63 B2
Solymár H 112 B2
Soma TR 186 C2
Somain F 78 B3
Somberek H 125 A4
Sombernon F 104 B3
Sombor SRB 125 B5
Sombreffe B 79 B4
Someren NL 80 A1
Somero FIN 8 B3
Somersham GB 44 A3
Somerton GB 43 A4
Sominy PL 68 A2
Somma Lombardo I 120 B1
Sommariva del Bosco I 119 C4
Sommarøy N 192 C2
Sommarset N 194 C6
Sommatino I 176 B2
Sommeilles F 91 C4
Sommen S 55 B5
Sommepy-Tahure F 91 B4
Sömmerda D 82 A3
Sommerfeld D 74 B2
Sommersted DK 59 C2
Sommesous F 91 C4
Somme-Tourbe F 91 B4
Sommières F 131 B3
Sommières-du-Clain F 115 B4
Somo E 143 A3
Somogyfajsz H 111 C4
Somogyjád H 111 C4
Somogysámson H 111 C4
Somogysárd H 125 A3
Somogyszil H 112 C2
Somogyszob H 124 A3
Somogyvár H 111 C4
Somontin E 164 B2
Somosiero E 151 A4
Somosköújifalu H 113 A3
Sompolno PL 76 B3
Sompuis F 91 C4
Son N 54 A1
Son Bou E 167 B4
Sonceboz CH 106 B2
Soncillo E 143 B3
Soncino I 120 B2
Sóndalo I 120 A3
Søndeled N 53 B5
Sønder Bjert DK 59 C2
Sønderborg DK 64 B2
Sønderby DK 64 B2
Sønder Felding DK 59 C1
Sønderho DK 59 C1
Sønder Hygum DK 59 C1
Sønder Omme DK 59 C1
Sondershausen D 82 A2
Søndersø DK 59 C3
Søndervig DK 59 B1
Søndre Enningdal Kappel N 54 B2
Sóndrio I 120 A2
Soneja E 159 B3
Son en Breugel NL 80 A1
Songe N 53 B5
Songeons F 90 B1
Sonkamuotka FIN 196 A6
Sonkovo RUS 9 D10
Sönnarslöv S 61 D4
Sonneberg D 82 B3
Sonnefeld D 82 B3
Sonnewalde D 84 A1
Sonnino I 169 B3
Sonogno CH 120 A1
Sonsbeck D 80 A2
Sonseca E 157 A4
Son Servera E 167 B3
Sønsterud N 49 B4
Sonstorp S 56 B1
Sonta SRB 125 B5
Sontheim D 94 C2
Sonthofen D 107 B5
Sontra D 82 A1
Sopelana E 143 A4
Sopje HR 125 B3
Šoporňa SK 111 A4
Sopot
PL 69 A3
SRB 127 C2
Sopotnica MK 182 B3
Sopron H 111 B3
Šor SRB 127 C1
Sora I 169 B3
Soragna I 120 C3
Soråker S 200 D3
Sorano I 168 A1
Sorbara I 121 C4
Sorbas E 164 B2
Sórbolo I 121 C3
Sörbygden S 200 D2
Sordal N 52 B3
Sordale GB 32 C3
Sore F 128 B2
Sörenberg CH 106 C3
Soresina I 120 B2
Sorèze F 146 A3
Sörforsa S 200 E3
Sorges F 115 C4
Sórgono I 179 B3
Sorgues F 131 A3
Sorgun TR 23 B8
Soria E 143 C4
Soriano Cálabro I 175 C2
Soriano nel Cimino I 168 A2
Sorihuela del Guadalimar E 164 A1
Sorisdale GB 34 B1
Sørkjosen N 192 C4
Sørli N 199 A10
Sormás H 111 C3
Sörmjöle S 200 C6
Sørmo N 194 B9
Sornac F 116 B2
Sorø DK 61 D1
Soroca MD 17 A8
Sørreisa N 194 A9
Sorrento I 170 C2
Sorsele S 195 E8
Sörsjön S 49 A5
Sorso I 178 B2
Sort E 146 B2
Sortavala RUS 9 B7
Sortino I 177 B4
Sortland N 194 B6
Sørum N 48 B2
Sørumsand N 48 C3
Sorunda S 57 A3
Sörup D 64 B2
Sørvågen N 194 C3
Sørvær N 192 B6
Sorvik S 50 B2
Sørvika N 199 C8
Sos F 128 B3
Sösdala S 61 C3
Sos del Rey Católico E 144 B2
Sošice HR 123 B4
Sośnica PL 75 A5
Sośnicowice PL 86 B2
Sośno PL 76 A2
Sosnovyy Bor RUS 9 C6
Sosnowiec PL 86 B3
Sospel F 133 B3
Šoštanj SLO 123 A4
Sotaseter N 198 D4
Sotillo de Adrada E 150 B3
Sotillo de la Ribera E 143 C3
Sotin HR 125 B5
Sotkamo FIN 3 D11
Sotobañado y Priorato E 142 B2
Soto de la Marina E 143 A3
Soto del Barco E 141 A4
Soto de los Infantes E 141 A4
Soto de Real E 151 B4
Soto de Ribera E 141 A5
Sotoserrano E 149 B3
Soto y Amío E 141 B5
Sotresgudo E 142 B2
Sotrondio E 142 A1
Sotta F 180 B2
Sottomarina I 122 B1
Sottrum D 72 A2
Sottunga FIN 51 B7
Sotuelamos E 158 B1
Souain F 91 B4
Soual F 146 A3
Soucy F 104 A2
Souda GR 185 D5
Soudron F 91 C4
Souesmes F 103 B4
Soufflenheim F 93 C3
Soufli GR 186 A1
Souillac F 129 B4
Souilly F 91 B5
Soulac-sur-Mer F 114 C2
Soulaines-Dhuys F 91 C4
Soulatgé F 146 B3
Soultz-Haut-Rhin F 106 B2
Soultz-sous-Forêts F 93 C3
Soumagne B 80 B1
Soumoulou F 145 A3
Souppes-sur-Loing F 103 A4
Souprosse F 128 C2
Sourdeval F 88 B3
Soure P 154 A2
Sournia F 146 B3
Souro Pires P 149 B2
Sourpi GR 182 D4
Sours F 90 C1
Sousceyrac F 116 C2
Sousel P 155 C3
Soustons F 128 C1
Söğüt
Bilecik TR 187 B5
Burdur TR 189 B4
Soutelo de Montes E 140 B2
Southam GB 44 A2
Southampton GB 44 C2
Southborough GB 45 B4
South Brent GB 42 B3
South Cave GB 40 B3
Southend GB 34 C2

Southend-on-Sea GB 45 B4
South Hayling GB 44 C3
South Molton GB 42 A3
South Ockendon GB 45 B4
South Petherton GB 43 B4
Southport GB 38 A3
South Shields GB 37 B5
South Tawton GB 42 B3
Southwell GB 40 B3
Southwold GB 45 A5
South Woodham Ferrers GB 45 B4
Söğütlu TR 187 B5
Souto P 148 B2
Soutochao E 141 C3
Souto da Carpalhosa P 154 B2
Souvigny F 104 C2
Souzay-Champigny F 102 B1
Soverato I 175 C2
Soveria Mannelli I 175 B2
Sövestad S 66 A2
Sovetsk RUS 12 A4
Sovići BIH 138 B3
Sovicille I 135 B4
Søvik N 198 C3
Sowerby GB 37 B5
Soyaux F 115 C4
Sozopol BG 17 D7
Spa B 80 B1
Spadafora I 177 A4
Spaichingen D 107 A3
Spakenburg NL 70 B2
Spalding GB 41 C3
Spálené Poříčí CZ 96 B1
Spalt D 94 B2
Spangenberg D 82 A1
Spangereid N 52 B3
Spantekow D 74 A2
Sparanise I 170 B2
Sparbu N 199 B8
Sparkær DK 58 B2
Sparkford GB 43 A4
Sparreholm S 56 A2
Sparta = Sparti GR 184 B3
Spartà I 177 A4
Sparti = Sparta GR 184 B3
Spean Bridge GB 34 B3
Speicher D 92 B2
Speichersdorf D 95 B3
Speke GB 38 A4
Spello I 136 C1
Spenge D 72 B1
Spennymoor GB 37 B5
Spentrup DK 58 B3
Sperenberg D 74 B2
Sperlinga I 177 B3
Sperlonga I 169 B3
Spetalen N 54 A1
Spetses GR 184 B4
Speyer D 93 B4
Spézet F 100 A2
Spezzano Albanese I 174 B2
Spezzano della Sila I 174 B2
Spiddle IRL 28 A2
Spiegelau D 96 C1
Spiekeroog D 71 A4
Spiez CH 106 C2
Spigno Monferrato I 133 A4
Spijk NL 71 A3
Spijkenisse NL 79 A4
Spilamberto I 135 A4
Spili GR 185 D5
Spilimbergo I 122 A1
Spilsby GB 41 B4
Spinazzola I 172 B2
Spincourt F 92 B1
Spind N 52 B2
Spindleruv-Mlyn CZ 84 B3
Spinoso I 174 A1
Špišić Bukovica HR 124 B3
Spišská Belá SK 99 B4
Spišská Nová Ves SK 99 C4
Spisská Stará Ves SK 99 B4
Spišské-Hanušovce SK 99 B4
Spišské Podhradie SK 99 C4
Spišské Vlachy SK 99 C4
Spišský-Štvrtok SK 99 C4
Spital A 110 B1
Spital am Semmering A 110 B2
Spittal an der Drau A 109 C4
Spittle of Glenshee GB 35 B4
Spitz A 97 C3
Spjald DK 59 B1
Spjærøy N 54 A1
Spjelkavik N 198 C3
Spjutsbygd S 63 B3
Split HR 138 B2
Splügen CH 107 C4
Spodsbjerg DK 65 B3
Spofforth GB 40 B2
Spohle D 71 A5
Spoleto I 136 C1
Spoltore I 169 A4
Spondigna I 108 C1
Sponvika N 54 A2
Spornitz D 73 A4
Spotorno I 133 A4
Spraitbach D 94 C1
Sprakensehl D 72 B3
Spręcowo PL 69 B5
Spremberg D 84 A2
Spresiano I 122 B1
Sprimont B 80 B1
Springe D 72 B2
Sproatley GB 41 B3
Spydeberg N 54 A2
Spytkowice PL 99 B3
Squillace I 175 C2
Squinzano I 173 B4
Sračinec HR 124 A2
Srbac BIH 124 B3
Srbobran SRB 126 B1
Srebrenica BIH 127 C1
Srebrenik BIH 125 C4
Sredets BG 17 D7
Središče SLO 124 A2
Śrem PL 76 B2
Sremska Mitrovica SRB 127 C1
Sremski Karlovci SRB 126 B1
Srní CZ 96 B1
Srnice Gornje BIH 125 C4
Srock PL 86 A3
Środa Śląska PL 85 A4
Środa Wielkopolski PL 76 B2
Srpska Crnja SRB 126 B2
Srpski Itebej SRB 126 B2
Srpski Miletić SRB 125 B5
Staatz A 97 C4
Stabbursnes N 193 B8
Staberdorf D 65 B4
Stabroek B 79 A4
Stachy CZ 96 B1
Staðarfell IS 190 B3
Stade D 72 A2
Staden B 78 B3
Stadl an der Mur A 109 B4
Stadskanaal NL 71 B3
Stadtallendorf D 81 B5
Stadthagen D 72 B2
Stadtilm D 82 B3
Stadtkyll D 80 B2
Stadtlauringen D 82 B2
Stadtlengsfeld D 82 B2
Stadtlohn D 71 C3
Stadtoldendorf D 82 A1
Stadtroda D 83 B3
Stadtsteinach D 82 B3
Stäfa CH 107 B3
Staffanstorp S 61 D3
Staffelstein D 82 B2
Staffin GB 31 B2
Stafford GB 40 C1
Stainach A 110 B1
Staindrop GB 37 B5
Staines-upon-Thames GB 44 B3
Stainville F 91 C5
Stainz A 110 C2
Staithes GB 37 B6
Staíti I 175 D2
Stäket S 57 A3
Stakroge DK 59 C1
Štalcerji SLO 123 B3
Stalden CH 119 A4
Stalham GB 41 C5
Stalheim N 46 B3
Stallarholmen S 56 A3
Ställberg S 50 C1
Ställdalen S 50 C1
Stallhofen A 110 B2
Stalon S 195 F6
Stalowa Wola PL 12 C5
Stamford GB 40 C3
Stamford Bridge GB 40 B3
Stamnes N 46 B2
Stams A 108 B1
Stamsried D 95 B4
Stamsund N 194 B4
Stanford le Hope GB 45 B4
Stånga S 57 C4
Stange N 48 B3
Stanghella I 121 B4
Stanhope GB 37 B4
Stanišić SRB 125 B5
Staňkov CZ 95 B5
Stankovci HR 137 B4
Stanley GB 37 B5
Stans CH 106 C3
Stansted Mountfitchet GB 45 B4
Stanzach A 108 B1
Stapar SRB 125 B5
Staphorst NL 70 B3
Staplehurst GB 45 B4
Stąporków PL 87 A4
Stara Baška HR 123 C3
Starachowice PL 87 A5
Stara Fužina SLO 122 A2
Stara Kamienica PL 84 B3
Stara Kiszewa PL 68 B3
Stará L'ubovnă SK 99 B4
Stara Moravica SRB 126 B1
Stara Novalja HR 137 A3
Stara Pazova SRB 127 C2
Stará Turá SK 98 C1
Staraya Russa RUS 9 D7
Stara Zagora BG 17 D6
Stärbsnäs S 51 C6
Starčevo SRB 127 C2
Stare Dłutowo PL 77 A4
Staré Hamry CZ 98 B2
Stare Jabłonki PL 69 B5
Staré Město CZ 98 B1
Stare Pole PL 69 A4
Stare Sedlo CZ 96 B2
Stare Strącze PL 85 A4
Stargard Szczeciński PL 75 A4
Stårheim N 198 D2
Stari Banovci SRB 127 C2
Starigrad
Ličko-Senjska HR 123 C3
Splitsko-Dalmatinska HR 138 B2
Stari Gradac HR 124 B3
Starigrad-Paklenica HR 137 A4
Stari Jankovci HR 125 B4
Stari Majdan BIH 124 C2
Stari-Mikanovci HR 125 B4
Staritsa RUS 9 D9
Starkenbach A 108 B1
Starnberg D 108 B2
Starogard PL 75 A4
Starogard Gdański PL 69 B3
Starokonstyantyniv UA 13 D7
Staro Petrovo Selo HR 124 B3
Staro Selo
HR 124 B1
SRB 127 C3
Stary Brzozów PL 77 B5
Stary Dzierzgoń PL 69 B4
Starý Hrozenkov CZ 98 C1
Stary Jaroslaw PL 68 A1
Stary Plzenec CZ 96 B1
Stary Sącz PL 99 B4
Starý Smokovec SK 99 B4
Staryy Chartoriysk UA 13 C6
Staškov SK 98 B2
Stassfurt D 82 A3
Staszów PL 87 B5
Stathelle N 53 A5
Staufen D 106 B2
Staunton GB 39 C4
Stavang N 46 A2
Stavanger N 52 B1
Stavåsnäs S 49 B4
Stavby S 51 B5
Staveley GB 40 B2
Stavelot B 80 B1
Stavenisse NL 79 A4
Stavern N 53 B6
Stavnäs S 55 A3
Stavoren NL 70 B2
Stavros
CY 181 A1
GR 183 C5
Stavroupoli GR 183 B6
Stavseng N 47 A6
Stavsiø N 48 B2
Stavsnäs S 57 A4
Stawiszyn PL 76 C3
Steane N 53 A4
Steblevë AL 182 B2
Stechelberg CH 106 C2
Štechovice CZ 96 B2
Stechow D 73 B5
Steckborn CH 107 B3
Stede Broek NL 70 B2
Steeg A 107 B5
Steenbergen NL 79 A4
Steenvoorde F 78 B2
Steenwijk NL 70 B3
Štefanje HR 124 B2
Steffisburg CH 106 C2
Stegaurach D 94 B2
Stege DK 65 B5
Stegelitz D 74 A2
Stegersbach A 111 B3
Stegna PL 69 A4
Steimbke D 72 B2
Stein GB 31 B2
Steinach
A 108 B2
Baden-Württemberg D 106 A3
Bayern D 82 B2
Thüringen D 82 B3
Stein an Rhein CH 107 B3
Steinau
Bayern D 81 B5
Niedersachsen D 64 C1
Steinbeck D 74 B2
Steinberg am Rofan A 108 B2
Steindorf A 109 C5
Steine N 46 B2
Steinen D 106 B2
Steinfeld
A 109 C4
D 71 B5
Steinfurt D 71 B4
Steingaden D 108 B1
Steinhagen D 72 B1
Steinheid D 82 B3
Steinheim
Bayern D 107 A5
Nordrhein-Westfalen D 81 A5
Steinhöfel D 74 B3
Steinhorst D 72 B3
Steinigtwolmsdorf D 84 A2
Steinkjer N 199 A8
Steinsholt N 53 A5
Stekene B 79 A4
Stelle D 72 A3
Stellendam NL 79 A4
Stenåsa S 63 B4
Stenay F 91 B5
Stenberga S 62 A3
Stendal D 73 B4
Stenhammar S 55 B4
Stenhamra S 57 A3
Stenhousemuir GB 35 B4
Stenlose DK 61 D2
Stensätra S 50 B3
Stensele S 195 E8
Stenstorp S 55 B4
Stenstrup DK 65 A3
Stenudden S 195 D8
Stenungsund S 54 B2
Štěpánov CZ 98 B1
Stephanskirchen D 108 B3
Stepnica PL 74 A3
Stepojevac SRB 127 C2
Stepping DK 59 C2
Sterbfritz D 82 B1
Sternberg D 65 C4
Šternberk CZ 98 B1
Sterup D 64 B2
Stes Maries-de-la-Mer F 131 B3
Stęszew PL 75 B5
Štěti CZ 84 B2
Stevenage GB 44 B3
Stewarton GB 36 A2
Steyerburg D 72 B2
Steyning GB 44 C3
Steyr A 110 A1
Stężyca PL 68 A2
Stezzano I 120 B2
Stia I 135 B4
Stibb Cross GB 42 B2
Sticciano Scalo I 135 C4
Stidsvig S 61 C3
Stiens NL 70 A2
Stige DK 59 C3
Stigen S 54 B3
Stigliano I 174 A2
Stigtomta S 56 B2
Stilida GR 182 E4
Stilla N 192 C7
Stillington GB 40 A2
Stilo I 175 C2
Stintino I 178 B2
Stio I 172 B1
Štip MK 182 B4
Stira GR 185 A5
Stirling GB 35 B4
Štítnik SK 99 C4
Štíty CZ 97 B4
Stjärnhov S 56 A3
Stjärnsund S 50 B3
Stjørdalshalsen N 199 B7
Stobnica PL 87 A3
Stobno PL 75 A5
Stobreč HR 138 B2
Stochov CZ 84 B1
Stockach D 107 B4
Stöckalp CH 106 C3
Stockaryd S 62 A2
Stockbridge GB 44 B2
Stockerau A 97 C4
Stockheim D 82 B3
Stockholm S 57 A4
Stockport GB 40 B1
Stocksbridge GB 40 B2
Stockton-on-Tees GB 37 B5
Stod CZ 96 B1
Stöde S 200 D2
Stødi N 195 D6
Stöðvarfjörður IS 191 C12
Stoer GB 32 C1
Stoholm DK 58 B2
Stoke Ferry GB 41 C4
Stoke Fleming GB 43 B3
Stoke Mandeville GB 44 B3
Stoke-on-Trent GB 40 B1
Stokesley GB 37 B5
Stokke N 54 A1
Stokkemarke DK 65 B4
Stokken N 53 B4
Stokkseyri IS 190 D4
Stokkvågen N 195 D4
Stokmarknes N 194 B5
Štoky CZ 97 B3
Stolac BIH 139 B3
Stølaholmen N 46 A3
Stolberg D 80 B2
Stolin BY 13 C7
Stollberg D 83 B4
Stöllet S 49 B5
Stollhamm D 71 A5
Stolno PL 76 A3
Stolpen D 84 A2
Stolzenau D 72 B2
Stompetoren NL 70 B1
Ston HR 139 C3
Stonařov CZ 97 B3
Stone GB 40 C1
Stonehaven GB 33 E4
Stonehouse GB 36 A3
Stongfjorden N 46 A2
Stonndalen N 47 B4
Stony Stratford GB 44 A3
Stopnica PL 87 B4
Storå S 56 A1
Storås N 198 B6
Storby FIN 51 B6
Stordal
Møre og Romsdal N 198 C4
Nord-Trøndelag N 199 B8
Store GB 33 B4
Storebø N 46 B2
Storebro S 62 A3
Store Damme DK 65 B5
Store Heddinge DK 65 A5
Store Herrestad S 66 A2
Store Levene S 55 B3
Storelv N 192 B6
Store Molvik N 193 B12
Støren N 199 B7
Store Skedvi S 50 B2
Store Vika S 57 B3
Storfjellseter N 199 D7
Storfjord N 192 C3
Storfjorden N 198 C3
Storfors S 55 A5
Storforshei N 195 D5
Storhøliseter N 47 A6
Storjord N 195 D6
Storkow
Brandenburg D 74 B2
Mecklenburg-Vorpommern D 74 A3
Storli N 198 C6
Storlien S 199 B9
Stornara I 171 B3
Stornoway GB 31 A2
Storo I 121 B3
Storozhynets UA 17 A6
Storrington GB 44 C3
Storseleby S 200 B2
Storsjön S 50 A3
Storslett N 192 C5
Storsteinnes N 192 C3
Storsund S 196 D3
Storuman S 195 E8
Störvattnet S 199 C9
Storvik
N 195 D4
S 50 B3
Storvreta S 51 C4
Štos SK 99 C4
Stössen D 83 A3
Stotel D 72 A1
Stötten D 108 B1
Stotternheim D 82 A3
Stouby DK 59 C2
Stourbridge GB 40 C1
Stourport-on-Severn GB 39 B4
Støvring DK 58 B2
Stow GB 35 C5
Stowbtsy BY 13 B7
Stowmarket GB 45 A5
Stow-on-the-Wold GB 44 B2
Straach D 73 C5
Strabane GB 27 B3
Strachan GB 33 D4
Strachur GB 34 B2
Stracin MK 182 A4
Strackholt D 71 A4
Stradbally IRL 29 B1
Stradella I 120 B2
Straelen D 80 A2
Stragari SRB 127 C2
Strakonice CZ 96 B1
Strålsnäs S 55 B6
Stralsund D 66 B2
Strand N 48 A3
Stranda N 198 C3
Strandby DK 58 A3
Strandebarm N 46 B3
Strandhill IRL 26 B2
Strandlykkja N 48 B3
Strandvik N 46 B2
Strangford GB 27 B5
Strängnäs S 56 A3
Strångsjö S 56 B2
Stráni CZ 98 C1
Stranice SLO 123 A4
Stranorlar IRL 26 B3
Stranraer GB 36 B1
Strasatti I 176 B1
Strasbourg F 93 C3
Strasburg D 74 A2
Strašice CZ 96 B1
Stråssa S 56 A1
Strassburg A 110 C1
Strass im Steiermark A 110 C2
Strasskirchen D 95 C4
Strasswalchen A 109 B4
Stratford-upon-Avon GB 44 A2
Strathaven GB 36 A2
Strathdon GB 32 D3
Strathkanaird GB 32 D1
Strathpeffer GB 32 D2
Strathy GB 32 C3
Strathyre GB 34 B3
Stratinska BIH 124 C2
Stratton GB 42 B2
Straubing D 95 C4
Straulas I 178 B3
Straume N 53 A5
Straumen
Nordland N 194 C6
Nord-Trøndelag N 199 B8
Straumsjøen N 194 B5
Straumsnes N 194 C6
Straupitz D 74 C3
Strausberg D 74 B2
Straussfurt D 82 A3
Strawczyn PL 87 B4
Straža
SLO 123 B4
SRB 127 C3
Stražnad Nezárkou CZ 96 B2
Strážnice CZ 98 C1
Strážný CZ 96 C1
Stráž Pod Ralskem CZ 84 B2
Štrbské Pleso SK 99 B4
Strečno SK 98 B2
Street GB 43 A4
Strehla D 83 A5
Strekov SK 112 B2
Strem A 111 B3
Stremska-Rača SRB 127 C1
Strengberg A 110 A1
Strengelvåg N 194 B6
Stresa I 119 B5
Streufdorf D 82 B2
Strib DK 59 C2
Striberg S 55 A5
Stříbro CZ 95 B4
Strichen GB 33 D4
Strigno I 121 A4
Štrigova HR 111 C3
Strijen NL 79 A4
Strizivojna HR 125 B4
Strmica HR 138 A2
Strmilov CZ 97 B3
Ströhen D 72 B1
Strokestown IRL 28 A3
Stromberg
Nordrhein-Westfalen D 81 A4
Rheinland-Pfalz D 93 B3
Stromeferry GB 31 B3
Strömnäs S 200 B2
Stromness GB 33 C3
Strömsberg S 51 B4
Strömsbruk S 200 E3
Strömsfors S 56 B2
Strömsnäsbruk S 61 C3
Strömstad S 54 B2
Strömsund
Jämtland S 199 B12
Västerbotten S 195 E7
Stronachlachar GB 34 B3
Stróngoli I 174 B3
Stronie Śląskie PL 85 B4
Strontian GB 34 B2
Stroppiana I 119 B5
Stroud GB 43 A4
Stroumbi CY 181 B1
Stróża PL 99 B3
Strücklingen D 71 A4
Struer DK 58 B1
Struga MK 182 B2
Strugi Krasnyye RUS 9 C6
Strumica MK 182 B4
Strumien PL 98 B2
Struy GB 32 D2
Stružec HR 124 B2
Stryków PL 77 C4
Stryn N 198 D3
Stryy UA 13 D5
Strzałkowo PL 76 B2
Strzegocin PL 77 B5
Strzegom PL 85 B4
Strzegowo PL 77 B5
Strzelce PL 77 B4
Strzelce Krajeńskie PL 75 B4
Strzelce Kurowo PL 75 B4
Strzelce Opolskie PL 86 B2
Strzelin PL 85 B5
Strzelno PL 76 B3
Strzepcz PL 68 A3
Strzybnica PL 86 B2
Strzygi PL 77 A4
Stubbekøbing DK 65 B5
Stuben A 107 B5
Stubenberg A 110 B2
Stubline SRB 127 C2
Studená CZ 97 B3
Studenci HR 138 B3
Studenka CZ 98 B2
Studenzen A 110 B2
Studienka SK 98 C1
Studland GB 43 B5
Studley GB 44 A2
Studzienice PL 68 A2
Stuer D 73 A5
Stugudal N 199 C8
Stugun S 200 C1
Stuhr D 72 A1
Stukenbrock D 81 A4
Stülpe D 74 B2
Stupava SK 111 A4
Stupnik HR 124 B1
Stupsk PL 77 A5
Sturkö S 63 B3

Tegernsee D 108 B2
Teggiano I 172 B1
Tegoleto I 135 B4
Teichel D 82 B3
Teignmouth GB 43 B3
Teillay F 101 B4
Teillet F 130 B1
Teisendorf D 109 B3
Teistungen D 82 A2
Teixeiro E 140 A2
Tejada de Tiétar E 150 B2
Tejado E 152 A1
Tejares E 150 B2
Tejn DK 67 A3
Teke TR 187 A4
Tekirdağ TR 186 B2
Tekovské-Lužany SK 112 A2
Telavåg N 46 B1
Telč CZ 97 B3
Telese Terme I 170 B2
Telford GB 38 B4
Telfs A 108 B2
Telgárt SK 99 C4
Telgte D 71 C4
Tellingstedt D 64 B2
Telšiai LT 8 E3
Telti I 178 B3
Teltow D 74 B2
Tembleque E 157 A4
Temelin CZ 96 B2
Temerin SRB 126 B1
Temiño E 143 B3
Témpio Pausánia I 178 B3
Templederry IRL 28 B3
Templemore IRL 28 B4
Temple Sowerby GB 37 B4
Templin D 74 A2
Temse B 79 A4
Tenay F 118 B2
Ten Boer NL 71 A3
Tenbury Wells GB 39 B4
Tenby GB 39 C2
Tence F 117 B4
Tende F 133 A3
Tenhult S 62 A2
Tenja HR 125 B4
Tenneville B 92 A1
Tennevoll N 194 B8
Tensta S 51 B4
Tenterden GB 45 B4
Teo E 140 B2
Teora I 172 B1
Tepasto FIN 196 B7
Tepelenë AL 182 C2
Teplá CZ 95 B4
Teplice CZ 84 B1
Teplička nad Váhom SK 98 B2
Tepsa FIN 197 B8
Tera E 143 C4
Téramo I 169 A3
Ter Apel NL 71 B4
Terborg NL 71 C3
Terchová SK 99 B3
Terebovlya UA 13 D6
Teremia Mare RO 126 B2
Terena P 155 C3
Teresa de Cofrentes E 159 B2
Terešov CZ 96 B1
Terezín CZ 84 B2
Terezino Polje HR 124 B3
Tergnier F 90 B3
Teriberka RUS 3 B14
Terlizzi I 171 B4
Termas de Monfortinho P 155 A4
Terme di Súio I 169 B3
Terme di Valdieri I 133 A3
Termens E 145 C4
Termes F 116 C3
Términi Imerese I 176 B2
Terminillo I 169 A2
Térmoli I 170 B3
Termonfeckin IRL 27 C4
Ternberg A 110 B1
Terndrup DK 58 B3
Terneuzen NL 79 A3
Terni I 168 A2
Ternitz A 111 B3
Ternopil UA 13 D6
Terpni GR 183 C5
Terracina I 169 B3
Terråk N 195 E3
Terralba I 179 C2
Terranova di Pollino I 174 B2
Terranova di Sibari I 174 B2
Terras do Bouro P 148 A1
Terrasini I 176 A2
Terrassa E 147 C3
Terrasson-Lavilledieu F 129 A4
Terrazos E 143 B3
Terriente E 152 B2
Terrugem P 155 C3
Tertenía I 179 C3
Teruel E 152 B2
Tervola FIN 196 C7
Tervuren B 79 B4
Terzaga E 152 B2
Tešanj BIH 125 C3
Tesáske-Mlyňany SK 98 C2
Teslić BIH 125 C3
Tessin D 66 B1
Tessy-sur-Vire F 88 B2
Tét H 111 B4
Tetbury GB 43 A4
Teterchen F 92 B2
Teterow D 65 C5
Teteven BG 17 D6
Tetiyev UA 13 D8
Tetovo MK 182 A2
Tettau D 82 B3
Tettnang D 107 B4
Teublitz D 95 B4
Teuchern D 83 A4
Teulada
E 159 C4
I 179 D2
Teupitz D 74 B2
Teurajärvi S 196 C5
Teutschenthal D 83 A3
Tevel H 112 C2
Teviothead GB 36 A4
Tewkesbury GB 39 C4
Thale D 82 A3
Thalfang D 92 B2
Thalgau A 109 B4
Thalkirch CH 107 C4
Thalmässing D 95 B3
Thalwil CH 107 B3
Thame GB 44 B3
Thann F 106 B2
Thannhausen D 94 C2
Thaon-les-Vosges F 105 A5
Tharandt D 83 B5
Tharsis E 161 B2
Thasos GR 183 C6
Thatcham GB 44 B2
Thaxted GB 45 B4
Thayngen CH 107 B3
Theale GB 44 B2
The Barony GB 33 B3
Thebes = Thiva GR 185 A4
Theding-hausen D 72 B2
Theessen D 73 B5
The Hague = 's-Gravenhage NL 70 B1
Themar D 82 B2
The Mumbles GB 39 C3
Thénezay F 102 C1
Thenon F 129 A4
Therouanne F 78 B2
Thessaloniki = Salonica GR 182 C4
Thetford GB 45 A4
Theux B 80 B1
Thézar-les-Corbières F 146 A3
Thèze F 145 A3
Thiberville F 89 A4
Thibie F 91 C4
Thiéblemont-Farémont F 91 C4
Thiendorf D 84 A1
Thiene I 121 B4
Thierrens CH 106 C1
Thiers F 117 B3
Thiesi I 178 B2
Thiessow D 66 B2
Thiezac F 116 B2
Þingeyri IS 190 B2
Þingvellir IS 190 C4
Thionville F 92 B2
Thira GR 185 C6
Thiron-Gardais F 89 B4
Thirsk GB 37 B5
Thisted DK 58 B1
Thiva = Thebes GR 185 A4
Thivars F 90 C1
Thiviers F 115 C4
Thizy F 117 A4
Tholen NL 79 A4
Tholey D 92 B3
Thomas Street IRL 28 A3
Thomastown IRL 30 B1
Thônes F 118 B3
Thonnance-les-Joinville F 91 C5
Thonon-les-Bains F 118 A3
Thorame-Basse F 132 A2
Thorame-Haute F 132 A2
Thorens-Glières F 118 A3
Thorigny-sur-Oreuse F 91 C3
Thörl A 110 B2
Þorlákshöfn IS 190 D4
Thornaby on Tees GB 37 B5
Thornbury GB 43 A4
Thorne GB 40 B3
Thornhill
Dumfries & Galloway GB 36 A3
Stirling GB 35 B3
Thornthwaite GB 36 B3
Thornton-le-Dale GB 40 A3
Þórshöfn IS 191 A10
Thouarcé F 102 B1
Thouars F 102 C1
Thrapston GB 44 A3
Threlkeld GB 36 B3
Thrumster GB 32 C3
Thueyts F 117 C4
Thuin B 79 B4
Thuir F 146 B3
Thumau D 95 A3
Thun CH 106 C2
Thuret F 116 B3
Thurey F 105 C4
Thüringen A 107 B4
Thurins F 117 B4
Thürkow D 65 C5
Thurles IRL 29 B4
Thurmaston GB 40 C2
Thurø By DK 65 A3
Thursby GB 36 B3
Thurso GB 32 C3
Thury-Harcourt F 89 B3
Thusis CH 107 C4
Thyborøn DK 58 B1
Þykkvibær IS 190 D5
Thyregod DK 59 C2
Tibi E 159 C3
Tibro S 55 B5
Tidaholm S 55 B4
Tidan S 55 B5
Tidersrum S 62 A3
Tiedra E 150 A2
Tiefenbach D 95 B4
Tiefencastel CH 107 C4
Tiefenort D 82 B2
Tiefensee D 74 B2
Tiel NL 79 A5
Tielmes E 151 B4
Tielt B 78 A3
Tienen B 79 B4
Tiengen D 106 B3
Tiercé F 102 B1
Tierga E 152 A2
Tiermas E 144 B2
Tierp S 51 B4
Tierrantona E 145 B4
Tighina MD 17 B8
Tighnabruaich GB 34 C2
Tignes F 119 B3
Tigy F 103 B4
Tihany H 112 C1
Tijnje NL 70 A2
Tijola E 164 B2
Tikhvin RUS 9 C8
Tilburg NL 79 A5
Til Châtel F 105 B4
Tilh F 128 C2
Tillac F 145 A4
Tillberga S 56 A2
Tille F 90 B2
Tillicoultry GB 35 B4
Tilloy Bellay F 91 B4
Tilly F 115 B5
Tilly-sur-Seulles F 88 A3
Tim DK 59 B1
Timau I 109 C4
Timbaki GR 185 D5
Timi CY 181 B1
Timişoara RO 126 B3
Timmele S 60 B3
Timmendorfer Strand D 65 C3
Timmernabben S 62 B4
Timmersdala S 55 B4
Timoleague IRL 29 C3
Timolin IRL 30 B2
Timrå S 200 D3
Timsfors S 61 C3
Timsgearraidh GB 31 A1
Tinajas E 152 B1
Tinalhas P 155 B3
Tinchebray F 88 B3
Tincques F 78 B2
Tineo E 141 A4
Tinglev DK 64 B2
Tingsryd S 63 B2
Tingstäde S 57 C4
Tingvoll N 198 C5
Tinlot B 79 B5
Tinnoset N 53 A5
Tinos GR 185 B6
Tintagel GB 42 B2
Tinténiac F 101 A4
Tintern GB 39 C4
Tintigny B 92 B1
Tione di Trento I 121 A3
Tipperary IRL 29 B3
Tiptree GB 45 B4
Tirana = Tiranë AL 182 B1
Tiranë = Tirana AL 182 B1
Tirano I 120 A3
Tiraspol MD 17 B8
Tire TR 188 A2
Tires I 108 C2
Tiriez E 158 C1
Tirig E 153 B4
Tiriolo I 175 C2
Tirnavos GR 182 D4
Tirrénia I 134 B3
Tirschenreuth D 95 B4
Tirstrup DK 59 B3
Tirteafuera E 157 B3
Tisno HR 137 B4
Tišnov CZ 97 B4
Tisovec SK 99 C3
Tisselskog S 54 B3
Tistedal N 54 A2
Tistrup DK 59 C1
Tisvildeleje DK 61 C2
Tiszaalpár H 113 C3
Tiszabö H 113 B4
Tiszacsége H 113 B5
Tiszadorogma H 113 B4
Tiszaföldvár H 113 C4
Tiszafüred H 113 B4
Tiszajenö H 113 B4
Tiszakécske H 113 C4
Tiszakeszi H 113 B4
Tiszakürt H 113 C4
Tiszalök H 113 A5
Tiszalúc H 113 A5
Tiszanána H 113 B4
Tiszaörs H 113 B4
Tiszaroff H 113 B4
Tiszasüly H 113 B4
Tiszasziget H 126 A2
Tiszaszőlős H 113 B4
Tiszaújváros H 113 B5
Tiszavasvári H 113 B5
Titaguas E 159 B2
Titel SRB 126 B2
Titisee-Neustadt D 106 B3
Tito I 172 B1
Titova Korenica HR 123 C4
Titran N 198 B5
Tittling D 96 C1
Tittmoning D 109 A3
Titz D 80 A2
Tiurajärvi FIN 196 B7
Tived S 55 B5
Tiverton GB 43 B3
Tivisa E 153 A4
Tívoli I 168 B2
Tizsadob H 113 A5
Tjällmo S 56 B1
Tjåmotis S 195 D9
Tjæreborg DK 59 C1
Tjautjas S 196 B3
Tjøme N 54 A1
Tjong N 195 D4
Tjonnefoss N 53 B4
Tjörn IS 190 B5
Tjörnarp S 61 D3
Tjøtta N 195 E3
Tkon HR 137 B4
Tleń PL 68 B3
Tlmače SK 98 C2
Tłuchowo PL 77 B4
Tlumačov CZ 98 B1
Tóalmas H 112 B3
Toano I 134 A3
Toba D 82 A2
Tobarra E 158 C2
Tobermore GB 27 B4
Tobermory GB 34 B1
Toberonochy GB 34 B2
Tobha Mor GB 31 B1
Tobo S 51 B4
Tocane-St Apre F 129 A3
Tocha P 148 B1
Tocina E 162 A2
Töcksfors S 54 A2
Tocón E 163 A4
Todal N 198 C5
Todi I 136 C1
Todmorden GB 40 B1
Todorici BIH 138 A3
Todtmoos D 106 B3
Todtnau D 106 B2
Toén E 140 B3
Tofta
Gotland S 57 C4
Skaraborg S 55 B4
Toftbyn S 50 B2
Tofte N 54 A1
Töftedal S 54 B2
Tofterup DK 59 C1
Toftlund DK 59 C2
Tófű H 125 A4
Tohmo FIN 197 C10
Tokaj H 113 A5
Tokarnia PL 87 B4
Tokary PL 76 C3
Tokod H 112 B2
Tököl H 112 B2
Tolastadh bho Thuath GB 31 A2
Toledo E 151 C3
Tolentino I 136 B2
Tolfa I 168 A1
Tolg S 62 A2
Tolga N 199 C8
Tolkmicko PL 69 A4
Tollarp S 61 D3
Tollered S 60 B2
Tølløse DK 61 D1
Tolmachevo RUS 9 C6
Tolmezzo I 122 A2
Tolmin SLO 122 A2
Tolna H 112 C2
Tolnanémedi H 112 C2
Tolob GB 33 B5
Tolosa
E 144 A1
P 155 B3
Tolox E 162 B3
Tolpuddle GB 43 B4
Tolva
E 145 B4
FIN 197 C11
Tolve I 172 B2
Tomar P 154 B2
Tomaševac SRB 126 B2
Tomašica BIH 124 C2
Tomášikovo SK 111 A4
Tomašouka BY 13 C5
Tomášovce SK 99 C3
Tomaszów Mazowiecki PL 87 A4
Tomatin GB 32 D3
Tombeboeuf F 129 B3
Tomdoun GB 32 D1
Tomelilla S 66 A2
Tomellosa E 151 B5
Tomelloso E 157 A4
Tomiño E 140 C2
Tomintoul GB 32 D3
Tomislavgrad BIH 138 B3
Tomisław PL 84 A3
Tomisławice PL 76 B3
Tomnavoulin GB 32 D3
Tompa H 126 A1
Tompaládony H 111 B3
Tomra N 198 C3
Tomter N 54 A1
Tona E 147 C3
Tonara I 179 B3
Tonbridge GB 45 B4
Tondela P 148 B1
Tønder DK 64 B1
Tongeren B 79 B5
Tongue GB 32 C2
Tönisvorst D 80 A2
Tønjum N 47 A4
Tonkopuro FIN 197 C11
Tonnay-Boutonne F 114 C3
Tonnay-Charente F 114 C3
Tonneins F 129 B3
Tonnerre F 104 B2
Tonnes N 195 D4
Tönning D 64 B1
Tonsåsen N 47 B6
Tønsberg N 54 A1
Tonstad N 52 B2
Toomyvara IRL 28 B3
Toormore IRL 29 C2
Topares E 164 B2
Topas E 150 A2
Toplița RO 17 B6
Topola SRB 127 C2
Topolčani MK 182 B3
Topoľčany SK 98 C2
Topoľčianky SK 98 C2
Topolje HR 124 B2
Topólka PL 76 B3
Topoľniky SK 111 B4
Topolovățu Mare RO 126 B3
Toponár H 125 A3
Toporów PL 75 B4
Topsham GB 43 B3
Topusko HR 124 B1
Toques E 140 B3
Torà E 147 C2
Toral de los Guzmanes E 142 B1
Toral de los Vados E 141 B4
Torbalı TR 188 A2
Torbjörntorp S 55 B4
Torbole I 121 B3
Torchiarolo I 173 B4
Torcross GB 43 B3
Torcy-le-Petit F 89 A5
Torda SRB 126 B2
Tørdal N 53 A4
Tordehumos E 142 C1
Tordera E 147 C3
Tordesillas E 150 A2
Tordesilos E 152 B2
Töre S 196 D5
Töreboda S 55 B5
Toreby DK 65 B4
Torekov S 61 C2
Torella dei Lombardi I 170 C3
Torellò E 147 B3
Toreno E 141 B4
Torfou F 114 A2
Torgau D 83 A5
Torgelow D 74 A3
Torgueda P 148 A2
Torhamn S 63 B3
Torhop N 193 B11
Torhout B 78 A3
Torigni-sur-Vire F 88 A3
Torija E 151 B4
Toril E 152 B2
Torino = Turin I 119 B4
Toritto I 171 C4
Torkovichi RUS 9 C7
Torla E 145 B3
Tormac RO 126 B3
Törmänen FIN 193 D11
Tormestorp S 61 C3
Tórmini I 121 B3
Tornada P 154 B1
Tornal'a SK 99 C4
Tornavacas E 150 B2
Tornby DK 58 A2
Tornesch D 72 A2
Torness GB 32 D2
Torniella I 135 B4
Tornimparte I 169 A3
Torning DK 59 B2
Tornio FIN 196 D7
Tornjoš SRB 126 B1
Tornos E 152 B2
Toro E 150 A2
Törökszentmiklós H 113 B4
Toropets RUS 9 D7
Torpa S 61 C3
Torpè I 178 B3
Torphins GB 33 D4
Torpo N 47 B5
Torpoint GB 42 B2
Torpsbruk S 62 A2
Torquay GB 43 B3
Torquemada E 142 B2
Torralba de Burgo E 151 A5
Torralba de Calatrava E 157 A4
Torrão P 154 C2
Torre Annunziata I 170 C2
Torreblacos E 143 C4
Torreblanca E 153 B4
Torreblascopedro E 157 B4
Torrecaballeros E 151 A3
Torrecampo E 156 B3
Torre Canne I 173 B3
Torre Cardela E 163 A4
Torrecilla E 152 B1
Torrecilla de la Jara E 156 A3
Torrecilla de la Orden E 150 A2
Torrecilla del Pinar E 151 A3
Torrecilla en Cameros E 143 B4
Torrecillas de la Tiesa E 156 A2
Torre das Vargens P 154 B3
Torre de Coelheiros P 154 C3
Torre de Dom Chama P 149 A2
Torre de Juan Abad E 157 B4
Torre de la Higuera E 161 B3
Torre del Bierzo E 141 B4
Torre del Burgo E 151 B4
Torre del Campo E 163 A4
Torre del Greco I 170 C2
Torre del Lago Puccini I 134 B3
Torre dell'Orso I 173 B4
Torre del Mar E 163 B3
Torredembarra E 147 C2
Torre de Miguel Sesmero E 155 C4
Torre de Moncorvo P 149 A2
Torre de Santa Maria E 156 A1
Torredonjimeno E 163 A4
Torre do Terranho P 148 B2
Torre Faro I 177 A4
Torregrosa E 147 C1
Torreira P 148 B1
Torrejoncillo E 155 B4
Torrejón de Ardoz E 151 B4
Torrejón de la Calzada E 151 B4
Torrejón del Rey E 151 B4
Torrejon el Rubio E 156 A1
Torrelaguna E 151 B4
Torrelapaja E 152 A2
Torre la Ribera E 145 B4
Torrelavega E 142 A2
Torrelobatón E 150 A2
Torrelodones E 151 B4
Torre los Negros E 152 B2
Torremaggiore I 171 B3
Torremanzanas E 159 C3
Torremayor E 155 C4
Torremezzo di Falconara I 174 B2
Torremocha E 156 A1
Torremolinos E 163 B3
Torrenieri I 135 B4
Torrenostra E 153 B4
Torrenova I 168 B2
Torrent E 159 B3
Torrente de Cinca E 153 A4
Torrenueva
Ciudad Real E 157 B4
Granada E 163 B4
Torreorgaz E 155 B4
Torre Orsáia I 172 B1
Torre-Pacheco E 165 B4
Torre Péllice I 119 C4
Torreperogil E 157 B4
Torres E 163 A4
Torresandino E 143 C3
Torre Santa Susanna I 173 B3
Torres-Cabrera E 163 A3
Torres de la Alameda E 151 B4
Torres Novas P 154 B2
Torres Vedras P 154 B1
Torrevieja E 165 B4
Torricella I 173 B3
Torri del Benaco I 121 B3
Torridon GB 31 B3
Torriglia I 134 A2
Torrijos E 151 C3
Tørring DK 59 C2
Torrita di Siena I 135 B4
Torroal P 154 C2
Torroella de Montgr i E 147 B4
Torrox E 163 B4
Torrskog S 54 A3

Ulrika S 56 B1
Ulriksfors S 200 C1
Ulrum NL 71 A3
Ulsberg N 198 C6
Ulsta GB 33 A5
Ulsted DK 58 A3
Ulsteinvik N 198 C2
Ulstrup
Vestsjællands Amt. DK 59 C3
Viborg Amt. DK 59 B2
Ulsvåg N 194 B6
Ulubey TR 188 A4
Uluborlu TR 189 A5
Ulukışla TR 23 C8
Ulverston GB 36 B3
Ulvik N 46 B3
Umag HR 122 B2
Uman UA 13 D9
Umba RUS 3 C14
Umbértide I 135 B5
Umbriático I 174 B2
Umčari SRB 127 C2
Umeå S 200 C6
Umgransele S 200 B4
Umhausen A 108 B1
Umka SRB 127 C2
Umljanovic HR 138 B2
Umnäs S 195 E7
Umurbey TR 186 B1
Unaðsdalur IS 190 A3
Unapool GB 32 C1
Unari FIN 197 B8
Unbyn S 196 D4
Uncastillo E 144 B2
Undenäs S 55 B5
Undersaker S 199 B10
Undredal N 46 B4
Unešić HR 138 B2
Úněšov CZ 96 B1
Ungheni MD 17 B7
Unhais da Serra P 148 B2
Unhošt CZ 84 B2
Unichowo PL 68 A2
Uničov CZ 98 B1
Uniejów PL 76 C3
Unisław PL 76 A3
Unkel D 80 B3
Unken A 109 B3
Unna D 81 A3
Unnaryd S 60 C3
Unquera E 142 A2
Unterach A 109 B4
Unterägeri CH 107 B3
Unterammergau D 108 B2
Unterhaching D 108 A2
Unteriberg CH 107 B3
Unterkochen D 94 C2
Unter Langkampfen A 108 B3
Unterlaussa A 110 B1
Unterlüss D 72 B3
Untermünkheim D 94 B1
Unterschächen CH 107 C3
Unterschleissheim D 95 C3
Unterschwaningen D 94 B2
Untersiemau D 82 B2
Unter-steinbach D 94 B2
Unterweissenbach A 96 C2
Unterzell D 95 B4
Upavon GB 44 B2
Úpice CZ 85 B4
Upiłka PL 68 B2
Upphärad S 54 B3
Uppingham GB 40 C3
Upplands-Väsby S 57 A3
Uppsala S 51 C4
Uppsjøhytta N 48 A1
Upton-upon-Severn GB 39 B4
Ur F 146 B2
Uras I 179 C2
Uraz PL 85 A4
Urbánia I 136 B1
Urbino I 136 B1
Urçay F 103 C4
Urda E 157 A4
Urdax E 144 A2
Urdilde E 140 B2
Urdos F 145 B3
Urk NL 70 B2
Úrkút H 111 B4
Urla TR 188 A1
Urlingford IRL 30 B1
Urnäsch CH 107 B4
Urnes N 47 A4
Uroševac KOS 16 D4
Urracal E 164 B2
Urries E 144 B2
Urroz E 144 B2
Ursensollen D 95 B3
Urshult S 63 B2
Uršna Sela SLO 123 B4
Urszulewo PL 77 B4
Ury F 90 C2
Urziceni RO 17 C7
Urzulei I 178 B3
Usagre E 156 B1
Uşak TR 187 D4
Usedom D 66 C2
Useldange L 92 B1
Uséllus I 179 C2
Ushakovo RUS 69 A5
Usingen D 81 B4
Usini I 178 B2
Usk GB 39 C4
Uskedal N 46 C2
Üsküdar TR 186 A4
Uslar D 82 A1
Úsov CZ 97 B5
Usquert NL 71 A3
Ussássai I 179 C3
Ussé F 102 B2
Usséglio I 119 B4
Ussel
Cantal F 116 B2
Corrèze F 116 B2
Usson-du-Poitou F 115 B4
Usson-en-Forez F 117 B3
Usson-les-Bains F 146 B3
Ustaoset N 47 B5
Ustaritz F 144 A2
Uštěk CZ 84 B2
Uster CH 107 B3
Ústi CZ 98 B1
Ustikolina BIH 139 B4
Ústínad Labem CZ 84 B2
Ústínad Orlicí CZ 97 B4
Ustiprača BIH 139 B5
Ustka PL 68 A1
Ust Luga RUS 8 C6
Ustroń PL 98 B2
Ustronie Morskie PL 67 B4
Ustyuzhna RUS 9 C10
Uszód H 112 C2
Utåker N 52 A1
Utansjö S 200 D3
Utebo E 152 A3
Utena LT 13 A6
Utery CZ 95 B5
Uthaug N 198 B6
Utiel E 159 B2
Utne N 46 B3
Utö S 57 B4
Utrecht NL 70 B2
Utrera E 162 A2
Utrillas E 153 B3
Utsjoki FIN 193 C11
Utstein kloster N 52 A1
Uttendorf A 109 B3
Uttenweiler D 107 A4
Utterslev DK 65 B4
Uttoxeter GB 40 C2
Utvälinge S 61 C2
Utvorda N 199 A7
Uusikaarlepyy FIN 3 E8
Uusikaupunki FIN 8 B2
Uvaly CZ 96 A2
Uvdal N 47 B5
Uza F 128 B1
Uzdin SRB 126 B2
Uzdowo PL 77 A5
Uzein F 145 A3
Uzel F 100 A3
Uzerche F 116 B1
Uzès F 131 A3
Uzhhorod UA 12 D5
Uzhok UA 12 D5
Užice SRB 127 D1
Uznach CH 107 B3
Üzümlü
Konya TR 189 B6
Muğla TR 188 C4
Uzunköprü TR 186 A1

V

Vaalajärvi FIN 197 B9
Vaas F 102 B2
Vaasa FIN 8 A2
Vaasen NL 70 B2
Vabre F 130 B1
Vác H 112 B3
Vacha D 82 B2
Váchartyán H 112 B3
Väckelsång S 63 B2
Vacqueyras F 131 A3
Vad S 50 B2
Vada I 134 B3
Väddö S 51 C5
Väderstad S 55 B5
Vadheim N 46 A2
Vadillo de la Sierra E 150 B2
Vadillos E 152 B1
Vadla N 52 A2
Vado I 135 A4
Vado Lígure I 133 A4
Vadsø N 193 B13
Vadstena S 55 B5
Vadum DK 58 A2
Vaduz FL 107 B4
Vafos N 53 B5
Vág H 111 B4
Vågåmo N 198 D6
Væggerløse DK 65 B4
Vaggeryd S 62 A2
Vaghia GR 184 A4
Vaglia I 135 B4
Váglio Basilicata I 172 B1
Vagney F 106 A1
Vagnhärad S 57 B3
Vagnsunda S 57 A4
Vagos P 148 B1
Vai GR 185 D7
Vaiano I 135 B4
Vaiges F 102 A1
Vaihingen D 93 C4
Vaillant F 105 B4
Vailly-sur-Aisne F 91 B3
Vailly-sur Sauldre F 103 B4
Vairano Scalo I 170 B2
Vaison-la-Romaine F 131 A4
Vaite F 105 B4
Väjern S 54 B2
Vajszló H 125 B3
Vaksdal N 46 B2
Vál H 112 B2
Valaam RUS 9 B7
Valada P 154 B2
Vålådalen S 199 B10
Valadares P 148 A1
Valado P 154 B1
Valandovo MK 182 B4
Valaská SK 99 C3
Valaská Belá SK 98 C2
Valaská Dubová SK 99 B3
Valašská Polanka CZ 98 B1
Valašské Klobouky CZ 98 B2
Valašské Meziříčí CZ 98 B1
Valberg F 132 A2
Vålberg S 55 A4
Valbo S 51 B4
Valbom P 148 A1
Valbondione I 120 A3
Valbonnais F 118 C2
Valbuena de Duero E 142 C2
Vălcani RO 126 B2
Valdagno I 121 B4
Valdahon F 105 B5
Valdaracete E 151 B4
Valday RUS 9 D8
Valdealgorfa E 153 B3
Valdecaballeros E 156 A2
Valdecabras E 152 B1
Valdecarros E 150 B2
Valdeconcha E 151 B5
Valdeflores E 161 B3
Valdefresno E 142 B1
Valdeganga E 158 B2
Valdelacasa E 150 B2
Valdelacasa de Tajo E 156 A2
Valdelarco E 161 B3
Valdelosa E 149 A4
Valdeltormo E 153 B4
Valdelugeros E 142 B1
Valdemanco de Esteras E 156 B3
Valdemarsvik S 56 B2
Valdemorillo E 151 B3
Valdemoro E 151 B4
Valdemoro Sierra E 152 B2
Valdenoceda E 143 B3
Valdeobispo E 149 B3
Valdeolivas E 152 B1
Valdepeñas E 157 B4
Valdepeñas de Jaén E 163 A4
Valdepiélago E 142 B1
Valdepolo E 142 B1
Valderas E 142 B1
Valdérice I 176 A1
Valderrobres E 153 B4
Valderrueda E 142 B2
Val de San Lorenzo E 141 B4
Val de Santo Domingo E 150 B3
Val d'Esquières F 132 B2
Valdestillas E 150 A3
Valdetorres E 156 B1
Valdetorres de Jarama E 151 B4
Valdeverdeja E 150 C2
Valdevimbre E 142 B1
Valdieri I 133 A3
Valdilecha E 151 B4
Val-d'Isère F 119 B3
Valdobbiádene I 121 B4
Valdocondes E 143 C3
Valdoviño E 140 A2
Valea lui Mihai RO 16 B5
Vale de Açor
Beja P 160 B2
Portalegre P 154 B3
Vale de Agua P 160 B1
Vale de Cambra P 148 B1
Vale de Lobo P 160 B1
Vale de Prazeres P 148 B2
Vale de Reis P 154 C2
Vale de Rosa P 160 B2
Vale de Santarém P 154 B2
Vale de Vargo P 160 B2
Vale do Peso P 155 B3
Valega P 148 B1
Valéggio sul Mincio I 121 B3
Valeiro P 154 C2
Valença P 140 B2
Valençay F 103 B3
Valence
Charente F 115 C4
Drôme F 117 C4
Valence d'Agen F 129 B3
Valence d'Albigeois F 130 A1
Valence-sur-Baise F 129 C3
Valencia E 159 B3
Valencia de Alcántara E 155 B3
Valencia de Don Juan E 142 B1
Valencia de las Torres E 156 B1
Valencia del Ventoso E 161 A3
Valencia de Mombuey E 161 A2
Valenciennes F 79 B3
Valensole F 132 B1
Valentano I 168 A1
Valentigney F 106 B1
Valentine F 145 A4
Valenza I 120 B1
Valenzuela E 163 A3
Valenzuela de Calatrava E 157 B4
Våler
Hedmark N 48 B3
Østfold N 54 A1
Valera de Abajo E 158 B1
Valeria E 158 B1
Valestrand N 52 A1
Valestrandsfossen N 46 B2
Valevåg N 52 A1
Valfabbrica I 136 B1
Valflaunes F 131 B2
Valga EST 8 D5
Valgorge F 131 A3
Valgrisenche I 119 B4
Valguarnera Caropepe I 177 B3
Valhelhas P 148 B2
Valjevo SRB 127 C1
Valka LV 8 D4
Valkeakoski FIN 8 B4
Valkenburg NL 80 B1
Valkenswaard NL 79 A5
Valkó H 112 B3
Valla S 56 A2
Vallada E 159 C3
Vallado E 141 A4
Valladolid E 150 A3
Vallåkra S 61 D2
Vallata I 172 A1
Vallberga S 61 C3
Vall d'Alba E 153 B3
Valldemossa E 166 B2
Valle N 52 A3
Valle Castellana I 136 C2
Valle de Abdalajís E 163 B3
Valle de Cabuérniga E 142 A2
Valle de la Serena E 156 B2
Valle de Matamoros E 155 C4
Valle de Santa Ana E 155 C4
Valledolmo I 176 B2
Valledoria I 178 B2
Vallelado E 150 A3
Vallelunga Pratameno I 176 B2
Valle Mosso I 119 B5
Vallendar D 81 B3
Vallentuna S 57 A4
Vallerås S 49 B5
Valleraugue F 130 A2
Vallermosa I 179 C2
Vallet F 101 B4
Valletta M 175 C3
Valley GB 38 A2
Vallfogona de Riucorb E 147 C2
Valli del Pasúbio I 121 B4
Vallo della Lucánia I 172 B1
Valloire F 118 B3
Vallombrosa I 135 B4
Vallon-Pont-d'Arc F 131 A3
Vallorbe CH 105 C5
Vallouise F 118 C3
Valls E 147 C2
Vallset N 48 B3
Vallsta S 50 A3
Vallstena S 57 C4
Valmadrid E 153 A3
Valmiera LV 8 D4
Valmojado E 151 B3
Valmont F 89 A4
Valmontone I 169 B2
Valö S 51 B5
Valognes F 88 A2
Valonga P 148 B1
Valongo P 148 A1
Válor E 164 C1
Valoria la Buena E 142 C2
Valøy N 199 A7
Valozhyn BY 13 A7
Valpaços P 148 A2
Valpelline I 119 B4
Valpiana I 135 B3
Valpovo HR 125 B4
Valras-Plage F 130 B2
Valréas F 131 A3
Vals CH 107 C4
Valsavarenche I 119 B4
Vålse DK 65 B4
Valsequillo E 156 B2
Valsjöbyn S 199 A11
Vals-les-Bains F 117 C4
Valsonne F 117 B4
Valstagna I 121 B4
Val-Suzon F 105 B3
Valtablado del Rio E 152 B1
Valþjofsstaður IS 191 B11
Val Thorens F 118 B3
Valtice CZ 97 C4
Valtiendas E 151 A4
Valtierra E 144 B2
Valtopina I 136 B1
Valtorta I 120 B2
Valtournenche I 119 B4
Valverde E 144 C2
Valverde de Burguillos E 155 C4
Valverde de Júcar E 158 B1
Valverde de la Vera E 150 B2
Valverde de la Virgen E 142 B1
Valverde del Camino E 161 B3
Valverde del Fresno E 149 B3
Valverde de Llerena E 156 B2
Valverde de Mérida E 156 B1
Valvträsk S 196 C4
Vamberk CZ 85 B4
Vamdrup DK 59 C2
Våmhus S 50 A1
Vamlingbo S 57 D4
Vammala FIN 8 B3
Vamos GR 185 D5
Vámosmikola H 112 B2
Vámosszabadi H 111 B4
Vanault-les-Dames F 91 C4
Vandel DK 59 C2
Vandenesse F 104 C2
Vandenesse-en-Auxois F 104 B3
Vandóies I 108 C2
Väne-Åsaka S 54 B3
Vänersborg S 54 B3
Vänersnäs S 54 B3
Vang N 47 A5
Vänge S 51 C4
Vangsnes N 46 A3
Vänjaurbäck S 200 B4
Vännacka S 54 A3
Vannareid N 192 B3
Vännäs S 200 C5
Vannes F 101 B3
Vannsätter S 51 A3
Vannvåg N 192 B3
Vansbro S 49 B6
Vanse N 52 B2
Vantaa FIN 8 B4
Vanttauskoski FIN 197 C9
Vanviken N 199 B7
Vanyarc H 112 B3
Vaour F 129 B4
Vapnyarka UA 13 D8
Vaprio d'Adda I 120 B2
Vaqueiros P 160 B2
Vara S 55 B3
Varacieux F 118 B2
Varades F 101 B4
Varages F 132 B1
Varaldsøy N 46 B2
Varallo I 119 B5
Varangerbotn N 193 B12
Varano de'Melegari I 120 C3
Varaždin HR 124 A2
Varaždinske Toplice HR 124 A2
Varazze I 133 A4
Varberg S 60 B2
Vardal N 48 B2
Varde DK 59 C1
Vårdö FIN 51 B7
Vardø N 193 B15
Vardomb H 125 A4
Varejoki FIN 196 C7
Varel D 71 A5
Varėna LT 13 A6
Vårenes N 52 A1
Varengeville-sur-Mer F 89 A4
Varenna I 120 A2
Varennes-en-Argonne F 91 B5
Varennes-le-Grand F 105 C3
Varennes-St Sauveur F 105 C4
Varennes-sur-Allier F 117 A3
Varennes-sur-Amance F 105 B4
Vareš BIH 139 A4
Varese I 120 B1
Varese Ligure I 134 A2
Vârfurile RO 16 B5
Vårgårda S 60 A2
Vargas
E 143 A3
P 154 B2
Vargön S 54 B3
Varhaug N 52 B1
Variaş RO 126 A2
Variaşu Mic RO 126 A3
Varilhes F 146 A2
Varin SK 98 B2
Väring S 55 B4
Váriz P 149 A3
Varkaus FIN 8 A5
Varmahlíð IS 190 B6
Varmaland IS 190 C4
Värmlands Bro S 55 A4
Värmskog S 55 A3
Varna
BG 17 D7
SRB 127 C1
Värnamo S 60 B4
Varnhem S 55 B4
Varnsdorf CZ 84 B2
Värö S 60 B2
Varoška Rijeka BIH 124 B2
Városlöd H 111 B4
Várpalota H 112 B2
Varreddes F 90 C2
Vars F 118 C3
Varsi I 120 C2
Varsseveld NL 71 C3
Vårsta S 57 A3
Vartdal N 198 C3
Vartofta S 55 B4
Vårvik S 54 A3
Várvölgy H 111 C4
Varzi I 120 C2
Varzjelas P 148 B1
Varzo I 119 A5
Varzy F 104 B2
Vasad H 112 B3
Väse S 55 A4
Vašica SRB 125 B5
Vasilevichi BY 13 B8
Väskinde S 57 C4
Vaskút H 125 A4
Vaslui RO 17 B7
Vassbotn N 53 B4
Vassenden N 47 A6
Vassieux-en-Vercors F 118 C2
Vassmolösa S 63 B4
Vassy F 88 B3
Västansjö S 195 E6
Västanvik S 50 B1
Västerås S 56 A2
Västerby S 50 B2
Västerfärnebo S 50 C3
Västergarn S 57 C4
Västerhaninge S 57 A4
Västervik S 62 A4
Vasto I 170 A2
Västra Ämtervik S 55 A4
Västra-Bodarne S 60 B2
Västra Karup S 61 C2
Vasvár H 111 B3
Vasylkiv UA 13 C9
Vát H 111 B3
Vatan F 103 B3
Väte S 57 C4
Vathia GR 184 C3
Vatican City = Cittádel Vaticano I 168 B2
Vatili CY 181 A2
Vatin SRB 126 B3
Vatland N 52 B3
Vatnar N 53 A5
Vatnås N 48 C1
Vatne N 53 B3
Vatnestrøm N 53 B4
Vätö S 51 C5
Vatra-Dornei RO 17 B6
Vatry F 91 C4
Vattholma S 51 B4
Vättis CH 107 C4
Vauchamps F 91 C3
Vauchassis F 104 A2
Vaucouleurs F 92 C1
Vaudoy-en-Brie F 90 C3
Vaulen N 52 B1
Vaulruz CH 106 C1
Vaulx Vraucourt F 90 A2
Vaumas F 104 C2
Vausseroux F 115 B3
Vauvenargues F 132 B1
Vauvert F 131 B3
Vauvillers F 105 B5
Vaux-sur-Sure B 92 B1
Vawkavysk BY 13 B6
Vaxholm S 57 A4
Växjö S 62 B2
Våxtorp S 61 C3
Vayrac F 129 B4
Važec SK 99 B3
Veberöd S 61 D3
Vechelde D 72 B3
Vechta D 71 B5
Vecinos E 149 B4
Vecsés H 112 B3
Vedavågen N 52 A1
Veddige S 60 B2
Vedersø DK 59 B1
Vedeseta I 120 B2
Vedevåg S 56 A1
Vedra E 140 B2
Vedum S 55 B3
Veendam NL 71 A3
Veenendaal NL 70 B2
Vega
Asturias E 142 A1
Asturias E 142 A1